c. Overall conclusion/financial reporting objective
Based on your role in the case and the above information, conclude on whether the financial reporting will be more aggressive or conservative or somewhere in between. Note that aggressive accounting tends to overstate net income/assets and present the company in the best light. Conservative accounting ensures that net income/assets are not overstated and that all pertinent information (positive or negative) is disclosed.

2. Identification and analysis of financial reporting issues

a. Issue identification
Read the case and look for potential financial reporting issues. To do this, you need to know the accounting principles and rules and have an understanding of the business and the business transactions. Issues are usually about deciding whether or not to **recognize** something (revenues, liabilities etc.), deciding how to **measure** financial statement elements (leave them as they are or write them down or off), or how to **present/disclose** these items in the financial statements (treat them as current or long term, debt or equity, discontinued or continuing operations, etc.).

b. Ranking issues
Focus on the more important issues. In other words, focus first on the issues that are material to the users of the information (those that are more complex and/or those that affect any of the key numbers or ratios identified above). You should identify right away what you consider to be material.

c. Analysis
The analysis should consider both qualitative and quantitative aspects. It should also look at the issue from different perspectives. For example, in a revenue recognition issue, should the revenue be recognized now or later? Consider only the relevant alternatives.

Qualitative:

- Each perspective must be supported by making reference to GAAP and accounting theory (including the conceptual framework). For example, recognize the revenue now because... or recognize it later because...
- Make sure the analysis is case specific—i.e. that it refers to the facts of the specific case.
- Make strong arguments for both sides of the discussion. If the issue is a real issue, there is often more than one way to account for the transaction or event.
- Make sure that the analysis considers the substance of the transaction from a business and economic perspective.

Quantitative:

- Calculate the impact of the different perspectives on key financial statement numbers/ratios. Would this decision be relevant to users?
- Calculate what the numbers might look like under different accounting methods, if they are relevant.

3. Recommendations

After each issue is analyzed, conclude on how the items should be accounted for. Your conclusion should be based on your role and the financial reporting objective that you identified earlier.

WILEY PLUS for *Intermediate Accounting*, Eighth Canadian Edition

Check with your instructor to find out if you have access to *WileyPLUS*!

Study More Effectively with a Multimedia Text

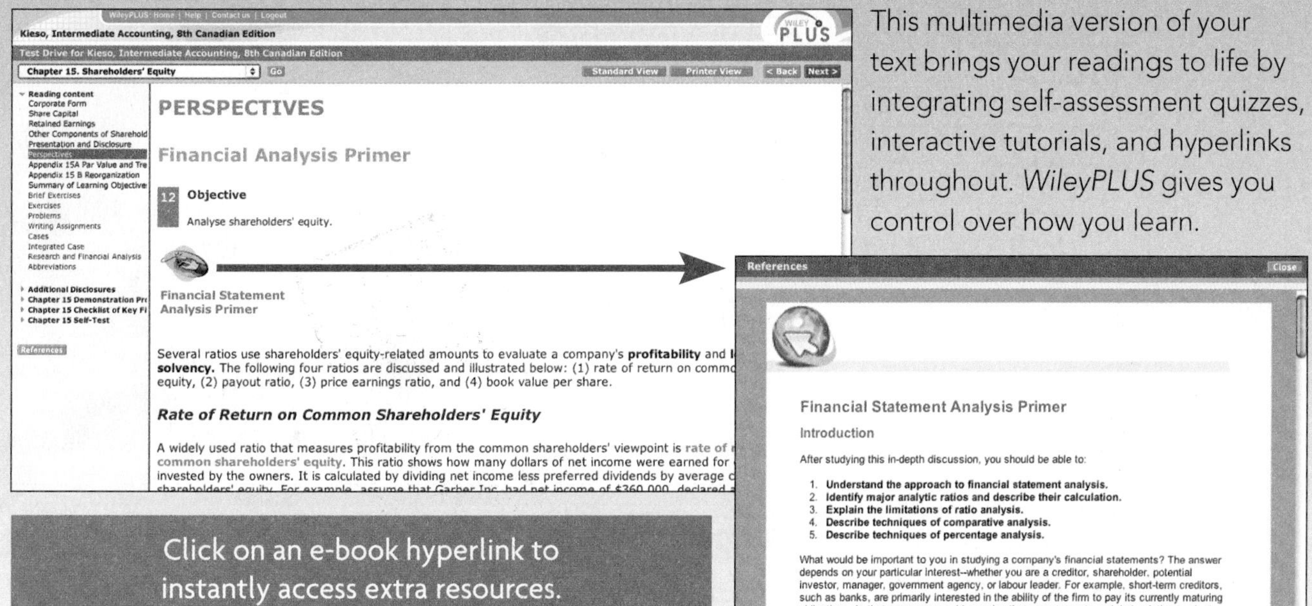

This multimedia version of your text brings your readings to life by integrating self-assessment quizzes, interactive tutorials, and hyperlinks throughout. *WileyPLUS* gives you control over how you learn.

Click on an e-book hyperlink to instantly access extra resources.

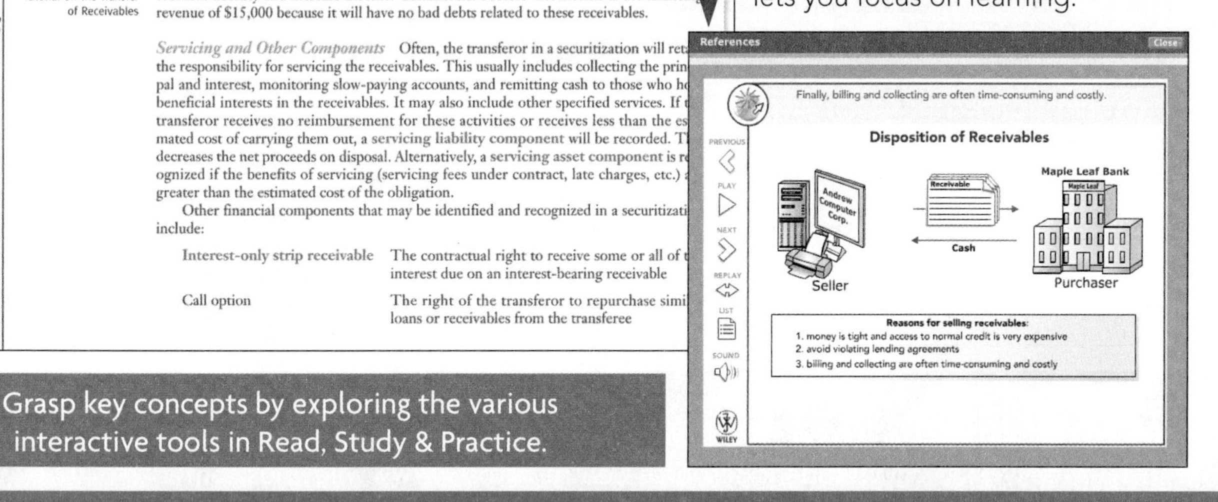

Preparing for a test has never been easier! *WileyPLUS* brings all of your course materials together and takes the stress out of organizing your study aids. A streamlined study routine saves you time and lets you focus on learning.

Grasp key concepts by exploring the various interactive tools in Read, Study & Practice.

John Wiley & Sons Canada, Ltd.

WILEY PLUS **for *Intermediate Accounting*, Eighth Canadian Edition**

Complete and Submit Assignments On-line Efficiently

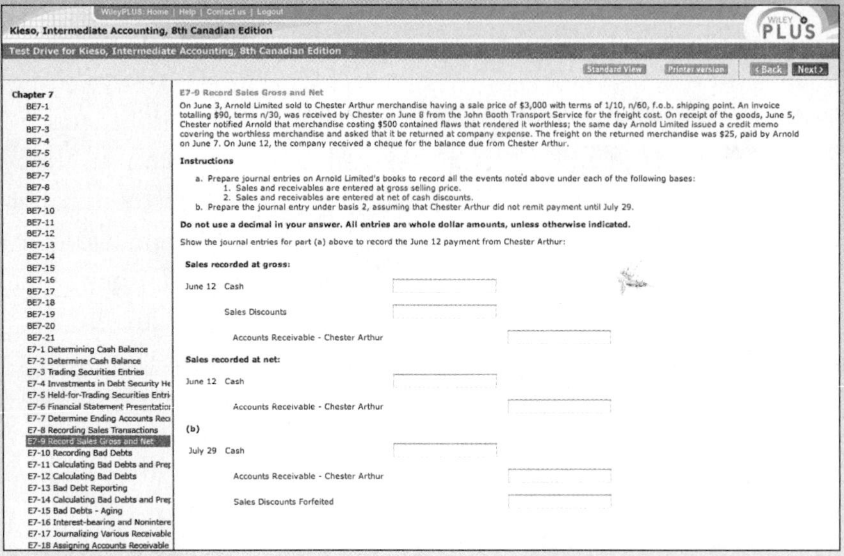

WileyPLUS: Home | Help | Contact us | Logout

Kieso, Intermediate Accounting, 8th Canadian Edition

Test Drive for Kieso, Intermediate Accounting, 8th Canadian Edition

Standard View | Printer version | ‹ Back | Next ›

Chapter 7
BE7-1
BE7-2
BE7-3
BE7-4
BE7-5
BE7-6
BE7-7
BE7-8
BE7-9
BE7-10
BE7-11
BE7-12
BE7-13
BE7-14
BE7-15
BE7-16
BE7-17
BE7-18
BE7-19
BE7-20
BE7-21
E7-1 Determining Cash Balance
E7-2 Determine Cash Balance
E7-3 Trading Securities Entries
E7-4 Investments in Debt Security He
E7-5 Held-for-Trading Securities Entri
E7-6 Financial Statement Presentatio
E7-7 Determine Ending Accounts Rec
E7-8 Recording Sales Transactions
E7-9 Record Sales Gross and Net
E7-10 Recording Bad Debts
E7-11 Calculating Bad Debts and Prep
E7-12 Calculating Bad Debts
E7-13 Bad Debt Reporting
E7-14 Calculating Bad Debts and Prep
E7-15 Bad Debts - Aging
E7-16 Interest-bearing and Nonintere
E7-17 Journalizing Various Receivable
E7-18 Assigning Accounts Receivable

E7-9 Record Sales Gross and Net

On June 3, Arnold Limited sold to Chester Arthur merchandise having a sale price of $3,000 with terms of 1/10, n/60, f.o.b. shipping point. An invoice totalling $90, terms n/30, was received by Chester on June 8 from the John Booth Transport Service for the freight cost. On receipt of the goods, June 5, Chester notified Arnold that merchandise costing $500 contained flaws that rendered it worthless; the same day Arnold Limited issued a credit memo covering the worthless merchandise and asked that it be returned at company expense. The freight on the returned merchandise was $25, paid by Arnold on June 7. On June 12, the company received a cheque for the balance due from Chester Arthur.

Instructions

a. Prepare journal entries on Arnold Limited's books to record all the events noted above under each of the following bases:
   1. Sales and receivables are entered at gross selling price.
   2. Sales and receivables are entered at net of cash discounts.
b. Prepare the journal entry under basis 2, assuming that Chester Arthur did not remit payment until July 29.

Do not use a decimal in your answer. All entries are whole dollar amounts, unless otherwise indicated.

Show the journal entries for part (a) above to record the June 12 payment from Chester Arthur:

Sales recorded at gross:

June 12 Cash
Sales Discounts
Accounts Receivable - Chester Arthur

Sales recorded at net:

June 12 Cash
Accounts Receivable - Chester Arthur

(b)

July 29 Cash
Accounts Receivable - Chester Arthur
Sales Discounts Forfeited

Your instructor can assign homework on-line for automatic grading and you can keep up-to-date on your assignments with your assignment list.

Your homework questions contain links to the relevant section of the multimedia text, so you know exactly where to go to get help solving each problem. In addition, use the Assignment area of *WileyPLUS* to monitor all of your assignments and their due dates.

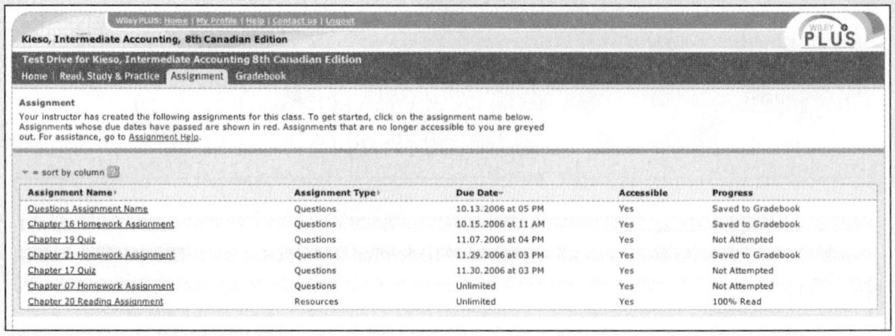

WileyPLUS: Home | My Profile | Help | Contact us | Logout

Kieso, Intermediate Accounting, 8th Canadian Edition

Test Drive for Kieso, Intermediate Accounting 8th Canadian Edition

Home | Read, Study & Practice | Assignment | Gradebook

Assignment

Your instructor has created the following assignments for this class. To get started, click on the assignment name below. Assignments whose due dates have passed are shown in red. Assignments that are no longer accessible to you are greyed out. For assistance, go to Assignment Help.

= sort by column

Assignment Name	Assignment Type	Due Date	Accessible	Progress
Questions Assignment Name	Questions	10.13.2006 at 05 PM	Yes	Saved to Gradebook
Chapter 16 Homework Assignment	Questions	10.15.2006 at 11 AM	Yes	Saved to Gradebook
Chapter 19 Quiz	Questions	11.07.2006 at 04 PM	Yes	Not Attempted
Chapter 21 Homework Assignment	Questions	11.29.2006 at 03 PM	Yes	Saved to Gradebook
Chapter 17 Quiz	Questions	11.30.2006 at 03 PM	Yes	Not Attempted
Chapter 07 Homework Assignment	Questions	Unlimited	Yes	Not Attempted
Chapter 20 Reading Assignment	Resources	Unlimited	Yes	100% Read

Keep Track of Your Progress

WileyPLUS: Home | My Profile | Help | Contact us | Logout

Kieso, Intermediate Accounting, 8th Canadian Edition

Test Drive for Kieso, Intermediate Accounting 8th Canadian Edition

Home | Read, Study & Practice | Assignment | Gradebook

Gradebook

These are results for all the assignments you have been given as homework. If an assignment due date has passed, then the assignment name is shown in red. If the instructor has allowed you to continue to work on assignments that are past due, your results will be shown in red. Assignments that are grayed out are no longer accessible to you. For more information, go to Gradebook Help.

= sort by column

Assignment Name	Assignment Type	Due Date	Progress	Score	Details	Accessible
Chapter 07 Homework Assignment	Questions	Unlimited	-	-/64	Not Attempted; Due Date Not Reached	Yes
Chapter 16 Homework Assignment	Questions	10.15.2006 11:00 AM	-	33/35	Attempted; Due Date Reached	Yes
Questions Assignment Name	Questions	10.13.2006 05:00 PM	-	2/2	Attempted; Due Date Reached	Yes
Chapter 20 Reading Assignment	Resources	Unlimited	100%	-		Yes
Chapter 21 Homework Assignment	Questions	11.29.2006 03:00 PM	-	48/48	Attempted; Due Date Not Reached	Yes
Chapter 17 Quiz	Questions	11.30.2006 03:00 PM	-	-/4	Not Attempted; Due Date Not Reached	Yes
Chapter 19 Quiz	Questions	11.07.2006 04:00 PM	-	-/10	Not Attempted; Due Date Not Reached	Yes
		Total	100%	83/163		

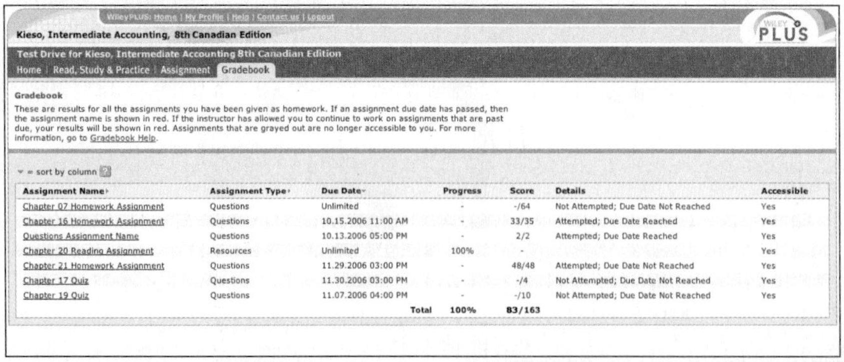

Your personal Gradebook lets you review your answers and results from past assignments as well as any feedback your instructor may have for you.

Keep track of your progress and review your completed questions at any time.

Technical Support: http://higheredwiley.custhelp.com
Student Resource Centre: http://www.wileyplus.com

For further information regarding *WileyPLUS* and other Wiley products, please visit www.wiley.ca

Intermediate Accounting

EIGHTH CANADIAN EDITION

Intermediate Accounting

Donald E. Kieso, PhD, CPA
KPMG Peat Marwick Emeritus Professor of Accounting
Northern Illinois University
DeKalb, Illinois

Jerry J. Weygandt, PhD, CPA
Arthur Andersen Alumni Professor of Accounting
University of Wisconsin
Madison, Wisconsin

Terry D. Warfield, PhD
Associate Professor
University of Wisconsin
Madison, Wisconsin

Nicola M. Young, MBA, FCA
Saint Mary's University
Halifax, Nova Scotia

Irene M. Wiecek, FCA
University of Toronto
Toronto, Ontario

John Wiley & Sons Canada, Ltd.

Library and Archives Canada Cataloguing in Publication
Intermediate accounting / Donald E. Kieso ... [et al.]. — 8th Canadian ed.

ISBN 978-0-470-83979-9 (v. 1)

ISBN 978-0-470-83980-5 (v. 2)

1. Accounting—Textbooks. I. Kieso, Donald E.

HF5635.I573 2007 657'.044 C2007-900378-8

Production Credits
Editorial Manager: Karen Staudinger
Publishing Services Director: Karen Bryan
Marketing Manager: Aida Krneta
Developmental Editor: Daleara Hirjikaka
Editorial Assistant: Sheri Coombs
Formatting: Emerson Group (Gail Ferreira Ng-A-Kien)
Cover and design: Interrobang Graphic Design Inc.
Cover Photo: Michael Ryan/Graphistock Photography/Veer
Wiley Bicentennial Logo: Richard J. Pacifico
Printing and Binding: Quebecor World—Dubuque

Printed and bound in the United States of America

3 4 5 6 7 QW 12 11 10 09 08

John Wiley and Sons Canada Ltd.
6045 Freemont Blvd.
Mississauga, Ontario L5R 4J3
Visit our website at www.wiley.ca

Dedicated to our husbands

John and George

and to our children

Hilary

Tim

Megan

Nicholas, and

Katherine

for their support, encouragement, and tolerance
throughout the writing of this book;
and to the many wonderful students who have passed
through our Intermediate Accounting classrooms.
We, too, have learned from you.

ABOUT THE AUTHORS

Canadian Edition

Nicola (Nickie) M. Young, MBA, FCA, is a Professor of Accounting in the Sobey School of Business at Saint Mary's University in Halifax, Nova Scotia, where her teaching responsibilities have varied from the introductory offering to final year advanced financial courses to the survey course in the Executive MBA program. She is the recipient of teaching awards, and has contributed to the academic and administrative life of the university through chairing the Department of Accounting, membership on the Board of Governors, and the Pension and other Committees. Nickie was associated with the Atlantic School of Chartered Accountancy for over twenty-five years in a variety of roles, including program and course development, teaching, and program reform. In addition to contributions to the accounting profession at the provincial level, Nickie has served on national boards of the Canadian Institute of Chartered Accountants (CICA) dealing with licensure and education. For the last fifteen years, she has worked with the CICA's Public Sector Accounting Board (PSAB) as an Associate, as a member and chair of the Board, and as a chair and member of PSAB Task Forces.

Irene M. Wiecek, FCA, is a faculty member of the University of Toronto at Mississauga and is cross-appointed to the Joseph L. Rotman School of Management. She teaches financial reporting in various programs including the Commerce Program (Accounting Specialist) and the Master of Management & Professional Accounting Program (MMPA). The Associate Director of the MMPA Program for many years, she co-founded and is Co-Director of the ICAO/Rotman Centre for Innovation in Accounting Education, which supports and facilitates innovation in accounting education. Irene has been involved in professional accounting education for over twenty years both at the Institute of Chartered Accountants of Ontario and the CICA, teaching and developing case/program material in various programs including the ICAO School of Accountancy. She helped create and currently directs the CICA In-depth GAAP Program. In the area of standard setting, she is Chair of the Canadian Academic Accounting Association Financial Accounting Exposure Draft Response Committee (since 2002). Irene is a member of the CICA Qualifications Committee which provides leadership, direction, and standards for admission into the CA profession. She is the recipient of the MMPA Faculty of the Year award for 2004 and 2006.

U.S. Edition

Donald E. Kieso, Ph.D., C.P.A., received his bachelor's degree from Aurora University and his doctorate in accounting from the University of Illinois. He has served as chairman of the Department of Accountancy and is currently the KPMG Emeritus Professor of Accountancy at Northern Illinois University. He has public accounting experience with Price Waterhouse & Co. (San Francisco and Chicago) and Arthur Andersen & Co. (Chicago) and research experience with the Research Division of the American Institute of Certified Public Accountants (New York). He has done postdoctorate work as a Visiting Scholar at the

University of California at Berkeley and is a recipient of NIU's Teaching Excellence Award and four Golden Apple Teaching Awards. Professor Kieso is the author of other accounting and business books and is a member of the American Accounting Association, the American Institute of Certified Public Accountants, and the Illinois CPA Society. He is the recipient of the Outstanding Accounting Educator Award from the Illinois CPA Society, the FSA's Joseph A. Silvoso Award of Merit, the NIU Foundation's Humanitarian Award for Service to Higher Education, the Distinguished Service Award from the Illinois CPA Society, and the Community Citizen of the Year Award from Rotary International.

Jerry J. Weygandt, Ph.D., C.P.A., is Arthur Andersen Alumni Professor of Accounting at the University of Wisconsin-Madison. He holds a Ph.D. in accounting from the University of Illinois. His articles have appeared in *Accounting Review*, *Journal of Accounting Research*, *Accounting Horizons*, *Journal of Accountancy*, and other academic and professional journals. Professor Weygandt is the author of other accounting and financial reporting books and is a member of the American Accounting Association, the American Institute of Certified Public Accountants, and the Wisconsin Society of Certified Public Accountants. He is the recipient of the Wisconsin Institute of CPAs's Outstanding Educator's Award and the Lifetime Achievement Award. In 2001, he received the American Accounting Association's Outstanding Accounting Educator Award.

Terry D. Warfield, Ph.D., is Associate Professor of Accounting at the University of Wisconsin-Madison. He received a B.S. and M.B.A. from Indiana University and a Ph.D. in accounting from the University of Iowa. Professor Warfield's area of expertise is financial reporting, and prior to his academic career, he worked for five years in the banking industry. He served as the Academic Accounting Fellow in the Office of the Chief Accountant at the U.S. Securities and Exchange Commission in Washington, D.C., from 1995–1996. Professor Warfield's primary research interests concern financial accounting standards and disclosure policies. He has published scholarly articles in *The Accounting Review*, *Journal of Accounting and Economics*, *Research in Accounting Regulation*, and *Accounting Horizons*, and he has served on the editorial boards of *The Accounting Review*, *Accounting Horizons*, and *Issues in Accounting Education*. Professor Warfield has served on the Financial Accounting Standards Committee of the American Accounting Association (Chair 1995–1996) and the AAA-FASB Research Conference Committee. Professor Warfield has received teaching awards at both the University of Iowa and the University of Wisconsin, and he was named to the Teaching Academy at the University of Wisconsin in 1995. Professor Warfield has developed and published several case studies based on his research for use in accounting classes. These cases have been selected for the AICPA Professor-Practitioner Case Development Program and have been published in *Issues in Accounting Education.*

PREFACE

The first Canadian edition of *Intermediate Accounting* made its appearance in 1982. In the 25 years since, it has changed, as have the many students who have used it. However, its goal has always been to help students understand, prepare, and use financial information by linking their accounting education with the "real-world" accounting environment. This continues to be the case with this new edition.

As always, we have aimed for a balanced discussion of concepts and procedures so that these elements reinforce one another. We have focused on the rationale behind transactions before discussing the accounting and reporting for those transactions. As with previous editions, we have thoroughly updated and revised every chapter to include coverage of all of the latest developments in the accounting profession and practice. In addition, we have included features to make all of this coverage even more understandable and relevant to today's accounting student. We have continued to refine the look of the text, added new pedagogical features and enhanced the technology package that accompanies the text, and we continue to emphasize the use of company data and examples so that students easily relate what they are learning to the real world of business.

Based on reviews by and feedback from intermediate accounting instructors and students from across the country, we have worked to help students prepare for the future, understand, and practise what they have learned. We strove to make the text as relevant for today's students as it was for those who used the first edition 25 years ago and are practising accountants today.

New Features

Helping Students Prepare for the Future

As Canada moves toward convergence of its GAAP and international standards, students need an increased understanding of the international reporting environment. To aid in building this awareness, we have introduced new sections comparing Canadian and international GAAP and discussing upcoming changes related to these differences. We also continue to feature marginal International Insights, marked with the icon shown here, to compare specific standards or terminology.

Helping Students Understand

Today's classroom is a diverse one and, with this in mind, this text has undergone a review by an instructor of English as a Second Language, who implemented changes throughout. This is especially evident in the earlier chapters. This increased readability will help all students, no matter what their background may be with the transition from introductory accounting to the more complex intermediate accounting course.

We have continued to refine the design of the text and have enhanced the four-colour design introduced in the seventh edition. Photos have been added to bring the opening stories to life and "infographics" have been redrawn for a more modern and colourful look.

Helping Students Practise

In the seventh edition we introduced all-new cases to the end-of-chapter material. These included "Integrated Cases" that draw material from several chapters in order to help students build issue identification skills. In this edition we have increased their number, adding at least 20 more cases overall. Further, a new summary guiding students through the case study method now appears inside the front cover of this text. This is in addition to the full Case Study Primer available on the Student Website.

Analysis doesn't have to be just part of the cases though. Our new Digging Deeper feature asks students to look more closely at the results they obtain in the problems and exercises. For instance, they might then be asked to comment on results or determine how things might be different if one of the original variables were to change. Digging Deeper questions are identified using the icon shown here.

Continuing Features

Many things have contributed to the success of Kieso over the quarter century. The following points outline just a few.

Real-World Emphasis

Since intermediate accounting is a course in which students must understand the application of accounting principles and techniques in practice, we strive to include as many real-world examples as possible.

Reinforcement of the Concepts

What Do the Numbers Mean?

Throughout each chapter students are asked "What Do the Numbers Mean?" and are presented with discussions applying accounting concepts to business contexts. This feature builds on the opening feature stories in making the accounting concepts relevant to students. Through current examples of how accounting is applied, students are better able to relate to and understand the material. In addition, a "Perspectives" section is present in most chapters. This section discusses the effect on the financial statements of many of the accounting choices made by corporate management, alerting students to look behind the numbers. Finally, the accounting equation appears in the margin next to key journal entries to help students understand the impact of each transaction on the financial position and cash flows of the company.

Integration of Ethics Coverage

Rather than featuring ethics coverage and problem material in isolation, we use an ethics icon to highlight ethical issues as they are discussed within each chapter. This icon also appears beside each exercise, problem, or case where ethical issues must be dealt with in relation to all kinds of accounting situations.

A Complete Package

Kieso continues to provide the most comprehensive and useful technology package available for the intermediate course. Its Student Website continues to expand with new tutorials on bad debts, bonds, and inventory methods. Also featured are a case primer, demonstration problems, expanded ethics coverage, and more. The site can be accessed at www.wiley.com/canada/kieso.

A key feature of every accounting package produced by John Wiley & Sons Canada, Ltd. is *WileyPLUS*. This online suite of resources that includes a complete multimedia version of the text will help your students come to class better prepared for lectures, and allows you to track their progress throughout the course more easily. They can take advantage of tools such as self-assessment quizzes and animated tutorials to help them study more efficiently. *WileyPLUS* is designed to provide instant feedback as students practise on their own. They can work through assignments with automatic grading or review custom-made class presentations featuring reading assignments, PowerPoint slides, and interactive simulations.

Currency and Accuracy

Accounting changes at a rapid pace—a pace that has increased in recent years. An up-to-date book is more important than ever. As in past editions, we have endeavoured to make this edition the most up-to-date and accurate text available. We have also ensured that new material subject to uncertainty has been vetted by subject matter experts.

The following list outlines the revisions and improvements made in the chapters of this volume.

Chapter 1 The Canadian Financial Reporting Environment

- New illustration showing stakeholders and what is at stake for each one.
- Increased emphasis on the transition to and rising importance of International Accounting Standards.
- Content on the CICA AcSB's strategic plan to transition to international standards.

Chapter 2 Conceptual Framework Underlying Financial Reporting

- More emphasis on international standards and where GAAP is headed including discussion of principles and concepts in transition (matching, revenue recognition), and going concern.
- Additional learning objective on material jointly created by the IASB and FASB regarding a new conceptual framework.

Chapter 3 The Accounting Information System

- Minor changes made.

Chapter 4 Reporting Financial Performance

- Increased emphasis on comprehensive income to reflect the new *CICA Handbook* Section 1530.
- Additional clarification on the treatment of held-for-sale assets.
- New *CICA Handbook* Section on accounting changes incorporated.
- Discussion of IASB/FASB work on the financial statement project.

Chapter 5 Financial Position and Cash Flows

- New sections showing how to calculate cash from operations and reviewing the IASB/FASB project on financial statements.
- Rewritten portions on monetary assets and liabilities, and investments
- Updated material on inventories to reflect new *CICA Handbook* Section 3031.

Chapter 6 Revenue Recognition

- More detailed guidance from *CICA Handbook* EIC141.
- Expanded section on barter transactions—updated for new *CICA Handbook* Section 3831.
- Expanded discussion on multiple element arrangements (bundled transactions) incorporating *CICA Handbook* EIC142.
- New section covering international perspective.

Chapter 7 Cash and Receivables

- Held-for-trading financial instruments transferred to chapter on investments.
- Loans and notes receivable now covered here rather than the investments chapter.
- *Handbook* changes: coverage of *CICA Handbook* Sections 3855 and 3862; *CICA Handbook* Section 3010 has been withdrawn and *CICA Handbook* Section 3861 superseded by *CICA Handbook* Section 3862.
- Reinforcement of the idea that the best measures of assets and liabilities result in the best matching.
- New learning objective and section compares Canadian and international standards.
- In the Valuation of Accounts Receivable section, the direct write-off method downplayed and discussed at the end rather than as a method of recording uncollectible accounts.
- Greater emphasis on basing the Allowance on the period-end accounts receivable as recommended in *CICA Handbook* Section 3020.
- New section in the loans discussion on accounting treatment when the fair value of the loan is not equal to the cash consideration.

Chapter 8 Inventory

- Previous Chapters 8 and 9 combined into one chapter.
- Appendices added: 8A: Retail Inventory Method and 8B: Application of the U.S. LCM rule, and LIFO.
- Chapter reflects new *CICA Handbook* Section 3031 on Inventories.
- Discussion of the U.S. method of applying LCM has been reduced and transferred to Appendix 8B.
- Coverage of *CICA Handbook* Section 3031; there is more discussion on a variety of types of inventory, including a short section on service providers' WIP; the section on variable and absorption costing has been removed; basket purchases and joint product costs are discussed together; a section has been added on capitalization of borrowing costs.
- Identification of specific and expanded disclosures.
- New section on a comparison of international and Canadian accounting standards.
- Reduced coverage of the inventory issues associated with special sales agreement.
- New section on accounting for vendor rebates.
- Reduced discussion of standard costs.

Chapter 9 Investments

- Loans and notes receivable material has been moved to Chapter 7.
- Held-for-trading investments have been moved from Chapter 7 to this chapter.
- Chapter now organized by classification of investment and therefore, accounting treatment: held-for-trading, held-to-maturity, available-for-sale, and strategic investments —significant influence, and control.
- Material now reflects new *CICA Handbook* Section 3855 (Financial Instruments—Recognition and Measurement) now in place and standards expected in outstanding Exposure Draft on Section 3862 (Financial Instruments—Disclosure).
- Coverage of equity method expanded to include need to identify and subsequently account for fair value differences and goodwill.
- New material on comparison of Canadian and international GAAP.

Chapter 10 Acquisition of Property, Plant, and Equipment

- Concept of "depletion base" introduced in section on natural resources, and its link to inventory more fully explained.
- Restoration/asset retirement costs added as one of the types of capitalizable costs of natural resource properties.
- Likelihood of Canada requiring interest capitalization is raised due to IASB change to require this approach.

- Cash discounts differentiated from purchase discounts on inventory purchases.
- For nonmonetary exchanges, simplified into one general principle using fair values and, in limited circumstances, one exception using book values.
- Section on Contributed Assets restructured.

Chapter 11 Amortization, Impairment, and Disposition

- Comparison of Canadian and international GAAP with discussion of when changes are expected in Canadian standards.
- More explicit statement that a change in depreciation method is a change in prior estimates of the pattern in which the asset benefits are expected by the company—and therefore, treated as a change in estimate, i.e., prospectively
- Discussion about increasing charge method of amortization changed to indicate that it is appropriate only in very limited circumstances.
- Property, plant, and equipment to be disposed of *by sale* now covered under Impairment, instead of under Dispositions.
- The topic of assets to be disposed of *other than by sale* is no longer addressed separately as the accounting requirements are similar to those *held for use*.

Chapter 12 Goodwill and Other Intangible Assets

- Comparison of differences between Canadian and international GAAP and when changes are expected in Canadian standards are provided.
- Reduced usage of the term "deferred charges" and more use of the term "internally developed intangible assets."
- In-process R&D explained.

Acknowledgments

We thank the users of our seventh edition, including the many instructors, faculty and students who contributed to this revision through their comments and instructive criticism. Special thanks are extended to the reviewers of and contributors to our eighth edition manuscript and supplements.

Manuscript reviewers for this eighth edition were:

Wayne Campbell
Seneca College

Esther Deutsch
Ryerson University

Don Dougherty
Saint Mary's University

Helen Farkas
McMaster University

Ian Feltmate
Acadia University

George Fisher
Thomson Rivers University

Harold Greenspon
McGill University

Mary Heisz
University of Western Ontario

Wayne Irvine
Mount Royal College

Michael Kaine
Sheridan College

Doug Leatherdale
Georgian College

Bruce McConomy
Wilfrid Laurier University

David McConomy
Queen's University

Tom Pippy
Conestoga College

Wendy Roscoe
Concordia University

Don Smith
Georgian College

John Varga
George Brown College

Patricia Zima
Mohawk College

Appreciation is also extended to colleagues at the Rotman School of Management, University of Toronto and the Sobey School of Business, Saint Mary's University, who provided input, suggestions and support, especially Joel Amernic and Dick Chesley, who have provided inspiration through many high-spirited debates on financial reporting theory and practice, Peter Thomas, for his professionalism and wisdom; Dan Segal, for his unique perspective on teaching the material and his contribution to the ever-expanding body of knowledge (including case material); and Laura Cumming, whose thoughtful reading of the text and problems provided excellent input.

It takes many people and co-ordinated efforts to get an edition off the ground. Many thanks to the team at John Wiley and Sons Canada, Ltd., who are superb: Editorial Manager Karen Staudinger, who has been an integral part of the last four editions; Karen Bryan, Publishing Services Director, for her incredible efforts over this and previous editions; Elsa Passera-Berardi, Media Editor, for managing this increasingly important aspect of the text; and Aida Krneta, Marketing Manager. The editorial contributions of David Schwinghamer, Zofia Laubitz, and Alison Arnot are also very much appreciated. A special thank you goes to Daleara Hirjikaka, our Developmental Editor, who dealt with us on an almost daily basis and kept everything on track.

We are also very grateful for the efforts of Cécile Laurin, Maria Belanger, Helen Farkas, Patricia Zima, Andrea Chance, and Miguel Minutti who contributed so much to the related supplements.

We appreciate the continuing co-operation of the accounting standards group at the Canadian Institute of Chartered Accountants and of Ron Salole, Vice-President of Standards. The Director and Principals of the Accounting Standards Board have been as open and helpful as possible in all our dealings with them. A special thank you is owed for this eighth edition to Ian Hague and Kate Ward. We also thank the CICA itself for allowing us to quote from their materials and Stantec Inc. for permitting us to use its 2005 Annual Report for our specimen financial statements.

Finally, on the occasion of the 25th anniversary of Kieso in Canada, we want to remember and thank Bruce Irvine and Harold Silvester who, through the first five editions of this text, set such a strong foundation. Their enthusiasm for intermediate accounting and their sharing of it with so many students set a high standard for us to follow.

If this book helps teachers instill in their students an appreciation of the challenges, value, and limitations of accounting, if it encourages students to evaluate critically and understand financial accounting theory and practice, and if it prepares students for advanced study, professional examinations, and the successful and ethical pursuit of their careers in accounting or business, then we will have attained our objective.

Suggestions and comments from users of this book are always appreciated. We have striven to produce an error-free text, but if anything has slipped through the variety of checks undertaken, please let us know so that corrections can be made to subsequent printings.

Irene M. Wiecek
TORONTO, ONTARIO

Nicola M. Young
HALIFAX, NOVA SCOTIA

February 2007

BRIEF CONTENTS

CONTENTS

Financial Fallout

Five years after Enron collapsed in an accounting scandal that rocked the business world and forced changes to financial reporting requirements worldwide, the dust is finally beginning to settle for the doomed company's bankers.

After seeing their investments in Enron disappear, shareholders launched a $40-billion class action lawsuit against several banks that Enron worked with, including the Royal Bank of Canada, Toronto-Dominion Bank, and the Canadian Imperial Bank of Commerce. The CIBC is one of five banks that settled with the group of shareholders, paying out $2.4 billion. RBC and TD, on the other hand, decided to do battle in court and put aside $800 million to cover possible losses.

They were encouraged in July 2006 when a judge tossed out an Enron lawsuit against Barclays Bank PLC. The U.S. district court judge ruled that the investors had no claim against the London-based bank since the bank is not alleged to have deceived the public. Under U.S. securities laws, there is no private right of action for aiding and abetting.

While TD and RBC immediately applied to have their own cases dismissed, the judge said that she would look at each bank's case individually to determine whether it had violated any securities laws.

RBC and TD took part in Enron's deals in much the same way as Barclays. TD worked with Barclays and two other banks on several "prepay transactions" that Enron allegedly used to disguise billions of dollars in loans as commodity trades. CIBC and Barclays were among a group of banks involved in helping Enron set up "special purpose entities," which the company also allegedly used to disguise billions of dollars in loans.

Scandals like Enron and the years of financial fallout they create make it very clear that accounting standards are necessary. With accounting being watched over more carefully and the creation of a global set of accounting standards, perhaps situations like these will no longer occur. ■

Source: Andrew Willis and Paul Waldie, "RBC, TD Buoyed by Enron Ruling," *The Globe and Mail*, September 8, 2006.

chapter 1

The Canadian Financial Reporting Environment

Learning Objectives

After studying this chapter, you should be able to:

1. Describe the essential characteristics of accounting.
2. Explain how accounting makes it possible to use scarce resources more efficiently.
3. Explain the meaning of "stakeholder" and identify key stakeholders in financial reporting and what is at stake for each one.
4. Identify the objective of financial reporting.
5. Explain the notion of management bias in financial reporting.
6. Understand the importance of user needs in the financial reporting process.
7. Explain the need for accounting standards.
8. Identify the major entities that influence the standard-setting process and explain how they influence financial reporting.
9. Explain the meaning of generally accepted accounting principles (GAAP).
10. Explain the significance of professional judgement in applying GAAP.
11. Understand issues related to ethics and financial accounting.
12. Identify some of the challenges facing accounting.

Preview of Chapter 1

North American financial reporting systems are among the best in the world. Our commitment to keeping our financial reporting systems strong is as intense as ever, because in this changing business world, information must be relevant and reliable for our capital markets to work efficiently. In the past several years, our financial reporting systems have been overhauled and strengthened in important ways. This chapter explains the environment of financial reporting and the many factors that affect it.

The chapter is organized as follows:

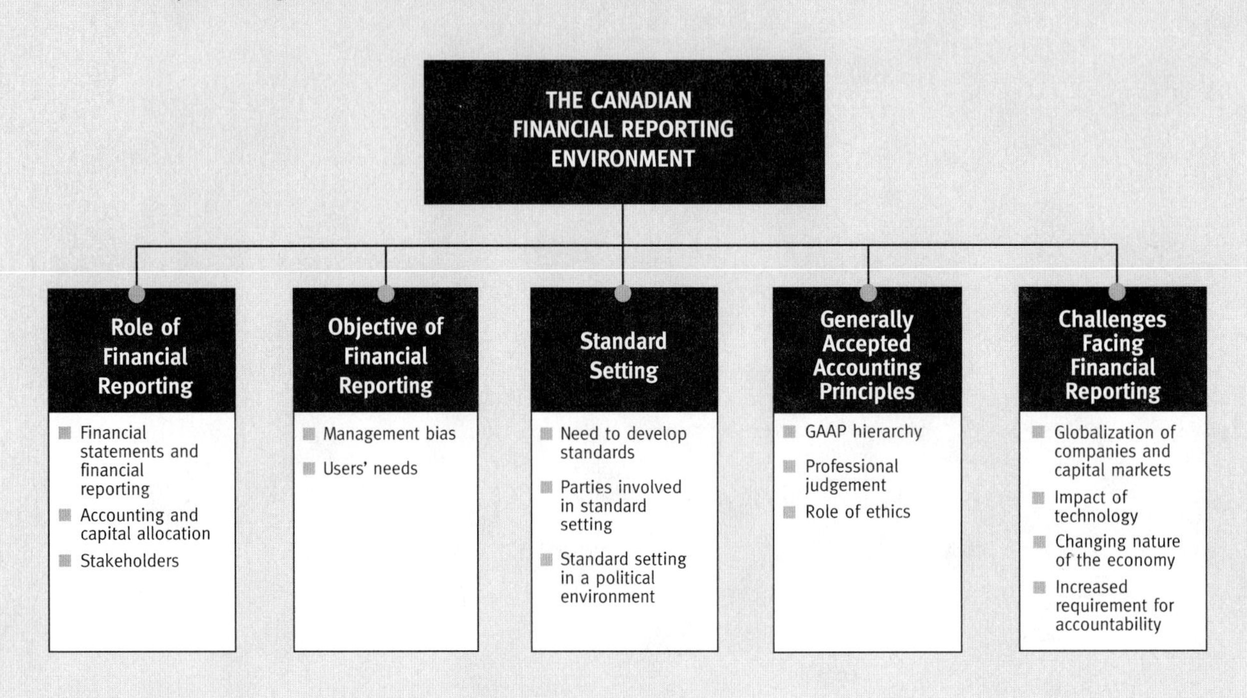

ROLE OF FINANCIAL REPORTING

Like other human activities and disciplines, accounting is largely a product of its environment. This environment includes conditions, restraints, and influences that are social, economic, political, and legal, which change over time. As a result, accounting objectives and practices are not the same today as they were in the past. **Accounting theory and practice have evolved and will continue to evolve to meet changing demands and influences.**

Over the past several years, the accounting landscape has changed dramatically, being shaped by such spectacular business failures as WorldCom Inc., Enron, and Arthur Andersen. The telecom giant WorldCom had pre-bankruptcy assets of over U.S. $100 billion and is the largest company to file for bankruptcy protection in U.S. history. Enron was an energy trader and at one time the seventh largest corporation in America. It was also the second largest company ever to file for bankruptcy protection in the U.S. Both

WorldCom and Enron misrepresented their financial position and results of operations in their financial statements. Andersen, meanwhile, was one of the five largest public accounting firms in the world. The firm ended up closing its doors in 2002 after it was charged with obstruction of justice relating to Enron, one of its largest clients at the time. The accounting profession is still dealing with the aftermath from these events.

Accounting is defined best by describing its three essential characteristics: it is the (1) **identification, measurement, and communication of financial information about** (2) **economic entities to** (3) **interested persons**. These characteristics have described accounting for hundreds of years. Yet, in the last 30 years, the size and complexity of economic entities have increased so much, and the interested persons have become so numerous and diverse, that the responsibility placed on the accounting profession is greater today than ever before.

1 Objective
Describe the essential characteristics of accounting. (3)

Financial Statements and Financial Reporting

Financial accounting (financial reporting) is the process that culminates in the preparation of financial reports that cover all of the enterprise's business activities and which are used by both **internal and external** parties. Users of these financial reports include investors, creditors, and others. In contrast, **managerial accounting** is the process of identifying, measuring, analyzing, and **communicating financial information** to **internal** decision-makers. This information may take varied forms, such as cost-benefit analyses and forecasts that management uses to plan, evaluate, and control an organization's operations.

Financial statements are the principal way of communicating financial information to those who are outside an enterprise. These statements give the firm's history, quantified in terms of money. The most frequently provided financial statements are (1) the **balance sheet**, (2) the **income statement**, (3) the **statement of cash flows**, and (4) the **statement of owners' or shareholders' equity**. In addition, **note disclosures** are an important part of each financial statement.

most freq provided fin stmt

Some financial information cannot be expressed in the financial statements or is better expressed through other means. Examples include the president's letter and supplementary schedules in the corporate annual report, prospectuses, reports filed with government agencies, news releases, management forecasts, and descriptions of an enterprise's social or environmental impact. Such information may be required by an authoritative pronouncement or regulatory rule[1] or custom, or because management wants to disclose it voluntarily. The main focus of this textbook is the basic financial statements.

Accounting and Capital Allocation

2 Objective
Explain how accounting makes it possible to use scarce resources more efficiently.

Because **resources** are limited, people try to conserve them, use them effectively, and identify and encourage those who can make efficient use of them. Through an **efficient use of resources**, our standard of living increases.

Markets, free enterprise, and competition determine whether a business will succeed and thrive. The accounting profession has the highly important responsibility of **measuring company performance** accurately and fairly on a timely basis. The information provided by accounting enables investors and creditors to **compare** the income and assets of companies and thus **assess the relative risks and returns** of different investment

[1] All public companies must disclose certain information under provincial securities law. This information is captured by the provincial securities commissions under the Canadian umbrella organization, the Canadian Securities Administrators (CSA), and is available electronically at www.sedar.com.

opportunities. Based on their assessments, investors and creditors can then channel their resources (i.e., invest in these companies or lend them money) more effectively. Illustration 1-1 shows the process of **capital allocation**.

Illustration 1-1
Capital Allocation Process

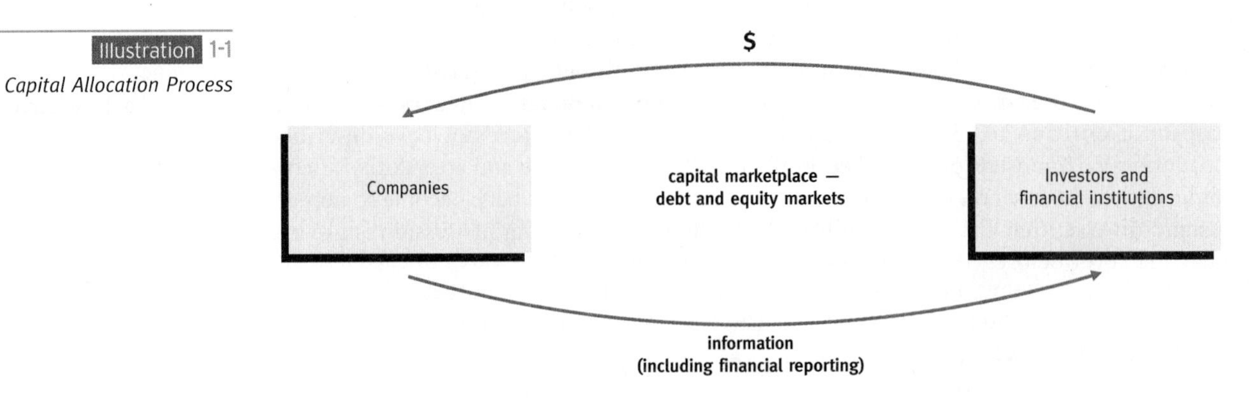

In Canada, the primary exchange mechanisms for allocating resources are **debt and equity markets**[2] as well as **financial institutions** such as banks.[3] The debt and equity marketplace includes both public stock markets/exchanges and private sources.

Illustration 1-2 shows the sources of capital in Canada for various stages of company growth.

Illustration 1-2
Sources of Capital

Financing Growth Companies

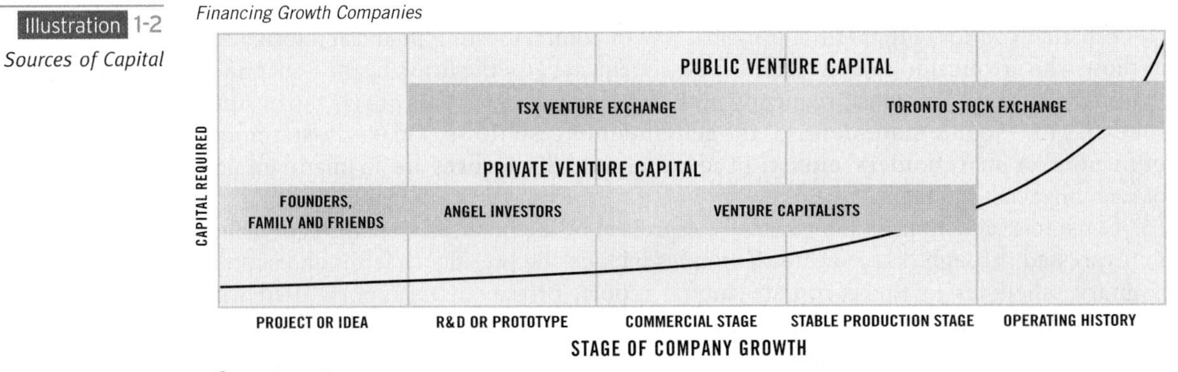

Source: www.tsx.com

An effective process of capital allocation is critical to a healthy economy as this promotes productivity, encourages innovation, and provides an efficient and liquid market for buying and selling securities and obtaining and granting credit.[4] Unreliable and irrelevant information leads to **poor capital allocation**, which has a negative impact on the securities markets and economic growth. The accounting numbers that companies report affect the **transfer of resources** among companies and individuals. Consider the fact that stock prices generally rise when positive news (including financial information) is expected

[2] The largest, most senior equity market in Canada is the Toronto Stock Exchange (TSX). The junior market—the TSX Venture Exchange (formerly the CDNX Stock Market)—was created in 2001 to handle startup companies. The Montreal Exchange, known as the Canadian Derivatives Exchange, is the main market for derivatives and futures trading.

[3] According to the Canadian Bankers Association website, based on total assets as at October 31, 2005, the six largest banks in Canada, from largest to smallest, are RBC Financial Group, TD Bank Financial Group, Scotiabank, Canadian Imperial Bank of Commerce, BMO Financial Group, and National Bank of Canada.

[4] AICPA Special Committee on Financial Reporting, "Improving Business Reporting: A Customer Focus," supplement in *Journal of Accountancy* (October 1994).

or released. In addition, **credit rating agencies** use accounting and other information to rate companies' financial stability.[5] This gives investors and creditors **additional independent information** to use when making decisions. For companies, a good rating can mean greater access to capital and at lower costs.

Stakeholders

3 Objective
Explain the meaning of "stakeholder" and identify key stakeholders in financial reporting and what is at stake for each one.

Stakeholders are parties who have something at risk in the financial reporting environment, e.g., their salary, job, investment, or reputation. Key stakeholders in the financial reporting environment include **traditional users** of financial information as well as others. In the stakeholder context, **users** may be more broadly defined to include not only parties who are relying directly on the financial information for resource allocation (such as investors and creditors) but also others who help in the efficient allocation of resources (such as financial analysts and regulators).

The broader definition of users includes anyone who **prepares, relies on, reviews, audits, or monitors financial information**. It includes investors, creditors, analysts, managers, employees, customers, suppliers, industry groups, unions, government departments and ministers, the public in general (e.g., consumer groups), regulatory agencies, other companies, and standard setters, as well as auditors, lawyers, and others. Illustration 1-3 shows the relationships among these stakeholders.

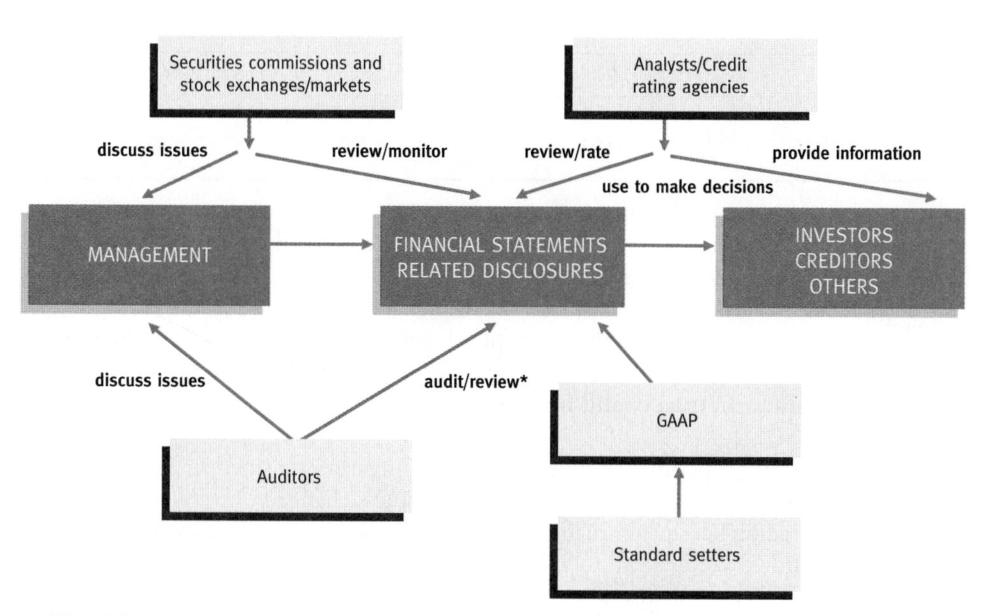

Illustration 1-3
Selected Key Stakeholders in the Financial Reporting Environment

Not all financial statements are required to be audited. In general, all companies whose shares or debt are **publicly traded must have an audit and therefore comply with GAAP. Other companies may have their statements audited and/or comply with GAAP depending on **user needs**.*

Various stakeholders have specific functions in the financial reporting environment. Company management **prepares** the financial statements. It has the best insight into the business and therefore knows what should be included in the financial statements. The statements are then **audited and reviewed** by auditors, who may discuss with management how economic events and transactions have been communicated in the financial statements. The value that auditors add to the statements lies in the auditors' independence.

[5] For example, institutions such as Dominion Bond Rating Service, Moody's, and Standard and Poor's rate issuers of bonds and preferred shares in the Canadian and global marketplaces.

They act on behalf of the shareholders to ensure that management is accounting properly for the economic transactions. The auditors also **review** the information to ensure that it reflects sound accounting choices.

Investors and creditors **rely on** the financial statements to make decisions. It is up to these parties to carefully examine the information given. Standard setters **set generally accepted accounting principles (GAAP),** which are often used to prepare the financial statements. GAAP helps **reduce management bias** by providing direction as to how events should be accounted for. Securities commissions and stock exchanges **monitor** the financial statements to ensure full and plain disclosure of material information and to determine whether the companies may continue to list their shares on stock exchanges. Finally, the credit rating agencies and analysts **monitor and analyze** the information produced by the company, looking for signs of change, i.e., an improved or weakened financial condition.

Illustration 1-4 identifies what is at stake for each stakeholder. This is not meant to be a complete list. Rather, it identifies the major stakeholder groups.

Illustration 1-4
What Is at Stake for Each Stakeholder?

STAKEHOLDER	WHAT IS AT STAKE?
Investors/creditors	Investment/loan
Management	Job, bonus, reputation, salary increase, access to capital markets by company
Securities commissions and stock exchanges	Reputation, effective and efficient capital marketplace
Analysts and credit rating agencies	Reputation, profits
Auditors	Reputation, profits (companies are their clients)
Standard setters	Reputation
Others	Various

As noted in Illustration 1-3, the system provides **checks and balances** to ensure that the people with capital—the investors and creditors—have good information to use when deciding where best to invest or allocate their capital. The system does not always work, however. Because the system involves people, human behaviour is often a key unpredictable variable. People often act in their own **self-interest** rather than in the **best interest of the capital marketplace, and by extension, the economy**.

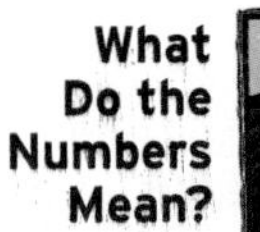

Consider the much-publicized case of Enron. Enron was formed in 1985 through a merger, and began its life as a pipeline company. Its business changed over the years as energy wholesaling and trading became more important than the pipeline operations. Revenues grew exponentially to more than U.S. $100 billion and the company reported profits of just under U.S. $1 billion by 2000. Its shares were also trading at over U.S. $80. All this came to a sudden stop when the company declared bankruptcy in December 2001 and its shares were delisted by the New York Stock Exchange in January 2002. Since then, thousands of people have been affected by the fall of Enron, losing investments, jobs, and pensions.

Arthur Andersen, one of the top five **public accounting firms** in the world, was a direct casualty of the Enron bankruptcy as it closed its offices later in 2002 after being convicted of obstructing justice in the government investigations that followed the Enron collapse. **Credit rating agencies** such as Moody's Investor Services and **analysts** also came under scrutiny. The government wanted to know why the rating agencies had not been able to determine much earlier that Enron was overextended.[6] Finally, **investment banks**

[6] In January 2002, a U.S. Governmental Affairs Committee launched a broad investigation into the collapse. This committee studied the role of stakeholders—mainly the watchdogs in the capital marketplace—to determine what went wrong.

such as Citigroup and J.P. Morgan Chase were criticized for helping Enron set up the very aggressive financing schemes that eventually led to its downfall.[7]

Why did the financial reporting system not function properly in this case? How did the capital marketplace allow so much capital to be channelled into a company that went bankrupt soon after? Where were the checks and balances? In hindsight, almost every player in the financial reporting system was at fault. **Self-interest** was a key factor.

Enron management overstated the company's financial health, thus personally benefiting from bonuses and stock options. The **auditors** gave the financial statements an unqualified audit report, indicating that Enron's financial statements were fairly presented. During the time that they were doing the audit, they also earned millions of dollars in consulting fees. Were they truly independent? The **analysts** and **credit rating agencies** did not recognize and signal that the company was financially unsound (or recognized it but did not signal it in a timely manner to the marketplace). Here also there was the issue of independence: many of the analysts worked for banks that were providing financing and were selling other services to Enron. Could the analysts be objective in assessing Enron when they were working for institutions that were earning large fees and other forms of income from the company?

The **Securities and Exchange Commission**, although it collected the financial information from the company on a timely basis, failed to detect any problem. Finally, the **investors and creditors** invested their capital without really understanding what they were investing in. They did not really understand the significant risk that they were taking. Most of these stakeholders were too excited about being involved with such a large, apparently successful company. They did not stop to ask whether Enron was just too good to be true. In hindsight, it was.

OBJECTIVE OF FINANCIAL REPORTING

4 Objective
Identify the objective of financial reporting.

To help establish a foundation for financial accounting and reporting, the accounting profession has put into words an overall **objective of financial reporting** by business enterprises. This is presented in Illustration 1-5.

Illustration 1-5
Objective of Financial Reporting

"The objective of financial statements is to communicate information that is useful to investors, members, contributors, creditors, and other users in making their resource allocation decisions and/or assessing management stewardship. Consequently, financial statements provide information about:

(a) an entity's economic resources, obligations, and equity/net assets;

(b) changes in an entity's economic resources, obligations, and equity/net assets; and

(c) the economic performance of the entity."

Source: *CICA Handbook*, Section 1000.15

International Insight

The objectives of financial reporting are different from nation to nation. Historically, the primary objective of accounting in many continental European nations and in Japan was conformity with the law. In contrast, Canada, the U.S., and countries following the new international accounting standards hold the view that the main objective is to provide information for investors. Insights into international standards and practices will be presented throughout the text.

Note the emphasis on **resource (or capital) allocation** decisions and the **assessment of management stewardship.**[8] In order to make resource allocation decisions, users look for information about **an enterprise's ability to earn income and generate future cash flows**, as these are needed to meet obligations and generate a return on investment. In order to assess management stewardship, users traditionally look at **historical data** to **determine (in hindsight)** whether the decisions that management made in obtaining and using the company's resources are acceptable and **optimize shareholder wealth and**

[7] *U.S. Senate Permanent Subcommittee on Investigations Staff Report on Fishtail, Bacchus, Sundance and Slapshot: Four Enron Transactions Funded and Facilitated by U.S. Financial Institutions*, (December 11, 2002).

[8] Management's duty to manage assets with care and trust is also called its fiduciary responsibility.

value. Users may also try to **predict** the impact of current management decisions on the company's future financial health.

Management Bias

As previously mentioned, company **management** is responsible for preparing the financial statements and normally states this fact at the beginning of the financial statements. At Stantec Inc., Tony Franceschini, president and chief executive officer, and Tom Wilson, vice president and chief financial officer, have both signed such a statement for the Stantec financial statements, which are shown in Appendix 5B. This statement is usually included at the beginning of the financial statements, just before the auditors' report.

Increasingly, companies have been accused of preparing **biased information**, which is information that presents the company in its best light, as in the Enron case mentioned earlier. This is sometimes referred to as **aggressive financial reporting** (as compared with **conservative financial reporting**) and might take the form of overstated assets and/or net income, understated liabilities and/or expenses, or carefully selected note disclosures that emphasize only positive events.[9]

There are many reasons why financial statements might be affected by management bias. These include the fact that the statements give information to users about **management stewardship**, as previously mentioned, and the fact that managers are often compensated (i.e., paid) based on the company's net income or share value. There is also a strong desire to **meet financial analysts' expectations** as this affects a company's access to capital markets. Financial analysts monitor earnings announcements carefully and compare them with their earlier expectations. They and others (including certain stock markets) post what they refer to as "**earnings surprises**" each day on their websites. Earnings surprises occur when a company reports net income figures that are different from what the market expects (prior expectations). The focus is on net income or earnings. If net income is lower than expected, this is a negative earnings surprise and the market will generally react unfavourably, resulting in declining share prices.[10]

Objective 5
Explain the notion of management bias in financial reporting.

Another reason that management could have for financial reporting bias is **to comply with contracts** that the company has. Many lending agreements and contracts require that certain benchmarks be met, and these often relate to financial stability or liquidity. These requirements often state that the company must maintain certain minimum financial ratios. The lenders then monitor if the company is respecting the contract by reviewing periodic financial statements that the company must submit.

For instance, according to note 8 in the financial statements of Stantec Inc. (Appendix 5B), the company recently signed a revolving credit facility agreement with its bank for $160 million. Under the terms of the agreement, the company must maintain certain debt to earnings and earnings to debt service ratios or the credit facility will be

[9] David Brown, chairman of the Ontario Securities Commission (OSC), spoke at length on this topic in a speech in 1999 entitled "Public Accounting at a Crossroads." Arthur Levitt, chair of the Securities and Exchange Commission (SEC), discussed his concerns over this issue in "Numbers Game," a major address to New York University in 1998. Both the OSC and the SEC review financial statements and financial reporting practices to ensure that investors have "full and plain disclosure" of all material facts that are needed to make investment decisions. In their speeches, Mr. Brown and Mr. Levitt both cited specific cases where they felt that financial reporting practices were problematic.

[10] For instance, for quarterly earnings numbers released on July 26, 2006, the Nasdaq website notes that there were 97 positive earnings surprises and 43 negative earnings surprises. Three companies met the expectations of analysts (no surprise). Positive earnings surprises included Corning Inc. and Altria Group Inc. Selected negative earnings surprises noted for the same day included Colgate-Palmolive Company and 3M Company, with Colgate missing its target by less than three-tenths of one cent.

withdrawn or changed. These ratios and the numbers that go into calculating them are therefore very sensitive and key numbers for the company.

Users' Needs

6 Objective
Understand the importance of user needs in the financial reporting process.

The objective of financial reporting is to **provide useful information to users.** As noted in Illustration 1-3, investors and creditors are among the key users of financial information. Providing information that is useful to users is a challenging task since they have **different needs and levels of knowledge. Institutional investors**[11] hold an increasing percentage of equity share holdings[12] and generally put a lot of their resources into managing their investment portfolios. Can those who prepare financial information therefore assume that the average individual investor has the same needs and knowledge level as an institutional investor when it comes to business and financial reporting? Likely not.

Meeting all user needs is made more challenging when linked with the potential for management bias. If the financial statements are aggressively prepared, they might be misleading to potential investors, who may want to see a company in its worst light **before** they decide to invest (as opposed to after). Generally accepted accounting principles assume that users have a **reasonable knowledge** of business and accounting.

STANDARD SETTING

Need to Develop Standards

7 Objective
Explain the need for accounting standards.

The main controversy in financial reporting is this: "Whose rules should we play by, and what should they be?" The answer is not immediately clear. This is because the users of financial statements have both **coinciding and conflicting needs** for information of various types. A **single set** of general-purpose financial statements is therefore prepared with the **expectation** that the majority of these needs will be met by the statements. These statements are also expected to present the enterprise's financial operations fairly.

As a result, accounting professions in various countries have tried to develop a **set of standards** that are **generally accepted** and **universally practised.** Without these standards, each enterprise would have to develop its own standards, and readers of financial statements would have to become familiar with every company's particular accounting and reporting practices. It would be almost impossible to prepare statements that could be compared.

This common set of standards and procedures is called **generally accepted accounting principles (GAAP).** The term "generally accepted" means either that an

---

[11] Institutional investors are corporate investors such as insurance companies, pension plans, mutual funds, and others. They are considered a separate class of investors because of their size and financial expertise, and the large size of the investments that they hold in other companies. In general, for the reasons just mentioned, institutional investors have greater power than the average investor.

[12] The Canadian Coalition for Good Governance (CCGG) is a group of institutional investors that controls over $940 billion in investments (up from $350 billion in 2003). Its members include many significant pension funds in Canada such as Alberta Teachers' Retirement Fund, Ontario Teachers' Pension Plan, OPSEU Pension Trust, and Ontario Municipal Employees Retirement Board, as well as many significant mutual funds and financial institutions such as Mackenzie Financial Corp., RBC Asset Management Inc., and TD Asset Management Inc. According to its website (www.ccgg.ca), CCGG was started in 2002 "to represent Canadian institutional shareholders in the promotion of corporate governance practices that best align the interests of boards and management with those of the shareholder." By working together, these shareholders, who represent many individual shareholders, can initiate positive change.

authoritative rule-making body in accounting has created a reporting principle in a particular area or that, over time, a specific practice has been accepted as appropriate because it is used universally.[13] Although principles and practices have resulted in both debate and criticism, most members of the financial community recognize them as the standards that over time have proven to be most useful. A more detailed discussion of GAAP is presented later in this chapter.

Parties Involved in Standard Setting

Objective 8
Identify the major entities that influence the standard-setting process and explain how they influence financial reporting.

Before 1900, single ownership was the most common form of business organization in our economy. Financial reports emphasized **solvency and liquidity** and were only for **internal use** or for banks and other lending institutions to examine. From 1900 to 1929, the growth of large corporations and their absentee ownership led to **increasing investment and speculation** in corporate stock. When the stock market crashed in 1929, this contributed to the Great Depression. These events emphasized the need for **standardized and increased corporate disclosures** that would allow shareholders to make informed decisions.

Several organizations play a role in developing financial reporting standards in Canada. The major organizations are:

1. Canadian Institute of Chartered Accountants (CICA) www.cica.ca
2. Provincial securities commissions such as the Ontario Securities Commission (OSC) www.osc.gov.on.ca
3. The Financial Accounting Standards Board (FASB) www.fasb.org and the Securities and Exchange Commission (SEC) www.sec.gov
4. International Accounting Standards Board (IASB) www.iasb.org

1. Canadian Institute of Chartered Accountants (CICA)

International Insight

The Canadian and U.S. legal systems are based on English common law, in which the government generally allows professionals to make the rules. These rules (standards) are therefore developed in the private sector. In contrast, some countries follow codified law, which leads to government-run accounting systems.

The first official recommendations on standards of financial statement disclosure were not published until 1946. Today, the **Accounting Standards Board (AcSB)** of the **Canadian Institute of Chartered Accountants (CICA)** has primary responsibility for setting GAAP in Canada[14] and produces a variety of authoritative material, including the most important source of GAAP, the ***CICA Handbook***. The *CICA Handbook* was originally published in 1968 and now consists of several volumes of accounting and assurance guidance.[15]

The AcSB's mission is as follows:

> to contribute to enhanced decision-making by continuously improving the quality of financial and other information about organizational performance reported by Canadian entities including profit oriented enterprises and not-for-profit organizations. The AcSB shall serve the public interest by developing and establishing standards and guidance

[13] The terms "principle" and "standard" are used interchangeably in practice and throughout this textbook.

[14] The *Canada Business Corporations Act and Regulations* (CBCA) Part XIV Financial Disclosure and Part 8 of the regulation (paras. 70 and 71), as well as provincial corporations acts, require that most companies incorporated under these acts prepare financial statements in accordance with GAAP as prepared by the CICA.

[15] The *Handbook* is also available to students in CD format and to members on-line at www.cica.ca. With the rapid pace of change in standard setting, most members use the on-line source as their main source of GAAP.

governing financial accounting and reporting domestically and by contributing to the development of internationally accepted standards.[16]

Two basic premises underlie the process of establishing financial accounting standards: (1) the AcSB should **respond to the needs and viewpoints** of the **entire economic community**, not just the public accounting profession, and (2) it should **operate in full public view** through a "**due process**" system that gives interested persons enough opportunity to make their views known. The **Accounting Standards Oversight Council (AcSOC)** oversees AcSB activities: its activities include setting the agenda and reporting to the public, among other things. Members of the AcSB and the AcSOC come from a wide range of groups that are interested or involved in the financial reporting process.[17]

Illustration 1-6
Evolution of a New or Revised Standard

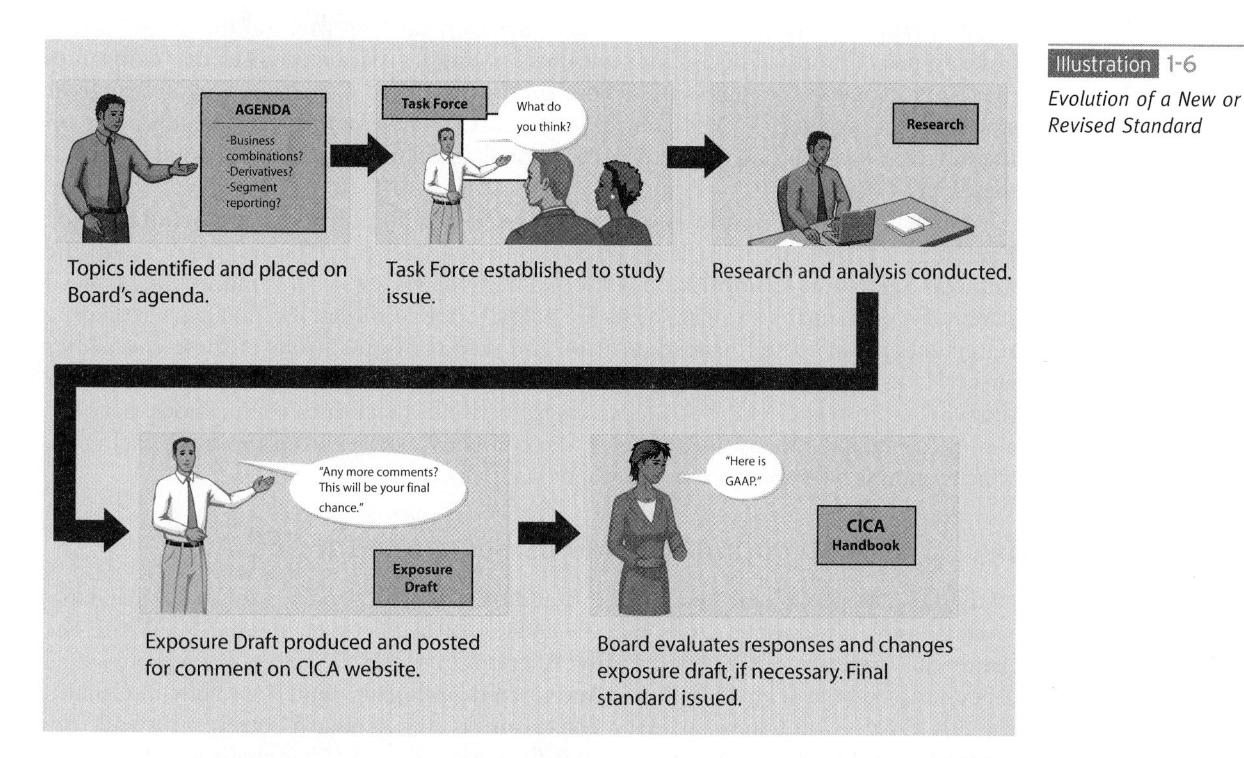

The steps in Illustration 1-6 show the evolution of a typical addition or amendment to the *CICA Handbook*.

Due process, by definition, is a lengthy process. To react more quickly to current financial reporting issues, the AcSB established the **Emerging Issues Committee (EIC)**. The EIC is a standing committee which meets several times each year. It studies issues that are presented to it by interested parties, such as companies that need a ruling on an accounting issue that may not be in the *Handbook*. It also studies and clarifies *Handbook* wording and how and when rules apply. After careful consideration, the EIC produces **EIC Abstracts**, which are then incorporated into the *Handbook*. EIC Abstracts are considered a major source of GAAP.

[16] www.acsbcanada.org

[17] According to the CICA website, AcSOC membership consists of senior members from business, finance, government, academe, the accounting and legal professions, regulators, and the financial analyst community. The members have a broad perspective on the complex issues facing standard setters. The goal is to achieve full representation across the spectrum of stakeholders.

2. Provincial Securities Commissions

International Insight

The International Organization of Securities Commissions (IOSCO) is a group of more than 100 securities regulatory agencies or securities exchanges from all over the world. IOSCO has existed since 1987. Collectively, its members represent a large proportion of the world's capital markets.

Provincial securities commissions[18] oversee and monitor the capital marketplace. They ensure that participants in the capital markets (e.g., companies, auditors, brokers and dealers, and investors) respect securities law and legislation so that, ultimately, the marketplace is fair. For instance, the British Columbia Securities Commission (www.bcsc.bc.ca) acknowledges that its mission is to protect and promote the public interest by fostering:

- A securities market that is fair and warrants public confidence.
- A dynamic and competitive securities industry that provides investment opportunities and access to capital.

As part of ensuring that investors have access to the information that they need in order to make informed decisions, securities law and legislation requires that companies that issue shares to the public and whose shares trade on a Canadian stock exchange or stock market produce GAAP financial statements.[19] The commissions generally rely on the CICA to develop GAAP and on professional accountants to use sound judgement as they apply GAAP.

Ontario is home to the largest stock exchange in Canada, the **Toronto Stock Exchange (TSX)**, and most large public companies are therefore registered with the **Ontario Securities Commission (OSC)**. The OSC reviews and monitors the financial statements of companies whose shares are publicly traded so that it can judge whether the statements present the financial position and results of operations of these companies fairly.[20] It also issues its own disclosure requirements, which inform companies about how the OSC interprets GAAP.[21] Stock exchanges, as well as securities commissions, have the ability to fine a company and/or delist the company's shares from the stock exchange, which removes a company's access to capital markets.

3. Financial Accounting Standards Board and the SEC

In the U.S., the **Financial Accounting Standards Board (FASB)** is the major standard-setting body, although it does not have final authority over standards. While the **American Institute of Certified Public Accountants (AICPA)** is the main professional accounting body for Certified Public Accountants, unlike its equivalent body in Canada, the AICPA does not have primary responsibility for standard setting—instead, the **Securities and Exchange Commission (SEC)** does. The SEC has confirmed its support

---

[18] In Canada, securities regulation is carried out by each province, with each of the 10 provinces and three territories being responsible for the companies in its jurisdiction. Many critics feel that this is cumbersome and costly, and are therefore lobbying for a national securities commission. There has been some movement in this direction. The provincial and territorial regulators have formed the Canadian Securities Administrators (CSA). The CSA is mainly responsible for developing a harmonized approach to securities regulation across the country (www.csa-acvm.ca). For now, the CSA collects and archives all filings that are required under the securities regulations of each province and territory (www.sedar.com).

[19] For instance, *Ontario Securities Act*, Sections 75 to 83.

[20] The OSC has a Continuous Disclosure Team that regularly reviews public companies' financial statements and other regulatory findings. The team plans to review each company at least every four years. Results of the review are published on the OSC website.

[21] For instance, Rules 51-501 and 52-501 were issued in 2000 and deal with disclosures for annual and interim financial statements. In 2002, Staff Accounting Notice 52-303 on "Non-GAAP Earnings Measures" was issued.

for the FASB by stating that financial statements which conform to FASB standards will be presumed to have substantial authoritative support. The SEC has also indicated in its reports to the U.S. government that it continues to believe that the private sector should stay responsible for establishing and improving accounting standards, although the commission must oversee any changes. Like the Canadian securities commissions, it also indicates what its position is on various financial reporting issues through what it calls Financial Reporting Releases.

The FASB has a substantial impact on Canadian financial reporting. Firstly, since Canadian GAAP is based on principles and is fairly open to interpretation, **accounting professionals often rely on the more rule-oriented, specific guidance** noted in the FASB pronouncements. Secondly, many Canadian companies are also listed on U.S. stock markets and exchanges such as Nasdaq (National Association of Securities Dealers Automated Quotation) and the NYSE (New York Stock Exchange). To be listed on a U.S. exchange, these companies **must follow U.S. GAAP** or at least provide a reconciliation between Canadian and U.S. GAAP in their financial statements. As we move toward international harmonization in accounting standards, the U.S. standards will continue to influence Canadian and international standards due to the significant capital pool of these markets.[22]

4. International Accounting Standards Board (IASB)

Most countries agree that more uniform standards are needed. As a result, the International Accounting Standards Committee (IASC) was formed in 1973 to try to lessen the areas of difference. The IASC's objective in terms of standard setting was to work generally to improve and harmonize regulations, accounting standards, and procedures relating to the presentation of financial statements. Eliminating differences is not easy: the financial reporting objectives in each country are different; the institutional structures are often not comparable; and there are strong national tendencies in most countries. Nevertheless, much progress has been made since the IASC's early days. In 2001, a new **International Accounting Standards Board (IASB)** was created. Its aims are as follows:

(a) to develop, in the public interest, a single set of high-quality, understandable, and enforceable global accounting standards that require high-quality, transparent, and comparable information in financial statements and other financial reporting to help participants in the world's capital markets and other users make economic decisions;

(b) to promote the use and rigorous application of those standards;

(c) in fulfilling the objectives associated with (a) and (b), to take account of, as appropriate, the special needs of small and medium-sized entities and emerging economies; and

(d) to bring about convergence of national accounting standards and International Financial Reporting Standards (IFRS) to high-quality solutions.

The IASB is quickly becoming the dominant standard-setting body in the world. By the year 2005, over 7,000 companies in over 100 countries had adopted IASB standards. Illustration 1-7 shows the countries that have adopted or permit the use of IFRS and the countries that are working towards convergence.

---

[22] In October 2002, the FASB and IASB signed an agreement (the Norwalk Agreement) which formalizes their commitment to converge U.S. and international accounting standards. In the mean time, Canadian companies who list shares on a U.S. exchange/stock market are allowed to report their financial statements in accordance with U.S. GAAP (subject to any reporting requirements under the company's incorporating legislation) per OSC National Instrument 52-107.

Illustration 1-7
Countries That Allow or Use IFRS or Are Seeking Convergence

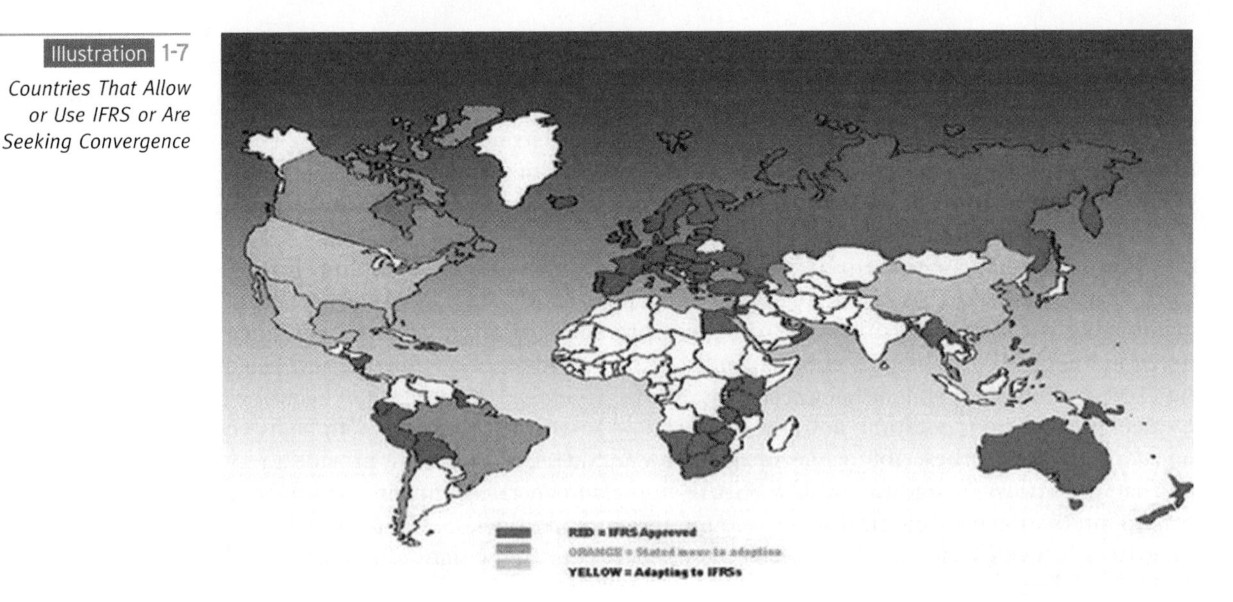

In its January 2006 Strategic Plan, the Canadian AcSB outlined separate strategies for three major categories of reporting issuers as follows:

Publicly accountable issuers—adoption of IFRS by 2011

Non–publicly accountable issuers—complete further research into user needs. In the meantime, these entities will continue to follow Canadian GAAP, including the differential reporting option (*CICA Handbook*, Section 1300)

Not-for-profit organizations—further consultation with the not-for-profit sector to determine whether they should follow IFRS or the same GAAP as non–publicly accountable enterprises

For the short term, Canadian GAAP will continue to exist in its present form. By 2011, however, it will change quite dramatically, as noted above. In the meantime, the AcSB is following a convergence strategy which will ensure that Canadian GAAP is converging with IFRS over the next few years. For publicly accountable enterprises, this means that the principles should be the same or close. Thus, by the time of the switchover to IFRS, while the *CICA Handbook* will then be an IFRS handbook, the content should be very similar to Canadian GAAP.

Expanded discussion of International Accounting
www.wiley.com/canada/kieso

Throughout this textbook, international considerations are presented to help you understand the international reporting environment.

Standard Setting in a Political Environment

When it comes to influencing the development of accounting standards, the most powerful force may be the stakeholder. Standard-setting stakeholders are the parties who are most interested in or affected by accounting standards, rules, and procedures. Like lobbyists in the provincial and national government arena, stakeholders play a significant role. **Accounting standards result as much from political action as they do from careful logic or empirical findings.** As part of its mandate, the AcSB includes all stakeholders as its members, giving them a **formal voice** in the process. Furthermore, through due process, all interested parties can comment on proposed changes or new standards.

Stakeholders may want particular economic events to be accounted for or reported in a particular way, and they fight hard to get what they want. They know that the most effective way to influence the standards that dictate accounting practice is to participate in formulating them or to try to influence or persuade the formulator.

Should politics play a role in setting financial accounting and reporting standards? The AcSB does not exist in isolation. Standard setting is part of the real world, and it cannot escape politics and political pressures. That is not to say that politics in standard setting is necessarily bad. Since many accounting standards do have economic consequences,[23] it is not surprising that special interest groups become vocal and critical (some supporting, some opposing) when standards are being formulated. Given this reality, a standard-setting body must pay attention to the economic consequences of its actions; at the same time, however, it should not issue pronouncements that are motivated mainly by politics. While paying attention to its constituencies, the AcSB should base its standards on sound research and a conceptual framework that is grounded in economic reality.

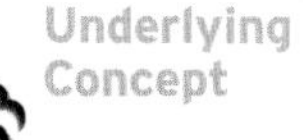

Underlying Concept

Options issued under ESOPS are stock options in **legal form**; however, many argue that the **economic substance** is that they are operating costs. They should therefore be recorded as a payroll expense.

An example of an accounting issue that has an economic consequence is the turmoil caused by employee stock option plan (ESOP) accounting. Historically, stock options issued under ESOPs have been treated as **capital transactions** and the related accounting therefore **did not affect net income**. More recently, however, the profession has supported treating options issued under these plans as **operating transactions** since they represent employee remuneration. In many cases, these plans provide benefits instead of a salary, and since salary is recorded as an **expense**, it is logical to record ESOPs as an expense.

Initially, when the AcSB issued the new *Handbook* Section 3870 on stock-based compensation, it allowed a **choice** in the way the options were accounted for—it **did not mandate treating the related costs as operating transactions**. This was due to the tremendous pressure put on the AcSB by companies that felt that expensing these options would affect their net income and, because of this, their ability to raise capital and its cost. Many felt that the costs associated with the options were not operating costs and therefore should not have an impact on the income statement. The AcSB has since revised this section to **mandate expensing costs associated with stock options**. With the current focus on transparency in financial reporting, many stakeholders are now more willing to accept this position.

GENERALLY ACCEPTED ACCOUNTING PRINCIPLES

9 Objective
Explain the meaning of generally accepted accounting principles (GAAP).

GAAP as developed by the AcSB has significant authoritative support through the Canadian and provincial business corporations acts and through securities legislation also. All companies whose shares or debt is traded in a public market must follow GAAP. Most other incorporated companies also follow GAAP as it gives the most useful information.

[23] "Economic consequences" in this context means the impact of accounting reports on the wealth positions of issuers and users of financial information and the decision-making behaviour resulting from that impact. The resulting behaviour of these individuals and groups could have harmful financial effects on the providers of the financial information (enterprises). For a more detailed discussion of this phenomenon, see Stephen A. Zeff, "The Rise of Economic Consequences," *Journal of Accountancy*, (December 1978), pp. 56–63.

GAAP Hierarchy

GAAP includes **not only specific rules, practices, and procedures** for particular circumstances but also **broad principles and conventions that apply generally**, including underlying concepts. GAAP is divided into **primary sources** and **other sources**, which is known as the **GAAP hierarchy**. Based on *Handbook* Section 1100, the **primary** sources of GAAP (in descending order of authority) are as follows:

- ***Handbook* Sections** 1300 to 4460, including Appendices and Board Notices[24]
- **Accounting Guidelines**, including Appendices and Board Notices
- **Background Information** and **Basis for Conclusions** documents, including Appendices
- Abstracts of Issues discussed by the Emerging Issues Committee (**EIC Abstracts**), including Appendices
- Illustrative examples of those pronouncements noted above
- **Implementation Guides** authorized by the Board

Other sources noted in Section 1100 include:

- **Pronouncements** by accounting standard-setting bodies in other jurisdictions
- **Research studies**
- Accounting **textbooks, journals, studies, and articles**
- Other

In general, primary sources must be looked at **first** for how to treat an issue. If primary sources do not deal with the specific issue, the entity should use accounting policies that are **consistent with the primary sources** as well as the concepts in Section 1000 (the **conceptual framework**). As business is constantly changing and new business transactions and contracts are regularly being entered into, the other listed sources are also important sources of GAAP.

Professional Judgement

Objective 10
Explain the significance of professional judgement in applying GAAP.

Professional judgement plays an especially important role in Canada. This is due to the basic philosophy of Canadian accountants on standard setting: the idea that **there cannot be a rule for every situation**. Canadian standards are therefore based primarily on **general principles** rather than **specific rules**. The basic premise is that professional accountants with significant education and experience will be able to apply these principles appropriately to any situation.

Role of Ethics

Objective 11
Understand issues related to ethics and financial accounting.

In accounting, as in other areas of business, **ethical dilemmas** are common. Some of these dilemmas are simple and easy to resolve. Many, however, are complex, and solutions are not obvious. Management biases—either internally prompted (e.g., to maximize bonuses)

[24] Board Notices, Background Information, Basis for Conclusion, and Implementation Guide documents have not technically been part of the *Handbook* in the past. Since the *Handbook* is now available electronically, this means that an expanded body of knowledge can now be made available on CD or on the CICA website. By including these other sources as primary sources of GAAP, the body of knowledge has expanded significantly and will continue to do so.

or externally prompted (e.g., to meet analysts' earnings expectations)—are the starting point of many ethical dilemmas. These biases sometimes lead to an emphasis on short-term results over long-term results and place accountants (both inside and outside the company) in an environment of conflict and pressure. Basic questions such as "Is this way of communicating financial information transparent?", "Does it provide useful information?", and "What should I do in this circumstance?" cannot always be answered by simply staying with GAAP or following the rules of the profession. Technical competence is not enough when decisions have an ethical side.

Doing the **right thing** and making the right decision is not always easy. What is right is not always evident and the pressures to "bend the rules," "play the game," or "just ignore it" can be considerable. In these cases, self-interest must be balanced with the interests of others. The decision is more difficult because no consensus has emerged among business professionals as to what constitutes a comprehensive ethical system.

Expanded discussion of Ethical Issues in Financial Accounting

www.wiley.com/canada/kieso

This whole process of **ethical sensitivity** and choosing among alternatives can also be complicated by time pressures, job pressures, client pressures, personal pressures, and peer pressure. Throughout this textbook, ethical considerations are presented to make you aware of the types of situations that you may encounter in your professional responsibility.

CHALLENGES FACING FINANCIAL REPORTING

12 Objective
Identify some of the challenges facing accounting.

In North America, we have the most liquid, deep, secure, and efficient public capital markets of any country at any time in history. One reason for this success is that our financial statements and related disclosures have captured and organized financial information in a useful and reliable way. However, much still needs to be done. During 2001 and 2002, the future of the capital market system was challenged by several major corporate scandals, as mentioned earlier in this chapter. The resulting turmoil gave all stakeholders a chance to re-examine their roles in the capital marketplace and to question if and how they add value to the system.

In the United States, where many of the problems occurred, the end result was to increase government regulation in the capital marketplace. The *Sarbanes-Oxley Act* **(SOX)**, enacted in 2002, gave more resources to the SEC to fight fraud and poor reporting practices.[25] The SEC was able to **increase its policing efforts** and approve **new auditor independence rules** and **materiality guidelines** for financial reporting. In addition, the SOX introduced sweeping changes to the institutional structure of the accounting profession. The following are some of the legislation's key provisions:

- An accounting oversight board was established and given oversight and enforcement authority. It was mandated to establish auditing, quality control, and independence standards and rules, and is known as the **Public Company Accounting Oversight Board** or **PCAOB**.
- Stronger **independence rules** were made for auditors. Audit partners, for example, are required to rotate every five years.
- CEOs and CFOs must **forfeit bonuses and profits** if there is an accounting restatement.
- CEOs and CFOs are required to **certify** that the financial statements and company disclosures are appropriate and fairly presented.
- Company management must report on **the effectiveness of the financial reporting internal control systems** and the auditors must assess and report on these internal controls.

[25] *Sarbanes-Oxley Act of 2002*, H. R. Rep. No. 107-610 (2002).

- **Audit committees** need independent members and members with financial expertise.
- Companies must disclose whether they have a **code of ethics** for their senior financial officers.

Stakeholders in the capital marketplace were faced with the question of whether similar reforms should be put in place in Canada. Companies that issue shares in the United States are bound by the SOX[26] and these companies therefore have no choice. Many stakeholders feel that unless Canada matches the standard set by SOX, Canadian capital markets will be seen as inferior. As a result, many of the SOX requirements have now been put in place, or are soon to be put in place, as follows:

- The **Canadian Public Accountability Board** (www.cpab-ccrc.ca) has been formed to look after similar issues as the PCAOB.
- The **OSC** has issued rules that, among other things, require company management to take responsibility for the appropriateness and fairness of the financial statements; public companies to have independent audit committees; and public accounting firms to be subject to the Canadian Public Accountability Board.[27]
- The **CSA** has issued a harmonized statement that requires much greater disclosures, including ratings from rating agencies, payments by companies to stock promoters, legal proceedings, and details about directors, including their previous involvement with bankrupt companies.[28]
- The **province of Ontario** has made amendments to its *Securities Act*.
- A **parliamentary committee of the federal government** issued a report recommending that similar regulatory reforms be introduced into federal legislation.

The impact of these reforms on the North American capital marketplace has been to put **more emphasis on government regulation** and less on **self-regulation**.

Globalization of Companies and Capital Markets

Many companies list on foreign stock exchanges. Larger stock exchanges are encouraging these listings as on-line trading has made these markets (and through the markets, the companies) more accessible to investors. Trading now happens around the clock. The move is thus toward global markets and global investors. The financial reporting environment is no longer limited by Canadian borders and is not simply influenced by Canadian stakeholders.

As mentioned in this chapter, Canadian, U.S., and international accounting standards are becoming increasingly interrelated. All parties are committed to a convergence of standards, but there are still many issues that standard setters must deal with. One key issue is the **principles versus rules** debate regarding GAAP.

The **United States uses a rules-based approach**. In a rules-based approach—much like the Canadian tax system—there is a rule for most things. The result is that the body of knowledge is significantly larger. There is also a tendency for companies to interpret the rules literally. Many companies take the view that if there is no rule for a particular situation, they are free to choose whatever treatment they think is appropriate. Similarly, many believe that as long as they comply with a rule, even in a narrow sense, they are in accordance with GAAP. Unfortunately, this does not always provide the best information for users.

In the past, the AcSB had been harmonizing with U.S. standards, which resulted in much of the U.S. wording being used in current Canadian GAAP. Thus, **Canadian GAAP**

[26] *Sarbanes-Oxley Act of 2002*, Section 106 (2002).

[27] OSC Multilateral Instrument 52-109, 52-110, and 52-108.

[28] CSA revised National Instrument 51-102, "Continuous Disclosure Obligations."

as it now stands is a mixture of the principle-and rule-based approaches. Since the IASB standards are more principles-based, Canadian GAAP (for public companies at least) will return toward a principles-based approach by 2011.[29]

Impact of Technology

Accountants are **providers of information.** They **identify, measure, and communicate useful information to users.** Technology affects this process in many profound ways. In its Report of the Inter-Institute Vision Task Force, the CICA concluded that we are presently in the third wave of computer technology. The first wave related to mainframes and the second wave related to personal computers. The third wave is driven by the use of networks and a convergence of computers and telecommunications technologies. Companies are now connected electronically to their banks, their suppliers, and regulatory agencies. The task force notes that in this third wave, automation focuses on stakeholders, distribution, and consumption. This gives stakeholders easy access to a significant amount of very timely company information.

As technology continues to advance at a dramatic pace, giving users **greater access to more and more information more and more rapidly**, the requirement for information that is more timely than annual and quarterly financial statements will rise sharply. Will this lead to **on-line real-time and/or continuous reporting**? Will this make users rely less on annual financial statements because they are not as timely and therefore relevant? Will this change the role of the public accountant?

The Internet's flexibility allows users to take advantage of tools such as search engines and hyperlinks and quickly find related information about a company. Financial reports are more relevant because the Internet allows companies to disclose more detail, which the user can then aggregate and analyze. From the company's perspective, providing information over the Internet gives the company access to a much larger group of users. Information can also be targeted to specific users, and costs are greatly reduced as well.

Some of the main drawbacks concern accessibility: will all users have the knowledge and ability to access the information? Equal access is certainly important for a fair playing field. Another issue is the quality and reliability of the information, especially since the information may not be audited. Would certain sites and content be more reliable than others? Finally, would making information available in this way leave companies open to computer hackers?

A continuous reporting model is already being developed in the capital markets arena. Securities commissions and stock markets already require ongoing disclosures from public companies and also monitor these disclosures. Companies can now file required disclosures electronically with securities commissions. Investors can log on to a website and tap into conversations, including earnings calls, briefings with analysts, and interviews with senior management and market regulators. In the past, these conversations were not accessible to the average investor.

Changing Nature of the Economy

Much of North America is transforming from an economy based on traditional manufacturing and resource extraction to what has become known in the past decade as a **"knowledge-based" economy.**[30] In terms of the market value of their publicly traded shares, such

---

[29] Until then, the FASB is working on a codification project to try to deal with what has become an excessively large and complex body of knowledge. Under the terms of the project, the FASB is trying to rewrite and combine the various sources of U.S. GAAP into a more manageable format—one that will hopefully reduce the size and complexity of U.S. GAAP.

[30] R. McLean, *The Canadian Performance Reporting Initiative* (Toronto: Ontario Premier's Council and the CICA, ongoing), Chapter 2.

companies as Microsoft, Cisco, Intel, Lucent, AT&T, and IBM dominate the North American markets. What these companies all have in common is that a large percentage of the value given to their shares is linked to such factors as their **relationships with customers and suppliers, knowledge base or intellectual assets, ability to adapt to a changing technological environment, and skillful leadership**. This is different from the more traditional manufacturing and resource-based economy, where value was more closely linked to physical and tangible assets and financing.

Most of the assets of these "new economy" companies cannot be seen in the balance sheet, yet they are mostly responsible for the company value. As noted by the CICA:

> In light of these shifts [i.e., in the economy], to maintain its relevancy, the [accounting] profession must move beyond interpreting the past. Increasingly what matters is the ability for organizational decision-makers to be positioned for the future. This ability to look forward is driven by one's ability to measure organizational performance along an increasingly broad spectrum of measures, both financial and non-financial... Chartered Accountants must provide decision-makers with the tools necessary to measure and report on organizational performance in all its aspects, not just the historical and financial.[31]

The knowledge-based companies that are beginning to dominate capital markets need **more relevant models for measuring and reporting value in order to create assets that are currently not recognized on the balance sheet**. There has been little progress in this area so far because of the difficulty of objectively valuing these assets and their potential impact on future earnings. Despite this difficulty, underwriting firms such as CIBC World Markets are in fact valuing these types of companies all the time when there are securities offerings or mergers and acquisitions. The market also values these assets, and the companies that house them, through share prices. How, if at all, can these values be shown in the financial statements?

Increased Requirement for Accountability

There is a **growing number of institutional investors**, partly because more and more capital is being invested in pension plans and mutual funds. The impact is that investors have become **more sophisticated in terms of knowledge levels**. Institutional investors, because of their size, have **greater representation in corporate boardrooms** and are thus more involved in running the companies they invest in. As a result, companies are being pushed toward **increased accountability**.

Financial performance is rooted in a company's business model (i.e., the earnings process, how companies finance the process, and what resources companies invest in). While, historically, this has not always been the focus of financial accounting, a company's ability to articulate its strategic vision and carry out that vision affects financial performance. The accounting information system is also part of a larger system of information management—a system that contains a significant amount of non-financial information.

Will investors move **beyond the financial reporting model** to a more **all-inclusive model of business reporting**—one that includes not only financial information but other key indicators and measurements that help predict value creation and monitor an organization's performance? The CICA AcSB mandate includes a push to **develop and support frameworks for measuring and reporting information that is used for evaluating and improving an organization's performance.**[32] Changes in these directions would broaden the focus from financial reporting to business reporting.

---

[31] *Report of the Inter-Institute Vision Task Force* (Toronto: CICA, 1996), p. 9.

[32] J. Waterhouse and A. Svendsen, *Strategic Performance Monitoring and Management: Using Non-Financial Measures to Improve Corporate Governance* (CICA,1998); and A. Willis and J. Desjardins, *Environmental Performance: Measuring and Managing What Matters* (CICA, 2001).

The CICA also has several other initiatives in this area:

- The CICA's **Risk Management and Governance Board** (formerly the Criteria of Control Board) focuses on a practical, commercial approach to risk management and governance.
- The CICA's **Canadian Performance Reporting Board** has issued standards on Management Discussion and Analysis disclosures.

These and other initiatives take a broader view of an all-inclusive model of business reporting.

Related to this theme of "business reporting" is the development of a business strategy model called the **balanced scorecard**.[33] Used quite widely, this model notes that **financial measures are only one component of useful information that decision-makers need in order to make effective decisions about the company**. The model views the company from four perspectives: financial, customer, internal processes, and learning and growth. These four perspectives are linked to the company's strategic vision, and objectives are developed within each perspective. The objectives help the company achieve its strategic vision. Measures are also developed to determine whether the objectives are being met.

Illustration 1-8

The Balanced Scorecard Model

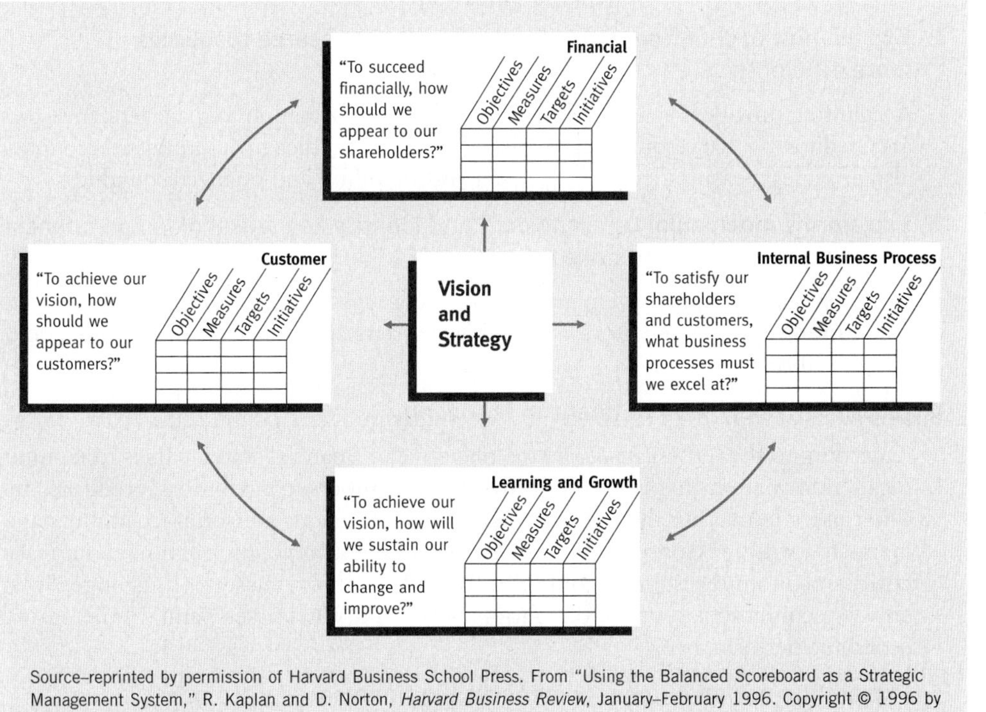

Source–reprinted by permission of Harvard Business School Press. From "Using the Balanced Scoreboard as a Strategic Management System," R. Kaplan and D. Norton, *Harvard Business Review*, January–February 1996. Copyright © 1996 by the Harvard Business School Publishing Corportion: all rights reserved.

Illustration 1-8 shows a **balanced scorecard model**. This model is used to help focus a company's internal efforts more effectively on meeting its strategic goals. The question is whether external users of financial statements also need to monitor these measures and whether companies should give external parties access to this information. If the information is important for company management in making decisions, is it not also important for external users?

We believe that the challenges presented by these changes must be met in order for the accounting profession to continue to provide the type of information that is needed for an efficient capital allocation process.

[33] R. Kaplan and D. Norton, *The Balanced Scorecard* (Boston: Harvard Business School Press, 1996).

Conclusion

Financial reporting is standing at the threshold of some significant changes. Is the accounting profession up to the challenge? At present, we believe that the profession is reacting responsibly and effectively to correct the shortcomings that have been identified and to move forward with a new vision. Because of its great resources and expertise, the profession should be able to develop and maintain high standards and meet its mandate. This is and will continue to be a difficult process that requires time, logic, and diplomacy. Through a well-chosen mix of these three ingredients, however, and a measure of luck, the accounting profession will continue to be a leader on the global business stage.

Summary of Learning Objectives

Student Website

Glossary

www.wiley.com/canada/kieso

KEY TERMS

Accounting Standards Board (AcSB), 12
Accounting Standards Oversight Council (AcSOC), 13
American Institute of Certified Public Accountants (AICPA), 14
Canadian Institute of Chartered Accountants (CICA), 12
capital allocation, 6
CICA Handbook, 12
due process, 13
EIC Abstracts, 13
Emerging Issues Committee (EIC), 13
ethical dilemmas, 18
financial accounting, 5
Financial Accounting Standards Board (FASB), 14
financial reporting, 5
financial statements, 5
GAAP hierarchy, 18
generally accepted accounting principles (GAAP), 11
International Accounting Standards Board (IASB), 15
management bias, 10
management stewardship, 9

1 Describe the essential characteristics of accounting.

The essential characteristics of accounting are the (1) identification, measurement, and communication of financial information about (2) economic entities to (3) interested persons.

2 Explain how accounting makes it possible to use scarce resources more efficiently.

Accounting provides reliable, relevant, and timely information to managers, investors, and creditors so that resources are allocated to the most efficient enterprises. Accounting also provides measurements of efficiency (profitability) and financial soundness.

3 Explain the meaning of "stakeholder" and identify key stakeholders in financial reporting and what is at stake for each one.

Investors, creditors, management, securities commissions, stock exchanges, analysts, credit rating agencies, auditors, and standard setters are some of the major stakeholders. See Illustration 1-4.

4 Identify the objective of financial reporting.

According to the *CICA Handbook*, the objective of financial statements is to communicate information that is useful to investors, members, contributors, creditors, and other users in making their resource allocation decisions and/or assessing management stewardship. Consequently, financial statements give information about (a) an entity's economic resources, obligations, and equity/net assets; (b) changes in an entity's economic resources, obligations, and equity/net assets; and (c) the entity's economic performance.

5 Explain the notion of management bias in financial reporting.

Management bias implies that the financial statements are not neutral: in other words, the preparers of the financial information are presenting the information in a manner that may overemphasize the positive and underemphasize the negative.

6 Understand the importance of user needs in the financial reporting process.

The financial reporting process is based on ensuring that users receive information that is relevant to decisions. This is a challenge as different users have different knowledge levels and needs. Management bias can make financial information less useful.

7 Explain the need for accounting standards.

The accounting profession has tried to develop a set of standards that is generally accepted and universally practised. Without this set of standards, each enterprise would have to develop its own standards, and readers of financial statements would have to become familiar with every company's particular accounting and reporting practices. As a result, it would be almost impossible to prepare statements that could be compared.

8 Identify the major entities that influence the standard-setting process and explain how they influence financial reporting.

The CICA AcSB is the main standard-setting body in Canada. Its mandate is from the CBCA as well as provincial acts of incorporation. Public companies are required to follow GAAP in order to access capital markets which are monitored by provincial securities commissions. The FASB and IASB are also important as they influence Canadian standard setting. Canada is committed to international harmonization of GAAP.

9 Explain the meaning of generally accepted accounting principles (GAAP).

Generally accepted accounting principles are either principles that have substantial authoritative support, such as the *CICA Handbook*, or specific practices that have been accepted as appropriate over time because they are being applied universally.

10 Explain the significance of professional judgement in applying GAAP.

Professional judgement plays an important role in Canadian GAAP since much of GAAP is based on general principles, which need to be interpreted.

11 Understand issues related to ethics and financial accounting.

When performing their professional duties, financial accountants are expected to note moral considerations and to make ethical decisions. Doing this is more difficult because no consensus has emerged among business professionals as to what constitutes a comprehensive ethical system.

12 Identify some of the challenges facing accounting.

Some of the challenges are globalization, leading to a requirement for international harmonization of standards; increased technology, resulting in the need for more timely information; the move to a new economy, resulting in a focus on measuring and reporting non-traditional assets that create value; and an increased requirement for accountability, resulting in the creation of new measurement and reporting models that look at business reporting as a whole.

Brief Exercises

BE1-1 Explain generally how financial accounting and managerial accounting differ from each other. **(LO1)**

BE1-2 How does accounting help the capital allocation process? **(LO2)**

BE1-3 What is the difference between "financial statements" and "financial reporting"? **(LO1,4)**

BE1-4 What are the major objectives of financial reporting? **(LO4)**

BE1-5 What is the value of having a common set of standards in financial accounting and reporting? **(LO7)**

BE1-6 What is the likely limitation of "general-purpose financial statements"? **(LO7)**

BE1-7 Which organization is currently dominant in the world for setting accounting standards? **(LO8)**

BE1-8 What are some of the developments or events that occurred between 1900 and 1930 that helped bring about changes in accounting theory or practice? **(LO8)**

BE1-9 In what direction is Canadian GAAP going in the future? **(LO8)**

(LO8) **BE1-10** Explain the role of the Emerging Issues Committee in establishing generally accepted accounting principles.

(LO8) **BE1-11** What is the role of the Ontario Securities Commission in standard setting?

(LO8) **BE1-12** What are some possible reasons why another organization, such as the OSC or SEC, should not issue financial reporting standards?

(LO8) **BE1-13** What are the sources of pressure that change and influence the development of accounting principles and standards?

(LO8) **BE1-14** Some individuals have argued that the AcSB needs to be aware of the economic consequences of its pronouncements. What is meant by "economic consequences"? What are some of the dangers if politics play too much of a role in the development of financial reporting standards?

(LO9) **BE1-15** If you were given complete authority to decide this, how would you propose that accounting principles or standards be developed and enforced?

(LO9) **BE1-16** If you had to explain or define "generally accepted accounting principles," what essential characteristics would you include in your explanation?

(LO9) **BE1-17** Explain the difference between primary and other sources of GAAP.

(LO10) **BE1-18** The chairman of the FASB at one time noted that "the flow of standards can only be slowed if (1) producers focus less on quarterly earnings per share and tax benefits and more on quality products, and (2) accountants and lawyers rely less on rules and law and more on professional judgement and conduct." Explain his comment.

(LO11) **BE1-19** One writer recently noted that 99.4% of all companies prepare statements that are in accordance with GAAP. Why, then, is there such concern about fraudulent financial reporting?

(LO11) **BE1-20** Some foreign countries have reporting standards that are different from standards in Canada. What are some of the main reasons why reporting standards are often different among countries?

(LO11) **BE1-21** How are financial accountants pressured when they need to make ethical decisions in their work? Is having technical mastery of GAAP enough to practise financial accounting?

(LO12) **BE1-22** What are some of the major challenges facing the accounting profession?

Writing Assignments

WA1-1 Some critics argue that having different organizations establish accounting principles is wasteful and inefficient. Instead of mandating accounting standards, each company could voluntarily disclose the type of information it considered important. If an investor wanted additional information, the investor could contact the company and pay to receive the information that is wanted.

Instructions

Comment on the appropriateness of this viewpoint.

WA1-2 Some accountants have said that the development and acceptance of generally accepted accounting principles (i.e., standard setting) is undergoing a "politicization." Some use the term "politicization" in a narrow sense to mean the influence by government agencies, particularly the securities commissions, on the development of generally accepted accounting principles. Others use it more broadly to mean the compromise that results when the bodies that are responsible for developing generally accepted accounting principles are pressured by interest groups (securities commissions, stock exchanges, businesses through their various organizations, financial analysts, bankers, lawyers, etc.).

Instructions

(a) What are the arguments in favour of the politicization of accounting standard setting?

(b) What are the arguments against the politicization of accounting standard setting?

(CMA adapted)

WA1-3 Three models for setting accounting standards follow:

1. The purely political approach, where national legislative action decrees accounting standards
2. The private, professional approach, where financial accounting standards are set and enforced by private, professional actions only

3. The public/private mixed approach, where standards are set by private-sector bodies that behave as though they were public agencies and the standards are mostly enforced through government agencies

Instructions

(a) Which of these three models best describes standard setting in Canada? Explain your choice.

(b) Why are companies, financial analysts, labour unions, industry trade associations, and others actively interested in standard setting?

(c) Cite an example of a group other than the AcSB that tries to establish accounting standards. Speculate on why such a group might want to set its own standards.

WA1-4 The increased availability and accessibility of computers and the Internet have had a major impact on the process of financial reporting. Most companies have websites and make a significant amount of financial information available to stakeholders, including annual reports and other financial data. This has sparked the question of whether companies should use a continuous reporting model instead of the current discrete model, where financial statements are generally issued only quarterly and annually. Under a continuous reporting model, the company would make more information available to users in real time or perhaps on a "delayed" real-time basis (e.g., weekly).

Instructions

What are the pros and cons of a continuous reporting model? Consider the various stakeholders in the capital marketplace.

WA1-5 The chapter mentions Enron and WorldCom, two companies that were accused of misstating their financial statements. The auditors for each company signed audit reports in which they stated that the financial statements of each company were fairly presented.

Instructions

How is it possible that a company can misrepresent its financial statements and still receive a "clean" audit opinion from the auditors?

WA1-6 The following information is from the Ontario Securities Commission (OSC) Statement of Allegation dated August 30, 2000, against Philip Services Corp. (Philip). The allegation is about information in the company prospectus that included audited financial statements for the years ended December 31, 1995 and 1996.

The prospectus included an unqualified audit opinion, meaning that the auditors had concluded in the audit report that the financial statements presented the company's financial position and results of operations fairly and in accordance with GAAP. At the time, the company was a leading integrated service provider of ferrous scrap processing, brokerage, and industrial outsourcing services. The OSC alleged that the company failed to provide full, true, and plain disclosure in the prospectus of material facts about the company's restructuring and special charges.

Instructions

(a) Explain the meaning of the term "GAAP" as it is used in the audit report.

(b) Explain how to determine whether or not an accounting principle is generally accepted.

(c) Discuss the sources of evidence for determining whether an accounting principle has substantial authoritative support.

(d) Discuss how the auditors were likely able to issue a clean audit opinion even though the OSC alleges that the company did not fully disclose all material facts.

WA1-7 As mentioned in the chapter, the capital marketplace's reaction to recent corporate failures has been to increase the amount of government regulation.

Instructions

(a) Identify what steps Canada and the United States have taken to increase government regulation.

(b) What other options to strengthen the capital marketplace might have been available to stakeholders?

(c) What are the strengths and weaknesses of government regulation?

Cases

Refer to the Case Primer on the Student Website to help you answer these cases.

Student Website
www.wiley.com/canada/kieso

CA1-1 When the AcSB issues new standards, the implementation date is usually 12 months after the issue date, but early implementation is encouraged. In this case, Paula Popovich, controller, is discussing with her financial vice-president the need for early implementation of a standard that would result in a fairer presentation of the company's financial condition and earnings. When the financial vice-president determines that early implementation of the standard will lower the reported net income for the year, he discourages Popovich from implementing the standard until it is required.

Instructions
Discuss the ethical issues.

(CMA adapted)

CA1-2 The T. Eaton Company (Eaton's) was a private Canadian company that experienced cash flow difficulties and hired new management to turn the company around. The company then went public and the shares sold at $15. Within months, however, the share price plummeted and Sears bought out Eaton's when it was on the threshold of bankruptcy.

Instructions
Who are the stakeholders in this situation? Explain what was at stake and why and how they were affected when the share price plummeted.

CA1-3 In a *Financial Post* article dated September 17, 2002, it was reported that Standard and Poor's downgraded Quebecor Media Inc.'s credit rating by two levels from BB to B+. The credit rating agency was concerned about the company's ability to refinance portions of its debt. Both BB and B+ are considered "junk" bonds and are below the BBB− category, which is the lowest grade that many pension and mutual funds are allowed to hold.

In the article, analysts said the company's financial profile had weakened due to tight debt covenants and resulting cash flow restrictions.

Instructions
Discuss whether Standard and Poor's is a stakeholder from Quebecor Media Inc.'s perspective. Discuss any bias that Quebecor might have when it issues its financial statements.

Research and Financial Analysis

RA1-1 Ontario Securities Commission (1)

The Ontario Securities Commission (OSC) has agreed that:

1. Canadian companies shall be allowed to follow U.S. GAAP when they file documents with the OSC
2. U.S. companies shall be allowed to file only U.S. GAAP statements to satisfy OSC requirements

Instructions
Research and prepare an essay in which you consider the following:

(a) Hypothesize about why the OSC might have taken these positions.

(b) How might Canadian investors benefit if U.S. standards become Canadian GAAP? How might they be disadvantaged?

(c) How do Canadian and U.S. standards differ in general?

(d) Review the financial statements of large Canadian companies whose shares trade on the TSX as well as a U.S. exchange. (Hint: look at www.sedar.com under "Company Profile" then "View this company's documents" then "Annual financial statements.") These companies generally include a note to the financial statements in which net income under Canadian GAAP is reconciled to net income under U.S. GAAP. Choose five companies and calculate the dollar and percentage difference between the Canadian and U.S. numbers. Discuss the implications of reporting two separate net income numbers.

RA1-2 Ontario Securities Commission (2)

As part of its Continuous Review Process, the OSC does annual reviews of companies that list on the TSX. In August 2002, the OSC issued a report on its activities for the previous year ended March 31, 2002. As part of its review, the OSC reviewed 137 Ontario-based TSX companies and looked specifically at their disclosure and reporting of non-GAAP earnings measures.

Instructions

(a) Define what is meant by "non-GAAP earnings measures."

(b) Summarize the OSC findings.

(c) List and briefly explain the reporting requirements in OSC Staff Notice 52-303 (www.osc.gov.on.ca).

(d) Why was this Staff Notice issued?

(e) Based on the report, is the reporting of "non-GAAP earnings measures" a problem?

RA1-3 IASB

Michael Sharpe, then deputy chairman of the International Accounting Standards Committee, made the following comments before the Financial Executives International 63rd Annual Conference: "There is an irreversible movement toward the harmonization of financial reporting throughout the world. The international capital markets require an end to:

1. The confusion caused by international companies announcing different results depending on the set of accounting standards applied. Recent announcements by Daimler-Benz (now DaimlerChrysler) highlight the confusion that this causes.
2. Companies in some countries obtaining unfair commercial advantages from the use of particular national accounting standards.
3. The complications in negotiating commercial arrangements for international joint ventures caused by different accounting requirements.
4. The inefficiency of international companies having to understand and use myriad accounting standards depending on the countries in which they operate and the countries in which they raise capital and debt. Executive talent is wasted on keeping up to date with numerous sets of accounting standards and the never-ending changes to them.
5. The inefficiency of investment managers, bankers, and financial analysts as they seek to compare financial reporting drawn up in accordance with different sets of accounting standards.
6. Failure of many stock exchanges and regulators to require companies subject to their jurisdiction to provide comparable, comprehensive, and transparent financial reporting frameworks giving international comparability.
7. Difficulty for developing countries and countries entering the free market economy, such as China and Russia, in accessing foreign capital markets because of the complexity of and differences between national standards.
8. The restriction on the mobility of financial service providers across the world as a result of different accounting standards.

Clearly, eliminating these inefficiencies by having comparable high-quality financial reporting used across the world would benefit international businesses."

Instructions

Research the issue using the Internet and answer the following questions:

(a) What is the International Accounting Standards Board and what is its relationship with the International Accounting Standards Committee?

(b) Which stakeholders might benefit from the use of international accounting standards?

(c) What do you believe are some of the major obstacles to harmonization?

RA1-4 Canadian Coalition for Good Governance

The Canadian Coalition for Good Governance was formed in 2002 and represents a significant number of institutional investors in Canada.

Instructions

(a) How does an institutional investor differ from other investors?

(b) In your opinion, what impact would the presence of a large number of investors have on management's financial reporting decisions?

(c) Go to the coalition's website www.ccgg.ca and identify the coalition's three largest members.

(d) Go to these companies' websites and identify their major investments.

RA1-5 SOX

In 2002, the *Sarbanes-Oxley Act* (SOX) was passed in the U.S. to strengthen the capital marketplace. In the following year, there were many debates in Canada about whether the securities commissions in Canada should adopt the same regulations. In the end, Canada did adopt a similar level of regulation.

Instructions

(a) Why was the SOX issued and what are its key components?

(b) What do you expect will be the SOX's impact on the U.S. capital marketplace?

(c) Do some research on the Internet and discuss the pros and cons of Canada adopting the same rules for companies listed on the TSX and TSX Venture Exchange. (Hint: look on the websites of the provincial securities commissions, the CICA, the TSX, and the *Globe and Mail* and *Financial Post*. Key words might be "SOX," "corporate accountability," and "post Enron.")

RA1-6 Principles versus Rules

Canadian and U.S. accounting standards are based on different philosophies. Canada uses a principles-based approach while the U.S. uses a rules-based approach. The U.S. is currently studying the merits of the principles-based approach. Note that IFRS are principles-based.

Instructions

(a) Identify the main factor that motivated the FASB to at least consider switching to the principles-based approach.

(b) Download and review the FASB Issues Proposal for a Principles-Based Approach to U.S. Accounting Standard Setting.

(c) In your own words, state the differences between a rules-based approach and a principles-based approach.

(d) Comment on which approach would be better for Canada.

RA1-7 Impact of Technology

The following is a quote from the foreword to *The Impact of Technology on Financial and Business Reporting*, a research study published by the CICA in 1999:

> Changes in technology have had, and are continuing to have, a profound effect on how information is captured, summarized, and communicated.

Instructions

Discuss the quote by referring to the research report and current real-life examples.

RA1-8 Financial Reporting Pressures

What follows is part of the testimony from Troy Normand in the WorldCom case. He was a manager in the corporate reporting department and is one of five individuals who pleaded guilty. He testified in the hope of receiving no prison time when he is ultimately sentenced.

Q: Mr. Normand, if you could just describe for the jury how the meeting started and what was said during the meeting?

A: I can't recall exactly who initiated the discussion, but right away Scott Sullivan acknowledged that he was aware we had problems with the entries, David Myers had informed him, and we were considering resigning.

He said that he respected our concerns but that we weren't being asked to do anything that he believed was wrong. He mentioned that he acknowledged that the company had lost focus quite a bit due to the preparations for the Sprint merger, and that he was putting plans in place and projects in place to try to determine where the problems were, why the costs were so high.

He did say he believed that the initial statements that we produced, that the line costs in those statements could not have been as high as they were, that he believed something was wrong and there was no way that the costs were that high.

I informed him that I didn't believe the entry we were being asked to do was right, that I was scared, and I didn't want to put myself in a position of going to jail for him or the company. He responded that he didn't believe anything was wrong, nobody was going to be going to jail, but that if it later was found to be wrong, that he would be the person going to jail, not me.

He asked that I stay, don't jump off the plane, let him land softly, that's basically how he put it. And he mentioned that he had a discussion with Bernie Ebbers asking Bernie to reduce projections going forward and Bernie had refused.

Q: Mr. Normand, you said that Mr. Sullivan said something about don't jump out of the plane. What did you understand him to mean when he said that?

A: Not to quit.

Q: During this meeting, did Mr. Sullivan say anything about whether you would be asked to make entries like this in the future?

A: Yes, he made a comment that from that point going forward we wouldn't be asked to record any entries, high-level late adjustments, that the numbers would be the numbers.

Q: What did you understand that to mean, the numbers would be the numbers?

A: That after the preliminary statements were issued, with the exception of any normal transactions, valid transactions, we wouldn't be asked to be recording any more late entries.

Q: I believe you testified that Mr. Sullivan said something about the line cost numbers not being accurate. Did he ask you to conduct any analysis to determine whether the line cost numbers were accurate?

A: No, he did not.

Q: Did anyone ever ask you to do that?

A: No.

Q: Did you ever conduct any such analysis?

A: No, I didn't.

Q: During this meeting, did Mr. Sullivan ever provide any accounting justification for the entry you were asked to make?

A: No, he did not.

Q: Did anything else happen during the meeting?

A: I don't recall anything else.

Q: How did you feel after this meeting?

A: Not much better actually. I left his office not convinced in any way that what we were asked to do was right. However, I did question myself to some degree after talking with him wondering whether I was making something more out of what was really there.

Instructions

Answer the following questions:

1. What appear to be the ethical issues in this case?
2. Is Troy Normand acting improperly or immorally?
3. What would you do if you were Troy Normand?
4. Who are the major stakeholders in this case?

Soaring Profits

After a decade in the air, WestJet Airlines has evolved from an innovative newcomer to industry leader. WestJet's 2005 fiscal year end saw a $24-million profit, and year-to-date numbers for 2006 were also predicting profits for the Calgary-based airline. Janice Paget, CGA, WestJet's vice-president, controller, and co-CFO, credits the company's success to sound business planning and financial management.

"We have a strong focus on strategic planning," Paget explains. "We're extremely focused on our budgeting process and monitoring our revenues and expenses and making sure that we're in line with our business plan."

The management discussion and analysis (MD&A) that accompanies WestJet's financial statements provides shareholders with information on the airline's fleet plan, the average cost for fuel, the number of employees, current financial results, and an explanation of why the numbers are up or down.

What WestJet doesn't provide is projections for the future, unlike other public companies. "We work in a volatile industry in an extremely volatile environment," Paget says. "We do not want to be in a position where we give guidance indicating X amount of earnings per share by the end of the year and then coming back to the market and saying, no, it's going to be more or less. To us, that's not our role. Our role is to provide as much information as we can and then allow the investing community to decide what they believe our performance will be over the next 12 months."

Transparency has always been a priority for WestJet's financial management. From its 1996 startup, the airline has acted like a public company, providing quarterly and annual reports to its shareholders. In 1998, it became a reporting issuer, coming under the jurisdiction of the provincial securities commission. It was listed on the Toronto Stock Exchange in July 1999.

Now offering flights across Canada and to several U.S. cities, WestJet had grown at an average of 50 percent a year until the end of 2004, when its expansion began to slow. "Once you hit a certain size, you can't continually keep growing at 50 percent," says Paget, who expects the airline to be averaging about 10 to 15 percent growth from here on in. ■

Conceptual Framework Underlying Financial Reporting

chapter 2

Learning Objectives

After studying this chapter, you should be able to:

1. Describe the usefulness of a conceptual framework.
2. Describe the main components of the conceptual framework for financial reporting.
3. Understand the objective of financial reporting.
4. Identify the qualitative characteristics of accounting information.
5. Define the basic elements of financial statements.
6. Describe the basic foundational concepts and constraints of accounting.
7. Explain the factors that contribute to choice in financial reporting decisions.
8. Identify the four types of financial reporting issues and what makes certain issues more important than others.
9. Explain the practice of financial engineering.
10. Identify factors that contribute to fraudulent financial reporting.
11. Recognize how similar Canadian GAAP is to international GAAP.

Preview of Chapter 2

Users of financial statements need relevant and reliable information. To help develop this type of financial information, accountants use a conceptual framework that guides financial accounting and reporting. In this chapter, we discuss the basic concepts that underlie this conceptual framework.

The chapter is organized as follows:

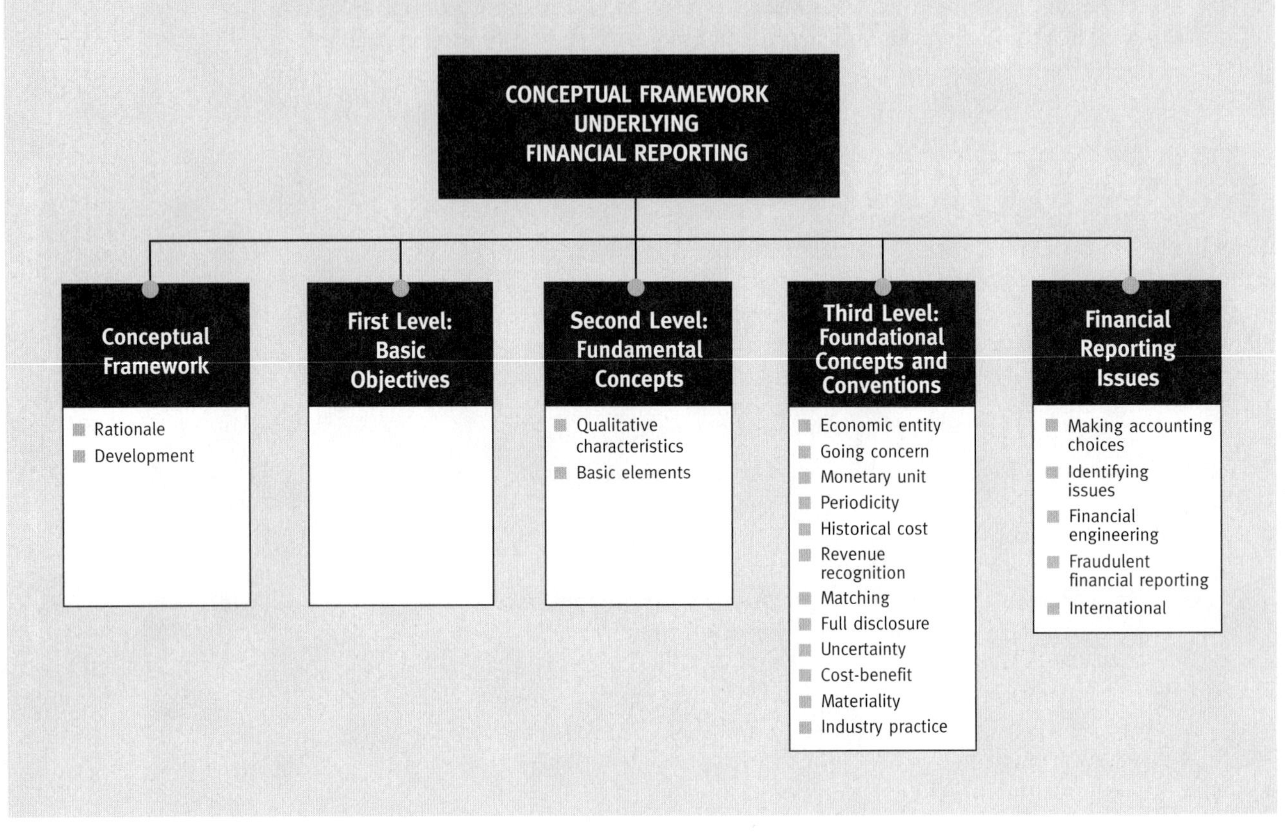

CONCEPTUAL FRAMEWORK

A **conceptual framework** is like a constitution: it is a "coherent system of interrelated objectives and fundamentals that can lead to consistent standards and that prescribes the nature, function, and limits of financial accounting and financial statements."[1] Many observers believe that the real contribution of standard-setting bodies, and even their continued existence, depends on the quality and usefulness of the conceptual framework.

Objective 1
Describe the usefulness of a conceptual framework.

Rationale for Conceptual Framework

Why is a conceptual framework necessary? First, to be useful, **standard setting should build on an established body of concepts and objectives.** Having a soundly developed

[1] "Conceptual Framework for Financial Accounting and Reporting: Elements of Financial Statements and Their Measurement," FASB discussion memorandum, (Stamford, Conn.: FASB, 1976), page 1 of the "Scope and Implications of the Conceptual Framework Project" section.

conceptual framework as its starting point, the AcSB is then able to issue additional **useful and consistent** standards over time. The result is a **coherent** set of standards and rules as they have all been built upon the same foundation. It is important that such a framework **increase** financial statement users' **understanding** of and **confidence** in financial reporting, and that it **enhance the comparability** of different companies' financial statements.

Second, by referring to an existing framework of basic theory, it should be possible to solve **new and emerging practical problems** more quickly. It is difficult, if not impossible, for the AcSB to quickly state the proper accounting treatment for highly complex situations. Practising accountants, however, must solve such problems on a day-to-day basis. By using **good judgement** and with the help of a **universally accepted conceptual framework**, it is hoped that accountants will be able to decide against certain alternatives quickly and to focus instead on a logical and acceptable treatment.

Development of the Conceptual Framework

Over the years, many organizations, committees, and interested individuals have developed and published their own conceptual frameworks, but no single framework has been universally accepted and relied on in practice. Realizing there was a need for a generally accepted framework, in 1976 the FASB issued a three-part discussion memorandum entitled "Conceptual Framework for Financial Accounting and Reporting: Elements of Financial Statements and Their Measurement." It stated the major issues that would need to be addressed in establishing a conceptual framework for setting accounting standards and resolving financial reporting controversies. Based on this, six "Statements of Financial Accounting Concepts" were then published. A seventh, on accounting measurement, was added in 2000. The AcSB followed the FASB example and issued *CICA Handbook* Section 1000—Financial Statement Concepts.

2 Objective
Describe the main components of the conceptual framework for financial reporting.

International Insight

In July 2006, the FASB and IASB issued a jointly developed discussion paper on objectives and qualitative characteristics. This document will eventually lead to a new harmonized conceptual framework.

Illustration 2-1 shows an overview of a conceptual framework.[2] At the first level, the objectives identify accounting's **goals and purposes**: these are the conceptual framework's building blocks. At the second level are the **qualitative characteristics** that make accounting information useful and the **elements of financial statements** (assets, liabilities, equity, revenues, expenses, gains, losses, and other comprehensive income).[3] At the third or final level are the **foundational principles and conventions** used in establishing and applying accounting standards. These include **assumptions**, **principles**, and **constraints** that describe the present reporting environment.

FIRST LEVEL: BASIC OBJECTIVES

As we discussed in Chapter 1, the **objective of financial reporting** according to *CICA Handbook* Section 1000 is to communicate information that is **useful** to investors, creditors, and other users in making their **resource allocation** decisions and/or **assessing management stewardship**. Consequently, financial statements provide information about all of the following:

3 Objective
Understand the objective of financial reporting.

(a) an entity's economic resources, obligations, and equity/net assets

(b) changes in an entity's economic resources, obligations, and equity/net assets

(c) the economic performance of the entity[4]

[2] Adapted from William C. Norby, *The Financial Analysts Journal*, March/April 1982, p. 22.

[3] It is debatable whether other comprehensive income is a separate element of financial statements as it simply contains other elements such as revenues, expenses, gains, and losses. It is considered by some to be a subclassification of the income statement.

[4] *CICA Handbook*, Section 1000.15.

Illustration 2-1

Conceptual Framework for Financial Reporting

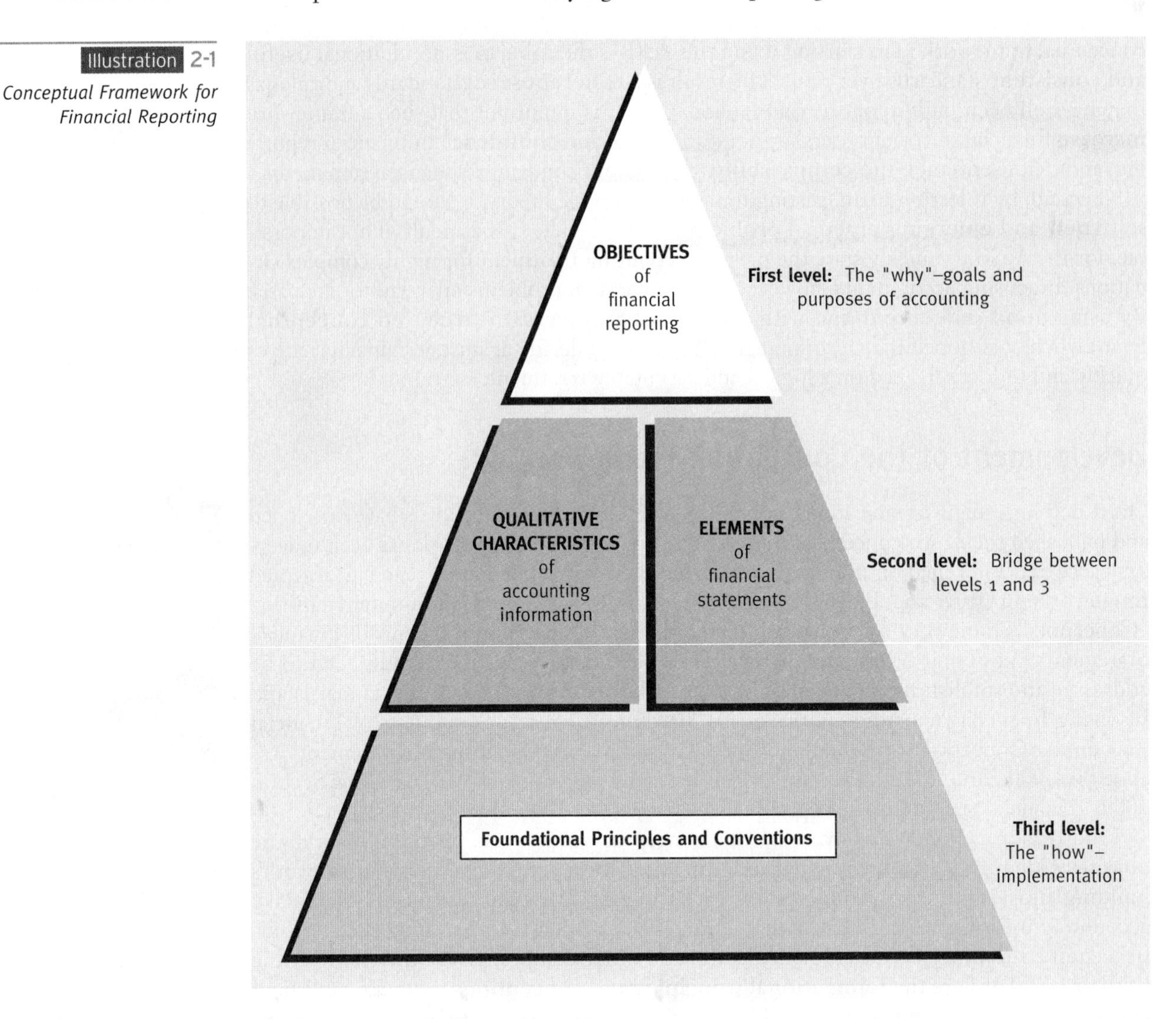

The accounting profession provides this information to users of financial statements through **general-purpose financial statements.** These are basic financial statements that give information that meets the needs of **key** users.[5] The statements are intended to provide the **most useful information possible in a manner whereby benefits exceed costs** to the different kinds of users.

Underlying these objectives is the notion that users need to have **reasonable knowledge** of business and financial accounting matters in order to understand the information in financial statements. This point is important: it means that preparers of financial statements can assume that users are reasonably competent at reading, interpreting, and understanding the information that is presented. This assumption affects both how information is reported and how much is reported.[6]

[5] Normally investors and creditors, according to the *CICA Handbook*, Section 1000.11.

[6] Users are presumed to have a reasonable understanding of business and economic activities and accounting as well as a willingness to study the information with reasonable diligence according to the *CICA Handbook*, Section 1000.19.

SECOND LEVEL: FUNDAMENTAL CONCEPTS

The objectives (the first level) are about accounting's **goals and purposes**. Later, we will discuss how these goals and purposes are **implemented** (the third level). Between these two levels is another level: the second level is necessary as it provides certain **conceptual building blocks** that explain the **qualitative characteristics** of accounting information and define the **elements of financial statements**. These conceptual building blocks form a bridge between the why of accounting (the objectives) and the how of accounting (recognition and measurement).

International Insight

In Switzerland, Germany, Korea, and other nations, capital is provided to business mainly by large banks. Creditors have very close ties to firms and can obtain information directly from them. Creditors do not need to rely on publicly available information, and financial information is focused on creditor protection. This process of capital allocation, however, is changing. It is likely that the need for publicly available information will also change.

Qualitative Characteristics of Accounting Information

Choosing an acceptable accounting method, the amount and types of information to be disclosed, and the format in which information should be presented involves determining **which alternative gives the most useful information for decision-making purposes** (**decision usefulness**). The conceptual framework has identified the **qualitative characteristics** of accounting information that distinguish information that is better (more useful) for making decisions from information that is inferior (less useful). These characteristics are explained next.

4 Objective
Identify the qualitative characteristics of accounting information.

Decision-Makers (Users) and Understandability

Decision-makers vary widely in the types of decisions they make, the decision-making methods they use, the information they already have or can obtain from other sources, and their ability to process the information. For information to be useful, there must be a connection between these users and the decisions they make. This connection, **understandability**, is the quality that allows reasonably informed users to see the information's significance. Fair presentation is achieved by applying GAAP, which includes providing enough information in a manner that is clear and understandable.[7]

Relevance and Reliability

Relevance and **reliability** are qualities that make accounting information useful for decision-making.

Relevance. To be relevant, accounting information must **make a difference in a decision**.[8] If a piece of information has no impact on a decision, it is irrelevant to that decision. Relevant information helps users make predictions about the final outcome of past, present, and future events; that is, it has **predictive value**. Relevant information also helps users confirm or correct their previous expectations; it has **feedback value**.

What Do the Numbers Mean?

For example, when a company issues an interim earnings announcement, this information is considered relevant because it provides a basis for forecasting **annual** earnings. It also gives feedback value as to how the company is performing to date. In February 2001, **Nortel Networks Corp.** announced that it would miss earlier projected financial targets for the year by 50 percent, a significant amount. When they received the information, users revised their expectations of the company's annual earnings.

For information to be relevant, it must also be **available** to decision-makers before it loses its ability to influence their decisions. Thus **timeliness** is a major ingredient.

[7] *CICA Handbook*, Section 1400.04.

[8] *CICA Handbook*, Section 1000.20.

If Nortel did not report its interim results until six months after the end of the period, the information would be much less useful for decision-making. In fact, when Nortel made the February announcements, there was some concern over whether the information could have been released even earlier. The announcement came two days after Nortel had finalized a deal to purchase a Zurich-based subsidiary from JDS Uniphase. As part of the deal, Nortel paid 65.7 million of its shares, and these ended up being worth substantially less once the earnings announcement was made.

The following chart shows the rapid price fall of Nortel stock from mid-year 2000 to mid-year 2001. Note the significant decline in February 2001.

Reliability. Accounting information is reliable to the extent that it is **verifiable**, is a **faithful representation** of the underlying economic reality, and is reasonably free of error and bias (i.e., it is **neutral**). Reliability is necessary for individuals who do not have the time or expertise to evaluate the information's factual content.

Verifiability exists when **independent** measurers, using the **same measurement methods**, get similar results. If outside parties arrive at different conclusions using the same measurement methods, then the statements are not verifiable. Auditors cannot render an opinion on such statements. Some numbers are more easily verified than others, e.g., cash can be verified by confirming with the bank where the deposit is held. Other numbers—such as accruals for environmental cleanup costs—are more difficult (although not necessarily impossible) to verify, as many assumptions are made to arrive at an estimate. Numbers that are easy to verify with a reasonable degree of accuracy are often referred to as "hard" numbers. Those that have more measurement uncertainty are called "soft."

Representational faithfulness means that the numbers and descriptions **represent what really exists or happened.** In other words, they present **the economic reality**. This means that the accounting numbers and descriptions must agree with the resources or events that these numbers and descriptions are supposed to represent. Numbers and financial statements are thought to be representationally faithful when they are **transparent** and when they reflect the **economic substance** of an underlying event or arrangement **rather than the legal form.**

What Do the Numbers Mean?

An excerpt follows from the notes to the financial statements of Enron Corp. for the year ended December 31, 2000. The complexity of the business arrangements makes it difficult to understand the nature of the underlying transactions. It contributes to a set of financial statements that lack transparency. The choice of words also makes the note difficult to read.

> In 2000 and 1999, Enron sold approximately $632 million and $192 million, respectively, of merchant investments and other assets to Whitewing. Enron recognized no gains or losses in connection with these transactions. Additionally, in 2000, ECT Merchant Investments Corp., a wholly-owned Enron subsidiary, contributed two pools of merchant investments to a limited partnership that is a subsidiary of Enron. Subsequent to the contributions, the partnership issued partnership interests representing 100% of the beneficial, economic interests in

> the two asset pools, and such interests were sold for a total of $545 million to a limited liability company that is a subsidiary of Whitewing. See Note 3. These entities are separate legal entities from Enron and have separate assets and liabilities. In 2000 and 1999, the Related Party, as described in Note 16, contributed $33 million and $15 million, respectively, of equity to Whitewing. In 2000, Whitewing contributed $7.1 million to a partnership formed by Enron, Whitewing and a third party. Subsequently, Enron sold a portion of its interest in the partnership through a securitization. See Note 3.[9]

Neutrality means that information cannot be selected to **favour one set of stakeholders over another**. Factual, truthful, unbiased information needs to be the overriding consideration when preparing financial information.

What Do the Numbers Mean?

Livent Inc. was a Canadian company that produced and presented large Broadway-style musicals. In 1993, the company went public, listing its shares on the TSX. By 1998, it filed for bankruptcy protection while it was being accused of accounting irregularities, and in 2001 it was investigated by the Ontario Securities Commission. The following excerpt is from the OSC Notice of Hearing and Allegation about manipulation of the financial statements:

> ... at the end of each financial reporting period, Livent accounting staff circulated to the Respondents a management summary reflecting actual results (including net income, on a show-by-show basis, compared to budget), as well as any improper adjustments carried forward from a prior financial period in connection with each show. Having regard to the actual results, the Respondents then provided instructions, directly or indirectly, to the Livent accounting staff specifying changes to be made to the actual results reflected in the company's books and records. In order to give effect to the Respondents' instructions, Livent accounting staff manipulated Livent's books and records by various means which did not accord with GAAP. The effect of the manipulations was to improve the presentation of Livent's financial results for the reporting period. Draft financial statements would then be generated for the reporting period incorporating the manipulations. These draft financial statements were then distributed to the Livent audit committee and, thereafter the Livent board of directors, for their review and approval. The Respondents attended meetings of the audit committee and the board of directors where these draft financial statements were discussed and ultimately approved. The Respondents did not disclose to the audit committee or the board of directors that, to their knowledge, the financial statements were false or misleading.

Among other things, management was charged with deliberately and systematically biasing the information. This contributed to the company's eventual downfall.

In practice, management needs to use many assumptions because of uncertainty in financial reporting. When choosing these assumptions, management must use its best estimates (management best estimate). How does the concept of **neutrality** fit with another key concept, **conservatism**?

Few conventions in accounting are as misunderstood as the concept of conservatism. In situations involving uncertainty and professional judgement, conservatism dictates that **net assets and net income not be overstated**. Does this represent a bias? Not necessarily. It is simply a default guideline. It acknowledges a **pre-existing tendency** of companies to overstate net assets and net income. Therefore it acts to counterbalance this tendency. An example of conservatism in accounting is the use of the lower of cost and net realizable value approach in valuing inventories.

---

[9] Consolidated financial statements of Enron Corp. for the year ended December 31, 2000.

Users of financial statements are more tolerant of understated net assets and net income than overstated balances. Therefore, if there is doubt about the numbers, it is better to understate than overstate net income and net assets. Of course, if there is no doubt, there is no need to apply this constraint. As you will see at the end of this chapter, biased information is tolerated much less now than in the past and the trend in financial reporting is away from any bias—including conservatism.

There is also another aspect to neutrality: neutrality in standard setting. Some observers argue that standards should not be issued if they cause undesirable economic effects on an industry or company (the **economic consequences argument,** which was mentioned in Chapter 1). This has been the long-standing argument against full recognition of employee stock option costs. Standards must be free from bias, however, or we will no longer have **credible financial statements**. Standard setters must therefore choose the best standards and acknowledge that users may change their decisions based on the new information that results from the new standard. While standard setters do not necessarily intend such changes in decisions, the fact that these changes occur shows the importance of ensuring that decision-relevant information is provided. Without credible financial statements, individuals will no longer use this information.

Comparability and Consistency

Information about an enterprise is more useful if it can be compared with similar information about another enterprise (**comparability**) and with similar information about the same enterprise at other points in time (**consistency**).[10]

Comparability. Information that has been measured and reported in a similar way for different enterprises is considered comparable. Comparability enables users to **identify the real similarities and differences in economic phenomena** because these have not been obscured by accounting methods that cannot be compared. For example, the accounting for pensions is different in North America and Japan. In Canada and the United States, pension costs are recorded as incurred, whereas in Japan there is little or no charge to income for these costs. As a result, it is difficult to compare and evaluate the financial results of General Motors or Ford with those of Nissan or Honda. It is important to remember therefore that **resource allocation decisions involve evaluations of alternatives** and a valid evaluation can only be made if comparable information is available. Although it is not a substitute for comparable information, a full disclosure of information sometimes allows users to overcome inconsistencies in how information is presented.

Consistency. When an entity uses the **same accounting treatment for similar events, from period to period**, the entity is considered to be consistent in its use of accounting standards. This does not mean that companies cannot switch from one accounting method to another. Companies can change methods, but such changes are only allowed when they are required by a primary source of GAAP or the change results in the financial statements providing reliable and more relevant information.[11] In these cases, the nature and effect of an accounting change, and the reasons for it, must be **disclosed** in the financial statements for the period in which the change is made.[12]

[10] Since the accounting environment is continually changing, comparability and consistency are difficult to achieve in practice. Tax laws change, new industries appear, new financial instruments are created, and mergers and divestitures occur.

[11] *CICA Handbook*, Section 1506.14.

[12] *CICA Handbook*, Section 1506.29.

When a company has made a change in **accounting principle**, the auditor need not refer to it in the audit report as long as the new policy is in accordance with GAAP. Changes in the financial statements (whether due to changes in policy or correction of errors) introduce uncertainty in the capital market place and undermine the financial reporting process.

What Do the Numbers Mean?

In 2006, Nortel announced yet again that it would be restating its results for the past four years and delaying the filing of its annual report to no later than April 30. The restatement was in addition to the two previous restatements. In response to the announcement, there was a corresponding decrease in share price, as is normal when negative news is reported by a company. The previous restatements had occurred in November 2003 and January 2005. According to a newspaper article,[13] an analyst asked whether there were any additional skeletons in the company's closet. Nortel stated that the restatements did not affect the cash flows of the company—rather, just the period that revenues were recognized in.

Toward the end of April, information about the restated financial statements was released and noted further adjustments. Interestingly, the share price did not decline as expected. The continuous restatements may have undermined the reliability or believability of the financial statements and made them less decision-relevant.

Trade-Offs

It is not always possible for financial information to have all the qualities of useful information. Sometimes a choice must be made about which quality is more important. **Relevant** information must have **feedback value**, **predictive value**, and be **timely**. **Reliable** information is **verifiable**, **representative of reality**, and **neutral**. Given that companies must issue annual financial statements, how long after the year-end date should they be issued? Financial statements are often released several weeks or months after year end. Issuing them earlier meets the timeliness criterion but issuing them at a later date allows time for management and auditors to check the statements to ensure that they are reliable. At some point in time, however, the information becomes irrelevant due to its lack of timeliness. Which is more important, timeliness or reliability? Each situation must be evaluated separately based on the facts available and the needs of the users.

The accounting profession is continually striving to produce financial information that meets all of the qualitative characteristics of useful information.

Basic Elements

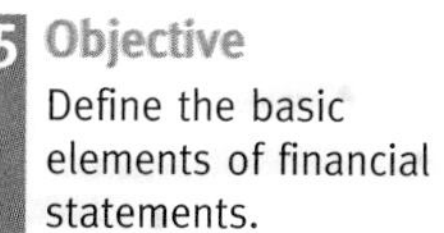
5 Objective
Define the basic elements of financial statements.

An important aspect of developing any theoretical structure is the body of basic elements or definitions to be included in the structure. At present, accounting uses many terms that have specific meanings. These terms make up the **language of accounting and business.** There are many elements that users expect to find on the financial statements, including **assets, liabilities, equity, revenues, gains, expenses, losses,** and **other comprehensive income**. In addition, with in each of these categories there are many subcategories, such as **current** and **noncurrent** assets, cash, inventory, and so on. The conceptual framework defines the basic elements so that users have a common understanding of the main items presented on the financial statements.

One important term is **asset.** Is an asset something we own? How do we define "own"? Is it based on **legal title** or **possession**? If ownership is based on legal title, can we assume that any leased asset would not be shown on the balance sheet? Is an asset something we have the **right to use**, or is it anything of value that is used by the enterprise to generate revenues? If the answer is the latter, should the enterprise's management then be considered an asset?

[13] "Nortel Accounting Woes Continue," *Toronto Star*, March 11, 2006.

The elements of financial statements that are most directly related to measuring an enterprise's performance and financial status are listed below. Each of these elements will be explained and examined in more detail in later chapters.

Elements of Financial Statements[14]

Assets are probable future economic benefits that have been obtained or are controlled by a particular entity as a result of past transactions or events. They have three essential characteristics:

1. They embody a **future benefit**.
2. The entity can **control access** to this benefit.
3. The **transaction** or event that gives the entity access to this benefit **has occurred**.

Generally, if a company has access to and control over substantially all of the **risks and rewards** of ownership, the asset should be recognized.

Liabilities are probable future sacrifices (of an economic benefit) that arise from a present duty or responsibility to others as a result of past transactions or events, where there is little or no discretion to avoid the obligation. Liabilities also have three essential characteristics:

1. They embody a **duty or responsibility**.
2. The entity has **little or no discretion to avoid** the duty.
3. The **transaction** or event that obligates the entity **has occurred.**

Equity/Net Assets is a **residual interest** in the assets of an entity that remains after deducting its liabilities (i.e., the net worth). In a business enterprise, the equity is the **ownership** interest.

Revenues are increases in economic resources, either by inflows or other enhancements of an entity's assets or settlement of its liabilities, which result from an entity's **ordinary activities.**

Expenses are decreases in economic resources, either by outflows or reductions of assets or the incurrence of liabilities, which result from an entity's **ordinary revenue-generating activities.**

Gains are increases in equity (net assets) from an entity's **peripheral or incidental transactions** and from all other transactions and other events and circumstances affecting the entity during a period, except those that result from revenues or investments by owners.

Losses are decreases in equity (net assets) from an entity's **peripheral or incidental transactions** and from all other transactions and other events and circumstances affecting the entity during a period, except those that result from expenses or distributions to owners.

Other Comprehensive Income[15] is made up of revenues, expenses, and gains and losses that, in accordance with primary sources of GAAP, are recognized in comprehensive income, but excluded from net income.

The financial statements include the following:

1. Income statement
2. Balance sheet
3. Statement of retained earnings
4. Statement of cash flows

---

[14] Taken from *CICA Handbook*, Section 1000.25 to .40 and Section 1530.03.

[15] Currently, the *Handbook* does not treat this as a separate element. There is also a question as to whether cash inflows and outflows might be considered to be separate elements of the cash flow statement. They are not listed as elements either.

5. Statement of comprehensive income (which may be incorporated into one of the other statements but must be displayed with the same prominence)[16]

The term **comprehensive income** is a relatively new income concept and includes more than the traditional notion of net income. It includes net income and all other changes in equity except for owners' investments and distributions. For example, the following would be included as **other comprehensive income** in the new comprehensive income statement:

- unrealized holding gains and losses on certain securities
- certain gains and losses related to foreign exchange instruments
- gains and losses related to certain types of hedges
- other

Note that although the information must be presented in the statements, the *Handbook* does not require companies to use the terms "Comprehensive Income" or "Other Comprehensive Income." This will be discussed further in Chapter 4.

THIRD LEVEL: FOUNDATIONAL CONCEPTS AND CONSTRAINTS

The framework's third level consists of **foundational concepts and constraints** that implement the basic objectives of level one. These concepts help explain which, when, and how financial elements and events should be **recognized**, **measured**, and **presented** by the accounting system. They act as guidelines for developing rational responses to controversial financial reporting issues. They have evolved over time and the specific accounting standards issued by the AcSB are based on these concepts in a fundamental way.

6 Objective
Describe the basic foundational concepts and constraints of accounting.

Basic **foundational concepts and constraints** underlying the financial accounting structure also include assumptions, principles and conventions. It is often difficult to put one of these labels onto the items noted below (and practice is varied) and so we have grouped them together under one heading. The specific label is not important—it is the substance of the concept and how it provides a solid foundation for accounting standard setting that is important. The following is a list of foundational concepts and constraints that helps shape accounting standards:

1. **economic entity**
2. **going concern**
3. **monetary unit**
4. **periodicity**
5. **historical cost**
6. **revenue recognition**
7. **matching**
8. **full disclosure**
9. **uncertainty**
10. **cost-benefit**
11. **materiality**
12. **industry practice**

Economic Entity

The **economic entity assumption** (or entity concept) means that economic activity can be **identified** with a particular **unit of accountability** (e.g., a company). In other words, a

[16] *CICA Handbook*, Section 1400.10.

company's business activity can be kept separate and distinct from its owners and any other business unit. If all the economic events that occur could not be separated in a meaningful way, there would be no basis for accounting.

The **entity concept** does not only apply to segregating the activities of different **business enterprises**. An individual, a department or division, or an entire industry can be considered a separate entity if we decide to define the unit in this way. Thus, the entity concept **does not necessarily always refer to a legal entity**. For tax and legal purposes, the **legal entity** is the relevant unit for a company. GAAP, however, requires that a parent company **consolidate** the financial statements of its subsidiaries with its own. A parent and its subsidiaries are separate **legal entities**, but merging their activities for accounting and reporting purposes gives more meaningful information.[17] Thus, the consolidated financial statements are prepared from the perspective of the **economic entity**. This allows the company to group together the assets, liabilities, and other financial statement elements that are under the parent's **control** into one set of statements. Control has historically been viewed as depending on the number of common shares held.[18]

Illustration 2-2 shows the notion of economic entity in regard to consolidated financial statements.

Illustration 2-2

Economic Entity as Defined for Consolidated Financial Statements

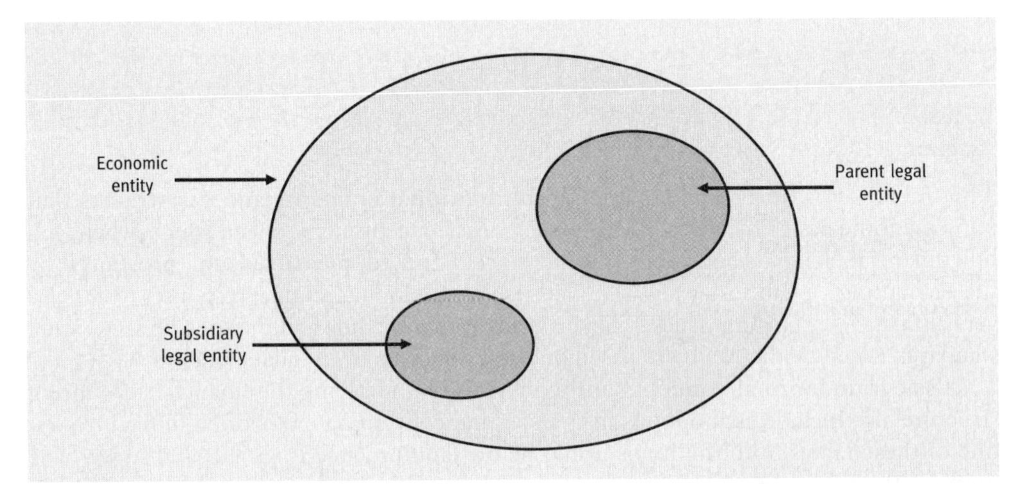

What Do the Numbers Mean?

It is important to first **define the entity** for financial reporting purposes. Many companies use what are known as Special Purpose Entities ("SPE") or Variable Interest Entities ("VIE"). These are legal entities set up for a specific purpose, e.g., to hold leases, pension funds, or perhaps certain investments. Are SPEs part of the economic entity for consolidated financial reporting purposes? This was the centre of much of the controversy for **Enron**. Enron had many SPEs that it did not include in its definition of economic entity and therefore excluded from its consolidated financial statements. As it turned out, Enron should have included them since the liabilities and losses of these SPEs ended up being liabilities and losses of Enron in the end. Enron's accounting had the impact of understating liabilities as well as overstating income. Subsequently, the AcSB has issued new standards on including VIE as part of the economic entity.[19]

---

[17] The concept of the entity is changing. For example, it is now harder to define the outer edges of companies. There are public companies with multiple public subsidiaries, each with joint ventures, licensing arrangements, and other affiliations and strategic alliances. Increasingly, loose affiliations of enterprises in joint ventures or customer-supplier relationships are formed and dissolved in a matter of months or weeks. These virtual companies raise accounting issues about how to account for the entity. See Steven H. Wallman, "The Future of Accounting and Disclosure in an Evolving World: The Need for Dramatic Change," *Accounting Horizons*, September 1995.

[18] That is, if the parent owns more than 50% of the (voting) common shares, it can exercise voting control.

[19] *CICA Handbook*, Accounting Guideline 15.

Going Concern

Most accounting methods are based on the **going concern assumption**. This is the assumption that a business enterprise will **continue to operate for the foreseeable future**—i.e., that it will not be forced to end its operations. Although there are many business failures, experience indicates that companies do have a fairly high continuance rate. While accountants do not believe that business firms will last indefinitely, they do expect them to last long enough to fulfill their objectives and commitments. Management must assess the ability of the company to continue as a going concern and take into account all available information, looking out at least twelve months from the balance sheet date.[20]

The implications of this assumption are profound. The **historical cost principle** would have limited usefulness if **liquidation** were assumed to be likely. Under a liquidation approach, for example, asset values are better stated at **net realizable value** (sales price less costs of disposal) than at **acquisition cost**. Amortization and amortization policies are justifiable and appropriate only if we assume some permanence to the enterprise; this is what justifies allocating the costs of the amortized assets to future periods to match them against future revenues. If a liquidation approach were adopted, the **current versus noncurrent classification** of assets and liabilities would lose much of its significance. Labelling anything a **fixed or long-term** asset would be difficult to justify. Indeed, listing liabilities according to their likely liquidation would be more reasonable.

The going concern assumption applies in most business situations. The only time when the assumption does not apply is when **there is intent to liquidate the net assets of the company and cease operations or trading in the company's shares or when the company has no realistic alternative but to liquidate or cease operations.**[21] In these cases, a total **revaluation** of assets and liabilities can provide information that closely approximates the entity's **net realizable value**. The accounting problems that arise when an enterprise is in liquidation are presented in advanced accounting courses. In order to illustrate the going concern concept and the question of liquidation, consider the situation of Air Canada.

What Do the Numbers Mean?

On April 1, 2003, **Air Canada** filed for bankruptcy protection under the *Companies' Creditors Arrangement Act* (CCAA) due to cash flow difficulties. The CCAA provides a safe harbour for companies in distress, giving them the opportunity to reorganize their financial affairs in an organized manner while at the same time holding off creditors. Air Canada's protection was granted for the period ending June 30. This was subsequently extended to September 30, 2003. In the meantime, the company issued its first quarter results.

Should the statements have been prepared on a **liquidation basis** or a **going concern basis**? Air Canada prepared the statements on a going concern basis using certain assumptions:

1. that management was in the process of developing a plan to restructure operations under the CCAA,
2. that it had been able to obtain "debtor in possession" financing from **General Electric Canada Finance Inc.**, and
3. that it expected the company to continue operating as a going concern.

The financial statements fully disclosed these facts. As it turns out, the company successfully emerged from bankruptcy protection and is still operating today. Companies are required to disclose any material uncertainties that may cast doubt upon the company's ability to continue on as a going concern.

Monetary Unit

The **monetary unit assumption** means that money is the common denominator of economic activity and is an appropriate **basis for accounting measurement** and analysis.

[20] *CICA Exposure Draft*, Going Concern (Amendments to Section 1400).

[21] Ibid.

International Insight

Due to their experiences with persistent inflation, several South American countries produce "constant currency" financial reports. Typically, a general price-level index is used to adjust the data for the effects of inflation so that the information becomes comparable from year to year.

This assumption implies that the monetary unit is the most effective way of expressing to interested parties changes in capital and exchanges of goods and services. The monetary unit is relevant, simple, universally available, understandable, and useful. Applying this assumption depends on the even more basic assumption that **quantitative data** are useful in communicating economic information and in making rational economic decisions.

In Canada and the United States, accountants have chosen generally to ignore the phenomenon of **price-level change** (inflation and deflation) by assuming that the unit of measure, the dollar, remains reasonably **stable**. This assumption about the monetary unit has been used to justify adding 1970 dollars to 2003 dollars without any adjustment. Only if circumstances change dramatically (such as if Canada or the United States were to experience high inflation similar to that in many South American countries) would the AcSB and FASB consider "inflation accounting."

IAS note

IAS 29 states certain requirements for entities that are reporting in a hyperinflationary economy.

Periodicity

The most accurate way to measure the results of an enterprise's activity would be to do the measurement at the time of the enterprise's eventual liquidation. At that point, there is complete certainty about all of the company's cash flows. Business, government, investors, and various other user groups, however, cannot wait that long for such information. Users need to be informed about performance and economic status on a **timely basis** so that they can evaluate and compare firms. For this reason, information must be reported periodically. The **periodicity assumption** (or time period assumption) implies that an enterprise's economic activities can be divided into **artificial time periods**. These time periods vary, but the most common are one month, one quarter, and one year.

The shorter the time period, the more difficult it becomes to **determine the proper net income** for the period. A month's results are usually less reliable than a quarter's results, and a quarter's results are likely less reliable than a year's results. This is because more estimates are needed to accrue costs and revenues in accrual accounting when the time period is shorter. Investors want and demand information that has been quickly processed and distributed; yet the more quickly the information is released, the more likely errors become.

The question of what time period is appropriate is becoming more serious because product cycles are shorter and products become obsolete more quickly. Many observers believe that, given the advances in technology, more on-line, **real-time financial information** needs to be provided to ensure that relevant information is available. The issue of continuous financial reporting was introduced in Chapter 1.

Historical Cost—Valuation Principles in Transition

Transactions can only be recognized when they have an appropriate basis of measurement and there is reasonable assurance as to the amount.[22] Once recognized, transactions and events result in financial statement elements. Transactions are initially measured at the amount of cash (or cash equivalents) that was paid or received or the fair value that was ascribed to the transactions when they took place. This is often called the **historical cost principle**.[23] The historical cost principle has three basic assumptions:

1. It represents a value at a **point in time**.
2. It results from a **reciprocal exchange** (i.e., a two-way exchange).
3. The exchange includes **an outside party**.

[22] *CICA Handbook*, Section 1000.44.

[23] *CICA Handbook*, Section 1000.53.

Initial recognition.

For non-financial assets, the value includes any **laid-down costs**—i.e., any cost that is incurred to get the asset ready (whether for sale or for generating income by using it). Inventory, for instance, might include the **cost of material, labour, and a reasonable allocation of overhead.**[24] Similarly, for a self-constructed asset, cost would include any cost incurred to get the asset **ready for its intended use,** including transportation and installation costs.[25]

Sometimes it is not possible to determine **cost or fair value**. Transactions that have some or all of the following characteristics present challenges:

- **Non-monetary or barter transactions** where **no cash or monetary consideration** is exchanged. Here it may be more difficult to determine the value of the assets exchanged.
- **Non-monetary, non-reciprocal transactions** where there is **no exchange**, such as donations.
- **Related party transactions** where the parties to the transaction are not acting at arm's length (i.e., there is **no outside party**). In these cases, the exchange price may not reflect the true value of the assets exchanged.

In such cases, an attempt is made to estimate the **fair value** if possible.

The historical cost principle also applies to financial instruments. Bonds, notes, and accounts payable and receivable are issued by a business enterprise in exchange for assets, or perhaps services, that have an **agreed-upon exchange price** or **economic value**. This price, established by the exchange transaction, is the "cost" of the financial instrument and gives the figure at which the instrument should be recognized in the financial statements as long as it is equal to fair value.

Subsequent remeasurement

Historical cost has an important advantage over other valuation methods: it is **reliable**. Because it generally comes from an **arm's-length transaction** or exchange, it represents a bargained, fairly arrived at value at a specific point in time. When it is first recognized, cost usually represents fair value. Over time, however, it often becomes irrelevant in terms of **predictive value**. Later remeasurements also have limitations, however. They can be based on different measurement values, such as fair value, and give information that is more relevant, but they often involve **measurement uncertainty.** Furthermore, because there is often no external exchange (i.e., exchange with an outside party), the values may be **subjective**.

Despite these limitations, the trend is toward an increasingly **mixed valuation model**. What used to be primarily a **historical cost–based model**, modified by the application of conservatism (i.e., revaluations occurred if the asset's value declined below cost), is moving more toward a **market valuation model**. The current **mixed valuation model** is shown in Illustration 2-3.

ASSET	BASIS OF VALUATION	MANAGEMENT INTENT
Accounts receivable	Lower of cost and net realizable value	To collect
Marketable securities held for trading	Fair value (normally market value)	To sell in near term for profit (part of trading portfolio)
Financial assets available for sale, e.g., securities	Fair value (where available—otherwise at cost)	To sell but not necessarily actively trade

Illustration 2-3

Valuation of Selected Balance Sheet Elements: A Mixed Valuation Model

[24] *CICA Handbook*, Section 3030.06. See also proposed Section 3031.10 to .14.

[25] *CICA Handbook*, Section 3061.05.

Inventories	Lower of cost and net realizable value	To sell and replace
Capital assets	Lower of cost and fair value (if cost not recoverable)	To hold to produce revenues
Financial assets held to maturity, e.g., bonds receivable	Lower of amortized cost and net realizable value	To hold for longer term and collect face value and interest
Liabilities	Historical cost	To repay

Illustration 2-3 identifies basic elements that are found on many balance sheets and provides the basis for valuation. As noted in the illustration, the existing **mixed attribute system** allows the following measurements to be used:

1. Historical cost
2. Amortized cost
3. Fair value consisting of any of the following:
   (a) market value
   (b) discounted cash flows
   (c) net present value/net realizable value
   (d) other
4. Lower of cost/amortized cost and fair value (conservatism)

The main emphasis in the model is on **relevance,** which is why many financial statement elements consider market or fair value in some way. Note that the **basis for valuation is usually tied to management's intent** for the asset. Management intent gives more insight into which value might be more relevant. As a general principle, **where current values are available** and they give more relevant information (in terms of what management intends to do with the asset or liability), they should be used as long as the **levels of measurement uncertainty are acceptable.**[26]

As will be seen in subsequent chapters, GAAP for financial instruments allows an entity to value any financial instrument at fair value regardless of intent. This option provides further evidence of the fair value trend.

Revenue Recognition

A crucial question for many enterprises is when revenue should be recognized. Revenue is generally recognized when the following three conditions are all true:

1. Performance is achieved (**earned**).
2. **Measurability is reasonably certain.**
3. **Collectibility is reasonably assured** (realized or realizable).[27]

This is referred to as the **revenue recognition principle**. As with the historical cost principle, the basic presumptions are that the transaction:

[26] Although using management intent allows greater transparency, it also allows bias and therefore, standard setters seek not to base the accounting on management intent.

[27] *CICA Handbook*, Section 1000.47.

- results from a **reciprocal exchange** (i.e., a two-way exchange) and
- the exchange includes **an outside party**.[28]

Revenues are **realized** when products (goods or services), merchandise, or other assets are **exchanged** for cash or claims to cash. Revenues are **realizable** if the assets received or held can be readily converted into cash or claims to cash. Assets are readily convertible if they can be sold or interchanged in an active market at prices that are readily determinable and there is no significant additional cost.

Performance

Revenues are considered earned when the entity has substantially accomplished what it must do to be entitled to the benefits that the revenues represent. In other words, revenue is recognized when the **earnings process is substantially complete**. When the earnings process is a **discrete earnings process**—i.e., with one main or **critical event**—the revenue recognition point is objective. In this case, revenue would normally be recognized when the **risks and rewards of ownership** pass to the buyer. When the earnings process lasts over a longer period and has more than one significant event—i.e., it is a **continuous earnings process**—revenue recognition becomes more difficult. An example of a continuous earnings process is a long-term construction contract. In these cases, revenue is recognized as it is earned, over the life of the contract.

Measurability and collectibility

When **measurement or collection is uncertain**, revenue recognition should be delayed until these uncertainties have been resolved or reduced to an acceptable level. For collectibility issues, either the **instalment** or **cost recovery** methods may be used to facilitate measurement of income that may be realized. These methods recognize profits as cash is received (often after the company has finished performing its side of the transaction).

Matching—Another Concept in Transition

Assets such as long-lived assets contribute to a company's ability to generate revenues. Therefore, accounting attempts to match these costs with the revenues that they produce. This practice is called **matching** because it dictates that effort (expenses) be matched with accomplishment (revenues) whenever this is reasonable and can be done. It also illustrates the **cause and effect relationship** between the money spent to earn revenues and the revenues themselves.

It may be difficult to establish exactly how much of a contribution is made to each period, however, and so often an estimation technique must be used. GAAP requires that a **rational and systematic** allocation policy be used that will approximate the asset's contribution to the revenue stream. Selection of a rational and systematic allocation technique involves making assumptions about the benefits that are being received as well as the costs associated with those benefits. The cost of a long-lived asset, for example, must be allocated over all accounting periods during which the asset is used because the asset contributes to revenue generation throughout its useful life.

[28] When the two parties are related, additional care needs to be taken to ensure that a bona fide transaction exists from the entity's perspective and that the basis for measurement is appropriate.

Costs are often classified into two groups: **product costs** and **period costs**. Product costs such as material, labour, and overhead attach to the product and are carried into future periods as inventory (if not sold) since inventory meets the definition of an asset. Period costs such as officers' salaries and other administrative expenses are recognized immediately—even though the benefits associated with these costs occur in the future—because no direct relationship between cost and revenue can be established and more importantly because the costs do not meet the definition of an asset.

In the past, accountants have argued that costs associated with producing revenues should be deferred, and recognized in the income statement when the related revenues are recognized. The following scenario provides an illustration of this.

What Do the Numbers Mean?

Livent Inc., mentioned earlier, followed the policy of deferring preproduction costs for the creation of each separate show until the show was opened. On opening night, the show would start to produce revenues and then the costs were amortized and matched with those revenues. Such costs included advertising, publicity and promotions, set construction, props, costumes, and salaries paid to the cast, crew, musicians, and creative constituents during rehearsal. In short, anything to do with the production was deferred.

On the one hand, one might argue that this was a bit aggressive. One could also argue that this treatment was acceptable because of the direct and incremental nature of these costs in terms of the future production revenues. The trouble began when the company started to reclassify some of these costs as fixed assets and also to reallocate these costs to different and unrelated shows that had higher revenue. The company even had spreadsheets to keep track of actual results as compared with those that were publicly reported.[29]

There are debates about whether or not "matching" is conceptually valid in terms of providing support for cost deferrals. A major concern is that matching permits certain costs to be **deferred and treated as assets** on the balance sheet when in fact these costs may not meet the definition of assets (no future benefits). If abused, matching can be used by a company to turn the balance sheet into a dumping ground for unmatched costs. The new conceptual frameworks being developed by the IASB and the FASB define financial statement elements (e.g., assets and liabilities). There are no grounds for recognizing assets and liabilities that do not specifically meet the definitions of these elements. If a cost or expenditure does not meet the definition of an asset, it is expensed (matching notwithstanding). In Canada, this changing emphasis is happening in part because of accounting abuses such as the one noted above at Livent Inc. and will be reflected in proposed changes to Sections 1000 and 3062 of the *Handbook*.

Accounting standard setters are moving towards ensuring that the balance sheet elements are properly recognized and measured as a basis for measuring income. Thus the concept of matching is not as central as it would be if the income statement were the main focus.

Full Disclosure

Anything that is relevant to decisions should be included in the financial statements. This is referred to as the **full disclosure principle**. The principle recognizes that the nature and amount of information included in financial reports reflects a series of judgemental trade-offs. These trade-offs aim for information that is:

- **detailed enough** to disclose matters that make a difference to users, but
- **condensed enough** to make the information understandable, and also appropriate in terms of the **costs** of preparing and using it.

[29] OSC Notice of Hearing and Statement of Allegations concerning Livent Inc., July 3, 2001.

More information is not always better. Too much information may result in a situation where the user is unable to digest or process the information. This is called **information overload**. Information about a company's financial position, income, cash flows, and investments can be found in one of three places:

1. In the **main body of financial statements**
2. In the **notes to the financial statements**
3. As supplementary information, including the **Management Discussion and Analysis** (MD&A)

The financial statements are a **formalized, structured way of communicating financial information**. Disclosure is not a substitute for proper accounting.[30] Certain numbers, such as earnings per share, send signals to the capital marketplace. For example, cash basis accounting for cost of goods sold is misleading, even if accrual-based amounts have been disclosed in the notes to the financial statements. As mentioned in Chapter 1, and earlier in this chapter with regard to Nortel, the market watches and listens for signals about earnings in particular and does not always react well to earnings surprises—especially negative ones.

The **notes to financial statements** generally **amplify or explain** the items presented in the main body of the statements. If the information in the main body of the statements gives an incomplete picture of the enterprise's performance and position, additional information that is needed to complete the picture should be included in the notes.

Information in the notes does not have to be quantifiable, nor does it need to qualify as an element. Notes can be partially or totally narrative. Examples of notes are:

- **descriptions** of the accounting policies and methods used in measuring the elements reported in the statements
- **explanations** of uncertainties and contingencies
- **statistics and details** that are too voluminous to include in the statements

The notes are not only helpful to understanding the enterprise's performance and position—they are essential.

Supplementary information may include details or amounts that present a different perspective from what appears in the financial statements. They may include quantifiable information that is high in relevance but low in reliability, or information that is helpful but not essential. One example of supplementary information is the data and schedules provided by oil and gas companies: typically they give information on proven reserves as well as the related discounted cash flows.

Supplementary information also includes management's explanation of the financial information and a discussion of its significance in the **MD&A**. The CICA MD&A *Guidance on Preparation and Disclosure* lays out six general disclosure principles. "MD&A's should:

- enable readers to **view the company through the eyes of management**;
- **complement** as well as **supplement** financial statements;
- be **reliable, complete, fair, and balanced**, providing material information—that is, information important to an investor, acting reasonably, in making a decision to invest or continue to invest in the company;
- have a **forward-looking** orientation;

[30] According to *CICA Handbook* Section 1000.42, recognition means including an item in one or more individual statements and does not mean disclosure in the notes to the financial statements. Some critics might argue, however, that if markets are assumed to be efficient, then as long as the information is disclosed, the market will absorb and use the information in pricing the shares.

- focus on **management's strategy for generating value** for investors over time;
- be **written in plain language**, with candour and without exaggeration, and embody the qualities of understandability, relevance, comparability, and consistency over reporting periods."

Thus, the MD&A is a step toward a more broadly based business reporting model that also contains forward-looking information. The Guideline also includes a framework that identifies five key elements that should be included in the MD&A:

1. The company's **vision, core businesses, and strategy**
2. **Key performance drivers**
3. **Capabilities** (capital and other resources) to achieve the desired results
4. **Results**—historical and prospective
5. **Risks** that may shape and/or affect the achievement of results

Hopefully, these additional disclosures will give users of the financial information a greater insight into the company's business.[31]

The content, arrangement, and display of financial statements, along with other facets of full disclosure, are discussed specifically in Chapters 4, 5, and 23, and more generally throughout the text.

Uncertainty

Uncertainty is considered a constraint because too much uncertainty may make it inappropriate to recognize a financial statement element. As a general rule, **elements** are **recognized** in the financial statements if they arise from events that are **likely or probable** and **measurable** (i.e., amounts may be reasonably estimated).[32] Management must assess the likelihood of outcomes (e.g., whether a company will lose a lawsuit) based on history and supporting evidence. Often, companies rely on specialists such as lawyers and engineers for help with such assessments.

Measurability is a big issue for many financial statement elements. When there is a **variance** between the recognized amount and another reasonably possible amount, this is called **measurement uncertainty**.[33] Accountants are continually working to develop and make use of **measurement tools** such as the Black-Scholes option pricing model, net present value model, and discounted cash flow models, as well as others. When observable values are not available (e.g., market prices, cost), these models are used as a way of dealing with measurement uncertainty.[34] There is a trade-off with uncertainty. Too much measurement uncertainty undermines the reliability of the financial statements. However, if the element is not recognized at all in the financial statements, then all relevant information has not been included. A compromise is to measure and recognize the elements in

---

[31] Although MD&A disclosures are mandated for public companies, the CICA Guidance, in its executive summary, notes that the MD&A can also be used by other organizations to communicate more effectively.

[32] *CICA Handbook*, Section 3290.12. and Section 1000.44.

[33] *CICA Handbook*, Section 1508.03.

[34] FASB Statement of Financial Accounting Concepts 7 addresses the use of cash flow and present value techniques in measurement. In Canada, these concepts are also being incorporated in the *Handbook*. See for instance Section 3025 on Impaired loans, Section 3063 on Impairment of long-lived assets, and other sections such as leases and employee future benefits. The AcSB, FASB, and IASB are all working on this issue with the goal of producing a converged standard.

the body of the financial statements and to disclose the measurement uncertainty and its significance in the notes to the financial statements.

Cost-Benefit Relationship

Too often, users assume that information is a cost-free commodity. But preparers and providers of accounting information know this is not true. This is why the **cost-benefit relationship** must be considered: the costs of providing the information must be weighed against the benefits that can be had from using the information. Standard-setting bodies and government agencies now use cost-benefit analysis before making their information requirements final. In order to justify requiring a particular measurement or disclosure, the benefits that are expected to come from it must be greater than the costs of making it.

The difficulty in cost-benefit analysis is that the costs and, especially, the benefits are not always evident or measurable. The costs are of several kinds, including the costs of:

- collecting and processing
- distributing
- auditing
- potential litigation
- disclosure to competitors
- analysis and interpretation

The benefits are enjoyed by both preparers (in terms of greater management control and access to capital) and users (in terms of allocation of resources, tax assessment, and rate regulation). Benefits, however, are generally more difficult to quantify than costs. The CICA has taken some steps to reduce the cost of providing information by developing a Differential Reporting model. This model allows smaller, private companies to follow a simplified version of GAAP based on cost-benefit considerations.[35] The AcSB is also studying how to deal with private companies (many of which are smaller) once there is international convergence with respect to international accounting standards for public companies.

Materiality

Materiality relates to an item's impact on a firm's overall financial operations. An item is material if including it or leaving it out would influence or change the judgement of a reasonable person.[36] It is immaterial and, therefore, irrelevant if it would have no impact on a decision-maker. In short, it must make a difference; otherwise, it does not have to be disclosed. The point involved here is about **relative size** and **importance**. If the amount involved is significant when compared with the other revenues and expenses, assets and liabilities, or net income of the entity, sound and acceptable standards should be followed. If the amount is so small that it is quite unimportant when compared with other items, applying a particular standard may be considered less important.

It is hard to give firm guidelines that decide when an item is or is not material because materiality depends on both a relative amount and relative importance.

[35] *CICA Handbook*, Section 1300.

[36] FASB Statement of Financial Accounting Concepts No. 2 (par. 132) sets forth the essence of materiality: "The omission or misstatement of an item in a financial report is material if, in light of surrounding circumstances, the item's magnitude is such that it is probable that the judgement of a reasonable person relying upon the report would have been changed or influenced by the item's inclusion or correction." This same concept of materiality has been adopted by the CICA. See *CICA Handbook*, Section 1000.17.

For example, the two sets of numbers in Illustration 2-4 show relative size.

Illustration 2-4
Materiality Comparison

	Company A	Company B
Sales	$10,000,000	$100,000
Costs and expenses	9,000,000	90,000
Income from operations	1,000,000	10,000
Unusual gain	20,000	5,000

During the particular period, the revenues and expenses, and therefore the net incomes, of Company A and Company B have been proportional. Each has also had an unusual gain.

In looking at the abbreviated income figures for Company A, it does not appear significant whether the amount of the unusual gain is presented separately or is merged with the regular operating income. It is only 2 percent of the operating income and, if merged, would not seriously distort the income figure. Company B has had an unusual gain of only $5,000, but it is relatively much more significant than the larger gain realized by A. For Company B, an item of $5,000 amounts to 50 percent of its operating income. Obviously, including such an item in ordinary operating income would affect the amount of that income materially. In this example, we can therefore see the importance of an item's relative size in determining its materiality.

Most companies and their auditors have adopted the general rule of thumb that anything above **5 percent of income from continuing operations** (after tax) is considered material.[37] This is a fairly simplistic and one-dimensional view of materiality, however, and needs further examination. The impact of the items on other factors, for instance on key financial statement ratios and management compensation—in short, on **any sensitive number on the financial statements**—should also be considered. Both **quantitative** and **qualitative** factors must be considered in determining whether an item is material.[38] Qualitative factors might include illegal acts, failure to comply with regulations, or inadequate or inappropriate description of an accounting policy. Materiality is also a factor in a large number of internal accounting decisions. The amount of classification required in a subsidiary expense ledger, the degree of accuracy required in prorating expenses among the departments of a business, and the extent to which adjustments should be made for accrued and deferred items are examples of judgements that should finally be determined based on reasonableness and practicability—i.e., on the materiality constraint sensibly applied. Only by exercising good judgement and professional expertise can reasonable and appropriate answers be found.

Industry Practice

A final consideration is **industry practice**. The peculiar nature of some industries and business concerns sometimes requires unique accounting. In these cases, it is important to ensure that the practices are consistent with the primary sources of GAAP and the conceptual framework.[39]

Illustration 2-5 presents the conceptual framework discussed in this chapter. It is similar to Illustration 2-1, except that it gives additional information for each level. We cannot overemphasize the usefulness of this conceptual framework in helping to understand many of the problem areas that are examined in later chapters.

[37] CICA Assurance and Related Services Guideline 31.

[38] *CICA Handbook*, Section 5142.06.

[39] *CICA Handbook*, Section 1100.31.

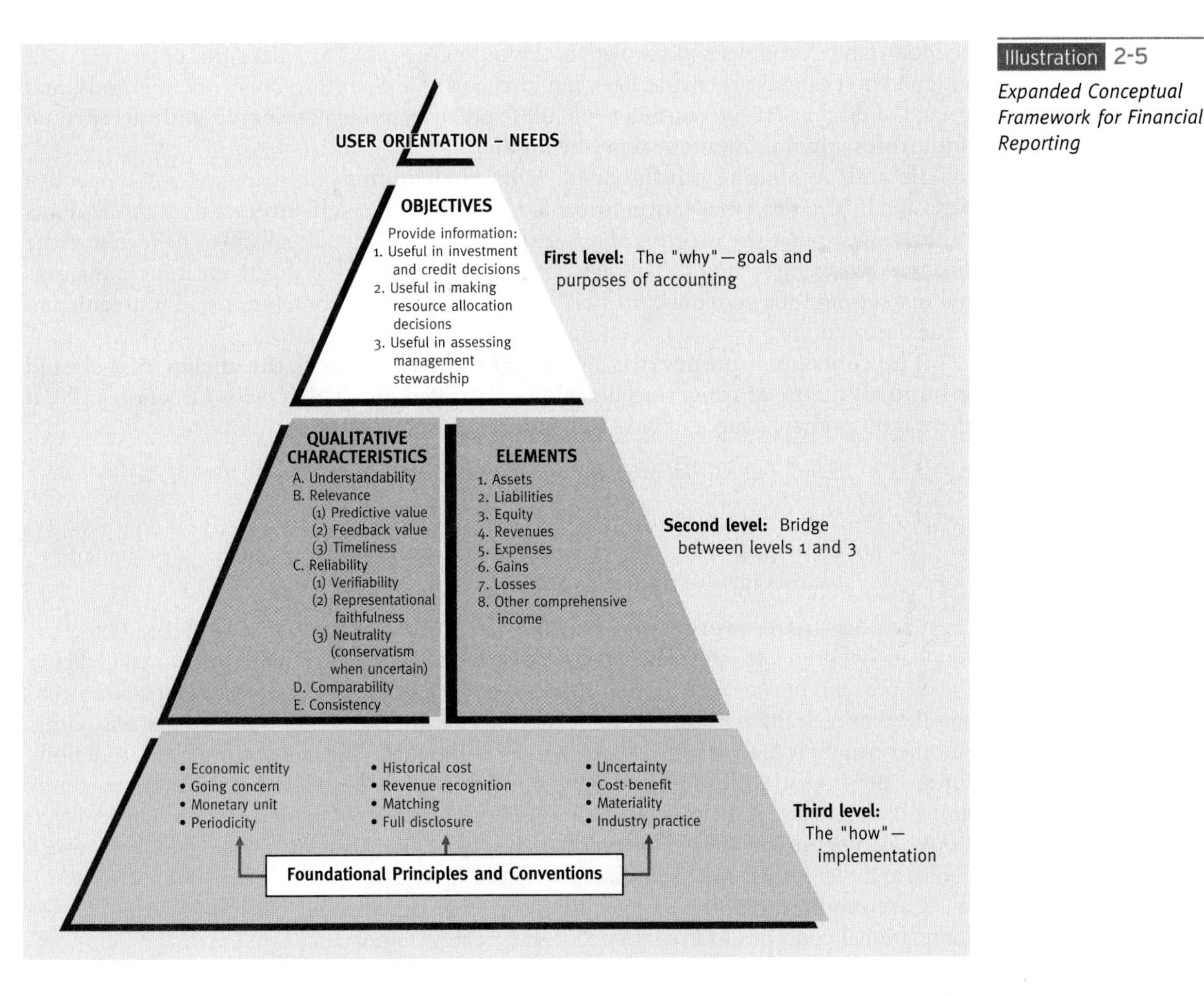

Illustration 2-5

Expanded Conceptual Framework for Financial Reporting

FINANCIAL REPORTING ISSUES

7 **Objective**
Explain the factors that contribute to choice in financial reporting decisions.

Making financial reporting decisions is a complex process. This section examines the factors that make this process challenging.

Making Accounting Choices

Many factors lead to there being choice in financial reporting. These include:

1. GAAP in Canada being **principles-based** and therefore requiring the use of professional judgement
2. **Measurement uncertainty**
3. **The complexity** of business transactions

   The role of each of these will be examined next.

Principles-Based Approach

As mentioned earlier in the chapter, the main objective of financial reporting is to **provide reliable decision-relevant financial information** to users so that they can make well-informed capital allocation decisions. Capital that is invested in good investments fuels the economy and encourages job growth and wealth creation. To achieve this objective, well-judged choices must be made between alternative accounting concepts, methods, and means of disclosure. Accounting principles and rules must be **selected and interpreted and professional judgement must be applied**.

Because accounting is **influenced by its environment** (in many cases in a negative way) and by decisions made by individuals who often act in **self-interest** or in the interests of the company (at the expense of other stakeholders), it is unrealistic to believe that the financial reporting system will always work properly. Instead of wealth creation in the capital markets and the economy, financial reporting decisions sometimes lead to wealth and value destruction.

The conceptual framework developed in this chapter is the anchor that should ground all financial reporting decisions. As noted in *CICA Handbook* Section 1100, if there is no primary source of GAAP to guide a decision,

> ... an entity should adopt accounting policies that are:
>
> (a) consistent with the primary sources of GAAP; and
>
> (b) **developed** through the exercise of professional judgement and the application of the concepts described in ... Section 1000.[40]

Canadian GAAP is **principles-based**—that is, most of the *Handbook* is based on a few foundational principles and concepts like those in the conceptual framework noted earlier in the chapter and in *Handbook* Section 1000.[41] The benefit of this approach is that all decisions should theoretically be **consistent** if they start from the same foundational reasoning. Another benefit is that principles-based GAAP is **flexible**. The most appropriate accounting for any new situation or novel business transaction may be arrived at through reason by going back to these principles (sometimes referred to as **first principles**). Principles-based GAAP is sometimes criticized for being too flexible. Some critics feel that it allows too much choice and therefore results in **lack of comparability**.

Care should therefore be taken to ensure that this flexibility is not abused. The key foundational concept of **neutrality** is of the greatest importance.

Measurement Uncertainty

Because **accrual accounting** is followed, many estimates must be used when preparing financial statements. In addition, uncertainty in valuation is one of the most prevalent measurement uncertainties. Fundamental principles and assumptions such as the **periodicity assumption**, the **going concern assumption**, the **matching principle**, the **revenue recognition principle**, and others also contribute to measurement uncertainty. Most numbers on a balance sheet and income statement are in fact quite "soft" and inexact. Measurement uncertainty was discussed earlier under the heading Constraints. The key for accountants is to **determine an acceptable level of uncertainty**, use **measurement tools** that help deal with the uncertainty, and **disclose enough information** to signal the uncertainty.

Unusual and Complex Transactions

The business environment is ever-changing and becoming increasingly complex. It is difficult for the AcSB to keep on top of all of these changes and impossible to write standards that consider all possible transactions. Therefore, accountants must often sort through the complexities and determine the most appropriate treatment. This involves a large amount of choice. Principles-based standards are more flexible than transactions-based standards and therefore preferable in dealing with this problem.

---

[40] *CICA Handbook*, Section 1100.04.

[41] As noted in Chapter 1, due to the AcSB prior commitment to harmonize with U.S. GAAP, Canadian GAAP was becoming increasingly rules-based. The AcSB current mandate is to adopt International GAAP for public companies. International GAAP is principles-based.

Identifying issues

When making financial reporting choices, some issues are more difficult to analyze and resolve than others. This is because there is more than one possible solution for how to account for the item. All issues fall into one of four categories:

8 Objective
Identify the four types of financial reporting issues and what makes certain issues more important than others.

(a) **Recognition**—Should the element be recorded or not in the general ledger (and hence in the income statement or balance sheet)? For example, revenue recognition, accrual of a liability, recognition of an asset.

(b) **Measurement**—If it is recognized, how much should the element be recorded at, i.e., what is its value or cost? For example, how should an accrual for environmental damages be measured? How should a particular asset be valued?

(c) **Presentation**—Where on the key financial statements should the item be shown? For example, as debt or equity, as an extraordinary item or discontinued operations.

(d) **Disclosure**—How much detail should be given in the financial reports?

Not all financial reporting decisions are the same—some are more important or material to a user's decisions. How do we determine the relative importance of an issue? While accountants must ensure the completeness, authorization, and accuracy of **all** transactions in the accounting system, they must ensure in particular that **important or material issues** receive special attention.

As previously noted, accounting decisions are not made in a vacuum. Many stakeholders depend on the information to make key decisions. As a result, some numbers in the financial statements have a **higher profile and visibility** than others since they become the **focus for decision-making**.

Contractual and regulatory focal points. As an example, many creditors structure lending agreements so that the borrower is required to maintain certain numbers for such liquidity and solvency ratios as current and debt-to-equity ratios. The company must calculate these ratios periodically and report to the lender on whether the company is respecting the loan agreement's requirements. These requirements are often referred to as **debt covenants**. If a company does not meet the requirement, the consequence is that the loan could become a demand loan and the lender could then insist that it be repaid immediately. Thus, any ratios that are mentioned in key business agreements become important ratios and any transactions that affect these ratios become important focal points.

Similarly, ratios and key numbers are used in **management remuneration arrangements**, such as bonuses that depend on earnings. Sometimes there are regulatory restrictions that emphasize certain key numbers or ratios. Accountants must be aware of all of these pressure points and factor them into their decision-making.

Key capital market focal points. Participants in capital markets focus on **earnings** and earnings per share. As discussed in Chapter 1, negative earnings surprises are not well received by the marketplace and affect a company's share price and ability to raise capital. For this reason, decisions that impact earnings are also important.

Any transactions or balances that affect key numbers or ratios by a material amount become important and significant. This is not to say that accountants should bias the accounting; rather, they need to **be aware of the impact** of their decisions on stakeholders.

Financial Engineering

A practice known as **financial engineering** became more visible during the past decade. Financial engineering is the process of legally structuring a business arrangement or transaction so that it meets the company's financial reporting objective (e.g., to maximize earn-

9 Objective
Explain the practice of financial engineering.

ings, minimize a debt-to-equity ratio, or other). This is often done by creating complex legal arrangements and financial instruments. These arrangements and instruments are created so that the resulting accounting meets the desired objective within GAAP. For example, a company that is raising debt financing might want the instrument structured so that it meets the GAAP definition of equity rather than debt. In this way, the debt-to-equity ratio is not affected.

Many financial institutions developed and marketed these products to their clients. These arrangements are often called structured financings. Since Enron, this practice has been reduced. Is financial engineering and the practice of structured financings acceptable under GAAP? Financial engineering has moved from being an accepted (saleable) practice and commodity to a potentially fraudulent activity.

Illustration 2-6 looks at the various shades of grey in accounting for transactions.

Illustration 2-6
Choice in Accounting Decision-Making

- Accounting for bona fide business transactions in a transparent way–no bias
- Using professional judgement to account for transactions, while keeping in mind critical financial statement numbers or ratios
- Aggressively interpreting GAAP so that the impact on critical financial statement numbers or ratios is minimal
- Structuring bona fide business transactions to minimize their impact on debt covenants
- Entering into specific business transactions for the sole purpose of making the financial statements look a certain way

→ **FRAUDULENT FINANCIAL REPORTING**

Fraudulent Financial Reporting

Objective 10
Identify factors that contribute to fraudulent financial reporting.

The role of accountants who are responsible for preparing a company's financial records is to capture business and economic events and transactions as they occur and communicate them to interested parties. They should not use the financial statements to portray something that is not there. Similarly, good financial reporting should be a result of **well reasoned and supported analysis** that is grounded in a conceptual framework. It should not be influenced by external pressures. Pressures in the capital marketplace are everywhere, however, and their potentially negative impact on financial reporting must be acknowledged. Pressures may arise from various sources, including the ones discussed below.

Economic or Business Environment

Sometimes a company experiences sudden drops in revenue or market share. The underlying reason may be unique to the company and due to some poor strategic and business decisions or it may result from an industry or economic downturn. This may put pressures on a company to "prop up" its revenues. There may be pressure to recognize revenues before they should be or to defer the recognition of some expenses.

Some companies use an industry or economic downturn as an opportunity to clean up their books and generally take large writedowns of assets such as inventory or goodwill. The markets expect a loss and the company's share price is therefore not overly affected in a negative way. This "purging" of the balance sheet has the positive impact of making future earnings look better.

Other Pressures

Budgets put tremendous pressure on company management. Since bonuses and even jobs depend on meeting budgets, sometimes this negative influence leaks inappropriately into accounting decisions.

Sometimes strong pressures build up because of debt covenants or analysts' expectations. These can be significant and may cause management to make biased decisions and misrepresent the company's financial position and operations.

If they are not monitored and controlled properly, these pressures are a major problem. In order to lessen the chances of fraudulent financial reporting, various controls and a solid governance structure may be put in place by a company. These could include:

(a) vigilant, knowledgeable top management

(b) an independent audit committee

(c) an internal audit function

(d) other internal controls at lower levels

International

11 Objective
Recognize how similar Canadian GAAP is to international GAAP.

Canadian and international GAAP are fundamentally similar since they are both principles-based. The IASB and FASB are currently working on a joint project to produce a common conceptual framework. As previously mentioned, they have produced the first part of the framework, which deals with the objectives of financial reporting and qualitative characteristics of useful information.

The draft document is currently out for comment and is very similar to the Canadian conceptual framework. The following points are worth noting:

1. The Canadian framework lists "**assessing resource allocation**" and "**management stewardship**" as key separate decisions that financial statement users need information for.[42] The IASB/FASB document notes that "resource allocation" is the main decision. It was felt that the information that is needed to assess stewardship is similar and that information necessary for users to make resource allocation decisions would encompass that necessary for users to assess management stewardship. No incremental information would be necessary to assess stewardship. For this reason, assessing stewardship was not listed as a separate decision.

2. The IASB/FASB document formally acknowledges that **neutrality** is incompatible with the concept of conservatism since the latter implies bias. The concept of conservatism is therefore excluded. In contrast, the Canadian standard allows that conservatism and neutrality can exist side by side when conditions are uncertain.

3. An additional characteristic of useful information was added—**completeness**. The IASB/FASB authors felt that this was an important characteristic and that information which faithfully represents economic reality must include all information that is necessary to describe the event. Under the Canadian standard, this concept is implied in the wording, but it is not explicitly identified.

4. In terms of the **trade-offs between qualitative characteristics**, whereas the Canadian standard discusses having to achieve an appropriate balance and leaves it

[42] *CICA Handbook*, Section 1000.15.

open to judgement, the IASB/FASB standard offers a bit more guidance. It notes that relevance must be dealt with first, then faithful representation, and finally comparability and understandability. It also notes that relevance deals with deciding which information to include, and representational faithfulness with how to present the information so that it best represents the underlying economic phenomena. Finally, once all the key economic events have been identified and decisions have been made about how best to represent them, it is time to ensure that the information is presented in a way that is comparable and understandable.

5. The term faithful representation was elevated to replace the term reliability. The concern was that the term reliability was being misread to imply that if numbers are volatile, they are not reliable.

   The document entitled "Revisiting the Concepts" issued jointly by the IASB and FASB provides an excellent discussion of some of the issues faced when authoring a harmonized conceptual framework.

Student Website

Glossary

www.wiley.com/canada/kieso

Summary of Learning Objectives

1 Describe the usefulness of a conceptual framework.

A conceptual framework is needed to (1) create standards that build on an established body of concepts and objectives, (2) provide a framework for solving new and emerging practical problems, (3) increase financial statement users' understanding of and confidence in financial reporting, and (4) enhance comparability among different companies' financial statements.

2 Describe the main components of the conceptual framework for financial reporting.

The first level deals with the objective of financial reporting. The second level includes the qualitative characteristics of useful information and elements of financial statements. The third level includes foundational principles and conventions.

3 Understand the objective of financial reporting.

The objective of financial reporting is to provide information that is useful to individuals making investment and credit decisions.

4 Identify the qualitative characteristics of accounting information.

The overriding criterion by which accounting choices can be judged is decision usefulness; that is, the goal is to provide the information that is the most useful for decision-making. Understandability, relevance, reliability, comparability, and consistency are the qualities that make accounting information useful for decision-making.

5 Define the basic elements of financial statements.

The basic elements of financial statements are (1) assets, (2) liabilities, (3) equity, (4) revenues, (5) expenses, (6) gains, and (7) losses. An additional element is other comprehensive income.

6 Describe the basic foundational concepts and constraints of accounting.

(1) Economic entity: the assumption that the activity of a business enterprise can be kept separate and distinct from its owners and any other business unit. (2) Going concern: the assumption that the business enterprise will have a long life. (3) Monetary unit: the assumption that money is the common denominator by which economic activity is conducted, and that the monetary unit gives an appropriate basis for meas-

KEY TERMS

assets, 42
basic elements, 41
comparability, 40
comprehensive income, 43
conceptual framework, 34
conservatism, 39
consistency, 40
continuous earnings process, 49
cost-benefit relationship, 53
critical event (earnings), 49
debt covenants, 57
decision usefulness, 37
discrete earnings process, 49
earned (revenue), 48
economic entity assumption, 43
economic substance over legal form, 38
equity/net assets, 42
expenses, 42
feedback value, 37
financial engineering, 57
first principles, 56
full disclosure principle, 50
gains, 42

urement and analysis. (4) Periodicity: the assumption that an enterprise's economic activities can be divided into artificial time periods to facilitate timely reporting.

(5) Historical cost principle: existing GAAP requires that many assets and liabilities be accounted for and reported based on their acquisition price. Many assets are later revalued. (6) Revenue recognition: revenue is generally recognized when it is (a) earned and measurable and (b) collectible (realizable). (7) Matching assists in the measurement of income by ensuring that costs (relating to long-lived assets) incurred in earning revenues are booked in the same period as the revenues earned. (8) Full disclosure principle: accountants follow the general practice of providing information that is important enough to influence an informed user's judgement and decisions.

(9) Uncertainty: excessive uncertainty makes recognition difficult or impossible. (10) Cost-benefit relationship: the costs of providing the information must be weighed against the benefits that can be had from using the information. (11) Materiality: sound and acceptable standards should be followed if the amount involved is significant when compared with the other revenues and expenses, assets and liabilities, or net income of the entity. (12) Industry practice: sometimes the unique nature of a specific industry requires unique accounting. Care should be taken to ensure that the resulting statements are consistent with primary sources of GAAP and the conceptual framework.

7 Explain the factors that contribute to choice in financial reporting decisions.

Choice is the result of many things, including (1) GAAP being principles-based, (2) measurement uncertainty, and (3) increasingly complex business transactions. The conceptual framework is the foundation that GAAP is built on. If there is no primary source of GAAP for a specific decision, then professional judgement must be used, making sure that the accounting policies chosen are consistent with the primary sources of GAAP and the conceptual framework. A principles-based approach allows flexibility, but this can lead to inconsistencies. Accrual-based accounting requires that transactions be recognized when incurred, which often involves estimations. This leads to measurement uncertainty. The AcSB is unable to keep pace with the increasingly complex nature of business and the business environment, and accountants must therefore decide how to account for complex transactions.

8 Identify the four types of financial reporting issues and what makes certain issues more important than others.

The four types of issues are (1) recognition, (2) measurement, (3) presentation, and (4) disclosure. Any transactions or balances that affect key numbers or ratios by a material amount become important and significant.

9 Explain the practice of financial engineering.

Financial engineering is the process of legally structuring a business arrangement or transaction so that it meets the company's financial reporting objective. This is a dangerous practice since it often results in biased information.

10 Identify factors that contribute to fraudulent financial reporting.

Fraudulent financial reporting often results from pressures on individuals or the company. These pressures may come from various sources, including worsening company, industry, or economic conditions, unrealistic internal budgets, and financial statement focal points related to contractual, regulatory, or capital market expectations. Weak internal controls and governance also contribute to fraudulent financial reporting.

11 Recognize how similar Canadian GAAP is to international GAAP.

The conceptual frameworks dealing with objectives and qualitative characteristics are very similar in that they are both principles-based. The differences include:

general-purpose financial statements, 36
going concern/ assumption, 45
historical cost principle, 46
industry practice, 54
information overload, 51
laid-down costs, 47
liabilities, 42
losses, 42
management best estimate, 39
matching, 49
materiality, 53
measurement uncertainty, 52
monetary unit assumption, 45
neutrality, 39
non-monetary/barter transactions, 47
non-monetary/ non-reciprocal transactions, 47
notes to financial statements, 51
objective of financial reporting, 35
other comprehensive income, 42
periodicity assumption, 46
predictive value, 37
qualitative characteristics, 37
realizable (revenue), 49
realized (revenue), 49
reciprocal exchange, 46
related party transactions,47
relevance, 37
reliability, 37
representational faithfulness, 38
revenue recognition principle, 48
revenues, 42
supplementary information, 51
timeliness, 37
transparent, 38
understandability, 37
verifiability, 38

- how assessment of management stewardship is dealt with
- how conservatism is dealt with (it is seen as incompatible with the concept of neutrality in the IASB/FASB standard)
- the addition of one more characteristic—completeness
- there being more guidance in the IASB/FASB standard on how to deal with trade-offs between qualitative characteristics
- the elevation of representational faithfulness

Brief Exercises

(LO 4) BE2-1 Discuss whether the changes described in each of the cases below violates the consistency characteristic (assume that the amounts are material):

(a) After three years of calculating amortization under an accelerated method for income tax purposes and under the straight-line method for reporting purposes, the company adopted an accelerated method for reporting purposes.

(b) The company disposed of one of the two subsidiaries that were included in its consolidated statements for prior years.

(c) The estimated remaining useful life of plant property was reduced because of obsolescence.

(d) The company is using an inventory valuation method that is different from the one used by other companies in its industry.

(LO 4) BE2-2 Identify which qualitative characteristic of accounting information is best described in each item below. (Do not use relevance and reliability.)

(a) The annual reports of Laurin Corp. are audited by public accountants.

(b) Reed Corp. and Moodie, Inc. both use the straight-line depreciation method.

(c) Baker Corp. has used straight-line amortization since it began operations.

(d) Swann Corp. issues its quarterly reports immediately after each quarter ends.

(LO 4, 6) BE2-3 What concept(s) from the conceptual framework does Accra Limited use in each of the following situations?

(a) Accra uses the lower of cost and net realizable value basis to value inventories.

(b) Accra was involved in litigation with Kinshasa Ltd. over a product malfunction. This litigation is disclosed in the financial statements.

(c) Accra allocates the cost of its depreciable (amortizable) assets over the period when it expects to receive revenue from these assets.

(d) Accra records the purchase of a new PC at its cash equivalent price.

(LO 5) BE2-4 Explain how you would decide whether to record each of the following expenditures as an asset or an expense. Assume all items are material.

(a) Legal fees of $1,500 are paid in purchasing land.

(b) Bratt, Inc. pays $21,000 to have the driveway to the office building paved.

(c) A meat market purchases a meat-grinding machine at a cost of $345.

(d) On June 30, Doctors Alan and Chung pay six months' office rent to cover the month of June and the next five months.

(e) Taylor's Hardware Company pays $9,000 in wages to labourers for construction of a building to be used in the business.

(f) Kwan's Florists pays wages of $2,100 for November to an employee who drives its delivery truck.

(LO 5) BE2-5 For each item that follows, indicate which element of the financial statements it belongs to:

(a) Retained earnings

(b) Sales

(c) Goodwill

(d) Inventory

(e) Amortization

(f) Loss on sale of equipment

(g) Interest payable
(h) Dividends
(i) Gain on sale of investment
(j) Issuance of common shares
(k) Unrealized holding gain on available-for-sale securities

BE2-6 For each item that follows, identify the foundational concept/constraint of accounting that best describes it: **(LO 6)**

(a) For its annual reports, Weksberg Corp divides its economic activities into 12-month periods.

(b) Ortiz, Inc. does not adjust amounts in its financial statements for the effects of inflation.

(c) Liu Ltd. reports current and noncurrent classifications in its balance sheet.

(d) The economic activities of Babin Corporation and its subsidiaries are merged for accounting and reporting purposes.

BE2-7 For each item that follows, identify the foundational concept/constraint of accounting that best describes it: **(LO 6)**

(a) Jolan Corporation reports revenue in its income statement when it is earned instead of when the cash is collected.

(b) Barre Enterprise recognizes amortization expense for a machine over the five-year period during which that machine helps the company earn revenue.

(c) Gonzalez, Inc. reports information about pending lawsuits in the notes to its financial statements.

(d) Douglas Farms reports land on its balance sheet at the amount paid to acquire it, even though the estimated fair market value is higher.

BE2-8 For each item that follows, indicate the foundational concept/constraint of accounting information that it illustrates: **(LO 6)**

(a) Zip's Farms, Inc. reports agricultural crops on its balance sheet at market value.

(b) Crimson Corporation does not accrue a contingent lawsuit gain of $650,000.

(c) Wildcat Ltd. does not disclose any information in the notes to its financial statements unless the value of the information to financial statement users is more than the cost of gathering it.

(d) Xu Corporation expenses the cost of wastebaskets in the year they are acquired.

BE2-9 Four concepts that were discussed in this chapter follow: **(LO 6)**

(a) Periodicity assumption

(b) Historical cost principle

(c) Conservatism

(d) Full disclosure principle

Match these concepts to the following accounting practices. Each letter can be used only once.

1. ________ Preparing financial statements on a quarterly basis.
2. ________ Using the lower of cost and market method for inventory valuation.
3. ________ Recording equipment at its purchase price.
4. ________ Using notes and supplementary schedules in the financial statements.

BE2-10 Four different transactions related to materiality follow. Explain whether you would classify these transactions as being material. **(LO 6)**

(a) Marcus Corp. has reported a positive trend in earnings over the last three years. In the current year, it reduces its bad debt allowance to ensure another positive earnings year. The impact of this adjustment is equal to 3% of net income.

(b) Sosa Ltd. has an extraordinary gain of $3.1 million on the sale of plant assets and a $3.3 million loss on the sale of investments. It decides to net the gain and loss because the net effect is considered immaterial. Sosa Ltd.'s income for the current year was $10 million.

(c) Mohawk Inc. expenses all capital equipment under $25,000 because it considers the amount immaterial. The company has followed this practice for several years.

(d) Hinckley Corporation follows a policy of expensing all capital purchases under $2,000 as it considers the amount immaterial. The company has followed this policy for many years and in prior years the impact of this decision has been less than 4% of net income. Due to a downturn in the economy, applying the policy in the current year would cause a misstatement of net income by 6%.

(LO 6) BE2-11 If the going concern assumption did not apply in accounting, how would this affect the amounts shown in the financial statements for the following items?

(a) Land

(b) Unamortized bond premium

(c) Amortization expense on equipment

(d) Merchandise inventory

(e) Prepaid insurance

Exercises

(LO 4) E2-1 (Qualitative Characteristics) The conceptual framework identifies the qualitative characteristics that make accounting information useful. Questions related to these qualitative characteristics and underlying constraints follow:

1. What is the quality of information that makes it possible for users to confirm or correct prior expectations?
2. Identify the pervasive constraints.
3. The SEC chairman once noted that if it becomes accepted or expected that accounting principles are determined or modified in order to achieve goals that do not involve economic measurement, we risk a serious loss in confidence in the credibility of our financial information system. Which qualitative characteristic of accounting information should ensure that this situation will not occur? (Do not use reliability.)
4. Owens Corp. switches from weighted average cost to FIFO over a two-year period. Which qualitative characteristic of accounting information is not followed?
5. Assume that the financial services profession allows its industry to defer losses on investments that it sells, because recognizing such losses immediately could have adverse economic consequences on the industry. Which qualitative characteristic of accounting information is not followed? (Do not use relevance or reliability.)
6. What are the qualities that make accounting information useful for decision-making?
7. Chapman, Inc. does not issue its first-quarter report until after the second quarter's results are reported. Which qualitative characteristic of accounting information is not followed? (Do not use relevance.)
8. Predictive value is an ingredient of which qualitative characteristics of useful information?
9. Victoria, Inc. is the only company in its industry to amortize its plant assets on a straight-line basis. Which qualitative characteristic of accounting information may not be followed? (Do not use industry practice.)
10. Joliet Corp. has tried to determine the replacement cost of its inventory. Three different appraisers arrive at substantially different amounts for this value. The president then decides to use the middle value for external reports. Which qualitative characteristic of information is lacking in this data? (Do not use reliability or representational faithfulness.)

(LO 4) E2-2 (Qualitative Characteristics) The qualitative characteristics that make accounting information useful for decision-making purposes are as follows:

Relevance	Timeliness	Representational faithfulness
Reliability	Verifiability	Comparability
Predictive value	Neutrality	Consistency
Feedback value	Understandability	Conservatism

Instructions

Match the appropriate qualitative characteristic(s) to each item that follows:

1. The qualitative characteristic that is being used when companies in the same industry use the same accounting principles.
2. A quality that information has when it confirms users' earlier expectations.
3. The imperative for comparing of a firm from period to period.
4. Ignores the economic consequences of a standard or rule.
5. Requires a high degree of consensus among individuals on a specific measurement.
6. Predictive value is an ingredient of this primary quality of information.
7. Neutrality is an ingredient of this primary quality of accounting information.

8. Two primary qualities that make accounting information useful for decision-making purposes.
9. Issuing interim reports is an example of what primary ingredient of relevance?

E2-3 (Elements of Financial Statements) Eight interrelated elements that are most directly related to measuring an enterprise's performance and financial status follow: **(LO 5)**

Assets	Expenses	Liabilities
Gains	Equity	Revenues
Losses	Other comprehensive income	

Instructions

Match the element(s) to each of the items that follow:

1. Arises from peripheral or incidental transactions.
2. Obliges a transfer of resources because of a past transaction.
3. Increases the ownership interest.
4. Declares and pays cash dividends to owners.
5. Increases net assets in the period from non-owner sources.
6. Characterizes items by their service potential or future economic benefit.
7. Is the increase in assets less liabilities during the year, after adding distributions to owners and subtracting investments by owners.
8. Decreases assets during the period for the payment of taxes.
9. Arises from income-generating activities that are the entity's ongoing major or central operations.
10. Is the residual interest in the enterprise's assets after deducting its liabilities.
11. Increases assets during the period through the sale of a product.
12. Decreases assets during the period by purchasing the company's own shares.
13. Includes all changes in equity during the period, except those resulting from investments by owners and distributions to owners.

E2-4 (Foundational Concepts and Constraints) The foundational concepts and constraints used in this chapter follow: **(LO 6)**

(a) Economic entity assumption	**(e)** Historical cost principle	**(i)** Materiality
(b) Going concern assumption	**(f)** Matching principle	**(j)** Industry practices
(c) Monetary unit assumption	**(g)** Full disclosure principle	**(k)** Revenue recognition
(d) Periodicity assumption	**(h)** Conservatism	

Instructions

For each situation that follows, identify by letter the foundational concept or constraint that best describes it. Do not use a letter more than once.

1. Allocates expenses to revenues in the proper period.
2. Indicates that market value changes after the purchase are not recorded in the accounts. (Do not use revenue recognition principle.)
3. Ensures that all relevant financial information is reported.
4. Is why plant assets are not reported at their liquidation value. (Do not use historical cost principle.)
5. Anticipates all losses, but reports no gains.
6. Indicates that personal and business record keeping should be separately maintained.
7. Separates financial information into time periods for reporting purposes.
8. Permits the use of market value valuation in certain specific situations.
9. Requires that information that is significant enough to affect the decision of reasonably informed users should be disclosed. (Do not use full disclosure principle.)
10. Assumes that the dollar is the measuring stick for reporting on financial performance.

(LO 6) E2-5 **(Foundational Concepts and Constraints)** The following are operational guidelines and practices that have developed over time.

1. Price-level changes are not recognized in the accounting records.
2. Financial information is presented so that reasonably prudent investors will not be misled.
3. Property, plant, and equipment are capitalized and amortized over the periods that they benefit.
4. Repair tools are expensed when they are purchased.
5. Market value is used by brokerage firms for the valuation of all marketable securities.
6. Each enterprise is kept as a unit that is distinct from its owner or owners.
7. All significant post–balance sheet events are reported.
8. Revenue is recorded at the point of sale.
9. All important aspects of bond indentures are presented in financial statements.
10. The rationale for accrual accounting is stated.
11. The use of consolidated statements is justified.
12. Reporting must be done at defined time intervals.
13. An allowance for doubtful accounts is established.
14. Goodwill is recorded only at the time of purchase.
15. Sales commission costs are charged to expense.

Instructions

Select the foundational concept or constraint that best justifies these procedures and practices.

(LO 6) E2-6 **(Foundational Concepts and Constraints)** Several operational guidelines used by accountants follow:

1. The treasurer of Farhan Corp. would like to prepare financial statements only during downturns in the company's wine production, which occur periodically when the rhubarb crop fails. He states that it is at such times that the statements could be most easily prepared. The company would never allow more than 30 months to pass without statements being prepared.
2. The Lachine Power & Light Inc. has purchased a large amount of property, plant, and equipment over several years. It has decided that because the general price level has changed materially over the years, it will issue only price-level-adjusted financial statements.
3. Miron Manufacturing Ltd. decided to manufacture its own widgets because it would be cheaper than buying them from an outside supplier. In an attempt to make its statements more comparable with those of its competitors, Miron charged its inventory account for what it felt the widgets would have cost if they had been purchased from an outside supplier. (Do not use the revenue recognition principle.)
4. Couturier's Discount Centres buys its merchandise by the truck-and train-car-load. Couturier does not defer any transportation costs in calculating the cost of its ending inventory. Such costs, although they vary from period to period, are always material in amount.
5. Grab & Run, Inc., a fast-food company, sells franchises for $100,000, accepting a $5,000 down payment and a 50-year note for the remainder. Grab & Run promises for three years to assist in site selection, building, and management training. Grab & Run records the $100,000 franchise fee as revenue in the period in which the contract is signed.
6. Musema Corp. faces a possible expropriation (i.e., takeover) of its foreign facilities and possible losses on sums that are owed by various customers who are almost bankrupt. The company president has decided that these possibilities should not be noted on the financial statements because Musema still hopes that these events will not take place.
7. Mike Hood, manager of College Bookstore, Inc., bought a computer for his own use. He paid for the computer by writing a cheque on the bookstore chequing account and charged the Office Equipment account.
8. Brock, Inc. recently completed a new 60-storey office building that houses its home offices and many other tenants. All the office equipment for the building that had a per item or per unit cost of $1,000 or less was expensed as immaterial, even though the office equipment has an average life of 10 years. The total cost of such office equipment was approximately $26 million. (Do not use the matching principle.)
9. Brokers and other dealers in securities generally value investments at their market or fair value for financial reporting purposes. The brokerage firm of Atreya and Hariri, Inc. continues to value its trading and investment accounts at cost or market, whichever is lower.

10. A large lawsuit has been filed against Mahoney Corp. by Perry Inc. Mahoney has recorded a loss and related estimated liability that is equal to the maximum possible amount that it feels it might lose. Mahoney is confident, however, that either it will win the suit or it will owe a much smaller amount.

Instructions

For each of the situations, list the foundational concept or constraint that has been violated. List only one term for each case.

E2-7 (Accounting Principles—Comprehensive) The following are transactions recorded by Maple Corporation during the current year: **(LO 6)**

(a) Ordinary repairs on capital assets were recorded as follows:

Capital Assets	10,000	
Accounts Payable		10,000

(b) The company collected $20,000 cash in advance for merchandise that will be shipped during the next accounting year.

Cash	20,000	
Sales Revenue		20,000

(c) On the last day of the year, the company declared a dividend to be paid in the next accounting year.

Dividend Expense	30,000	
Dividend Payable		30,000

(d) On the last day of the accounting period, a 12-month insurance policy was purchased. The insurance coverage is for the next accounting year.

Insurance Expense	4,000	
Cash		4,000

Instructions

For each transaction, determine which element of the conceptual framework was violated (if any) and give the entry that should have been recorded if there was a violation.

(CGA-Canada adapted)

E2-8 (Full Disclosure Principle) Facts related to Zhang, Inc. follow. Assume that none of these facts were mentioned in the financial statements and the related notes. **(LO 6)**

(a) To be more concise, the company decided that only net income should be reported on the income statement. Details on revenues, cost of goods sold, and expenses were omitted.

(b) Equipment purchases of $170,000 were partly financed during the year by issuing a $110,000 note payable. The company offset the equipment against the note payable and reported plant assets at $60,000.

(c) During the year, an assistant controller for the company embezzled $15,000. Zhang's net income for the year was $2.3 million. Neither the assistant controller nor the money have been found.

(d) Zhang has reported its ending inventory at $2.1 million in the financial statements. No other information on inventories is presented in the financial statements and related notes.

(e) The company changed its method of amortizing equipment from the double-declining balance to the straight-line method. This change is not mentioned anywhere in the financial statements.

Instructions

Assume that you are the auditor of Zhang, Inc. and that you have been asked to explain the appropriate accounting and related disclosure that is necessary for each of these items. Write your responses.

E2-9 (Comprehensive) Information related to Brooks, Inc. follows: **(LO 6)**

(a) Amortization expense on the building for the year was $60,000. Because the building was increasing in value during the year, the controller decided to charge the amortization expense to retained earnings instead of to net income. The following entry was recorded:

Retained Earnings	60,000	
Accumulated Amortization—Buildings		60,000

(b) Materials were purchased on January 1, 2008, for $120,000 and this amount was entered in the Materials account. On December 31, 2008, the materials would have cost $141,000, so the following entry was made:

Inventory	21,000	
Gain on Inventories		21,000

(c) During the year, the company sold certain equipment for $285,000, recognizing a gain of $69,000. Because the controller believed that new equipment would be needed in the near future, the controller decided to defer the gain and amortize it over the life of the new equipment that would soon be purchased.

(d) An order for $61,500 has been received from a customer for products on hand. This order was shipped on January 9, 2009. The company made the following entry in 2008:

Accounts Receivable	61,500	
Sales		61,500

Instructions

Comment on the appropriateness of Brooks, Inc's accounting procedures.

(LO 6) **E2-10** **(Accounting Principles—Comprehensive)** Transactions from Fresh Horses, Inc.'s current year follow:

(a) The president of Fresh Horses, Inc. used his expense account to purchase a new Suburban SUV for personal use only. The following journal entry was made:

Miscellaneous Expense	29,000	
Cash		29,000

(b) Merchandise inventory that cost $620,000 was reported on the balance sheet at $690,000, which is the expected selling price less estimated selling costs. The following entry was made to record this increase in value:

Merchandise Inventory	70,000	
Revenue		70,000

(c) The company is being sued for $500,000 by a customer who claims damages for personal injury that was apparently caused by a defective product. Company attorneys feel extremely confident that the company will have no liability for damages resulting from the situation. Nevertheless, the company decides to make the following entry:

Loss from Lawsuit	500,000	
Liability for Lawsuit		500,000

(d) Because the general level of prices increased during the current year, Fresh Horses, Inc. determined that there was a $16,000 understatement of amortization expense on its equipment and decided to record it in its accounts. The following entry was made:

Amortization Expense	16,000	
Accumulated Amortization		16,000

(e) Fresh Horses, Inc. has been concerned about whether intangible assets could generate cash in case of liquidation. As a result, goodwill arising from a purchase transaction during the current year and recorded at $800,000 was written off as follows:

Retained Earnings	800,000	
Goodwill		800,000

(f) Because of a "fire sale," equipment that was obviously worth $200,000 was acquired at a cost of $155,000. The following entry was made:

Equipment	200,000	
Cash		155,000
Revenue		45,000

Instructions

In each of the situations, discuss the appropriateness of the journal entries in terms of generally accepted accounting principles.

(LO 6) **E2-11** **(Revenue Recognition Principle)** The following independent situations require professional judgement for determining when to recognize revenue from the transactions:

(a) Air Temiskaming sells you an advance purchase airline ticket in September for your flight home at Christmas.

(b) Giant Lion's Furniture Stores Inc. sells you a home theatre on a "no money down, no interest, and no payments for one year" promotional deal.

(c) The Centurions Baseball Team sells season tickets to games on-line. Fans can purchase the tickets at any time, although the season doesn't officially begin until April. It runs from April through October.

(d) The Montreal Dominion Bank lends you money in August. The loan and the interest are repayable in full in November.

(e) In September, Citi College collects tuition revenue for the term from new and returning students. The term runs from September through December.

(f) Belle Vallée Wools sells you a sweater. In August, you placed the order using Belle Vallée's on-line catalogue. The sweater arrives in September and you charge it to your Belle Vallée credit card. You receive and pay the Belle Vallée bill in October.

Instructions

Identify when revenue should be recognized in each of the above situations.

Problems

P2-1 Accounting information provides useful information about business transactions and events. The people who provide and use financial reports must often select and evaluate accounting alternatives. The conceptual framework that was developed in this chapter examines the characteristics of accounting information that make it useful for decision-making. It also points out that various limitations that are part of the measurement and reporting process can make it necessary to trade-off or sacrifice some of the characteristics of useful information.

Instructions

(a) For each of the following pairs of information characteristics, give an example of a situation in which one of the characteristics may be sacrificed for a gain in the other:

1. Relevance and reliability.
2. Relevance and consistency.
3. Comparability and consistency.
4. Relevance and understandability.

(b) What criterion should be used to evaluate trade-offs between information characteristics?

P2-2 You are hired to review the accounting records of McDowell Corporation before it closes its revenue and expense accounts as December 31, the end of its current fiscal year. The following information comes to your attention.

1. During the current year, McDowell Corporation changed its policy on expensing purchases of small tools. In the past, these purchases had always been expensed because they amounted to less than 2% of net income, but the president has decided that they should be capitalized and then amortized from now on. It is expected that purchases of small tools will not change greatly from year to year.
2. McDowell Corporation built a warehouse at a cost of $1 million. The company had been amortizing the asset on a straight-line basis over 10 years. In the current year, the controller doubled the amortization expense because the warehouse replacement cost had increased significantly.
3. When the balance sheet was prepared, detailed information about the amount of cash on deposit in each of several banks was omitted. Only the total amount of cash under a caption "Cash in banks" was presented.
4. On July 15 of the current year, McDowell Corporation purchased an undeveloped piece of land for $320,000. The company spent $80,000 in subdividing the land and getting it ready for sale. A property appraisal at the end of the year indicated that the land was now worth $500,000. Although none of the lots were sold, the company recognized revenue of $180,000, less related expenses of $80,000, for a net income on the project of $100,000.
5. For several years, the company used the FIFO method for inventory valuation purposes. During the current year, the president noted that all the other companies in the industry had switched to the moving average method. The company decided not to switch to moving average because net income would decrease by $830,000.

Instructions

State whether or not you agree with the decisions made by McDowell Corporation. Explain your reasoning and, wherever possible, support your answers by referring to the generally accepted principles, assumptions, and constraints that apply to the circumstances.

P2-3 The following transactions fall somewhere in the continuum of accounting decision-making that is shown in Illustration 2-6.

1. The company president approached one of the company's major suppliers to ask him to modify the payment terms on regular purchases so that they extend beyond the current year. This would make the liabilities long-term rather than short-term and would improve the company's current ratio.

2. The controller determines that significant amounts of capital assets are impaired and should be written off. Coincidentally, the company is currently showing lower levels of net income, but expects better results in the following years.
3. The company management decides to amortize machinery on a unit-of-production approach to better match its machinery cost to the revenues that are generated.
4. The vice-president of finance decides to capitalize interest during the self-construction of one of the company's warehouses. This policy will increase net income and several profitability ratios.
5. The business owner enters into an arrangement with a business associate whereby they will buy each other's merchandise before year-end. The merchandise will then be shipped to customers after year-end from the holding company's warehouse.

Instructions
For each situation, state where it falls in the continuum.

P2-4 After you finish presenting your report on the financial statements of Scott Publishing Corp. to its board of directors, one of the new directors expresses surprise. She finds it odd that the income statement assumes that an equal proportion of the revenue is earned with the publication of each issue of the company's magazine. She feels that the critical event in the process of earning revenue in the magazine business is the cash sale of the subscription. She says that she does not understand why most of the revenue cannot be recognized in the period of the sale.

Instructions
Discuss whether or not it would be appropriate to time the recognition of revenue in Scott Publishing Corp.'s account with:

1. The cash sale of the magazine subscription.
2. The publication of the magazine every month.
3. Both events, by recognizing a portion of the revenue with the cash sale of the magazine subscription and a portion of the revenue with the publication of the magazine every month.

P2-5 On June 5, 2008, McCoy Corporation signed a contract with Sandov Associates. Under the terms of the contract Sandov agreed (1) to construct an office building on land owned by McCoy, (2) to accept responsibility for obtaining financing for the project and finding tenants, and (3) to manage the property for 35 years.

The annual net income from the project, after paying debts for the year, was to be divided equally between McCoy Corporation and Sandov Associates. Sandov was to accept its share of future net income as full payment for its services in construction, obtaining finances and tenants, and project management.

By May 31, 2009, the project was nearly completed and tenants had signed leases to occupy 90% of the available space at annual rents adding up to $4 million in total. It is estimated that, after operating expenses and debt service, the annual net income will amount to $1.5 million. The management of Sandov Associates believed that (a) the economic benefit derived from the contract with McCoy should be reflected on Sandov's financial statements for the fiscal year ended May 31, 2009, and issued a directive that revenue be accrued in an amount that is equal to the commercial value of the services that Sandor had rendered during the year, (b) this amount be carried in contracts receivable, and (c) all related expenditures be charged against the revenue.

Instructions

(a) Explain the main difference between the economic concept of business income that Sandov's management seems to have and the measurement of income under generally accepted accounting principles.

(b) Discuss the factors that need to be considered in determining when revenue should be recognized in terms of measuring periodic income.

(c) Does Sandov management's belief accord with generally accepted accounting principles for the measurement of revenue and expense for the year ended May 31, 2009? Support your opinion by discussing how the factors to be considered in asset measurement and revenue and expense recognition apply to this case.

(AICPA adapted)

P2-6 Carl Schneider sells and erects shell houses. These are frame structures that are completely finished on the outside but are unfinished on the inside except for flooring, partition studding, and ceiling joists. Shell houses are sold mainly to customers who are handy with tools and who have time to do the interior wiring, plumbing, wall completion and finishing, and other work that has to be done to make the shell houses liveable dwellings.

Schneider buys shell houses from a manufacturer in unassembled packages consisting of all the lumber, roofing, doors, windows, and similar materials that are needed to complete a shell house. When he begins operations in a new area, Schneider buys or leases land as a site for his local warehouse, field office, and display houses. Sample display houses are erected at a total cost of $20,000 to $29,000, including the cost of the unassembled packages. The chief cost of the display houses is the unassembled packages, as erecting the shell is a short, low-cost operation. Old sample models are torn down or altered into new models every three to seven years. Sample display houses have little salvage value because dismantling and moving costs amount to almost as much as the cost of an unassembled package.

Instructions

(a) A choice must be made between (1) expensing the costs of sample display houses in the periods in which the expenditure is made and (2) spreading the costs over more than one period. Discuss the advantages of each method.

(b) Would it be preferable to amortize the cost of display houses based on (1) the passage of time or (2) the number of shell houses sold? Explain.

(AICPA adapted)

P2-7 Recently, your Uncle Waldo, who knows that you always have your eye out for a profitable investment, has discussed the possibility of your purchasing some corporate bonds that he just learned of. He suggests that you may wish to get in on the ground floor of this deal. The bonds being issued by Cricket Corp. are 10-year debentures, which promise a 40% rate of return. Cricket manufactures novelty and party items.

You have told Uncle Waldo that unless you can take a look at Cricket's financial statements, you would not feel comfortable about such an investment. Thinking that this is the chance of a lifetime, Uncle Waldo has obtained a copy of Cricket's most recent, unaudited financial statements, which are a year old. These statements were prepared by Mrs. John Cricket. You look over these statements, and they are quite impressive.

The balance sheet showed a debt-to-equity ratio of .10 and, for the year shown, the company reported net income of $2,424,240.

The financial statements are not shown in comparison with amounts from other years. In addition, there are no significant note disclosures about inventory valuation, amortization methods, loan agreements, and so on.

Instructions

Write a letter to Uncle Waldo explaining why it would be unwise to base an investment decision on the financial statements that he has given you. Refer to the concepts developed in this chapter.

P2-8 Hinckley Nuclear Power Plant will be "mothballed" at the end of its useful life (approximately 20 years) at great expense. Historically, matching has required that expenses be matched to revenue. Accountants Jana Kingston and Pete Henning are arguing whether it is better to allocate the expense of mothballing over the next 20 years or ignore it until mothballing occurs.

Instructions

Discuss the issues, taking the stakeholders' perspectives into consideration.

Writing Assignments

WA2-1 Roger Chang has some questions about the theoretical framework in which standards are set. He knows that standard-setters have been trying to develop a conceptual framework for the formulation of accounting theory. Yet Roger's supervisors have said that these theoretical frameworks have little value in the practical sense—in the real world. Roger did notice that accounting standards seem to be established after the fact rather than before—i.e., after problems occur. He thought this meant the theory could be poorly structured but he never really questioned the process at school because he was too busy doing the homework.

Roger thinks that he might feel less anxious about accounting theory and accounting semantics (the terminology) if he could identify the basic concepts and definitions that are accepted by the profession and then consider them in light of his current work. By doing this, he hopes to develop an appropriate connection between theory and practice.

Instructions

Help Roger recognize the purpose and benefit of a conceptual framework.

WA2-2 Gordon and Medford are discussing various aspects of *CICA Handbook* Section 1000—Financial Statement Concepts. Gordon points out that this pronouncement provides little, if any, guidance to the practising professional on how to resolve accounting controversies. He believes that the statement gives such broad guidelines that it would be impossible to apply the objectives to present-day reporting problems. Medford admits this may be true but he still feels that objectives are needed as a starting point in helping to improve financial reporting.

Instructions

Discuss.

WA2-3 An accountant must be familiar with the concepts involved in determining the earnings of a business entity. The amount of earnings that is reported for a business entity depends on the proper recognition, in general, of revenues and expenses for a specific time period. In some situations, costs are recognized as expenses at the time of product sale; in other situations, guidelines have been developed for recognizing costs as expenses or losses by other criteria.

Instructions

(a) Explain the rationale for recognizing costs as expenses at the time of product sale.

(b) What is the rationale that makes it appropriate to treat costs as expenses of a period instead of assigning them to an asset? Explain.

(c) In what general circumstances would it be appropriate to treat a cost as an asset instead of as an expense? Explain.

(d) Some expenses are assigned to specific accounting periods based on a systematic and rational allocation of asset cost. Explain the rationale for recognizing expenses in this way.

(e) Identify the conditions in which it would be appropriate to treat a cost as a loss.

(AICPA adapted)

WA2-4 Financial statements include a significant amount of soft information.

Instructions

Define what is meant by "soft" versus "hard" information. Discuss the factors that contribute to soft numbers in financial reporting.

WA2-5 Many Canadian companies include in the notes to their financial statements a note that reconciles Canadian GAAP net income to U.S. GAAP net income.

Instructions

Discuss this in regard to the conceptual framework.

Student Website

www.wiley.com/canada/kieso

Cases

Refer to the Case Primer on the Student Website to help you answer these cases.

CA2-1 Bre-X Minerals (Bre-X), a small mining company, announced in the early 1990s that it had discovered a fairly significant gold deposit in Indonesia. The company's shares skyrocketed from pennies a share to over $280 per share. Subsequently, it was discovered that the company had been "salting the samples"[43] and that there was little, if any, gold there. This information was not disclosed to the market until long after it was discovered that there was no gold. Certain parties who had access to this information benefited; however, many investors lost a significant amount of money.

Lawsuits that relate to the misrepresentations are ongoing as at September 2006. John Felderhof, who formerly worked for Bre-X, faces penalties ranging from a fine of $1 million to imprisonment for two years plus additional penalties of up to three times any profits from insider trading. He has been accused of selling $84 million worth of Bre-X stock between April and October 1996 while having information that was not disclosed to investors.

Instructions

Using the conceptual framework, identify and analyze the financial reporting issues.

CA2-2 Bennett Environmental Inc. operates in North America. Its basic business is high temperature treatment services for the remediation of contaminated soils and other PCB-contaminated construction debris, according to its 2002 annual report. In 2002, its annual revenues were $48,103,845 (more than double the previous year). In June 2003, the company successfully bid on a $200-million, three-year contract to treat contaminated soils from a large site in New Jersey.

The cleanup site was previously operated by Federal Creosote, which made treated railroad ties until the mid-1950s. In 1997, homes in the surrounding area discovered that the creosote, which has now been determined to be carcinogenic, was leaking into their basements. As a temporary solution, the waste will be shipped to Quebec, where it will be

[43] The term "salting" refers to the practice of someone tampering with the samples (and adding in some, or more, gold).

incinerated. The company has almost completed work on its New Brunswick plant where the rest of the waste will ultimately be incinerated.[44]

Instructions

The company's year end is December 31. Discuss the financial reporting issues that the company would have faced after work began on the clean-up site in early 2004.

CA2-3 The statement that follows about Weyerhaeuser Company appeared in a financial magazine:

> The land and timber holdings are now carried on the company's books at a mere $422 million (U.S.). The value of the timber alone is variously estimated at $3 billion to $7 billion and is rising all the time. The understatement of the company is pretty severe, conceded Charles W. Bingham, a senior vice-president. Adds Robert L. Schuyler, another senior vice-president: We have a whole stream of profit nobody sees and there is no way to show it on our books.

Instructions

Act as an analyst and discuss the financial reporting issues.

[44] Based on the June 3, 2003, article from the *Globe and Mail*, "Bennet Wins N. J. Tainted Soil Contract."

Research and Financial Analysis

RA2-1 Teck Cominco

Obtain the (restated) 2005 financial statements of Teck Cominco Limited from the Student website and answer the following questions:

Instructions

(a) Using the notes to the consolidated financial statements, determine the company's revenue recognition policy. Comment on whether the company uses an aggressive or conservative method for reporting revenue.

(b) Give two examples of where historical cost information is reported on the financial statements and related notes. Give two examples where fair value information is reported in either the financial statements or related notes.

(c) Why did the company restate the financial statements? Comment on this. Argue both sides of the reporting issue, in other words, how they treated the item before and after the restatement. (Hint: See the definition of cash and cash equivalents in the *Handbook*.)

(v) Read note 3(e) (i) regarding stripping costs. Argue both sides of the argument on how to treat stripping costs. Comment on the impact of both treatments on the financial statements.

RA2-2 Abitibi-Consolidated Inc. versus Domtar Inc.

Instructions

Go to the Student website and find the annual reports for Abitibi-Consolidated Inc. and Domtar Inc. for the year ended December 31, 2005. Use them to answer the following questions:

(a) What are the main lines of business of these two companies as shown in their notes to the financial statements? What are the key business risks?

(b) Which company has the dominant position in paper product sales? Explain how you used information in the financial statements to answer this.

(c) Review the key accounting policies for revenues, inventories, fixed assets, and environmental costs. How comparable are these two sets of statements?

(d) Domtar also reports in U.S. dollars. Why do you think it does this?

(e) Which company is more profitable and why? Support your answer.

RA2-3 Retrieval of Information on Public Company

There are several commonly available indexes and reference products that help individuals locate articles that previously appeared in business publications and periodicals. Articles can generally be searched by company or by subject matter. Several common sources are *Canadian Business and Current Affairs* (*CBCA Fulltext Business*), *Investex Plus*, *The Wall Street Journal Index*, *Business Abstracts* (formerly the *Business Periodical Index*), and *ABI/Inform*.

Instructions

Use one of these resources to find an article about a company that interests you. Read the article and answer the following questions. (Note: Your library may have hard copy or CD-ROM versions of these sources or they may be available through your library's electronic database.)

(a) What is the article about?

(b) What specific information about the company is included in the article?

(c) Identify any accounting-related issues that are discussed in the article.

RA2-4 Concepts and Quantitative Guidelines—Materiality

In 2002, the AcSB issued a guideline entitled "Applying Materiality and Audit Risk Concepts in Conducting an Audit." Materiality is used to determine whether a transaction or event has decision relevance for financial reporting purposes. Materiality can be determined either quantitatively or qualitatively.

Instructions

Summarize and discuss the quantitative and qualitative thresholds that are expressed in the guideline. Compare your findings to current guidance in the *CICA Handbook*.

RA2-5 Research Study on Mining Company Disclosures

PricewaterhouseCoopers (PwC) completed a study in 2002 on disclosures in the petroleum industry that was entitled "Drilling Deeper." It showed that most oil and gas companies were not disclosing enough information about their companies, and the result was that 80 percent of the companies in the survey felt that their share prices did not reflect the company's true value.

An excerpt from the study follows:

> More than ever, investors are on guard against corporate reports that may be technically correct, but fail to provide a true picture of a company's health and prospects. The need for reporting measures and techniques that fully communicate the potential of a company's strategy and operations and promote trust is possibly greater than ever before. Petroleum companies have built solid relationships with investors but, as this survey shows, there is potential for fine-tuning and deepening communication to deliver more value for investors and companies alike.
>
> The debate is intensifying. In the rush, post-Enron, to scrutinise reporting practices, it is inevitable that the oil and gas industry will be high on the list for politicians and regulators. The danger for companies is that such scrutiny may be driven disproportionately by political factors rather than insight and understanding of the industry, its strategies and its processes.
>
> *Drilling deeper* identifies the industry-specific indicators that companies believe are critical to manage the value of their business, and contrasts these with the reporting priorities of investors and analysts. It is clear that there is potential both for companies to educate the investment community on the significance of certain indicators, and for the investment community's priorities to be matched by better reporting progress against those indicators.
>
> The potential benefits for companies are two-fold. By increasing disclosure, companies have the prospect of deepening relationships with long-term investors, reducing stock volatility and maximising share value. It also provides a clear platform for influencing and educating the regulatory climate.

Instructions

1. Download and read the report from the PwC website at www.pwc.com. (Hint: Look under "energy, utilities and mining," and then under publications.)
2. Explain how oil and gas companies earn income. What is the earnings process?
3. Why might the shares be undervalued?
4. Discuss the financial reporting principles that are at issue here.
5. Explain how this situation might contribute to problems in the industry.

Cable Connections

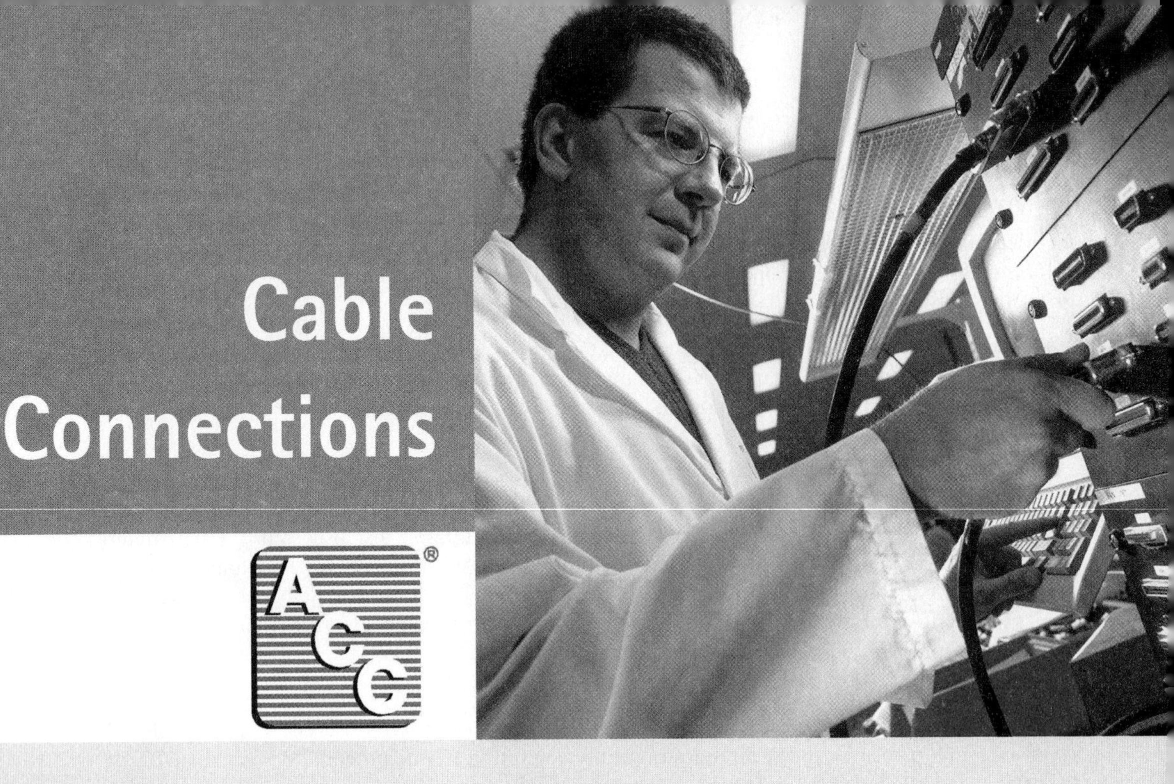

In 1984, certified general accountant Louise Nesterenko was vice-president of finance for a Calgary computer company that had received a shipment of new personal computers. The computers arrived without any cables, and to order new ones from Ontario would take three weeks. The enterprising woman saw a hole in the Western marketplace—and a year later, she launched Alberta Computer Cable Inc. (ACC).

The company has since grown from a single staff member and first-year revenues of less than $60,000 to 70 full-time employees and more than $4 million in revenue in 2006.

ACC manufactures and distributes cables and other computer connectivity products—from a single cable to orders in the thousands, often within 24 hours. This efficiency is thanks to one thing: "The accounting system was crucial to our success," Nesterenko says.

Effective cash management is important because, from the start, Nesterenko did not look for any outside funding. She relies on a good payables system. "We notify all our vendors that payments will always be made, regardless, the third Monday of the month," she says.

The accounts receivable system is also tightly run, with statements faxed to clients on a regular basis. "Our bad debts are so insignificant, they don't register on a scale," Nesterenko says. Out of $7.5 million in sales, bad debts totalled $2,330 for 2006. In addition, Nesterenko ensures that no account represents more than 12 percent of the company's business.

The sophistication of the record keeping has increased with the company's growth. ACC originally used a custom software package that was updated at the end of each day. Now, it runs "Made-2-Manage" software, which updates all components—the general ledger, bank, accounts payable and receivable—instantaneously. In addition, the use of digital photography in receiving reduces the risk of errors in managing shipments, and scanning inventory products into the software as soon as they come out of production has made them available much sooner. ■

The Accounting Information System

Learning Objectives

After studying this chapter, you should be able to:

1. Understand basic accounting terminology.
2. Explain double-entry rules.
3. Identify the steps in the accounting cycle.
4. Record transactions in journals, post journal entries to ledger accounts, and prepare a trial balance.
5. Explain the reasons for preparing adjusting entries.
6. Prepare closing entries.
7. Explain how inventory accounts are adjusted at year end.
8. Prepare a 10-column work sheet and financial statements.

After studying the appendix, you should be able to:

9. Identify adjusting entries that may be reversed.

Preview of Chapter 3

As the story of ACC shows, all companies need a reliable information system. The purpose of this chapter is to explain and illustrate the features of an accounting information system. Even though most companies have sophisticated computerized and automated accounting systems, it is still important to understand the mechanics of bookkeeping. How do transactions get captured in the system and how and when are the financial statements produced?

The chapter is organized as follows:

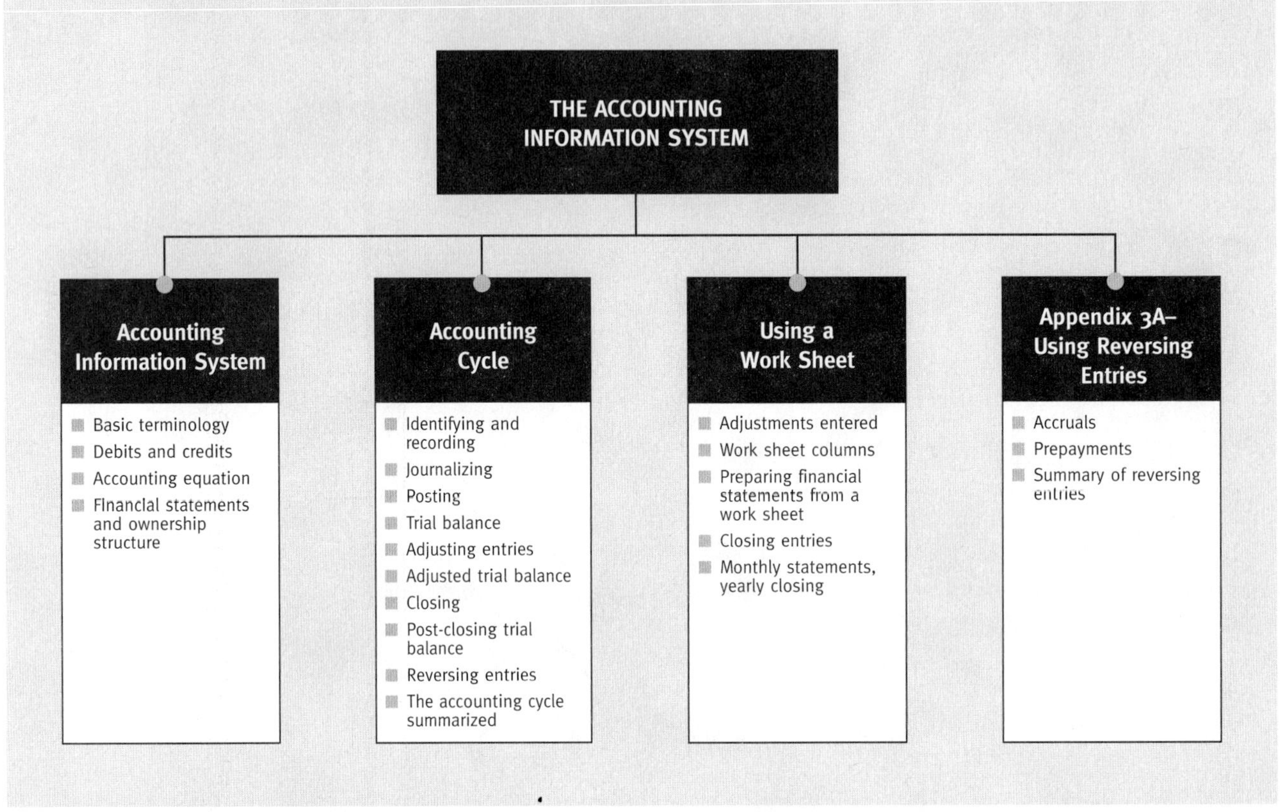

ACCOUNTING INFORMATION SYSTEM

The system of collecting and processing transaction data and making financial information available to interested parties is known as the **accounting information system**.

Accounting information systems can be very different from one business to another. Many factors shape these systems, including the type of business and kinds of transactions it engages in, the firm's size, the amount of data that is handled, and the kind of information that management and others need to get from the system.

Basic Terminology

Financial accounting is built on a set of concepts (discussed in Chapters 1 and 2) for identifying, recording, classifying, and interpreting transactions and other events relating to enterprises. It is important to understand the **basic terminology** that is used in **collecting** accounting data.

1 Objective
Understand basic accounting terminology.

BASIC TERMINOLOGY

Event. A happening of consequence. An **event** is generally the source or cause of changes in assets, liabilities, and equity. Events can be external or internal.

Transaction. An **external event** involving a transfer or exchange between two or more entities or parties.

Account. A systematic arrangement that accumulates transactions and other events. A separate **account** is kept for each asset, liability, revenue, and expense, and for gains, losses, and capital (owners' equity).

Permanent and temporary accounts. **Permanent** (real) **accounts** are asset, liability, and equity accounts; they appear on the balance sheet. **Temporary** (nominal) **accounts** are revenue, expense, and dividend accounts; except for dividends, they appear on the income statement. Temporary accounts are periodically closed; permanent accounts are left open.

Ledger.[1] The book (or electronic database) containing the accounts. Each account usually has a separate page. A **general ledger** is a collection of all the asset, liability, owners' equity, revenue, and expense accounts. A **subsidiary ledger** contains the details of a specific general ledger account.

Journal. The book of original entry where transactions and other selected events are first recorded. Various amounts are transferred to the ledger from the book of original entry, the **journal**.

Posting. The process of transferring the essential facts and figures from the book of original entry to the ledger accounts.

Trial balance. A list of all open accounts in the ledger and their balances. A **trial balance** that is taken immediately after all adjustments have been posted is called an **adjusted trial balance**. A trial balance taken immediately after closing entries have been posted is known as a **post-closing** or **after-closing trial balance**. A trial balance can be prepared at any time.

Adjusting entries. Entries that are made at the end of an accounting period to bring all accounts up to date on an accrual accounting basis so that correct financial statements can be prepared.

Financial statements. Statements that reflect the collecting, tabulating, and final summarizing of the accounting data. Four **financial statements** are involved: (1) the **balance sheet**, which shows the enterprise's financial condition at the end of a period; (2) the **income statement**, which measures the results of operations during the period; (3) the **statement of cash flows**, which reports the cash provided and used by operating, investing, and financing activities during the period; and (4) the

[1] Most companies use accounting software systems instead of manual systems. The software allows the data to be entered into a database and various reports can then be generated, such as journals, trial balances, ledgers, and financial statements.

statement of retained earnings, which reconciles the balance of the retained earnings account from the beginning to the end of the period. Comprehensive income may be shown in a separate statement—the **statement of comprehensive income**—or as part of the income statement.

Closing entries. The formal process for reducing temporary accounts to zero and then determining net income or net loss and transferring it to an owners' equity account. This is also known as "closing the ledger," "closing the books," or merely "closing."

Debits and Credits

Objective 2
Explain double-entry rules.

The terms **debit** and **credit** refer to the left and right sides of a general ledger account, respectively. They are commonly abbreviated as Dr. for debit and Cr. for credit. These terms do not mean "increase" or "decrease". The terms debit and credit are used repeatedly in the recording process to describe where entries are made. For example, the act of entering an amount on the left side of an account is called **debiting** the account. Making an entry on the right side is **crediting** the account. When the totals of the two sides are compared, an account will have a debit balance if the total of the debit amounts is more than the credits. Conversely, an account will have a credit balance if the credit amounts exceed the debits. The procedure of having debits on the left and credits on the right is an accounting custom. We could function just as well if debits and credits were reversed. However, the custom of having debits on the left side of an account and credits on the right side (like the custom of driving on the right-hand side of the road) has been adopted in Canada. This rule applies to all accounts.

The equality of debits and credits is the basis for the double-entry system of recording transactions (also sometimes called double-entry bookkeeping). Under the **double-entry accounting** system, which is used everywhere, the two-sided (dual) effect of each transaction is recorded in appropriate accounts. This system gives a logical method for recording transactions. It also offers a way of proving the accuracy of the recorded amounts. If every transaction is recorded with equal debits and credits, then the sum of all the debits to the accounts must equal the sum of all the credits.

Illustration 3-1
Double-Entry (Debit and Credit) Accounting System

Normal Balance– Debit

Asset Accounts

Debit	Credit
+ (increase)	–(decrease)

Expense and Dividend Accounts

Debit	Credit
+ (increase)	–(decrease)

Normal Balance– Credit

Liability Accounts

Debit	Credit
–(decrease)	+ (increase)

Shareholders' Equity Accounts

Debit	Credit
– (decrease)	+ (increase)

Revenue Accounts

Debit	Credit
–(decrease)	+ (increase)

All **asset** and **expense** accounts are increased on the left (or debit side) and decreased on the right (or credit side). Conversely, all **liability** and **revenue** accounts are increased on the right (or credit side) and decreased on the left (or debit side). Shareholders' equity accounts, such as Common Shares and Retained Earnings, are increased on the credit side, whereas Dividends is increased on the debit side. The basic guidelines for an accounting system are presented in Illustration 3-1.

Accounting Equation

In a double-entry system, for every debit there must be a credit, and vice versa. This leads us to the basic accounting equation shown in Illustration 3-2.

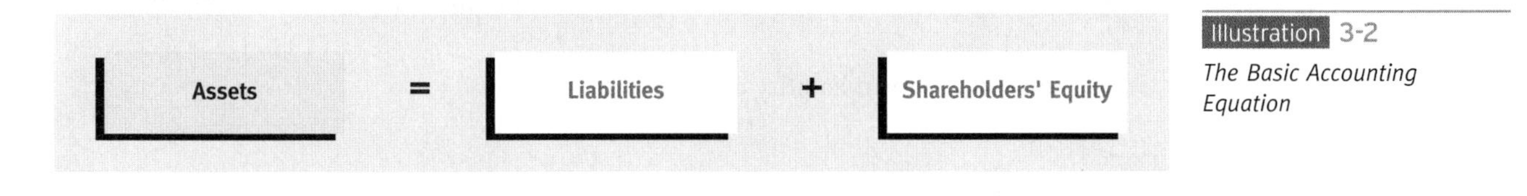

Illustration 3-2
The Basic Accounting Equation

Illustration 3-3 expands this equation to show the accounts that compose shareholders' equity. In addition, the debit/credit rules and effects on each type of account are shown. Study this diagram carefully. It will help you understand the fundamentals of the double-entry system. Like the basic equation, the expanded basic equation must balance (total debits **must** equal total credits).

Illustration 3-3
Expanded Basic Equation and Debit/Credit Rules and Effects

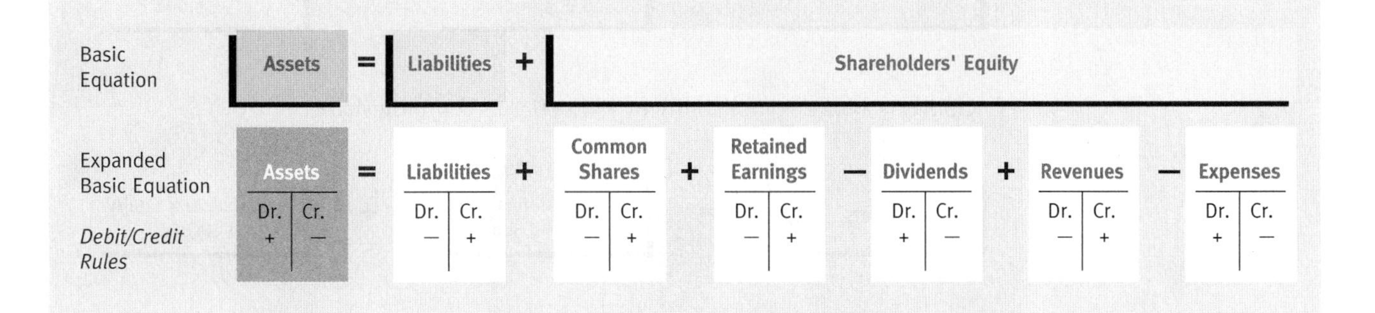

Every time a transaction occurs, the elements in the equation change, but the basic equality of the two sides remains. To illustrate, here are eight different transactions for Perez Inc.:

1 Owners invest $40,000 in exchange for common shares:

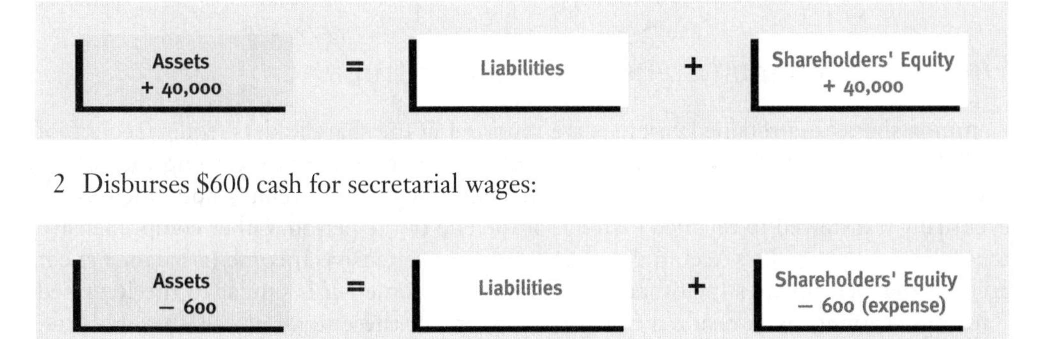

2 Disburses $600 cash for secretarial wages:

3 Purchases office equipment priced at $5,200, giving a 10% promissory note in exchange:

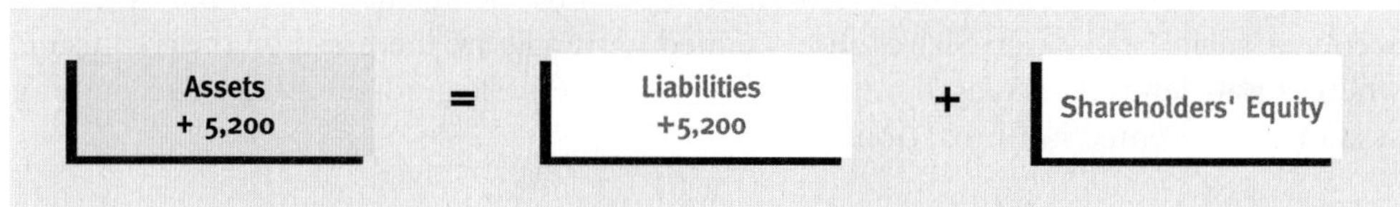

4 Receives $4,000 cash for services rendered:

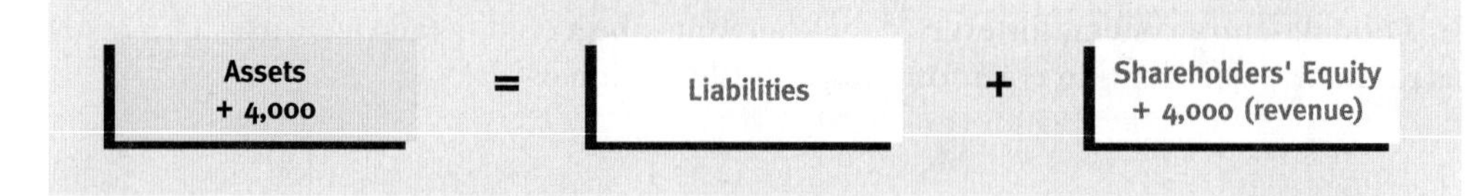

5 Pays off a short-term liability of $7,000:

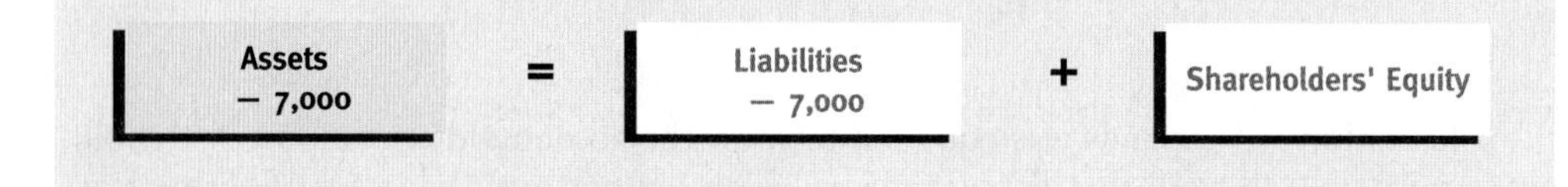

6 Declares a cash dividend of $5,000:

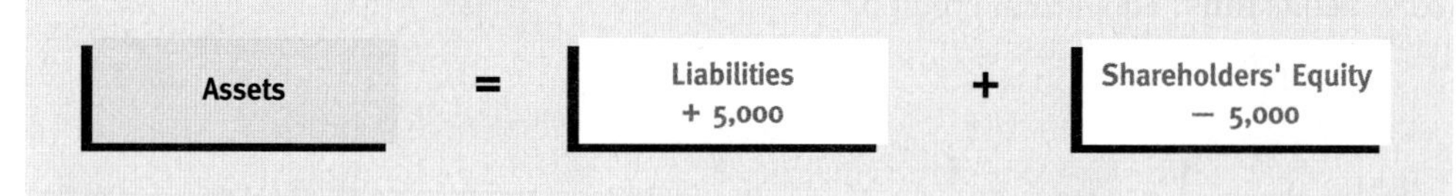

7 Converts a long-term liability of $80,000 into common shares:

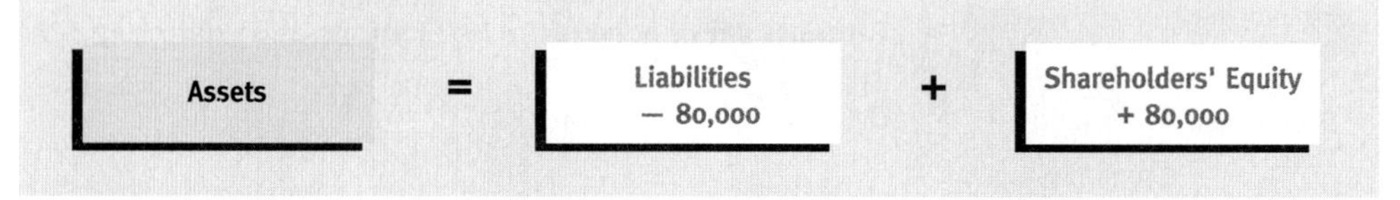

8 Pays $16,000 cash for a delivery van:

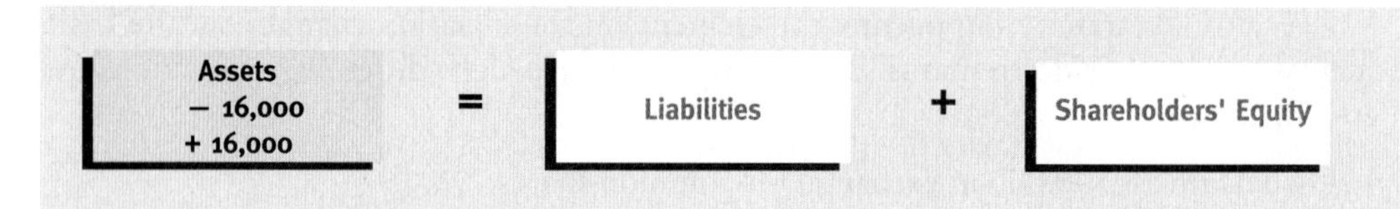

Financial Statements and Ownership Structure

Common shares and retained earnings are reported in the shareholders' equity section of the balance sheet. Dividends are reported on the statement of retained earnings. Revenues and expenses are reported on the income statement. Dividends, revenues, and expenses are eventually transferred to retained earnings at the end of the period. Other comprehensive income is transferred to Accumulated Other Comprehensive Income (a balance sheet account that accumulates the other comprehensive income—it is similar to the Retained Earnings account). As a result, a change in any one of these items affects shareholders' equity. The relationships to shareholders' equity are shown in Illustration 3-4.

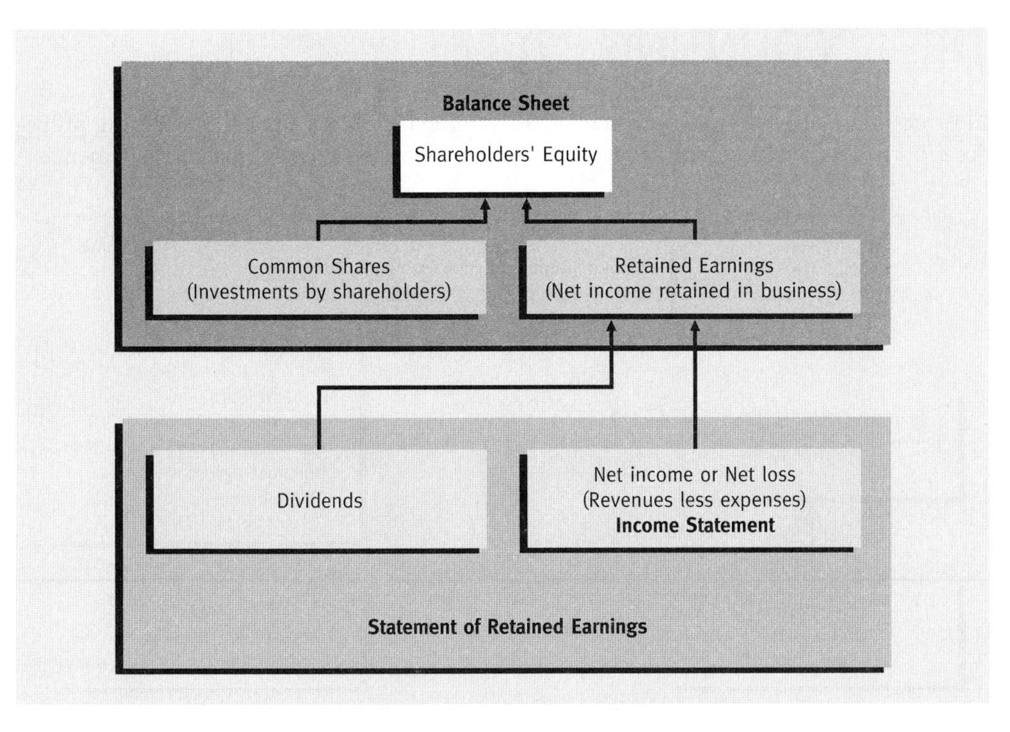

Illustration 3-4
Financial Statements and Ownership Structure

The type of ownership structure that a business enterprise uses determines the types of accounts that are part of the equity section or that affect it. In a **corporation**,[2] **Common Shares, Contributed Surplus, Dividends**, and **Retained Earnings** are commonly used accounts. In a **proprietorship** or **partnership**, a **Capital** account is used to indicate the owner's or owners' investment in the company. A **Drawings** or withdrawal account may be used to indicate withdrawals by the owner(s). These two accounts are grouped or netted under **Owners' Equity**.

Illustration 3-5 summarizes the transactions that affect shareholders' equity and relates them to the temporary and permanent account classifications and to the types of business ownership.

Illustration 3-5
Effects of Transactions on Owners' or Shareholders' Equity Accounts

		Ownership Structure			
		Proprietorships and Partnerships		Corporations	
Transactions Affecting Owners' Equity	Impact on Owners' Equity	Temporary Accounts	Permanent Accounts	Temporary Accounts	Permanent Accounts
Investment by owner(s)	Increase		Capital		Common Shares and related accounts
Revenues earned	Increase	Revenue		Revenue	
Expenses incurred	Decrease	Expense	Capital	Expense	Retained Earnings
Withdrawal by owner(s)	Decrease	Drawings		Dividend	

[2] Corporations are incorporated under a government act such as the *Canada Business Corporations Act*. The main reason for incorporation is to limit the liability for the owners if the corporation gets sued or goes bankrupt. When companies are incorporated, shares are issued to owners and the company becomes a separate legal entity (separate and distinct from its owners).

THE ACCOUNTING CYCLE

Objective 3
Identify the steps in the accounting cycle.

Illustration 3-6 charts the steps in the **accounting cycle**. These are the accounting procedures normally used by enterprises to record transactions and prepare financial statements.

Illustration 3-6
The Accounting Cycle

Student Website
Accounting Cycle Tutorial
www.wiley.com/canada/kieso

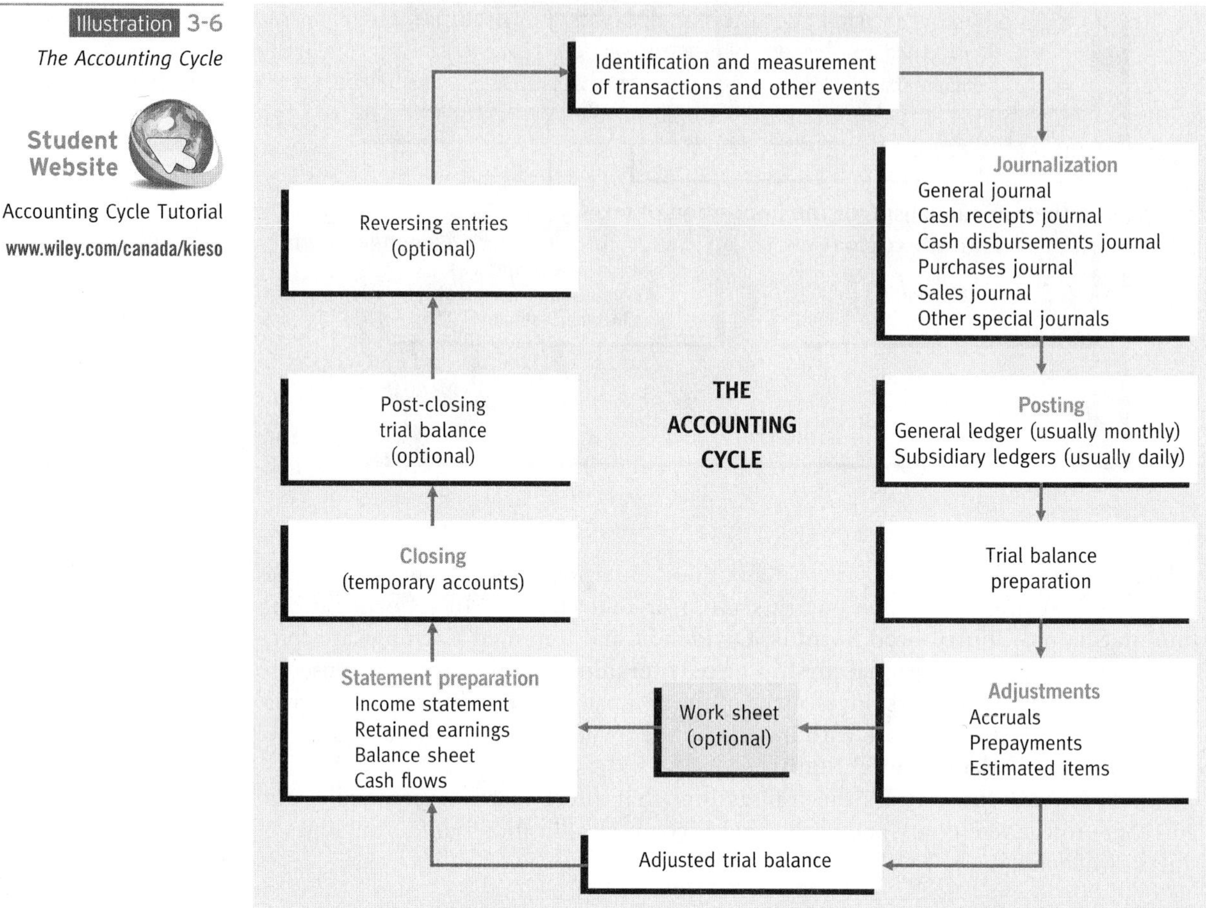

When the steps have been completed, the sequence starts over again in the next accounting period.

Identifying and Recording Transactions and Other Events

The first step in the accounting cycle is to **analyze transactions** and other selected **events**. The problem is determining **what to record**. There are no simple rules for whether an event should be recorded. It is generally agreed that changes in personnel, changes in managerial policies, and the value of human resources, though important, should not be recorded in the accounts. On the other hand, when the company makes a cash sale or purchase—no matter how small—it should be recorded. The treatment relates to the accounting concepts presented in Chapter 2. An item should be **recognized** in the financial statements if it is an **element**, is **measurable**, and for assets and liabilities, is **probable**.

The phrase "transactions and other events and circumstances that affect a business enterprise" is used to describe the sources or causes of changes in an entity's assets, liabilities, and equity.[3] Events are of two types:

[3] Elements of Financial Statements of Business Enterprises, Statement of Financial Accounting Concepts No. 6 (Stamford, Conn.: FASB, 1985), pp. 259–260.

- **External events** involve interaction between an entity and its environment, such as a **transaction** with another entity, a change in the price of a product or service that an entity buys or sells, a flood or earthquake, or an improvement in technology by a competitor.
- **Internal events** occur within an entity, such as using buildings and machinery in its operations or transferring or consuming raw materials in production processes.

Many events have **both** external and internal elements. For example, acquiring the services of employees or others involves exchange transactions, which are external events. The employee provides services and the company remunerates the employee. Using those services (labour), often from the moment they are acquired, is part of production, which is internal. Events may be initiated and controlled by an entity, such as the purchase of merchandise or the use of a machine, or they may be beyond its control, such as an interest rate change, a theft or vandalism, or the imposition of taxes.

As a particular kind of **external event**, a **transaction** can be an exchange in which each entity both receives and gives up value, such as a purchase or sale of goods or services. Alternatively, a transaction can be a transfer in one direction (i.e., be non-reciprocal) in which an entity incurs a liability or transfers an asset to another entity without directly receiving (or giving up) value in exchange. Examples include distributions to owners, the payment of taxes, gifts, charitable contributions, casualty losses, and thefts.

In short, as many events as possible that affect the enterprise's financial position are recorded. Some events are not recorded because of tradition or because measuring them is too complex. The accounting profession in recent years has shown signs of breaking with age-old traditions and is more receptive than ever to accepting the challenge of measuring and reporting events and phenomena that were previously viewed as too complex and immeasurable.[4] These areas will be studied in further depth in the rest of the textbook.

Journalizing

4 Objective
Record transactions in journals, post journal entries to ledger accounts, and prepare a trial balance.

The varied effects of transactions on the basic business elements (assets, liabilities, and equities) are categorized and collected in accounts. The **general ledger** is a collection of all the asset, liability, shareholders' equity, revenue, and expense accounts. A **T account** (as shown in Illustration 3-8) is a convenient method for showing the effect of transactions on particular asset, liability, equity, revenue, and expense items.

In practice, transactions and other selected events are not first recorded in the ledger. This is because each transaction affects two or more accounts, and since each account is on a different page in the ledger, it would be inconvenient to record each transaction this way. The risk of error would also be greater.[5] To overcome this limitation and to have a complete record of each transaction or other selected event in one place, a journal (the book of original entry) is used. The simplest journal form is a chronological listing of transactions and other events that expresses the transactions and events as debits and credits to particular accounts. This is called a **general journal**. The following transactions are presented in the general journal illustration that follows them:

Nov. 11 Buys a new delivery truck on account from Auto Sales Inc., $22,400.

Nov. 13 Receives an invoice from the *Evening Graphic* for advertising, $280.

Nov. 14 Returns merchandise to Canuck Supply for credit, $175.

Nov. 16 Receives a $95 debit memo from Confederation Ltd., indicating that freight on a purchase from Confederation Ltd. was prepaid but is the company's obligation.

[4] Examples of these include accounting for defined future benefit pension plans and stock-based employee compensation. These will be covered in Chapters 20 and 17, respectively.

[5] The transition to electronic bookkeeping systems and databases has dramatically changed the way bookkeeping is carried out. Much of the terminology and visual layout of the reports have been retained, however.

Expanded Discussion of Special Journals

www.wiley.com/canada/kieso

Each general journal entry has four parts:

1. The accounts and amounts to be debited (Dr.)
2. The accounts and amounts to be credited (Cr.)
3. A date
4. An explanation

Debits are entered first, and then followed by the credits, which are slightly indented. The explanation begins below the name of the last account to be credited and may take one or more lines. The Reference column is completed when the accounts are posted.

In some cases, businesses use **special journals** in addition to the general journal. Special journals summarize transactions that have a common characteristic (e.g., cash receipts, sales, purchases, cash payments), which saves time in doing the various bookkeeping tasks.

Illustration 3-7

General Journal with Sample Entries

GENERAL JOURNAL PAGE 12

Date 2007	Account Title and Explanation	Ref.	Amount Debit	Credit
Nov. 11	Delivery Equipment	8	$22,400	
	Accounts Payable	34		$22,400
	(Purchased delivery truck on account)			
Nov. 13	Advertising Expense	65	280	
	Accounts Payable	34		280
	(Received invoice for advertising)			
Nov. 14	Accounts Payable	34	175	
	Purchase Returns	53		175
	(Returned merchandise for credit)			
Nov. 16	Transportation-In	55	95	
	Accounts Payable	34		95
	(Received debit memo for freight on merchandise purchased)			

Posting

The items entered in a general journal must be transferred to the general ledger. This procedure is called **posting** and is part of the summarizing and classifying process.

For example, the November 11 entry in the general journal in Illustration 3-7 showed a debit to Delivery Equipment of $22,400 and a credit to Accounts Payable of $22,400. The amount in the debit column is posted from the journal to the debit side of the ledger account Delivery Equipment. The amount in the credit column is posted from the journal to the credit side of the ledger account Accounts Payable.

The numbers in the Ref. column of the general journal refer to the ledger accounts to which the items are posted. For example, the 34 placed in the column to the right of Accounts Payable indicates that this $22,400 item was posted to Account No. 34 in the ledger.

The general journal posting is completed when all the posting reference numbers have been recorded opposite the account titles in the journal. This means that the number in the posting reference column serves two purposes: (1) it indicates the ledger account number of the account involved, and (2) it indicates that the posting has been completed for that item. Each business enterprise chooses its own numbering system for its ledger accounts. One practice is to begin numbering with asset accounts and to follow with liabilities, shareholders' equity, revenue, and expense accounts, in that order.

The various ledger accounts in Illustration 3-8 are shown after the posting process is completed. The source of the data that has been transferred to the ledger account is indicated by the reference GJ 12 (General Journal, page 12).

Delivery Equipment No. 8

Date	Ref.	Debit	Date	Ref.	Credit
Nov. 11	GJ 12	$22,400			

Accounts Payable No. 34

Date	Ref.	Debit	Date	Ref.	Credit
Nov. 14	GJ 12	$175	Nov. 11	GJ 12	$22,400
			13	GJ 12	280
			16	GJ 12	95

Purchase Returns No. 53

Date	Ref.	Debit	Date	Ref.	Credit
			Nov. 14	GJ 12	$175

Transportation-In No. 55

Date	Ref.	Debit	Date	Ref.	Credit
Nov. 16	GJ 12	$95			

Advertising Expense No. 65

Date	Ref.	Debit	Date	Ref.	Credit
Nov. 13	GJ 12	$280			

Illustration 3-8
Ledger Accounts, in T Account Format

Trial Balance

A **trial balance** is a list of accounts and their balances at a specific time. Customarily, a trial balance is prepared at the end of an accounting period. The accounts are listed in the order in which they appear in the ledger, with debit balances listed in the left column and credit balances in the right column. The totals of the two columns must agree.

The main purpose of a trial balance is to prove the mathematical equality of debits and credits after posting. Under the double-entry system, this equality will occur when the sum of the debit account balances equals the sum of the credit account balances. A trial balance also uncovers errors in journalizing and posting. In addition, it is useful when preparing financial statements. The procedures for preparing a trial balance consist of:

1. Listing the account titles and their balances
2. Totalling the debit and credit columns
3. Proving the equality of the two columns

Illustration 3-9 shows the trial balance prepared from the ledger of Pioneer Advertising Agency Inc.

PIONEER ADVERTISING AGENCY INC.
Trial Balance
October 31, 2007

	Debit	Credit
Cash	$ 80,000	
Accounts Receivable	72,000	
Advertising Supplies	25,000	
Prepaid Insurance	6,000	
Office Equipment	50,000	
Notes Payable		$ 50,000
Accounts Payable		25,000

Illustration 3-9
Trial Balance (Unadjusted)

Unearned Service Revenue		12,000
Common Shares		100,000
Dividends	5,000	
Service Revenue		100,000
Salaries Expense	40,000	
Rent Expense	9,000	
	$287,000	$287,000

Note that the total debits, $287,000, equal the total credits, $287,000. In the trial balance, the account numbers of the account titles are also often shown to the left of the titles.

A trial balance does not prove that all transactions have been recorded or that the ledger is correct. Even though the trial balance columns agree, there can still be many errors. For example, the trial balance may still balance when:

1. a transaction is not journalized,
2. a correct journal entry is not posted,
3. a journal entry is posted twice,
4. incorrect accounts are used in journalizing or posting, or
5. offsetting errors are made in recording a transaction amount.

In other words, as long as equal debits and credits are posted, even to the wrong account or in the wrong amount, the total debits will equal the total credits.

Adjusting Entries

Objective 5 Explain the reasons for preparing adjusting entries.

In order for revenues to be recorded in the period in which they are earned, and for expenses to be recognized in the period in which they are incurred, **adjusting entries** are made at the end of the accounting period. In short, **adjustments are needed to ensure that the revenue recognition principle is followed and proper matching occurs.**

The use of adjusting entries makes it possible to report on the balance sheet the appropriate assets, liabilities, and owners' equity at the statement date and to report on the income statement the proper net income (or loss) for the period. However, the trial balance—the first pulling together of the transaction data—may not contain up-to-date and complete data. This is true for the following reasons:

1. Some events are **not journalized daily** because it is not efficient to do so. Examples are the consumption of supplies and the earning of wages by employees.
2. Some costs are not journalized during the accounting period because these costs **expire with the passage of time** rather than as a result of recurring daily transactions. Examples of such costs are building and equipment deterioration and rent and insurance.
3. Some items may be **unrecorded**. An example is a utility service bill that will not be received until the next accounting period.

Adjusting entries are required every time financial statements are prepared. The starting point is to analyze each trial balance account to determine whether it is complete and up to date for financial statement purposes. The analysis requires a thorough understanding of the company's operations and the relationships between its accounts. Preparing adjusting entries is often a complicated process that requires the services of a skilled professional. In accumulating the adjustment data, the company may need to take inventory counts of supplies and repair parts. It may also be desirable to prepare supporting schedules of insurance policies, rental agreements, and other contractual commitments. Adjustments are often prepared after the balance sheet date, but the entries are dated as at the balance sheet date.

Types of Adjusting Entries

Adjusting entries can be classified as either **prepayments** or **accruals**. Each of these classes has two subcategories as follows:

PREPAYMENTS	ACCRUALS
1. **Prepaid Expenses.** Expenses paid in cash and recorded as assets before they are used or consumed.	3. **Accrued Revenues.** Revenues earned but not yet received in cash or recorded.
2. **Unearned Revenues.** Revenues received in cash and recorded as liabilities before they are earned.	4. **Accrued Expenses.** Expenses incurred but not yet paid in cash or recorded.

Specific examples and explanations of each type of adjustment are given later in this chapter. Each example is based on the October 31 trial balance of Pioneer Advertising Agency Inc. (Illustration 3-9). We assume that Pioneer Advertising uses an accounting period of one month. Thus, monthly adjusting entries will be made. The entries will be dated October 31.

Adjusting Entries for Prepayments

As mentioned above, prepayments are either **prepaid expenses** or **unearned revenues.** Adjusting entries for prepayments are required at the statement date to record the portion of the prepaid expense or unearned revenue that was actually incurred or earned in the current accounting period. Assuming an adjustment is needed for both types of prepayments, the asset and liability involved are overstated and the related expense and revenue are understated. For example, in the trial balance, the balance in the asset account Advertising Supplies shows only supplies purchased. This balance is overstated; the related expense account, Advertising Supplies Expense, is understated because the cost of supplies used has not been recognized. Thus, the adjusting entry for prepayments will decrease a balance sheet account and increase an income statement account. Illustration 3-10 shows the effects of adjusting entries for prepayments.

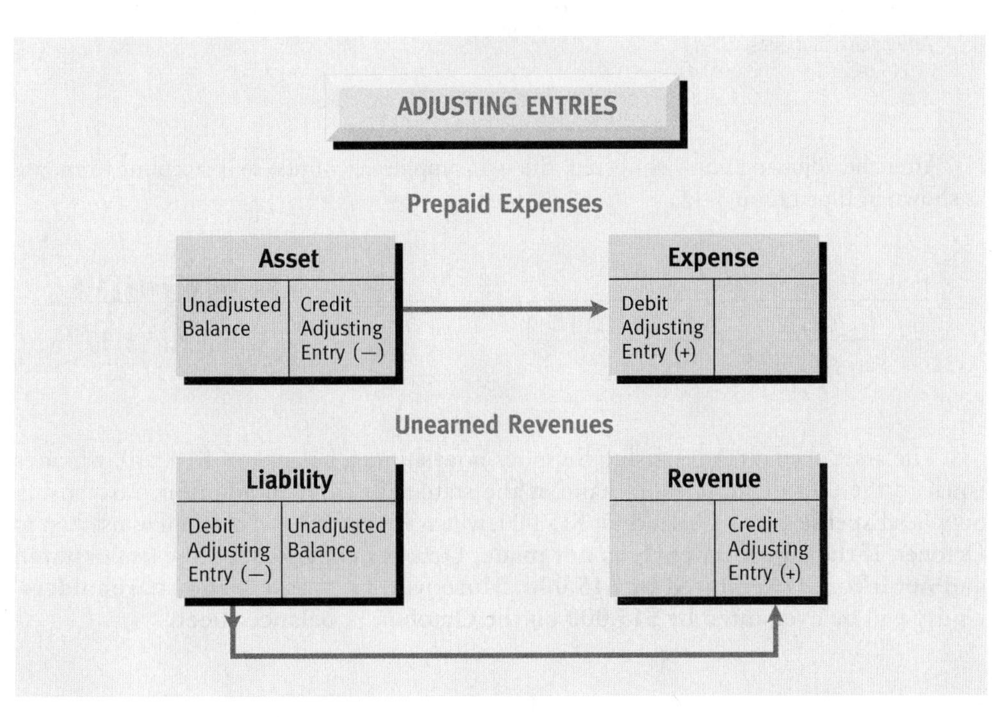

Illustration 3-10
Adjusting Entries for Prepayments

Prepaid Expenses. As previously stated, expenses that have been paid in cash and recorded as assets before they are used or consumed are identified as **prepaid expenses.** When a cost is incurred, an asset account is debited to show the service or benefit that will be received in the future. Prepayments often occur for such things as insurance, supplies, advertising, and rent.

Prepaid expenses expire either with the passage of time (e.g., rent and insurance) or by being used and consumed (e.g., supplies). The expiration of these costs does not require an entry each day, which would be unnecessary and impractical. Instead, it is customary to postpone the recognition of such cost expirations until financial statements are prepared. At each statement date, adjusting entries are made to record the expenses that apply to the current accounting period and to show the remaining unexpired costs in the asset accounts.

Before adjustment, assets are overstated and expenses are understated. **Thus, the prepaid expense adjusting entry results in a debit to an expense account and a credit to an asset account.**

Supplies. Several different types of supplies are used in businesses. For example, a CA firm will have office supplies such as stationery, envelopes, and accounting paper. In contrast, an advertising firm will have advertising supplies such as graph paper, video film, and poster paper. Supplies are generally debited to an asset account when they are acquired. During the course of operations, supplies are depleted or entirely consumed. However, recognition of the used-up supplies is deferred until the adjustment process when a physical inventory (a count) of supplies is taken. The difference between the balance in the Supplies account (the asset) and the cost of supplies on hand represents the supplies used up for the period (the expense).

Pioneer Advertising Agency purchased advertising supplies costing $25,000 on October 5. The debit was made to the asset Advertising Supplies, and this account shows a balance of $25,000 in the October 31 trial balance. An inventory count at the close of business on October 31 reveals that $10,000 of supplies is still on hand. Thus, the cost of supplies used is $15,000 ($25,000 – $10,000), and the following adjusting entry is made:

A	= L +	SE
−15,000		−15,000

Cash flows: No effect

Oct. 31		
Advertising Supplies Expense	15,000	
Advertising Supplies		15,000
(To record supplies used)		

After the adjusting entry is posted, the two supplies accounts, in T account form, are as shown in Illustration 3-11.

Illustration 3-11
Supplies Accounts after Adjustment

Advertising Supplies			
10/5	$25,000	10/31 Adj.	$15,000
10/31 Bal.	$10,000		

Advertising Supplies Expense		
10/31 Adj.	$15,000	

The asset account Advertising Supplies now shows a balance of $10,000, which is equal to the cost of supplies on hand at the statement date. In addition, Advertising Supplies Expense shows a balance of $15,000, which equals the cost of supplies used up in October. **If the adjusting entry is not made, October expenses will be understated and net income overstated by $15,000. Moreover, both assets and shareholders' equity will be overstated by $15,000 on the October 31 balance sheet.**

Insurance. Most companies have fire and theft insurance on merchandise and equipment, personal liability insurance for accidents suffered by customers, and automobile insurance on company cars and trucks. The cost of insurance protection is the amount paid as insurance premiums. The term (duration) and coverage (what the company is insured against) are specified in the insurance policy. The minimum term is usually one year, but three- to five-year terms are available and offer lower annual premiums. Insurance premiums are normally charged to the asset account Prepaid Insurance when they are paid. At the financial statement date, it is necessary to debit Insurance Expense and credit Prepaid Insurance for the cost that has expired during the period.

On October 4, Pioneer Advertising Agency Inc. paid $6,000 for a one-year fire insurance policy. The coverage began as of October 1. The premium was charged to Prepaid Insurance when it was paid, and this account shows a balance of $6,000 in the October 31 trial balance. An analysis of the policy reveals that $500 of insurance expires each month ($6,000/12). Thus, the following adjusting entry is made:

Insurance

Oct. 4

Insurance purchased; record asset

Insurance Policy			
Oct $500	Nov $500	Dec $500	Jan $500
Feb $500	March $500	April $500	May $500
June $500	July $500	Aug $500	Sept $500
1 YEAR $6,000			

Oct. 31 Insurance expired; record insurance expense

Oct. 31		
Insurance Expense	500	
Prepaid Insurance		500
(To record insurance expired)		

A	=	L	+	SE
−500				−500

Cash flows: No effect

After the adjusting entry is posted, the accounts are as in Illustration 3-12.

Illustration 3-12

Insurance Accounts after Adjustment

Pre-paid Insurance				Insurance Expense		
10/4	$6,000	10/31 Adj.	$500	10/31 Adj.	$500	
10/31 Bal.	$5,500					

The asset Prepaid Insurance shows a balance of $5,500, which represents the unexpired cost of the 11 months of remaining coverage. At the same time, the balance in Insurance Expense is equal to the insurance cost that has expired in October. **If this adjustment is not made, October expenses will be understated by $500 and net income overstated by $500. Moreover, both assets and owners' equity will also be overstated by $500 on the October 31 balance sheet.**

Amortization/Depreciation. Companies typically own a variety of productive facilities such as buildings, equipment, and motor vehicles. These assets provide a service for many years. The term of service is commonly referred to as the asset's **useful life. Because an asset such as a building is expected to provide service for many years, it is recorded as an asset, rather than an expense, in the year it is acquired.** Such assets are recorded at cost, as required by the cost principle.

Underlying Concept

The historical cost principle requires that depreciable assets be recorded at cost. Matching allows this cost to be allocated to future periods.

In order to match the cost of the asset with the revenues that it is generating, a portion of the cost of a long-lived asset should be reported as an expense during each period of the asset's useful life. **Amortization** is the process of **allocating the cost of an asset** to expense over its useful life in a rational and systematic manner.

From an accounting standpoint, when productive facilities are acquired, the transaction is viewed essentially as a long-term prepayment for services. Periodic adjusting entries for amortization are therefore needed for the same reasons described earlier for other prepaid expenses; that is, it is necessary to recognize the cost that has expired during the period (the expense) and to report the unexpired cost at the end of the period (the asset).

In determining a productive facility's useful life, there are three main causes of amortization:

- actual use
- deterioration due to the elements
- obsolescence

When an asset is acquired, the effects of these factors cannot be known with certainty, so they must instead be estimated. Thus, you should recognize that amortization is an estimate rather than a factual measurement of the cost that has expired. A common procedure in calculating amortization expense is to divide the asset's cost by its useful life. For example, if the cost is $10,000 and the useful life is expected to be 10 years, annual amortization is $1,000.

For Pioneer Advertising, amortization on the office equipment is estimated at $4,800 a year (cost of $50,000 less a salvage value of $2,000 divided by a useful life of 10 years), or $400 per month. Accordingly, amortization for October is recognized by the following adjusting entry:

A	=	L	+	SE
−400				−400

Cash flows: No effect

Oct. 31		
Amortization Expense	400	
Accumulated Amortization—Office Equipment		400
(To record monthly amortization)		

After the adjusting entry is posted, the accounts show that the balance in the accumulated amortization account will increase by $400 each month.

Illustration 3-13

Accounts after Adjustment for Amortization

Office Equipment

Debit	Credit
10/5 $50,000	

Accumulated Amortization—Office Equipment

Debit	Credit
	10/31 Adj. $400

Amortization Expense

Debit	Credit
10/31 Adj. $400	

Therefore, after journalizing and posting the adjusting entry at November 30, the balance will then be $800 in the accumulated amortization account.

Accumulated Amortization—Office Equipment is a contra asset account. A **contra asset account** is an account that is offset against an asset account on the balance sheet. In the case of accumulated amortization, this account is offset against Office Equipment on the balance sheet and its normal balance is therefore a credit. This account is used instead of crediting Office Equipment so that the original cost of the equipment and the total cost that has expired to date can both be disclosed. In the balance sheet, Accumulated Amortization—Office Equipment is deducted from the related asset account (which is normally a debit), as shown in Illustration 3-14.

Illustration 3-14

Balance Sheet Presentation of Accumulated Amortization

Office equipment	$50,000	
Less: Accumulated amortization—office equipment	400	$49,600

The difference between any depreciable asset's cost and its related accumulated amortization is known as its **book value**. In Illustration 3-14, the equipment's book or carrying value at the balance sheet date is $49,600. It is important to realize that the asset's **book value and market value are generally two different values.**

Note also that amortization expense identifies that portion of the asset's cost that has expired in October. As in the case of other prepaid adjustments, **if this adjusting entry is not made, then total shareholders' equity and net income will be overstated and amortization expense will be understated.**

If additional equipment is involved, such as delivery or store equipment, or if the company has buildings, amortization expense is recorded on each of these items. Related accumulated amortization accounts also are created. These accumulated amortization accounts would be described in the ledger as follows: Accumulated Amortization—Delivery Equipment; Accumulated Amortization—Store Equipment; and Accumulated Amortization—Buildings.

Unearned Revenues. As stated earlier, revenues that have been received in cash and recorded as liabilities before they are earned are called **unearned revenues**. Such items as rent, magazine subscriptions, and customer deposits for further service may result in unearned revenues. Airlines such as **Air Canada** and **United Airlines** treat receipts from the sale of tickets as unearned revenue until the flight service is provided. Similarly, tuition fees received by a university before the start of a semester are considered unearned revenue. Unearned revenues are the opposite of prepaid expenses. Indeed, unearned revenue on the books of one company is likely to be a prepayment on the books of the company that has made the advance payment. For example, if identical accounting periods are assumed, a landlord will have unearned rent revenue when a tenant has prepaid rent.

When the payment is received for services that will be provided in a future accounting period, an unearned revenue account (a liability) should be credited to recognize the obligation that exists. Unearned revenues are later earned by performing the service for the customer (which discharges the liability). During the accounting period, it may not be practical to make an entry each day as the revenue is earned. In such cases, the recognition of earned revenue is delayed until the adjustment process. At that time, an adjusting entry is then made to record the revenue that has been earned and to show the liability that remains. In the typical case, liabilities are overstated and revenues are understated prior to adjustment. Thus, the adjusting entry for unearned revenues results in a debit (decrease) to a liability account and a credit (increase) to a revenue account.

Pioneer Advertising Agency received $12,000 on October 2 from R. Knox for advertising services that are expected to be completed by December 31. The payment was credited to Unearned Service Revenue, and this account shows a balance of $12,000 in the October 31 trial balance. When analysis reveals that $4,000 of these services have been earned in October, the following adjusting entry is made:

Oct. 31		
Unearned Service Revenue	4,000	
Service Revenue		4,000
(To record revenue for services provided)		

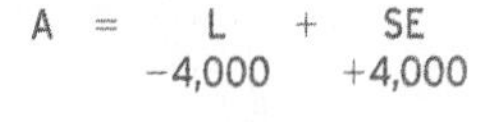

Cash flows: No effect

After the adjusting entry is posted, the accounts are as shown in Illustration 3-15.

Illustration 3-15
Service Revenue Accounts after Prepayments Adjustment

Unearned Service Revenue (Dr.)	Unearned Service Revenue (Cr.)	Service Revenue (Dr.)	Service Revenue (Cr.)
10/31 Adj. $4,000	10/2 $12,000		10/31 Bal. $100,000
	10/31 Bal. $8,000		10/31 Adj. 4,000
			10/31 Bal. $104,000

Underlying Concept

The revenue recognition principle requires revenue to be recognized when it is earned (when the company has discharged any liabilities to the customer).

The account Unearned Service Revenue now shows a balance of $8,000, which represents the remaining advertising services that are expected to be performed in the future. At the same time, Service Revenue shows total revenue earned in October of $104,000. **If this adjustment is not made, revenues and net income will be understated by $4,000 in the income statement. Moreover, liabilities will be overstated and shareholders' equity will be understated by $4,000 on the October 31 balance sheet.**

Alternative Method for Adjusting Prepayments

So far, the assumption has been that an asset (e.g., prepaid rent) or liability (e.g., unearned revenue) is recorded when the company initially pays or receives the cash. An alternative treatment is to record the initial entry through the related income statement account and adjust it later. For example, if Pioneer Advertising Agency Inc. paid $6,000 for a one-year fire insurance policy on October 1, it could initially have recorded the whole amount in Insurance Expense. Thus at October 31, the adjusting entry would be as follows:

A	= L +	SE
+5,500		+5,500

Cash flows: No effect

Oct. 31		
Prepaid Insurance	5,500	
Insurance Expense		5,500
(To record unexpired insurance)		

The same could be done for other prepayments, such as supplies and revenues.

Adjusting Entries for Accruals

The second category of adjusting entries is **accruals**. Adjusting entries for accruals are required in order to record revenues earned and expenses incurred in the current accounting period that have not been recognized through daily entries. If an accrual adjustment is needed, the revenue account (and the related asset account) and/or the expense account (and the related liability account) are understated. Thus, the adjusting entry for accruals will increase both a balance sheet and an income statement account. Adjusting entries for accruals are shown in Illustration 3-16.

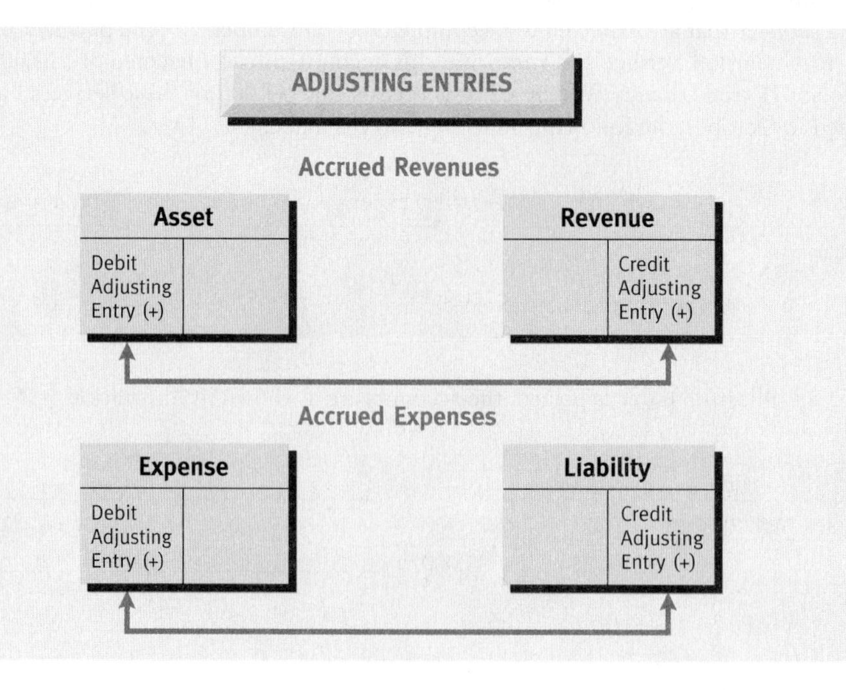

Illustration 3-16
Adjusting Entries for Accruals

Accrued Revenues. As explained earlier, revenues that have been **earned but not yet received** in cash or recorded at the statement date are **accrued revenues**. Accrued revenues may **accumulate (accrue) with the passing of time**, as in the case of interest revenue and rent revenue. Or they may result from services that have been performed but neither billed nor collected, as in the case of commissions and fees. The former are unrecorded because earning interest and rent does not involve daily transactions; the latter may be unrecorded because only a portion of the total service has been provided.

An adjusting entry is required in order to show the receivable that exists at the balance sheet date and to record the revenue that has been earned during the period. Before adjustment, both assets and revenues are understated. Accordingly, an adjusting entry for accrued revenues results in a debit (increase) to an asset account and a credit (increase) to a revenue account.

In October, Pioneer Advertising Agency earned $2,000 for advertising services that were not billed to clients before October 31. Because these services have not yet been billed, they have not been recorded in any way. Thus, the following adjusting entry is made:

Oct. 31		
Accounts Receivable	2,000	
Service Revenue		2,000
(To record revenue for services provided)		

A	= L +	SE
+2,000		+2,000

Cash flows: No effect

Illustration 3-17 shows the accounts after the adjusting entry is posted.

Accounts Receivable

Debit	Credit
10/31 $72,000	
10/31 Adj. 2,000	
10/31 Bal. $74,000	

Service Revenue

Debit	Credit
	10/31 $100,000
	10/31 4,000
	10/31 Adj. 2,000
	10/31 Bal. $106,000

Illustration 3-17
Receivable and Revenue Accounts after Accrual Adjustment

The asset Accounts Receivable shows that $74,000 is owed by clients at the balance sheet date. The balance of $106,000 in Service Revenue is the total revenue earned during the month ($100,000 + $4,000 + $2,000). If the adjusting entry is not made, assets and shareholders' equity on the balance sheet, and revenues and net income on the income statement, will all be understated.

Accrued Expenses. As indicated earlier, expenses that have been incurred but not yet paid or recorded at the statement date are called **accrued expenses**. Interest, rent, taxes, and salaries can be accrued expenses. Accrued expenses result from the same causes as accrued revenues. In fact, an accrued expense on the books of one company is accrued revenue to another company. For example, the $2,000 accrual of service revenue by Pioneer is an accrued expense to the client that received the service.

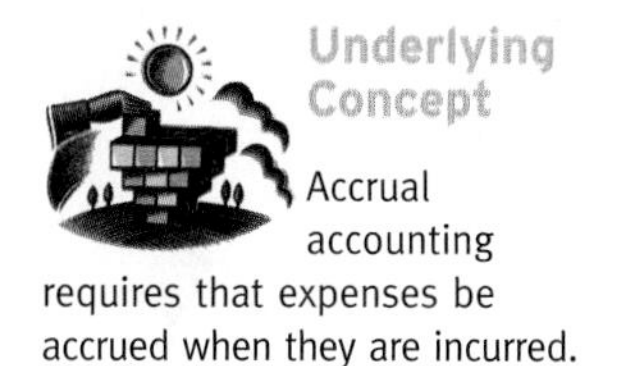

Accrual accounting requires that expenses be accrued when they are incurred.

Adjustments for accrued expenses are necessary in order to record the obligations that exist at the balance sheet date and to recognize the expenses that apply to the current accounting period. Before adjustment, both liabilities and expenses are understated. Therefore, the adjusting entry for accrued expenses results in a debit (increase) to an expense account and a credit (increase) to a liability account.

Accrued Interest. Pioneer Advertising Agency signed a three-month note payable for $50,000 on October 1. The note requires interest at an annual rate of 12 percent. The interest accumulation amount is determined by three factors:

- the note's face value
- the interest rate, which is always expressed as an annual rate
- the length of time the note is outstanding

In this instance, the total interest due on the $50,000 note at its due date three months later is $1,500 ($50,000 × 12% × 3/12), or $500 for one month. The formula for calculating interest and how it applies to Pioneer Advertising Agency for the month of October are shown in Illustration 3-18.

Illustration 3-18
Formula for Calculating Interest

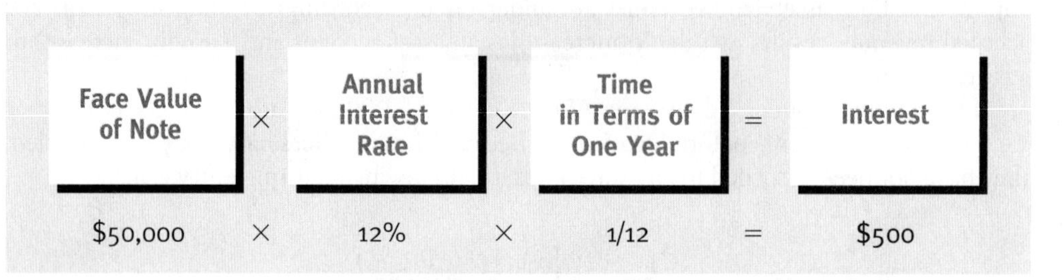

Note that the time period is expressed as a fraction of a year. The accrued expense adjusting entry at October 31 is as follows:

A	=	L	+	SE
		+500		−500

Cash flows: No effect

Oct. 31		
Interest Expense	500	
Interest Payable		500
(To record interest on notes payable)		

After this adjusting entry is posted, the accounts are as shown in Illustration 3-19.

Illustration 3-19
Interest Accounts after Adjustment

Interest Expense			Interest Payable	
10/31	$500		10/31	$500

Interest Expense shows the interest charges that apply to the month of October. The amount of interest owed at the statement date is shown in Interest Payable. It will not be paid until the note comes due at the end of three months. The Interest Payable account is used instead of crediting Notes Payable in order to disclose the two types of obligations (interest and principal) in the accounts and statements. **If this adjusting entry is not made, liabilities and interest expense will be understated, and net income and shareholders' equity will be overstated.**

Accrued Salaries. Some types of expenses, such as employee salaries and commissions, are paid for after the services have been performed. At Pioneer Advertising, salaries were last paid on October 26; the next payment of salaries will not occur until November 9. As shown in the calendar that follows, three working days remain in October (October 29, 30, and 31).

At October 31, the salaries for these days represent an accrued expense and a related liability to Pioneer Advertising. The employees receive total salaries of $10,000 for a five-

	S	M	Tu	W	Th	F	S
October							
		1	2	3	4	5	6
	7	8	9	10	11	12	13
Start of pay period → 15	14	15	16	17	18	19	20
	21	22	23	24	25	26 (Payday)	27
	28	29	30	31			

Adjustment period (Oct. 29–31)

S	M	Tu	W	Th	F	S
November						
				1	2	3
4	5	6	7	8	9 (Payday)	10
11	12	13	14	15	16	17
18	19	20	21	22	23	24
25	26	27	28	29	30	

day workweek, or $2,000 per day. Thus, accrued salaries at October 31 are $6,000 ($2,000 times 3), and the adjusting entry is:

Oct. 31		
Salaries Expense	6,000	
Salaries Payable		6,000
(To record accrued salaries)		

A	=	L	+	SE
		+6,000		−6,000

Cash flows: No effect

After this adjusting entry is posted, the accounts are as shown in Illustration 3-20.

Illustration 3-20
Salary Accounts after Adjustment

Salaries Expense

		Debit	Credit
10/26		$40,000	
10/31	Adj.	6,000	
10/31	Bal.	$46,000	

Salaries Payable

Debit			Credit
	10/31	Adj.	$6,000

After this adjustment, the balance in Salaries Expense of $46,000 (23 days times $2,000) is the actual salary expense for October. The balance in Salaries Payable of $6,000 is the amount of liability for salaries owed as of October 31. **If the $6,000 adjustment for salaries is not recorded, Pioneer's expenses will be understated by $6,000, and its liabilities will be understated by $6,000.**

At Pioneer Advertising, salaries are payable every two weeks. Consequently, the next payday is November 9, when total salaries of $20,000 will again be paid. The payment consists of $6,000 of salaries payable at October 31 plus $14,000 of salaries expense for November (7 working days as shown in the November calendar x $2,000). Therefore, the following entry is made on November 9:

Nov. 9		
Salaries Payable	6,000	
Salaries Expense	14,000	
Cash		20,000
(To record November 9 payroll)		

A	=	L	+	SE
−20,000		−6,000		−14,000

Cash flows: ↓ 20,000 outflow

This entry eliminates the liability for Salaries Payable that was recorded in the October 31 adjusting entry and records the proper amount of Salaries Expense for the period November 1 to November 9.

Bad Debts. **In order to properly match revenues with expenses, a bad debt must be recorded as an expense of the period in which the revenue was earned instead of being recorded in the period when the accounts or notes are written off. So that the receivable balance shows its proper value, uncollectible, worthless receivables must be recognized.** Proper matching and valuation therefore require an adjusting entry.

At the end of each period, an estimate is made of the amount of current period revenue on account that will later be uncollectible. The estimate is based on the amount of bad debts experienced in past years, general economic conditions, how long the receivables are past due, and other factors that indicate uncollectibility. Usually it is expressed as a percentage of the revenue on account for the period. Or it may be calculated by adjusting the Allowance for Doubtful Accounts to a certain percentage of the trade accounts receivable and trade notes receivable at the end of the period.

Underlying Concept

According to contingency accounting, bad debt expense must be recognized when a loss is likely and measurable.

To illustrate, assume that experience shows that a reasonable estimate for bad debt expense for the month is $1,600. The adjusting entry for bad debts is:

Oct. 31		
Bad Debt Expense	1,600	
Allowance for Doubtful Accounts		1,600
(To record monthly bad debt expense)		

A	= L +	SE
−1,600		−1,600

Cash flows: No effect

Illustration 3-21 shows the accounts after the adjusting entry is posted.

Illustration 3-21
Accounts after Adjustment for Bad Debt Expense

Accounts Receivable

Debit			Credit
10/1		$72,000	
10/31	Adj.	2,000	
10/31	Bal.	$74,000	

Allowance for Doubtful Accounts

Debit	Credit
	10/31 Adj. $1,600

Bad Debt Expense

Debit	Credit
10/31 Adj. $1,600	

Adjusted Trial Balance

After all adjusting entries have been journalized and posted, another trial balance is prepared from the ledger accounts. This trial balance is called an **adjusted trial balance**. It shows the balance of all accounts, including those that have been adjusted, at the end of the accounting period. The purpose of an adjusted trial balance is to show the effects of all financial events that have occurred during the accounting period.

Illustration 3-22
Trial Balance (Adjusted)

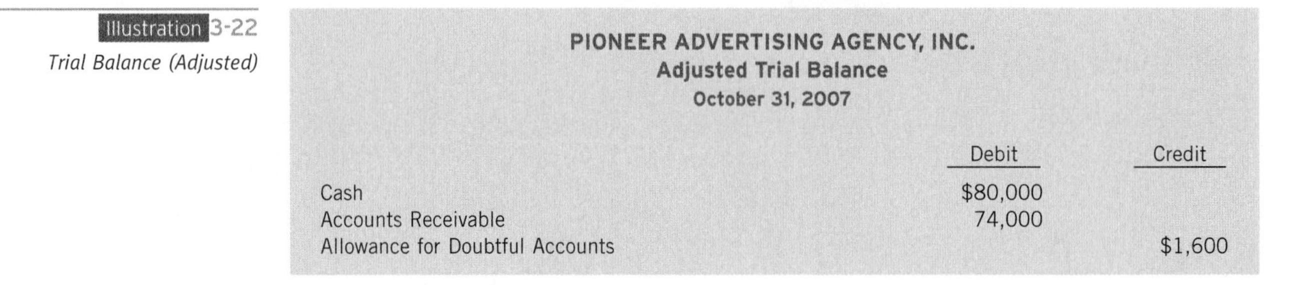
PIONEER ADVERTISING AGENCY, INC.
Adjusted Trial Balance
October 31, 2007

	Debit	Credit
Cash	$80,000	
Accounts Receivable	74,000	
Allowance for Doubtful Accounts		$1,600

Advertising Supplies	10,000	
Prepaid Insurance	5,500	
Office Equipment	50,000	
Accumulated Amortization—Office Equipment		400
Notes Payable		50,000
Accounts Payable		25,000
Interest Payable		500
Unearned Service Revenue		8,000
Salaries Payable		6,000
Common Shares		100,000
Dividends	5,000	
Service Revenue		106,000
Salaries Expense	46,000	
Advertising Supplies Expense	15,000	
Rent Expense	9,000	
Insurance Expense	500	
Interest Expense	500	
Amortization Expense	400	
Bad Debt Expense	1,600	
	$297,500	$297,500

Closing

Basic Process

6 Objective
Prepare closing entries.

The procedure that reduces the balance of temporary accounts to zero in order to prepare the accounts for the next period's transactions is known as the **closing process**. In the closing process, all of the revenue and expense account balances (income statement items) are transferred to a clearing or suspense account called **Income Summary**, which is used only at year end. Revenues and expenses are matched in the Income Summary account, and the net result of this matching (which is the net income or net loss for the period) is then transferred to an owners' equity account (retained earnings for a corporation and normally capital accounts or owners' equity for proprietorships and partnerships). All closing entries are posted to the appropriate general ledger accounts.

For example, assume that the revenue accounts of Collegiate Apparel Shop Inc. have the following balances, after adjustments, at year end:

Sales Revenue	$280,000
Rental Revenue	27,000
Interest Revenue	5,000

These revenue accounts would be closed and the balances transferred by the following closing journal entry:

Sales Revenue	280,000	
Rental Revenue	27,000	
Interest Revenue	5,000	
Income Summary		312,000
(To close revenue accounts to Income Summary)		

A	=	L	+	SE
				−312,000
				+312,000

Cash flows: No effect

Assume that the expense accounts, including Cost of Goods Sold, have the following balances, after adjustments, at year end:

적발녀

Cost of Goods Sold	$206,000
Selling Expenses	25,000
General and Administrative Expenses	40,600
Interest Expense	4,400
Income Tax Expense	13,000

These expense accounts would be closed and the balances transferred through the following closing journal entry:

A = L + SE
−289,000
+289,000

Cash flows: No effect

Income Summary	289,000	
Cost of Goods Sold		206,000
Selling Expenses		25,000
General and Administrative Expenses		40,600
Interest Expense		4,400
Income Tax Expense		13,000
(To close expense accounts to Income Summary)		

The Income Summary account now has a credit balance of $23,000, which is net income. **The net income is then transferred to retained earnings by closing the Income Summary account to Retained Earnings** as follows:

A = L + SE
−23,000
+23,000

Cash flows: No effect

Income Summary	23,000	
Retained Earnings		23,000
(To close Income Summary to Retained Earnings)		

Assuming that dividends of $7,000 were declared and distributed during the year, the Dividends account is closed directly to Retained Earnings as follows:

A = L + SE
−7,000
+7,000

Cash flows: No effect

Retained Earnings	7,000	
Dividends		7,000
(To close Dividends to Retained Earnings)		

After the closing process is completed, each income statement account is balanced out to zero and is ready to be used in the next accounting period. Illustration 3-23 shows the closing process in T account form.

Inventory and Cost of Goods Sold

Objective 7
Explain how inventory accounts are adjusted at year end.

The closing procedures just shown assume that a perpetual inventory system is being used. With a **perpetual inventory system**, purchases and sales are recorded directly in the inventory account as they occur. Therefore, the balance in Inventory should represent the ending inventory amount, and no adjusting entries are needed. To be sure that the inventory amount is accurate, a **physical count** of the items in the inventory is generally done each year.

In the perpetual inventory system, since all purchases are debited directly to the Inventory account, there are no separate Purchases accounts. However, a Cost of Goods Sold account is used to accumulate what is issued from inventory. That is, when inventory items are sold, the cost of the sold goods is credited to Inventory and debited to Cost of Goods Sold.

Illustration 3-23

The Closing Process

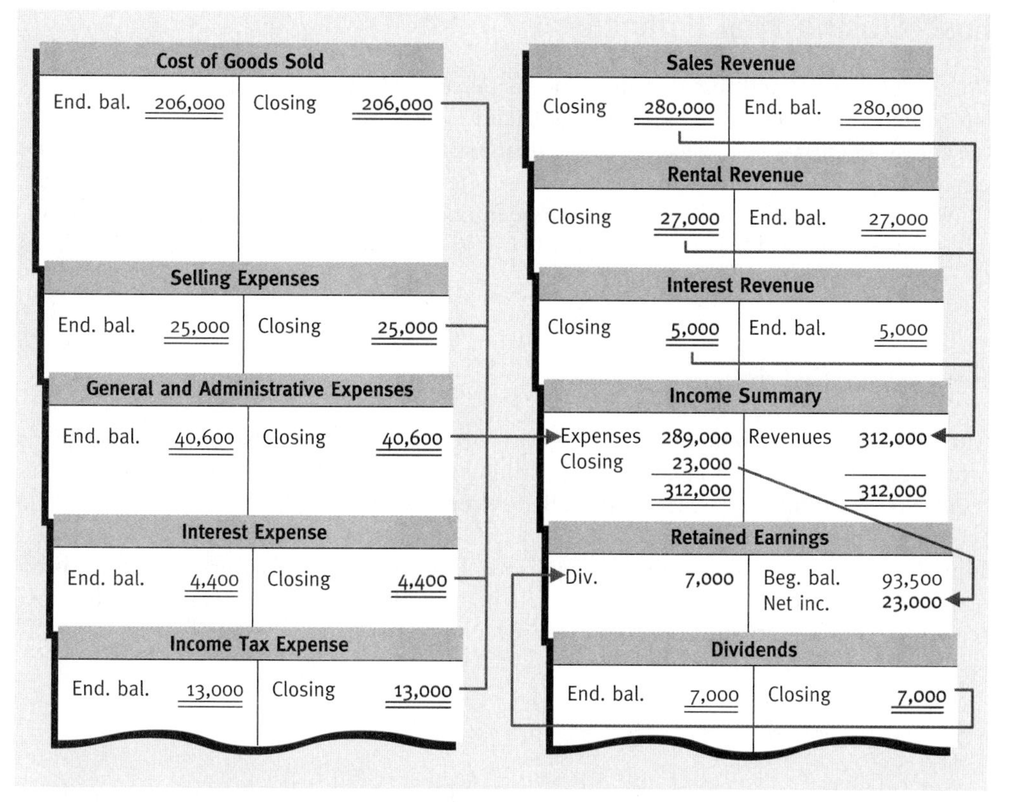

With a **periodic inventory system**, a Purchases account is used, and the Inventory account is unchanged during the period. The Inventory account therefore represents the beginning inventory amount throughout the period. At the end of the accounting period, the Inventory account must be adjusted by **closing out the beginning inventory amount** and **recording the ending inventory amount**. The ending inventory is determined by physically counting the items on hand and valuing them at cost or at the lower of cost or market. Under the periodic inventory system, cost of goods sold is therefore determined by adding the beginning inventory to net purchases and deducting the ending inventory.

To illustrate how cost of goods sold is calculated with a periodic inventory system, assume that Collegiate Apparel Shop has a beginning inventory of $30,000; purchases of $200,000; transportation-in of $6,000; purchase returns and allowances of $1,000; purchase discounts of $3,000; and ending inventory of $26,000. The calculation of cost of goods sold is as shown in Illustration 3-24.

Underlying Concept

Using a periodic inventory system instead of a perpetual one is an application of the cost-benefit concept since it is cheaper to maintain a periodic inventory system. Computers have greatly reduced the costs of maintaining a perpetual inventory system, however.

Illustration 3-24

Calculation of Cost of Goods Sold

Beginning inventory			$30,000
Purchases		$200,000	
Less: Purchase returns and allowances	$1,000		
Less: Purchase discounts	3,000	4,000	
Net purchases		196,000	
Plus: Transportation-in		6,000	
Cost of goods purchased			202,000
Cost of goods available for sale			232,000
Less: Ending inventory			26,000
Cost of goods sold			$206,000

Cost of goods sold will be the same whether the perpetual or periodic method is used.

Post-Closing Trial Balance

We already mentioned that a trial balance is taken after the period's regular transactions have been entered and that a second trial balance (the adjusted trial balance) is taken after the adjusting entries have been posted. A third trial balance may be taken after posting the closing entries. The trial balance after closing, often called the **post-closing trial balance**, shows that equal debits and credits have been posted to the Income Summary account. The post-closing trial balance consists only of asset, liability, and owners' equity accounts (i.e., the permanent accounts).

Reversing Entries

After the financial statements have been prepared and the books have been closed, it is often helpful to reverse some of the adjusting entries before recording the next period's regular transactions. Such entries are called **reversing entries**. A reversing entry is made at the beginning of the next accounting period and is the exact opposite of the related adjusting entry made in the previous period. The recording of reversing entries is an optional step in the accounting cycle that may be done at the beginning of the next accounting period. Appendix 3A discusses reversing entries in more detail.

The Accounting Cycle Summarized

The steps in the accounting cycle follow a logical sequence of the accounting procedures that are used during a fiscal period:

1. Enter the period's transactions in appropriate journals.
2. Post from the journals to the ledger (or ledgers).
3. Take an unadjusted trial balance (trial balance).
4. Prepare adjusting journal entries and post to the ledger(s).
5. Take a trial balance after adjusting (adjusted trial balance).
6. Prepare the financial statements from the second trial balance.
7. Prepare closing journal entries and post to the ledger(s).
8. Take a trial balance after closing (post-closing trial balance).
9. Prepare reversing entries (optional) and post to the ledger(s).

This list of procedures forms the complete accounting cycle that is normally performed in every fiscal period.

USING A WORK SHEET

Objective 8
Prepare a 10-column work sheet and financial statements.

To make the end-of-period (monthly, quarterly, or annually) accounting and reporting process easier, a work sheet is often used. A **work sheet** is a sheet of paper with columns (or computer spreadsheet) that is used to adjust the account balances and prepare the financial statements. Using a work sheet helps accountants prepare financial statements on a more timely basis. It is not necessary to delay preparing the financial statements until the adjusting and closing entries are journalized and posted. The **10-column work sheet** shown in this chapter (Illustration 3-25) has columns for the first trial balance, adjustments, adjusted trial balance, income statement, and balance sheet.

The work sheet does not replace the financial statements. Instead, it is an informal device for accumulating and sorting the information that is needed for the financial statements. Completing the work sheet makes it more certain that all of the details of the end-of-period accounting and statement preparation have been brought together properly.

Adjustments Entered on the Work Sheet

The following items, (a) through (f), are the basis for the adjusting entries made in the work sheet in Illustration 3-25:

(a) Furniture and equipment are amortized at the rate of 10% per year based on an original cost of $67,000.

(b) Estimated bad debts are 0.25% of sales ($400,000).

(c) Insurance of $360 expired during the year.

(d) Interest of $800 accrued on notes receivable as December 31.

(e) The Rent Expense account contains $500 of rent paid in advance, which is applicable to next year.

(f) Property taxes of $2,000 accrued to December 31.

The adjusting entries shown on the December 31, 2007, work sheet are as follows:

	Account	Debit	Credit
(a)	Amortization Expense—Furniture and Equipment	6,700	
	Accumulated Amortization—Furniture and Equipment		6,700
(b)	Bad Debt Expense	1,000	
	Allowance for Doubtful Accounts		1,000
(c)	Insurance Expense	360	
	Prepaid Insurance		360
(d)	Interest Receivable	800	
	Interest Revenue		800
(e)	Prepaid Rent Expense	500	
	Rent Expense		500
(f)	Property Tax Expense	2,000	
	Property Tax Payable		2,000

These adjusting entries are transferred to the work sheet's Adjustments columns and each column can be named by letter. The accounts that are set up from the adjusting entries and which are not already in the trial balance are listed below the totals of the trial balance, as shown on the work sheet. The Adjustments columns are then totalled and balanced.

Work Sheet Columns

Trial Balance Columns

Data for the trial balance are obtained from the ledger balances of Uptown Cabinet Corp. at December 31. The amount for Merchandise Inventory, $40,000, is the year-end inventory amount under a perpetual inventory system.

Adjustments Columns

After all adjustment data are entered on the work sheet, the equality of the adjustment columns is established. The balances in all accounts are then extended to the adjusted trial balance columns.

Adjusted Trial Balance

The adjusted trial balance shows the balance of all accounts after adjustment at the end of the accounting period. For example, the $2,000 shown opposite Allowance for Doubtful Accounts in the Trial Balance Cr. column is added to the $1,000 in the Adjustments Cr. column. The $3,000 total is then extended to the Adjusted Trial Balance Cr. column.

Illustration 3-25
Work Sheet

UPTOWN CABINET CORP.
Ten-Column Work Sheet
For the Year Ended December 31, 2007

	Trial Balance		Adjustments		Adjusted Trial Balance		Income Statement		Balance Sheet	
Accounts	Dr.	Cr.	Dr.	Cr.	Dr.	Cr.	Dr.	Cr.	Dr.	Cr.
Cash	1,200				1,200				1,200	
Notes receivable	16,000				16,000				16,000	
Accounts receivable	41,000				41,000				41,000	
Allowance for doubtful accounts		2,000		(b)1,000		3,000				3,000
Merchandise inventory	40,000				40,000				40,000	
Prepaid insurance	900			(c)360	540				540	
Furniture and equipment	67,000				67,000				67,000	
Accumulated amortization—furniture and equipment		12,000		(a)6,700		18,700				18,700
Notes payable		20,000				20,000				20,000
Accounts payable		13,500				13,500				13,500
Bonds payable		30,000				30,000				30,000
Common shares		50,000				50,000				50,000
Retained earnings, Jan. 1, 2007		14,200				14,200				14,200
Sales		400,000				400,000		400,000		
Cost of goods sold	316,000				316,000		316,000			
Sales salaries expense	20,000				20,000		20,000			
Advertising expense	2,200				2,200		2,200			
Travelling expense	8,000				8,000		8,000			
Salaries, office and general	19,000				19,000		19,000			
Telephone and Internet expense	600				600		600			
Rent expense	4,800			(e)500	4,300		4,300			
Property tax expense	3,300		(f)2,000		5,300		5,300			
Interest expense	1,700				1,700		1,700			
Totals	541,700	541,700								
Amortization expense—furniture and equipment			(a)6,700		6,700		6,700			
Bad debt expense			(b)1,000		1,000		1,000			
Insurance expense			(c)360		360		360			
Interest receivable			(d)800		800				800	
Interest revenue				(d)800		800		800		
Prepaid rent expense			(e)500		500				500	
Property tax payable				(f)2,000		2,000				2,000
Totals			11,360	11,360	**552,200**	**552,200**	**385,160**	**400,800**		
Income before income taxes							15,640			
Totals							400,800	400,800		
Income before income taxes								15,640		
Income tax expense			(g)3,440				3,440			
Income tax payable				(g) 3,440						3,440
Net income							12,200			12,200
Totals							**15,640**	**15,640**	**167,040**	**167,040**

Similarly, the $900 debit opposite Prepaid Insurance is reduced by the $360 credit in the Adjustments column. The result, $540, is shown in the Adjusted Trial Balance Dr. column.

Income Statement and Balance Sheet Columns

All the debit items in the Adjusted Trial Balance columns are extended into the Income Statement or Balance Sheet columns to the right. All the credit items are also extended. The next step is to total the Income Statement columns; the amount that is needed in order to balance the debit and credit columns is the pretax income or loss for the period. The income before income taxes of $15,640 is shown in the Income Statement Dr. column because revenues exceeded expenses by that amount.

Income Taxes and Net Income

The federal and provincial income tax expense and related tax liability are calculated next. The company assumes a tax rate of 22% to arrive at $3,440. Because the Adjustments columns have been balanced, this adjustment is entered in the Income Statement Dr. column as Income Tax Expense and in the Balance Sheet Cr. column as Income Tax Payable. The following adjusting journal entry is recorded on December 31, 2007, posted to the general ledger, and then entered on the work sheet:

	Dr.	Cr.
(g) Income Tax Expense	3,440	
Income Tax Payable		3,440

Next, the Income Statement columns are balanced with the income taxes included. The $12,200 difference between the debit and credit columns in this illustration represents net income. The net income of $12,200 is entered in the Income Statement Dr. column to achieve equality and in the Balance Sheet Cr. column as the increase in retained earnings.

Preparing Financial Statements from a Work Sheet

The work sheet gives the information that is needed to prepare financial statements without referring to the ledger or other records. In addition, the data have been sorted into appropriate columns, which makes it easier to prepare the statements.

The financial statements prepared from the 10-column work sheet are as follows: **Income Statement for the Year Ended December 31, 2007 (Illustration 3-26), Statement of Retained Earnings for the Year Ended December 31, 2007 (Illustration 3-27), and Balance Sheet as at December 31, 2007 (Illustration 3-28).**

Income Statement

The income statement in the illustration is for a trading or merchandising concern; if a manufacturing concern were illustrated, three inventory accounts would be used: raw materials, work in process, and finished goods.

Statement of Retained Earnings

The net income earned by a corporation may be retained in the business or distributed to shareholders by paying dividends. In Illustration 3-27, the net income earned during the year was added to the balance of Retained Earnings on January 1, increasing the balance to $26,400 on December 31. No dividends were declared during the year.

Illustration 3-26
Income Statement

UPTOWN CABINET CORP.
Income Statement
For the Year Ended December 31, 2007

Net sales			$400,000
Cost of goods sold			316,000
Gross profit on sales			84,000
Selling expenses			
Sales salaries expense		$20,000	
Advertising expense		2,200	
Travelling expense		8,000	
Total selling expenses		30,200	
Administrative expenses			
Salaries, office, and general	$19,000		
Telephone and Internet expense	600		
Rent expense	4,300		
Property tax expense	5,300		
Amortization expense—furniture and equipment	6,700		
Bad debt expense	1,000		
Insurance expense	360		
Total administrative expenses		37,260	
Total selling and administrative expenses			67,460
Income from operations			16,540
Other revenues and gains			
Interest revenue			800
			17,340
Other expenses and losses			
Interest expense			1,700
Income before income taxes			15,640
Income taxes			3,440
Net income			$ 12,200
Earnings per share			**$ 1.22**

Illustration 3-27
Statement of Retained Earnings

UPTOWN CABINET CORP.
Statement of Retained Earnings
For the Year Ended December 31, 2007

Retained earnings, Jan. 1, 2007	$14,200
Add net income for 2007	12,200
Retained earnings, Dec. 31, 2007	**$26,400**

Balance Sheet

The balance sheet prepared from the 10-column work sheet has new items created by year-end adjusting entries. Interest receivable, unexpired insurance, and prepaid rent expense are included as current assets. These assets are considered current because they will be converted into cash or consumed in the ordinary routine of the business in a relatively short period of time. The amount of Allowance for Doubtful Accounts is deducted from the total of accounts, notes, and interest receivable because it is estimated that only $54,800 of $57,800 will be collected in cash.

In the property, plant, and equipment section, the accumulated amortization is deducted from the cost of the furniture and equipment; the difference in the two amounts is the book or carrying value of the furniture and equipment.

Illustration 3-28
Balance Sheet

UPTOWN CABINET CORP.
Balance Sheet
As at December 31, 2007

Assets			
Current assets			
Cash			$ 1,200
Notes receivable	$16,000		
Accounts receivable	41,000		
Interest receivable	800	$57,800	
Less: Allowance for doubtful accounts		3,000	54,800
Merchandise inventory			40,000
Prepaid insurance			540
Prepaid rent			500
Total current assets			97,040
Property, plant, and equipment			
Furniture and equipment		67,000	
Less: Accumulated amortization		18,700	
Total property, plant, and equipment			48,300
Total assets			$145,340
Liabilities and Shareholders' Equity			
Current liabilities			
Notes payable			$ 20,000
Accounts payable			13,500
Property tax payable			2,000
Income tax payable			3,440
Total current liabilities			38,940
Long-term liabilities			
Bonds payable, due June 30, 2009			30,000
Total liabilities			68,940
Shareholders' equity			
Common shares, issued and outstanding, 10,000 shares		$50,000	
Retained earnings		26,400	
Total shareholders' equity			76,400
Total liabilities and shareholders' equity			$145,340

Property tax payable is shown as a current liability because it is an obligation that is payable within a year. Other short-term accrued liabilities would also be shown as current liabilities.

The bonds payable, due in 2009, are long-term liabilities and are shown in a separate section. (Interest on the bonds was paid on December 31.)

Because Uptown Cabinet Corp. is a corporation, the balance sheet's capital section, called the shareholders' equity section in Illustration 3-28, is a bit different from the capital section for a proprietorship. Total shareholders' equity consists of the common shares, which represent the original investment by shareholders, and the earnings retained in the business.

Closing Entries

The entries for the closing process are on the following page.

GENERAL JOURNAL
December 31, 2007

Interest Revenue	800	
Sales	400,000	
Cost of Goods Sold		316,000
Sales Salaries Expense		20,000
Advertising Expense		2,200
Travelling Expense		8,000
Salaries, Office, and General		19,000
Telephone and Internet Expense		600
Rent Expense		4,300
Property Tax Expense		5,300
Amortization Expense—Furniture and Equipment		6,700
Bad Debt Expense		1,000
Insurance Expense		360
Interest Expense		1,700
Income Tax Expense		3,440
Income Summary		12,200
(To close revenues and expenses to Income Summary)		
Income Summary	12,200	
Retained Earnings		12,200
(To close Income Summary to Retained Earnings)		

Monthly Statements, Yearly Closing

Using a work sheet at the end of each month or quarter makes it possible to prepare interim financial statements even though the books are closed only at the end of each year. For example, assume that a business that closes its books on December 31 wants monthly financial statements. At the end of January, a work sheet similar to the one illustrated in this chapter can be prepared to supply the information that is needed for statements for January. At the end of February, a work sheet can be used again. Note that because the accounts were not closed at the end of January, the income statement taken from the work sheet on February 28 will present the net income for two months. To obtain an income statement for only the month of February, the items in the January income statement are simply subtracted from the same items in the income statement for the months of January and February together.

It is also possible to have a statement of retained earnings for February only by subtracting the January items. The balance sheet prepared from the February work sheet, however, shows assets, liabilities, and shareholders' equity as at February 28, the specific date for which a balance sheet is desired.

The March work sheet would show the revenues and expenses for three months, and the subtraction of the revenues and expenses for the first two months could be made to supply the amounts needed for an income statement for the month of March only, and so on throughout the year.

Student Website

Glossary
www.wiley.com/canada/kieso

Summary of Learning Objectives

KEY TERMS

account, 79
accounting cycle, 84
accounting information system, 78

1 Understand basic accounting terminology.

It is important to understand the following terms: (1) event, (2) transaction, (3) account, (4) permanent and temporary accounts, (5) ledger, (6) journal, (7) posting, (8) trial balance, (9) adjusting entries, (10) financial statements, (11) closing entries.

2 Explain double-entry rules.

The left side of any account is the debit side; the right side is the credit side. All asset and expense accounts are increased on the left or debit side and decreased on the right or credit side. Conversely, all liability and revenue accounts are increased on the right or credit side and decreased on the left or debit side. Shareholders' equity accounts, Common Shares, and Retained Earnings are increased on the credit side, whereas Dividends is increased on the debit side.

3 Identify the steps in the accounting cycle.

The basic steps in the accounting cycle are (1) identification and measurement of transactions and other events; (2) journalizing; (3) posting; (4) the unadjusted trial balance; (5) adjustments; (6) the adjusted trial balance; (7) statement preparation; and (8) closing.

4 Record transactions in journals, post journal entries to ledger accounts, and prepare a trial balance.

The simplest journal form is a chronological listing of transactions and events that are expressed as debits and credits to particular accounts. The items entered in a general journal must be transferred (posted) to the general ledger. An unadjusted trial balance should be prepared at the end of a specific period after the entries have been recorded in the journal and posted to the ledger.

5 Explain the reasons for preparing adjusting entries.

Adjustments achieve a proper matching of revenues and expenses, which is necessary in order to determine the correct net income for the current period and to achieve an accurate statement of the end-of-the-period balances in assets, liabilities, and owners' equity accounts.

6 Prepare closing entries.

In the closing process, all of the revenue and expense account balances (income statement items) are transferred to a clearing account called Income Summary, which is used only at the end of the fiscal year. Revenues and expenses are matched in the Income Summary account. The net result of this matching, which represents the net income or net loss for the period, is then transferred to a shareholders' equity account (retained earnings for a corporation and capital accounts for proprietorships and partnerships).

7 Explain how inventory accounts are adjusted at year end.

Under a perpetual inventory system, the balance in the Inventory account should represent the ending inventory amount. When the inventory records are maintained in a periodic inventory system, a Purchases account is used; the Inventory account is unchanged during the period. The Inventory account balance represents the beginning inventory amount throughout the period. At the end of the accounting period, the inventory account must be adjusted by closing out the beginning inventory amount and recording the ending inventory amount.

8 Prepare a 10-column work sheet and financial statements.

The 10-column work sheet provides columns for the first trial balance, adjustments, adjusted trial balance, income statement, and balance sheet. The work sheet does not replace the financial statements. Instead, it is the accountant's informal device for accumulating and sorting the information that is needed for the financial statements.

Appendix 3A

Using Reversing Entries

Objective 9
Identify adjusting entries that may be reversed.

The purpose of reversing entries is to make it easier to record transactions in the next accounting period. The use of reversing entries does not change the amounts reported in the previous period's financial statements.

ILLUSTRATION OF REVERSING ENTRIES—ACCRUALS

Reversing entries are usually used for reversing two types of adjusting entries: accrued revenues and accrued expenses. To illustrate the optional use of reversing entries for accrued expenses, we will use the following transaction and adjustment data:

1. October 24 (initial salary entry): $4,000 of salaries expense incurred between October 1 and October 24 is paid.
2. October 31 (adjusting entry): $1,200 of salaries expense is incurred between October 25 and October 31. This will be paid in the November 8 payroll.
3. November 8 (subsequent salary entry): $2,500 of salaries expense is paid. Of this amount, $1,200 applies to accrued wages payable at October 31 and $1,300 was incurred between November 1 and November 8.

The comparative entries are shown in Illustration 3A-1.

Illustration 3-A-1
Comparison of Entries for Accruals, with and without Reversing Entries

Reversing Entries Not Used				Reversing Entries Used			
Initial Salary Entry							
Oct. 24	Salaries Expense	4,000		Oct. 24	Salaries Expense	4,000	
	Cash		4,000		Cash		4,000
Adjusting Entry							
Oct. 31	Salaries Expense	1,200		Oct. 31	Salaries Expense	1,200	
	Salaries Payable		1,200		Salaries Payable		1,200
Closing Entry							
Oct. 31	Income Summary	5,200		Oct. 31	Income Summary	5,200	
	Salaries Expense		5,200		Salaries Expense		5,200
Reversing Entry							
Nov. 1	**No entry is made.**			**Nov. 1**	**Salaries Payable**	**1,200**	
					Salaries Expense		**1,200**
Subsequent Salary Entry							
Nov. 8	**Salaries Payable**	**1,200**		**Nov. 8**	**Salaries Expense**	**2,500**	
	Salaries Expense	**1,300**			**Cash**		**2,500**
	Cash		**2,500**				

The illustration shows that the first three entries are the same whether or not reversing entries are used. The last two entries, however, are different. The November 1 reversing entry eliminates the $1,200 balance in Salaries Payable that was created by the October 31 adjusting entry. The reversing entry also creates a $1,200 credit balance in the Salaries Expense account. As you know, it is unusual for an expense account to have a credit balance; however, the balance is correct in this instance. It is correct because the entire amount of the first salary payment in the new accounting period will be debited to Salaries Expense. This debit will eliminate the credit balance, and the resulting debit balance in the expense account will equal the salaries expense incurred in the new accounting period ($1,300 in this example).

When reversing entries are made, all cash payments of expenses can be debited to the expense account. This means that on November 8 (and every payday), Salaries Expense can be debited for the amount paid without having to consider any accrued salaries payable. Being able to make the same entry each time simplifies the recording process in an accounting system.

ILLUSTRATION OF REVERSING ENTRIES—PREPAYMENTS

Up to this point, we have assumed that all prepayments are recorded as prepaid expenses or unearned revenues. In some cases, prepayments are recorded directly in expense or revenue accounts. When this occurs, prepayments may also be reversed. To illustrate the use of reversing entries for prepaid expenses, we will use the following transaction and adjustment data:

December 10 (initial entry): $20,000 of office supplies are purchased for cash.

December 31 (adjusting entry): $5,000 of office supplies are on hand.

The comparative entries are shown in Illustration 3A-2.

Illustration 3A-2

Comparison of Entries for Prepayments, with and without Reversing Entries

Reversing Entries Not Used				Reversing Entries Used			
Initial Purchase of Supplies Entry							
Dec. 10	Office Supplies	20,000		Dec. 10	Office Supplies Expense	20,000	
	Cash		20,000		Cash		20,000
Adjusting Entry							
Dec. 31	Office Supplies Expense	15,000		Dec. 31	Office Supplies	5,000	
	Office Supplies		15,000		Office Supplies Expense		5,000
Closing Entry							
Dec. 31	Income Summary	15,000		Dec. 31	Income Summary	15,000	
	Office Supplies Expense		15,000		Office Supplies Expense		15,000
Reversing Entry							
Jan. 1	No entry			Jan. 1	Office Supplies Expense	5,000	
					Office Supplies		5,000

After the adjusting entry on December 31 (with or without reversing entries), the asset account Office Supplies shows a balance of $5,000 and Office Supplies Expense shows a balance of $15,000. If Office Supplies Expense was debited when the supplies were first purchased, a reversing entry is made to return to the expense account the cost of the still unused supplies. The company then continues to debit Office Supplies Expense for additional purchases of office supplies during the next period.

It could be asked why all prepaid items are not simply entered originally into real accounts (assets and liabilities), as this would make reversing entries unnecessary. Sometimes this practice is followed. Doing this is particularly useful for items that need to be apportioned over several periods (e.g., supplies and parts inventories). However, items that do not follow this regular pattern and that may or may not involve two or more periods are usually first entered in revenue or expense accounts. The revenue and expense accounts may not require adjusting and are systematically closed to Income Summary. Using the temporary accounts adds consistency to the accounting system and makes the recording more efficient, especially when a large number of such transactions occur during the year. For example, the bookkeeper knows that when an invoice is received for anything except a capital asset acquisition, the amount is expensed. This way, when the invoice is received, the bookkeeper does not have to worry about whether or not the item will result in a prepaid expense at the end of the period, because adjustments will be made at that time.

SUMMARY OF REVERSING ENTRIES

The guidelines for reversing entries can be summarized as follows:

1. All accrued items should be reversed.
2. All prepaid items for which the original cash transaction was debited or credited to an expense or revenue account should be reversed.
3. Adjusting entries for amortization and bad debts are not reversed.

Although reversing entries reduce potential errors and are therefore often used, they do not have to be used. Many accountants avoid them entirely. Reversing entries add an extra step to the bookkeeping process. Also, there may be instances where it does not make sense to use them. Assume a company with a December 31 year end has accrued six months' worth of interest on a bond (June 30 interest payment date) at year end. If the company releases financial information monthly, it would not make sense to reverse the entry in January since this would show a credit balance when the monthly reports are prepared.

Summary of Learning Objective for Appendix 3A

9 Identify adjusting entries that may be reversed.

Reversing entries are usually used for reversing two types of adjusting entries: accrued revenues and accrued expenses. Prepayments may also be reversed if the initial entry to record the transaction is made to an expense or revenue account.

Note: All assignment material with an asterisk (*) relates to the appendix to the chapter.

Brief Exercises

BE3-1 For the following accounts, what differences are there between the trial balance before closing and the trial balance after closing? **(LO 3)**

(a) Accounts Payable

(b) Expense accounts

(c) Revenue accounts

(d) Retained Earnings

(e) Cash

BE3-2 Transactions for Angel Limited for the month of May follow. Prepare journal entries for each transaction. (You may leave out explanations.) **(LO 4)**

May	1	Owners invest $9,000 cash in exchange for common shares of Angel Limited, a small welding corporation.
	3	Buy equipment on account for $1,100.
	13	Pay $400 to landlord for May rent.
	21	Bill Noble Corp. $500 for welding work done.

BE3-3 Fancy Repair Shop Inc. had the following transactions during the first month of business. Journalize the transactions. **(LO 4)**

August	2	Invested $12,000 cash and $2,500 of equipment in the business.
	7	Purchased supplies on account for $600. (Debit asset account.)
	12	Performed services for clients, collecting $1,300 in cash and billing the clients $670 for the remainder.
	15	Paid August rent, $600.
	19	Counted supplies and determined that only $270 of the supplies purchased on August 7 are still on hand.

BE3-4 On July 1, 2009, Blondy Ltd. pays $18,000 to Hindi Insurance Ltd. for a three-year insurance contract. Both companies have fiscal years ending December 31. Prepare two sets of journal entries for Blondy for the July 1 entry and the adjusting entry on December 31. Treat the expenditure as an asset in the first set and as an expense in the second. **(LO 4)**

BE3-5 Using the data in BE3-4, journalize the entry on July 1 and the adjusting entry on December 31 for Hindi Insurance Ltd. Hindi uses the accounts Unearned Insurance Revenue and Insurance Revenue. Prepare two sets of journal entries—one where the initial cash receipt is treated as Unearned Insurance Revenue and one where it is treated as Insurance Revenue. **(LO 4)**

BE3-6 On August 1, Bell Limited paid $12,600 in advance for two years of insurance coverage. Prepare Bell's August 1 journal entry and the annual adjusting entry on December 31. Prepare two sets of journal entries, treating the initial August 1 expenditure as an asset in the first set and as an expense in the second. **(LO 4)**

BE3-7 Modigliani Corporation owns a warehouse. On November 1, it rented storage space to a lessee (tenant) for three months for a total cash payment of $3,000 received in advance. Prepare Modigliani's November 1 journal entry and the December 31 annual adjusting entry. Prepare a second set of journal entries, assuming that the initial cash receipt on November 1 is treated as revenue. **(LO 4)**

BE3-8 Janeway Corp.'s weekly payroll totals $10,000 and is paid on Fridays. Employees work a five-day week. Prepare Janeway's adjusting entry on Wednesday, December 31, and the journal entry to record the $10,000 cash payment on Friday, January 2. **(LO 4)**

BE3-9 Included in Mascot Corp.'s December 31 trial balance is a note receivable of $20,000. The note is a four-month, 9% note dated October 1. Prepare Mascot's December 31 adjusting entry to record $450 of accrued interest, and the February 1 journal entry to record a receipt of $20,600 from the borrower. **(LO 5)**

BE3-10 Prepare the following adjusting entries at December 31 for DeGroot Ltd.: **(LO 5)**

1. Interest on notes payable of $200 is accrued.
2. Fees earned but unbilled total $1,300.
3. Salaries earned of $700 have not been recorded.
4. Bad debt expense for the year is $900.

Use the following account titles: Service Revenue, Accounts Receivable, Interest Expense, Interest Payable, Salaries Expense, Salaries Payable, Allowance for Doubtful Accounts, and Bad Debt Expense.

(LO 5) **BE3-11** At the end of Rafael Limited's first year of operations, its trial balance shows Equipment $20,000; Accumulated Amortization—Equipment $0; and Amortization Expense $0. Amortization for the year is estimated to be $4,000. Prepare the adjusting entry for amortization at December 31, and indicate the balance sheet presentation for the equipment at December 31.

(LO 5) **BE3-12** If a computer and printer are purchased for office use for $3,900 and the purchase is recorded as a debit to Purchases, what would be the effect of this error on the balance sheet and income statement of the same period as the purchase?

(LO 5) **BE3-13** Atanak Apartments receives $800 from a tenant as one month's rent in advance for the month of May.

(a) Assuming the company records all prepayments in (permanent) balance sheet accounts:

1. Prepare the original journal entry Atanak should record when it receives the rent on May 1.
2. Prepare the adjusting journal entry Atanak should record at the end of May, when the month's rent has been earned.

(b) Assuming the company records all prepayments in (temporary) income statement accounts:

1. Prepare the original journal entry Atanak should record when it receives the rent on May 1.
2. Prepare the adjusting journal entry Atanak should record at the end of May, when the month's rent has been earned.

(c) Compare and comment upon the ending account balances for each alternative, (a) and (b).

(LO 6) **BE3-14** Manny Molitar is the maintenance supervisor for Blue Jay Insurance Co. and has recently purchased a riding lawnmower and accessories that will be used in caring for the grounds around corporate headquarters. He sent the following information to the accounting department:

Cost of mower and accessories	$2,800	Date purchased	7/1/08
Estimated useful life	4 yrs.	Monthly salary of groundskeeper	$1,100
		Estimated annual fuel cost	$150

Calculate the amount of amortization expense (for the mower and accessories) that should be reported on Blue Jay's December 31, 2008, income statement. Assume straight-line amortization.

(LO 7) **BE3-15** Willis Corporation has beginning inventory $76,000; Purchases $486,000; Freight-in $16,200; Purchase Returns $5,800; Purchase Discounts $5,000; and ending inventory $69,500. Calculate its cost of goods sold.

(LO 6) **BE3-16** Karen Inc. has the following year-end account balances: Sales $538,900; Interest Revenue $13,500; Cost of Goods Sold $356,200; Operating Expenses $89,000; Income Tax Expense $35,100; and Dividends $11,900. Prepare the year-end closing entries.

(LO 9) ***BE3-17** Pelican Inc. made a December 31 adjusting entry to debit Salaries Expense and credit Salaries Payable for $2,700. On January 2, Pelican paid the weekly payroll of $5,000. Prepare Pelican's (a) January 1 reversing entry, (b) January 2 entry (assuming the reversing entry was prepared), and (c) January 2 entry (assuming the reversing entry was not prepared).

Exercises

(LO 4) **E3-1 (Transaction Analysis—Service Company)** Charlie Ainsworth is a licensed CA. During the first month of operations of his business (a sole proprietorship), the following events and transactions occurred:

April	2	Invested $12,000 cash and equipment valued at $14,000 in the business.
	2	Hired a secretary-receptionist at a salary of $340 per week payable monthly.
	3	Purchased $800 of supplies on account. (Debit an asset account.)
	7	Paid office rent of $600 for the month.
	11	Completed a tax assignment and billed the client $1,100 for services rendered. (Use the service revenue account.)
	12	Received a $4,200 advance on a management consulting engagement.
	17	Received cash of $2,900 for services completed for Botticelli Limited.
	21	Paid insurance expense of $110.
	30	Paid the secretary-receptionist $1,360 for the month.

30 A count of supplies indicated that $220 of supplies had been used.
30 Purchased a new computer for $4,100 with personal funds. (The computer will only be used for business purposes.)

Instructions

Journalize the transactions in the general journal (omit explanations).

E3-2 (Corrected Trial Balance) The trial balance of Wanda Landowska Company, a sole proprietorship, does not balance. Your review of the ledger reveals the following: (a) each account had a normal balance; (b) the debit footings in Prepaid Insurance, and Property Tax Expense were each understated by $100, and Accounts Payable was overstated $100; (c) transposition errors were made in Accounts Receivable and Service Revenue, and the correct balances are $2,750 and $6,690, respectively; (d) a debit posting to Advertising Expense of $300 was omitted; and (e) a $1,500 cash drawing by the owner was debited to Wanda Landowska, Capital, and credited to Cash. **(LO 4)**

WANDA LANDOWSKA COMPANY
Trial Balance
April 30, 2008

	Debit	Credit
Cash	$ 4,800	
Accounts Receivable	2,570	
Prepaid Insurance	700	
Equipment		$ 8,000
Accounts Payable		4,500
Property Tax Payable	560	
Wanda Landowska, Capital		11,200
Service Revenue	6,960	
Salaries Expense	4,200	
Advertising Expense	1,100	
Property Tax Expense		800
	$20,890	$24,500

Instructions

Prepare a correct trial balance.

E3-3 (Corrected Trial Balance) The trial balance of Blues Corner Corporation does not balance. **(LO 4)**

BLUES CORNER CORPORATION
Trial Balance
April 30

	Debit	Credit
Cash	$ 5,912	
Accounts Receivable	5,240	
Supplies on Hand	2,967	
Furniture and Equipment	6,100	
Accounts Payable		$ 7,044
Common Shares		8,000
Retained Earnings		2,000
Service Revenue		5,200
Office Expense	4,320	
	$24,539	$22,244

An examination of the ledger shows these errors:

1. Cash received from a customer on account was recorded (both debit and credit) as $1,380 instead of $1,830.
2. The purchase on account of a computer costing $3,200 was recorded as a debit to Office Expense and a credit to Accounts Payable.

3. Services that were performed for $2,250 on account for a client were recorded as a $2,250 debit to Accounts Receivable and a $225 credit to Service Revenue.
4. A payment of $95 for telephone charges was entered as a debit to Office Expense and a debit to Cash.
5. The Service Revenue account was totalled at $5,200 instead of $5,280.

Instructions

Use the information to prepare a correct trial balance.

(LO 4) **E3-4 (Corrected Trial Balance)** The trial balance of Chris Cross Inc. does not balance.

CHRIS CROSS INC.
Trial Balance
June 30, 2009

	Debit	Credit
Cash		$ 2,870
Accounts Receivable	$ 3,231	
Supplies	800	
Equipment	3,800	
Accounts Payable		2,666
Unearned Service Revenue	1,200	
Common Shares		6,000
Retained Earnings		3,000
Service Revenue		2,380
Wages Expense	3,400	
Office Expense	940	
	$13,371	$16,916

Each of the listed accounts has a normal balance for the general ledger. An examination of the ledger and journal reveals the following errors:

1. Cash received from a customer on account was debited $570 to Accounts Receivable and credited to cash for the same amount. The amount collected was actually $750.
2. The purchase of a computer printer on account for $500 was recorded as a $500 debit to Supplies and a $500 credit to Accounts Payable.
3. Services were performed on account for a client for $890. Accounts Receivable was debited $890 and Service Revenue was credited $89.
4. A payment of $65 for telephone charges was recorded as a $65 debit to Office Expense and a $65 debit to Cash.
5. When the Unearned Service Revenue account was reviewed, it was found that $325 of the balance was earned before June 30.
6. A debit posting to Wages Expense of $670 was omitted.
7. A payment on account for $206 was credited to Cash for $206 and credited to Accounts Payable for $260.
8. A dividend of $575 was debited to Wages Expense for $575 and credited to Cash for $575.
9. Each account has a normal balance.

Instructions

Prepare a correct trial balance. (Note: It may be necessary to add one or more accounts to the trial balance.)

(LO 4) **E3-5 (Transactions of a Corporation, Including Investment and Dividend)** Scratch Miniature Golf and Driving Range Inc. was opened on March 1 by Scott Verplank. The following selected events and transactions occurred during March:

Mar.	1	Invested $50,000 cash in the business in exchange for common shares.
	3	Purchased Lee Janzen's Golf Land for $38,000 cash. The price consists of land, $10,000; building, $22,000; and equipment, $6,000. (Make one compound entry.)
	5	Advertised the opening of the driving range and miniature golf course, paying advertising expenses of $1,600.
	6	Paid $1,650 cash for a one-year insurance policy.
	10	Purchased golf equipment for $2,500 from Sluman Ltd., payable in 30 days.
	18	Received golf fees of $1,700 cash.

25 Declared and paid a $500 cash dividend.
30 Paid wages of $900.
30 Paid Sluman Ltd. in full.
31 Received $750 of fees in cash.

Verplank uses the following accounts for his company: Cash; Prepaid Insurance; Land; Buildings; Equipment; Accounts Payable; Common Shares; Dividends; Service Revenue; Advertising Expense; and Wages Expense.

Instructions

Journalize the March transactions.

E3-6 **(Alternative Treatment of Prepayment)** At Martin Ltd., prepaid costs are debited to expense when paid, and unearned revenues are credited to revenue when the cash is received. During January of the current year, the following transactions occurred: **(LO 5)**

Jan. 2 Paid $2,400 for casualty insurance protection for the year.
10 Paid $1,700 for supplies.
15 Received $5,100 for services to be performed in the future.

On January 31, it is determined that $1,500 of the service revenue has been earned and that there are $800 of supplies on hand.

Instructions

(a) Journalize and post the January transactions. Use T accounts.

(b) Journalize and post the adjusting entries at January 31.

(c) Determine the ending balance in each of the accounts.

E3-7 **(Alternative Treatment of Prepayment)** Earlton Recreation Ltd. initially records all prepaid costs as expenses and all revenue collected in advance as revenues. The following information is available for the year ended December 31, 2009: **(LO 5)**

1. Purchased a one-year insurance policy on May 1, 2009, for $4,620 cash.
2. Paid $6,875 for five months' rent in advance on October 1, 2009.
3. On September 15, 2009, received $3,600 cash from a corporation that sponsors a game each month for the most improved student attending a nearby school. The $3,600 was for nine games on the first Friday of each month starting October 1, 2009.
4. Signed a contract for cleaning services starting December 1, 2009, for $1,050 per month. Paid for the first three months on December 1, 2009.
5. During the year, sold $1,500 of gift certificates. Determined that on December 31, 2009, $475 of these gift certificates had not been redeemed.

Instructions

(a) For each of the above, prepare a journal entry to record the initial transaction.

(b) Post each of the above transactions. Use T accounts (ignore the Cash account).

(c) Journalize and post the adjusting entries at December 31, 2009.

(d) Determine the ending balance in each of the accounts.

(e) How would the balances at December 31, 2009 be affected by Earlton's deciding to initially record the payment of prepaid costs as assets and revenues collected in advance as liabilities?

***E3-8** **(Adjusting and Reversing Entries)** On December 31, adjusting information for Lyman Corporation is as follows: **(LO 5, 9)**

1. The estimated amortization on equipment is $1,400.
2. Property taxes amounting to $525 have accrued but are unrecorded and unpaid.
3. Employee wages that are earned but unpaid and unrecorded amount to $1,900.
4. The Unearned Service Revenue balance includes $1,500 that has been earned.
5. Interest of $200 on a $25,000 note receivable has accrued.

Instructions

(a) Prepare adjusting journal entries.

(b) Prepare reversing journal entries.

(LO 5, 9) ***E3-9 (Closing and Reversing Entries)** On December 31, the adjusted trial balance of Cree Inc. shows the following selected data:

Accounts Receivable	$5,700	Service Revenue	$110,000
Interest Expense	7,800	Interest Payable	2,400

Analysis shows that adjusting entries were made for (a) $5,700 of services performed but not billed, and (b) $2,400 of accrued but unpaid interest.

Instructions

(a) Prepare the closing entries for the temporary accounts at December 31.

(b) Prepare the reversing entries on January 1.

(c) Enter the adjusted trial balance data in the four accounts. Post the entries in (a) and (b) and rule and balance the accounts. (Use T accounts.)

(d) Prepare the entries to record (1) the collection of the accrued service revenue on January 10, and (2) the payment of all interest due ($3,000) on January 15.

(e) Post the entries in (d) to the temporary accounts.

(LO 5, 9) ***E3-10 (Adjusting and Reversing Entries)** When the accounts of Barenboim Inc. are examined, the following adjusting data are uncovered on December 31, the end of a fiscal year:

1. The Prepaid Insurance account shows a debit of $5,880 for the cost of a two-year fire insurance policy dated August 1 of the current year.
2. On November 1, Rental Revenue was credited $2,400 for revenue from a sublease for a three-month period beginning on that date.
3. Purchases of advertising materials for $1,200 during the year were recorded in the Advertising Expense account. On December 31, advertising materials of $290 are on hand.
4. Interest of $770 has accrued on notes payable.

Instructions

(a) Prepare in general journal form (i) the adjusting entry for each item and (ii) the reversing entry for each item, where appropriate.

(b) Is it possible to ignore the use of reversing entries altogether? What purpose do they serve and why would management decide to use them? If management decides to use them, do they have to use them in all possible situations where reversing entries could be used?

(LO 5) **E3-11 (Adjusting Entries)** The ledger of Deng Rental Agency Ltd. on March 31 of the current year includes the following selected accounts before adjusting entries have been prepared:

	Debit	Credit
Prepaid Insurance	$ 3,600	
Supplies	2,800	
Equipment	25,000	
Accumulated Amortization—Equipment		$ 8,400
Notes Payable		20,000
Unearned Rent Revenue		9,300
Rent Revenue		60,000
Interest Expense	-0-	
Wages Expense	14,000	

An analysis of the accounts shows the following:

1. The equipment amortization is $350 per month.
2. One-half of the unearned rent was earned during the quarter.
3. Interest of $550 is accrued on the notes payable.
4. Supplies on hand total $950.
5. Insurance expires at the rate of $300 per month.

Instructions

Prepare the adjusting entries at March 31, assuming that adjusting entries are made quarterly. Additional accounts are Amortization Expense, Insurance Expense, Interest Payable, and Supplies Expense.

E3-12 **(Adjusting Entries)** Karen Pain, D.D.S., opened a dental practice on January 1, 2008. During the first month of operations, the following transactions occurred: **(LO 5)**

1. Performed services for patients who had dental plan insurance. At January 31, $1,350 of such services was earned but not yet billed to the insurance companies.
2. Utility expenses incurred but not paid before January 31 totalled $1,520.
3. Purchased dental equipment on January 1 for $80,000, paying $20,000 in cash and signing a $60,000, three-year note payable. The equipment amortization is $400 per month. Interest is $500 per month.
4. Purchased a one-year malpractice insurance policy on January 1 for $12,000.
5. Purchased $3,800 of dental supplies. On January 31, determined that $500 of supplies were on hand.

Instructions

(a) Prepare the adjusting entries on January 31. Account titles are Accumulated Amortization—Dental Equipment; Amortization Expense; Service Revenue; Accounts Receivable; Insurance Expense; Interest Expense; Interest Payable; Prepaid Insurance; Supplies; Supplies Expense; Utilities Expense; and Utilities Payable. Assume that the company first records prepayments to assets.

(b) Prepare the adjusting entries on January 31 assuming that the company first records prepayments through the related income statement accounts (i.e., it uses the alternative method).

E3-13 **(Analyze Adjusted Data)** A partial adjusted trial balance of Pansy Limited at January 31, 2007, shows the following: **(LO 5)**

PANSY LIMITED
Adjusted Trial Balance
January 31, 2007

	Debit	Credit
Supplies	$ 600	
Prepaid Insurance	2,400	
Salaries Payable		$ 800
Unearned Revenue		1,000
Supplies Expense	950	
Insurance Expense	400	
Salaries Expense	1,800	
Service Revenue		3,000

Instructions

Answer the following questions, assuming the company's fiscal year begins January 1:

(a) If the amount in Supplies Expense is the January 31 adjusting entry, and $650 of supplies was purchased in January, what was the balance in Supplies on January 1?

(b) If the amount in Insurance Expense is the January 31 adjusting entry, and the original insurance premium was for one year, what was the total premium and when was the policy purchased?

(c) If $2,500 of salaries was paid in January, what was the balance in Salaries Payable at December 31, 2006?

(d) If $1,600 was received in January for services performed in January, what was the balance in Unearned Revenue at December 31, 2006?

E3-14 **(Adjusting Entries)** Benson Balladucci is the new owner of Ace Computer Services Inc. At the end of August 2008, his first month of ownership, Mr. Balladucci is trying to prepare monthly financial statements. Information follows for unrecorded expenses that the business incurred in August: **(LO 5)**

1. At August 31, Mr. Balladucci owed his employees $4,500 in wages that would be paid on September 1.
2. At the end of the month, he had not yet received the month's utility bill. Based on previous experience, he estimated the bill would be $700.
3. On August 1, Mr. Balladucci borrowed $60,000 from a local bank on a 10-year mortgage. The annual interest rate is 5%.
4. A telephone bill of $117 for August charges is unpaid at August 31.

Instructions
Use the information to prepare the adjusting journal entries as of August 31, 2008.

(LO 5) E3-15 (Adjusting Entries) Selected accounts of Urdu Limited follow:

Supplies

Beg. Bal.	800	10/31	470

Accounts Receivable

10/17	2,400		
10/31	1,650		

Salaries Expense

10/15	800		
10/31	600		

Salaries Payable

		10/31	600

Unearned Service Revenue

10/31	400	10/20	650

Supplies Expense

10/31	470		

Service Revenue

		10/17	2,400
		10/31	1,650
		10/31	400

Instructions
From an analysis of the T accounts, reconstruct (a) the October transaction entries, and (b) the adjusting journal entries that were made on October 31, 2008.

(LO 5) E3-16 (Adjusting Entries) The trial balance for Greco Resort Limited on August 31 is as follows:

GRECO RESORT LIMITED
Trial Balance
August 31, 2008

	Debit	Credit
Cash	$ 6,700	
Prepaid Insurance	3,500	
Supplies	1,800	
Land	20,000	
Cottages	142,000	
Furniture	16,000	
Accounts Payable		$ 4,800
Unearned Rent Revenue		4,600
Loan Payable		77,000
Common Shares		81,000
Retained Earnings		9,000
Dividends	5,000	
Rent Revenue		76,200
Salaries Expense	44,800	
Utilities Expense	9,200	
Repair Expense	3,600	
	$252,600	$252,600

Other data:

1. The balance in Prepaid Insurance is a one-year premium paid on June 1, 2008.
2. An inventory count on August 31 shows $450 of supplies on hand.
3. Annual amortization rates are cottages 4% and furniture 10%. The residual value is estimated to be 10% of the cost.
4. Unearned Rent Revenue of $3,800 was earned prior to August 31.
5. Salaries of $375 were unpaid at August 31.
6. Rental fees of $800 were due from tenants at August 31.
7. The loan interest rate is 8% per year.

Instructions

(a) Journalize the adjusting entries on August 31 for the three-month period June 1 to August 31.

(b) Prepare an adjusted trial balance as at August 31.

E3-17 **(Closing Entries)** The adjusted trial balance of Lopez Limited shows the following data on sales at the end of its fiscal year October 31, 2008: Sales $850,000; Freight-out $12,000; Sales Returns and Allowances $14,000; and Sales Discounts $5,000. **(LO 6)**

Instructions

(a) Prepare the sales revenue section of the income statement.

(b) Prepare separate closing entries for (1) sales and (2) the contra accounts to sales.

E3-18 **(Closing Entries)** Information follows for Gonzales Corporation for the month of January 2007: **(LO 6)**

Cost of Goods Sold	$228,000	Salary Expense	$ 61,000
Freight-out	9,000	Sales Discounts	7,000
Insurance Expense	12,000	Sales Returns and Allowances	1,000
Rent Expense	20,000	Sales	364,000

Instructions

Prepare the necessary closing entries.

E3-19 **(Closing Entries)** Selected account balances follow for Winslow Inc. as of December 31, 2009: **(LO 6)**

Merchandise Inventory	$ 60,000	Cost of Goods Sold	$222,700
Common Shares	75,000	Selling Expenses	26,000
Retained Earnings	45,000	Administrative Expenses	31,000
Dividends	18,000	Income Tax Expense	30,000
Sales Returns and Allowances	2,000		
Sales Discounts	5,000		
Sales	390,000		

Instructions

Prepare closing entries for Winslow Inc. on December 31, 2009.

E3-20 **(Missing Amounts)** Financial information follows for two different companies: **(LO 7)**

	Alatorre Ltd.	Eduardo Inc
Sales	$92,000	(d)
Sales returns	(a)	$ 6,000
Net sales	81,000	95,000
Cost of goods sold	55,500	(e)
Gross profit	(b)	37,000
Operating expenses	15,000	23,000
Net income	(c)	14,000

Instructions

Calculate the missing amounts.

E3-21 **(Find Missing Amounts—Periodic Inventory)** Financial information follows for four different companies: **(LO 7)**

	Pamela's Cosmetics Inc.	Dean's Grocery Inc.	Anderson Wholesalers Ltd.	Baywatch Supply Ltd.
Sales	$98,000	(c)	$144,000	$120,000
Sales returns	(a)	$ 5,000	12,000	9,000
Net sales	74,000	101,000	132,000	(g)
Beginning inventory	21,000	(d)	44,000	24,000
Purchases	63,000	105,000	(e)	90,000
Purchase returns	6,000	10,000	8,000	(h)
Ending inventory	(b)	48,000	30,000	28,000
Cost of goods sold	64,000	72,000	(f)	72,000
Gross profit	10,000	29,000	18,000	(i)

Instructions

Determine the missing amounts for (a) to (i). Show all calculations.

(LO 8) E3-22 (Work Sheet) Selected accounts follow for Algonquin Inc. as reported in the work sheet at the end of May 2008:

Accounts	Adjusted Trial Balance		Income Statement		Balance Sheet	
	Dr.	Cr.	Dr.	Cr.	Dr.	Cr.
Cash	9,000					
Merchandise Inventory	80,000					
Sales		480,000				
Sales Returns and Allowances	10,000					
Sales Discounts	5,000					
Cost of Goods Sold	290,000					

Instructions

Complete the work sheet by extending the amounts reported in the adjusted trial balance to the appropriate columns in the work sheet. Do not total individual columns.

(LO 8) E3-23 (Cost of Goods Sold Section—Periodic Inventory) The trial balance of Maori Limited at the end of its fiscal year, August 31, 2009, includes the following accounts: Merchandise Inventory $14,300; Purchases $151,600; Sales $200,000; Freight-in $4,000; Sales Returns and Allowances $4,000; Freight-out $1,000; and Purchase Returns and Allowances $2,000. The ending merchandise inventory is $21,500.

Instructions

Prepare a cost of goods sold section for the year ending August 31.

(LO 8) E3-24 (Work Sheet Preparation) The trial balance of Potter Roofing Inc. at March 31, 2009, is as follows:

POTTER ROOFING INC.
Trial Balance
March 31, 2009

	Debit	Credit
Cash	$ 1,800	
Accounts Receivable	2,600	
Roofing Supplies	600	
Equipment	6,000	
Accumulated Amortization—Equipment		$ 400
Accounts Payable		1,100
Unearned Service Revenue		500
Common Shares		6,400
Retained Earnings		600
Service Revenue		2,600
Salaries Expense	500	
Miscellaneous Expense	100	
	$11,600	$11,600

Other data:

1. A physical count reveals only $520 of roofing supplies on hand.
2. Equipment is amortized at a rate of $120 per month.
3. Unearned service revenue amounted to $100 on March 31.
4. Accrued salaries are $850.

Instructions

Enter the trial balance on a work sheet and complete the work sheet, assuming that the adjustments relate only to the month of March. (Ignore income taxes.)

E3-25 **(Work Sheet and Balance Sheet Presentation)** The adjusted trial balance of Widijat Company's work sheet for the month ended April 30, 2008, contains the following: **(LO 8)**

WIDIJAT COMPANY
Work Sheet (partial)
For the Month Ended April 30, 2008

Account Titles	Adjusted Trial Balance		Income Statement		Balance Sheet	
	Dr.	Cr.	Dr.	Cr.	Dr.	Cr.
Cash	$17,672					
Accounts Receivable	8,520					
Prepaid Rent	3,280					
Equipment	18,050					
Accumulated Amortization		$ 4,895				
Notes Payable		6,700				
Accounts Payable		4,472				
Bradley, Capital		34,960				
Bradley, Drawings	6,250					
Service Revenue		13,190				
Salaries Expense	8,040					
Rent Expense	2,260					
Amortization Expense	145					
Interest Expense	83					
Interest Payable		83				

Instructions
Complete the work sheet and prepare a balance sheet as illustrated in this chapter.

E3-26 **(Partial Work Sheet Preparation)** Jurassic Inc. prepares monthly financial statements from a work sheet. Selected parts of the January work sheet showed the following data: **(LO 8)**

JURASSIC INC.
Work Sheet (partial)
For the Month Ended January 31, 2009

Account Titles	Trial Balance		Adjustments		Adjusted Trial Balance	
	Dr.	Cr.	Dr.	Cr.	Dr.	Cr.
Supplies	3,256			(a)1,500	1,756	
Accumulated Amortization		6,682		(b) 257		6,939
Interest Payable		100		(c) 50		150
Supplies Expense			(a)1,500		1,500	
Amortization Expense			(b) 257		257	
Interest Expense			(c) 50		50	

During February, no events occurred that affected these accounts. At the end of February, the following information was available and relates to the adjustments identified by letter in the work sheet:

(a) Supplies on hand, $1,115

(b) Monthly amortization, $257

(c) Accrued interest, $50

Instructions
Reproduce the data that would appear in the February work sheet and indicate the amounts that would be shown in the February income statement.

Problems

P3-1 Transactions follow for Isao Aoki, D.D.S., for the month of September:

Sept.	1	Aoki begins practice as a dentist and invests $18,000 cash.
	2	Purchases furniture and dental equipment on account from Green Jacket Limited for $17,280.
	4	Pays rent for office space, $680 for the month.
	4	Employs a receptionist, Michael Bradley.
	5	Purchases dental supplies for cash, $792.
	8	Receives cash of $1,690 from patients for services performed.
	10	Pays miscellaneous office expenses, $430.
	14	Bills patients $4,740 for services performed.
	18	Pays Green Jacket Limited on account, $3,600.
	19	Withdraws $4,000 cash from the business for personal use.
	20	Receives $980 from patients on account.
	25	Bills patients $1,870 for services performed.
	30	Pays the following expenses in cash: office salaries, $1,400; and miscellaneous office expenses, $85.
	30	Dental supplies used during September amount to $330.

Instructions

(a) Enter the transactions in appropriate general ledger accounts, using the following account titles: Cash; Accounts Receivable; Supplies on Hand; Furniture and Equipment; Accumulated Amortization; Accounts Payable; Isao Aoki, Capital; Isao Aoki, Drawings; Service Revenue; Rent Expense; Miscellaneous Office Expense; Office Salaries Expense; Supplies Expense; Amortization Expense; and Income Summary. Allow 10 lines for the Cash and Income Summary accounts, and five lines for each of the other accounts that are needed. Record amortization using a five-year life on the furniture and equipment, the straight-line method, and no residual value.

(b) Prepare an adjusted trial balance.

(c) Prepare an income statement, balance sheet, and statement of owners' equity.

(d) Close the ledger. Post directly to the general ledger account without writing out the journal entry.

(e) Prepare a post-closing trial balance.

P3-2 Yancy Advertising Agency Limited was founded by Tang Min in January of 2003. Presented below are both the adjusted and unadjusted trial balances as of December 31, 2007:

YANCY ADVERTISING AGENCY LIMITED
Trial Balance
December 31, 2007

	Unadjusted		Adjusted	
	Dr.	Cr.	Dr.	Cr.
Cash	$ 11,000		$ 11,000	
Accounts Receivable	20,000		22,500	
Art Supplies	8,400		5,000	
Prepaid Insurance	3,350		1,900	
Printing Equipment	60,000		60,000	
Accumulated Amortization		$ 28,000		$ 35,000
Accounts Payable		5,000		5,000
Interest Payable		-0-		150
Notes Payable		5,000		5,000
Unearned Advertising Revenue		7,400		5,600
Salaries Payable		-0-		2,000
Common Shares		10,000		10,000
Retained Earnings		3,500		3,500
Advertising Revenue		58,200		62,500
Salaries Expense	10,000		12,000	
Insurance Expense			1,450	
Interest Expense	350		500	
Amortization Expense			7,000	
Art Supplies Expense			3,400	
Rent Expense	4,000		4,000	
	$117,100	$117,100	$128,750	$128,750

Instructions

(a) Journalize the annual adjusting entries that were made.

(b) Prepare an income statement and a statement of retained earnings for the year ending December 31, 2007, and a balance sheet at December 31.

(c) Answer the following questions:

1. If the note has been outstanding three months, what is its annual interest rate?
2. If the company paid $13,500 in salaries in 2007, what was the balance in Salaries Payable on December 31, 2006?

P3-3 A review of the ledger of Okanagen Inc. at December 31, 2009, produces the following data for the preparation of annual adjusting entries:

1. Salaries Payable $0. There are eight salaried employees. Salaries are paid every Friday for the current week. Five employees receive a salary of $1,200 each per week, and three employees earn $800 each per week. December 31 is a Tuesday. Employees do not work weekends. All employees worked the last two days of December.
2. Unearned Rent Revenue $415,200. The company began subleasing office space in its new building on November 1. Each tenant has to make a $5,000 security deposit that is not refundable until occupancy is ended. At December 31, the company had the following rental contracts that are paid in full for the entire term of the lease:

Date	Term (in months)	Monthly Rent	Number of Leases
Nov. 1	6	$ 4,100	5
Dec. 1	6	$10,300	4

3. Prepaid Advertising $16,200. This balance consists of payments on two advertising contracts. The contracts provide for monthly advertising in two trade magazines. The terms of the contracts are as follows:

Contract	Date	Amount	Number of Magazine Issues
A650	May 1	$7,200	12
B974	Oct. 1	9,000	24

The first advertisement runs in the month in which the contract is signed.

4. Notes Payable $80,000. This balance consists of a note for one year at an annual interest rate of 9%, dated June 1.

Instructions

Prepare the adjusting entries at December 31, 2009. (Show all calculations.)

P3-4 The completed financial statement columns of the work sheet for Zhou Limited follow:

ZHOU LIMITED
Work Sheet
For the Year Ended December 31, 2008

		Income Statement		Balance Sheet	
Account No.	Account Titles	Dr.	Cr.	Dr.	Cr.
101	Cash			8,000	
112	Accounts Receivable			7,500	
130	Prepaid Insurance			1,800	
157	Equipment			28,000	
167	Accumulated Amortization				8,600
201	Accounts Payable				11,600
212	Salaries Payable				3,600
301	Common Shares				20,000
306	Retained Earnings				6,800
400	Service Revenue		42,000		
622	Repair Expense	3,200			
711	Amortization Expense	2,800			
722	Insurance Expense	1,200			
726	Salaries Expense	36,600			
732	Utilities Expense	3,500			
	Totals	47,300	42,000	45,300	50,600
	Net Loss		5,300	5,300	
		47,300	47,300	50,600	50,600

Instructions

(a) Prepare an income statement, retained earnings statement, and classified balance sheet. Zhou's shareholders purchased additional shares in the business for $4,000 investment in the business during 2008.

(b) Prepare the closing entries.

(c) Post the closing entries and rule and balance the accounts. Use T accounts. Income Summary is No. 350.

(d) Prepare a post-closing trial balance.

P3-5 Noah's Ark has a fiscal year ending on September 30. Selected data from the September 30 work sheet follow:

NOAH'S ARK
Work Sheet
For the Year Ended September 30, 2008

	Trial Balance		Adjusted Trial Balance	
	Dr.	Cr.	Dr.	Cr.
Cash	37,400		37,400	
Supplies	18,600		1,500	
Prepaid Insurance	31,900		3,600	
Land	80,000		80,000	
Equipment	120,000		120,000	
Accumulated Amortization		36,200		41,000
Accounts Payable		14,600		14,600
Unearned Admissions Revenue		2,700		1,700
Mortgage Payable		50,000		50,000
N.Y. Berge, Capital		109,700		109,700
N.Y. Berge, Drawings	14,000		14,000	
Admissions Revenue		278,500		279,500
Salaries Expense	109,000		109,000	
Repair Expense	30,500		30,500	
Advertising Expense	9,400		9,400	
Utilities Expense	16,900		16,900	
Property Taxes Expense	18,000		21,000	
Interest Expense	6,000		12,200	
Totals	491,700	491,700		
Insurance Expense			28,300	
Supplies Expense			17,100	
Interest Payable				6,200
Amortization Expense			4,800	
Property Taxes Payable				3,000
Totals			505,700	505,700

Instructions

(a) Prepare a complete work sheet.

(b) Prepare a classified balance sheet. (Note: In the next fiscal year, $10,000 of the mortgage payable is due for payment.)

(c) Journalize the adjusting entries, using data in the work sheet.

(d) Journalize the closing entries, using data in the work sheet.

(e) Prepare a post-closing trial balance.

P3-6 The trial balance of Bhopal Fashion Centre Inc. contained the following accounts at November 30, the company's fiscal year end:

BHOPAL FASHION CENTRE INC.
Trial Balance
November 30, 2008

	Debit	Credit
Cash	$ 29,200	
Accounts Receivable	34,200	
Merchandise Inventory	45,000	
Store Supplies	5,500	
Store Equipment	85,000	
Accumulated Amortization—Store Equipment		$ 18,000
Delivery Equipment	48,000	
Accumulated Amortization—Delivery Equipment		6,000
Notes Payable		41,000
Accounts Payable		58,500
Common Shares		100,000
Retained Earnings		8,000
Sales		750,200
Sales Returns and Allowances	4,200	
Cost of Goods Sold	497,400	
Salaries Expense	140,000	
Advertising Expense	26,400	
Utilities Expense	14,000	
Repair Expense	12,100	
Delivery Expense	16,700	
Rent Expense	24,000	
	$981,700	$981,700

Adjustment data:

1. Store supplies on hand totalled $3,100.
2. Amortization is $9,000 on the store equipment and $7,000 on the delivery equipment.
3. Interest of $ 6,000 is accrued on notes payable at November 30.

Other data:

1. Salaries expense is 70% selling and 30% administrative.
2. Rent expense and utilities expense are 80% selling and 20% administrative.
3. Of the notes payable, $30,000 is due for payment next year.
4. Repair expense is 100% administrative.

Instructions

(a) Enter the trial balance on a work sheet and complete the work sheet.

(b) Prepare a multiple-step income statement and retained earnings statement for the year and a classified balance sheet as at November 30, 2008.

(c) Journalize the adjusting entries.

(d) Journalize the closing entries.

(e) Prepare a post-closing trial balance.

P3-7 Hardisty Department Store Inc. is located near the shopping mall. At the end of the company's fiscal year on December 31, 2009, the following accounts appeared in two of its trial balances:

	Unadjusted	Adjusted
Accounts Payable	$ 79,300	$ 79,300
Accounts Receivable	95,300	95,300
Accumulated Amortization—Building	42,100	52,500
Accumulated Amortization—Equipment	29,600	42,900
Building	190,000	190,000
Cash	68,000	68,000
Common Shares	160,000	160,000
Retained Earnings	16,600	16,600
Cost of Goods Sold	412,700	412,700
Amortization Expense—Building		10,400
Amortization Expense—Equipment		13,300
Dividends	28,000	28,000
Equipment	110,000	110,000
Insurance Expense		7,200
Interest Expense	3,000	11,000
Interest Payable		8,000
Interest Revenue	4,000	4,000
Merchandise Inventory	75,000	75,000
Mortgage Payable	80,000	80,000
Office Salaries Expense	32,000	32,000
Prepaid Insurance	9,600	2,400
Property Taxes Expense		4,800
Property Taxes Payable		4,800
Sales Salaries Expense	76,000	76,000
Sales	718,000	718,000
Sales Commissions Expense	11,000	14,500
Sales Commissions Payable		3,500
Sales Returns and Allowances	8,000	8,000
Utilities Expense	11,000	11,000

Analysis reveals the following additional data:

1. Insurance expense and utilities expense are 60% selling and 40% administrative.
2. In the next year, $20,000 of the mortgage payable will be due for payment.
3. Property tax expense and amortization on the building are administrative expenses; amortization on the equipment is a selling expense.

Instructions

(a) Prepare a multiple-step income statement, retained earnings statement, and classified balance sheet.

(b) Journalize the adjusting entries that were made.

(c) Journalize the closing entries that are necessary.

P3-8 The following accounts appeared in the December 31 trial balance of Alexander Theatre:

	Debit	Credit
Equipment	$216,000	
Accumulated Amortization—Equipment		$ 60,000
Notes Payable		92,000
Admissions Revenue		380,000
Advertising Expense	13,680	
Salaries Expense	57,600	
Interest Expense	1,400	

Instructions

(a) From the account balances above and the information that follows, prepare the annual adjusting entries necessary on December 31:

1. The equipment has an estimated life of 16 years and a residual value of $40,000. (Use the straight-line method.)
2. The note payable is a 90-day note given to the bank on October 20 and bearing interest at 10%.
3. In December, 2,000 coupon admission books were sold at $25 each; they can be used for admission any time after January 1.
4. Of the Advertising Expense balance, $1,100 is paid in advance.
5. Salaries accrued but unpaid are $4,700.

(b) What amounts should be shown for each of the following on the income statement for the year?

1. Interest expense
2. Admissions revenue
3. Advertising expense
4. Salaries expense

P3-9 The trial balance and the other information for consulting engineer Muhammad Moamar follow:

MUHAMMAD MOAMAR, CONSULTING ENGINEER
Trial Balance
December 31, 2009

	Debit	Credit
Cash	$ 31,500	
Accounts Receivable	49,600	
Allowance for Doubtful Accounts		$ 750
Engineering Supplies Inventory	1,960	
Unexpired Insurance	1,100	
Furniture and Equipment	25,000	
Accumulated Amortization—Furniture and Equipment		6,250
Notes Payable		7,200
Muhammad Moamar, Capital		35,010
Service Revenue		100,000
Rent Expense	9,750	
Office Salaries Expense	28,500	
Heat, Light, and Water Expense	1,080	
Miscellaneous Office Expense	720	
	$149,210	$149,210

1. Fees received in advance from clients, $6,900.
2. Services performed for clients that were not recorded by December 31, $7,300.
3. Bad debt expense for the year, $1,430.
4. Insurance expired during the year, $480.
5. Furniture and equipment is being amortized at 9% per year.
6. Muhammad gave the bank a 90-day, 12% note for $7,200 on December 1, 2009.
7. Rent is $750 per month. The rent for 2009 and for January 2010 has been paid.
8. Office salaries earned but unpaid at December 31, 2009, $2,510.

Instructions

(a) From the trial balance and other information given, prepare annual adjusting entries as at December 31, 2009.

(b) Prepare an income statement for 2009, a balance sheet, and a statement of owners' equity. Muhammad Moamar withdrew $17,000 cash for personal use during the year.

P3-10 Andrew Advertising Corporation was founded by Jan Andrew in January 2001. The adjusted and unadjusted trial balances as of December 31, 2008, follow:

ANDREW ADVERTISING CORPORATION
Trial Balance
December 31, 2008

	Unadjusted		Adjusted	
	Dr.	Cr.	Dr.	Cr.
Cash	$ 7,000		$ 7,000	
Accounts Receivable	19,000		25,800	
Art Supplies	8,500		5,500	
Prepaid Insurance	3,250		2,500	
Printing Equipment	60,000		60,000	
Accumulated Amortization		$ 27,000		$ 33,750
Accounts Payable		5,000		5,000
Interest Payable				150
Notes Payable		5,000		5,000
Unearned Service Revenue		7,000		5,600
Salaries Payable				1,500
Common Shares		10,000		10,000
Retained Earnings		4,500		4,500
Service Revenue		58,600		66,800
Salaries Expense	10,000		11,500	
Insurance Expense			750	
Interest Expense	350		500	
Amortization Expense			6,750	
Art Supplies Expense	5,000		8,000	
Rent Expense	4,000		4,000	
	$117,100	$117,100	$132,300	$132,300

Instructions

(a) Journalize the annual adjusting entries that were made.

(b) Prepare an income statement and statement of retained earnings for the year ending December 31, 2008, and a balance sheet at December 31.

(c) Answer the following questions:

1. If the useful life of equipment is eight years, what is the expected residual value?
2. If the note has been outstanding three months, what is the annual interest rate on that note?
3. If the company paid $12,500 in salaries in 2008, what was the balance in Salaries Payable on December 31, 2007?

P3-11 The following information relates to Joachim Anderson, Realtor, at the close of the fiscal year ending December 31:

1. Joachim paid the local newspaper $335 for an advertisement to be run in January of the next year, and charged it to Advertising Expense.
2. On November 1, Joachim signed a 90-day, 10% note to borrow $15,000 from Yorkville Bank.
3. The following salaries and wages are due and unpaid at December 31: sales, $1,420; office clerks, $1,060.
4. Interest of $500 has accrued to date on a note that Joachim holds from Grant Muldaur.
5. The estimated loss on bad debts for the period is $1,560.
6. Stamps and stationery are charged to the Stationery and Postage Expense account when purchased; $110 of these supplies remain on hand.
7. Joachim has not yet paid the December rent of $1,000 on the building his business uses.
8. Insurance was paid on November 1 for one year and charged to Prepaid Insurance, $1,170.
9. Property taxes accrued, $1,670.

10. On December 1, Joachim gave Laura Palmer a 60-day, 15% note for $6,000 on account.

11. On October 31, Joachim received $2,580 from Douglas Raines in payment of six months' rent for Raines's office space in the building and credited Unearned Rent Revenue.

12. On September 1, he paid six months' rent in advance on a warehouse, $8,300, and debited the asset account Prepaid Rent Expense.

13. The bill from Light & Power Limited for December has been received but not yet entered or paid, $510.

14. The estimated amortization on furniture and equipment is $1,400.

Instructions

Prepare annual adjusting entries as at December 31.

P3-12 The trial balance follows of the Millcraft Golf Club, Inc. as at December 31. The books are closed annually on December 31.

MILLCRAFT GOLF CLUB, INC.
Trial Balance
December 31

	Debit	Credit
Cash	$115,000	
Accounts Receivable	13,000	
Allowance for Doubtful Accounts		$ 1,100
Land	350,000	
Buildings	120,000	
Accumulated Amortization—Buildings		38,400
Equipment	150,000	
Accumulated Amortization—Equipment		70,000
Unexpired Insurance	9,000	
Common Shares		500,000
Retained Earnings		82,000
Dues Revenue		200,000
Green Fees Revenue		8,100
Rental Revenue		15,400
Utilities Expense	54,000	
Salaries Expense	80,000	
Maintenance Expense	24,000	
	$915,000	$915,000

Instructions

(a) Enter the balances in ledger accounts. Allow five lines for each account.

(b) From the trial balance and the information that follows, prepare annual adjusting entries and post to the ledger accounts:

1. The buildings have an estimated life of 26 years with no salvage value (the company uses the straight-line method).
2. The equipment is amortized at 10% per year.
3. Insurance expired during the year, $5,300.
4. The rental revenue is the amount received for 11 months for dining facilities. The December rent has not yet been received.
5. It is estimated that 24% of the accounts receivable will be uncollectible.
6. Salaries earned but not paid by December 31 amount to $3,600.
7. Dues paid in advance by members total $9,900.

(c) Prepare an adjusted trial balance.

(d) Prepare closing entries and post to the ledger.

P3-13 The December 31 trial balance of Drew Boutique Inc. follows:

DREW BOUTIQUE INC.
Trial Balance
December 31

	Debit	Credit
Cash	$ 18,500	
Accounts Receivable	42,000	
Allowance for Doubtful Accounts		$ 700
Inventory, December 31	80,000	
Furniture and Equipment	84,000	
Accumulated Amortization—Furniture and Equipment		35,000
Prepaid Insurance	5,100	
Notes Payable		28,000
Common Shares		80,600
Retained Earnings		10,000
Sales		600,000
Cost of Goods Sold	398,000	
Sales Salaries Expense	50,000	
Advertising Expense	6,700	
Administrative Salaries Expense	65,000	
Office Expense	5,000	
	$754,300	$754,300

Instructions

(a) Create T accounts and enter the balances shown.

(b) Prepare adjusting journal entries for the following and post to the T accounts. Open additional T accounts as necessary. (The books are closed yearly on December 31.)

1. Bad debts are estimated to be $1,700 (percentage of sales method is used).
2. Furniture and equipment is amortized based on a six-year life and no residual value.
3. Insurance expired during the year, $2,700.
4. Interest accrued on notes payable, $3,420.
5. Sales salaries earned but not paid are $2,400.
6. Advertising paid in advance is $750.
7. Office supplies on hand total $1,500 and were charged to Office Expense when they were purchased.

(c) Prepare closing entries and post to the accounts.

P3-14 The unadjusted trial balance of Clancy Inc. at December 31, 2008, is as follows:

	Dr.	Cr.
Cash	$ 39,740	
Accounts Receivable	103,000	
Allowance for Doubtful Accounts		$ 3,500
Merchandise Inventory	60,000	
Prepaid Insurance	2,620	
Investment in Casper Inc. Bonds (9%)	40,000	
Land	30,000	
Building	124,000	
Accumulated Amortization—Building		11,810
Equipment	33,600	
Accumulated Amortization—Equipment		5,600
Goodwill	26,600	
Accounts Payable		101,050
Bonds Payable (20-year, 7%)		180,000
Common Shares		121,000
Retained Earnings		21,950
Sales		200,000
Rental Income		10,800
Advertising Expense	22,500	
Supplies Expense	10,800	

Purchases	98,000	
Purchase Discounts		900
Office Salary Expense	17,500	
Sales Salary Expense	36,000	
Interest Expense	12,250	
	$656,610	$656,610

Additional information:

1. Actual advertising costs amounted to $1,500 per month. The company has already paid for advertisements in *Montezuma Magazine* for the first quarter of 2009.
2. The building was purchased and occupied on January 1, 2006, with an estimated life of 21 years. (The company uses straight-line amortization.)
3. Prepaid insurance contains the premium costs of two policies: Policy A, cost of $960, one-year term taken out on Sept. 1, 2007; Policy B, cost of $1,980, three-year term taken out on April 1, 2008.
4. A portion of Clancy's building has been converted into a snack bar that has been rented to the Ono Food Corp. since July 1, 2007, at a rate of $7,200 per year payable each July 1.
5. One of the company's customers declared bankruptcy on December 30, 2008. It is now certain that the $2,700 the customer owes will never be collected. This fact has not been recorded. In addition, Clancy estimates that 4% of the Accounts Receivable balance on December 31, 2008, will become uncollectible.
6. An advance of $600 to a salesperson on December 31, 2008, was charged to Sales Salary Expense.
7. On November 1, 2006, Clancy issued 180 $1,000 bonds at par value. Interest is paid semi-annually on April 30 and October 31.
8. The equipment was purchased on January 1, 2006, and has an estimated life of 12 years. (The company uses straight-line amortization.)
9. On August 1, 2008, Clancy purchased at par value 40 $1,000, 9% bonds maturing on August 31, 2010. Interest is paid on July 31 and January 31.
10. The inventory on hand at December 31, 2008, was $90,000 after a physical inventory count.

Instructions

(a) Prepare adjusting and correcting entries for December 31, 2008, using the information given. (In solving this problem, record the adjustment for inventory in the same entry that records the Cost of Goods Sold for the year.)

(b) Indicate which of the adjusting entries could be reversed.

P3-15 The unadjusted trial balance of Lentil Ltd. at December 31, 2008, is as follows:

	Dr.	Cr.
Cash	$ 10,850	
Accounts Receivable	56,500	
Allowance for Doubtful Accounts		$ 750
Inventory	58,000	
Prepaid Insurance	2,940	
Prepaid Rent	13,200	
Investment in Legume Inc. Bonds	18,000	
Land	10,000	
Plant and Equipment	104,000	
Accumulated Amortization		18,000
Accounts Payable		9,310
Bonds Payable		50,000
Common Shares		100,000
Retained Earnings		80,660
Sales		223,310
Rent Revenue		10,200
Purchases	170,000	
Purchase Discounts		2,400
Transportation-out	9,000	
Transportation-in	3,500	
Salaries and Wages Expense	31,000	
Interest Expense	6,750	
Miscellaneous Expense	890	
	$494,630	$494,630

Additional information:

1. On November 1, 2008, Lentil received $10,200 rent from its lessee for a 12-month lease beginning on that date. This was credited to Rent Revenue.
2. Lentil estimates that 7% of the Accounts Receivable balances on December 31, 2008, will be uncollectible. On December 28, 2008, the bookkeeper incorrectly credited Sales for a receipt of $1,000 on account. This error had not yet been corrected on December 31.
3. After a physical count, inventory on hand at December 31, 2008, was $77,000.
4. Prepaid insurance contains the premium costs of two policies: Policy A, cost of $1,320, two-year term, taken out on September 1, 2008; Policy B, cost of $1,620, three-year term, taken out on April 1, 2008.
5. The regular rate of amortization is 10% of cost per year. Acquisitions and retirements during a year are amortized at half this rate. There were no retirements during the year. On December 31, 2007, the balance of Plant and Equipment was $90,000.
6. On April 1, 2008, Lentil issued at par value 50 $1,000, 11% bonds maturing on April 1, 2013. Interest is paid on April 1 and October 1.
7. On August 1, 2008, Lentil purchased at par value 18 $1,000, 12% Legume Inc. bonds, maturing on July 31, 2010. Interest is paid on July 31 and January 31.
8. On May 30, 2008, Lentil rented a warehouse for $1,100 per month and debited Prepaid Rent for an advance payment of $13,200.

Instructions

(a) Prepare the year-end adjusting and correcting entries in general journal form using the information given. Record the adjusting entry for inventory by using a Cost of Goods Sold account.

(b) Indicate the adjusting entries that could be reversed.

P3-16 Eric Mayers, CGA, was retained by Downtown TV Repair Ltd. to prepare financial statements for the month of March 2009. Mayers accumulated all the ledger balances from the business records and found the following:

DOWNTOWN TV REPAIR LTD.
Trial Balance
March 31, 2009

	Debit	Credit
Cash	$ 6,000	
Accounts Receivable	3,800	
Supplies	900	
Equipment	11,400	
Accumulated Amortization—Equipment		$ 1,815
Accounts Payable		3,000
Salaries Payable		600
Unearned Fees Revenue		935
Common Shares		10,000
Retained Earnings		4,160
Repair Service Revenue		6,450
Salaries Expense	2,900	
Advertising Expense	800	
Utilities Expense	310	
Amortization Expense	700	
Repair Expense	150	
	$26,960	$26,960

Eric Mayers reviewed the records and found the following errors:

1. Cash received from a customer on account was recorded as $750 instead of $570.
2. The purchase, on account, of a scanner that cost $375 was recorded as a debit to Supplies and a credit to Accounts Payable for $375.
3. A payment of $30 for advertising expense was entered as a debit to Utilities Expense $30 and a credit to Cash, $30.

4. The first salary payment this month was for $1,800, which included $600 of salaries payable on February 28. The payment was recorded as a debit to Salaries Expense, $1,800 and a credit to Cash of $1,800. The business does not use reversing entries.
5. A cash payment for repair expense on equipment for $90 was recorded as a debit to Equipment, $90, and a credit to Cash, $90.

Instructions

(a) Prepare an analysis of each error that shows (1) the incorrect entry, (2) the correct entry, and (3) the correcting entry.

(b) Prepare a corrected trial balance.

P3-17 Samuels Corp. began operations on January 1, 2009. Its fiscal year end is December 31. Samuels has decided that prepaid costs are debited to expense when paid, and unearned revenues are credited to revenue when the cash is received. During 2009, the following transactions occurred.

1. On January 1, 2009, Samuels bought office supplies for $4,100 cash. A physical count at December 31, 2009, revealed $900 of supplies still on hand.
2. Samuels bought a $3,780 one-year insurance policy for cash on August 1, 2009. The policy came into effect on this date.
3. On November 15, 2009, Samuels received a $1,200 advance cash payment from a client for architectural services to be provided in the future. As at December 31, 2009, one quarter of these services had not been performed.
4. On December 15, 2009, Samuels rented out excess office space for a six-month period starting on this date, and received a $540 cheque for the first month's rent.

Instructions

(a) For each of the above transactions, prepare the journal entry for the original transaction and any adjusting journal entry required at December 31, 2009.

(b) In a business where there are several divisions or office locations where accounting is performed, is it possible that prepayments would be treated as assets in some offices and as expenses in others when initially recorded? Does the business have to have a consistent approach in all of its offices?

Research and Financial Analysis

RA 3-1 Stantec Inc.

The financial statements of Stantec Inc. are presented in Appendix 5B. Complete the following instructions by referring to these financial statements and the accompanying notes.

Instructions

(a) What were the company's total assets at year end for the two years that are presented?

(b) How much cash (and cash equivalents) did the company have at year end?

(c) What were the company's total revenues for the current and preceding year? What are the three main sources of revenues and how profitable are they?

(d) Using the financial statements and related notes, identify the items that may result in adjusting entries for prepayments and accruals.

(e) The company presents certain numbers as "net" on the income statement (revenues and interest). Discuss why this may be appropriate.

RA 3-2 Saputo Inc.

Saputo Inc. is one of the top 20 dairy producers in the world, with 8,400 employees and 44 plants worldwide. Go to Saputo's 2006 annual report on the Student Website and complete the following instructions.

Instructions

(a) On page 1 of the annual report, the company reports certain numbers that are meant to give an overview of the company's financial results. Are the numbers prepared in accordance with GAAP? In your answer, also discuss why the company would present the information in this way and whether the information is more or less useful to financial statement users because of its presentation.

(b) On page 41, there are two statements. One is signed by company management and the other by the auditors. Briefly summarize the content of each statement and discuss why these statements provide important information to users. How much responsibility does top management have for the creation and monitoring of the accounting information systems that produce the financial information?

RA 3-3 Financial Statement Dates

Companies normally issue their annual financial statements within weeks of year end.

Instructions

(a) Identify the top five companies (by revenue) in the following industries. (Hint: Look on the Student Website for a link to the Top 1000 Canadian Companies from the *Report on Business*.)

1. Banks
2. Insurance
3. Real Estate
4. Biotech and pharmaceutical

(b) For each company, identify its year-end date and the date that the financial statements were produced (look at the auditor's report). You will have to go to the company websites or SEDAR (www.sedar.com) to find the statements.

(c) What is the likely reason that the banks have a different year end than the others?

(d) How many days does it take for the companies to produce the statements after year end? Look at the average time for each industry. Within each industry, how close are the issue dates among companies? Comment on your findings.

RA 3-4 ERP

Enterprise Resource Planning (ERP) software systems include bookkeeping systems as well as systems to monitor and manage human resource functions, quality control functions, and many other aspects of business. The software runs off a centralized database that services all company departments and functions.

Instructions

Research and write a one- to two-page summary that gives details about what ERPs are and why they have gained so much attention. Why do companies find them so useful? What are the pros and cons to these systems? (Hint: Search for "Enterprise Resource Planning" on the Internet.)

Doing Well by Doing Good

When reporting their performance, many companies see much more than their financial results. They look at the triple bottom line: the social, environmental, and economic impact of their operations. One of these companies is B.C.'s Vancity credit union.

Vancity states that one of its aims is to strengthen its long-term business while contributing to the well-being of its members, staff, communities, and the environment. Indeed, it clearly embraces corporate social responsibility on its website: "For us, corporate social responsibility goes beyond donating money or volunteering time to worthy causes. It's about operating in a way that is responsible to our members and our staff, that is respectful of the environment, and that is supportive of the communities in which we live and work."

In addition to providing effective financial management and ensuring that Vancity is a great place to work, the credit union is committed to leading by example and using its resources and expertise to make positive changes in the community. It does this by being a model and supporter of socially and environmentally responsible business practices and by looking for business partners that have progressive employee relations, contribute to the well-being of their communities, and respect the environment. Vancity also invests back into the community. Each year, it shares 30 percent of its profits with its members and communities, including the $1-million Vancity Award.

"We believe that accountability and transparency are keys to building a strong financial services sector—one that is responsive to the needs of consumers, and socially and environmentally responsible in its business decisions," says CEO Dave Mowatt.

Vancity publishes an Accountability Report, which is verified externally to assure that it is a reliable, balanced, and reasonable account of Vancity's social and environmental performance. Vancity then uses key findings from this social audit in its business planning process to set targets and action plans that ensure that it continually improves its performance. ■

Reporting Financial Performance

Learning Objectives

After studying this chapter, you should be able to:

1. Identify the uses and limitations of an income statement.
2. Prepare a single-step income statement.
3. Prepare a multiple-step income statement.
4. Explain how irregular items are reported.
5. Measure and report results of discontinued operations.
6. Explain intraperiod tax allocation.
7. Explain where earnings per share information is reported.
8. Prepare a retained earnings statement.
9. Explain how comprehensive income is reported.

After studying Appendix 4A, you should be able to:

10. Explain the differences between the cash basis of accounting and the accrual basis of accounting.

Preview of Chapter 4

The way items are reported in the income statement can affect how useful it is to users. Although the net income number (the bottom line) is a key focal point for many users, the other elements in the income statement have significant information content as well. This chapter examines the many different types of revenues, expenses, gains, and losses that are represented in the income statement and related information.

The chapter is organized as follows:

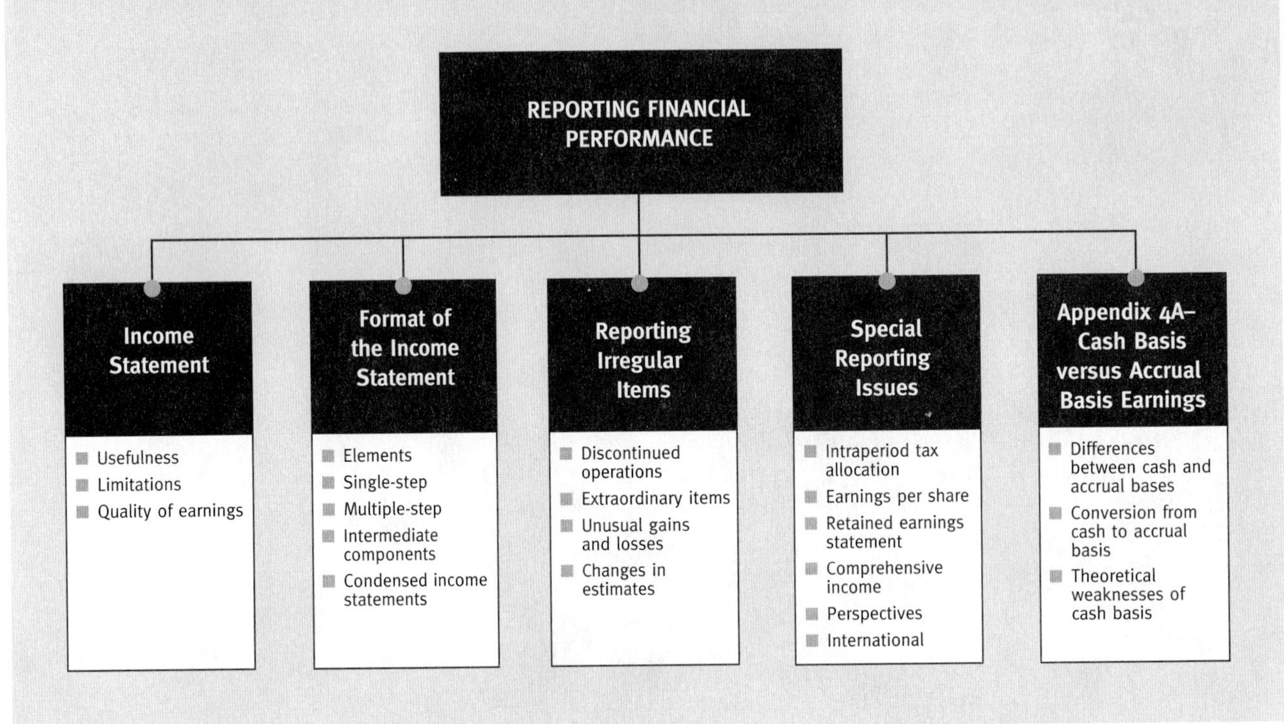

All business is based on the **business model** of getting cash, investing it in resources, and then using these resources to generate profits. This model can be broken down into three distinct types of activities:

1. **Financing:** Obtaining cash funding, often by borrowing, issuing shares, or (in established companies) retaining profits. Financing activities also involve the repayment of debt and/or repurchase of shares.
2. **Investing:** Using the funding to buy assets and invest in people. Investing activities also include divestitures.
3. **Operating:** Using the assets and people to earn profits.

In performing these three types of activities, companies take on different levels of **risk** and find different **opportunities**. Companies must **manage** these risks in order to get the best performance and returns. Better companies develop strategies that will allow them to react to the best opportunities in order to maximize shareholder value. **Value creation** is central in any business model.

Since the objective of financial reporting is to communicate to interested stakeholders what the company is doing, the financial statements should capture these **fundamental**

business activities and communicate them appropriately. In general, the information is captured and communicated as follows:

- The **balance sheet** aims to capture the **financing and investing activities**.
- The **income statement** aims to capture the **operating and performance-related activities**.
- The **cash flow statement** looks at the **interrelationship** between the activities.

Illustration 4-1 presents this overview of the business model.

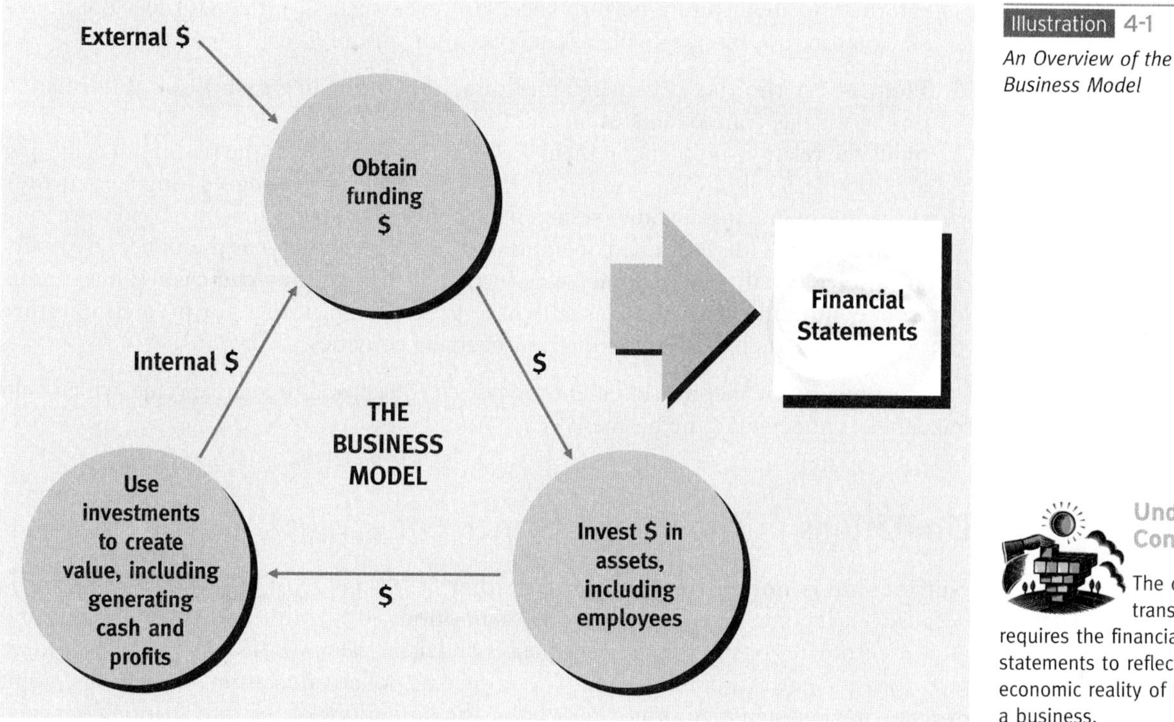

Illustration 4-1
An Overview of the Business Model

Underlying Concept

The concept of transparency requires the financial statements to reflect the economic reality of running a business.

INCOME STATEMENT

The **income statement**, often called the statement of earnings or statement of income,[1] is the report that measures the success of a company's operations for a specific time period. The business and investment communities use this report to determine profitability, investment value, and creditworthiness. It provides investors and creditors with information that helps them allocate resources and assess management stewardship.

1 Objective
Identify the uses and limitations of an income statement.

Usefulness of the Income Statement

There are several ways in which the income statement helps financial statement users decide where to invest their resources and evaluate how well management is using a

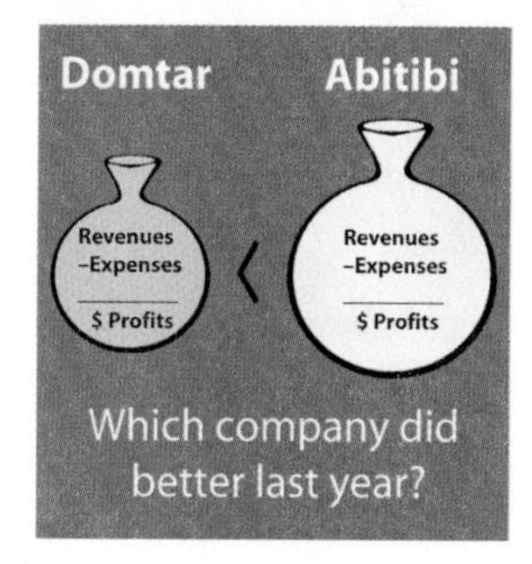

[1] *Financial Reporting in Canada, 2005* (Toronto, CICA), Chapter 11, indicates that for the 200 companies surveyed, 80 used "earnings," 64 used "income," and 51 used "operations" in their title for this statement. The term "income" is becoming more popular.

company's resources.[2] For example, investors and creditors can use the information in the income statement to:

1. **Evaluate the enterprise's past performance and profitability.** By examining revenues, expenses, gains, and losses, users can see how the company (and management) performed and compare the company's performance with its competitors. (Balance sheet information is also useful in assessing profitability, e.g., by calculating return on assets. See Appendix 5A.)
2. **Provide a basis for predicting future performance.** Information about past performance can be used to determine important trends that, if they continue, provide information about future performance. However, success in the past does not necessarily mean the company will have success in the future.
3. **Help assess the risk or uncertainty of achieving future cash flows.** Information on the various components of income—revenues, expenses, gains, and losses—highlights the relationships among them and can be used to assess the risk of not achieving a particular level of cash flows in the future. For example, segregating a company's recurring **operating** income (results from continuing operations) from nonrecurring income sources (discontinued operations, extraordinary items) is useful because **operations are usually the primary way to generate revenues and cash.** Thus, results from continuing operations usually have greater significance for predicting future performance than do results from nonrecurring activities.

In summary, the income statement provides feedback and predictive value, which help stakeholders understand the business.

Limitations of the Income Statement

Net income is not a point estimate. Rather, it is a range of possible values. This is because net income is based on several assumptions. By definition, accrual accounting requires estimates of such things as expenses and asset values to be recorded. Because we report net income as a point estimate (i.e., a specific dollar value estimate at a single point in time), income statement users must know the limitations of the information contained in the income statement. The income statement includes a mix of **hard** numbers (which are easily measured with a reasonable level of certainty, e.g., cash sales) and **soft** numbers (which are more difficult to measure, e.g., provision for bad debt). Specifically, the income statement has the following shortcomings:

1. **Items that cannot be measured reliably are not reported in the income statement.** Currently, companies are not allowed to include certain items in the determination of income even though these items arguably affect an entity's performance from one point in time to another. For example, contingent gains may not be recorded in income, as there is uncertainty about whether the gains will ever be realized.

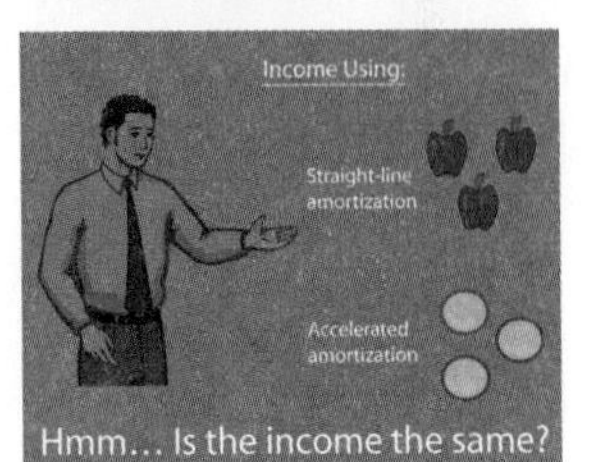

2. **Income numbers are affected by the accounting methods that are used.** For example, one company may choose to depreciate or amortize its plant assets on an accelerated basis; another may choose straight-line amortization. Assuming all other factors are equal, the first company's income will be lower even though the two companies are essentially the same. The result is that we are comparing apples with oranges.
3. **Income measurement involves the use of estimates.** For example, one company may estimate in good faith that an asset's useful life is 20 years while another company uses a 15-year estimate for the same type of asset. Similarly, some companies may

[2] Showing that income information is useful, accounting researchers have documented that the market prices of companies change when income is reported to the market. See W.H. Beaver, "Perspectives on Recent Capital Markets Research," *The Accounting Review* (April 2002), pp. 453–474.

make overly optimistic estimates of future warranty returns and bad debt write-offs, which would result in lower expenses and higher income. As mentioned above, when there is significant measurement uncertainty, the resulting numbers that are captured in the financial statements are called "soft numbers."

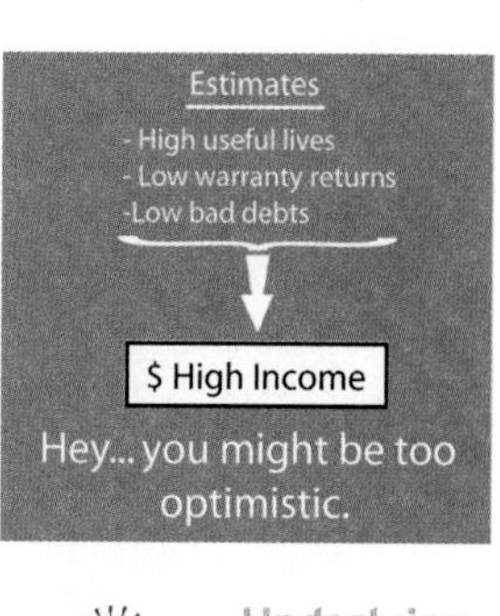

Quality of Earnings

Users need **good information** about a company's earnings to make decisions; however, not all income statements provide this. We began to look at this issue above (through limitations of the income statement) and will examine it further here. When analyzing earnings information, there are two aspects that must be considered:

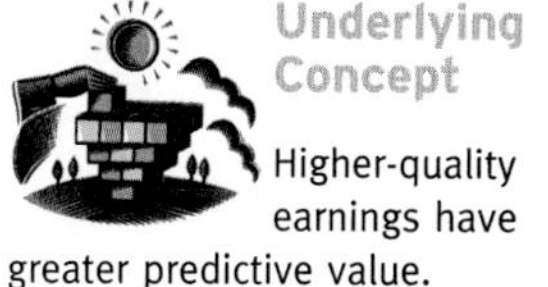

Underlying Concept

Higher-quality earnings have greater predictive value.

1. **Content**, which includes
   (a) the **integrity of the information,** including whether it reflects the underlying business fundamentals, and
   (b) the **sustainability of the earnings**
2. **Presentation**, which means a clear, concise manner that makes it easy to use and understandable

The **nature of the content** and the **way it is presented** are referred to as the **quality of earnings**.

From an accountant's perspective, the emphasis is on ensuring that the information **is unbiased, reflects reality, and is transparent and understandable**. From a capital market perspective, these factors are also important, but the real focus is on whether the **earnings are sustainable**. With its current business model, can the company continue to generate or sustain these earnings in the future? Note that accountants acknowledge this additional perspective by segregating earnings on the income statement between those that are expected to continue and those that are not. Even though the underlying business might be accurately reflected and understandable in the financial statements, the quality of the earnings might be judged to be low because the earnings are not sustainable.[3]

As suggested, earnings numbers may be judged to be of a **higher** quality or, conversely, a **lower** quality. Higher-quality earnings are more reliable, with a lower margin of potential misstatement, and are more representative of the underlying business and economic reality.

Companies with higher-quality earnings are attributed higher values by the markets, all other things being equal. Earnings that cannot be replicated and/or appear significantly biased are discounted by the markets.

Illustration 4-2 presents some attributes of high quality earnings.

Illustration 4-2

Some Attributes of High-Quality Earnings

High-quality earnings have the following characteristics:

1. Content
   - **Unbiased**, as numbers are not manipulated, and **objectively determined**. (Consider the need to estimate, the accounting choices, and the use of professional judgement.)
   - **Reflects the economic reality** as all transactions and events are appropriately captured.
   - **Reflects primarily the earnings generated from ongoing core business activities** instead of earnings from one-time gains or losses.
   - **Closely correlates with cash flows from operations.** Earnings that convert to cash more quickly provide a better measure of real earnings as there is little or no uncertainty about whether they will be realized.
   - **Based on sound business strategy and business model.** (Consider the riskiness of the business, business strategy, industry, and the economic and political environments. Identify the effect of these on earnings stability, volatility, and sustainability.)

[3] In assessing whether earnings are sustainable, a strategic analysis of the company's positioning within the industry must be performed, as well as an assessment of the business model's viability. This is beyond the scope of this course.

2. Presentation
   - **Transparent**, as no attempt is made to disguise or mislead. It reflects the underlying business fundamentals.
   - **Understandable**

Can management control the quality of earnings? Looking at Illustration 4-2, we see that there are some factors that are under management control, such as the integrity of the information, i.e., what information is captured and **recognized**, how it is **measured**, and how it is **presented and disclosed**. Management may also have some control over how quickly cash is generated from operations and how closely this correlates with reported earnings, e.g., through the choice of sales and payment terms. Factors such as the economic and political environment are beyond the control of management for the most part, although management may certainly develop strategies to identify and minimize risks that lead to volatile earnings.

Earnings management may be defined as the process of **targeting certain earnings levels** (whether current or future) or desired earnings trends and then **working backwards to determine what has to be done to ensure that these targets are met** (which can involve the selection of accounting and other company policies, the use of estimates, and even the execution of transactions). In many cases, earnings management is used to increase income in the current year by reducing income in future years. For example, companies may prematurely recognize sales before they are complete in order to boost earnings. Some companies may enter into transactions only so that the statements look better, and thus incur unnecessary transaction costs.

Earnings management can also be used to decrease current earnings in order to increase future income. Reserves may be established by using aggressive assumptions to estimate items such as sales returns, loan losses, and warranty returns. These reserves can then be reduced in the future to increase income. Earnings management activities have a negative effect on the quality of earnings. As long as there is full disclosure, an efficient market should see through these attempts to mask the underlying economic reality. Unfortunately, companies do not always disclose all important information and markets do not always operate efficiently.

Although many users do not believe that management intentionally misrepresents accounting results, there is concern that much of the information that companies distribute is too promotional and that troubled companies take great pains to present their results in the best light. Preparers of financial statements must strive to present information that is of the highest quality. Users of this information must assess the quality of earnings before making their decisions.

FORMAT OF THE INCOME STATEMENT

Elements of the Income Statement

International Insight

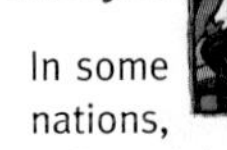

In some nations, financial reporting is prepared on the same basis as tax returns. In such cases, companies have incentives to minimize reported income.

Net income results from revenue, expense, gain, and loss transactions. These transactions are summarized in the income statement. This view of the income statement is **transactions-based** because it focuses on the income-related activities that have occurred during the period.[4] Income can be further classified by customer, product line, or function, or by

[4] The most common alternative to the transaction approach is the **capital maintenance approach** to income measurement. Under this approach, income for the period is determined based on the **change in equity**, after adjusting for capital contributions (e.g., investments by owners) or distributions (e.g., dividends). In other words, net income is a residual calculation. If the company is better off at the end of the year (excluding shareholder transactions), the excess is income—no matter what the source is. Canada is currently moving toward a combination of the two approaches with the new standards on **comprehensive income**. In addition, the IASB and FASB currently have a joint project on financial presentation that deals with the definition of "income." Comprehensive income and the IASB/FASB project will be discussed later in the chapter.

operating and non-operating, continuing and discontinued, and regular and irregular categories.[5] The income statement presentation and classifications will be discussed later in the chapter.

More formal definitions of income-related items, referred to as the major **elements** of the income statement, are as follows:

ELEMENTS OF FINANCIAL STATEMENTS[6]

Revenues. **Increases in economic resources**, either by:

1. Inflows
2. Enhancements of an entity's assets
3. Settlements of liabilities resulting from the entity's ordinary activities

Expenses. **Decreases in economic resources**, either by:

1. Outflows
2. Reductions of assets
3. Creation of liabilities, resulting from an entity's ordinary revenue-generating activities

Gains. **Increases in equity (net assets)** from **peripheral** or **incidental transactions** of an entity and from all other transactions and other events and circumstances affecting the entity during a period except those that result from revenues or investment by owners

Losses. **Decreases in equity (net assets)** from **peripheral** or **incidental transactions** of an entity and from all other transactions and other events and circumstances affecting the entity during a period except those that result from expenses or distributions to owners

Other comprehensive income.[7] Revenues, gains, and losses that, in accordance with primary sources of GAAP, are **recognized in comprehensive income, but excluded from net income**

These are the same **elements** identified in Chapter 2 and the conceptual framework. **Revenues** take many forms, such as sales, fees, interest, dividends, and rents. **Expenses** also take many forms, such as cost of goods sold, amortization, interest, rent, salaries and wages, and taxes. **Gains** and **losses** also are of many types, resulting from the sale of investments, sale of plant assets, settlement of liabilities, write-offs of assets due to obsolescence or casualty, and theft. **Other comprehensive income** includes unrealized gains and losses on certain securities, certain foreign exchange gains or losses, and other gains and losses.

Underlying Concept
The business model should be transparent.

The **distinction** between revenues and gains (and expenses and losses) depends to a great extent on how the enterprise's **ordinary** or **typical business activities** are defined. It is therefore critical to understand an enterprise's typical business activities. For example, when McDonald's sells a hamburger, the selling price is recorded as **revenue**. However, when McDonald's sells a french-fryer, any excess of the selling price over the book value would be recorded as a **gain**. This difference in treatment results because the hamburger sale is part of

[5] The term "irregular" is used for transactions and other events that come from developments that are outside the normal business operations.

[6] *CICA Handbook*, Sections 1000.37–.40 and 1530.03.

[7] As noted in Chapter 2, there is some discussion as to whether other comprehensive income is a separate financial statement element because it includes only other elements.

McDonald's regular operations while the french-fryer sale is not. Only when a manufacturer of french-fryers sells a fryer, therefore, would the sale proceeds be recorded as **revenue**.

The importance of properly presenting these elements should not be underestimated. For many decision-makers, the **parts of a financial statement may be more useful than the whole**. A company must be able to generate cash flows from its **normal ongoing core business activities** (revenues minus expenses). Having income statement elements shown in some detail and in a format that shows the data from prior years allows decision-makers to better assess whether a company does indeed **generate cash flows** from its normal ongoing core business activities and **whether it is getting better or worse at it**.

In arriving at income or loss before discontinued operations and extraordinary items, companies are required to present the following items in the income statement:[8]

- revenues
- amount of inventories recognized as expense for the period
- income from investments
- finance income
- income from leases
- government assistance
- amortization
- goodwill impairment
- research and development costs
- exchange gains or losses
- interest expense
- unusual items
- income taxes

Annual Reports
www.wiley.com/canada/kieso

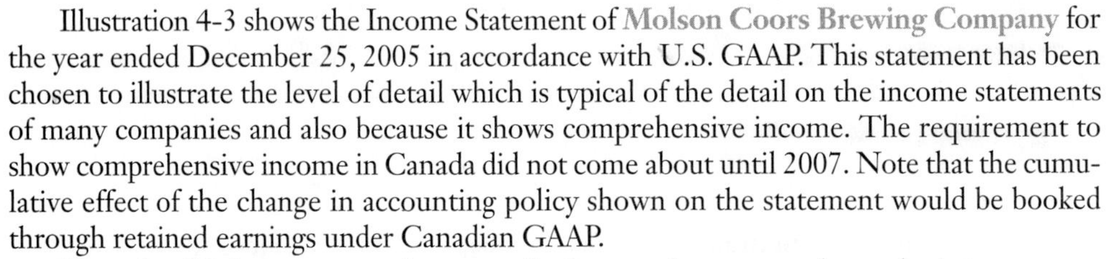
Illustration 4-3 shows the Income Statement of Molson Coors Brewing Company for the year ended December 25, 2005 in accordance with U.S. GAAP. This statement has been chosen to illustrate the level of detail which is typical of the detail on the income statements of many companies and also because it shows comprehensive income. The requirement to show comprehensive income in Canada did not come about until 2007. Note that the cumulative effect of the change in accounting policy shown on the statement would be booked through retained earnings under Canadian GAAP.

Note that Molson presents the **cost of sales** number separately on the income statement. This is now required under Canadian GAAP.

Single-Step Income Statements

Objective 2
Prepare a single-step income statement.

In reporting revenues, gains, expenses, and losses, a format known as the **single-step income statement** is often used. In the single-step statement, only two main groupings are used: **revenues** and **expenses**. Expenses and losses are deducted from revenues and gains to arrive at net income or loss before discontinued operations and extraordinary items. The expression "single-step" comes from the single subtraction that is needed to arrive at net income before discontinued operations and extraordinary items. Frequently, income tax is reported separately as the last item before net income before discontinued operations and extraordinary items to indicate its relationship to income before income tax.

---

[8] *CICA Handbook*, Sections 1520 and 3031.

Illustration 4-3

Molson Coors Brewing Company's Statement of Earnings

MOLSON COORS BREWING COMPANY AND SUBSIDIARIES

CONSOLIDATED STATEMENTS OF INCOME

AND COMPREHENSIVE INCOME

(IN THOUSANDS, EXCEPT SHARE DATA)

	For the Years Ended		
	December 25, 2005	December 26, 2004	December 28, 2003
Sales	$ 7,417,702	$ 5,819,727	$ 5,387,220
Excise taxes	(1,910,796)	(1,513,911)	(1,387,107)
Net sales	5,506,906	4,305,816	4,000,113
Cost of goods sold	(3,306,949)	(2,741,694)	(2,586,783)
Gross profit	2,199,957	1,564,122	1,413,330
Other operating expenses:			
Marketing, general and administrative	(1,632,516)	(1,223,219)	(1,105,959)
Special items, net (Note 8)	(145,392)	7,522	—
Total other operating expenses	(1,777,908)	(1,215,697)	(1,105,959)
Operating income	422,049	348,425	307,371
Other (expense) income:			
Interest income	17,503	19,252	19,245
Interest expense	(131,106)	(72,441)	(81,195)
Other (expense) income, net (Note 5)	(13,245)	12,946	8,397
Total other expense	(126,848)	(40,243)	(53,553)
Income from continuing operations before income taxes and minority interests	295,201	308,182	253,818
Income tax expense	(50,264)	(95,228)	(79,161)
Minority interests	(14,491)	(16,218)	—
Income from continuing operations	230,446	196,736	174,657
Loss from discontinued operations, net of tax (Note 3)	(91,826)	—	—
Income before cumulative effect of change in accounting principle (Note 1)	138,620	196,736	174,657
Cumulative effect of change in accounting principle, net of tax	(3,676)	—	—
Net income	$ 134,944	$ 196,736	$ 174,657
Other comprehensive income, net of tax:			
Foreign currency translation adjustments	122,971	123,011	147,803
Unrealized (loss) gain on derivative instruments	(19,276)	(217)	282
Minimum pension liability adjustment	(6,203)	(24,048)	(15,031)
Reclassification adjustments	(8,404)	(4,686)	4,235
Comprehensive income	$ 224,032	$ 290,796	$ 311,946
Basic income (loss) per share:			
From continuing operations	2.90	5.29	4.81
From discontinued operations	(1.16)	—	—
Cumulative effect of change in accounting principle	(0.04)	—	—
Basic net income per share	$ 1.70	$ 5.29	$ 4.81
Diluted income (loss) per share:			
From continuing operations	2.88	5.19	4.77
From discontinued operations	(1.15)	—	—
Cumulative effect of change in accounting principle	(0.04)	—	—
Diluted net income per share	$ 1.69	$ 5.19	$ 4.77
Weighted average shares—basic	79,403	37,159	36,338
Weighted average shares—diluted	80,036	37,909	36,596

Illustration 4-4 shows the single-step income statement of DeGrootes Corporation.

Illustration 4-4
Single-Step Income Statement

DEGROOTES CORPORATION
Income Statement
For the Year Ended December 31, 2007

Revenues	
Net sales	$3,972,413
Rental revenue	171,410
Total revenues	4,143,823
Expenses	
Cost of goods sold	1,982,541
Selling expenses	453,028
Administrative expenses	350,771
Interest expense	126,060
Income tax expense	369,427
Total expenses	3,281,827
Income before discontinued operations and extraordinary item	$ 861,996
Loss from discontinued operations (net of tax – see note X)	130,000
Income before extraordinary item	$ 731,996
Extraordinary gain (net of tax – see note XX)	45,500
Net income	$ 777,496
Income per common share before discontinued operations and extraordinary gain	$.43
Net income per common share (see note XXX)	$.39

The single-step form of income statement is widely used in financial reporting in smaller, private companies. The **multiple-step** form described below is used almost exclusively among public companies.[9]

The main advantages of the single-step format are that the **presentation is simple** and **no one type of revenue or expense item is implied to have priority over any other**. Potential classification problems are thus eliminated.

Multiple-Step Income Statements

Objective 3
Prepare a multiple-step income statement.

Some users argue that **presenting other important revenue and expense data separately** makes the income statement more informative and more useful. These further classifications include:

1. A separation of the company's operating and non-operating activities. For example, enterprises often present an income from operations figure and then sections entitled **other revenues and gains** and **other expenses and losses**. These other categories include interest revenue and expense, gains or losses from sales of miscellaneous items, and dividends received.

2. A classification of expenses **by functions**, such as merchandising or manufacturing (cost of goods sold), selling, and administration. This makes it possible to immediately **compare** costs of previous years and costs of different departments during the same year.

[9] Chapter 11, *Financial Reporting in Canada, 2005* (Toronto, CICA). Of the 200 companies surveyed, 98 percent used the multiple-step form.

A **multiple-step income statement** is used to recognize these additional relationships. This statement separates **operating** transactions and **non-operating** transactions and **matches** costs and expenses with related revenues. It also highlights certain intermediate components of income that are used to calculate ratios for assessing the enterprise's performance (i.e., gross profit/margin).

To illustrate, DeGrootes Corporation's multiple-step income statement is presented in Illustration 4-5. Note, for example, that in arriving at net income before discontinued operations and extraordinary items, at least three main subtotals are presented: net sales revenue, gross profit, and income from operations. The disclosure of net sales revenue is useful because regular revenues are reported as a separate item. Irregular or incidental revenues are disclosed elsewhere in the income statement. As a result, trends in revenue from continuing operations (typical business activities) should be easier to identify, understand, and analyze. Similarly, the reporting of gross profit provides a useful number for evaluating performance and assessing future earnings. A study of the trend in gross profits may show **how successfully a company uses its resources** (prices paid for inventory, costs accumulated, wastage); it may also be a basis for **understanding how profit margins have changed** as a result of competitive pressure (which may limit the prices that the company is able to charge for its products and services). Gross profit percentage is a very important ratio in the retail business.

Finally, disclosing income from operations **highlights the difference between regular and irregular or incidental activities**. Disclosure of operating earnings may help in comparing different companies and assessing their operating efficiencies. Note that if Degrootes had **discontinued operations or extraordinary items**, these would be added to the bottom of the statement and shown separately. These items are by definition **atypical and/or nonrecurring** and therefore have **little predictive value**. They do, however, give **feedback value** on past decisions made by management. Net income that consists mainly of net income from continuing operations would be viewed as **higher quality**.

Underlying Concept

This disclosure helps users recognize that incidental or irregular activities are **unlikely to continue at the same level (i.e. it enhances predictive value).**

Illustration 4-5

Multiple-Step Income Statement

DEGROOTES CORPORATION
Income Statement
For the Year Ended December 31, 2007

Sales Revenue			
Sales			$4,053,081
Less: Sales discounts		$ 24,241	
Less: Sales returns and allowances		56,427	80,668
Net sales revenue			3,972,413
Cost of Goods Sold			
Merchandise inventory, Jan. 1, 2007		461,219	
Purchases	$1,989,693		
Less: Purchase discounts	19,270		
Net purchases	1,970,423		
Freight and transportation-in	40,612	2,011,035	
Total merchandise available for sale		2,472,254	
Less: Merchandise inventory, Dec. 31, 2007		489,713	
Cost of goods sold			1,982,541
Gross profit on sales			1,989,872
Operating Expenses			
Selling expenses			
Sales salaries and commissions	202,644		
Sales office salaries	59,200		
Travel and entertainment	48,940		
Advertising expense	38,315		
Freight and transportation-out	41,209		
Shipping supplies and expense	24,712		
Postage and stationery	16,788		
Amortization of sales equipment	9,005		
Telephone and Internet expense	12,215	453,028	

Administrative expenses			
Officers' salaries	186,000		
Office salaries	61,200		
Legal and professional services	23,721		
Utilities expense	23,275		
Insurance expense	17,029		
Amortization of building	18,059		
Amortization of office equipment	16,000		
Stationery, supplies, and postage	2,875		
Miscellaneous office expenses	2,612	350,771	803,799
Income from operations			1,186,073
Other Revenues and Gains			
Rental revenue			171,410
Other Expenses and Losses			
Interest on bonds and notes			126,060
Income before income tax, discontinued operations and extraordinary item			1,231,423
Income tax			369,427
Income before discontinued operations and extraordinary item			861,996
Discontinued Operations (see note X)			
Loss from operations (net of taxes of $34,000)		80,000	
Loss from disposal of division (net of taxes of $21,000)		50,000	130,000
Income before extraordinary item			731,996
Extraordinary gain (net of taxes of $19,500 – see note XX)			45,500
Net income			$ 777,496
Income per common share before discontinued operations and extraordinary gain			$.43
Net income per common share (see note XXX)			$.39

Intermediate Components of the Income Statement

When a multiple-step income statement is used, some or all of the following sections or subsections may be prepared:

INCOME STATEMENT SECTIONS

1. *Continuing Operations*
   (a) Operating Section. A report of the **revenues and expenses** of the company's principal operations.
      i. Sales or Revenue Section. A subsection presenting sales, discounts, allowances, returns, and other related information. Its purpose is to arrive at the net amount of sales revenue.

ii. Cost of Goods Sold Section. A subsection that shows the cost of goods that were sold to produce the sales.

iii. Selling Expenses. A subsection that lists expenses resulting from the company's efforts to make sales.

iv. Administrative or General Expenses. A subsection reporting expenses of general administration.

(b) Non-Operating Section. A report of revenues and expenses resulting from the company's secondary or auxiliary activities. In addition, special gains and losses that are infrequent or unusual, but not both, are normally reported in this section. Generally these items break down into two main subsections:

i. Other Revenues and Gains. A list of the revenues earned or gains incurred from non-operating transactions, and generally net of related expenses.

ii. Other Expenses and Losses. A list of the expenses or losses incurred from non-operating transactions, and generally net of any related income.

(c) Income Tax. A short section reporting income taxes on income from continuing operations.

2. *Discontinued Operations.* Material gains or losses resulting from the disposition of a part of the business (net of taxes).

3. *Extraordinary Items.* Atypical and infrequent material gains and losses beyond the control of management (net of taxes).

4. *Other Comprehensive Income.* Other gains/losses that are not required by primary sources of GAAP to be included in net income. This section includes all other changes in equity that do not relate to shareholder transactions.

Although the **content** of the operating section is generally the same, the **presentation** or organization of the material does not need to be as described above.

Usually, financial statements that are provided to external users have **less detail** than internal management reports. The latter tend to have more expense categories, and they are usually grouped along lines of responsibility. This detail allows top management to judge staff performance.

Whether a single-step or multiple-step income statement is used, **irregular transactions** such as discontinued operations and extraordinary items are **required to be reported separately**, following income from continuing operations.

Condensed Income Statements

In some cases it is impossible to present all the desired expense detail in a single income statement of convenient size. This problem is solved by including only the totals of expense groups in the statement of income and preparing **supplementary schedules** of expenses to support the totals. With this format, the income statement itself may be reduced to a few lines on a single sheet. In such instances, readers who want to study all the reported data on operations must give their attention to the supporting schedules.

Underlying Concept

This contributes to understandability as it reduces "information overload."

The income statement shown in Illustration 4-6 for DeGrootes Corporation is a condensed version of the more detailed multiple-step statement presented earlier and is more typical of what is done in actual practice.

Illustration 4-6
Condensed Income Statement

DEGROOTES CORPORATION
Income Statement
For the Year Ended December 31, 2007

Sales		$3,972,413
Cost of goods sold		1,982,541
Gross profit		1,989,872
Selling expenses (see Note D)	453,028	
Administrative expenses	350,771	803,799
Income from operations		1,186,073
Other revenues and gains		171,410
Other expenses and losses		126,060
Income before income tax		1,231,423
Income tax		369,427
Income before discontinued operations and extraordinary item		$ 861,996
Loss from discontinued operations (net of tax – see note X)		130,000
Income before extraordinary item		$ 731,996
Extraordinary gain (net of tax – see note XX)		45,500
Net income		$ 777,496
Income per common share before discontinued operations and extraordinary gain		$.43
Net income per common share (see note XXX)		$.39

An example of a supporting schedule, cross-referenced as Note D and detailing the selling expenses, is shown in Illustration 4-7.

Illustration 4-7
Sample Supporting Schedule

Note D: Selling expenses	
Sales salaries and commissions	$202,644
Sales office salaries	59,200
Travel and entertainment	48,940
Advertising expense	38,315
Freight and transportation-out	41,209
Shipping supplies and expense	24,712
Postage and stationery	16,788
Amortization of sales equipment	9,005
Telephone and Internet expense	12,215
Total selling expenses	$453,028

Underlying Concept

This is an example of a trade-off between understandability and full disclosure.

Deciding **how much detail** to include in the income statement is always a problem. On the one hand, a simple, summarized statement allows a reader to quickly discover important factors. On the other hand, disclosure of the results of all activities provides users with detailed relevant information. Certain basic elements are always included, but they may be presented in various formats.

REPORTING IRREGULAR ITEMS

4 Objective
Explain how irregular items are reported.

Either the **single-step** or the **multiple-step** income statement may be used for financial reporting purposes, which means there is some flexibility in presenting the income components. In two important areas, however, specific guidelines have been developed. These two areas relate to what is included in income and how certain unusual or irregular items are reported.

What should be included in net income has been a controversy for many years. For example, should irregular gains and losses, corrections of revenues and prior year's expenses, and non-operating changes in equity be treated differently from ongoing revenues and expenses from operating activities? One option is to book these items directly to retained earnings or a separate equity section, i.e., not book them through the income statement.

Currently, income measurement follows a modified **all-inclusive approach**. This approach indicates that most items, even irregular ones, are recorded in income.[10] Some exceptions include:

1. **Errors** in the income measurement of prior years
2. **Changes in accounting policies that are applied retroactively**

Because these items relate to earnings that were already reported in a prior period, they are not included in current income. Rather, they are recorded as adjustments to retained earnings.[11] Note that certain other items are included in other comprehensive income, which is excluded from the net income calculation but included in comprehensive income.

Illustration 4-8 identifies the most common types of irregular items and numbers of each that were reported in a survey of 200 large companies.[12] As indicated, unusual items, which often contain write-offs and other one-time items, were reported by more than 80 percent of the surveyed firms. About 34 percent of the surveyed firms reported discontinued operations. Thus, developing a framework for reporting irregular items is important to ensure that financial statement users have relevant, high-quality income information.[13]

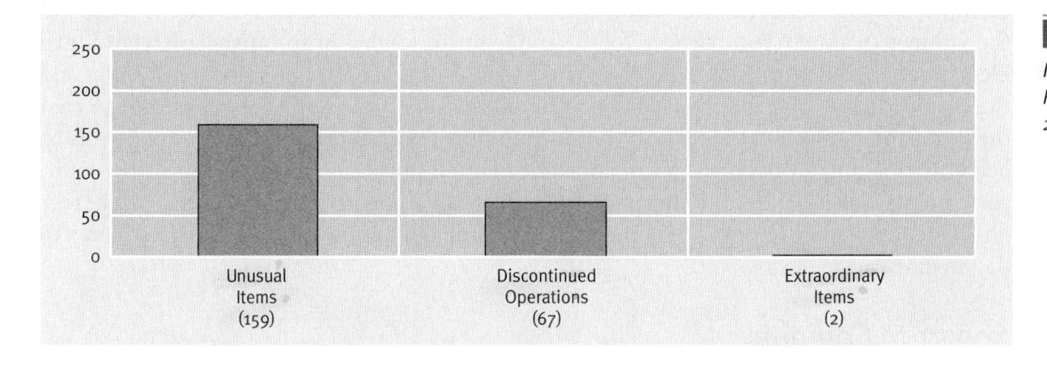

Illustration 4-8
Number of Irregular Items Reported in 2004 by 200 Public Companies

[10] *CICA Handbook*, Section 1000.27. The modified all-inclusive approach is substantially consistent with a **capital maintenance approach** to measuring income since net income is equal to a change in net assets excluding capital transactions. *CICA Handbook* Section 1000.55 notes that financial statements are prepared with capital maintenance measured in financial terms.

[11] *CICA Handbook*, Section 1506.31.

[12] Chapters 11, 39, and 40, *Financial Reporting in Canada*, 2005 (Toronto, CICA).

[13] As noted earlier, the AcSB, IASB, and FASB are currently working on projects dealing with financial statement presentation. The objective is to improve the quality of information presented in the income and cash flow statements. The work completed thus far supports the all-inclusive or comprehensive income approach.

Some users support a **current operating performance approach** to income reporting. They argue that the most useful income measures are the ones that reflect only regular and recurring revenue and expense elements—i.e., normalized, sustainable earnings. Irregular items do not reflect an enterprise's future earning power since, by definition, they are irregular and atypical or non-recurring. Operating income supporters believe that including one-time items such as write-offs and restructuring charges reduces the income measure's basic **predictive value**.

In contrast, others warn that a focus on operating income potentially misses important information about a firm's performance. Any gain or loss that is experienced by the firm, whether it is directly or indirectly related to operations, contributes to the firm's long-run profitability. As one analyst notes, "write-offs matter .... They speak to the volatility of (past) earnings."[14] In other words, they have **feedback value**. As a result, some non-operating items can be used to assess the riskiness of future earnings—and therefore have **predictive value**. Furthermore, determining which items are (regular) **operating** items and which are **irregular** requires judgement and this could lead to differences in the treatment of irregular items and to possible manipulation of income measures.

Discontinued Operations

As indicated in Illustration 4-8, one of the most common types of irregular items relates to **discontinued operations**. Discontinued operations include **components of an enterprise** that have been **disposed of** (by sale, abandonment, or spin-off) **or** are classified as **held for sale**, where:

- the **operations and cash flows** have been, or will be, **eliminated**, and
- the enterprise will **not have any continuing involvement**.[15]

What Do the Numbers Mean?

Companies might discontinue operations as part of a downsizing strategy to improve their operating results, to focus on core operations, or even to generate cash flows. For example, Napster Inc. (formerly Roxio Inc.), whose shares trade on Nasdaq Canada, was the subject of much controversy for helping music lovers swap music for free. Until December 17, 2004, the company had two divisions—the consumer software division and the on-line music distribution division. The consumer software division was sold so that the company could focus solely on the on-line music distribution business. Its goal is to become a leading global provider of consumer digital music services. Currently, the company boasts that it is the only legal on-line advertising supported service that offers free on-demand music listening. Since the sale, the company has devoted all of its resources to the on-line music business.

Separate Component

In order to qualify for separate presentation on the income statement, the discontinued business must be a **component of an entity** (a **business component**) where the **operations, cash flows, and financial elements are clearly distinguishable** from the rest of the enterprise. A component can be any one of the following:

- A **reportable** or **operating segment** as defined in *CICA Handbook* Section 1701—Segmented Reporting
- A **reporting unit** as defined in *CICA Handbook* Section 3062 in testing for goodwill impairment

---

[14] D. McDermott, "Latest Profit Data Stir Old Debate between Net and Operating Income," *The Wall Street Journal*, May 3, 1999.

[15] *CICA Handbook*, Section 3475.27.

- A **subsidiary**
- An **asset group** as defined in *CICA Handbook* Section 3063 for impairment of long-lived assets[16]

Student Toolkit—Additional Disclosures

Basically, a component consists of a **unit of operation**, which may be as small as a hotel or an apartment building that is being rented out, or as large as a major subsidiary. In terms of discontinued operations, when does the **disposal of an asset** constitute a **disposal of a component? The key elements are that the asset or group of assets generates its own net cash flows and is operationally distinct (i.e., it operates as a separate unit).**

Illustration 4-9 gives a conceptual view of what constitutes a component in terms of discontinued operations.

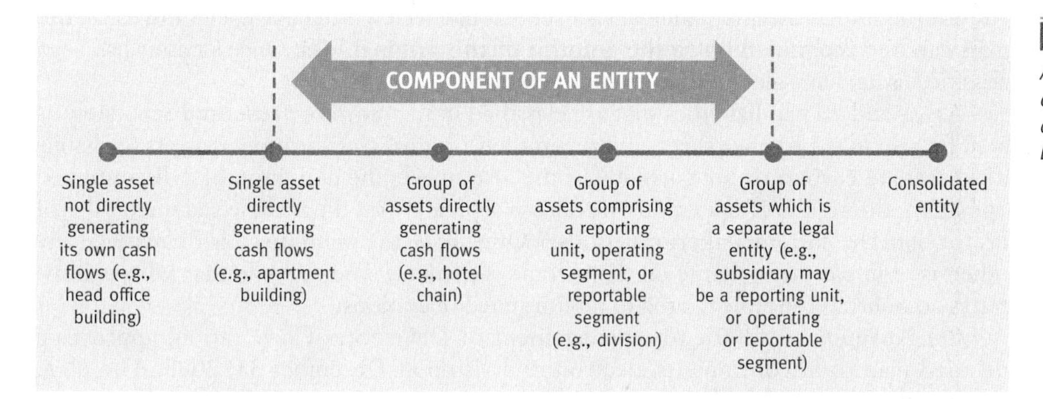

Illustration 4-9

A Conceptual View of a Component of an Entity in Terms of Discontinued Operations

As noted above, the operations and cash flows from the component must be eliminated from the ongoing operations and the entity must not have continuing involvement. Generally, this will be the case in a straight-forward sale.[17]

Assets Held for Sale

If the component is not yet disposed of, an additional condition must be met before the transaction can be given a different presentation on the income statement. This condition is that the assets relating to the component must be considered to be **held for sale** by the company. Assets are considered to be held for sale when all of the following criteria are met:

- There is an **authorized plan** to sell.
- The asset is **available for immediate sale** in its current state.
- There is an **active program** to find a buyer.
- Sale is **probable** within one year.
- The asset is **reasonably priced** and actively marketed.
- **Changes** to the plan are **unlikely**.[18]

---

[16] *CICA Handbook*, Section 3475.28.

[17] EIC Abstract 153 discusses this issue in greater detail. Cash flows might not be seen to be eliminated for instance, where the entity continues to sell products to the disposed component or to its customers. Continuing involvement might be evidenced where the entity retains an ownership interest in the disposed component or where it provides management services. Consideration would be given to the significance of the cash flows or continuing involvement.

[18] *CICA Handbook*, Section 3475.08.

In summary, for accounting purposes, assets may be considered as held for sale when there is a **formal plan** to dispose of the component. This ensures that only assets for which management has a detailed, approved plan for disposal get treated as discontinued operations. Note that assets that are held for sale might not (and do not need to) meet the definition of discontinued operations. Where this is the case, these assets, as noted below, would be measured and presented the same way (as if they were discontinued operations) on the balance sheet, but any related gains or losses would be recorded as part of income from continuing operations.

Measurement and Presentation

When an asset is held for sale regardless of whether it meets the definition of a discontinued operation, the asset is **remeasured** to the lower of its carrying value and fair value less its cost to sell.[19] Note that if the value of an asset that has been written down later increases, **the gain can be recognized up to the amount of the original loss**. Once an asset has been classified as held for sale, **no further depreciation is recognized**.

Assets and related liabilities that are classified in this way are **presented** separately as held for sale in the balance sheet, and retain their original classification as assets (or liabilities) that are current or noncurrent.[20] If the asset meets the definition of a discontinued operation, the results of operations are shown separately on the income statement, net of tax for both the current and prior periods.[21] Otherwise, the write-down is treated like any other asset impairment charge on the income statement. The example that follows illustrates accounting concepts related to discontinued operations.

On November 1, 2007, top management of DeGrootes Corporation, approves a detailed plan to discontinue its electronics division at December 31, 2008. The plan, among other things, identifies steps to find a buyer and includes a timeline for disposition, along with a calculation of the expected gain or loss on disposition. The business is available for sale immediately.

As top management has approved the disposal and has stated in reasonable detail which assets are to be disposed of and how, a **formal plan** exists. The division is a separate business (being a division) that is therefore operationally distinct, with separate cash flows. Since it is a division, it will also have separate financial information and is thus a business component. Separate financial information is critical so that the gain or loss from discontinued operations can be properly **measured**. The company will have no continuing involvement in the electronics division after it is sold.

Assume that during the year, the electronics division for Degrootes lost $80,000 (net of tax of $34,000) and that the assets were sold the following year at a loss of $50,000 (net of tax of $21,000). The assets and liabilities relating to the division would be segregated on the balance sheet as follows, according to their exact nature:

- current assets: as "current assets held for sale/related to discontinued operations"
- noncurrent assets: as "noncurrent assets held for sale/related to discontinued operations"
- current liabilities: as "current liabilities related to assets held for sale/discontinued"
- long-term liabilities: as "long-term liabilities related to assets held for sale/discontinued"

Assume that the company had estimated that the asset impairment as at year end was $50,000 net of tax. The information would be shown as in Illustration 4-5 on the current year's annual income statement.

---

[19] *CICA Handbook*, Section 3475.13.

[20] *CICA Handbook*, Section 3475.33.

[21] *CICA Handbook*, Section 3475.30.

The company would then stop recording depreciation on the division's assets and, in the following year, would show any operating losses or profits and/or revised gain or loss on disposal as discontinued operations. Estimated future losses would not be included in the loss from operations since they would already be implied (and therefore included) in the fair value estimate of the assets held for sale or sold. Note that the phrase "Income from continuing operations" is only used when gains or losses on discontinued operations or extraordinary items occur. Note that the company would, in addition to the detail shown on the income statement, make additional note disclosures including a description of the disposal. The detail shown on the face of the income statement (breakdown between earnings/loss from operations and gain/loss from sale) could also be shown in the notes.[22]

5 Objective
Measure and report results of discontinued operations.

International Insight

The classification of items as "extraordinary" differs across nations. Even in countries where the criteria for identifying extraordinary items are similar, these criteria are not interpreted identically. Thus, what is extraordinary in North America is not necessarily extraordinary elsewhere.

Extraordinary Items

Extraordinary items are material, non-recurring items that are significantly different from the entity's typical business activities.[23] They are presented separately on the income statement in order to provide enough detail to have predictive value. The three criteria that must all be met for items to be considered extraordinary are as follows. They must:

1. be **infrequent**
2. be **atypical** of normal business activities of the company
3. not depend mainly on **decisions or determinations by management** or owners[24]

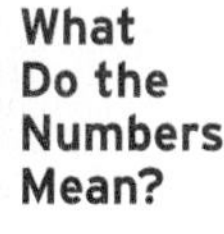

What Do the Numbers Mean?

Professional judgement must be used when deciding whether these three criteria are met; indeed, because of the third criterion, very few extraordinary items are actually reported. How infrequent is infrequent, the first criterion? Consideration should be given to how often an event has occurred in the past and may recur in the future. For instance, in 2001, a fibre optics cable supplying 315,000 high-speed Internet customers of **Rogers Cable Inc.** (Rogers) was damaged. This was the second time that it had been damaged in a month. Twice in one month would appear to meet the criterion of frequency for the current year; however, a review of the existence of past damage would confirm whether this was a frequent occurrence for the company over time.

The second criterion to determine whether or not an event is atypical also involves the use of professional judgement. As a starting point, **typical business activities** should be identified. What is the company's business and what are typical activities and business risks? Consider the Rogers example above. Rogers is a subsidiary of **Rogers Communications Inc.** and is in the business of supplying high-speed cable access to homes and industry for cable television and Internet services. Fixed assets, which include land and distribution cable, account for 51 percent of the company's total assets, which is pretty significant. Is damage to high-speed fibre optics cables considered a typical business risk? The cables are normally buried and therefore less likely to be damaged by animals and vandals; however, in this case, they were exposed as they were being repaired. One factor to consider is whether the company insures itself against such losses. If so, this may be an acknowledgement that the company feels that this risk is typical and significant enough to cover with insurance.

If a company was completely insured against every possible risk, no loss would ever occur from extraordinary items; however, sometimes companies are not able to obtain

[22] *CICA Handbook*, Section 3475.36 and .37.

[23] It is often difficult to determine what is extraordinary, because assessing the materiality of individual items requires judgement. However, in making materiality judgements, extraordinary items should be considered individually, and not together (*CICA Handbook*, Section 3480.09).

[24] *CICA Handbook*, Section 3480.02.

insurance for complete coverage. In such cases, if a loss occurs, part of it will be borne by the company itself. Also, even if a company can get complete coverage, the costs to completely insure against all risks are too high to be acceptable. Thus, a company must make decisions about what to insure itself against.

What Do the Numbers Mean?

No recent event better illustrates the difficulties of determining whether a transaction meets the definition of extraordinary than the financial impact of the terrorist attacks on the World Trade Center on September 11, 2001. To many, this event, which resulted in the tragic loss of lives, jobs, and in some cases, entire businesses, clearly meets the criteria for unusual and infrequent. For example, airlines, insurance companies, and other businesses recorded major losses due to property damage, business disruption, and the suspension of airline travel and of securities trading. But, to the surprise of many, extraordinary item reporting was not permitted for losses arising from the terrorist attacks.

The reason? After much deliberation, the Emerging Issues Task Force (EITF) of the FASB decided that measuring the possible loss was too difficult. Take the airline industry as an example. What portion of the airlines' losses after September 11 was related to the terrorist attack, and what portion was due to the ongoing recession? There was also concern that some companies would use the attacks as a reason for reporting as extraordinary some losses that had little direct relationship to the attacks. For example, shortly after the attacks, energy company AES and shoe retailer Footstar, both of which were experiencing profit pressure before the attacks, put some of the blame for their poor performance on the attacks.[25]

The third criterion looks at **management involvement**. The event must not depend on or result from a management or owner decision. This third criterion ensures that items that are classified as extraordinary items are beyond management control. Thus, decisions to sell assets at losses, or to downsize or restructure, and other similar expenses are not considered extraordinary.

For further clarification, the CICA specifies that the following gains and losses are **not** extraordinary items:

1. Losses and provisions for losses from bad debt and inventories
2. Gains and losses from fluctuations in foreign exchange rates
3. Adjustments on contract prices
4. Gains and losses from write-downs or the sale of property, plant and equipment, or other investments
5. Income tax reductions that are created by claiming losses from prior periods or reversal of previously recorded tax benefits
6. Changes in income tax rates or laws[26]

The items listed above are not considered extraordinary, because they are **usual in nature** and may be **expected to recur** as a consequence of customary and continuing business activities.

In determining whether an item is extraordinary, the environment in which the entity operates is very important. The environment includes such factors as industry characteristics, geographic location, and the nature and amount of government regulations. Thus, a loss from hail damage is only treated as an extraordinary item for a tobacco grower's crops if severe damage from hailstorms is rare where the grower is located. Thus, frost damage to a citrus grower's crop in Florida does not qualify as extraordinary, because frost damage

[25] J. Creswell, "Bad News Bearers Shift the Blame," *Fortune* (October 15, 2001), p. 44.

[26] *CICA Handbook*, Section 3480.04.

is normally experienced there every three or four years. In this environment, the criterion of infrequency is not met.

Extraordinary items are shown **net of taxes** in a separate section in the income statement, usually just before net income.[27]

Unusual Gains and Losses

Because of the restrictive criteria for extraordinary items, financial statement users must carefully examine the financial statements for items that meet only some of the criteria for presentation as an extraordinary item, but not all three. As indicated earlier, items such as write-downs of inventories and gains and losses from fluctuations of foreign exchange are not considered extraordinary items. Thus, these items are sometimes shown with the normal, recurring revenues, costs, and expenses. If they are not material in amount, they are combined with other items in the income statement. If they are material, they are disclosed separately, but are shown above "income (loss) before extraordinary items."

For example, in the last three years, Teck Cominco Limited, a diversified mining and refining company, presented an unusual charge for an investment write-down as well as an unusual gain on disposition of property, as shown in Illustration 4-10.

Illustration 4-10

Income Statement Presentation of Unusual Charges

Consolidated Statements of Earnings
Years ended December 31

($ in millions, except share data)	2005	2004	2003
Revenues	**$ 4,415**	$ 3,428	$ 2,228
Operating expenses	**(2,135)**	(2,029)	(1,735)
Depreciation and amortization	**(274)**	(275)	(223)
Operating profit	**2,006**	1,124	270
Other expenses			
General, administration and marketing	**(89)**	(68)	(55)
Interest on long-term debt (Note 17)	**(69)**	(61)	(65)
Exploration	**(70)**	(42)	(30)
Research and development	**(13)**	(14)	(14)
Other income (Note 18)	**155**	24	1
Writedown of investment (Note 7)	–	(64)	–
Gain on disposition of Los Filos property (Note 4(f))	–	–	58
	1,920	899	165
Provision for income and resource taxes (Note 19)	**(575)**	(305)	(50)
Equity earnings (Note 4(e))	–	–	10
Net earnings from continuing operations	**1,345**	594	125
Net earnings from discontinued operation (Note 4(c))	–	23	9
Net earnings	**$ 1,345**	$ 617	$ 134
Basic earnings per share (Note 16(k))	**$ 6.62**	$ 3.18	$ 0.71
Basic earnings per share from continuing operations	**$ 6.62**	$ 3.06	$ 0.66
Diluted earnings per share	**$ 6.22**	$ 2.99	$ 0.68
Diluted earnings per share from continuing operations	**$ 6.22**	$ 2.88	$ 0.64
Weighted average shares outstanding (millions)	**202.5**	193.0	184.8
Shares outstanding at the end of the year (millions)	**203.4**	201.4	186.5

Student Toolkit—Additional Disclosures

www.wiley.com/canada/kieso

[27] CICA *Handbook* Section 1581, *Business Combinations*, allows part of the excess of the fair value of acquired net assets over their cost in a business combination to be treated as an extraordinary item even though it might not necessarily meet the definition of an extraordinary item. In essence, the excess represents a type of windfall to the company, with the company presumed to have received greater value than what it paid when acquiring the other company. The resulting gain is therefore separated from the other income and expense items on the income statement.

As indicated in Illustration 4-8, unusual items have been common in recent years. There has been a tendency to report unusual items in a separate section just above income from operations before income taxes and extraordinary items.[28]

Changes in Estimates

Another type of change involves changes in estimates. Estimates are inherent in the accounting process. Estimates are made, for example, of useful lives and salvage values of depreciable assets, of uncollectible receivables, of inventory obsolescence, and of the number of periods that a particular expenditure is expected to benefit. Often enough, as time passes, as circumstances change, or as additional information is obtained, even estimates that were originally made in good faith must be changed. Such **changes in estimates** are accounted for in the period of change if they affect only that period, or in the period of change and future periods if the change affects both.

To illustrate a change in estimate that affects only the period of change, assume that DuPage Materials Corp. has consistently estimated its bad debt expense at 1% of credit sales. In 2007, however, DuPage's controller determines that the estimate of bad debts for the current year's credit sales must be revised upward to 2%, or double the previous year's percentage. Using 2% results in a bad debt charge of $240,000, or double the amount using the 1% estimate for prior years. The expense is recorded at December 31, 2007, as follows:

A	= L +	SE
−240,000		−240,000

Cash flows: No effect

Bad Debt Expense	240,000	
Allowance for Doubtful Accounts		240,000

The entire change in estimate is included in the 2007 income because it reflects decisions made and information available in the current year and no future periods are affected by the change. Changes in estimate are not handled retroactively; that is, they are not carried back to adjust prior years.

All accounting changes (including corrections of errors) will be examined further in Chapter 21.

SPECIAL REPORTING ISSUES

Intraperiod Tax Allocation

Objective 6
Explain intraperiod tax allocation.

As previously noted, certain irregular items are shown on the income statement net of tax, which is a more informative disclosure to statement users. This procedure of allocating tax balances within a period is called **intraperiod tax allocation**. Intraperiod tax allocation relates the income tax expense or benefit of the fiscal period to the underlying income statement items and events that are being taxed. Intraperiod tax allocation is used for the following items: (1) income from continuing operations, (2) discontinued operations, (3) extraordinary items, and (4) other comprehensive income (which will be discussed later in this chapter).

The income tax expense that is attributed to income from continuing operations is calculated by finding the income tax expense related to the revenue and expense transactions

[28] Some companies report items such as restructuring charges every year as unusual items. Research on the market reaction to income containing one-time items indicates that the market discounts the earnings of companies that report a series of non-recurring items. Such evidence supports the argument that these elements reduce the quality of earnings. See J. Elliot and D. Hanna, "Repeat Accounting Write-Offs and the Information Content of Earnings," *Journal of Accounting Research* (Supplement, 1996).

that are used in determining this income. In this tax calculation, the tax consequences of the items that are excluded from the determination of income from continuing operations are not considered. A separate tax effect is then associated with each irregular item.

In applying the concept of intraperiod tax allocation, assume that Schindler Corp. has income before income tax and extraordinary item of $250,000 and an extraordinary gain from the expropriation of land by the government of $100,000. If the income tax rate is assumed to be 40%, the information in Illustration 4-11 is presented on the income statement.

Income before income tax and extraordinary item	$250,000
Income tax	100,000
Income before extraordinary item	150,000
Extraordinary gain net of applicable taxes of (40,000)	60,000
Net income	$210,000

Illustration 4-11
Intraperiod Tax Allocation, Extraordinary Gain

The income tax of $100,000 ($250,000 × 40%) that is attributed to income before income tax and extraordinary item is determined from the revenue and expense transactions related to this income. In this income tax calculation, the tax consequences of items excluded from the determination of income before income tax and extraordinary item are not considered. The "extraordinary gain" then shows a separate tax effect of $40,000.

Earnings per Share

7 **Objective**
Explain where earnings per share information is reported.

Typically, the results of a company's operations are summed up in one important figure: net income. As if this simplification were not enough, the financial world has widely accepted an even more distilled and compact figure as its most significant business indicator: **earnings per share**. Many users focus primarily on the earnings per share number (rightly or wrongly) as a key indicator of the company's performance. While the earnings per share number yields significant information, it does not tell the whole story. This undue emphasis on earnings per share makes it a very sensitive number for companies.

The calculation of earnings per share is usually straightforward. Net income minus preferred dividends (income available to common shareholders) is divided by the weighted average number of common shares outstanding to arrive at earnings per share. To illustrate, assume that Lancer Inc. reports net income of $350,000 and declares and pays preferred dividends of $50,000 for the year. The weighted average number of common shares outstanding during the year is 100,000 shares. Earnings per share is $3.00, as calculated in Illustration 4-12.

$$\frac{\text{Net Income} - \text{Preferred Dividends}}{\text{Weighted Average Number of Common Shares Outstanding}}$$

$$= \text{Earnings per Share (EPS)}$$

$$= \frac{\$350{,}000 - 50{,}000}{100{,}000}$$

$$= \$3.00$$

Illustration 4-12
Sample Calculation of Earnings per Share

Note that the EPS figure measures the number of dollars earned by each common share but not the dollar amount paid to shareholders in the form of dividends.

"Net income per share" or "earnings per share" is a ratio that commonly appears in prospectuses, proxy material, and annual reports to shareholders. It is also highlighted in

Student Toolkit—Additional Disclosures

www.wiley.com/canada/kieso

the financial press, by statistical services like **Standard & Poor's**, and by Bay Street securities analysts. Because of its importance, companies are required to disclose earnings per share on the face of their income statement. In addition, a company that reports a discontinued operation or an extraordinary item must report earnings per share for income before discontinued operations and extraordinary items as well as per share amounts for these line items either on the face of the income statement or in the notes to the financial statements.[29] Illustration 4-10 shows how earnings per share may be presented.

Many corporations have simple capital structures that include only common shares. For these companies, a presentation such as earnings per common share is appropriate on the income statement. In many instances, however, companies' earnings per share are subject to dilution (reduction) in the future because existing contingencies allow future issues of additional common shares. These corporations would present both basic EPS and fully diluted EPS.[30]

In summary, the simplicity and availability of figures for per share earnings lead inevitably to their being used widely. Because of the excessive importance that the public—even the well-informed public—attaches to earnings per share, this information must be made as meaningful as possible.

Retained Earnings Statement

Objective 8
Prepare a retained earnings statement.

Retained earnings is affected by many variables and can be presented in may different ways. Net income increases retained earnings and a net loss decreases retained earnings. Both cash and share dividends decrease retained earnings. Retroactively applied changes in accounting principles and corrections of errors may either increase or decrease retained earnings. Information on retained earnings, including the changes it has undergone, can be shown in different ways. For example, many companies prepare a separate retained earnings statement,[31] as shown in Illustration 4-13.

Illustration 4-13
Retained Earnings Statement

WOODS INC.
Retained Earnings Statement
For the Year Ended December 31, 2008

Balance, January 1, as reported		$1,050,000
Correction for understatement of net income in prior period (inventory error) (net of taxes of $35,000)		50,000
Balance, January 1, as adjusted		1,100,000
Add: Net income		360,000
		1,460,000
Less: Cash dividends	$100,000	
Less: Stock dividends	200,000	300,000
Balance, December 31		$1,160,000

The reconciliation of the beginning to the ending balance in retained earnings provides information about why net assets increased or decreased during the year. The association of dividend distributions with net income for the period indicates what management

[29] *CICA Handbook*, Section 3500.60 and .61.

[30] Earnings per share will be covered in significant detail in Chapter 17.

[31] Chapter 6 of *Financial Reporting in Canada, 2005* (Toronto, CICA) notes that in 2004, 148 out of 200 public companies presented the statement of retained earnings as a separate statement.

is doing with earnings: it may be plowing part or all of the earnings back into the business, distributing all current income, or distributing current income plus the accumulated earnings of prior years. Note that the retained earnings statement may be combined with the income statement by adding it to the bottom of the income statement. Illustration 4-14 shows such a combined statement.

Illustration 4-14

Combined Income and Retained Earnings Statement for Tenke Mining Corp.

TENKE MINING CORP.
CONSOLIDATED STATEMENTS OF OPERATIONS AND DEFICIT
(In US Dollars)

	Year ended December 31, 2005	Year ended December 31, 2004
Expenses		
Amortization	1,027	792
General exploration and project investigation	293,815	133,870
Interest and bank charges	9,227	8,319
Management fees (Note 8(a))	145,431	120,086
Consulting	50,161	45,833
Donation	10,545	9,771
Office and general	32,923	10,001
Professional fees	281,347	204,995
Promotion and public relations	427,350	113,413
Stock based compensation (Note 6(b))	167,056	943,869
Stock exchange and filing fees	96,340	67,767
Telephone and facsimile	17,304	9,381
Transfer agent and shareholder information	43,747	22,785
Travel	578,633	19,779
Wages and benefits	289,746	118,137
	2,444,652	1,828,798
Other (income) expenses		
Interest income	(224,331)	(87,902)
Foreign exchange gain	(71,742)	(337,628)
Write-off of mineral property interests	551,219	760,466
Loss for the year	2,699,798	2,163,734
Deficit, beginning of the year	133,994,244	131,830,510
Deficit, end of the year	$ 136,694,042	$ 133,994,244
Basic and diluted loss per common share	$ 0.06	$ 0.05
Weighted average number of shares outstanding	48,553,949	45,297,770

Changes in Accounting Principle

Underlying Concept

Retroactive application ensures consistency.

Changes in accounting occur frequently in practice, because important events or conditions may be in dispute or uncertain at the statement date. One type of accounting change is when a different accounting principle is adopted to replace the one previously used. **Changes in accounting principle** would include, for example, a change in the method of inventory pricing from FIFO to average cost. Accounting changes are only allowed if they are required by a primary source of GAAP or if they result in reliable and more relevant information.[32]

Changes in accounting principle are generally recognized through **retrospective restatement**, which involves determining the effect of the policy change on the income of prior periods that are affected. The financial statements for all prior periods that are

[32] *CICA Handbook*, Section 1506.14.

presented for comparative purposes should be restated except when the effect cannot be determined reasonably. If all comparative years are not disclosed, a cumulative amount would instead be calculated and adjusted through the opening retained earnings amount.

To illustrate, Gaubert Inc. decided in March 2007 to change from the FIFO method of valuing inventory to the weighted average method. If prices are rising, cost of sales would be higher and ending inventory lower for the preceding period.

Illustration 4-15 shows what should be presented in the 2007 financial statements.

Illustration 4-15
Income Statement Presentation of a Change in Accounting Principle

Retained earnings, January 1, 2007 as previously reported	$120,000
Cumulative effect on prior years of retrospective application of new inventory costing method (net of $9,000 tax)	14,000
Adjusted balance of retained earnings, January 1, 2007	$106,000

The journal entry would be:

A	= L +	SE
−14,000		−14,000

Cash flows: No effect

Taxes Receivable	9,000	
Retained Earnings	14,000	
Inventory		23,000

The example in the illustration assumes that no comparative data for prior years are shown. A note describing the change and its impact would also be required.

Comprehensive Income

Objective 9
Explain how comprehensive income is reported.

Comprehensive income includes all changes in equity during a period except for the changes that result from investments by owners and distributions to owners. Comprehensive income therefore includes all revenues and gains and expenses and losses reported in net income, and, in addition, gains and losses that bypass net income but affect shareholders' equity. These items that bypass the income statement are recorded in an account called **Other Comprehensive Income**. Comprehensive income is equal to net income plus other comprehensive income.

Student Toolkit–Additional Disclosures

www.wiley.com/canada/kieso

An example of one of the items that is included in other comprehensive income is unrealized gains and losses on available-for-sale securities.[33] Why are they excluded from net income? Because disclosing them separately (1) highlights the impact on net income due to fluctuations in fair value, and (2) informs the financial statement user of the gain or loss that would be incurred if the securities were sold at fair value. There is otherwise little theoretical justification for segregating items such as this from net income. Over time, comprehensive income will likely become net income. The creation of this separate and distinct category outside of net income serves to transition GAAP over to a more all inclusive concept of net income.

The AcSB decided that the components of other comprehensive income must be displayed in a financial statement with the same prominence as other key financial statements.[34]

[33] Available-for-sale securities are further discussed in Chapter 9. Other examples of comprehensive items are certain translation gains and losses on foreign currency and unrealized gains and losses on certain hedging transactions.

[34] *CICA Handbook*, Section 1530.04.

This may be done, for instance, by expanding the income statement or the statement of shareholders' equity, or by adding another separate statement.[35] Regardless of the format, net income must be added to other comprehensive income to arrive at comprehensive income. Earnings per share information related to comprehensive income is not required.[36]

Note that a company is not required to use the terms "Other comprehensive income" or "Comprehensive income."

Combined Income and Comprehensive Income Statement

To illustrate these presentation formats, assume that V. Gill Inc. reports the following information for 2008: sales revenue $800,000; cost of goods sold $600,000; operating expenses $90,000; and an unrealized holding gain on available-for-sale securities of $30,000, net of tax.

The combined income statement format is shown in Illustration 4-16 below. The relationship of the traditional income statement to the comprehensive income statement is apparent because net income is the starting point in the comprehensive income statement.

Illustration 4-16

Combined Income and Comprehensive Income Statement

V. GILL INC.
Statement of Income and Comprehensive Income
For the Year Ended December 31, 2008

Sales revenue	$800,000
Cost of goods sold	600,000
Gross profit	200,000
Operating expenses	90,000
Net income	110,000
Other comprehensive income	
Unrealized holding gain, net of tax	30,000
Comprehensive income	$140,000

The combined statement has the advantage of not requiring the creation of a new financial statement. However, burying net income in a subtotal on the statement is a disadvantage.

Statement of Shareholders' Equity

The statement of shareholders' equity reports the changes in each shareholder's equity account and in total shareholders' equity during the year, including comprehensive income. The statement of shareholders' equity is often **prepared in columnar form** with columns for each account and for total shareholders' equity.

To illustrate its presentation, assume the same information for V. Gill Inc. and that the company had the following shareholders' equity account balances at the beginning of 2008: Common Shares $300,000; Retained Earnings $50,000; and Accumulated Other Comprehensive Income $60,000. No changes in the Common Shares account occurred during the year. A statement of shareholders' equity for V. Gill Inc. is shown in Illustration 4-17.

[35] *CICA Handbook*, Section 1530.08.

[36] A company is required to display the components of other comprehensive income and related tax effects.

Illustration 4-17

Presentation of Comprehensive Income Items in Shareholders' Equity Statement

V. GILL INC.
Statement of Shareholders' Equity
For the Year Ended December 31, 2008

	Total	Common Shares	Comprehensive Income	Retained Earnings	Accumulated Other Comprehensive Income
Beginning balance	$410,000	$300,000		$ 50,000	$60,000
Net income	110,000		$110,000	110,000	
Other comprehensive income					
Unrealized holding gain, net of tax	30,000		30,000		30,000
Comprehensive income			$140,000		
Ending balance	$550,000	$300,000		$160,000	$90,000

Because many companies already provide a statement of shareholders' equity, adding additional columns to display information related to comprehensive income is not costly. The other comprehensive income is accumulated in an account called Accumulated Other Comprehensive Income, as shown in Illustration 4-18. This account acts like a second Retained Earnings account.

Balance Sheet Presentation

Regardless of the display format chosen, the **accumulated other comprehensive income** of $90,000 is reported in the shareholders' equity section of the balance sheet of V. Gill Inc. as shown in Illustration 4-18.

Illustration 4-18

Presentation of Accumulated Other Comprehensive Income in the Balance Sheet

V. GILL INC.
Balance Sheet
As at December 31, 2008
(Shareholders' Equity Section)

Shareholders' equity	
Common shares	$300,000
Retained earnings	160,000
Accumulated other comprehensive income	90,000
Total shareholders' equity	$550,000

By providing information on the components of comprehensive income as well as total accumulated other comprehensive income, the company communicates information about all changes in net assets.[37] With this information, users will be better able to understand the quality of the company's earnings. This information should help users predict the amounts, timing, and uncertainty of future cash flows.

Perspectives

Financial analysts assess quality of earnings and factor it into their decisions. They are often looking to see what additional information the income statements provide in terms

[37] Note that prior period adjustments and the cumulative effect of changes in accounting principle are not considered other comprehensive income items.

of valuing the company's shares. When valuing the shares, analysts look at how good the numbers are at the financial statement date and then they determine whether the company can continue to produce similar or better earnings in the future.

Some attributes of high-quality earnings were expressed in Illustration 4-2. To assess the quality of earnings, look for and analyze the following:

- **accounting policies**—aggressive accounting policies, soft numbers
- **notes to financial statements**—unrecognized liabilities and asset overstatement and, in general, measurement uncertainty
- **financial statements** as a whole—complexity of presentation or language (which may obscure the company's performance or financial position)
- **income statement**—percentage of net income derived from ongoing operations, to see whether the company can produce profits mainly from its core business
- **cash flow statement**—cash from operating activities versus net income, to get a sense of whether net income is backed by cash or not
- **balance sheet**—to see how the company is financed and what the revenue-generating assets are
- **other**—environmental factors such as the industry and economy. How is the company doing compared with its competitors? How is it positioning itself to take advantage of opportunities and manage risk? Where is the industry going? Are current earnings likely to be repeated in the future?

Companies often try to help users assess the results of operations and their financial position by providing modified GAAP information such as **pro forma earnings**. Pro forma earnings start with GAAP net income and add back or deduct nonrecurring or non-operating items to arrive at an adjusted net income number. Pro forma earnings are not bad per se. If the calculation of the pro forma earnings is **clearly disclosed and explained**, and is also reconciled to net income, it can add value to the decision-making process. The danger with these numbers is that there are no standards to ensure that the calculation is **consistently** prepared and **comparable** between companies.

International

The IASB has been working on its *Performance Reporting* project since September 2001. In October 2001, the FASB also began to work on a similar project. There was concern that the two projects were diverging in focus, and so, in April of 2004, the IASB and FASB decided to work together to come up with a joint, converged standard. In March of 2006, the name of the project was changed to *Financial Statement Presentation* and it now consists of three phases as follows:

Phase A—What constitutes a complete set of financial statements

Phase B—Presentation of information on the face of the statements

Phase C—Interim financial reporting

Phase A brings the IAS in line with the U.S. and Canadian standards on comprehensive income. The exposure draft was issued in March of 2006 for comment by July 2006. Working principles for Phase B which have been agreed upon state that the financial statements should:

- provide a cohesive financial picture of an entity;
- provide information to help users assess the liquidity of an entity;

- separate the financing activities from other activities;
- provide information about the measurement of assets and liabilities; and
- disaggregate information and present subtotals and totals.

The IASB plans to issue a discussion paper/exposure draft by the first quarter of 2007. A final standard is expected two years after that.

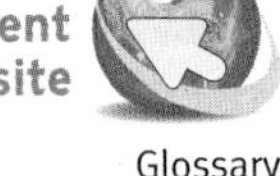

Glossary

www.wiley.com/canada/kieso

Summary of Learning Objectives

1 Identify the uses and limitations of an income statement.

The income statement provides investors and creditors with information that helps them predict the amounts, timing, and uncertainty of future cash flows. It also helps users determine the risk (level of uncertainty) of not achieving particular cash flows. The limitations of an income statement are that (1) the statement does not include many items that contribute to the general growth and well-being of an enterprise; (2) income numbers are often affected by the accounting methods that are used; and (3) income measures are often estimates.

2 Prepare a single-step income statement.

In a single-step income statement, there are two main groupings: revenues and expenses. Expenses are deducted from revenues to arrive at net income or loss before discontinued operations and extraordinary items—i.e., only a single subtraction is made. Frequently, income tax is reported separately as the last item before net income before discontinued operations and extraordinary items to indicate its relationship to income before income tax.

3 Prepare a multiple-step income statement.

A multiple-step income statement shows two additional classifications: (1) a separation of operating results from the results obtained through the subordinate or nonoperating activities of the company; and (2) a classification of expenses by functions, such as merchandising or manufacturing, selling, and administration.

4 Explain how irregular items are reported.

Irregular gains or losses or nonrecurring items are generally closed to Income Summary and are included in the income statement. They are treated in the income statement as follows: (1) Discontinued operation of a business component is classified as a separate item, after continuing operations. (2) The unusual, material, non-recurring items that are significantly different from the customary business activities and beyond the control of management are shown in a separate section for extraordinary items, below discontinued operations. (3) Other items that are material in amount, are unusual or nonrecurring, and are not considered extraordinary are separately disclosed and are included as part of continuing operations.

5 Measure and report results of discontinued operations.

The gain or loss on disposal of a business component involves the sum of: (1) the income or loss from operations to the financial statement date, and (2) the gain or loss on the disposal of the business component. These items are reported net of tax among the irregular items in the income statement.

6 Explain intraperiod tax allocation.

The tax expense for the year should be related, where possible, to specific items on the income statement in order to give a more informative disclosure to statement

KEY TERMS

all-inclusive approach, 153
business component, 154
capital maintenance approach, 144
changes in accounting principle, 163
changes in estimates, 160
comprehensive income, 164
current operating performance approach, 154
discontinued operations, 154
earnings management, 144
earnings per share, 161
extraordinary items, 157
formal plan, 156
income statement, 141
intraperiod tax allocation, 160
multiple-step income statement, 149
pro forma earnings, 167
quality of earnings, 143
single-step income statement, 146
typical business activities, 157

users. This procedure is called intraperiod tax allocation—i.e., allocation within a period. Its main purpose is to relate the income tax expense for the fiscal period to the following items that affect the amount of the tax provisions: (1) income from continuing operations, (2) discontinued operations, (3) extraordinary items, and (4) other comprehensive income.

7 Explain where earnings per share information is reported.

Because of its importance, and despite the dangers of focusing attention solely on earnings per share, the profession has concluded that earnings per share must be disclosed on the face of the income statement. A company that reports a discontinued operation or an extraordinary item must report per share amounts for these line items either on the face of the income statement or in the notes to the financial statements.

8 Prepare a retained earnings statement.

The retained earnings statement should disclose net income (loss), dividends, prior period adjustments, and transfers to and from retained earnings (appropriations).

9 Explain how comprehensive income is reported.

Comprehensive income may be presented by expanding the income statement or the statement of shareholders' equity or by adding another separate statement that is presented as equally important.

Appendix 4A

Cash Basis versus Accrual Basis Earnings

Differences between Cash and Accrual Bases

Objective 10
Explain the differences between the cash basis of accounting and the accrual basis of accounting.

Most companies use the **accrual basis** of accounting: they recognize revenue when it is earned and recognize expenses in the period when they are incurred, which means that the time when cash is received or paid is not a factor in recognizing the transaction. Some small enterprises and the average individual taxpayer, however, use a strict or modified cash basis approach. Under the **strict cash basis** of accounting, revenue is recorded only when the cash is received and expenses are recorded only when the cash is paid. On the cash basis, income is determined based on the actual collection of revenues and payment of expenses, and the revenue recognition and matching principles are ignored. Consequently, cash basis financial statements do not conform with generally accepted accounting principles.

To illustrate and contrast accrual basis accounting and cash basis accounting, assume that Quality Contractor signs an agreement to build a garage for $22,000. In January, Quality Contractor begins construction, incurs costs of $18,000 on credit, and by the end of January delivers a finished garage to the buyer. In February, Quality Contractor collects $22,000 cash from the customer. In March, Quality pays the $18,000 that is owed to the creditors. Illustrations 4A-1 and 4A-2 show the net income for each month under cash basis accounting and accrual basis accounting.

Illustration 4A-1
Income Statement–Cash Basis

QUALITY CONTRACTOR
Income Statement Cash Basis
For the Month of

	January	February	March	Total
Cash receipts	$-0-	$22,000	$ -0-	$22,000
Cash payments	-0-	-0-	18,000	18,000
Net income (loss)	$-0-	$22,000	$(18,000)	$ 4,000

Illustration 4A-2
Income Statement–Accrual Basis

QUALITY CONTRACTOR
Income Statement Accrual Basis
For the Month of

	January	February	March	Total
Revenues	$22,000	$-0-	$-0-	$22,000
Expenses	18,000	-0-	-0-	18,000
Net income (loss)	$ 4,000	$-0-	$-0-	$ 4,000

For the three months combined, total net income is the same under both cash basis accounting and accrual basis accounting; the difference is in the timing of net income. The balance sheet is also affected by the basis of accounting. For instance, if cash basis accounting were used, Quality Contractor's balance sheets at each month end would appear as in Illustration 4A-3.

Illustration 4A-3
Balance Sheets–Cash Basis

QUALITY CONTRACTOR
Balance Sheets Cash Basis
As at

	January 31	February 28	March 31
Assets			
Cash	$-0-	$22,000	$4,000
Total assets	$-0-	$22,000	$4,000
Liabilities and Owners' Equity			
Owners' equity	$-0-	$22,000	$4,000
Total liabilities and owners' equity	$-0-	$22,000	$4,000

Illustration 4A-4 shows what Quality Contractor's balance sheets at each month end would look like if accrual basis accounting were used.

Illustration 4A-4
Balance Sheets–Accrual Basis

QUALITY CONTRACTOR
Balance Sheets Accrual Basis
As at

	January 31	February 28	March 31
Assets			
Cash	$ -0-	$22,000	$4,000
Accounts receivable	22,000	-0-	-0-
Total assets	$22,000	$22,000	$4,000
Liabilities and Owners' Equity			
Accounts payable	$18,000	$18,000	$ 0
Owners' equity	4,000	4,000	4,000
Total liabilities and owners' equity	$22,000	$22,000	$4,000

An analysis of the preceding income statements and balance sheets shows the following ways in which cash basis accounting is inconsistent with basic accounting theory:

1. The cash basis understates revenues and assets from the construction and delivery of the garage in January. It ignores the $22,000 of accounts receivable, which is a near-term future cash inflow.
2. The cash basis understates the expenses incurred with the construction of the garage and the liability outstanding at the end of January. It ignores the $18,000 of accounts payable, which is a near-term future cash outflow.
3. The cash basis understates owners' equity in January by not recognizing the revenues and the asset until February, and it overstates owners' equity in February by not recognizing the expenses and liability until March.

In short, cash basis accounting violates the theory underlying the elements of financial statements.

The **modified cash basis**, a mixture of cash basis and accrual basis, is the method often followed by professional services firms (doctors, lawyers, accountants, consultants) and by retail, real estate, and agricultural operations. It is the pure cash basis of accounting with modifications that have substantial support, such as capitalizing and amortizing plant assets or recording inventory.[38]

Conversion from Cash Basis to Accrual Basis

Fairly often, a cash basis or a modified cash basis set of financial statements needs to be converted to the accrual basis so it can be presented to investors and creditors. To illustrate this conversion, assume that Dr. Diane Windsor keeps her accounting records on a cash basis. In the year 2008, Dr. Windsor received $300,000 from her dental patients and paid $170,000 for operating expenses, resulting in an excess of cash receipts over disbursements of $130,000 ($300,000 – $170,000). At January 1 and December 31, 2008, she has the accounts receivable, unearned service revenue, accrued liabilities, and prepaid expenses shown in Illustration 4A-5.

Illustration 4A-5
Excerpt from General Ledger

	January 1, 2008	December 31, 2008
Accounts receivable	$12,000	$9,000
Unearned service revenue	-0-	4,000
Accrued liabilities	2,000	5,500
Prepaid expenses	1,800	2,700

Service Revenue Calculation

To convert the amount of cash received from patients to service revenue on an accrual basis, changes in accounts receivable and unearned service revenue during the year must be considered. Accounts receivable at the beginning of the year represent revenues earned last year that are collected this year. Ending accounts receivable indicate revenues earned this year that are not yet collected. Therefore, beginning accounts receivable are subtracted and ending accounts receivable added to arrive at revenue on an accrual basis, as shown in Illustration 4A-6.

Illustration 4A-6
Conversion of Cash Receipts to Revenue–Accounts Receivable

Cash receipts from customers	(– Beginning accounts receivable) (+ Ending accounts receivable)	=	Revenue on an accrual basis

Using similar analysis, beginning unearned service revenue represents cash received last year for revenues earned this year. Ending unearned service revenue results from collections this year that will be recognized as revenue next year. Therefore, beginning unearned service revenue is added and ending unearned service revenue is subtracted to arrive at revenue on an accrual basis, as shown in Illustration 4A-7.

[38] A cash or modified cash basis might be used in the following situations:

1. A company that is primarily interested in cash flows (for example, a group of physicians that distributes cash basis earnings for salaries and bonuses)
2. A company that has a limited number of financial statement users (a small, closely held company with little or no debt)
3. A company that has operations that are relatively straightforward (small amounts of inventory, long-term assets, or long-term debt)

Cash receipts from customers	(+ Beginning unearned service revenue) (– Ending unearned service revenue)	=	Revenue on an accrual basis

Illustration 4A-7
Conversion of Cash Receipts to Revenue—Unearned Service Revenue

Cash collected from customers, therefore, is converted to service revenue on an accrual basis, as Illustration 4A-8 shows.

Cash receipts from customers		$300,000
Beginning accounts receivable	$(12,000)	
Ending accounts receivable	9,000	
Beginning unearned service revenue	–0–	
Ending unearned service revenue	(4,000)	(7,000)
Service revenue (accrual)		$293,000

Illustration 4A-8
Conversion of Cash Receipts to Service Revenue

Operating Expense Calculation

To convert cash paid for operating expenses during the year to operating expenses on an accrual basis, you must consider changes in prepaid expenses and accrued liabilities during the year. Beginning prepaid expenses should be recognized as expenses this year. (The cash payment occurred last year.) Therefore, the beginning prepaid expenses balance is added to cash paid for operating expenses to arrive at operating expense on an accrual basis.

Conversely, ending prepaid expenses result from cash payments made this year for expenses to be reported next year. (The expense recognition is deferred to a future period.) As a result, ending prepaid expenses are deducted from cash paid for expenses, as shown in Illustration 4A-9.

Cash paid for operating expenses	(+ Beginning prepaid expenses) (– Ending prepaid expenses)	=	Expenses on an accrual basis

Illustration 4A-9
Conversion of Cash Payments to Expenses—Prepaid Expenses

Using similar analysis, beginning accrued liabilities result from expenses recognized last year that require cash payments this year. Ending accrued liabilities relate to expenses recognized this year that have not been paid. Beginning accrued liabilities, therefore, are deducted and ending accrued liabilities are added to cash paid for expenses to arrive at expenses on an accrual basis, as shown in Illustration 4A-10.

Cash paid for operating expenses	(– Beginning accrued liabilities) (+ Ending accrued liabilities)	=	Expenses on an accrual basis

Illustration 4A-10
Conversion of Cash Payments to Expenses—Accrued Liabilities

For Dr. Diane Windsor, therefore, cash paid for operating expenses is converted to operating expenses on an accrual basis as in Illustration 4A-11.

Cash paid for operating expenses		$170,000
Beginning prepaid expense	$ 1,800	
Ending prepaid expense	(2,700)	
Beginning accrued liabilities	(2,000)	
Ending accrued liabilities	5,500	2,600
Operating expenses (accrual)		$172,600

Illustration 4A-11
Conversion of Cash Paid to Operating Expenses

Illustration 4A-12 shows how this entire conversion can be presented in a work sheet.

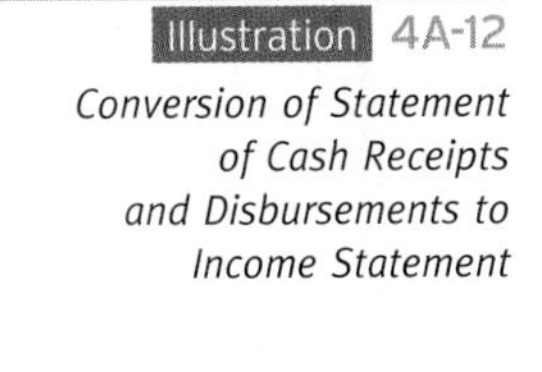

Conversion of Statement of Cash Receipts and Disbursements to Income Statement

DIANE WINDSOR, D.D.S.
Conversion of Income Statement Data from Cash Basis to Accrual Basis
For the Year 2008

		Adjustments		
	Cash Basis	Add	Deduct	Accrual Basis
Collections from customers	$300,000			
− Accounts receivable, Jan. 1			$12,000	
+ Accounts receivable, Dec. 31		$9,000		
+ Unearned service revenue, Jan. 1		—	—	
− Unearned service revenue, Dec. 31			4,000	
Service revenue				$293,000
Disbursement for expenses				
+ Prepaid expenses, Jan. 1		1,800		
− Prepaid expenses, Dec. 31			2,700	
− Accrued liabilities, Jan. 1			2,000	
+ Accrued liabilities, Dec. 31	170,000	5,500		
Operating expenses				172,600
Excess of cash collections over disbursements—cash basis	$130,000			
Net income—accrual basis				$120,400

Using this approach, collections and disbursements on a cash basis are adjusted to revenue and expenses on an accrual basis to arrive at accrued net income. In any conversion from the cash basis to the accrual basis, depreciation or amortization expense is an expense in arriving at net income on an accrual basis.

Theoretical Weaknesses of the Cash Basis

Underlying Concept

Accrual-based net income is a good predictor of future cash flows.

The cash basis does report exactly when cash is received and when cash is disbursed. To many people, that information represents something solid, something concrete. Isn't cash what it's all about? Does it make sense to invent something, design it, produce it, market and sell it, if you aren't going to get cash for it in the end? If so, then what is the merit of accrual accounting?

Today's economy is based more on credit than cash. And the accrual basis, not the cash basis, recognizes all aspects of credit. Investors, creditors, and other decision-makers seek timely information about an enterprise's future cash flows. Accrual basis accounting provides this information by reporting the cash inflows and outflows associated with earnings activities as soon as these cash flows can be estimated with an acceptable degree of certainty. Receivables and payables are forecasters of future cash inflows and outflows. In other words, accrual basis accounting aids in predicting future cash flows by reporting transactions and other events with cash consequences at the time the transactions and events occur, rather than when the cash is received and paid.

Summary of Learning Objective for Appendix 4A

Glossary

www.wiley.com/canada/kieso

KEY TERMS

accrual basis, 170
modified cash basis, 172
strict cash basis, 170

10 Explain the differences between the cash basis of accounting and the accrual basis of accounting.

Accrual basis accounting provides information about cash inflows and outflows associated with earnings activities as soon as these cash flows can be estimated with an acceptable degree of certainty. That is, accrual basis accounting aids in predicting future cash flows by reporting transactions and events with cash consequences at the time the transactions and events occur, rather than when the cash is received and paid. The cash basis focuses rather on when the cash is received or dispersed and therefore it is not the best predictor of future cash flows if the company has irregular cash flow patterns.

Note: All assignment material with an asterisk (*) relates to the appendix to the chapter.

Brief Exercises

BE4-1 Portables Inc. had sales revenue of $890,000 in 2008. Other items recorded during the year were: **(LO 2)**

Cost of goods sold	$395,000
Wage expense	120,000
Income tax expense	115,000
Increase in value of company reputation	35,000
Other operating expenses	10,000
Unrealized gain on value of patents	20,000

Prepare a single-step income statement for Portables for 2008. Portables has 100,000 common shares outstanding.

BE4-2 Alley Corporation had net sales of $2,780,000 and investment revenue of $103,000 in 2008. Its 2008 expenses were: cost of goods sold $2,190,000; selling expenses $272,000; administrative expenses $211,000; interest expense $76,000; and income tax expense $40,000. Prepare a single-step income statement for Alley Corporation, which has 10,000 common shares outstanding. **(LO 2)**

BE4-3 Use the information in BE4-2 for Alley Corporation to prepare a multiple-step income statement. **(LO 3)**

BE4-4 Green Corporation had income from continuing operations of $12.6 million in 2008. During 2008, it disposed of its restaurant division at an after-tax loss of $89,000. Before the disposal, the division operated at a loss of $315,000 (net of tax) in 2008. Green had 10 million common shares outstanding during 2008. Prepare a partial income statement for Green beginning with income from continuing operations. **(LO 5)**

BE4-5 Boyz Corporation had income before income taxes for 2008 of $7.3 million. In addition, it suffered an unusual and infrequent pre-tax loss of $1,770,000 from a volcano eruption. Of this amount, $500,000 was insured. The corporation's tax rate is 30%. Prepare a partial income statement for Boyz beginning with income before income taxes. The corporation had 5 million common shares outstanding during 2008. **(LO 4)**

BE4-6 Patty's Pancakes (PP) is a franchisor that operates several corporate owned restaurants as well as several franchised restaurants. The franchisees pay 3% of their sales revenues to PP in return for advertising and support. During the year, PP sold its corporate owned stores to a franchisee. PP continues to monitor quality control in its franchised operations and franchisees must buy all product from them. Would this qualify for discontinued operations treatment? **(LO 4)**

BE4-7 DougieDoug Limited reports the following for 2007: sales revenues $700,000; cost of sales $500,000; operating expenses $80,000; and an unrealized holding loss on available-for-sale securities for 2007 of $60,000. The company has January 1, 2007, balances in common shares of $350,000; accumulated other comprehensive income $80,000; and retained earnings of $90,000. It issued no shares during 2007. Prepare a statement of shareholders' equity. **(LO 9)**

(LO 7) BE4-8 Geddes Limited had 40,000 common shares on January 1, 2008. On April 1, 8,000 shares were repurchased. On August 31, 12,000 shares were issued. Calculate the number of shares at December 31, 2008, and the weighted average number of shares for 2008.

(LO 7) BE4-9 In 2009, Puckett Corporation reported net income of $1.2 million. It declared and paid preferred share dividends of $250,000. During 2009, Puckett had a weighted average of 190,000 common shares outstanding. Calculate Puckett's 2009 earnings per share.

(LO 8) BE4-10 Global Corporation had retained earnings of $529,000 at January 1, 2008. Net income in 2008 was $1,646,000 and cash dividends of $660,000 were declared and paid. Prepare a 2008 retained earnings statement for Global Corporation.

(LO 8) BE4-11 Use the information in BE4-10 to prepare a retained earnings statement for Global Corporation, assuming that in 2008 Global discovered that it had overstated 2006 amortization by $25,000 (net of tax).

(LO 9) BE4-12 On January 1, 2007, Farrey Corp. had cash and common shares of $60,000. At that date, the company had no other asset, liability, or equity balances. On January 2, 2007, it purchased for cash $20,000 of equity securities that it classified as available-for-sale investments. It received cash dividends of $8,000 during the year on these securities. In addition, it has an unrealized holding gain on these securities of $5,000 net of tax. Determine the following amounts for 2007: (a) net income; (b) comprehensive income; (c) other comprehensive income; and (d) accumulated other comprehensive income (end of 2007).

(LO 10) *BE4-13 Smith Corp. had cash receipts from customers in 2008 of $152,000. Cash payments for operating expenses were $97,000. Smith has determined that at January 1, accounts receivable were $13,000 and prepaid expenses were $17,500. At December 31, accounts receivable were $18,600 and prepaid expenses were $23,200. Calculate (a) the service revenue and (b) the operating expenses.

Exercises

(LO 1) E4-1 (Calculation of Net Income) The following are all changes in the account balances of Glesen Ltd. during the current year, except for Retained Earnings:

	Increase (Decrease)		Increase (Decrease)
Cash	$ 74,000	Accounts payable	$(56,000)
Accounts receivable (net)	45,000	Bonds payable	82,000
Inventory	137,000	Common shares	125,000
Investments in trading securities	(47,000)	Contributed surplus	13,000

Instructions

Calculate the net income for the current year, assuming that there were no entries in the Retained Earnings account except for net income and a dividend declaration of $19,000, which was paid in the current year.

(LO 1) E4-2 (Calculation of Net Income) Selected information follows for Videohound Video Company during 2008:

Cash balance, January 1	$ 23,000
Accounts receivable, January 1	19,000
Collections from customers during year	200,000
Capital account balance, January 1	38,000
Total assets, January 1	75,000
Cash investment added, July 1	5,000
Total assets, December 31	101,000
Cash balance, December 31	20,000
Accounts receivable, December 31	36,000
Merchandise taken for personal use	11,000
Total liabilities, December 31	41,000

Instructions

Calculate the net income for 2008.

E4-3 (Income Statement Items) Certain account balances follow for Paczki Products Corp.: **(LO 1)**

Rental revenue	$ 6,500	Sales discounts	$ 7,800
Interest expense	12,700	Selling expenses	99,400
Beginning retained earnings	114,400	Sales	390,000
Ending retained earnings	134,000	Income tax	31,000
Dividends earned	71,000	Cost of goods sold	184,400
Sales returns	12,400	Administrative expenses	82,500

Instructions

Based on the balances, calculate the following: (a) total net revenue, (b) net income, and (c) dividends declared during the current year.

E4-4 (Single-Step Income Statement) The financial records of Geneva Inc. were destroyed by fire at the end of 2008. Fortunately, the controller had kept the following statistical data related to the income statement: **(LO 2)**

1. The beginning merchandise inventory was $84,000 and it decreased 20% during the current year.
2. Sales discounts amounted to $15,000.
3. There were 15,000 common shares outstanding for the entire year.
4. Interest expense was $20,000.
5. The income tax rate was 35%.
6. Cost of goods sold amounted to $420,000.
7. Administrative expenses were 20% of cost of goods sold but only 4% of gross sales.
8. Four-fifths of the operating expenses related to sales activities.

Instructions

Based on the available data, prepare a single-step income statement for the year 2008.

E4-5 (Multiple-Step and Single-Step) Two accountants for the firm of Elwes and Wright are arguing about the merits of presenting an income statement in a multiple-step versus a single-step format. The discussion involves the following 2008 information for Singh Corp. (in thousands): **(LO 2, 3)**

Administrative expense	
Officers' salaries	$ 3,900
Amortization of office furniture and equipment	3,560
Cost of goods sold	58,570
Rental revenue	15,230
Selling expense	
Transportation-out	2,290
Sales commissions	7,280
Amortization of sales equipment	6,480
Sales	106,500
Income tax	9,070
Interest expense on bonds payable	1,860

Instructions

(a) Prepare an income statement for the year 2008 using the multiple-step form. Common shares outstanding for 2008 total 30,550,000.

(b) Prepare an income statement for the year 2008 using the single-step form.

(c) Which format do you prefer? Explain why.

E4-6 (Multiple-Step and Single-Step—Periodic Inventory Method) Income statement information for Ying-Wai Corporation for the year 2008 follows: **(LO 2, 3, 4)**

Administrative expenses		Transportation-in	$ 14,000
Officers' salaries	$ 39,000	Purchase discounts	10,000
Amortization expense—building	28,500	Inventory (beginning)	120,000
Office supplies expense	9,500	Sales returns and allowances	15,000
Inventory (ending)	137,000	Selling expenses	
Flood damage (pre-tax extraordinary item)	50,000	Sales salaries	71,000
Purchases	600,000	Amortization expense—store equipment	18,000
Sales	930,000	Store supplies expense	9,000

In addition, the corporation has other revenue from dividends received of $20,000 and other interest expense on notes payable of $9,000. There are 20,000 common shares outstanding for the year. The total effective tax rate on all income is 34%.

Instructions

(a) Prepare a multiple-step income statement for 2008.

(b) Prepare a single-step income statement for 2008.

(c) Discuss the merits of the two income statements, compared to each other.

(LO 2, 4, 5, 8) **E4-7 (Combined Single-Step)** The following information was taken from the records of Evelyn Roberts Inc. for the year 2008:

Extraordinary gain from expropriation	$ 95,000
Loss on discontinuance of Micron Division	75,000
Administrative expenses	240,000
Rent revenue	40,000
Extraordinary loss—flood	60,000
Cash dividends declared	70,000
Retained earnings, January 1, 2008	600,000
Cost of goods sold	850,000
Selling expenses	300,000
Sales	1,900,000

The following additional information was also available: income tax applicable to income from continuing operations, $187,000; income tax applicable to loss on discontinuance of Micron Division, $25,000; income tax applicable to extraordinary gain from expropriation, $29,000; income tax applicable to extraordinary loss from a flood, $18,000. Shares outstanding during 2008 were 25,000.

Instructions

(a) Prepare a single-step income statement for 2008.

(b) Prepare a combined single-step income and retained earnings statement.

(LO 3, 4) **E4-8 (Multiple-Step and Extraordinary Items)** The following balances were taken from the books of Voisine Corp. on December 31, 2008:

Interest revenue	$ 86,000	Accumulated amortization—equipment	$ 40,000
Cash	51,000	Accumulated amortization—building	28,000
Sales	1,380,000	Notes receivable	155,000
Accounts receivable	150,000	Selling expenses	194,000
Prepaid insurance	20,000	Accounts payable	170,000
Sales returns and allowances	150,000	Bonds payable	100,000
Allowance for doubtful accounts	7,000	Administrative and general expenses	97,000
Sales discounts	45,000	Accrued liabilities	32,000
Land	100,000	Interest expense	60,000
Equipment	200,000	Notes payable	100,000
Building	140,000	Loss from earthquake damage (extraordinary item)	150,000
Common shares	500,000	Retained earnings	21,000
Cost of Goods Sold	621,000		

Assume the total effective tax rate on all items is 44%.

Instructions

Prepare a multiple-step income statement, assuming 200,000 common shares were outstanding during the year.

(LO 3, 4) **E4-9 (Condensed Income Statement—Periodic Inventory Method)** The following are selected ledger accounts of Sooyoun Corporation at December 31, 2007:

Cash	$ 185,000	Travel and entertainment	$ 69,000
Merchandise inventory	535,000	Accounting and legal services	33,000
Sales	4,275,000	Insurance expense	24,000
Advances from customers	117,000	Advertising	54,000
Purchases	2,786,000	Transportation-out	93,000
Sales discounts	34,000	Amortization of office	48,000
Purchase discounts	27,000	Amortization of sales equipment	36,000
Sales salaries	284,000	Telephone sales	17,000
Office salaries	346,000	Utilities—office	32,000
Purchase returns	15,000	Miscellaneous office expenses	8,000

Sales returns	$ 79,000	Rental revenue	$240,000
Transportation-in	72,000	Extraordinary loss (before tax)	70,000
Accounts receivable	142,500	Interest expense	176,000
Sales commissions	83,000	Common shares	900,000

Sooyoun's effective tax rate on all items is 34%. A physical inventory indicates that the ending inventory is $686,000. The number or common shares outstanding is 90,000.

Instructions

Prepare a condensed 2007 income statement for Sooyoun Corporation.

E4-10 (Multiple-Step Statement with Retained Earnings) Information follows for Gottlieb Corp. for the year 2008: **(LO 3, 4, 8)**

Net sales	$1,300,000	Write-off of inventory due to obsolescence	$ 80,000
Cost of goods sold	780,000	Amortization expense omitted by accident in 2007	55,000
Selling expenses	65,000	Casualty loss (extraordinary item) before taxes	50,000
Administrative expenses	48,000	Dividends declared	45,000
Dividend revenue	20,000	Retained earnings at December 31, 2007	980,000
Interest revenue	7,000		

The effective tax rate is 44% on all items. Assume that 40,000 common shares are outstanding.

Instructions

(a) Prepare a multiple-step income statement for 2008.

(b) Prepare a separate retained earnings statement for 2008.

(c) Prepare the journal entry to record the amortization expense omitted by accident in 2007.

(d) Prepare a combined multiple-step statement of income and retained earnings for 2008.

(e) What are the advantages and disadvantages to the users of financial statements of the combined presentation of the statements of income and retained earnings?

E4-11 (Discontinued Operations) Assume that Shengru Inc. decides to sell CBTV, its television subsidiary, on September 30, 2007. There is a formal plan to dispose of the subsidiary and the sale qualifies for discontinued operations treatment. Pertinent data on the operations of the TV subsidiary are as follows: loss from operations from beginning of year to September 30, $1,900,000 (net of tax); loss from operations from September 30 to end of 2007, $700,000 (net of tax); estimated loss on sale of net assets on disposal date June 1, 2008, $150,000 (net of tax). The year end is December 31. **(LO 5)**

Instructions

(a) What is the net income/loss from discontinued operations reported in 2007? In 2008?

(b) Prepare the discontinued operations section of the income statement for the year ended 2007.

(c) If the amount reported in 2008 as a gain or loss from disposal of the subsidiary by Shengru Inc. becomes materially incorrect, when and how is the correction reported, if at all?

E4-12 (Discontinued Operations) On October 5, 2008, Marzook Inc.'s board of directors decided to dispose of the Song and Elwood Division. A formal plan was approved. Marzook is a real estate firm with approximately 25% of its income coming from its management of apartment complexes. The Song and Elwood Division gets contracts to clean apartments after tenants move out of the Marzook complexes and several others. The board decided to dispose of the division because of unfavourable operating results. **(LO 5)**

Net income for Marzook was $91,000 after tax (assume a 30% rate) for the fiscal year ended December 31, 2008. The Song and Elwood Division accounted for only $4,200 (after tax) of this amount. The average number of common shares outstanding was 20,000 for the year.

Because of the unfavourable results and the extreme competition, the board believes that it cannot sell the business intact. Its final decision is to auction off the cleaning equipment on May 10, 2009. The equipment is the only asset of the division and has a carrying value of $25,000 at October 5, 2008. The board believes that proceeds from the sale will be approximately $5,000 after the auction expenses. Currently, the estimated fair value of the equipment is $10,000.

Instructions

(a) Prepare the income statement and the appropriate footnotes that relate to the Song and Elwood Division for 2008. The income statement should begin with income from continuing operations before income taxes. Earnings per share calculations are not required.

(b) Explain how the assets would be valued and presented on the balance sheet.

(LO 7) **E4-13 (Earnings per Share)** The shareholders' equity section of Tkachuk Corporation as of December 31, 2009, follows:

8% cumulative preferred shares, 100,000 shares authorized, 80,000 shares outstanding	$ 4,500,000
Common shares, 10 million shares authorized and issued	10,000,000
Contributed surplus	10,500,000
	25,000,000
Retained earnings	177,000,000
	$202,000,000

Net income of $43 million for 2009 reflects a total effective tax rate of 44%. Included in the net income figure is a loss of $15 million (before tax) as a result of a major casualty.

Instructions
Calculate earnings per share data as they should appear on the financial statements of Tkachuk Corporation.

(LO 7) **E4-14 (Earnings per Share)** At December 31, 2007, Naoya Corporation had the following shares outstanding:

10% cumulative preferred shares, 107,500 shares outstanding	$10,750,000
Common shares, 4,000,000 shares outstanding	20,000,000

During 2008, Naoya's only share transaction was the issuance of 400,000 common shares on April 1. During 2008, the following also occurred:

Income from continuing operations before taxes	$23,650,000
Discontinued operations (loss before taxes)	$ 3,225,000
Preferred dividends declared	$ 1,075,000
Common dividends declared	$ 2,200,000
Effective tax rate	35%

Instructions
Calculate earnings per share data as they should appear in the 2008 income statement of Naoya Corporation.

(LO 8) **E4-15 (Retained Earnings Statement)** Holiday Corporation began operations on January 1, 2005. During its first three years of operations, Holiday reported net income and declared dividends as follows:

	Net income	Dividends declared
2005	$ 55,000	$ -0-
2006	135,000	$30,000
2007	160,000	$50,000

The following information is for 2008:

Income before income tax	$340,000
Prior period adjustment: understatement of 2006 amortization expense (before taxes)	$ 57,000
Cumulative increase in prior year's income from change in inventory methods (before taxes)	$ 37,000
Dividends declared (of this amount, $25,000 will be paid on January 15, 2009)	$100,000
Effective tax rate	39%

Instructions
Prepare a 2008 retained earnings statement for Holiday Corporation.

(LO 9) **E4-16 (Comprehensive Income)** Rosy Randall Corporation reported the following for 2007: net sales $1,200,000; cost of sales $750,000; selling and administrative expenses $320,000; and unrealized holding gains on available-for-sale securities $18,000.

Instructions
Prepare a statement of comprehensive income. Ignore taxes and EPS.

(LO 9) **E4-17 (Comprehensive Income)** Kelly Corporation had the following balances at December 31, 2007 (all amounts in thousands): preferred shares $1,526; common shares $2,591; contributed surplus $2,425; retained earnings $13,692; and accumulated other comprehensive income $2,006.

During the year ended December 31, 2008, the company earned net income of $4,352, generated an unrealized holding loss on available-for-sale securities of $348; sold common shares of $170; and paid out dividends of $23 and $7 to preferred and common shareholders, respectively.

Instructions

Prepare a statement of shareholders' equity for the year ended December 31, 2008, as well as the shareholders' equity section of the Kelly Corporation balance sheet at December 31, 2008.

***E4-18 (Cash and Accrual Basis)** Portmann Corp. maintains its financial records on the cash basis of accounting. As it would like to secure a long-term loan from its regular bank, the company asks you, as an independent CA, to convert its cash basis income statement data to the accrual basis. You are provided with the following summarized data for 2007, 2008, and 2009: **(LO 10)**

	2007	2008	2009
Cash receipts from sales:			
On 2007 sales	$320,000	$160,000	$ 30,000
On 2008 sales	–0–	355,000	90,000
On 2009 sales	–0–		408,000
Cash payments for expenses:			
On 2007 expenses	185,000	67,000	25,000
On 2008 expenses	40,000[a]	135,000	55,000
On 2009 expenses	–0–	45,000[b]	218,000

[a]Prepayments of 2008 expense
[b]Prepayments of 2009 expense

Instructions

Using the data above, prepare abbreviated income statements for the years 2007 and 2008 on:

(a) the cash basis

(b) the accrual basis

Problems

P4-1 Information for 2008 follows for Barkley Corp.:

Retained earnings balance, January 1, 2008	$ 1,980,000
Sales for the year	36,500,000
Cost of goods sold	28,500,000
Interest revenue	170,000
Selling and administrative expenses	4,700,000
Write-off of goodwill (not tax deductible)	520,000
Assessment for additional 2006 income taxes (normal, recurring)	500,000
Gain on sale of investments in trading securities (normal, recurring)	110,000
Loss due to flood damage—extraordinary item (net of tax)	390,000
Loss on disposition of wholesale division (net of tax)	440,000
Operating loss for wholesale division (net of tax)	90,000
Dividends declared on common shares	250,000
Dividends declared on preferred shares	70,000

Instructions

Prepare a multiple-step income statement and a retained earnings statement. Barkley decided to discontinue its entire wholesale operations and to keep its manufacturing operations. On September 15, Barkley sold the wholesale operations to Portmann Corp. During 2008, there were 800,000 common shares outstanding all year. Assume Barkley's tax rate is 30%.

P4-2 The trial balance follows for McLean Corporation at December 31, 2009:

MCLEAN CORPORATION
Trial Balance
Year Ended December 31, 2009

	Debits	Credits
Purchase discounts		$ 10,000
Cash	$ 205,100	
Accounts receivable	105,000	
Rent revenue		18,000
Retained earnings		260,000
Salaries payable		18,000
Sales		1,400,000
Notes receivable	110,000	
Accounts payable		49,000
Accumulated amortization—equipment		28,000
Sales discounts	14,500	
Sales returns	17,500	
Notes payable		70,000
Selling expenses	432,000	
Administrative expenses	99,000	
Common shares		300,000
Income tax expense	38,500	
Cash dividends	45,000	
Allowance for doubtful accounts		5,000
Supplies	14,000	
Freight-in	20,000	
Land	70,000	
Equipment	140,000	
Bonds payable		100,000
Gain on sale of land		30,000
Accumulated amortization—building		19,600
Merchandise inventory	89,000	
Building	98,000	
Purchases	810,000	
Totals	$2,307,600	$2,307,600

A physical count of inventory on December 31 resulted in an inventory amount of $124,000.

Instructions

Prepare a single-step income statement and a retained earnings statement. Assume that the only changes in retained earnings during the current year were from net income and dividends. There were 30,000 common shares outstanding the entire year.

P4-3 Charyk Inc. reported income from continuing operations before taxes during 2008 of $1,790,000. Additional transactions occurring in 2008 but not considered in the $1,790,000 are as follows:

1. The corporation experienced an insured flood loss (extraordinary) of $80,000 during the year.
2. At the beginning of 2006, the corporation purchased a machine for $54,000 (residual value of $9,000) that had a useful life of six years. The bookkeeper used straight-line amortization for 2006, 2007, and 2008 but failed to deduct the residual value in calculating the amortization base amount.
3. The sale of securities held as a part of its portfolio resulted in a loss of $107,000 (before taxes).
4. When its president died, the corporation gained $100,000 from an insurance policy. The cash surrender value of this policy had been carried on the books as an investment in the amount of $46,000 (the gain is non-taxable).
5. The corporation disposed of its recreational division at a loss of $115,000 before taxes. Assume that this transaction meets the criteria for discontinued operations.
6. The corporation decided to change its method of inventory pricing from average cost to the FIFO method. The effect of this change on prior years is to increase 2006 income by $60,000 and decrease 2007 income by $20,000 before taxes. The FIFO method has been used for 2008.

Instructions

(a) Prepare an income statement for the year 2008 starting with income from continuing operations before taxes. Calculate earnings per share as it should be shown on the face of the income statement. There were 80,000 common shares outstanding for the year. (Assume a tax rate of 40% on all items, unless they are noted as being non-taxable.)

(b) Assume beginning retained earnings for 2008 is $2,540,000 and that dividends of $175,000 were declared during the year. Prepare the statement of retained earnings for 2008.

(c) How do the GAAP classification rules for the statements of income and retained earnings assist in the assessment of the quality of earnings?

P4-4 The following account balances were included in the trial balance of Reid Corporation at June 30, 2008:

Sales	$1,928,500	Amortization of office furniture and equipment	$ 7,250
Sales discounts	31,150	Real estate and other local taxes	7,320
Cost of goods sold	1,071,770	Bad debt expense—selling	4,850
Sales salaries	56,260	Building expense—prorated to administration	9,130
Sales commissions	97,600	Miscellaneous office expenses	6,000
Travel expense—salespersons	28,930	Sales returns	62,300
Freight-out	21,400	Dividends received	38,000
Entertainment expense	14,820	Bond interest expense	18,000
Telephone and Internet—sales	9,030	Income taxes	133,000
Amortization of sales equipment	4,980	Amortization understatement due to error—	
Building expense—prorated to sales	6,200	2006 (net of tax)	17,700
Miscellaneous selling expenses	4,715	Dividends declared on preferred shares	9,000
Office supplies used	3,450	Dividends declared on common shares	32,000
Telephone and Internet—administration	2,820		

The Retained Earnings account had a balance of $292,000 at June 30, 2008, before closing. There are 180,000 common shares outstanding.

Instructions

(a) Using the multiple-step form, prepare an income statement and retained earnings statement for the year ended June 30, 2008.

(b) Using the single-step form, prepare an income statement for the year ended June 30, 2008.

P4-5 A combined single-step income and retained earnings statement for Pereira Corp. follows for 2009 (amounts in thousands):

Net sales		$640,000
Costs and expenses		
Cost of goods sold		500,000
Selling, general, and administrative expenses		66,000
Other, net		17,000
		583,000
Income before income tax		57,000
Income tax		19,400
Net income		37,600
Retained earnings at beginning of period, as previously reported	141,000	
Adjustment required for correction of error	(7,000)	
Retained earnings at beginning of period, as restated		134,000
Dividends on common shares		(12,200)
Retained earnings at end of period		$159,400

Additional facts are as follows:

1. "Selling, general, and administrative expenses" for 2009 included a usual but infrequently occurring charge of $10.5 million for a write-down of inventory.
2. "Other, net" for 2009 included an extraordinary item charge of $9 million. If the extraordinary item charge had not occurred, income taxes for 2009 would have been $22.4 million instead of $19.4 million.

3. "Adjustment required for correction of an error" resulted from a change in estimate as the useful life of certain assets was reduced to eight years and a catch-up adjustment was made.
4. Pereira Corp. disclosed earnings per common share for net income in the notes to the financial statements.

Instructions

(a) Determine from these additional facts whether the presentation of the facts in the Pereira income and retained earnings statement is appropriate. If the presentation is not appropriate, describe the appropriate presentation and discuss the theory that supports this change.

(b) Prepare a revised combined statement of income and retained earnings for Pereira Corp.

P4-6 A combined statement of income and retained earnings for Olive Miller Ltd. for the year ended December 31, 2008, follows. Also presented are three unrelated situations involving accounting changes and the classification of certain items as ordinary or extraordinary. Each situation is based on the combined statement of income and retained earnings of Olive Miller Ltd. and makes it necessary to revise the statement.

OLIVE MILLER LTD.
Combined Statement of Income and Retained Earnings
For the Year Ended December 31, 2008

Sales	$5,700,000
Cost of goods sold	2,900,000
Gross margin	2,800,000
Selling, general, and administrative expenses	1,800,000
Income before income tax	1,000,000
Income tax	300,000
Income before extraordinary item	700,000
Extraordinary item (net of applicable taxes of $210,000)	490,000
Net income	210,000
Retained earnings, January 1	700,000
Retained earnings, December 31	$ 910,000

Situation A. In late 2008, the company discontinued its apparel fabric division. The loss on sale of this discontinued division amounted to $620,000. This amount was included as part of selling, general, and administrative expenses. Before its disposal, the division reported the following for 2008: sales of $1,200,000; cost of goods sold of $600,000; and selling, general, and administrative expenses of $450,000.

The extraordinary item in the combined statement of income and retained earnings for 2008 was for a loss sustained as a result of damage to the company's merchandise caused by a tornado that struck its main warehouse in Lethbridge. This natural disaster was considered an unusual and infrequent occurrence for that area.

Situation B. At the end of 2008, the company's management decided that the estimated loss rate on uncollectible accounts receivable was too low. The loss rate used for the years 2007 and 2008 was 1.2% of total sales, and owing to an increase in the write-off of uncollectible accounts, the rate was raised to 3% of total sales. The amount recorded in Bad Debts Expense under the heading Selling, General, and Administrative Expenses for 2008 was $68,400 and for 2007 was $75,000.

The extraordinary item in the combined statement of income and retained earnings of 2008 was for a loss incurred when outmoded equipment was abandoned. The equipment was used in the business in the past.

Situation C. On January 1, 2006, the company acquired machinery at a cost of $500,000. The company adopted the double-declining balance method of depreciation for this machinery, and had been recording depreciation over an estimated life of 10 years, with no residual value. At the beginning of 2008, a decision was made to adopt the straight-line method of depreciation for this machinery to provide more relevant information. By mistake, however, the double-declining balance method was used for 2008. For financial reporting purposes, depreciation was included in selling, general, and administrative expenses.

The extraordinary item in the combined statement of income and retained earnings was for shutdown expenses incurred by the company during a major strike in 2008 by its operating employees.

Instructions

For each of the three unrelated situations, prepare a revised combined statement of income and retained earnings for Olive Miller Ltd. The company has a 30% income tax rate. Ignore earnings per share calculations.

P4-7 The retained earnings account for the year 2008 for Byron Corp. follows:

Retained earnings, January 1, 2008		$257,600
Add		
Gain on sale of investments in trading securities (net of tax)	$ 41,200	
Net income	129,500	
Refund on litigation with government (net of tax)	21,600	
Recognition of income earned in 2007, but omitted from income statement in that year (net of tax)	25,400	217,700
		475,300
Deduct		
Loss on discontinued operations (net of tax)	25,000	
Write-off of goodwill (net of tax)	60,000	
Cumulative effect on income in changing from straight-line amortization to accelerated amortization in 2008	18,200	
Cash dividends declared	32,000	135,200
Retained earnings, December 31, 2008		$340,100

Instructions

(a) Prepare a corrected retained earnings statement. Byron Corp. normally sells investments like the ones mentioned above.

(b) State where the items that do not appear in the corrected retained earnings statement should be shown.

P4-8 Hamad Corporation commenced business on January 1, 2005. Recently the corporation has had several unusual accounting problems related to the presentation of its income statement for financial reporting purposes.

You are the CA for Hamad and have been asked to examine the following data:

HAMAD CORPORATION
Income Statement
For the Year Ended December 31, 2008

Sales	$9,500,000
Cost of goods sold	5,900,000
Gross profit	3,600,000
Selling and administrative expense	1,300,000
Income before income tax	2,300,000
Income tax (30%)	690,000
Net income	$1,610,000

This additional information was also provided:

1. The controller mentioned that the corporation has had difficulty in collecting on several of its receivables. For this reason, the bad debt write-off was increased from 1% to 2% of sales. The controller estimates that if this rate had been used in past periods, an additional $83,000 worth of expense would have been charged. The bad debt expense for the current period was calculated using the new rate and is part of selling and administrative expense.
2. There were 400,000 common shares outstanding at the end of 2008. No additional shares were purchased or sold in 2008.
3. The following items were not included in the income statement:
   1. Inventory in the amount of $112,000 was obsolete.
   2. The major casualty loss suffered by the corporation was an extraordinary item. It was partially uninsured and cost $162,000, net of tax.
4. Retained earnings as at January 1, 2008, were $2.8 million. Cash dividends of $700,000 were paid in 2008.
5. In January 2008, Hamad changed its method of accounting for plant assets from the straight-line method to the accelerated method (double-declining balance). The controller has prepared a schedule that shows what the amortization expense would have been in previous periods if the double-declining method had been used. Assume that this change results in more reliable and relevant presentation.

	Amortization Expense under Straight-Line	Amortization Expense under Double-Declining	Difference
2005	$ 75,000	$150,000	$ 75,000
2006	75,000	112,500	37,500
2007	75,000	84,375	9,375
	$225,000	$346,875	$121,875

6. In 2008, Hamad discovered that in 2007 it had failed to record $20,000 as an expense for sales commissions. The sales commissions for 2007 were included in the 2008 expenses.

Instructions

(a) Prepare the income statement for Hamad Corporation in accordance with professional pronouncements. Do not prepare notes to the financial statements. The effective tax rate for past years was 30%.

(b) Prepare a combined statement of net income and retained earnings.

(c) From the perspective of the reader of the financial statements, what is the purpose of intraperiod tax allocation for the statements of income and retained earnings?

P4-9 Fadime Corp. has 100,000 common shares outstanding. In 2008, the company reports income from continuing operations before taxes of $2,710,000. Additional transactions not considered in the $2,710,000 are as follows:

1. In 2008, Fadime Corp. sold equipment for $140,000. The machine had originally cost $80,000 and had accumulated amortization of $36,000. The gain or loss is considered ordinary.
2. The company discontinued operations of one of its subsidiaries during the current year at a loss of $290,000 before taxes. Assume that this transaction meets the criteria for discontinued operations. The loss on operations of the discontinued subsidiary was $90,000 before taxes; the loss on disposal of the subsidiary was $200,000 before taxes.
3. The sum of $520,000 was received as a result of a lawsuit for a breached 2004 contract. Before the decision, legal counsel was uncertain about the outcome of the suit and had not established a receivable.
4. In 2008, the company reviewed its accounts receivable and determined that $54,000 of accounts receivable that had been carried for years appeared unlikely to be collected. No allowance for doubtful accounts was previously set up.
5. An internal audit discovered that amortization of intangible assets was understated by $35,000 (net of tax) in a prior period. The amount was charged against retained earnings.

Instructions

Analyze the above information and prepare an income statement for the year 2008, starting with income from continuing operations before income taxes. Calculate earnings per share as it should be shown on the face of the income statement. (Assume a total effective tax rate of 38% on all items, unless otherwise indicated.)

P4-10 Campbell Corporation management formally decided to discontinue operation of its Rocketeer Division on November 1, 2007. Campbell is a successful corporation with earnings of $150 million or more before taxes for each of the past five years. The Rocketeer Division is being discontinued because it has not contributed to this profitable performance.

The main assets of this division are the land, plant, and equipment used to manufacture engine components. The land, plant, and equipment had a net book value of $96 million on November 1, 2007.

Campbell's management has entered into negotiations for a cash sale of the division for $87 million. The expected sale date and final disposal of the division is July 1, 2008. Campbell Corporation has a fiscal year ending May 31. The results of operations for the Rocketeer Division for the 2007–2008 fiscal year and the estimated results for June 2008 are presented below. The before-tax losses after October 31, 2007, are calculated without amortization on the plant and equipment because the net book value as at November 1, 2007, is being used as a basis for negotiating the sale.

Period	Before-Tax Loss
June 1, 2007 to October 31, 2007	$(6,100,000)
November 1, 2007 to May 31, 2008	$(3,900,000)
June 1–30, 2008 (estimated)	$(750,000)

The Rocketeer Division will be accounted for as a discontinued operation on Campbell's 2007–2008 fiscal year financial statements. Campbell's tax rate is 40% on operating income and all gains and losses.

Instructions

(a) Explain how the Rocketeer Division's assets would be reported on Campbell Corporation's balance sheet as at May 31, 2008.

(b) Explain how the discontinued operations and pending sale of the Rocketeer Division would be reported on Campbell Corporation's income statement for the year ended May 31, 2008.

(c) On July 5, 2008, Campbell Corporation disposes of the division assets at an adjusted price of $84 million. Explain how the discontinued operations and sale of the Rocketeer Division would be reported on Campbell Corporation's income statement for the year ended May 31, 2009. The estimated loss of operations of $750,000 was accurate.

(d) Assume that Campbell Corporation management was debating whether the sale of the Rocketeer Division qualified under GAAP for discontinued operations treatment. List specific factors or arguments that management would use to suggest that the treatment should be as a discontinued operation. List specific factors or arguments that management would use to avoid the treatment as a discontinued operation. Why would management have a particular preference about which treatment is given? From an external user's perspective, what relevance does the presentation of the discontinued operation have for the interpretation of the financial results?

(CMA adapted)

P4-11 Amos Corporation was incorporated and began business on January 1, 2007. It has been successful and now requires a bank loan for additional working capital to finance an expansion. The bank has requested an audited income statement for the year 2007. The accountant for Amos Corporation provides you with the following income statement, which Amos plans to submit to the bank:

AMOS CORPORATION
Income Statement

Sales		$850,000
Dividends		32,300
Gain on recovery of insurance proceeds from earthquake loss (extraordinary)		27,300
Unrealized holding gain on available-for-sale securities		5,000
		914,600
Less:		
Selling expenses	$100,100	
Cost of goods sold	510,000	
Advertising expense	13,700	
Loss on obsolescence of inventories	34,000	
Loss on discontinued operations	48,600	
Administrative expense	73,400	779,800
Income before income tax		134,800
Income tax		53,920
Net income		$ 80,880

There are 100,000 common shares outstanding during the year.

Instructions

(a) Indicate the deficiencies in the income statement as it currently is. Assume that the corporation wants a single-step income statement.

(b) Prepare a revised single-step statement of income and comprehensive income.

P4-12 The following is from a recent income statement for Baring Corp.:

Sales	$21,924,000,000
Costs and expenses	20,773,000,000
Income from operations	1,151,000,000
Other income	22,000,000
Interest and debt expense	(130,000,000)
Earnings before income taxes	1,043,000,000
Income taxes	(287,000,000)
Net income	$ 756,000,000

It includes only five separate numbers (which are in billions of dollars), two subtotals, and the net earnings figure.

Instructions

(a) Indicate the deficiencies in the income statement.

(b) What recommendations would you make to the company to improve the usefulness of its income statement?

(c) Why do some businesses provide only a minimal disclosure of financial statement elements on their income statement?

P4-13 Stan Foxworthy, vice-president of finance for Hand Corp., has recently been asked to discuss with the company's division controllers the proper accounting for extraordinary items. Foxworthy prepared the situations that follow to use as examples in the discussion:

1. An earthquake destroys one of the oil refineries owned by a large multinational oil company. Earthquakes are rare in this location.
2. A publicly held company has incurred a substantial loss in the unsuccessful registration of a bond issue.
3. A large portion of a cigarette manufacturer's tobacco crops are destroyed by a hailstorm. Severe damage from hailstorms is rare in this locality.
4. A large diversified company sells a block of shares from its portfolio of securities that were acquired for investment purposes. The securities are presently treated as available for sale.
5. A company sells a block of common shares of a publicly traded company. The block of shares, which represents less than 10% of the publicly held company, is the only security investment that the company has ever owned. The securities are treated as available-for-sale securities.
6. A company that operates a chain of warehouses sells the extra land surrounding one of its warehouses. When the company buys property for a new warehouse, it usually buys more land than it needs for the warehouse because it expects the land to increase in value. Twice during the past five years the company sold excess land.
7. A textile manufacturer with only one plant moves to another location and incurs relocation costs of $725,000.
8. A company experiences a material loss in the repurchase of a large bond issue that has been outstanding for three years. The company regularly repurchases bonds of this type.
9. A railroad experiences an unusual flood loss to part of its track system. Flood losses normally occur every three or four years.
10. A machine tool company sells the only land it owns. The land was acquired 10 years ago for future expansion, but shortly after the purchase the company abandoned all plans for expansion and decided to keep the land as an investment that would appreciate in value.

Instructions

For each situation, determine whether the item should be classified as extraordinary. Explain the reasons for your position.

P4-14 In recent years, Grace Inc. has reported steadily increasing income. The company reported income of $20,000 in 2005, $25,000 in 2006, and $30,000 in 2007. Several market analysts have recommended that investors buy Grace Inc. shares because they expect the steady growth in income to continue. Grace is approaching the end of its 2008 fiscal year, and it looks to be a good year once again. However, it has not yet recorded warranty expense.

Based on prior experience, this year's warranty expense should be around $5,000, but some top managers have approached the controller to suggest a larger, more conservative warranty expense should be recorded this year. Income before warranty expense is $43,000. Specifically, by recording an $8,000 warranty accrual this year, Grace could report an income increase for this year and still be in a position to cover its warranty costs in future years.

Instructions

(a) What is earnings management?

(b) What would be the effect of the proposed accounting in 2008? In 2009?

(c) What is the appropriate accounting in this situation?

P4-15 Andy Neville, controller for Tatooed Heart Inc., recently prepared the company's income statement for 2008. Mr. Neville believes that the statement is a fair presentation of Tatooed Heart's financial progress during the current period, but he also admits that he has not examined any recent professional pronouncements on accounting.

TATOOED HEART INC.
Income Statement
For the Year Ended December 31, 2008

Sales			$377,852
Less: Sales returns and allowances			16,320
Net sales			361,532
Cost of goods sold:			
Inventory, January 1, 2008		$ 50,235	
Purchases	$192,143		
Less: Purchase discounts	3,142	189,001	
Cost of goods available for sale		239,236	
Inventory, December 31, 2008		41,124	
Cost of goods sold			198,112
Gross profit			163,420
Selling expenses		41,850	
Administrative expenses		32,142	73,992
Income before income tax			89,428
Other revenues and gains			
Dividends received			40,000
			129,428
Income tax			43,900
Net income			$ 85,528

TATOOED HEART INC.
Retained Earnings Statement
For the Year Ended December 31, 2008

Retained earnings, January 1, 2008			$216,000
Add:			
Net income for 2008	$85,528		
Gain from casualty (net of tax)	10,000		
Gain on sale of plant assets	21,400	$116,928	
Deduct:			
Loss on expropriation (net of tax)	13,000		
Correction of mathematical error (net of tax)	17,186	(30,186)	86,742
Retained earnings, December 31, 2008			$302,742

Instructions

(a) Determine whether these statements are prepared under the current operating concept of income or the all-inclusive concept of income. Cite specific details to support your answer.

(b) Which method do you favour and why?

(c) Which method must be used, and how should the information be presented? Prepare revised income and retained earnings statements for Tatooed Heart Inc. There were 50,000 common shares outstanding for the year. For questionable items, use the classification that would normally be appropriate.

P4-16 The following financial statement was prepared by employees of Klein Corporation:

KLEIN CORPORATION
Income Statement
Year Ended December 31, 2007

Revenues	
Gross sales, including sales taxes	$1,044,300
Less: Returns, allowances, and cash discounts	56,200
Net sales	988,100
Dividends, interest, and purchase discounts	30,250
Recoveries of accounts written off in prior years	13,850
Total revenues	1,032,200
Costs and expenses	
Cost of goods sold	465,900
Salaries and related payroll expenses	60,500
Rent	19,100
Freight-in and freight-out	3,400
Bad debt expense	24,000
Addition to reserve for possible inventory losses	3,800
Total costs and expenses	576,700
Income before extraordinary items	455,500
Extraordinary items	
Loss on discontinued styles (Note 1)	37,000
Loss on sale of trading securities (Note 2)	39,050
Loss on sale of warehouse (Note 3)	86,350
Tax assessments for 2006 and 2005 (Note 4)	34,500
Total extraordinary items	196,900
Net income	$ 258,600
Net income per common share	$ 2.30

Note 1: New styles and rapidly changing consumer preferences resulted in a $37,000 loss on the disposal of discontinued styles and related accessories.

Note 2: The corporation sold an investment in trading securities at a loss of $39,050. The corporation normally sells securities of this type.

Note 3: The corporation sold one of its warehouses at an $86,350 loss (net of taxes).

Note 4: The corporation was charged $34,500 for additional income taxes resulting from a settlement in 2007. Of this amount, $17,000 was for 2006, and the balance was for 2005. This type of litigation recurs frequently at Klein Corporation.

Instructions

Identify and discuss the weaknesses in classification and disclosure in the single-step income statement above. You should explain why these treatments are weaknesses and what the proper presentation of the items would be in accordance with recent professional pronouncements.

***P4-17** On January 1, 2008, Jill Monroe and Jenni Meno formed a computer sales and service enterprise in Montreal by investing $90,000 cash. The new company, Razorback Sales and Service, has the following transactions in January:

1. Paid $6,000 in advance for three months' rent of office, showroom, and repair space.
2. Purchased 40 personal computers at a cost of $1,500 each, 6 graphics computers at a cost of $3,000 each, and 25 printers at a cost of $450 each, paying cash on delivery.
3. Sales, repair, and office employees earned $12,600 in salaries during January, of which $3,000 was still payable at the end of January.
4. Sold 30 personal computers for $2,550 each, 4 graphics computers for $4,500 each, and 15 printers for $750 each; of the sales amounts, $75,000 was received in cash in January and $30,750 was sold on a deferred payment plan.
5. Other operating expenses of $8,400 were incurred and paid for during January; $2,000 of incurred expenses were payable at January 31.

Instructions

(a) Using the transaction data above, prepare (1) a cash basis income statement and (2) an accrual basis income statement for the month of January.

(b) Using the transaction data above, prepare (1) a cash basis balance sheet and (2) an accrual basis balance sheet as of January 31, 2008.

(c) Identify the items in the cash basis financial statements that make cash basis accounting inconsistent with the theory underlying the elements of financial statements.

***P4-18** Dr. John Gleason, M.D., maintains the accounting records of Bones Clinic on a cash basis. During 2008, Dr. Gleason collected $146,000 in revenues and paid $55,470 in expenses. At January 1, 2008, and December 31, 2008, he had accounts receivable, unearned service revenue, accrued expenses, and prepaid expenses as follows (all long-lived assets are rented):

	January 1	December 31
Accounts receivable	$9,250	$16,100
Unearned service revenue	2,840	1,620
Accrued expenses	3,435	2,200
Prepaid expenses	2,000	1,775

Instructions

Last week, Dr. Gleason asked you, his CA, to help him determine his income on the accrual basis. Write a letter to him explaining what you did to calculate net income on the accrual basis. Be sure to state net income on the accrual basis and to include a schedule of your calculations.

Writing Assignments

WA4-1 Information about a corporation's operations is presented in an income statement or in a combined income and retained earnings statement. Income statements are prepared on either a current operating performance basis or an all-inclusive basis. Users of these income statements have different opinions about how material, nonrecurring charges and credits should be treated.

Instructions

(a) Define "current operating performance" and "all-inclusive" as they are used above.

(b) Explain the differences in content and organization of a current operating performance income statement and an all-inclusive income statement. Include a discussion of the proper treatment of material, nonrecurring charges and credits.

(c) Give the main arguments in support of each of the three statements: all-inclusive income statement, current operating performance income statement, and a combined income and retained earnings statement.

(d) Discuss what the category Other Comprehensive Income is based on as a concept.

(AICPA adapted)

***WA4-2** Ernest Banks is the manager and accountant for a small company that is privately owned by three individuals. Banks has always given the owners cash-based financial statements. The owners are not accountants and do not understand how financial statements are prepared. Recently, the business has experienced strong growth, and inventory, accounts receivable, and capital assets have become more significant company assets. Banks understands generally accepted accounting principles and knows that net income would be lower if he prepared accrual-based financial statements. He is afraid, however that if he gave the owners financial statements prepared on an accrual basis, they would think he is not managing the business well—they might even decide to fire him.

Instructions

Discuss the issues.

WA4-3 Anikan Limited has approved a formal plan to sell its head office tower to an outside party. A detailed plan has been approved by the board of directors. The building is on the books at $50 million (net book value). The estimated selling price is $49 million. The company will continue to use the building until the new head office is complete. Construction has not yet started on the new building.

Instructions

Discuss the financial reporting issues.

Cases

Student Website
www.wiley.com/canada/kieso

Refer to the Case Primer on the Student Website to help you answer these cases.

CA4-1 Allen Corp. is an entertainment firm that earns approximately 30% of its income from the Casino Royale Division, which manages gambling facilities. As auditor for Allen Corp., you have recently overheard the following discussion between the controller and financial vice-president:

VICE-PRESIDENT: If we sell the Casino Royale Division, it seems ridiculous to segregate the results of the sale in the income statement. Separate categories tend to be absurd and confusing to the shareholders. I believe we should simply report the gain on the sale as other income or expense without any details.

CONTROLLER: Professional pronouncements would require that we disclose this information separately in the income statement. If a sale of this type relates to a separate component and there's a formal plan to dispose of it, it has to be reported as a discontinued operation.

VICE-PRESIDENT: What about the walkout we had last month when our employees were upset about their commission income? Wouldn't this situation also be an extraordinary item?

CONTROLLER: I'm not sure whether that would be reported as extraordinary or not.

VICE-PRESIDENT: Oh well, it doesn't make any difference because the net effect of all these items is immaterial, so no disclosure is necessary.

Instructions

Discuss.

CA4-2 Anderson Corp. is a major manufacturer of foodstuffs whose products are sold in grocery and convenience stores throughout Canada. The company's name is well known and respected because its products have been marketed nationally for over 50 years.

In April 2008, the company was forced to recall one of its major products. Thirty-five people in Okotoles were treated for severe intestinal pain, and three people eventually died from complications. They had all consumed the same Anderson product.

The product causing the problem was traced to one specific lot or batch. Anderson keeps samples from all lots of foodstuffs. After thorough testing, Anderson and the legal authorities confirmed that the product had been tampered with after it had left the company's plant and was no longer under the company's control.

All of the product was recalled from the market—the only time an Anderson product had been recalled nationally and the only incident of tampering. People who still had the product in their homes, even though it was not from the affected lot, were encouraged to return the product for credit or refund. A media campaign was designed and implemented by the company to explain what had happened and what the company was doing to minimize any chance of recurrence. Anderson decided to continue the product with the same trade name and same wholesale price. However, the packaging was redesigned completely to be tamper-resistant and safety-sealed. This required the purchase and installation of new equipment.

The corporate accounting staff recommended that the costs associated with the tampered product be treated as an extraordinary charge on the 2008 financial statements. Corporate accounting was asked to identify the various costs that could be associated with the tampered product and related recall. These costs are as follows (in thousands):

1. Credits and refunds to stores and consumers	$30,000
2. Insurance to cover lost sales and idle plant costs for possible future recalls	5,000
3. Transportation costs and off-site warehousing of returned product	2,000
4. Future security measures for other Anderson products	4,000
5. Testing of returned product and inventory	900
6. Destruction of returned product and inventory	2,400
7. Public relations program to re-establish brand credibility	4,200
8. Communication program to inform customers, answer inquiries, prepare press releases, etc.	1,600
9. Higher cost arising from new packaging	800
10. Investigation of possible involvement of employees, former employees, competitors, etc.	500
11. Packaging redesign and testing	2,000

12. Purchase and installation of new packaging equipment	$ 6,000
13. Legal costs for defence against liability suits	750
14. Lost sales revenue due to recall	32,000

Anderson's estimated earnings before income taxes and before consideration of any of the above items for the year ending December 31, 2008, are $225 million.

Instructions
Play the role of the company controller and discuss the issues.

CA4-3 As a reviewer for the Ontario Securities Commission, you are in the process of reviewing the financial statements of public companies. The following items have come to your attention:

1. A merchandising company incorrectly overstated its ending inventory two years ago by a material amount. Inventory for all other periods is correctly calculated.
2. An automobile dealer sells for $137,000 an extremely rare 1930 S type Invicta, which it purchased for $21,000 10 years ago. The Invicta is the only such display item that the dealer owns.
3. During the current year, a drilling company extended the estimated useful life of certain drilling equipment from 9 to 15 years. As a result, amortization for the current year was materially lowered.
4. A retail outlet changed its calculation for bad debt expense from 1% to 0.5% of sales because of changes in its clientele.
5. A mining company sells a foreign subsidiary that does uranium mining, although the company continues to mine uranium in other countries.
6. A steel company changes from straight-line amortization to accelerated amortization in accounting for its plant assets.
7. A construction company, at great expense to itself, prepares a major proposal for a government loan. The loan is not approved.
8. A water pump manufacturer has had large losses resulting from a strike by its employees early in the year.
9. Amortization for a prior period was incorrectly understated by $950,000. The error was discovered in the current year.
10. A large sheep rancher suffered a major loss because the provincial government required that all sheep in the province be killed to halt the spread of a rare disease. Such a situation has not occurred in the province for 20 years.
11. A food distributor that sells wholesale to supermarket chains and to fast-food restaurants (two major classes of customers) decides to discontinue the division that sells to one of the two classes of customers.

Instructions
Discuss the issues.

CA4-4 You are working on the audit team for December Inc., a client with multiple divisions and annual sales of $90 million. The company mainly sells electronic transistors to small customers and has one division (the October Division) that deals in acoustic transmitters for Navy submarines. The October Division has approximately $18 million in sales.

It is an evening in late February 2008, and the audit work for the year ended December 31, 2007, is complete. You are working in the client's office on the report, when you overhear a conversation among the financial vice-president, the treasurer, and the controller. They are discussing the sale of the October Division, which is expected to happen in June of this year, and the related reporting problems.

The vice-president thinks that the sale does not need to be segregated in the income statement because separate categories tend to be abused and they confuse the shareholders. The treasurer disagrees. He feels that if an item is unusual or infrequent, it should be classified as an extraordinary item, and that this applies to the sale of the October Division. The controller counters that an item must be both infrequent and unusual to be extraordinary, not one or the other. He therefore feels the sale of the October Division should be shown separately, but not as an extraordinary item. Another alternative is to show pro forma income that excludes the October Division.

The sale is not news to you because you read about it in the minutes of the December 16, 2007, board of directors meeting. The minutes indicated plans to sell the transmitter plant and equipment by June 30, 2008, to the company's major competitor, who seems interested. The board estimates that net income and sales will remain constant until the sale, on which the company expects a $700,000 profit.

You also hear the controller disagree with the vice-president about the results of the strike last year and the sale of old transistor ovens. The ovens were formerly used in manufacturing, and the vice-president believes that both the effects of the strike and the sale of the ovens should be extraordinary items. In addition, the treasurer thinks that the government regulation issued last month which made much of their inventory of raw material useless would also be extraordinary. The regulations set beta emission standards at levels lower than those in the raw materials supply, and there is no alternative use for the materials.

After a long discussion that seems to be getting nowhere, the controller finally claims that the discussion is really just academic anyway. Since the net effect of all three items is immaterial, no disclosure is required, he says.

Instructions
Discuss the issues.

CA4-5 United Manufacturing Company (UMC) recently filed for bankruptcy protection. The company manufactures downhill skis and its shares trade on the TSX. With the increased popularity of such alternative winter sports as snow boarding and tubing, sales of skis are sagging. The company has decided to start a new line of products that focuses on the growing industry surrounding snow tubing and snow boarding. At present, however, the company needs interim financing to pay suppliers and its payroll. It also needs a significant amount of cash so that it can reposition itself in the marketplace. Management is planning to go to the bank with draft financial statements to discuss additional financing. The company's year end is December 31, 2007, and it is now January 15, 2008. Current interest rates for loans are 5%, but because it is in bankruptcy protection, UMC feels that it will likely have to pay at least 15% on any loan. There is concern that the bank will turn the company down.

At a recent management meeting, the company decided to convert its ski manufacturing facilities into snow board manufacturing facilities. It will no longer produce skis. Management is unsure if the company will be able to recover the cost of the ski inventory. Although the conversion will result in significant expenditures, the company feels that this is justified if UMC wants to remain a viable business. The shift in strategic positioning will not result in any layoffs as most employees will work in the retrofitted plant. The remaining employees will be trained in the new business.

The conversion to snow board manufacturing facilities would not require selling the ski manufacturing machines as these machines can be used to produce snow boards. The company estimates the results and cash flows from its operation of selling skis to be a $20-million loss.

On December 15, 2007, the company entered into an agreement with LKT to sell its entire inventory in ski bindings to LKT. Under the terms of the deal, LKT paid $10 million cash for the inventory (its regular selling price at the time). The cost to UMC of this inventory was $6 million and so a profit of $4 million was booked pre-tax. In a separate deal, UMC agreed to buy back the inventory in January for $10,125,000.

Before filing for bankruptcy protection, the company was able to buy a large shipment of snow tubes wholesale for a bargain price of $7 million from a supplier that was in financial trouble. The value of the inventory is approximately $10 million. The inventory was sitting in the UMC manufacturing facility taking up a lot of space. Because the manufacturing facility was being renovated, UMC reached an agreement with its leading competitor, MMN. According to the contract, MMN agreed to purchase the snow tubes from UMC for $8 million and UMC shipped the inventory on December 31 to arrive on January 5. The inventory was shipped f.o.b. shipping point. UMC normally reimburses its customers if the inventory is damaged in transit. UMC has a tentative verbal agreement that it will repurchase the snow tubes that MMN does not sell by the time the renovations are complete (in approximately six months). The buyback price will include an additional amount that will cover storage and insurance costs.

The company pays taxes at a rate of 40%.

Instructions
Adopt the role of Ray Romano—the company controller—and discuss the financial reporting issues related to the preparation of the financial statements for the year ended December 31, 2007.

Research and Financial Analysis

RA4-1 Stantec Inc.

The financial statements and accompanying notes of Stantec Inc. are presented in Appendix 5B as they appear in the company's annual report.

Instructions

Refer to the statements and notes to answer the following questions.

(a) What type of income statement format does the company use?

(b) What business is the company in? How is this reflected in the balance sheet and income statement?

(c) Has the company adopted the new set of accounting standards on comprehensive income and financial instruments? What is or will be the impact on the financial statements of adopting these standards?

RA4-2 Royal Bank of Canada

Obtain the 2006 annual report for the Royal Bank of Canada from the Student Website. Note that financial reporting for Canadian banks is also constrained by the *Bank Act* and monitored by the Office of the Superintendent of Financial Institutions.

Instructions

(a) Revenues and expenses are defined as arising from ordinary activities of the business. What are the ordinary activities (core business activities) of the bank? What normal expenses must the bank incur in order to generate core revenues?

(b) Are the core business activities reflected in the income statement? (Hint: Look at the classification between revenues and other income/gains and expenses and other costs/losses.)

(c) Calculate the percentage of the various revenues/income streams to total revenues/income. Discuss the trends from year to year. In other words, are these revenue/income streams increasing as a percentage of the total revenue/income or decreasing? What are the main sources of the revenues/income?

RA4-3 Trizec Canada Inc. and Mainstreet Equity Corp.

Instructions

Go to the Student Website, and use the annual reports of Trizec Canada Inc. and Mainstreet Equity Corp. to answer the following questions related to the years ended December 31, 2005, and September 30, 2005, respectively.

(a) What type of income statement format(s) do these two companies use? Identify any differences in income statement format between the two companies.

(b) Look at the Management Discussion and Analysis and the annual report in general. What business are both companies in?

(c) What are the main sources of revenues for both companies? Are these increasing or decreasing?

(d) Is the nature of each business reflected in its balance sheet? (Hint: What is the main asset and what percentage of total assets is this asset?)

(e) Identify the irregular items reported by these two companies in their income statements over the two-year period. Do these irregular items appear to be significant? Comment on both presentations.

RA4-4 Canadian Securities Administrators

The Canadian Securities Administrators (CSA), an umbrella group of Canadian provincial securities commissions, accumulates all documents that public companies are required to file under securities law. This electronic database may be accessed from the following website: www.sedar.com. Company financial statements may also be accessed through the company websites.

Instructions
Visit the CSA website and find the company documents for Bank of Montreal and Royal Bank of Canada. Answer the following questions:

(a) What types of company documents may be found here that provide useful information for investors who are making investment decisions?

(b) Locate the Annual Information Form. Explain the nature of the information that it contains. As a financial statement analyst, is this information useful to you? Why?

(c) Who are the auditors of both banks?

(d) Which stock exchange(s) do the banks trade on?

(e) Go to the company websites directly (www.bmo.com and www.royalbank.com). Look under Investor relations. What type of information is on these websites and how is it different from what is found on the CSA website (www.sedar.com)? Should these websites contain the same information as the CSA website?

RA4-5 Reporting Financial Performance/Financial Statement Presentation

The IASB and FASB are currently studying the issue of reporting financial performance. As noted in the chapter, Phase A of the project is almost complete and the standard setters are currently working on Phase B.

Instructions
Go to the FASB website and download and read the material on financial statement presentation.

(a) Identify the working principles established for Phase B of the project.

(b) What are the main income statement categories that are being proposed? Discuss whether these categories will improve financial reporting.

(c) How will Other Comprehensive Income be treated? Do you agree with this treatment?

RA4-6 Quality of Earnings Research

Quality of earnings analysis is a very important tool in assessing the value of a company and its shares. The chapter presents a framework for evaluating quality of earnings.

Instructions
Do an Internet search on the topic and write a critical essay discussing the usefulness of the quality of earnings assessment.

RA4-7 Alliance Atlantis Communications Inc.

An excerpt from the annual report of Alliance Atlantis Communications Inc. is shown below. The excerpt shows a calculation of Earnings Before Interest, Tax, Depreciation, and Amortization (EBITDA)—a non-GAAP earnings measure.

Instructions

Discuss the pros and cons of management's decision to report additional earnings numbers outside of the traditional audited financial statements. In the case of this company, in your opinion, do you think that this presentation provides good, useful information?

Extra Cash Grows Company

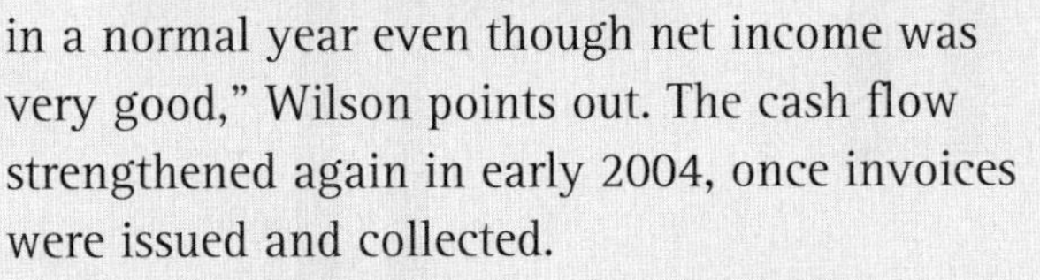

Stantec Inc. provides planning, engineering, architecture, surveying, and management for a wide variety of facilities and infrastructure projects across North America. "We provide services in five different practice areas—buildings, environment, industrial, transportation, and urban land—and we focus on professional services," says Don Wilson, Stantec's vice-president and chief financial officer.

Headquartered in Edmonton, the firm has been successful at providing these professional services, turning a profit every year since its establishment in 1954.

Consistent profits, however, do not necessarily mean consistent levels of cash flow. "In most years, we have seen differences between operating cash flow and net income," says Wilson. For example, in October 2003, Stantec's implementation of a new project management and financial system resulted in delays in issuing invoices to clients in the last quarter of the year. "The cash flow in that last quarter was less than in a normal year even though net income was very good," Wilson points out. The cash flow strengthened again in early 2004, once invoices were issued and collected.

A similar scenario occurred in 2005 when a U.S. acquisition, The Keith Companies, slowed the pace of invoicing. This situation corrected itself in early 2006.

Stantec uses most of its positive cash flow to reinvest in growing the business with acquisitions. "We use cash to buy other firms, or to pay out debt incurred in acquisitions," Wilson explains.

The company does not pay dividends to shareholders. "We have continued to generate increasing earnings for shareholders by reinvesting that cash in the growth of our company," says Wilson. In fact, Stantec's compound annual growth rate in revenue for the 10 years ended 2005 was just over 20 percent, while the compound annual growth rate in net income for the same period was over 28 percent. ■

Financial Position and Cash Flows

chapter 5

Learning Objectives

After studying this chapter, you should be able to:

1. Identify the uses and limitations of a balance sheet.
2. Identify the major classifications of a balance sheet.
3. Prepare a classified balance sheet.
4. Identify balance sheet information that requires supplemental disclosure.
5. Identify major disclosure techniques for the balance sheet.
6. Indicate the purpose of the statement of cash flows.
7. Identify the content of the statement of cash flows.
8. Prepare the cash from operating activities section of the statement of cash flows.
9. Understand the usefulness of the statement of cash flows.

After studying Appendix 5A, you should be able to:

10. Identify the major types of financial ratios and what they measure.

Preview of Chapter 5

The **balance sheet** and **statement of cash flows** complement the income statement, offering information about the company's financial position and how the firm generates and uses cash. This chapter examines the many different types of assets, liabilities, and shareholders' equity items that affect the balance sheet and the statement of cash flows.

The chapter is organized as follows:

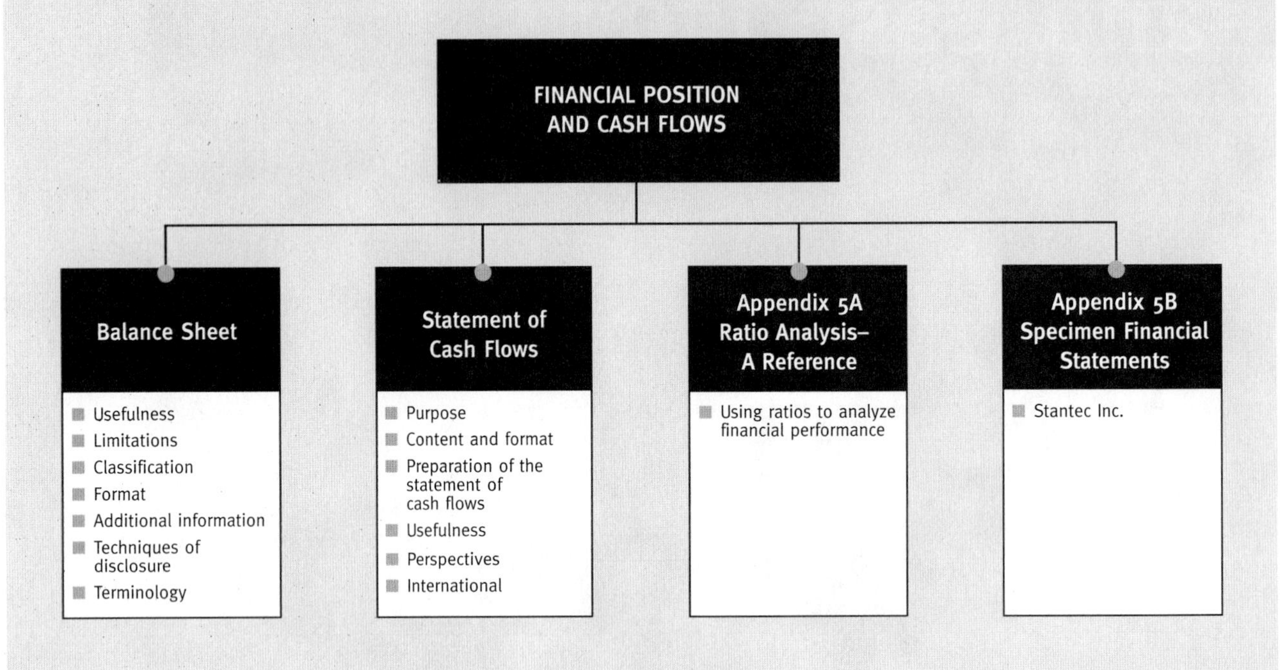

SECTION 1—BALANCE SHEET

The **balance sheet**, sometimes referred to as the **statement of financial position**, reports a business enterprise's assets, liabilities, and shareholders' equity at a specific date. This financial statement provides information about the nature and amounts of the following: investments in enterprise resources, obligations to creditors, and the owners' equity in net resources.[1] It therefore helps in predicting the amounts, timing, and uncertainty of future cash flows.

Usefulness of the Balance Sheet

Objective 1
Identify the uses and limitations of a balance sheet.

Containing information about assets, liabilities, and shareholders' equity, the balance sheet becomes a basis for calculating rates of return on invested assets and evaluating the enterprise's

[1] Chapter 6 of *Financial Reporting in Canada, 2005* (Toronto, CICA) indicates that approximately 90 percent of the companies surveyed used the term "balance sheet." The term "statement of financial position" is used very little, although it does communicate the concept well. Note that in the Financial Statement project, the IASB and FASB recently proposed that enterprises use the title "Statement of Financial Position," but would not make this title mandatory.

capital structure. Information in the balance sheet is also used to assess business risk[2] and future cash flows. In this regard, **the balance sheet is useful for analyzing a company's liquidity, solvency, and financial flexibility**, as described below, and helps also in analyzing profitability (even though this is not the main focus of the statement).

Liquidity looks at the **amount of time that is expected to pass until an asset is realized** (converted into cash or other monetary asset) or until a liability has to be paid. Does the company have enough cash on hand and cash coming in to cover its short-term liabilities? Certain ratios help assess overall liquidity, including the **current ratio, quick or acid test ratio**, and **current cash debt coverage ratio**. The liquidity of certain assets, such as receivables and inventory, is assessed through **turnover ratios**.[3] These ratios look at how fast the receivables or inventories are being collected or sold. Creditors are interested in **short-term** liquidity ratios, because these ratios indicate whether the enterprise will have the resources to pay its current and maturing obligations. Similarly, shareholders assess liquidity to evaluate the possibility of future cash dividends or the buyback of shares. In general, the greater the liquidity, the lower the risk of enterprise or business failure.[4]

Solvency refers to an **enterprise's ability to pay its debts and related interest**. For example, when a company carries a high level of long-term debt compared to its assets, it is at higher risk for insolvency than a similar company with less long-term debt. Companies with higher debt are more risky because more of their assets will be required to meet these fixed obligations (such as interest and principal payments). Certain ratios help assess solvency. These are often called "coverage" ratios as they refer to a company's ability to cover its interest and long-term debt payments.

Liquidity and solvency affect an entity's **financial flexibility**, which measures the **"ability of an enterprise to take effective actions to alter the amounts and timing of cash flows so it can respond to unexpected needs and opportunities."**[5] For example, a company may become so loaded with debt—so financially inflexible—that its cash sources to finance expansion or to pay off maturing debt are limited or non-existent. An enterprise with a high degree of financial flexibility is better able to survive bad times, to recover from unexpected setbacks, and to take advantage of profitable and unexpected investment opportunities. Generally, the greater the financial flexibility, the lower the risk of enterprise or business failure.

What Do the Numbers Mean?

As mentioned in Chapter 2, **Air Canada** filed for bankruptcy protection in April 2003. Factors such as outbreaks of severe acute respiratory syndrome (SARS), the Iraq war, and terrorism threats had severely reduced airline travel, and therefore airlines' cash inflows. At that time, Air Canada's total debt exceeded its total assets by $2,558 million, leaving it very little flexibility to react to changes in its environment. It was therefore very vulnerable to the decreasing demand for its services. Its current liabilities exceeded its current assets by $1,386 million, resulting in an inability to cover its day-to-day operating costs. By the end of the second quarter, the company had taken steps, while under bankruptcy protection, to ease the cash flow problems and increase flexibility. These included:

1. arranging for interim financing (called debtor in possession [DIP] financing) with General Electric Capital Canada Inc. (GE),
2. restructuring union contracts, and
3. renegotiating aircraft leases for 106 planes (with GE).

---

[2] Risk means the unpredictability of the enterprise's future events, transactions, circumstances, and results.

[3] The formulas for these ratios and other ratios are summarized in Appendix 5A.

[4] Liquidity measures are important inputs to bankruptcy prediction models, such as those developed by Altman and others. See G. White, A. Sondhi, and D. Fried, *The Analysis of Financial Statements* (New York: John Wiley & Sons, 2003), Chapter 18.

[5] "Reporting Income, Cash Flows, and Financial Position of Business Enterprises," *Proposed Statement of Financial Accounting Concepts* (Stamford, Conn.: FASB, 1981), par. .25.

This DIP financing provided the company with an additional $700-million line of credit while the other two significant renegotiations helped reduce immediate cash needs for salaries and lease/rent payments. Note that the line of credit, while providing short-term relief, increases total debt when it is used. The company announced that it hoped to emerge from bankruptcy protection by the end of 2003. It did not quite meet this target but did eventually emerge from bankruptcy protection on September 30, 2004. With a new strategy that included a competitive cost structure, a redesigned network, a new revenue model, and a new corporate structure, the company managed to turn a $258-million profit for its year end 2005 despite the increase in fuel prices. As at December 31, 2005, the long-term debt to equity ratio was still high at 6.6:1; however, this was a significant improvement over the previous year when the ratio was 32:1.

Limitations of the Balance Sheet

Timber at Historical Cost | Timber at Current Value

If we sell that land, we could get more than we paid.

Because the income statement and the balance sheet are interrelated, it is not surprising that the balance sheet has many of the same limitations as the income statement. Here are some of the major limitations of the balance sheet:

1. Many assets and liabilities are stated at their historical cost. As a result, the information that is reported in the balance sheet has higher reliability but it can be criticized as being less relevant than the current fair value would be. Use of historical cost and other valuation methods was discussed in Chapter 2. As noted there, we are moving towards greater use of fair value, specifically for derivatives and investments.

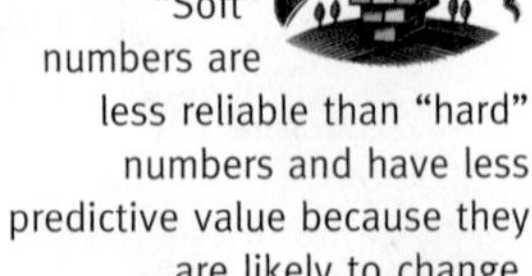

Underlying Concept

"Soft" numbers are less reliable than "hard" numbers and have less predictive value because they are likely to change.

2. Judgements and estimates are used in determining many of the items reported in the balance sheet. This recalls the issue identified in Chapter 4 when discussing income statement limitations. As was stated there, the financial statements include many "soft" numbers—i.e., numbers that are significantly uncertain.

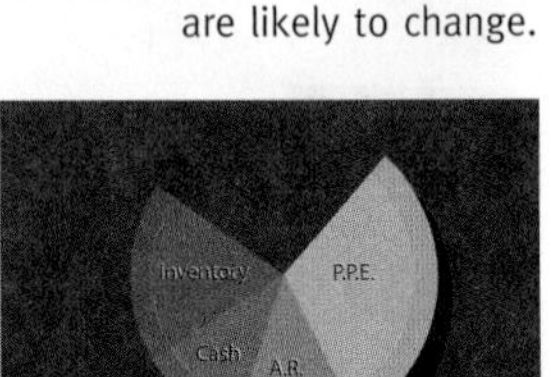

3. The balance sheet necessarily **leaves out many items** that are of financial value to the business but cannot be recorded objectively.[6] These may be either assets or liabilities. Recall again the discussion from Chapter 4. Because liquidity and solvency ratios worsen when liabilities are recognized, a company may be biased against including liabilities in the financial statements. Knowing this, analysts habitually look for and capitalize[7] many liabilities that may be "off-balance sheet" before they calculate key liquidity and solvency ratios. For example, when valuing a company, specialists in mergers and acquisitions consider off–balance sheet obligations such as lease commitments. The information that is disclosed in the notes to the financial statements and the analyst's knowledge of the business and industry become critical in this context, as they make it possible to identify and measure off–balance sheet items that often represent either additional risk to the company or unrecognized assets (for instance goodwill).

Classification in the Balance Sheet

Underlying Concept

Disclosing too much detail often obscures important information by creating information overload.

Objective 2
Identify the major classifications of a balance sheet.

Balance sheet accounts are **classified** (like the income statement) so that **similar items are grouped together** to arrive at significant subtotals. The material is also arranged so that important relationships are shown.

As is true of the income statement, the balance sheet's parts and subsections can be more informative than the whole. Individual items should be separately reported and classified in enough detail so that users can assess the amounts, timing, and uncer-

[6] Several of these omitted items (such as internally generated goodwill and certain commitments) are discussed in later chapters.

[7] While the term "capitalize" is often used in the context of recording costs as assets, it is sometimes used differently: in the context here, it means recognizing the liabilities on the balance sheet.

tainty of future cash flows, and evaluate the company's liquidity and financial flexibility, profitability, and risk.

Classification in financial statements helps analysts and other financial statement users by **grouping items with similar characteristics** and **separating items with different characteristics**. In this regard, the balance sheet has additional information content. Recall that many users use the information in financial statements to assess risk, including the company's financial flexibility, as noted earlier. Consider how the following groupings of assets and liabilities provide additional insight:

International Insight

The IASB and FASB are working on the next phase of the Financial Statements project, which is to establish consistent principles for aggregating information and to identify the totals and subtotals that should be reported.

1. Assets that are of a different type or that have a different **function** in the activities of the company should be reported as separate items. For example, merchandise inventories should be reported separately from property, plant, and equipment. Inventory will be sold and property, plant, and equipment will be used. In this way, investors can see how fast inventory is turning over or being sold.
2. Liabilities with **different implications for the enterprise's financial flexibility** should be reported as separate items. For example, long-term liabilities should be reported separately from current liabilities, and debt should be separate from equity.
3. Assets and liabilities with different **general liquidity characteristics** should be reported as separate items. For example, cash should be reported separately from accounts receivable.
4. Certain assets, liabilities, and equity instruments have **attributes that allow them to be measured or valued more easily**. Reporting these separately takes advantage of this characteristic. Financial instruments and monetary assets and liabilities are two such groupings. Each will be discussed separately below.

Monetary Assets and Liabilities **Monetary assets** represent either money itself **or claims to future cash flows that are fixed and determinable in amounts and timing.**[8] Because of these characteristics, they are said to be easier to measure, and generally are. In addition, their carrying values (which approximate net realizable value) are more representative of reality as they normally are close to the amount of cash that the company will receive in the future. Examples are accounts and notes receivable. Likewise, liabilities which require **future cash outflows that are fixed and determinable in amounts and timing**[9] are also considered to be monetary and thus easier to measure. Accounts and notes payable and long-term debt are examples. In contrast, other assets—such as inventory, property, plant and equipment, certain investments, and intangibles—are **non-monetary assets** because their value in terms of a monetary unit such as dollars is not fixed. There is therefore additional measurement uncertainty. These assets are often recorded at their historical cost (or amortized cost), which does not reflect their true value.

Underlying Concept

With non-monetary assets, historical cost is often a more reliable measure.

Financial Instruments **Financial instruments** are contracts between two or more parties. They are often marketable or tradable, and therefore easy to measure.[10] Many financial instruments are also monetary assets or liabilities. They include the following:

- **cash**
- **contractual rights to receive, or obligations to deliver, cash or another financial instrument**
- **investments in other companies** [11]

[8] *CICA Handbook*, Section 3831.05.

[9] Ibid.

[10] Markets often exist or can be created for these instruments because of their nature and measurability. Liabilities are included because they represent the other side of an asset contract—e.g., accounts payable to one company represents accounts receivable to another. Accounts receivable contracts or pools are often bought and sold.

[11] See *CICA Handbook* Section 3855.19 for more complete definitions.

Contractual rights to **receive** cash or other financial instruments are assets, whereas contractual obligations to **pay** are liabilities. Cash, investments, accounts receivable, and all payables or debt are examples of financial instruments. These instruments are all monetary. Shares are also financial instruments. Current accounting standards on financial instruments require fair value accounting for certain types of financial instruments, including certain types of investments.[12] This is due to the fact that fair value (often market value) is fairly easy to obtain and represents an objective view of the measurement of the instrument. The accounting and reporting of financial instruments is discussed more extensively in Chapters 7, 9, 13, 14, 15, and 16. Derivatives, a more complex type of financial instrument, will be covered in Chapter 16. Most monetary assets and liabilities are financial instruments.

The three general classes of items that are included in the balance sheet are assets, liabilities, and equity. They are defined below.

ELEMENTS OF THE BALANCE SHEET

1. *Assets.* Probable **future economic benefits** obtained or **controlled by** a particular entity as a result of **past transactions** or events.
2. *Liabilities.* Probable future sacrifices of economic benefits because of a present **duty or responsibility** to others that was created by **past transactions** or events, and where there **is little or no discretion to avoid** the obligation.
3. *Equity/Net Assets.* The **residual interest** in an entity's assets that remains after deducting its liabilities. In a business enterprise, the equity is the ownership interest.

These are the same definitions from Chapter 2 and the conceptual framework. Illustration 5-1 shows the general format for presenting the balance sheet.

Illustration 5-1
Balance Sheet Classifications

Assets	Liabilities and Shareholders' Equity
Current assets	Current liabilities
Long-term investments	Long-term debt
Property, plant, and equipment	Shareholders' equity
Intangible assets	Capital shares
Other assets	Contributed surplus
	Retained earnings
	Accumulated other comprehensive income

Although the balance sheet can be classified in some other way, in actual practice these major subdivisions are closely followed, with exceptions in certain industries. When the balance sheet is for a proprietorship or partnership, the classifications in the owners' equity section are presented a little differently, as will be shown later in the chapter.

Student Website

Analyst Toolkit—Financial Statement Analysis Primer

www.wiley.com/canada/kieso

These standard classifications make it easier to calculate important ratios such as the current ratio for assessing liquidity and debt-to-equity ratios for assessing solvency. Because total assets are broken down into categories, users can easily calculate which assets are more significant than others and how these relationships change over

[12] *CICA Handbook*, Section 3855.55.

time.[13] This gives insight into management's strategy and stewardship. Illustration 5-2 shows a classified balance sheet for **Petro-Canada**.

Illustration 5-2

Classified Balance Sheet–Excerpt from Petro-Canada

CONSOLIDATED BALANCE SHEET

(stated in millions of Canadian dollars)

As at December 31,	2005	2004 *(Note 3)*
ASSETS		
CURRENT ASSETS		
Cash and cash equivalents *(Note 13)*	$ 721	$ –
Accounts receivable *(Note 10)*	1,617	1,086
Inventories *(Note 14)*	596	549
Assets of discontinued operations *(Note 3)*	237	387
	3,171	2,022
PROPERTY, PLANT AND EQUIPMENT, NET *(Note 15)*	15,921	14,318
GOODWILL *(Note 16)*	737	853
DEFERRED CHARGES AND OTHER ASSETS *(Note 17)*	415	345
ASSETS OF DISCONTINUED OPERATIONS *(Note 3)*	411	598
	$ 20,655	$ 18,136
LIABILITIES AND SHAREHOLDERS' EQUITY		
CURRENT LIABILITIES		
Outstanding cheques less cash and cash equivalents *(Note 13)*	$ –	$ 36
Accounts payable and accrued liabilities	2,854	2,188
Income taxes payable	82	272
Liabilities of discontinued operations *(Note 3)*	102	133
Short-term notes payable	–	299
Current portion of long-term debt	7	6
	3,045	2,934
LONG-TERM DEBT *(Note 18)*	2,906	2,275
OTHER LIABILITIES *(Note 19)*	1,888	646
ASSET RETIREMENT OBLIGATIONS *(Note 20)*	923	834
FUTURE INCOME TAXES *(Note 7)*	2,405	2,708
COMMITMENTS AND CONTINGENT LIABILITIES *(Note 25)*		
SHAREHOLDERS' EQUITY		
Common shares *(Note 21)*	1,362	1,314
Contributed surplus *(Note 21)*	1,422	1,743
Retained earnings	7,018	5,408
Foreign currency translation adjustment	(314)	274
	9,488	8,739
	$ 20,655	$ 18,136

See accompanying Notes to Consolidated Financial Statements

Approved on behalf of the Board of Directors

Ron A. Brenneman
Director

Brian F. MacNeill
Director

46 PETRO-CANADA

[13] This type of comparison is done by performing a **vertical analysis**, which calculates the percentage that a specific asset represents when divided by total assets. This number may then be compared with the same percentage from past years. The latter comparison is generally called **horizontal or trend analysis**. Horizontal and vertical analyses are discussed further on the Student Website under Financial Statement Analysis.

Note that the current ratio changed significantly from 2004 to 2005. The calculations for the current ratio are as follows.

2004 = $2,022 million/$2,934 million = 0.69 to 1

2005 = $3,171 million/$3,045 million = 1.04 to 1

The improving current ratio means that Petro-Canada's liquidity position has grown stronger. Understanding the company's changing business and business environment is key in interpreting this. According to the annual report, the overall improvement in the company's business was due to strong commodities prices, improved margins (i.e., higher gross profits) in refining, and solid overall operations. The change in ratio was from higher accounts receivable due to increased revenues (which were offset partially by increased accounts payable). In addition, a closer look at the financial statements reveals that the company spent less on property, plant, and equipment and exploration, as well as less on acquisitions. This resulted in additional cash on hand, which also helped improve the ratio.

Current Assets

Objective 3
Prepare a classified balance sheet.

Current assets are **cash and other assets that will ordinarily be realized within one year from the date of the balance sheet or within the normal operating cycle if the cycle is longer than a year.**[14] The operating cycle is the average time between the acquisition of materials and supplies and the realization of cash. Cash is realized through sales of the product that is created from the materials and supplies. The cycle begins with cash and then moves through inventory, production, and receivables, and back to cash. When there are several operating cycles within one year, the one-year period is used. If the operating cycle is more than one year, the longer period is used. Illustration 5-3 shows the operating cycle for manufacturing companies.

Illustration 5-3
The Business Operating Cycle for Manufacturing Companies

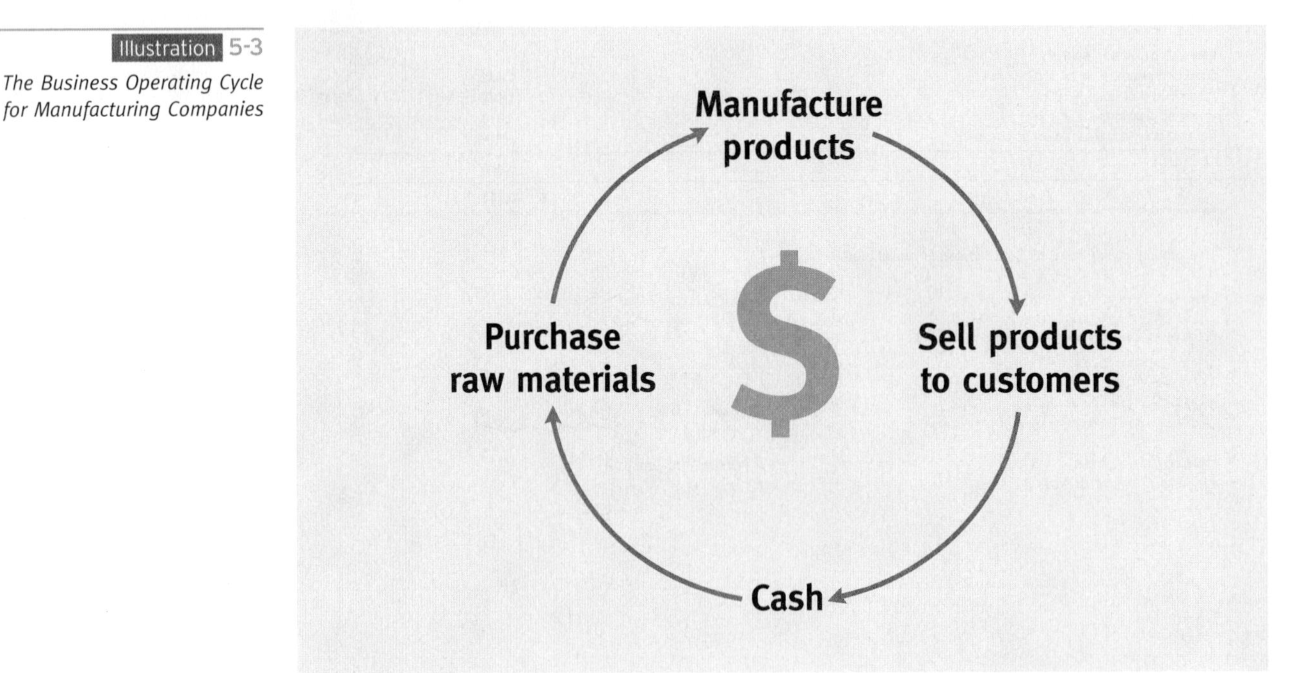

[14] *CICA Handbook*, Section 1510.01.

For most industries, current assets are generally segregated and presented in the balance sheet in order according to their liquidity.[15] The five major items that are found in the current assets section are cash, short-term investments (can be referred to as held-for-trading or available-for-sale investments), receivables, inventories, and prepayments. Cash is included at its stated value; investments are valued at their fair value;[16] accounts receivable are stated at the estimated amount that is collectible; inventories generally are included at the lower of cost and net realizable value; and prepaid items are valued at cost.

Underlying Concept

Grouping these similar items together reduces the amount of redundant information on the balance sheet and therefore makes the information easier to understand.

Cash Cash is often grouped with other cash-like liquid assets and reported as **cash and cash equivalents**.[17] Cash and cash equivalents are defined as **cash, demand deposits, and short-term, highly liquid investments that are readily convertible into known amounts of cash and have an insignificant risk of changing in value.**[18] Illustration 5-4 details the cash and cash equivalents for Stantec Inc. The company defines its cash and cash equivalents as cash and unrestricted investments that have initial maturities of less than three months.

Illustration 5-4

Balance Sheet Presentation of Cash and Cash Equivalents—Excerpt from the December 31, 2005, Financial Statements of Stantec Inc. (in thousands of dollars)

ASSETS *[note 8]*		
Current		
Cash and cash equivalents	**28,143**	37,890
Restricted cash *[note 2]*	**21,312**	–
Accounts receivable, net of allowance for doubtful accounts of $16,053 in 2005 ($21,095 – 2004)	**137,928**	112,476
Costs and estimated earnings in excess of billings	**66,172**	40,861
Prepaid expenses	**5,420**	4,165
Future income tax assets *[note 14]*	**14,827**	8,532
Other assets *[note 6]*	**6,569**	4,831
Total current assets	**280,371**	208,755

Any restrictions on the general availability of cash or any commitments on how it is likely to be used must be disclosed. As noted in Illustration 5-4, Stantec presents restricted cash separately. Cash that is not available for current purposes should be excluded from current assets.[19]

Student Website

Student Toolkit—Additional Disclosures

www.wiley.com/canada/kieso

How much cash should a company hold? In general, a company needs enough liquid assets, including cash, to be able to settle its current liabilities in a timely manner; however,

[15] The real estate industry is an example that does not follow this approach. This is because the industry feels that a more meaningful presentation results when the most important assets are presented first. In most real estate development companies, the most important and largest asset is revenue-producing properties. This asset includes hotels, shopping centres, leased buildings, and so on that generate revenue or profits for the company. Brookfield Properties Corporation records this asset first on its balance sheet. On the liabilities side, the corresponding debt related to the properties is recorded. For Brookfield, this asset represents 78 percent of total assets. Real estate companies are bound by GAAP and also by specialized industry GAAP (Real Estate GAAP as published by the Real Properties Association of Canada [REALpac]; see www.realpac.ca). For different reasons, Bombardier Inc. does not classify its balance sheet. It operates in two distinct segments (aerospace and transportation) that have differing operating cycles and, because of this, the company feels that classification would not add value.

[16] Historically, in most industries these financial instruments have been valued mainly at their historical cost. *CICA Handbook* Section 3855 on financial instruments now requires investments that are classified as held for trading or available for sale to be valued at their fair value.

[17] According to a survey of 200 companies, 137 reported cash and cash equivalents (up from 112 in 2001) and an additional 28 reported that they grouped cash with short-term deposits or investments (CICA, *Financial Reporting in Canada, 2005*, Chapter 18).

[18] *CICA Handbook*, Section 1540.06.

[19] *CICA Handbook*, Section 3000.01.

it must also ensure that its assets do not sit idle. Cash itself is generally non-interest-bearing and so does not contribute to net income. Too much cash can make a company a more likely target for a takeover bid.

Short-Term Investments Investments in debt and equity securities are grouped into three separate portfolios for their valuation and presentation. These portfolios may be categorized as follows:[20]

Held-to-maturity: Debt securities that the company intends to hold to maturity and has the ability to do so.

Held-for-trading: Financial instruments that have any of the following characteristics and are not loans or receivables:

1. They are acquired for the purpose of selling them in the near term.
2. They are part of a portfolio of identified financial instruments that are managed together and for which there is evidence of a recent actual pattern of short-term profit taking.
3. They are derivatives.[21]

Available-for-sale: Debt and equity securities that are not classified as held-to-maturity or held-for-trading securities.

Note that these labels do not need to be used. However, when they are used correctly they are a useful way of categorizing investments because they allow users to understand management's intentions.[22] Held-for-trading securities should normally be recorded as current assets. Available-for-sale and held-to-maturity securities should be classified as current or non-current depending on the nature of the investment and management intent. All of these securities should be measured at their fair value, except for the held-to-maturity securities, which are measured at their amortized cost. This is not a hard rule, however, as GAAP does allow a company to value any financial instrument at its fair value. This is known as the "fair value option" and will be discussed in greater detail in Chapter 9.

Companies that have excess cash often have significant amounts of short-term investments. While deciding what to do with the money, they will temporarily invest it so as to generate some profits (instead of letting the funds sit idle as non-interest-bearing cash. In addition, the way a company does business can result in higher levels of investments. For instance, the business models of insurance companies, pension funds, and banks result in significant amounts of temporary as well as long-term investments. Insurance companies collect premiums up front and invest the money so that they have funds available to pay out future claims that arise under the insurance policies. Pension plans likewise collect money up front (through pension contributions from individuals) and invest it for future payout when the contributors retire. Money is a bank's inventory. The bank must decide how much of it should be invested and in which investments.

Receivables Accounts receivable should be segregated to show **ordinary trade accounts**, amounts owing by **related parties**, and other **unusual items** of a substantial amount.[23] Anticipated losses due to uncollectibles should be accrued. The amount and nature of any nontrade receivables, and any receivables that have been designated or pledged as collateral, should be disclosed.[24] Accounts receivable are valued at their net

[20] *CICA Handbook*, Section 3855.19. Since this section only became effective in 2006 for public companies, there are currently very few Canadian examples of this balance sheet presentation before 2006. More detail will be presented in Chapter 9.

[21] Derivatives will be discussed further in Chapter 16.

[22] *CICA Handbook*, Section 3855.35.

[23] *CICA Handbook*, Section 3020.01.

[24] *CICA Handbook*, Section 1400.14.

realizable value. Illustration 5-5 shows how QLT Inc. reported its receivables in note 4 to its financial statements.

4. ACCOUNTS RECEIVABLE

(in thousands of U.S. dollars)	2005	2004
Visudyne®	$34,188	$42,983
Royalties	5,358	4,173
Contract research and development	1,176	3,801
Income taxes receivable	—	2,068
Eligard®	1,859	1,532
Foreign exchange contracts	—	164
Trade and other	2,078	1,879
Allowance for doubtful accounts	(673)	—
	$43,986	$56,600

Accounts receivable – Visudyne represents amounts due from Novartis Ophthalmics and consists of our 50% share of pre-tax profit on sales of Visudyne, amounts due from the sale of bulk Visudyne to Novartis Ophthalmics and reimbursement of specified royalty and other costs. The allowance for doubtful accounts has been provided for specifically identified accounts primarily related to our dental business.

Balance Sheet Presentation of Securities—Excerpt from QLT Inc.'s December 31, 2005, Financial Statements

Student Website

Student Toolkit—Additional Disclosures

www.wiley.com/canada/kieso

QLT is a biotechnology company that specializes in the discovery, development, and commercialization of drugs, including light-activated drugs such as Visudyne. Visudyne is marketed through Novartis Ophthalmics (Novartis), the company's co-development partner. The companies share the earnings from distribution of the drug. Because of the relationship between QLT and Novartis, the latter is considered a related party[25] and the accounts receivable are therefore disclosed separately. Note also that because the company markets and distributes its main product through Novartis, almost all of its receivables come from one source and this creates a credit risk concentration. This is important information and is thus highlighted in note 20 to the financial statements, which deals with financial instruments and concentration of credit risk. The category "Contract research and development" represents work done for other companies. Ordinary trade and other receivables represent a very small part of QLT's total receivables.

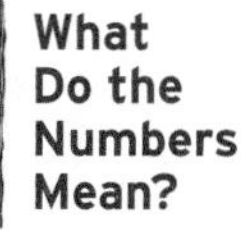

What Do the Numbers Mean?

Inventories Inventories are assets:

1. **held for sale in the ordinary course of business;**
2. **in the process of production for such sale; or**
3. **in the form of materials or supplies to be consumed in the production process or in the rendering of service.**[26]

They are valued at the lower of cost and net realizable value, with cost being determined using a **cost formula** such as first-in, first-out (FIFO), weighted average cost, or specific identification (where items are not ordinarily interchangeable). It is important to disclose these details as this information helps users understand the amount of judgement that was used in measuring this asset. For a manufacturer, the stage of the inventories' completion is also indicated (raw materials, work in process, and finished goods). Illustration 5-6 shows the breakdown of QLT's inventory.

Underlying Concept

The use of the lower of cost and net realizable value to value inventory is an example of conservatism in accounting.

International Insight

The IASB and FASB formally acknowledge that **neutrality** is incompatible with the concept of **conservatism** since the latter implies bias. Therefore, the concept of conservatism is no longer included in their conceptual framework.

[25] The identification and measurement of related parties and related-party transactions will be covered in Chapter 23.

[26] Proposed *CICA Handbook*, Section 3031.06.

Illustration 5-6

Balance Sheet Presentation of Inventories–Excerpt from QLT Inc.'s December 31, 2005, Financial Statements

5. INVENTORIES

(in thousands of U.S. dollars)	2005	2004
Raw materials and supplies	$22,046	$14,340
Work-in-process	29,083	30,864
Finished goods	390	2,152
Reserve for obsolete inventory	(1,452)	—
Provision for non-completion of product inventory	(3,828)	(1,457)
	$46,239	$45,899

We record a provision for non-completion of product inventory to provide for the potential failure of inventory batches in production to pass quality inspection. During the year ended December 31, 2005, we incurred charges to the provision for non-completion of $0.8 million (2004 – $2.2 million).

What Do the Numbers Mean?

QLT also discloses the following in its Significant Accounting Policy note:

Inventories

Raw materials and supplies inventories are carried at the of actual lower cost and net realizable value. Finished goods and work-in-process inventories are carried at the lower of weighted average cost and net realizable value. We record a provision for non-completion of product inventory to provide for potential failure of inventory batches in production to pass quality inspection. The provision is calculated at each stage of the manufacturing process. We estimate our non-completion rate based on past production and adjust our provision quarterly based on actual production volume and actual non-completion experience. We maintain a reserve for obsolescence for product expiration and obsolescence. Inventory that is obsolete or expired is written down to its market value if lower than cost.

The **nature of the inventory is important in assessing value.** QLT's inventory consists mainly of manufactured pharmaceuticals, which must be made according to very high standards and demanding specifications. Because of this, QLT acknowledges the risk that the manufactured batches might not pass quality inspection. The company also has a provision for obsolescence since products may become "off-code"—i.e., unusable due to their age. Retailers would consider theft and out-of-date stock in assessing the value of their inventory. High-tech companies would consider obsolescence.

Which types of companies are likely to have significant inventory? Companies that sell and manufacture goods will normally carry inventory (as compared with companies that offer services only). How much inventory is enough or, conversely, how much inventory is too much? Companies must have at least enough inventory to meet customer demands. On the other hand, inventory ties up significant amounts of cash flows, creates storage costs, and subjects the company to risk of theft, obsolescence, and so on. Many companies operate on a just-in-time philosophy, meaning that they streamline their production and supply channels so that they can order the raw materials and produce the product in a very short time. Car manufacturers often follow this philosophy, thus freeing up working capital and reducing the need for storing inventory.

Prepaid Expenses **Prepaid expenses** included in current assets are **expenditures already made for benefits (usually services) that will be received within one year or the operating cycle**, whichever is longer. These items are current assets because cash does not need to be used for them again in the current year or operating cycle as they have already been paid for. A common example is the payment in advance for an insurance policy. It is classified as a prepaid expense at the time of the expenditure because the payment occurs before the coverage benefit is received. Prepaid expenses are reported at the amount of the unexpired or unconsumed cost. Other common prepaid expenses include rent, advertising, taxes, and office or operating supplies.

Companies often include insurance and other prepayments for two or three years in current assets even though part of the advance payment applies to periods beyond one year or the current operating cycle. This is done by convention even though it is inconsistent with the definition of current assets.

Non-Current Investments

Non-current investments, often simply called investments, normally consist of one of the types shown in Illustration 5-7.

Illustration 5-7

Types of Non-Current Investments

TYPES OF NON-CURRENT INVESTMENTS	MEASUREMENT
Debt Securities	
Available for sale	Fair value
Held to maturity	Amortized cost
Equity Securities	
Available for sale	Fair value (unless not available and then at cost)
Significant influence investments	Equity method
Non-consolidated subsidiaries	Equity method or at cost
Other	
Sinking funds, tangible assets held as investments, other	Generally at cost

Long-term investments are usually presented on the balance sheet just below current assets in a separate section called "Investments." Many securities that are properly shown among long-term investments are, in fact, readily marketable. They are not included as current assets unless management intends to convert them to cash in the short term, that is, within a year or the operating cycle, whichever is longer.

Management may be holding some of these investments for strategic reasons (e.g., significant influence investments or non-consolidated subsidiaries). Investments that are held for strategic reasons are generally held for longer periods of time and are accounted for using the equity method (or at cost).[27] This will be seen in greater detail in Chapter 9.

The value of an investment may be considered impaired when there is objective evidence of a decline in value that is not temporary. This might occur, for example, when the market value of common shares has been less than their carrying value for several years. This will also be covered in greater detail in Chapter 9.

The excerpt in Illustration 5-8 from the financial statements of **Fairmont Hotels & Resorts Inc.** (Fairmont) reports various types of investments in partnership units, shares, investment trusts, and land separately after current assets.

Illustration 5-8

Balance Sheet Presentation of Long-Term Investments–Excerpt from Fairmont Hotels and Resorts Inc.'s December 31, 2005, Financial Statements

CONSOLIDATED BALANCE SHEETS

As at December 31 *(in millions of U.S. dollars)*	2005	2004
ASSETS		
Current assets		
Cash and cash equivalents	$ 279.2	$ 99.1
Accounts receivable (net of allowance for doubtful accounts of $1.8; 2004–$1.0)	91.7	90.2
Inventory	13.7	15.5
Prepaid expenses and other	14.6	11.2
	399.2	216.0
Investments in partnerships and corporations *(note 5)*	155.1	160.7
Non-hotel real estate *(note 7)*	100.2	100.3
Property and equipment *(note 8)*	1,308.8	1,435.5
Goodwill *(notes 4 and 9)*	164.8	162.8
Intangible assets *(notes 5 and 9)*	284.8	245.0
Other assets and deferred charges *(note 10)*	111.0	82.3
	$ 2,523.9	$ 2,402.6

[27] *CICA Handbook*, Sections 1590.26 and 3051.06.

Fairmont's presentation shows the investment in partnerships and corporations (which are mostly all accounted for by the equity method) separately from the investment in non-hotel real estate.

Property, Plant, and Equipment

Property, plant, and equipment are tangible capital assets—i.e., properties of a durable nature—which are **used in ongoing business operations to generate income**. These assets consist of physical or tangible property such as land, buildings, machinery, furniture, tools, and wasting resources (e.g., timberland, minerals). They are carried at their cost or amortized cost. With the exception of land, most assets are either depreciable (such as buildings) or depletable (such as timberlands or oil reserves).

ClubLink Corporation has significant capital assets. In fact, in 2005, capital assets represented 94 percent of the corporation's total assets. This is not surprising as the company is one of Canada's largest golf club developers and operators. The bulk of these assets are in land (golf courses) and buildings. Illustration 5-9 shows the detailed breakdown of these assets as presented in note 4 to ClubLink's financial statements.

Illustration 5-9

Balance Sheet Presentation of Property, Plant, and Equipment–Excerpt from ClubLink Corporation's December 31, 2005, Financial Statements

3. Capital Assets

(thousands of dollars)	Cost	Accumulated Amortization	2005 Net	2004 Net
Operating capital assets				
Golf course lands	$ 253,519	$ –	$ 253,519	$ 246,077
Leased lands	13,218	1,283	11,935	11,164
Buildings	142,094	21,534	120,560	117,140
Roads, cart paths and irrigation	72,118	16,245	55,873	52,177
Maintenance equipment	28,053	15,905	12,148	12,533
Clubhouse equipment	27,430	13,221	14,209	15,162
Golf carts	13,223	5,259	7,964	8,516
Office and computer equipment	5,319	2,100	3,219	3,028
	$ 554,974	$ 75,547	479,427	465,797
Development capital assets				
Properties under construction			6,240	7,437
Properties held for future development			29,142	32,427
			35,382	39,864
			$ 514,809	$ 505,661

What Do the Numbers Mean?

Note that ClubLink further segregates its capital assets into **operating** and **development** assets. This helps users understand which assets are already producing revenues and which ones will be coming on stream to produce additional future revenues, and are therefore the company's current growth potential. The basis of valuing the property, plant, and equipment, any liens against the properties, and accumulated amortization should be disclosed, usually in notes to the statements.

Aside from companies in the golf club business, those based in real estate, manufacturing, resources, or pharmaceuticals also have large amounts of capital assets on their balance sheets. These types of companies are often referred to as being **capital-intensive** since they require large amounts of capital to invest in their long-term revenue-generating assets.

Intangible Assets

Intangible assets are capital assets that have no physical substance and usually have a higher degree of uncertainty about their future benefits. They include patents, copyrights, franchises, goodwill, trademarks, trade names, and secret processes. These intangibles are initially recorded at cost and are divided into two groups for accounting purposes:

- those with finite lives
- those with indefinite lives

The former are amortized to expense over their useful lives. The latter are not amortized. Both are tested for impairment.

Intangibles can amount to significant economic resources, yet financial analysts often ignore them. This is because their **valuation and measurement are difficult**. Many intangible assets, especially those that are **internally generated** (e.g., goodwill), are never recognized at all on the balance sheet.

As Illustration 5-10 shows, a significant portion of Biovail Corporation's total assets is composed of goodwill and intangibles (50 percent).

Illustration 5-10

Balance Sheet Presentation of Goodwill and Intangible Assets–Excerpt from Biovail Corporation's Financial Statements (amounts in thousands of U.S. dollars)

	At December 31 2005	2004
ASSETS		
Current		
Cash and cash equivalents	$ 445,289	$ 34,324
Marketable securities	505	5,016
Accounts receivable	132,699	148,762
Assets of discontinued operation held for sale	1,893	—
Inventories	89,473	110,154
Deposits and prepaid expenses	14,923	16,395
	684,782	314,651
Long-term assets of discontinued operation held for sale	1,107	—
Marketable securities	6,859	—
Long-term investments	66,421	68,046
Property, plant and equipment, net	199,567	186,556
Intangible assets, net	910,276	978,073
Goodwill	100,294	100,294
Other assets, net	59,506	63,440
	$2,028,812	$1,711,060

What Do the Numbers Mean?

A further look at the detail behind the amount for intangibles shows that Biovail's intangibles include trademarks and product rights for several pharmaceutical products. It makes sense that the company would have a large amount of money invested in intangibles since Biovail is in the business of developing products in the controlled-release drug-delivery sector. The drugs are patented by the company and become main revenue generators. Having stated this, the true value of **internally generated** patents is generally not reflected in the balance sheet. Instead, it is most often the **purchased** rights to drugs that show up as intangible assets since the value of these rights is measured through their acquisition. For instance, in 2000, Biovail acquired the rights to Cardizem, a drug for the treatment of hypertension and angina. This drug still accounts for 40 percent of the balance in intangible assets before amortization.

Other Assets

The items included in the section Other Assets vary widely in practice. Some of the items that are commonly included (if they are not included anywhere else) are non-current receivables, intangible assets, assets in special funds, future income tax assets, property held for sale, and advances to subsidiaries. The company should be careful to disclose these assets in enough detail for users to get a better idea of their nature.

Future income tax assets represent the taxes that may be avoided or saved due to deductions that a company may take when it prepares its **future** tax returns. For instance, when a company buys an asset, it is allowed to deduct the cost of the asset from future taxable income. This represents a benefit, which is tax effected and recognized on the balance sheet. Future income taxes will be discussed in greater detail in Chapter 18.

Current Liabilities

Current liabilities are the **obligations that are due within one year from the date of the balance sheet or within the operating cycle, where this is longer**.[28] This concept includes:

1. Payables resulting from the acquisition of goods and services: trade accounts payable, wages payable, taxes payable
2. Collections received in advance for the delivery of goods or the performance of services, such as unearned rent revenue or unearned subscriptions revenue
3. Other liabilities whose liquidation will take place within the operating cycle, such as the portion of long-term bonds to be paid in the current period, or short-term obligations arising from a purchase of equipment
4. Short-term financing that is payable on demand (such as a line of credit or overdraft)
5. Derivative financial instruments

At times, a liability that is payable within the year may not be included in the current liabilities section. This may occur either when the debt will be refinanced through another long-term issue,[29] or when the debt is retired out of non-current assets. This approach is justified because the liquidation of the liability does not result from the use of current assets or the creation of other current liabilities.

Current liabilities are not reported in any consistent order. The items that are most commonly listed first are accounts payable, accrued liabilities, or short-term debt; those that are most commonly listed last are income taxes payable, current maturities of long-term debt, or other current liabilities. Any secured liability—for example, notes payable that have shares held as collateral for them—is fully described in the notes so that the assets providing the security can be identified.

The excess of total current assets over total current liabilities is referred to as working capital (sometimes called net working capital). Working capital is thus the net amount of a company's relatively liquid resources. That is, it is the liquid buffer (or cushion) that is available to meet the operating cycle's financial demands. Working capital as an amount is rarely disclosed on the balance sheet, but it is calculated by bankers and other creditors as an indicator of a company's short-run liquidity. To determine the actual liquidity and availability of working capital to meet current obligations, however, one must analyze the current assets' composition and analyze their nearness to cash.

Long-Term Debt/Liabilities

Underlying Concept

Information about covenants and restrictions gives insight into the entity's financial flexibility and is therefore disclosed in respect of the full disclosure principle.

Long-term liabilities are **obligations that are not reasonably expected to be liquidated within the normal operating cycle but instead are payable at some later date**. Bonds payable, notes payable, some future income tax liabilities, lease obligations, and pension obligations are the most common examples. Generally, extensive supplementary disclosure is needed for this section, because most long-term debt is subject to various covenants and restrictions in order to protect lenders.[30] Long-term liabilities that mature

[28] *CICA Handbook*, Section 1510.05.

[29] In Chapter 13, there is a more detailed discussion of debt that is expected to be refinanced and how this is classified in the balance sheet.

[30] The rights and privileges of the various securities that are outstanding (both debt and equity) are usually explained in the notes to the financial statements. Examples of information that should be disclosed are dividend and liquidation preferences, participation rights, call prices and dates, conversion or exercise prices or rates and pertinent dates, sinking fund requirements, unusual voting rights, and significant terms of contracts to issue additional shares (*CICA Handbook*, Sections 3210 and 3240. See also the requirements of *CICA Handbook* Section 3862).

within the current operating cycle are classified as current liabilities if current assets will be used to liquidate them.

Generally, long-term liabilities are of three types:

1. Obligations arising from **specific financing situations**, such as the issuance of bonds, long-term lease obligations, and long-term notes payable
2. Obligations arising from **ordinary enterprise operations**, such as pension obligations, future income tax liabilities, and deferred or unearned revenues
3. Obligations that **depend on the occurrence or non-occurrence of one or more future events to confirm the amount payable**, the payee, or the date payable, such as service or product warranties and other contingencies

It is desirable to report any premium or discount separately as an addition to, or subtraction from, the bonds payable. The terms of all long-term liability agreements (including the maturity date or dates, interest rates, nature of the obligation, and any security pledged to support the debt) are frequently described in notes to the financial statements. **Future income tax liabilities** are future amounts that the company will owe to the government for income taxes. Deferred or unearned revenues are often treated as liabilities because a service or product is owed to the customer. They may be classified as long-term or current.

The excerpt from **Sobeys Inc.** in Illustration 5-11 is an example of the liabilities section of the balance sheet.

Illustration 5-11

Balance Sheet Presentation of Long-Term Debt–Excerpt from Sobeys Inc.'s May 6, 2006, Balance Sheet (in millions

Liabilities		
Current		
Accounts payable and accrued liabilities	$ 1,158.8	$ 1,083.3
Future tax liabilities (Note 7)	46.1	52.4
Long-term debt due within one year	25.0	194.9
	1,229.9	1,330.6
Long-term debt (Note 6)	465.0	262.9
Long-term lease obligation (Note 17)	20.8	12.3
Employee future benefits obligation (Note 14)	96.0	92.2
Future tax liabilities (Note 7)	44.1	33.1
Deferred revenue	3.3	3.0
Minority interest (Note 1t v)	45.2	29.6
	1,904.3	1,763.7
Shareholders' equity		
Capital stock (Note 8)	904.8	901.4
Contributed surplus	0.9	0.4
Retained earnings	928.6	780.3
	1,834.3	1,682.1
	$ 3,738.6	$ 3,445.8

Contingent liabilities (see Note 13)

See accompanying notes to the consolidated financial statements.

Approved on behalf of the Board

Bill McEwan
Director

Peter C. Godsoe
Director

Sobeys Inc. 2006 Annual Report

Note that the company's long-term liabilities are mainly composed of long-term debt. The deferred revenues consist of revenues from long-term supplier purchase agreements and rental revenue from the sale of subsidiaries. These revenues are being recognized throughout the terms of the related agreements (which are greater than one year).

Owners' Equity

The **owners' equity** (shareholders' equity) section is one of the most difficult sections to prepare and understand. This is due to the complexity of capital share agreements and the various restrictions on residual equity that are imposed by corporation laws, liability agreements, and boards of directors. The section is usually divided into four parts:[30a]

1. **Share Capital**, which represents the exchange value of shares that have been issued
2. **Contributed Surplus**, which includes premiums on shares issued and other
3. **Retained Earnings**, which includes undistributed earnings, and is sometimes referred to as earned surplus
4. **Accumulated Other Comprehensive Income**, which includes unrealized gains and losses on available-for-sale securities, certain gains or loses from hedging activities, non-shareholder and non-government donations, and other

The major disclosure requirements for capital shares (or stock) are their authorized, issued, and outstanding amounts. Contributed surplus is usually presented as one amount. Retained earnings, also presented as one amount, is positive if the company has undistributed accumulated profits. Otherwise, it will be a negative number and labelled "Deficit." Any capital shares that have been reacquired by the company (treasury stock) are shown as a reduction of shareholders' equity.[31]

A corporation's ownership or shareholders' equity accounts are quite different from the equivalent accounts in a partnership or proprietorship. Partners' permanent capital accounts and the balance in their temporary accounts (drawings accounts) are shown separately. Proprietorships ordinarily use a single capital account that handles all of the owners' equity transactions.

Illustration 5-12 presents the shareholders' equity section from **Alliance Atlantis Communications Inc.** (Alliance Atlantis).

Illustration 5-12

Balance Sheet Presentation of Shareholders' Equity—Excerpt from Alliance Atlantis December 31, 2005, Balance Sheet (in millions of dollars)

Shareholder's Equity		
Share capital and other (*note 12*)	**732.7**	725.7
Deficit	**(310.3)**	(372.5)
Cumulative translation adjustments (*note 14*)	**(9.1)**	(0.5)
	413.3	352.7
	1,586.9	1,620.9

Commitments and contingencies (*note 24*). Approved by the Board of Directors

Note that the Retained Earnings account is in a deficit position and hence is called Deficit. The company had losses in 2003 but has been profitable for the last two years. Thus, the deficit is declining. Alliance Atlantis has chosen to show the details on the number of shares issued and authorized as well as other details in the notes to the financial statements. This leaves the balance sheet itself uncluttered. Illustration 5-13 shows (for a different company) how this information might be presented on the face of a balance sheet. The Cumulative Translation Adjustment account would be renamed Accumulated Other Comprehensive Income under the new accounting standard.

[30a] *The CICA Handbook* requires retained earnings and accumulated other comprehensive income to be presented separately along with a total of the two. In addition, share capital, contributed surplus and any reserves are presented separately.

[31] In Canada, under the CBCA, shares that are reacquired must be cancelled. However, some provincial jurisdictions and other countries (e.g., the United States) still allow treasury shares to exist.

Balance Sheet Format

One method of presenting a classified balance sheet is to list assets by sections on the left side and liabilities and shareholders' equity by sections on the right side. The main disadvantage of this format is that it requires two facing pages. To avoid the use of facing pages, another format, shown in Illustration 5-13, lists liabilities and shareholders' equity directly below assets on the same page.

See the Student Website for additional annual reports and examples of balance sheets.

www.wiley.com/canada/kieso

Illustration 5-13

Classified Balance Sheet

SCIENTIFIC PRODUCTS, INC.
Balance Sheet
December 31, 2008

Assets			
Current assets			
Cash		$ 42,485	
Investments—trading		28,250	
Accounts receivable	$165,824		
Less: Allowance for doubtful accounts	1,850	163,974	
Notes receivable		23,000	
Inventories—at lower of average cost and NRV		489,713	
Supplies on hand		9,780	
Prepaid expenses		16,252	
Total current assets			$ 773,454
Long-term investments—available for sale			87,500
Property, plant, and equipment			
Land—at cost		125,000	
Buildings—at cost	975,800		
Less: Accumulated amortization	341,200	634,600	
Total property, plant, and equipment			759,600
Intangible assets			
Goodwill			100,000
Total assets			$1,720,554
Liabilities and Shareholders' Equity			
Current liabilities			
Accounts payable		$247,532	
Accrued interest		500	
Income taxes payable		62,520	
Accrued salaries, wages, and other liabilities		9,500	
Deposits received from customers		420	
Total current liabilities			$ 320,472
Long-term debt			
Twenty-year 12% debentures, due January 1, 2011			500,000
Total liabilities			820,472
Shareholders' equity			
Paid in on capital shares			
Preferred, 7%, cumulative—authorized, issued, and outstanding, 30,000 shares	$300,000		
Common—authorized, 500,000 shares; issued and outstanding, 400,000 shares	400,000		
Contributed surplus	37,500	737,500	
Retained earnings	102,333		
Accumulated other comprehensive income	60,249	162,582	
Total shareholders' equity			900,082
Total liabilities and shareholders' equity			$1,720,554

Most public Canadian companies use this format.[32]

[32] In a survey of 200 Canadian companies, the CICA found that 197 out of the 200 used this format (CICA, *Financial Reporting in Canada, 2005*, Chapter 6).

Additional Information Reported

Objective 4
Identify balance sheet information that requires supplemental disclosure.

The balance sheet is not complete simply because the assets, liabilities, and shareholders' equity accounts have been listed. Supplemental information is also highly important. This can be information that is not presented elsewhere in the statement, or it can be more detail about items in the balance sheet or limitations on them (qualifications). There are normally five types of information that are supplemental to the account titles and amounts that are presented in the balance sheet.

SUPPLEMENTAL BALANCE SHEET INFORMATION

1. *Contingencies:* material events that have an uncertain outcome
2. *Accounting Policies:* explanations of the valuation methods that are used or the basic assumptions that are made for inventory valuations, amortization methods, investments in subsidiaries, etc.
3. *Contractual Situations:* explanations of certain restrictions or covenants that are attached to specific assets or, more likely, to liabilities
4. *Additional Detail:* expanded details on specific balance sheet line items
5. *Subsequent Events:* events that happened after the balance sheet data were compiled

Contingencies

A **contingency** is defined as an **existing situation in which there is uncertainty about whether a gain (gain contingency) or loss (loss contingency) will occur and that will finally be resolved when one or more future events occur or fail to occur.**[33] In short, contingencies are material events that have an uncertain future. Examples of gain contingencies are tax operating loss carry-forwards or company litigation against another party. Typical loss contingencies relate to litigation against the company, environmental issues, possible tax assessments, or government investigation. The accounting and reporting requirements for contingencies are examined fully in Chapter 13.

Accounting Policies

CICA Handbook Section 1505 recommends disclosure for all significant accounting principles and methods that management has chosen from among alternatives or that are peculiar to a particular industry. For instance, inventories can be calculated under different cost formulas (such as weighted average and FIFO); plant and equipment can be amortized under several accepted methods of cost allocation (such as double declining-balance, straight-line, and other); and investments can be carried at different valuations (such as cost, fair value, or using the equity method). Users of financial statements who are more informed know of these possibilities and examine the statements closely to determine the methods that are used and their impact on net income and key ratios.

Companies are also required to disclose information about their use of estimates in preparing the financial statements.[34] The disclosure of significant accounting principles and methods and of risks and uncertainties is particularly useful when this information is given as the first note or when it is presented in a separate summary that precedes the notes to the financial statements.

---

[33] *CICA Handbook*, Section 3290.02.

[34] *CICA Handbook*, Section 1508 and various other sections.

Contractual Situations

In addition to contingencies and different valuation methods, contractual situations should also be disclosed in the notes to the financial statements when they are significant. It is mandatory, for example, that the essential provisions of guarantees, lease contracts, pension obligations, and stock option plans be clearly stated in the notes. The analyst who examines a set of financial statements wants to know not only the liability amounts but also how the different contractual provisions (i.e., the terms and conditions) are affecting the company now, and will in the future.

5 Objective
Identify major disclosure techniques for the balance sheet.

Underlying Concept
The basis for including additional information is the full disclosure principle; that is, the information needs to be important enough to influence the decisions of an informed user.

Commitments that oblige a company to maintain a certain amount of working capital, limit its payment of dividends, restrict its use of assets, or require it to maintain certain financial ratios must all be disclosed if they are material. Considerable judgement is necessary to determine whether leaving out such information is misleading. The axiom in this situation is, "When in doubt, disclose." It is better to disclose a little too much information than not enough.

The accountant's judgement should include ethical considerations, because the way of disclosing the accounting principles, methods, and other items that have important effects on the enterprise may reflect the interests of a particular stakeholder in subtle ways that are at the expense of other stakeholders. A reader, for example, may benefit from having certain information highlighted in comprehensive notes, whereas the company—not wanting to emphasize that information—may choose to provide limited (rather than comprehensive) information in its notes.

Additional Detail

For many balance sheet items, further detail is disclosed to make them clearer. This has already been discussed under the various headings of the balance sheet assets, liabilities, and equity.

Subsequent Events

Several weeks or months may pass after the end of the year before the financial statements are issued. This time is used to count and price inventory, reconcile subsidiary ledgers with controlling accounts, prepare necessary adjusting entries, ensure all transactions for the period have been entered, and obtain an audit of the financial statements.

Underlying Concept
There is a trade-off here. Timely information is more relevant but may not be as reliable.

During this period, important transactions and events may occur that materially affect the company's financial position or operating situation. These events are known as **subsequent events**. Notes to the financial statements should explain any significant financial events that occur after the formal balance sheet date but before the financial statements have been issued.

According to Section 3820 of the *CICA Handbook*, subsequent events fall into two types or categories:

1. Events that provide further evidence of **conditions that existed** at the balance sheet date (financial statements must be adjusted for these)
2. Events that indicate **conditions that occurred after** the financial statement date (these must be disclosed in notes if the condition causes a significant change to assets or liabilities, and/or it will have a significant impact on future operations)

These will be covered in further detail in Chapter 23.

Techniques of Disclosure

The additional information that is reported should be disclosed as completely and as intelligently as possible. The following methods of disclosing pertinent information are available:

explanations in parentheses, notes, cross references and contra items, and supporting schedules, as will be explained next.

Parenthetical Explanations

Additional information is often provided by explanations in parentheses that follow the item. For example, shareholders' equity may be shown as it is in Illustration 5-14 in the financial statements of Imax Corporation.

Illustration 5-14

Parenthetical Explanations–Excerpt from Imax Corporation's December 31, 2005, Financial Statements (in thousands of U.S dollars)

Shareholders' equity (deficit)		
Capital stock (note 17) Common shares – no par value. Authorized – unlimited number. Issued and outstanding – 40,213,542 (2004 – 39,446,964)	121,674	116,281
Other equity	1,758	3,227
Deficit	(144,347)	(160,945)
Accumulated other comprehensive income (loss)	(2,128)	(939)
Total shareholders' deficit	(23,043)	(42,376)
Total liabilities and shareholders' equity (deficit)	$ 243,411	$ 230,853

(the accompanying notes are an integral part of these condensed consolidated financial statements)

Using the parentheses makes it possible to disclose additional balance sheet information that is pertinent and adds clarity and completeness. It has an advantage over a note because it brings the additional information into the body of the statement where it is less likely to be missed. Of course, lengthy parenthetical explanations that might distract the reader from the balance sheet information must be used carefully.

Notes

Notes are used if additional explanations cannot be shown conveniently as parenthetical explanations or to reduce the amount of detail on the face of the statement. For example, the details for various other accounts of Telesat Canada that it classifies as current liabilities are shown in note 12 to its financial statements rather than on the face of the statement, as Illustration 5-15 shows. Because Telesat Canada's total liabilities and shareholders' equity are more than $1.6 billion, these smaller amounts are not considered significant enough to be disclosed separately line by line on the face of the balance sheet.

Illustration 5-15

Note Disclosure–Excerpt from Notes to the Financial Statements of Telesat Canada (in thousands of dollars)

12. Other current liabilities

	2005	**2004**
Deferred revenues and deposits (see note 16)	**30,314**	24,193
Deferred milestone payments (see note 16)	**32,276**	52,029
Capital lease liabilities (see note 16)	**4,748**	846
Income taxes payable	**16,895**	16,408
Satellite performance incentive payments (see note 16)	**10,569**	9,130
Dividends payable	**449**	—
Other liabilities	**15,993**	9,232
	111,244	111,838

The notes must present all essential facts as completely and concisely as possible. Loose wording can mislead readers instead of helping them. Notes should add to the total information that is made available in the financial statements, not raise unanswered questions or contradict other parts of the statements.

Cross References and Contra Items

When there is a direct relationship between an asset and a liability, this can be cross referenced on the balance sheet. For example, in the current assets section of a balance sheet dated as at December 31, 2008, this might be shown:

Cash on deposit with sinking fund trustee for redemption of bonds payable—see Current liabilities	$800,000

In the same balance sheet, in the current liabilities section, would be the amount of bonds payable to be redeemed within one year:

Bonds payable to be redeemed in 2009—see Current assets	$2,300,000

This cross reference points out that $2.3 million of bonds payable are to be redeemed currently, and thus far only $800,000 in cash has been set aside for the redemption. This means, therefore, that the additional cash will need to come from unrestricted cash, from sales of investments, from profits, or from some other source. The same information can be shown in parentheses if this technique is preferred.

Another common procedure is to establish contra or adjunct accounts. A **contra account** on a balance sheet is an item that reduces an asset, liability, or owners' equity account. Examples include Accumulated Amortization and Discount on Bonds Payable. Contra accounts provide some flexibility in presenting the financial information. Use of the Accumulated Amortization account, for example, allows a statement reader to see the asset's original cost and its amortization to date.

An **adjunct account**, on the other hand, increases an asset, liability, or owners' equity account. An example is Premium on Bonds Payable, which, when added to the Bonds Payable account, describes the enterprise's total bond liability.

Supporting Schedules

Often a separate schedule is needed to present more detailed information about certain assets or liabilities because the balance sheet only provides a single summary item. Illustration 5-16 shows an example with both the balance sheet item and supporting schedule.

Illustration 5-16
Disclosure through Use of Supporting Schedules

Property, plant, and equipment Land, buildings, equipment, and other fixed assets, net (see Schedule 3)	$643,300

A separate schedule then might be presented as follows.

SCHEDULE 3
Land, Buildings, Equipment, and Other Fixed Assets

	Total	Land	Buildings	Equipment	Other Fixed Assets
Balance January 1, 2008	$740,000	$46,000	$358,000	$260,000	$76,000
Additions in 2008	161,200		120,000	38,000	3,200
	901,200	46,000	478,000	298,000	79,200
Assets retired or soldin 2008	31,700			27,000	4,700
Balance December 31, 2008	869,500	46,000	478,000	271,000	74,500

Amortization taken to January 1, 2008	196,000		102,000	78,000	16,000
Amortization taken in 2008	56,000		28,000	24,000	4,000
	252,000		130,000	102,000	20,000
Amortization on assets retired in 2008	25,800			22,000	3,800
Amortization accumulated December 31, 2008	226,200		130,000	80,000	16,200
Book value of assets	$643,300	$46,000	$348,000	$191,000	$58,300

Terminology

International Insight

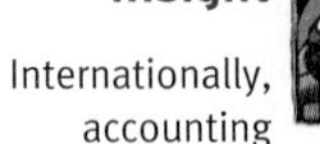

Internationally, accounting terminology is problematic. For example, Canadian and U.S. investors normally think of "stock" as "equity" or "ownership," but the British refer to inventory as "stocks." In Canada and the U.S., "fixed assets" generally refers to "property, plant, and equipment," while in Britain, this category includes more items.

Account titles in the general ledger often use terms that are not very helpful for a balance sheet. Account titles are often brief and include technical terms that are understood only by accountants. Balance sheets, meanwhile, are examined by many people who are not familiar with the technical vocabulary of accounting. Thus, balance sheets should contain descriptions that will be generally understood and less likely to be misinterpreted.

SECTION 2—STATEMENT OF CASH FLOWS

Objective 6
Indicate the purpose of the statement of cash flows.

The balance sheet, the income statement, and the statement of shareholders' equity each present information about an enterprise's cash flows during a period, but they do this to a limited extent and in a fragmented manner. For instance, comparative balance sheets might show what new assets have been acquired or disposed of and what liabilities have been incurred or liquidated. The income statement presents information about the resources provided by operations, but not exactly the cash that has been provided. The statement of retained earnings shows the amount of dividends declared. None of these statements presents a detailed summary of all the cash inflows and outflows, or the sources and uses of cash during the period. To satisfy this need, the **statement of cash flows** (also called the cash flow statement) is required.[35]

The statement's value is that it helps users evaluate liquidity, solvency, and financial flexibility, as previously defined. The material in Chapter 5 is introductory as it reviews the statement of cash flows' existence, usefulness and the mechanics of calculating cash-flows from operations. Note that Chapter 22 deals with the preparation and content of the statement of cash flows in greater detail.

Purpose of the Statement of Cash Flows

International Insight

Statements of cash flows are not required in all countries. Some nations require a statement that reports the sources and applications of "funds" (often defined as working capital); others have no requirement for either cash or funds flow statements.

The main purpose of a statement of cash flows is to allow users to **assess the enterprise's capacity to generate cash and cash equivalents and its needs for cash resources.**[36]

Reporting the sources, uses, and net increase or decrease in cash helps investors, creditors, and others know what is happening to a company's most liquid resource. Because most people maintain their cheque book and prepare their tax return on a cash basis, they can relate to and understand the statement of cash flows as it shows the causes and effects of cash inflows and outflows and the net increase or decrease in cash. The statement of cash flows answers the following simple but important questions:

[35] According to the *CICA Handbook*, Section 1540.03, the cash flow statement should be presented as an integral part of the financial statements.

[36] *CICA Handbook*, Section 1540.01.

1. Where did cash come from during the period?
2. What was cash used for during the period?
3. What was the change in the cash balance during the period?

Content and Format of the Statement of Cash Flows

Cash receipts and cash payments during a period are classified in the statement of cash flows into three different activities: **operating, investing**, and **financing** activities. These are the main types of activities that companies engage in. These classifications are defined as follows:

7 Objective
Identify the content of the statement of cash flows.

1. **Operating activities** are the enterprise's main revenue-producing activities and all other activities that are not related to investing or financing.
2. **Investing activities** are the acquisitions and disposals of long-term assets and other investments that are not included in cash equivalents.
3. **Financing activities** are activities that result in changes in the size and composition of the enterprise's equity capital and borrowings.[37]

With cash flows classified into each of these categories, the statement of cash flows has assumed the basic format shown in Illustration 5-17.

Statement of Cash Flows	
Cash flows from operating activities	$XXX
Cash flows from investing activities	XXX
Cash flows from financing activities	XXX
Net increase (decrease) in cash	XXX
Cash at beginning of year	XXX
Cash at end of year	$XXX

Illustration 5-17
Basic Format of Cash Flow Statement

Student Website

See the Student Website for additional examples of annual reports and cash flow statements.

www.wiley.com/canada/kieso

Illustration 5-18 shows the inflows and outflows of cash classified by activity.

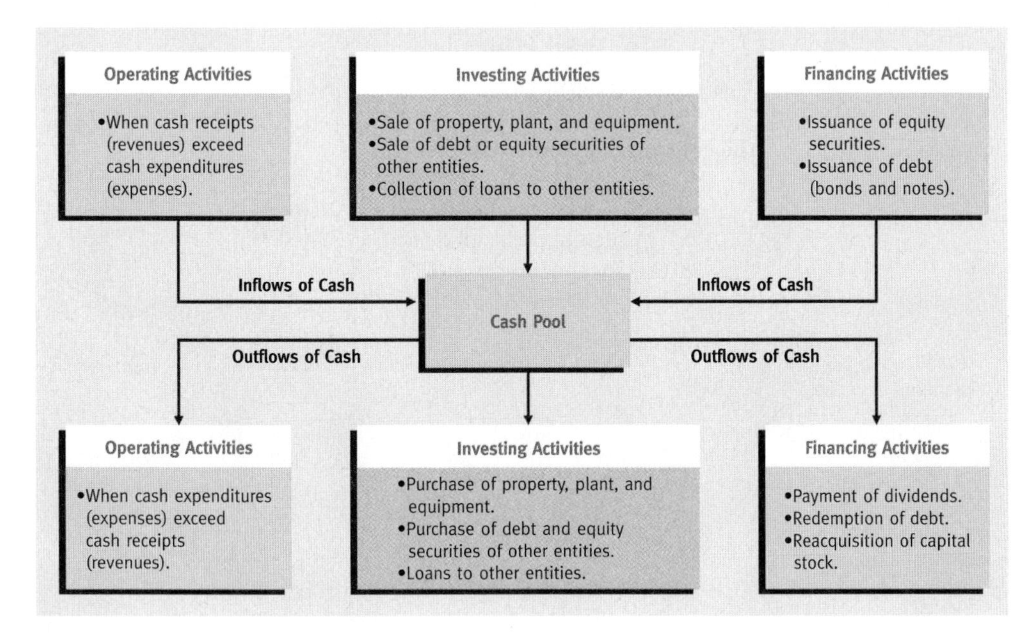

Illustration 5-18
Cash Inflows and Outflows

[37] *CICA Handbook*, Section 1540.06.

Preparation of the Statement of Cash Flows

Objective 8
Prepare the cash from operating activities section of the statement of cash flows.

Companies obtain the information to prepare a statement of cash flows from a variety of sources. These include the balance sheet, income statement, and selected transaction data—normally data in the general ledger Cash account. Because the statement is intended to include all cash transactions, the Cash account is an important source of information. Preparation of the statement requires the following steps:

1. Determine the cash provided by or used in operating, investing, and financing activities.
2. Determine the change (increase or decrease) in cash during the period.
3. Reconcile the change in cash with the beginning and ending cash balances.

In this chapter, we will use the following simple example to look briefly at how to calculate the cash provided by or used in operating activities. Assume that on January 1, 2007, in its first year of operations, Telemarketing Inc. issued 50,000 shares for $50,000 cash. The company then rented its office space, furniture, and telecommunications equipment and performed marketing services throughout the year. In June 2007, the company also purchased land for $15,000. Finally, it paid cash dividends of $14,000 during the year. Illustration 5-19 shows the company's comparative balance sheets at the beginning and end of 2007.

Illustration 5-19
Comparative Balance Sheets for Telemarketing Inc.

TELEMARKETING INC.
Balance Sheets

Assets	Dec. 31, 2007	Jan. 1, 2007	Increase/Decrease
Cash	$31,000	$-0-	$31,000 Increase
Accounts receivable	41,000	-0-	41,000 Increase
Land	15,000	-0-	15,000 Increase
Total	$87,000	$-0-	
Liabilities and Shareholders' Equity			
Accounts payable	$12,000	$-0-	12,000 Increase
Common shares	50,000	-0-	50,000 Increase
Retained earnings	25,000	-0-	25,000 Increase
Total	$87,000	-0-	

Illustration 5-20 shows the company's income statement.

Illustration 5-20
Income Statement for Telemarketing Inc.

TELEMARKETING INC.
Income Statement
For the Year Ended December 31, 2007

Revenues	$172,000
Operating expenses	120,000
Income before income tax	52,000
Income tax	13,000
Net income	$ 39,000

Additional information:
Dividends of $14,000 were paid during the year.

Cash provided by operating activities is the excess of cash receipts over cash payments for operating activities. Companies determine this amount by converting net income on an accrual basis to a cash basis. To do this, they add to or deduct from net income those items in the income statement that do not affect cash, such as credit sales, accrued expenses, amortizations, and non-cash gains/losses. They then adjust net income for the items that affected the current year's cash but are related to the operating activities of prior years, such as the collection of the previous year's credit sales or payment of the previous year's accrued expenses. This procedure requires that a company analyze not only the current year's income statement but also the comparative balance sheet and selected transaction data (especially items affecting the Cash account). This analysis is important since, for instance, credit sales from last year that are collected this year (and were previously recorded as accounts receivable) will increase cash.

Analysis of Telemarketing's comparative balance sheets reveals two items that will affect the calculation of net cash provided by operating activities:

1. The increase in accounts receivable is a non-cash increase of $41,000 in revenues from credit sales. This amount would be included in net income as sales and so must be deducted in arriving at cash from operations.
2. The increase in accounts payable is a non-cash increase of $12,000 in expenses due to accruals. This amount would have been deducted in arriving at net income but, since these expenses did not require a cash outlay, they will be added back in arriving at cash from operations.

Therefore, to arrive at cash from operations, Telemarketing Inc. deducts from net income the increase in accounts receivable ($41,000) and it adds back to net income the increase in accounts payable ($12,000). Note that since there were no operations in the previous year, there is no need to adjust for items accrued last year that may affect cash this year. Furthermore, there are no non-cash gains/losses and no amortization. As a result of these adjustments, the company determines that cash provided by operations amounted to $10,000, as calculated in Illustration 5-21.

Illustration 5-21
Calculation of Net Cash Provided by Operations

Net income		$39,000
Adjustments to reconcile net income to net cash provided by operating activities:		
Increase in accounts receivable	$(41,000)	
Increase in accounts payable	12,000	(29,000)
Net cash provided by operating activities		$10,000

Telemarketing Inc.'s only investing activity was a land purchase. It has two financing activities: (1) the increase of $50,000 in common shares resulting from the issuance of these shares, and (2) the payment of $14,000 in cash dividends. Illustration 5-22 presents Telemarketing Inc.'s statement of cash flows for 2007.

Illustration 5-22
Statement of Cash Flows

TELEMARKETING INC.
Statement of Cash Flows
For the Year Ended December 31, 2007

Cash flows from operating activities		
Net income		$39,000
Adjustments to reconcile net income to net cash provided by operating activities:		
Increase in accounts receivable	$(41,000)	
Increase in accounts payable	12,000	(29,000)

Net cash provided by operating activities		10,000
Cash flows from investing activities		
Purchase of land	(15,000)	
Net cash used by investing activities		(15,000)
Cash flows from financing activities		
Issuance of common shares	50,000	
Payment of cash dividends	(14,000)	
Net cash provided by financing activities		36,000
Net increase in cash		31,000
Cash at beginning of year		-0-
Cash at end of year		$31,000

The increase in cash of $31,000 that is reported in the statement of cash flows agrees with the increase in cash that was calculated from the comparative balance sheets. Note that not all of a company's activities involve cash, for example, the conversion of bonds to shares, an issuance of debt to purchase assets, and non-monetary exchanges. These activities should not be included in the body of the cash flow statement but should be disclosed elsewhere in the financial statements.

Note that the net cash provided by operating activities section begins with net income and reconciles to cash. This presentation is called the indirect method of presenting cash flows from operating activities. Another option is the direct method. The direct method normally presents the following information in the operations portion of the statement (the rest of the statement remains the same in both methods):

1. Cash received from customers
2. Cash paid to suppliers and employees
3. Interest paid/received
4. Taxes paid
5. Other

Under GAAP, either method is acceptable although the direct method is preferred. See Chapter 22 for a more detailed discussion.

Usefulness of the Statement of Cash Flows

Objective 9
Understand the usefulness of the statement of cash flows.

Although net income provides a long-term measure of a company's success or failure, cash is a company's lifeblood. Without cash, a company will not survive. For small and newly developing companies, cash flow is the single most important element of survival. Even medium and large companies indicate that controlling cash flow is a major concern.

Creditors examine the statement of cash flows carefully because they are concerned about being paid. A good starting point in their examination is to find **net cash provided by operating activities**. A high amount of net cash provided by operating activities indicates that a company was able to generate enough cash internally from operations in the most recent period to pay its bills without further borrowing. Conversely, a low or negative amount of net cash provided by operating activities indicates that a company did not generate enough cash internally from its operations and, therefore, had to borrow or issue equity securities to acquire additional cash.

Just because a company was able to generate cash flows from operating activities in the most recent period, however, this does not mean that it will be able to do so again in future periods. Consequently, creditors look for answers to the following questions in the company's statement of cash flows:

1. How successful is the company in generating net cash provided by operating activities?
2. What are the trends in net cash flow provided by operating activities over time?
3. What are the major reasons for the positive or negative net cash provided by operating activities?
4. Are the cash flows sustainable or renewable—i.e., can they be repeated over time?

It is important to recognize that companies can fail even though they are profitable. The difference between net income and net cash provided by operating activities can be substantial. One of the main reasons for the difference between a positive net income and a negative net cash provided by operating activities is major increases in receivables and/or inventory. To illustrate, assume that in its first year of operations Hinchcliff Inc. reported net income of $80,000. Its net cash provided by operating activities, however, was a negative $95,000, as shown in Illustration 5-23.

HINCHCLIFF INC.
Net Cash Flow from Operating Activities

Net income		$ 80,000
Adjustments to reconcile net income to net cash provided by operating activities:		
Increase in receivables	$ (75,000)	
Increase in inventories	(100,000)	(175,000)
Net cash provided by operating activities		$ (95,000)

Illustration 5-23
Negative Net Cash Provided by Operating Activities

Note that the negative net cash provided by operating activities occurred for Hinchcliff even though it reported a positive net income. The company could easily experience a "cash crunch" because it has tied up its cash in receivables and inventory. If problems in collecting receivables occur or inventory is slow-moving or becomes obsolete, the company's creditors may have difficulty collecting on their loans.

Companies that are expanding often experience this type of "cash crunch" as they must buy increasing inventory amounts to meet increasing sales demands. This means that the cash outflow to purchase the inventory occurs before the cash inflow from the customer for sale of that product. This is often referred to as a "lead-lag" factor. The cash outflow leads (occurs first) and the cash inflow from sales lags (occurs later). The lead-lag factor requires the company to use up any excess cash that it has on hand or to borrow more funds. Refer back to Illustration 5-3 on the business operating cycle.

As mentioned earlier in the chapter, financial flexibility may be assessed by using information from the financial statements. The cash flow statement is especially good for providing this type of information.

Financial Liquidity

One ratio that is used to assess liquidity is the **current cash debt coverage ratio**. It indicates whether the company can pay off its current liabilities for the year from its operations. The formula for this ratio is shown in Illustration 5-24.

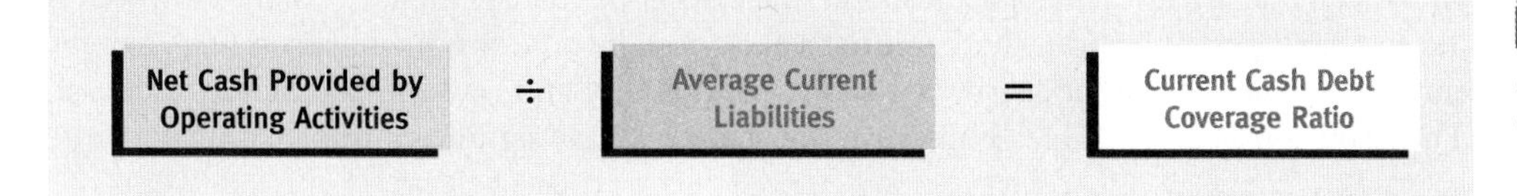

Illustration 5-24
Formula for Current Cash Debt Coverage Ratio

The higher this ratio is, the less likely it is that a company will have liquidity problems. For example, a ratio of at least 1:1 is good because it indicates that the company can meet all of its current obligations from internally generated cash flow. To compare this ratio to a benchmark number, it can be compared with the ratios for similar companies in the industry (or with the ratios of prior years for the company itself).

Financial Flexibility

A more long-run measure that provides information on financial flexibility is the **cash debt coverage ratio**. This ratio indicates a company's ability to repay its liabilities from net cash provided by operating activities without having to liquidate the assets that it uses in its operations. Illustration 5-25 presents the formula for this ratio.

Illustration 5-25
Formula for Cash Debt Coverage Ratio

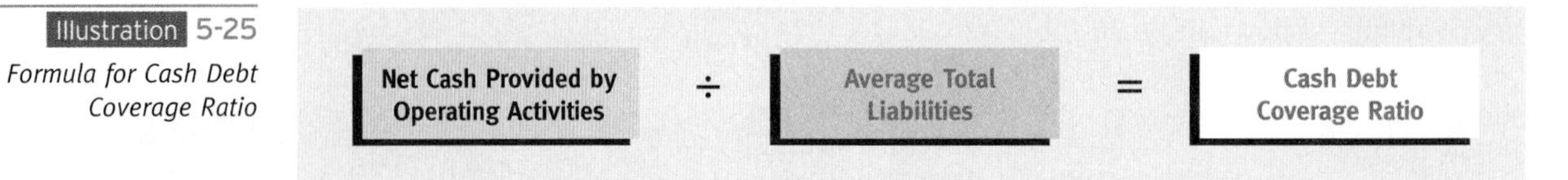

The higher this ratio, the less likely it is that the company will experience difficulty in meeting its obligations as they come due. As a result, this ratio signals whether the company can pay its debts and survive if external sources of funds become limited or too expensive.

Perspectives

Cash Flow Patterns

Please refer to Illustration 5-22 showing the full statement of cash flows for Telemarketing Inc. The cash flow statement can yield some interesting results when users look at the various patterns between cash inflows and outflows for the following subtotals on the statement: operating, investing, and financing cash flows. For instance, Telemarketing Inc. has positive cash flows/cash inflows ("+") from operating activities of $10,000; negative cash flows/cash outflows ("−") from investing activities of $15,000; and positive cash flows/cash inflows ("+") from financing activities of $31,000. Together these numbers thus yield a "+" "−" "+" pattern.

Interpreting this, the company is getting its cash from operations (which is a very good sign) and also from the issuance of common shares. It is investing this cash to expand the business. The fact that the company is able to raise funds in the capital markets by issuing shares indicates that the capital markets have faith in the company's ability to prosper. The fact that the bulk of the money being used to finance the assets is generated from operations means that the company does not have to increase its solvency risk by issuing debt or further diluting its shareholders' equity by issuing more shares. Telemarketing Inc. appears to be a successful company in an expansionary mode.

Companies that generate cash from investing activities may be selling off long-term assets. This pattern generally goes with a company that is in a downsizing or restructuring mode. If the assets that are being disposed of are excess or redundant assets, then it makes sense to free up the capital that is tied up. Similarly, if the assets being disposed of relate to operations that are not profitable, disposal reflects a good management decision. However, if the company is in a position where it **must** sell off core income-producing assets (e.g., to generate cash), then it may be sacrificing future profitability and revenue-producing potential. This is obviously undesirable. Thus, cash flow patterns have significant information content.

Free Cash Flow

A more sophisticated way to examine a company's financial flexibility is to develop a **free cash flow** analysis. This analysis starts with net cash provided by operating activities and ends with free cash flow, which is calculated as net cash provided by operating activities less capital expenditures and dividends.[38] Free cash flow is the amount of discretionary cash flow that a company has for purchasing additional investments, retiring its debt, purchasing treasury stock, or simply adding to its liquidity. This measure indicates a company's level of financial flexibility. Questions that a free cash flow analysis answers include these:

1. Is the company able to pay its dividends without the help of external financing?
2. If business operations decline, will the company be able to maintain its needed capital investment?
3. What is the free cash flow that can be used for additional investments, retirement of debt, purchases of treasury stock, or additions to liquidity?

Illustration 5-27 shows a free cash flow analysis for Nestor Corporation.

Illustration 5-26
Free Cash Flow Analysis

NESTOR CORPORATION
Free Cash Flow Analysis

Net cash provided by operating activities	$ 411,750
Less: Capital expenditures	(252,500)
Dividends	(19,800)
Free cash flow	$ 139,450

This analysis shows that Nestor has a positive, and substantial, net cash provided by operating activities of $411,750. Nestor reports on its statement of cash flows that it purchased equipment of $182,500 and land of $70,000 for total capital spending of $252,500. This amount is subtracted from net cash provided by operating activities because, without continued efforts to maintain and expand its facilities, it is unlikely that Nestor can continue to maintain its competitive position. Capital spending is deducted first on the analysis above to indicate it is generally the least discretionary expenditure that a company makes. Dividends are then deducted to arrive at free cash flow.

Nestor has more than enough cash flow to meet its dividend payment and therefore has satisfactory financial flexibility. Nestor used its free cash flow to redeem bonds and add to its liquidity. If it finds additional investments that are profitable, it can increase its spending without putting its dividend or basic capital spending in jeopardy. Companies that have strong financial flexibility can take advantage of profitable investments even in tough times. In addition, strong financial flexibility frees companies from worry about survival in poor economic times. In fact, those with strong financial flexibility often do better in poor economic times because they can take advantage of opportunities that other companies cannot.

Caution

As more and more complex financial instruments are created, this results in presentation issues for financial statement preparers. Many instruments have attributes of both debt

[38] In determining free cash flow, some companies do not subtract dividends, because they believe these expenditures are discretionary.

and equity. This is significant for analysts since a misclassification will affect key ratios. Note disclosure of the details of the instruments helps analysts and other users in assessing a company's liquidity and solvency. This issue will be discussed further in subsequent chapters on liabilities and equities.

International

As was first mentioned in Chapter 4, the IASB/FASB Financial Statement Presentation project will define what constitutes a complete set of financial statements and what should be presented on the face of the statements. To date, the following decisions have been made that differ from Canadian GAAP:

- A statement of changes in equity would be required (replacing the statement of retained earnings). Currently in Canada, financial statements include a statement of retained earnings and detailed disclosures are required for changes in the share capital accounts (these are normally provided as a note to the financial statements). This change is a necessary one due to the addition of the accumulated other comprehensive income account. With this new statement, changes in all equity accounts would be shown including share capital, contributed surplus, retained earnings, and accumulated other comprehensive income. This creates greater transparency. Changes in equity due to non-owner transactions would be presented separately (changes in retained earnings and accumulated other comprehensive income).
- The names of the financial statements would be as follows:
    - Statement of financial position (balance sheet)
    - Statement of recognized income and expense (income statement). This statement could be presented in one or two statements (with the second separating out what is basically comprehensive income)
    - Statement of changes in equity (statement of changes in retained earnings)
    - Statement of cash flows (cash flow statement)

  (Note that these titles would not be mandatory and are mostly named in this way for descriptive purposes.)

The IASB/FASB discussions are ongoing.

Student Website

Glossary

www.wiley.com/canada/kieso

KEY TERMS

adjunct account, 221
available-for-sale securities, 208
balance sheet, 200
cash and cash equivalents, 207

Summary of Learning Objectives

1 Identify the uses and limitations of a balance sheet.

The balance sheet provides information about the nature and amounts of investments in enterprise resources, obligations to creditors, and the owners' equity in net resources. The balance sheet contributes to financial reporting by providing a basis for (1) calculating rates of return, (2) evaluating the enterprise's capital structure, and (3) assessing the enterprise's liquidity, solvency, and financial flexibility. The limitations of a balance sheet are as follows: (1) The balance sheet often does not reflect current value, because accountants have adopted a historical cost basis in valuing and reporting assets and liabilities. (2) Judgements and estimates must be used in preparing a balance sheet. The collectibility of receivables, the saleability of inventory, and the useful life of long-term tangible and intangible assets are difficult to determine. (3) The balance sheet leaves out many items that are of financial value to the business but cannot be recorded objectively, such as its human resources, customer base, and reputation.

2 Identify the major classifications of a balance sheet.

The balance sheet's general elements are assets, liabilities, and equity. The major classifications within the balance sheet on the asset side are current assets; investments; property, plant, and equipment; intangible assets; and other assets. The major classifications of liabilities are current and long-term liabilities. In a corporation, shareholders' equity is generally classified as shares, contributed surplus, retained earnings, and accumulated other comprehensive income.

3 Prepare a classified balance sheet.

The most common format lists liabilities and shareholders' equity directly below assets on the same page.

4 Identify balance sheet information that requires supplemental disclosure.

Five types of information are normally supplemental to account titles and amounts presented in the balance sheet. (1) Contingencies: Material events that have an uncertain outcome. (2) Accounting policies: Explanations of the valuation methods that are used or the basic assumptions that are made for inventory valuation, amortization methods, investments in subsidiaries, etc. (3) Contractual situations: Explanations of certain restrictions or covenants that are attached to specific assets or, more likely, to liabilities. (4) Detailed information: Clarification by giving more detail about the composition of balance sheet items. (5) Subsequent events: Events that happen after the balance sheet date.

5 Identify major disclosure techniques for the balance sheet.

There are four methods of disclosing pertinent information in the balance sheet: (1) Parenthetical explanations: Additional information or description is often provided by giving explanations in parentheses that follow the item. (2) Notes: Notes are used if additional explanations or descriptions cannot be shown conveniently as parenthetical explanations. (3) Cross references and contra items: A direct relationship between an asset and a liability is cross referenced on the balance sheet. (4) Supporting schedules: Often a separate schedule is needed to present more detailed information about certain assets or liabilities because the balance sheet provides just a single summary item.

6 Indicate the purpose of the statement of cash flows.

The main purpose of a statement of cash flows is to provide relevant information about an enterprise's cash receipts and cash payments during a period. Reporting the sources, uses, and net increase or decrease in cash lets investors, creditors, and others know what is happening to a company's most liquid resource.

7 Identify the content of the statement of cash flows.

Cash receipts and cash payments during a period are classified in the statement of cash flows into three different activities: (1) Operating activities: Involve the cash effects of transactions that enter into the determination of net income. (2) Investing activities: Include making and collecting loans and acquiring and disposing of investments (both debt and equity) and property, plant, and equipment. (3) Financing activities: Involve liability and owners' equity items and include (a) obtaining capital from owners and providing them with a return on their investment and (b) borrowing money from creditors and repaying the amounts borrowed.

cash debt coverage ratio, 228
contingency, 218
contra account, 221
current assets, 206
current cash debt coverage ratio, 227
current liabilities, 214
financial flexibility, 201
financial instruments, 203
financing activities, 223
free cash flow, 229
future income tax assets, 213
future income tax liabilities, 215
held-for-trading securities, 208
held-to-maturity securities, 208
intangible assets, 212
investing activities, 223
liquidity, 201
long-term liabilities, 214
monetary assets, 203
non-current investments, 211
non-monetary assets, 203
operating activities, 223
other assets, 213
owners' (shareholders') equity, 216
prepaid expenses, 210
property, plant, and equipment/capital assets, 212
solvency, 201
statement of cash flows, 222
statement of financial position, 200
subsequent events, 218
working capital, 214

8 Prepare the cash from operating activities section of the statement of cash flows.

This involves starting with net income and adjusting it for non-cash activities, such as credit sales, accrued expenses, amortization, and gains/losses. It is important to look carefully at prior years' operating activities that might affect cash this year, such as cash collected this year from last year's credit sales and cash spent this year for last year's accrued expenses.

9 Understand the usefulness of the statement of cash flows.

Creditors examine the statement of cash flows carefully because they are concerned about being paid. The amount and trend of net cash flow provided by operating activities in relation to the company's liabilities is helpful in making this assessment. In addition, measures such as a free cash flow analysis provide creditors and shareholders with a better picture of the company's financial flexibility.

Appendix 5A

Ratio Analysis—A Reference

Using Ratios to Analyze Financial Performance

Companies expose themselves to many risks in doing business. Strategically, the goal is to identify these risks and then manage them in order to take advantage of opportunities and maximize shareholder value. How do users know whether a company is managing its risks in a manner that will create the most shareholder value? Illustration 5A-1 shows the business

10 Objective
Identify the major types of financial ratios and what they measure.

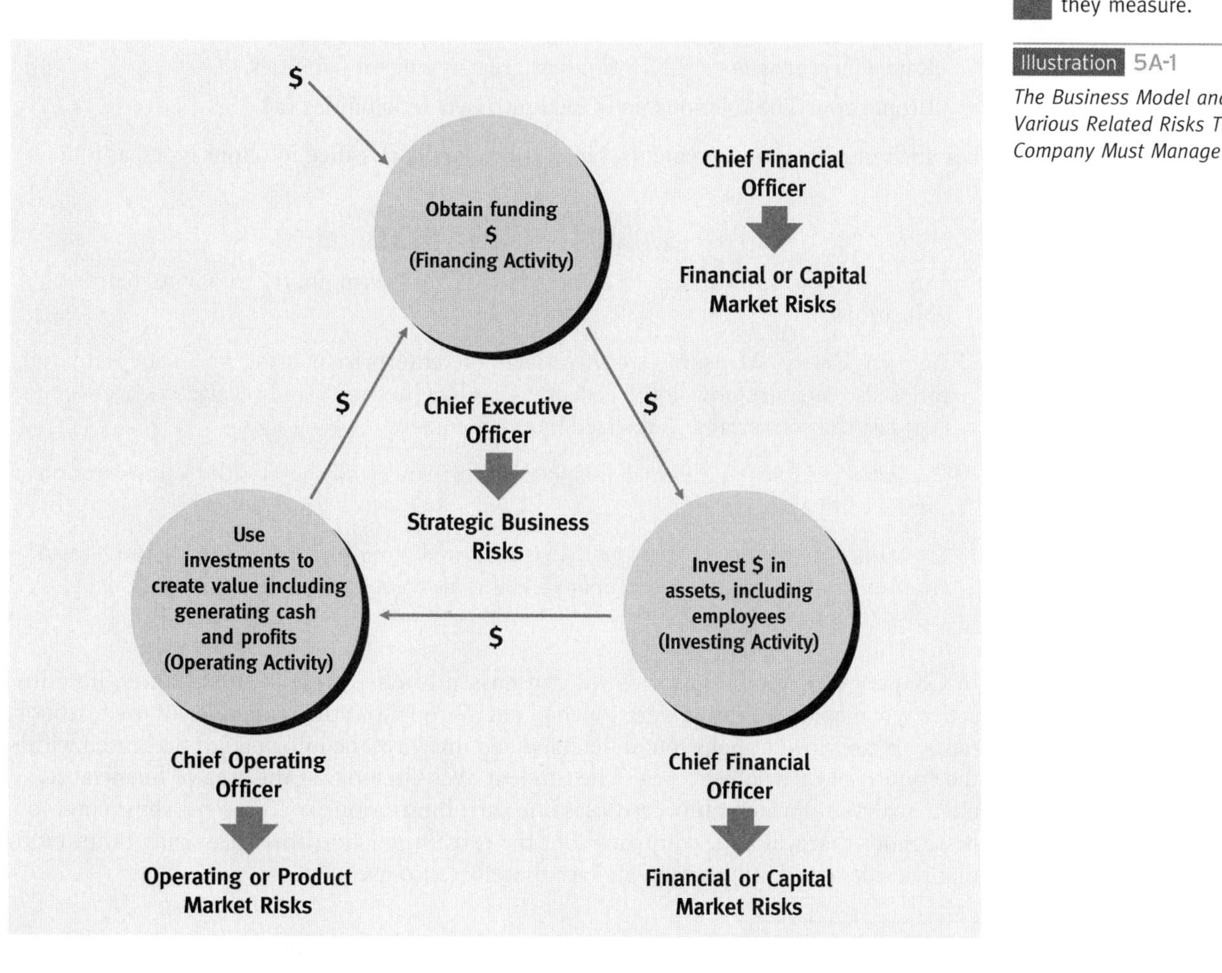

Illustration 5A-1

The Business Model and Various Related Risks That a Company Must Manage

model that was originally introduced in Chapter 4. Now risks have been added to the model along with the key management personnel who are responsible for managing the risks.[39]

Financial or capital market risks are related to financing and investing activities. For example, when a company borrows funds, it might increase its solvency and liquidity risk. **Operating or product market risks** are related to operating activities. For instance, when it manufactures a drug, there is a risk that a company might not be able to produce quality products on time or successfully target the appropriate market for sale of the drug.

Information about risks is useful and much of this information is included in the annual report both within the financial statements and in other parts. The financial statements give information about financing, investing, and operating activities and therefore provide indirect feedback on how related risks are being managed and how this in turn affects performance. A solvent company that constantly generates cash from operations has a solid business model where risks and opportunities are well managed to create value. Companies usually disclose explicit information about risks and risk management policies in the MD&A section of the annual report.

Ratio analysis helps in assessing operating and financial risks by **expressing the relationship between selected financial statement data**. Qualitative information from financial statements is gathered by **examining relationships** between items on the statements and **identifying trends** in these relationships. Relationships are often expressed in terms of either a percentage, a rate, or a simple proportion.

To illustrate, recently Stantec Inc. had current assets of $280.4 million and current liabilities of $157.8 million. The relationship is determined by dividing current assets by current liabilities. The alternative means of expression are:

Percentage: Current assets are 178% of current liabilities.

Rate: Current assets are 1.78 times as great as current liabilities.

Proportion: The relationship of current assets to liabilities is 1.78:1.

For analyzing financial statements, ratios are generally classified into four types, as follows:

MAJOR TYPES OF RATIOS

Liquidity Ratios. Measure the enterprise's short-term ability to pay its maturing obligations.

Activity Ratios. Measure how effectively the enterprise is using its assets. Activity ratios also measure how liquid certain assets like inventory and receivables are—i.e., how fast the asset's value is realized by the company.

Profitability Ratios. Measure financial performance and shareholder value creation for a specific time period.

Coverage or Solvency Ratios. Measure the degree of protection for long-term creditors and investors or a company's ability to meet its long-term obligations.

Analyst Toolkit–Financial Statement Analysis Primer

www.wiley.com/canada/kieso

In Chapter 4, profitability ratios were discussed briefly, while in this chapter, liquidity, activity, and coverage ratios were touched on. Throughout the remainder of the textbook, ratios are provided to help you understand and interpret the information presented within the context of each subject area. The Student Website looks at the area of financial statement analysis, of which ratio analysis is one part. Illustration 5A-2 presents some common, basic ratios that will be used throughout the text. In practice, there are many other ratios that provide useful information and are therefore also used.

[39] This is a brief overview only. It is meant to link risk with the business model and with the use of financial statements in communicating information about risk management. A thorough review of risk models and risk management is beyond the scope of this text.

Illustration 5A-2
A Summary of Financial Ratios

RATIO	FORMULA	PURPOSE OR USE
I. Liquidity		
1. Current ratio	Current assets / Current liabilities	Measures short-term debt-paying ability
2. Quick or acid-test ratio	Cash, marketable securities, and receivables (net) / Current liabilities	Measures immediate short-term liquidity
3. Current cash debt coverage ratio	Net cash provided by operating activities / Average current liabilities	Measures a company's ability to pay off its current liabilities in a specific year from its operations
II. Activity		
4. Receivables turnover	Net sales / Average trade receivables (net)	Measures liquidity of receivables
5. Inventory turnover	Cost of goods sold / Average inventory	Measures liquidity of inventory
6. Asset turnover	Net sales / Average total assets	Measures how efficiently assets are used to generate sales
III. Profitability		
7. Profit margin on sales	Net income / Net sales	Measures net income generated by each dollar of sales
8. Rate of return on assets	Net income / Average total assets	Measures overall profitability of assets
9. Rate of return on common share equity	Net income minus preferred dividends / Average common shareholders' equity	Measures profitability of owners' investment
10. Earnings per share	Net income minus preferred dividends / Weighted average shares outstanding	Measures net income earned on each common share
11. Price earnings ratio	Market price of shares / Earnings per share	Measures ratio of the market price per share to earnings per share
12. Payout ratio	Cash dividends / Net income	Measures percentage of earnings distributed as cash dividends
IV. Coverage		
13. Debt to total assets	Total debt / Total assets	Measures the percentage of total assets provided by creditors
14. Times interest earned	Income before interest charges and taxes / Interest charges	Measures ability to meet interest payments as they come due
15. Cash debt coverage ratio	Net cash provided by operating activities / Average total liabilities	Measures company's ability to repay its total liabilities in a specific year from its operations
16. Book value per share	Common shareholders' equity / Outstanding shares	Measures the amount each share would receive if the company were liquidated at the amounts reported on the balance sheet

The key to a refined, information-rich analysis is having a good **understanding of the business, business risks, and industry** before calculating and interpreting any ratios. Specialized industries focus on different ratios depending on the critical success factors in their business. As discussed throughout the chapter, different companies and businesses would be expected to have different types of assets and capital structures. Furthermore, they would be expected to have different types of costs, revenue streams, and business models.

Success in the retail industry, for instance, is in the ability to set prices and target customers in a way that gets maximum market penetration. Also critical is the ability to minimize inventory shrinkage (there is a high risk of theft) and keep inventory moving so that it does not become obsolete or out of fashion. A company's ability to achieve this, or its failure to do so, is reflected in the gross profit margin (a ratio). This is calculated by dividing gross profit by revenues. Companies must achieve a gross profit that is high enough to cover other costs. A stable gross profit margin is a positive sign that management is dealing with all of the above issues.

Once ratios are calculated, they must then be examined and the information interpreted. Examining ratios by themselves provides very little insight. Instead, the **ratios must be compared with or benchmarked against similar ratios, perhaps for the same company from prior periods or, alternatively, for similar companies in the same industry**.

When benchmarking is done against industry numbers, it may be necessary to create industry benchmarks if they are not available. To do this, select several companies that have a similar business model and are in the same industry. Companies that are the same size are better comparators.

Note that average amounts may be approximated by taking opening and closing balances and dividing by two.

Glossary

www.wiley.com/canada/kieso

Summary of Learning Objective for Appendix 5A

10 Identify the major types of financial ratios and what they measure.

Ratios express the mathematical relationship between one quantity and another, in terms of either a percentage, a rate, or a proportion. Liquidity ratios measure the short-run ability to pay maturing obligations. Activity ratios measure how effectively assets are being used. Profitability ratios measure an enterprise's success or failure. Coverage ratios measure the degree of protection for long-term creditors and investors.

KEY TERMS

activity ratios, 234
coverage ratios, 234
liquidity ratios, 234
profitability ratios, 234
ratio analysis, 234
solvency ratios, 234

Appendix 5B

Specimen Financial Statements

The following pages contain the financial statements and accompanying notes from the 2005 annual report of **Stantec Inc.** (Stantec). The full text of the annual report in PDF format, can be found on the Student Website. Stantec provides design and consulting services in planning, engineering, architecture, interior design, landscape architecture, surveying, and project management. The company offers consulting services through all phases of business, starting with the idea or concept stage and focusing on providing sustainable solutions that have a positive impact on the world. Stantec has 5,500 employees with offices throughout North America and the Caribbean. In 2005, the company completed its acquisition of The Keith Companies, adding 800 employees and many new offices. The company also listed on the NYSE in 2005.

The Business

The company's business model focuses on continuing growth and profitability while controlling risk. Its goal is to become a top 10 global design firm. Stantec operates in five areas: buildings, environment, industrial and project management, transportation, and urban land. Its projects include the following, among others:

1. Creation of environmentally friendly building designs that minimize the impact on the surrounding areas, including wetlands
2. Design of a water treatment plant needed to clean up acid mine drainage from a large former copper mine
3. Development of wind farms
4. Conversion of landfill gas into useable energy

We do not expect that you will understand everything in the company's financial statements and accompanying notes when you first read them. Instead, we expect that by the time you complete the material in this text, your level of understanding and ability to interpret will have grown significantly.

At this point, we recommend that you take 20 to 30 minutes to scan the statements and notes to familiarize yourself with the contents and accounting elements. Throughout the following chapters, when you are asked to refer to specific parts of Stantec's financials, do so. Then, when you have completed reading this book, we challenge you to reread Stantec's financials to see how much greater and more sophisticated your understanding of them has become.

Management Report

The annual report, including the consolidated financial statements, is the responsibility of the management of the Company. The consolidated financial statements were prepared by management in accordance with Canadian generally accepted accounting principles. Where alternative accounting methods exist, management has chosen those it considers most appropriate in the circumstances. The significant accounting policies used are described in note 1 to the consolidated financial statements. Certain amounts in the financial statements are based on estimates and judgments relating to matters not concluded by year-end. The integrity of the information presented in the financial statements is the responsibility of management. Financial information presented elsewhere in this annual report has been prepared by management and is consistent with the information in the consolidated financial statements.

Management is responsible for the development and maintenance of systems of internal accounting and administrative controls of high quality. Such systems are designed to provide reasonable assurance that the financial information is accurate, relevant, and reliable and that the Company's assets are appropriately accounted for and adequately safeguarded.

The Board of Directors is responsible for ensuring that management fulfills its responsibilities and for final approval of the annual consolidated financial statements. The Board has appointed an Audit Committee comprising three Directors, none of whom is an officer or employee of the Company or its subsidiaries. The Audit Committee meets at least four times each year to discharge its responsibilities under a written mandate from the Board of Directors. The Audit Committee meets with management and with the external auditors to satisfy itself that they are properly discharging their responsibilities, reviews the consolidated financial statements and the Auditors' Report, and examines other auditing and accounting matters. The Audit Committee has reviewed the audited consolidated financial statements with management, including a discussion of the quality of the accounting principles as applied and significant judgments affecting the Company's consolidated financial statements. The Audit Committee has discussed with the external auditors the external auditors' judgments of the quality of those principles as applied and judgments noted above. The consolidated financial statements and Management's Discussion and Analysis have been reviewed by the Audit Committee and approved by the Board of Directors of Stantec Inc.

The consolidated financial statements have been examined by the shareholders' auditors, Ernst & Young LLP, Chartered Accountants. The Auditors' Report outlines the nature of their examination and their opinion on the consolidated financial statements of the Company. The external auditors have full and unrestricted access to the Audit Committee, with or without management being present.

Tony Franceschini P.Eng.
President & CEO
February 10, 2006

Don Wilson CA
Vice President & CFO
February 10, 2006

Auditors' Report

To the Shareholders of
Stantec Inc.

We have audited the consolidated balance sheets of **Stantec Inc.** as at December 31, 2005 and 2004 and the consolidated statements of income and retained earnings and cash flows for each of the years in the three-year period ended December 31, 2005. These financial statements are the responsibility of the Company's management. Our responsibility is to express an opinion on these financial statements based on our audits.

We conducted our audits in accordance with Canadian generally accepted auditing standards. Those standards require that we plan and perform an audit to obtain reasonable assurance whether the financial statements are free of material misstatement. An audit includes examining, on a test basis, evidence supporting the amounts and disclosures in the financial statements. An audit also includes assessing the accounting principles used and significant estimates made by management, as well as evaluating the overall financial statement presentation.

In our opinion, these consolidated financial statements present fairly, in all material respects, the financial position of the Company as at December 31, 2005 and 2004 and the results of its operations and its cash flows for each of the years in the three-year period ended December 31, 2005 in accordance with Canadian generally accepted accounting principles.

Ernst & Young LLP

Chartered Accountants
Edmonton, Canada
February 10, 2006

Stantec Inc.
Consolidated Balance Sheets

	As at December 31	
	2005	2004
	$	$
	(In thousands of Canadian dollars)	
ASSETS *[note 8]*		
Current		
Cash and cash equivalents	**28,143**	37,890
Restricted cash *[note 2]*	**21,312**	–
Accounts receivable, net of allowance for doubtful accounts of $16,053 in 2005 ($21,095 – 2004)	**137,928**	112,476
Costs and estimated earnings in excess of billings	**66,172**	40,861
Prepaid expenses	**5,420**	4,165
Future income tax assets *[note 14]*	**14,827**	8,532
Other assets *[note 6]*	**6,569**	4,831
Total current assets	**280,371**	208,755
Property and equipment *[note 3]*	**58,519**	48,262
Goodwill *[note 4]*	**242,674**	84,694
Intangible assets *[note 5]*	**27,304**	6,278
Future income tax assets *[note 14]*	**6,814**	6,357
Other assets *[note 6]*	**13,097**	7,754
Total assets	**628,779**	362,100
LIABILITIES AND SHAREHOLDERS' EQUITY		
Current		
Accounts payable and accrued liabilities *[note 7]*	**106,757**	78,718
Billings in excess of costs and estimated earnings	**24,251**	18,832
Income taxes payable	**4,441**	5,732
Current portion of long-term debt *[note 8]*	**4,813**	12,820
Future income tax liabilities *[note 14]*	**17,552**	10,653
Total current liabilities	**157,814**	126,755
Long-term debt *[note 8]*	**81,886**	21,155
Other liabilities *[note 9]*	**24,764**	16,818
Future income tax liabilities *[note 14]*	**16,262**	8,316
Total liabilities	**280,726**	173,044
Commitments and contingencies *[notes 2, 8, 10, and 11]*		
Shareholders' equity		
Share capital *[note 12]*	**210,604**	87,656
Contributed surplus *[note 12]*	**5,522**	2,544
Cumulative translation account *[note 13]*	**(25,575)**	(19,018)
Deferred stock compensation	**(833)**	–
Retained earnings	**158,335**	117,874
Total shareholders' equity	**348,053**	189,056
Total liabilities and shareholders' equity	**628,779**	362,100

See accompanying notes

On behalf of the Board:

Director

Director

Stantec Inc.
Consolidated Statements of Income and Retained Earnings

	Years Ended December 31		
	2005	2004	2003
	$	$	$
	(In thousands of Canadian dollars, except per share amounts)		
Income			
Gross revenue	**618,020**	520,879	459,942
Less subconsultant and other direct expenses	**93,468**	71,728	68,546
Net revenue	**524,552**	449,151	391,396
Direct payroll costs	**234,553**	205,513	183,471
Gross margin	**289,999**	243,638	207,925
Administrative and marketing expenses	**212,633**	183,739	154,788
Depreciation of property and equipment	**12,389**	11,986	9,912
Amortization of intangible assets	**2,542**	927	925
Net interest expense *[note 8]*	**571**	2,805	2,637
Share of income from associated companies	**(187)**	(385)	(580)
Foreign exchange (gains) losses	**(449)**	(94)	615
Income before income taxes	**62,500**	44,660	39,628
Income taxes *[note 14]*			
Current	**21,735**	18,065	10,050
Future	**143**	(3,595)	4,508
Total income taxes	**21,878**	14,470	14,558
Net income for the year	**40,622**	30,190	25,070
Retained earnings, beginning of the year	**117,874**	88,266	64,240
Shares repurchased *[note 12]*	**(161)**	(582)	(1,044)
Retained earnings, end of the year	**158,335**	117,874	88,266
Earnings per share *[note 15]*			
Basic	**2.04**	1.63	1.37
Diluted	**1.98**	1.59	1.31

See accompanying notes

Stantec Inc.
Consolidated Statements of Cash Flows

	Years Ended December 31		
	2005	2004	2003
	$	$	$
	(In thousands of Canadian dollars)		
CASH FLOWS FROM (USED IN) OPERATING ACTIVITIES			
Cash receipts from clients	**637,391**	568,897	465,114
Cash paid to suppliers	**(200,445)**	(169,573)	(156,460)
Cash paid to employees	**(355,621)**	(313,321)	(274,444)
Dividends from equity investments	**550**	300	–
Interest received	**6,531**	6,426	2,710
Interest paid	**(6,551)**	(8,639)	(4,462)
Income taxes paid	**(28,882)**	(10,530)	(18,142)
Income taxes recovered	**4,341**	3,791	2,577
Cash flows from operating activities *[note 16]*	**57,314**	77,351	16,893
CASH FLOWS FROM (USED IN) INVESTING ACTIVITIES			
Business acquisitions, including cash acquired and bank indebtedness assumed *[note 2]*	**(100,383)**	(18,845)	(6,046)
Cash of joint venture held for sale	**–**	–	(369)
Restricted cash used for acquisitions *[note 2]*	**9,000**	–	–
Increase in investments held for self-insured liabilities	**(7,295)**	(9,562)	–
Proceeds on disposition of investments	**522**	55	195
Collection of notes receivable from disposition of Technology and Design Build segments	**406**	1,014	–
Purchase of property and equipment	**(17,005)**	(17,488)	(28,713)
Proceeds on disposition of property and equipment	**155**	34,672	1,444
Cash flows used in investing activities	**(114,600)**	(10,154)	(33,489)
CASH FLOWS FROM (USED IN) FINANCING ACTIVITIES			
Repayment of long-term debt	**(46,875)**	(35,546)	(20,592)
Proceeds from long-term borrowings	**95,929**	13,960	–
Net change in bank indebtedness financing	**–**	(17,151)	17,151
Repurchase of shares for cancellation *[note 12]*	**(195)**	(720)	(1,392)
Share issue costs *[note 12]*	**(1,969)**	–	–
Proceeds from issue of share capital *[note 12]*	**961**	3,490	651
Cash flows from (used in) financing activities	**47,851**	(35,967)	(4,182)
Foreign exchange loss on cash held in foreign currency	**(312)**	(683)	(1,081)
Net increase (decrease) in cash and cash equivalents	**(9,747)**	30,547	(21,859)
Cash and cash equivalents, beginning of the year	**37,890**	7,343	29,202
Cash and cash equivalents, end of the year	**28,143**	37,890	7,343

See accompanying notes

Stantec Inc.
Notes to the Consolidated Financial Statements

1. Summary of Significant Accounting Policies

Stantec Inc. (the Company) is a provider of comprehensive professional services in the area of infrastructure and facilities for clients in the public and private sectors. The Company's services include planning, engineering, architecture, interior design, landscape architecture, surveying and geomatics, environmental sciences, and project economics.

Generally accepted accounting principles

The Company prepares its consolidated financial statements in accordance with Canadian generally accepted accounting principles (GAAP). These financial statements have, in management's opinion, been properly prepared within reasonable limits of materiality and within the framework of the accounting policies summarized below. The effects of differences between the application of Canadian and United States GAAP on the financial statements of the Company are described in note 20.

Effective January 1, 2005, the Company adopted Accounting Guideline 15 (AcG-15)—"Consolidation of Variable Interest Entities" (VIEs) of the Canadian Institute of Chartered Accountants (CICA) Handbook. VIEs are those entities that are subject to control on a basis other than ownership of voting interests. AcG-15 provides guidance for identifying VIEs and requires the primary beneficiary of a VIE to consolidate the VIE. These consolidated financial statements include all VIEs for which the Company is the primary beneficiary. The initial adoption of this accounting guideline on a prospective basis did not have an impact on the Company's consolidated financial statements.

Effective January 1, 2004, the Company adopted the recommendations of Section 1100 of the CICA Handbook, "Generally Accepted Accounting Principles." This section establishes standards for financial reporting in accordance with GAAP. It describes what constitutes GAAP and its sources and states that an entity should apply every primary source of GAAP that deals with the accounting and reporting in financial statements of transactions or events it encounters. The initial adoption of these recommendations on a prospective basis on January 1, 2004, did not have an impact on the Company's consolidated financial statements.

Use of estimates

The preparation of financial statements in conformity with GAAP requires management to make estimates and assumptions that affect the reported amounts of assets and liabilities at the date of the financial statements and the reported amounts of revenues and expenses during the reporting period. Significant estimates used in the preparation of these consolidated financial statements include the percentage of completion of fixed fee and variable fee with ceiling contracts, provisions for losses on incomplete contracts, allowances for doubtful accounts receivable, provision for legal claims, provision for self-insured liabilities, the fair value of stock-based awards, the fair value of identifiable intangible assets acquired in business acquisitions, liabilities for lease exit activities, and future cash flows used to estimate the fair value of reporting units for goodwill impairment purposes. Actual results may differ from these estimates.

During the 2005 fiscal year, management revised its estimate of the allowance for doubtful accounts based on improved information available on historical loss experience. This revision was applied prospectively and reduced the allowance for doubtful accounts and administrative and marketing expenses at the time of the revision by $4,000,000.

Principles of consolidation

The consolidated financial statements include the accounts of the Company, its subsidiary companies, and all VIEs for which the Company is the primary beneficiary. All significant intercompany accounts and transactions have been eliminated. The results of the operations of subsidiaries acquired during the year are included from their respective dates of acquisition.

Joint ventures and partnerships are accounted for on the proportionate consolidation basis, which results in the Company recording its pro rata share of the assets, liabilities, revenues, and expenses of each of these entities.

Cash and cash equivalents

Cash and cash equivalents include cash and unrestricted investments with initial maturities of three months or less. Such investments are carried at the lower of cost or market value.

Investments

Investments in associated companies over which the Company is able to exercise significant influence, but not control, are accounted for using the equity method, which reflects the Company's investment at original cost plus its share of earnings (losses) net of dividends received. These investments include Teshmont Consultants Inc. (50%), SSBV Consultants Inc. (33.3%), and Planning & Stantec Limited (50%).

Other investments, including investments held for self-insured liabilities, are recorded at cost. When a loss in the value of such investments occurs that is other than temporary, the investment is written down to recognize the loss.

Property and equipment

Property and equipment is recorded at cost less accumulated depreciation. Depreciation is calculated at annual rates designed to write off the costs of assets over their estimated useful lives as follows:

Engineering equipment	20–30%	declining balance
Business information systems		straight-line over 3–5 years
Office equipment	20–30%	declining balance
Automotive equipment	30%	declining balance
Leasehold improvements		straight-line over term of lease plus one renewal period to a maximum of 15 years or the improvement's economic life
Buildings	4–5%	declining balance

Leases

Leases that transfer substantially all the risks and benefits of ownership of assets to the Company are accounted for as capital leases. Assets under capital leases are recorded at the inception of the lease together with the related long-term obligation to reflect the purchase and financing thereof. Rental payments under operating leases are expensed as incurred.

From time to time, the Company enters into or renegotiates premises operating leases that result in the receipt of lease inducement benefits. These benefits are accounted for as a reduction of rental expense over the terms of the associated leases.

Goodwill and intangible assets
The cost of intangible assets with finite lives is amortized over the period in which the benefits of such assets are expected to be realized, principally on a straight-line basis. The Company's policy is to amortize client relationships with determinable lives over periods ranging from 10 to 15 years. Contract backlog is amortized over estimated contractual lives of generally less than one and a half years. Other intangible assets include technology, non-compete agreements, and advantageous leasehold commitments, which are amortized over estimated lives of one to five years. Goodwill is not amortized but is evaluated annually for impairment by comparing the fair value of the reporting unit, determined on a discounted after-tax cash flow basis, to the carrying value. An impairment loss would be recognized if the carrying value of the goodwill were to exceed its fair value.

Long-lived assets
The Company monitors the recoverability of long-lived assets, including property and equipment and intangible assets with finite lives, using factors such as expected future asset utilization, business climate, and future undiscounted cash flows expected to result from the use of the related assets. An impairment loss would be recognized if the carrying value of the long-lived asset were to exceed its fair value.

Accrual and investments held for self-insured liabilities
The Company self-insures certain risks related to professional liability and automobile physical damages. The accrual for self-insured liabilities includes estimates of the costs of reported claims (including potential claims that are probable of being asserted) and is based on estimates of loss using assumptions made by management, including consideration of actuarial projections. The accrual for self-insured liabilities does not include unasserted claims where assertion by a third party is not probable.

The Company invests funds to support the accrual for self-insured liabilities. These investments are classified in other assets as investments held for self-insured liabilities.

Forward contracts
The Company may enter into forward currency exchange contracts to manage risk associated with net operating assets denominated in US dollars. The Company's policy is to not utilize derivative financial instruments for trading or speculative purposes. These derivative contracts, which are not accounted for as hedges, are marked to market, and any changes in the market value are recorded in income or expense when the changes occur. The fair value of such instruments is recorded as either accounts receivable or payable.

Non-interest-bearing debt
Non-interest-bearing debt is carried at its present value using discount rates based on the bank prime rate prevailing at the time the debt was issued. The discount is applied over the term of the debt and is charged to interest expense.

Fair value of financial instruments
The carrying amounts of cash and cash equivalents, restricted cash, accounts receivable, bank loans, and accounts payable and accrued liabilities approximate their fair values because of the short-term maturity of these instruments. The carrying amount of bank loans approximates its fair value because the applicable interest rate is based on variable reference rates. The carrying values of other financial assets and financial liabilities approximate their fair values except as otherwise disclosed in the financial statements.

Credit risk

Financial instruments that subject the Company to credit risk consist primarily of cash and cash equivalents, investments held for self-insured liabilities, and accounts receivable. The Company maintains an allowance for estimated credit losses and mitigates the risk of its investment in bonds through the overall quality and mix of its bond portfolio. The Company provides services to diverse clients in various industries and sectors of the economy, and its credit risk is not concentrated in any particular client, industry, economic, or geographic sector.

Interest rate risk

The Company is subject to interest rate risk to the extent that its credit facilities are based on floating rates of interest. In addition, the Company is subject to interest rate pricing risk to the extent that its investments held for self-insured liabilities contain fixed rate government and corporate bonds. The Company has not entered into any derivative agreements to mitigate these risks.

Revenue recognition

In the course of providing its services, the Company incurs certain direct costs for subconsultants and other expenditures that are recoverable directly from clients. These direct costs are included in the Company's gross revenue. Since such direct costs can vary significantly from contract to contract, changes in gross revenue may not be indicative of the Company's revenue trends. Accordingly, the Company also reports net revenue, which is gross revenue less subconsultant and other direct expenses.

Revenue from fixed fee and variable fee with ceiling contracts is recognized using the percentage of completion method. Contract revenue is recognized on the ratio of contract costs incurred to total estimated costs. Provisions for estimated losses on incomplete contracts are made in the period in which the losses are determined. Revenue from time and material contracts without stated ceilings and from short-term projects is recognized as costs are incurred. Revenue is calculated based on billing rates for the services performed. Costs and estimated earnings in excess of billings represents work in progress that has been recognized as revenue but not yet invoiced to clients. Billings in excess of costs and estimated earnings represents amounts that have been invoiced to clients but not yet recognized as revenue.

Employee benefit plans

The Company contributes to group retirement savings plans and an employee share purchase plan based on the amount of employee contributions subject to maximum limits per employee. The Company accounts for such defined contributions as an expense in the period in which the contributions are made. The expense recorded in 2005 was $8,436,000 (2004 – $7,311,000; 2003 – $5,980,000). The Company does not provide postemployment or postretirement benefits.

Foreign currency translation

Transactions denominated in a foreign currency and the financial statements of foreign subsidiaries (excluding US-based subsidiaries) included in the consolidated financial statements are translated as follows: monetary items at the rate of exchange in effect at the balance sheet date; non-monetary items at historical exchange rates; and revenue and expense items (except depreciation and amortization, which are translated at historical exchange rates) at the average exchange rate for the year. Any resulting gains or losses are included in income in the year incurred.

The Company's US-based subsidiaries are designated as self-sustaining operations. The financial statements of these subsidiaries are translated using the current rate method. Under this method, assets and liabilities are translated at the rate of exchange in effect at the balance sheet date, and revenue and expense items (including depreciation and amortization) are translated at the average rate of exchange for the year. The resulting exchange gains and losses are deferred and included as a separate component of shareholders' equity in the cumulative translation account.

Stock-based compensation and other stock-based payments
The Company has one share option plan, which is described in note 12, and accounts for grants under this plan in accordance with the fair value-based method of accounting for stock-based compensation. Compensation expense for stock options awarded under the plan is measured at the fair value at the grant date using the Black-Scholes valuation model and is recognized over the vesting period of the options granted. In years prior to January 1, 2002, the Company recognized no compensation expense when shares or stock options were issued.

Investment tax credits
Investment tax credits arising from qualifying scientific research and experimental development efforts are recorded as a reduction of the applicable administrative and marketing expenses when there is reasonable assurance of their ultimate realization. Investment tax credits of $1,239,000 (2004 – $426,000; 2003 – $237,000) were recorded and reduced administrative and marketing expenses in 2005.

Income taxes
The Company uses the liability method to account for income taxes. Under this method, future income tax assets and liabilities are determined based on differences between financial reporting and the tax bases of assets and liabilities and measured using the substantively enacted tax rates and laws that will be in effect when these differences are expected to reverse.

Earnings per share
Basic earnings per share is computed based on the weighted average number of common shares outstanding during the year. Diluted earnings per share is computed using the treasury stock method, which assumes that the cash that would be received on the exercise of options is applied to purchase shares at the average price during the year and that the difference between the shares issued on the exercise of options and the number of shares obtainable under this computation, on a weighted average basis, is added to the number of shares outstanding. The impact of outstanding restricted shares, on a weighted average basis, is also added to the number of shares outstanding. Antidilutive options are not considered in computing diluted earnings per share.

Allowance for doubtful accounts
The Company maintains an allowance for doubtful accounts for estimated losses resulting from the inability to collect on its accounts receivable. The Company uses estimates in arriving at its allowance for doubtful accounts that are based, primarily, on the age of the outstanding accounts receivable and on its historical collection and loss experience.

Recent accounting pronouncements
In January 2005, the CICA released the new handbook Section 1530, "Comprehensive Income," and Section 3251, "Equity," effective for annual and interim periods beginning on or after October 1, 2006. These pronouncements further aligned Canadian GAAP with US GAAP (note 20). Section 1530 establishes standards for the reporting and display of comprehensive income. Comprehensive income is defined to include revenues, expenses, gains, and losses that, in accordance with primary sources of GAAP, are recognized in comprehensive income but excluded from net income. Section 1530 does not address issues

of recognition or measurement for comprehensive income and its components. Section 3251, "Equity," establishes standards for the presentation of equity and changes in equity during the reporting period. The requirements set out in Section 3251 are in addition to those established in Section 1530 and require that an enterprise present separately the components of equity: retained earnings, accumulated other comprehensive income, the total for retained earnings and accumulated other comprehensive income, contributed surplus, share capital, and reserves. Upon initial adoption of these recommendations in fiscal 2007, unrealized losses on the translation of self-sustaining foreign operations will be included in comprehensive income. Currently, these unrealized losses are reflected in the Company's cumulative translation account.

In January 2005, the CICA released the new handbook Section 3855, "Financial Instruments—Recognition and Measurement," effective for annual and interim periods beginning on or after October 1, 2006. This pronouncement further aligned Canadian GAAP with US GAAP (note 20). The section provides standards for the classification of financial instruments and related interest, dividends, gains, and losses. It prescribes when a financial instrument should be stated at fair value and when it would be valued using cost-based measures. Financial instruments are defined to include accounts receivable and payable, loans, investments in debt and equity securities, and derivative contracts. Upon initial adoption of these recommendations in fiscal 2007, the Company's investments held for self-insured liabilities will be reflected as investments held for sale, and the resulting unrealized gains or losses will be reflected through other comprehensive income until realized, at which time the gains or losses will be recognized in net income. This new standard is not expected to have a material effect on the results of the Company's operations.

2. Business Acquisitions

Acquisitions are accounted for under the purchase method of accounting, and the results of operations since the respective dates of acquisition are included in the consolidated statements of income. From time to time, as a result of the timing of acquisitions in relation to the Company's reporting schedule, certain of the purchase price allocations may not be finalized at the initial time of reporting. Purchase price allocations are completed after the vendors' final financial statements and income tax returns have been prepared and accepted by the Company. Such preliminary purchase price allocations are based on management's best estimates of the fair value of the acquired assets and liabilities. Upon finalization, adjustments to the initial estimates may be required, and these adjustments may be material. The purchase prices of acquisitions are generally subject to price adjustment clauses included in the purchase agreements. Such purchase price adjustments generally result in an increase or reduction to the promissory note consideration recorded at acquisition to reflect either more or less non-cash working capital realized than was originally expected. These purchase price adjustments, therefore, have no net effect on the original purchase price allocations. In the case of some acquisitions, additional consideration may be payable based on future performance parameters. As at December 31, 2005, the maximum contingent consideration that may be payable in 2006 and future years is approximately $9,000. This additional consideration is recorded as additional goodwill in the period in which the contingency is resolved.

Acquisitions in fiscal 2005

On August 3, 2005, the Company acquired the shares and business of CPV Group Architects & Engineers Ltd. for cash consideration. This acquisition strengthens the Company's architecture and interior design presence in Canada.

On September 15, 2005, the Company acquired the shares and business of The Keith Companies, Inc. (Keith) for a combination of cash consideration and Stantec common shares. Under the terms of the agreement, the number of common shares issued (3,328,776) as consideration was based on the average sale price of the Stantec common stock on the Toronto Stock Exchange for each of the 20 trading days ending on the second trading day prior to the closing of the merger, converted to US dollars for each trading day at the noon buying rate quoted by the Federal Reserve Bank of New York on such trading day. In order for the Keith transaction to qualify as a reorganization under the provisions of Section 368(a) of the U.S. Internal Revenue Code of 1986, a portion of Keith's cash, at the time of acquisition, is subject to restrictions on its use. Generally, the restricted cash can be used to fund further acquisitions as well as future capital expenditures. The acquisition of Keith supplements the Company's urban land development services group and increases the breadth and depth of the Company's multidiscipline engineering and consulting services by adding employees and offices throughout the western and midwestern United States.

On October 1, 2005, the Company acquired the shares and business of Keen Engineering Co. Ltd. for cash consideration and promissory notes. This acquisition supplements the Company's building design services in Canada and the western United States.

The purchase price allocations for the CPV Group Architects & Engineers Ltd., Keith, and Keen Engineering Co. Ltd. acquisitions have not yet been finalized. The Company expects to finalize the purchase price allocations for the CPV Group Architects & Engineers Ltd. and Keith acquisitions during the first quarter of 2006 and for the Keen Engineering Co. Ltd. acquisition during the second quarter of 2006.

During 2005, the Company paid additional contingent consideration in connection with the Cosburn Patterson Mather Limited (2002) acquisition and finalized the purchase price allocations for The Sear-Brown Group, Inc. (2004), GBR Architects Limited (2004), and Dunlop Architects Inc. (2004) acquisitions. In addition, the Company adjusted the purchase price on the Ecological Services Group Inc. (2003), GBR Architects Limited (2004), and Dunlop Architects Inc. (2004) acquisitions pursuant to price adjustment clauses included in the purchase agreements.

Acquisitions in fiscal 2004

During 2004, the Company acquired the shares and business of The Sear-Brown Group, Inc. (April 2, 2004), GBR Architects Limited (May 31, 2004), and Dunlop Architects Inc. (October 8, 2004) and the assets and business of Shaflik Engineering (November 26, 2004). The Sear-Brown Group, Inc. acquisition opened up a new geographic market for the Company in the northeastern United States and a new service in the bio/pharmaceuticals industry. The acquisition of GBR Architects Limited and of Dunlop Architects Inc. supplemented the Company's architecture and interior design practice while increasing its presence in Winnipeg and the Greater Toronto Area, respectively. The Shaflik Engineering acquisition strengthened the Company's capabilities for upcoming Olympic projects in British Columbia with its strong involvement in sports facilities and transportation systems.

During 2004, the Company also adjusted the purchase price in connection with the Cosburn Patterson Mather Limited (2002), The Spink Corporation (2001), the APAI Architecture Inc. and Mandalian Enterprises Limited (2003), the Graeme & Murray Consultants Ltd. (2002), the Ecological Services Group Inc. (2003), and The RPA Group (2002) acquisitions pursuant to price adjustment clauses included in the purchase agreements.

Aggregate consideration paid

Details of the aggregate consideration given and of the fair values of net assets acquired or adjusted for are as follows:

	Keith 2005 $000s	Other 2005 $000s	Total 2005 $000s	Total 2004 $000s
Cash consideration	**107,062**	**11,200**	**118,262**	12,432
Share consideration	**125,540**	–	**125,540**	–
Promissory notes	–	**2,753**	**2,753**	1,487
Purchase price	**232,602**	**13,953**	**246,555**	13,919
Assets and liabilities acquired at fair values				
Cash acquired (bank indebtedness assumed)	**22,075**	**(4,196)**	**17,879**	(6,413)
Restricted cash acquired	**30,882**	–	**30,882**	–
Non-cash working capital	**9,747**	**3,929**	**13,676**	6,057
Property and equipment	**5,751**	**991**	**6,742**	3,211
Investments	**32**	–	**32**	87
Goodwill	**149,844**	**12,218**	**162,062**	18,425
Other long-term assets	**554**	–	**554**	–
Intangible assets				
Client relationships	**17,476**	**947**	**18,423**	1,357
Contract backlog	**3,995**	**1,053**	**5,048**	301
Other	**669**	**(139)**	**530**	500
Other long-term liabilities	**(1,380)**	**243**	**(1,137)**	(1,642)
Long-term debt	–	**(745)**	**(745)**	(8,414)
Future income taxes	**(8,226)**	**(348)**	**(8,574)**	450
Deferred stock compensation	**1,183**	–	**1,183**	–
Net assets acquired	**232,602**	**13,953**	**246,555**	13,919

All of the goodwill is non-deductible for income tax purposes.

At the time of acquisition, management estimates the exit costs to downsize or close offices occupied by the acquired entity. These costs are accrued in other long-term liabilities as part of the purchase price allocation (note 9).

Pro forma data

The following unaudited pro forma data presents information as if the acquisitions of The Sear-Brown Group, Inc., GBR Architects Limited, Dunlop Architects Inc., Shaflik Engineering Ltd., CPV Group Architects & Engineers Ltd., Keith, and Keen Engineering Co. Ltd. had occurred on January 1, 2004. This unaudited pro forma data is provided for information purposes only and is based on historical information. This unaudited pro forma data does not necessarily reflect the actual results of operations that would have occurred had these acquired entities and Stantec Inc. comprised a single entity during the periods, nor is it necessarily indicative of the future results of the operations of the combined entities.

	2005 $000s	2004 $000s
	(Unaudited)	
Pro forma gross revenue	**753,291**	726,827
Pro forma net revenue	**646,614**	628,844
Pro forma net income	**49,098**	39,563
Basic pro forma earnings per share	**2.20**	1.81
Diluted pro forma earnings per share	**2.15**	1.77

3. Property and Equipment

	2005		2004	
	Cost $000s	Accumulated Depreciation $000s	Cost $000s	Accumulated Depreciation $000s
Engineering equipment	**42,560**	**22,736**	33,622	19,058
Business information systems	**11,475**	**4,237**	9,681	1,796
Office equipment	**23,030**	**10,071**	19,953	7,519
Automotive equipment	**5,263**	**2,867**	4,254	2,578
Leasehold improvements	**14,226**	**2,053**	11,994	2,031
Buildings	**4,204**	**704**	1,901	594
Land	**429**	–	433	–
	101,187	**42,668**	81,838	33,576
Net book value	**58,519**		48,262	

In 2004 the Company completed the sale of its Edmonton office building (included in buildings and land) for cash proceeds of $34,500,000. Concurrent with the sale, the Company leased the property back for a period of 15 years. The lease is accounted for as an operating lease. The resulting gain of $7,103,000 was deferred and is being amortized over the lease term (note 9).

Included in leasehold improvements is construction work in progress in the amount of $337,000 (2004 – buildings – $89,000) on which depreciation has not started.

4. Goodwill

	2005 $000s	2004 $000s
Goodwill, beginning of the year	**84,694**	69,696
Current year acquisitions	**160,840**	18,006
Additional purchase price payments	**700**	–
Other purchase price adjustments	**522**	419
Impact of foreign exchange	**(4,082)**	(3,427)
Goodwill, end of the year	**242,674**	84,694

5. Intangible Assets

	2005		2004	
	Gross Carrying Amount $000s	Accumulated Amortization $000s	Gross Carrying Amount $000s	Accumulated Amortization $000s
Client relationships	**24,914**	**2,232**	6,859	1,195
Contract backlog	**4,900**	**1,219**	339	290
Other	**1,218**	**277**	750	185
	31,032	**3,728**	7,948	1,670
Carrying amount	**27,304**		6,278	

Once an intangible asset is fully amortized, the gross carrying amount and related accumulated amortization are removed from the accounts. Other than goodwill, the Company has not recognized any intangible assets with indefinite lives. For intangible assets held as of December 31, 2005, the estimated aggregate amortization expense for each of the next five years is as follows:

	$000s
2006	5,762
2007	3,154
2008	2,609
2009	2,541
2010	2,403
Thereafter	10,835
	27,304

6. Other Assets

	2005 $000s	2004 $000s
Investments held for self-insured liabilities	**16,857**	9,562
Investments in associated companies	**1,545**	1,909
Investments – other	**710**	1,114
Other	**554**	–
	19,666	12,585
Less current portion of investments held for self-insured liabilities	**6,569**	4,831
	13,097	7,754

The investments held for self-insured liabilities consist of government and corporate bonds of $14,013,000 (2004 – $8,740,000) and equity securities of $2,844,000 (2004 – $822,000). The bonds bear interest at rates ranging from 3.0 to 6.8% per annum (2004 – 3.5 to 8.6%). The estimated fair value of the bonds at December 31, 2005, was $13,721,000 (2004 – $8,761,000) and of the equities was $3,406,000 (2004 – $839,000). The term to maturity of the bond portfolio is $373,000 due within one year and $13,640,000 due from one to 10 years.

7. Accounts Payable and Accrued Liabilities

	2005 $000s	2004 $000s
Trade accounts payable	**26,784**	21,651
Employee and payroll liabilities	**52,314**	37,188
Accrued liabilities	**27,659**	19,879
	106,757	78,718

8. Long-Term Debt

	2005 $000s	2004 $000s
Non-interest-bearing note payable	**122**	111
Other non-interest-bearing notes payable	**5,643**	7,862
Bank loan	**79,035**	23,997
Mortgages payable	**1,706**	1,765
Other	**193**	240
	86,699	33,975
Less current portion	**4,813**	12,820
	81,886	21,155

The non-interest-bearing note payable is due November 1, 2027, in the amount of $933,000. The note's carrying value of $122,000 is determined using a discount rate of 9.75%. If the non-interest-bearing note payable were discounted at interest rates in effect at December 31, 2005, the fair value of the note would be $184,000 (2004 – $177,000).

The carrying values of the other non-interest-bearing notes payable have been calculated using a weighted average rate of interest of 5.58% and are supported by promissory notes. The notes are due at various times from 2006 to 2008. The aggregate maturity value of the notes is $5,985,000 (2004 – $8,336,000). As at December 31, 2005, there were no US-dollar non-interest-bearing notes outstanding. As at December 31, 2004, $47,000 of the notes' carrying value was payable in US funds (US$39,000). The carrying value of the other non-interest-bearing notes payable approximates their fair value based on interest rates in effect at December 31, 2005.

During 2005, the Company replaced its existing revolving credit facility with a revolving credit facility in the amount of $160 million due on August 31, 2008. This facility is available for acquisitions, working capital needs, capital expenditures, and general corporate purposes. At December 31, 2005, the facility was accessed to finance a portion of the Keith acquisition. Depending on the form under which the credit facility is accessed, rates of interest will vary between Canadian prime, US base rate, or LIBOR rate or bankers acceptance rates plus 65 or 85 basis points. As at December 31, 2005, $29,075,000 of the bank loan was payable in US funds (US$25,000,000). Repayment of loans under the credit facility may be made from time to time at the option of the Company. The average interest rate applicable at December 31, 2005, was 4.34% (2004 – 3.47%). The credit facility agreement contains restrictive covenants, including, but not limited to, debt to earnings ratio and earnings to debt service ratio. The Company was in compliance with all covenants under this agreement as at December 31, 2005. All assets of the Company are held as collateral under a general security agreement for the bank loan.

The mortgages payable bear interest at a weighted average rate of 7.67% and are supported by first mortgages against land and buildings. Subsequent to the year-end, the mortgages payable were paid out in full.

Other long-term debt bears interest at a weighted average rate of 3.5% and is due at dates ranging from 2006 to 2007. No assets are pledged in support of this debt.

Principal repayments required on long-term debt in each of the next five years and thereafter are as follows:

	$000s
2006	4,813
2007	1,661
2008	80,103
2009	–
2010	–
Thereafter	122
	86,699

The interest incurred on long-term debt in 2005 was $2,000,000 (2004 – $2,219,000; 2003 – $2,681,000). In 2005 total interest expense, net of interest income, was $571,000 (2004 – $2,805,000; 2003 – $2,637,000). At December 31, 2005, the Company had issued and outstanding letters of credit totaling $1,070,000.

9. Other Liabilities

	2005 $000s	2004 $000s
Provision for self-insured liabilities	**12,866**	5,236
Deferred gain on sale leaseback	**6,624**	7,073
Lease inducement benefits	**7,997**	4,742
Liabilities on lease exit activities	**2,251**	2,817
Other	**1,021**	–
	30,759	19,868
Less current portion included in accrued liabilities	**5,995**	3,050
	24,764	16,818

Provision for self-insured liabilities

Effective August 1, 2003, the Company began self-insuring a portion of its estimated liabilities that may arise in connection with reported legal claims (note 11). This provision is based on the results of an actuarial review performed in 2005 and 2004, with the current and long-term portion determined based on the actuarial estimate provided. At December 31, 2005, the long-term portion was $10,288,000 (2004 – $4,731,000).

	2005 $000s	2004 $000s
Provision, beginning of the year	**5,236**	2,410
Current year provision	**9,764**	2,826
Payment for claims settlement	**(2,134)**	–
Provision, end of the year	**12,866**	5,236

The self-insured liability increased during 2005, primarily due to new claims incurred and reported since the end of 2004. Claim settlements of $2,134,000 were made in 2005. The timing of such settlement payments is dependent upon the resolution of case-specific matters and may extend over several months or years.

Liabilities on lease exit activities

Charges are accrued when management closes offices in existing operations or finalizes plans to downsize offices in locations assumed from an acquiree upon a business acquisition. Included in the liability is the present value of the remaining lease payments, reduced by estimated sublease rentals that can reasonably be obtained.

	2005 $000s	2004 $000s
Liability, beginning of the year	**2,817**	–
Current year provision:		
Established for existing operations	**609**	936
Resulting from acquisitions	**276**	3,465
Payment or reductions:		
Impacting net income	**(1,103)**	(1,375)
Impacting the purchase price allocation	**(325)**	–
Impact of foreign exchange	**(23)**	(209)
Liability, end of the year	**2,251**	2,817

10. Commitments

Commitments for annual basic premises rent under long-term leases and for equipment and vehicle operating leases for the next five years are as follows:

	$000s
2006	34,794
2007	31,248
2008	25,240
2009	21,936
2010	18,910
Thereafter	79,585
	211,713

The premise rental expense for the year ended December 31, 2005, was $29,282,000 (2004 – $25,116,000; 2003 – $19,321,000).

11. Contingencies

In the normal conduct of operations, various legal claims are pending against the Company alleging, among other things, breaches of contract or negligence in connection with the performance of consulting services. The Company carries professional liability insurance, subject to certain deductibles and policy limits, and has a captive insurance company that provides insurance protection against such claims. In some cases, parties are seeking damages that substantially exceed the Company's insurance coverage. Based on advice and information provided by legal counsel, the Company's previous experience with the settlement of similar claims, and the results of the annual actuarial review, management believes that the Company has recognized adequate provisions for probable and reasonably estimable liabilities associated with these claims and that their ultimate resolutions will not materially exceed insurance coverages or have a material adverse effect on the Company's consolidated financial position or annual results of operations. Management cannot estimate the extent to which losses exceeding those already recorded in the financial statements may be incurred.

12. Share Capital

Authorized

Unlimited Common shares, with no par value

Unlimited Preferred shares issuable in series with attributes designated by the Board of Directors

Common shares issued and outstanding

	Capital Stock						Contributed Surplus		
	2005		2004		2003		2005	2004	2003
	Shares #	$000s	Shares #	$000s	Shares #	$000s	$000s	$000s	$000s
Balance, beginning of the year	**18,871,085**	**87,656**	18,327,284	84,281	18,282,720	83,973	**2,544**	1,842	1,247
Share options exercised for cash	**120,070**	**961**	573,101	3,490	119,264	651			
Stock-based compensation expense							**963**	725	600
Shares repurchased under normal course issuer bid.	**(6,800)**	**(33)**	(29,300)	(134)	(74,700)	(343)	**(1)**	(4)	(5)
Reclassification of fair value of stock options previously expensed		**159**		19		–	**(159)**	(19)	–
Shares issued on acquisition	**3,328,776**	**123,365**	–	–	–	–			
Restricted shares issued on acquisition							**2,175**	–	–
Share issue costs		**(1,504)**		–		–			
Balance, end of the year	**22,313,131**	**210,604**	18,871,085	87,656	18,327,284	84,281	**5,522**	2,544	1,842

During 2005, 6,800 common shares (2004 – 29,300; 2003 – 74,700) were repurchased for cancellation pursuant to an ongoing Normal Course Issuer Bid at a cost of $195,000 (2004 – $720,000; 2003 –

$1,392,000). Of this amount, $33,000 and $1,000 (2004 – $134,000 and $4,000; 2003 – $343,000 and $5,000) reduced the share capital and contributed surplus accounts, respectively, with $161,000 (2004 – $582,000; 2003 – $1,044,000) being charged to retained earnings.

During 2005, the Company incurred share issue costs of $1,969,000 less a future tax recovery of $465,000.

During 2005, the Company recognized a stock-based compensation expense of $1,814,000 (2004 – $1,014,000; 2003 – $706,000) in administrative and marketing expenses. Of the amount expensed, $963,000 related to the fair value of the options granted (2004 – $725,000; 2003 – $600,000); $519,000 related to deferred share unit compensation (2004 – $289,000; 2003 – $106,000), and $332,000 related to the restricted shares issued on the Keith acquisition. The fair value of the options granted was reflected through contributed surplus; the deferred share unit compensation was reflected through accrued liabilities; and the restricted shares were reflected through deferred stock compensation. Upon the exercise of share options for which a stock-based compensation expense has been recognized, the cash paid together with the related portion of contributed surplus is credited to share capital. Upon the vesting of restricted shares for which a stock-based compensation expense has been recognized, the related portion of contributed surplus is credited to share capital.

Share options

Under the Company's share option plan, options to purchase common shares may be granted by the Board of Directors to directors, officers, and employees. Options are granted at exercise prices equal to or greater than fair market value at the issue date, generally vest evenly over a three-year period, and have contractual lives that range from five to 10 years. The aggregate number of common shares reserved for issuance that may be purchased upon the exercise of options granted pursuant to the plan shall not exceed 996,003 common shares. At December 31, 2005, 57,739 options were available for issue.

The Company has granted share options to directors, officers, and employees to purchase 938,264 shares at prices between $3.50 and $27.10 per share. These options expire on dates between March 14, 2006, and January 2, 2013.

	2005		2004		2003	
	Shares #	Weighted Average Exercise Price $	Shares #	Weighted Average Exercise Price $	Shares #	Weighted Average Exercise Price $
Share options, beginning of the year	**1,071,333**	**13.34**	1,479,100	9.28	1,296,200	6.09
Granted	–	–	167,000	24.50	307,500	21.29
Exercised	**(120,070)**	**8.00**	(573,101)	6.09	(119,264)	5.46
Cancelled	**(12,999)**	**23.69**	(1,666)	18.40	(5,336)	12.62
Share options, end of the year	**938,264**	**13.88**	1,071,333	13.34	1,479,100	9.28

The Company had issued options to directors, officers, and employees at December 31, 2005, as follows:

	Options Outstanding			Options Exercisable	
Range of Exercise Prices $	Outstanding #	Weighted Average Remaining Contractual Life in Years	Weighted Average Exercise Price $	Shares Exercisable #	Weighted Average Exercise Price $
3.50 – 3.60	**347,500**	**0.8**	**3.56**	**347,500**	**3.56**
5.20 – 7.00	**40,550**	**0.8**	**6.05**	**40,550**	**6.05**
14.50 – 18.85	**159,400**	**4.1**	**15.62**	**159,400**	**15.62**
21.00 – 27.10	**390,814**	**5.8**	**23.17**	**148,654**	**22.22**
3.50 – 27.10	**938,264**	**3.4**	**13.88**	**696,104**	**10.45**

The fair value of options granted subsequent to January 1, 2002, is determined at the date of grant using the Black-Scholes option-pricing model. The Black-Scholes option valuation model was developed for use in estimating the fair value of traded options that have no vesting restrictions and are fully transferable. In addition, option valuation models require the input of highly subjective assumptions, including expected stock price volatility. Because the Company's employee stock options have characteristics that are significantly different from those of traded options, and because changes in subjective input assumptions can materially affect the fair value estimate, in management's opinion the existing models do not necessarily provide a reliable single measure of the fair value of the Company's employee stock options.

The estimated fair value of options granted both at the share market price on the grant date and in excess of the share market price on the grant date was determined using the weighted average assumptions indicated below. No options were granted in 2005.

	2004	2003	
	Granted at Market	Granted at Market	Granted in Excess of Market
Risk-free interest rate (%)	4.07	4.48	5.04
Expected hold period to exercise (years)	6.0	6.2	9.1
Volatility in the price of the Company's shares (%) ...	26.1	27.4	28.5
Weighted average fair value per option ($)	8.46	7.40	6.04

13. Cumulative Translation Account

The foreign currency cumulative translation account represents the unrealized gain or loss on the Company's net investment in self-sustaining US-based operations. The change in the cumulative translation account during the year relates to the fluctuation in the value of the Canadian dollar relative to the US dollar. Balance sheet accounts denominated in US dollars have been translated to Canadian dollars at the rate of 1.1630 (2004 – 1.2020; 2003 – 1.2965).

	2005 $000s	2004 $000s	2003 $000s
Cumulative translation account, beginning of the year	**(19,018)**	(13,861)	1,966
Current year deferred translation adjustment	**(6,557)**	(5,157)	(15,827)
Cumulative translation account, end of the year	**(25,575)**	(19,018)	(13,861)

14. Income Taxes

The effective income tax rate in the consolidated statements of income differs from statutory Canadian tax rates as a result of the following:

	2005 %	2004 %	2003 %
Income tax expense at statutory Canadian rates	**34.8**	34.7	36.8
Increase (decrease) resulting from:			
Income from associated companies	**(0.1)**	(0.3)	(0.6)
Rate differential on foreign income	**0.7**	(2.0)	0.6
Non-deductible expenses:			
Meals and entertainment	**1.1**	1.4	1.4
Stock compensation	**0.5**	0.6	0.6
Non-taxable foreign income net of non-creditable withholding taxes	**(1.6)**	(1.3)	(1.6)
Other	**(0.4)**	(0.7)	(0.5)
	35.0	32.4	36.7

Since the Company operates in several tax jurisdictions, its income is subject to various rates of taxation. The details of income before income taxes are as follows:

	2005 $000s	2004 $000s	2003 $000s
Domestic	**61,323**	48,111	36,583
Foreign	**1,177**	(3,451)	3,045
Total income before income taxes	**62,500**	44,660	39,628

Details of the income tax expense (recovery) are as follows:

		2005 $000s	2004 $000s	2003 $000s
Current:	Domestic	**21,172**	17,724	9,474
	Foreign	**563**	341	576
Total current expense		**21,735**	18,065	10,050
Future:	Domestic	**5**	(566)	3,532
	Foreign	**138**	(3,029)	976
Total future expense		**143**	(3,595)	4,508
Total:	Domestic	**21,177**	17,158	13,006
	Foreign	**701**	(2,688)	1,552
Total income tax expense		**21,878**	14,470	14,558

Significant components of the Company's future income tax assets and liabilities are as follows:

	2005 $000s	2004 $000s
Future income tax assets		
Differences in timing of deductibility of expenses	**13,470**	9,434
Loss carryforwards	**4,670**	2,316
Share issue and other financing costs	**519**	237
Tax cost of property and equipment in excess of carrying value	**357**	684
Deferred gain on sale of building	**1,513**	1,518
Other	**1,112**	700
	21,641	14,889
Less current portion	**14,827**	8,532
	6,814	6,357

	2005 $000s	2004 $000s
Future income tax liabilities		
Cash to accrual adjustments on acquisitions of US subsidiaries	–	2,091
Differences in timing of taxability of revenues	**15,287**	7,702
Carrying value of property and equipment in excess of tax cost	**7,304**	5,025
Carrying value of intangible assets in excess of tax cost	**10,625**	2,016
Other	**598**	2,135
	33,814	18,969
Less current portion	**17,552**	10,653
	16,262	8,316

At December 31, 2005, loss carryforwards of approximately $3,374,000 are available to reduce the taxable income of certain Canadian subsidiaries. These losses expire as set out below:

	$000s
2007	194
2008	1,454
2009	66
2010	978
2014	664
2015	18
	3,374

In addition, the Company has loss carryforwards of approximately $10,625,000 available to reduce the taxable income of certain US subsidiaries that expire at varying times over the next 20 years.

The potential income tax benefits that will result from the application of Canadian and US tax losses have been recognized in these financial statements.

15. Earnings Per Share

The number of basic and diluted common shares outstanding, as calculated on a weighted average basis, is as follows:

	2005 #	2004 #	2003 #
Basic shares outstanding	**19,920,117**	18,499,598	18,329,960
Share options (dilutive effect of 938,264 options; 2004 – 1,041,333; 2003 – 1,419,100)	**533,792**	507,691	788,056
Restricted shares (dilutive effect of 58,696 restricted shares)	**17,207**	–	–
Diluted shares outstanding	**20,471,116**	19,007,289	19,118,016

16. Cash Flows From (Used In) Operating Activities

Cash flows from operating activities determined by the indirect method are as follows:

	2005 $000s	2004 $000s	2003 $000s
CASH FLOWS FROM OPERATING ACTIVITIES			
Net income for the year	**40,622**	30,190	25,070
Add (deduct) items not affecting cash:			
Depreciation of property and equipment	**12,389**	11,986	9,912
Amortization of intangible assets	**2,542**	927	925
Future income tax	**143**	(3,595)	4,508
Loss (gain) on dispositions of investments and property and equipment	**562**	(504)	57
Stock-based compensation expense	**1,814**	894	706
Provision for self-insured liability	**9,764**	2,826	–
Other non-cash items	**(1,332)**	(1,065)	–
Share of income from equity investments	**(187)**	(385)	(580)
Dividends from equity investments	**550**	300	–
	66,867	41,574	40,598
Change in non-cash working capital accounts:			
Accounts receivable	**15,748**	(1,542)	(1,252)
Costs and estimated earnings in excess of billings	**(19,572)**	30,218	(35,239)
Prepaid expenses	**487**	496	113
Accounts payable and accrued liabilities	**(2,697)**	(6,350)	13,944
Billings in excess of costs and estimated earnings	**1,664**	1,600	4,951
Income taxes payable/recoverable	**(5,183)**	11,355	(6,222)
	(9,553)	35,777	(23,705)
Cash flows from operating activities	**57,314**	77,351	16,893

17. Joint Ventures

The Company participates in joint ventures with other parties as follows:

	Percentage Owned		
	2005	2004	2003
	%	%	%
yyC.T. Joint Venture	**20**	20	20
Stantec – S&L Partnership	**50**	50	50
Colt Stantec Joint Venture	**n/a**	50	50
Edmonton International Airports Joint Venture	**33**	33	33
Pine Creek Consultants Joint Venture	**33**	33	33
Dunlop Joint Ventures	**33–80**	33–80	n/a
Stantec Architecture Ltd./J.L. Richards & Associates Joint Venture	**50**	n/a	n/a

As part of the acquisition of Dunlop Architects Inc. (Dunlop), the Company acquired the interests of 13 joint ventures entered into by Dunlop. The interest held in these joint ventures ranges from 33 to 80%, and each is project specific.

A summary of the assets, liabilities, revenues, expenses, and cash flows included in the consolidated financial statements related to joint ventures is as follows:

	2005	2004	2003
	$000s	$000s	$000s
Statement of income			
Gross revenue	**5,941**	1,186	11,949
Subconsultant and other direct expenses	**5,072**	894	9,611
Administrative and marketing expenses	**147**	217	776
Net income for the year	**722**	75	1,562
Balance sheets			
Current assets	**3,743**	3,445	1,547
Current liabilities	**2,842**	2,822	1,583
Statement of cash flows			
Cash flows used in operating activities	**(488)**	(274)	(86)

18. Segmented Information

The Company provides comprehensive professional services in the area of infrastructure and facilities throughout North America and internationally. The Company considers the basis on which it is organized, including geographic areas and service offerings, in identifying its reportable segments. Operating segments of the Company are defined as components of the Company for which separate financial information is available that is evaluated regularly by the chief operating decision maker in allocating resources and assessing performance. The chief operating decision maker is the Chief Executive Officer (CEO) of the Company, and the Company's operating segments are based on its regional geographic areas.

During 2003, the Company had seven operating segments, of which five were aggregated into the Consulting Services reportable segment. The two remaining operating segments (Design Build and Technology), which were below the quantitative thresholds in the recommendations of the CICA, were disclosed in the Other reportable segment. In addition to the above-noted operating segments, corporate administration groups reported to the CEO and were included in the Other reportable segment. In the second quarter of 2004, an additional operating segment was added upon the acquisition of The Sear-Brown Group, Inc. This new segment has been aggregated into the Consulting Services reportable segment.

The Design Build operating segment consisted of the operations of the Company's 50% share of Lockerbie Stanley Inc. that, at December 31, 2003, was reflected as assets held for sale pending the finalization of an agreement to sell the Company's interest. The sale was completed in 2004. In addition, during 2004, the Company sold the operations related to its Technology segment. Operations sold during the year have not been presented as discontinued operations, because the amounts are not material.

Effective 2004, because the operations that comprised the Company's Design Build and Technology segments were sold and because the Company's corporate administration groups are not material, all operations of the Company are included in one reportable segment as Consulting Services.

Geographic information

	Property and Equipment, Goodwill, Intangible Assets	
	2005 $000s	**2004 $000s**
Canada	**104,463**	86,731
United States	**223,593**	52,032
International	**441**	471
	328,497	139,234

Geographic information

	Gross Revenue		
	2005 $000s	**2004 $000s**	**2003 $000s**
Canada	**380,471**	325,844	290,413
United States	**233,428**	190,362	161,655
International	**4,121**	4,673	7,874
	618,020	520,879	459,942

Gross revenue is attributed to countries based on the location of work performed.

Practice area information

	Gross Revenue		
	2005 $000s	**2004 $000s**	**2003 $000s**
Consulting Services			
Environment	**104,437**	105,471	91,758
Buildings	**159,233**	107,465	89,943
Transportation	**92,146**	92,631	80,519
Urban Land	**208,903**	168,876	159,941
Industrial	**53,301**	45,371	33,304
	618,020	519,814	455,465
Other	–	1,065	4,477
	618,020	520,879	459,942

Customers

The Company has a large number of clients in various industries and sectors of the economy. Gross revenue is not concentrated in any particular client.

19. Forward Contracts

The Company had no forward contracts outstanding at December 31, 2005. As at December 31, 2004, the Company had entered into foreign currency forward contracts that provided for the sale of US$10.0 million at rates ranging from 1.2050 to 1.2386 per US dollar. The fair values of these contracts, estimated using market rates at December 31, 2004, were $229,000. During 2004, net unrealized gains of $229,000 relating to derivative financial instruments were recorded in foreign exchange (gains) losses.

20. United States Generally Accepted Accounting Principles

The consolidated financial statements of the Company are prepared in Canadian dollars in accordance with accounting principles generally accepted in Canada (Canadian GAAP) that, in most respects, conform to accounting principles generally accepted in the United States (US GAAP). The following adjustments and disclosures would be required in order to present these consolidated financial statements in accordance with US GAAP. Investments in joint ventures are accounted for using the equity method under US GAAP, whereas Canadian GAAP requires the proportionate consolidation method. As permitted by the Securities and Exchange Commission, no disclosure of the effect of this difference is required.

a) Net income and comprehensive income

There are no identifiable material items that would result in a change in net income presented under Canadian and US GAAP.

The Company accounts for leases in accordance with Statement of Financial Accounting Standards No. 13, "Accounting for leases" (SFAS 13). SFAS 13 requires leasehold improvements in an operating lease to be amortized over the shorter of their economic lives or the lease term, as defined in SFAS 13. As a result, SFAS 13 requires the amortization period for leasehold improvements to be shorter than that applied by the Company under Canadian GAAP. The incremental amortization has been determined to be immaterial to the years presented.

Under US GAAP, the Company's investments held for self-insured liabilities would be classified as investments available for sale and recorded at fair value (note 6). The difference between the recorded and fair value of these investments has been determined to be immaterial to the years presented.

Comprehensive income is measured in accordance with Statement of Financial Accounting Standards No. 130, "Reporting Comprehensive Income" (SFAS 130). This standard defines comprehensive income as all changes in equity other than those resulting from investments by owners and distributions to owners and includes adjustments arising on the translation of self-sustaining foreign operations. Canadian GAAP does not yet require similar disclosure.

Statement of Comprehensive Income

	2005 $000s	2004 $000s	2003 $000s
Net income under Canadian and US GAAP	**40,622**	30,190	25,070
Other comprehensive income, net of tax:			
Unrealized foreign exchange loss on translation of self-sustaining foreign operations	**(6,557)**	(5,157)	(15,827)
Comprehensive Income	**34,065**	25,033	9,243
Accumulated other comprehensive income, beginning of year	**(19,018)**	(13,861)	1,966
Unrealized foreign exchange loss on translation of self-sustaining foreign operations	**(6,557)**	(5,157)	(15,827)
Accumulated other comprehensive income, end of the year	**(25,575)**	(19,018)	(13,861)

b) Other disclosure requirements

i) Allowance for doubtful accounts

	2005 $000s	2004 $000s	2003 $000s
Balance, beginning of the year	**21,095**	16,952	17,316
Acquired balances	**7,298**	5,294	651
Provision for doubtful accounts	**73**	6,632	4,544
Deductions	**(12,164)**	(7,152)	(4,221)
Impact on foreign exchange	**(249)**	(631)	(1,338)
Balance, end of the year	**16,053**	21,095	16,952

ii) Long-term contracts

Included in accounts receivable are holdbacks on long-term contracts of $1,431,000 in 2005 and of $3,653,000 in 2004.

21. Comparative Figures

Certain comparative figures have been reclassified to conform to the presentation adopted for the current year.

Note: All assignment material with an asterisk (*) relates to Appendix 5A.

Brief Exercises

(LO 1) **BE5-1** One of the weaknesses or limitations of the balance sheet is that it leaves out financial statement elements if they cannot be objectively recorded. Name three examples of items that are omitted because of this limitation.

(LO 2) **BE5-2** Broncho Corporation has the following accounts included in its December 31, 2008, trial balance: Accounts Receivable $221,000; Inventories $190,000; Allowance for Doubtful Accounts $8,000; Patents $92,000; Prepaid Insurance $9,700; Accounts Payable $88,000; and Cash $9,000. Prepare the balance sheet's current assets section, listing the accounts in proper sequence. Identify which items are monetary.

(LO 2) **BE5-3** The following accounts are in Daily Limited's December 31, 2008, trial balance: Prepaid Rent $1,300; Long-Term Investments in Common Shares $62,000; Unearned Fees $7,000; Land Held for Investment $139,000; and Long-Term Receivables $45,000. Prepare the long-term investments section of the balance sheet. Identify which items are financial instruments.

(LO 2) **BE5-4** Azalea Corp.'s December 31, 2008, trial balance includes the following accounts: Inventories $20,000; Buildings $308,000; Accumulated Amortization—Equipment $119,000; Equipment $209,000; Land Held for Investment $146,000; Accumulated Amortization—Buildings $45,000; Land $273,000; Machinery under Capital Leases $270,000; and Accumulated Amortization—Machinery under Capital Leases $100,000. Prepare the balance sheet's property, plant, and equipment section.

(LO 2) **BE5-5** Mai Corporation has the following accounts included in its December 31, 2008, trial balance: Trading Securities $124,000; Goodwill $266,000; Prepaid Insurance $112,000; Patents $20,000; and Franchises $124,000. Prepare the balance sheet's intangible assets section.

(LO 2) **BE5-6** Included in Euclid Limited's December 31, 2008, trial balance are the following accounts: Accounts Payable $251,000; Obligations under Long-Term Capital Leases $175,000; Discount on Bonds Payable $142,000; Advances from Customers $141,000; Bonds Payable $600,000; Wages Payable $127,000; Interest Payable $142,000; and Income Taxes Payable $9,000. Prepare the current liabilities section of the balance sheet. Identify which items are monetary.

(LO 2) **BE5-7** Use the information presented in BE5-6 for Euclid Limited to prepare the long-term liabilities section of the balance sheet.

(LO 2) **BE5-8** Tong Corp.'s December 31, 2008, trial balance includes the following accounts: Investment in Common Shares $185,000; Retained Earnings $349,000; Trademarks $87,000; Preferred Shares $279,000; Common Shares $67,000; Future Income Taxes $191,000; and Contributed Surplus $4,000. Prepare the shareholders' equity section of the balance sheet.

(LO 8, 10) **BE5-9** Midwest Beverage Company reported the following items in the most recent year:

Net income	$40,000
Dividends paid	5,000
Increase in accounts receivable	10,000
Increase in accounts payable	5,000
Purchase of equipment	8,000
Amortization expense	4,000
Issue of notes payable for cash	20,000

Calculate net cash provided by operating activities.

(LO 8) **BE5-10** Kes Company reported 2008 net income of $151,000. During 2008, accounts receivable increased by $13,000 and accounts payable increased by $9,500. Amortization expense was $39,000. Prepare the cash flows from operating activities section of the statement of cash flows.

(LO 8) **BE5-11** Yorkis Perez Corporation engaged in the following cash transactions in 2008:

Sale of land and building	$181,000
Repurchase of company's own shares	40,000
Purchase of land	37,000
Payment of cash dividend	85,000
Purchase of equipment	53,000
Issuance of common shares	147,000
Retirement of bonds payable	100,000

Calculate the net cash provided by investing activities.

BE5-12 Use the information from BE5-11 for Yorkis Perez Corporation to calculate the net cash from financing activities. **(LO 8)**

***BE5-13** Using the information from BE5-11, determine Yorkis Perez's free cash flow, assuming that the corporation reported net cash from operating activities of $400,000. Calculate the dividend payout ratio for Yorkis Perez for the year. **(LO 10)**

Exercises

E5-1 (Balance Sheet Classifications) Several balance sheet accounts of SooYoun Inc. follow: **(LO 2)**

1. Investment in Preferred Shares
2. Common Shares Distributable
3. Cash Dividends Payable
4. Accumulated Amortization
5. Warehouse in Process of Construction
6. Petty Cash
7. Accrued Interest on Notes Payable
8. Accrued Interest on Notes Receivable
9. Deficit
10. Investments—Trading Securities
11. Income Taxes Payable
12. Unearned Subscription Revenue
13. Work-in-Process
14. Accrued Vacation Pay
15. Customer Deposits

Instructions

For each account, indicate the proper balance sheet classification. In the case of borderline items, indicate the additional information that would be required to determine the proper classification. (Refer to Illustration 5-1 as a guideline.) Also, identify which items are monetary and which are financial instruments.

E5-2 (Classification of Balance Sheet Accounts) The classifications of Findlay Limited's balance sheet follow: **(LO 2)**

1. Current assets
2. Long-term investments
3. Property, plant, and equipment
4. Intangible assets
5. Other assets
6. Current liabilities
7. Non-current liabilities
8. Capital shares
9. Contributed surplus
10. Retained earnings
11. Accumulated other comprehensive income

Instructions

Indicate by number where each of the following accounts would be classified:

(a) Preferred Shares
(b) Goodwill
(c) Wages Payable
(d) Trade Accounts Payable
(e) Buildings
(f) Trading Securities
(g) Current Portion of Long-Term Debt
(h) Premium on Bonds Payable
(i) Allowance for Doubtful Accounts
(j) Accounts Receivable
(k) Demand Bank Loan
(l) Notes Payable (due next year)
(m) Office Supplies
(n) Mortgage Payable
(o) Land
(p) Bond Sinking Fund
(q) Inventory
(r) Prepaid Insurance
(s) Bonds Payable
(t) Taxes Payable
(u) Unrealized Gain on Derivatives
(v) Donation of Artwork (from unrelated customer)

E5-3 (Classification of Balance Sheet Accounts) Assume that Macy Inc. uses the following headings on its balance sheet: **(LO 2)**

1. Current assets
2. Long-term investments
3. Property, plant, and equipment
4. Intangible assets
7. Long-term liabilities
8. Capital shares
9. Contributed surplus
10. Retained earnings

5. Other assets
6. Current liabilities
11. Accumulated other comprehensive income

Instructions

Indicate by number how each of the following should usually be classified. If an item should appear in a note to the financial statements, use the letter N to indicate this. If an item need not be reported at all on the balance sheet, use the letter X. Indicate also whether an item is monetary and/or represents a financial instrument.

(a) Unexpired insurance
(b) Shares owned in affiliated companies
(c) Unearned subscriptions
(d) Advances to suppliers
(e) Unearned rent
(f) Copyrights
(g) Petty cash fund
(h) Sales tax payable
(i) Accrued interest on notes receivable
(j) Twenty-year issue of bonds payable that will mature within the next year (no sinking funds exist, and refunding is not planned)
(k) Machinery retired from use and held for sale
(l) Fully amortized machine still in use
(m) Held-to-maturity investment in bonds
(n) Accrued interest on bonds payable
(o) Salaries that company budget shows will be paid to employees within the next year
(p) Accumulated amortization
(q) Accumulated unrealized gains on available for sale securities
(r) Bank demand loan
(s) Land held for speculation

(LO 2, 3, 10) E5-4 **(Preparation of Corrected Balance Sheet)** Sibongilie Corp. has decided to expand its operations. The bookkeeper recently completed the following balance sheet in order to obtain additional funds for expansion:

SIBONGILIE CORP.
Balance Sheet
For the Year Ended December 31, 2008

Current assets	
Cash (net of bank overdraft of $30,000)	$ 540,000
Accounts receivable (net)	150,000
Inventories at lower of average cost or net realizable value	322,000
Trading securities at cost (fair value $120,000)	140,000
Property, plant, and equipment	
Building (net)	1,570,000
Office equipment (net)	450,000
Land held for future use	2,375,000
Intangible assets	
Goodwill	180,000
Held-to-maturity investment in bonds	90,000
Prepaid expense	12,000
Current liabilities	
Accounts payable	505,000
Notes payable (due next year)	135,000
Pension obligation	72,000
Rent payable	49,000
Premium on bonds payable	53,000
Long-term liabilities	
Bonds payable	500,000

Shareholders' equity	
Common shares, unlimited authorized, 290,000 issued	290,000
Contributed surplus	160,000
Retained earnings	?

Instructions

(a) Prepare a revised balance sheet using the available information. Assume that the bank overdraft relates to a bank account held at a different bank than the account with the cash balance. Assume that the accumulated amortization balance for the buildings is $560,000 and for the office equipment, $105,000. The allowance for doubtful accounts has a balance of $17,000. The pension obligation is considered a long-term liability.

(b) What effect, if any, does the classification of the bank overdraft have on the working capital and current ratio of Sibongilie Corp.? What is the likely reason that the bank overdraft was given that particular classification?

E5-5 (Correction of Balance Sheet) The bookkeeper for Nguyen Corp has prepared the following balance sheet as at July 31, 2008: **(LO 2, 3, 10)**

NGUYEN CORP.
Balance Sheet
As at July 31, 2008

Cash	$ 69,000	Notes and accounts payable	$ 44,000
Accounts receivable (net)	40,500	Long-term liabilities	99,000
Inventories	60,000	Shareholders' equity	155,500
Equipment (net)	84,000		$298,500
Patents	45,000		
	$298,500		

The following additional information is provided:

1. Cash includes $1,200 in a petty cash fund and $15,000 in a bond sinking fund.
2. The net accounts receivable balance is composed of the following three items: (a) accounts receivable debit balances $52,000; (b) accounts receivable credit balances $8,000; (c) allowance for doubtful accounts $3,500.
3. Inventory costing $5,300 was shipped out on consignment on July 31, 2008. The ending inventory balance does not include the consigned goods. Receivables of $5,300 were recognized on these consigned goods.
4. Equipment had a cost of $112,000 and an accumulated amortization balance of $28,000.
5. Taxes payable of $6,000 were accrued on July 31. Nguyen Corp, however, had set up a cash fund to meet this obligation. This cash fund was not included in the cash balance, but was offset against the taxes payable amount.

Instructions

(a) Use the information available to prepare a corrected classified balance sheet as at July 31, 2008 (adjust the account balances based on the additional information).

(b) What effect, if any, does the treatment of the credit balances in accounts receivable of $8,000 have on the working capital and current ratio of Nguyen Corp.? What is the likely reason that the credit balances in accounts receivable were given that particular classification? What is the likely cause of the credit balances in accounts receivable?

E5-6 (Preparation of Classified Balance Sheet) Assume that Dion Inc. has the following accounts at the end of the current year: **(LO 3)**

1. Common Shares
2. Raw Materials
3. Preferred Share Investments, Long-Term
4. Unearned Rent
5. Work-in-Process
6. Copyrights (net)
7. Buildings
8. Notes Receivable, Short-Term
9. Cash
10. Accrued Salaries Payable
11. Accumulated Amortization—Buildings
12. Cash Restricted for Plant Expansion
13. Land Held for Future Plant Site
14. Allowance for Doubtful Accounts
15. Retained Earnings
16. Unearned Subscriptions
17. Receivables from Officers (due in one year)
18. Finished Goods
19. Accounts Receivable
20. Bonds Payable (due in four years)

Instructions
Prepare a classified balance sheet in good form (no monetary amounts are necessary).

(LO 3, 4, 5) **E5-7 (Current Assets Section of Balance Sheet)** Selected accounts follow of Kawabata Limited at December 31, 2008:

Finished Goods	$152,000	Cost of Goods Sold	$2,100,000
Revenue Received in Advance	90,000	Notes Receivable	40,000
Bank Overdraft	8,000	Accounts Receivable	161,000
Equipment	453,000	Raw Materials	207,000
Work-in-Process	134,000	Supplies Expense	60,000
Cash	97,000	Allowance for Doubtful Accounts	12,000
Trading Securities	51,000	Licences	18,000
Customer Advances	36,000	Contributed Surplus	88,000
Cash Restricted for Plant Expansion	150,000	Common Shares	22,000

The following additional information is available:

1. Inventories are valued at lower of cost and net realizable value using FIFO.
2. Equipment is recorded at cost. Accumulated amortization, calculated on a straight-line basis, is $50,600.
3. The trading securities have a fair value of $129,000.
4. The notes receivable are due April 30, 2009, with interest receivable every April 30. The notes bear interest at 12%. (Hint: Accrue interest due on December 31, 2008.)
5. The allowance for doubtful accounts applies to the accounts receivable. Accounts receivable of $50,000 are pledged as collateral on a bank loan.
6. Licences are recorded net of accumulated amortization of $14,000.

Instructions

(a) Prepare the current assets section of Kawabata Limited's December 31, 2008, balance sheet, with appropriate disclosures.

(b) Outline the other ways or methods that can be used to disclose the details that are required under GAAP for the financial statement elements in part (a).

(LO 3) **E5-8 (Current vs. Long-Term Liabilities)** Chopin Corporation is preparing its December 31, 2007, balance sheet. The following items may be reported as either a current or long-term liability:

1. On December 15, 2007, Chopin declared a cash dividend of $2.50 per share to shareholders of record on December 31. The dividend is payable on January 15, 2008. Chopin has issued 1 million common shares.
2. Also on December 31, Chopin declared a 10% stock dividend to shareholders of record on January 15, 2008. The dividend will be distributed on January 31, 2008. Chopin's common shares have a market value of $54 per share.
3. At December 31, bonds payable of $100 million are outstanding. The bonds pay 7% interest every September 30 and mature in instalments of $25 million every September 30, beginning September 30, 2008.
4. At December 31, 2006, customer advances were $12 million. During 2007, Chopin collected $40 million of customer advances, and advances of $25 million were earned.
5. At December 31, 2007, retained earnings set aside for future inventory losses is $22 million.
6. At December 31, 2007, Chopin has an operating line of credit with a balance of $3.5 million. For several years now, Chopin has successfully met all the conditions of this bank loan. If Chopin defaults on any of the loan conditions in any way, the bank has the right to demand payment on the loan.

Instructions
For each item above, indicate the dollar amounts to be reported as a current liability and as a long-term liability, if any.

(LO 3, 10) **E5-9 (Current Assets and Current Liabilities)** The current assets and current liabilities sections of the balance sheet of Scarlatti Corp. are as follows:

SCARLATTI CORP.
Balance Sheet (partial)
December 31, 2007

Cash		$ 957,000	Accounts payable	$1,028,000
Accounts receivable	$1,189,000		Notes payable	853,000
Allowance for doubtful accounts	197,000	992,000		$1,881,000
Inventories		957,000		
Prepaid expenses		19,000		
		$2,925,000		

The following errors have been discovered in the corporation's accounting:

1. January 2008 cash disbursements that were entered as of December 2007 included payments of accounts payable in the amount of $741,000, on which a cash discount of 2% was taken.
2. The inventory included $127,000 of merchandise that was received at December 31 but with no purchase invoices received or entered. Of this amount, $14,500 was received on consignment; the remainder was purchased f.o.b. destination, terms 2/10, n/30.
3. Sales for the first four days in January 2008 in the amount of $447,000 were entered in the sales book as at December 31, 2007. Of these, $121,500 were sales on account and the remainder were cash sales.
4. Cash, not including cash sales, collected in January 2008 and entered as at December 31, 2007, totalled $135,324. Of this amount, $123,324 was received on account after cash discounts of 2% had been deducted; the remainder was proceeds on a bank loan.

Instructions

(a) Restate the balance sheet's current assets and liabilities sections. (Assume that both accounts receivable and accounts payable are recorded gross.)

***(b)** Calculate the current ratio before and after the corrections prepared in part (a). Did the restatement improve or worsen this ratio?

(c) State the net effect of your adjustments on Scarlatti Corp.'s retained earnings balance.

E5-10 (Preparation of Balance Sheet) The trial balance of Kwanzu Corporation at December 31, 2007, follows: **(LO 3)**

	Debits	Credits
Cash	$ 205,000	
Sales		$ 7,960,000
Trading Securities	153,000	
Cost of Goods Sold	4,800,000	
Held-to-Maturity Investment in Bonds	299,000	
Long-Term Investments in Shares—Available for Sale (market $345,000)	277,000	
Short-Term Notes Payable		98,000
Accounts Payable		545,000
Selling Expenses	1,860,000	
Investment Gains		63,000
Land	260,000	
Buildings	1,040,000	
Dividends Payable		136,000
Accrued Liabilities		96,000
Accounts Receivable	515,000	
Accumulated Amortization—Buildings		152,000
Allowance for Doubtful Accounts		25,000
Administrative Expenses	900,000	
Interest Expense	211,000	
Inventories	687,000	
Extraordinary Gain		160,000
Correction of Prior Year's Error	140,000	
Long-Term Notes Payable		900,000
Equipment	600,000	

Bonds Payable		$ 1,000,000
Accumulated Amortization—Equipment		60,000
Franchise	$ 160,000	
Common Shares		809,000
Patent	195,000	
Retained Earnings		218,000
Accumulated Other Comprehensive Income		80,000
Totals	$12,302,000	$12,302,000

Instructions

(a) Prepare a classified balance sheet at December 31, 2007. Ignore income taxes.

(b) Is there any situation where it would make more sense to have a balance sheet that is not classified?

(LO 3, 8) **E5-11 (Preparation of Balance Sheet)** Worldly Corporation's balance sheet at the end of 2006 included the following items:

Current assets	$1,105,000	Current liabilities	$1,020,000
Land	30,000	Bonds payable	1,100,000
Building	1,120,000	Common shares	180,000
Equipment	320,000	Retained earnings	174,000
Accum. amort.—build.	(130,000)	Total	$2,474,000
Accum. amort.—equip.	(11,000)		
Patents	40,000		
Total	$2,474,000		

The following information is available for 2007:

1. Net income was $391,000.
2. Equipment (cost of $20,000 and accumulated amortization of $8,000) was sold for $10,000.
3. Amortization expense was $4,000 on the building and $9,000 on equipment.
4. Patent amortization expense was $3,000.
5. Current assets other than cash increased by $229,000. Current liabilities increased by $213,000.
6. An addition to the building was completed at a cost of $31,000.
7. A long-term investment in shares (no quoted market value) was purchased for $20,500.
8. Bonds payable of $75,000 were issued.
9. Cash dividends of $180,000 were declared and paid.

Instructions

(a) Prepare a balance sheet at December 31, 2007.

(b) Prepare a statement of cash flows for the year ended December 31, 2007.

(LO 6, 8, 9) **E5-12 (Prepare Statement of Cash Flows)** A comparative balance sheet for Nicholson Industries Inc. follows:

NICHOLSON INDUSTRIES INC.
Balance Sheet

	December 31	
Assets	2007	2006
Cash	$ 21,000	$ 34,000
Accounts receivable	104,000	54,000
Inventories	220,000	189,000
Land	71,000	110,000
Equipment	260,000	200,000
Accumulated amortization—equipment	(69,000)	(42,000)
Total	$607,000	$545,000

Liabilities and Shareholders' Equity		
Accounts payable	$ 52,000	$ 59,000
Bonds payable	150,000	200,000
Common shares	214,000	164,000
Retained earnings	91,000	22,000
Accumulated other comprehensive income	100,000	100,000
Total	$607,000	$545,000

Additional information:

1. Net income for the fiscal year ending December 31, 2007, was $129,000.
2. Cash dividends of $60,000 were declared and paid.
3. Bonds payable amounting to $50,000 were retired through issuance of common shares.
4. Land was sold at book value.

Instructions

(a) Prepare a statement of cash flows using the indirect format for cash flows from operations.

(b) Comment in general on the results reported in the statement of cash flows.

E5-13 **(Statement of Cash Flows—Classifications)** The major classifications of activities reported in the statement of cash flows are operating, investing, and financing. For this question, assume the following: **(LO 7)**

(a) The direct format is being used.

(b) The indirect format is being used.

Instructions

Classify each of the transactions in the lettered list that follows as:

1. Operating activity
2. Investing activity
3. Financing activity
4. Not reported as a cash flow

Transactions:

(a) Issuance of common shares

(b) Purchase of land and building

(c) Redemption of bonds

(d) Proceeds on sale of equipment

(e) Amortization of machinery

(f) Amortization of patent

(g) Issuance of bonds for plant assets

(h) Payment of cash dividends

(i) Exchange of furniture for office equipment

(j) Loss on sale of equipment

(k) Increase in accounts receivable during year

(l) Decrease in accounts payable during year

E5-14 **(Prepare Statement of Cash Flows)** The comparative balance sheet of Marubeni Corporation for the fiscal year ending December 31, 2008, follows: **(LO 8, 9)**

MARUBENI CORPORATION
Balance Sheet

	December 31	
Assets	2008	2007
Cash	$ 29,000	$ 14,000
Accounts receivable	106,000	88,000
Equipment	30,000	21,000
Less: Accumulated amortization	(17,000)	(11,000)
Total	$148,000	$112,000
Liabilities and Shareholders' Equity		
Accounts payable	$ 29,000	$ 16,000
Common shares	100,000	80,000
Retained earnings	19,000	16,000
Total	$148,000	$112,000

Net income of $44,000 was reported and dividends of $41,000 were paid in 2008. New equipment was purchased and none was sold.

Instructions

Prepare a statement of cash flows using the indirect format for cash flows from operations.

(LO 8) **E5-15** **(Prepare Partial Statement of Cash Flows—Operating Activities)** The income statement of Sanford Delivery Inc. for the year ended December 31, 2008, reported the following condensed information:

SANFORD DELIVERY INC.
Income Statement
Year Ended December 31, 2008

Revenue		$545,000
Operating expenses		370,000
Income from operations		175,000
Other revenues and expenses		
Gain on sale of equipment	$25,000	
Interest expense	10,000	15,000
Income before income taxes		190,000
Income taxes		42,000
Net income		$148,000

Sanford's balance sheet contained the following comparative data at December 31:

	2008	2007
Accounts receivable	$50,000	$60,000
Prepaid insurance	8,000	5,000
Accounts payable	30,000	41,000
Interest payable	2,000	750
Income taxes payable	8,000	4,500
Unearned revenue	10,000	14,000

Additional information:
Operating expenses include $70,000 in amortization expense.

Instructions

(a) Prepare the operating activities section of the cash flow statement for the year ended December 31, 2008, using the indirect format.

(b) Prepare the operating activities section of the cash flow statement for the year ended December 31, 2008, using the direct format.

(LO 10) ***E5-16** **(Analysis)** Use the information in E5-14 for Marubeni Corporation.

Instructions

(a) Calculate the current ratio and debt to total assets ratio as at December 31, 2007 and 2008.

(b) Based on the analysis in (a), comment on the company's liquidity and financial flexibility.

(LO 10) ***E5-17** **(Analysis)** Use the information in E5-12 for Nicholson Industries.

Instructions

(a) Calculate the current and acid-test ratios for 2006 and 2007.

(b) Calculate Nicholson's current cash debt coverage ratio for 2007.

(c) Based on the analyses in (a) and (b), comment on Nicholson's liquidity and financial flexibility.

Problems

P5-1 A list of accounts in alphabetical order follows:

Accounts Receivable
Accrued Wages
Accumulated Amortization—Buildings
Accumulated Amortization—Equipment
Accumulated Other Comprehensive Income
Advances to Employees
Advertising Expense
Allowance for Doubtful Accounts
Available-for-Sale Securities—Non-Current
Bonds Payable
Buildings
Cash in Bank
Cash on Hand
Commission Expense
Common Shares
Copyright (net of amortization)
Dividends Payable
Equipment
Gain on Sale of Equipment
Interest Receivable
Inventory—Beginning
Inventory—Ending
Land
Land for Future Plant Site
Loss from Flood
Notes Payable—Current
Patent (net of amortization)
Pension Obligations
Petty Cash
Preferred Shares
Premium on Bonds Payable
Prepaid Rent
Purchase Returns and Allowances
Purchases
Notes Receivable (due in five years)
Retained Earnings
Sales
Sales Discounts
Sales Salaries Expense
Taxes Payable
Trading Securities
Transportation-in
Unearned Subscriptions
Unrealized Gain/Loss on Available-for-Sale Securities

Instructions

Prepare a classified balance sheet in good form, without monetary amounts.

P5-2 Balance sheet items for Li Inc. follow for the current year, 2008:

Goodwill	$ 215,000	Accumulated amortization-equipment	$ 292,000
Payroll taxes payable	177,591	Inventories	314,800
Bonds payable	300,000	Rent payable (short-term)	45,000
Discount on bonds payable	15,000	Taxes payable	188,362
Cash	410,000	Long-term rental obligations	480,000
Land	480,000	Common shares (20,000 shares issued)	200,000
Notes receivable	545,700	Preferred shares (15,000 shares issued)	150,000
Notes payable to banks (demand)	340,000	Prepaid expenses	87,920
Accounts payable	640,000	Equipment	1,470,000
Retained earnings	?	Trading securities	121,000
Income taxes receivable	97,630	Accumulated amortization—building	170,200
Unsecured notes payable (long-term)	1,600,000	Building	1,640,000

Instructions

(a) Prepare a classified balance sheet in good form. The numbers of authorized shares are as follows: 400,000 common and 20,000 preferred. Assume that notes receivable and notes payable are short-term, unless stated otherwise. Cost and fair value of temporary investments are the same.

(b) What additional disclosures would you expect to provide for the long-term rental obligations?

P5-3 The trial balance of Klix Inc. and other related information for the year 2008 follows:

KLIX INC.
Trial Balance
December 31, 2008

	Debits	Credits
Cash	$ 105,000	
Accounts Receivable	363,500	
Allowance for Doubtful Accounts		$ 58,700
Prepaid Insurance	5,900	
Inventory	308,500	
Long-Term Investments—Available for Sale	339,000	
Land	71,000	
Construction Work in Progress	124,000	
Patents	36,000	
Equipment	400,000	
Accumulated Amortization—Equipment		326,000
Unamortized Discount on Bonds Payable	20,000	
Accounts Payable		162,000
Accrued Expenses		49,200
Notes Payable		94,000
Bonds Payable		400,000
Common Shares		500,000
Accumulated Other Comprehensive Income		45,000
Retained Earnings		138,000
	$1,772,900	$1,772,900

Additional information:

1. The inventory has a net realizable value of $360,000. The FIFO method of inventory valuation is used.
2. The fair value of the investments is $577,000.
3. The amount of the Construction Work in Progress account represents the costs to date on a building in the process of construction. (The company is renting factory space at the present time while waiting for the new building to be completed.) The land that the building is being constructed on cost $71,000, as shown in the trial balance.
4. The patents were purchased by the company at a cost of $40,000 and are being amortized on a straight-line basis.
5. Of the unamortized discount on bonds payable, $2,000 will be amortized in 2009.
6. The notes payable represent bank loans that are secured by long-term investments carried at $120,000. These bank loans are due in 2009.
7. The bonds payable bear interest at 11% payable every December 31, and are due January 1, 2013.
8. For common shares, 600,000 are authorized and 500,000 are issued and outstanding.

Instructions

Prepare a balance sheet as at December 31, 2008, so that all important information is fully disclosed.

P5-4 The balance sheet of Cruise Corporation as of December 31, 2008, is as follows:

CRUISE CORPORATION
Balance Sheet
December 31, 2008

Assets	
Goodwill (Note 2)	$ 70,000
Buildings (Note 1)	1,640,000
Inventories	312,100
Trading securities (Note 4)	100,000
Land	650,000
Accounts receivable	170,000
Long-term investments—available for sale (Note 4)	87,000
Cash on hand	175,900

Assets allocated to trustee for plant expansion	
Cash in bank	120,000
Treasury notes, at cost and fair value	138,000
	$3,463,000

Equities	
Notes payable (Note 3)	$ 600,000
Common shares, unlimited authorized, 1,000,000 issued	1,150,000
Retained earnings	456,000
Accumulated other comprehensive income	252,000
Appreciation capital (Note 1)	520,000
Income taxes payable	75,000
Reserve for amortization of building	410,000
	$3,463,000

Note 1: Buildings are stated at cost, except for one building that was recorded at its appraised value. The excess of the appraisal value over cost was $520,000. Amortization has been recorded based on cost.
Note 2: Goodwill in the amount of $70,000 was recognized because the company believed that book value was not an accurate representation of the company's fair market value. The gain of $70,000 was credited to Retained Earnings.
Note 3: Notes payable are long-term except for the current instalment due of $190,000.
Note 4: Trading securities have a market value of $75,000 and available-for-sale securities have a market value of $200,000.

Instructions

Prepare a corrected classified balance sheet in good form. The notes above are for information only.

P5-5 The balance sheet of Krause Corporation follows for the current year, 2008:

KRAUSE CORPORATION
Balance Sheet
December 31, 2008

Current assets	$ 138,000	Current liabilities	$ 330,000
Investments	927,000	Long-term liabilities	990,000
Property, plant, and equipment	1,720,000	Shareholders' equity	1,770,000
Intangible assets	305,000		
	$3,090,000		$3,090,000

The following additional information is available:

1. The current assets section includes the following: cash $23,000; accounts receivable $115,000, less $10,000 allowance for doubtful accounts; inventories $15,000; and unearned revenue $5,000. The cash balance is composed of $27,000, less a bank overdraft of $4,000. Inventories are stated at the lower of FIFO cost or net realizable value.
2. The investments section includes the following: notes receivable from a related company, due in 2014, $27,000; temporary investments in common shares of another company—trading, $280,000 (fair value $280,000); long-term available-for-sale securities $140,000 (fair value $240,000); bond sinking fund $250,000; and patents $130,000.
3. Property, plant, and equipment includes buildings $1,040,000, less accumulated amortization $360,000; equipment $450,000, less accumulated amortization $180,000; land $500,000; and land held for future use $270,000.
4. Intangible assets include the following: franchise $165,000; goodwill $100,000; and discount on bonds payable $40,000.
5. Current liabilities include the following: accounts payable $103,000; notes payable, short-term $80,000, long-term $107,000; and taxes payable $40,000.
6. Long-term liabilities are composed solely of 10% bonds payable due in 2010.
7. Shareholders' equity has 70,000 preferred shares (200,000 authorized), which were issued for $450,000, and 100,000 common shares (400,000 authorized), which were issued at an average price of $10 per share. In addition, the corporation has retained earnings of $120,000 and accumulated other comprehensive income of $200,000.

Instructions

(a) Prepare a balance sheet in good form (adjust the amounts in each balance sheet classification based on the additional information).

(b) What makes the condensed format of the original balance sheet inadequate in terms of the amount of detail that needs to be disclosed under GAAP?

P5-6 Cooke Inc. had the following balance sheet at the end of operations for 2006:

COOKE INC.
Balance Sheet
December 31, 2006

Cash	$ 20,000	Accounts payable	$ 30,000
Accounts receivable	21,200	Long-term notes payable	41,000
Investments—trading	32,000	Common shares	100,000
Plant assets (net)	81,000	Retained earnings	23,200
Land	40,000		
	$194,200		$194,200

During 2007, the following occurred:

1. Cooke Inc. sold part of its investment portfolio for $19,000. This transaction resulted in a gain of $3,400 for the firm. The company often sells and buys securities of this nature.
2. A tract of land was purchased for $18,000 cash.
3. Long-term notes payable in the amount of $17,000 were retired before maturity by paying $17,000 cash.
4. An additional $26,000 in common shares was issued.
5. Dividends totalling $9,200 were declared and paid to shareholders.
6. Net income for 2007 was $32,000 after allowing for amortization of $12,000.
7. Land was purchased through the issuance of $30,000 in bonds.
8. At December 31, 2007, cash was $41,000; accounts receivable were $41,600; and accounts payable remained at $30,000.

Instructions

(a) Prepare a statement of cash flows for the year ended December 31, 2007.

(b) Prepare the balance sheet as it would appear at December 31, 2007.

(c) How might the statement of cash flows help the user of the financial statements?

*(d) Calculate the following ratios:

1. Free cash flow
2. Current cash debt coverage ratio
3. Cash debt coverage ratio

(e) What is the cash flow pattern for Cooke? Discuss any areas of concern.

P5-7 Anne Spier has prepared baked goods for sale since 1991. She started a baking business in her home and has been operating in a rented building with a storefront since 1996. Spier incorporated the business as MAS Inc. on January 1, 2007, with an initial share issue of 1,000 common shares for $2,500. Anne Spier is the principal shareholder of MAS Inc.

Sales have increased by 30% annually since operations began at the present location, and additional equipment is needed for the continued growth that is expected. Spier wants to purchase some additional baking equipment and to finance the equipment through a long-term note from a commercial bank. Kelowna Bank & Trust has asked Spier to submit an income statement for MAS Inc. for the first five months of 2007 and a balance sheet as at May 31, 2007.

Spier assembled the following information from the corporation's cash basis records to use in preparing the financial statements that the bank wants to see:

1. The bank statement showed the following 2007 deposits through May 31:

Sale of common shares	$ 2,500
Cash sales	22,770
Rebates from purchases	130
Collections on credit sales	5,320
Bank loan proceeds	2,880
	$33,600

2. The following amounts were disbursed through May 31, 2007:

Baking materials	$14,400
Rent	1,800
Salaries and wages	5,500
Maintenance	110
Utilities	4,000
Insurance premium	1,920
Equipment	3,600
Principal and interest payment on bank loan	298
Advertising	424
	$32,052

3. Unpaid invoices at May 31, 2007, were as follows:

Baking materials	$256
Utilities	270
	$526

4. Customer records showed uncollected sales of $4,336 at May 31, 2007.

5. Baking materials costing $2,075 were on hand at May 31, 2007. There were no materials in process or finished goods on hand at that date. No materials were on hand or in process and no finished goods were on hand at January 1, 2007.

6. The note for the three-year bank loan is dated January 1, 2007, and states a simple interest rate of 8%. The loan requires quarterly payments on April 1, July 1, October 1, and January 1. Each payment is to consist of equal principal payments plus accrued interest since the last payment.

7. Anne Spier receives a salary of $750 on the last day of each month. The other employees have been paid through May 25, 2007, and are due an additional $270 on May 31, 2007.

8. New display cases and equipment costing $3,600 were purchased on January 2, 2007, and have an estimated useful life of five years. These are the only fixed assets that are currently used in the business. Straight-line amortization is used for book purposes.

9. Rent was paid for six months in advance on January 2, 2007.

10. A one-year insurance policy was purchased on January 2, 2007.

11. MAS Inc. is subject to an income tax rate of 20%.

12. Payments and collections from the unincorporated business through December 31, 2006, were not included in the corporation's records, and no cash was transferred from the unincorporated business to the corporation.

Instructions

(a) Using the accrual basis of accounting, prepare an income statement for the five months ended May 31, 2007.

(b) Using the accrual basis, prepare a balance sheet as at May 31, 2007.

(CMA adapted)

P5-8 Mansbridge Inc. had the following balance sheet at the end of operations for 2006:

MANSBRIDGE INC.
Balance Sheet
December 31, 2006

Cash	$ 20,000	Accounts payable	$ 30,000
Accounts receivable	21,200	Bonds payable	41,000
Investments—trading	32,000	Common shares	100,000
Plant assets (net)	81,000	Retained earnings	23,200
Land	40,000		
	$194,200		$194,200

During 2007, the following occurred:

1. Mansbridge liquidated its investment portfolio at a loss of $5,000.

2. A parcel of land was purchased for $43,000.
3. An additional $32,000 worth of common shares was issued.
4. Dividends totalling $12,000 were declared and paid to shareholders.
5. Net income for 2007 was $35,000, including $12,000 in amortization expense.
6. Land was purchased through the issuance of $30,000 in additional bonds.
7. At December 31, 2007, Cash was $65,200; Accounts Receivable was $42,000; and Accounts Payable was $40,000.
8. The fair value of the investments is equal to their cost.

Instructions

(a) Prepare the balance sheet as it would appear at December 31, 2007.

(b) Prepare a statement of cash flows for the year ended December 31, 2007.

*(c) Calculate the current and acid-test ratios for 2006 and 2007.

*(d) Calculate Mansbridge's current cash debt coverage ratio for 2007.

(e) What is the cash flow pattern? Discuss where the cash comes from and where it goes.

P5-9 In an examination of Acevedo Corporation as at December 31, 2007, you have learned about the following situations. No entries have been made in the accounting records for these items.

1. The corporation erected its present factory building in 1991. Amortization was calculated using the straight-line method, based on an estimated life of 35 years. Early in 2007, the board of directors conducted a careful survey and estimated that the factory building had a remaining useful life of 25 years as at January 1, 2007.
2. An additional assessment of 2006 income taxes was levied and paid in 2007.
3. When calculating the accrual for officers' salaries at December 31, 2007, it was discovered that the accrual for officers' salaries for December 31, 2006, had been overstated.
4. On December 15, 2007, Acevedo Corporation declared a common shares dividend of $1 per share on its issued common shares outstanding, payable February 1, 2008, to the common shareholders of record on December 31, 2007.
5. Acevedo Corporation, which is on a calendar-year basis, changed its inventory cost flow formula as at January 1, 2007. The inventory for December 31, 2006, was costed by the weighted average method, and the inventory for December 31, 2007, was costed by the FIFO method.
6. On January 15, 2008, Acevedo's warehouse containing raw materials was damaged by a flash flood.
7. During December 2007, the former president retired and a new president was appointed.

Instructions

Describe fully how each item above should be reported in the financial statements of Acevedo Corporation for the year 2007.

P5-10 The balance sheet of Bellemy Corporation follows (in thousands):

BELLEMY CORPORATION
Balance Sheet
December 31, 2008

Assets		
Current assets		
Cash	$26,000	
Marketable securities—trading	18,000	
Accounts receivable	25,000	
Merchandise inventory	20,000	
Supplies inventory	4,000	
Investment in subsidiary company	20,000	$113,000
Investments		
Marketable securities		25,000
Property, plant, and equipment		
Buildings and land	91,000	
Less: Reserve for amortization	31,000	60,000

Other assets		
Held-to-maturity investment in bonds		19,000
		$217,000
Liabilities and Equity		
Current liabilities		
Accounts payable	$22,000	
Reserve for income taxes	15,000	
Customer accounts with credit balances	1	$ 37,001
Deferred credits		
Unamortized premium on bonds payable		2,000
Long-term liabilities		
Bonds payable		60,000
Total liabilities		99,001
Shareholders' equity		
Common shares issued	85,000	
Earned surplus	24,999	
Cash dividends declared	8,000	117,999
		$217,000

Instruction

Evaluate the balance sheet. Briefly describe the proper treatment of any item that you find incorrect.

Writing Assignments

WA5-1 The partner in charge of the Spencer Corporation audit comes by your desk and leaves a letter he has started to the CEO and a copy of the statement of cash flows for the year ended December 31, 2008. Because he must leave on an emergency, he asks you to finish the letter by explaining (1) the difference between the net income and cash flow amounts; (2) the importance of operating cash flow; (3) the sustainable source(s) of cash flow; and (4) possible suggestions to improve the cash position.

SPENCER CORPORATION
Statement of Cash Flows
For the Year Ended December 31, 2008

Cash flows from operating activities		
Net income		$ 100,000
Adjustments to reconcile net income to net cash provided by operating activities:		
Amortization expense	$ 11,000	
Loss on sale of fixed assets	5,000	
Increase in accounts receivable (net)	(40,000)	
Increase in inventory	(35,000)	
Decrease in accounts payable	(41,000)	(100,000)
Net cash provided by operating activities		-0-
Cash flows from investing activities		
Sale of plant assets	25,000	
Purchase of equipment	(100,000)	
Purchase of land	(200,000)	
Net cash used by investing activities		(275,000)
Cash flows from financing activities		
Payment of dividends	(10,000)	
Redemption of bonds	(100,000)	
Net cash used by financing activities		(110,000)
Net decrease in cash		(385,000)
Cash balance, January 1, 2008		400,000
Cash balance, December 31, 2008		$ 15,000

Date
James Spencer III, CEO
Spencer Corporation
125 Bay Street
Toronto, ON

Dear Mr. Spencer:

I have good news and bad news about the financial statements for the year ended December 31, 2008. The good news is that net income of $100,000 is close to what we predicted in the strategic plan last year, indicating strong performance this year. The bad news is that the cash balance is seriously low. Enclosed is the Statement of Cash Flows, which best illustrates how both of these situations occurred at the same time...

Instructions
Complete the letter to the CEO, including the four elements that the partner asked for.

WA5-2 Andrea Pafko, corporate comptroller for Nicholson Industries, is trying to decide how to present "Property, plant, and equipment" in the balance sheet. She realizes that the statement of cash flows will show that the company made a significant investment in purchasing new equipment this year, but overall she knows the company's plant assets are rather old. She feels that she can disclose one amount for the title "Property, plant, and equipment, net of amortization," and the result will be a low figure. However, it will not disclose the assets' age. If she chooses to show the cost less accumulated amortization, the assets' age will be visible. She proposes the following:

Property, plant, and equipment, net of amortization	$ 10,000,000

rather than

Property, plant, and equipment	$ 50,000,000
Less: Accumulated amortization	(40,000,000)
Net book value	$ 10,000,000

Instructions
Discuss the financial reporting issues, including any ethical issues.

WA5-3 Brookfield Properties Corporation (BPC) reported net income of $164 million for the year ended December 31, 2005, which is up 19% from the prior year. The company owns, develops, and manages North American office properties and its shares trade on both the New York and Toronto stock exchanges. The company takes pride in its strong financial position and in providing a foundation for growth.

The company's balance sheet follows:

Consolidated Balance Sheet

December 31 (US Millions)	Note	2005	2004[1]
Assets			
Commercial properties	5	$ 7,430	$ 6,555
Development properties	6	615	716
Receivables and other	7	955	739
Restricted cash and deposits	8	316	297
Marketable securities	9	58	285
Cash and cash equivalents		64	112
Assets related to discontinued operations	10	75	96
		$ 9,513	$ 8,800
Liabilities			
Commercial property debt	11	$ 5,216	$ 4,754
Accounts payable and other liabilities	12	626	452
Future income tax liability	13	188	96
Liabilities related to discontinued operations	10	51	64
Capital securities	14	1,101	1,069
Non-controlling interests	15	59	53
Preferred equity - subsidiaries	16	329	320
Shareholders' equity			
Preferred equity - corporate	17	45	45
Common equity	18	1,898	1,947
		$ 9,513	$ 8,800

[1] Certain comparative information has been restated to conform with current year presentation – see Notes 2, 8 and 10
See accompanying notes to the consolidated financial statements

Instructions
Play the role of a financial analyst and critically evaluate the balance sheet presentation. Discuss alternative presentations and recommend the presentation format that would provide the best transparency for the company's business and the message that it wants to communicate.

Student Website

www.wiley.com/canada/kieso

Cases

Refer to the Case Primer on the Student Website to help you answer these cases.

CA5-1 Fairmont Hotels and Resorts Inc. (FHR) operates in the resort industry and owns and/or operates and manages luxury and first class hotels and resorts. In 2001, the predecessor company Canadian Pacific Limited completed a major reorganization, which split the predecessor company into five separate public companies including FHR, (which housed the hotel and resort business). In 2002, although revenues increased, profits dropped dramatically. FHR's shares trade on both the TSX and NYSE, which means the financial statements are required to include a reconciliation between Canadian and U.S. GAAP.

In the reconciliation note, the following was stated: "Under Canadian GAAP, computer systems development costs for internal use software are capitalized when the project is expected to be of continuing benefit to FHR and otherwise expensed. U.S. GAAP standards require that certain costs of computer software developed for internal use be capitalized and amortized."

In addition, the following was noted under the "Changes in accounting policy" note: "In 2002, revenues and expenses from managed and franchised properties were included in the consolidated statements of income in response to a recent CICA Emerging Issues abstract. The 2001 and 2000 revenues and expenses have been reclassified to conform with the presentation adopted for 2002. They were previously recorded in a net basis."

Instructions
Discuss the alternative treatments and recommend which treatment reflects reality. Hint: Use the conceptual framework identified in Chapter 2.

CA5-2 In the late 1990s, CIBC helped Enron structure 34 "loans" that appeared in the financial statements as cash proceeds from sales of assets. Enron subsequently went bankrupt in 2001 and left many unhappy investors and creditors with billions of dollars lost. In December 2003, CIBC settled four regulatory investigations with the SEC, U.S. Federal Reserve, U.S. Justice Department, and Canadian Office of the Superintendent of Financial Institutions. The settlement, which amounted to U.S. $80 million, is one of the largest regulatory penalties against a Canadian bank. The regulatory authorities felt that CIBC had aided Enron in boosting its earnings and hiding debt. CIBC set aside a $109-million reserve in early 2003 in preparation for this settlement. No additional reserves were set aside.

As part of the settlement, CIBC agreed to get rid of its structured financing line of business (where all of these "loans" were created). Bank management noted that the decision to get rid of the structured financing business would reduce annual earnings by 10 cents a share. The bank had previously reported annual earnings of $5.21 per share. In addition, the bank had to accept the appointment of an outside monitor whose role, among other things, would be to review the bank's compliance with the settlement. Strategically, the bank had already reduced its emphasis on corporate lending (having suffered heavy losses in 2002) in favour of an increased focus on earnings from branch banking operations.

At the end of 2003, CIBC was still owed $213 million from Enron. There were many additional Enron-related lawsuits pending against the bank, but the bank announced that the lawsuits were without merit. The bank had insurance against many of these claims and noted that it planned to vigorously defend itself.

Instructions
Adopt the role of the company's auditors and discuss any financial reporting issues.

(Information sources: "Canadian Bank to Pay Fine and Drop Unit in Enron Case," *New York Times*, Dec. 23, 2003; "CIBC to Pay US80M over Enron," *National Post*, Dec. 23, 2003; and "Enron Cost CIBC $80M," *Toronto Star*, Dec. 23, 2003.)

Integrated Case

IC5-1 Franklin Drug Ltd. (FDL) is a global public company that researches, develops, markets, and sells prescription drugs. Revenues and net income are down this year partly because one of the company's competitors, Barney Drug Inc. (BDI), has created and is selling generic versions of two of FDL's best-selling drugs. The drugs, known as FD1 and FD2, are still protected by patents which will not expire for another three years. Normally, when a drug is patented, other drug companies are not legally allowed to sell generic versions of the drug. This practice of patenting new drugs allows the companies that develop the drugs enough time to recover their large investment in research and development of the drugs.

In recent years, however, generic drug companies have become more aggressive in producing and selling generic copies of the drugs before patents expire. FDL refers to this practice as "launching the generic products at risk" because, legally, the competitors are not allowed to sell them while the patent is still in force. Currently, FDL has about $2 million in development costs capitalized on the balance sheet. It has launched a lawsuit against BDI to cease and desist selling the generic drugs. These types of lawsuits are usually long and very expensive. By the time the lawsuit is settled one way or the other, the patents will have expired. So far, legal costs incurred for the lawsuits are $300,000.

During the year, the patent on a third drug, FD3, expired and several competitor drug companies began actively marketing generic replacements. FDL still has $500,000 worth of development costs on the balance sheet. Although the increased competition may result in this asset being impaired, FDL feels that it can hold its market share based on the past success of FD3 in treating patients. So far, sales of FD3 have only declined 3%. On the other hand, the company's share price has declined significantly because of the uncertainty surrounding future sales. Company management is not happy with the drop in share price, because a significant portion of their remuneration is based on stock options.

The company gives volume rebates to some of its larger customers. Under the terms of the sales agreements, the more purchases that a customer makes in a certain time frame, the larger the rebate percentage is on these purchases. The length of the time frame varies. Three large contracts are currently outstanding at year end with new customers. The time frames on these contracts extend beyond year end. FDL must estimate the volume rebates by considering what the total sales will be under these contracts. The company has a history of basing this estimate on past experience.

It is now early January and the auditors are coming in for an audit planning meeting.

Instructions

In preparation for the meeting, you, as audit senior on the job, have done some preliminary research on the company. Write a memo that outlines the potential financial reporting issues.

Research and Financial Analysis

RA5-1 Stantec Inc.

The financial statements for 2005 of Stantec Inc. appear in Appendix 5B.

Instructions

(a) What alternative formats could the company have used for its balance sheet? Which format did it adopt?

(b) Identify the various techniques of disclosure that the company could have used to disclose additional financial information that is pertinent. Which techniques does it use in its financials?

(c) Which presentation method does the company use for its statement of cash flows (direct or indirect method)? What were the company's cash flows from its operating, investing, and financing activities for 2005? What were its trends in net cash provided by operating activities over the period 2003–2005? Is the cash generated from operating activities significantly different from net earnings in all three years? Suggest why this might happen.

(d) Calculate the company's (1) current cash debt coverage ratio, (2) cash debt coverage ratio, and (3) free cash flow for 2005. What do these ratios indicate about the company's financial condition?

RA5-2 Magna International Inc.

The financial statements for Magna International Inc. may be found on the Student Website

Instructions

(a) Calculate the ratios identified in Appendix 5A for both years that are presented in the financial statements.

(b) Comment on the company's liquidity, solvency, and profitability.

(c) Review the cash flow patterns on the statements of cash flows and comment on where the company is getting its cash from and where it is spending it.

(d) Perform a "vertical analysis" of the assets. (Calculate each asset as a percentage of total assets.) How has this result changed from year to year?

RA5-3 Maple Leaf Foods Inc.

The financial statements for Maple Leaf Foods Inc. may be found on the Student Website.

Instructions

(a) Calculate the liquidity and solvency ratios identified in Appendix 5A for both years that are presented in the financial statements.

(b) Comment on the company's financial flexibility.

(c) Review the cash flow patterns on the statements of cash flows and comment on where the company is getting its cash from and where it is spending it. (Hint: Identify the cash flow pattern and explain what information the pattern provides.)

(d) Perform a "horizontal analysis" for working capital. How has this result changed from year to year and what are the implications for the company's financial health?

RA5-4 Goldcorp Inc.

The 2001 annual report for Goldcorp Inc. may be found on the student website. Read the material leading up to the financial statements and answer the following questions:

(a) Explain how the company's business changed from 2000 to 2001. What significant events occurred?

(b) What was the impact on key ratios of the event(s) identified in part (a)?

RA5-5 Abitibi-Consolidated Inc. versus Domtar Inc.

The financial statements for Abitibi Consolidated Inc. and Domtar Inc. may be found on the Student Website.

Instructions

(a) Is Domtar a good benchmark for comparing against? Explain.

(b) Identify three other companies that might be used for comparisons.

(c) Calculate industry averages for these five companies for the current and debt-to-total assets ratios.

(d) Based on this very brief analysis, which company is in better shape in terms of liquidity and solvency? How do these companies compare with the other three companies?

(e) Review the statement of cash flows. Describe the cash flow patterns for each company.

(f) Comment on these cash flow patterns, noting changes over the past two to three years.

RA5-6 Industry analysis

The following is an excerpt from a recent issue of "The Top 1000 Canadian Companies" published by the *Globe and Mail.*

Gold Producers

COMPANY AND YEAR END	REVENUE $000	REVENUE % CH'GE	PROFIT $000	PROFIT % CH'GE	RETURN ON CAPITAL 1-YR %	RETURN ON CAPITAL 5-YR %	GOLD RECOVERED OZ. (000)	CASH COST $ PER OZ.	PROVEN AND PROBABLE RESERVES TONS (000)	PROVEN AND PROBABLE RESERVES CONTAINED OZ. (000)
Barrick Gold(De02)[1]	(US)2,108,000	52	(US)229,000	-15	4.49	1.91	5,695	(US)177	1,229,152	86,927
Placer Dome(De02)[1]	(US)1,289,000	0	(US)119,000	163	7.02	0.18	2,823	(US)180	462,292	52,891
Kinross Gold(De02)[1]	(US)274,600	-2	(US)-30,900	15	-4.30	-18.58	889	(US)201	510,451	13,166
Echo Bay Mines(De02)[1]	(US)206,970	-13	(US)-7,690	-35	-5.11	-4.20	539	(US)237	114,930	3,400
Cambior Inc.(De02)[1]	(US)204,203	-33	(US)-8,052	37	-2.37	-17.06	569	(US)223	72,668	4,216
Goldcorp Inc.(De02)[1]	(US)189,215	9	(US)65,643	24	41.29	17.93	608	(US)93	16,298	5,537
Meridian Gold(De02)[1]	(US)135,441	14	(US)41,516	7	16.38	5.27	436	(US)87	14,661	4,281
Agnico-Eagle Mines(De02)[1]	(US)111,044	10	(US)4,023	176	2.48	-0.30	260	(US)182	41,692	4,022
Northgate Exploration(De02)[1]	(US)110,992	14	(US)-14,243	-46	-5.48	-0.37	282	(US)204	120,549	2,503
Iamgold Corp.(De02)[1]	(US)90,709	7	(US)5,535	-49	5.40	9.46	290	(US)178	236,335	3,600

1. Company reports in U.S. dollars.

Instructions

(a) Review the data provided for the top 10 gold producers. What is the average production cost per ounce of gold for the 10 companies?

(b) Identify the two companies that have significantly lower costs per ounce. What is the relationship between gold cost and profit? (Look at all 10 companies.)

(c) Research the gold industry and explain why gold production costs are different for each company. (Hint: read the annual reports of several gold-producing companies.)

(d) How are gold selling prices determined? Comment on their stability.

(e) Identify the financial risks that are associated with gold production. How do companies manage these risks and what is the impact of risk management on profitability?

Counting on Cable

Montreal-based Cogeco Cable Inc. provides analogue and digital television, telephony, and high-speed Internet services to clients all over Ontario, but mainly in southern Ontario, and throughout Quebec outside the Montreal and Quebec City areas. It has also expanded internationally, with the recent acquisition of a cable telecommunications company in Portugal.

Cogeco recognizes revenue from all its monthly services at the time when the service is provided. "We have multiple cycle billings," explains Pierre Maheux, Cogeco's corporate controller. If a customer is billed from the 1st to 31st, Cogeco recognizes a full month of revenue for that customer. If a customer is connected on the 15th, the company has partial service revenue for that month from the 15th to 31st. The customer's bill will then be from the 15th to the 14th of the following month going forward, and the company will recognize the monthly service revenue only according to the month in which the service is provided.

"Customer billing and revenue recognition are two separate things," Maheux points out. "A customer could request to be billed for several months in advance, but Cogeco will still recognize service revenue on a monthly basis." If a customer cancels service after making an advance payment, Cogeco will reimburse the customer for the period that it has not yet provided service for. This refund will not affect the company's revenue figures since Cogeco has not yet recognized revenue for this service.

Cogeco has no formal contract or written agreement with customers, so they can request to cancel their service at any time. For cancellations, the company stops service and billing, and recognizes partial monthly service revenue up to the cancellation date.

"Our general policy, which is the same for most companies in our industry, is to bill customers one month in advance," says Maheux. "That way, we have better control of bad debts. If we need to disconnect service for non-payment, the company avoids significant bad debt expenses."

chapter 6

Revenue Recognition

Learning Objectives

After studying this chapter, you should be able to:

1. Apply the revenue recognition principle.
2. Describe the accounting issues associated with revenue recognition for sales of goods.
3. Explain the accounting for consignment sales.
4. Describe the accounting issues related to revenue recognition for services and long-term contracts.
5. Apply the percentage-of-completion method for long-term contracts.
6. Apply the completed-contract method for long-term contracts.
7. Account for losses on long-term contracts.
8. Understand when to book sales net versus gross.
9. Discuss how to deal with measurement uncertainty.
10. Discuss how to deal with collection uncertainty.
11. Explain and apply the instalment sales method of accounting.
12. Explain and apply the cost recovery method of accounting.

After studying Appendix 6A, you should be able to:

13. Explain revenue recognition for franchises.

Preview of Chapter 6

When should revenue be recognized? As mentioned in the opening vignette on Cogeco, the company must earn it before it is recognized—even if it is paid in advance. Revenue recognition is a complex issue, but the answer to the question can be found by analyzing the earnings process. This chapter presents the general principles that are used in recognizing revenues for most business transactions.

The chapter is organized as follows:

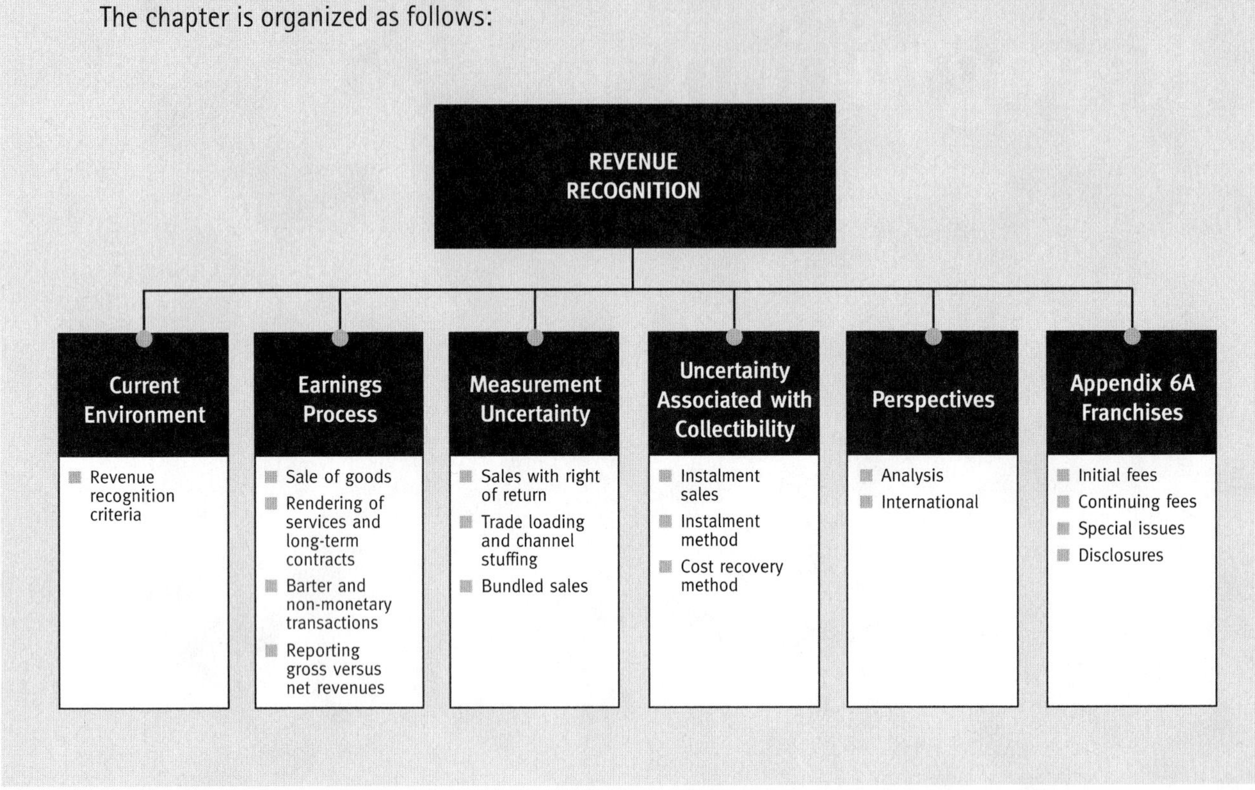

THE CURRENT ENVIRONMENT

Student Toolkit–Additional Disclosures

www.wiley.com/canada/kieso

The issue of when to recognize revenue receives constant and considerable attention. A series of highly publicized cases of companies that were recognizing revenue too soon has caused the OSC and SEC to increase their enforcement actions in this area.[1]

[1] The OSC completed a review of revenue recognition practices in 2001 and again in 2002 as it felt that some users were placing too much emphasis on revenue growth as a key indicator of value and performance. The review targeted 75 public companies in both years. The 2001 survey findings indicated that there was a need for improving the nature and extent of disclosure. The OSC identified cases that were later investigated to determine whether financial reporting practices related to revenue recognition appeared to apply relevant GAAP appropriately. The 2002 survey showed improvement, with only one company having to restate its financial statements and 29 making additional enhanced disclosures. The OSC's most recent continuous disclosure review covered 395 companies and found that a significant number of them failed to disclose the specific triggers for revenue recognition. Problems were also found with accounting for upfront fees and arrangements when there were rights of return.

Revenue Recognition Criteria

Objective 1
Apply the revenue recognition principle.

Revenues are **realized** when goods and services are exchanged for cash or claims to cash (receivables). Realization is "the process of converting noncash resources and rights into money and is most precisely used in accounting and financial reporting to refer to sales of assets for cash" or claims to cash.[2] Revenue recognition is "the process of including an item in the financial statements of an entity."[3] It is governed by general principles and there is therefore a wide range of practical applications. Different companies interpret these principles in different ways.[4] Revenues are recognized according to the **revenue recognition principle**. Under this principle, revenue is recognized when **performance** is substantially complete and when **collection is reasonably assured.**[5]

Underlying Concept
The related costs must be measurable and recognized at the same time as revenues to help measure net income appropriately.

Performance occurs when the entity can **measure** the revenue and when it has substantially accomplished what it must do to be entitled to the benefits of the revenues—that is, the **earnings process must be complete or substantially complete.**[6] Both of these components are important. If a company cannot measure the transaction, then either there is too much uncertainty surrounding the transaction or the company has not completed all that it has to do to earn the revenues. The determination of whether the earnings process is complete or substantially complete depends on whether the entity has sold a product or provided a service (or both), so it is important to first determine what the revenue is for. Each of these situations will be examined further in the following pages. Although the *CICA Handbook* does not specifically mention **cost** measurability, this is also very important.

Underlying Concept
Revenues are increases in economic resources resulting from ordinary activities, which arise due to increases in assets or reductions in/settlement of liabilities

In short, revenues are recognized when the following criteria are met:

1. **Performance is achieved, which means**
   a. **risks and rewards are transferred and/or the earnings process** is substantially complete, and
   b. **measurability** is reasonably assured.
2. **Collectibility** is reasonably assured.

EIC 141 further clarifies the meaning of **performance**. The standard states that performance is regarded as being achieved when:

- **persuasive evidence of an arrangement** exists (i.e., the terms of a business deal or contract are agreed upon and finalized),
- **delivery** has occurred or the service has been rendered, and
- the seller's **price** to the buyer is **fixed and determinable.**[7]

---

[2] SFAC No. 6, par. 143.

[3] *CICA Handbook*, Section 1000. Recognition is not the same as realization, although the two are sometimes used interchangeably in accounting literature and practice.

[4] Because of this, and in part also because of the increased profile of revenue recognition issues with the securities commissions, companies generally disclose the revenue recognition method in the notes to their financial statements. Out of a survey of 200 companies, 93 percent disclosed their revenue recognition policies in 2004. (*Financial Reporting in Canada, 2005* [Toronto: CICA], Chapter. 7).

[5] *CICA Handbook*, Section 3400.06.

[6] *CICA Handbook*, Section 3400.07.

[7] The EIC was issued in order to harmonize the Canadian standard with the U.S. standard in accordance with the mandate at that time to converge with U.S. accounting standards. The SEC, through its SAB 101 statement on revenue recognition, had previously provided more specific guidance because general criteria are often difficult to interpret. EIC 141 acknowledges SAB 101 as being consistent with *CICA Handbook* Section 3400, noting that it should be referred to as interpretive guidance. Note that there was a debate at the time about how convergence/harmonization would be made to happen. The committee felt that the wording in the EIC needed to be very close or identical to the U.S. standard so as not to create any additional Canadian/U.S. GAAP differences. Do not be fooled by the nature of the U.S. standard and, by extension, EIC 141, which appear to give clear rules. Significant judgement is still needed in interpreting the standard.

Note that the second and third points above are similar to *CICA Handbook* Section 3400 even though the wording is slightly different. In determining whether there is **persuasive evidence of an arrangement,** the following should be considered, among other factors:

1. **Customary business practice**—This refers to how and when the entity considers that the terms of the arrangement are finalized. If the company normally requires a signed contract, then this would be needed before any revenue recognition. Alternatively, if the entity considers that a customer has accepted an Internet transaction as soon as the customer submits a credit card number, then the submission would be enough. Each business is different, so the business model and earnings process must first be carefully understood. For example, with a company that sells over the internet, an e-mail to the customer with a transaction code might signal the existence of an arrangement.

2. **Side arrangements**—Sometimes an entity enters into additional agreements with the customer which may modify the original transaction. Side agreements that modify the main sales agreement may indicate that, contrary to what was thought before, the arrangement was not final and that revenue should not have been recognized or at least, that the two deals should be viewed as one for revenue recognition purposes. Therefore, all related agreements must be reviewed together before revenue is recognized. Consider the example of an electronics store that sells a cell phone and then immediately sells a service contract so that the customer can use the phone. These transactions are clearly related.

3. **Economic substance**—The transaction may be a **consignment** or **financing type of transaction** (as opposed to a sale), in which case no revenue will be recognized, at least initially. Consignment accounting will be examined in further detail later in this chapter.[8]

Underlying Concept

Even though a transaction may be legally structured as a sale, as accountants we must look at the underlying economic substance. Substance is what determines the accounting–i.e., economic substance takes precedence over (legal) form

The earnings process is examined in more detail next.

International Insight

IAS 18 also requires measurability of both the revenues and related costs.

EARNINGS PROCESS

Objective 2
Describe the accounting issues associated with revenue recognition for sales of goods.

What does the company do to create valuable products or services that customers will pay for? How does it add value? **Earnings process** is a term that refers to the actions that a company takes to add value. It is an important part of the business model as it focuses on the operating activities.[9] The earnings process is unique to each company and each industry. Different industries add value in different ways. For example, companies that sell goods have vastly differing earnings processes than those that sell services. Companies that are in the biotechnology business have models that are different from real estate companies. For this reason, it is important to begin with an understanding of the earnings process.

Sale of Goods

The manufacturing company **Magnotta Winery Corporation** makes wine (among other products). Its business involves the steps shown in Illustration 6-1.

[8] If it was determined that the transaction represented a financing transaction, the credit would be booked to a liability account instead of a sales account and the inventory would remain on the books. Significant judgement would be required in this latter case. See also the discussion on sales with buybacks later in this chapter.

[9] A view of the business model was introduced in Chapters 4 and 5. Note that much of Canadian and U.S. GAAP relating to revenue recognition is current based on defining the earnings process and assessing whether the revenues have been earned. As noted later in this Chapter under the heading "International" we will see that the IASB is moving away from this view as it is felt that the analysis is too subjective.

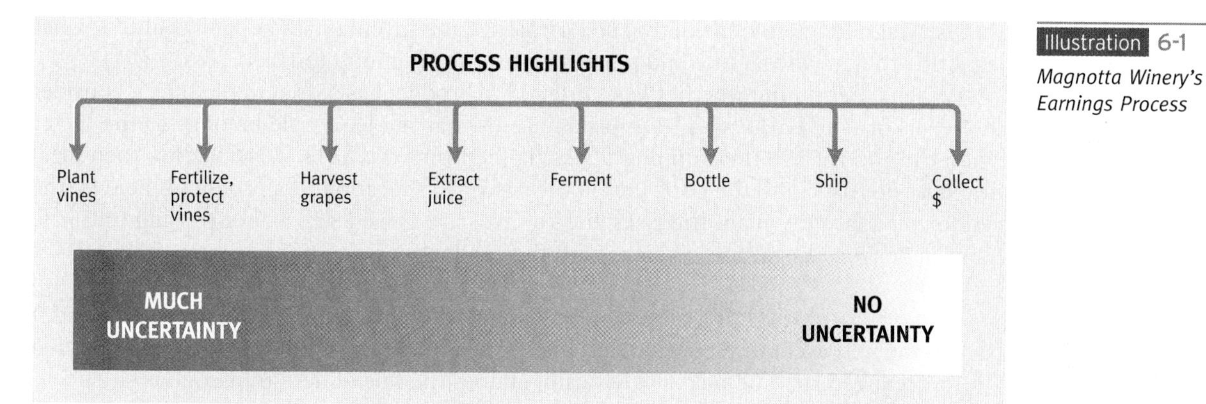

Illustration 6-1
Magnotta Winery's Earnings Process

Magnotta must perform all of the acts in the illustration in order to earn the revenues from sales of its wine. At the early points in the earnings process, there is significant uncertainty about how much product will be produced and its quality. What if the vines get diseased? What if temperatures are too low or there is excess rainfall? What if there is no market for the product? Moving along the earnings process timeline (from left to right), the conditions creating the uncertainty resolve themselves. At the far right-hand side of the earnings process, once the product is shipped and paid for, all uncertainty is eliminated about delivery of the product, measurability of both its costs and revenues, and collectibility of those revenues.

Often, there is one main act or **critical event** in the earnings process that signals **substantial completion** or **performance**. At this point, although there remains some uncertainty, its level is acceptable and revenues can be recognized under accrual accounting. In businesses that sell goods, this is normally at the **point of delivery**. This is generally when the **risks and rewards of ownership** pass. If the earnings process has a critical event, it is often referred to as a **discrete earnings process**.

Risks and Rewards of Ownership

The concept of risks and rewards (benefits) of ownership is a core concept in financial reporting. It helps establish ownership and when ownership passes from one party to another.[10]

Illustration 6-2 presents some of the risks and rewards associated with the sale of wine at Magnotta.

Illustration 6-2
Risks and Rewards of Ownership–Case of Wine

Risks	Rewards
— wine will age poorly and therefore decline in value	— wine will age well and appreciate in value
— wine will be stolen/vandalized	— wine can be consumed by owner or buyer
	— wine inventory may be used as collateral for bank loan
— wine will be stored improperly	— wine may be sold for cash

In determining who has the risks and rewards of ownership and, therefore, whether a sale has occurred at the point of delivery, it is important to look at who has **possession** of the goods and who has **legal title**. The risks and rewards usually start from these two factors;

[10] That is, in order to recognize an asset on the balance sheet, a company must prove that it has the risks and rewards of ownership. If it no longer has the risks and rewards, they have been passed on to another party and a disposition has occurred.

that is, Magnotta is not entitled to sell or pledge the inventory as collateral unless it has legal title to it, and legal title and possession expose Magnotta to risk of loss.

When determining whether legal title to the product has passed to the buyer, consider the terms of sale. **F.o.b. shipping point** means that the legal title belongs to the buyer when the goods leave the shipping docks. If the terms are **f.o.b. destination**, then legal title does not pass until the goods reach the customer's location. If a product is held by the vendor on a layaway plan, the risks and rewards are considered as not passing until the point of delivery. Legal title remains with the vendor, who also has possession.

Underlying Concept

Legal title has transferred in this situation, but the economic substance of the transaction is that the **seller retains the risks of ownership.**

Sales with Buyback If a company sells inventory in one period and agrees to buy it back in the next accounting period, has the company sold the product? In essence, this is a 100-percent return. The buyback basically undoes the sale. These transactions should be looked at together and professional judgement must be used to determine what the economic substance is.

When there is a repurchase agreement at a set price and this price covers all costs of the inventory plus related holding costs, the inventory and related liability remain on the seller's books since the seller retains the price risk.[11] As mentioned earlier, the economic substance of the transaction might indicate that this is a financing type of transaction where the company used the inventory as collateral in order to obtain some short-term financing.

Bill and Hold Transactions Sometimes a company will sell inventory to a customer but not ship it. This is called a **bill and hold** transaction. Why would a company do this? There are many reasons. Perhaps the customer does not have room in its warehouse in the short term, or perhaps the customer's receiving department is on strike. These two reasons are examples of bona fide business reasons for not shipping the inventory. There is a risk, however, that bill and hold sales are instead the result of aggressive selling practices and the question is then whether they represent a real sale.

EIC 141 requires that certain additional analysis be completed before recognizing revenues in these situations. In particular, the following things must all be evident:

- The customer must be the one who requests the bill and hold and must have a business reason for making the request.
- There must be a fixed commitment (written or electronic) including a delivery schedule.
- The goods must be segregated from other inventory in the warehouse and be ready to ship.

In addition, the company should consider past bill and hold transactions (that is, whether the inventory was eventually delivered), which party is insuring the inventory against loss (as evidence of who has the risks and rewards of ownership), and whether there are special payment terms (e.g., terms that would have encouraged the customer to enter into the deal even if it did not want the inventory or intend to take delivery of it). This would be in addition to meeting the regular revenue recognition criteria.

Transactions with Customer Acceptance Provisions It is important to be careful when one of the provisions of the deal (i.e., a condition) is that the customer has the right to accept or reject the inventory. Customer acceptance provisions are considered to be

[11] *CICA Handbook*, EIC Abstract 141. Accounting Guideline "Transfer of Receivables" allows recognition of a sale of accounts receivables when control over the assets is surrendered. Surrendering of control occurs when the assets are isolated from the transferor, the transferee can pledge or exchange the assets, and the transferor will not repurchase the assets. *CICA Handbook* EIC Abstract 121 deals with accounting for wash sales of financial assets other than receivables, that is, the transfer of financial assets with the intent to reacquire them. The EIC requires the application of the Guideline test to other financial assets. These GAAP sources could also be used for guidance on sales of non-financial assets.

substantive and bargained for. Illustration 6-3 summarizes the different types of acceptance provisions and their accounting treatment according to EIC 141.

Type of acceptance provision	Accounting treatment
Trial or evaluation basis	No sale until evaluation period lapses or customer accepts
Right of return based on subjective criteria, e.g., colour not liked	Okay to recognize sale as long as company can estimate returns (perhaps based on historical trends?)
Right of return based on seller's or customer's objective specifications, e.g., the product has to meet certain size requirements	Recognize sale when specifications are achieved or customer sign-off (signature or verbal okay) is obtained.

Illustration 6-3
Customer Acceptance Provisions

Note that significant professional judgement is required in the last two types.

Disposition of Assets Other Than Inventory The risks-and-rewards concept does not apply only to sales of inventory, as in the case of Magnotta's wine inventory. It also applies to items that are disposed of through sales that are not part of the normal earnings process—e.g., sales of income-producing or capital assets. In these cases, a gain[12] is generated (instead of revenues). It is important to carefully establish that, in substance, a disposition has actually occurred. In certain cases, a company may sell a fixed asset and receive a note receivable that is secured by the asset itself. If very little other consideration is received, has the asset really been sold? Have the risks and rewards really passed?

If the purchaser does not pay, legal title to the asset may return to the vendor **at little or no loss to the purchaser**. This indicates that the risks and rewards may still be with the vendor. In general, the purchaser must demonstrate substantial commitment to pay. This normally is proven when the purchaser makes a commitment with a fair value of not less than 15 percent of the consideration's fair value. An example of this is when the purchaser pays non-refundable cash equal to at least 15 percent of the total consideration.[13]

Underlying Concept

Legally, a transaction may be structured as a sale. However, analysis of the economic substance might show it to be something else.

Consignment Sales In some distribution arrangements, the vendor **retains legal title** to the goods. In such cases, the point of delivery is therefore not proof of full performance. This specialized method of marketing for certain types of products uses what is known as a **consignment**. Under this arrangement, the **consignor** (e.g., a manufacturer) ships merchandise to the **consignee** (e.g., a dealer), who acts as an agent for the consignor in selling the merchandise. Both consignor and consignee are interested in selling: the former to make a profit or develop a market, the latter to make a commission on the sales.

3 Objective
Explain the accounting for consignment sales.

The consignee accepts the merchandise and agrees to exercise due diligence (or care) in looking after the inventory and selling it. When the merchandise is sold, cash received from customers is then remitted to the consignor by the consignee, after deducting a sales commission and any chargeable expenses. Revenue is recognized only after the consignor receives notification of the sale. For the entire time of the consignment, the merchandise is carried as the consignor's inventory and is separately classified as Merchandise on Consignment. It is not recorded as an asset on the consignee's books.

Upon sale of the merchandise, the consignee has a liability for the net amount that it must remit to the consignor. The consignor periodically receives from the consignee a

[12] Gains (as contrasted with revenues) commonly result from transactions and other events that do not involve an earnings process. For gain recognition, being earned is generally less important than being realized or realizable.

[13] *CICA Handbook*, EIC Abstract 79.

report that shows the merchandise received, merchandise sold, expenses chargeable to the consignment, and cash remitted.

To illustrate consignment accounting entries, assume that Sohail Manufacturing Corp. ships merchandise costing $36,000 on consignment to Chosky Stores. Sohail pays $3,750 of freight costs and Chosky pays $2,250 for local advertising costs that are reimbursable from Sohail. By the end of the period, two-thirds of the consigned merchandise has been sold for $40,000 cash. Chosky notifies Sohail of the sales, retains a 10% commission, and remits the cash due to Sohail. The journal entries in Illustration 6-4 would be made by the consignor (Sohail) and the consignee (Chosky).

Illustration 6-4
Entries for Consignment Sales

Sohail Mfg. Corp. (Consignor)			Chosky Stores (Consignee)		
Shipment of consigned merchandise					
Inventory on Consignment	36,000		No entry (record memo of merchandise received)		
Finished Goods Inventory		36,000			
Payment of freight costs by consignor					
Inventory on Consignment	3,750		No entry.		
Cash		3,750			
Payment of advertising by consignee					
No entry until notified.			Receivable from Consignor	2,250	
			Cash		2,250
Sales of consigned merchandise					
No entry until notified.			Cash	40,000	
			Payable to Consignor		40,000
Notification of sales and expenses and remittance of amount due					
Cash	33,750		Payable to Consignor	40,000	
Advertising Expense	2,250		Receivable from Consignor		2,250
Commission Expense	4,000		Commission Revenue		4,000
Revenue from Consignment Sales		40,000	Cash		33,750
Adjustment of inventory on consignment for cost of sales					
Cost of Goods Sold	26,500		No entry.		
Inventory on Consignment [2/3 ($36,000 + $3,750) = $26,500]		26,500			

Why would companies use consignment to sell their goods? The company selling the goods will often use this type of distribution mechanism to encourage consignees to take their goods and sell them. Under the consignment arrangement, the manufacturer (consignor) retains the risk that the merchandise might not sell and frees the dealer (consignee) from having to commit part of its working capital to inventory. Presumably, if the products sell very well to third parties, the consignor could push for the consignee to actually purchase the goods outright. A variety of different systems and account titles are used to record consignments, but they all share the common goal of postponing the recognition of revenue until it is known that a sale to a third party (the customer) has occurred.

Non-Refundable Fees Fees that are paid up front should not be recognized as revenues unless the earnings process is substantially complete, that is, unless the company has earned them. This is true even if the fees are non-refundable.

Continuing Managerial Involvement In some cases, the vendor **retains some involvement in the product sold**, such as the responsibility to fix the product if it breaks or to provide ongoing product support to the customer.

For instance, in order to encourage a sale, the company might promise that the purchaser will receive a certain amount if the purchaser resells the asset (guaranteed minimum resale value). In this case, the seller still retains the risk of losing value, so it is important to consider whether or not a sale should be recognized.[14] Alternatively, the vendor may promise certain cash flows from the purchased asset. In the case of a sold building, for example, certain cash flows might be promised from rent. Has a real sale occurred? As a general rule, in order to recognize revenues, the seller should not retain a degree of continuing managerial involvement in the transferred goods or effective control over them that would normally be associated with ownership.[15] Professional judgement must be used in determining whether or not continuing managerial involvement in a particular case prevents revenue recognition.

Completion of Production In some cases, revenue may be recognized at the completion of production even though there is no specific customer for the finished product at that point. Examples of such situations can be found in the forestry and agricultural industries where the products have assured prices and ready markets. Revenue may be recognized when the timber is cut or the crops are harvested if the sales price is reasonably assured, the units are interchangeable, and no significant costs are involved in distributing the product.[16] Even if there are additional costs, the costs may be accrued if they are measurable. Thinking back to Illustration 6-1, the argument is that earlier recognition is acceptable under accrual accounting as there is little or no uncertainty about measurement (price) or finding a customer. Performance is substantially complete even though the risks and rewards of ownership still rest with the company.

Rendering of Services and Long-Term Contracts

4 Objective
Describe the accounting issues related to revenue recognition for services and long-term contracts.

In the earnings process for sales of goods, the benchmark or critical event for revenue recognition is normally delivery. The focus is different, however, in the earnings process for providing services. When services are provided, the focus is on **performance of the service**, and the earnings process often has **numerous significant events** instead of just one critical event or discrete act. The earnings process is said to be an ongoing or **continuous earnings process** as opposed to a discrete earnings process.

As an example, consider a public accounting firm where an auditor accepts a contract to provide assurance to a company's shareholders about the accuracy and fairness of the company's financial position and operations. The earnings process is noted in Illustration 6-5.

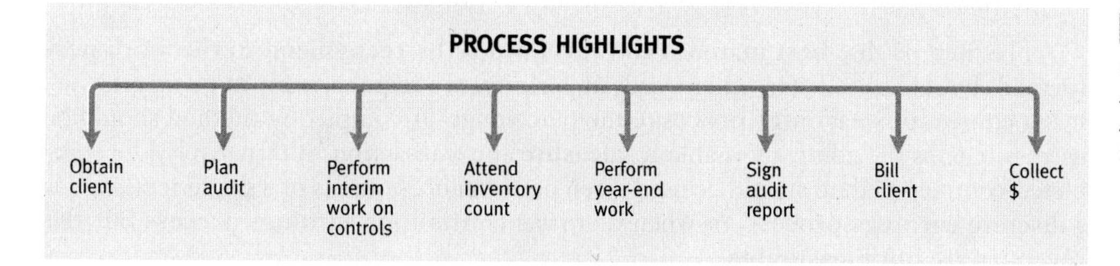

Illustration 6-5
Earnings Process of Public Accounting Firm in Providing Assurance to Client on Financial Statements

[14] *CICA Handbook*, EIC Abstract 84 suggests that no sale should be recognized.

[15] *CICA Handbook*, Section 3400.07.

[16] In its Background Information and Basis for Conclusion documents relating to the Exposure Draft on Inventories, the CICA noted that the mining industry now measures its inventory at cost instead of market or net realizable value, which used to be the common measurement.

Businesses that provide services are different from businesses that sell goods, since the customer is usually identified before the services are performed. (In a sale of goods, as noted in Illustration 6-1, the goods are produced and then a customer is found). Often a contract to set the terms of the relationship or engagement is signed up front. This contract establishes the nature of the services to be provided and the value of the services, among other things. In the case of the auditor, an engagement letter would be signed up front and serve as the contract.

Consider the performance "test." When does performance occur in the earnings process noted in Illustration 6-5? Should the company wait until the audit report is signed (i.e., until the engagement is completed) before recognizing the revenue? There is no easy answer. This may be seen as a **continuous earnings process** with many significant events, including the planning and the interim work. As such, it might make sense to recognize revenues bit by bit as each significant event is performed (as long as it is collectible). Judgement is required.

The issue becomes even more complicated if the process is a **long-term process** (as many service contracts are), since the services are performed over longer periods of time, often spanning one or more fiscal year ends. With these types of contracts, there may also be a "service" component and a "goods" component, e.g., a construction company building a road for the government.

Long-term contracts such as construction-type contracts, development of military and commercial aircraft, weapons delivery systems, and space exploration hardware frequently provide that the seller (builder) may invoice the purchaser at intervals, as various points in the project are reached. These invoices are referred to as **billings**. When the project has separable units, such as a group of buildings or kilometres of roadway, the passage of title and billing may occur at previously stated stages of completion, such as the completion of each building unit or every 10 kilometres of road. Such contract provisions provide for delivery in instalments, and the accounting records may reflect this by recording sales when instalments are "delivered."

Two quite different methods of accounting for long-term construction contracts are currently recognized:[17]

1. **Percentage-of-Completion Method.** Revenues and gross profit are recognized each period based on the construction progress—in other words, the percentage of completion. Construction costs plus gross profit earned to date are accumulated in an inventory account (Construction in Process), and progress billings are accumulated in a contra inventory account (Billings on Construction in Process).

2. **Completed-Contract Method.** Revenues and gross profit are recognized only when the contract is completed. Construction costs are accumulated in an inventory account (Construction in Process), and progress billings are accumulated in a contra inventory account (Billings on Construction in Process).

The method that **best matches the revenues to be recognized to the work performed** should be used.[18] In other words, if performance requires many ongoing acts (i.e., it is a **continuous earnings process**), the percentage-of-completion method should be used as long as the company is able to **measure** the transaction. Alternatively, the completed-contract method should be used when performance consists of a single act (i.e., it is a **discrete earnings process**) or when there is a **continuous earnings process but the revenues are not measurable**.

The rationale for using percentage-of-completion accounting is that under most of these contracts, the buyer and seller have obtained **enforceable rights**. The buyer has the legal right to require specific performance on the contract; the seller has the right to require

[17] *CICA Handbook*, Section 3400.08.

[18] *CICA Handbook*, Section 3400.08.

progress payments that provide evidence of the buyer's ownership interest. As a result, a **continuous sale** occurs as the work progresses, and revenue should be recognized accordingly.

The presumption is that percentage of completion is the better method and that the completed-contract method should be used only when the percentage-of-completion method is inappropriate.[19]

Percentage-of-Completion Method

The percentage-of-completion method recognizes revenues, costs, and gross profit as progress is made toward completion on a long-term contract. If recognition of these items were deferred until the entire contract was complete, the efforts (costs) and accomplishments (revenues) of the interim accounting periods would be misrepresented. In order to apply the percentage-of-completion method, however, there has to be a basis or standard for measuring the progress toward completion at particular interim dates.

Measuring progress toward completion requires significant judgement. Costs, labour hours worked, tonnes produced, and other such measures are often used. The various measures are identified and classified as either input or output measures.[20] **Input measures** (costs incurred, labour hours worked) measure the efforts that have been devoted to a contract. **Output measures** (tonnes produced, storeys of a building completed, kilometres of a highway completed) measure results. Neither of these measures can be applied to all long-term projects; instead, the measure needs to be carefully tailored to the circumstances, which means that judgement is essential.

Underlying Concept

Both input and output measures have measurement uncertainty.

Whichever method is used, there are some disadvantages with input and output measures. The input measure is based on an established relationship between a unit of input and productivity. If inefficiencies cause the productivity relationship to change, inaccurate measurements result. Another potential problem, called front-end loading, produces higher estimates of completion because significant costs are incurred up front. Some early-stage construction costs should therefore be ignored if they do not relate directly to the actual performance of the contract; these include, for example, the costs of uninstalled materials or the costs of subcontracts that have not yet been performed.

Output measures can also result in inaccurate measures if the units that are used are not comparable in time, effort, or cost to complete. For example, using storeys completed can be deceiving; completing the first storey of an eight-storey building may require more than one-eighth of the total cost because of the substructure and foundation construction.

One of the more popular input measures that is used to determine the progress toward completion is cost, sometimes referred to as the **cost-to-cost basis**. Under the cost-to-cost basis, the percentage of completion is measured by comparing costs incurred to date with the most recent estimate of the total costs to complete the contract. The formula for this is shown in Illustration 6-6.

$$\frac{\text{Costs incurred to date}}{\text{Most recent estimate of total costs}} = \text{percent complete}$$

Illustration 6-6

Formula for Percentage of Completion, Cost-to-Cost Basis

The percentage of costs incurred out of total estimated costs is then applied to the total revenue or the estimated total gross profit on the contract to arrive at the revenue or the gross profit amounts to be recognized to date. Illustration 6-7 shows this formula.

[19] *Accounting Trends and Techniques – 2004* reports that, of the 119 of its 600 sample companies that referred to long-term construction contracts, 110 used the percentage-of-completion method and 9 used the completed-contract method.

[20] *CICA Handbook*, EIC Abstract 78.

Illustration 6-7
Formula for Total Revenue to Be Recognized to Date

Percent complete	×	Estimated total revenue (or gross profit)	=	Revenue (or gross profit) to be recognized to date

To find the amount of revenue and gross profit that will be recognized in each period, we would need to subtract the total revenue or gross profit that has been recognized in prior periods, as shown in Illustration 6-8.

Illustration 6-8
Formula for Amount of Current Period Revenue, Cost-to-Cost Basis

Revenue (or gross profit) to be recognized to date	–	Revenue (or gross profit) recognized in prior periods	=	Current period revenue (or gross profit)

Objective 5
Apply the percentage-of-completion method for long-term contracts.

Illustration of Percentage-of-Completion Method, Cost-to-Cost Basis To illustrate the percentage-of-completion method, assume that Hardhat Construction Ltd. has a contract starting July 2008 to construct a $4.5-million bridge that is expected to be completed in October 2010, at an estimated cost of $4 million. Illustration 6-9 shows the data for the entire construction period (note that by the end of 2009 the estimated total cost has increased from $4 million to $4,050,000).

Illustration 6-9
Application of Percentage-of-Completion Method, Cost-to-Cost Basis

	2008	2009	2010
Costs to date	$1,000,000	$2,916,000	$4,050,000
Estimated costs to complete	3,000,000	1,134,000	—
Progress billings during the year	900,000	2,400,000	1,200,000
Cash collected during the year	750,000	1,750,000	2,000,000

The percent complete would be calculated as follows.

	2008	2009	2010
Costs incurred to date			
Contract price	$4,500,000	$4,500,000	$4,500,000
Less estimated cost:			
Costs to date	1,000,000	2,916,000	4,050,000
Estimated costs to complete	3,000,000	1,134,000	
Estimated total costs	4,000,000	4,050,000	4,050,000
Estimated total gross profit	$ 500,000	$ 450,000	$ 450,000
Percent complete	25% ($1,000,000) ($4,000,000)	72% ($2,916,000) ($4,050,000)	100% ($4,050,000) ($4,050,000)

International Insight

When the outcome of a construction contract cannot be estimated reliably, IAS 11 requires that costs and an equal amount of revenues be recognized, as long as the revenues are recoverable or collectible.

Based on the data above, the entries in Illustration 6-10 would be prepared to record (1) the costs of construction, (2) progress billings, and (3) collections. These entries appear as summaries of the many transactions that would be entered individually as they occur during the year.

Illustration 6-10
Journal Entries–Percentage-of-Completion Method, Cost-to-Cost Basis

	2008		2009		2010	
To record cost of construction:						
Construction in Process	1,000,000		1,916,000		1,134,000	
Materials, Cash, Payables, etc.		1,000,000		1,916,000		1,134,000
To record progress billings:						
Accounts Receivable	900,000		2,400,000		1,200,000	
Billings on Construction in Process		900,000		2,400,000		1,200,000
To record collections:						
Cash	750,000		1,750,000		2,000,000	
Accounts Receivable		750,000		1,750,000		2,000,000

In this illustration, the costs incurred to date as a proportion of the estimated total costs to be incurred on the project are a measure of the extent of progress toward completion.

The estimated revenue and gross profit to be recognized for each year are calculated in Illustration 6-11.

Illustration 6-11

Percentage of Completion, Revenue and Gross Profit by Year

	2008	2009	2010
Revenue recognized in:			
2008 $4,500,000 × 25%	$1,125,000		
2009 $4,500,000 × 72%		$3,240,000	
Less: Revenue recognized in 2008		1,125,000	
Revenue in 2009		$2,115,000	
2010 $4,500,000 × 100%			$4,500,000
Less: Revenue recognized in 2008 and 2009			3,240,000
Revenue in 2010			$1,260,000
Gross profit recognized in:			
2008 $500,000 × 25%	$ 125,000		
2009 $450,000 × 72%		$ 324,000	
Less: Gross profit recognized in 2008		125,000	
Gross profit in 2009		$ 199,000	
2010 $450,000 × 100%			$ 450,000
Less: Gross profit recognized in 2008 and 2009			$ 324,000
Gross profit in 2010			$ 126,000

The entries to recognize revenue and gross profit each year and to record the completion and final approval of the contract are shown in Illustration 6-12.

Illustration 6-12

Journal Entries to Recognize Revenue and Gross Profit and to Record Contract Completion–Percentage-of-Completion Method, Cost-to-Cost Basis

	2008		2009		2010	
To recognize revenue and gross profit:						
Construction in Process (gross profit)	125,000		199,000		126,000	
Construction Expenses	1,000,000		1,916,000		1,134,000	
Revenue from Long-Term Contract		1,125,000		2,115,000		1,260,000
To record completion of the contract:						
Billings on Construction in Process					4,500,000	
Construction in Process						4,500,000

Note that the gross profit that was calculated above is debited to Construction in Process, while Revenue from Long-Term Contract is credited for the amounts calculated above. The difference between the amounts that are recognized each year for revenue and gross profit is debited to a nominal account, Construction Expenses (similar to cost of goods sold in a manufacturing enterprise), which is reported in the income statement. That amount (the difference) is the actual cost of construction incurred in that period. For example, for Hardhat Construction the actual costs of $1 million in 2008 are used to calculate both the gross profit of $125,000 and the percent complete (25%).

Costs continue to be accumulated in the Construction in Process account so that there is a record of total costs incurred (plus recognized profit) to date. Although, theoretically, the percentage-of-completion method reflects a **series of sales,** the related inventory cost cannot be removed until the construction is completed and transferred to the new owner. The Construction in Process account would include the summary entries over the term of the construction project that are shown in Illustration 6-13.

Illustration 6-13

Content of Construction in Process Account–Percentage-of-Completion Method

Construction in Process				
2008 construction costs	$1,000,000	12/31/10	to close completed project	$4,500,000
2008 recognized gross profit	125,000			
2009 construction costs	1,916,000			
2009 recognized gross profit	199,000			
2010 construction costs	1,134,000			
2010 recognized gross profit	126,000			
Total	$4,500,000	Total		$4,500,000

The Hardhat illustration contains a change in estimate in the second year, 2009, when the estimated total costs increased from $4 million to $4,050,000. By adjusting the percent completed to the new estimate of total costs, and then deducting the amount of revenues and gross profit that has been recognized in prior periods from revenues and gross profit calculated for progress to date, the change in estimate is accounted for in a cumulative catch-up manner. That is, the change in estimate is accounted for in the period of change so that the balance sheet at the end of that period and the accounting in subsequent periods are the same as if the revised estimate had been the original estimate.

Financial Statement Presentation—Percentage-of-Completion Generally, when a receivable from a sale is recorded, the Inventory account is reduced. In the percentage-of-completion method, however, both the receivable and the inventory continue to be carried. Subtracting the balance in the Billings account from Construction in Process avoids double-counting the inventory. During the life of the contract, the difference between the Construction in Process and the Billings on Construction in Process accounts is reported in the balance sheet as a current or non-current asset (if the amount is a debit) or liability (if it is a credit).

When the costs incurred plus the gross profit recognized to date (the balance in Construction in Process) are more than the billings, this excess is reported as a current asset entitled "Cost and Recognized Profit in Excess of Billings." The unbilled portion of the revenue recognized to date can be calculated at any time by subtracting the billings to date from the revenue recognized to date, as shown for 2008 for Hardhat in Illustration 6-14.

Illustration 6-14

Calculation of Unbilled Contract

Amount at Dec. 31, 2008	
Contract revenue recognized to date: $4,500,000 × $\frac{\$1,000,000}{\$4,000,000}$ =	$1,125,000
Billings to date	900,000
Unbilled revenue	$ 225,000

When the billings are more than the costs incurred and gross profit to date, this excess is reported as a liability entitled "Billings in Excess of Costs and Recognized Profit." Separate disclosures of the dollar amounts of billings and costs are preferred, rather than a summary presentation of the net difference.

Using data from the previous illustration, Hardhat would report the status and results of its long-term construction activities under the percentage-of-completion method as in Illustration 6-15.

Illustration 6-15

Financial Statement Presentation–Percentage-of-Completion Method

HARDHAT CONSTRUCTION LTD.

Income Statement		2008	2009	2010
Revenue from long-term contracts		$1,125,000	$2,115,000	$1,260,000
Costs of construction		1,000,000	1,916,000	1,134,000
Gross profit		$ 125,000	$ 199,000	$ 126,000

Balance Sheet (12/31)		2008	2009
Current assets			
Accounts receivable		$ 150,000	$ 800,000
Inventories			
Construction in process	$1,125,000		
Less: Billings	900,000		
Costs and recognized profit in excess of billings		$ 225,000	
Current liabilities			
Billings ($3,300,000) in excess of costs and recognized profit ($3,240,000)			$ 60,000

Note 1. Summary of significant accounting policies.

LONG-TERM CONSTRUCTION CONTRACTS. The company recognizes revenues and reports profits from long-term construction contracts, its principal business, under the percentage-of-completion method of accounting. These contracts generally extend for periods in excess of one year. The amounts of revenues and profits that are recognized each year are based on the ratio of costs incurred to the total estimated costs. Costs included in construction in process include direct materials, direct labour, and project-related overhead. Corporate general and administrative expenses are charged to the periods as incurred and are not allocated to construction contracts.

Completed-Contract Method

6 Objective
Apply the completed-contract method for long-term contracts.

In the completed-contract method, revenue and gross profit are recognized when the contract is completed. Costs of long-term contracts in process and current billings are accumulated, but there are no interim charges or credits to income statement accounts for revenues, costs, and gross profit.

The main advantage of the completed-contract method is that reported revenue is based on final results rather than on estimates of unperformed work. Its major disadvantage is that it does not reflect current performance when the period of a contract is longer than one accounting period. Although operations may be fairly steady during the contract period, revenue is not reported until the year of completion, which creates a distortion of earnings.[21]

The annual entries to record costs of construction, progress billings, and collections from customers would be identical to those illustrated under the percentage-of-completion method, but with the very important exclusion of the recognition of revenue and gross profit. For Hardhat Construction's bridge project illustrated on the preceding pages, the following entries are made in 2010 under the completed-contract method to recognize revenue and costs and to close out the inventory and billing accounts:

Billings on Construction in Process	4,500,000	
Revenue from Long-Term Contracts		4,500,000
Costs of Construction	4,050,000	
Construction in Process		4,050,000

A = L + SE
−$450,000 +$450,000

Cash flows: No effect

[21] *CICA Handbook* EIC Abstract 65 states that law firms must use the percentage-of-completion method, as the completed-contract method is inappropriate. The abstract further notes that other professional service firms could use the abstract for guidance in similar revenue recognition situations.

Illustration 6-16 compares how Hardhat would have recognized gross profit on the same bridge project under the two methods.

Illustration 6-16
Comparison of Gross Profit Recognized under Different Methods

	Percentage-of-Completion	Completed-Contract
2008	$125,000	$ 0
2009	199,000	0
2010	126,000	$450,000

Hardhat would report its long-term construction activities as in Illustration 6-17.

Illustration 6-17
Financial Statement Presentation–Completed-Contract Method

HARDHAT CONSTRUCTION LTD.

Income Statement		2008	2009	2010
Revenue from long-term contracts		—	—	$4,500,000
Costs of construction		—	—	4,050,000
Gross profit		—	—	$ 450,000
Balance Sheet (12/31)		2008	2009	
Current assets				
Accounts receivable		$150,000	$800,000	
Construction in process	$1,000,000			
Less: Billings	900,000			
Unbilled contract costs		$100,000		
Liabilities				
Billings ($3,300,000) in excess of contract costs ($2,916,000)			$384,000	

Note 1. Summary of significant accounting policies.

LONG-TERM CONSTRUCTION CONTRACTS. The company recognizes revenues and reports profits from long-term construction contracts, its principal business, under the completed-contract method. These contracts generally extend for periods in excess of one year. Contract costs and billings are accumulated during the periods of construction, but no revenues or profits are recognized until contract completion. Costs included in construction in process include direct material, direct labour, and project-related overhead. Corporate general and administrative expenses are charged to the periods as incurred and are not allocated to construction contracts.

Long-Term Contract Losses

Objective 7
Account for losses on long-term contracts.

Two types of losses can occur under long-term contracts:

1. **Loss in Current Period on a Profitable Contract.** This condition occurs when there is a significant increase in the estimated total contract costs during construction but the increase does not eliminate all profit on the contract. Under the percentage-of-completion method only, the increase in the estimated cost requires an adjustment in the current period for the excess gross profit that was recognized on the project in prior periods. This adjustment is recorded as a loss in the current period because it is a change in accounting estimate (discussed in Chapter 21).

2. **Loss on an Unprofitable Contract.** Cost estimates at the end of the current period may indicate that a loss will result once the contract is completed. Under both the percentage-of-completion and the completed-contract methods, the entire loss that is expected on the contract must be recognized in the current period.

The treatment above for unprofitable contracts is consistent with the accounting custom of anticipating foreseeable losses to avoid overstating current and future income (conservatism).

Loss in Current Period To illustrate a loss in the current period on a contract that is expected to be profitable upon completion, assume that on December 31, 2009, Hardhat estimates the costs to complete the bridge contract at $1,468,962 instead of $1,134,000. Assuming all other data are the same as before, Hardhat would calculate the percent complete and recognize the loss as shown in Illustration 6-18. Compare these calculations with those for 2009 in Illustration 6-9. The percent complete has dropped from 72% to 66½% due to the increase in estimated future costs to complete the contract.

The 2009 loss of $48,500 is a cumulative adjustment of the excessive gross profit that was recognized on the contract in 2008. Instead of restating the prior period, the prior period misstatement is absorbed entirely in the current period. In this illustration, the adjustment was large enough to result in recognition of a loss.

Conservatism justifies recognizing the losses immediately. Loss recognition does not require realization; it only requires evidence that an impairment of asset value has occurred.

Illustration 6-18
Calculation of Recognizable Loss, 2009–Loss in Current Period

Cost to date (12/31/09)	$2,916,000
Estimated costs to complete (revised)	1,468,962
Estimated total costs	$4,384,962
Percent complete ($2,916,000/$4,384,962)	66½%
Revenue recognized in 2009	
($4,500,000 × 66½%) − $1,125,000	$1,867,500
Costs incurred in 2009	1,916,000
Loss recognized in 2009	$ 48,500

Hardhat would record the loss in 2009 as follows:

Construction Expenses	1,916,000	
Construction in Process (loss)		48,500
Revenue from Long-Term Contract		1,867,500

A = L + SE
−$48,500 −$48,500
Cash flows: No effect

The loss of $48,500 will be reported on the 2009 income statement as the difference between the reported revenues of $1,867,500 and the costs of $1,916,000.[22] Under the completed-contract method, no loss is recognized in 2009, because the contract is still expected to result in a profit that will be recognized in the year of completion.

Loss on an Unprofitable Contract To illustrate the accounting for an overall loss on a long-term contract, assume that at December 31, 2009, Hardhat estimates the costs to complete the bridge contract at $1,640,250 instead of $1,134,000. Revised estimates on the bridge contract appear as follows:

	2008 Original Estimates	2009 Revised Estimates
Contract price	$4,500,000	$4,500,000
Estimated total cost	4,000,000	4,556,250*
Estimated gross profit	$ 500,000	
Estimated loss		$ (56,250)

*($2,916,000 + $1,640,250)

[22] In 2010, Hardhat will recognize the remaining 33½% of the revenue ($1,507,500), with costs of $1,468,962 as expected, and report a gross profit of $38,538. The total gross profit over the three years of the contract would be $115,038 [$125,000 (2008) – $48,500 (2009) + $38,538 (2010)], which is the difference between the total contract revenue of $4,500,000 and the total contract costs of $4,384,962.

Under the percentage-of-completion method, $125,000 of gross profit was recognized in 2008 (see Illustration 6-11). This $125,000 must be offset in 2009 because it is no longer expected to be realized. In addition, the total estimated loss of $56,250 must be recognized in 2009 since losses must be recognized as soon as they can be estimated. Therefore, a total loss of $181,250 ($125,000 + $56,250) must be recognized in 2009.

Illustration 6-19 shows the calculation for the revenue to be recognized in 2009.

Illustration 6-19
Calculation of Revenue Recognizable, 2009–Unprofitable Contract

Revenue recognized in 2009		
Contract price		$4,500,000
Percent complete		× 64%*
Revenue recognizable to date		2,880,000
Less: Revenue recognized prior to 2009		1,125,000
Revenue recognized in 2009		$1,755,000
Cost to date (12/31/09)	$2,916,000	
Estimated cost to complete	1,640,250	
Estimated total costs	$4,556,250	

*Percent complete: $2,916,000/$4,556,250 = 64%

To calculate the construction costs to be expensed in 2009, we add the total loss to be recognized in 2009 ($125,000 + $56,250) to the revenue to be recognized in 2009.

This calculation is shown in Illustration 6-20.

Illustration 6-20
Calculation of Construction Expense, 2009–Unprofitable Contract

Revenue recognized in 2009 (calculated above)		$1,755,000
Total loss recognized in 2009:		
Reversal of 2004 gross profit	$125,000	
Total estimated loss on the contract	56,250	181,250
Construction cost expensed in 2009		$1,936,250

Hardhat would record the long-term contract revenues, expenses, and loss in 2009 as follows:

A	= L +	SE
−$181,250		−$181,250

Cash flows: No effect

Construction Expenses	1,936,250	
Construction in Process (Loss)		181,250
Revenue from Long-Term Contracts		1,755,000

As Illustration 6-21 shows, Construction in Process has a balance of $2,859,750 at the end of 2009.[23]

[23] If the costs in 2010 are $1,640,250 as projected, at the end of 2010 the Construction in Process account will have a balance of $1,640,250 + $2,859,750, or $4,500,000, which is equal to the contract price. When the revenue remaining to be recognized in 2010 of $1,620,000 [$4,500,000 (total contract price) – $1,125,000 (2008) – $1,755,000 (2009)] is matched with the construction expense to be recognized in 2010 of $1,620,000 [total costs of $4,556,250 less the total costs recognized in prior years of $2,936,250 (2008, $1,000,000; 2009, $1,936,250)], a zero profit results. Thus, the total loss has been recognized in 2009, the year in which it first became evident.

2008 Construction costs	$1,000,000		
	Construction in Process		
2008 Construction costs	$1,000,000		
2008 Recognized gross profit	125,000		
2009 Construction costs	1,916,000	2009 Recognized loss	$181,250
Balance	2,859,750		

Illustration 6-21

Content of Construction in Process Account at End of 2009–Unprofitable Contract

Under the completed-contract method, the contract loss of $56,250 is also recognized in the year in which it first became evident. The following entry is therefore made in 2009:

Loss from Long-Term Contracts	56,250	
Construction in Process (Loss)		56,250

A	= L +	SE
−$56,250		−$56,250

Cash flows: No effect

Just as the Billings for Construction in Process account balance cannot be higher than the contract price, neither can the balance in Construction in Process exceed the contract price. In circumstances where the Construction in Process balance is more than the Billings for Construction in Process amount, the recognized loss may be deducted on the balance sheet from the construction costs that have accumulated in Construction in Process. That is, under both the percentage-of-completion and the completed-contract methods, the provision for the loss (the credit) may be combined with Construction in Process, thereby reducing the balance. In circumstances where the billings are more than the accumulated costs (as in the 2009 illustration above), the amount of the estimated loss must be reported separately on the balance sheet as a current liability. That is, under both the percentage-of-completion and the completed-contract methods, the amount of the loss of $56,250, as estimated in 2009, would be taken from the Construction in Process account and reported separately as a current liability entitled Estimated Liability from Long-Term Contracts.

Disclosures In addition to making the financial statement disclosures that all businesses are required to make, construction contractors usually make some unique disclosures. Generally these additional disclosures are made in the notes to the financial statements. For example, a construction contractor should disclose the method of recognizing revenue, the basis that is used to classify assets and liabilities as current (the nature and length of the operating cycle), the basis for recording inventory, the effects of any revision of estimates, the amount of backlog on uncompleted contracts, and the details about receivables (billed and unbilled, maturity, interest rates, and significant individual or group concentrations of credit risk).

Barter and Non-Monetary Transactions

Barter transactions are transactions where few or no monetary assets are received as consideration when goods or services are sold. For instance, a computer manufacturing company might sell a computer but instead of receiving cash as consideration, the company might receive another type of asset, such as office furniture. Is this still a sale? Is the earnings process substantially complete? How should the transaction be measured?

As a **general rule,** the transaction may be treated as a sale and should be recorded at the **value that can be measured more reliably: the fair value of the asset given up or the fair value of the asset received.**[24]

[24] *CICA Handbook*, Section 3831.06.

More specifically, the transaction is treated as a sale and measured at fair value unless any of the following is true:

1. It lacks **commercial substance** (this will be explained further below).
2. It is an exchange of a product or property held for sale in the ordinary course of business for a product or property to be sold in the same line of business to facilitate sales to customers who are not parties to the exchange (e.g., a car dealership exchanging a blue car for a black car with another dealership in order to facilitate a sale to a customer).
3. The fair value is not reliably measurable.
4. It is a non-monetary, non-reciprocal transfer to owners (for instance, a spinoff of an operating division to the shareholders).[25]

What does the term commercial substance mean? It means that the transaction is a bona fide purchase and sale and that the entity has entered into the transaction for business purposes, exchanging one type of asset or service for another. After the transaction, the entity will be in a different position and its future cash flows are expected to change significantly as a result of the transaction (in terms of timing, amount, and/or riskiness).[26] This topic will be seen in further detail in Chapter 10.

Reporting Gross versus Net Revenues

Although net income does not change if a company chooses to report revenues as the **gross** amount billed to the customer (as well as the related cost of goods sold) instead of the **net** amount retained, the revenues number changes. Since revenue is the focus of many financial statement users, this is an important issue.

What Do the Numbers Mean?

Consider Priceline.com, the U.S. company that allows "naming your own price" for airline tickets and hotel rooms. In its third-quarter SEC filings for 1999, Priceline reported that it earned $152 million in revenues. But that included the full amount that customers paid for tickets, hotel rooms, and rental cars. Traditional travel agencies call that amount "gross bookings," not revenues. And much like regular travel agencies, Priceline keeps only a small portion of gross bookings—namely, the spread between the customers' accepted bids and the price it paid for the merchandise. The rest, which Priceline calls "product costs," are paid to the airlines and hotels that supply the tickets and rooms. In a recent quarter, those costs came to $134 million, leaving Priceline just $18 million of what it calls "gross profit" and what most other companies would call revenues. And that amount is before all of Priceline's other costs—like advertising and salaries—which netted out to a loss of $102 million. The difference is not academic: Priceline stock traded at about 23 times its reported revenues but at a mind-boggling 214 times its "gross profits."

Source: Jeremy Kahn, "Presto Chango! Sales Are Huge," *Fortune* (March 20, 2000), p. 44.

---

[25] *CICA Handbook*, Section 3831.06. Note that this involves non-controlling shareholders only and the transaction would be valued at the carrying value of the operating division. If the spinoff is to a **controlling shareholder**, it is a related-party transaction and *CICA Handbook* Section 3840 applies. Related-party transactions will be discussed further in Chapter 23.

[26] When determining whether the cash flows have changed significantly, the "entity-specific" value is sometimes examined. The entity-specific value is the value of the assets to the company (versus the value on the open market). This might be different because companies use the assets differently and there may be synergies in one company which do not exist at another. Thus, the asset would be more valuable to the first company. The company's cash flows would be said to change significantly when the entity-specific value of the asset that is received is different from the value of the asset received per *CICA Handbook* Section 3831.11.

In analyzing this issue (which is essentially a **presentation** issue), the following factors should be considered:

8 Objective
Understand when to book sales net versus gross.

1. whether the company acts as a **principal** in the transaction or an **agent or broker** (who is buying and selling an item for commission)
2. whether the company takes **title to the goods** being sold
3. whether the company has the **risks and rewards of ownership** of the goods being sold[27]

For example, a real estate agent acts as a **broker** or **agent**, finding a house for a customer and then taking a **commission** on the sale. The agent does not take **title** to the house nor does he or she have the **risks and rewards** associated with ownership of the house. Revenues associated with the sale of a house would be recorded net as commissions. On the other hand, a company such as Mattamy Homes Limited, which builds houses and then sells them to customers, acts as a **principal**. It has the risks and rewards of ownership of the house before selling it (including legal title). When Mattamy sells a house, it would record the house's market value as revenue and the cost to build it as cost of goods sold.

MEASUREMENT UNCERTAINTY

Measurement uncertainty results from an inability to measure the consideration itself—in some barter transactions, for example—or an inability to measure returns. Barter transactions were dealt with in the prior section.

9 Objective
Discuss how to deal with measurement uncertainty.

Sales with Right of Return

Whether cash or credit sales are involved, there is a special problem with claims for returns and allowances. In Chapter 7, the accounting treatment for normal returns and allowances is presented. However, certain companies experience such a high rate of returns—the ratio of returned merchandise to sales—that they find it necessary to postpone reporting sales until the return privilege has substantially expired. The length of the return period and historical rates of returns should therefore be considered. External factors such as obsolescence, business or economic cycles, the financial health of customers, and the arrival of a competitor's products that may cause the company's products to become obsolete also affect rates of return.

What Do the Numbers Mean?

For example, in the publishing industry, the rate of return approaches 25 percent for hardcover books and 65 percent for some magazines. The high rate of return is a function of two factors: (1) the publishers want to induce sales and therefore over-ship and (2) retailers have more power in the industry. Chapters Inc., formed through the merger between Smithbooks and Coles in 1995, engaged in very aggressive return activities after the merger. In 2001, Indigo Books & Music, Inc. became Canada's largest book retailer as a result of an amalgamation between Indigo and Chapters Inc.

Since this deal created an even greater concentration in the retail book industry in Canada, the deal was reviewed by the federal Competition Tribunal. The Tribunal concluded, among other things, that the deal could go through as long as 24 Chapters stores were sold to an unrelated party and the new company adhered to a business code of conduct. The code of conduct stipulated that returns would be limited and payments to publishers would have to be made within a reasonable time frame.

Returns in many industries are frequently done either through a right of contract or as a matter of practice, involving guaranteed sales agreements or consignments.

[27] *CICA Handbook*, EIC Abstract 123.

Three alternative revenue recognition treatments are available when the seller is exposed to continued risks of ownership through return of the product. These are (1) not recording a sale until all return privileges have expired; (2) recording the sale, but reducing sales by an estimate of future returns; and (3) recording the sale and accounting for the returns as they occur. The second treatment is only an option when returns are measurable, but it is the preferred treatment under accrual accounting.

The following situations may prevent revenue recognition when there is a **right of return** even though title to the goods has passed:[28]

1. If the price is not fixed or determinable.
2. If the buyer's obligation to pay is excused until the buyer resells, consumes, or uses the product.
3. If the buyer's obligation would change in the event of theft, damage, or destruction of the product.
4. If the returns are not estimable.

These situations create measurement uncertainty, and there is a question as to who has the risks and rewards of ownership.

In some cases, the company may offer **price protection** to the customer, that is, if the purchase price goes down before the customer has resold the product, the vendor will provide a cash refund. This is to stop the customer from returning the product and repurchasing it at the lower price. In these cases, the company must estimate and recognize the potential loss due to cash refunds.[29] If this cannot be measured, revenue might not be recognizable.

Fully refundable fees may be recognized as revenues as long as the entity is able to estimate the amount of refunds and the estimates are being made for a large pool of homogeneous items (presumably to make it easier to measure the refunds). Finally, revenues related to **cancellable sales arrangements** should not be recognized until the cancellation privileges have expired, because the cancellation period is seen as a trial period.

Trade Loading and Channel Stuffing

The domestic cigarette industry at one time used a distribution practice known as trade loading. Producers would induce their wholesale customers, known as the trade, to buy more product than they could resell. As a result, the wholesalers would return significant amounts of product in the following period. In the computer software industry, this same practice is referred to as channel stuffing. Software producers would offer deep discounts to their distributors, who would then overbuy and not be able to subsequently resell.

Trade loading and channel stuffing overstate sales in one period and distort operating results. If it is used without an appropriate allowance for sales returns, channel stuffing is a classic example of booking tomorrow's revenue today. The problem is the motivating factors that lie beneath these transactions. It is not a problem to use aggressive selling practices as long as they are sustainable and result in revenues that are realizable. The danger is to use these and similar types of transactions for the sole purpose of booking more revenues.

Bundled Sales

When the sale creates multiple deliverables, such as a product and service or several products and/or services, the revenue should be allocated between the deliverables. These types of sales are sometimes referred to as **bundled sales** or **multiple element**

[28] *CICA Handbook*, EIC Abstract 141.

[29] *CICA Handbook*, EIC Abstract 141.

arrangements. Revenue recognition criteria should be considered separately for each deliverable or unit. For instance, a cellular telephone company might sell a phone plus a monthly service (to provide airtime).

A deliverable may be treated as a **separate unit of accounting** if the following are all true:[30]

1. Each deliverable has **value to the customer on a stand-alone basis (i.e., on its own)**.
2. The *undelivered* deliverable has a **value that can be determined objectively** (e.g., fair value).
3. If there is a general right of return, **completion of the contract is probable and within the control of the vendor**.

In our example above, as long as the phone and service meet all three criteria, they can be treated as separate units in revenue recognition. Does the phone have value on a stand-alone basis (i.e., without the service)? It might if the customer can use the phone with another service or buy the service separately. Can we measure the value of the service? Possibly, if the service is sold separately.[31] Finally, if there is a right of return, is it likely that the contract will not be cancelled? A company might look at its past history with the product and customer to determine this.

Once we establish whether there are separate units, we would then allocate the overall price to each unit. Ideally, the **relative fair value method** would be used: in this method, the fair value of each item is determined and then the purchase price is allocated based on the relative fair values. Alternatively, the **residual value method** could be used: in this method, the fair value of the **undelivered** item would be subtracted from the overall purchase price. The residual value would then be used to value the delivered item (in this case the telephone).

For example, assume that Jason Inc. sells a product and service bundled together. Assume further that the separate deliverables meet the GAAP criteria for treatment as separate units. The fair value of the product is \$100 and the fair value of the service is \$200. In order to make the sale, Jason Inc. sold the bundle at a discount for \$250. Under the fair value method, the amount that is allocated to the product would be \$83.33 [\$100 ÷ (\$100 + \$200) × \$250] and the value attributed to the service would be \$166.67 [\$200 ÷ (\$100 + \$200) × \$250]. If the residual value method is used, the service would be valued at \$200 and the product at \$50 (\$250 − \$200).

Once we allocate the purchase price to each unit, we then follow GAAP to see if the revenue for each unit should be recognized. The revenue for the phone would be recognized upon delivery, and the revenue for the airtime would be recognized as the service is provided (or the airtime is used up).

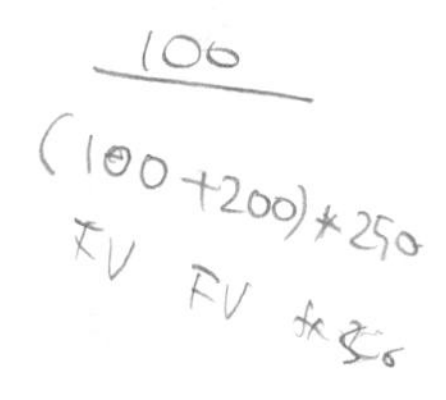

If it is not possible to measure each part, then revenue recognition criteria must be applied to the whole bundled sale as though it were one product or service.[32]

UNCERTAINTY ASSOCIATED WITH COLLECTIBILITY

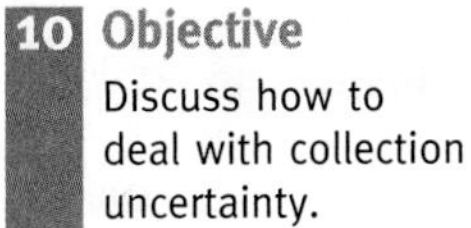

10 Objective
Discuss how to deal with collection uncertainty.

At the point of sale, if it is reasonably sure that collection of the receivable will ultimately occur, revenues are recognized.[33] Note that as long as it is possible to estimate uncollectible amounts at the point of sale (perhaps based on historical data), the sale is booked and the

[30] *CICA Handbook*, EIC Abstract 142.

[31] Note the emphasis on the undelivered item. It is important to be able to value the undelivered item to ensure that the revenue is not overstated for the delivered item (conservatism).

[32] *CICA Handbook*, EIC Abstract 142.

[33] *CICA Handbook*, Section 3400.16.

potential uncollectible amount is accrued. Alternatively, when **collectibility** cannot be reasonably assured, revenues cannot be recognized. In these cases, it is presumed that if collectibility is not established at the time of sale, then in substance no real sale has been made.

Certain types of sales transactions—such as sales that require or allow payment over longer periods—create greater collectibility risk. Instalment sales are an example of this type of sale. If collectibility is established but the uncollectible amounts cannot be estimated, one of two methods is generally used to defer income recognition until the cash is received:

1. **Instalment sales method**
2. **Cost recovery method**

In some situations, cash is received before delivery or transfer of the property. When this occurs, the amount is recorded as a deposit because the sale transaction is incomplete.

Instalment Sales

The expression "instalment sales" is generally used to describe any type of sale which requires payment of the amount owed in periodic instalments over an extended period of time. It is used in retailing, where all types of farm and home equipment and furnishings are sold on an instalment basis. It is also sometimes used in the heavy equipment industry, in which machine installations are paid for over a long period.

Because of the greater risk to **collectibility**, various devices are used to protect the seller. In merchandising, the two most common devices are (1) the use of a **conditional sales contract** that provides that title to the item sold does not pass to the purchaser until all payments have been made, and (2) use of **notes secured by a chattel** (personal property) mortgage on the article sold. Both of these devices permit the seller to repossess the goods sold if the purchaser defaults on one or more payments. The repossessed merchandise is then resold at whatever price it can be sold for in order to compensate the seller for the uncollected instalments and the expense of repossession.

Objective 11
Explain and apply the instalment sales method of accounting.

Instalment Method

The **instalment sales method** is one way of dealing with sales agreements that allow extended payment terms. It emphasizes collection rather than a sale, recognizing income in the collection periods rather than the sale period. This method is justified as follows: when there is no reasonable approach for estimating the degree of collectibility, income should not be recognized until cash is collected.

Underlying Concept

Realization is a critical part of revenue recognition. Thus, if there is a high degree of uncertainty about collectibility, revenue recognition must

International Insight

IAS 18 gives more extensive application guidance–i.e., revenue is measured at the PV of future cash flows when settlement of cash is deferred.

Under the instalment sales method of accounting, income recognition is deferred until the period of cash collection. Both revenues and costs of sales are recognized in the period of sale but the related gross profit is deferred to the periods in which cash is collected. Thus, instead of the sale being deferred to the future periods of anticipated collection and then related costs and expenses being deferred, only the proportional gross profit is deferred.

Other expenses, such as selling and administrative expense, are not deferred. Thus, the theory that costs and expenses should be matched against sales is applied in instalment sales transactions through the gross profit figure, but no further. Companies that use the instalment sales method of accounting generally record their operating expenses without considering that a portion of the year's gross profit will be deferred. This practice is often justified on the basis that (1) these expenses do not follow sales as closely as does the cost of goods sold, and (2) accurately dividing the expenses between the periods would be so difficult that it could not be justified by the benefits that would be gained.

Procedures for Deferring Income

To defer income for any specific year, do the following:

1. During the year, record both sales and cost of sales in the regular way, using the special accounts described later, and calculate the rate of gross profit on instalment sales transactions.
2. At year end, apply the rate of gross profit to the cash collections of the current year's instalment sales to arrive at the realized gross profit.
3. The gross profit that has not been realized should be deferred to future years.

International Insight

In Japan, instalment method accounting is frequently used whenever the collection period is more than two years, whether or not there is uncertainty about the collectibility of cash.

For sales made in prior years, the gross profit rate of each year's sales must be applied against cash collections of accounts receivable from that year's sales to arrive at the realized gross profit.

From the discussion above of the general practice that is followed in recording income from instalment sales, it is apparent that special accounts must be used. These accounts provide certain special information that is needed in order to determine the realized and unrealized gross profit in each year of operations. The requirements for special accounts are as follows:

1. Instalment sales transactions must be kept separate in the accounts from all other sales.
2. The gross profit on instalment sales must be determinable.
3. The amount of cash that is collected on accounts receivable from instalment sales must be known, and the total collected on the current year's and on each preceding year's sales must be determinable.
4. It must be possible to carry forward each year's deferred gross profit.

In each year, ordinary operating expenses are charged to expense accounts and are closed to the Income Summary account, just as under customary accounting procedure. Thus, the only specific difference in calculating net income under the instalment sales method, as it is generally applied, is the deferral of gross profit until it is realized by accounts receivable collections.

To illustrate the instalment sales method in accounting for the sales of merchandise, assume the following data:

	2008	2009	2010
Instalment sales	$200,000	$250,000	$240,000
Cost of instalment sales	150,000	190,000	168,000
Gross profit	$ 50,000	$ 60,000	$ 72,000
Rate of gross profit on sales	25% (a)	24% (b)	30% (c)
Cash receipts			
2008 sales	$ 60,000	$100,000	$ 40,000
2009 sales		100,000	125,000
2010 sales			80,000

(a) $50,000 ÷ 200,000 (b) $60,000 ÷ 250,000 (c) $72,000 ÷ 240,000

To simplify the illustration, interest charges are not included. Summary entries in general journal form for the year 2008 are as follows:

2008		
Instalment Accounts Receivable, 2008	200,000	
Instalment Sales		200,000
(To record sales made on instalment in 2008)		
Cash	60,000	
Instalment Accounts Receivable, 2008		60,000
(To record cash collected on instalment receivables)		
Cost of Instalment Sales	150,000	
Inventory (or Purchases)		150,000
(To record cost of goods sold on instalment in 2008 on either a perpetual or a periodic inventory basis)		
Deferred (unrealized) Gross Profit—current year (income statement)	35,000	
Deferred Gross Profit (balance sheet)		35,000
(to defer gross profit recognition for unrealized gross profits [25% ($200,000 − 60,000)])		

The summary entries in journal form for year 2 (2009) are:

2009		
Instalment Accounts Receivable, 2009	250,000	
Instalment Sales		250,000
(To record sales made on instalment in 2009)		
Cash	200,000	
Instalment Accounts Receivable, 2008		100,000
Instalment Accounts Receivable, 2009		100,000
(To record cash collected on instalment receivables)		
Cost of Instalment Sales	190,000	
Inventory (or Purchases)		190,000
(To record cost of goods sold on instalment in 2009)		
Deferred Gross Profit (balance sheet)	25,000	
Realized Gross Profit—prior year sales (income statement)		25,000
(to record 2008 realized gross profits [25% × $100,000])		
Deferred (unrealized) Gross Profit—current year (income statement)	36,000	
Deferred Gross Profit (balance sheet)		36,000
(to defer gross profit recognition for unrealized gross profits [24% ($250,000 − 100,000)])		

The two income statement accounts, Realized Gross Profit—Prior Year Sales and Deferred (unrealized) Gross Profit—Current Year, would generally be netted against each other. The entries in 2010 would be similar to those of 2009, and the gross profit realized on prior years' sales would be $40,000, as shown by the following calculations:

From 2008	\$ 40,000 × 25% =	\$10,000
From 2009	\$125,000 × 24% =	\$30,000
		\$40,000

Deferred gross profit on 2010 sales would be calculated as follows.

30% × ($240,000 − 80,000) = $48,000

Additional Problems of Instalment Sales Accounting

In addition to the problems of calculating the current realized and deferred gross profit, there are also other problems in accounting for instalment sales transactions. These problems relate to:

1. Interest on instalment contracts
2. Uncollectible accounts
3. Defaults and repossessions

Interest on Instalment Contracts Because the collection of instalment receivables is spread over a long period, it is customary to charge the buyer interest on the unpaid balance. A schedule of equal payments consisting of interest and principal is set up.

As Illustration 6-22 shows, a smaller amount of each successive payment is attributed to interest and a correspondingly larger amount is attributed to the principal. This illustration assumes that an asset costing $2,400 is sold for $3,000 with interest of 8% included in the three instalments of $1,164.10.

Illustration 6-22
Instalment Payment Schedule

Date	Cash (Debit)	Interest Earned (Credit)	Instalment Receivables (Credit)	Instalment Unpaid Balance	Realized Gross Profit (20%)
1/2/08	—	—		$3,000.00	—
1/2/09	$1,164.10(a)	$240.00(b)	$ 924.10(c)	2,075.90(d)	$184.82(e)
1/2/10	1,164.10	166.07	998.03	1,077.87	199.61
1/2/11	1,164.10	86.23	1,077.87	-0-	215.57
					$600.00

(a) Periodic payment ÷ Original unpaid balance / PV of an annuity of $1.00 for three periods at 8%; $1,164.10 = $3,000 ÷ 2.57710.
(b) $3,000.00 × .08 = $240.
(c) $1,164.10 − $240.00 = $924.10.
(d) $3,000.00 − $924.10 = $2,075.90.
(e) $924.10 × .20 = $184.82.

Interest should be accounted for separately from the gross profit recognized on the instalment sales collections during the period. It is recognized as interest revenue at the time of the cash receipt.

Uncollectible Accounts The problem of bad debts or uncollectible accounts receivable is somewhat different for businesses that sell on an instalment basis, because of a repossession feature that is often part of the sales agreement. This feature gives the selling company an opportunity to recoup any uncollectible accounts through repossession and resale of the repossessed merchandise. If the company knows from experience that its repossessions do not, as a rule, compensate for uncollectible balances, it may be advisable to provide for such losses by charging them to a special bad debt expense account just as is done for other credit sales.

Defaults and Repossessions Depending on the sales contract terms and credit department policy, the seller can repossess merchandise sold under an instalment arrangement if the purchaser fails to meet payment requirements. Repossessed merchandise may be reconditioned before it is offered for resale. It may be resold for cash or instalment payments.

The accounting for repossessions recognizes that the related instalment receivable account is not collectible and that it should be written off. Along with the account receivable, the applicable deferred gross profit must be removed from the ledger using the following entry:

Repossessed Merchandise (an inventory account)	XX	
Deferred Gross Profit (balance sheet)	XX	
Instalment Accounts Receivable		XX

The above entry assumes that the repossessed merchandise should be recorded on the books at exactly the amount of the uncollected account less the deferred gross profit applicable. This assumption may or may not be proper. The condition of the repossessed merchandise, the cost of reconditioning it, and the market for second-hand merchandise of that particular type must all be considered. The objective should be to put any asset acquired on the books at its fair value or, when fair value cannot be determined, at the best possible approximation of fair value. If the fair value of the repossessed merchandise is less than the uncollected balance less the deferred gross profit, a "loss on repossession" should be recorded at the repossession date.

To illustrate the required entry, assume that a refrigerator was sold to Marilyn Hunt for $500 on September 1, 2008. Terms require a down payment of $200 and $20 on the first of every month for 15 months, starting October 1, 2008. It is further assumed that the refrigerator cost $300 and that it is sold to provide a 40% rate of gross profit on the selling price. At the year end of December 31, 2008, a total of $60 should have been collected in addition to the original down payment.

If Hunt makes her January and February payments in 2009 and then defaults, the account balances that apply to Hunt at the time of default would be:

Instalment Account Receivable ($500 − $200 − $20 − $20 − $20 − $20 − $20) =	200 (dr.)
Deferred Gross Profit (Balance Sheet) [40% ($500 − $200 − $20 − $20 − $20)] =	96 (cr.)

The deferred gross profit on the Hunt account still has the December 31, 2008, balance ($96) because no entry has yet been made to recognize the gross profit realized by 2009 cash collections ($40 × 40% = $16). If the repossessed article's estimated fair value is set at $70, the following entry would be required to record the repossession. Assume that the $16 of realized gross profit will be recognized at year end with the regular entry to recognize realized gross profit.

A	=	L	+	SE
−$130		−$80		−$50

Cash flows: No effect

Deferred Gross Profit	80	
Repossessed Merchandise	70	
Loss on Repossession	50	
Instalment Account Receivable (Hunt)		200

The loss amount is determined by (1) subtracting the deferred gross profit from the amount of the account receivable, to determine the unrecovered cost (or book value) of the merchandise repossessed, and (2) subtracting the estimated fair value of the repossessed merchandise from the unrecovered cost, to get the amount of the loss on repossession.

Financial Statement Presentation of Instalment Sales Transactions If instalment sales transactions are a significant part of total sales, it is desirable to give full disclosure of instalment sales, the cost of instalment sales, and any expenses that are allocable to instalment sales. If, however, instalment sales transactions are an insignificant part of total sales, it may be satisfactory to include only the realized gross profit in the income statement as a special item following the gross profit on sales, as Illustration 6-23 shows.

Illustration 6-23
Disclosure of Instalment Sales Transactions–Insignificant Amount

HEALTH MACHINE CORP.
Statement of Income
For the Year Ended December 31, 2009

Sales	$620,000
Cost of goods sold	490,000
Gross profit on sales	130,000
Gross profit realized on instalment sales	51,000
Total gross profit on sales	$181,000

If more complete disclosure of instalment sales transactions is desired, a presentation similar to the one in Illustration 6-24 may be used.

Illustration 6-24
Disclosure of Instalment Sales Transactions–Significant Amount

HEALTH MACHINE CORP.
Statement of Income
For the Year Ended December 31, 2009

	Instalment Sales	Other Sales	Total
Sales	$248,000	$620,000	$868,000
Cost of goods sold	182,000	490,000	672,000
Gross profit on sales	66,000	130,000	196,000
Less: Deferred gross profit on instalment sales of this year	47,000		47,000
Realized gross profit on this year's sales	19,000	130,000	149,000
Add: Gross profit realized on instalment sales of prior years	32,000		32,000
Gross profit realized this year	$ 51,000	$130,000	$181,000

Underlying Concept

This level of detail might result in "information overload" for some users.

The apparent awkwardness of this presentation method is difficult to avoid if management wants to fully disclose the instalment sales transactions in the income statement. One solution, of course, is to prepare a separate schedule that shows instalment sales transactions and to then present only the final figure in the income statement.

In the balance sheet, it is generally considered desirable to classify instalment accounts receivable by their year of collectibility. There is debate about whether instalment accounts that are not collectible for two or more years should be included in current assets. If instalment sales are part of normal operations, they may be considered current assets because they are collectible within the business operating cycle. If this practice is followed, there should not be much confusion as long as the maturity dates are fully disclosed, as shown in Illustration 6-25.

Illustration 6-25
Disclosure of Instalment Accounts Receivable, by Year

Current assets		
Notes and accounts receivable		
Trade customers	$78,800	
Less: Allowance for doubtful accounts	3,700	
	75,100	
Instalment accounts collectible in 2009	22,600	
Instalment accounts collectible in 2010	47,200	$144,900

On the other hand, receivables from an instalment contract for a transaction that is not related to normal operations should be reported in the Other Assets section if the instalments are due beyond one year.

Repossessed merchandise is a part of inventory and should therefore be included as inventory in the Current Assets section of the balance sheet. Any gain or loss on repossessions should be included in the income statement in the "Other Revenues and Gains" or "Other Expenses and Losses" sections.

Deferred gross profit on instalment sales may be treated either as unearned revenue (current liability) or a contra asset account (as a valuation of instalment accounts receivable).

Cost Recovery Method

Objective 12
Explain and apply the cost recovery method of accounting.

Under the **cost recovery method**, no profit is recognized until cash payments by the buyer add up to more than the seller's cost for the merchandise sold. After all costs have been recovered, any additional cash collections are included in income. This method is therefore the most conservative method of recognizing income under accrual accounting.[34] The income statement for the period of the sale reports sales revenue, the cost of goods sold, and the gross profit—both the amount (if any) that is recognized during the period and the amount that is deferred. The deferred gross profit is either presented as unearned revenue or it is offset against the related receivable (reduced by collections) on the balance sheet. Subsequent income statements report the gross profit as a separate revenue item when it is recognized as earned.

To illustrate the cost recovery method, assume that early in 2008 Fesmire Manufacturing sells inventory with a cost of $25,000 to Higley Limited for $36,000, with payments receivable of $18,000 in 2008, $12,000 in 2009, and $6,000 in 2010. If the cost recovery method applies to this sale transaction and the cash is collected on schedule, then cash collections, revenue, cost, and gross profit are recognized as in Illustration 6-26.

Illustration 6-26
Calculation of Gross Profit–Cost Recovery Method

	2008	2009	2010
Cash collected	$18,000	$12,000	$6,000
Revenue	$36,000	-0-	-0-
Cost of goods sold	25,000	-0-	-0-
Deferred gross profit	$11,000	$11,000	$6,000
Recognized gross profit	-0-	5,000*	6,000
Deferred gross profit balance (end of period)	$11,000	$ 6,000	$-0-

*$25,000 − $18,000 = $7,000 of unrecovered cost at the end of 2008; $12,000 − $7,000 = $5,000, the excess of cash received in 2009 over unrecovered cost.

Under the cost recovery method, total revenue and cost of goods sold are reported in the period of sale, similar to the instalment sales method. However, unlike the instalment sales method, which recognizes income as cash is collected, the cost

[34] "Omnibus Opinion – 1966," *Opinions of the Accounting Principles Board No. 10* (New York: AICPA, 1969), p. 149, fn. 8; "Accounting for Franchise Fee Revenue," *Statement of Financial Accounting Standards No. 45* (Stamford, Conn.: FASB, 1981), par. 6; "Accounting for Sales of Real Estate," *Statement of Financial Accounting Standards No. 66*, pars. 62 and 63. In Canada, CICA Accounting Guideline No. 2 (franchise fee revenue) mentions that either the instalment method or cost recovery method may be used when there is no reasonable basis for estimating collectibility.

recovery method recognizes profit only when cash collections exceed the total cost of the goods sold.

The journal entry to record the deferred gross profit on this transaction at the end of 2008 (after the sale and the cost of sale were recorded in the normal manner) is as follows:

2008		
Deferred (unrealized) Gross Profit (income statement)	11,000	
Deferred Gross Profit (balance sheet)		11,000
(To record deferred gross profit on sales accounted for under the cost recovery method)		

A	=	L	+	SE
		+$11,000		−$11,000

Cash flows: No effect

In 2009 and 2010, the deferred gross profit becomes realized gross profit as the cumulative cash collections exceed the total costs. The following entries are recorded in these years:

2009		
Deferred Gross Profit (balance sheet)	5,000	
Realized Gross Profit (income statement)		5,000
(To recognize gross profit to the extent that cash collections in 2009 exceed costs)		

A	=	L	+	SE
		−$5,000		+5,000

Cash flows: No effect

2010		
Deferred Gross Profit (balance sheet)	6,000	
Realized Gross Profit (income statement)		6,000
(To recognize gross profit to the extent that cash collections in 2010 exceed costs)		

A	=	L	+	SE
		−$6,000		+6,000

Cash flows: No effect

PERSPECTIVES

Analysis

Although the revenues number is used in several key ratios, the most important revenue analysis is normally a trend analysis (changes in revenues from year to year). Due to the sensitivity and high profile of the revenues number on the income statement, there is a lot of pressure to report biased revenue numbers. Biased reporting is possible under both a principles-based accounting standards system (because there is less specific guidance) and a rules-based accounting standards system (by finding loopholes in the rules). Revenues are a key number that is used to judge management's job performance and they are a signal in the marketplace for sustainable growth potential. The value of firms in certain industries, such as Internet companies, is often based on revenues since many of these firms do not generate profits in their early years.

As mentioned in the opening statements of the chapter, this is one of the main areas of misrepresentation. Note that it is often difficult to spot these misrepresentations in financial statements since the note disclosures are often very general. It is therefore important to carefully understand the underlying business and business model of the company and to ensure that any changes in the business model are reflected appropriately in the statements. Care should also be taken to ensure that large and unusual transactions are entered into for bona fide business reasons (e.g., to add value to the shareholders) rather than to make the company's performance look better than it really is.

International

The IASB and FASB are currently working together on new revenue recognition standards. The following is an excerpt from the IASB website regarding the revenue recognition project:

> **Work on this project commenced in 2002. The main reasons for undertaking this project are as follows.**
>
> - Eliminate weaknesses in existing concepts and standards.
> - The revenue recognition requirements in IAS 18 focus on the occurrence of critical events rather than changes in assets and liabilities. Some believe that this approach leads to debits and credits that do not meet the definition of assets and liabilities being recognised on the balance sheet.
> - A practical weakness of IAS 18 is that it gives insufficient guidance on contracts that provide more than one good or service to the customer. It is unclear when contracts should be divided into components and how much revenue should be attributed to each component.
> - The International Financial Reporting Interpretations Committee (IFRIC) receives frequent requests for guidance on the application of IAS 18.
> - Converge IFRSs and US requirements.
> - There are approximately 200 sources of standards and guidance on revenue recognition in US GAAP. These are not all based on consistent concepts.
> - There are substantial differences between IFRSs and US requirements.[35]

From the IASB perspective, International GAAP does not provide enough guidance; and from the FASB perspective, US GAAP provides excessive and inconsistent guidance.

The boards have agreed on the following in principle:

1. Revenues would be recognized based on changes in assets and liabilities (performance obligations) arising from contracts with customers.
2. Whether the revenues are earned or realized will not be part of the analysis for whether or not revenues should be recognized. The problem with this approach is that it results in deferred debits and credits being recognized that do not meet the (new) definitions of assets and liabilities. Whether revenues are earned or realized is also difficult to determine, which leads to a lack of consistency. It is especially problematic with bundled sales.
3. In terms of measuring performance obligations, the Boards are considering the legal layoff amount (the amount that the entity would have to pay to have someone take the obligation off their hands) and/or the customer consideration amount (the amount that the customer would pay for the same service) as a basis for measurement. Only legally enforceable obligations would be considered.

Other matters that are being considered include whether all proceeds from sales should be recorded as revenues (distinguishing revenues from gains provides useful information, but it is difficult to make this distinction consistently) and whether performance obligations should be remeasured. The new approach emphasizes legal interpretation of changes in

[35] www.iasb.org.

the assets and liabilities of the company and it will be interesting to see where the standards end up. Accountants will have to have greater knowledge of the law and legal environment in order to apply the standards. Furthermore, since the laws will be different around the world, this approach may result in a lack of consistency.

Summary of Learning Objectives

Glossary

www.wiley.com/canada/kieso

KEY TERMS

barter transactions, 307
bill and hold, 294
billings, 298
bundled sales, 310
collectibility, 312
commercial substance, 308
completed-contract method, 298
consignment, 295
continuous earnings process, 297
continuous sale, 299
cost recovery method, 318
cost-to-cost basis, 299
critical event, 293
discrete earnings process, 293
earnings process, 292
f.o.b. destination, 294
f.o.b. shipping point, 294
input measures, 299
instalment sales method, 312
legal title, 293
measurement uncertainty, 309
multiple element arrangements, 310
output measures, 299
percentage-of-completion method, 298
performance, 291
persuasive evidence of an arrangement, 291
point of delivery, 293
possession, 293
realized, 291
relative fair value method, 311

1 Apply the revenue recognition principle.

The revenue recognition principle states that revenue should be recognized when (1) performance is substantially complete (and the transaction is measurable) and (2) collection is reasonably assured. Thus, revenue is earned when the entity has substantially accomplished what it must do to be entitled to the benefits represented by the revenues—that is, when the earnings process is complete or virtually complete. Revenues and costs must be measurable and it must be reasonably certain that the revenues will be collected.

2 Describe the accounting issues associated with revenue recognition for sales of goods.

Judgement must be applied in determining when the risks and rewards pass and whether the earnings process is substantially complete. The nature of the earnings process depends on the business model and both must be considered to determine if revenue and income are recognized. Different terms in the sales agreement must be analyzed to determine their impact on revenue recognition. Consider shipping terms, sales with buyback, bill and hold sales, customer acceptance provisions, and other such terms.

3 Explain the accounting for consignment sales.

The risks and rewards remain with the seller in this case and, therefore, a real sale does not occur until the goods are sold to a third party. Special accounts separate inventory on consignment.

4 Describe the accounting issues related to revenue recognition for services and long-term contracts.

The earnings process is more likely a continuous one, involving many significant events. Often, the customer is identified upfront, and revenue is therefore recognized throughout the earnings process.

5 Apply the percentage-of-completion method for long-term contracts.

To apply the percentage-of-completion method to long-term contracts, a basis is needed for measuring the progress toward completion at particular interim dates. One of the most popular input measures that is used to determine the progress toward completion is the cost-to-cost basis. Using this basis, the percentage of completion is measured by comparing costs incurred to date with the most recent estimate of the total costs to complete the contract. The percentage that the costs incurred amount to out of the total estimated costs is applied to the total revenue or the estimated total gross profit on the contract to arrive at the revenue or the gross profit amounts to be recognized to date.

6 Apply the completed-contract method for long-term contracts.

Under this method, revenue and gross profit are recognized only when the contract is completed. Costs of long-term contracts in process and current billings are accumulated, but there are no interim charges or credits to income statement accounts for revenues, costs, and gross profit. The annual entries to record costs of construction, progress billings, and collections from customers would be identical to those for the percentage-of-completion method, with one significant exception: revenue and gross profit are not recognized until the end of the contract.

7 Account for losses on long-term contracts.

Two types of losses can become evident under long-term contracts: (1) A loss in the current period on a profitable contract. Under the percentage-of-completion method only, the estimated increase in the cost requires a current period adjustment of excess gross profit that has been recognized on the project in prior periods. This adjustment is recorded as a loss in the current period because it is a change in an accounting estimate. (2) A loss on an unprofitable contract. Under both the percentage-of-completion and the completed-contract methods, the entire loss that is expected from the contract must be recognized in the current period.

8 Understand when to book sales net versus gross.

Transactions where the seller is acting as principal in the sale should be accounted for on a gross basis. Where the seller is acting as an agent (putting buyers and sellers together) the transaction should be booked on a net basis. Consideration should be given to whether the seller has the risks and rewards of ownership of the product being sold.

9 Discuss how to deal with measurement uncertainty.

Transactions that involve rights of return may require remeasurement. Remeasurement of the transaction may also be necessary when there is trade loading or channel stuffing. Bundled sales have special measurement issues as they may have to be separated into distinct units of accounting for revenue recognition. The selling price must be allocated to each unit.

10 Discuss how to deal with collection uncertainty.

Normally, if it can be estimated, a provision for uncollectible amounts is accrued. In certain types of sales arrangements, payment is extended over the longer term. In these cases, the instalments or cost recovery methods may be used. These methods allow revenue recognition upfront but gross profits are deferred.

11 Explain and apply the instalment sales method of accounting.

The instalment sales method recognizes income in the periods of collection rather than in the period of sale. The instalment method of accounting is justified on the basis that when there is no reasonable approach for estimating the degree of collectibility, revenue should not be recognized until cash is collected.

12 Explain and apply the cost recovery method of accounting.

Under the cost recovery method, no profit is recognized until cash payments by the buyer exceed the seller's cost of the merchandise sold. After all costs have been recovered, any additional cash collections are included in income. The income statement for the period of sale reports sales revenue, the cost of goods sold, and the gross profit—both the amount that is recognized during the period and the amount that is deferred. The deferred gross profit is treated as deferred or unearned revenues on the balance sheet or is offset against the related receivable on the balance sheet. Subsequent income statements report the gross profit as a separate income item when it is recognized as earned.

Appendix 6A

Franchises

13 **Objective**
Explain revenue recognition for franchises.

As is indicated throughout this chapter, revenue is recognized based on two criteria: **performance and collectibility.** These criteria are appropriate for most business activities. This appendix looks at how they apply to industries that are characterized by franchises.

There are many different types of franchise arrangements. They apply to some of the following well-known franchises:

Soft ice cream/frozen yogourt stores (Baskin Robbins, TCBY, Dairy Queen)
Food drive-ins (McDonald's, Tim Hortons, Burger King)
Restaurants (Swiss Chalet, Pizza Hut, Denny's)
Motels (Holiday Inn, Ramada, Best Western)
Auto rentals (Avis, Hertz, National)
Others (H & R Block, Mr. Lube, Mac's Convenience Stores)

There are two possible sources for revenues in franchise companies: (1) from the sale of initial franchises and related assets or services (**initial franchise fee**), and (2) from **continuing franchise fees** based on franchise operations. The franchisor (the party that grants business rights under the franchise) normally provides the franchisee (the party that operates the franchised business) with the following services:

1. Assistance in site selection
   (a) analyzing locations
   (b) negotiating a lease
2. Evaluation of potential income
3. Supervision of construction activity
   (a) obtaining financing
   (b) designing the building
   (c) supervising the contractor while building occurs
4. Assistance in the acquisition of signs, fixtures, and equipment
5. Bookkeeping and advisory services
   (a) setting up the franchisee's records
   (b) advising on income, real estate, and other taxes
   (c) advising on local regulations of the franchisee's business
6. Employee and management training
7. Quality control
8. Advertising and promotion

During the 1960s and early 1970s, it was standard accounting practice for franchisors to recognize the entire franchise fee at the date of sale whether the fee was received then or was collectible over a long period of time. Frequently, franchisors recorded the entire amount as revenue in the year of sale even though many of the services had not yet been performed and there was uncertainty about whether the entire fee would be collected.[36]

However, a franchise agreement may guarantee refunds to the franchisee if certain conditions are not met, and the profit from franchise fees can be reduced sharply by future costs of obligations and services that the franchisor is obliged to render.[37]

Initial Franchise Fees

The initial franchise fee is the consideration that the franchisor receives in exchange for establishing the franchise relationship and providing some initial services. Initial franchise fees are to be recorded as revenue only when the franchisor has established **substantial performance**[38]—i.e., the franchisor has substantially completed the services it is obligated to perform and collection of the fee is reasonably assured. Substantial performance occurs when the franchisor has no remaining obligation to refund any cash it has received or to excuse any non-payment of a note and it has substantially performed all significant initial services that the contract requires. The beginning of operations by the franchisee is normally considered to be the earliest point for assuming that substantial performance has occurred; this is true unless it can be demonstrated that substantial performance has occurred before that time.

Illustration of Entries for Initial Franchise Fee

To illustrate, assume that Dino's Pizza Inc. charges an initial franchise fee of $50,000 for the right to operate as a franchisee of Dino's Pizza. Of this amount, $10,000 is payable when the agreement is signed and the balance is payable in five annual payments of $8,000 each. In return for the initial franchise fee, the franchisor will help locate the site, negotiate the site lease or purchase, supervise the construction activity, and provide the bookkeeping services. The franchisee's credit rating indicates that money can be borrowed at 8%. The present value of an ordinary annuity of five annual receipts of $8,000 each, discounted at 8%, is $31,941.68. The discount of $8,058.32 represents the interest revenue to be accrued by the franchisor over the payment period.

1. If there is reasonable expectation that the down payment may be refunded and if substantial future services remain to be performed by Dino's Pizza Inc., the entry should be:

A	=	L	+ SE
+$41,942		+$41,942	

Cash flows: ↑ $10,000 inflow

Account	Debit	Credit
Cash	10,000	
Notes Receivable	40,000	
Discount on Notes Receivable		8,058
Unearned Franchise Fees		41,942

[36] In 1987 and 1988, the SEC ordered a half-dozen fast-growing startup franchisors, including Jiffy Lube International, Moto Photo, Inc., Swensen's, Inc., and LePeep Restaurants, Inc., to defer their initial franchise fee recognition until it was earned. See "Claiming Tomorrow's Profits Today," *Forbes*, October 17, 1988, p. 78.

[37] To reduce the abuses in revenue recognition that existed and to standardize the accounting and reporting practices in the franchise industry, the CICA issued an Accounting Guideline and the FASB issued Statement No. 45.

[38] *CICA Handbook*, Accounting Guideline No. 2.

2. If it is extremely unlikely that the initial franchise fee will need to be refunded, if the amount of future services to be provided to the franchisee is minimal, if collectibility of the note is reasonably assured, and if substantial performance has occurred, the entry should be:

Cash	10,000	
Notes Receivable	40,000	
Discount on Notes Receivable		8,058
Revenue from Franchise Fees		41,942

A	= L +	SE
+$41,942		+$41,942

Cash flows: ↑ $10,000 inflow

3. If the initial down payment is not refundable and is a fair measure of the services already provided, if there remains a significant amount of services still to be performed by the franchisor in future periods, and if collectibility of the note is reasonably assured, the entry should be:

Cash	10,000	
Notes Receivable	40,000	
Discount on Notes Receivable		8,058
Revenue from Franchise Fees		10,000
Unearned Franchise Fees		31,942

A	= L	+ SE
+$41,942	+$31,942	+$10,000

Cash flows: ↑ $10,000 inflow

4. If the initial down payment is not refundable and no future services are required by the franchisor, but collection of the note is so uncertain that recognition of the note as an asset is unwarranted, the entry should be:

Cash	10,000	
Revenue from Franchise Fees		10,000

A	= L +	SE
+$10,000		+$10,000

Cash flows: ↑ $10,000 inflow

5. Under the same conditions as those listed under 4 except that the down payment is refundable or substantial services still need to be performed, the entry should be:

Cash	10,000	
Unearned Franchise Fees		10,000

A	= L	+ SE
+$10,000	+$10,000	

Cash flows: ↑ $10,000 inflow

In cases 4 and 5—where collection of the note is extremely uncertain—cash collections may be recognized using the instalment method or the cost recovery method.

Continuing Franchise Fees

Continuing franchise fees are received in return for the continuing rights that are granted by the franchise agreement and for providing such services as management training, advertising and promotion, legal assistance, and other support. Continuing fees should be reported as revenue when they are earned and receivable from the franchisee, unless a portion of them has been designated for a particular purpose, such as providing a specified amount for building maintenance or local advertising. In that case, the portion that is deferred needs to be an amount that is enough to cover the estimated cost in excess of continuing franchise fees and to provide a reasonable profit on the continuing services.

Special Issues

Bargain Purchases

In addition to paying continuing franchise fees, franchisees often purchase some or all of their equipment and supplies from the franchisor. The franchisor would account for these sales as it would for any other product sales. Sometimes, however, the franchise agreement grants the franchisee the right to make bargain purchases of equipment or supplies after the initial franchise fee is paid. If the bargain price is lower than the normal selling price of the same product, or if it does not provide the franchisor a reasonable profit, then a portion of the initial franchise fee should be deferred. The deferred portion would be accounted for as an adjustment of the selling price when the franchisee subsequently purchases the equipment or supplies.

Options to Purchase

A franchise agreement may give the franchisor an option to purchase the franchisee's business. As a matter of management policy, the franchisor may reserve the right to purchase a profitable franchised outlet, or to purchase one that is in financial difficulty. If it is probable at the time when the option is given that the franchisor will ultimately purchase the outlet, then the initial franchise fee should not be recognized as revenue. It should instead be recorded as a liability. When the option is exercised (i.e., the franchisor purchases the outlet), the liability would reduce the franchisor's investment in the outlet.

Franchisor's Cost

Franchise accounting also includes proper accounting for the franchisor's cost. The objective is to match related costs and revenues by reporting them as components of income in the same accounting period. Ordinarily, franchisors should defer the recognition of direct costs of specific franchise sales if the revenue from these sales has not yet been recognized. Costs should not be deferred, however, if it is unlikely that they will lead to future, realizeable revenues.

Indirect costs that are regular and recurring, such as selling and administrative expenses, and are incurred regardless of the level of franchise sales should be expensed as they are incurred.

Disclosures of Franchisors

Franchisors must disclose all significant commitments and obligations created by franchise agreements and describe any services that have not yet been substantially performed. They should also disclose any resolution that eliminates uncertainties about the collectibility of franchise fees. Initial franchise fees should be segregated from other franchise fee revenue if they are significant. As much as possible, the revenues and costs of franchisor-owned outlets should be separated from the revenues and costs of franchised outlets.

Glossary

www.wiley.com/canada/kieso

Summary of Learning Objective for Appendix 6A

KEY TERMS

continuing franchise fees, 323
initial franchise fee, 323
substantial performance, 324

13 Explain revenue recognition for franchises.

In a franchise arrangement, the initial franchise fee is recorded as revenue only when the franchisor makes substantial performance of the services it is obligated to perform and collection of the fee is reasonably assured. Continuing franchise fees are recognized as revenue when they are earned and receivable from the franchisee.

Note: All assignment material with an asterisk (*) relates to the appendix to the chapter.

Brief Exercises

BE6-1 Two real estate developers own parcels of land of equal value at opposite ends of the Calgary suburbs. Each developer intends to resell or develop its parcel of land and has held the property for several years. Over the years, both properties have appreciated in value beyond their carrying values. Because each developer is already developing residential housing on land that is beside the other developer's undeveloped parcel of land, the two developers decide to exchange the parcels of land without adding any cash consideration in the exchange. The developers agree that the parcels of land are equivalent in their fair market value at the time of the exchange. Discuss how the revenue recognition principle should be applied to this exchange. What factors determine whether or not the property that was obtained can be recorded at its fair market value on the date of the exchange and whether corresponding revenues can be recorded on this date? **(LO 1, 7)**

BE6-2 TGI Corporation shipped $220,000 of merchandise on consignment to Thomas Company. TGI paid freight costs of $2,000. Thomas Company paid $500 for local advertising, which is reimbursable from TGI. By year end, 60% of the merchandise had been sold for $262,300. Thomas notified TGI, retained a 10% commission, and remitted the cash due to TGI. Prepare TGI's entry when the cash is received. **(LO 3)**

BE6-3 Boomer Inc. began work on a $5-million contract in 2008 to construct an office building. Boomer uses the percentage-of-completion method. At December 31, 2008, the balances in certain accounts were as follows: Construction in Process $750,000; Accounts Receivable $340,000; and Billings on Construction in Process $1 million. Indicate how these accounts would be reported in the company's December 31, 2008, balance sheet. **(LO 5)**

BE6-4 Wan Inc. began work on a $9.6-million contract in 2007 to construct an office building. During 2007, Wan Inc. incurred costs of $1.3 million, billed its customers for $2.1 million, and collected $960,000. At December 31, 2007, the estimated future costs to complete the project total $5 million. (a) Prepare Wan's 2007 journal entries using the percentage-of-completion method. (b) Prepare Wan's 2007 journal entries using the completed-contract method. **(LO 5, 6)**

BE6-5 Tower Construction Corp. began work on a $2,020,000 construction contract in 2007. During 2007, the company incurred costs of $588,000, billed its customer for $615,000, and collected $275,000. At December 31, 2007, the estimated future costs to complete the project total $532,000. Prepare Tower's journal entry to record any profit or loss for the year ended December 31, 2007, using (a) the percentage-of-completion method and (b) the completed-contract method. **(LO 7)**

BE6-6 Candeloro Inc. began work on a $5-million contract in 2008 to construct an office building. Candeloro uses the completed-contract method. At December 31, 2008, the balances in certain accounts were as follows: Construction in Process $1,165,000; Accounts Receivable $560,000; and Billings on Construction in Process $1,400,000. Indicate how these accounts would be reported in Candeloro's December 31, 2008, balance sheet. **(LO 6)**

BE6-7 Inexperienced construction company T&T Corp. signed a risky contract to build a sports facility at a fixed contract amount of $1.9 million. The work began in early 2007 and T&T incurred costs of $810,000. At December 31, 2007, the estimated future costs to complete the project totalled $990,000. During 2008, T&T ran into trouble with weather conditions and incurred costs of $890,000 and estimated that it would need to spend $300,000 to complete the project. During 2009, T&T reluctantly completed the project, incurring further costs of $320,000. Prepare a schedule to calculate the amount of revenues and gross profit or loss to be recognized by T&T Corp. during the three years of the contract using (a) the percentage-of-completion method and (b) the completed-contract method. Provide the entry to record any interim loss that needs to be accrued on the contract using the completed-contract method. **(LO 7)**

BE6-8 Manchrian Music sells CDs to retailers. In 2008, it recorded sales revenue of $500,000 and granted credit of $28,000 for CDs that retailers returned. Experience indicates that the normal return rate is 10%. Prepare the company's journal entries to record (a) the $28,000 of returns and (b) estimated returns at December 31, 2008. **(LO 9)**

BE6-9 Paradise Corporation began selling goods on an instalment basis on January 1, 2008. During 2008, Paradise had instalment sales of $700,000; cash collections of $254,000; and cost of instalment sales of $380,000. Prepare the company's entries to record instalment sales, cash collected, cost of instalment sales, deferral of gross profit, and gross profit recognized, using the instalment sales method. (Round the gross profit percentage to three decimal places.) **(LO 11)**

BE6-10 Shinsui Limited sells goods on the instalment basis and uses the instalment sales method. Due to a customer default on instalment payments, Shinsui repossessed merchandise that was originally sold for $2,100, and had resulted in a gross profit rate of 40%. At the time of repossession, the uncollected balance was $1,110, and the fair value of the repossessed merchandise was $1,725. Prepare Shinsui's entry to record the repossession. **(LO 11)**

(LO 11) **BE6-11** At December 31, 2009, Starskin Corporation had the following account balances:

Instalment Accounts Receivable, 2008	$245,000
Instalment Accounts Receivable, 2009	240,000
Deferred Gross Profit, 2008	103,400
Deferred Gross Profit, 2009	110,700

Most of Starskin's sales are made on a two-year instalment basis. Indicate how these accounts would be reported in the company's December 31, 2009, balance sheet. The 2009 accounts are collectible in 2011, and the 2008 accounts are collectible in 2010.

(LO 12) **BE6-12** Brew Corporation sold equipment to Mug Limited for $130,000. The equipment was on Brew's books at a net amount of $91,000. Brew collected $70,000 in 2008; $40,000 in 2009; and $20,000 in 2010. If Brew uses the cost recovery method, what amount of gross profit will be recognized in each year?

(LO 13) ***BE6-13** Raclette Inc. charges an initial franchise fee of $160,000 for the right to operate as a franchisee of Raclette. Of this amount, $32,000 is collected immediately. The remainder is collected in four equal annual instalments of $32,000 each. These instalments have a present value of $101,435. There is reasonable expectation that the down payment may be refunded and substantial future services will be performed by Raclette Inc. Prepare Raclette's journal entry to record the franchise fee.

Exercises

(LO 1) **E6-1 (Revenue Recognition—Various Industries)** The following are independent situations that require professional judgement for determining when to recognize revenue from the transactions:

1. Air Canada sells you an advance purchase airline ticket in September for your flight home in December.
2. Leon's Furniture sells you a home theatre on a "no money down, no interest, and no payments for one year" promotional deal.
3. The Toronto Blue Jays sell season tickets on-line to games in the Skydome. Fans can purchase the tickets at any time, although the season does not officially begin until April 1. The season runs from April 1 through October each year.
4. TD Canada Trust lends you money in August. The loan and interest are repayable in full in November.
5. In September, Centennial College collects tuition fees for the term from new and returning students. The term runs from September through December.
6. Sears sells you a sweater. In August, you place the order using Sears' on-line catalogue. The sweater arrives in September and you charge it to your Sears credit card. In October, you receive the Sears credit card statement and pay the amount due.

Instructions

(a) Identify when revenue should be recognized in each of the above situations. Support your choice by referring to the criteria for recognizing revenue.

(b) In the case of the Air Canada ticket, in item 1 above, would your answer to (a) be different if the ticket was non-transferrable and non-refundable and the trip could not be rescheduled?

(LO 1) **E6-2 (Revenue Recognition—Tree Farm)** Santa's Christmas Tree Farm Ltd. grows pine, fir, and spruce trees. The farm cuts and sells trees during the Christmas season and exports most of the trees to the U.S. The remaining trees are sold to local tree lot operators.

It normally takes 12 years for a tree to grow to a suitable size and the average selling price of a tree is $24. The president believes that the company should recognize revenue at the rate of $2 per year for each tree that it cuts. The biggest costs to the business are pest control, fertilizer, and pruning trees over the 12-year period. These costs average $12 per tree. The president believes the costs should be expensed as they are incurred over a 12-year period.

Instructions

(a) Do you agree with the president's proposed revenue recognition policy for Santa's Christmas Tree Farm Ltd.? If you disagree, propose an alternate method that is supported by the revenue recognition criteria.

(b) How should the costs of pest control, fertilizer, and pruning be recognized?

E6-3 (Bill and Hold Transaction) Dave Scotland Inc. (DSI) sold inventory to a new customer, CSI, on December 20, 2007. The sale was made at a significant discount to induce the customer to switch from its regular supplier. CSI asked DSI not to ship the inventory until January 2, 2008, because CSI's warehouse was shutting down for the holidays. DSI agreed and decided to leave the inventory on its warehouse shelves with unsold inventory. It was felt that the shipment would be in the way if it was left on the shipping docks and that the shipping department could easily get the inventory ready for shipment on January 2. **(LO 2)**

Instructions

Discuss whether the transaction should be booked as a sale in the December 31, 2007, financial statements.

E6-4 (Transactions with Customer Acceptance Provisions) Consider the following unrelated situations: **(LO 2)**

1. Book of the Week Limited sends out books to potential customers on a trial basis. If the customers do not like the books, they can return them at no cost.
2. Sea Clothing Company Inc. has a return policy that allows customers to return merchandise in good order for a full refund within 30 days of purchase.
3. Shivani Inc. sells machinery to manufacturers. Customers have the right to inspect the equipment upon delivery and may return it if certain specifications for size and weight are not met.

Instructions

Indicate the point at which these transactions may be recognized as sales. Explain your reasoning.

E6-5 (Consignment Calculations) On May 3, 2007, Branzei Limited consigned 80 freezers, costing $500 each, to Martino Inc. The cost of shipping the freezers was $840 and was paid by Branzei. On December 30, 2007, an account sales report was received from the consignee, reporting that 37 freezers had been sold for $700 each. A remittance was made by the consignee for the amount due, after deducting a commission of 6%, advertising costs of $200, and total installation costs of $320 on the freezers sold. **(LO 3)**

Instructions

(a) Calculate the inventory value of the unsold units that are in the hands of the consignee.

(b) Calculate the consignor's profit on the units sold.

(c) Calculate the amount of cash that will be remitted by the consignee.

E6-6 (Analysis of Percentage-of-Completion Method Financial Statements) In 2008, Gage Construction Corp. began construction work on a three-year, $10-million contract. Gage uses the percentage-of-completion method for financial accounting purposes. The income to be recognized each year is based on the proportion of costs incurred out of the total estimated costs for completing the contract. The financial statement presentations for this contract at December 31, 2008, are as follows: **(LO 5)**

Balance Sheet		
Accounts receivable construction contract billings		$996,500
Construction in progress	$2,015,000	
Less contract billings	1,236,500	
Cost of uncompleted contract in excess of billings		778,500
Income Statement		
Income (before tax) on the contract recognized in 2008		$863,629

Instructions

(a) How much cash was collected in 2008 on this contract?

(b) What was the initial estimated total gross profit before tax on this contract?

(c) What is the relationship between the balances in the Construction in Progress and Contract Billings accounts during the contract? Is one always more than the other? Is there a predictable ratio between the two account balances during the progress of the contract?

(AICPA adapted)

E6-7 (Gross Profit on Uncompleted Contract) On April 1, 2007, Buming Limited entered into a cost-plus-fixed-fee contract to construct an electric generator for Tian Corporation. At the contract date, Buming estimated that it would take two years to complete the project at a cost of $4,500,000. The fixed fee that is stipulated in the contract is $1,050,000. Buming chooses appropriately to account for this contract under the percentage-of-completion method. During 2007, Buming incurred costs of $1,700,000 related to the project. The estimated cost at December 31, 2007, to complete the contract is $3,250,000. Tian was billed $600,000 under the contract. **(LO 5)**

Instructions

Prepare a schedule to calculate the amount of gross profit that Buming should recognize under the contract for the year ended December 31, 2007. Show supporting calculations in good form.

(AICPA adapted)

(LO 5) E6-8 **(Recognition of Profit—Percentage-of-Completion Method)** In 2008, Rendezvous Construction Inc. agreed to construct an apartment building at a price of $12 million. Information on the costs and billings for this contract follows:

	2008	2009	2010
Costs incurred in the period	$3,180,000	$2,100,000	$1,785,000
Estimated costs yet to be incurred	5,300,000	2,700,000	-0-
Customer billings in the period	3,000,000	4,000,000	5,000,000
Collection of billings to date	2,000,000	4,000,000	6,000,000

Instructions

(a) Assuming that the percentage-of-completion method is used, (1) calculate the amount of gross profit to be recognized in 2008 and 2009, and (2) prepare journal entries for 2008 and 2009.

(b) For 2008 and 2009, show how the details related to this construction contract would be disclosed on the balance sheet and on the income statement.

(LO 5, 6) E6-9 **(Recognition of Profit on Long-Term Contracts and Entries)** During 2007, Pierette started a construction job with a contract price of $2.5 million. The job was completed in 2009 and information for the three years of construction is as follows:

	2007	2008	2009
Costs incurred to date	$1,070,000	$1,455,000	$1,785,000
Estimated costs to complete	830,000	275,000	-0-
Billings to date	1,000,000	1,900,000	2,500,000
Collections to date	770,000	1,810,000	2,500,000

Instructions

(a) Calculate the amount of gross profit that should be recognized each year under the percentage-of-completion method.

(b) Prepare all necessary journal entries for 2007, 2008, and 2009, including closing the contract accounts upon completion of the contract, assuming the percentage-of-completion method is used.

(c) Calculate the amount of gross profit that should be recognized each year under the completed-contract method.

(d) Prepare the necessary entry in 2009 to close the contract accounts and to recognize the revenues and costs upon completion, assuming the completed-contract method is used.

(LO 5, 6) E6-10 **(Recognition of Gross Profit on Long-Term Contract with Overall Loss and Entries)** During 2007, Houston Corporation started a construction job with a contract price of $4.2 million. Houston ran into severe technical difficulties during construction but managed to complete the job in 2009. The following information is available:

	2007	2008	2009
Costs incurred to date	$ 600,000	$2,000,000	$4,250,000
Estimated costs to complete	3,150,000	2,000,000	-0-

Instructions

(a) Calculate the amount of gross profit that should be recognized each year under the percentage-of-completion method.

(b) Prepare the journal entries for 2009 to recognize the revenue from the contract and close the contract accounts upon completion, assuming the percentage-of-completion method is used.

(c) Calculate the amount of gross profit or loss that should be recognized each year under the completed-contract method.

(d) Prepare the necessary entry in 2009 to close the contract accounts and to recognize the revenues and costs upon completion, assuming the completed-contract method is used.

E6-11 (Recognition of Revenue on Long-Term Contract and Entries) Van DeHoot Construction Corp. uses the percentage-of-completion method of accounting. In 2008, Van DeHoot began work under contract #E2-D2, which provided for a contract price of $5.2 million. Other details follow: **(LO 5, 6)**

	2008	2009
Costs incurred during the year	$1,680,000	$1,385,000
Estimated costs to complete, as at December 31	1,120,000	–0–
Billings during the year	2,420,000	2,780,000
Collections during the year	2,350,000	2,850,000

Instructions

(a) What portion of the total contract price would be recognized as revenue in 2008? In 2009?

(b) Assuming the same facts as those above except that the company uses the completed-contract method of accounting, what portion of the total contract price would be recognized as revenue in 2009?

(c) Prepare a complete set of journal entries for 2008 and 2009 under the percentage-of-completion method, including the entries for closing the contract.

(d) Prepare a complete set of journal entries for 2008 and 2009 under the completed-contract method.

E6-12 (Recognition of Profit and Balance Sheet Amounts for Long-Term Contracts) Adam Construction Corp. began operations on January 1, 2007. During the year, Adam entered into a contract with Dave Corp. to construct a manufacturing facility. At that time, Adam estimated that it would take five years to complete the facility at a total cost of $6.5 million. The total contract price to construct the facility is $10.3 million. During the year, Adam incurred $3,185,800 in construction costs on the project. The estimated cost to complete the contract is $4,204,200. Adam billed Dave for 30% of the contract price and Dave paid the amount. **(LO 5, 6)**

Instructions

Prepare schedules to calculate the amount of gross profit to be recognized for the year ended December 31, 2007, and the amount to be shown as cost of uncompleted contract in excess of related billings or billings on uncompleted contract in excess of related costs at December 31, 2007, under each of the following methods:

(a) completed-contract method

(b) percentage-of-completion method

Show supporting calculations in good form.

(AICPA adapted)

E6-13 (Long-Term Contract Reporting) Angela Construction Ltd. began operations in 2007. Construction activity for the first year follows. All contracts are with different customers, and any work remaining at December 31, 2007, is expected to be completed in 2008. **(LO 6, 7)**

Project	Total Contract Price	Billings through 12/31/07	Cash Collections through 12/31/07	Contract Costs Incurred through 12/31/07	Estimated Additional Costs to Complete
1	$2,360,000	$1,360,000	$1,040,000	$1,450,000	$1,040,000
2	2,670,000	1,220,000	1,210,000	1,126,000	504,000
3	500,000	500,000	440,000	330,000	–0–
	$5,530,000	$3,080,000	$2,690,000	$2,906,000	$1,544,000

Instructions

Prepare a partial income statement and balance sheet to indicate how the above information would be reported in the financial statement. Angela uses the completed-contract method.

E6-14 (Revenue Recognition on Book Sales with High Returns) Pebbles Publishing Inc. publishes college textbooks that are sold to bookstores on the following terms: Each title has a fixed wholesale price, is shipped f.o.b. shipping point, and payment is due 60 days after shipment. The retailer may return a maximum of 30% of an order at the retailer's expense. Sales are made only to retailers that have good credit ratings. Experience indicates that the normal return rate is 12% and the average collection period is 72 days. **(LO 1, 2, 9)**

Instructions

(a) Identify the different revenue recognition points that Pebbles could use for its textbook sales.

(b) Briefly discuss the reasoning for your answers in (a) above.

(c) In late July, Pebbles shipped books and sent an invoice for $5 million. Prepare the journal entry to record this event based on your previous answers.

(d) In October, $800,000 of the invoiced July sales were returned according to the return policy, and the remaining $4.2 million was paid. Prepare the entry to record the return and payment.

(e) In instances where the normal rate of return can vary from year to year, do you believe that management has an opportunity for smoothing income from year to year? Explain.

(LO 8) **E6-15 (Sales with Discounts)** On June 3, Rancourt Corp. sold $16,500 of merchandise to Kerry Randall, terms 2/10, n/60, f.o.b. shipping point. An invoice totalling $520, terms n/30, was received by Randall on June 8 from Olympic Transport Service for the freight cost. When it received the goods on June 5, Randall notified Rancourt that merchandise costing $4,000 contained flaws that made it worthless. The same day, Rancourt issued a credit memo covering the worthless merchandise and asked that it be returned at the company's expense. The freight on the returned merchandise was $124, and was paid by Rancourt on June 7. On June 12, the company received a cheque for the balance due from Randall.

Instructions

(a) Prepare journal entries on Rancourt's books to record all the events noted above under each of the following bases:
1. Sales and receivables are entered at gross selling price.
2. Sales and receivables are entered net of cash discounts.

(b) Prepare the journal entry under basis 2, assuming that Randall did not remit payment until August 5.

(c) Which method would give Rancourt's general manager better reports and details for managing the business?

(LO 8) **E6-16 (Revenue Recognition on Marina Sales with Discounts)** Wavy Marina has 500 slips that rent for $1,000 per season. Payments must be made in full at the start of the boating season, April 1. Slips may be reserved for the next season if they are paid for by December 31. Under a new policy, if payment is made by December 31, a 5% discount is allowed. The boating season ends October 31, and the marina has a December 31 year end. To provide cash flow for major dock repairs, the marina operator is also offering a 25% discount on the fees for a second season if the second season is also paid for before December 31 of the current year.

For the fiscal year ended December 31, 2008, all 500 slips were rented at full price. Two hundred slips were reserved and paid for in advance of the 2009 boating season, and 160 slips were reserved and paid for in advance of the 2010 boating season.

Instructions

(a) Prepare the appropriate journal entries for fiscal 2008.

(b) If Wavy Marina had not offered a discount of 25% for the 2010 boating season, it would have received the annual fee of $1,000 per slip on April 1, 2010. Calculate the real cost of the discount given by Wavy Marina. Express the cost as an annual percentage so that it can be compared fairly to alternative sources of financing.

(LO 9) **E6-17 (Bundled Sales)** Victor Cheung Inc. (VCI) purchased some telecommunications equipment in January of the current year. The equipment normally sells for $2,300. In order to induce VCI to close the deal, the salesman offered VCI related services that normally sell for $1,000. The services allow VCI to access the Internet for the next year. The equipment and services were bundled together and VCI was charged $2,700 for the whole thing—a great deal. There is a general right of return but VCI has already taken delivery of the equipment and has started using it. All is working well and VCI is very happy with the service.

Instructions

(a) Are the deliverables (the equipment and the related services) considered to be separate units for accounting purposes? Explain.

(b) If yes, allocate the overall price using the following methods:
1. Relative fair value method
2. Residual value method

E6-18 (Instalment Sales Method Calculations and Entries) Harder Corporation uses the instalment sales method of accounting to recognize income in its financial statements. The following information is available for 2008 and 2009: **(LO 11)**

	2008	2009
Instalment sales	$1,900,000	1,000,000
Cost of instalment sales	1,230,000	680,000
Cash collections on 2008 sales	670,000	350,000
Cash collections on 2009 sales	–0–	475,000

Instructions

(a) Calculate the amount of realized gross profit that should be recognized in each year.

(b) Prepare all journal entries required in 2008 and 2009.

E6-19 (Analysis of Instalment Sales Accounts) Humpback Ltd. uses the instalment sales method of accounting. On December 31, 2010, the books show balances as follows: **(LO 11)**

Instalment Receivables		Deferred Gross Profit (Balance Sheet Account)		Gross Profit on Sales	
2008	$101,000	2008	$ 71,000	2008	37%
2009	400,000	2009	260,000	2009	32%
2010	800,000	2010	995,000	2010	31%

Instructions

(a) Prepare the adjusting entry or entries required on December 31, 2010, to recognize the realized gross profit for 2010. (Instalment receivables have already been credited for cash receipts during 2010.)

(b) Calculate the amount of cash collected in 2010 on accounts receivable for each year.

E6-20 (Gross Profit Calculations and Repossessed Merchandise) Minutto Corporation, which began business on January 1, 2007, uses the instalment sales method of accounting. The following data were obtained for the years 2007 and 2008: **(LO 11)**

	2007	2008
Instalment sales	$2,100,000	$1,000,000
Cost of instalment sales	1,575,000	770,000
General and administrative expenses	170,000	84,000
Cash collections on sales of 2007	1,010,000	840,000
Cash collections on sales of 2008	–0–	400,000

Instructions

(a) Calculate the balance in the deferred gross profit balance sheet accounts on December 31, 2007, and December 31, 2008.

(b) A 2007 sale resulted in a default in 2008. At the date of default, the balance on the instalment receivable was $112,000, and the repossessed merchandise had a fair value of $80,000. Prepare the entry to record the repossession.

(AICPA adapted)

E6-21 (Interest Revenue from Instalment Sale) Badali Corporation sells farm machinery on an instalment plan. On July 1, 2007, Badali entered into an instalment sale contract with Kogan Inc. for a 10-year period. Equal annual payments of $200,000 are due under the instalment sale on each July 1. The first payment was made on July 1, 2007. More information follows: **(LO 11)**

1. The amount that would be realized on an outright sale of similar farm machinery is $1,650,000.
2. The cost of the farm machinery sold to Kogan Inc. is $1,050,000.
3. The financing charges for the entire instalment period are $650,000 based on a stated interest rate of 10%, which is appropriate.
4. Collection of the instalments that are due under the contract is reasonably assured.

Instructions

What income or loss before income taxes should Badali record for the year ended December 31, 2007, as a result of the above transaction?

(AICPA adapted)

(LO 11, 12) **E6-22** **(Instalment Method and Cost Recovery)** Cheung Corp., a capital goods manufacturing business that started on January 4, 2008, and operates on a calendar-year basis, uses the instalment method of profit recognition in accounting for all its sales. The following data were taken from the 2008 and 2009 records:

	2008	2009
Instalment sales	$1,480,000	$1,620,000
Gross profit as a percentage of sales	20%	21%
Cash collections on sales of 2008	$ 840,000	$ 240,000
Cash collections on sales of 2009	-0-	$1,080,000

The amounts for cash collections do not include amounts that were collected for interest charges.

Instructions

(a) Calculate the amount of realized gross profit that should be recognized on the 2009 income statement, assuming that it is prepared using the instalment method.

(b) State where the balance of Deferred Gross Profit would be reported on the financial statements for 2009.

(c) Calculate the amount of realized gross profit that should be recognized on the income statement, assuming that it is prepared using the cost recovery method.

(CIA adapted)

(LO 11, 12) **E6-23** **(Instalment Sales Method and Cost Recovery Method)** On January 1, 2008, Tihal Limited sold property for $250,000. The note will be collected as follows: $100,000 in 2008; $110,000 in 2009; and $40,000 in 2010. The property had cost Tihal $175,000 when it was purchased in 2006.

Instructions

(a) Calculate the amount of gross profit that is realized each year, assuming Tihal uses the cost recovery method.

(b) Calculate the amount of gross profit that is realized each year, assuming Tihal uses the instalment sales method.

(LO 11) **E6-24** **(Instalment Sales—Default and Repossession)** Jitsui Imports Inc. was involved in two default and repossession cases during the year:

1. A refrigerator was sold to Conrad White for $1,800, which resulted in a 35% gross margin. White made a down payment of 20% and 4 of the remaining 16 equal payments, and then defaulted on further payments. The refrigerator was repossessed, at which time the fair value was determined to be $800.
2. An oven that cost $1,200 was sold to Delilah Brown for $1,600 on the instalment basis. Brown made a down payment of $240 and paid $80 a month for six months, after which she defaulted. The oven was repossessed and the estimated value at the time of repossession was determined to be $750.

Instructions

Prepare the journal entries to record each of these repossessions. (Ignore interest charges.)

(LO 11) **E6-25** **(Instalment Sales—Default and Repossession)** Ku Inc. uses the instalment sales method in accounting for its instalment sales. On January 1, 2008, Ku had an instalment account receivable from Kristopher King with a balance of $1,800. During 2008, $750 was collected from King. When no further collection could be made, the merchandise sold to King was repossessed. The repossessed merchandise had a fair market value of $650 after the company spent $60 for reconditioning it. The merchandise was originally sold with a gross profit rate of 40%.

Instructions

Prepare the entries on the books of Ku to record all transactions related to King during 2008. (Ignore interest charges.)

(LO 12) **E6-26** **(Cost Recovery Method)** On January 1, 2008, Jacob Limited sold real estate that cost $110,000 to Kimberly Limited for $120,000. Kimberly agreed to pay for the purchase over three years by making three end-of-year equal payments of $52,557 that include 15% interest. Shortly after the sale, Jacob learns distressing news about Kimberly's financial circumstances. Because collection is now very uncertain, Jacob decides to account for the sale using the cost recovery method.

Instructions

Applying the cost recovery method, prepare a schedule that shows the amount of cash collected, the increase (decrease) in deferred interest revenue, the balance of the receivable, the balance of the unrecovered cost, the gross profit realized, and the interest revenue realized for each of the three years, assuming the payments are made as agreed.

E6-27 **(Cost Recovery Method)** On January 1, 2008, Richardson Inc. sells 200 acres of farmland for $600,000, taking in exchange a 10% interest-bearing note. Richardson purchased the farmland in 1987 at a cost of $100,000. The note will be paid in three instalments of $241,269 each on December 31, 2008, 2009, and 2010. Collectibility of the note is uncertain; Richardson therefore uses the cost recovery method. **(LO 12)**

Instructions

Prepare a three-year instalment payment schedule for Richardson (under the cost recovery method) that shows cash collections, deferred interest revenue, instalment receivable balances, unrecovered cost, realized gross profit, and realized interest revenue for each year.

***E6-28** **(Franchise Entries)** Sage Inc. charges an initial franchise fee of $170,000. Upon signing the agreement, a payment of $50,000 is due; thereafter, three annual payments of blended principal and interest of $40,000 are required. The franchisee's credit rating would result in paying 10% interest to borrow money. **(LO 13)**

Instructions

Prepare the entries to record the initial franchise fee on the franchisor's books under the following assumptions:

(a) The down payment is not refundable, no future services are required of the franchisor, and collection of the note is reasonably assured.

(b) The franchisor has substantial services to perform, the down payment is refundable, and collection of the note is very uncertain.

(c) The down payment is not refundable, collection of the note is reasonably certain, the franchisor still needs to perform a substantial amount of services, and the down payment is a fair measure of the services already performed.

***E6-29** **(Franchise Fee, Initial Down Payment)** On January 1, 2008, Susan Sali signed an agreement to operate as a franchisee of Short-Track Inc. for an initial franchise fee of $174,000. The amount of $30,000 was paid when the agreement was signed, and the balance is payable in six annual payments of $24,000 each, beginning January 1, 2009. Under the agreement, the down payment is not refundable and no future services are required of the franchisor. Sali's credit rating indicates that she can borrow money at 11% for a loan of this type. **(LO 13)**

Instructions

(a) How much should Short-Track record as revenue from franchise fees on January 1, 2008? At what amount should Sali record the franchise acquisition cost on January 1, 2008?

(b) What entry would be made by Short-Track on January 1, 2008, if the down payment is refundable and substantial future services still have to be performed by Short-Track?

(c) How much revenue from franchise fees would Short-Track record on January 1, 2008, under each of the following independent situations?

1. The initial down payment is not refundable, it is a fair measure of the services already provided, a significant amount of services is still to be performed by Short-Track in future periods, and collectibility of the note is reasonably assured.
2. The initial down payment is not refundable and no future services are required of the franchisor, but collection of the note is so uncertain that recognition of the note as an asset is not justified.
3. The initial down payment has not been earned and collection of the note is so uncertain that recognition of the note as an asset is not justified.

Problems

P6-1 Dunbar Construction Ltd. has entered into a contract beginning January 1, 2008, to build a parking complex. It has estimated that the complex will cost $6 million and will take three years to construct.

The complex will be billed to the purchasing company at $9 million. The following data are for the construction period:

	2008	2009	2010
Costs to date	$2,770,000	$5,320,000	$7,300,000
Estimated costs to complete	4,155,000	2,120,560	–0–
Progress billings to date	2,000,000	6,300,000	9,000,000
Cash collected to date	1,040,000	5,000,000	9,000,000

Instructions

(a) Using the percentage-of-completion method, calculate the estimated gross profit that would be recognized during each year of the construction period.

(b) Prepare all necessary journal entries for 2008, 2009, and 2010, including the entries for closing the contract accounts upon completion, assuming the percentage-of-completion method is used.

(c) Prepare a partial comparative income statement for the fiscal years ending December 31, 2008 and 2009.

(d) Prepare a balance sheet at December 31, 2008 and 2009, that shows the accounts related to the contract and includes their classifications assuming the percentage-of-completion method is used.

(e) Calculate the estimated gross profit that would be recognized during each year of the construction period if the completed-contract method is used. Prepare a partial income statement for the fiscal year ending December 31, 2010.

(f) Prepare the necessary entry in 2010 to close the contract accounts and to recognize the revenues and costs upon completion, assuming the completed-contract method is used.

(g) Prepare a balance sheet at December 31, 2008 and 2009, that shows the accounts related to the contract and includes their classifications assuming the completed-contract method is used.

P6-2 On March 1, 2007, Stevens Inc. entered into a contract to build an apartment building. It estimates that the building will cost $92 million and will take three years to complete. The contract price was $123 million. The following information is for the construction period:

	2007	2008	2009
Costs to date	$46,500,000	$68,600,000	$ 92,100,000
Estimated costs to complete	61,640,000	29,400,000	–0–
Progress billings to date	31,050,000	80,100,000	123,000,000
Cash collected to date	29,950,000	77,950,000	123,000,000

Instructions

(a) Calculate the amount of gross profit to be recognized each year under the percentage-of-completion method.

(b) Prepare all necessary journal entries for 2009, including the entries for closing the contract accounts upon completion.

(c) Prepare a partial balance sheet for December 31, 2008, showing the balances in the receivables and inventory accounts.

P6-3 Grant Construction Ltd. has entered into a contract beginning January 1, 2008, to build a bridge in Temiskaming Shores. It estimates that the bridge will cost $4.8 million and will take three years to construct.

The bridge will be billed to the municipality at $5.5 million. The following data are for the construction period:

	2008	2009	2010
Costs to date	$1,500,000	$5,020,000	$5,700,000
Estimated costs to complete	3,500,000	704,000	–0–
Progress billings to date	1,600,000	5,000,000	5,500,000
Cash collected to date	1,300,000	4,800,000	5,500,000

Instructions

(a) Using the percentage-of-completion method, calculate the estimated gross profit or loss that would be recognized during each year of the construction period.

(b) Prepare all necessary journal entries for 2008, 2009, and 2010, including the entries for closing the contract accounts upon completion, assuming the percentage-of-completion method is used.

(c) Prepare a partial comparative income statement for the fiscal years ending December 31, 2008 and 2009.

(d) Prepare a balance sheet at December 31, 2008 and 2009, that shows the accounts related to the contract and includes their classifications assuming the percentage-of-completion method is used.

(e) Calculate the estimated gross profit or loss that would be recognized during each year of the construction period under the completed-contract method. Prepare any necessary entries to accrue contract losses (note the year would be made) for the year ending December 31, 2008. Prepare partial income statements for the fiscal years ending December 31, 2010.

(f) Prepare the necessary entry in 2010 to close the contract accounts and to recognize the revenues and costs upon completion, assuming the completed-contract method is used.

(g) Prepare a balance sheet at December 31, 2008 and 2009, that shows the accounts related to the contract and includes their classifications assuming the completed-contract method is used.

P6-4 On February 1, 2008, Romance Inc. obtained a contract to build an athletic stadium. The stadium was to be built at a total cost of $15.4 million and was scheduled for completion by September 1, 2010. One clause of the contract stated that Romance was to deduct $105,000 from the $15.4-million billing price for each week that completion was delayed. Completion was delayed six weeks, which resulted in a $630,000 penalty. Data for the construction period are as follows:

	2008	2009	2010
Costs to date	$3,782,000	$ 8,850,000	$10,500,000
Estimated costs to complete	7,618,000	1,450,000	-0-
Progress billings to date	5,200,000	10,100,000	14,770,000
Cash collected to date	4,000,000	9,800,000	14,770,000

Instructions

(a) Using the percentage-of-completion method, calculate the estimated gross profit recognized in the years 2008 to 2010.

(b) Prepare a partial balance sheet for December 31, 2009, showing the balances in the receivable and inventory accounts.

(c) Is it better for a business to have progress billings in excess of the Construction in Process balance, or vice versa? How can the contractor manage the contract to get the preferred balance?

P6-5 Zheng Inc. was established in 1972 by Tian Zheng and initially operated under contracts to build customized homes of very high quality for specific buyers. In the 1980s, Zheng's two sons joined the firm and expanded the company's activities into the high-rise apartment and industrial plant markets. When the company's long-time financial manager retired, Zheng's sons hired Lance Ling as controller. Ling, a former university friend of Zheng's sons, had been working for a public accounting firm for the last six years.

When he reviewed the company's accounting practices, Ling noticed that the company followed the completed-contract method of revenue recognition, as it always had since the years when individual home building was the company's main focus. Several years ago, most of the company's activities had shifted to the high-rise and industrial building areas. From land acquisition to the completion of construction, most building contracts now cover several years. Under the circumstances, Ling believes that the company should follow the percentage-of-completion method of accounting. From a typical building contract, Ling developed the following data:

ZHENG INC.

Contract price: $10,000,000

	2007	2008	2009
Estimated costs	$2,010,000	$4,015,000	$1,675,000
Progress billings	2,000,000	2,500,000	5,500,000
Cash collections	1,800,000	2,300,000	5,900,000

Instructions

(a) Explain the difference between completed-contract revenue recognition and percentage-of-completion revenue recognition.

(b) Using the data provided for the Zheng Inc. and assuming the percentage-of-completion method of revenue recognition is used, calculate the company's revenue and gross profit for 2007, 2008, and 2009, under each of the following circumstances:

1. Assume that all costs are incurred, all billings to customers are made, and all collections from customers are received within 30 days of billing, as planned.
2. Further assume that, as a result of unforeseen local ordinances and the fact that the building site was in a wetlands area, the company had cost overruns of $1.2 million in 2007 to pay for changes to the site so that it would comply with the ordinances and overcome wetlands barriers to construction.
3. Further assume that, in addition to the cost overruns of $1.2 million for this contract, inflationary factors were greater than what was anticipated when the original contract cost was set and have caused an additional cost overrun of $1,240,000 in 2008. No cost overruns are expected to occur in 2009.

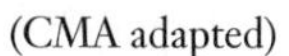

(CMA adapted)

P6-6 On March 1, 2008, Whellan Limited signed a contract to construct a factory building for Vottero Manufacturing Inc. for a total contract price of $9.4 million. The building was completed by October 31, 2010. The annual contract costs that were incurred, the estimated costs to complete the contract, and the accumulated billings to Vottero for 2008, 2009, and 2010 were as follows:

	2008	2009	2010
Contract costs incurred during the year	$1,600,000	$5,000,000	$2,200,000
Estimated costs to complete the contract at Dec. 31	4,800,000	2,084,000	–0–
Billings to Vottero during the year	2,000,000	5,100,000	2,300,000
Cash collections from Vottero during the year	1,950,000	4,900,000	2,550,000

Instructions

(a) Using the percentage-of-completion method, prepare schedules to calculate the profit or loss that should be recognized from this contract for the years ended December 31, 2008, 2009, and 2010.

(b) Using the completed-contract method, prepare schedules to calculate the profit or loss that should be recognized from this contract for the years ended December 2008, 2009, and 2010.

(c) Prepare all necessary journal entries for 2008, 2009, and 2010, including the entries to close the contract accounts upon completion, assuming the completed-contract method is used.

P6-7 On July 1, 2008, Wang Construction Company Inc. contracted to build an office building for Zhou Corp. for a total contract price of $1,850,000. On July 1, Wang estimated that it would take two or three years to complete the building. On December 31, 2010, the building was deemed substantially completed. The following data are for accumulated contract costs incurred, estimated costs to complete the contract, and accumulated billings to Zhou for 2008, 2009, and 2010:

	12/31/08	12/31/09	12/31/10
Contract costs incurred to date	$ 450,000	$1,200,000	$1,900,000
Estimated costs to complete the contract	1,350,000	800,000	–0–
Billings to Zhou during the year	300,000	1,100,000	450,000
Cash collections during the year	200,000	1,000,000	650,000

Instructions

(a) Using the percentage-of-completion method, prepare schedules to calculate the profit or loss that should be recognized from this contract for the years ended December 31, 2008, 2009, and 2010.

(b) Prepare all necessary journal entries for 2008, 2009, and 2010, including the entries to close the contract accounts upon completion, assuming the percentage-of-completion method is used.

(c) Using the completed-contract method, prepare schedules to calculate the profit or loss to be recognized from this contract for the years ended December 2008, 2009, and 2010.

(d) Prepare any necessary entry to accrue contract losses for the year ending December 31, 2009.

P6-8 Miron Construction Ltd. has entered into a contract beginning in February 2008 to build two warehouses in Timmins for Atlas Mines Ltd. The contract has a fixed price of $19 million. The following data are for the construction period:

	2008	2009	2010
Costs for the year	$8,100,000	$ 8,900,000	$ 2,600,000
Estimated costs to complete	9,900,000	2,540,000	–0–
Progress billings to date	7,000,000	15,200,000	19,000,000
Cash collected to date	6,200,000	14,500,000	18,700,000

Instructions

(a) Using the percentage-of-completion method, calculate the estimated gross profit that should be recognized during each year of the construction period.

(b) Prepare all necessary journal entries for 2008, 2009, and 2010, including the entries to close the contract accounts upon completion, assuming the percentage-of-completion method is used.

(c) Prepare a partial comparative income statement for the fiscal years ending December 31, 2008 and 2009, assuming the percentage-of-completion method is used.

(d) Prepare a balance sheet at December 31, 2008 and 2009, that shows the accounts related to the contract and includes their classifications, assuming the percentage-of-completion method is used.

(e) Calculate the estimated gross profit or loss that should be recognized during each year of the construction period, assuming the completed-contract method is used. Prepare any necessary entries to accrue contract losses (note the year the entry would be made). Prepare a partial income statement for the fiscal year ending December 31, 2010.

(f) Prepare the necessary entry in 2010 to close the contract accounts and to recognize the revenues and costs upon completion, assuming the completed-contract method is used.

(g) Prepare a balance sheet at December 31, 2008 and 2009, that shows the accounts related to the contract and includes their classifications, assuming the completed-contract method is used.

P6-9 You have been engaged by Shen Corp. to advise it on the proper accounting for a series of long-term contracts. Shen began doing business on January 1, 2007, and its construction activities for the first year of operations are shown below. All contract costs are with different customers, and any work that remains to be done at December 31, 2007, is expected to be completed in 2008.

Project	Total Contract Price	Billings through 12/31/07	Cash Collections through 12/31/07	Contract Costs Incurred through 12/31/07	Estimated Additional Costs to Complete
A	$ 300,000	$200,000	$180,000	$248,000	$ 67,000
B	350,000	110,000	105,000	67,800	271,200
C	280,000	280,000	255,000	186,000	-0-
D	200,000	35,000	25,000	123,000	87,000
E	240,000	205,000	200,000	185,000	15,000
	$1,370,000	$830,000	$765,000	$809,800	$440,200

Instructions

(a) Using the percentage-of-completion method, prepare a schedule to calculate gross profit or loss to be reported, unbilled contract costs and recognized profit, and billings in excess of costs and recognized profit.

(b) Prepare a partial income statement and balance sheet to show how the information would be reported for financial statement purposes.

(c) Repeat the requirements for part (a), assuming Shen uses the completed-contract method.

(d) Using information from your answers to the previous questions, prepare a brief report that compares the conceptual merits (both positive and negative) of the two revenue recognition approaches.

P6-10 Mahaher Inc. entered into a firm fixed-price contract with Nobes Clinic on July 1, 2005, to construct a four-storey office building. At that time, Mahaher estimated that it would take between two and three years to complete the project. The total contract price is $5.5 million. Mahaher chooses appropriately to account for this contract under the completed-contract method in its financial statements and for income tax reporting. The building was deemed substantially completed on December 31, 2007.

The estimated percentage of completion, accumulated contract costs incurred, estimated costs to complete the contract, and accumulated billings to the clinic under the contract were as follows for the years 2005, 2006, and 2007:

	December 31, 2005	December 31, 2006	December 31, 2007
Percentage of completion	30%	71.1%	100%
Contract costs incurred to date	$1,140,000	$4,055,000	$5,800,000
Estimated costs to complete the contract	$2,660,000	$1,645,000	-0-
Billings to Nobes Clinic	$1,500,000	$2,500,000	$5,500,000

Instructions

(a) Prepare schedules to calculate the amount to be shown as "cost of uncompleted contract in excess of related billings" or "billings on uncompleted contract in excess of related costs" at December 31, 2005, 2006, and 2007. Ignore income taxes. Show supporting calculations in good form.

(b) Prepare schedules to calculate the profit or loss that should be recognized from this contract for the years ended December 31, 2005, 2006, and 2007. Ignore income taxes. Show supporting calculations in good form.

(c) Assume a construction company had all of the information that it required to use the percentage-of-completion method for construction contracts. Why would this company want to account for contracts using the completed-contract method?

(AICPA adapted)

P6-11 The following is summarized information for Deng Corp., which sells merchandise on an instalment basis:

	2007	2008	2009
Sales (on instalment plan)	$360,000	$360,000	$300,000
Cost of sales	255,000	263,800	192,000
Gross Profit	$105,000	$ 96,200	$108,000
Collections from customers on:			
2007 instalment sales	$175,000	$100,000	$ 85,000
2008 instalment sales		200,000	120,000
2009 instalment sales			110,000

Instructions

(a) Calculate the realized gross profit for each of the years 2007, 2008, and 2009.

(b) Prepare all journal entries that are required in 2009 under the instalment sales method of accounting. (Ignore interest charges.)

P6-12 Spearing Inc. sells merchandise on open account and on instalment terms. Data follow for its first year of operations, 2008, and for the years 2009, and 2010:

	2008	2009	2010
Sales on account	$770,000	$426,000	$625,000
Instalment sales	640,000	275,000	480,000
Collections on instalment sales			
Made in 2008	220,000	90,000	80,000
Made in 2009		110,000	140,000
Made in 2010			125,000
Cost of sales			
Sold on account	540,000	277,000	441,000
Sold on instalment	428,800	167,750	224,200
Selling expenses	154,000	87,000	102,000
Administrative expenses	100,000	51,000	52,000

Instructions

From the data above, determine the net income for each year under the instalment sales method of accounting. (Ignore interest charges.)

P6-13 Shao Limited sells appliances for cash and on an instalment plan and makes entries to record its cost of sales every month. Its trial balance at December 31, 2008 follows:

SHAO LIMITED
Trial Balance
December 31, 2008

	Dr.	Cr.
Cash	$153,000	
Instalment Accounts Receivable, 2007	48,000	
Instalment Accounts Receivable, 2008	91,000	
Inventory—New Merchandise	123,200	
Inventory—Repossessed Merchandise	24,000	
Accounts Payable		$ 98,500
Deferred Gross Profit, 2007		45,600
Capital Shares		170,000
Retained Earnings		93,900
Sales		343,000
Instalment Sales		200,000

Cost of Sales	255,000	
Cost of Instalment Sales	128,000	
Gain or Loss on Repossessions	800	
Selling and Administrative Expenses	128,000	
	$951,000	$951,000

The accounting department has prepared the following analysis of cash receipts for the year:

Cash sales (including repossessed merchandise)	$424,000
Instalment accounts receivable, 2007	104,000
Instalment accounts receivable, 2008	109,000
Other	36,000
Total	$673,000

Repossessions recorded during the year are summarized as follows:

	2007
Uncollected balance	$8,000
Loss on repossession	800
Repossessed merchandise	4,800

Instructions
Based on the trial balance and accompanying information, complete the following:

(a) Calculate the rate of gross profit for 2007 and 2008.

(b) Prepare journal entries as of December 31, 2008, to record any deferred and/or realized profits under the instalment sales method of accounting.

(c) Prepare a statement of income for the year ended December 31, 2008, after taking into account the journal entries from (b).

P6-14 The following summarized information is for the instalment sales activity of Greenwood Inc. for the year 2007:

Instalment sales during 2007	$700,000
Costs of goods sold on instalment basis	462,000
Collections from customers	280,000
Unpaid balances on merchandise repossessed	24,000
Estimated value of merchandise repossessed	9,200

Instructions

(a) Prepare the journal entries at the end of 2007 to record the above data.

(b) Prepare the entry to record the gross profit realized during 2007.

P6-15 Racine Inc. sells merchandise for cash and on an instalment plan. Entries to record cost of goods sold are made at the end of each year.

In 2008, repossessions of merchandise that was sold in 2007 were recorded correctly and can be summarized by the following journal entry:

Deferred Gross Profit, 2007	7,200	
Repossessed Merchandise	8,000	
Loss on Repossessions	2,800	
Instalment Accounts Receivable, 2007		18,000

Some of the repossessed merchandise was sold for cash in 2008, and the sale was recorded by a debit to Cash and a credit to Sales.

The inventory amount for repossessed merchandise on hand at December 31, 2008, is $4,000; for new merchandise, $127,400. There was no repossessed merchandise on hand at January 1, 2008.

Collections on accounts receivable during 2008 were as follows:

Instalment Accounts Receivable, 2007	$80,000
Instalment Accounts Receivable, 2008	50,000

The cost of the merchandise sold under the instalment plan during 2008 was $117,000.

The rate of gross profit on 2007 and 2008 instalment sales can be calculated from the information given above. Racine's trial balance at December 31, 2008, follows:

RACINE INC.
Trial Balance
December 31, 2008

	Dr.	Cr.
Cash	$ 98,400	
Instalment Accounts Receivable, 2007	80,000	
Instalment Accounts Receivable, 2008	130,000	
Inventory, Jan. 1, 2008	120,000	
Repossessed Merchandise	8,000	
Accounts Payable		$ 47,200
Deferred Gross Profit, 2007		64,000
Common Shares		200,000
Retained Earnings		40,000
Sales		400,000
Instalment Sales		180,000
Purchases	380,000	
Loss on Repossessions	2,800	
Operating Expenses	112,000	
	$931,200	$931,200

Instructions

(a) From the trial balance and other information given above, prepare adjusting and closing entries as at December 31, 2008.

(b) Prepare an income statement for the year ended December 31, 2008.

P6-16 Selected transactions of Liping Limited follow:

1. A television set costing $560 is sold to Wycliffe on November 1, 2007, for $800. Wycliffe makes a down payment of $200 and agrees to pay $30 on the first of each month for 20 months thereafter.
2. Wycliffe pays the $30 instalment due on December 1, 2007.
3. On December 31, 2007, the appropriate entries are made to record profit realized on the instalment sales.
4. The first seven instalments in 2008 of $30 each are paid by Wycliffe. (Make one entry.)
5. In August 2008, the set is repossessed after Wycliffe fails to pay the August 1 instalment and indicates that he will be unable to continue the payments. The estimated fair value of the repossessed set is $100.

Instructions

Prepare journal entries to record the transactions above for Liping. Closing entries should not be made.

P6-17 On January 2, 2007, Truong Inc. entered into a contract with a manufacturing company to purchase room-size air conditioners. Truong then sold the units at retail on an instalment plan with collections over approximately 30 months and no carrying charges.

For income tax purposes, Truong decided to report income from its sales of air conditioners according to the instalment sales method.

Purchases and sales of new units were as follows:

	Units Purchased		Units Sold	
Year	Quantity	Price Each	Quantity	Price Each
2007	1,400	$130	1,100	$200
2008	1,200	112	1,500	170
2009	900	136	800	182

Collections on instalment sales were as follows:

	Collections Received		
	2007	2008	2009
2007 sales	$42,000	$88,000	$ 80,000
2008 sales		51,000	100,000
2009 sales			34,600

In 2009, 50 units from the 2008 sales were repossessed and sold for $80 each on the instalment plan. At the time of repossession, $1,440 had been collected from the original purchasers and the units had a fair value of $3,000 altogether.

General and administrative expenses for 2009 were $60,000. No charge has been made against current income for the applicable insurance expense from a three-year policy expiring June 30, 2010, costing $7,200, and for an advance payment of $12,000 on a new contract to purchase air conditioners beginning January 2, 2010.

Instructions

Assuming that the weighted-average method is used for determining the inventory cost, including the cost of repossessed merchandise, prepare schedules to calculate the following for 2007, 2008, and 2009:

(a) **1.** The cost of goods sold on instalments

2. The average unit cost of goods sold on instalment for each year

(b) The gross profit percentages for 2007, 2008, and 2009

(c) The gain or loss on repossessions in 2009

(d) The net income from instalment sales for 2009 (ignore income taxes)

(AICPA adapted)

Writing Assignments

WA6-1 Revenue is usually recognized at the point of delivery. Under special circumstances, however, there are also other bases that can be used for the timing of revenue recognition.

Instructions

(a) Why is the point of delivery usually used as the basis for the timing of revenue recognition?

(b) Discuss the validity of each of the following critiques of using the point of delivery for revenue recognition. (Disregard the special circumstances that allow other bases to be used instead of the point of delivery.)

1. It is too conservative because revenue is earned throughout the entire process of production.

2. It is not conservative enough because accounts receivable do not represent disposable funds, sales returns and allowances may be made, and collection and bad debt expenses may be incurred in a later period.

(c) Revenue may also be recognized (1) during production and (2) when cash is received. For each of these two bases of timing revenue recognition, give an example of the circumstances in which it is properly used and discuss the accounting merits of using this basis instead of the sales basis.

(AICPA adapted)

WA6-2 Currently, revenue is recognized as it is earned. A company must have performed its duties under the contract by either providing services or delivering goods or both. This is a transactions-based view of revenue recognition that focuses on the income statement. Alternatively, one might argue that revenues are to be recognized when assets are created or liabilities discharged. Discuss the theoretical validity of this balance sheet view of revenue recognition.

Instructions

(Hint: look at the work being done by the IASB and FASB)

Discuss.

Cases

Student Website

www.wiley.com/canada/kieso

Refer to the Case Primer on the Student Website to help you answer these cases.

CA6-1 Alexi Industries has three operating divisions: Figaro Mining, Manuel Paperbacks, and Oslo Protection Devices. Each division maintains its own accounting system and method of revenue recognition. During the year, Alexi was running short of cash due to a major expansion in Figaro Mining. Problems in the mining industry were also contributing to cash flow difficulties. Due to the buoyancy of the equity markets (markets had reached a 10-year high), prices of commodities such as gold, silver, and platinum were down. As a result, the company had approached the bank for a line of credit. Before making any adjustments, the company's draft financial statements are showing a break-even net income. The following information is available for each of the three operating divisions:

Figaro Mining
Figaro Mining specializes in the extraction of precious metals such as silver, gold, and platinum. During the fiscal year ended November 30, 2008, Figaro entered into contracts worth \$2.25 million and shipped metals worth \$2 million. A quarter of the shipments were made from inventories on hand at the beginning of the fiscal year, and the remainder were made from metals that were mined during the year. Mining production totals for the year, valued at market prices, were as follows: silver \$750,000; gold \$1.3 million; and platinum \$490,000. Figaro uses the completion-of-production method to recognize revenue.

Manuel Paperbacks
Manuel Paperbacks sells large quantities of novels to a few book distributors that in turn sell to several national chains of bookstores. Manuel allows distributors to return up to 30% of sales, and distributors give the same terms to bookstores. While returns from individual titles fluctuate greatly, the returns from distributors have averaged 20% in each of the past five years. A total of \$8 million of paperback novel sales were made to distributors during the fiscal year. On November 30, 2008, \$3.2 million of fiscal 2008 sales were still subject to return privileges over the next six months. The remaining \$4.8 million of fiscal 2008 sales had actual returns of 21%. Sales from fiscal 2008 totalling \$2.5 million were collected in fiscal 2008, with less than 18% of sales returned. Manuel records revenue at the point of sale.

Oslo Protection Devices
Oslo Protection Devices works through manufacturers' agents in various cities. Orders and down payments for alarm systems are forwarded from agents, and Oslo ships the goods f.o.b. shipping point. Customers are billed for the balance due plus actual shipping costs. The firm received orders for \$6 million of goods during the fiscal year ended November 30, 2008. Down payments of \$600,000 were received, and \$5 million of goods were billed and shipped. Actual freight costs of \$100,000 were also billed. Commissions at 10% of the product price were paid to manufacturers' agents after the goods were shipped to customers. Such goods are warranted for 90 days after shipment, and warranty returns have been about 1% of sales. Oslo also installs many of the systems as well as systems for other manufacturers. The installation is approximately 20% of the value of the sale. Oslo recognizes revenue at the point of sale.

Instructions
Assume the role of the assistant controller and prepare a report to the controller in which you discuss any financial reporting issues related to the three divisions. The controller needs this information before his upcoming meeting with the bank. He does not want any unpleasant surprises in the meeting.

CA6-2 Points International Ltd. ("Points") was formed on January 6, 1999, and currently trades on the TSX Venture Exchange. Sales in 2002 were \$2.4 million, with the Toronto-based company experiencing revenue growth of 240% compared to the prior year. Points is an on-line exchange that allows customers to combine, exchange, and purchase points or miles from various loyalty programs such as Aeroplan, American Airlines, eBay, and Priority Club. In its annual report, the company commented on the growth potential in the industry. It noted that, according to *The Economist*, global frequent flyer points are now worth approximately U.S. \$500 billion (with about 8.5 trillion unredeemed miles) and that frequent flyer points are arguably the second largest currency, after the U.S. dollar.

The company partners with several major airlines, such as Air Canada and American Airlines, and its business can therefore be affected by fluctuations in the airline industry. Points has responded to this risk by making it easier to exchange airline points for retail points and by consolidating points from various different programs.

The following excerpts from the company's Annual Information Form (filed with the securities commission) and Annual Report give details on the earnings process and related revenue recognition policy.

According to the company's Annual Information Form:

Revenue from the online exchange:

Commission fee revenue: Points retains a commission on all exchanges, based on a value of the loyalty currency tendered for exchange by the loyalty program member. Through the exchange model, the participating loyalty program sets a value on the currency tendered for "sale". Based on this valuation, a percentage is remitted to Points, and the remaining balance is used to purchase a currency of another participating loyalty program. The Corporation filed a U.S. Patent Application covering this exchange process.

Consumer exchange fees: The payment by a customer of an annual fee allows unlimited *pointsxchange* transactions. Alternately, customers can pay a service fee for a single exchange.

According to note 2 of the 2002 Annual Financial Statements:

Revenue recognition

Revenues from transaction processing are recognized as the services are provided under the terms of related contracts. Membership fees received in advance for services to be provided over a future period are recorded as deferred revenue and recognized as revenue evenly over the term of service. Related direct costs are also recognized over the term of the membership.

Revenues from the sales of loyalty program points are recorded net of costs, in accordance with Abstract 123 of the Emerging Issues Committee ("EIC") of the Canadian Institute of Chartered Accountants ("C.I.C.A."), "Reporting Revenue Gross as a Principal Versus Net as an Agent", when the collection of the sales proceeds is reasonably assured and other material conditions of the exchange are met. Gross proceeds received on the resale of loyalty program points, net of the commissions earned, are included in deposits in the attached consolidated balance sheet until remitted.

Nonrefundable partner sign-up fees with no fixed term, and for which the company is under no further obligations, are recognized as revenue when received.

Custom web site design revenues are recorded on the percentage-of-completion basis.

Although the company's revenues increased substantially in 2002, the company suffered a loss of over three times its revenues. This loss was $3.3 million less than the loss from 2001.

Instructions

Assume the role of a financial analyst and do a critical analysis of the revenue recognition policies. You are trying to establish whether you should issue a buy or sell order on these shares.

CA6-3 *Cutting Edge* is a monthly magazine that has been on the market for 18 months. It has a circulation of 1.4 million copies. Negotiations are underway to obtain a bank loan in order to update its facilities. It is producing close to capacity and expects to grow at an average of 20% per year over the next three years.

After reviewing the financial statements of Cutting Edge, Gary Hall, the bank loan officer, said that a loan could only be offered to Cutting Edge if it could increase its current ratio and decrease its debt-to-equity ratio to a specified level. Alexander Popov, the marketing manager of Cutting Edge, has devised a plan to meet these requirements. Popov indicates that an advertising campaign can be used to immediately increase circulation. The potential customers would be contacted after purchasing another magazine's mailing list. The campaign would include:

1. An offer to subscribe to *Cutting Edge* at three-quarters the normal price
2. A special offer to all new subscribers to receive the most current world atlas whenever requested at a guaranteed price of $2.00
3. An unconditional guarantee of a full refund for any subscriber who is dissatisfied with the magazine

Although the offer of a full refund is risky, Popov claims that few people will ask for a refund after receiving half of their subscription issues. Popov notes that other magazine companies have tried this sales promotion technique and experienced great success. Their average cancellation rate was 25%. On average, each company increased its initial circulation threefold and in the long run had increased circulation to twice the level that it was before the promotion. In addition, 60% of the new subscribers are expected to take advantage of the atlas premium. Popov feels confident that the increased subscriptions from the advertising campaign will increase the current ratio and decrease the debt-to-equity ratio.

In addition to the above, Popov has just signed a large deal with a newly opened store to take delivery of the current edition of the magazine. The new customer has asked that the magazines be held by *Cutting Edge* for a couple of weeks to a month.

Instructions

Assume the role of the controller and discuss the financial reporting issues.

CA6-4 Pankratov Lakes is a new real estate development that consists of 500 recreational lakefront and lake-view lots. As a special incentive to the first 100 buyers of lake-view lots, the developer is offering three years of free financing on 10-year, 12% notes, no down payment, and one week at a nearby established resort (a $1,200 value). The normal price per lot is $12,000. The cost to the developer for each lake-view lot is an estimated average of $2,000. The development costs continue to be incurred and the actual average cost per lot is not known at this time. The resort promotion cost is $700 per lot. Customers must have their lot inspected before taking legal title to it. Customers who do not like the developed property after its inspection may cancel the deal.

Instructions

Discuss the issues.

CA6-5 Nimble Health and Racquet Club (NHRC) operates eight clubs in the metropolitan area of a large city and offers one-year memberships. The members may use any of the eight facilities but must reserve racquetball court time and pay a separate fee before using the court. As an incentive to new customers, NHRC advertised that any customers who are not satisfied for any reason can receive a refund of the remaining portion of their unused membership fees. Membership fees are due at the beginning of the individual membership period; however, customers are given the option of financing the membership fee over the membership period at a 15% interest rate.

In the past, some customers had said they would like to take only the regularly scheduled aerobic classes and not pay for a full membership. During the current fiscal year, NHRC began selling coupon books for aerobic classes only to accommodate these customers. Each book is dated and contains 50 coupons that may be redeemed for any regularly scheduled aerobic class over a one-year period. After the one-year period, unused coupons are no longer valid.

During 2004, NHRC expanded into the health equipment market by purchasing a local company that manufactures rowing machines and cross-country ski machines. These machines are used in NHRC's facilities and are sold through the clubs and mail-order catalogues. Customers must make a 20% down payment when placing an equipment order; delivery is in 60 to 90 days after an order is placed. The machines are sold with a two-year unconditional guarantee. Based on experience, NHRC expects the costs to repair machines under guarantee to be 4% of sales.

NHRC is in the process of preparing financial statements as at May 31, 2009, the end of its fiscal year. James Hogan, corporate controller, expressed concern over the company's performance for the year and decided to review the preliminary financial statements prepared by Barbara Hardy, NHRC's assistant controller. After reviewing the statements, Hogan proposed that the following changes be reflected in the May 31, 2009, published financial statements:

1. Membership revenue should be recognized when the membership fee is collected.
2. Revenue from the coupon books should be recognized when the books are sold.
3. Down payments on equipment purchases and expenses associated with the guarantee on the rowing and cross-country machines should be recognized when they are paid.

Hardy indicated to Hogan that the proposed changes are not in accordance with generally accepted accounting principles, but Hogan insisted that the changes be made. Hardy believes that Hogan wants to manipulate income to delay any potential financial problems and increase his year-end bonus. At this point, Hardy is unsure what action to take.

Instructions

Discuss the financial reporting issues.

(CMA adapted)

CA6-6 The following is an excerpt from the financial statements of Saskatchewan Wheat Pool. Among other things, the pool buys grain from farmers and sells it to the Canadian Wheat Board.

Notes to the Consolidated Financial Statements July 31, 2002, in thousands

Revenue Recognition

Generally, sales are recognized upon shipment of products and other operating revenues are recognized when services are performed. A large portion of the company's Grain Handling and Marketing segment revenue is derived from Canadian Wheat Board ("Board") grains. The company assumes the risk of physical loss, while promoting the value of grain deliveries through blending and cleaning. Consequently, the value of Board grains handled is recorded as a sale, and the sale is recognized when it is delivered to the Board, typically at a port terminal. Other grain handling revenues are recognized when functions are performed in accordance with the company's contract with the Board. In the case of non-Board grains, sales are recognized when grain is shipped from the company's country or port terminals, or on transfer of ownership.

Changes in Accounting Policies—prior year 2001
The company changed its revenue recognition method for receipts of grain at its country elevators. Previously, the company's policy was to recognize a portion of the grain handling revenue as earned when grain was received and recognize the balance when grain was shipped. The new revenue recognition method recognized all of these revenues when the grain is shipped or title transfers to the customer. The effect of the change resulted in a $2.1 million after-tax increase to fiscal 2001 earnings. The cumulative effect of this change on prior year financial statements was to decrease retained earnings by $6.0 million.

The Wheat Pool had experienced two years of drought in its primary operating area and there were concerns about its ability to meet upcoming principal payments on debt. At the end of 2002, the company was experiencing cash outflows from operating activities and its 2002 loss of $92 million was more than double its loss from the prior year.

Instructions
In 2004, $150 million worth of debt was coming due. Adopt the role of the creditors and discuss the financial reporting issues.

Integrated Cases

IC6-1 Treetop Pharmaceuticals (TP) is in the business of research, development, and production of over-the-counter pharmaceuticals. During the year, it acquired 100% of the net assets of Treeroot Drugs Limited (TDL) for $200 million. The fair value of the identifiable assets at the time of purchase was $150 million (which included $120 million for patents). The company plans to sell the patents to a third party at the end of seven years even though, at that time, the remaining legal life of the patent will be five years. TP already has a commitment from a specific third party that has agreed to pay $50 million for the patents (in seven years).

In January, in an unrelated deal, the company acquired a trademark that has a remaining legal life of three years. The trademark is renewable every 10 years at little cost. TP is unsure if it will renew the trademark or not.

Because of the two acquisitions, TP has been a bit short of cash and has entered into the following arrangement with Drug Development Corporation (DDC). DDC paid $30 million to TP upfront when the contract was signed. Under the contract terms, the money is to be used to develop drugs and new channels to distribute them. TP has already spent a considerable portion of this money. TP agreed that it will pay DDC 2% of the revenues from the subsequent sale of the drugs (which are now close to the point of commercial production).

Because of the cash shortage, the company has also entered into negotiations with the bank to increase its line of credit. The bank has expressed concern about the company's liquidity. TP's top management has graciously agreed to take stock options instead of any bonuses or raises for the next two years in order to reduce cash flow constraints.

It is now year end and TP is getting ready to issue its financial statements. It is concerned about one of its major competitors, which has just come out with several new drugs that will compete directly with the drugs that TDL sells. Management is worried that this may severely erode the market for TDL's products. As a matter of fact, TP has had preliminary meetings to discuss selling TDL and has contacted a consultant to help find a buyer.

Jack Kimble, the controller, is preparing for a planning meeting with TP's auditors. The auditors are currently analyzing TP's draft financial statements to identify critical and high-risk areas. The draft financial statements show the company as barely breaking even. The chief financial officer has commented that the company's share price is likely to "take a tumble" since the company has always been profitable in past years and the company's competitors seem to be doing well currently. Kimble is also debating how to deal with the latest news from TP's lawyers. Apparently, the company is being sued in a class action lawsuit (i.e., by a significant number of people) for illness that was allegedly caused by one of TP's main pharmaceutical products. The claim is for an amount equal to revenues from last year. At this point, the lawyers have a concern that the case against TP may be successful and they are having trouble trying to estimate the potential loss to the company.

Instructions:
Adopt the role of the controller and prepare an analysis of all the financial reporting issues that TP is facing.

IC6-2 Recreational Vehicle Inc. (RVI) sells mid-sized to large, new and used motorized recreational vehicles. The company's only shareholder, Ronald Trump, manages the business. During the last two years, Canada's tourism industry has been hit hard by the appreciating Canadian dollar (much of the tourism depends on non-Canadians vacationing in Canada) and the threat of terrorism. Sales of RVs have therefore been slow.

RVI is located at the corner of two major highways, which gives it good visibility to people driving by. The facilities are very old, however, and in need of upgrading. Ronald has been thinking of building a new showroom and would like to go see the loan officer at Barrick Bank to get a loan. During construction, RVI will move its business to an adjacent building that it will rent.

The loan will also be used to pay for a new electronic billboard that can be seen from the highway. The billboard will cost $1 million but will allow RVI to display many different messages, including its sales and seasonal promotions. The cost of the billboard will be defrayed by renting out space on the billboard at times during the year when RVI is not using it. RVI has had many companies interested in this and is currently involved in a bidding process to determine which companies it will take on as advertising partners. So far, 10 companies have bid for the opportunity to advertise on the billboard and RVI has charged and collected a $25,000 fee from each of them. The $25,000 fee is non-refundable and represents the amount required by RVI for the privilege to bid on the billboard space only. RVI has not decided which bids it will accept yet. It cannot accept all of the bids but plans to accept three of them.

In his years in the business, Ronald has found that many potential RV owners/customers find the cost of the vehicle to be prohibitive. The RVs normally sell for about $90,000 each. With that in mind, several years ago he came up with the following program. Customers may buy the RV for as little as 10% down in cash as long as they also sign a marketing agreement with RVI. Under the terms of the agreement, RVI cares for the vehicle (storing it on its premises when not in use, providing repairs and maintenance), rents the vehicle to third parties, and advertises the availability of the unit. For instance, if the customer/owner decides to only use the RV for three weeks in the year, RVI will store the unit and try to rent it out the rest of the time. In return, RVI gets 40% of the rental fee. Once this program was in place, RVI found that sales of new RVs increased dramatically. As a result, it now has a substantial fleet which it rents out—hence the need to expand and upgrade the facilities.

Many of the potential RV owners/customers need financing, so RVI either provides the financing or helps negotiate a loan with Barrick Bank. Often, the customers make the loan payments out of the rental revenue that they earn under the rental program. If the customer does not make the loan payments, ownership of the RV reverts back to RVI. Ownership of several of these RVs has gone back to RVI in the past two years. When this happens, RVI either continues to rent the RV or tries to resell it.

The risk of theft is significant for these types of vehicles and RVI therefore ensures that owners have appropriate insurance coverage. Over the past three years, the insurance company has been complaining about excessive claims and losses, however, and in September it notified RVI and the RV owners that it would no longer allow the insured RVs to be rented out. Many of the owners switched insurance companies, but there are presently ten RVs on the lot with no insurance, and they are not covered by any other insurance. Ronald has not been able to get in touch with their owners.

It is now December, and Barrick Bank has loaned the company the money it needs to construct the new facilities. The old building has been demolished and the new facilities are under construction. The loan pays interest at prime plus 2% and requires that the company maintain a working capital ratio of 2:1, and maintain its profitability as well. The company must provide audited financial statements to the bank at least annually.

Instructions

Adopt the role of the auditors of RVI and discuss the financial reporting issues.

IC6-3 Comtel Incorporated (CI) is a leader in delivering communications capabilities that power global commerce and secure the world's most critical information. Its shares trade on the TSX and NYSE. The company had been experiencing unprecedented growth, but then, in 2001, industry demand for the company's services and products declined dramatically due to an industry realignment, an economic downturn, and a tightening in global capital and product markets. In 2003, after CI had downsized its operations considerably, the industry stabilized and the company began to enter a turnaround period.

In 2002, employee morale was very low because of all the downsizing. Many employees were being actively recruited away from CI. Management decided to deal with this by setting up bonus programs for employees who stayed to see the company through the difficult times and back to profitability. Under one plan, every employee would receive a bonus in the first quarter that the company achieved enough profit to cover the bonus costs. In order to help achieve profitability, the CFO met with the managers of his divisions and established profitability targets and what he referred to as "road maps" that showed how these targets could be achieved. The roadmaps included statements that the profits could only be achieved through the release from the balance sheet of excess provisions (i.e., provisions for obsolete inventory and bad debts). The provisions had been overprovided for in earlier years in an effort to "manage" profits.

However, in 2003, the company came under scrutiny from the SEC and OSC and received notification from the U.S. Attorney's office regarding a criminal investigation into alleged accounting irregularities. In addition, there were several lawsuits outstanding against the company by shareholders. These class action suits alleged that CI had provided misleading information to them in the financial statements for 2001 and 2002. Once news of this was released, credit rating agencies significantly downgraded their ratings of CI's securities. As a result of this negative activity, the company had not released its financial statements for 2003 and was now in breach of the TSX requirement to file financial statements. Although the TSX had not done so, it now had the power to delist the shares of CI.

The controller of CI is now at the point where he must finalize the financial statements and has come across the following information:

1. During the year, the company signed contracts to sell optical products which included software. Before year end, the company shipped out what it called an "interim product solution"—in other words, the optical product ordered by the company was not yet ready in its final form so the company shipped a beta or draft version of it. This interim product would then be followed shortly by the final version. Revenues were recognized upon shipment of the interim product solution as it was felt that the final version just needed minor refinements. The customers generally paid more than half of what was owed under the contract when they received the interim product solution. It was rare that customers backed out of this type of contract for any reason.
2. In 2003, CI had purchased a subsidiary of ABC Inc. and agreed to pay additional future consideration for the purchase (the consideration would take the form of additional CI shares). The additional consideration was a function of the profitability of the subsidiary. The more profitable the subsidiary, the more shares that CI would issue as consideration. Given that CI shares are highly volatile, CI and ABC agreed that the number of shares to be issued should be based on the average price per share in the three months prior to the future issuance date of the shares. So far, the subsidiary was performing above expectation.
3. By the end of 2003, CI was still restructuring in order to streamline operations and activities around its core activities. Part of the restructuring included the abandonment of the VOF (Voice Over Fiber) operations. The decision was made after it became clear that VOIP (Voice over Internet Protocol) would be the dominant technology in years to come. The operations would be closed down in early 2004, and this would involve workforce reductions and abandonment of plant and equipment.

Instructions

Analyze the financial reporting issues.

Research and Financial Analysis

RA6-1 Barrick Gold Corporation

Barrick Gold Corporation has its head office in Toronto. Its shares trade on the NYSE and TSX, as well as other exchanges.

Instructions

Refer to the company's financial statements and accompanying notes in the Student Website and answer the following questions.

(a) What were the company's gross revenues for 2003, 2004, and 2005? What is the percentage change?

(b) Based on your findings in (a), comment on the net income/loss of the company over the three-year period.

(c) Review the notes to the financial statements to determine the company's revenue recognition policy. Discuss the policy, considering the nature of the business and the industry.

(d) The company uses the U.S. dollar to present its Canadian financial statements and believes that this choice is justified because most of its activities take place in the United States or in U.S. dollars. Prove that its activities are mostly in U.S. dollars by giving evidence from the financial statements and annual report.

(e) Even though this is a Canadian company, its primary financial statements are prepared according to U.S. GAAP. What is the likely reason that it chooses to have its main financial statements according to U.S. GAAP and puts less focus on the Canadian GAAP financial statements? Can a similar case be made for the company to follow international GAAP?

RA6-2 Sears Canada Inc. and Hudson's Bay Company

Sears Canada Inc. and Hudson's Bay Company are two major retailers in North America, and they both have a significant presence in Canada. HBC's business strategy (through Zellers) is high volume, low cost. Sears' emphasis is on higher-price, higher-end products.

Instructions

Using the annual reports on the Student Website, answer the following:

(a) Calculate the "Earnings before interest and taxes" to "sales" percentage for each company for the most recent two years. Comment on the trend. Where do most HBC revenues come from?

(b) Identify any significant or unusual items that are affecting your calculations. Recalculate the percentage.

(c) Which company's strategy appears to be more successful? Consider the economic environment.

(d) Compare the income statements for each company for the most current year. Comment on their comparability.

RA6-3 IASB

As capital markets become more global, accounting standards are converging in the countries where the major capital markets exist.

Instructions

Go to the International Accounting Standards Board website (www.iasb.org) and research the current project on revenue recognition. Compare and contrast the proposed standard with the Canadian standards (*CICA Handbook* 3400).

RA6-4 Qwest Communications International

In the past several years, there have been many cases of companies that have overstated their revenues, particularly in the United States. The Securities and Exchange Commission (SEC) has been vigilant in tracking these companies down. Qwest Communications International is one such case where revenues were misstated several times.

Instructions

There are various sources for information about the Qwest Communications misstatements. Research the issue by visiting the company website (www.qwest.com) and the SEC website (www.sec.gov). List the main types of misstatements related to revenues and provide the amount of each misstatement. Discuss how the company had treated the revenues originally and in the restatement. How is it possible that the auditors gave the company a clean audit opinion for its original statements?

Sales Factor

HOLLYWOOD
THE JEAN PEOPLE

For its first 17 or so years, Montreal-based Hollywood Jeans made sure that its receivables would be paid by using factors—finance companies that insure any receivables. Eventually, however, the now 25-year-old design manufacturer of denim products decided that the cost of factoring was beginning to outweigh the benefits.

With the changing retail landscape and the consolidation of many factoring companies into fewer and larger companies, the criteria for insuring a company's receivables became more limiting. Hollywood Jeans found that the total annual cost of factoring exceeded the denim company's true losses. After a thorough analysis of its receivables performance, the company discovered that as long as it ran a strong credit team, good prior investigation, and a continuous investigation process, the total cost of maintaining support staff in the credit department would be less than what factoring costs.

To factor its U.S.-based accounts, Hollywood Jeans still uses Export Development Canada (EDC) to insure it receives payment for its export transactions. Its in-house credit staff handles all other accounts.

Although factoring is not cost-effective for Hollywood Jeans, the arrangement is essential for new apparel companies unless they have access to a lot of capital. In the apparel industry, there is a lot of risk with customer accounts. The company pays all the costs of buying the material, doing the sewing, and sending the shipment, and it then has to wait for its money, sometimes up to 90 days.

While factors consider the apparel industry to be high-risk generally, when collecting receivables becomes high-risk in other businesses, it may be due to poor preparation. When running a super sale, for example, companies sometimes blind themselves to possible credit risks.

Hollywood Jeans' philosophy—"It's only a sale when the money is in the bank"—helps its employees keep their eyes open to such risks. ■

chapter 7

Cash and Receivables

Learning Objectives

After studying this chapter, you should be able to:

1. Define financial assets.
2. Identify items that are considered cash and cash equivalents.
3. Indicate how cash and related items are reported.
4. Define receivables and identify the different types of receivables.
5. Account for and explain the accounting issues related to the recognition and measurement of accounts receivable.
6. Account for and explain the accounting issues related to the valuation of accounts receivable.
7. Account for and explain the accounting issues related to the recognition, measurement, and valuation of short-term notes receivable.
8. Account for and explain the accounting issues related to the recognition and measurement of long-term loans receivable.
9. Account for and explain the basic accounting issues related to the disposition of receivables.
10. Explain how receivables and loans are reported and analyzed.
11. Compare current Canadian and international GAAP.

After studying the appendix, you should be able to:

12. Explain common techniques for controlling cash.

Preview of Chapter 7

This chapter introduces and discusses the accounting for and reporting of a company's most liquid of financial assets—its cash and receivables. The accounting standards for financial instruments changed significantly when *CICA Handbook* Section 3855 became effective in October 2006. This chapter offers an overview of cash and cash equivalents and also covers another key financial asset—loans and receivables. Chapter 9 provides much more detail about other financial assets and the move toward fair value accounting.

The chapter is organized as follows:

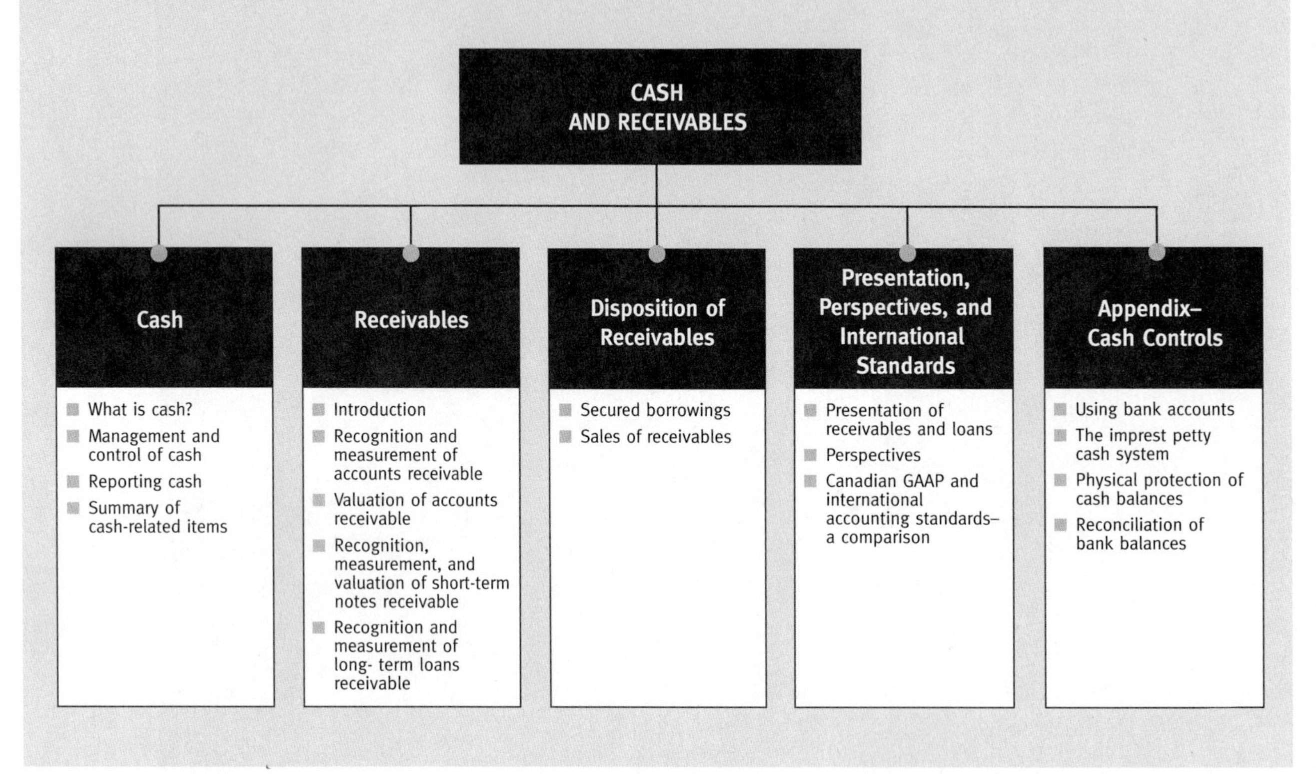

Objective 1
Define financial assets.

We now begin our detailed study of balance sheet accounts and the recognition and measurement concepts that apply to the different categories of assets, liabilities, and shareholders' equity. The first assets covered are generally the most liquid, and they are usually financial assets. A **financial asset** is defined by *CICA Handbook* Section 3855.19 as

> any asset that is:
>
> (i) cash;
>
> (ii) a contractual right to receive cash or another financial asset from another party;
>
> (iii) a contractual right to exchange financial instruments with another party under conditions that are potentially favourable to the entity; or
>
> (iv) an equity instrument of another entity.

Financial assets are covered in different chapters of this text. Chapter 7 deals with cash and cash equivalents, and with accounts, notes, and loans receivable. Chapter 9 covers other major categories of financial assets—mainly investments in the debt and equity instruments of other companies. The financial assets in these two chapters fit parts (i), (ii), and (iv) of the definition. The more complex instruments that fit part (iii), such as derivatives, along with financial liabilities and equity, are seen in Volume 2. Chapters 7 and 9 highlight the profession's recent movement away from the long-standing transactions-based historical cost model, toward one that relies more and more on fair values. Watch for references in other chapters as well for requirements to measure and disclose fair values.

CASH

What Is Cash?

2 Objective
Identify items that are considered cash and cash equivalents.

Cash is the most liquid asset and is the standard medium of exchange and the basis for measuring and accounting for all other items. It meets the definition of a financial asset, and is generally classified as a current asset. To be reported as a current asset, it must be readily available for paying current obligations, and must have no restrictions on it that limit how it can be used in satisfying debts.

Cash consists of coins, currency, and other available funds that are on deposit at a bank. Negotiable instruments such as money orders, certified cheques, cashier's cheques, personal cheques, and bank drafts are also viewed as cash. Although a company's bank may have a legal right to demand advance notice before it allows a withdrawal from a savings account, banks rarely ask for this notice and savings accounts are therefore also usually classified as cash.

It is more appropriate to classify money-market funds, certificates of deposit (CDs), and similar types of deposits and "short-term paper"[1] that allow investors to earn interest as **cash equivalents** or **short-term investments** than as cash. The reason is that there are usually restrictions or penalties on these securities when they are converted to cash. Money-market funds that give chequing account privileges, however, are usually classified as cash.

Certain items present classification problems: for example, postdated cheques from customers and IOUs are treated as receivables. It is proper to treat travel advances as receivables if the advances are to be collected from the employees or deducted from their salaries. Otherwise, it is more appropriate to classify the travel advance as a prepaid expense. Postage stamps on hand are classified as part of office supplies inventory or as a prepaid expense. Petty cash funds and change funds are included in current assets as cash because these funds are used to meet current operating expenses and to liquidate current liabilities.

---

[1] There are different types of short-term paper for investment. For example, CDs are issued by a bank as formal evidence of the bank's indebtedness. They must usually be held until maturity, although some CDs for over $100,000 are negotiable. Guaranteed investment certificates (GICs) are issued by trust companies and are similar time deposits. The short-term certificates mature in 30 to 360 days and generally pay interest at the short-term rate that is in effect on the date they are issued. In money-market funds, which are a variation of the mutual fund, the yield is determined by the mix of Treasury bills and commercial paper making up the fund's portfolio. Treasury bills are Canadian government obligations with 3-, 6-, and 12-month maturities; they are sold in denomination multiples of $1,000 (face value) at weekly government auctions. Commercial paper is short-term unsecured debt notes issued by corporations with good credit ratings, usually in minimum denominations of $100,000 and for terms of from one to 365 days.

Management and Control of Cash

Of all assets, cash is at the greatest risk of being used or diverted improperly. Management must overcome two problems in accounting for cash transactions: (1) it must establish proper controls to ensure that no unauthorized transactions are entered into by officers, employees, or others; and (2) it must ensure that the information that is needed in order to properly manage cash on hand and cash transactions is made available. Yet even with sophisticated control devices, errors can and do happen. *The Wall Street Journal* once ran a story entitled "A $7.8 Million Error Has a Happy Ending for a Horrified Bank," which described how **Manufacturers Hanover Trust Co.** mailed about $7.8 million too much in cash dividends to its shareholders. As the headline suggests, most of the money was eventually returned.

To safeguard cash and ensure the accuracy of the accounting records for this asset, effective internal control over cash is crucial. There are new challenges to maintaining control over liquid assets as more and more transactions are done with the swipe of a debit or credit card. For example, a recent survey conducted by the Bank for International Settlements reported that Canadians use debit cards more than people in any other country in the world, with 81.7 transactions per person in 2003, compared with 63.4 in the United States. The same survey also indicated that Canadians were the top automated bank machine (ABM) users with 43 such transactions per inhabitant in 2003 compared with 37.1 in the U.S. and 40 in the UK.[2] In addition, electronic commerce over the Internet continues to grow. Each of these trends contributes to the shift from cold cash to digital cash and brings new challenges for the control of cash. The appendix to this chapter discusses some basic control procedures that are used to ensure that cash is reported correctly.

Reporting Cash

Objective 3
Indicate how cash and related items are reported.

Although the reporting of cash is fairly straightforward, there are some issues that need special attention. They concern the reporting of:

1. restricted cash
2. cash in foreign currencies
3. bank overdrafts
4. cash equivalents

Restricted Cash

International Insight

Among others, one possible restriction that companies need to be aware of when they have cash in accounts outside Canada is whether regulations restrict the exportation of currency from the foreign country.

Petty cash and special payroll and dividend bank accounts are examples of cash that has been set aside for a particular purpose. In most situations, these fund balances are not material and therefore are not segregated from cash when it is reported in the financial statements. When an amount is material, restricted cash is segregated from regular cash for reporting purposes. The **restricted cash** is separately disclosed and reported in the Current Assets section or is classified separately in the Long-Term Assets section, depending on the date of availability or disbursement. In general, it should not be classified in current assets if there are restrictions that prevent it from being used for current purposes, unless the restricted cash offsets a current liability.[3] Cash that is classified in the long-term section has often been set aside for investment or financing purposes, such as for a plant expansion, long-term debt retirement, or as collateral.

[2] Canadian Bankers Association, "Taking a Closer Look: Electronic Banking," May 2005, <http://www.cba.ca> (July 26, 2006).

[3] *CICA Handbook*, Section 3000.01.

Some lending institutions require customers who borrow money from them to keep minimum cash balances in their chequing or savings accounts. These minimum balances are called **compensating balances**, and are defined as the portion of any demand deposit (or any time deposit or certificate of deposit) that a corporation keeps as support for its existing borrowing arrangements with a lending institution.[4] By requiring a compensating balance, the bank gets an effective interest rate on its loan that is higher than the stated rate because it can use the restricted amount that must remain on deposit. In the U.S., where banks more often require compensating balances, the accounting practice is to report in current assets any legally restricted deposits that are held as compensating balances against short-term borrowing arrangements.

To ensure that investors are not misled about the amount of cash that is available to meet recurring obligations, legally restricted balances have to be reported separately in current assets or noncurrent assets, as appropriate. In practice, many companies prefer to disclose the restriction rather than report it separately.

Cash in Foreign Currencies

Many companies have bank accounts in other countries, especially if they have recurring transactions in that country's currency. The foreign currency is translated into Canadian dollars at the exchange rate on the balance sheet date and, in situations where there is no restriction on the transfer of those funds to the Canadian company, it is included as cash in current assets. If there are restrictions on the flow of capital out of a country, the cash is reported as restricted. The classification of the cash as current or noncurrent is based on the circumstances and, in extreme cases, restrictions may be so severe that the foreign balances do not even qualify for recognition as assets.

Bank Overdrafts

Bank overdrafts occur when cheques are written for more than the amount in the cash account. Overdrafts are reported in the Current Liabilities section, and companies often do this by adding the amount to what is reported as accounts payable. If the overdraft amount is material, it should be disclosed separately either on the face of the balance sheet or in the related notes.

In general, bank overdrafts should not be offset against the Cash account. A major exception is when there is available cash in another account at the same bank where the overdraft is. Offsetting in this case is appropriate.

Cash Equivalents

Cash is often reported with the asset category called cash equivalents. **Cash equivalents** are defined as "short-term, highly liquid investments that are readily convertible to known amounts of cash and which are subject to an insignificant risk of changes in value."[5] Companies usually hold cash equivalents for meeting upcoming cash requirements. Generally, only investments with **original maturities** of three months or less qualify under the definition, and equity investments are excluded. Examples of cash equivalents are Treasury bills, commercial paper, and money-market funds.

International Insight

IAS 7 allows some equity investments, such as preferred shares that are close to their redemption date, to be included as cash equivalents.

In some circumstances, bank overdrafts may be deducted when the amount of cash and cash equivalents is being determined. If overdrafts are part of the firm's cash management activities, they are repayable on demand, and the bank balance fluctuates often

[4] *Accounting Series Release No. 148*, "Amendments to Regulations S-X and Related Interpretations and Guidelines Regarding the Disclosure of Compensating Balances and Short-Term Borrowing Arrangements," Securities and Exchange Commission, November 13, 1973.

[5] *CICA Handbook*, Section 1540.06(b).

between a positive and negative balance, the overdraft may be considered part of cash and cash equivalents.[6]

Because some companies report investments that qualify as cash equivalents in other categories of current assets, such as short-term or held-for-trading investments, it is important for them to disclose their reporting policy in a note to the financial statements.

CICA Handbook Section 3855, "Financial Instruments—Recognition and Measurement," requires cash equivalents to be measured at their fair value. Because investments that are classified as cash equivalents are very short-term, their cost—or cost plus accrued interest to the balance sheet date—is generally the same as their fair value.

Illustration 7-1 shows the information that Ottawa-based **Zarlink Semiconductor Inc.** reports in its 2006 financial statements.

Illustration 7-1

Reporting of Cash and Cash Equivalents—Zarlink Semiconductor Inc.

ASSETS	March 31, 2006	March 25, 2005
	(in millions of U.S. dollars)	
Current assets:		
Cash and cash equivalents	$ 90.7	$ 19.4
Short-term investments	24.6	39.6
Restricted cash	14.0	13.9

NOTES TO THE CONSOLIDATED FINANCIAL STATEMENTS

2. ACCOUNTING POLICIES

(C) CASH, CASH EQUIVALENTS AND SHORT-TERM INVESTMENTS

All highly liquid investments with original maturities of three months or less are classified as cash and cash equivalents. The fair value of cash equivalents approximates the amounts shown in the financial statements. Short-term investments comprise highly liquid corporate debt instruments that are held to maturity with terms of not greater than one year. Short-term investments are carried at amortized cost, which approximates their fair value.

(D) RESTRICTED CASH

Restricted cash consists of cash and cash equivalents pledged as security toward the Company's Swedish pension liability, and as collateral for various letters of credit, as required under the terms of the Company's credit facilities.

Student Website

Student Toolkit—Additional Disclosures

www.wiley.com/canada/kieso

Summary of Cash-Related Items

Cash and cash equivalents include currency and most negotiable instruments. If the item cannot be converted to coin or currency on short notice, it is classified separately as an investment, receivable, or prepaid expense. Cash that is not available for paying liabilities that are currently maturing is classified in the long-term assets section. Illustration 7-2 summarizes the classification of cash-related items.

Illustration 7-2

Classification of Cash-Related Items

Classification of Cash, Cash Equivalents, and Noncash Items

Item	Classification	Comment
Cash	Cash	If unrestricted, report it as cash. If restricted, identify and report it as a current or noncurrent asset.
Petty cash and change funds	Cash	Report them as cash.

[6] *CICA Handbook*, Section 1540.10.

Short-term paper	Cash equivalents	Are investments with a maturity of less than three months, and are often combined with cash.
Short-term paper	Short-term investments	Are investments with a maturity of 3 to 12 months.
Postdated cheques and IOUs	Receivables	Are assumed to be collectible.
Travel advances	Receivables or prepaid expenses	Are assumed to be collectible from employees or deducted from their salaries, or spent on travel in the future.
Postage on hand (as stamps or in postage meters)	Prepaid expenses	May also be classified as office supplies inventory.
Bank overdrafts	Current liability	If there is a right of offset, they reduce cash.
Compensating balances	Cash classified separately as a deposit that is maintained as a compensating balance	Classify as current or noncurrent in the balance sheet. Disclose details of the arrangement.

RECEIVABLES

Introduction

4 Objective
Define receivables and identify the different types of receivables.

In general, receivables are claims that a company has against customers and others for money, goods, or services. As we saw in the introduction to this chapter, when the claim is a **contractual** right to receive cash or other financial assets from another party, the receivable is a financial asset. On the balance sheet, receivables are classified as either current (short-term) or noncurrent (long-term). Current receivables are expected to be collected within a year or during the current operating cycle, whichever is longer. All other receivables are classified as noncurrent.

These financial assets are generally referred to in a more specific way as loans or receivables, with loans being a type of receivable, as explained below. Both **loans and receivables** result from "the delivery of cash or other assets by a lender to a borrower in return for a promise to repay on a specified date or dates, or on demand, usually with interest."[7] Although similar to loans and receivables, *Handbook* Section 3855.33 does not allow "investments in government debt, corporate bonds, convertible debt, commercial paper" and other securitized debt instruments to be classified as loans and receivables.

Loans and receivables can be further classified. **Trade receivables** are amounts owed by customers who the company has sold goods or delivered services to as part of its normal business operations; that is, they are amounts that result from operating transactions. They can be either open accounts receivable or notes receivable. Open **accounts receivable** are short-term extensions of credit that are based on a purchaser's **oral** promise to pay for goods and services that have been sold. They are normally collectible within 30 to 60 days, but credit terms may be longer—or shorter—depending on the industry. **Notes receivable** are **written** promises to pay a certain amount of money on a specified future date. They may arise from sales of goods and services, or from other transactions.

[7] *CICA Handbook*, Section 3855.19(h). Note that some loans and receivables are not financial assets. They are excluded when the claim does not result from a contractual commitment, such as income taxes receivable, which result from government legislation; or when the claim is not for cash or another financial asset.

As the term "loan" suggests, **loans receivable** are created when one party advances cash or other assets to a borrower and receives a promise to be repaid later. Loans tend to result from financing transactions by borrowers and investing transactions by lenders. When there is a written document that gives the terms and conditions of the loan receivable, the loan is then also called a note receivable.

Nontrade receivables are created by a variety of transactions and can be written promises either to pay cash or to deliver other assets. Nontrade receivables include the following, among other items:

1. Advances to officers and employees, or to subsidiaries or other companies
2. Amounts owing from a purchaser on the sale of capital assets or investments where delayed payment terms have been agreed on
3. Amounts receivable from the government: income taxes paid in excess of the amount owed, GST payments recoverable, investment tax credits, or other tax rebates receivable
4. Dividends and interest receivable
5. Claims against insurance companies for casualties the company has suffered; against common carriers for damaged or lost goods; against creditors for returned, damaged, or lost goods; or against customers for returnable items (crates, containers, etc.)

Because of their special nature, nontrade receivables are generally classified and reported as separate items in the balance sheet or in a note that is cross-referenced to the balance sheet. Illustration 7-3 shows the balance sheet and separate reporting of trade and nontrade receivables in Note 2 to the financial statements of **Four Seasons Hotels Inc.** Note 3 (not shown) gives extensive detail on Four Seasons' holdings of long-term secured and unsecured loans receivable.

Illustration 7-3

Receivables Reporting–Four Seasons Hotels Inc.

December 31, 2005 and 2004
(In thousands of US dollars (note 1(a))

	2005	2004
Assets		
Current assets:		
Cash and cash equivalents	$ 242,178	$ 226,377
Receivables (note 2)	69,690	81,541
Inventory	7,326	1,439
Prepaid expenses	2,950	2,981
	322,144	312,338
Long-term receivables (note 3)	175,374	179,060

2. **Receivables:**

	2005	2004
Trade accounts of consolidated hotels	$ 1,526	$ 4,331
Receivables from hotel partnerships, affiliates and managed hotels	52,684	56,674
Receivables relating to stock options exercised (note 11(a))	–	5,708
Taxes receivable	6,647	2,735
Other	8,833	12,093
	$ 69,690	$ 81,541

Receivables at December 31, 2005 are recorded net of an allowance for doubtful accounts of $2,792 (2004 - $2,535). The net bad debt expense for the year ended December 31, 2005 was $18 (2004 - $10).

Note that the following discussion of **accounts and notes receivable** assumes that they are short-term trade receivables, and that the discussion of **loans receivable** is based on long-term nontrade loans or notes. In addition, it is assumed that they all are financial assets. The basic accounting issues—**recognition, measurement, valuation, and disposition**—are discussed in the following order, and the references to sections of the *Handbook* indicate the relevant accounting standards.

	Handbook Section	
	Short-Term Trade	Other Accounts, Notes, and Loans
1. Recognition and measurement of accounts receivable	3855	3855
2. Valuation of accounts receivable	3020	3025
3. Recognition, measurement, and valuation of short-term notes receivable	3855, 3020	
4. Recognition and measurement of long-term loans receivable		3855
5. Valuation (impairment in value) of long-term loans receivable		3025
6. Disposition of receivables		AcG12
7. Statement presentation and disclosures	3020, 3862	3020, 3025, 3862

Recognition and Measurement of Accounts Receivable

5 Objective
Account for and explain the accounting issues related to the recognition and measurement of accounts receivable.

The accounting standards for the recognition and measurement of accounts receivable are found in *CICA Handbook* Section 3855:

- recognize an account receivable when the entity becomes a party to the contractual provisions of the financial instrument (para. .39);
- when recognized initially, measure the receivable at its fair value[8] (para. .55); and
- subsequently, measure receivables at amortized cost using the effective interest method. (para. .66(b))

The entity only becomes a party to the contractual provisions of the financial instrument when it has a legal claim to receive cash or other financial assets. While a commitment to sell goods or services to a customer might be made when a customer's order is received, there is no legal claim until one of the parties to the contract has performed under the agreement.

Recognizing receivables initially at their fair value is not as straightforward as it might seem. This is because fair value may not be the same as the exchange price that the parties agreed on. The **exchange price, the amount due** from the customer or borrower, is generally indicated on a business document, usually an invoice. Two factors can make measuring the fair value of short-term receivables more complicated: (1) the availability of discounts (trade and cash discounts) and (2) the length of time between the sale and the payment due date (the interest element).

Trade Discounts

Customers are often quoted prices based on list or catalogue prices that may have trade or quantity discounts. **Trade discounts** are used to avoid frequent changes in catalogues, to

[8] Receivables that are created by related party transactions may be an exception. Chapter 23 discusses the issues underlying the related party transactions.

quote different prices for different quantities purchased, or to hide the true invoice price from competitors.

Trade discounts are commonly quoted in percentages. For example, if your textbook has a list price of $90 and the publisher sells it to college and university bookstores for list less a 30-percent trade discount, the receivable recorded by the publisher is $63 per textbook. The normal practice is simply to deduct the trade discount from the list price and recognize the net amount as the receivable and revenue.

Cash Discounts (Sales Discounts)

Cash discounts or **sales discounts** are offered to encourage fast payment. They are expressed in specific terms: for example, 2/10, n/30 means there is a 2-percent discount if the invoice is paid within 10 days and that the gross amount is due in 30 days; while 2/10, E.O.M., net 30, means there is a 2-percent discount if the invoice is paid before the 10th day of the following month, with full payment due by the 30th of the following month.

Companies that buy goods or services but fail to take sales discounts are usually not using their money as effectively as they could. An enterprise that receives a 1-percent reduction in the sales price for paying within 10 days when the total payment is due within 30 days is basically earning 18.25 percent interest (0.01 divided by 20/365) because of the discount—or, more technically, it is at least avoiding that rate of interest included in the undiscounted invoice price. For this reason, companies usually take the discount unless their cash is severely limited.

Theoretically, the receivable and the sale should both be recognized at the net amount or fair value, that is, the present value of the future cash flows. Under this approach, customers who pay within the discount period purchase at the cash price; those who pay after the discount period expires are penalized for not paying quickly. The discounts that are not taken are penalties added to the fair value of the transaction. They are reported separately as Sales Discounts Forfeited, similar to interest or financing revenue.

The most commonly used method of recording short-term receivables and related sales, however, is to record the gross amounts of the receivable and sale—i.e., at the full amount assuming no discount will be taken. Under this method, sales discounts are recognized in the accounts only when payment is received within the discount period. Sales discounts are then shown in the income statement as a deduction from sales to arrive at net sales.

The entries in Illustration 7-4 show the difference between the gross and net methods.

Illustration 7-4

Entries under Gross and Net Methods of Recording Cash (Sales) Discounts

Gross Method			Net Method		
Sales of $10,000, terms 2/10, n/30:					
Accounts Receivable	10,000		Accounts Receivable	9,800	
Sales		10,000	Sales		9,800
Payment of $4,000 received within discount period:					
Cash	3,920		Cash	3,920	
Sales Discounts	80		Accounts Receivable		3,920
Accounts Receivable		4,000			
Payment of $6,000 received after discount period:					
Cash	6,000		Accounts Receivable	120	
Accounts Receivable		6,000	Sales Discounts Forfeited		120
			Cash	6,000	
			Accounts Receivable		6,000

If the gross method is used, sales discounts are reported as a deduction from sales in the income statement. Proper asset valuation requires that a reasonable estimate be made of discounts that are expected to be taken after the balance sheet date and that the amount be recognized if it is material. Allowance for Sales Discounts, a contra account to Accounts Receivable on the balance sheet, is credited for such amounts and the Sales Discounts account on the income statement is increased or debited. If the net method is used, the receivables are already at their realizable value so no further adjustment is needed. The Sales Discounts Forfeited account is recognized as an item of "Other revenue" on the income statement.[9]

While the net method is theoretically preferred, it is rarely used. This is because it requires more analysis and bookkeeping for the additional adjusting entries to record sales discounts forfeited on accounts receivable that have passed the discount period. Using the gross method, along with the added requirement to estimate and record discounts that are expected to be taken after the balance sheet date, satisfies the Section 3855 standard which requires accounts receivable to be recognized at their fair value.

Nonrecognition of Interest Element

Ideally, receivables should be measured initially at their fair value represented by their present value; that is, the amount of cash that would be required at the date of sale to satisfy the outstanding claim.[10] As mentioned in the previous section, this is equivalent to the discounted value of the cash that will be received in the future. When expected cash receipts require a waiting period, the face amount of the receivable is not a good measure of the debt that exists at the current moment because the face value would be discounted if the debt were paid off immediately.

Underlying Concept

Materiality means it must make a difference to a decision-maker. Standard setters believe that interest and present value concepts do not need to be strictly applied if omitting them results in financial statements that are not materially different.

To illustrate, assume that a company makes a sale on account for \$1,000. The applicable annual interest rate is 12%, and cash is to be received at the end of four months. The receivable's present value is not \$1,000 but \$961.54 (\$1,000 × 0.96154, Table A-2; $n = 1$, $i = 4\%$).[11] In other words, \$1,000 to be received in four months is equivalent to \$961.54 received today.

Theoretically, the discounted amount of \$961.54 is the fair value of the receivable and sales revenue, and any additional amount received after the sale is interest revenue. **In practice, accountants have generally chosen to ignore this for accounts receivable because the discount amount is not usually material when compared to the net income for the period.** Generally, receivables that are created by normal business transactions with customers and that are due in the short term are not accounted for using present value considerations.[12]

Valuation of Accounts Receivable

6 Objective

Account for and explain the accounting issues related to the valuation of accounts receivable.

When financial statements are prepared, financial statement presentation has to be addressed. The decisions for reporting receivables involve their classification and valuation on the balance sheet.

To classify the receivables, the length of time that each receivable will be outstanding needs to be determined. For companies that present classified balance sheets, receivables that are expected to be collected within a year or the operating cycle, whichever is longer, are classified as current; all other receivables are classified as long-term.

---

[9] Because discounts not taken can be viewed as a short-term financing charge, some critics argue that an interest income account should be used to record these amounts.

[10] Chapter 9 discusses fair value considerations more fully.

[11] Present and future value tables are provided immediately following Chapter 12.

[12] *CICA Handbook*, Section 3020, "Accounts and Notes Receivable," is silent on the issue of interest. However, in the U.S., *APB Opinion No. 21*, "Interest on Receivables and Payables," states that all receivables are subject to present value measurement techniques.

The valuation of receivables is more complex, but the goal is to report them on the balance sheet at their net realizable value. **Net realizable value**—the net amount expected to be received in cash—is not necessarily the amount that is legally receivable. To determine the net realizable value, estimates are needed of both the uncollectible receivables and any returns, allowances, or cash discounts that may be granted.

Uncollectible Accounts Receivable

As one accountant so aptly noted, the credit manager's idea of heaven would probably be a place where everyone (eventually) paid his or her debts.[13] Illustration 7-5 shows the recent experience of **Sears Canada Inc.**, and how important credit sales can be for many companies. Interestingly, the use of debit cards and third-party credit cards such as Visa and MasterCard is increasing at Sears while cash and company credit cards are being used less.

Illustration 7-5
Sears Canada Customer Method of Payment

	2005	2001
Sears Card or Sears MasterCard	54.4%	60.5%
Third Party Credit Cards	20.5%	15.6%
Debit Cards	12.4%	8.5%
Cash	12.7%	15.4%
Total	100.0%	100.0%

Source: Sears Canada Inc. 2005 and 2002 Annual Reports

Except for cash sales, it is possible that the full amount of the sale will never be collected. An uncollectible account receivable needs to be properly recorded in the accounts. It is a loss of revenue that requires a decrease in the asset Accounts Receivable and a related decrease in income and shareholders' equity. The decrease in income is recognized by recording bad debt expense.

The main issue in recording uncollectible accounts receivable is their timing: When should Accounts Receivable be reduced? When should the bad debt loss be recognized? Section 3020 is clear—the **allowance method** is required. In this method, an estimate is made of the expected uncollectible amounts from all sales made on account or from the total of outstanding receivables. This estimate is entered as an expense and a reduction in accounts receivable (through an increase in the Accounts Receivable **contra account** Allowance for Doubtful Accounts) **in the same period as when the sale is recorded**. A contra allowance account is used because the Accounts Receivable account is supported by a subsidiary ledger of each customer's balance owing and management does not know yet which specific accounts will result in non-collection and bad debt losses.

Allowance Method

The **allowance method** reports receivables at their estimated realizable value and uses an estimate to recognize bad debt losses as an expense in the same accounting period as when the sales on account are made. Supporters of the allowance method believe that these two effects—a proper carrying value for receivables on the balance sheet and the resulting matching of expenses and revenues in the same period—are the reasons to use it. They believe that although estimates are involved, the percentage of sales that will not be collected can be predicted based on past experience, present market conditions, and an

[13] William J. Vatter, *Managerial Accounting* (Englewood Cliffs, N.J.: Prentice-Hall, 1950), p. 60.

analysis of the outstanding balances. Many companies set their credit policies to allow for a certain percentage of uncollectible accounts. In fact, many feel that if the percentage is not reached, sales are being lost because of credit policies that are too strict.

Within the allowance method, there are two approaches to estimating bad debt expense. The estimate is normally based on either (1) the level of sales or (2) the outstanding receivables.

Percentage-of-Sales (Income Statement) Approach. If there is a fairly stable relationship between previous years' credit sales and bad debts, then that relationship can be turned into a percentage and used to determine the current year's bad debt expense.

Underlying Concept

The percentage-of-sales method is a good illustration of using the matching concept, which relates expenses to revenues earned.

The **percentage-of-sales approach** matches costs with revenues because it relates the charge (the expense) to the period in which the sale is recorded. To illustrate, assume that Dockrill Corp. estimates from past experience that about 2% of net credit sales become uncollectible. If Dockrill Corp. has net credit sales of $400,000 in 2007, the entry to record bad debt expense in 2007 using the percentage-of-sales method is as follows:

Bad Debt Expense	8,000	
Allowance for Doubtful Accounts		8,000

A	= L +	SE
−8,000		−8,000

Cash flows: No effect

Allowance for Doubtful Accounts is a valuation account (i.e., a contra asset) and is subtracted from receivables on the balance sheet.[14] The amount of bad debt expense and the related credit to the allowance account are not affected by any balance that is already in the allowance account. Because the bad debt expense estimate is related to a nominal account (Sales), and any balance in the allowance is ignored, this method is often called the **income statement approach**. It achieves an excellent matching of cost and revenues.

Percentage-of-Receivables (Balance Sheet) Approach. Alternatively, a company can use its past experience to estimate the percentage of its outstanding receivables that will become uncollectible, without identifying specific accounts. This procedure gives a reasonably accurate estimate of the receivables' realizable value, but does a poorer job of relating bad debt expense directly to the sales of the period. Its objective instead is to report receivables on the balance sheet at their net realizable values; for this reason, it is referred to as the **percentage-of-receivables** (or **balance sheet**) **approach**.

The percentage that is used in this approach may be a combined rate that reflects an overall estimate of the uncollectible receivables. Another approach is to set up an **aging schedule**, which is more sensitive to the actual status of the accounts receivable. This approach determines the age of each account receivable and applies a different percentage to each of the various age categories, based on past experience. In practice, aging schedules are often used. They show which accounts need special attention by highlighting how long various accounts receivable have been outstanding. The schedule of Wilson & Co. in Illustration 7-6 is an example.

This analysis tells us that Wilson & Co. expects to receive $547,000 less $37,650, or $509,350 net cash receipts, from the December 31 amounts owed, and that this should be the amount reported on the balance sheet for net accounts receivable. To do this, the balance in Allowance for Doubtful Accounts must equal $37,650. **Assuming that there is no**

[14] In the past, many Canadian companies did not disclose the amount of their allowance for doubtful accounts. Unless the opposite was stated, it was assumed that an adequate allowance had been made for potentially uncollectible accounts. Under *Handbook* Section 3862, which was recently released, companies now have to disclose all changes in the allowance account during the period.

Illustration 7-6
Accounts Receivable Aging Schedule

WILSON & CO.
Aging Schedule

Name of Customer	Balance Dec. 31	Under 60 days	61–90 days	91–120 days	Over 120 days
Western Stainless Steel Corp.	$ 98,000	$ 80,000	$18,000		
Brockville Steel Company	320,000	320,000			
Freeport Sheet & Tube Co.	55,000				$55,000
Manitoba Iron Works Ltd.	74,000	60,000		$14,000	
	$547,000	$460,000	$18,000	$14,000	$55,000

Summary

Age	Amount	Percentage Estimated to Be Uncollectible	Required Balance in Allowance
Under 60 days old	$460,000	4%	$18,400
61–90 days old	18,000	15%	2,700
91–120 days old	14,000	20%	2,800
Over 120 days	55,000	25%	13,750
Year-end balance of Allowance for Doubtful Accounts should =			$37,650

previous balance in the allowance account before this adjustment, the entry for bad debt expense for the current year is:

A = L + SE
−37,650 −37,650
Cash flows: No effect

Bad Debt Expense	37,650	
Allowance for Doubtful Accounts		37,650

To change the illustration slightly, **assume that the allowance account already had a credit balance of $800 before adjustment**. In this case, the amount to be added to the account to bring it to the desired balance of $37,650 is $36,850 ($37,650 − $800), and the following entry is made:

A = L + SE
−36,850 −36,850
Cash flows: No effect

Bad Debt Expense	36,850	
Allowance for Doubtful Accounts		36,850

The balance in the allowance account is therefore reported at $37,650. **If instead the balance before adjustment was a debit balance of $200**, then the amount to be recorded for bad debt expense would be $37,850 ($37,650 desired balance + $200 debit balance). In the percentage-of-receivables method, the balance that is already in the allowance account before the adjusting entry is made **cannot be ignored**; it has to be considered because it is used to calculate the amount needed for the adjustment.

Aging schedules are not just prepared in order to determine the amount needed in the allowance account for bad debt expense. They are prepared also as an internal control measure that breaks down the receivables into categories and identifies delinquent accounts. The estimated loss percentage for each category is based on previous loss experience and the advice of credit department personnel. Regardless of whether a combined rate or an aging schedule is used, the main purpose of the percentage-of-receivables method for financial statement purposes is to report receivables in the balance sheet at their net realizable value. While it does result in bad debt expense being recognized, it does not do as good a job as the percentage-of-sales method at relating bad debt expense to the period in which the sale takes place.

The allowance for doubtful accounts as a percentage of receivables varies considerably, depending on the industry and recent economic conditions. Stantec Inc., a professional engineering services firm, for example, reported an allowance for doubtful accounts of more than 10 percent of its accounts receivable at December 31, 2005, while Potash Corporation of Saskatchewan Inc., an integrated fertilizer and related industrial and feed products company, reported an allowance of only 1.1 percent of its receivables. Look again at Illustration 7-3 to see how Four Seasons Hotels Inc. reports its receivables net of the allowance account.

In summary, the percentage-of-receivables method results in a better valuation of receivables on the balance sheet. In terms of matching, however, the percentage-of-sales approach gives the better results. Illustration 7-7 relates these methods to these two criteria.

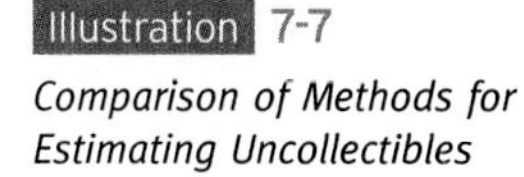
Illustration 7-7
Comparison of Methods for Estimating Uncollectibles

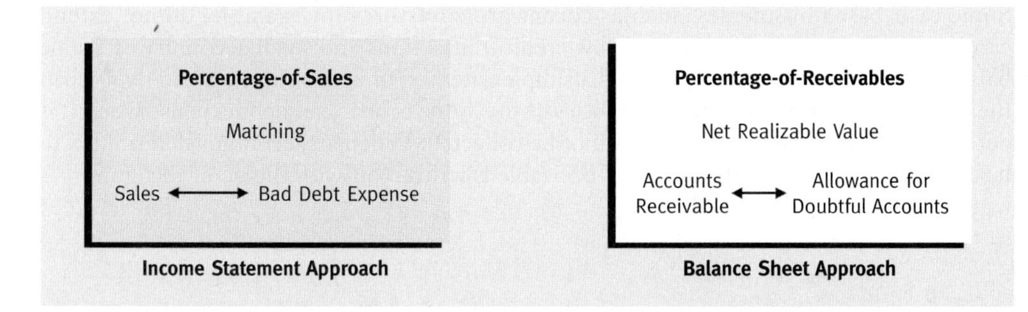

Which approach should be used? *Handbook* Section 3020.12 requires that short-term receivables be valued at "the best possible estimate of the amount for which reasonable assurance of collection exists, in the light of current conditions and assuming the continuation of the business as a 'going concern.'" This focus on asset measurement is consistent with the conceptual framework and the definition of expenses as "decreases in economic resources." Many companies use the percentage-of-sales method throughout the year, but make their year-end adjustment based on year-end receivable balances.

Accounts Receivable Written Off Under the allowance method, when a **specific account** is determined to be uncollectible, its balance is removed from Accounts Receivable and Allowance for Doubtful Accounts is reduced. For example, assuming the account of Brown Ltd. of $550 is considered uncollectible, the write-off entry is as follows:

Allowance for Doubtful Accounts	550	
Accounts Receivable		550

A	=	L	+	SE
0		0		0

Cash flows: No effect

Note that there is no effect on the income statement **from writing off an account,** nor should there be. This is because bad debt expense was **previously** estimated, recognized, and matched with revenue **in the period of the sale**. There is also no effect on the net amount of the receivables because Accounts Receivable and its contra account are **both** reduced by equal amounts.

Collection of an Account Previously Written Off If a collection is made on a receivable that was previously written off, the procedure is to **first** re-establish the receivable by reversing the write-off entry, and **then** recognize the cash inflow as a regular receipt on account. To illustrate, assume that Brown Ltd. eventually remits $300, but indicates that this is all that will be paid. The entries to record this transaction are as follows:

A = L + SE
0 0 0

Cash flows: No effect

Accounts Receivable	300	
Allowance for Doubtful Accounts		300
(To reinstate the account written off and now determined to be collectible.)		
Cash	300	
Accounts Receivable		300
(To record the receipt of cash on account from Brown Ltd.)		

A = L + SE
0 0 0

Cash flows: ↑ 300 inflow

Direct Write-Off Method

Some cash-based businesses, such as corner grocery stores for example, do not extend credit often and therefore have very few credit transactions and small accounts receivable balances. For such businesses, there is a simpler method of accounting for bad debts than the allowance method. The **direct write-off method** records bad debt expense when it is determined that a specific account cannot be collected. When an account is determined to be uncollectible, the specific account receivable is written off with the debit recognized as bad debt expense:

A = L + SE
−$$ −$$

Cash flows: No effect

Bad Debt Expense	$$	
Accounts Receivable		$$

If amounts are later collected on an account that was previously written off, a notation is made in the customer's record, and the amount collected is recognized through entries in Cash and a revenue account entitled Uncollectible Amounts Recovered:

A = L + SE
+$$ +$$

Cash flows: ↑ $$ inflow

Cash	$$	
Uncollectible Amounts Recovered		$$

No allowance account is used.

From a practical standpoint, this method is simple and convenient. The direct write-off method is theoretically weak, however, because it usually does not match the period's costs with revenues. It also fails to show receivables at their estimated realizable value on the balance sheet. **As a result, the direct write-off method is not considered appropriate, except when the uncollectible amount is immaterial.**

Sales Returns and Allowances To properly measure sales revenues and receivables, it is sometimes necessary to use additional allowance accounts. Probable sales returns and price reductions are estimated and deducted as contra accounts against sales on the income statement and accounts receivable on the balance sheet. This results in net sales and the net realizable amount of accounts receivable being properly reported on the financial statements.

This procedure is followed so that the sales returns or price allowances (called **sales returns and allowances**) are reported in the same period as the sales that they relate to. If this adjustment is not made, however, the amount of mismatched returns and allowances is usually not material as long as the items are handled consistently from year to year. The situation changes when a company completes a few special orders for large amounts near the end of its accounting period: in this case, sales returns and allowances should be anticipated and recognized in the period of the sale to avoid distorting the current period's income statement. There are some companies that by their nature have significant returns and therefore usually have an allowance for sales returns.

As an example, assume that Astro Corporation estimates that approximately 5 percent of its $1 million of trade receivables outstanding will be returned or some adjustment will be made to the sale price. Leaving out a $50,000 charge could have a material effect on net income for the period. The entry to show expected sales returns and allowances is:

Sales Returns and Allowances	50,000	
Allowance for Sales Returns and Allowances		50,000

A	= L +	SE
−50,000		−50,000

Cash flows: No effect

The account Sales Returns and Allowances is reported as an offset to Sales Revenue in the income statement. Returns and price allowances are accumulated separately (instead of being debited directly to the Sales account) so that better information is available to management and statement readers. Allowance for Sales Returns and Allowances is an asset valuation account (contra asset) similar to Allowance for Doubtful Accounts and is deducted from total accounts receivable.

In most cases, it is acceptable to report in the income statement all returns and allowances that were made during a period, even if they are not related to the current period's sales. Doing this is justified by practicality and immateriality.[15]

Recognition, Measurement, and Valuation of Short-Term Notes Receivable

7 Objective

Account for and explain the accounting issues related to the recognition, measurement, and valuation of short-term notes receivable.

A note receivable is similar to an account receivable, with one difference: the note is supported by a formal **promissory note**, which is a **written** promise to pay a specific sum of money at a specific future date, and this makes a note receivable a negotiable instrument. The note is signed by a **maker** in favour of a designated **payee** who can then legally and readily sell or transfer the note to others. **Notes always contain an interest element** because of the time value of money, but they may be classified as interest-bearing or non–interest-bearing. **Interest-bearing notes** have a stated rate of interest that is payable in addition to the face value of the note; **zero-interest-bearing notes** (or **non–interest-bearing notes**) also include interest, but it is equal to the difference between the amount that was borrowed (the proceeds) and the higher face amount that will be paid back. The rate may not be stated explicitly.

Companies often accept notes receivable from customers who need to extend the payment period of an outstanding receivable. Notes are also sometimes required from high-risk or new customers. In addition, notes are often used in loans to employees and subsidiaries and in sales of property, plant, and equipment. In some industries (e.g., the pleasure and sport boat industry), all credit sales are supported by notes. Most notes, however, are created by lending transactions. The basic issues in accounting for notes receivable are the same as those for accounts receivable: recognition, measurement, valuation, and disposition. This section discusses only short-term notes. Long-term notes and loans receivable are covered later in this chapter.

To illustrate the accounting for notes receivable, assume that on March 14, 2008, Prime Corporation agreed to allow its customer, Gouneau Ltd., to substitute a six-month note for the account receivable of $1,000 that Gouneau was unable to pay when it came

[15] An interesting sidelight to the entire problem of returns and allowances is determining when a sale is a sale. In certain circumstances, the seller is exposed to such a high risk of ownership through possible return of the property that the sale is not recognized. Such situations have developed, particularly in sales to related parties. This subject is discussed in more detail in Chapter 6.

due for payment. This means that Gouneau is basically borrowing $1,000 from Prime for six months. It was agreed that **the note would bear interest** at a rate of 6%. Prime's entries to record the substitution and payment of the note are as follows:

A	= L	+ SE
0	0	0

Cash flows: No effect

March 14, 2008		
Note Receivable	1,000	
Account Receivable		1,000

A	= L	+ SE
+30		+30

Cash flows: ↑ 1,030 inflow

September 14, 2008		
Cash	1,030	
Note Receivable		1,000
Interest Income		30*
*$1,000 × .06 × 6/12		

Alternatively, a note could be accepted in exchange for lending money to an employee or subsidiary company, for example, in a **non–interest-bearing note** situation. In this case, the interest is the difference between the amount of cash that is borrowed and the face or maturity value of the note receivable. Assume that the president of Ajar Ltd. borrowed money from the company on February 23, 2008, and signed a promissory note for $5,000 repayable in nine months' time. An interest rate of 8% is appropriate for this type of loan. Instead of borrowing $5,000 and repaying this amount with 8% interest added on at the maturity date, the president receives only $4,717 on February 23. The $283 difference between the $4,717 borrowed and the $5,000 repaid represents 8% interest for the nine-month period that the note is outstanding: $4,717 × 8% × 9/12 = $283. Ajar's entries are as follows:[16]

A	= L	+ SE
0	0	0

Cash flows: ↓ 4,717 outflow

February 23, 2008		
Note Receivable	4,717	
Cash		4,717

A	= L	+ SE
+283		+283

Cash flows: ↑ 5,000 inflow

November 23, 2008		
Cash	5,000	
Note Receivable		4,717
Interest Income		283*
*4,717 × .08 × 9/12		

In both cases, if financial statements are prepared while the note receivable is still outstanding, interest must be accrued to the balance sheet date.

Like accounts receivable, **short-term notes receivable** that are created by the sale of goods and services are recorded and reported at their net realizable value—i.e., at their

[16] Alternatively, the entries could initially recognize the note's maturity value in Note Receivable and the discount in Discount on Note Receivable, a contra account to Note Receivable:

Feb. 23	Note Receivable	5,000	
	Cash		4,717
	Discount on Note Receivable		283
Nov. 23	Cash	5,000	
	Note Receivable		5,000
	Discount on Note Receivable	283	
	Interest Income		283

The effects on the balance sheet and cash flows are identical, regardless of the entries made. If financial statements were prepared while this note is still outstanding, the discount would be reduced and interest income earned to the balance sheet date would be recognized in the account Interest Income.

face amount less all necessary allowances. The main notes receivable allowance account is Allowance for Doubtful Accounts. The calculations and estimates in valuing short-term notes receivable and in recording bad debt expense and the related allowance **are exactly the same as for trade accounts receivable**, which were explained above.

Recognition and Measurement of Long-Term Loans Receivable

8 Objective
Account for and explain the accounting issues related to the recognition and measurement of long-term loans receivable.

Since some form of promissory note is often the proof that a loan exists, the above explanation of notes receivable applies equally well to loans receivable. The examples of loans receivable that are illustrated below assume that a note is the basis for each transaction. What changes as we move from short-term notes to long-term loans is the length of time to maturity and the importance of interest in measuring and accounting for the financial instrument.

The accounting standards for the recognition and measurement of loans receivable are the same as those identified above for accounts receivable:

- recognize a loan receivable when the entity becomes a party to the contractual provisions of the financial instrument;
- when recognized initially, measure the loan receivable at its fair value;[17] and
- subsequently, measure loans receivable at amortized cost using the effective interest method.

The **fair value** of a note or loan receivable is defined in Section 3855 as "the amount of the consideration that would be agreed upon in an arm's length transaction between knowledgeable, willing parties who are under no compulsion to act." This definition of fair value is used throughout Canadian accounting standards. Applied specifically to financial instruments, fair value is estimated as **the present value of the cash amounts that are expected to be collected in the future, with the amounts discounted at the market rate of interest that is appropriate for a loan with similar risk and other characteristics.**[18] When the interest stated on an interest-bearing note is the same as the effective (market) rate of interest, the note's fair value is equal to its **face value**.[19] When the stated rate is not the same as the market rate, the note's cost (or **present value**, or **fair value**) is different from the note's **face value**. The difference between the price for the note now and its maturity value—resulting in either a discount or a premium—is then amortized over the note's life so that the interest income that is reported approximates the effective or market rate. The procedure for this is illustrated further below.

Transaction costs that are incurred in acquiring a loan or note receivable, such as commissions, can be treated in one of two ways:

1. they can be recognized as an expense when they are incurred, or
2. they can be added to the fair value of the instrument, which then increases the original amount that is recognized as an asset at acquisition. In this case, the transaction costs are an adjustment to the discount or premium that will be amortized over the life of the loan, and the effective rate of interest is recalculated.

[17] Loans that are created in related party transactions may be an exception. Chapter 23 discusses the issues in related party transactions.

[18] *CICA Handbook* Section 3855.A55-A61 indicates that there are two approaches to estimating the present value of projected cash flows: a discount rate adjustment approach and a cash flow adjustment approach. These two methods are discussed more fully in Appendix 16C of this text.

[19] The **stated interest rate**, also referred to as the **face rate** or the **coupon rate**, is the rate that is part of the note contract. The **effective interest rate**, also referred to as the **market rate** or the **yield rate**, is the rate that is used in the market to determine the note's value—i.e., the discount rate that is used to determine its present value.

Companies are required to disclose the policy they follow for transaction costs.

After the initial recognition of loans and receivables, they are later measured at their amortized cost.[20] **Amortized cost** is the amount that was recognized when the instrument was acquired, reduced by any principal payments received, and adjusted for the amortization of any discount or premium, if appropriate, and write-downs for impairment or uncollectibility. Let's see how this works!

International Insight

Accounting for loans and receivables at amortized cost is consistent with both U.S. GAAP and IAS 39.

Notes Issued at Face Value

To illustrate an interest-bearing note issued at face value, assume that Bigelow Corp. lends Scandinavian Imports $10,000 in exchange for a $10,000, three-year note bearing interest at 10% payable annually. The market rate of interest for a note of similar risk is also 10%. The first step is always to identify the amounts and timing of the cash flows. For our example, the following diagram shows both the interest and principal cash flows:

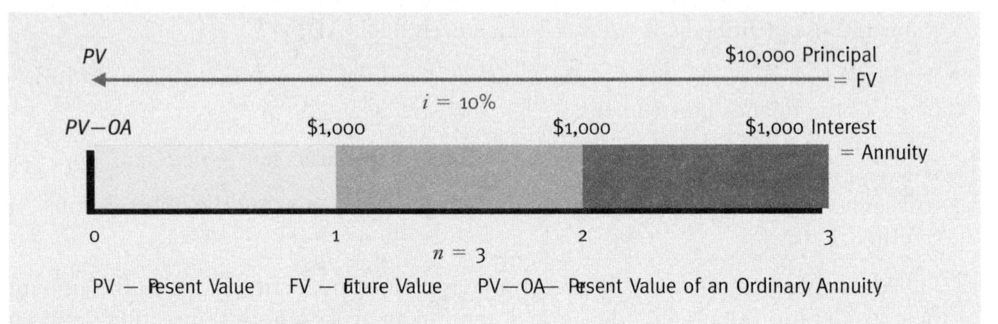

The note's present value or exchange price is calculated as in Illustration 7-8.

Illustration 7-8
Present Value of Note–Stated and Market Rates the Same

Face value of the note		$10,000
Present value of the lump sum principal:		
$10,000 (PVF*$_{3,10\%}$) = $10,000 (0.75132) (Table A-2)	$7,513	
Present value of the interest annuity:		
$1,000 (PVF*–OA$_{3,10\%}$) = $1,000 (2.48685) (Table A-4)	2,487	
Present value of the note		10,000
Difference		$ -0-

*Present Value Factors found in Tables A1–A5

In this case, the note's fair value, present value, and face value are the same ($10,000) **because the effective and stated interest rates are the same.** Bigelow Corp. records its acquisition of the note as follows:

A	= L	+ SE
0	0	0

Cash flows: ↓ 10,000 outflow

Notes Receivable	10,000	
Cash		10,000

[20] This is the usual basis of measurement. Companies are allowed to designate loans and receivables as **held for trading** or **available for sale**, in which case they are measured after acquisition at their fair value. Chapter 9 explains this option in more detail.

Bigelow Corp. later recognizes the interest earned each year ($10,000 × 0.10) as follows:

Cash	1,000	
Interest Income		1,000

A	= L +	SE
+1,000		+1,000

Cash flows: ↑ 1,000 inflow

Notes Not Issued at Face Value

Zero-Interest-Bearing Notes If a zero-interest-bearing note is received in exchange for cash, its present value is usually the cash paid to the issuer. Because both the note's future amount and present value are known, the interest rate can be calculated, i.e., it is implied. The **implicit interest rate** is the rate that equates the cash paid with the amounts receivable in the future. The difference between the future (face) amount and the present value (cash paid) is a discount and this amount is amortized to interest income over the life of the note using the effective interest method. In most cases, the implicit interest rate is the market rate. This is because the transaction is usually carried out between two parties who are "at arm's length" and acting in their own best interests.[21]

To illustrate, assume Jeremiah Company receives a three-year, $10,000 zero-interest-bearing note, and the present value is known to be $7,721.80. The implicit rate of interest of 9% (assumed to approximate the market rate) can be determined as in Illustration 7-9.

$$\text{PV of note} = \text{PV of future cash flows}$$
$$\text{PV of note} = \text{FV of note} \times PVF_{3,\ ?\%} \text{ (Table A-2)}$$
$$\$7{,}721.80 = \$10{,}000 \times PVF_{3,\ ?\%}$$
$$PVF_{3,\ ?\%} = \frac{\$7{,}721.80}{\$10{,}000}$$
$$PVF_{3,\ ?\%} = 0.77218$$

Table A-2: Where n = 3 and PVF = 0.77218, i = 9%

Illustration 7-9
Determination of Implicit Interest Rate

Thus, the implicit rate that makes the total cash to be received at maturity ($10,000) equal to the present value of the future cash flows ($7,721.80) is 9%. Note that if any two of the three variables on the second line of the equation in Illustration 7-9 are known, the third variable can be determined. For example, if the note's maturity value (**face value**) and **present value factor (*i* and *n*)** are known, the note's **present value** can be determined.

The time diagram for the single cash flow of Jeremiah's note is as follows:

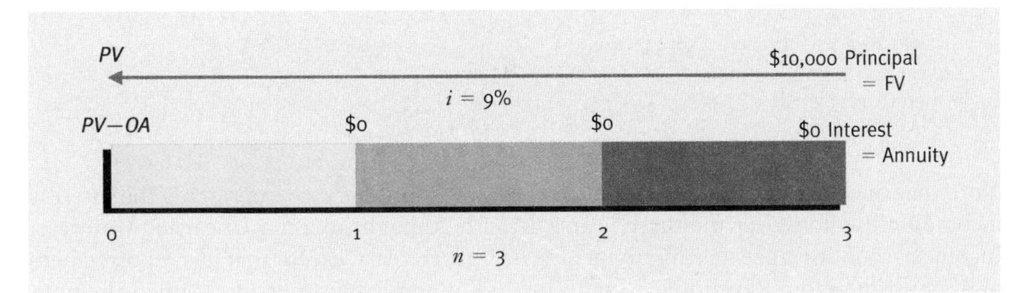

[21] There may be situations when the implicit interest rate is not the market rate; that is, when the fair value of the loan differs from the cash consideration. This circumstance is dealt with later in this chapter.

The entry to record the transaction is:

A = L + SE
0 0 0

Cash flows: ↓ 7,721.80 outflow

Notes Receivable	10,000.00	
Discount on Notes Receivable ($10,000 – $7,721.80)		2,278.20
Cash		7,721.80

Discount on Notes Receivable is reported on the balance sheet as a contra asset account to Notes Receivable. Each year, the discount is amortized using the **effective interest method** to recognize the interest income.[22] This method requires that the effective interest or yield rate be calculated at the time when the investment is made. This rate is then later used to calculate interest income by applying it to the carrying amount (book value) of the investment for each interest period. The note's carrying amount changes as it is increased by the amount of discount amortized or decreased by the amount of premium amortized in each period. **Thus, the net carrying amount is always equal to the present value of the note's remaining cash flows (principal and interest payments) discounted by the market rate at acquisition.** Jeremiah's three-year discount amortization and interest income schedule is shown in Illustration 7-10.

Illustration 7-10
Discount Amortization Schedule–Effective Interest Method

SCHEDULE OF NOTE DISCOUNT AMORTIZATION
Effective Interest Method
0% Note Discounted at 9%

	Cash Received	Interest Income	Discount Amortized	Carrying Amount of Note[a]
Date of issue				$ 7,721.80
End of year 1	$ -0-	$ 694.96[b]	$ 694.96[c]	8,416.76[d]
End of year 2	-0-	757.51	757.51	9,174.27
End of year 3	-0-	825.73[e]	825.73	10,000.00
	$ -0-	$2,278.20	$2,278.20	

[a] Note Receivable less Discount on Note Receivable
[b] $7,721.80 × 0.09 = $694.96
[c] $694.96 – 0 = $694.96
[d] $7,721.80 + $694.96 = $8,416.76 or $10,000 – ($2,278.20 – $694.96) = $8,416.76
[e] 5¢ adjustment for rounding

Interest income at the end of the first year using the effective interest method is recorded as follows:

A = L + SE
+694.96 +694.96

Cash flows: No effect

Discount on Notes Receivable	694.96	
Interest Income ($7,721.80 × 9%)		694.96

Note that the amount of the total discount, $2,278.20 in this case, represents the interest income on the note over the three years. It can be thought of as an Unearned (Interest) Income account that gets taken into income over three years, except that it is reported netted against the Note Receivable account instead of as a liability account. When the note receivable comes due at the end of Year 3, the accounts have the following balances: Notes

[22] *CICA Handbook* Section 3855.66(b).

Receivable, $10,000.00; Discount on Notes Receivable, $0.00. When Jeremiah Company receives the cash at the end of Year 3, it makes the following entry:

Cash	10,000	
Note Receivable		10,000

A	=	L	+	SE
0		0		0

Cash flows: ↑ 10,000 inflow

Interest-Bearing Notes The stated rate of a note and its effective rate are often different, as they were in the zero-interest-bearing case above.

To illustrate a different situation, assume that Morgan Corp. made a loan to Marie Co. and received in exchange a $10,000, three-year note bearing interest at 10% annually. The market rate of interest for a note of similar risk is 12%. The time diagram for all cash flows is as follows:

Underlying Concept

Using a simpler method that gives similar results to the effective interest method is an application of the materiality concept.

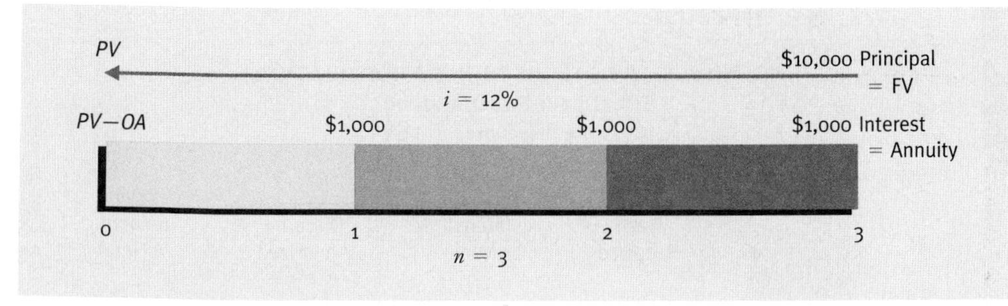

Note that the interest cash flows are determined by the stated rate (10%) but that **all cash flows are discounted at the market rate** (12%) in determining the note's present value. The present value ($9,520) of the two streams of cash is calculated in Illustration 7-11.[23]

Illustration 7-11

Calculation of Present Value—Effective Rate Different from Stated Rate

Face value of the note		$10,000
Present value of the principal:		
$10,000 (PVF*$_{3,12\%}$) = $10,000 (0.71178)	$7,118	
Present value of the interest:		
$1,000 (PVF*–OA$_{3,12\%}$) = $1,000 (2.40183)	2,402	
Present value of the note		9,520
Difference		$ 480

*Present Value Factor

Because the **effective interest rate** or **market interest rate** (12%) is greater than the [...] that the note actually pays (10%), you would expect the note's present value (also its [...]alue) to be less than its face value; that is, the note should be exchanged at a **discount**. [...]makes intuitive sense. If you were to invest in a note that promises 10 percent when [...]ould get 12 percent elsewhere in the market at the same level of risk, you would not [...] willing to pay face value for the note.

rate
fair v
This i
you c
be

[23] Be alert to the fact that "n" equals the number of interest periods, **not one year**, and that "i" is the interest rate **for the period defined by "n."** If interest were paid semi-annually in this example, "n" would be 6, not 3, and "i" would be 6%, not 12%, and these would be used to discount both the maturity amount **and** the interest flows. The interest cash flow used in the present value calculation would be $500, not $1,000.

The receipt of the note in exchange for cash equal to its fair value is recorded by Morgan as follows:

A	= L	+ SE
0	0	0

Cash flows: ↓ 9,520 outflow

Notes Receivable	10,000	
Discount on Notes Receivable		480
Cash		9,520

When the note matures, Morgan will thus receive $480 more than it invested in the note, and this discount effectively increases the return on the investment from 10 percent to 12 percent. The discount is amortized each period and the amount of interest income that is recognized is greater than the $1,000 received each year. Morgan's three-year discount amortization and interest income schedule is shown in Illustration 7-12.

Illustration 7-12
Discount Amortization Schedule–Effective Interest Method

SCHEDULE OF NOTE DISCOUNT AMORTIZATION
Effective Interest Method
10% Note Discounted at 12%

	Cash Received	Interest Income	Discount Amortized	Carrying Amount of Note[a]
Date of issue				$ 9,520
End of year 1	$1,000[b]	$1,142[c]	$142[d]	9,662[e]
End of year 2	1,000	1,159	159	9,821
End of year 3	1,000	1,179	179	10,000
	$3,000	$3,480	$480	

[a] Note Receivable less Discount on Note Receivable
[b] $10,000 × 10% = $1,000
[c] $9,520 × 12% = $1,142
[d] $1,142 − $1,000 = $142
[e] $9,520 + $142 = $9,662 or $10,000 − ($480 − $142) = $9,662

On the date of issue, the note has a present value of $9,520. Its unamortized discount—the interest income that will be spread over the three-year life of the note—is $480.

At the end of Year 1, Morgan receives $1,000 in cash, but the interest income is $1,142 ($9,520 × 12%). The difference between $1,000 and $1,142 is the discount to be amortized, $142. Morgan records the annual interest received and amortization of the discoun[illegible] for the first year as follows:

A	= L	+ SE
+1,142		+1,142

Cash flows: ↑ 1,000 inflow

Cash	1,000	
Discount on Notes Receivable	142	
Interest Income		1,142

The note's carrying amount is now $9,662 ($9,520 + $142), or the balance in the [illegible] Receivable account of $10,000 reduced by the adjusted balance of the Discount on No[illegible] Receivable account of $338 ($480 – $142). This process is repeated until the end of Year 3.

When the stated rate is greater than the effective interest rate, the note's fair value (its present value) is more than its face value and the note is exchanged at a **premium**. The premium on a note receivable is recorded as a debit and amortized using the effective interest method over the life of the note through annual reductions in the amount of interest income that is recognized.

Notes Received for Property, Goods, or Services

When property, goods, or services are sold and a long-term note is received as the consideration instead of cash or a short-term receivable, there may be an issue in determining the selling price. If an appropriate market rate of interest is known for the note, or for a note of similar risk, there is no problem. The sale's proceeds are equal to the present value of the cash flows promised by the note, discounted at the market rate of interest. **Remember that if the stated rate and the market rate are the same, the note's face value and fair value are the same.** It is when the two rates are not the same that the note's fair value must be determined by discounting the cash flows at the market rate.

If an appropriate market rate is not known, two approaches can be used:

1. The fair value of the property, goods, or services that are given up can be used instead of the fair value of the note received. In this case, because the note's present value, the actual cash flow amounts, and the timing of the cash flows are all known, the market or yield interest rate can be determined. This is needed in order to amortize any resulting discount or premium on the note.

2. An appropriate interest rate can be imputed. **Imputation** is the process of determining an appropriate interest rate, and the resulting rate is called an **imputed interest rate.** The objective for calculating the appropriate interest rate is to approximate the rate that would have been agreed on if an independent borrower and lender had negotiated a similar transaction. The choice of a rate is affected by the prevailing rates for similar instruments of issuers with similar credit ratings. It is also affected by such factors as restrictive covenants, collateral, the payment schedule, and the existing prime interest rate.

To illustrate, assume that Oasis Corp. sold land in exchange for a five-year note that has a maturity value of $35,247 and no stated interest rate. The property originally cost Oasis $14,000. What are the proceeds on disposal of the land; that is, what selling price should be recorded in this transaction?

Situation 1: Assume that the market rate of interest of 12% is known. In this case, the proceeds from the sale are equal to the present value of the note, which is $20,000. This is a non-interest-bearing note, so the only cash flow is the $35,247 received in five periods' time: $35,247 × .56743 (Table A-2) = $20,000. The entry to record the sale is:

Notes Receivable	35,247	
Discount on Notes Receivable ($35,247 – $20,000)		15,247
Land		14,000
Gain on Sale of Land ($20,000 – $14,000)		6,000

A	= L +	SE
+6,000		+6,000

Cash flows: No effect

Situation 2: Assume that the market rate of interest is unknown, but that the land has been appraised recently for $20,000. In this case, the property's fair value determines the amount of the proceeds and the note's fair value. The entry is the same as in Situation 1. To amortize the discount, however, the implicit interest rate must be determined. This is done by finding the interest rate that makes the present value of the future cash flow amount of $35,247 equal to its present value of $20,000. The procedure is as follows: First the present value factor is calculated: $20,000 ÷ $35,247 = .56742. Table A-2 then identifies the interest rate for five periods and a factor of .56742 as 12%.

Situation 3: Assume that neither the market rate nor the land's fair value is known. In this case, a market rate must be imputed and then used to determine the note's present value. It will also be used to recognize interest income over the five years and amortize the discount. If a 12% rate is estimated for Oasis, then the entry will be the same as in Situation 1. If a different rate results, the discount on the note and the gain on sale will be different as well.

Fair Value Not Equal to Cash Consideration

Accountants need to be alert when recognizing and measuring loans receivable. Sometimes, the cash that is exchanged when the loan is made may not be the same as the fair value of the loan. In this situation, the substance of the transaction must be determined and accounted for. Imagine a situation where a company advances $20,000 to an officer of the company, charges no interest on the advance, and makes it repayable in four years. Assuming a market rate of 6%, the fair value of the loan receivable is $15,842 ($20,000 × .79209, the PV factor for $n = 4$ and $i = 6$), resulting in a discount of $4,158. Although the fair value of the loan is $15,842, the officer of the company actually received $20,000. This $4,158 difference must then be recognized and accounted for according to its nature—in this case, additional compensation. The entry to record this transaction is as follows.

A	=	L	+	SE
−4,158				−4,158

Cash flows: ↓ 20,000 outflow

Note/Loan Receivable	20,000	
Compensation Expense	4,158	
Discount on Note/Loan Receivable		4,158
Cash		20,000

Impairment in Value of Long-Term Loans Receivable

While the valuation of short-term notes receivable is exactly the same as for short-term trade accounts receivable, special standards have been developed for the valuation of impaired long-term loans receivable. A company considers a note receivable as **impaired** when collecting all the amounts that are due—both principal and interest—will likely not occur. Banks particularly, but not exclusively, have had problems with loans that they are unable to collect from real estate ventures, less-developed countries, technology companies, and others. We discuss impairments in detail, as well as restructurings of loans and debts, in Appendix 14A.

DISPOSITION OF RECEIVABLES

Objective 9
Account for and explain the basic accounting issues related to the disposition of receivables.

In the normal course of events, accounts and notes receivable are collected when they are due and then removed from the books. However, as credit sales and receivables have grown in size and significance, this "normal course of events" has evolved. **In order to receive cash more quickly from receivables, owners now often transfer accounts or loans receivable to another company for cash.**

There are various reasons for this early transfer. First, for competitive reasons, providing sales financing for customers is almost mandatory in many industries. In the sale of durable goods, such as automobiles, trucks, industrial and farm equipment, computers, and appliances, a large majority of sales are on an instalment contract basis. This means that the seller is financing the purchase by allowing the buyer to pay for it over time, usually in equal periodic payments or instalments. Many major companies in these and other industries have created wholly owned subsidiaries that specialize in receivables financing. For example, Canadian Tire Corporation, Limited's Financial Services segment incorporated a federally regulated bank, Canadian Tire Bank. This wholly owned subsidiary manages and finances Canadian Tire's MasterCard and retail credit card and personal loan portfolios.

Second, the **holder** may sell receivables because money is tight and access to normal credit is not available or is far too expensive. A firm may have to sell its receivables, instead of borrowing, to avoid violating the terms of its current lending agreements. In addition, the billing and collecting of receivables is often time-consuming and costly. Credit card companies such as MasterCard, VISA, and other finance companies take over the collection process and provide merchants with immediate cash in exchange for a fee to cover their collection and bad debt costs. There are also **purchasers** of receivables, who buy the receivables to obtain the legal protection of ownership rights that are given to a purchaser of assets instead of the lesser rights that a secured creditor like Visa or MasterCard has. In addition, banks and other lending institutions may be forced to purchase receivables because of legal lending limits; that is, they may not be allowed to make any additional loans but still be able to buy receivables and charge a fee for this service.

Receivables can be used to generate immediate cash for a company in two ways. Often referred to as **asset-based financing**, these ways are:

1. Secured borrowings
2. Sales of receivables

Secured Borrowings

Like many other assets, receivables are often used as collateral in borrowing transactions. A creditor may require that the debtor assign or pledge receivables as security for a loan, but leave the receivables under the control of the borrowing company. The note or loan payable, a liability, is reported on the balance sheet and, if it is not paid when it is due, the creditor has the right to convert the collateral to cash; that is, to collect the receivables.

Accounting Guideline 12 recommends that, after the transfer, a company should account for the transferred assets in a **secured borrowing** **in the same way as it did before the borrowing**, and that it account for the liability according to accounting policies for similar liabilities.[24] The debtor thus recognizes interest expense on the borrowed amount, and may have to pay an additional finance charge, which is expensed.

In addition to recording the collection of receivables, the company must also recognize all discounts, returns and allowances, and bad debts. Each month, the proceeds from collecting accounts receivable are used to retire the loan obligation.

Sales of Receivables

Sales of receivables have increased greatly in recent years. One common type is a sale to a factor. **Factors** are finance companies or banks that buy receivables from businesses for a fee and then collect the amounts owed directly from the customers. **Factoring receivables** was traditionally associated with the garment trade in Montreal, but it is now common in other industries as well, such as furniture, consumer electronics, and automotive aftermarkets. Illustration 7-13 shows a factoring arrangement.

It is becoming more and more common to **transfer receivables** through a process known as **securitization**. Securitization is defined as the transformation of financial assets such as loans and receivables into securities, which are then often called **asset-backed securities**. The process takes a pool of assets that produces interest and principal payments, such as credit card receivables, mortgage receivables, or car loan receivables, and sells shares in these pools. The result is securities that are backed by pools of assets. Almost every asset that has a payment stream (i.e., that produces payments) and has a long-term payment history is a candidate for securitization.

For example, Canadian Tire Corporation, Limited's 2005 Management Discussion & Analysis reports that instead of owning all of its receivables throughout the collection period, it sells customer credit card and personal loan receivables to Glacier Credit Card Trust

[24] *CICA Handbook*, "Transfers of Receivables."

Illustration 7-13
Basic Procedures in Factoring

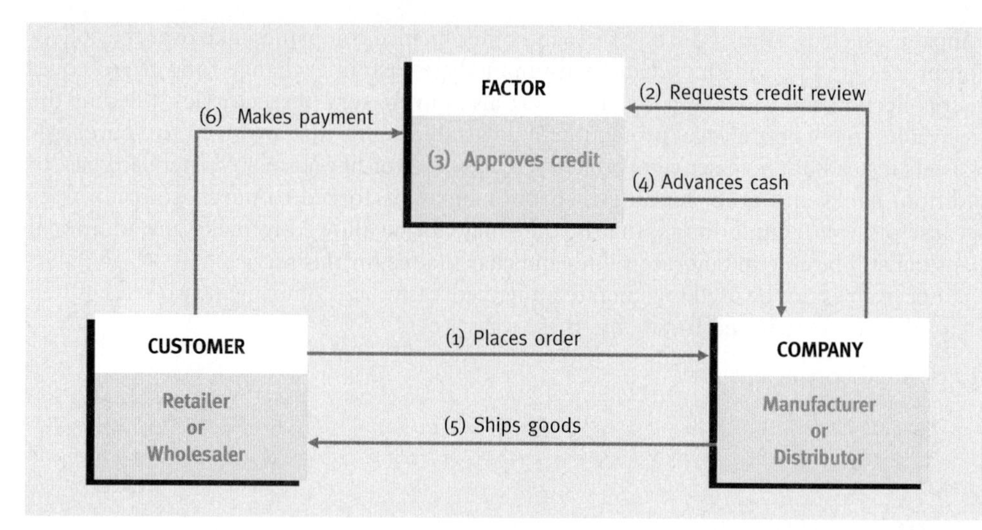

and another independent third party trust. Glacier Credit Card Trust was formed to hold the receivables as an investment, and is financed by the issue of debt securities to third party investors. By this process, ownership of the receivables is transformed into securities being held by a **special purpose entity (SPE)**, the trust.

The arrangements that are made in a securitization transaction differ from company to company. Canadian Tire, for example, sells pools of these receivables for cash and some retained interest in or components of the receivables. The components it gets back include the right to the interest portion of the receivables (but not the principal), a subordinated interest in the loans sold, and a securitization reserve. Canadian Tire also continues to service the receivables; that is, it manages the accounts, including the responsibility to collect the amounts due. The relevant notes to the company's financial statements are provided in Illustration 7-18, presented later in the chapter.

What Do the Numbers Mean?

What is the motivation for this type of transaction? Basically, it is a financing transaction that gives companies a more attractive way to raise funds than by issuing a corporate bond or note. The credit risk for a bond or note issued by a company is higher than the credit risk of a special purpose entity that holds the company's receivables. For example, Sears Canada Inc.'s annual report recently reported a credit rating of AAA and R-1 (High) **for its trust securitized debt issues and commercial paper**, respectively, which are the highest possible ratings for these debt classifications. Compare these with BBB and BBB (High) ratings for Sears' **senior unsecured debt**. The higher credit rating is due to the fact that receivables transferred to an SPE are often credit enhanced[25] and the cash flows to the SPE are much more predictable than the cash flows to the operating company because there are no operating risks for an SPE. When the risk is less, the cost of financing is also less. The net result is that the company that transfers its receivables gets access to lower-cost financing that it can then use to pay off debt that has a higher cost of capital.

The differences between factoring and securitization are that **factoring** usually involves a sale to only one company, fees are relatively high, the quality of the receivables may be lower, and the seller does not usually service the receivables afterward. In a **securitization**, many investors are involved, margins are tight, the receivables are of higher quality, and the seller usually continues to service the receivables. When the company making the transfer continues to be involved in some way with the transferred assets, and measurement of the underlying transaction amounts involves some uncertainty, many disclosures are required in the financial statements.

[25] Credit enhancements include guaranteeing payment through recourse to the company selling the receivables or third party guarantee provisions, the use of cash reserve accounts, or overcollateralization—i.e., providing security with a greater fair value than the amount that is at risk.

Underlying Principles

Before identifying the criteria that need to exist for a transaction to be treated as a sale, it is important to understand two basic concepts that underlie the decisions of the Accounting Standards Board. The first principle, which is applied in many similar situations, is that only assets that an **entity can control** should be recognized on its balance sheet. Once control is given up, the asset should no longer be recognized—it should be derecognized. The second concept, which has been applied to assets such as accounts receivable only recently, is that receivables can be disaggregated (or separated) into a variety of financial components. This approach makes it possible to assign values to such components as the rights to the principal cash flows and/or interest cash flows, a recourse provision, servicing rights, agreements to reacquire, and rights to returns in excess of specified limits, for example. Previous standards treated receivables as an inseparable unit that could only be "entirely sold or entirely retained."[26]

Criteria for Treatment as a Sale

Before the Accounting Standards Board published *Accounting Guideline 12*, companies tended to account for many transactions as **sales** of receivables, even when they had a major continuing interest in and control over the transferred receivables. Doing this resulted in their financial statements showing a reduction in receivables, no additional debt, and often a gain on sale. The purpose of *Accounting Guideline 12* is to identify when a transfer of receivables qualifies for **being treated as a sale**, and when it is merely a **secured borrowing**. In addition, it covers how to account for **the sale of receivables**, particularly when the transferor (the company selling the receivables) continues to have an interest in the transferred assets.

International Insight

The IASB has a similar approach to the sale of receivables, although it allows more flexibility in implementation.

The AcSB concluded that a sale occurs when the seller surrenders control of all or a portion of the receivables to the buyer and receives in exchange a consideration that does not include a beneficial interest in the transferred asset. A **beneficial interest** is basically a debt or equity claim to the cash flows of the party that acquired the receivables. The following three conditions must be met **before a sale can be recorded:**

1. The transferred assets have been isolated from the transferor—i.e., put beyond the reach of the transferor and its creditors, even in bankruptcy or receivership.
2. Each transferee (the party that receives the assets) has the right to pledge or exchange the assets (or beneficial interests) that it received, and there are no conditions that either (1) limit the transferee's ability to take advantage of this right or (2) give more than a trivial benefit to the transferor.
3. The transferor does not maintain effective control over the transferred assets through either an agreement to repurchase or redeem them before their maturity or through an ability to unilaterally cause the holder to return specific assets.[27]

If all three conditions **are not met**, the transferor records the transfer as a secured borrowing. **Only when all three conditions are satisfied** is control over the assets assumed to be given up, and the transaction accounted for as a sale. If accounting for the transaction as a sale is appropriate, the specific asset components that were obtained need to be identified, as well as the liability components that were incurred. The general rules of accounting for transfers of receivables are summarized in Illustration 7-14.

Applying the accounting and disclosure guidance for transfers of receivables becomes more complex because of specialized contracts with different terms and conditions

[26] *Accounting Guideline 12*, par. 6.

[27] *Accounting Guideline 12*, par. 9.

Illustration 7-14
Accounting for Transfers of Receivables

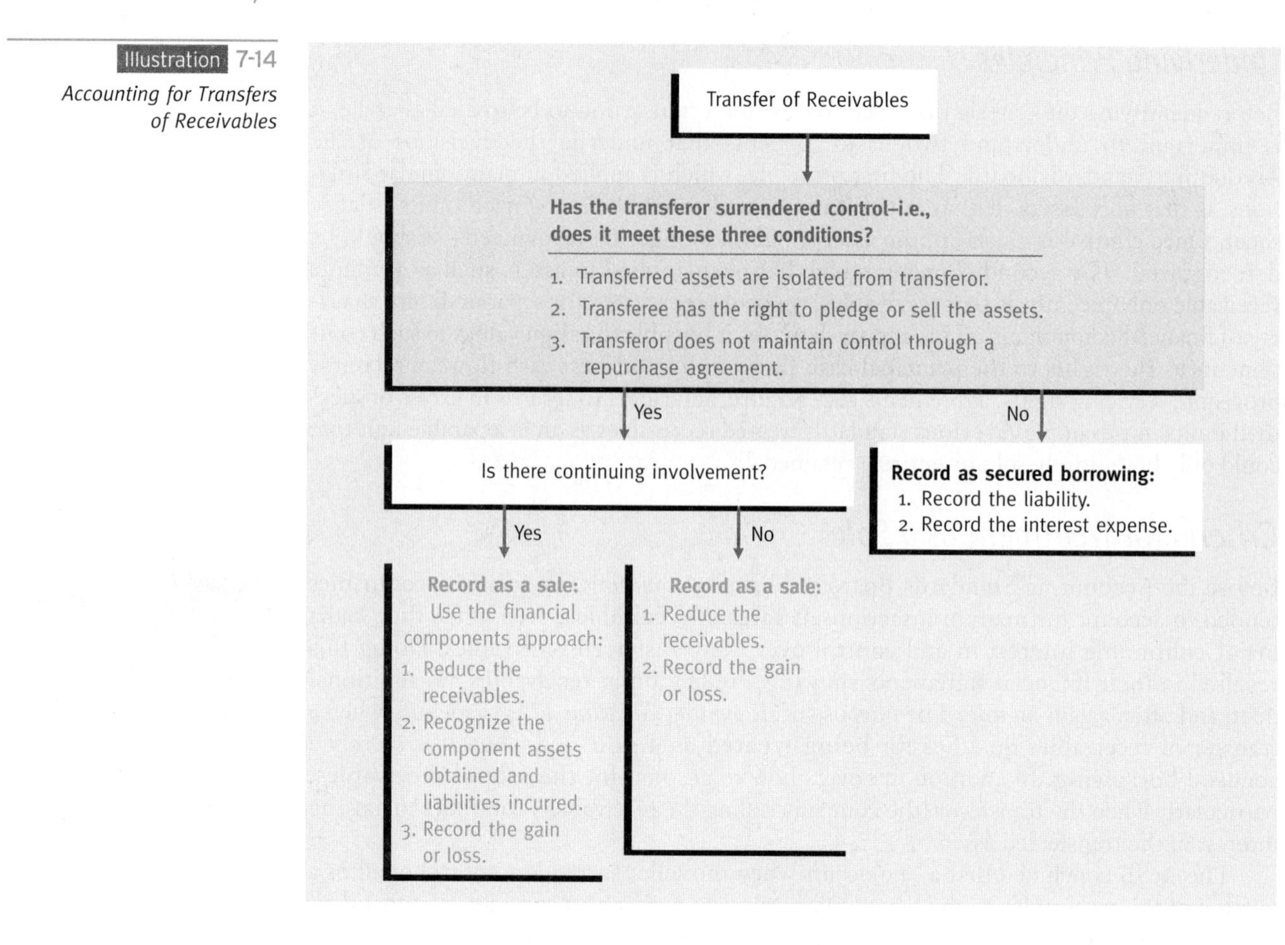

between companies, the securitization of receivables, and special purpose entities. The illustrations that follow are somewhat simplified to make the basic process of accounting for such transactions easier to follow.

Sale with No Continuing Involvement by Transferor

The most straightforward situation is when the receivables are sold outright to another unrelated party, such as a factor, and they are sold without recourse.

When receivables are sold **without recourse**, the purchaser assumes the risk of collection and absorbs any credit losses.[28] The transfer of accounts receivable in a non-recourse transaction is an outright sale of the receivables both in form (the title is transferred) and substance (control is transferred). In non-recourse transactions, as in any sale of assets, Cash is debited for the proceeds. Accounts Receivable is credited for the receivables' face value. The difference, reduced by any provision for probable adjustments (discounts, returns, allowances, etc.), is recognized in the account Gain or Loss on the Sale of Receivables. When appropriate, the seller uses a Due from Factor account (reported as a receivable) to account for the proceeds that are retained by a factor in order to cover probable sales discounts, sales returns, and sales allowances.

To illustrate, Crest Textiles Ltd. factors $500,000 of accounts receivable with Commercial Factors, Inc. on a **without recourse** basis. The receivables records are

[28] *Accounting Guideline 12* defines "recourse" as "the right of a transferee of receivables to receive payment from the transferor of those receivables for failure of debtors to pay when due, the effects of prepayments, or adjustments resulting from defects in the eligibility of the transferred receivables."

transferred to Commercial Factors, Inc., which takes over full responsibility for the collections. Commercial Factors assesses a finance charge of 3% of the amount of accounts receivable and withholds an initial amount equal to 5% of the accounts receivable. Illustration 7-15 shows the journal entries for both Crest Textiles and Commercial Factors for this receivables transfer without recourse.

Illustration 7-15
Entries for Sale of Receivables without Recourse

Crest Textiles Ltd.			Commercial Factors, Inc.		
Cash	460,000		Accounts (Notes) Receivable	500,000	
Due from Factor	25,000*		Due to Crest Textiles		25,000
Loss on Sale of Receivables	15,000**		Financing Revenue		15,000
Accounts (Notes) Receivable		500,000	Cash		460,000

*(5% × $500,000)
**(3% × $500,000)

To recognize the sale of all the financial components of the receivables, Crest Textiles records a loss of $15,000. The factor's net income will be the difference between the financing revenue of $15,000 and the amount of any uncollectible receivables.

Sale with Continuing Involvement by Transferor

Recourse Component Retained If receivables are sold **with recourse**, the seller or transferor guarantees payment to the purchaser if the customer fails to pay. A **financial components approach** is used to record this type of transaction because the seller has a continuing involvement with the receivable. Each party to the sale recognizes the components (assets and liabilities) that it controls after the sale and stops recognizing the assets and liabilities that were sold or extinguished.

To illustrate, assume the same information as in Illustration 7-15 for Crest Textiles and Commercial Factors except that the receivables are sold **with recourse**. Crest Textiles estimates that the recourse obligation (a liability) has a fair value of $6,000. This is the company's estimate of the fair value of the cost of its agreement in the contract to pay the amount of any receivables that debtors fail to pay. To determine the loss on the sale of Crest Textiles' receivables, the net proceeds from the sale are calculated and compared with the carrying amount of the assets that were sold, as Illustration 7-16 shows. Net proceeds are cash or other assets received in a sale less any liabilities incurred.

Illustration 7-16
Calculation of Net Proceeds and Loss on Sale

Calculation of net proceeds:		
Cash received (an asset)	$460,000	
Due from factor (an asset)	25,000	$485,000
Less: Recourse obligation (a liability)		6,000
Net proceeds		$479,000
Calculation of loss on sale:		
Carrying (book) amount		$500,000
Net proceeds		479,000
Loss on sale of receivables		$ 21,000

Illustration 7-17 shows the journal entries for both Crest Textiles and Commercial Factors for the receivables sold with a recourse component being retained.

Illustration 7-17
Entries for Sale of Receivables with Recourse Component Retained

Crest Textiles Ltd.			Commercial Factors, Inc.		
Cash	460,000		Accounts Receivable	500,000	
Due from Factor	25,000		Due to Crest Textiles		25,000
Loss on Sale of Receivables	21,000		Financing Revenue		15,000
Accounts (Notes)			Cash		460,000
Receivable		500,000			
Recourse Liability		6,000			

Tutorial on the Transfer of Receivables

www.wiley.com/canada/kieso

In this case, Crest Textiles recognizes a loss of $21,000. In addition, a liability of $6,000 is recorded to indicate the probable payment to Commercial Factors for uncollectible receivables. If all the receivables are collected, Crest Textiles would eliminate its recourse liability and increase income. Commercial Factors' net income is the financing revenue of $15,000 because it will have no bad debts related to these receivables.

Servicing and Other Components Often, the transferor in a securitization will retain the responsibility for servicing the receivables. This usually includes collecting the principal and interest, monitoring slow-paying accounts, and remitting cash to those who hold beneficial interests in the receivables. It may also include other specified services. If the transferor receives no reimbursement for these activities or receives less than the estimated cost of carrying them out, a **servicing liability component** will be recorded. This decreases the net proceeds on disposal. Alternatively, a **servicing asset component** is recognized if the benefits of servicing (servicing fees under contract, late charges, etc.) are greater than the estimated cost of the obligation.

Other financial components that may be identified and recognized in a securitization include:

Interest-only strip receivable	The contractual right to receive some or all of the interest due on an interest-bearing receivable
Call option	The right of the transferor to repurchase similar loans or receivables from the transferee

Disclosure

Accounting Guideline 12 requires many disclosures for securitized receivables that are accounted for as sales. The goal is to inform readers about the fair value measurements and key assumptions that were used, the characteristics of the securitizations, cash flows between the special purpose entity and the transferor, the balances and risk of servicing the assets and liabilities, and some sensitivity analysis. Illustration 7-18 in the next section of the chapter gives an example of the main securitization disclosures made by **Canadian Tire Corporation, Limited** for its year ended December 31, 2005.

PRESENTATION, PERSPECTIVES, AND INTERNATIONAL STANDARDS

Presentation of Receivables and Loans

Objective 10
Explain how receivables and loans are reported and analyzed.

Trade accounts and notes receivable require the following reporting:

1. Segregate the different types of receivables so that ordinary trade accounts, amounts owing by related parties, and other significant amounts are separately reported.

2. Indicate the amounts and maturity dates of instalment accounts with a maturity of more than one year.
3. Report in current assets the amounts that are receivable within one year from the balance sheet date, or the operating cycle, if longer.
4. Disclose the nature and carrying value of receivables that have been designated or pledged as collateral for the liabilities.[29]

The requirements in *Handbook* Section 3862, "Financial Instruments—Disclosure,"[30] also apply to receivables and loans. The purpose of the disclosures is to provide information about how significant these financial assets are to the organization's position and performance and to allow users to assess the nature and extent of the associated risks. This standard requires much more information than previously about the risks that a company faces through its financial instruments and how they are managed. This new input is useful in evaluating a company's position and performance and its prospects for future returns and cash flows, which are evident from the disclosures required.

International Insight

When receivables that will be paid in a foreign currency are being held, there is a risk that the exchange rate may move against the company and cause a decrease in the amount collected in terms of Canadian dollars. Companies that have cross-border transactions often "hedge" these receivables by buying contracts to exchange currencies at specified amounts at future dates.

The major disclosures about the significance of loans and receivables to a company's financial position and performance are as follows:

1. Their carrying amount on the balance sheet
2. The terms and conditions and carrying amount of those pledged as collateral
3. A reconciliation of changes during the period in any allowance account that is used for recording impairments due to credit losses
4. Gains or losses, total interest income, interest income on impaired loans, and any impairment losses reported on the income statement
5. Their fair value, and information about how the fair values were determined. Short-term receivables with insignificant differences between the carrying and fair values are excluded from this requirement.[31]

The disclosures about the nature and extent of risks arising from loans and receivables require the following:

1. **Qualitative** information for each type of risk,[32] such as the exposures to risk and the origin of each risk, how the entity manages and measures each risk, and any changes from the previous period
2. **Quantitative** measures that management uses for each type of risk, ensuring that any concentrations of risk are identified
3. The amount of the entity's maximum exposure to credit risk; a description of any collateral being held; and specific information about amounts not yet past due or impaired, and separate information for those that are
4. A sensitivity analysis and explanations about the market risk factors

Extensive excerpts from the December 31, 2005, balance sheet of Canadian Tire Corporation, Limited and the notes cross-referenced to the balance sheet are presented in Illustration 7-18. This illustration shows most of the disclosures that are required for

[29] *CICA Handbook*, Sections 1400.14, 1510.01, and 3020.01, .02.
[30] This new standard is effective October 1, 2007.
[31] *CICA Handbook*, Sections 3862.07A to .30A.
[32] *Handbook* Section 3862.05A identifies and defines the various types of risks: credit risk, market risk (currency, interest-rate, and other types of price risk), and liquidity risk.

receivables and loans. Note that these financial statements were prepared before the requirements of Section 3862 were released.

Illustration 7-18

Canadian Tire Corporation, Limited Disclosures of Receivables and Loans

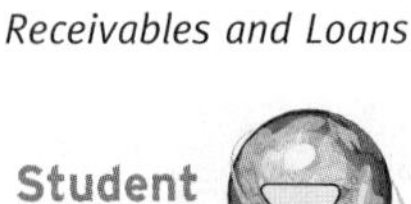

Student Toolkit—Additional Disclosures

www.wiley.com/canada/kieso

Consolidated Balance Sheets

As at (Dollars in millions)		**December 31, 2005**		January 1, 2005
ASSETS				
Current assets				
Cash and cash equivalents (Note 12)	$	**838.0**	$	802.2
Accounts receivable (Note 12)		**652.8**		370.7
Loans receivable (Note 2)		**728.7**		592.4
Merchandise inventories		**675.5**		620.6
Prepaid expenses and deposits		**42.4**		24.1
Future income taxes (Note 11)		**43.6**		24.6
Total current assets		**2,981.0**		2,434.6
Long-term receivables and other assets (Note 3)		**132.1**		129.7

1. SIGNIFICANT ACCOUNTING POLICIES (Excerpts)

Loans receivable Loans receivable include credit card and personal loans receivable. Loans receivable are recorded at cost net of unearned interest income and of allowances established for credit losses. Interest income is recorded on an accrual basis, except for impaired loans, the treatment of which is described below.

An allowance for credit losses is calculated using the historical loss experience of account balances based on aging and arrears status, with certain adjustments for other relevant circumstances influencing the recoverability of the loans.

Effective July 1, 2001, the Company adopted the CICA's Accounting Guideline 12 ("AcG-12"), "Transfers of Receivables". Under this policy, the Company is required to recognize gains or losses on its loans receivable securitizations subsequent to June 30, 2001 that qualify as sales. The gain or loss on the sale of the loans receivable depends in part on the previous carrying amount of the loans involved in the sale. The carrying amount is allocated between the assets sold and the retained interests based on their relative fair values at the date of sale. The Company estimates fair value based on the present value of future expected cash flows using management's estimates of the key assumptions (see Note 2).

2. LOANS RECEIVABLE

The Company sells pools of loans receivable ("the Loans") to third party trusts ("the Trusts") in transactions known as securitizations. Loans include both credit card and personal loans receivable. The transactions are accounted for as sales in accordance with Accounting Guideline 12, "Transfers of Receivables" ("AcG-12"), and the Loans are removed from the Consolidated Balance Sheets. The Company retains the interest-only strip, and for the personal loan securitization, a subordinated interest in the loans sold (the "seller's interest") and cash deposited with one of the Trusts (the "securitization reserve"), all of which are retained interests. The seller's interest and securitization reserve provide that Trust with a source of funds in the event that the interest and principal collected on the Loans is not sufficient to pay the Trust's creditors. The Trusts' recourse to the Company is limited to the retained interests. The Company also assumes responsibility for servicing the Loans, for which it does not receive any direct compensation.

The proceeds of the sale are deemed to be the cash received, interest-only strip and securitization reserve, less any servicing obligation assumed. The proceeds are allocated between the Loans, interest-only strip, seller's interest and securitization reserve based on their relative fair value at the date of sale, with any excess or deficiency recorded as a gain or loss on sale respectively. The Company estimates fair values by discounting future cash flows or comparing the appropriate yield curves to matching maturity terms. Retained interests are measured at fair value and are reviewed for impairment on a quarterly basis. For the year ended December 31, 2005, the Company recognized pre-tax gains of $19.9 million (2004 - $22.6 million) on the securitization of the Loans.

As the Company does not control the Trusts, they have not been consolidated in these financial statements.

Quantitative information about loans receivable managed and securitized by the Company is as follows:

	Total principal amount of receivables[1]		Average balances[1]	
(Dollars in millions)	**2005**	2004	**2005**	2004
Total net managed credit card portfolio	**$ 3,143.4**	$ 2,789.2	**$ 2,818.2**	$ 2,512.6
Credit card receivables sold	**(2,422.8)**	(2,209.3)	**(2,224.2)**	(1,889.5)
Credit card receivables held	**720.6**	579.9	**594.0**	623.1
Total net managed personal loan portfolio[2]	**215.8**	64.0	**190.0**	29.6
Personal loans sold[3]	**(176.3)**	-	**(7.3)**	-
Personal loans held	**39.5**	64.0	**182.7**	29.6
Total loans receivable	**760.1**	643.9	**$ 776.7**	$ 652.7
Less: long-term portion[4]	**31.4**	51.5		
Current portion of loans receivable[5]	**$ 728.7**	$ 592.4		

[1] Amounts shown are net of allowance for credit losses.
[2] Personal loans are unsecured loans that are provided to qualified existing credit cardholders for terms of three to five years. Personal loans have fixed monthly payments of principal and interest; however, the personal loans can be repaid at any time without penalty.
[3] Personal loans totaling $205.4 million were sold, net of the seller's interest on securitization of $29.1 million.
[4] The long-term portion of loans receivable is included in "Long-term receivables and other assets". It includes the long-term portion of the seller's interest on securitization of $21.2 million (2004 - nil).
[5] The current portion of loans receivable includes the current portion of the seller's interest on securitization of $7.9 million (2004 - nil).

Net credit losses for the year ended December 31, 2005, were $182.1 million (2004 - $149.6 million). Net credit losses are charge-offs net of recoveries and are based on the total managed portfolio of loans receivable.

The book value and fair value of the retained interests based on future cash flows are as follows:

	2005		2004	
(Dollars in millions)	**Book value**	**Fair value**	Book value	Fair value
Credit card loans	**$ 91.7**	**$ 92.6**	$ 80.5	$ 81.3
Personal loans	**47.2**	**50.1**	-	-
Total fair value of retained interests	**$ 138.9**	**$ 142.7**	$ 80.5	$ 81.3

For both the credit card and personal loans, the retained interests include the allowance on securitized receivables and the interest-only strip. For the personal loan securitization, retained interests also include the seller's interest and the securitization reserve.

The following tables show the key economic assumptions used in measuring the fair value of retained interests at the date of securitization. The tables also display the sensitivity of the current fair value of residual cash flows to immediate 10 percent and 20 percent adverse changes in those assumptions at year end.

Credit card loans

	Assumptions	Impact of adverse changes on fair value of retained interest[1]		Assumptions
(Dollars in millions)	**2005**	10%	20%	2004
Yield[2]	**16.55%**	$ (12.9)	$ (25.7)	16.50%
Liquidation rate[3]	**24.05%**	(10.3)	(18.9)	23.01%
Expected credit losses[2]	**6.01%**	(0.1)	(0.3)	5.60%
Discount rate[2]	**12.00%**	(1.5)	(3.1)	12.00%
Servicing rate[2,4]	**2.00%**	(0.1)	(0.2)	2.00%

Personal loans

	Assumptions	Impact of adverse changes on fair value of retained interest[1]		Assumptions
(Dollars in millions)	**2005**	10%	20%	2004
Yield[2]	**12.53%**	$ (3.0)	$ (6.0)	N/A
Pre-payment rate[3]	**55.48%**	(0.4)	(0.7)	N/A
Expected credit losses[2]	**3.60%**	(0.8)	(1.7)	N/A
Discount rate[2]	**8.00%**	(0.3)	(0.6)	N/A
Servicing rate[2,4]	**1.00%**	(0.1)	(0.2)	N/A

[1] These sensitivities are hypothetical and should be used with caution. As the figures indicate, changes in fair value based on a 10 percent or 20 percent variation in assumptions generally cannot be extrapolated because the relationship of the change in assumption to the change in fair value may not be linear. Also, in these tables, the effect of a variation in a particular assumption on the fair value of the retained interest is calculated without changing any other assumption; in reality, changes in one factor may result in changes in another (for example, increases in market interest rates may result in lower payments and increased credit losses), which might magnify or counteract the sensitivities.

[2] Yield, expected credit losses and discount and servicing rates are based on historical patterns.

[3] Based on historical patterns, credit card loans are estimated to be collected in 12 months. Personal loans are collected over terms of three to five years.

[4] The servicing liability as at December 31, 2005 was $18.2 million (2004 - $13.5 million).

Details of cash flows from securitizations:

(Dollars in millions)	**2005**	2004
Proceeds from new securitizations	**$ 541.1**	$ 625.0
Proceeds from collections reinvested in previous securitizations	**6,723.0**	5,601.0
Other cash flows received on retained interests	**1,286.7**	1,335.3

3. LONG-TERM RECEIVABLES AND OTHER ASSETS

(Dollars in millions)	**2005**	2004
Interest-only strip	**$ 55.6**	$ 41.3
Personal loans (Note 2)	**31.4**	51.5
Other assets	**24.0**	15.3
Other receivables	**11.9**	12.2
Long-term debt issue costs	**7.5**	7.5
Mortgages receivable	**1.7**	1.9
	$ 132.1	$ 129.7

12. NOTES TO THE CONSOLIDATED STATEMENTS OF CASH FLOWS (Excerpts)

Sale of Associate Dealer receivables During 2005 and 2004, the Company sold certain Associate Dealer receivables to independent investors. According to the terms of the sale, the Company retained full servicing responsibilities for which it received no compensation. For the year ended December 31, 2005, the Company recognized a loss of $0.1 million (2004 - $2.1 million) on the sale of Associate Dealer receivables, which assumes no expected credit losses and a servicing liability of 1.0 percent. Quantitative information about accounts receivable managed by the Company is as follows:

	Total principal amount of receivables	
(Dollars in millions)	**2005**	2004
Associate Dealer receivables	**$ 570.2**	$ 543.3
Associate Dealer receivables sold	**(47.9)**	(323.2)
Other accounts receivable	**130.5**	150.6
Accounts receivable	**$ 652.8**	$ 370.7

15. FINANCIAL INSTRUMENTS (Excerpts)

The fair values of other financial instruments are as follows:

(Dollars in millions)	2005 Book value	2005 Fair value	2004 Book value	2004 Fair value
Financial assets and liabilities				
Interest-only strip	$ 55.6	$ 60.1	$ 41.3	$ 42.2
Long-term personal loans, mortgages and other receivables	45.0	41.8	65.6	59.1
Equity derivative contracts	11.8	20.6	6.8	8.4
Securitization reserve	4.1	3.4	—	—

The fair values of the interest-only strip, long-term personal loans, mortgages and other receivables, securitization reserve, long-term debt (excluding current portion) and interest rate swap contracts were estimated based on: quoted market prices (when available); discounted cash flows, using discount rates based on prevailing market interest rates and the Company's credit rating; or by comparing the appropriate yield curves to matching maturity terms as at year end.

Interest rate risk The following table identifies the Company's financial assets and liabilities which are sensitive to interest rate movements and those which are non-interest rate sensitive as they are either non-interest bearing or bear interest at fixed rates.

(Dollars in millions)	2005 Interest sensitive	2005 Non-interest sensitive	2004 Interest sensitive	2004 Non-interest sensitive
Cash and cash equivalents	$ 838.0	$ -	$ 802.2	$ -
Loans receivable	-	728.7	-	592.4
Long-term personal loans, mortgages and other receivables	-	45.0	-	65.6
Long-term debt (including current portion)	-	(1,375.6)	-	(1,087.4)
	$ 838.0	$ (601.9)	$ 802.2	$ (429.4)

Credit risk The Company's exposure to concentrations of credit risk is limited. Accounts receivable are primarily from Associate Dealers who individually comprise less than one percent of the total balance outstanding and are spread across Canada. Similarly, loans receivable are generated by credit card and personal loan customers, a large and geographically dispersed group. Current credit exposure is limited to the loss that would be incurred if all of the Company's counterparties were to default at the same time.

Perspectives

Analysts often calculate financial ratios to evaluate the liquidity of a company's accounts receivable. To assess the receivables' liquidity, the **receivables turnover ratio** is used. This ratio measures the number of times, on average, that receivables are collected during the period. The ratio is calculated by dividing net sales by average receivables (net) outstanding during the year. Theoretically, the numerator should include only credit sales, but this information is often not available. As long as the relative amounts of credit and cash sales stay fairly constant, however, the trend indicated by the ratio will still be valid. Unless seasonal factors are significant, average receivables outstanding can be calculated from the beginning and ending balances of net trade receivables.

To illustrate, **Canadian Utilities Limited** reported 2005 revenue of $2,515.8 million and accounts receivable balances at December 31, 2004 and 2005, of $372.8 million and $351.3 million, respectively. Its accounts receivable turnover ratio is calculated in Illustration 7-19.

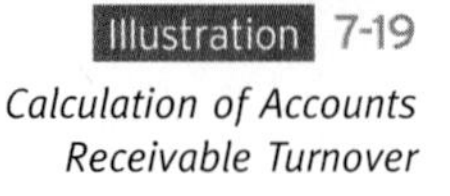

Illustration 7-19

Calculation of Accounts Receivable Turnover

$$\text{Accounts Receivable Turnover} = \frac{\text{Net Sales/Revenue}}{\text{Average trade receivables (net)}}$$

$$= \frac{\$2,515.8}{(\$372.8 + \$351.3)/2}$$

$$= 6.95 \text{ times, or every 53 days } (365 \text{ days} \div 6.95)^{33}$$

[33] Often the receivables turnover is converted to "days to collect accounts receivable" or "days sales outstanding"—i.e., to an average collection period. In this case, 6.95 is divided into 365 days to obtain 53 days. Several figures other than 365 could be used here; a common alternative is 360 days because it is divisible by 30 (days) and 12 (months). Please use 365 days in any homework calculations.

The results give information about the quality of the receivables. They also give an idea of how successful the firm is in collecting its outstanding receivables, particularly when compared with prior periods, industry standards, the credit terms offered by the company, or targets set internally. Management would also prepare an aging schedule to determine how long specific receivables have been outstanding. It is possible that a satisfactory receivables turnover may have resulted because certain receivables were collected quickly though others have been outstanding for a relatively long time. An aging schedule would reveal such patterns.

Underlying Concept

Providing information that will help users assess an enterprise's current liquidity and potential future cash flows is one of the main objectives of accounting.

Because the estimated expense for uncollectible accounts is subject to a large degree of judgement, there is always some concern that companies can use this judgement to manage earnings. By overestimating the amount of uncollectible loans in a good earnings year, a bank, for example, can "save for a rainy day." In future, less profitable periods, the bank will then be able to reduce its overly conservative allowance for its loan loss account and increase earnings as a result.[34]

Further analysis should be done on changes in the basic related accounts. Ordinarily, sales, accounts receivable, and the allowance for doubtful accounts should all move in the same direction. Higher sales should generate more receivables and an increased allowance. If sales have increased as well as receivables, but the allowance has not increased proportionately, the reader should be alert to the possibility of earnings management. If the allowance grows faster than receivables, particularly when sales have not increased, this could indicate deterioration in credit quality. Alternatively, perhaps the company has built up its allowance account so that there is a cushion for poorer performing years ahead. The answers are not always obvious, but this type of analysis can identify concerns.

With the increased practice of selling receivables through securitization transactions, especially where a company retains servicing (such as collection) responsibilities, the financial ratios have to be calculated and interpreted carefully. Consider the following:

- While the company has sold its receivables and received cash earlier than if the receivables were collected in the ordinary course of business, the cash flows are actually from financing transactions, not operating activities.
- Growth in sales should not be compared to growth in receivables on the balance sheet when calculating the receivables turnover and days sales uncollected. Adjustments are needed to the receivable balances for the sold but uncollected accounts. Companies are required to provide this information through note disclosures.
- Securitization is "off–balance sheet" since the sold receivables are removed from the current assets and the amount "borrowed" is not reported in current liabilities. This therefore affects liquidity ratios such as the current and quick ratios. Even though the same dollar amount is missing from the assets and liabilities, the ratios can be significantly affected.

Securitization transactions can be complex, making it necessary to be very cautious when interpreting basic financial statement ratios. Companies are increasingly required by regulators to provide a full discussion in the MD&A of critical issues like liquidity, especially if the company depends on such off–balance sheet financing arrangements.

Canadian GAAP and International Accounting Standards—A Comparison

11 Objective
Compare current Canadian and international GAAP.

As of 2007, Canadian accounting standards in the area of cash and loans and receivables were converged with those of the IASB. **Convergence** means that an entity that applies Canadian

[34] Recall from the earnings management discussion in Chapter 4 that increasing or decreasing income through management manipulation reduces the quality of financial reports.

standards would also be complying **substantially** with the international standards—although a specific method may need to be applied when there is a choice or additional disclosures may be necessary. While there may be differences in vocabulary and guidance between the two sets of standards, the differences do not change the intent of the standard. Illustration 7-20 sets out the major primary sources of GAAP for cash, loans, and receivables.

Illustration 7-20
Primary Sources of GAAP

Canada	International[35]
Section 1540: Cash flow statements	IAS 7: Cash flow statements
Section 3000: Cash	No corresponding IFRS
Section 3020: Accounts and notes receivable Section 3025: Impaired loans Section 3855: Financial instruments—recognition and measurement	IAS 39: Financial instruments: recognition and measurement
Section 3862: Financial instruments—disclosures	IFRS 7: Financial instruments: disclosures

The following differences are noted:

Definitions. Unlike *Handbook* Section 3855, IAS 39 does not allow loans that are quoted in an active market to be classified in the "loans and receivables" category of financial assets.

Initial recognition—transaction costs. IAS 39 does not allow a choice of methods in accounting for transaction costs. Transaction costs that can be directly attributed to the acquisition or issue of loans and receivables are added to the initial carrying amount of the item. Section 3855 allows companies to choose between this approach and one that expenses the costs immediately.

Financial instruments transferred between related parties. International pronouncements, like those in the U.S., have no special accounting standards for transactions between related parties. In Canada, Section 3855 covers the accounting for transfers of financial instruments between related parties, and is consistent with *Handbook* Section 3840 on related party transactions.[36]

Impairment. IAS 39 addresses the impairment of loans and accounts receivable, whereas Section 3855 sends the reader to *Handbook* Section 3020 for the standards on impairment of short-term trade accounts and notes receivable, and to Section 3025 for impaired loans. Generally, IAS 39 "is more stringent regarding general loan loss allowances."[37]

Derecognition.[38] IAS 39 identifies the situations that require a derecognition of loans and receivables. *Handbook* 3855 does not specifically cover the derecognition of such assets. *Accounting Guideline 12*, "Transfers of Receivables," does address the derecognition of certain financial assets, but is much more limited in scope than IAS 39. The international standard focuses on the transfer of the risks and rewards of ownership rather than on "legal isolation" aspects, as required in *Accounting Guideline* 12.[39]

[35] The International Accounting Standards Board (IASB) publishes its accounting standards as International Financial Reporting Standards—IFRS. The Board also adopted the standards that were issued by its predecessor, the International Accounting Standards Committee (IASC), and these are known as International Accounting Standards or IAS. See Chapter 1 for a fuller discussion.

[36] *CICA Handbook* Section 3840, "Related Party Transactions." See Chapter 23 for coverage of this topic.

[37] CICA, *Implementation Plan for Incorporating International Financial Reporting Standards into Canadian GAAP*, July 31, 2006, p. 38.

[38] **Derecognition** is defined in Section 3855.19(m) as "the removal of a previously recognized financial asset or liability from an entity's balance sheet."

[39] CICA, *Implementation Plan for Incorporating International Financial Reporting Standards into Canadian GAAP*, July 31, 2006, p. 34.

Disclosures. The paragraphs of the newly released *Handbook* Section 3862 closely match those of IFRS 7, a step toward the adoption of international standards as GAAP for Canadian public companies in the future. Because of differences in their scope (or issues not related to this chapter), different derecognition and impairment models, and the related-party transaction guidelines and differential reporting standards that are specific to Canada, some IFRS paragraphs are not used or additional paragraphs are included in the *Handbook* section.

Before the change over to international standards in 2011, the Accounting Standards Board in Canada expects that IAS projects, or joint projects with them, will eliminate many outstanding differences. The FASB is also working closely on harmonization.

Summary of Learning Objectives

1 Define financial assets.

Financial assets are a major type of asset defined as cash, a contractual right to receive cash or another financial asset, an equity holding in another company, or a contractual right to exchange financial instruments under potentially favourable conditions.

2 Identify items that are considered cash and cash equivalents.

To be reported as cash, an asset must be readily available to pay current obligations and not have any contractual restrictions that would limit how it can be used in satisfying debts. Cash consists of coins, currency, and available funds on deposit at a bank. Negotiable instruments such as money orders, certified cheques, cashier's cheques, personal cheques, and bank drafts are also viewed as cash. Savings accounts are usually classified as cash. Cash equivalents include highly liquid short-term investments (i.e., maturing less than three months from the date of purchase) that can be exchanged for known amounts of cash and have an insignificant chance of changing in value. Examples include Treasury bills, commercial paper, and money-market funds. In certain circumstances, temporary bank overdrafts may be deducted in determining the balance of cash and cash equivalents.

3 Indicate how cash and related items are reported.

Cash is reported as a current asset in the balance sheet, with foreign currency balances reported at their Canadian dollar equivalent at the balance sheet date. The reporting of other related items is as follows: (1) Restricted cash: Legally restricted deposits that are held as compensating balances against short-term borrowing should be stated separately among the cash and cash equivalent items in Current Assets. Restricted deposits that are held against long-term borrowing arrangements should be separately classified as noncurrent assets in either the Investments or Other Assets sections. (2) Bank overdrafts: These are reported in the Current Liabilities section and may be added to the amount reported as accounts payable. (3) Cash equivalents: This item is often reported together with cash as "cash and cash equivalents."

4 Define receivables and identify the different types of receivables.

Receivables are claims held against customers and others for money, goods, or services. Most receivables are financial assets. The receivables are classified into three types: (1) current or noncurrent; (2) trade or nontrade; and (3) accounts receivable or notes receivable.

5 Account for and explain the accounting issues related to the recognition and measurement of accounts receivable.

Two issues that may complicate the measurement of accounts receivable are (1) the availability of discounts (trade and cash discounts) and (2) the length of time between

Student Website

Glossary

www.wiley.com/canada/kieso

KEY TERMS

accounts receivable, 359
aging schedule, 365
allowance method, 364
amortized cost, 406
asset-backed securities, 379
asset-based financing, 379
balance sheet approach, 365
bank overdrafts, 357
beneficial interest, 381
cash, 365
cash discounts, 362
cash equivalents, 357
compensating balances, 357
contra account, 364
convergence, 389
coupon rate, 371
derecognition, 390
direct write-off method, 368
discount, 375
effective interest method, 374
effective interest rate, 371
face rate, 371
face value, 371
factoring receivables, 379
fair value, 371
financial asset, 354
financial components approach, 383
implicit interest rate, 373
imputed interest rate, 377

income statement approach, 365
interest-bearing notes, 369
interest-only strip receivable, 384
loans receivable, 360
loans and receivables, 359
market rate, 371
net realizable value, 364
non-interest-bearing notes, 369
nontrade receivables, 360
notes receivable, 359
percentage-of-receivables approach, 365
percentage-of-sales approach, 365
premium, 376
promissory note, 369
receivables turnover ratio, 388
restricted cash, 356
sales discounts, 362
sales returns and allowances, 368
secured borrowing, 379
securitization, 379
servicing asset component, 384
servicing liability component, 384
short-term notes receivable, 370
stated interest rate, 371
trade discounts, 361
trade receivables, 359
with recourse, 383
without recourse, 382
yield rate, 371
zero-interest-bearing notes, 369

the sale and the payment due dates (the interest element). Ideally, receivables should be measured initially at their fair value, which is either their present value or the discounted value of the cash to be received in the future. Receivables that are created by normal business transactions and are due in the short term are excluded from present value considerations.

6 Account for and explain the accounting issues related to the valuation of accounts receivable.

Short-term receivables are valued and reported at their net realizable value—the net amount that is expected to be received in cash, which is not necessarily the amount that is legally receivable. Determining net realizable value requires estimating uncollectible receivables and any future returns or allowances and discounts that are expected to be taken. The adjustments to the asset account also affect the income statement amounts of bad debt expense, sales returns and allowances, and sales discounts.

7 Account for and explain the accounting issues related to the recognition, measurement, and valuation of short-term notes receivable.

The accounting issues related to short-term notes receivable are identical to those of accounts receivable. However, because notes always contain an interest element, interest income must be properly recognized. Notes receivable either bear interest on the face amount (interest-bearing) or have an interest element that is the difference between the amount lent and the maturity value (non-interest-bearing).

8 Account for and explain the accounting issues related to the recognition and measurement of long-term loans receivable.

Long-term loans and receivables are recognized initially at their fair value (the present value of the future cash flows), with a choice of capitalizing or expensing any direct transaction costs. After their acquisition, they are accounted for at their amortized cost. This requires amortizing any discount if the item was issued at less than its face value, or any premium if it was issued for an amount greater than its face value, using the effective interest method. The difference between interest income earned and the "cash" interest received is the amount of discount or premium to be amortized.

9 Account for and explain the basic accounting issues related to the disposition of receivables.

To accelerate the receipt of cash from receivables, the owner may transfer the receivables to another entity for cash. The transfer of receivables to a third party for cash may be done in one of two ways: (1) Secured borrowing: A creditor often requires that the debtor designate or pledge receivables as security for the loan. (2) Sales (factoring or securitization) of receivables: Factors are finance companies or banks that buy receivables from businesses and then collect the remittances directly from the customers. Securitization is the transfer of receivables to a special purpose entity that is mainly financed by highly rated debt instruments. In many cases, transferors have some continuing involvement with the receivables they sold. A financial components approach is used to record this type of transaction: this approach breaks the receivables down into a variety of asset and liability components, and the sold components are accounted for separately from the retained ones.

10 Explain how receivables and loans are reported and analyzed.

Disclosure of receivables requires that valuation accounts be appropriately offset against receivables, that the receivables be appropriately classified as current or noncurrent, and that pledged or designated receivables be identified. As financial instruments, specific disclosures are required for receivables so that users can determine their significance to the company's financial position and performance and can assess the nature and extent of associated risks and how these risks are managed and measured. Receivables are analyzed in terms of their turnover and age (number of days outstanding), and in terms of relative changes in the related sales, receivables, and allowance accounts.

11 Compare current Canadian and international GAAP.

Canadian accounting standards in the area of cash and loans and receivables are substantially converged with those of the IASB. Some minor differences remain. There are Canadian standards with no IASB pronouncements, as well as the reverse. Projects on the agendas of both standard-setting bodies and the FASB will limit further outstanding differences before the expected changeover date in 2011.

Appendix 7A

Cash Controls

Objective 12
Explain common techniques for controlling cash.

As indicated in the chapter, cash creates many management and control problems. The purpose of this appendix is to identify some of the basic controls related to cash.

Using Bank Accounts

International Insight

Multinational corporations often have cash accounts in more than one currency. For financial statement purposes, these currencies are typically translated into Canadian dollars using the exchange rate in effect at the balance sheet date.

To meet its control objectives, a company may use different banks in different locations and different types of bank accounts. For large companies that operate in multiple locations, the location of bank accounts can be important. Having collection accounts in strategic locations can speed up the flow of cash into the company by shortening the time between a customer's payment mailing and the company's use of the cash. Multiple collection centres are generally used to reduce the size of a company's **collection float**, which is the difference between the amount on deposit according to the company's records and the amount of collected cash according to the bank record.

The **general chequing account** is the main bank account in most companies and often the only bank account in small businesses. Cash is deposited in and disbursed from this account as all transactions are cycled through it. Deposits from and disbursements to all other bank accounts are made through the general chequing account.

Imprest bank accounts are used to make a specific amount of cash available for a limited purpose. The account acts as a clearing account for a large volume of cheques or for a specific type of cheque. The specific and intended amount to be cleared through the imprest account, such as for a payroll, is deposited by transferring that amount from the general chequing account or other source. Imprest bank accounts are also used for disbursing dividend cheques, commissions, bonuses, confidential expenses (e.g., officers' salaries), and travel expenses.

Lockbox accounts are often used by large companies with multiple locations to make collections in cities where most of their customer billing occurs. The company rents a local post office box and authorizes a local bank to pick up the remittances mailed to that box number. The bank empties the box at least once a day and immediately credits the company's account for collections. The greatest advantage of a lockbox is that it accelerates the availability of collected cash. Generally, in a lockbox arrangement, the bank microfilms the cheques for record purposes and provides the company with a deposit slip, a list of collections, and any customer correspondence. If the control over cash is improved and if the income generated from accelerating the receipt of funds is more than what the lockbox system costs, it is considered worthwhile to use it.

Companies are increasing their use of systems that electronically transfer funds from customers and to suppliers. While these advances will make many of the controls in a system based on paper cheque transactions obsolete, companies will still always need to improve the effectiveness of the controls that are part of their information and processing systems.

The Imprest Petty Cash System

Almost every company finds it necessary to pay small amounts for a great many things, such as employee lunches, taxi fares, minor office supplies, and other miscellaneous expenses. It is usually impractical to require that such disbursements be made by cheque, but it remains important to have some control over them. A simple method of obtaining reasonable control, and which follows the rule of disbursement by cheque, is the **petty cash** system, particularly an imprest system.

This is how the system works:

1. Someone is designated as the petty cash custodian and given a small amount of currency from which to make small payments. The transfer of funds from the bank account to petty cash is recorded as follows, assuming a $300 transfer:

Petty Cash	300	
Cash		300

A	=	L	+	SE
0		0		0

Cash flows: No effect

2. As payments are made out of this fund, the petty cash custodian gets signed receipts from each individual who receives cash from the fund. If possible, evidence of the disbursement should be attached to the petty cash receipt. Petty cash transactions are not recorded in the accounts until the fund is reimbursed, and they are recorded by someone other than the petty cash custodian.

3. When the cash in the fund runs low, the custodian presents to the general cashier a request for reimbursement that is supported by the petty cash receipts and other disbursement evidence. The custodian receives a company cheque to replenish the fund. At this point, transactions are recorded in the accounting system based on the petty cash receipts. For example:

Office Supplies Expense	42	
Postage Expense	53	
Entertainment Expense	76	
Cash Over and Short	2	
Cash		173

A	=	L	+	SE
−173				−173

Cash flows: ↓ 173 outflow

4. If it is decided that the balance of the fund is too high, an adjustment may be made and the surplus amount is then deposited back into the bank account. The following adjustment lowers the fund balance from $300 to $250:

Cash	50	
Petty Cash		50

A	=	L	+	SE
0		0		0

Cash flows: No effect

Note that entries are made to the Petty Cash account only to increase or decrease the size of the fund.

A **Cash Over and Short** account is used when the cash in the petty cash fund plus the dollar amount of the receipts does not add up to the imprest petty cash amount. When this occurs, it is usually due to an error, such as a failure to provide correct change, overpayment of an expense, a lost receipt, etc. If cash is short (i.e., the sum of the receipts and cash in the fund is less than the imprest amount), the shortage is debited to the Cash Over and Short account. If there is more cash than there should be, the overage is credited to Cash

Over and Short. This account is left open until the end of the year, when it is closed and generally shown on the income statement as an "other expense or revenue."

Unless a reimbursement has just been made, there are usually expense items in the fund. This means that, if accurate financial statements are wanted, the fund needs to be reimbursed at the end of each accounting period in addition to when it is nearly empty.

Under an **imprest system**, the petty cash custodian is responsible at all times for the amount of the fund on hand, whether the amount is in cash or signed receipts. These receipts are the evidence that the disbursing officer needs in order to issue a reimbursement cheque. Two additional procedures are followed to obtain more complete control over the petty cash fund:

1. Surprise counts of the fund are made from time to time by a superior of the petty cash custodian to determine that the fund is being accounted for satisfactorily.
2. Petty cash receipts are cancelled or mutilated after they have been submitted for reimbursement so that they cannot be used for a second reimbursement.

Physical Protection of Cash Balances

It is not only cash receipts and cash disbursements that need to be safeguarded through internal control measures. Cash on hand and in banks must also be protected. Because receipts become cash on hand and disbursements are made from the cash in banks, adequate control of receipts and disbursements is part of protecting cash balances. Certain other procedures, however, should also be considered.

The physical protection of cash is such an elementary necessity that it requires little discussion. Every effort should be made to minimize the cash on hand in the office. A petty cash fund, the current day's receipts, and perhaps funds for making change should be the only funds on hand at any time. As much as possible, these funds should be kept in a vault, safe, or locked cash drawer. Each day's receipts should be transmitted **intact** to the bank as soon as is practical. Intact means that the total receipts are accounted for together and no part of the amount is used for other purposes. This leaves a clear trail from the receipts activity to the bank. Accurately stating the amount of available cash, both in internal management reports and in external financial statements, is also extremely important.

Every company has a record of cash received and disbursed, and the cash balance. Because of the many cash transactions, however, errors or omissions can occur in keeping this record. It is therefore necessary to periodically prove the balance shown in the general ledger. Cash that is actually present in the office—petty cash, change funds, and undeposited receipts—can be counted and compared with the company records. Cash on deposit is not available for count and is proved by preparing a bank reconciliation, which is a reconciliation of the company's record and the bank's record of the company's cash.

Reconciliation of Bank Balances

At the end of each calendar month, the bank sends each customer a bank statement (a copy of the bank's account with the customer) together with the customer's cheques that were paid by the bank during the month.[40] (Less and less hard copy will be returned as banks provide companies with electronic access to this information.) If no errors were made by the bank or the customer, if all deposits made and all cheques drawn by the customer reached the bank within the same month, and if no unusual transactions occurred that

[40] As mentioned in the chapter, use of paper cheques continues to be a popular means of payment. However, easy access to desktop publishing software and hardware has created new opportunities for cheque fraud in the form of duplicate, altered, or forged cheques. At the same time, new fraud-fighting technologies, such as ultraviolet imaging, high-capacity barcodes, and biometrics are being developed. These technologies convert paper documents into document files that are processed electronically, thereby reducing the risk of fraud.

affected either the company's or the bank's record of cash, the balance of cash reported by the bank to the customer will be the same as the balance in the customer's own records. This rarely occurs, because of one or more of the following:

RECONCILING ITEMS

1. **Deposits in Transit.** End-of-month deposits of cash that are recorded on the depositor's books in one month are received and recorded by the bank in the following month.
2. **Outstanding Cheques.** Cheques written by the depositor are recorded when they are written but may not be recorded by (or "clear") the bank until the next month.
3. **Bank Charges.** Charges are recorded by the bank against the depositor's balance for such items as bank services, printing cheques, **not-sufficient-funds (NSF) cheques**,[41] and safe-deposit box rentals. The depositor may not be aware of these charges until the bank statement is received.
4. **Bank Credits.** Collections or deposits by the bank for the depositor's benefit may not be known to the depositor until the bank statement is received. These are reconciling items as long as they have not yet been recorded on the company's records. Examples are note collections for the depositor, interest earned on interest-bearing chequing accounts, and direct deposits by customers and others.
5. **Bank or Depositor Errors.** Errors by either the bank or the depositor cause the bank balance to disagree with the depositor's book balance.

For these reasons, differences between the depositor's record of cash and the bank's record are usual and expected. The two records therefore need to be reconciled to determine the reasons for the differences between the two amounts.

A **bank reconciliation** is a schedule that explains any differences between the bank's and the company's records of cash. If the difference results only from transactions not yet recorded by the bank, the company's record of cash is considered correct. But if some part of the difference is due to other items, the bank's records or the company's records must be adjusted.

Two forms of bank reconciliation can be prepared. One form reconciles from the bank statement balance to the book balance or vice versa. The other form reconciles both the bank balance and the book balance to a correct cash balance. This latter form is more popular. A sample of this form and its common reconciling items is shown in Illustration 7A-1.

Illustration 7A-1

Bank Reconciliation Form and Content

Balance per bank statement (end of period)		$$$
Add: Deposits in transit	$$	
Undeposited receipts (cash on hand)	$$	
Bank errors that understate the bank statement balance	$$	$$
		$$$
Deduct: Outstanding cheques	$$	
Bank errors that overstate the bank statement balance	$$	$$
Correct cash balance		**$$$**
Balance per company's books (end of period)		$$$
Add: Bank credits and collections not yet recorded in the books	$$	
Book errors that understate the book balance	$$	$$
		$$$
Deduct: Bank charges not yet recorded in the books	$$	
Book errors that overstate the book balance	$$	$$
Correct cash balance		**$$$**

[41] An NSF cheque is a cheque received by a company, included in its cash receipts, and deposited in its bank account. Later, the bank discovers that the cheque writer's bank account did not have enough cash in it to honour the cheque.

This form of reconciliation has two sections: (1) the "Balance per bank statement" and (2) the "Balance per company's books." Both sections end with the same correct cash balance. The correct cash balance is the amount that the books must be adjusted to and is the amount reported on the balance sheet. **Adjusting journal entries are prepared for all the addition and deduction items that appear in the "Balance per company's books" section.** The bank should be notified immediately about any errors that it has made.

To illustrate, Nugget Mining Company's books show a cash balance at the Ottawa National Bank on November 30, 2008, of $20,502. The bank statement covering the month of November shows an ending balance of $22,190. An examination of Nugget's accounting records and the November bank statement identified the following reconciling items:

1. A deposit of $3,680 was taken to the bank late on November 30 but does not appear on the bank statement.
2. Cheques written in November but not charged to (deducted from) the November bank statement are:

Cheque #7327	$ 150
#7348	4,820
#7349	31

3. Nugget has not yet recorded the $600 of interest collected by the bank on November 20 on Sequoia Co. bonds held by the bank for Nugget.
4. Bank service charges of $18 are not yet recorded on Nugget's books.
5. A $220 cheque for Nugget from a customer was returned with the bank statement and marked "NSF." The bank, having originally recognized this as part of one of Nugget's deposits, now deducted this bad cheque as a disbursement from Nugget's account.
6. Nugget discovered that cheque #7322, written in November for $131 in payment of an account payable, had been incorrectly recorded in its books as $311.
7. A cheque written on Nugent Oil Co.'s account for $175 had been incorrectly charged to Nugget Mining and was included with the bank statement.

Illustration 7A-2 shows the reconciliation of the bank and book balances to the correct cash balance of $21,044.

Illustration 7A-2
Sample Bank Reconciliation

NUGGET MINING COMPANY
Bank Reconciliation
Ottawa National Bank, November 30, 2008

Balance per bank statement, November 30/08			$22,190
Add: Deposit in transit	(1)	$3,680	
Bank error—incorrect cheque charged to account by bank	(7)	175	3,855
			26,045
Deduct: Outstanding cheques	(2)		5,001
Correct cash balance, November 30/08			$21,044
Balance per books, November 30/08			$20,502
Add: Interest collected by the bank	(3)	$ 600	
Error in recording cheque #7322	(6)	180	780
			21,282
Deduct: Bank service charges	(4)	18	
NSF cheque returned	(5)	220	238
Correct cash balance, November 30/08			$21,044

The journal entries to adjust and correct Nugget Mining's books in early December 2008 are taken from the items in the "Balance per books" section and are as follows:

Cash	600	
Interest Income		600
(To record interest on Sequoia Co. bonds, collected by bank)		
Cash	180	
Accounts Payable		180
(To correct error in recording amount of cheque #7322)		
Office Expense—Bank Charges	18	
Cash		18
(To record bank service charges for November)		
Accounts Receivable	220	
Cash		220
(To record customer's cheque returned NSF)		

A	= L	+ SE
+762	+180	+582

Cash flows: ↑ 542 inflow

Alternatively, one summary entry could be made with a net $542 debit to Cash, which is the difference between the balance before adjustment of $20,502 and the correct balance of $21,044. When the entries are posted, Nugget's cash account will have a balance of $21,044. Nugget should return the Nugent Oil Co. cheque to Ottawa National Bank, informing the bank of the error.

Summary of Learning Objective for Appendix 7A

Glossary

www.wiley.com/canada/kieso

12 Explain common techniques for controlling cash.

The common techniques that are used to control cash are as follows: (1) Using bank accounts: A company can vary the number and location of banks and the types of accounts to meet its control objectives. (2) The imprest petty cash system: It may be impractical to require small amounts of various expenses to be paid by cheque, yet some control over them is important. (3) Physical protection of cash balances: Adequate control of receipts and disbursements is part of protecting cash balances. Every effort should be made to minimize the cash on hand in the office. (4) Reconciliation of bank balances: Cash on deposit is not available for counting and is proved by preparing a bank reconciliation.

KEY TERMS

bank reconciliation, 397
deposits in transit, 397
imprest system, 396
intact, 396
not-sufficient-funds (NSF) cheques, 399
outstanding cheques, 397
petty cash, 395

Note: All assignment material with an asterisk (*) relates to the appendix to the chapter.

Brief Exercises

(LO 2) BE7-1 Stowe Enterprises owns the following assets at December 31, 2008:

Cash in bank savings account	68,500	Chequing account balance	20,500
Cash on hand	14,800	Postdated cheque from Yu Co.	450
Cash refund due, overpayment of income taxes	31,400	Certificates of deposit (180-day)	90,000

What amount should be reported as cash?

(LO 5) BE7-2 Civic Company made sales of $20,000 with terms 1/10, n/30. Within the discount period, it received $15,000 in payments from customers; after the discount period, it received $5,000 in payments from customers. Assuming Civic uses the gross method of recording sales, prepare journal entries for the above transactions.

(LO 5) BE7-3 Use the information for Civic Company in BE7-2, but assume instead that Civic uses the net method of recording sales. Prepare the journal entries for the transactions.

(LO 5) BE7-4 Yoshi Corp. uses the gross method to record sales made on credit. On June 1, the company made sales of $45,000 with terms 1/15, n/45. On June 12, Yoshi received full payment for the June 1 sale. Prepare the required journal entries for Yoshi Corp.

(LO 5) BE7-5 Use the information from BE7-4, assuming Yoshi Corp. uses the net method to account for cash discounts. Prepare the required journal entries for Yoshi Corp.

(LO 6) BE7-6 Battle Tank Limited had net sales in 2008 of $1.1 million. At December 31, 2008, before adjusting entries, the balances in selected accounts were as follows: Accounts Receivable $250,000 debit; Allowance for Doubtful Accounts $2,800 credit. Assuming Battle Tank estimates that 2% of its net sales will become uncollectible, prepare the December 31, 2008, journal entry to record bad debt expense.

(LO 6) BE7-7 Information for Battle Tank Limited is provided in BE7-6. (a) Instead of estimating the uncollectibles at 2% of net sales, assume it is expected that 8% of accounts receivable will prove to be uncollectible. Prepare the entry to record bad debt expense. (b) Instead of estimating uncollectibles at 2% of net sales, assume Battle Tank prepares an aging schedule that estimates total uncollectible accounts at $21,000. Prepare the entry to record bad debt expense.

(LO 7) BE7-8 Addams Family Importers sold goods to Acme Decorators for $20,000 on November 1, 2008, accepting Acme's $20,000, six-month, 6% note. (a) Prepare Addams' November 1 entry, December 31 annual adjusting entry, and May 1 entry for the collection of the note and interest. (b) Prepare any appropriate reversing entry at January 1, 2009, and the May 1, 2009, entry for the collection of the note and interest.

(LO 7) BE7-9 Aero Acrobats lent $25,243 to Afterburner Limited, accepting Afterburner's $26,000, three-month, zero-interest-bearing note. The implied interest is 12%. Prepare Aero's journal entries for the initial transaction and the collection of $26,000 at maturity assuming (a) the Note Receivable account was debited for $25,243, and (b) the Note Receivable account was debited for $26,000.

(LO 8) BE7-10 Lin Du Corp. lent $15,944 to Prefax Ltd., accepting Prefax's $20,000, two-year, zero-interest-bearing note. The implied interest is 12%. (a) Prepare Lin Du's journal entries for the initial transaction, recognition of interest each year, and the collection of $20,000 at maturity. (b) Use time value of money tables, a financial calculator or Excel functions to prove that the note will yield 12%.

(LO 8) BE7-11 Bartho Products sold used equipment with a cost of $15,000 and a carrying amount of $2,500 to Vardy Corp. in exchange for a $5,000, three-year note receivable. Although no interest was specified, the market rate for a loan of that risk would be 9%. Prepare the entries to (a) record the sale of Bartho's equipment and receipt of the note, (b) the recognition of interest each year, and (c) the collection of the note at maturity.

(LO 9) BE7-12 On October 1, 2008, Akira, Inc. assigns $1 million of its accounts receivable to Alberta Provincial Bank as collateral for a $750,000 loan evidenced by a note. The bank's charges are as follows: a finance charge of 4% of the assigned receivables and an interest charge of 13% on the loan. Prepare the October 1 journal entries for both Akira and Alberta Provincial Bank.

BE7-13 Landstalker Enterprises sold $750,000 of accounts receivable to Leander Factors, Inc. on a without recourse basis. The transaction meets the criteria for a sale, and no asset or liability components of the receivables are retained by Landstalker. Leander Factors assesses a finance charge of 4% of the amount of accounts receivable and retains an amount equal to 5% of accounts receivable. Prepare journal entries for both Landstalker and Leander. **(LO 9)**

BE7-14 Use the information for Landstalker Enterprises in BE7-13 and assume instead that the receivables are sold with recourse. Prepare the journal entry for Landstalker to record the sale, assuming the recourse obligation has a fair value of $9,000. **(LO 9)**

BE7-15 Keyser Woodcrafters sells $200,000 of receivables with a fair value of $210,000 to Keyser Trust in a securitization transaction that meets the criteria for a sale. Keyser Woodcrafters receives full fair value for the receivables and agrees to continue to service the receivables, estimating that the fair value of this service liability component is $11,000. Prepare the journal entry for Keyser Woodcrafters to record the sale. **(LO 9)**

BE7-16 The financial statements of Andrés Wines Ltd. report net sales of $167,634 thousand for its year ended March 31, 2005. Accounts receivable are $14,132 thousand at March 31, 2005, and $12,801 thousand at March 31, 2004. Calculate the company's accounts receivable turnover ratio and the average collection period for accounts receivable in days. **(LO 10)**

BE7-17 Refer to Illustration 7-19 in Chapter 7 for the information about Canadian Utilities Limited. Given that the company's accounts receivable balance at December 31, 2003, was $540.6 million and 2004 sales were $3,011.4 million, calculate the company's accounts receivable turnover ratio for 2004. Did it improve in 2005? **(LO 10)**

***BE7-18** Genesis Ltd. designated Alexa Kidd as petty cash custodian and established a petty cash fund of $350. The fund is reimbursed when the cash in the fund is at $11. Petty cash receipts indicate that funds were disbursed for $174 of office supplies and $167 of freight charges on inventory purchases. Genesis uses a perpetual inventory system. Prepare journal entries for the establishment of the fund and the reimbursement. **(LO 12)**

***BE7-19** Use the information in BE7-18. Assume that Genesis decides (a) to increase the size of the petty cash fund to $450 immediately after the reimbursement, and (b) to reduce the size of the petty cash to $200 immediately after the reimbursement. Prepare the entries that are necessary to record the (a) and (b) transactions. **(LO 12)**

***BE7-20** Jaguar Corporation is preparing a bank reconciliation and has identified the following potential reconciling items. For each item, indicate if it is (1) added to the balance per bank statement, (2) deducted from the balance per bank statement, (3) added to the balance per books, or (4) deducted from the balance per books. **(LO 12)**

(a) Deposit in transit of $5,500
(b) Interest credited to Jaguar's account of $31
(c) Bank service charges of $20
(d) Outstanding cheques of $7,422
(e) NSF cheque returned of $260

***BE7-21** Use the information for Jaguar Corporation in BE7-20. Prepare any entries that are necessary to make Jaguar's accounting records correct and complete. **(LO 12)**

Exercises

E7-1 **(Determining Cash Balance)** The controller for Eastwood Co. is trying to determine the amount of cash to report on the December 31, 2008, balance sheet. The following information is provided: **(LO 2)**

1. A commercial savings account with $600,000 and a commercial chequing account balance of $900,000 are held at First National Bank. There is also a bank overdraft of $35,000 in a chequing account at the Royal Scotia Bank. No other accounts are held at the Royal Scotia Bank.
2. Eastwood has agreed to maintain a cash balance of $100,000 at all times in its chequing account at First National Bank to ensure that credit is available in the future.
3. It has a $5-million investment in a Commercial Bank of Montreal money-market mutual fund. This fund has chequing account privileges.
4. There are travel advances of $18,000 for executive travel for the first quarter of next year (employees will complete expense reports after they travel).
5. A separate cash fund in the amount of $1.5 million is restricted for the retirement of long-term debt.

6. There is a petty cash fund of $3,000.
7. A $1,900 IOU from Marianne Koch, a company officer, will be withheld from her salary in January 2009.
8. There are 20 cash floats for retail operation cash registers: 8 at $75, and 12 at $100.
9. The company has two certificates of deposit, each for $500,000. These certificates of deposit each had a maturity of 120 days when they were acquired. One was purchased October 15 and the other on December 27.
10. Eastwood has received a cheque dated January 12, 2009, in the amount of $25,000 from a customer owing funds at December 31. It has also received a cheque dated January 8, 2009, in the amount of $11,500 from a customer as an advance on an order that was placed on December 29 and will be delivered February 1, 2009.
11. Eastwood holds $2.1 million of commercial paper of Sergio Leone Co., which is due in 60 days.
12. Currency and coin on hand amounted to $7,700.
13. Eastwood acquired 1,000 shares of Sortel for $3.90 per share in late November and is holding these for trading. The shares are still on hand at year end and have a market value of $4.10 per share on December 31, 2008.

Instructions

(a) Calculate the amount of cash to be reported on Eastwood Co.'s balance sheet at December 31, 2008.

(b) Indicate the proper way to report items that are not reported as cash on the December 31, 2008, balance sheet.

(LO 2) E7-2 (Determine Cash Balance) Several independent situations follow. For each situation, determine the amount that should be reported as cash. If the item(s) is (are) not reported as cash, explain why.

1. Chequing account balance $625,000; certificate of deposit $1.1 million; cash advance to subsidiary $980,000; utility deposit paid to gas company $180.
2. Chequing account balance $500,000; overdraft in special chequing account at same bank as normal chequing account $17,000; cash held in bond sinking fund $200,000; petty cash fund $300; coins and currency on hand $1,350.
3. Chequing account balance $540,000; postdated cheque from customer $11,000; cash restricted to maintain compensating balance requirement $100,000; certified cheque from customer $9,800; postage stamps on hand $620.
4. Chequing account balance at bank $57,000; money-market balance at mutual fund (has chequing privileges) $38,000; NSF cheque received from customer $800.
5. Chequing account balance $700,000; cash restricted for future plant expansion $500,000; short-term (60-day) Treasury bills $180,000; cash advance received from customer $900 (not included in chequing account balance); cash advance of $7,000 to company executive, payable on demand; refundable deposit of $26,000 paid to federal government to guarantee performance on construction contract.

(LO 4) E7-3 (Financial Statement Presentation of Receivables) Gleason Inc. shows a balance of $228,640 in the Accounts Receivable account on December 31, 2008. The balance consists of the following:

Instalment accounts due in 2009	$ 23,000
Instalment accounts due after 2009	34,000
Overpayments to creditors	2,640
Due from regular customers, of which $40,000 represents accounts pledged as security for a bank loan	85,000
Advances to employees	3,000
Advance to subsidiary company (made in 2003)	81,000
	$228,640

Instructions

Show how the information above should be presented on the balance sheet of Gleason Inc. at December 31, 2008.

(LO 5) E7-4 (Determine Ending Accounts Receivable) Your accounts receivable clerk, Mitra Adams, to whom you pay a salary of $1,500 per month, has just purchased a new Cadillac. You have decided to test the accuracy of the accounts receivable balance of $86,500 shown in the ledger.

The following information is available for your first year in business:

1. Collections from customers $198,000
2. Merchandise purchased $320,000

3. Ending merchandise inventory $99,000

4. Goods are marked to sell at 40% above cost.

Instructions

Estimate the ending balance of accounts receivable from customers that should appear in the ledger and any apparent shortages. Assume that all sales are made on account.

E7-5 **(Recording Sales Transactions)** Information from Perez Computers Ltd. follows: **(LO 5)**

July	1	Sold $20,000 of computers to Robertson Corp., terms 2/15, n/60.
	5	Robertson Corp. returned for full credit one computer with an invoice price of $2,200.
	10	Perez received payment from Robertson for the full amount owed from the July transactions.
	17	Sold $220,000 in computers and peripherals to Clarkson Store, terms 2/10, n/30.
	26	Clarkson Store paid Perez for half of its July purchases.
Aug.	30	Clarkson Store paid Perez for the remaining half of its July purchases.

Instructions

(a) Prepare the entries for Perez Computers Ltd., assuming the gross method is used to record sales and cash discounts.

(b) Prepare the entries for Perez Computers Ltd., assuming the net method is used to record sales and cash discounts.

E7-6 **(Record Sales Gross and Net)** On June 3, Arnold Limited sold to Chester Arthur merchandise having a sale price of $3,000 with terms 3/10, n/60, f.o.b. shipping point. A $90 invoice, terms n/30, was received by Chester on June 8 from John Booth Transport Service for the freight cost. When it received the goods on June 5, Chester notified Arnold that $500 of the merchandise contained flaws that rendered it worthless; the same day Arnold Limited issued a credit memo covering the worthless merchandise and asked that it be returned to them at their expense. The freight on the returned merchandise was $25, which Arnold paid on June 7. On June 12, the company received a cheque for the balance due from Chester Arthur. **(LO 5)**

Instructions

(a) Prepare journal entries on Arnold Limited's books to record all of the above transactions under each of the following independent bases:

1. Sales and receivables are entered at gross selling price.

2. Sales and receivables are entered at net of cash discounts.

(b) Prepare the journal entry under basis 2, assuming that Chester Arthur did not pay until July 29.

E7-7 **(Journalizing Various Receivable Transactions)** Information on Janut Corp. follows: **(LO 5, 9)**

July	1	Janut Corp. sold to Harding Ltd. merchandise having a sales price of $9,000, terms 3/10, net/60. Janut records its sales and receivables net.
	3	Harding Ltd. returned defective merchandise having a sales price of $700.
	5	Accounts receivable of $19,000 (gross) are factored with Jackson Credit Corp. without recourse at a financing charge of 9%. Cash is received for the proceeds and collections are handled by the finance company. (These accounts were subject to a 2% discount and were all past the discount period.)
	9	Specific accounts receivable of $15,000 (gross) are pledged to Landon Credit Corp. as security for a loan of $11,000 at a finance charge of 3% of the loan amount plus 9% interest on the outstanding balance. Janut will continue to make the collections. All the accounts receivable are past the discount period and were originally subject to a 2% discount.
Dec.	29	Harding Ltd. notifies Janut that it is bankrupt and will pay only 10% of its account. Give the entry to write off the uncollectible balance using the allowance method. (Note: First record the increase in the receivable on July 11 when the discount period passed.)

Instructions

Prepare all necessary entries in general journal form for Janut Corp.

E7-8 **(Recording Bad Debts)** At the end of 2007, Juan Corporation has accounts receivable of $800,000 and an allowance for doubtful accounts of $47,000. On January 16, 2008, Juan determined that its $6,000 receivable from Maximillian Ltd. will not be collected, and management has authorized its write-off. **(LO 6)**

Instructions

(a) Prepare the journal entry for Juan Corporation to write off the Maximillian receivable.

(b) What is the net realizable value of Juan's accounts receivable before and after the write-off of the Maximillian receivable? What is the book value of Juan's accounts receivable before and after the write-off?

(LO 6) E7-9 **(Summary Entries for Accounts Receivable)** The balance sheets of Traverse Corp. on December 31, 2007 and 2008, showed gross accounts receivable of $8,450 and $9,275, respectively. The balances in Allowance for Doubtful Accounts at December 31, 2007 and 2008, after recording the bad debt expense were $725 and $796, respectively. The income statement for Traverse for the fiscal years ending December 31, 2007 and 2008, showed bad debts expenses of $420 and $455 respectively, which is equal to 1% of sales. All sales are on account.

Instructions

Prepare summary journal entries for 2008 to record the bad debts expense, sales on account, accounts receivable write-offs, and collections on account.

(LO 6) E7-10 **(Calculating Bad Debts)** At January 1, 2008, the credit balance of Amos Corp.'s Allowance for Doubtful Accounts was $400,000. For 2008, the bad debt expense entry was based on a percentage of net sales. Net sales for 2008 were $71 million. Based on the latest available facts at the time, the 2008 bad debt expense was estimated to be 0.8% of net sales. During 2008, uncollectible receivables amounting to $500,000 were written off against the allowance for doubtful accounts.

Instructions

Prepare a schedule calculating the balance in Amos' Allowance for Doubtful Accounts at December 31, 2008.

(LO 6) E7-11 **(Bad Debt Reporting)** The chief accountant for Dickinson Corporation provides you with the following list of accounts receivable that were written off in the current year:

Date	Customer	Amount
Mar. 31	Eli Masters Ltd.	$ 7,700
June 30	Crane Associates	6,800
Sept. 30	Annie Lowell's Dress Shop	12,000
Dec. 31	Richard Frost	6,830

Dickinson Corporation follows the policy of debiting Bad Debt Expense as accounts are written off. The chief accountant maintains that this procedure is appropriate for financial statement purposes.

All of Dickinson Corporation's sales are on a 30-day credit basis. Sales for the current year total $3.2 million, and research has determined that bad debt losses approximate 2% of sales.

Instructions

(a) Do you agree or disagree with Dickinson Corporation's policy on recognizing bad debt expense? Why or why not?

(b) By what amount would net income differ if bad debt expense was calculated using the allowance method and percentage-of-sales approach?

(c) Under what conditions is using the direct write-off method justified?

(LO 6) E7-12 **(Calculating Bad Debts and Preparing Journal Entries)** The trial balance before adjustment of Chloe Inc. shows the following balances:

	Dr.	Cr.
Accounts Receivable	$105,000	
Allowance for Doubtful Accounts	1,950	
Sales (all on credit)		$684,000
Sales Returns and Allowances	30,000	

Instructions

Give the entry for bad debt expense for the current year assuming:

(a) the allowance should be 4% of gross accounts receivable.

(b) historical records indicate that 1% of net sales will not be collected.

(c) Allowance for Doubtful Accounts has the same amount but it is a credit balance and the allowance should be 4% of gross accounts receivable.

(d) Allowance for Doubtful Accounts has the same amount but it is a credit balance and historical records indicate that 1% of net sales will not be collected.

E7-13 (Bad Debts—Aging) Gerard Manley, Inc. has the following account among its trade receivables: **(LO 6)**

Hopkins Co.

1/1	Balance forward	850	1/28	Cash (#1710)	1,100
1/20	Invoice #1710	1,100	4/2	Cash (#2116)	1,350
3/14	Invoice #2116	1,350	4/10	Cash (1/1 Balance)	155
4/12	Invoice #2412	2,110	4/30	Cash (#2412)	1,000
9/5	Invoice #3614	490	9/20	Cash (#3614 and part of #2412)	790
10/17	Invoice #4912	860	10/31	Cash (#4912)	860
11/18	Invoice #5681	2,000	12/1	Cash (#5681)	1,250
12/20	Invoice #6347	800	12/29	Cash (#6347)	800

Instructions

Age the Hopkins Co. account and specify any items that may need particular attention at year end.

E7-14 (Interest-Bearing and Non-Interest-Bearing Notes) Saleh Corp. was experiencing cash flow problems and was unable to pay its $35,000 account payable to Amirkal Corp. when it fell due on September 30, 2007. Saleh agreed to substitute a one-year note for the open account. The following two options were presented to Saleh by Amirkal Corp.: **(LO 7)**

Option 1 A one-year note for $35,000 due September 30, 2008. Interest at a rate of 8% would be payable at maturity.

Option 2 A one-year non-interest-bearing note for $37,800. The implied rate of interest is 8%.

Assume that Amirkal Corp. has a December 31 year end.

Instructions

(a) Assuming Saleh Corp. chooses Option 1, prepare the entries required on Amirkal Corp.'s books on September 30, 2007, December 31, 2007, and September 30, 2008.

(b) Assuming Saleh Corp. chooses Option 2, prepare the entries required on Amirkal Corp.'s books on September 30, 2007, December 31, 2007, and September 30, 2008.

(c) Compare the amount of interest income earned by Amirkal Corp. in 2007 and 2008 under both options. Comment briefly.

(d) From management's perspective, does one option provide better liquidity for Amirkal at December 31, 2007? Does one option provide better cash flows than the other?

E7-15 (Notes Receivable with Zero and Unrealistic Interest Rates) On July 1, 2008, Agincourt Inc. made two sales: **(LO 8)**

1. It sold excess land having a fair market value of $700,000 in exchange for a four-year, non-interest-bearing promissory note in the face amount of $1,101,460. The land's carrying value is $590,000.
2. It rendered services in exchange for an eight-year promissory note having a face value of $400,000. Interest at a rate of 3% is payable annually.

The customers in the above transactions have credit ratings that require them to borrow money at 12% interest. Agincourt recently had to pay 8% interest for money it borrowed from British National Bank.

On July 1, 2008, Agincourt also agreed to accept an instalment note from one of its customers in partial settlement of accounts receivable that were overdue. The note calls for four equal payments of $20,000, including the principal and interest due, on the anniversary of the note. The implied interest rate on this note is 10%.

Instructions

(a) Prepare the journal entries to record the three notes receivable transactions of Agincourt Inc. on July 1, 2008.

(b) Prepare an effective-interest amortization table for the instalment note obtained in partial collection of accounts receivable. From Agincourt's perspective, what are the advantages of an instalment note compared to a non-interest-bearing note?

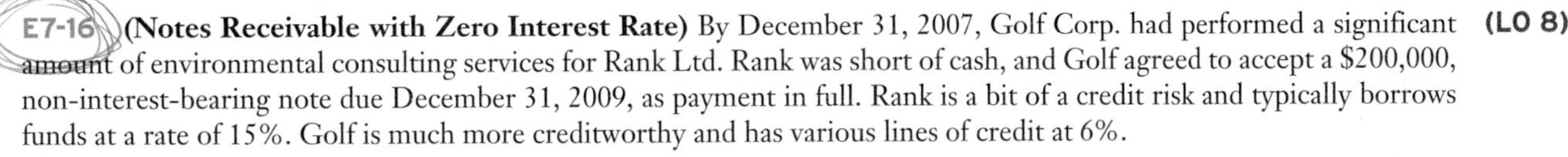

E7-16 (Notes Receivable with Zero Interest Rate) By December 31, 2007, Golf Corp. had performed a significant amount of environmental consulting services for Rank Ltd. Rank was short of cash, and Golf agreed to accept a $200,000, non-interest-bearing note due December 31, 2009, as payment in full. Rank is a bit of a credit risk and typically borrows funds at a rate of 15%. Golf is much more creditworthy and has various lines of credit at 6%. **(LO 8)**

Instructions

(a) Prepare the journal entry to record the transaction of December 31, 2007, for Golf Corp.

(b) Assuming Golf Corp.'s fiscal year end is December 31, prepare the journal entry required at December 31, 2008.

(c) Assuming Golf Corp.'s fiscal year end is December 31, prepare the journal entry required at December 31, 2009.

(d) What are the amount and classification of the note on Golf Corp.'s balance sheet as at December 31, 2008?

(LO 9) E7-17 **(Assigning Accounts Receivable)** On April 1, 2008, Rasheed Corporation assigns $400,000 of its accounts receivable to First Provincial Bank as collateral for a $200,000 loan that is due July 1, 2008. The assignment agreement calls for Rasheed to continue to collect the receivables. First Provincial Bank assesses a finance charge of 3% of the accounts receivable, and interest on the loan is 10%, a realistic rate for a note of this type.

Instructions

(a) Prepare the April 1, 2008, journal entry for Rasheed Corporation.

(b) Prepare the journal entry for Rasheed's collection of $350,000 of the accounts receivable during the period April 1 to June 30, 2008.

(c) On July 1, 2008, Rasheed paid First Provincial Bank the entire amount that was due on the loan.

(LO 9) E7-18 **(Transfer of Receivables with Recourse)** Quartet Ltd. factors receivables with a carrying amount of $220,000 to Joffrey Company for $170,000 on a with recourse basis.

Instructions

The recourse provision has a fair value of $1,000. Assuming this transaction should be recorded as a sale, prepare the appropriate journal entry to record the transaction on the books of Quartet Ltd.

(LO 9) E7-19 **(Transfer of Receivables with Recourse)** Houseman Corporation factors $180,000 of accounts receivable with Battle Financing, Inc. on a with recourse basis. Battle Financing will collect the receivables. The receivable records are transferred to Battle Financing on August 15, 2008. Battle Financing assesses a finance charge of 2% of the amount of accounts receivable and also reserves an amount equal to 4% of accounts receivable to cover probable adjustments.

Instructions

(a) What conditions must be met for a transfer of receivables to be accounted for as a sale?

(b) Assume the conditions from part (a) are met. Prepare the journal entry on August 15, 2008, for Houseman to record the sale of receivables, assuming the recourse obligation has a fair value of $2,000.

(c) What effect will the factoring of receivables have on calculating the accounts receivable turnover for Houseman? Comment briefly.

(LO 9) E7-20 **(Transfer of Receivables with Servicing Retained)** Lute Retail Ltd. transfers $355,000 of its accounts receivable to an independent trust in a securitization transaction on July 11, 2008, receiving 96% of the receivables balance as proceeds. Lute will continue to manage the customer accounts, including their collection. Lute estimates this obligation has a liability value of $12,500. In addition, the agreement includes a recourse provision with an estimated value of $9,900. The transaction is to be recorded as a sale.

Instructions

(a) Prepare the journal entry on July 11, 2008, for Lute Retail Ltd. to record the securitization of the receivables.

(b) What effect will the securitization of receivables have on Lute Retail Ltd.'s accounts receivable turnover? Comment briefly.

(LO 10) E7-21 **(Analysis of Receivables)** Information follows for Jones Company:

1. The beginning of the year Accounts Receivable balance was $15,000.
2. Net sales for the year were $210,000. (Credit sales were $100,000 of the total sales.) Jones does not offer cash discounts.
3. Collections on accounts receivable during the year were $70,000.

Instructions

(a) Prepare summary journal entries to record the items noted above.

(b) Calculate Jones Company's accounts receivable turnover ratio for the year. How old is the average receivable?

(c) Use the turnover ratio calculated in (b) to analyze Jones Company's liquidity. The turnover ratio last year was 4.85.

(LO 10) E7-22 **(Receivables Turnover)** The Becker Milk Company Limited, a real estate management company since November 1996, reports the following information in its financial statements for the years ended April 30, 2006, 2005, and 2004:

Accounts receivable, net of allowance for doubtful accounts	April 30, 2006	$ 60,898
	April 30, 2005	121,432
	April 30, 2004	96,154
Revenue (note 6), year ended	April 30, 2006	3,727,695
	April 30, 2005	3,662,708
	April 30, 2004	3,525,883

Note 6: Revenue
As of April 30, 2006, the company's largest single tenant, Alimentation Couche-Tard Inc., accounted for 82% of the revenue. It accounted for 86% of the revenue in 2005.

Instructions

(a) Calculate the receivables turnover and days sales outstanding (or average age of receivables) for the two most recent years provided.

(b) Comment on your results.

***E7-23 (Petty Cash)** Keene, Inc. decided to establish a petty cash fund to help ensure internal control over its small cash expenditures. The following information is available for the month of April: **(LO 12)**

1. On April 3, a petty cash fund is established in the amount of $250.

2. A summary of the petty cash expenditures made by the petty cash custodian as of April 13 is as follows:

Delivery charges paid on merchandise purchased	$60.00
Supplies purchased and used	25.00
Postage expense	33.00
IOUs from employees	17.00
Miscellaneous expenses	36.00

The petty cash fund was replenished on April 13. The balance in the fund was $77.

3. The petty cash fund balance was increased by $50 to $300 on April 20.

Instructions

Prepare the journal entries to record the transactions related to petty cash for the month of April.

***E7-24 (Petty Cash)** The petty cash fund of Luigi's Auto Repair Service, a sole proprietorship, contains the following: **(LO 12)**

1. Coins and currency		$ 15.20
2. An IOU from Bob Cunningham, an employee, for a cash advance		63.00
3. A cheque payable to Luigi's Auto Repair from Pat Webber, an employee, marked NSF		34.00
4. Vouchers for the following:		
Stamps	$ 21.00	
Two NHL playoff tickets for Al Luigi	150.00	
A printer cartridge	14.35	185.35
		$297.55

The general ledger account Petty Cash has a balance of $300.00.

Instructions

Prepare the journal entry to record the reimbursement of the petty cash fund.

***E7-25 (Bank Reconciliation and Adjusting Entries)** Ling Corp. deposits all receipts intact and makes all payments by cheque. The following information is available from the cash records: **(LO 12)**

	April 30 Bank Reconciliation
Balance per bank	$ 7,120
Add: Deposits in transit	1,540
Deduct: Outstanding cheques	(2,000)
Balance per books	$ 6,660

Month of May Results

	Per Bank	Per Books
Balance on May 31	$8,760	$9,370
May deposits	5,000	5,810
May cheques	4,000	3,100
May note collected (not included in May deposits)	1,000	—
May bank service charge	25	—
May NSF cheque from a customer, returned by the bank (recorded by the bank as a charge)	335	—

Instructions

(a) Keeping in mind the time lag between deposits and cheques being recorded in the books and when they are recorded by the bank, determine the amount of outstanding deposits and outstanding cheques at May 31.

(b) Prepare a bank reconciliation going from the balance per bank and balance per books to the correct cash balance.

(c) Prepare the general journal entry or entries to correct the Cash account at May 31.

(LO 12) ***E7-26 (Bank Reconciliation and Adjusting Entries)** Bruno Corp. has just received its August 31, 2008, bank statement, which is summarized as follows:

National Bank of Ottawa	Disbursements	Receipts	Balance
Balance, August 1			$ 9,369
Deposits during August		$32,200	41,569
Note collected for depositor, including $40 interest		1,040	42,609
Cheques cleared during August	$34,500		8,109
Bank service charges	20		8,089
Balance, August 31			8,089

The general ledger Cash account contained the following entries for the month of August:

Cash

Balance, August 1	10,050	Disbursements in August	34,903
Receipts during August	35,000		

Deposits in transit at August 31 are $3,800, and cheques outstanding at August 31 total $1,050. Cash on hand at August 31 is $310. The bookkeeper improperly entered one cheque in the books at $146.50. The cheque was actually written for $164.50 for supplies (expense) and cleared the bank during the month of August.

Instructions

(a) Prepare a bank reconciliation dated August 31, 2008, proceeding to a correct balance.

(b) Prepare any entries that are needed to make the books correct and complete.

(c) What amount of cash should be reported in the August 31 balance sheet?

Problems

P7-1 Mainet Equipment Corp. usually closes its books on December 31, but at the end of 2008 it held its cash book open so that a more favourable balance sheet could be prepared for credit purposes. Cash receipts and disbursements for the first 10 days of January were recorded as December transactions.

The following information is given:

1. January cash receipts recorded in the December cash book totalled $41,140. Of that amount, $23,500 was for cash sales and $17,640 was for collections on account for which cash discounts of $360 were given.
2. January cash disbursements that were recorded in the December cheque register were for payments on account totalling $28,450 of accounts payable on which discounts of $250 were taken.
3. The ledger has not been closed for 2008.
4. The amount shown as inventory was determined by a physical count on December 31, 2008.

Instructions

(a) Prepare any entries that you consider necessary to correct Mainet Equipment Corp.'s accounts at December 31.

(b) To what extent was Mainet Equipment Co. able to show a more favourable balance sheet at December 31 by holding its cash book open? (Use ratio analysis.) Assume that the balance sheet that was prepared by the company showed the following amounts:

	Dr.	Cr.
Cash	$39,000	
Receivables	42,000	
Inventories	67,000	
Accounts payable		$45,000
Other current liabilities		14,200

P7-2 A series of unrelated situations follow:

1. Atlantic Inc.'s unadjusted trial balance at December 31, 2008, included the following accounts:

	Debit	Credit
Allowance for doubtful accounts	$ 4,000	
Sales		$1,900,000
Sales returns and allowances	67,000	
Sales discounts	2,300	

2. An analysis and aging of Central Corp.'s accounts receivable at December 31, 2008, disclosed the following:

Amounts estimated to be uncollectible	$ 160,000
Accounts receivable	1,790,000
Allowance for doubtful accounts (per books)	125,000

3. Western Co. provides for doubtful accounts based on 3% of credit sales. The following data are available for 2008:

Credit sales during 2008	$2,100,000
Allowance for doubtful accounts 1/1/08	17,000
Collection of accounts written off in prior years (customer credit was re-established)	8,000
Customer accounts written off as uncollectible during 2008	26,000

4. At the end of its first year of operations, December 31, 2008, Pacific Inc. reported the following information:

Accounts receivable, net of allowance for doubtful accounts	$950,000
Customer accounts written off as uncollectible during 2008	24,000
Bad debt expense for 2008	92,000

5. The following accounts were taken from Northern Inc.'s unadjusted trial balance at December 31, 2008:

	Debit	Credit
Sales (all on credit)		$750,000
Sales discounts	$ 11,400	
Allowance for doubtful accounts	14,000	
Accounts receivable	410,000	

Instructions

(a) For situation 1, Atlantic estimates its bad debt expense to be 1.5% of net sales. Determine its bad debt expense for 2008.

(b) For situation 2, what is the net realizable value of Central Corp.'s receivables at December 31, 2008?

(c) For situation 3, what is the balance in Allowance for Doubtful Accounts at December 31, 2008?

(d) For situation 4, what is the balance in accounts receivable at December 31, 2008, before subtracting the allowance for doubtful accounts?

(e) For situation 5, if doubtful accounts are 7% of accounts receivable, what is the bad debt expense amount to be reported for 2008?

P7-3 Paderewski Corporation operates in an industry that has a high rate of bad debts. Before any year-end adjustments, the balance in Paderewski's Accounts Receivable account was $625,000 and Allowance for Doubtful Accounts had a credit balance of $35,000. The year-end balance reported in the balance sheet for Allowance for Doubtful Accounts will be based on the following aging schedule:

Days Account Outstanding	Amount	Probability of Collection
Less than 16 days	$355,000	97%
Between 16 and 30 days	115,000	92%
Between 31 and 45 days	80,000	80%
Between 46 and 60 days	40,000	75%
Between 61 and 75 days	20,000	40%
Over 75 days	15,000	0%

Instructions

(a) What is the appropriate balance for Allowance for Doubtful Accounts at year end?

(b) Show how accounts receivable would be presented on the balance sheet.

(c) What is the dollar effect of the year-end bad debt adjustment on the before-tax income?

P7-4 From its first day of operations to December 31, 2008, Madden Corporation provided for uncollectible accounts receivable under the allowance method: entries for bad debt expense were made monthly based on 2% of credit sales; bad debts that were written off were charged to the allowance account; recoveries of bad debts previously written off were credited to the allowance account; and no year-end adjustments were made to the allowance account. Madden's usual credit terms were net 30 days, and remain unchanged.

The balance in Allowance for Doubtful Accounts was $154,000 at January 1, 2008. During 2008, credit sales totalled $9.4 million; interim entries for bad debt expense were based on 2% of credit sales; $95,000 of bad debts were written off; and recoveries of accounts previously written off amounted to $15,000. Madden upgraded its computer facility in November 2008, and an aging of accounts receivable was prepared for the first time as at December 31, 2008. A summary of the aging analysis follows:

Classification by Month of Sale	Balance in Each Category	Estimated % Uncollectible
November–December 2008	$1,080,000	6%
July–October 2008	650,000	10%
January–June 2008	420,000	35%
Before January 1, 2008	150,000	75%
	$2,300,000	

Based on a review of how collectible the accounts really are in the "Before January 1, 2008" aging category, additional receivables totalling $69,000 were written off as at December 31, 2008. The 75% uncollectible estimate therefore only applies to the remaining $81,000 in the category. Finally, beginning with the year ended December 31, 2008, Madden adopted a new accounting method for estimating the allowance for doubtful accounts: it now uses the amount indicated by the year-end aging analysis of accounts receivable.

Instructions

(a) Prepare a schedule that analyzes the changes in Allowance for Doubtful Accounts for the year ended December 31, 2008. Show supporting calculations in good form. (Hint: In calculating the allowance amount at December 31, 2008, subtract the $69,000 write-off.)

(b) Prepare the journal entry for the year-end adjustment to the Allowance for Doubtful Accounts balance as at December 31, 2008.

(AICPA adapted)

P7-5 The following information relates to Shea Inc.'s Accounts Receivable for the 2008 fiscal year:

1. An aging schedule of the accounts receivable as at December 31, 2008, is as follows:

Age	Net Debit Balance	% to Be Applied after Write Off Is Made
Under 60 days	$172,342	1%
61–90 days	136,490	3%
91–120 days	39,924*	7%
Over 120 days	23,644	$4,200 definitely uncollectible; 20% of remainder is estimated uncollectible
	$372,400	

*The $2,740 write-off of receivables (see item 4 below) is related to the 91–120-day category.

2. The Accounts Receivable control account has a debit balance of $372,400 on December 31, 2008.

3. Two entries were made in the Bad Debts Expense account during the year: (1) a debit on December 31 for the amount credited to Allowance for Doubtful Accounts, and (2) a credit for $2,740 on November 3, 2008, and a debit to Allowance for Doubtful Accounts because of a bankruptcy.

4. Allowance for Doubtful Accounts is as follows for 2008:

Allowance for Doubtful Accounts					
11/3	Uncollectible accounts written off	2,740	1/1	Beginning balance	8,750
			12/31	5% of $372,400	18,620

5. There is a credit balance in Accounts Receivable (61–90 days) of $4,840, which represents an advance on a sales contract.

Instructions
Assuming that the books have not been closed for 2008, make the necessary correcting entries.

P7-6 The balance sheet of Reynolds Corp. at December 31, 2007, includes the following:

Notes receivable	$ 26,000	
Accounts receivable	182,100	
Less: Allowance for doubtful accounts	(17,300)	$190,800

Transactions in 2008 include the following:

1. Accounts receivable of $138,000 were collected. This amount includes gross accounts of $40,000 on which 2% sales discounts were allowed.
2. An additional $6,700 was received in payment of an account that was written off in 2005.
3. Customer accounts of $19,500 were written off during the year.
4. At year end, Allowance for Doubtful Accounts was estimated to need a balance of $21,000. This estimate is based on an analysis of aged accounts receivable.

Instructions
Prepare all necessary journal entries to reflect the information above.

(AICPA adapted)

P7-7 On October 1, 2008, Farm Equipment Corp. sold a harvesting machine to Stead Industries. Instead of a cash payment, Stead Industries gave Farm Equipment a $100,000, two-year, 12% note, which is a realistic rate for a note of this type. The note required interest to be paid annually on October 1. Farm Equipment's financial statements are prepared on a calendar-year basis.

Instructions

(a) Assuming that no reversing entries are used and that Stead Industries fulfills all the terms of the note, prepare the necessary journal entries for Farm Equipment Corp. for the entire term of the note.

(b) Repeat the journal entries under the assumption that Farm Equipment Corp. uses reversing entries.

P7-8 On December 31, 2008 Zhang Ltd. rendered services to Beggy Corp. at an agreed price of $91,844.10. In payment, Zhang accepted $36,000 cash and agreed to receive the balance in four equal instalments of $18,000 that are due each December 31. An interest rate of 11% is applicable.

Instructions

(a) Prepare the entries recorded by Zhang Ltd. for the sale and for the receipts including interest on the following dates:

1. December 31, 2008
2. December 31, 2009
3. December 31, 2010
4. December 31, 2011
5. December 31, 2012

(b) From Zhang Ltd.'s perspective, what are the advantages of an instalment note compared to a non-interest-bearing note?

P7-9 Desrosiers Ltd. had the following long-term receivable account balances at December 31, 2007:

Note receivable from sale of division	$1,800,000
Note receivable from officer	400,000

Transactions during 2008 and other information relating to Desrosiers' long-term receivables were as follows:

(a) The $1.8-million note receivable is dated May 1, 2007, bears interest at 9%, and represents the balance of the consideration received from the sale of Desrosiers's electronics division to New York Company. Principal payments of $600,000 plus appropriate interest are due on May 1, 2008, 2009, and 2010. The first principal and interest payment was made on May 1, 2008. Collection of the note instalments is reasonably assured.

(b) The $400,000 note receivable is dated December 31, 2007, bears interest at 8%, and is due on December 31, 2010. The note is due from Mark Cumby, president of Desrosiers Ltd., and is secured by 10,000 Desrosiers common shares. Interest is payable annually on December 31, and the interest payment was made December 31, 2008. The quoted market price of Desrosiers's common shares was $45 per share on December 31, 2008.

(c) On April 1, 2008, Desrosiers sold a patent to Pinot Company in exchange for a $200,000 non-interest-bearing note due on April 1, 2010. There was no established exchange price for the patent, and the note had no ready market. The prevailing rate of interest for a note of this type at April 1, 2008, was 12%. The present value of $1 for two periods at 12% is 0.79719 (use this factor). The patent had a carrying amount of $40,000 at January 1, 2008, and the amortization for the year ended December 31, 2008, would have been $8,000. The collection of the note receivable from Pinot is reasonably assured.

(d) On July 1, 2008, Desrosiers sold a parcel of land to Harris Inc. for $200,000 under an instalment sale contract. Harris made a $60,000 cash down payment on July 1, 2008, and signed a four-year, 11% note for the $140,000 balance. The equal annual payments of principal and interest on the note will be $45,125 payable on July 1, 2009, through July 1, 2012. The land could have been sold at an established cash price of $200,000. The cost of the land to Desrosiers was $150,000. Collection of the instalments on the note is reasonably assured.

Instructions

(a) For each note:

1. Describe the relevant cash flows in terms of amount and timing.
2. Determine the amount of interest income that should be reported in 2008.
3. Determine the portion of the note and any interest that should be reported in current assets at December 31, 2008.
4. Determine the portion of the note that should be reported as a long-term investment at December 31, 2008.

(b) Prepare the long-term receivables section of Desrosiers's balance sheet at December 31, 2008.

(c) Prepare a schedule showing the current portion of the long-term receivables and accrued interest receivable that would appear in Desrosiers's balance sheet at December 31, 2008.

(d) Determine the total interest income from the long-term receivables that would appear on Desrosiers's income statement for the year ended December 31, 2008.

P7-10 Logo Limited manufactures sweatshirts for sale to athletic-wear retailers. The following summary information was available for Logo for the year ended December 31, 2007:

Cash	$20,000
Trade accounts receivable (net)	40,000
Inventories	85,000
Accounts payable	65,000
Other current liabilities	15,000

Part 1

During 2008, Logo had the following transactions:

1. Total sales were $465,000. Of the total sales amount, $215,000 was on a credit basis.
2. On June 30, a $50,000 account receivable of a major customer was settled with Logo accepting a $50,000, one-year, 11% note, with the interest payable at maturity.
3. Logo collected $160,000 on trade accounts receivable during the year.
4. At December 31, 2008, Cash had a balance of $15,000, Inventories had a balance of $80,000, accounts payable were $70,000, and other current liabilities were $16,000.

Instructions

(a) Prepare summary journal entries to record the items noted above.

(b) Calculate the current ratio and the receivables turnover ratio for Logo at December 31, 2008. Use these measures to assess Logo's liquidity. The receivables turnover ratio last year was 4.75.

Part 2

Now assume that at year end 2008, Logo enters into the following transactions related to the company's receivables:

1. Logo sells the note receivable to Prairie Bank for $50,000 cash plus accrued interest. Given the creditworthiness of Logo's customer, the bank accepts the note without recourse and assesses a finance charge of 3.5%. Prairie Bank will collect the note directly from the customer.

2. Logo factors some accounts receivable at the end of the year. Accounts totalling $40,000 are transferred to First Factors, Inc., with recourse. First Factors retains 6% of the balances and assesses a finance charge of 4% on the transfer. First Factors will collect the receivables from Logo's customers. The fair value of the recourse obligation is $4,000.

Instructions

(c) Prepare the journal entry to record the transfer of the note receivable to Prairie Bank.

(d) Prepare the journal entry to record the sale of receivables to First Factors.

(e) Calculate the current ratio and the receivables turnover ratio for Logo at December 31, 2008. Use these measures to assess Logo's liquidity. The receivables turnover ratio last year was 4.85.

(f) Discuss how the ratio analysis in (e) would be affected if Logo had transferred the receivables in secured borrowing transactions.

P7-11 In 2008, Ibran Corp. required additional cash for its business. Management therefore decided to use accounts receivable to raise the additional cash and has asked you to determine the income statement effects of the following transactions:

1. On July 1, 2008, Ibran assigned $400,000 of accounts receivable to Provincial Finance Corporation as security for a loan. Ibran received an advance from Provincial of 85% of the assigned accounts receivable less a commission of 3% on the advance. Before December 31, 2008, Ibran collected $220,000 on the assigned accounts receivable, and remitted $232,720 to Provincial Finance. Of the latter amount, $12,720 was interest on the advance from Provincial.
2. On December 1, 2008, Ibran sold $300,000 of accounts receivable to Wunsch Corp. for $250,000. The receivables were sold outright on a without recourse basis and Ibran has no continuing interest in the receivables.
3. On December 31, 2008, an advance of $120,000 was received from First Bank by pledging $160,000 of Ibran's accounts receivable. Ibran's first payment to First Bank is due on January 30, 2009.

Instructions

Prepare a schedule showing the income statement effects of the above transactions for the year ended December 31, 2008.

P7-12 The Cormier Corporation sells office equipment and supplies to many organizations in the city and surrounding area on contract terms of 2/10, n/30. In the past, over 75% of the credit customers have taken advantage of the discount by paying within 10 days of the invoice date. However, the number of customers taking the full 30 days to pay has increased within the last year. It now appears that less than 60% of the customers are taking the discount. Bad debts as a percentage of gross credit sales have risen from the 1.5% of past years to about 4% in the current year.

The controller responded to a request for more information on the deterioration in collections of accounts receivable by preparing the following report:

THE CORMIER CORPORATION
Finance Committee Report—Accounts Receivable Collections
May 31, 2008

The fact that some credit accounts will prove uncollectible is normal. Annual bad debt write-offs have been 1.5% of gross credit sales over the past five years. During the last fiscal year, this percentage increased to slightly less than 4%. The current Accounts Receivable balance is $1.6 million. The condition of this balance in terms of age and probability of collection is as follows:

Proportion of Total	Age Categories	Probability of Collection
68%	not yet due	99%
15%	less than 30 days past due	96.5%
8%	30 to 60 days past due	95%
5%	61 to 120 days past due	91%
2.5%	121 to 180 days past due	70%
1.5%	more than 180 days past due	20%

Allowance for Doubtful Accounts had a credit balance of $43,300 on June 1, 2007. The Cormier Corporation has provided for a monthly bad debt expense accrual during the current fiscal year based on the assumption that 4% of gross credit sales will be uncollectible. Total gross credit sales for the 2007–08 fiscal year amounted to $4 million. Write-offs of bad accounts during the year totalled $145,000.

Instructions

(a) Prepare an accounts receivable aging schedule for The Cormier Corporation using the age categories identified in the controller's report to the Finance Committee. Show (1) the amount of accounts receivable outstanding for each age category and in total, and (2) the estimated amount that is uncollectible for each category and in total.

(b) Calculate the amount of the year-end adjustment that is needed to bring Allowance for Doubtful Accounts to the balance indicated by the age analysis. Then prepare the necessary journal entry to adjust the accounting records.

(c) Assuming that the economy is currently in recession with tight credit and high interest rates:

1. Identify steps that the Cormier Corporation might consider to improve the accounts receivable situation.
2. Evaluate each step you identify in terms of the risks and costs that it involves.

(CMA adapted)

P7-13 The Divine Corporation manufactures sweaters for sale to athletic-wear retailers. The following information was available on Divine for the years ended December 31, 2007 and 2008:

	December 31, 2007	December 31, 2008
Cash	$ 20,000	$ 15,000
Accounts receivable	40,000	?
Allowance for doubtful accounts	5,500	?
Inventories	85,000	80,000
Current liabilities	80,000	86,000
Total credit sales	480,000	550,000
Collections on accounts receivable	440,000	500,000

During 2008, Divine had the following transactions:

1. On June 1, 2008, sales of $50,000 to a major customer were settled with Divine accepting a $50,000, one-year note bearing 9% interest that is payable at maturity. The $50,000 is not included in the total credit sales amount above.
2. Divine factors some accounts receivable at the end of the year. Accounts totalling $40,000 are transferred to First Factors Inc., with recourse. First Factors will receive the collections from Divine's customers and retain 6% of the balances. Divine is assessed a finance charge of 4% on this transfer. The fair value of the recourse obligation is $4,000.
3. Divine wrote off $2,300 of accounts receivable during 2008.
4. Based on the latest available information, the 2008 bad debt expense is estimated to be 0.8% of credit sales.

Additional information:

Included in the cash balance at December 31, 2008, are the following: a chequing account with a balance of $9,600; postage stamps of $100; petty cash of $300; coins and currency on hand of $3,000; and post-dated cheques from customers of $2,000.

Instructions

(a) Prepare the journal entry for the factoring of the accounts receivable to First Factors Inc.

(b) Based on the above transactions and additional information, determine the balances of Accounts Receivable and Allowance for Doubtful Accounts at December 31, 2008.

(c) Prepare the current assets section of Divine's balance sheet at December 31, 2008.

(d) Calculate the current ratios for Divine for 2007 and 2008.

(e) Calculate the receivables turnover ratio for Divine for 2008. Divine's receivables turnover ratio for 2007 was 13.4 times.

(f) Comment on Divine's liquidity and ability to collect accounts receivable. Comment also on the improvement or deterioration of the current and receivables turnover ratios.

(g) Discuss the effect on the current and accounts receivable turnover ratios if Divine had decided to assign $40,000 of accounts receivable instead of factoring them to First Factors Inc. Recalculate the ratios to support your conclusions.

***P7-14** Joseph Howe is reviewing the cash accounting for Connolly Corporation, a local mailing service. Howe's review will focus on the petty cash account and the bank reconciliation for the month ended May 31, 2008. He has collected the following information from Connolly's bookkeeper:

Petty Cash

1. The petty cash fund was established on May 10, 2008, in the amount of $300.
2. Expenditures from the fund by the custodian as at May 31, 2008, were evidenced by approved receipts for the following:

Postage expense	$33.00
Mailing labels and other supplies	40.00
Coffee supplies (milk, sugar, cups)	35.00
IOUs from employees	30.00
Shipping charges	57.45
Newspaper advertising	22.80
Miscellaneous expenses	15.35

On May 31, 2008, the petty cash fund was replenished and increased to $400; currency and coin in the fund at that time totalled $64.99.

Bank Reconciliation

SCOTIA IMPERIAL BANK
Bank Statement

	Disbursements	Receipts	Balance
Balance, May 1, 2008			$8,769
Deposits		$28,000	
Note payment, direct from customer (interest of $30)		930	
Cheques cleared during May	$ 31,150		
Bank service charges	37		
Balance, May 31, 2008			$6,512

Connolly's Cash Account

Balance, May 1, 2008	$ 9,150
Deposits during May 2008	31,000
Cheques written during May 2008	(31,835)

Deposits in transit are determined to be $3,000, and cheques outstanding at May 31 total $550. Cash on hand (besides petty cash) at May 31, 2008, is $246.

Instructions

(a) Prepare the journal entries to record the transactions related to the petty cash fund for May.

(b) Prepare a bank reconciliation dated May 31, 2008, proceeding to a correct balance, and prepare the journal entries to make the books correct and complete.

(c) What amount of cash should be reported in the May 31, 2008, balance sheet?

***P7-15** The cash account of Villa Corp. shows a ledger balance of $3,969.85 on June 30, 2008. The bank statement as at that date indicates a balance of $4,150. When the statement was compared with the cash records, the following facts were determined:

1. There were bank service charges for June of $25.00.
2. A bank memo stated that Bao Dai's note for $900 and interest of $36 had been collected on June 29, and the bank had made a charge of $5.50 on the collection. (No entry had been made on Villa's books when Bao Dai's note was sent to the bank for collection.)
3. Receipts for June 30 of $2,890 were not deposited until July 2.
4. Cheques outstanding on June 30 totalled $2,136.05.
5. On June 29, the bank had charged Villa Corp.'s account for a customer's uncollectible cheque amounting to $453.20.
6. A customer's cheque for $90 had been entered as $60 in the cash receipts journal by Villa Corp. on June 15.
7. Cheque no. 742 in the amount of $491 had been entered in the cashbook as $419, and cheque no. 747 in the amount of $58.20 had been entered as $582. Both cheques were issued to pay for purchases of equipment.
8. In May 2008, the bank had charged a $27.50 Wella Corp. cheque against the Villa Corp. account. The June bank statement indicated that the bank had reversed this charge and corrected its error.

Instructions

(a) Prepare a bank reconciliation dated June 30, 2008, proceeding to a correct cash balance.

(b) Prepare any entries that are needed to make the books correct and complete.

***P7-16** Information related to Bonzai Books Ltd. is as follows: balance per books at October 31, $41,847.85; November receipts, $173,528.91; November disbursements, $166,193.54; balance per bank statement at November 30, $56,270.20. The following cheques were outstanding at November 30:

#1224	$1,635.29
#1230	2,468.30
#1232	3,625.15
#1233	482.17

Included with the November bank statement and not recorded by the company were a bank debit memo for $31.40 covering bank charges for the month, a debit memo for $572.13 for a customer's cheque returned and marked NSF, and a credit memo for $1,400 representing bond interest collected by the bank in the name of Bonzai Books Ltd. Cash on hand at November 30 that had been recorded and was not yet deposited amounted to $1,920.40.

Instructions

(a) Prepare a bank reconciliation to the correct balance at November 30 for Bonzai Books Ltd.

(b) Prepare any journal entries that are needed to adjust the Cash account at November 30.

***P7-17** Information follows on Quartz Industries Ltd.:

QUARTZ INDUSTRIES LTD.
Bank Reconciliation
May 31, 2008

Balance per bank statement		$30,928.46
Less: Outstanding cheques		
No. 6124	$2,125.00	
No. 6138	932.65	
No. 6139	960.57	
No. 6140	1,420.00	5,438.22
		25,490.24
Add deposit in transit		4,710.56
Balance per books (correct balance)		$30,200.80

CHEQUE REGISTER—JUNE

Date		Payee	No.	Invoice Amount	Discount	Cash
June	1	Ren Mfg.	6141	$ 237.50		$ 237.50
	1	Stimpy Mfg.	6142	915.00	$ 9.15	905.85
	8	Rugrats Co., Inc.	6143	122.90	2.45	120.45
	9	Ren Mfg.	6144	306.40		306.40
	10	Petty Cash	6145	89.93		89.93
	17	Muppet Babies Photo	6146	706.00	14.12	691.88
	22	Hey Dude Publishing	6147	447.50		447.50
	23	Payroll Account	6148	4,130.00		4,130.00
	25	Dragnet Tools, Inc.	6149	390.75	3.91	386.84
	28	Dare Insurance Agency	6150	1,050.00		1,050.00
	28	Get Smart Construction	6151	2,250.00		2,250.00
	29	M M T, Inc.	6152	750.00		750.00
	30	Lassie Co.	6153	400.00	8.00	392.00
				$11,795.98	$37.63	$11,758.35

PROVINCIAL BANK
Bank Statement
General Chequing Account of Quartz Industries–June, 2008

Debits			Date	Credits	Balance
					$30,928.46
$2,125.00	$ 237.50	$ 905.85	June 1	$4,710.56	32,370.67
932.65	120.45		12	1,507.06	32,824.63
1,420.00	447.50	306.40	23	1,458.55	32,109.28
4,130.00	11.05*		26		27,968.23
89.93	2,250.00	1,050.00	28	4,157.48	28,735.78

*Bank charges

Cash received on June 29 and 30 and deposited in the mail on June 30 for the general chequing account amounted to $4,607.96. Because the Cash account balance at June 30 is not given, it must be calculated based on other information in the problem.

Instructions
Prepare a bank reconciliation to the correct balance as of June 30, 2008, for Quartz Industries.

Writing Assignments

WA7-1 The trial balance of Imotex Ltd. contains the following accounts:

(a) Accounts receivable, trade

(b) Accounts receivable, related company

(c) Accounts receivable, to be exchanged for shares in another company

(d) Note receivable, receivable in grams of a precious metal

(e) Cash

(f) Investment in Royal Bank common shares (long-term investment)

(g) Interest rate swap: contract to receive fixed rate (at 8%) and to pay variable rate (current rates are 6%) on debenture debt

(h) U.S. dollar cash holdings in a U.S. subsidiary's bank account

Instructions
For (a) to (h), indicate whether the item is or is not a financial asset. Give an explanation for each of your choices.

WA7-2 Sib Mukandi runs a wholesale merchandising business that sells approximately 5,000 items per month with a total monthly average sales value of $250,000. The company's annual bad debt ratio has been approximately 1.5% of sales. In recent discussions with her bookkeeper, Ms. Mukandi has become confused by all the alternatives that are apparently available in handling the allowance for doubtful accounts. The following information has been shown to her:

1. An allowance can be set up (a) based on a percentage of sales or (b) based on a valuation of all past due or otherwise questionable accounts receivable—with accounts that are considered uncollectible being charged to the allowance at the close of the accounting period, or specific items being charged off directly against (1) Gross Sales, or to (2) Bad Debt Expense in the year in which they are determined to be uncollectible.
2. Collection agency fees, legal fees, and so on incurred in connection with the attempted recovery of bad debts can be charged to (a) Bad Debt Expense, (b) Allowance for Doubtful Accounts, (c) Legal Expense, or (d) General Expense.
3. Debts previously written off in whole or in part but currently recovered can be credited to (a) Other Revenue, (b) Bad Debt Expense, or (c) Allowance for Doubtful Accounts.

Instructions
Which of the methods would you recommend to Ms. Mukandi for (1) allowances and charge-offs, (2) collection expenses, and (3) recoveries? State briefly and clearly the reasons that support your recommendations.

WA7-3 Soon after beginning the year-end audit work on March 10 at Arkin Corp., the auditor has the following conversation with the controller:

Controller: The year ended March 31 should be our most profitable in history and, because of this, the Board of Directors has just awarded the officers generous bonuses.

Auditor: I thought profits were down this year in the industry, at least according to your latest interim report.

Controller: Well, they were down, but 10 days ago we closed a deal that will give us a substantial increase for the year.

Auditor: Oh, what was it?

Controller: Well, you remember a few years ago our former president bought shares of Hi-Tek Enterprises Ltd. because he had those grandiose ideas about becoming a conglomerate? For six years, we weren't able to sell the shares. They cost us $3 million and hadn't paid a nickel in dividends. Thursday we sold the shares to Campbell Inc. for $4 million. So, we'll have a gain of $700,000 ($1 million pre-tax) which will increase our net income for the year to $4 million, compared with last year's $3.8 million. As far as I know, we'll be the only company in the industry to register an increase in net income this year. That should help the market value of our shares!

Auditor: Do you expect to receive the $4 million in cash by March 31, your fiscal year end?

Controller: No. Although Campbell Inc. is an excellent company, they're a little tight for cash because of their rapid growth. So they're going to give us a $4-million non-interest-bearing note with $400,000 due each year for the next 10 years. The first payment is due March 31 of next year.

Auditor: Why is the note non-interest-bearing?

Controller: Because that's what everybody agreed to. Since we don't have any interest-bearing debt, the funds invested in the note don't cost us anything and besides, we weren't getting any dividends on the Hi-Tek Enterprises shares.

Instructions

Prepare the auditor's written report to the controller on how this transaction should be accounted for, and how any corrections that are necessary will affect the reported results for the current year ended March 31.

WA7-4 Rudolph Corp. is a subsidiary of Huntley Corp. The controller believes that the yearly charge for doubtful accounts for Rudolph should be 2% of net credit sales. The president, nervous that the parent company might expect the subsidiary to sustain its 10% growth rate, suggests that the controller increase the charge for doubtful accounts to 3% yearly. The president thinks that the lower net income, which reflects a 6% growth rate, will be a more sustainable rate for Rudolph.

Instructions

(a) Should the controller be concerned with Rudolph Corp.'s growth rate in estimating the allowance? Explain your answer.

(b) Does the president's request pose an ethical dilemma for the controller? Give your reasons for why it does or does not.

WA7-5 Who would have thought that musicians David Bowie and James Brown had anything to do with accounting? Asset- or artist-backed financing vehicles have been used by these performers and others as a means of securitizing royalties and rights to other intellectual property.

Instructions

Perform an Internet search on "Bowie bonds" or on David Pullman, who created them. Write a brief report explaining how this securitization works and what similarities it has to accounts receivable securitization.

Cases

www.wiley.com/canada/kieso

Refer to the Case Primer on the Student Website to help you answer these cases.

CA7-1 Hanley Limited (HL) manufactures camera equipment. The company plans to list its shares on the TSX Venture Exchange. To do so, it must meet all of the following initial listing requirements (among others):

1. Net tangible assets must be at least $500,000.
2. Pre-tax earnings must be $50,000.
3. The company must have adequate working capital.

Hanley has experienced significant growth in sales and is having difficulty estimating its bad debt expense. During the year, the sales team has been extending credit on a more aggressive basis in order to increase commissions revenues. Under the percentage-of-receivables approach using past percentages, the estimate is $50,000. Hanley has performed an aging and estimates the bad debts at $57,000. Finally, using a percentage of sales, the expense is estimated at $67,000. Before booking the allowance, net tangible assets are approximately $550,000. The controller decides to accrue $50,000, which results in pre-tax earnings of $60,000.

Instructions
Adopt the role of the TSX Venture exchange staff and decide whether the company meets the financial aspects of the initial requirements for listing on the TSX Venture Exchange.

CA7-2 Telus Corporation (Telus) is one of Canada's largest telecommunications companies and provides both products and services. Its shares are traded on the Toronto and New York stock exchanges. Verizon owns 21% of Telus' voting and non-voting shares and 73% are widely held. In its 2002 management discussion and analysis, Telus noted that its business plans could be negatively affected if its current financing became insufficient. Its plan was to finance future capital requirements with internally generated funds and to also use its bank line of credit. Because of disruptions in the capital market and reduced lending to the telecommunications sector, as well as downgradings and negative outlooks on Telus debt, additional borrowing is not really an option.

According to the 2002 Annual Report:

> On July 26, 2002, Telus entered into an agreement with an arms-length securitization trust under which it is able to sell an interest in certain of its trade receivables up to a maximum of $650 million. As at December 31, 2002, Telus had received aggregate cash proceeds of $475 million. Under the program, Telus is required to maintain at least a BBB (low) credit rating by Dominion Bond Rating Service. In the event this rating is not maintained, the Company may be required to wind down the program. A change in credit rating could impact Telus' cost of and access to capital.

Under the terms of the agreement, Telus will still service the receivables. In structuring the transaction, the following assumptions were made:

Expected credit loss	2.4%
Discount rate	4.2%
Servicing costs	1.0%

Instructions
Adopt the role of the controller of Telus and discuss the financial reporting issues.

Integrated Cases

IC7-1 Franklyn's Furniture (FF) is a mid-sized owner-operated business that was started 25 years ago by Fred Franklyn. The retail furniture business is cyclical, with business dropping off in times of economic downturn, as is the case currently. In order to encourage sales, the store offers its own credit cards to good customers. FF has run into a bit of a cash crunch and is planning to go to the bank to obtain an increase in its line of credit in order to replenish and expand the furniture stock. At present, the line of credit is capped at (i.e., limited to) 70% of the credit card receivables and inventory. The receivables and inventory have been pledged as security for the loan.

Fred Franklyn has identified two possible sources of the cash shortage—outstanding credit card receivables and a buildup in old inventory. He has come up with two strategies to deal with the problem:

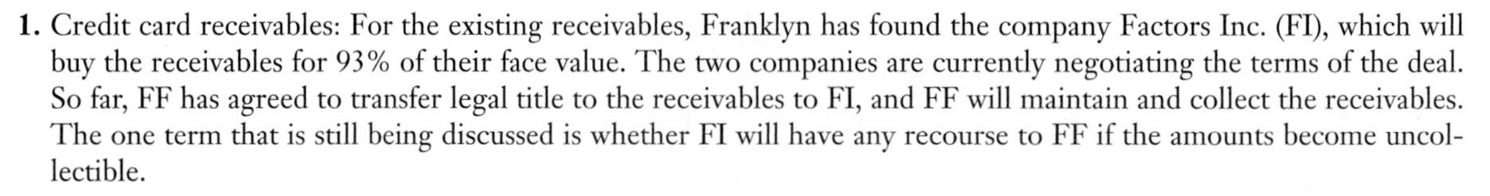

1. Credit card receivables: For the existing receivables, Franklyn has found the company Factors Inc. (FI), which will buy the receivables for 93% of their face value. The two companies are currently negotiating the terms of the deal. So far, FF has agreed to transfer legal title to the receivables to FI, and FF will maintain and collect the receivables. The one term that is still being discussed is whether FI will have any recourse to FF if the amounts become uncollectible.

2. Excess inventory: A new sales promotion has been advertised in the newspaper for the past two months. Under the terms of the promotion, customers do not pay anything up front and will be able to take the furniture home and begin payments the following year. Response to the advertisement has been very good and a significant amount of inventory has been moved to date, leaving room for new inventory once the bank financing comes through.

Instructions

Assume the role of Fred Franklyn's bookkeeper and advise him about the impact of the strategies on the company's financial reporting.

IC7-2 Bowearth Limited (BL) is in the lumber business. The company sells pulp and paper products as well as timber and lumber. It has over one million acres of timberland which it either owns or leases. The company's shares trade on the "Public Stock Exchange" (the PSE). Net income for the past few years has been positive and increasing, and it has averaged approximately $1 million over the past five years. This year, however, due to various factors, the company is just expecting to break even.

During the year, the company announced an exclusive licensing agreement with Lindor Inc. (LI), an unrelated company. Under the terms of the agreement, the company will have exclusive sales and distribution rights for LI's technology and products. In return, it will pay LI royalties. The technology and products target the pulp and paper industry. During the first five years of the agreement, royalty payments that must be paid by BL to LI are 3% of sales in the first year, 2% in the second, and 1% thereafter. There is a minimum royalty of $500,000 that must be paid regardless of the level of sales. LI has been in business many years and the technology is proven and in great demand. It is therefore very likely that BL will have to pay.

The U.S. government has recently levied anti-dumping fees of 8% on all softwood lumber shipped to the U.S., as well as countervailing duties of 20%. The amounts must be paid by the company to the U.S. government in order to continue to sell in the U.S.A. The Canadian government has challenged the right of the U.S. government to charge this amount and has appealed to the World Trade Organization. Canada feels that under the North American Free Trade Agreement (NAFTA), such charges cannot be legally levied. In the meantime, BL has been accruing and setting the amounts aside in cash deposits with the bank just in case the appeal is unsuccessful. The amounts accrued and set aside to date are approximately $3 million. The U.S. government is continuing to allow the company to ship lumber as long as the cash is set aside in the bank. To date, the appeal process is going well and the Canadian government feels that the fees/duties will at least be reduced significantly, if not completely eliminated. There are rumours that the fees/duties may be cancelled next year.

The company is currently being sued by a former major shareholder for providing misleading financial statements. The lawsuit alleges that net income was materially misstated. The case has not yet gone to court. BL feels that the case is not very strong but has nonetheless fired the president, William Waters, to be on the safe side. As a result, BL is also being sued for wrongful dismissal by its former president. Waters is suing for a lost bonus of $300,000 as well as lost future income in the amount of $10 million. BL is investigating the claim of overstated net income and, to date, has not found anything that indicates a material misstatement.

The controller, Fred Flame, is unsure of how to book all of the above in the financial statements (or if he even should). He has a meeting with the bank next week to discuss increasing the company's line of credit. He is hopeful that once the ruling comes down from the World Trade Organization, the increased line of credit will not be needed. In the meantime, the bank has signalled that it will be looking at the company's liquidity very closely. The auditors will also be coming in to review the statements in the next month.

Instructions

Adopt the role of Fred Flame and discuss the financial reporting issues.

Research and Financial Analysis

RA7-1 Maple Leaf Foods Inc.

Selected excerpts from the financial statements of Maple Leaf Foods Inc. for the year ended December 31, 2005, follow:

Consolidated Balance Sheet

(In thousands of Canadian dollars)

As at December 31	2005	2004
Current assets		
Cash and cash equivalents	**$ 80,502**	$111,770
Accounts receivable (note 3)	**247,014**	292,462

Consolidated Statement of Earnings

(In thousands of Canadian dollars)

Years ended December 31	2005	2004
Sales	**$6,462,581**	$6,364,983

Notes to the consolidated financial statements

3. Accounts receivable

Under revolving securitization programs, the Company has sold certain of its trade accounts receivable to financial institutions. The Company retains servicing responsibilities and retains a limited recourse obligation for delinquent receivables. At December 31, 2005, trade accounts receivable being serviced under this program amounted to $230.1 million (2004—$209.7 million).

In addition, the company reported accounts receivable of $242,306 thousand at December 31, 2003; fiscal year 2003 sales of $5,041,896 thousand; and securitized receivables of $186.8 million at December 31, 2003.

Instructions

(a) Calculate the accounts receivable turnover for 2004 and 2005 and the average age of the accounts receivable at December 31, 2004 and 2005, without taking the additional securitized receivables into account. Comment on your results.

(b) Calculate the percentage growth in sales and accounts receivable in 2004 and 2005 without taking the securitized receivables into account. Comment on your results.

(c) Explain how the securitized receivables should be taken into account in the calculations in (a) and (b) above, or not taken into account at all. Recalculate your ratios and percentages. Did the securitizations have an effect on your assessment of the company? Explain.

RA7-2 Canadian Tire Corporation, Limited

Canadian Tire Corporation, Limited is one of Canada's best-known retailers. The company operates over 460 "hard-goods" retail stores through Associate Dealers, and over 330 corporate and franchise stores under its subsidiary Mark's Work Wearhouse, and has about 260 independently operated gasoline sites. It offers financial services through its branded credit cards and now provides personal loans and a variety of insurance and warranty products.

Instructions

Access the financial statements of Canadian Tire Corporation, Limited for its year ended December 31, 2005, either on the Student website or the SEDAR website (www.sedar.com). Refer to these financial statements and their accompanying notes to answer the following questions:

(a) How does Canadian Tire define cash and cash equivalents on its balance sheet?

(b) What criteria does the company use to determine what short-term investments to include in this category?

(c) Review the financial statements and notes and identify all the assets reported by Canadian Tire that qualify as loans and receivables. Be specific. Does the company disclose the amount of its allowance for doubtful accounts?

(d) Accounting standards require companies to disclose information about their exposure to credit risk. What is credit risk? What does Canadian Tire report? What is your assessment of its exposure to credit risk?

(e) Canadian Tire uses its accounts receivable to generate cash before the receivables are due. Briefly describe the form of "transfer" activities that the company uses. Are the receivables used as security for loans, are they sold outright with no continuing interest, or does Canadian Tire have a continuing relationship with the accounts? What financial components does it retain, if any?

RA7-3 Stantec Inc.

Stantec Inc., according to its 2005 Annual Report, "provides design and consulting services in planning, engineering, architecture, interior design, landscape architecture, surveying, and project management," and is a leader in sustainable solutions. With a head office in Edmonton, Alberta, the company employs over 5,500 employees in more than 60 locations in North America and the Caribbean. Stantec's financial statements are provided for you in Appendix 5B.

Instructions

(a) Identify all items on the company's December 31, 2005, balance sheet that qualify as cash, cash equivalents, and loans and receivables.

(b) What is included in "cash and cash equivalents"?

(c) Identify why the company reports restricted cash. Should it be reported as a current asset or a noncurrent asset? Comment.

(d) Prepare a T account of Allowance for Doubtful Accounts covering the year ended December 31, 2005. (Hint: Details are given in Note 20.) As much as possible, reconstruct the journal entries that were made to this account during the year.

(e) Which year—2004 or 2005—recognized the higher amount of bad debt expense? Explain briefly how you determined your answer. Can you suggest why that year's amount is higher?

RA7-4 Sears Canada Inc. versus Hudson's Bay Company

Instructions

Hudson's Bay Company has been ranked as the fifth largest retailer in Canada (by total revenue) by *The Globe and Mail's Report on Business Magazine* (July 2006). Sears Canada Inc. was ranked seventh.

Access both companies' financial statements for the year 2005, either on the Student website or on SEDAR (www.sedar.com). Use this information to answer the following questions.

(a) Compare how the two companies report cash and cash equivalents on the statement of financial position. What is included in the cash and cash equivalents of each? Is there any restricted cash reported by either company? If yes, have both companies reported it in a similar way?

(b) What types of receivables do Sears and Hudson's Bay have? Do both companies have the same ones?

(c) What amounts of "trade" accounts receivable (net) do Sears and Hudson's Bay have? Can you tell which company reports the greater allowance for doubtful accounts (amount and percentage of gross receivables) at the end of the most recent year?

(d) Does either company dispose of receivables before their due date to generate cash? Comment.

(e) Calculate, compare, and comment on the accounts receivable turnover ratio for both companies for the most recent year. How does securitization of receivables affect this ratio? Be specific.

RA7-5 Research Issue

Financial Reporting in Canada, published annually by the Canadian Institute of Chartered Accountants, is a survey of 200 Canadian company annual reports to shareholders. The survey is of companies chosen from the group included in the S&P/TSX composite index.

Instructions

Find the report and examine the sections about cash, and accounts and notes receivable. Write a short report that summarizes how Canadian companies are reporting these financial assets and what the general trend is in Canada.

Tracking Sales

BROCK'S

The first Brock's general store opened in Port Perry, Ontario, in 1881. Now the fifth generation of Brocks, sisters Marina and Juliana, run both the original store, now a large department store selling brand-name fashion and footwear, and another satellite store in Fenelon Falls in Ontario's Kawartha Lakes region.

Brock's uses the retail inventory method to estimate its inventory. Computer software keeps track of inventory by season, department, and class of item, such as sportswear or outerwear.

"We run an on-hand inventory value report at month end," Marina Brock says. "We try to get as close to a realizable value as possible, so the current season inventory is taken at full value, and then as we go back we discount it slightly to reflect that it would be harder to sell at market value." The computer allocates the percentages of the merchandise from the current and previous seasons to get a clearer picture of the entire stock's value.

"Each sale is recorded and the cost of the goods is recorded at the time of sale," Brock explains. "It's taken out of the inventory at that time at the original cost. Everything is done on an individual transaction basis, then summarized at the end of the day."

The Brocks take a physical inventory each January, scanning each item with hand-held scanners. All returns are manually transferred out of the computer records. The computer then updates the inventory records and creates a variance, indicating the inventory's actual value versus its book value. Brock says the store's variance had usually indicated a shrinkage of about 1 percent of sales, due to clerical errors and shoplifting, although a new electronically tagged merchandise system has reduced the percentage of shrinkage to 0.75 percent.

Keeping close tabs on the value of the store's inventory helps control the investment in merchandise, which is critical to business success. The computer program Softwear POS tracks the inventory very accurately. "We know pretty much to the dollar what we've got everywhere," Brock says. ■

chapter 8

Inventory

Learning Objectives

After studying this chapter, you should be able to:

1. Define and identify categories of inventory.
2. Distinguish between basic perpetual and periodic inventory systems and account for them.
3. Identify the decisions that are needed to determine the inventory value to report on the balance sheet.
4. Determine which inventory items should be included on an enterprise's balance sheet.
5. Identify the effects of inventory errors on the financial statements and adjust for them.
6. Determine what is included in inventory cost.
7. Identify GAAP cost formula options and indicate when each cost formula is appropriate.
8. Explain why inventory is measured at the lower of cost and net realizable value.
9. Identify and apply the lower of cost and net realizable value standard for inventory.
10. Explain the accounting issues for purchase commitments.
11. Apply the gross profit method of estimating inventory.
12. Identify the inventory disclosures required by GAAP.
13. Explain how inventory analysis provides useful information.
14. Compare current Canadian and international GAAP.

After studying the appendices you should be able to:

15. Apply the retail method of estimating inventory.
16. Identify and apply U.S. inventory standards that differ from Canadian and international GAAP.

Preview of Chapter 8

Inventories are often a major part of a company's total assets. As the opening story showed, accounting and reporting for this asset can have a material effect on both the income statement and balance sheet. Many decisions go into determining the final amounts to be reported for inventory on the balance sheet and for cost of goods sold on the income statement: the quantity of inventory on hand, which costs are included in inventory cost, what cost formula is used, and whether valuation at cost is the appropriate measure on the balance sheet.

This chapter introduces the basic issues related to the recognition, measurement, and reporting of inventory and cost of goods sold, including what choices are available under GAAP. Accounting for long-term construction contract inventories is a closely related topic that was examined in Chapter 6. Two appendices cover the related topic of determining inventory cost using the retail inventory method and a discussion of two ways in which U.S. GAAP for inventories is different from Canadian GAAP.

The chapter is organized as follows:

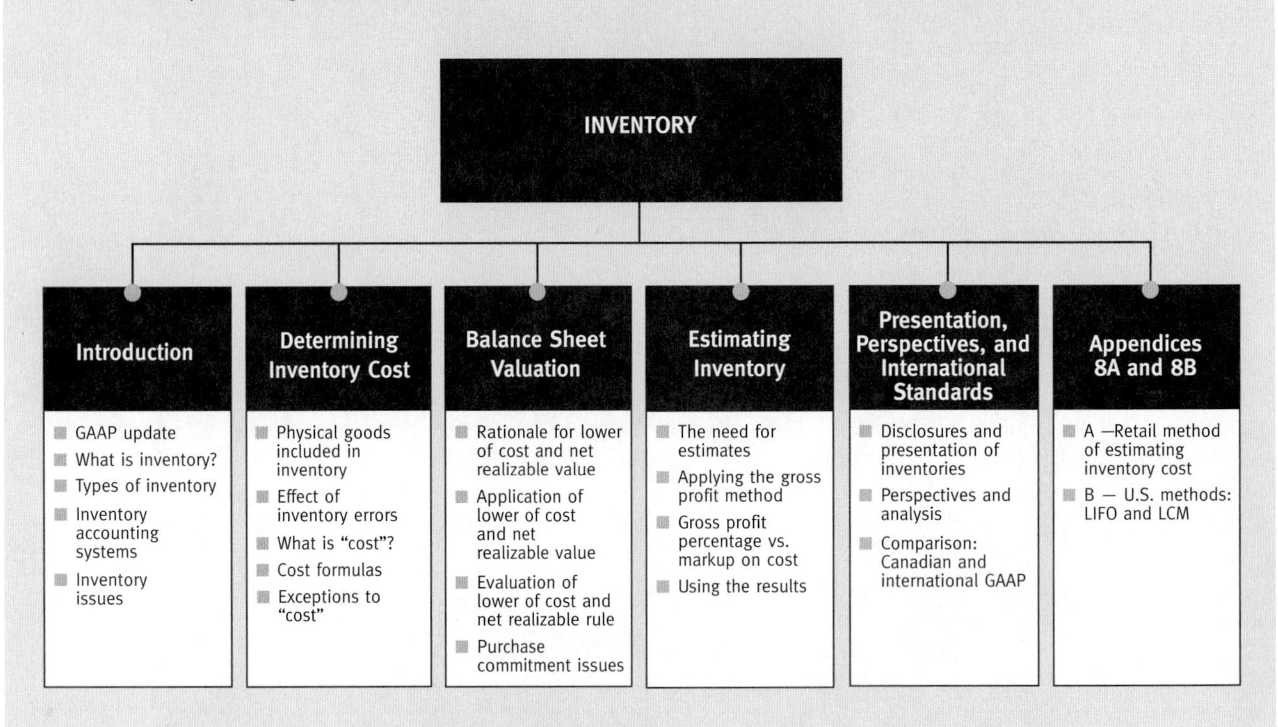

INTRODUCTION

GAAP Update

Until *CICA Handbook* Section 3031 was issued in 2007, Section 3030 titled "Inventories" had guided Canadian accountants for almost 40 years. Section 3031, also entitled

"Inventories," is based on IAS 2, the international inventory standard. The Canadian AcSB's strategy with the new section was to "avoid a second round of changes in the proposed transition" to international accounting standards in 2011.[1]

The new standard offers more guidance on what "cost" is and what "net realizable value" is, and it codifies many aspects of current Canadian practice. The major changes required by Section 3031 are as follows:

- LIFO (last-in, first-out) is no longer an acceptable "cost formula" or cost flow choice.
- Inventory is required to be measured at the lower of cost and net realizable value. Previously, companies used a variety of definitions of "market" in applying the LCM or lower of cost and market rule.
- Additional disclosures are now required, including separate reporting of the cost of goods sold.

The next sections of this chapter give more detail about these recommendations.

What Is Inventory?

1 Objective
Define and identify categories of inventory.

Inventories are defined in Section 3031.06 as "assets:

(a) held for sale in the ordinary course of business;

(b) in the process of production for such sale; or

(c) in the form of materials or supplies to be consumed in the production process or in the rendering of services."

Sometimes there is a fine line between what is inventory and what is better classified as property, plant, and equipment. Minor spare parts and servicing equipment, for example, are included as inventory unless their use is restricted to an item of property, plant, and equipment. Major spare parts and standby equipment, on the other hand, are recognized as capital assets if they are expected to be used over more than one period.[2] Professional judgement is needed whenever the situation is not obvious.

Inventory comes in many forms. Securities held by an investment dealer, land and other property held by developers for resale, unbilled employee and partner time spent on client files in a law office or professional accounting practice, grain in silos, salmon in a fish farming operation and long-term construction projects are all examples of inventory. Some of these, however, are not covered by the new accounting standards.

Handbook Section 3031 specifically excludes construction work in process and inventories that qualify as financial instruments.[3] Other categories of inventory are excluded from the **measurement** standards in Section 3031, but must still meet the **expense recognition** and **disclosure** standards.[4]

---

[1] CICA, "Inventories, Section 3031," Exposure Draft, June 2006, p. i.

[2] *CICA Handbook*, Section 3061.04.

[3] Refer to Chapter 6 for a discussion of construction work-in-process inventories.

[4] *CICA Handbook*, Section 3031.03–.05. Excluded are inventories held by agricultural and forest product producers, agricultural produce after harvest, and minerals and mineral products, all to the extent that they are measured at their net realizable value in accordance with well-established practices in those industries; inventories of broker-traders who buy or sell commodities and measure them at their fair value less costs to sell; and biological assets (i.e., living plants or animals) related to agricultural activity and agricultural produce at the point of harvest.

Types of Inventory

The identification, measurement, and disclosure of inventories must be done carefully because the investment in inventories is frequently the largest current asset of merchandising (retail) and manufacturing businesses. Hudson's Bay Company, for example, reported almost $1.5 billion of inventory at January 31, 2006. This accounted for 70.5 percent of its current assets and almost 39 percent of total assets! Like other **merchandising concerns,** The Bay usually purchases its merchandise in a form that is ready for sale. It reports the cost assigned to unsold units left on hand as **merchandise inventory**. As Illustration 8-1 shows, only one inventory account, Merchandise Inventories, appears in its financial statements.

Domtar Inc., like many of the largest Canadian businesses—Bombardier, General Motors of Canada, and Magna International Inc., for example—is a manufacturer. At December 31, 2005, Domtar reported inventories amounting to 62 percent of its current assets. Although the products that they produce can be quite different, manufacturers normally have three inventory accounts: Raw Materials, Work in Process, and Finished Goods. Amounts for goods and materials that are on hand but have not yet gone into production are reported as **raw materials inventory**. Raw materials include the wood to make a baseball bat, for example, or the steel to make a car. These materials can be traced directly to the end product. At any point in a continuous production process, some units are not completely processed. The cost of the raw material on which production has started but is not yet complete, plus the direct labour cost applied specifically to this material and its applicable share of manufacturing overhead costs, constitutes the **work-in-process inventory**. The costs associated with the completed but still unsold units on hand are reported as **finished goods inventory**.

The current assets sections in Illustration 8-1 contrast the financial statement presentation of inventories of a merchandising company and of a manufacturing company.

Illustration 8-1

Comparison of Inventory Presentation for Merchandising and Manufacturing Companies

MERCHANDISING COMPANY
Hudson's Bay Company
Balance Sheet, January 31, 2006

(thousands of dollars)	Notes	2006	2005
Current assets			
Cash in stores		$ 7,730	$ 7,713
Short-term deposits		117,426	254,908
Credit card receivables	3	331,066	427,443
Other accounts receivable		100,841	119,497
Merchandise inventories		1,465,606	1,412,320
Prepaid expenses and other current assets		57,411	65,439
		$2,080,080	$2,287,320

MANUFACTURING COMPANY
Domtar Inc.
Balance Sheet, December 31, 2005

(in millions of Canadian dollars)	2005	2004
Assets		
Current assets		
Cash and cash equivalents	$ 83	$ 52
Receivables (Note 10)	294	226
Inventories (Note 11)	715	723
Prepaid expenses	11	12

Income and other taxes receivable	$ 16	$ 17
Future income taxes (Note 8)	38	87
	$1,157	$1,117
Note 11		
Inventories		
Work in process and finished goods	$ 376	$ 390
Raw materials	182	157
Operating and maintenance supplies	157	176
	$ 715	$ 723

Manufacturing companies also sometimes include a manufacturing or factory supplies inventory account, as **Domtar** does. It is for such items as machine oils, nails, cleaning materials, and so on that are used in production but are not the primary materials being processed. As Illustration 8-2 shows, the flow of costs for merchandising and manufacturing companies is different.

The Cost of Goods Manufactured statement that is referred to in Illustration 8-2 is mainly for internal use. Illustration 8-3 shows a sample **cost of goods manufactured statement**, which presents a level of detail that is rarely found in published financial statements. Note that **the cost of goods manufactured during the year is similar to the cost of goods purchased in a merchandising company**. Each is the major source of the cost of goods available for sale in the period.

Underlying Concept

Because inventory provides future economic benefits to the company (i.e., the revenue from sales), it meets the definition of an asset. Inventory costs are therefore matched against revenue in the period when the inventory is sold.

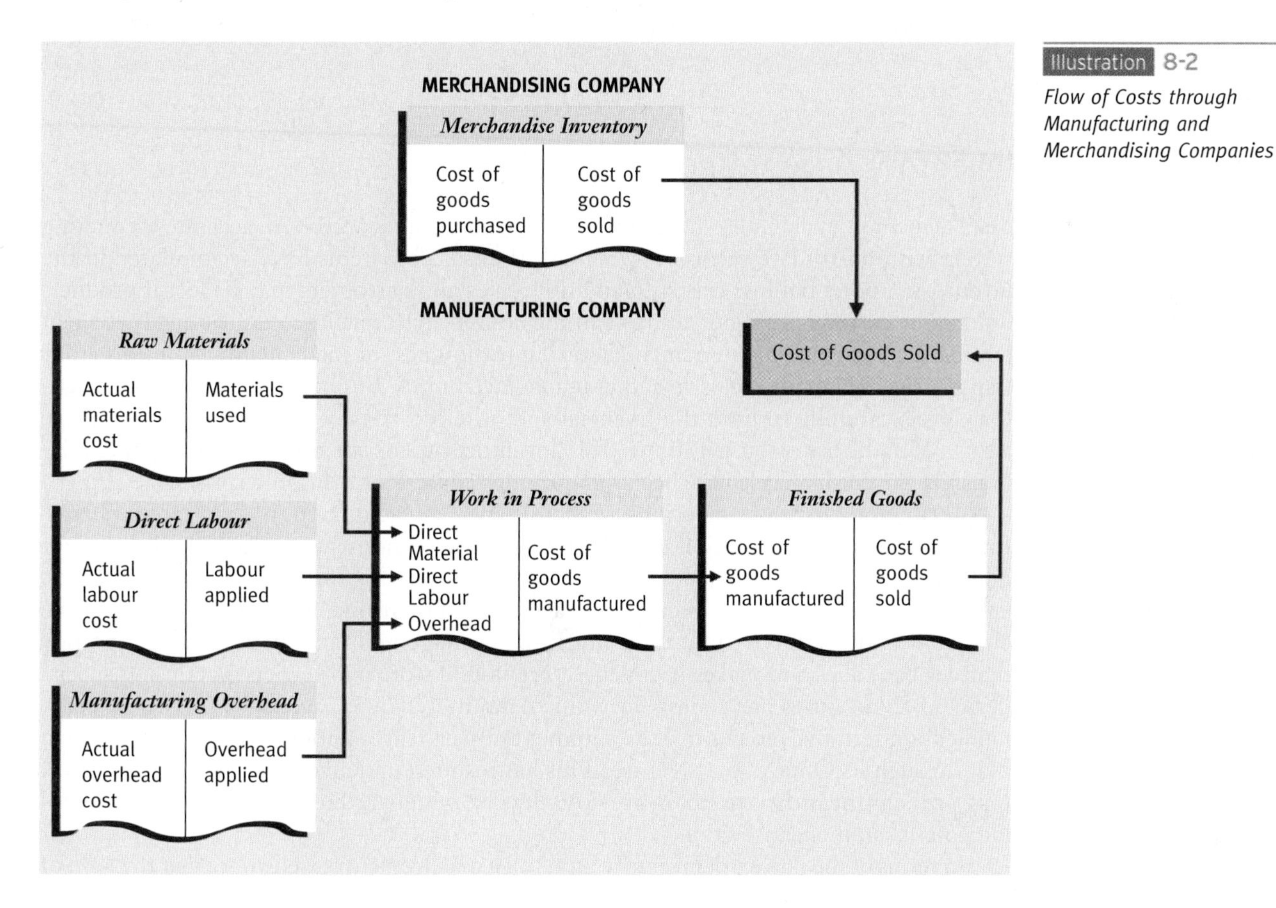

Illustration 8-2

Flow of Costs through Manufacturing and Merchandising Companies

Illustration 8-3
Statement of Cost of Goods Manufactured

STATEMENT OF COST OF GOODS MANUFACTURED
For the Year Ended December 31, 2008

Raw materials consumed			
Raw materials inventory, Jan. 1, 2008			$ 14,000
Add net purchases:			
Purchases		$126,000	
Less: Purchase returns and allowances	$1,800		
Purchase discounts	1,200	3,000	123,000
Raw material available for use			137,000
Less **raw materials inventory, Dec. 31, 2008**			17,000
Cost of raw materials consumed			120,000
Direct labour			200,000
Manufacturing overhead			
Supervisors' salaries		$ 63,000	
Indirect labour		20,000	
Factory supplies used		18,000	
Heat, light, power, and water		13,000	
Amortization of building and equipment		27,000	
Tools expense		2,000	
Patent amortization		1,000	
Miscellaneous factory expenses		6,000	150,000
Total manufacturing costs for the period			470,000
Work-in-process inventory, Jan. 1, 2008			33,000
Total manufacturing costs			503,000
Less **work-in-process inventory, Dec. 31, 2008**			28,000
Cost of goods manufactured during the year			**$475,000**

Inventory Accounting Systems

Management is vitally interested in inventory planning and control. An accurate accounting system with up-to-date records is essential. If unsaleable items have accumulated in the inventory, a potential loss exists. In addition, sales and customers may be lost if products ordered by customers are not available in the desired style, quality, and quantity. Inefficient purchasing procedures, faulty manufacturing techniques, or inadequate sales efforts may trap management with excessive and unusable inventories. Businesses must monitor inventory levels carefully to limit the financial and other costs associated with carrying these assets. With the use of "just-in-time" (JIT) inventory order systems and better supplier relationships, inventory levels have been significantly reduced for many enterprises.

What Do the Numbers Mean?

Technology has played an important role in the development of inventory systems. Radio-frequency identification data (RFID) communications systems for warehouses, for example, have helped companies such as Hospital Logistics Inc., Eli Lilly Canada Inc., and BC Hot House Foods increase the accuracy of their inventory information and the efficiency and productivity of their inventory management activities. This technology replaces bar codes and makes it possible to remotely store and retrieve data using special devices. Toyota uses bar codes, electronic data interchange, and radio-frequency communication terminals to control the shipment of parts throughout North America, much of it through its Ontario parts centre. This has resulted in delivery times and safety stock that are significantly less than previous levels, which reduces costs and errors and increases customer satisfaction.

In terms of the impact of inventory on results, management is well aware that the level of year-end inventory can materially affect the amount of current assets, total assets, net income, and therefore, retained earnings. As indicated in Chapter 2, **these amounts, or totals that**

include them, are used to calculate ratios that are then used to evaluate management's performance (e.g., calculations of bonuses) and adherence to debt restrictions (e.g., to not exceed a specified debt-to-total-asset ratio or dividend payout ratio).

For these and other reasons, management is very interested in having an inventory accounting system that gives accurate, up-to-date information on quantities. As will be seen later in this chapter, the choice of a cost formula to value inventories is also an important factor.

Perpetual System

2 Objective
Distinguish between basic perpetual and periodic inventory systems and account for them.

As indicated in Chapter 3, inventory records can be kept on a perpetual basis or periodic basis. Under a **perpetual inventory system, a continuous or perpetual record of inventory changes is maintained in the Inventory account**. This means that the dollar cost of all purchases and the cost of the items sold (or issued out of inventory) are recorded directly in the Inventory account as the purchases and sales occur. The accounting features of a perpetual inventory system are as follows:

1. Purchases of merchandise for resale or raw materials for production are debited to Inventory rather than to Purchases.
2. Freight-in, purchase returns and allowances, and purchase discounts are debited to Inventory instead of being accounted for in separate accounts.
3. Cost of goods sold is recognized at the time of each sale by debiting Cost of Goods Sold and crediting Inventory.
4. Inventory is a control account that is supported by a subsidiary ledger of individual inventory records. The subsidiary records show the quantity and cost of each type of inventory on hand.

The perpetual inventory system provides a continuous record of the balances in both the Inventory account and the Cost of Goods Sold account.

In a computerized record-keeping system, whenever inventory is added or issued, the change can be recorded almost instantaneously. The popularity and affordability of computerized accounting software have made the perpetual system cost-effective for many kinds of businesses. It is now common for most retail stores, big or small, to use optical scanners at the cash register that record sales as part of the store's perpetual inventory system.

Periodic System

In a **periodic inventory system**, the quantity of inventory on hand is determined, as the name implies, only periodically. Each acquisition of inventory during the accounting period is recorded by a debit to the Purchases account. The total in the Purchases account at the end of the accounting period is added to the cost of the inventory on hand at the beginning of the period to determine the total cost of the goods available for sale during the period. The cost of ending inventory is subtracted from the cost of goods available for sale to calculate the cost of goods sold.

Note that under a periodic inventory system, the cost of goods sold is a residual amount that depends on separately calculating the cost of the ending inventory. This can be based either on a physically counted ending inventory that is costed appropriately, or on an estimate of the cost of the ending inventory, as explained later in this chapter.

If it is based on a physical count of the inventory, the count is done only once a year, at year end. However, most companies need more current information about their inventory levels to avoid stockouts and overpurchasing, and to help prepare monthly or quarterly financial data. As a consequence, many companies use a **modified perpetual inventory system** in which **increases and decreases in quantities—not dollar amounts—**are kept in a detailed inventory record. **Not recorded as part of the double-entry system, this is just a record of quantities that helps determine the level of inventory at any point in time.**

Whether a company maintains a perpetual inventory in quantities and dollars, in quantities only, or has no perpetual inventory record at all, it probably takes a physical inventory once a year. No matter what type of inventory records are used or how well-controlled the procedures for recording purchases and requisitions are, the danger of loss and errors is always present. Waste, breakage, theft, improper entry, failure to prepare or record requisitions, and many other similar possibilities can cause the inventory records to be different than the actual inventory on hand. For these reasons, it is necessary to periodically verify the inventory records by actually counting, weighing, or measuring the actual inventory on hand. **These counts are compared with the detailed inventory records, and the records are then corrected so that they agree with the quantities actually on hand.**

As far as possible, the physical inventory should be taken near the end of a company's fiscal year so that correct inventory quantities can be used in preparing annual accounting reports and statements. Because this is not always possible, physical inventories that are taken within two or three months of the year end are considered satisfactory **as long as the detailed inventory records are maintained with a fair degree of accuracy.**

To illustrate the difference between a perpetual and a periodic system, assume that Fesmire Limited had the following balances and transactions during the current year:

Beginning inventory	100 units at $ 6 = $ 600
Purchases	900 units at $ 6 = $5,400
Defective units returned to the supplier	50 units at $ 6 = $ 300
Sales	600 units at $12 = $7,200
Ending inventory	350 units at $ 6 = $2,100

The entries to record these transactions during the current year are shown in Illustration 8-4.

Illustration 8-4

Comparative Entries–Perpetual vs. Periodic

Perpetual Inventory System			Periodic Inventory System		
1. Beginning Inventory, 100 units at $6:					
The inventory account shows the inventory on hand at $600.			The inventory account shows the inventory on hand at $600.		
2. Purchase 900 units at $6:					
Inventory	5,400		Purchases	5,400	
Accounts Payable		5,400	Accounts Payable		5,400
3. Return 50 defective units:					
Accounts Payable	300		Accounts Payable	300	
Inventory		300	Purchase returns and allowances		300
4. Sale of 600 units at $12:					
Accounts Receivable	7,200		Accounts Receivable	7,200	
Sales		7,200	Sales		7,200
Cost of Goods Sold (600 at $6)	3,600				
Inventory		3,600	(No entry)		
5. End-of-period entries for inventory accounts, 350 units at $6 = $2,100:					
No entry necessary.			Purchase returns and allowances	300	
The account, Inventory, shows the ending balance of $2,100			Inventory (ending, by count)	2,100	
($600 + $5,400 − $300 − $3,600).			Cost of Goods Sold	3,600	
			Purchases		5,400
			Inventory (beginning)		600

When a perpetual inventory system is used and there is a difference between the perpetual inventory balance and the physical inventory count, a separate entry is needed to adjust the perpetual inventory account. To illustrate, assume that at the end of the reporting period the perpetual inventory account reported an inventory balance of $4,000, but a physical count indicated $3,800 was actually on hand. The adjusting entry is:

Inventory Over and Short	200	
Inventory		200

A	=	L	+	SE
−200				−200

Cash flows: No effect

Perpetual inventory overages and shortages may be recorded as an adjustment of (i.e., closed to) Cost of Goods Sold. This would be appropriate if they were caused by incorrect record keeping. Alternatively, the Inventory Over and Short account may be reported in the Other Revenues and Gains or Other Expenses and Losses section, depending on its balance. When this is done, the overage or shortage is not a component of Cost of Goods Sold, and the gross profit percentage is not distorted by such things as shrinkage, breakage, and theft. **Note that in a periodic inventory system, the account Inventory Over and Short is not used since there are no accounting records that can be compared to the physical count.** Thus, inventory overages and shortages are buried in cost of goods sold in the periodic inventory system.

Inventory Issues

3 Objective
Identify the decisions that are needed to determine the inventory value to report on the balance sheet.

Because the goods that are sold or used during an accounting period almost never correspond exactly with the goods that were bought or produced during that period, the physical inventory either increases or decreases. In addition, the cost of the same number of items could be higher or lower at the end of the period than at the beginning. The cost of all the goods that are available for sale or use has to be allocated between the goods that were sold or used and those that are still on hand. The **cost of goods available for sale or use** is the total of (1) the cost of the goods on hand at the beginning of the period and (2) the cost of the goods acquired or produced during the period. The **cost of goods sold** is the difference between those available for sale during the period and those on hand at the end of the period, as shown in Illustration 8-5.

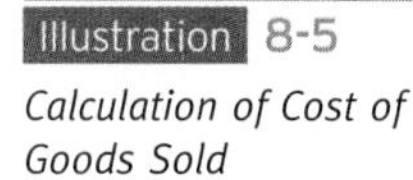
Illustration 8-5
Calculation of Cost of Goods Sold

Beginning inventory, Jan. 1	$100,000
Cost of goods acquired or produced during the year	800,000
Total cost of goods available for sale	**900,000**
Ending inventory, Dec. 31	200,000
Cost of goods sold during the year	**$700,000**

Determining the cost of ending inventory takes several steps. It can be a complex process that requires answers to each of the following questions:

1. **Which physical goods should be included as part of inventory?** Who owns inventory still in transit at the balance sheet date, or inventory on consignment? What about inventory under special sales agreements?

2. **What costs should be included as part of inventory cost?** Consider purchase discounts and vendor rebates, product versus period costs, capacity considerations in allocating overhead, and standard costs.

3. **What cost formula should be used?** Consider specific identification, average cost, or FIFO.

Determining the value that should be reported on the balance sheet requires one additional question to be answered:

4. **Has there been an impairment in value of any of the inventory items?** Inventory cannot be reported on the balance sheet at more than the net cash amount that is expected to be recovered from its sale or use.

We will now explore each of these four basic issues one at a time.

DETERMINING INVENTORY COST

Physical Goods Included in Inventory

Objective 4
Determine which inventory items should be included on an enterprise's balance sheet.

Technically, purchases should be recorded when legal title to the goods passes to the buyer, as this is usually when the risks and rewards of ownership are transferred. In practice, however, acquisitions are generally recorded when the goods are received because it is difficult for the buyer to determine the exact time when title legally passes to the buyer for every purchase. In addition, it is unlikely that a material error will result from this practice if it is done consistently. Illustration 8-6 gives the general guidelines for determining whether the seller or the buyer should report an item as inventory.

Illustration 8-6
Guidelines for Determining Who Reports the Inventory

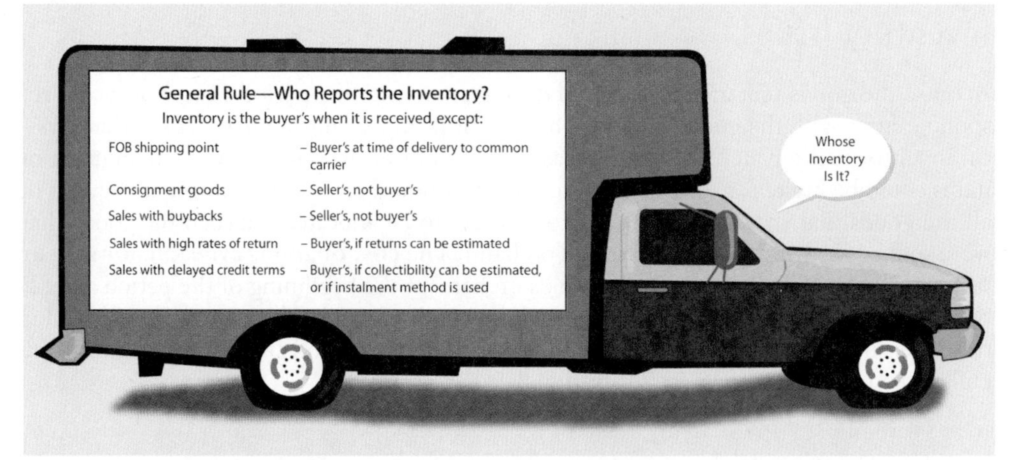

Goods in Transit

Sometimes purchased merchandise is in transit—i.e., not yet received—at the end of a fiscal period. **The accounting for these goods depends on who owns them**. This can be determined by applying the "transfer of risks and rewards" test. If the goods are shipped **f.o.b. shipping point**, the risks and rewards of ownership, which usually go with having legal title, pass to the buyer when the seller delivers the goods to the common carrier (transporter), who then acts as an agent for the buyer. (The abbreviation "f.o.b." stands for "free on board.") If the goods are shipped **f.o.b. destination**, ownership and its associated risks and rewards do not pass until the goods reach the destination. "Shipping point" and "destination" are often indicated by naming a specific location, for example, f.o.b. Medicine Hat.[5]

[5] Terms other than f.o.b. shipping point or f.o.b. destination (e.g., CIF for "cost, insurance, freight") are often used to identify when legal title passes. The f.o.b. terms are used in this text to reflect that an agreement on when title passes must be reached between the buyer and seller in the purchase-sale contract. In a particular situation, the terms of the sale contract are examined to determine when the risks and rewards of ownership pass from the seller to the buyer.

Goods in transit at the end of a fiscal period that were sent f.o.b. shipping point are recorded by the buyer as purchases of the period and should be included in ending inventory. **If these purchases are ignored, the result is understated inventories and accounts payable in the balance sheet, and understated purchases and ending inventories when calculating cost of goods sold for the income statement.**

The accountant normally prepares a purchase **cut-off schedule** for the end of a period to ensure that goods received from suppliers around the end of the year are recorded in the appropriate period. Cut-off procedures can be extensive and include the following controls:

- Curtailing and controlling the receipt and shipment of goods around the time of the count
- Marking freight and shipping documents as "before" and "after" the inventory count
- Ensuring that receiving reports on goods received before the count are linked to invoices that are also recorded in the same period

Because goods that are bought f.o.b. shipping point may still be in transit when a period ends, the cut-off schedule is not completed until a few days after the period's end date since this gives enough time for goods shipped at year end to be received. In cases where there is some doubt about whether or not title has passed, the accountant uses professional judgement by considering the sales agreement's intent, the policies of the parties involved, industry practices, and any other available information.

Consigned Goods

In Chapter 6, the nature of consignment shipments and accounting for consignment sales was discussed. In terms of accounting for inventory, **it is important to recognize that goods out on consignment remain the consignor's property and are included in the consignor's inventory** at their purchase price or production cost plus the cost of handling and shipping the goods to the consignee. When the consignee sells the **consigned goods**, the revenue, less a selling commission and expenses incurred in accomplishing the sale, is remitted to the consignor.

Occasionally, the inventory out on consignment is shown as a separate item or is reported in notes, but unless the amount is large, there is little need for this. For the consignee, no entry is made to adjust its Inventory account for the goods it received, because the goods remain the consignor's property. In addition, the consignee should be extremely careful not to include any consigned goods in its inventory count.

Special Sales Agreements

While the transfer of legal title is a general guideline for determining whether the risks and rewards of ownership have passed from a seller to a buyer, **transfer of legal title and the underlying economic substance of the situation (i.e., the passage of risks and rewards) do not always match.** For example, it is possible for legal title to pass to the purchaser but for the seller of the goods to still retain the risks of ownership. Conversely, it is also possible for legal title to remain with the seller but for the risks and rewards of ownership to be transferred to the purchaser.

Underlying Concept

Recognizing revenue when the inventory is "parked" violates the revenue recognition principle. This principle requires that the earnings process be substantially completed, with the risks and rewards of ownership transferred to the purchaser.

Three special sale situations that were discussed in Chapter 6 from a revenue recognition perspective will now be briefly reviewed for their inventory implications.

Sales with Buyback Agreement Sometimes an enterprise finances its inventory without reporting either the liability or the inventory on its balance sheet. This approach—often referred to as a **product financing arrangement**—usually involves a "sale" with either an implicit or explicit "buyback" agreement. These are sometimes called "parking transactions" because the seller simply parks the inventory on another enterprise's balance sheet for a short period of time, agreeing to repurchase it in the future. **If the risks and rewards of ownership have not been transferred, the inventory should remain on the seller's books.**

Sales with High Rates of Return There are often formal or informal agreements in such industries as publishing, music, toys, and sporting goods that allow a buyer to return inventory for a full or partial refund. **An acceptable accounting treatment is that if a reasonable prediction of the returns can be established, then the goods should be considered sold and an allowance for returns should be recognized.** Conversely, if the returns are unpredictable, these goods should not be removed from the Inventory account.

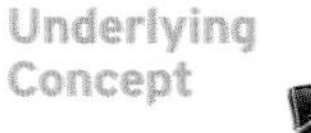

Underlying Concept

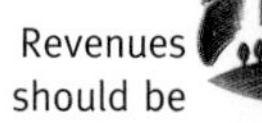

Revenues should be recognized in this situation because they have been substantially earned and are reasonably estimable. The basic risks and rewards of ownership have been transferred. Collection is not the most critical event and bad debts can be reasonably estimated.

Sales with Delayed Payment Terms Because the risk of losses from uncollectibles is higher in delayed payment sales than in other sales transactions, the seller often retains legal title to the merchandise until all payments have been received. Should the inventory be considered sold, even though legal title has not passed? **The goods should be removed from the seller's inventory and the sale should be recorded if the cost of the outstanding risk (i.e., the bad debts) can be reasonably estimated and matched with the related revenue.** For revenue that is reported using the instalment method, **inventory is removed from the balance sheet and the gross profit is recognized over time in proportion to the cash collected.** These issues are raised here to illustrate that in some cases, goods are removed from inventory even though legal title may not have passed.

Effect of Inventory Errors

Objective 5
Identify the effects of inventory errors on the financial statements and adjust for them.

Items that have been incorrectly included or excluded in determining the ending inventory amount create errors in both the income statement and balance sheet. Decisions that are based on financial statement amounts affected by such errors (e.g., bonuses paid to management based on net income) would therefore be in error and comparability would also be impaired. Let's look at two cases and the effects on the financial statements.

Ending Inventory Misstated

What would happen if the beginning inventory and purchases are recorded correctly, but some items are excluded from ending inventory by mistake (e.g., they were on the premises but were missed in the physical count, or they were out on consignment)? In this situation, the effects on the financial statements at the end of the period are as shown in Illustration 8-7.

Illustration 8-7
Financial Statement Effects of Understated Ending Inventory

Balance Sheet		Income Statement	
Inventory	Understated	Cost of goods sold	Overstated
Retained earnings	Understated	Net income	Understated
Working capital (current assets less current liabilities)	Understated		
Current ratio (Current assets divided by current liabilities)	Understated		

Working capital and the current ratio are understated because a portion of the ending inventory is omitted; net income is understated because cost of goods sold is overstated.

To illustrate the effect on net income over a two-year period, assume that the ending inventory of Weiseman Ltd. is understated by $10,000 and that all other items are stated correctly. The effect of this error is an understatement of net income in the current year and an overstatement of net income in the following year. The error affects the following year because the beginning inventory of that year is understated, thereby causing net income to be overstated. Both net income figures are misstated, but the total for the two years is correct as the two errors will be counterbalanced (offset), as shown in Illustration 8-8.

When inventory is misstated, its presentation lacks representational faithfulness.

Illustration 8-8

Effect of Ending Inventory Error on Two Periods

WEISEMAN LTD.

	Incorrect Recording		Correct Recording	
	2007	2008	2007	2008
Revenues	$100,000	$100,000	$100,000	$100,000
Cost of goods sold				
Beginning inventory	25,000	20,000	25,000	30,000
Purchased or produced	45,000	60,000	45,000	60,000
Goods available for sale	70,000	80,000	70,000	90,000
Less: Ending inventory*	20,000	40,000	30,000	40,000
Cost of goods sold	50,000	40,000	40,000	50,000
Gross profit	50,000	60,000	60,000	50,000
Administrative and selling expenses	40,000	40,000	40,000	40,000
Net income	$ 10,000	$ 20,000	$ 20,000	$ 10,000
	Total income for two years = $30,000		Total income for two years = $30,000	

*Ending inventory understated by $10,000 in 2007; correct amount is $30,000.

If the error were discovered in 2007 just before the books were closed, the correcting entry in 2007 would be:

Inventory	10,000	
Cost of Goods Sold		10,000

A = L + SE
+10,000 +10,000

Cash flows: No effect

If the error were not discovered until 2008, after the books were closed for 2007, the correcting entry in 2008 would be:

Inventory	10,000	
Retained Earnings		10,000

A = L + SE
+10,000 +10,000

Cash flows: No effect

If the error were discovered after the books for 2008 were closed, **no entry is required as the error is self-correcting over the two-year period.** The inventory on the balance sheet at the end of 2008 is correct, as is the total amount of retained earnings. **However, whenever comparative financial statements are prepared that include 2007 or 2008, the inventory and net income for those years would be adjusted and reported at the correct figures.**

If ending inventory is **overstated**, the reverse effect occurs. Inventory, working capital, current ratio, and net income are overstated and cost of goods sold is understated.

The error's effect on net income will be counterbalanced in the next year, but both years' net income figures are incorrect, which would distort any analysis of trends in earnings and ratios.

Purchases and Inventory Misstated

Suppose that certain goods that the company owns are not recorded as a purchase and are not counted in ending inventory. Illustration 8-9 shows the effect on the financial statements, assuming this is a purchase on account.

Illustration 8-9
Financial Statement Effects of Understated Purchases and Inventory

Balance Sheet		Income Statement	
Inventory	Understated	Purchases	Understated
Retained earnings	No effect	Inventory (ending)	Understated
Accounts payable	Understated	Cost of goods sold	No effect
Working capital	No effect	Net income	No effect
Current ratio	Overstated		

Omitting goods from purchases and inventory results in understated inventory and accounts payable on the balance sheet, and understated purchases and ending inventory on the income statement. **Net income for the period is not affected by omitting such goods, because purchases and ending inventory are both understated by the same amount—i.e., the error offsets itself in cost of goods sold.**[6] Total working capital is unchanged, but the **current ratio** is overstated (assuming it was greater than 1 to 1) because equal amounts were omitted from inventory and accounts payable.

To illustrate the effect on the current ratio, assume that a company understated its accounts payable and ending inventory by $40,000. The understated and correct data are shown in Illustration 8-10.

Illustration 8-10
Effects of Purchases and Ending Inventory Errors

Purchases and Ending Inventory Understated		Purchases and Ending Inventory Correct	
Current assets	$120,000	Current assets	$160,000
Current liabilities	$ 40,000	Current liabilities	$ 80,000
Current ratio	3 to 1	Current ratio	2 to 1

The correct current ratio is 2 to 1 rather than 3 to 1. Thus, understating accounts payable and ending inventory can lead to a "window dressing" of the current ratio—i.e., it can appear better than it really is.

If purchases (on account) and ending inventory are both overstated, then the effects on the balance sheet are exactly the reverse: inventory and accounts payable are overstated, the current ratio is understated, and the amount of working capital is not affected. Cost of goods sold and net income are also unaffected because the errors offset each other. The preceding examples show some of the errors that can occur and their consequences, but

[6] To correct the error in the year of the error before the books are closed, and assuming inventories are adjusted before the closing entries, the following entries are needed:

Periodic Method			**Perpetual Method**		
Purchases	$x		Inventory	$x	
Accounts Payable		$x	Accounts Payable		$x
Inventory	$x				
Cost of Goods Sold		$x			

there are also many other types of possible errors: not recording a purchase but counting the new inventory; not recording a sale in the current period although the items have been delivered; omitting the adjusting entry to update the account Allowance for Future Returns in situations where the sales are known to have a high rate of return, and others.

The importance of accurately calculating purchases and inventory cannot be overemphasized since having reliable amounts in the financial statements depends on an accurate inventory amount. One has only to read the financial press to learn how misstating inventory can generate high income numbers. For example, in the past some Canadian farm equipment manufacturers treated deliveries to dealers as company sales (thus reducing their inventory), even though sales to the ultimate consumer did not occur as quickly as the deliveries to the dealers. The result was a significantly inflated reported income for the manufacturers.

As Chapter 5 showed, when an error from a prior period is corrected it is accounted for retroactively as an adjustment to retained earnings. Full disclosure requires a description of the error, and a statement of the effect on the current and prior period financial statements.

What Is "Cost"?

6 **Objective**
Determine what is included in inventory cost.

After knowing what goods are to be included in ending inventory, the next issue is determining their cost. **Inventories, like other non-financial assets, are generally recognized initially on the basis of cost.** How is cost determined, and what should be included in "cost"?

Handbook Section 3031.10 indicates that inventory cost is made up of "all costs of purchase, costs of conversion and other costs incurred in bringing the inventories to their present location and condition." This includes any costs associated with transporting the goods and other direct costs of acquisition such as non-recoverable taxes and duties. Other related issues are discussed next.

Purchase Discounts

When suppliers offer cash discounts to purchasers, there are two possible methods to account for the purchases: the gross method and the net method. Under the **gross method, both the purchases and payables are recorded at the gross amount of the invoice, and any purchase discounts that are later taken are credited to a Purchase Discount account.** This account is reported as a contra account to Purchases, as a reduction in the cost of purchases.

The alternative approach, called the **net method, is to record the purchases and accounts payable initially at an amount net of the cash discounts.** If the account payable is paid within the discount period, the cash payment is exactly equal to the amount originally set up in the payable account. **If the account payable is paid after the discount period is over, the discount that is lost is recorded in a Purchase Discounts Lost account.** Recording the loss makes it possible for the company to assign responsibility for the loss to a specific employee. This treatment is considered more theoretically appropriate because it (1) provides a correct reporting of the asset cost and related liability,[7] and (2) makes it possible to measure the inefficiency of financial management if the discount is not taken. Illustration 8-11 illustrates the difference between the gross and net methods.

[7] *CICA Handbook* Section 3031.11 indicates that trade discounts are deducted in determining the cost of inventory purchases. Section 3031.18 also indicates that, to the extent that the purchase arrangement contains a financing element, the amount paid in excess of the normal credit terms should be recognized as interest expense over the period that the account payable is outstanding.

Illustration 8-11
Entries under Gross and Net Methods

Gross Method			Net Method		
Purchase cost of $10,000, terms 2/10, net 30:					
Purchases	10,000		Purchases	9,800	
Accounts Payable		10,000	Accounts Payable		9,800
Invoices of $4,000 are paid within discount period:					
Accounts Payable	4,000		Accounts Payable	3,920	
Purchase Discounts		80	Cash		3,920
Cash		3,920			
Invoices of $6,000 are paid after discount period:					
Accounts Payable	6.000		Accounts Payable	5,880	
Cash		6,000	Purchase Discounts Lost	120	
			Cash		6,000

Under the gross method, purchase discounts are deducted from purchases in determining cost of goods sold. If the net method is used, purchase discounts lost are considered a financial expense and are reported in the income statement's Other Expenses section. Many believe that the difficulty in using the somewhat more complicated net method is not worth its benefits. Also, some critics contend that management is reluctant to report the amount of purchase discounts lost in the financial statements. These reasons may explain why the less theoretically correct, but simpler, gross method is so popular. If the discounts are material, however, the net method should be used.

Vendor Rebates

Assume that Johnston Corp., with a June 30 year end, has been purchasing more and more inventory from Roster Limited in recent years. Roster offers its customers a special **vendor rebate** of $0.10 per unit on each unit purchased if the volume of purchases in the calendar year (i.e., from January 1 to December 31) is more than 100,000 units. This year, for the first time, Johnston management expects to pass the 100,000 unit volume—60,000 units have been purchased in the first six months of the current year and forecasted purchases for the next six months are over 50,000 units. Should Johnston recognize the anticipated rebate in its current year ended June 30? If so, how much should be recognized, and how does this affect the financial statements?

Underlying Concept

Revenues and expenses are defined in terms of changes in assets and liabilities. Therefore, if an asset does not exist or cannot be recognized in this situation, an expense recovery cannot be recognized either.

Cash rebates that are received are generally a reduction of the purchase cost of inventory. The following accounting guidance is based on whether any "rebate receivable" meets the definition of an asset and its recognition criteria:[8]

- If the rebate is at the supplier's discretion, no rebate should be recognized until it is paid or the vendor becomes obligated to make a payment.
- If the rebate is **probable** and can be **reasonably estimated**, recognize it as a reduction of the cost of purchases for the period. To the extent that the goods remain in inventory, the inventory cost is reduced. To the extent that the goods have been sold, cost of goods sold is reduced.
- The amount of the rebate to recognize is based on the proportion of the total rebate that is expected relative to the transactions to date.

If the rebate offered by Roster Limited is not discretionary, and if it is probable that Johnston will purchase 110,000 units by December 31 and management is able to make a reasonable estimate of the total rebate for the calendar year, Johnston should recognize the rebate as follows for its current year ended June 30:

[8] *EIC-144*, "Accounting by a Customer (Including a Reseller) for Certain Consideration Received from a Vendor," CICA, December 1, 2005.

Rebate Receivable	6,000	
Inventory (5,000 units)		500
Cost of Goods Sold (55,000 units)		5,500

110,000 units × $0.10 = $11,000; 60,000/110,000 × $11,000 = $6,000
or 60,000 units × $0.10 = $6,000

A	=	L	+	SE
+5,500				+5,500

Cash flows: No effect

The amount recognized is split between Inventory on the balance sheet and Cost of Goods Sold on the income statement in proportion to where the costs of the 60,000 units purchased between January 1 and June 30 are at June 30.

What Do the Numbers Mean?

Offering promotional payments is very common in the world of retail. Eager to meet their sales targets or promote their products through shelf placements and in store advertisements, vendors have been happy to grease the palms of retailers with rebates, allowances, and price breaks. The question is, "How should retailers account for these payments?" For a while, a variety of methods were used, but some questionable practices changed that.

Recently, the Securities and Exchange Commission in the U.S. sued three executives of Kmart Holding and some Kmart vendors for their role in a $24-million accounting fraud that booked vendor allowances early. The scheme apparently allowed some Kmart managers to meet internal profit-margin targets. Similarly, Royal Ahold, a large Dutch supermarket operator, discovered that its U.S. Foodservice unit had improperly accounted for vendor payments, resulting in overstated earnings of at least $500 million (later revised upward to $800 million). Other subsidiaries were also found to have inflated profits for similar reasons.

Not surprisingly, standard setters have now issued guidelines to curb the previous flexibility in accounting for these promotional payments.

Source: C. Schneider, "Retailers and Vendor Allowances," *CFO.com* (August 13, 2003).

Product Costs

Product costs are those costs that "attach" to the inventory and are recorded in the inventory account. These costs are directly connected with bringing goods to the buyer's place of business and converting such goods to a saleable condition. They include freight charges on goods purchased, other direct costs of acquisition, and labour and other production costs that are incurred in processing the goods until they are sold.

Underlying Concept

Product costs are a direct application of the historical cost principle.

Non-recoverable taxes (e.g., some provincial sales taxes) paid on goods that are purchased for resale or manufacturing purposes are a cost of inventory. Since value-added taxes (e.g., the federal Goods and Services Tax) can be recovered by a manufacturer, wholesaler, or retailer, they are not normally treated as a cost of inventory. Chapter 13 discusses this type of tax.

Conversion costs include direct labour and an allocation of the fixed and variable production overhead costs that are incurred in processing direct materials into finished goods. The allocation of fixed production costs is based on the company's normal production capacity so that costs of idle capacity or low production levels do not end up in inventory. They are charged instead to expense as they are incurred. Alternatively, if production levels are abnormally high, the fixed costs are spread out over the larger number of units that is produced so that inventory is not measured at a higher amount than its cost. Actual production levels can be used if close to normal levels, and actual levels are used to charge variable costs to production.[9]

[9] *CICA Handbook*, Section 3031. Section 3031.13 defines normal capacity as "the production expected to be achieved on average over a number of periods or seasons under normal circumstances, taking into account the loss of capacity resulting from planned maintenance."

International Insight

IAS 41 on agricultural activity recommends that agricultural production at the point of harvest be measured at its fair value less the estimated costs to sell it. This value becomes the "cost" of inventory for the expense and disclosure standards in Section 3031.

It would be theoretically correct to allocate to inventories a share of any buying costs or expenses of a purchasing department, insurance costs in transit, and other costs that are incurred in handling the goods before they are sold because such costs are incurred in "bringing the inventories to their present location and condition." However, because it is difficult in actual practice to allocate such costs and expenses, these items are not ordinarily included in inventory cost.

Standard Costs A company that uses a **standard cost system** predetermines the unit costs for material, labour, and manufacturing overhead. Usually the standard costs are based on the costs that should be incurred per unit of finished goods when the plant is operating at normal capacity. When the actual costs are not the same as the standard costs, the differences are recorded in variance accounts, which management can then examine and follow up on by taking appropriate action to achieve greater control over costs.

For financial statement purposes, reporting inventories at standard cost is acceptable when it is calculated using "normal levels of materials and supplies, labour, efficiency and capacity utilization." Unallocated overheads are expensed as they are incurred.[10]

Service Providers' Work in Process Companies that provide services rather than manufacture products may have a large amount of work-in-process inventories. These, too, are measured at their production costs. For service providers, the major "production" costs are for service personnel and overhead costs associated with this "direct labour." Supervisory costs and other overheads are allocated using the same principles as for manufactured products.

Costs Excluded from Inventory Some costs are closely related to acquiring and converting a product, but they are not considered to be product costs. These include storage costs (unless they are necessary because the product must be held before the next stage of production); abnormal spoilage or wastage of materials, labour, or other production costs; and interest costs when inventory is purchased on delayed payment terms.

Selling expenses and, under ordinary circumstances, **general and administrative expenses** are not considered directly related to the acquisition or conversion of goods and, therefore, are not considered a part of inventories. Such costs are **period costs**. Why are these costs not considered part of inventory? Selling expenses are generally thought of as being more directly related to the cost of goods sold than to the unsold inventory. In most cases, these costs are so unrelated or indirectly related to the actual production process that any allocation would be completely arbitrary.

Borrowing Costs

Underlying Concept

In capitalizing interest, the constraints of materiality and cost/benefit are both applied.

Interest or **borrowing costs** that are associated with getting inventories ready for sale are usually expensed when they are incurred. A major argument for this approach is that interest costs are a cost of financing. Others have argued, however, that because interest costs are incurred to finance activities that help bring inventories to a condition and place ready for sale, they are therefore as much a cost of the asset as materials, labour, and overhead, and should therefore be capitalized.[11] While the FASB has ruled that interest costs related to assets that are constructed for internal use or assets that are produced as discrete projects (such as ships or real estate projects) for sale or lease should be capitalized, the *CICA*

---

[10] *CICA Handbook*, Section 3031.13 and 21.

[11] The reporting rules on interest capitalization have their greatest impact in accounting for property, plant, and equipment and, therefore, are discussed in detail in Chapter 10. This brief overview presents the basic issues when inventories are involved.

Handbook requires only that, **if interest is capitalized, this policy and the amount that is capitalized in the current period be disclosed.**[12]

Interestingly, the IASB just recently changed its standard on borrowing costs (IAS 23) to harmonize it with the FASB standard as part of its short-term convergence project. This means that the Canadian standard is likely to move in the same direction in the future so that interest costs that can be attributed directly to the acquisition, construction, or production of a qualifying asset are treated as product costs. However, this may not occur until 2011.[13]

International Insight

Applying the FASB and IASB standards on borrowing costs is still compatible with the Canadian standard.

"Basket" Purchases and Joint Product Costs

A special problem occurs when a group of units with different characteristics is purchased at a single lump sum price—i.e., in what is called a **basket purchase**. Assume that Woodland Developers purchases land for $1 million and it can be subdivided into 400 lots. These lots are of different sizes and shapes but can be roughly sorted into three groups graded A, B, and C. The purchase cost of $1 million must be allocated among the lots so that the cost of the lots that are later sold (cost of goods sold) and those remaining on hand (ending inventory) can be calculated.

It is inappropriate to use the average lot cost of $2,500 (the total cost of $1 million divided by the 400 lots) because the lots vary in size, shape, and attractiveness. When this kind of situation occurs—and it is not at all unusual—the most reasonable practice is to allocate the total cost among the various units **based on their relative sales value**. For our example, the cost allocation is shown in Illustration 8-12.

Illustration 8-12

Allocation of Costs, Using Relative Sales Value

Lots	Number of Lots	Sales Price Per Lot	Total Sales Value	Relative Sales Value	Total Cost	Cost Allocated to Lots	Cost Per Lot
A	100	$10,000	$1,000,000	100/250	$1,000,000	$ 400,000	$4,000
B	100	6,000	600,000	60/250	1,000,000	240,000	2,400
C	200	4,500	900,000	90/250	1,000,000	360,000	1,800
			$2,500,000			$1,000,000	

The cost per lot is then used in calculating the cost of ending inventory as well as the cost of lots sold. **Brookfield Properties Corporation**, which owns, develops, and manages properties—including The World Financial Center in New York and First Canadian Place and The Exchange Tower in Toronto—includes in its financial statements the following accounting policy note on its residential development properties: "Costs are allocated to the saleable acreage of each project or subdivision in proportion to the anticipated revenue."

This method, the **relative sales value method**, is rational, can be applied consistently, and is commonly used whenever there is a **joint cost** that needs to be allocated. Other examples include when two or more products are produced at the same time and the costs for each product cannot be distinguished. The petroleum industry uses it to value (at cost) the many products and by-products obtained from a barrel of crude oil, as does the food processing industry, where different cuts of meat of varying value are "split off" from one animal carcass. When the value of a by-product is relatively minor, it is often measured at its net realizable value and deducted from the cost of the major product.

[12] *CICA Handbook*, Section 3850.03.

[13] IAS 23 excludes inventories that are routinely manufactured or produced in large quantities on a repetitive basis from the scope of IAS 23.

Illustration 8-13 shows **Brookfield Properties Corporation**'s accounting policy note on its inventory of properties under development from its December 31, 2005, financial statements.

Illustration 8-13
Development Property Joint Inventory Costs

NOTE 1: SUMMARY OF ACCOUNTING POLICIES

(d) Capitalized costs
Costs capitalized to commercial and residential properties which are under development and other properties held for sale include all direct and directly attributable expenditures incurred in connection with the acquisition, development, construction and initial predetermined leasing period. Costs directly attributable to development projects include interest and salaries and benefits of employees directly associated with the development projects, such as architects, engineers, designers and development project managers. Ancillary income relating specifically to such properties during the development period is treated as a reduction of costs.

NOTE 6: DEVELOPMENT PROPERTIES

Development properties include commercial developments, primarily for office development and residential land under and held for development. A breakdown of development properties is as follows:

(Millions)	2005	2004
Commercial developments	$ 224	$ 399
Residential development land	391	317
Total	$ 615	$ 716

Commercial developments include commercial land which represents developable land and construction costs. Residential development land includes fully entitled lots and land in processing. The company capitalizes interest and administrative and development costs to both commercial and residential development properties. During 2005, the company capitalized a total of $50 million (2004 - $55 million) of costs. Included in this amount is $18 million (2004 - $6 million) related to redevelopment costs, $17 million (2004 - $35 million) of construction and related costs and $15 million (2004 - $14 million) of interest capitalized to the company's commercial development sites.

The company, through its subsidiaries, is contingently liable for obligations of its joint venture associates in its residential development land joint ventures. The amount of such obligations at December 31, 2005 is $1 million (2004 - $1 million). In each case, all of the assets of the joint venture are available first for the purpose of satisfying these obligations, with the balance shared among the participants in accordance with the pre-determined joint venture arrangements.

Cost Formulas

Objective 7
Identify GAAP cost formula options and indicate when each cost formula is appropriate.

Two issues have now been addressed in determining inventory cost—which inventory items to include, and which costs to include in (or exclude from) the product cost. The next issue is this: **if inventories need to be priced at cost and many purchases have been made at different unit costs, which of the various cost prices should be assigned to Inventory on the balance sheet and which costs should be charged to Cost of Goods Sold on the income statement?**

Conceptually, the specific identification of the actual items sold and unsold seems ideal, but doing this is often too expensive or simply impossible to achieve. Consequently, companies must choose another acceptable inventory **cost formula**.[14] A cost formula is a method of assigning inventory costs incurred during the accounting period to inventory that is still on hand at the end of the period (ending inventory) and to inventory that was sold during the period (cost of goods sold).

Illustration 8-14 provides data that will be used in this discussion of the inventory cost formula choice. The data summarize the inventory-related activities of Call-Mart Inc. for the month of March. Note that the company experienced increasing unit costs for its purchases throughout the month.

[14] Before the release of *Handbook* Section 3031 in 2007, the term "cost flow assumption" was used instead of cost formula.

Illustration 8-14

Data Used to Illustrate Inventory Calculation: Cost Formula Choice

CALL-MART INC.

Date	Purchases	Sold or Issued	Balance
March 1	(beginning inventory) 500 @ $3.80		500 units
March 2	1,500 @ $4.00		2,000 units
March 15	6,000 @ $4.40		8,000 units
March 19		4,000	4,000 units
March 30	2,000 @ $4.75		6,000 units
	10,000	4,000	

From this information, we see that there were 10,000 units available for sale, made up of 500 units in opening inventory and 9,500 purchased during the month. Of the 10,000 available, 4,000 were sold, leaving 6,000 units in ending inventory.

The **cost of goods available for sale** can also be calculated:

500 units @ $3.80 =	$ 1,900
1,500 units @ $4.00 =	6,000
6,000 units @ $4.40 =	26,400
2,000 units @ $4.75 =	9,500
10,000 units	$43,800

Having this information, the real question now is: **which price or prices should be assigned to the 6,000 units of ending inventory and which to the 4,000 units sold?** The answer depends on which cost formula is chosen.

Primary sources of GAAP recognize three acceptable cost formulas, which will be discussed next:

1. Specific identification
2. First-in, first-out (FIFO)
3. Weighted average cost

Specific Identification

In **specific identification**, each item that is sold and each item in inventory needs to be identified. The costs of the specific items that are sold are included in the cost of goods sold, and the costs of the specific items on hand are included in the ending inventory. This method is appropriate and required for goods that are not ordinarily interchangeable, and for goods and services that are produced and segregated for specific projects.[15] It is used most often in situations where a relatively small number of costly, easily distinguishable items (e.g., by their physical characteristics, serial numbers, or special markings) are handled. In the retail trade, this includes some types of jewellery, fur coats, automobiles, and some furniture. In manufacturing, it includes special orders and many products manufactured under a job cost system.

International Insight

The Canadian standard is now the same as the IASB requirements in IAS 2.

[15] *CICA Handbook*, Section 3031.23.

To illustrate this method, assume that Call-Mart Inc.'s inventory items are distinguishable and that the 6,000 units of ending inventory consist of 100 units from the opening inventory, 900 from the March 2 purchase, 3,000 from the March 15 purchase, and 2,000 from the March 30 purchase. The ending inventory and cost of goods sold are calculated as shown in Illustration 8-15.

Illustration 8-15
Specific Identification Cost Formula

Units from	No. of Units	Unit Cost	Total Cost
Beginning inventory	100	$3.80	$ 380
March 2 purchase	900	4.00	3,600
March 15 purchase	3,000	4.40	13,200
March 30 purchase	2,000	4.75	9,500
Ending inventory	**6,000**		**$26,680**

Cost of goods available for sale (beginning inventory + purchases)	$43,800
Deduct: Ending inventory	26,680
Cost of goods sold	**$17,120**

Conceptually, this method appears ideal because actual costs are matched against actual revenue, and ending inventory items are reported at their specific cost. In fact, the requirement that this method **only be used for goods that are not ordinarily interchangeable** is an attempt to make sure this benefit is achieved and to prevent management from manipulating the amount of net income.

Consider the following two examples of what might happen if businesses were allowed to use this method more generally. Assume, for instance, that a wholesaler purchases identical plywood early in the year at three different prices. When the plywood is sold, the wholesaler can choose either the lowest or the highest price to charge to expense simply by choosing which plywood is delivered to the customer. This means that a manager can manipulate net income simply by delivering to the customer the higher- or lower-priced item, depending on whether lower or higher reported income is wanted for the period.

Another problem with the broader use of the specific identification cost formula is that allocating certain costs can become arbitrary when the inventory items are interchangeable. In some circumstances, **it is difficult to directly relate shipping charges, storage costs, discounts, and other blanket charges to a specific inventory item.** The only option, then, is to allocate these costs somewhat arbitrarily, which eliminates some of the benefits offered by the specific identification method.[16]

Weighted Average Cost

As its name implies, an average cost formula prices inventory items based on the average cost of the goods that are available for sale during the period. The **weighted average cost formula** takes into account that the volume of goods purchased at each price is different.

[16] A good illustration of the cost allocation problem occurs in the motion picture industry. Often actors and actresses receive a percentage of net income for a particular movie or television program. Some actors who have had these arrangements have alleged that their programs have been extremely profitable to the motion picture studios but they have received little in the way of profit-sharing. Actors contend that the studios allocate additional costs to successful projects to ensure that there will be no profits to share. Such contentions illustrate the type of problem that can emerge when contracts are based on accounting numbers that include arbitrary allocations. One way to help overcome such problems is to establish specific measurement rules on how the accounting numbers are to be determined. This should be done before the contract is signed so that all parties clearly understand what they are getting into.

To illustrate, assuming that Call-Mart Inc. uses the periodic inventory method (or a perpetual system in units only), the ending inventory and cost of goods sold would be calculated as in Illustration 8-16.

Illustration 8-16
Weighted Average Cost Formula–Periodic Inventory

	Date	No. Units	Unit Cost	Total Cost
Inventory	Mar. 1	500	$3.80	$ 1,900
Purchases	Mar. 2	1,500	4.00	6,000
Purchases	Mar. 15	6,000	4.40	26,400
Purchases	Mar. 30	2,000	4.75	9,500
Total goods available		10,000		$43,800

Weighted average cost per unit	$43,800 / 10,000 = $4.38	
Ending inventory in units	6,000	
Cost of ending inventory	**6,000 × $4.38 = $26,280**	
Cost of goods available for sale	$43,800	
Deduct ending inventory	26,280	
Cost of goods sold	$17,520	(= 4,000 × $4.38)

Note that the beginning inventory units and cost are both included in calculating the average cost per unit.

Another weighted average cost method is the **moving-average cost formula**. This method is used with **perpetual** inventory records that are **kept in both units and dollars**. Use of the moving-average cost method for full perpetual records is shown in Illustration 8-17.

Illustration 8-17
Moving-Average Cost Formula–Perpetual Inventory

Date	Purchased		Sold or Issued	Balance*	
Mar. 1	Beginning inventory			(500 @ $3.80)	$ 1,900
Mar. 2	(1,500 @ $4.00)	$ 6,000		(2,000 @ $3.95)	7,900
Mar. 15	(6,000 @ $4.40)	26,400		(8,000 @ $4.2875)	34,300
Mar. 19			(4,000 @ $4.2875) $17,150	(4,000 @ $4.2875)	17,150
Mar. 30	(2,000 @ $4.75)	9,500		(6,000 @ $4.4417)	26,650

***Calculation of moving-average cost per unit:**

After March 2 purchase
= Cost of units available / Units available
= [$1,900 + (1,500 × $4.00)] / (500 + 1,500)
= ($1,900 + $6,000) / 2,000
= $7,900 / 2,000
= $3.95

After March 15 purchase
= [$7,900 + (6,000 × $4.40)] / (2,000 + 6,000)
= $34,300 / 8,000
= $4.2875

After March 30 purchase
= [17,150 + (2,000 × $4.75)] / (4,000 + 2,000)
= $26,650 / 6,000
= $4.4417

In this method, a **new average unit cost is calculated each time** a purchase is made **because the cost of goods sold at average cost has to be recognized at the time of each sale.** On March 15, after 6,000 units are purchased for $26,400, 8,000 units with a total cost of $34,300 ($7,900 plus $26,400) are on hand. The average unit cost is $34,300 divided by 8,000, or $4.2875. This unit cost is used in costing withdrawals of inventory until another purchase is made, when a new average unit cost is calculated. Accordingly, the cost of each of the 4,000 units withdrawn on March 19 is shown at $4.2875, which makes a total cost of goods sold of $17,150. On March 30, following the purchase of 2,000 units for $9,500, a new unit cost of $4.4417 is determined for an ending inventory of $26,650.

Justification for using the average cost method is that the costs it assigns to inventory and cost of goods sold closely follow the actual physical flow of many inventories that are interchangeable. While it is impossible to measure the specific physical flow of inventory, it is reasonable to cost items based on an average price. There are also practical reasons that support this method. It is simple to apply, objective, and not very open to income manipulation. This argument is particularly persuasive when the inventory involved is relatively homogeneous in nature. In terms of achieving financial statement objectives, an average cost method results in an average of costs being used to determine the cost of goods sold in the income statement and ending inventory in the balance sheet.

First-In, First-Out (FIFO)

The **FIFO cost formula** assigns costs based on the assumption that goods are used in the order in which they are purchased. In other words, it assumes that **the first goods purchased are the first ones used** (in a manufacturing concern) **or sold** (in a merchandising concern). The inventory remaining, therefore, must come from the most recent purchases.

To illustrate, assume that Call-Mart Inc. uses the periodic inventory system (or a perpetual system in units only), where the inventory cost is calculated only at the end of the month. **The ending inventory's cost for the 6,000 units remaining is calculated by taking the cost of the most recent purchase and working back until all units in the ending inventory are accounted for.** The ending inventory and cost of goods sold are determined as shown in Illustration 8-18.

Illustration 8-18
FIFO Cost Formula–Periodic Inventory

Date	No. Units	Unit Cost	Total Cost
March 30	2,000	$4.75	$ 9,500
March 15	4,000	4.40	17,600
Ending inventory	6,000		$27,100
Cost of goods available for sale	$43,800		
Deduct: Ending inventory	27,100		
Cost of goods sold	$16,700		

If a perpetual inventory system **in quantities and dollars** is used, a cost figure is attached to each withdrawal from inventory when the units are sold. In the example, the cost of the 4,000 units removed on March 19 is made up first from the items in the beginning inventory, then the items purchased on March 2, and finally from the March 15 purchases. The inventory record under FIFO and **a perpetual system** for Call-Mart Inc. is shown in Illustration 8-19, which also results in an ending inventory of $27,100 and a cost of goods sold of $16,700.

Notice that in these two FIFO examples, the cost of goods sold and ending inventory are the same. **In all cases where FIFO is used, the inventory and cost of goods sold are the same at the end of the month whether a perpetual or periodic system is used.** This is true because the same costs will always be first in and, therefore, first out: so this is true whether cost of goods sold is calculated as goods are sold throughout the accounting period (the perpetual system) or based on what remains at the end of the accounting period (the periodic system).

Illustration 8-19
FIFO Cost Formula–Perpetual Inventory

Date	Purchased	Sold or Issued	Balance	
Mar. 1	Beginning inventory		500 @ $3.80	$ 1,900
Mar. 2	(1,500 @ $4.00) $ 6,000		500 @ 3.80 1,500 @ 4.00	7,900
Mar. 15	(6,000 @ $4.40) 26,400		500 @ 3.80 1,500 @ 4.00 6,000 @ 4.40	34,300
Mar. 19		500 @ $3.80 1,500 @ 4.00 2,000 @ 4.40 **$16,700**	4,000 @ 4.40	17,600
Mar. 30	(2,000 @ $4.75) 9,500		4,000 @ 4.40 2,000 @ 4.75	27,100

One objective of FIFO is to roughly follow the actual physical flow of goods. When the physical flow of goods really is first-in, first-out, the FIFO method approximates the use of specific identification. At the same time, it does not permit manipulation of income because the enterprise is not free to choose a certain cost to be charged to expense.

Another advantage of the FIFO method is that the ending inventory is close to its current cost. Because the costs of the first goods in are transferred to cost of goods sold, the ending inventory amount is made up of the most recent purchases. This approach generally provides a cost that is close to the replacement cost for inventory on the balance sheet, particularly when the inventory turnover is rapid and/or price changes have not occurred since the most recent purchases.

The FIFO method's basic disadvantage is that current costs are not matched against current revenues on the income statement. The oldest costs are charged against current revenue, which can lead to distortions in gross profit and net income when prices are changing rapidly.

What Happened to Last-In, First-Out (LIFO)?

International Insight

Until recently, LIFO was an allowed alternative in IAS 2. As it is no longer permitted as a cost formula by the international standard, there is now a difference between international and U.S. GAAP.

The **LIFO** cost formula assigns costs based on the assumption that the cost of the most recent purchase is the first cost to be charged to cost of goods sold. When prices are rising, the income statement (i.e., Cost of Goods Sold) is charged with the higher, more recent costs. The cost assigned to the inventory remaining would therefore come from the earliest acquisitions (i.e., "first-in, still-here") and is made up of the "oldest" costs.

New *CICA Handbook* Section 3031, however, contrary to Section 3030 which it replaces, does not identify last-in, first-out as an acceptable cost formula. The document *Background Information and Basis for Conclusions* (July 2006), which underlies Section 3031, explains why the AcSB accepted the decision of the IASB to eliminate this method:

(a) Assigning the oldest costs to ending inventory does not represent actual inventory flows reliably.

(b) Under LIFO, the cost of ending inventory is not a fair representation of the recent cost of inventories on hand. Although LIFO results in a natural adjustment to reported income when prices are rising, it results in an unacceptable distortion of the measure of the inventory on the balance sheet.

(c) Use of LIFO can result in serious distortions of reported income, especially when old inventory cost "layers" are expensed in the period. (See Appendix 8B.)

The Canada Revenue Agency has never allowed companies to use LIFO to calculate their income for tax purposes. As a result, this method has not been widely used in Canada.

The AcSB intends to permit Canadian public companies that are listed on U.S. exchanges as well as Canadian stock exchanges to prepare their financial statements under U.S. GAAP. For this reason, a fuller discussion of LIFO is included in Appendix 8B.

Choice of Cost Formula

The new inventory standards limit the ability of preparers to choose a cost formula. Specific identification is required when inventory is made up of goods that are not ordinarily interchangeable, and when goods and services are produced and segregated for specific projects. Otherwise, the choice is between a weighted average method and FIFO. The choice is further restricted as one more requirement is imposed: the same cost formula must be used "for all inventories having a similar nature and use to the entity."[17]

The overriding objectives that underlie the inventory standards are as follows:

Underlying Concept

The standards result in measures that are representationally faithful, increasing their reliability.

1. Chose an approach that corresponds as closely as possible to the physical flow of goods. This is a major change from the past, where the goal was to choose the method that resulted "in the fairest matching of costs against revenues regardless of whether or not the method corresponds to the physical flow of goods."[18]
2. Report an inventory cost on the balance sheet that is representative of the inventory's recent cost.
3. Use the same method for all inventory assets that have similar economic characteristics for the entity.

The new requirements are consistent with standard setters' recent emphasis on assets and liabilities as concepts whose definitions and measurements become the basis for determining the amounts and timing of revenues and expenses. Companies, on the other hand, tend to be more interested in the income numbers that result, particularly because of investor expectations. Income taxes are also a consideration. Methods that permit a lower ending inventory valuation result in lower income and reduced cash outflows for taxes.

Compared to the FIFO cost formula, an average cost formula results in recent costs being reflected more in the cost of goods sold and older costs in ending inventory. In a period of rising prices, there may be tax advantages to the average cost formula.

It can be seen that the freedom to switch from one inventory costing method to another would permit a wide range of possible net income figures for a particular company for a particular period. This would affect the comparability of the financial statements. The choice of methods has been limited in order to support appropriate financial reporting. Companies must now choose the costing formula that is most suitable to their particular circumstances and, once selected, apply it consistently from then on. If conditions indicate that another accounting policy would result in a reliable and more relevant presentation in the financial statements, a change may be made. Such a change is accounted for retroactively, is clearly explained, and its effect is disclosed in the financial statements.[19]

Underlying Concept

Consistent application of the same formula enhances the comparability of the financial statements.

Exceptions to "Cost"

For most companies and in most situations, inventory is recorded at cost or the lower of cost and net realizable value. Some critics believe that inventory should always be valued at its **net realizable value**—i.e., the estimated selling price in the ordinary course of business

[17] *CICA Handbook*, Section 3031.25.

[18] *CICA Handbook*, Section 3030.09, withdrawn in 2007.

[19] *CICA Handbook*, Section 1506.

less the estimated costs of completion and disposal[20]—because that is the net amount that will be collected in cash from the inventory in the future. In certain restricted circumstances, it is possible to record inventory at its net realizable value even if that amount is above cost. Chapter 6 identified the two criteria that must both be met for valuation above cost and revenue to be recognized before the point of sale:

1. There is an active and controlled market with a quoted price that applies to all quantities.
2. The costs of disposal are not significant.

Inventories of certain minerals (rare metals especially) are often reported at selling prices because there is often a controlled market without significant costs of disposal. A similar treatment is used for agricultural products that are immediately marketable at quoted prices. This is consistent with the recognition of revenue when production is complete. The Saskatchewan Wheat Pool Inc. reports such a policy in the notes to its 2005 financial statements, shown in Illustration 8-20.

As mentioned earlier in the chapter, inventories in certain specialized industries do not have to follow the measurement requirements of the inventory standards. The exclusions are for industries where revenue recognition criteria are met before the point of sale, and the result is that their inventory is reported with a profit element incorporated in the amount recognized. These inventories include agricultural and forest products, minerals and mineral products, and commodities of broker-traders that are often measured at their net realizable value or related measures.

Illustration 8-20

Inventory Valued at Net Realizable Value–Saskatchewan Wheat Pool Inc.

Inventories

Grain inventories in the Grain Handling and Marketing segment include both hedgable and non-hedgable commodities. Hedgable grain inventories are valued on the basis of closing market quotations less freight and handling costs and also reflect gains and losses on open grain purchase and sale contracts. Non-hedgable grain inventories are valued at the lower of cost and net realizable value. Agri-products and other inventories which consist of raw materials, work in progress and finished goods are valued at the lower of cost and net realizable value.

This method of valuation is also sometimes used when cost figures are too difficult to obtain. In some cases, marketable by-products are produced where the costs are indistinguishable. As indicated earlier in the chapter, instead of the company attempting a costly exercise of arbitrary cost allocation, the by-products are measured at the market price of the by-product less any costs to bring them to market.

BALANCE SHEET VALUATION

Rationale for Lower of Cost and Net Realizable Value

8 Objective
Explain why inventory is measured at the lower of cost and net realizable value.

In addition to requiring that the carrying amount of inventories be "recognized as an expense in the period in which the related revenue is recognized," the accounting standard requires any loss of inventory or impairment in its value to be recognized as an expense in the period when the loss or impairment occurs.[21]

As indicated earlier, inventories are initially recorded at cost. However, a departure from the historical cost principle occurs if inventory declines in value below its original cost. This reduction in value may be due to the inventory itself (e.g., obsolete or damaged goods), a reduction in its selling price, or an increase in its disposal cost. **The cost**

[20] *CICA Handbook*, Section 3031.06.

[21] *CICA Handbook*, Section 3031.34.

principle is overridden when the asset's future utility (its ability to generate net cash flows) is no longer as great as its carrying amount. Inventories that experience a decline in utility are therefore valued based on the lower of cost and net realizable value, instead of on the original cost.

Underlying Concept

Using the lower of cost and net realizable value for measurement is an excellent example of proper asset valuation, the conservatism constraint, and matching.

A departure from cost is justified for two main reasons. First, readers presume that **current assets can be converted into at least as much cash as the value reported for them on the balance sheet**; and second, **a loss of utility should be deducted from (i.e., matched with) revenues in the period in which the loss occurs**, not in the period in which the inventory is sold. In addition, this is a **conservative approach to inventory valuation**. That is, when there is doubt about an asset's value, it is preferable to report it closer to its expected realizable value than to overvalue it.

Objective 9

Identify and apply the lower of cost and net realizable value standard for inventory.

Until *Handbook* Section 3031 became effective in 2007, the Canadian standard for inventory valuation was more flexible. Previously, inventory was valued at the lower of cost and market—or LCM. The term **market** in the phrase "the lower of cost and market" has several different meanings. It could mean replacement cost, net realizable value, or net realizable value less a normal profit margin. These terms are described and illustrated more fully in Appendix 8B.

The option of choosing a meaning of "market" has been eliminated in the new standard. The lower of cost and market is still part of GAAP in Canada, but market is now defined as net realizable value. As this was the definition most commonly used in Canada in the past, the change in standard may not have a significant effect on the financial statements of Canadian companies.[22] Why has there been such support for this method?

International Insight

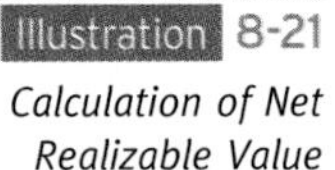

The IAS 2 standard is also net realizable value. The FASB requires a "rule" to be applied that incorporates all the definitions of "market."

The use of replacement cost as "market" is based on the assumption that a decline in an item's replacement cost usually results in a decline in its selling price. While replacement cost may be appropriate in a few specific circumstances, it is not reasonable to assume that prices will fall in the same proportion as input costs fell, or that they will fall below inventory cost, or that such market conditions exist for all products.

The choice between net realizable value (NRV) and NRV less a normal profit margin fell to NRV because NRV less a normal profit margin has the effect of arbitrarily shifting profits from one period to another. To see the effects of reducing the carrying value of inventory under these two methods, assume that a company has unfinished inventory at December 31, 2008, with a cost of $760, a completed sales value of $1,000, estimated cost of completion of $275, and a normal profit margin of 10% of sales. Illustration 8-21 shows the calculation of "market" based on each of these definitions.

Illustration 8-21
Calculation of Net Realizable Value

Inventory—sales value	$1,000
Less: Estimated cost of completion and disposal	275
Net realizable value	**725**
Less: Allowance for normal profit margin (10% of sales)	100
Net realizable value less a normal profit margin	**$ 625**

Illustration 8-22 first summarizes the effects of using net realizable value as the definition of market, and then shows the effects of using the more conservative net realizable value less a normal profit margin.

[22] *Financial Reporting in Canada*, 2005 (Toronto: CICA, 2005) reports that, of the interpretations of "market" disclosed in the 2004 financial statements of 156 of the surveyed companies, 77 used only net realizable value or estimated net realizable value, 12 used only replacement cost, 2 used only net realizable value less a normal profit margin, and 1 reported another single method. Sixty-two companies used more than one method, and of these, 54 used replacement cost, and most often with net realizable value as well. Only 4 companies did not disclose how they defined "market."

Illustration 8-22
Income Statement Effects of Using Different Definitions of "Market"

	Inventory Value December 31, 2008 Balance Sheet	Profit (loss) recognized in 2008	in 2009
If definition of NRV used:			
Cost = $760			
Market = $725			
LCM =	$725		
Effect on 2008 Income Statement:			
$760 – $725 (inventory write-down)		$(35)	
Effect on 2009 Income Statement:			
Revenue			$1,000
Cost of Goods Sold (carrying value, Dec. 31/08)			(725)
Completion costs incurred in 2009			(275)
			$0
If definition of NRV less a normal profit margin used:			
Cost = $760			
Market = $625			
LCM =	$625		
Effect on 2008 Income Statement:			
$760 – $625 (inventory writedown)		$(135)	
Effect on 2009 Income Statement:			
Revenue			$1,000
Cost of Goods Sold (carrying value, Dec. 31/08)			(625)
Completion costs incurred in 2009			(275)
			$ 100

When the inventory is written down to net realizable value, a $35 loss is recognized in 2008 and the company breaks even on the sale of the item in 2009. Compare this with the results when the inventory is written down to the lower NRV less a normal profit margin amount. In this case, a $135 loss is absorbed in 2008 and a profit of $100 is reported the following year. Although the net result is the same—a $35 loss between the two years—the second method arbitrarily penalizes 2008 and shifts profit into the year of the sale. Because of the lack of justification for the arbitrary shifting of profit between years, net realizable value is now used.

Application of the U.S. approach to lower of cost and market is discussed briefly in Appendix 8B.

What Is Net Realizable Value?

Net realizable value is an estimate. Unlike inventory cost, which usually remains at a determined value, net realizable value changes over time for a variety of reasons. Inventory may deteriorate or become obsolete with time; selling prices fluctuate with changes in supply and demand; substitute products become available; and input costs to complete and sell, liquidate, or otherwise dispose of the product vary with conditions and the specific markets that the inventory is sold into.

Underlying Concept

Regardless of the definition of "market" that is used, the intent is the same: current assets should not be reported at more than their realizable value to the company.

Estimates of NRV are based on the best evidence available at and shortly after the balance sheet date. The objective is to determine the most likely (net) realizable value of the product on hand at the end of the accounting period given the specific circumstances of the particular entity. A new assessment is required at each balance sheet date. If economic circumstances change and the estimate of the net realizable value changes from the previous estimate, the revised amount is used in determining the lower of cost and NRV.

Application of Lower of Cost and Net Realizable Value

The **lower of cost and net realizable value** standard requires that inventory be valued at cost unless NRV is lower than cost, in which case the inventory is valued at NRV. To apply this:

1. Determine the cost.
2. Determine the net realizable value.
3. Compare the two.
4. Use the lower value for inventory on the financial statements.

To demonstrate, consider the information in Illustration 8-23 for the inventory of Regner Foods Limited.

Illustration 8-23

Determining the Lower of Cost and NRV

Food	Cost	Net Realizable Value	Lower of Cost and NRV
Spinach	$ 80,000	$120,000	$ 80,000
Carrots	100,000	100,000	100,000
Cut beans	50,000	40,000	40,000
Peas	90,000	72,000	72,000
Mixed vegetables	95,000	92,000	92,000
Final inventory value			$384,000

To establish the value of each item of inventory, compare the net realizable value in the middle column of Illustration 8-23 with cost. The lower of the two values is then chosen. Cost is the lower amount for spinach; net realizable value is lower for cut beans, peas, and mixed vegetables; and cost and NRV are identical for carrots. The inventory value reported on Regner Foods' balance sheet is therefore $384,000.

Usually, this analysis is only applied to losses in value that occur in the normal course of business from such causes as style changes, a shift in demand, or regular shop wear. Damaged or deteriorated goods are reduced directly to net realizable value. If the amount is significant, such goods may be carried in separate inventory accounts.

In the previous illustration for Regner Foods, we assumed that the lower of cost and net realizable value rule was applied to each item of food. Indeed, **the new accounting standards specify that the comparison is usually applied on an item-by-item basis.** However, the standards recognize that it may be appropriate in some circumstances to group similar or related items and then compare their cost and NRV as a group. Grouping inventory for this purpose is appropriate only when the following three conditions are all met:

1. The items are closely related in terms of their end use.
2. The items are produced and marketed in the same geographical area.
3. The items cannot be evaluated separately from other items in the product line in a practical or reasonable way.[23]

[23] *CICA Handbook*, Section 3031.29.

The guidance specifies that major segmentation, such as grouping all finished goods inventory, or all inventory within a geographic area, or all inventory that is specific to an industry, is not appropriate.

Grouping inventory and then comparing only the subtotals of cost and net realizable value can affect the amount of inventory that is reported on the balance sheet. To illustrate, assume that Regner Foods separates its food products into "frozen" and "canned" categories.

As indicated in Illustration 8-24, if the lower of cost and NRV rule is applied to the subtotals of these groups, the valuation of inventory is $394,000; if it is applied to individual items, it is $384,000. The reason for the difference is that realizable values lower than cost are offset against realizable values higher than cost when the major categories approach is adopted. For example, the lower NRVs for cut beans, peas, and mixed vegetables are partially offset by the higher NRV for spinach. **The item-by-item approach** is always the more conservative method because net realizable values above cost are never included in the valuation.

Illustration 8-24
Grouping Inventory Categories

	Cost	NRV	Lower of Cost and NRV by: Individual Items	Related Products
Frozen				
Spinach	$ 80,000	$120,000	$ 80,000	
Carrots	100,000	100,000	100,000	
Cut beans	50,000	40,000	40,000	
Total frozen	230,000	260,000		$230,000
Canned				
Peas	90,000	72,000	72,000	
Mixed vegetables	95,000	92,000	92,000	
Total canned	185,000	164,000		164,000
Total			$384,000	$394,000

The Canada Revenue Agency dictates that "in comparing 'cost' and 'fair market value' in order to determine which is the lower, the comparison should be made separately and individually in respect of each item (or each usual class of items if specific items are not readily distinguishable) in the inventory." A comparison of total cost and total market is only permitted as an exception when the cost of the specific items (using specific identification, FIFO, or average cost) is not known and only an average cost is available.[24]

International Insight

The tax rules in the United States also require that the basis for valuation be individual items unless doing so involves practical difficulties.

Recording the Lower of Cost and Net Realizable Value

Two methods are used for recording inventory at the lower market amount. One method, referred to as the **direct method**, records the NRV of the inventory directly in the Inventory account at year end if the amount is lower than cost. No loss is reported separately in the income statement because the loss is buried in cost of goods sold. The second method does not change the Inventory account itself. Instead it keeps the inventory amount at cost and establishes a separate contra asset account to Inventory on the balance sheet and a loss account in the income statement to record the write-off. This latter approach is referred to as the **indirect method** or **allowance method**.

The following data are the basis for Illustrations 8-25 and 8-26, which show the entries under both methods:

[24] *CRA Interpretation Bulletin*—473R, December 21, 1998, on "Inventory Valuation," par. .3.

Inventory	At Cost	At NRV
Beginning of the period	$65,000	$65,000
End of the period	82,000	70,000

The entries in Illustration 8-25 assume the use of a **periodic** inventory system. Those in Illustration 8-26 assume a **perpetual** inventory system.

Illustration 8-25

Accounting for the Reduction of Inventory to NRV–Periodic Inventory System

Ending Inventory Recorded at NRV (Direct Method)			Ending Inventory Recorded at Cost and Reduced to NRV Using an Allowance		
To transfer out beginning inventory balance:					
Cost of Goods Sold (or Income Summary)	65,000		Cost of Goods Sold (or Income Summary)	65,000	
Inventory		65,000	Inventory		65,000
To record ending inventory:					
Inventory	70,000		Inventory	82,000	
Cost of Goods Sold (or Income Summary)		70,000	Cost of Goods Sold (or Income Summary)		82,000
To write down inventory to lower NRV:					
No entry			Loss Due to Decline in NRV of Inventory*	12,000	
			Allowance to Reduce Inventory to NRV		12,000

*A debit to Cost of Goods Sold is also acceptable.

Illustration 8-26

Accounting for the Reduction of Inventory to NRV–Perpetual Inventory System

Direct Method			Indirect or Allowance Method		
To reduce inventory from cost to NRV:					
Cost of Goods Sold	12,000		Loss Due to Decline in NRV of Inventory*	12,000	
Inventory		12,000	Allowance to Reduce Inventory to NRV		12,000

*A debit to Cost of Goods Sold is also acceptable.

The advantage of identifying the loss due to the decline in net realizable value separately is that it may be reported in Other Expenses and Losses, and therefore not distort the cost of goods sold for the year. It thus clearly discloses the loss resulting from the market decline of inventory prices instead of burying it in the cost of goods sold. The advantage of using an allowance account on the balance sheet is that inventory cost numbers are retained in both the Inventory control and subsidiary ledger accounts.

Although using an allowance account makes it possible to disclose the inventory at cost and at the lower of cost and NRV on the balance sheet, it raises the problem of how to dispose of the new account balance in the following period. If the particular merchandise is still on hand, the allowance account should be retained. Otherwise, beginning inventory and cost of goods available for sale will be overstated. But if the goods have been sold, then the account should be closed. A new allowance account balance is then established for any decline in inventory value that exists at the end of the next accounting period.

Many accountants leave the allowance account on the books and merely adjust its balance at the next balance sheet date to agree with the discrepancy between cost and the lower of cost and NRV at that time. Thus, if prices are falling, a loss is recorded. If prices are rising, a loss recorded in prior years is recovered and a gain (which is not really a gain, but **a recovery of a previously recognized loss**) is recorded, as shown in Illustration 8-27.

Date	Inventory at Cost	Inventory at NRV	Amount Required in Allowance Account	Adjustment of Allowance Account Balance	Effect on Net Income
Dec. 31, 2006	$188,000	$176,000	$12,000 cr.	$12,000 increase	Loss
Dec. 31, 2007	194,000	187,000	7,000 cr.	5,000 decrease	Gain
Dec. 31, 2008	173,000	174,000	0	7,000 decrease	Gain
Dec. 31, 2009	182,000	180,000	2,000 cr.	2,000 increase	Loss

Illustration 8-27

Effect on Net Income of Adjustments to the Allowance Account

Any net "gain" can be thought of as the excess of the credit effect of closing the beginning allowance balance over the debit effect of setting up the current year-end allowance account. Recovering the loss up to the original cost is permitted, **but it may not exceed the original cost.**

Underlying Concept

The balance sheet presentation of inventory is an example of the trade-off between relevance and reliability. NRV is more relevant than cost, and cost is more reliable than NRV. Apparently, relevance takes precedence in a down market, and reliability is more important in an up market.

Evaluation of the Lower of Cost and Net Realizable Value Rule

Measuring inventories at the lower of cost and NRV has some conceptual and practical deficiencies. Recognizing net realizable values only when they are lower than cost is an inconsistent treatment that can lead to distortions in reported income. The accounting values that are reported are not neutral and unbiased measures of income and net assets. Because NRV is an estimate, company management has the opportunity to over- or underestimate realizable values, depending on the results it would like to report for the period. Others feel that any accounting method that arbitrarily transfers income from one period to another reduces the quality of earnings.

On the other hand, many financial statement users appreciate the lower of cost and net realizable value requirement because they at least know that inventory and income are not overstated. Supporters contend that accounting measurement has not reached a level of sophistication that enables us to provide acceptably reliable (i.e., verifiable) fair values for inventory above cost.

Purchase Commitment Issues

10 Objective

Explain the accounting issues for purchase commitments.

In many lines of business, a firm's survival and continued profitability depend on having enough merchandise in stock to meet all customer demands. Consequently, it is quite common for a company to agree to buy inventory weeks, months, or even years in advance. Such arrangements may be made based on either estimated or firm sales commitments from the company's customers. Generally, title to the merchandise or materials described in these **purchase commitments** has not passed to the buyer. Indeed, the goods may exist only as natural resources or, in the case of commodities, as unplanted seed, or in the case of a product, as work in process.

Usually, it is both unnecessary and incorrect for the buyer to make entries for commitments to purchase goods that have not been shipped by the seller. Ordinary orders, where the prices are determined at the time of shipment and **the buyer or seller can still cancel the order**, do not represent either an asset or a liability to the buyer. They are therefore not recorded in the books or reported in the financial statements.

Even with formal, **non-cancellable purchase contracts**, no asset or liability is recognized on the date when the contract takes effect, **because the contract is "executory" in nature**: in other words, neither party has performed (or fulfilled) its part of the contract. However, if the amounts are material, such contract details should be disclosed in the buyer's balance sheet in a note, as shown in Illustrations 8-28 and 8-29.

Illustration 8-28
Disclosure of Purchase Commitments– Cameco Corporation

24. Commitments and Contingencies

c) Commitments

At December 31, 2005, Cameco's purchase commitments, the majority of which are fixed-price uranium and conversion purchase arrangements, were as follows:

	(Millions (US))
2006	$ 141
2007	126
2008	136
2009	126
2010	114
Thereafter	413
Total	**$1,056**

Illustration 8-29
Disclosure of Purchase Commitment

Note 1: Contracts for the purchase of raw materials in 2008 have been executed in the amount of $600,000. The market price of such raw materials on December 31, 2007, is $640,000.

In Illustration 8-29, the contracted price is less than the market price at the balance sheet date. **If the contracted price is higher than the market price and losses are reasonably determinable and likely to occur at the time of purchase, losses should be recognized in the period during which such declines in price take place.** For example, if purchase contracts for delivery in 2008 have been executed at a firm price of $640,000 and the material's market price on the company's year end of December 31, 2007, is $600,000, the following entry is made on December 31, 2007:

A	=	L	+	SE
		+40,000		−40,000

Cash flows: No effect

Loss on Purchase Contracts	40,000	
Accrued Liability on Purchase Contracts		40,000

The loss is shown on the income statement under Other Expenses and Losses. The Accrued Liability on Purchase Contracts is reported in the balance sheet's liability section. When the goods are delivered in 2008, the entry (in a perpetual system) is:

A	=	L	+ SE
+600,000		+600,000	

Cash flows: No effect

Inventory	600,000	
Accrued Liability on Purchase Contracts	40,000	
Accounts Payable		640,000

Underlying Concept

Reporting the loss is conservative. However, reporting the decline in market price is debatable because no asset is recorded and the accrued liability on purchase contracts is not a present obligation. This area demonstrates the need for good definitions of assets and liabilities.

If the price has partially or fully recovered before the inventory is received, the Accrued Liability on Purchase Contracts amount is reduced. A resulting gain (Recovery of Loss) is then reported in the period of the price increase for the amount of the partial or full recovery. This accounting treatment almost mirrors recognizing an impairment in inventory value by recording such assets at the lower of cost and net realizable value.

Accounting for purchase commitments (indeed, for all executory contracts) is unsettled and controversial. Some argue that these contracts should be reported as assets and liabilities when the contract is signed; others believe that recognition at the delivery date is more appropriate. Clearly, the treatment of such contracts in particular situations requires judgement based on generally accepted accounting principles and experience.

International Insight

Unlike Canadian standards, IAS 37 addresses situations such as purchase commitments that may result in losses.

ESTIMATING INVENTORY

The Need for Estimates

11 Objective

Apply the gross profit method of estimating inventory.

Recall that the basic purpose of taking a physical inventory is to verify the accuracy of the perpetual inventory records, or, if there are no perpetual records, to arrive at an inventory amount. Sometimes, taking a physical inventory is impractical or impossible. In such cases, estimation methods are used to approximate inventory on hand. One such method is called the gross profit, or gross margin, method. This method is used in situations where only an estimate of inventory is needed (e.g., preparing interim reports or testing the reasonableness of the cost calculated by some other method) or where inventory has been destroyed by fire or some other catastrophe. It may also be used to provide a rough check on the accuracy of a physical inventory count. For example, the estimated amount is compared with the physical count amount to see if they are reasonably close; if they are not, a reason should be found.

Another method that is widely used with retail inventories is the retail inventory method. Like the gross profit method, it depends on establishing a relationship between selling (retail) prices and cost. Appendix 8A discusses this approach in detail.

Applying the Gross Profit Method

The **gross profit method** is based on three premises:

1. The beginning inventory plus purchases equals the **cost of goods available for sale**.
2. Goods not sold must be on hand **in the ending inventory**.
3. When an estimate of cost of goods sold is deducted from the cost of goods available for sale, the result is an estimate of ending inventory.

To illustrate, assume that a company has a beginning inventory of $60,000 and purchases of $200,000, both at cost. Sales at selling price amount to $280,000. The gross profit on the selling price is 30%. The gross margin method is applied as in Illustration 8-30.

Illustration 8-30

Application of Gross Profit Method

Beginning inventory (at cost)		$ 60,000
Purchases (at cost)		200,000
Goods available for sale (at cost)		260,000
Sales (at selling price)	$280,000	
Less: Gross profit (30% of $280,000)	84,000	
Sales at cost = Estimated cost of goods sold		196,000
Estimated inventory (at cost)		$ 64,000

Note that the estimated cost of goods sold could also have been calculated directly as 70% of sales, i.e., 100% less 30%. **The cost of goods sold percentage is always the complement of the gross profit percentage.**

All the information needed to estimate the inventory at cost, except for the gross profit percentage, is available in the current period's records. The gross profit percentage is determined by reviewing company policies and the records of prior periods. In some cases, this percentage must be adjusted if the prior periods are not considered representative of the current period.[25]

Gross Profit Percentage versus Markup on Cost

In most situations, the **gross profit percentage** is used and it is the gross profit as a percentage of the selling price. The previous illustration, for example, used a 30% gross profit on sales. Gross profit on selling price is the common method for quoting the profit for several reasons: (1) Most goods are stated on a retail basis, not a cost basis. (2) A profit quoted on the selling price is lower than one based on cost, and this lower rate gives a favourable impression to the consumer. (3) The gross profit based on selling price can never exceed 100%.[26]

In the previous example, the gross profit was given. But how was that figure derived? To see how a gross profit percentage is calculated, assume that an article cost $15.00 and sells for $20.00, a gross profit of $5.00. This markup of $5.00 is one-quarter or 25% of the selling price (i.e., the retail price) but is one-third or 33⅓% of cost (see Illustration 8-31).

Illustration 8-31
Gross Profit Percentage vs. Percentage of Markup on Cost

$$\frac{\text{Gross profit}}{\text{Selling price}} = \frac{\$\,5.00}{\$20.00} = 25\%\text{ of selling price} \qquad \frac{\text{Gross profit}}{\text{Cost}} = \frac{\$\,5.00}{\$15.00} = 33^1/_3\%\text{ of cost}$$

Although it is normal to calculate the gross profit based on the selling price, you should understand the basic relationship between this ratio and the percentage of **markup on cost**.

For example, assume that you were told that the **markup on cost** for a specific item is 25%. What, then, is the **gross profit on selling price**? To find the answer, assume that the item's selling price is $1.00. In this case, the following formula applies:

$$\begin{aligned} \text{Cost} + \text{Gross profit} &= \text{Selling price} \\ C + .25C &= \$1.00 \\ 1.25C &= \$1.00 \\ C &= \$0.80 \end{aligned}$$

The gross profit equals $0.20 ($1.00 – $0.80), and the rate of gross profit on selling price is therefore 20% ($0.20/$1.00).

---

[25] An alternative approach to estimating inventory using the gross profit percentage, considered by some to be less complicated than the method just shown, uses the standard income statement format as follows (assume the same data as in the illustration above):

Sales		$280,000		$280,000
Cost of sales				
Beginning inventory	$ 60,000		$ 60,000	
Purchases	200,000		200,000	
Goods available for sale	260,000		260,000	
Ending inventory	(3) ?		(3) 64,000 Est.	
Cost of goods sold		(2) ?		(2) 196,000 Est.
Gross profit on sales (30%)		(1) ?		(1)$ 84,000 Est.

Calculate the unknowns as follows: first the gross profit amount, then cost of goods sold, and then the ending inventory.

(1) $280,000 × 30% = $84,000 (gross profit on sales)
(2) $280,000 – $84,000 = $196,000 (cost of goods sold)
(3) $260,000 – $196,000 = $64,000 (ending inventory)

[26] The terms "gross profit percentage," "gross margin percentage," "rate of gross profit," and "rate of gross margin" are synonymous: they all reflect the relationship of gross profit to the selling price. The terms "percentage markup" or "rate of markup" are used to describe the relationship of gross profit to cost. It is very important to understand the difference.

Conversely, assume that you were told that the **gross profit on selling price** is 20%. What is the **markup on cost**? To find the answer, again assume that the selling price is \$1.00. The same formula can be used:

$$\begin{aligned} \text{Cost} + \text{Gross profit} &= \text{Selling price} \\ C + .20SP &= SP \\ C &= .80SP \\ C &= .80(\$1.00) \\ C &= \$0.80 \end{aligned}$$

Here, as in the example above, the markup or gross profit equals \$0.20 (\$1.00 – \$0.80), and the markup on cost is 25% (\$0.20/\$0.80).

Retailers use the formulas in Illustration 8-32 to express these relationships.

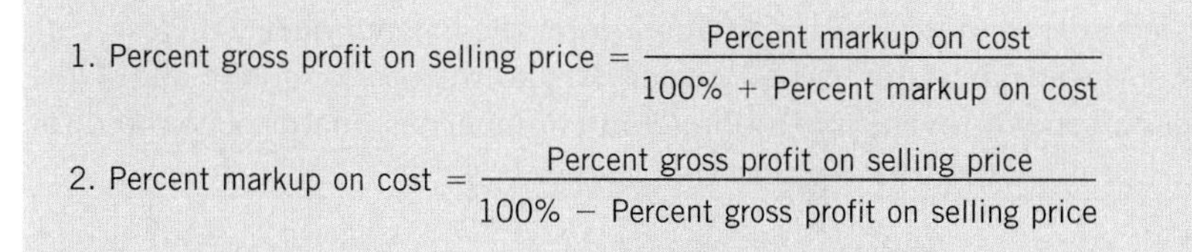

$$1.\ \text{Percent gross profit on selling price} = \frac{\text{Percent markup on cost}}{100\% + \text{Percent markup on cost}}$$

$$2.\ \text{Percent markup on cost} = \frac{\text{Percent gross profit on selling price}}{100\% - \text{Percent gross profit on selling price}}$$

Illustration 8-32

Formulas Relating to Gross Profit

Using the Results

What are the major disadvantages of the gross profit method? One is that **it provides an estimate** only. Second, the gross profit method uses **past percentages** in determining the markup. Although the future may be similar to the past, a current rate is more appropriate. It is important to emphasize that whenever significant fluctuations occur, the percentage should be adjusted appropriately. Third, **it may be inappropriate to apply a single gross profit rate**. Often, a store or department handles merchandise with very different rates of gross profit. In these situations, the gross profit method may have to be applied by subsections, lines of merchandise, or a similar basis that classifies merchandise according to its respective rates of gross profit.

Because the result is only an estimate, the gross profit method is **not normally acceptable for financial reporting purposes**. A physical inventory is needed as an additional verification that the inventory indicated in the records is actually on hand. Nevertheless, the gross profit method is used to estimate ending inventory for **interim** (monthly and quarterly) **reporting** and for **insurance purposes** (e.g., fire losses). Note that the results of applying the gross profit method will reflect the inventory method that is used (specific identification, FIFO, average cost) because this method is based on historical records.

PRESENTATION, PERSPECTIVES, AND INTERNATIONAL STANDARDS

Disclosures and Presentation of Inventories

12 **Objective**
Identify the inventory disclosures required by GAAP.

Inventories are one of the most significant assets of manufacturing and merchandising companies, and of many service enterprises. For this reason, companies are required to disclose additional information about these resources.

Some disclosures are similar to the ones required for other balance sheet items: the choice of accounting policies to measure the inventory, the carrying amount pledged as security for liabilities, and the amount of inventories recognized as an expense in the year.

This latter amount is usually reported as cost of goods sold, and includes unallocated and abnormal production costs. Other disclosures include the following:

- the carrying amount of the total inventory and each category of inventory as classified by the organization in a way that is appropriate for its nature (such as materials, work in process, finished goods, production supplies, etc.)
- the carrying amount of inventories of agricultural, forest product, mineral and mineral product producers carried at net realizable value; of commodity broker-traders carried at fair value less selling costs; and of certain biological assets
- the amount of any impairment or other inventory loss charged against income in the period, as well as any such amounts that are reversed, complete with reasons for the reversal

The excerpts in Illustration 8-33 from the financial statements of Magna International Inc. illustrate the company's disclosure of choices made in determining its inventory cost including the cost formula used, the basis of valuation on the balance sheet, the carrying value of major categories making up the total inventory, and the cost of goods sold. Note that Magna includes a type of inventory (tooling and engineering) that is accounted for under the completed contract method explained in Chapter 6.

Illustration 8-33
Inventory Disclosures–Magna International Inc.

Student Toolkit–Additional Disclosures

www.wiley.com/canada/kieso

Consolidated Balance Sheets

Magna International Inc.
[U.S. dollars in millions]

As at December 31,

	Note	2005	2004 [restated – note 2]
ASSETS			
Current assets			
Cash and cash equivalents		**$ 1,682**	$ 1,519
Accounts receivable		**3,436**	3,276
Inventories	7	**1,388**	1,376
Prepaid expenses and other		**97**	110
		6,603	6,281

Consolidated Statements of Income

Magna International Inc.
[U.S. dollars in millions, except per share figures]

Years ended December 31,

	Note	2005	2004 [restated – note 2]
Sales		**$ 22,811**	$ 20,653
Costs and expenses			
Cost of goods sold		**19,831**	17,696

1. SIGNIFICANT ACCOUNTING POLICIES

Inventories

Production inventories and tooling inventories manufactured in-house are valued at the lower of cost and net realizable value, with cost being determined substantially on a first-in, first-out basis. Cost includes the cost of materials plus direct labour applied to the product and the applicable share of manufacturing overhead.

Outsourced tooling inventories are valued at the lower of subcontracted costs and net realizable value.

7. INVENTORIES

Inventories consist of:

	2005	2004
Raw materials and supplies	**$ 449**	$ 474
Work-in-process	**208**	229
Finished goods	**201**	186
Tooling and engineering	**530**	487
	$ 1,388	$ 1,376

Tooling and engineering inventory represents costs incurred on separately priced tooling and engineering services contracts in excess of billed and unbilled amounts included in accounts receivable.

Perspectives and Analysis

13 Objective
Explain how inventory analysis provides useful information.

Because the amount of inventory that a company carries can have significant economic consequences, it is crucial that inventories be managed effectively. Inventory management is a double-edged sword. On the one hand, management wants to have a wide variety and high quantities on hand so customers have the greatest selection and always find what they want in stock. On the other hand, such an inventory policy may result in excessive carrying costs (e.g., in investment, storage, insurance, taxes, obsolescence, and damage). Low inventory levels, which have the lowest carrying costs, lead to stockouts, lost sales, and unhappy customers. Financial ratios can be used to help management chart a middle course between these two dangers and to help investors assess management's performance. Common ratios that are used to evaluate inventory levels are the inventory turnover and a related measure, average days to sell (or average age of) the inventory.

The **inventory turnover ratio** measures the number of times on average that the inventory was sold during the period. Its purpose is to measure the liquidity of the investment in inventory. A manager may use past turnover experience to determine how long the inventory now in stock will take to be sold. The inventory turnover is calculated by dividing the cost of goods sold by the average inventory on hand during the period.

Unless seasonal factors are significant, average inventory can be calculated from the beginning and ending inventory balances.[27] For example, **Magna International Inc.**, above, reported beginning inventory of $1,376 million, ending inventory of $1,388 million, and cost of goods sold of $19,831 million for its 2005 fiscal year. The calculation of the 2005 inventory turnover of Magna International is shown in Illustration 8-34.

Illustration 8-34
Inventory Turnover Ratio

$$\text{Inventory Turnover} = \frac{\text{Cost of Goods Sold}}{\text{Average Inventory}} = \frac{\$19{,}831}{\frac{\$1{,}376 + \$1{,}388}{2}} = 14.3 \text{ times}$$

A variant of the inventory turnover ratio is the **average days to sell inventory**, which represents the average age of the inventory on hand or the number of days it takes to sell inventory after it is purchased. For example, if Magna's inventory turns over 14.3 times per year, that means it takes, on average, 365 days divided by 14.3 or approximately 25.5 days to sell its average investment in inventory.

Is this a good turnover ratio? If the company sells fresh fruit and vegetables, you would know that this is not a good number. However, for other products, it is not as easy to come to a firm conclusion. For example, Magna provides components, systems, and complete vehicles to the automotive industry. Each industry has its norms, however, so the industry average is one standard that the company's ratio can be compared against. Because the choice of inventory cost formula may affect the inventory reported on the balance sheet and the cost of goods sold, these differences make adjustments necessary in any inter-company comparisons. This is true not only for turnover ratios but for any analysis that includes inventory: the amount of working capital, the working capital ratio, and the gross profit percentage, for example. Internally, company management compares these numbers with its goals and objectives for the year.

[27] Some seasonal variation is common in most companies. The fiscal year end is usually chosen at a low activity point in the year's operations, which means that inventories in the annual financial statements are usually at one of their lowest levels in the year. Internally, management has access to additional information and can make adjustments to use the average monthly inventory level. External users, without access to monthly financial reports, are limited to using the average between the opening and closing annual inventory balances. Public companies are required to report to shareholders on a quarterly basis. In this case, the average can be based on five inventory amounts throughout the year.

There is no absolute standard of comparison for most ratios, but generally speaking, companies that are able to keep their inventory at lower levels with higher turnovers than those of their competitors, and still satisfy customer needs, are the most successful.

Comparison: Canadian and International GAAP

Objective 14
Compare current Canadian and international GAAP.

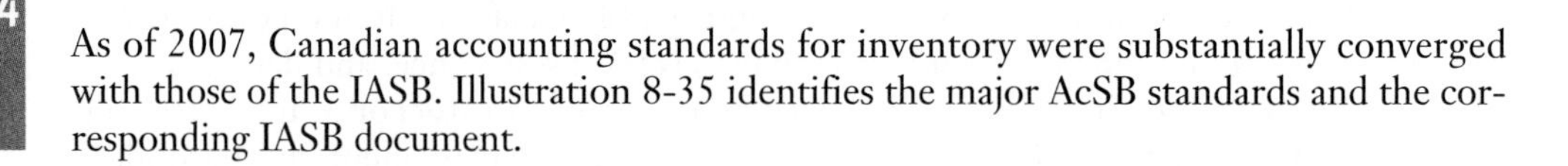

As of 2007, Canadian accounting standards for inventory were substantially converged with those of the IASB. Illustration 8-35 identifies the major AcSB standards and the corresponding IASB document.

Illustration 8-35
Primary Sources of GAAP

Canada	International
Section 3031: Inventories	IAS 2: Inventories
No corresponding section	IAS 41: Agriculture
No corresponding section	IAS 11: Construction contracts
Section 3850: Interest capitalization —disclosure considerations	IAS 23: Borrowing costs

The following significant differences are noted:

Scope. There is no equivalent Canadian standard to IAS 41 for the measurement of agricultural products. The AcSB decided to wait until the international community had more experience in applying fair value measures to this type of inventory. The FASB, IASB, and AcSB are jointly studying fair value measurement, and until they reach a decision, Canadian preparers apply *Handbook* Section 1100 on Generally Accepted Accounting Principles to determine the appropriate methods.

Construction contracts. There is no Canadian equivalent to IAS 11 for construction contracts, although Section 3400, "Revenues," refers to the use of the percentage-of-completion and completed-contract methods. IAS 11 does not permit the completed-contract method, and replaces it instead with the cost recovery method when percentage-of-completion is not appropriate.

Borrowing costs. IAS 23, now harmonized with the U.S. standard, requires interest to be capitalized for qualifying assets. *Handbook* Section 3850 only requires disclosure of the accounting method that has been chosen and the amount of interest capitalized, if applicable. Therefore, Canadian companies applying IAS 23 can also be in compliance with *Handbook* Section 3850.

Purchase commitments. IAS 2 includes a cross reference to IAS 37 in connection with possible liabilities arising from firm sales contracts and purchase commitments. IAS 37 requires that a present obligation under an onerous contract be recognized as a liability to the extent that the costs are higher than the economic benefits that are expected to be received under the contract.[28] Canadian standards do not directly discuss purchase commitments at prices in excess of fair value.

No major changes are expected in the general inventory standards internationally or in Canada in the near future as both standards are relatively new and substantially similar.

Student Website
Glossary
www.wiley.com/canada/kieso

Summary of Learning Objectives

KEY TERMS

allowance method, 455
average days to sell inventory, 463
basket purchase, 443

1 Define and identify categories of inventory.

Only one inventory account, Merchandise Inventory, appears in the financial statements of a merchandising concern. A manufacturer normally has three inventory

[28] According to IAS 37, paragraph 68, an onerous contract is a contract where "the unavoidable costs of meeting the obligations under the contract exceed the economic benefits expected to be received under it."

accounts: Raw Materials, Work in Process, and Finished Goods. There may also be an inventory account for factory or manufacturing supplies.

2 Distinguish between basic perpetual and periodic inventory systems and account for them.

Under a perpetual inventory system, a continuous record of changes in inventory is maintained in the Inventory account. That is, all purchases and transfers of goods into and out of the account (i.e., issues) are recorded directly in the Inventory account as they occur. No such record is kept under a periodic inventory system. Under the periodic system, year-end inventory is determined by a physical count; and the amount of ending inventory and cost of goods sold is based on this count. Even under the perpetual system, an annual count is needed to test the accuracy of the records.

3 Identify the decisions that are needed to determine the inventory value to report on the balance sheet.

To determine the balance sheet inventory amount, you need to decide which physical goods are included in inventory, what expenditures are included in "cost," what cost formula to apply, and finally, whether there has been any reduction in the inventory's value.

4 Determine which inventory items should be included on an enterprise's balance sheet.

Generally, inventory is included on the balance sheet of the enterprise that has legal title to the goods—i.e., the company that has the risks and rewards of ownership. Consigned goods remain the property of the consignor. Exceptions to the general rule of legal title are made when the risks and rewards associated with ownership have been transferred and title has not.

5 Identify the effects of inventory errors on the financial statements and adjust for them.

If the ending inventory is misstated, (1) the inventory, retained earnings, working capital, and current ratio in the balance sheet will be incorrect, and (2) the cost of goods sold and net income in the income statement will be incorrect. If purchases and inventory are misstated, (1) the inventory, accounts payable, and current ratio will be incorrect, and (2) purchases and ending inventory in the income statement will be incorrect.

6 Determine what is included in inventory cost.

Inventory costs include all costs of purchase, conversion, and other costs incurred in bringing the inventories to their present location and condition. Such charges include freight charges on goods purchased, other direct costs of acquisition, and labour and other direct production costs incurred in processing the goods up to the time of sale. Manufacturing overhead costs are allocated to inventory based on the normal capacity of the production facilities.

7 Identify GAAP cost formula options and indicate when each cost formula is appropriate.

The specific identification method is used to assign costs for items of inventory that are not ordinarily interchangeable or that are produced for specific projects. The weighted average or first-in, first-out cost formula is used to assign costs to other types of inventory. All inventory items that have a similar nature and use to the entity use the same cost formula.

8 Explain why inventory is measured at the lower of cost and net realizable value.

Current assets should not be reported on the balance sheet at a higher amount than the net cash that is expected to be generated from their use or sale. When this

consigned goods, 435
conversion costs, 441
cost formula, 444
cost of goods available for sale or use, 433
cost of goods manufactured statement, 429
cost of goods sold, 433
current ratio, 438
cut-off schedule, 435
direct method, 455
finished goods inventory, 428
first-in, first-out (FIFO) cost formula, 448
f.o.b. destination, 434
f.o.b. shipping point, 434
gross method, 439
gross profit method, 459
gross profit percentage, 460
indirect method, 455
inventories, 427
inventory turnover ratio, 463
joint cost, 443
LIFO, 449
lower of cost and net realizable value, 454
market, 452
markup on cost, 460
merchandise inventory, 428
modified perpetual inventory system, 431
moving-average cost formula, 447
net method, 439
net realizable value, 450
period costs, 442
periodic inventory system, 431
perpetual inventory system, 431
product costs, 441
product financing arrangement, 435
purchase commitments, 457
purchase discounts, 439
raw materials inventory, 428
relative sales value method, 443

amount is less than "cost," inventory is written down and the loss in value is recognized in the same period as the decline.

9 Identify and apply the lower of cost and net realizable value standard for inventory.

Net realizable value is the estimated selling price in the ordinary course of business reduced by the expected costs to complete and sell the goods. Ordinarily, each item's cost and NRV are compared and the lower value is chosen. However, items that are related to each other and have similar purposes, are produced and marketed in the same geographical area, and that cannot be evaluated separately from other items may be grouped and the lower of the group's cost and net realizable value is chosen.

10 Explain the accounting issues for purchase commitments.

Accounting for purchase commitments is controversial. Some critics argue that these contracts should be reported as assets and liabilities when the contract is signed; others believe that recognition at the delivery date is more appropriate. Generally, if purchase commitments are significant relative to the company's financial position and operations, they should be disclosed in a note to the financial statements. If a contract requires future payment of a price in excess of the market value at the balance sheet date, the contingent loss is recognized and offset by a liability.

11 Apply the gross profit method of estimating inventory.

Ending inventory can be determined by deducting an estimate of cost of goods sold from the actual cost of goods available for sale. Cost of goods sold is estimated by multiplying net sales by the percentage that cost of goods sold is of sales. This percentage is derived from the gross profit percent: 100 percent − gross profit percentage = cost of goods sold percentage.

12 Identify the inventory disclosures required by GAAP.

In addition to identifying how cost is determined, the amount of inventory that is pledged as security, and the amount charged to the income statement as expense in the period, disclosures are required of the inventories' carrying value by category; the carrying amounts of items with measurements based on NRV or fair value; write-downs and write-down recoveries in the period; and the circumstances responsible for any recovery in value.

13 Explain how inventory analysis provides useful information.

Common ratios that are used in the management and evaluation of inventory levels are the inventory turnover and a related measure, average days to sell the inventory, often called the average age of inventory. This is useful information as excessive investment in inventory is expensive to carry, yet too little inventory results in lost sales and dissatisfied customers.

14 Compare current Canadian and international GAAP.

Recent changes to both IAS 2 and *CICA Handbook* standards on inventory (Section 3031) result in Canadian and international standards being substantially harmonized. There are international but not Canadian standards on the measurement of agricultural and construction inventories, on the capitalization of borrowing costs on qualifying assets, and on purchase commitments, but not major differences in how these costs are accounted for between the two jurisdictions.

Appendix 8A

The Retail Method of Estimating Inventory Cost

15 **Objective**
Apply the retail method of estimating inventory.

Accounting for inventory in a retail operation presents several challenges. Retailers with certain types of inventory can use the specific identification method to value their inventories. As explained in the chapter, this approach makes sense when individual inventory units are significant, such as automobiles, pianos, or fur coats. However, imagine attempting to use such an approach at Canadian Tire, Zellers, or Sears—high-volume retailers that have many different types of merchandise at relatively low unit costs! It would be difficult to determine the cost of each sale, to enter cost codes on the tickets, to change the codes to reflect declines in value of the merchandise, to allocate costs such as transportation, and so on.

An alternative is to estimate inventory cost whenever necessary by taking a physical inventory at retail prices. In most retail businesses, there is an observable pattern between cost and selling prices. Retail prices can then be converted to cost simply by multiplying them by the cost-to-retail ratio. This method, called the **retail inventory method**, **requires that the following information be available: (1) the total cost and retail value of the goods purchased, (2) the total cost and retail value of the goods available for sale, and (3) the sales for the period.**

Here is how it works: The sales for the period are deducted from the retail value of the goods available for sale to produce an estimate of the inventory at retail or selling prices. The ratio of cost to retail for all goods passing through a department or company is determined by dividing the total goods available for sale at cost by the total goods available for sale at retail. The ending inventory valued at retail is then converted to ending inventory at cost by applying the **cost-to-retail ratio**. Use of the retail inventory method is very common. For example, Hart Stores Inc., Reitmans (Canada) Limited, and Hudson's Bay Company all report using the retail inventory method in determining their inventory cost. Reitmans' note disclosure of its policy is shown in Illustration 8A-1.

Illustration 8A-1
Example of Retail Inventory Method Note

Reitmans (Canada) Limited (from its 2006 annual report)

Merchandise inventories are valued at the lower of cost, determined principally on an average basis using the retail inventory method and net realizable value.

An example of how the retail inventory method works is shown in Illustration 8A-2.

Illustration 8A-2
Retail Inventory Method

	Cost	Retail
Beginning inventory	$14,000	$ 20,000
Purchases	63,000	90,000
Goods available for sale	$77,000	110,000
Deduct: Sales		85,000
Ending inventory, at retail		$ 25,000
Ratio of cost to retail ($77,000 ÷ $110,000)		70%
Ending inventory at cost (70% of $25,000)		$ 17,500

To avoid a potential misstatement of the inventory, periodic inventory counts are made, especially in retail operations where losses due to shoplifting and breakage are common. **When a physical count at retail is taken, the inventory cost is determined by multiplying the resulting amount at retail by the cost-to-retail ratio.** Differences between the records and the physical count require an adjustment to make the records agree with the count.

The retail method is approved by various retail associations and the accounting profession, and is allowed (except for methods approximating a LIFO valuation) by the Canada Revenue Agency. **One advantage of the retail inventory method is that the inventory balance can be approximated without a physical count.** This makes the method particularly useful when preparing interim reports. Insurance adjusters use this approach to estimate losses from fire, flood, or other types of casualty.

This method also acts as a control device because any deviations from a physical count at year end have to be explained. In addition, the retail method speeds up the physical inventory count at year end. The crew taking the inventory only needs to record the retail price of each item, which is often done using a scanner. There is no need to determine each item's invoice cost, thus saving time and expense.

Retail Method Terminology

The amounts shown in the Retail column of Illustration 8A-2 represent the original retail or selling prices (cost plus an original markup or mark-on), assuming no price changes.

Sales prices, however, are frequently marked up or down from the original sales price. For retailers, the term **markup** means an increase in the price above the original sales price. **Markup cancellations** are decreases in merchandise prices that had been marked up above the original retail price. Markup cancellations cannot be greater than markups. **Net markups** refer to markups less markup cancellations.

Markdowns are decreases in price below the original selling price. They are a common phenomenon and occur because of a decline in general price levels, special sales, soiled or damaged goods, overstocking, and competition. **Markdown cancellations** occur when the markdowns are later offset by increases in the prices of goods that had been marked down, such as after a one-day sale. A markdown cancellation cannot exceed the original markdown. Markdowns less markdown cancellations are known as **net markdowns**.

To illustrate these different concepts, assume that Designer Clothing Store recently purchased 100 dress shirts from a supplier. The cost for these shirts was $1,500, or $15 a shirt. Designer Clothing established the selling price on these shirts at $30 each. The manager noted that the shirts were selling quickly, so she added $5 to the price of each shirt. This markup made the price too high for customers and sales lagged. The manager then responded by reducing the price to $32. To this point, there has been a **markup of $5** and a **markup cancellation of $3** on the original selling price of a shirt. When the major marketing season ended, the manager set the price of the remaining shirts at $23. This price change constitutes a **markup cancellation of $2** and a **$7 markdown**. If the shirts are later priced at $24, a **markdown cancellation of $1** occurs.

Retail Inventory Method with Markups and Markdowns—Conventional Method

To determine the ending inventory figures using the retail inventory method, a decision must be made on the treatment of markups, markup cancellations, markdowns, and markdown cancellations **when calculating the ratio of cost to retail.**

To illustrate the different possibilities, consider the data for In-Fashion Stores Inc., shown in Illustration 8A-3. In-Fashion's ending inventory at cost can be calculated under two different cost-to-retail ratios.

Ratio A: Reflects a cost percentage that includes net markups but excludes net markdowns.

Ratio B: Reflects a cost ratio that incorporates both the net markups and net markdowns.

Illustration 8A-3

Retail Inventory Method with Markups and Markdowns: In-Fashion Stores Inc.

Information in Records

	Cost	Retail
Beginning inventory	$ 500	$ 1,000
Purchases (net)	20,000	35,000
Markups		3,000
Markup cancellations		1,000
Markdowns		2,500
Markdown cancellations		2,000
Sales (net)		25,000

Retail Inventory Method

	Cost		Retail	
Beginning inventory	$ 500		$ 1,000	
Purchases (net)	20,000		35,000	
Merchandise available for sale	20,500		36,000	
Add:				
Markups		$ 3,000		
Less: Markup cancellations		(1,000)		
Net markups	—		2,000	
	20,500		38,000	
Cost-to-retail ratio $\frac{\$20,500}{\$38,000} = 53.9\%$				(A)
Deduct:				
Markdowns		2,500		
Less: Markdown cancellations		(2,000)		
Net markdowns	—		500	
	$20,500		37,500	
Cost-to-retail ratio $\frac{\$20,500}{\$37,500} = 54.7\%$				(B)
Deduct: Sales (net)			25,000	
Ending inventory at retail			$12,500	

The calculations to determine the cost of ending inventory for In-Fashion Stores are therefore:

Ending inventory at retail × Cost ratio = Ending inventory, at cost	
Under **(A)**:	$12,500 × 53.9% = $6,737.50
Under **(B)**:	$12,500 × 54.7% = $6,837.50

Which percentage should be used to calculate ending inventory? The answer depends on whether you are trying to determine inventory "cost" or a more conservative "lower of cost and market" figure.

The **conventional retail inventory method** **uses the cost-to-retail ratio incorporating net markups but excluding net markdowns** as shown in the calculation of **ratio A. It is designed to approximate the lower of average cost and market, with market being defined as net realizable value less a normal profit margin.** To understand why net markups but not net markdowns are included in the cost-to-retail ratio, we must understand how a retail outlet operates. When a company has a net markup on an item, this normally indicates that the item's market value has increased. On the other hand, if the item has a net markdown, this means that the item's utility has declined. Therefore, to approximate the lower of cost and market, net markdowns are considered a current loss and are not included in calculating the cost-to-retail ratio. **This makes the denominator a larger number and the ratio a lower percentage.** With a lower cost-to-retail ratio, the result approximates a lower of cost and market amount.

To make this clearer, assume two different items were purchased for $5 each, and the original sales price was established at $10 each. One item was then marked down to a selling price of $2. Assuming no sales for the period, if markdowns are included in the cost-to-retail ratio (**ratio B** above), the ending inventory is calculated as shown in Illustration 8A-4.

Illustration 8A-4

Retail Inventory Method Including Markdowns–Cost Method

Markdowns Included in Cost-to-Retail Ratio

	Cost	Retail
Purchases	$10.00	$20.00
Deduct: Markdowns		8.00
Ending inventory, at retail		$12.00
Cost-to-retail ratio $\frac{\$10.00}{\$12.00} = 83.3\%$		
Ending inventory at average cost ($12.00 × .833) =		$10.00

This approach results in ending inventory at the average cost of the two items on hand without considering the loss on the one item.

If markdowns are excluded from the ratio (**ratio A** above), the result is ending inventory at the lower of average cost and market. The calculation is shown in Illustration 8A-5.

Illustration 8A-5

Retail Inventory Method Excluding Markdowns–Conventional Method (LCM)

Markdowns Not Included in Cost-to-Retail Ratio

	Cost	Retail
Purchases	$10.00	$20.00
Cost-to-retail ratio $\frac{\$10.00}{\$20.00} = 50\%$		
Deduct: Markdowns		8.00
Ending inventory, at retail		$12.00
Ending inventory at lower of average cost and market ($12 × .50) =		$6.00

The $6 inventory valuation includes two inventory items, one inventoried at $5 and the other at $1. Basically, for the item with the market decline, the sales price was reduced from $10 to $2 and the cost was reduced from $5 to $1.[29] Therefore, to approximate the lower of average cost and market, the cost-to-retail ratio is established by dividing the cost of goods available by the sum of the original retail price of these goods plus the net markups; the net markdowns are excluded from the ratio.

Many possible cost-to-retail ratios could be calculated, depending on whether or not the beginning inventory, net markups, and net markdowns are included. The schedule below summarizes some inventory valuation methods that are made approximate by the inclusion or exclusion of various items in the cost-to-retail ratio, since net purchases are always included in the ratio:

Beginning Inventory	Net Markups	Net Markdowns	Inventory Cost Formula and Valuation Method Approximated
Include	Include	Include	Average cost
Include	Include	Exclude	Lower of average cost and market (conventional method)
Exclude	Include	Include	FIFO cost
Exclude	Include	Exclude	Lower of FIFO cost and market

Using the FIFO cost formula, the estimated ending inventory (and its cost) will, by definition, come from the purchases of the current period. **Therefore, the opening inventory, at cost and retail, is excluded in determining the cost ratio.** The retail price of the opening inventory is then added to determine the total selling price of goods available for the period.

Handbook Section 3031 is clear that, for purposes of determining inventory **cost**, markdowns below the original sales price are included in determining the ratio. It also specifies that separate estimates are prepared for each retail department.

Special Items Relating to the Retail Method

The retail inventory method becomes more complicated when such items as freight-in, purchase returns and allowances, and purchase discounts are involved. **Freight costs** are treated as a part of the purchase cost. **Purchase returns and allowances** are ordinarily considered a reduction of the cost price and retail price, and **purchase discounts** are usually considered a reduction of the purchase cost. In short, the treatment for the items affecting the cost column of the retail inventory approach follows the calculation of cost of goods available for sale.

Note also that it is considered proper to treat **sales returns and allowances** as adjustments to gross sales; **sales discounts to customers**, however, are not recognized when sales are recorded gross. If the Sales Discount account were adjusted in such a situation, the ending inventory figure at retail would be overvalued.

In addition, a number of special items require careful analysis. **Transfers-in** from another department, for example, are reported in the same way as purchases from an outside enterprise. **Normal shortages** (breakage, damage, theft, shrinkage) are deducted in the retail column because these goods are no longer available for sale. These costs are

[29] The conventional method defines "market" as net realizable value less the normal profit margin. In other words, the sale price of the item marked down is $2, but after subtracting a normal profit of 50% of the selling price, the inventoriable amount becomes $1.

reflected in the selling price because a certain amount of shortage is considered normal in a retail enterprise. As a result, this amount is not considered in calculating the cost-to-retail percentage. Rather, it is shown as a deduction, similar to sales, to arrive at ending inventory at retail. **Abnormal shortages** are deducted from both the cost and retail columns before calculating the cost-to-retail ratio and are reported as a special inventory amount or as a loss. To do otherwise distorts the cost-to-retail ratio and overstates ending inventory. Finally, companies often provide their employees with special discounts to encourage loyalty, better performance, and so on. **Employee discounts** are deducted from the retail column in the same way as sales. These discounts should not be considered in the cost-to-retail percentage because they do not reflect an overall change in the selling price.

Illustration 8A-6 shows some of these treatments in more detail, using the conventional retail inventory method to determine the ending inventory at lower of average cost and market.

Illustration 8A-6

Conventional Retail Inventory Method–Special Items Included

	Cost		Retail
Beginning inventory	$ 1,000		$ 1,800
Purchases	30,000		60,000
Freight-in	600		—
Purchase returns	(1,500)		(3,000)
Totals	30,100		58,800
Net markups			9,000
Abnormal shrinkage	(1,200)		(2,000)
Totals	$28,900		65,800
Deduct:			
Net markdowns			1,400
Sales		$36,000	
Sales returns		(900)	35,100
Employee discounts			800
Normal shrinkage			1,300
Ending inventory at retail			$27,200

Cost-to-retail ratio $\frac{\$28,900}{\$65,800} = 43.9\%$

Ending inventory, lower of average cost and market (43.9% × $27,200) = $11,940.80

Evaluation of Retail Inventory Method

The retail inventory method of calculating inventory is used for these reasons:

1. To permit the calculation of net income without a physical count of inventory
2. As a control measure in determining inventory shortages
3. To control quantities of merchandise on hand
4. As a source of information for insurance and tax purposes

One characteristic of the retail inventory method is that it **has an averaging effect for varying rates of gross profit**. When it is applied to an entire business where rates of gross profit vary among departments, no allowance is made for a possible distortion of results because of these differences. Many companies refine the retail method in such conditions by calculating inventory separately by departments or by classes of merchandise with similar rates of gross profit. In addition, this method's reliability rests on the assumption that the distribution of inventory items is similar to the mix in the total goods available for sale.

Summary of Learning Objective for Appendix 8A

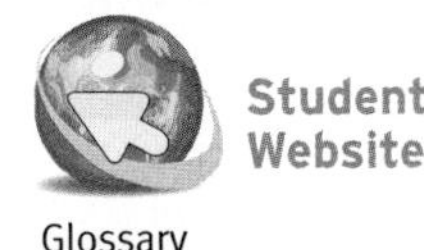

Glossary

www.wiley.com/canada/kieso

15 Apply the retail method of estimating inventory.

The retail inventory method is based on multiplying the retail price of ending inventory (determined by a count or from the accounting records) by a cost-to-retail percentage (derived from information in the accounting and supplementary records). To apply the retail inventory method, records must be kept of the costs and retail prices for beginning inventory, net purchases, and abnormal spoilage, as well as the retail amount of net markups, net markdowns, and net sales. Which items go into the numerator and denominator of the cost-to-retail ratio depends on the type of inventory valuation estimate that is wanted.

KEY TERMS

conventional retail inventory method, 470
cost-to-retail ratio, 467
markdown cancellations, 468
markdowns, 468
markup, 468
markup cancellations, 468
net markdowns, 468
net markups, 468
retail inventory method, 467

Appendix 8B

U.S. Methods: LIFO and LCM

Objective 16
Identify and apply U.S. inventory standards that differ from Canadian and international GAAP.

Application of the LIFO Cost Formula

As indicated in the chapter, U.S. inventory standards differ from the standards applied in Canada and internationally. One major difference is the additional option of using the "last-in, first-out" (LIFO) inventory cost formula. The **LIFO method** assigns costs on the assumption that the cost of the most recent purchase is the first cost to be charged to cost of goods sold. The cost assigned to the inventory remaining, therefore, comes from the earliest acquisitions (i.e., "first-in, still-here").

If a periodic inventory system (or a perpetual system in units only) is used, it is assumed that **the total quantity sold or issued during the period comes from the most recent purchases, even though such purchases may have been made after the actual date of sale.** Conversely, the ending inventory costs consist first of costs from the beginning inventory and then from purchases early in the period.

Illustration 8B-1
Data Used to Illustrate Inventory Calculation: Cost Formula Choice

CALL-MART INC.

Date	Purchases	Sold or Issued	Balance
March 1	(beginning inventory) 500 @ $3.80		500 units
March 2	1,500 @ $4.00		2,000 units
March 15	6,000 @ $4.40		8,000 units
March 19		4,000	4,000 units
March 30	2,000 @ $4.75		6,000 units
	10,000	4,000	

Using the chapter example for Call-Mart Inc., reproduced here as Illustration 8B-1, the assumption is made that the 4,000 units withdrawn and sold consisted of the 2,000 units purchased on March 30 and 2,000 of the 6,000 units purchased on March 15. Therefore, the cost of the ending inventory of 6,000 units is assumed to come from the cost of any beginning inventory (500 units) and then the earliest purchases in the period (1,500 units on March 2 and 4,000 units on March 15). The inventory and related cost of goods sold are calculated as shown in Illustration 8B-2. The cost of goods available for sale of $43,800 was calculated on page 445.

Illustration 8B-2
LIFO Cost Formula–Periodic Inventory

Date of Invoice	No. of Units	Unit Cost	Total Cost
Beginning inventory	500	$3.80	$ 1,900
Mar. 2 purchase	1,500	4.00	6,000
Mar. 15 purchase	4,000	4.40	17,600
Ending inventory	**6,000**		**$25,500**
Cost of goods available for sale	$43,800		
Deduct: Ending inventory	25,500		
Cost of goods sold	**$18,300**		

If a perpetual inventory system is kept in quantities and dollars, applying the last-in, first-out method results in different ending inventory and cost of goods sold amounts, as shown in Illustration 8B-3.

Illustration 8B-3
LIFO Cost Formula–Perpetual Inventory

Date	Purchased	Sold or Issued	Balance	
Mar. 1	Beginning inventory		500 @ $3.80	$ 1,900
Mar. 2	(1,500 @ $4.00) $ 6,000		500 @ 3.80 1,500 @ 4.00	7,900
Mar. 15	(6,000 @ $4.40) 26,400		500 @ 3.80 1,500 @ 4.00 6,000 @ 4.40	34,300
Mar. 19		(4,000 @ $4.40) **$17,600**	500 @ $3.80 1,500 @ 4.00 2,000 @ 4.40	16,700
Mar. 30	(2,000 @ $4.75) 9,500		500 @ $3.80 1,500 @ 4.00 2,000 @ 4.40 2,000 @ 4.75	26,200

The month-end **periodic** inventory calculation presented in Illustration 8B-2 (inventory of $25,500 and cost of goods sold of $18,300) shows a different amount from the **perpetual** inventory calculation (inventory of $26,200 and cost of goods sold of $17,600). This is because the periodic system matches the total withdrawals for the month with the total purchases for the month, whereas the perpetual system matches each withdrawal with the immediately preceding purchases. In effect, the periodic calculation assumed that the goods that were not purchased until March 30 were included in the sale or issue of March 19.

Evaluation of LIFO

Use of the LIFO cost formula is controversial. Arguments for and against the use of LIFO necessarily reflect an individual's view of many fundamental issues about financial accounting: What is relevant? Which financial statement element definitions are primary: assets and liabilities or revenues and expenses?

Reaching a conclusion about LIFO's acceptability in the U.S. is a matter of judgement. Careful reflection on its major advantages and disadvantages tends to indicate that, for most points, the advantages of LIFO become the disadvantages of other cost formula or cost flow methods (FIFO and average cost) and vice versa.

Advantages of LIFO

Matching Matching requires that we deduct costs in the same period as related revenues are recognized. **The principle, however, does not say which costs should be matched when alternatives are available.**

In LIFO, the more recent costs are matched against current revenues to provide what may be viewed as a more realistic measure of current earnings in periods of changing prices. For example, in the early 1990s, many Canadian oil companies changed to the LIFO method. The explanation was as follows in Petro-Canada's financial report: "The change was made to more closely match current costs with current revenues in determination of the results of the Company's operations."

During periods of rising prices, many critics challenge the quality of non-LIFO historical cost-based earnings, noting that by failing to match current costs against current revenues, **"paper"** or **"inventory profits"** are created. **Inventory profits** occur because old low inventory costs that are matched against sales are less than the recent, higher costs to replace the inventory. The cost of goods sold therefore is perceived to be understated and profit is overstated. By using LIFO, rather than FIFO or average cost, more recent costs are matched against revenues and inventory profits are therefore reduced.

Future Earnings Hedge With LIFO, in a period of rising prices, a company's future reported earnings will not be affected substantially by future price declines due to write-downs to a lower net realizable value. LIFO eliminates or substantially minimizes write-downs to market as a result of price decreases. The reason: since the most recent (higher cost) inventory is assumed to be sold first, the ending inventory value ordinarily will be lower than net realizable value. In contrast, inventory with a FIFO cost is more vulnerable to price declines, which can reduce net income substantially. When prices are declining, however, this aspect of LIFO becomes a disadvantage.

Disadvantages of LIFO

Reduced Earnings Many corporate managers view the lower profits that are reported under the LIFO method, compared to other methods, as a distinct disadvantage. They fear that the effect on net income from using LIFO may be misunderstood and that, as a result of the lower profits (assuming rising prices), the company's share price will fall. In fact, though, there is some evidence to refute this argument. Studies have indicated that users of financial data show a sophistication that enables them to recognize the impact on reported income from using LIFO compared with other methods and, as a consequence, consider this when they assess a company's share price.

Inventory Distortion Under LIFO, the inventory valuation on the balance sheet is normally outdated because the oldest costs remain in inventory. This results in several problems, especially in evaluating the amounts, ratios, and related trends that include the ending inventory. The extent of the problem depends on the degree and direction of the changes in price and the rate of inventory turnover.

Physical Flow LIFO does not approximate the items' physical flow except in a few situations.

Inventory Liquidation Use of LIFO raises the problem of **LIFO liquidation**. If the base or layers of old costs in beginning inventory are eliminated (e.g., when units sold during a period exceed the units purchased for a period), strange results can occur as extremely old, low costs get transferred into cost of goods sold.

Poor Buying Habits Because of the liquidation problem, LIFO may cause poor buying habits. A company may simply purchase more goods and match the cost of these goods against revenue to ensure that old costs are not charged to expense. Furthermore, the possibility always exists with LIFO that a company will try to manage (i.e., manipulate) its earnings at year end simply by altering its purchasing pattern.

Acceptability for Tax Purposes LIFO inventory valuation is not accepted by the Canada Revenue Agency for determining taxable income except in a few special circumstances. If Canadian companies want to use LIFO, they are required to maintain information on one of the acceptable methods as well, and use it on their tax return. In the U.S., this is not a concern as companies can use LIFO for tax purposes if they also use it for financial reporting purposes.

Current Cost Income Not Measured LIFO still falls short of measuring current cost (replacement cost) income. When measuring current cost income, the cost of goods sold should consist not of the most recently incurred costs but rather of the cost that will be incurred to replace the goods that have been sold. Using replacement cost is referred to as the next-in, first-out method, which is not currently acceptable for inventory valuation.

Lower of Cost and Market—U.S. Approach

The accounting profession in the United States applies a different approach to inventory valuation for balance sheet purposes—the **lower of cost and market** or lower-of-cost-or-market rule. (The latter term is used mainly in the U.S., while the former term is the Canadian preference.) "Market" could mean replacement cost, net realizable value, or net realizable value less a normal profit margin.

Replacement cost generally means the amount that would be needed to acquire an equivalent item in the normal course of business operations (i.e., buying from usual sources or manufacturing in normal quantities). As indicated earlier in the chapter, **net realizable value (NRV)** is the item's estimated selling price in the ordinary course of business, less the estimated future costs to complete and dispose of the item. **NRV less a normal profit margin** is determined by deducting a normal profit margin from the previously defined NRV amount.

For example, a retailer may have some calculator wristwatches on hand that cost $30.00 each when purchased. If the supplier's catalogue price is now $28.00, this is their replacement cost. If their selling price today is $50.00, and a 10% commission is paid on each sale, the net realizable value is $50.00 less $5.00, or $45.00. If a normal profit margin is 35% of the selling price, the net realizable value less a normal profit margin is $27.50 (i.e., $50 – $5 – [.35 × $50]). Consequently, in this example, the inventory cost is $30 per unit, but under the lower of cost and market rule the inventory could be reported at $28.00 or $30.00 or $27.50, depending on how a particular company defined "market."

Generally, "market" is the item's replacement cost. When applying the lower of cost and market rule, however, "market" cannot exceed net realizable value (a ceiling or upper limit value) or be less than net realizable value less a normal profit margin (a floor or lower limit value).[30] Therefore, the value designated as "market" is the middle value of these three possibilities. Once the designated market has been determined, it is compared with the cost and the lower amount is used for inventory valuation.

This approach is based on the assumption that declines in replacement cost reflect or predict a decline in selling price (realizable value). The ceiling and floor limits are introduced to protect against situations where this assumption is seriously wrong. Consequently, while the underlying objective of reflecting a decline in utility of inventory is common in both Canada and the United States, each country has reached a different conclusion as to how this is best accomplished.

Continuing with the Regner Foods example on pages 454 and 455, the first step is to calculate amounts for all three possible market values, as indicated in columns 2, 3, and 4 of Illustration 8B-4. Given these amounts, the **designated market value** is then chosen.

[30] "Restatement and Revision of Accounting Research Bulletins," *Accounting Research Bulletin No. 43*, (New York: AICPA, 1953), Ch. 4, par. 8.

The designated market value is always the middle value of three amounts: the replacement cost, net realizable value (the ceiling), and net realizable value less a normal profit margin (the floor).

The designated market value is then compared with cost (column 1) to determine the lower of cost and market. This is shown in the illustration.

Illustration 8B-4
Determining Inventory Value–U.S. Approach

Food	Cost	Replacement Cost	Net Realizable Value (Ceiling)	NRV Less a Normal Profit Margin (Floor)	**Designated Market Value**	Final Inventory Value
Spinach	$ 80,000	$ 88,000	$120,000	$104,000	**$104,000**	$ 80,000
Carrots	100,000	90,000	100,000	70,000	**90,000**	90,000
Cut beans	50,000	45,000	40,000	27,500	**40,000**	40,000
Peas	90,000	36,000	72,000	48,000	**48,000**	48,000
Mixed vegetables	95,000	105,000	92,000	80,000	**92,000**	92,000
						$350,000

Glossary

www.wiley.com/canada/kieso

KEY TERMS

designated market value, 477
LIFO method, 474
LIFO liquidation, 476
lower of cost and market (LCM), 477
net realizable value (NRV), 477
net realizable value less a normal profit margin, 477
replacement cost, 477

Summary of Learning Objective for Appendix 8B

16. Identify and apply U.S. inventory standards that differ from Canadian and international GAAP.

The FASB permits the use of the LIFO cost formula in determining inventory cost, and requires a specific formula in determining the lower of cost and market for balance sheet valuation. LIFO assumes that cost of goods sold is made up of the most recent costs and ending inventory of the oldest costs. Inventory is valued on the balance sheet at the lower of cost and market, but "market" is defined as replacement cost. In applying this rule, the value for replacement cost cannot be any higher than net realizable value or lower than NRV less a normal profit margin.

Note: All assignment material with an asterisk (*) relates to the appendices to the chapter.

Brief Exercises

(LO 1) BE8-1 The following assets are included in the December 31 trial balance of Joel Corp.:

Cash	$ 190,000	Work in process	$200,000
Equipment (net)	1,200,000	Receivables (net)	400,000
Prepaid insurance	41,000	Patents	210,000
Raw materials	335,000	Finished goods	150,000

Prepare the current assets section of the December 31 balance sheet.

(LO 2, 6) BE8-2 Alanis Ltd. uses a perpetual inventory system. Its beginning inventory consists of 50 units that cost $35 each. During June, the company purchased 150 units at $35 each, returned 6 units for credit, and sold 125 units at $55 each.

(a) Journalize the June transactions.

(b) Journalize the June transactions assuming that Alanis uses a periodic inventory system.

(c) Assume that Alanis uses a periodic system and prepares financial statements at the end of each month. An inventory count determines that there are 69 units of inventory remaining at June 30. Prepare the necessary adjusting entry at June 30.

BE8-3 Ahmed Corp. purchases inventory costing $5,000 on July 11 on terms 3/10, n/30, and pays the invoice in full on July 15. **(LO 2, 6)**

(a) Prepare the required entries to record the two transactions assuming Ahmed uses (1) the gross method of recording purchases, and (2) the net method of recording purchases. Assume the periodic method is used.

(b) Journalize the two transactions under (1) the gross method and (2) the net method assuming the invoice was paid on July 31 instead of July 15.

BE8-4 Mayberry Ltd. took a physical inventory on December 31 and determined that goods costing $200,000 were on hand. Not included in the physical count were $15,000 of goods purchased from Taylor Corporation, f.o.b. shipping point; and $27,000 of goods sold to Mount Pilot Ltd. for $35,000, f.o.b. destination. Both the Taylor purchase and the Mount Pilot sale were in transit at year end. What amount should Mayberry report as its December 31 inventory? **(LO 4)**

BE8-5 Bravo Ltd. purchases units of wood frames that have manufacturer's rebates from Traders Inc. The rebate requires Bravo to purchase a minimum number of units in a calendar year. The initial unit cost of each wood frame is $2.00 before any rebate. If more than 3,500 units are purchased, the rebate is $0.15 per unit for all units purchased beyond the base amount of 3,500 units. Bravo Ltd. has a June 30 fiscal year end. By June 30, 2008, Bravo had purchased 3,000 wood frames for the six-month period from January 1, 2008 to June 30, 2008. Bravo estimates that an additional 3,000 wood frames will be purchased from July 1, 2008 to December 31, 2008. Bravo's management is very confident that this estimate will be confirmed by future purchases from Traders. **(LO 4, 6)**

(a) Calculate the amount of any rebate that Bravo should accrue at June 30, 2008, assuming the rebate cannot be cancelled by Traders.

(b) Calculate the unit cost that Bravo should use in the costing of wood frames using the perpetual inventory system. (Round to four decimal places.)

BE8-6 Bryars Enterprises Ltd. reported cost of goods sold for 2008 of $1.4 million and retained earnings of $5.2 million at December 31, 2008. Bryars later discovered that its ending inventories at December 31, 2007 and 2008, were overstated by $135,000 and $65,000, respectively. Determine the correct amounts for 2008 cost of goods sold and December 31, 2008, retained earnings. **(LO 5)**

BE8-7 PC Plus buys 1,000 computer game CDs from a distributor that is discontinuing those games. The purchase price for the lot is $5,100. PC Plus will group the CDs into three price categories for resale, as follows: **(LO 6)**

Group	No. of CDs	Price per CD
1	100	$ 5.00
2	800	10.00
3	100	15.00

Determine the cost per CD for each group, using the relative sales value method.

BE8-8 Jose Zorilla Corp. uses a periodic inventory system. On April 19, the company sold 600 units. The following additional information is available: **(LO 7, 16)**

	Units	Unit Cost	Total Cost
April 1 inventory	250	$12	$ 3,000
April 15 purchase	400	14	5,600
April 23 purchase	350	15	5,250
	1,000		$13,850

(a) Calculate the April 30 inventory and the April cost of goods sold using the weighted average cost formula.

(b) Calculate the April 30 inventory and the April cost of goods sold using the FIFO formula.

*(c) Calculate the April 30 inventory and the April cost of goods sold using the LIFO formula.

BE8-9 Data on Jose Zorilla are presented in BE8-8. Assume that Zorilla uses a perpetual inventory system. **(LO 7, 16)**

(a) Calculate the April 30 inventory and the April cost of goods sold using (1) the moving average cost formula and (2) the FIFO cost formula.

*(b) Calculate the April 30 inventory and the April cost of goods sold using the LIFO cost formula.

(c) Prepare a table that summarizes the results of the amounts obtained in parts (a) and (b) above and those of BE8-8. The table should show the amounts arrived at for the amounts reported as inventory and cost of goods sold under the perpetual and periodic systems.

(d) Outline any conclusions or trends that you see based on the table prepared in part (c).

(LO 9) BE8-10 Robin Corporation has the following four items in its ending inventory:

Item	Cost	Net Realizable Value
Jokers	$1,820	$2,100
Penguins	5,000	4,900
Riddlers	4,290	4,625
Scarecrows	3,200	4,210

Determine the total lower of cost and net realizable value inventory value for the ending inventory on an individual item basis.

(LO 9) BE8-11 Battle Inc. uses a perpetual inventory system. At January 1, 2008, inventory was $214,000 at both cost and net realizable value. At December 31, 2008, the inventory was $311,000 at cost and $287,750 at net realizable value. Prepare the necessary December 31 entry under (a) the direct method and (b) the indirect method.

(LO 9) BE8-12 Golden Enterprises Ltd.'s records reported an inventory cost of $45,600 and a net realizable value of $44,000 at December 31, 2007. At December 31, 2008, the records indicated a cost of $64,700 and a net realizable value of $59,625.

(a) Assuming that Golden Enterprises uses a perpetual inventory system, prepare the necessary December 31, 2008, entry under (1) the direct method and (2) the indirect method.

(b) Assume that at December 31, 2009, the records indicate inventory with a cost of $60,000 and a net realizable value of $60,900. Prepare the necessary December 31, 2009, entry under (1) the direct method and (2) the indirect method.

(LO 10) BE8-13 Beaver Corp. signed a long-term non-cancellable purchase commitment with a major supplier to purchase raw materials in 2009 at a cost of $1 million. At December 31, 2008, the raw materials to be purchased have a market price of $965,000.

(a) Prepare any necessary December 31 entry.

(b) In 2009, Beaver paid $1 million to obtain the raw materials, which were worth $915,000. Prepare the entry to record the purchase.

(LO 11) BE8-14 Big Hunt Corporation's April 30 inventory was destroyed by fire. January 1 inventory was $210,000, and purchases for January through April totalled $580,000. Sales for the same period were $700,000. Big Hunt's normal gross profit percentage is 31%. Using the gross profit method, estimate Big Hunt's April 30 inventory that was destroyed by fire.

(LO 11) BE8-15 Refer to the information for Big Hunt Corporation in BE8-14. Assume that instead of a 31% gross profit rate, Big Hunt's markup on cost is 100%. Using the gross profit method, estimate Big Hunt's April 30 inventory that was destroyed by fire.

(LO 13) BE8-16 In its 2005 annual report, Costco Wholesale Corporation reported inventory of $4,014.7 million at the end of its 2005 fiscal year; $3,643.6 million at the end of its 2004 fiscal year; cost of goods sold of $46,347.0 million for the fiscal year 2005; and net sales of $52,935.2 million for fiscal year 2005. Calculate Costco's inventory turnover and the average days to sell inventory for the fiscal year 2005.

(LO 15) *BE8-17 Bikini Inc. had beginning inventory of $12,000 at cost and $20,000 at retail. Net purchases were $127,500 at cost and $185,000 at retail. Net markups were $10,000; net markdowns were $7,000; and sales were $164,500. Calculate the ending inventory at cost using the conventional retail method. Round the cost-to-retail ratio to two decimal places.

Exercises

E8-1 (Periodic versus Perpetual Entries) Fong Corporation sells one product, with information for January as follows: **(LO 2)**

Jan.	1	Inventory	100 units at $5 each
	4	Sale	80 units at $8 each
	11	Purchase	150 units at $6.50 each
	13	Sale	120 units at $8.75 each
	20	Purchase	160 units at $7 each
	27	Sale	100 units at $10 each

Fong uses the FIFO cost formula. All purchases and sales are on account.

Instructions

(a) Assume Fong uses a periodic system. Prepare all necessary journal entries, including the end-of-month adjusting entry to record cost of goods sold. A physical count indicates that the ending inventory for January is 110 units.

(b) Calculate gross profit using the periodic system.

(c) Assume Fong uses the periodic system, and a count on January 31 reports only 102 units in ending inventory. How would your entries in (a) change, if at all? Explain briefly.

(d) Assume Fong uses a perpetual system. Prepare all January journal entries.

(e) Calculate gross profit using the perpetual system.

(f) Assume Fong uses the perpetual system, and a count on January 31 reports only 102 units in ending inventory. How would your entries in (d) change, if at all? Explain briefly.

E8-2 (Determining Merchandise Amounts—Periodic) Two or more items are omitted in each of the following tabulations of income statement data. Fill in the amounts that are missing. **(LO 2)**

	2007	2008	2009
Sales	$315,000	$______	$415,000
Sales returns	11,000	13,000	______
Net sales	______	347,000	______
Beginning inventory	38,000	32,000	______
Ending inventory	______	______	______
Purchases	______	260,000	298,000
Purchase returns and allowances	5,000	8,000	10,000
Transportation-in	8,000	9,000	12,000
Cost of goods sold	233,000	______	293,000
Gross profit on sales	71,000	91,000	102,000

E8-3 (Purchases Recorded—Gross Method and Net Method) Transactions follow for Jennings Limited: **(LO 2, 6)**

May	10	Purchased goods billed at $15,000, terms 3/10, n/60.
	11	Purchased goods billed at $16,575, terms 1/15, n/30.
	19	Paid invoice of May 10.
	24	Purchased goods billed at $11,500, terms 3/10, n/30.

Instructions

(a) Prepare general journal entries for the transactions above, assuming that purchases are to be recorded at net amounts after cash discounts and that discounts lost are to be treated as a financial expense. Assume a periodic inventory system.

(b) Assuming there are no purchase or payment transactions other than the ones mentioned above, prepare the adjusting entry required on May 31 if financial statements are to be prepared as at that date.

(c) Prepare general journal entries for the transactions above, assuming that purchases are to be recorded using the gross method. Assume a periodic inventory system.

(d) Indicate whether there are entries required at May 31 in addition to those in (c) if financial statements are to be prepared. Explain.

(e) Which method would provide the general manager of Jennings with better details for managing the business?

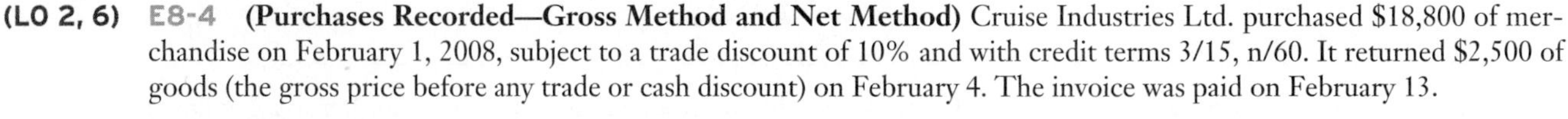

(LO 2, 6) E8-4 **(Purchases Recorded—Gross Method and Net Method)** Cruise Industries Ltd. purchased $18,800 of merchandise on February 1, 2008, subject to a trade discount of 10% and with credit terms 3/15, n/60. It returned $2,500 of goods (the gross price before any trade or cash discount) on February 4. The invoice was paid on February 13.

Instructions

(a) Assuming that Cruise uses the perpetual method for recording merchandise transactions, record the purchase, return, and payment using the gross method.

(b) Assuming that Cruise uses the periodic method for recording merchandise transactions:

1. Record the purchase, return, and payment using the gross method.
2. At what amount would the purchase on February 1 be recorded if the net method were used?

(c) Which method (gross or net) would provide the general manager of Cruise with the better details for managing the business?

(LO 4) E8-5 **(Inventoriable Costs)** In an annual audit of Majestic Company Limited, you find the following transactions near the company's year-end closing date, December 31, 2008:

1. A special machine was made to order for a customer and then specifically put aside in the back part of the shipping room on December 31, 2008. The customer was billed on that date and the machine was not included in inventory although it was not shipped until January 4, 2009.
2. Merchandise costing $2,800 was received on January 3, 2009, and the purchase invoice for it was recorded on January 5. The invoice showed that the shipment was made on December 29, 2008, f.o.b. destination.
3. A packing case containing a product costing $3,400 was in the shipping room when the physical inventory was taken. It was not included in the inventory, because it was marked "Hold for shipping instructions." Your investigation revealed that the customer's order was dated December 18, 2008, but that the case was shipped and the customer billed on January 10, 2009. The product was a stock item of your client.
4. Merchandise costing $680 and received on January 6, 2009, was entered in the purchase journal on January 7, 2009. The invoice showed that it was shipped f.o.b. supplier's warehouse on December 31, 2008. Because it was not on hand at December 31, it was not included in inventory.
5. Merchandise costing $720 was received on December 28, 2008, and the invoice was not recorded. You located it in the hands of the purchasing agent; it was marked "on consignment."

Instructions

Assuming that each amount is material, state whether the merchandise should be included in the client's inventory, and give the reason for your decision.

(LO 4) E8-6 **(Inventoriable Costs—Perpetual)** The Davis Machine Corporation maintains a general ledger account for each class of inventory, debiting the individual accounts for increases during the period and crediting them for decreases. The transactions that follow are for the Raw Materials inventory account, which is debited for materials purchased and credited for materials requisitioned for use:

1. An invoice for $13,600, terms f.o.b. destination, was received and entered January 2, 2009. The receiving report shows that the materials were received on December 28, 2008.
2. Materials costing $28,000, shipped f.o.b. destination, were not entered by December 31, 2008, because they were in a railroad car on the company's siding on that date and had not been unloaded.
3. Materials costing $7,300 were returned to the creditor f.o.b. shipping point on December 29, 2008. The return was entered on that date even though the materials were not expected to reach the creditor's place of business until January 6, 2009.
4. An invoice for $11,500, terms f.o.b. shipping point, was received and entered December 30, 2008. The receiving report shows that the materials were received on January 4, 2009, and the bill of lading shows that they were shipped January 2, 2009.
5. Materials costing $19,800 were received on December 30, 2008. No entry was made for them as of that date, however, because they were ordered with a specified delivery date of no earlier than January 10, 2009.

Instructions

(a) Prepare any correcting journal entries that are required at December 31, 2008, assuming that the books have not been closed. Also indicate which entries must be reversed after closing so that the next period's accounts will be correct.

(b) For item 4 above, what do you believe is the reason that the supplier issued an invoice to Davis Machine Corporation dated December 30, 2008, when the goods were only shipped on January 2, 2009? How should Davis deal with this situation with its supplier?

E8-7 (Inventoriable Costs—Error Adjustments) Craig Corporation asks you to review its December 31, 2008, inventory values and prepare the necessary adjustments to the books. The following information is given to you: **(LO 4, 5)**

1. Craig uses the periodic method of recording inventory. A physical count reveals $279,890 of inventory on hand at December 31, 2008, although the books have not yet been adjusted to reflect the ending inventory.
2. Not included in the physical count of inventory is $13,420 of merchandise purchased on December 15 from Browser. This merchandise was shipped f.o.b. shipping point on December 29 and arrived in January. The invoice arrived and was recorded on December 31.
3. Included in inventory is merchandise sold to Champy on December 30, f.o.b. destination. This merchandise was shipped after it was counted. The invoice was prepared and recorded as a sale on account for $12,800 on December 31. The merchandise cost $7,350, and Champy received it on January 3.
4. Included in inventory was merchandise received from Dudley on December 31 with an invoice price of $15,630. The merchandise was shipped f.o.b. destination. The invoice, which has not yet arrived, has not been recorded.
5. Not included in inventory is $16,040 of merchandise purchased from Glowser Industries. This merchandise was received on December 31 after the inventory had been counted. The invoice was received and recorded on December 30.
6. Included in inventory was $10,438 of inventory held by Craig on consignment from Jackel Industries.
7. Included in inventory is merchandise sold to Kemp, f.o.b. shipping point. This merchandise was shipped after it was counted on December 31. The invoice was prepared and recorded as a sale for $35,900 on December 31. The cost of this merchandise was $17,950, and Kemp received the merchandise on January 5.
8. Excluded from inventory was a carton labelled "Please accept for credit." This carton contains merchandise costing $1,500, which had been sold to a customer for $2,600. No entry had been made to the books to record the return, but none of the returned merchandise seemed damaged.

Instructions

(a) Determine the proper inventory balance for Craig Corporation at December 31, 2008.

(b) Prepare any adjusting entries to bring inventory to its proper amount at December 31, 2008. Assume the books have not been closed.

E8-8 (Inventoriable Costs) The following is a list of items that may or may not be reported as inventory in a company's December 31 balance sheet: **(LO 4, 6)**

1. Goods out on consignment at another company's store
2. Goods sold on an instalment basis
3. Goods purchased f.o.b. shipping point that are in transit at December 31
4. Goods purchased f.o.b. destination that are in transit at December 31
5. Goods sold to another company, and with our company having signed an agreement to repurchase the goods at a set price that covers all costs related to the inventory
6. Goods sold where large returns are predictable
7. Goods sold f.o.b. shipping point that are in transit at December 31
8. Freight charges on goods purchased
9. Freight charges on goods sold
10. Factory labour costs incurred on goods that are still unsold
11. Interest costs incurred for inventories that are routinely manufactured in large quantities
12. Costs incurred to advertise goods held for resale
13. Materials on hand and not yet placed into production by a manufacturing firm
14. Office supplies
15. Raw materials on which a manufacturing firm has started production, but which are not completely processed
16. Factory supplies
17. Goods held on consignment from another company
18. Goods held on consignment by another company
19. Costs identified with units completed by a manufacturing firm, but not yet sold

20. Goods sold f.o.b. destination that are in transit at December 31
21. Temporary investments in shares and bonds that will be resold in the near future
22. Costs of uncleared land to be developed by a property development company

Instructions

Indicate which of these items would typically be reported as inventory in the financial statements. If an item should not be reported as inventory, indicate how it should be reported in the financial statements.

(LO 5) E8-9 **(Inventory Errors—Periodic)** Martine Limited makes the following errors during the current year. Each error is an independent case.

1. Ending inventory is overstated by $120, but purchases are recorded correctly.
2. Both ending inventory and a purchase on account are understated. (Assume this purchase of $550 was recorded in the following year.)
3. Ending inventory is correct, but a purchase on account was not recorded. (Assume this purchase of $710 was recorded in the following year.)

Instructions

Indicate the effect of each error on working capital, current ratio (assume that the current ratio is greater than 1), retained earnings, and net income for the current year and the following year.

(LO 5) E8-10 **(Inventory Errors)** Walker Limited has a calendar-year accounting period. The following errors were discovered in 2008:

1. The December 31, 2006, merchandise inventory had been understated by $21,000.
2. Merchandise purchased on account in 2007 was recorded on the books for the first time in February 2008, when the original invoice for the correct amount of $5,430 arrived. The merchandise had arrived December 28, 2007, and was included in the December 31, 2007, merchandise inventory. The invoice arrived late because of a mix-up by the wholesaler.
3. Accrued interest of $1,300 at December 31, 2007, on notes receivable had not been recorded until the cash for the interest was received in March 2008.

Instructions

(a) Calculate the effect of each error on the 2007 net income.

(b) Calculate the effect, if any, that each error had on the related December 31, 2007, balance sheet items.

(LO 5) E8-11 **(Inventory Errors)** The net income per books of Patrice Limited was determined without any knowledge of the following errors. The 2003 year was Patrice's first year in business. No dividends have been declared or paid.

Year	Net Income per Books	Error in Ending Inventory	
2003	$50,000	Overstated	$ 6,000
2004	52,000	Overstated	9,000
2005	54,000	Understated	12,000
2006	56,000	No error	
2007	58,000	Understated	2,000
2008	60,000	Overstated	8,000

Instructions

(a) Prepare a work sheet to show the adjusted net income figure for each of the six years after taking into account the inventory corrections.

(b) Prepare a schedule that indicates both the original retained earnings balance reported at the end of each year and the corrected amount.

(c) Consider the trends in the increase in income from 2003 to 2008 as originally reported and as revised after the corrections. Would you suspect that the income is being manipulated by adjusting the ending balance in the inventory account?

(LO 5, 9, 13) E8-12 **(Lower of Cost and Net Realizable Value—Effect of Error)** Oickle Corporation uses the lower of FIFO cost and net realizable value method on an individual item basis, applying the direct method. The inventory at December 31, 2008, included product MX. Relevant per-unit data for product MX follow:

Estimated selling price	$45
Cost	40
Replacement cost	46
Estimated selling expense	14
Normal profit	9

There were 1,000 units of product MX on hand at December 31, 2008. Product MX was incorrectly valued at $35 per unit for reporting purposes. All 1,000 units were sold in 2009.

Instructions

(a) Was net income for 2008 overstated or understated? By how much (ignore income tax aspects)?

(b) Was net income for 2009 overstated or understated? By how much?

(c) Indicate whether the current ratio, inventory turnover ratio, and debt-to-total assets ratio would be overstated, understated, or not affected for the years ended December 31, 2008 and December 31, 2009. Explain briefly.

(d) Assume that management did not discover the error in inventory until after the end of the fiscal year but before the closing entries were made and the financial statements were released. Should the adjustment be recorded? How would the error be treated if it were discovered after the financial statements were released?

E8-13 (Relative Sales Value Method) Lu Realty Corporation purchased unimproved land for $55,000. The land was improved and subdivided into building lots at an additional cost of $34,460. These building lots were all the same size but, because of differences in location, were offered for sale at different prices as follows: **(LO 6)**

Group	No. of Lots	Price per Lot
1	9	$3,000
2	15	4,000
3	17	2,400

Operating expenses that were allocated to this project totalled $18,200 for the year. At year end, there were also unsold lots remaining, as follows:

Group 1	5 lots
Group 2	7 lots
Group 3	2 lots

Instructions

Determine the year-end inventory and net income of Lu Realty Corporation.

E8-14 (Cost Allocation and LC and NRV) During 2008, Trainor Furniture Limited purchased a carload of wicker chairs. The manufacturer of the chairs sold them to Trainor for a lump sum of $59,850, because it was discontinuing manufacturing operations and wanted to dispose of its entire stock. Three types of chairs are included in the carload. The three types and the estimated selling price for each are as follows: **(LO 6, 9)**

Type	No. of Chairs	Estimated Selling Price per Chair
Lounge chairs	400	$90
Armchairs	300	80
Straight chairs	700	50

Trainor estimates that the costs to sell this inventory would amount to $2 per chair. During 2008, Trainor sells 350 lounge chairs, 210 armchairs, and 120 straight chairs, all at the same prices as estimated. At December 31, 2008, the remaining chairs were put on sale: the lounge chairs at 25% off the regular price, the armchairs at 30% off, and the straight chairs at 40% off. All were expected to be sold at these prices.

Instructions

(a) What is the total cost of the chairs remaining in inventory at the end of 2008?

(b) What is the net realizable value of the chairs remaining in inventory?

(c) What is the appropriate inventory value to be reported on the December 31, 2008, balance sheet assuming the lower of cost and NRV is applied on an individual item basis?

E8-15 (FIFO and Weighted Average) B.C. Corporation is a multi-product firm. The following information concerns one of its products, the Hawkeye: **(LO 7)**

Date	Transaction	Quantity	Price/Cost
Jan. 1	Beginning inventory	1,000	$12
Feb. 4	Purchase	2,000	18
Feb. 20	Sale	2,500	30
Apr. 2	Purchase	3,000	23
Nov. 4	Sale	2,000	33

Instructions

Calculate cost of goods sold, assuming B.C. uses:

(a) a periodic inventory system and FIFO cost formula.

(b) a periodic inventory system and weighted average cost formula.

(c) a perpetual inventory system and moving average cost formula.

(LO 7) **E8-16** **(Alternative Inventory Methods)** Amos Corporation began operations on December 1, 2008. The only inventory transaction in 2008 was the purchase of inventory on December 10, 2008, at a cost of $20 per unit. None of this inventory was sold in 2008. Relevant information is as follows:

Ending inventory units:		
December 31, 2008		100
December 31, 2009, by purchase date		
—December 2, 2009	100	
—July 20, 2009	50	150

During 2009, the following purchases and sales were made:

Purchases		Sales	
Mar. 15	300 units at $24	Apr. 10	200
July 20	300 units at $25	Aug. 20	300
Sept. 4	200 units at $28	Nov. 18	150
Dec. 2	100 units at $30	Dec. 12	200

The company uses the periodic inventory method.

Instructions

Determine ending inventory under (1) specific identification, (2) FIFO, and (3) weighted average cost.

(LO 7, 16) ***E8-17** **(Calculate FIFO, LIFO, Weighted Average Cost—Periodic)** The following information is for the inventory of mini radios at Cleartone Company Limited for the month of July:

Date	Transaction	Units In	Unit Cost	Total	Units Sold	Unit Price	Total
July 1	Balance	100	$4.10	$ 410			
6	Purchase	800	4.20	3,360			
7	Sale				300	$7.00	$ 2,100
10	Sale				300	7.30	2,190
12	Purchase	400	4.50	1,800			
15	Sale				200	7.40	1,480
18	Purchase	300	4.60	1,380			
22	Sale				400	7.40	2,960
25	Purchase	500	4.58	2,290			
30	Sale				200	7.50	1,500
	Totals	2,100		$9,240	1,400		$10,230

Instructions

(a) Assuming that the periodic inventory method is used, calculate the inventory cost at July 31 under each of the following cost flow formulas:

1. FIFO
2. LIFO
3. Weighted average (Round the weighted average unit cost to the nearest one-tenth of one cent.)

(b) Answer the following questions:

1. Which of the cost flow formulas above will result in the lowest gross profit on the income statement? Explain why.
2. Which of the formulas will yield the highest current ratio? Explain why.

***E8-18 (Calculate FIFO, LIFO, Moving Average Cost—Perpetual)** Information is presented in E8-17 on the inventory of mini radios at Cleartone Company Limited for the month of July. **(LO 7, 16)**

Instructions

Assuming that the perpetual inventory method is used, calculate the inventory cost at July 31 under each of the following cost flow formulas:

(a) FIFO

(b) LIFO

(c) Moving average (Round all unit costs to the nearest one-tenth of one cent.)

(d) Indicate where the inventory costs that were calculated in this exercise are different from the ones in E8-17 and explain the possible reasons for these differences.

E8-19 (Lower of Cost and Net Realizable Value, Periodic Method—Journal Entries) As a result of its annual inventory count, Zinck Corp. determined its ending inventory at cost and at lower of cost and net realizable value at December 31, 2007, and December 31, 2008. This information is as follows: **(LO 9)**

	Cost	Lower of Cost and NRV
Dec. 31, 2007	$421,000	$383,250
Dec. 31, 2008	485,000	451,250

Instructions

(a) Prepare the journal entries required at December 31, 2007 and 2008, assuming that the inventory is recorded directly at market and a periodic inventory system is used.

(b) Prepare the journal entries required at December 31, 2007 and 2008, assuming that the inventory is recorded at cost and an allowance account is adjusted at each year end under a periodic system.

(c) Which of the two methods above provides the higher net income in each year?

E8-20 (Lower of Cost and NRV Valuation Account) The following information is for Candlebox Enterprises Ltd.: **(LO 9)**

	Jan. 31	Feb. 28	Mar. 31	Apr. 30
Inventory at cost	$15,000	$25,100	$27,000	$23,000
Inventory at the lower of cost and net realizable value	14,500	17,600	20,600	17,300
Purchases for the month		20,000	24,000	26,500
Sales for the month		29,000	35,000	40,000

Instructions

(a) Using the above information, prepare monthly income statements (as far as the data permit) in columnar form for February, March, and April. Show the inventory in the statement at cost, show the gain or loss due to fluctuations in NRV separately. Candlebox uses the indirect or allowance method.

(b) Prepare the journal entry that is needed to establish the valuation account at January 31 and the entries to adjust it at the end of each month after that.

E8-21 (Purchase Commitments) At December 31, 2008, Indigo Ltd. has outstanding non-cancellable purchase commitments for 36,000 litres of raw material at $3.50 per litre. The material will be used in Indigo's manufacturing process, and the company prices its raw materials inventory at cost or NRV, whichever is lower. **(LO 10)**

Instructions

(a) Assuming that the market price as at December 31, 2008, is $3.60 per litre, how would this commitment be treated in the accounts and statements? Explain.

(b) Assuming that the market price as at December 31, 2008, is $2.70 per litre instead of $3.60, how would you treat this commitment in the accounts and statements?

(c) Prepare the entry for January 2009, when the 36,000-litre shipment is received, assuming that the situation in (b) existed at December 31, 2008, and that the market price in January 2009 is $2.70 per litre. Explain your treatment.

(LO 11) E8-22 **(Gross Profit Method)** Terry Arthur Company Limited uses the gross profit method to estimate inventory for monthly reports. Information follows for the month of May:

Inventory, May 1	$ 160,000
Purchases	640,000
Freight-in	30,000
Sales	1,000,000
Sales returns	70,000
Purchase discounts	12,000

Instructions

(a) Calculate the estimated inventory at May 31, assuming that the gross profit is 30% of sales.

(b) Calculate the estimated inventory at May 31, assuming that the markup on cost is 30%. Round the gross profit percentage to four decimal places.

(LO 11) E8-23 **(Gross Profit Method)** Mahon Corporation's retail store and warehouse closed for the entire weekend while the year-end inventory was counted. When the count was finished, the controller gathered all the count books and information from the clerical staff, completed the ending inventory calculations, and prepared the following partial income statement for the general manager for Monday morning:

Sales		$2,500,000
Beginning inventory	$ 600,000	
Purchases	1,500,000	
Total goods available for sale	2,100,000	
Less ending inventory	550,000	
Cost of goods sold		1,550,000
Gross profit		$ 950,000

The general manager called the controller into her office after quickly reviewing the preliminary statements. "You've made an error in the inventory," she stated. "My pricing all year has been carefully controlled to provide a gross profit of 42%, and I know the sales are correct."

Instructions

(a) How much should the ending inventory have been?

(b) If the controller's ending inventory amount was due to an error, suggest where the error might have occurred.

(LO 13) E8-24 **(Analysis of Inventories)** The financial statements of The Forzani Group Ltd. for the 52 weeks ended January 29, 2006, January 30, 2005, and February 1, 2004, disclose the following information (in thousands):

	Jan. 29, 2006	Jan. 30, 2005	Feb. 1, 2004
Inventory	$278,002	$278,631	$268,519

	52 weeks ended	
	Jan. 29, 2006	Jan. 30, 2005
Sales	$1,129,404	$985,054
Gross margin	383,091	333,896
Net income	13,757	21,545

Instructions

(a) Calculate Forzani Group's (1) inventory turnover and (2) average days to sell inventory for each of the two years ending in 2006 and 2005.

(b) Calculate Forzani Group's gross profit percentage and percentage markup on cost for each fiscal year.

(c) Is the growth in inventory levels over the last year consistent with the increase in sales? Explain your answer.

E8-25 **(Ratios)** Partial information follows for a Canadian manufacturing company: **(LO 13)**

	Year 6	Year 5	Year 4
Sales	$19,331.9	$______	$11,870.0
Cost of goods sold	______	8,701.5	7,881.1
Gross margin	______	2,739.8	______
Ending inventory	1,877.8	______	1,341.0
Gross profit %	24.9%	______	______
Inventory turnover	6.85	______	
Days sales in inventory	______	______	

Instructions

(a) Enter the missing amounts where indicated for Years 4, 5, and 6 in the above schedule.

(b) Comment on the profitability and inventory management trends, and suggest possible reasons for these results.

***E8-26** **(Retail Inventory Method)** The records of Elena's Boutique report the following data for the month of April: **(LO 15)**

Sales	$115,425	Purchases (at cost)	$ 57,000
Sales returns	2,000	Purchases (at sales price)	102,600
Additional markups	10,000	Purchase returns (at cost)	2,000
Markup cancellations	1,500	Purchase returns (at sales price)	3,000
Markdowns	9,300	Beginning inventory (at cost)	30,000
Markdown cancellations	2,800	Beginning inventory (at sales price)	46,500
Freight on purchases	2,400		

Instructions

(a) Estimate the ending inventory using the conventional retail inventory method.

(b) Assuming that a physical count of the inventory determined that the actual ending inventory at retail prices at the end of April was $33,700, estimate the loss due to shrinkage and theft.

(c) Identify four reasons that the estimate of inventory may be different from the actual inventory at cost.

***E8-27** **(Lower of Cost and Market)** Singing Pump Corp. uses the lower of cost and market method on an individual item basis in pricing its inventory items. The inventory at December 31, 2008, consists of products D, E, F, G, H, and I. Relevant per-unit data for these products follow: **(LO 16)**

	Item D	Item E	Item F	Item G	Item H	Item I
Estimated selling price	$136	$110	$95	$95	$110	$93
Cost	83	80	80	82	50	37
Replacement cost	120	72	70	30	70	30
Estimated selling expense	30	30	30	25	30	30
Normal profit	20	20	20	20	20	20

Instructions

(a) Determine the proper unit value to report on the balance sheet at December 31, 2008, for each inventory item, in accordance with the Canadian accounting standards of reporting.

(b) Use the lower of cost and market rule in accordance with the U.S. methods to determine market values and determine the proper unit value to report on the balance sheet at December 31, 2008, for each inventory item.

Problems

P8-1 The following independent situations relate to inventory accounting:

1. Jag Co. purchased goods with a list price of $210,000, having trade discounts of 20% and 10%, and no cash discounts.
2. Francis Company's inventory of $1.1 million at December 31, 2008, was based on a physical count of goods priced at cost and before any year-end adjustments relating to the following items:
   (a) Goods shipped f.o.b. shipping point on December 24, 2008, from a vendor at an invoice cost of $69,000 to Francis Company were received on January 4, 2009.

(b) The physical count included $29,000 of goods billed to Sakic Corp., f.o.b. shipping point, on December 31, 2008. The carrier picked up these goods on January 3, 2009.

3. Messier Corp. had 1,500 units on hand of part 54169 on May 1, 2008, with a cost of $21 per unit. Messier uses a periodic inventory system. Purchases of part 54169 during May were as follows:

	Units	Unit Cost
May 9	2,000	$22.00
17	3,500	23.00
26	1,000	24.00

A physical count on May 31, 2008, shows 2,100 units of part 54169 on hand.

4. Lindros Ltd., a retail store chain, had the following information in its general ledger for the year 2008:

Merchandise purchased for resale	$909,400
Interest on notes payable to vendors	8,700
Purchase returns	16,500
Freight-in	22,000
Freight-out	17,100
Cash discounts on purchases	6,800

Instructions

Answer the following questions for the situations above and explain your answer in each case:

(a) For situation 1, how much should Jag Co. record as the cost of these goods?

(b) For situation 2, what should Francis report as its inventory amount on its balance sheet?

(c) For situation 3, using the FIFO method, what is the inventory cost of part 54169 at May 31, 2008? Using the weighted average cost formula, what is the inventory cost?

(d) For situation 4, what is Lindros' inventoriable cost for 2008?

P8-2 On February 1, 2008, Goodtime Ltd. began selling scooters that it purchased exclusively from United Motors Inc. United Motors offers vendor rebates based on the volume of annual sales to its customers, and calculates and pays the rebates at its fiscal year end, December 31. Goodtime has a September fiscal year end and uses a perpetual inventory system. The rebate offer that Goodtime received is for a $100 rebate on each scooter that is purchased in excess of 175 units in the calendar year ending December 31. An additional rebate of $40 is given for all units purchased in excess of 200 units in the same year. By September 30, 2008, Goodtime had purchased 190 units from United Motors and had sold all but 35. Although it only made its first purchase on February 1, 2008, Goodtime expects to purchase a total of 250 scooters from United Motors by December 31, 2008. Before arriving at the estimate of 250 scooters, Goodtime's management looked carefully at trends in purchases by its competitors and the strong market for sales of scooters in the coming months. Management is very confident the 250 scooters will be purchased by December 31, 2008.

Instructions

(a) Based on the conceptual framework, discuss the reasoning that Goodtime should use in how it treats the rebate that it expects to receive from United Motors.

(b) Would your opinion change if the rebate that is expected from United Motors had been discretionary?

(c) Discuss some of the factors that management should consider in arriving at a reasonable estimate of its amount of purchases to December 31, 2008.

(d) Calculate the amount of any accrued rebate to be recorded by Goodtime at September 30, 2008, assuming that the rebate is not discretionary and that management has a high degree of confidence in its estimate of the amount of purchases that will occur by December 31, 2008.

(e) Record the accruals that are necessary at Goodtime's fiscal year end of September 30, 2008.

P8-3 Kirk Limited, a manufacturer of small tools, provided the following information from its accounting records for the year ended December 31, 2008:

Inventory at December 31, 2008 (based on physical count of goods in Kirk's plant, at cost, on December 31, 2008)	$1,520,000
Accounts payable at December 31, 2008	1,200,000
Total current assets	2,380,000
Total current liabilities	1,400,000
Net sales (sales less sales returns)	8,150,000

Additional information:

1. Included in the physical count were tools billed to a customer f.o.b. shipping point on December 31, 2008. These tools had a cost of $31,000 and were billed at $43,000. The shipment was on Kirk's loading dock waiting to be picked up by the common carrier.
2. Goods were in transit from a vendor to Kirk on December 31, 2008. The invoice cost was $71,000, and the goods were shipped f.o.b. shipping point on December 29, 2008.
3. Work-in-process inventory costing $38,000 was sent to an outside processor for plating on December 30, 2008.
4. Tools that were returned by customers and awaiting inspection in the returned goods area on December 31, 2008, were not included in the physical count. On January 8, 2009, these tools costing $40,000 were inspected and returned to inventory. Credit memos totalling $55,000 were issued to the customers on the same date.
5. Tools shipped to a customer f.o.b. destination on December 26, 2008, were in transit at December 31, 2008, and had a cost of $21,000. When it was notified that the customer received the goods on January 2, 2009, Kirk issued a sales invoice for $42,000.
6. Goods with an invoice cost of $27,000 that were received from a vendor at 5 p.m. on December 31, 2008, were recorded on a receiving report dated January 2, 2009. The goods were not included in the physical count, but the invoice was included in accounts payable at December 31, 2008.
7. Goods that were received from a vendor on December 26, 2008, were included in the physical count. However, the vendor invoice of $56,000 for these goods was not included in accounts payable at December 31, 2008, because the accounts payable copy of the receiving report was lost.
8. On January 3, 2009, a monthly freight bill in the amount of $7,000 was received. The bill specifically related to merchandise purchased in December 2008, and half of this merchandise was still in the inventory at December 31, 2008. The freight charges were not included in either the inventory account or accounts payable at December 31, 2008.

Instructions

(a) Using the format shown below, prepare a schedule of adjustments to the initial amounts in Kirk's accounting records as at December 31, 2008. Show separately the effect, if any, of each of the eight transactions on the December 31, 2008, amounts. If the transaction has no effect on the initial amount that is shown, write "NONE."

	Inventory	Accounts Payable	Net Sales
Initial amounts	$1,520,000	$1,200,000	$8,150,000
Adjustments increase (decrease)			
1.			
2.			
3.			
4.			
5.			
6.			
7.			
8.			
Total adjustments			
Adjusted amounts	$	$	$

(b) After you arrive at the adjusted balance for part (a) above, determine if the following ratios have improved or if they have deteriorated:

1. Working capital
2. Current ratio
3. Gross profit
4. Profit margin

(AICPA adapted)

P8-4 Capeland Boats Limited, which began operations in 2005, always values its inventories at their current net realizable value. Its annual inventory figure is arrived at by taking a physical count and then pricing each item in the physical inventory at current resale prices. The condensed income statements for the company's past four years are as follows:

	2005	2006	2007	2008
Sales	$850,000	$880,000	$950,000	$990,000
Cost of goods sold	560,000	590,000	630,000	650,000
Gross profit	290,000	290,000	320,000	340,000
Operating expenses	190,000	180,000	200,000	210,000
Income before taxes	$100,000	$110,000	$120,000	$130,000

Instructions

(a) Comment on the procedures that Capeland uses for valuing inventories.

(b) Prepare corrected condensed income statements using an acceptable method of inventory valuation, assuming that the inventory at cost and as determined by the corporation (using net realizable value) at the end of each of the four years is as follows:

Year	At Cost	Net Realizable Value
2005	$130,000	$144,000
2006	144,000	162,000
2007	185,000	172,000
2008	150,000	159,000

(c) Compare the trend in income for the four years using the corporation's approach to valuing ending inventory and using a method that is acceptable under GAAP.

(d) Calculate the cumulative effect of the difference in the valuation of inventory on the ending balance of retained earnings from 2005 through 2008.

(e) Comment on the differences that you observe after making the corrections to the inventory valuation over the four years.

P8-5 Some of the transactions of Dubois Corp. during August follow. Dubois uses the periodic inventory method.

August 10	Purchased merchandise on account, $14,000, terms 2/10, n/30.
13	Returned $1,200 of the purchase of August 10 and received a credit on account.
15	Purchased merchandise on account, $12,000, terms 2/10, n/60.
25	Purchased merchandise on account, $20,000, terms 2/10, n/30.
28	Paid the invoice of August 15 in full.

Instructions

(a) Assuming that purchases are recorded at gross amounts and that discounts are to be recorded when taken:

1. Prepare general journal entries to record the transactions.
2. Describe how the various items would be shown in the financial statements.

(b) Assuming that purchases are recorded at net amounts and that discounts lost are treated as financial expenses:

1. Prepare general journal entries to enter the transactions.
2. Prepare the adjusting entry that is necessary on August 31 if financial statements are prepared at that time.
3. Describe how the various items would be shown in the financial statements.

(c) Which method results in a higher reported gross profit ratio? Explain.

(d) Which of the two methods do you prefer and why?

P8-6 Digby Limited stocks a variety of sports equipment for sale to institutions. The following stock record card for footballs was taken from the records at the December 31, 2008, year end:

Date	Voucher	Terms	Units Received	Unit Invoice Cost	Gross Invoice Amount
January 1	balance	Net 30	90	$20.00	$1,800.00
15	10624	Net 30	50	20.00	1,000.00
March 15	11437	1/5, net 30	65	16.00	1,040.00
June 20	21332	1/10, net 30	90	15.00	1,350.00
September 12	27644	1/10, net 30	84	12.00	1,008.00
November24	31269	1/10, net 30	76	11.00	836.00
	Totals		455		$7,034.00

A physical inventory on December 31, 2008, reveals that 100 footballs were in stock. The bookkeeper informs you that all the discounts were taken. Assume that Digby Limited uses a periodic inventory system and records purchases at their invoice price less discounts. During 2008, the average sales price per football was $21.50.

Instructions

(a) Calculate the December 31, 2008, inventory using the FIFO formula.

(b) Calculate the December 31, 2008, inventory using the weighted average cost formula. (Round unit costs to the nearest cent.)

(c) Prepare income statements for the year ended December 31, 2008, as far as the gross profit line under each of the FIFO and weighted average methods, and calculate the gross profit rate for each. Comment.

(d) If the selling prices for the footballs that were sold follow the same pattern as their wholesale prices from the supplier, might this have an effect on the inventory cost that is reported on the December 31, 2008, balance sheet? (Hint: Review your answers to parts [a] to [c].)

P8-7 The summary financial statements of DeliMart Ltd. on December 31, 2008, are as follows:

DELIMART LTD.
Balance Sheet, December 31, 2008

Assets	
Cash	$ 2,000
Accounts and notes receivable	36,000
Inventory	60,000
Property, plant, and equipment (net)	100,000
	$198,000
Liabilities and Shareholders' Equity	
Accounts and notes payable	$ 50,000
Long-term debt	50,000
Common shares	50,000
Retained earnings	48,000
	$198,000

The following errors were made by the inexperienced accountant on December 31, 2007, and were not corrected:

The inventory was overstated by $15,000. A prepaid expense of $2,400 was omitted (it was fully expensed in 2007). Accrued revenue of $2,500 was omitted (it was recognized when cash was received in 2008). A supplier's invoice for $1,700 for purchases made in 2007 was not recorded until 2008.

On December 31, 2008, there were further errors:

The inventory was understated by $18,000. A prepaid expense of $800 was omitted. Accrued December 2008 salaries of $1,100 were not recognized. Unearned income of $2,300 was recorded in the 2008 revenue. In addition, it was determined that $20,000 of the accounts payable were long-term, and that a $500 dividend was reported as dividend expense and deducted in calculating net income.

The net income reported on the books for 2008 was $55,000.

Instructions

(a) Calculate the working capital, current ratio, and debt-to-equity ratio for DeliMart Ltd. based on the original balance sheet information provided above.

(b) Calculate the corrected net income for 2008.

(c) Prepare a corrected balance sheet at December 31, 2008.

(d) Using the corrected data, recalculate the ratios in part (a). Comment.

P8-8 John Potter established Dilemma Co. as a sole proprietorship on January 5, 2008. At the company's year end of December 31, 2008, the accounts had the following balances (in thousands):

Current assets, excluding inventory	$ 10
Other assets	107
Current liabilities	30
Long-term bank loan	50
Owner's investment (excluding income)	40
Purchases during year	
Jan. 2: 5,000 @ $11	
June 30: 8,000 @ $12	
Dec. 10: 6,000 @ $16	247
Sales	284
Other expenses	40

A count of ending inventory on December 31, 2008, showed there were 4,000 units on hand.

Potter is now preparing financial statements for the year. He is aware that inventory may be costed using the FIFO or weighted average cost formula. He is unsure of which one to use and asks for your assistance. In discussions with Potter, you learn the following:

1. Suppliers to Dilemma provide goods at regular prices as long as Dilemma's current ratio is at least 2 to 1. If this ratio is lower, the suppliers increase their price by 10% in order to compensate for what they consider to be a substantial credit risk.
2. The terms of the long-term bank loan include the bank's ability to demand immediate repayment of the loan if the debt-to-total-assets ratio is greater than 45%.
3. Potter thinks that, for the company to be a success, the rate of return on total assets should be at least 30%.
4. Potter has an agreement with the company's only employee that, for each full percentage point above a 25% rate of return on total assets, she will be given an additional one day off with pay in the following year.

Instructions

(a) Prepare an income statement and a year-end balance sheet assuming the company applies:
1. the FIFO cost formula
2. the weighted average cost formula

(b) Identify the advantages of each formula in (a).

(c) Identify the disadvantages of each formula in (a).

(d) Which method do you recommend? Explain briefly.

(e) Considering the choice of inventory cost formulas that are available, do the ratios that Potter uses adequately measure the financial performance of Dilemma?

P8-9 Bateman Company determined its ending inventory at cost and at lower of cost and market at December 31, 2007, 2008, and 2009, as follows:

	Cost	Lower of Cost and Net Realizable Value
Dec. 31, 2007	$680,000	$680,000
Dec. 31, 2008	880,000	818,400
Dec. 31, 2009	900,000	830,000

Instructions

(a) Prepare the journal entries that are required at December 31, 2008 and 2009, assuming that a periodic inventory system and the direct method of adjusting to NRV are used.

(b) Prepare the journal entries that are required at December 31, 2008 and 2009, assuming that a periodic inventory system is used, with inventory recorded at cost and reduced to NRV through the use of an allowance account.

P8-10 Rashid Corp. lost most of its inventory in a fire in December just before the year-end physical inventory was taken. The corporation's books disclosed the following:

Beginning inventory	$340,000	Sales	$1,300,000
Purchases for the year	780,000	Sales returns	48,000
Purchase returns	60,000	Gross margin on sales	40%

Merchandise with a selling price of $42,000 remained undamaged after the fire. Damaged merchandise with an original selling price of $30,000 had a net realizable value of $10,600.

Instructions

(a) Calculate the amount lost due to the fire, assuming that the corporation had no insurance coverage.

(b) Prepare the journal entry to record the loss and account for the damaged inventory in a separate Damaged Inventory account. In the same entry, record cost of goods sold for the year ended December 31.

(c) How would the loss be classified on the income statement of Rashid Corp.?

(d) While the gross profit percentage has averaged 40% over the past five years, it has been as high as 42% and as low as 37.5%. Given this information, should a range of possible loss amounts be provided instead of a single figure? Explain.

P8-11 Brooks Specialty Corp., a division of FH Inc., manufactures three models of gear shift components for bicycles that are sold to bicycle manufacturers, retailers, and catalogue outlets. Since beginning operations in 1969, Brooks has used normal absorption costing and has assumed a first-in, first-out cost flow in its perpetual inventory system. Except for overhead, manufacturing costs are accumulated using actual costs. Overhead is applied to production using predetermined overhead rates. The balances of the inventory accounts at the end of Brooks' fiscal year, September 30, 2008, follow. The inventories are stated at cost before any year-end adjustments.

Finished goods	$647,000
Work in process	112,500
Raw materials	240,000
Factory supplies	69,000

The following information relates to Brooks' inventory and operations:

1. The finished goods inventory consists of these items:

	Cost	Market
Down tube shifter		
Standard model	$ 67,500	$ 67,000
Click adjustment model	94,500	87,000
Deluxe model	108,000	110,000
Total down tube shifters	270,000	264,000
Bar end shifter		
Standard model	83,000	90,050
Click adjustment model	99,000	97,550
Total bar end shifters	182,000	187,600
Head tube shifter		
Standard model	78,000	77,650
Click adjustment model	117,000	119,300
Total head tube shifters	195,000	196,950
Total finished goods	$647,000	$648,550

2. Half of the finished goods inventory of head tube shifters is at catalogue outlets on consignment.
3. Three-quarters of the finished goods inventory of bar end shifters has been pledged as collateral for a bank loan.
4. Half of the raw materials balance is for derailleurs acquired at a contracted price that is 20% above the current market price. The market value of the rest of the raw materials is $127,400.
5. The total market value of the work-in-process inventory is $108,700.
6. Included in the cost of factory supplies are obsolete items with a historical cost of $4,200. The market value of the remaining factory supplies is $65,900.

7. Brooks applies the lower of cost and net realizable value method to each of the three types of shifters in finished goods inventory. For each of the other three inventory accounts, Brooks applies the lower of cost and net realizable value method to the total of each inventory account.
8. Consider all of the amounts presented above as being material amounts in relation to Brooks' financial statements as a whole.

Instructions

(a) Prepare the inventory section of Brooks' statement of financial position as at September 30, 2008, including any required note(s).

(b) Regardless of your answer to (a), assume that the net realizable value of Brooks' inventories is less than cost. Explain how this decline would be presented in Brooks' income statement for the fiscal year ended September 30, 2008.

(c) Assume that Brooks has a firm purchase commitment for the same type of derailleur that is included in the raw materials inventory as at September 30, 2008, and that the purchase commitment is at a contracted price that is 15% higher than the current market price. These derailleurs are to be delivered to Brooks after September 30, 2008. Discuss the impact, if any, that this purchase commitment would have on Brooks' financial statements prepared for the fiscal year ended September 30, 2008.

(CMA adapted)

***P8-12** The Pendse Wood Corporation manufactures desks. Most of the company's desks are standard models that are sold at catalogue prices. At December 31, 2008, the following finished desks appear in the company's inventory:

Finished Desks	Type A	Type B	Type C	Type D
2008 catalogue selling price	$460	$490	$890	$1,040
FIFO cost per inventory list, Dec. 31, 2008	410	450	830	960
Estimated current cost to manufacture (at Dec. 31, 2008 and early 2009)	460	440	790	1,000
Sales commissions and estimated other costs of disposal	45	60	90	130
2009 catalogue selling price	550	550	870	1,210
Quantity on hand	5	17	13	10

The 2008 catalogue was in effect through November 2008, and the 2009 catalogue is effective as of December 1, 2008. All catalogue prices are net of the usual discounts. Generally, the company tries to obtain a 20% gross margin on the selling price and has usually been successful in achieving this.

Instructions

(a) Assume that the company has adopted a lower of FIFO cost and net realizable value approach for the valuation of inventories and applies it on an individual inventory item basis. At what total inventory value will the desks appear on the company's December 31, 2008, balance sheet?

(b) Assume that 78% of the shares of Pendse Wood were acquired during 2008 by Shripad Inc., a U.S. wood products company that is listed on the Toronto and New York Stock exchanges. The controller of Shripad advises that, for consolidation purposes, Pendse's inventory valuation methods must be consistent with those of the parent company. Shripad uses the U.S. rules for determining the lower of cost and market, and applies its approach on an individual item basis. What inventory value should Pendse's controller be allowed to report to the parent company while still adhering to Canadian GAAP?

(c) Explain the rationale for using the lower of cost and market rule for inventories.

(d) As the controller of Pendse, write a memo to its president in which you explain the accounting and reporting implications of using the valuation determined in (b) for reporting under Canadian GAAP.

(e) What would be the effect on key financial ratios of implementing the U.S. LCM approach?

***P8-13** The records for the Clothing Department of Dar's Discount Store are summarized as follows for the month of January:

Inventory, January 1: at retail, $25,000; at cost, $17,000

Purchases in January: at retail, $142,990; at cost, $90,500

Freight-in: $7,000

Purchase returns: at retail, $3,000; at cost, $2,300

Purchase allowances: $2,200

Transfers in from suburban branch: at retail, $13,000; at cost, $9,200

Net markups: $8,000

Net markdowns: $4,000

Inventory losses due to normal breakage, etc.: at retail, $400

Sales at retail: $117,000

Sales returns: $2,400

Instructions

(a) Estimate the inventory for this department as at January 31 at (1) retail and (2) the lower of average cost and market. Round the cost-to-retail ratio to two decimal places.

(b) Assume that a physical inventory count taken at retail prices after the close of business on January 31 indicated an inventory amount that is $450 less than what was estimated in (a) part (1). What could have caused this discrepancy?

***P8-14** Some of the information found on a detailed inventory card for Leif Letter Ltd. for January is as follows:

	Received		Issued	Balance
Date	No. of Units	Unit Cost	No. of Units	No. of Units
Jan. 1 (opening balance)	150	$2.90		150
2	1,050	3.00		1,200
7			700	500
10	600	3.20		1,100
13			500	600
18	1,000	3.30	300	1,300
20			1,100	200
23	1,300	3.40		1,500
26			800	700
28	1,500	3.60		2,200
31			1,300	900

Instructions

(a) From the above data, calculate the ending inventory based on each of the following cost formulas. Assume that perpetual inventory records are kept in units only. Carry unit costs to the nearest cent and ending inventory to the nearest dollar.

1. First-in, first-out (FIFO)
2. Last-in, first-out (LIFO)
3. Weighted average cost

(b) Based on your results in part (a), and assuming that the average selling price per unit during January was $6.75, prepare partial income statements up to the "gross profit on sales" line. Calculate the gross profit percentage under each inventory cost formula. Comment on your results.

(c) Assume the perpetual inventory record is kept in dollars, and costs are calculated at the time of each withdrawal. Recalculate the amounts under this revised assumption, carrying average unit costs to four decimal places. Would the ending inventory amounts under each of the three cost formulas above be the same? Explain.

Writing Assignments

WA8-1 Jack McDowell, the controller for McDowell Lumber Corporation, has recently hired you as assistant controller. He wishes to determine your expertise in the area of inventory accounting and therefore asks you to answer the following unrelated questions.

Instructions

Write a memo to him that answers each of his questions:

(a) A company is involved in the wholesaling and retailing of automobile tires for foreign cars. Most of the inventory is imported, and it is valued on the company's records at the actual inventory cost plus freight-in. At year end, the warehousing costs are prorated over cost of goods sold and ending inventory. Are warehousing costs considered a product cost or a period cost?

(b) A certain portion of a company's inventory consists of obsolete items. Should obsolete items that are not currently consumed in the production of goods or services to be available for sale be classified as part of inventory?

(c) A company purchases airplanes for sale to others. However, until they are sold, the company charters and services the planes. What is the proper way to report these airplanes in the company's financial statements?

(d) A company wants to buy coal deposits but does not want the financing for the purchase to be reported on its financial statements. The company therefore establishes a trust to acquire the coal deposits. The company agrees to buy the coal over a certain period of time at specified prices. The trust is able to finance the coal purchase and then pay off the loan when it is paid by the company for the minerals. How should this transaction be reported?

WA8-2 Local Drilling Inc. is a Canadian drilling-site company. All of the company's drilling material is purchased by the head office and stored at a local warehouse before being shipped to the drilling sites. The price of drilling material has been steadily decreasing over the past few years. Upon request of the site manager, the drilling material is sent to various sites where it is stored and then used in drilling. When the material is sent, managers are charged the inventory cost based on the cost assigned to the item in the head office records. At any particular time, it is estimated that about one-half of the company's drilling material inventory will be at the local warehouse. Part of each site manager's performance evaluation is based on the net income reported for the site.

Instructions

With the choices of the specific identification, FIFO, and moving-average cost formulas and use of a perpetual inventory system:

(a) Which costing method would you, as a site manager, want to see used? Why?

(b) If FIFO were used, as a site manager what could you do that would help your evaluation when you request inventory? Why, and what might the implications be for the company as a whole?

(c) As the decision-maker at head office, which method would you recommend if you wanted the results to be fair for all site managers? Why?

(d) Which method would you recommend for determining the company's taxable income? Why?

(e) Which method would you recommend for financial statement purposes? Why?

WA8-3 Two of the criteria for evaluating management's performance at Norway Corporation are the inventory turnover ratio and the number of days sales in inventory. The market value of Norway Corporation's inventory has recently declined below its cost. The controller, Harry Fiord, has suggested to management that it may want to switch from the direct method to the allowance method in applying the lower of cost and market rule because it more clearly discloses the decline in market value, and it does not distort the cost of goods sold. The financial vice-president, Krista Mallot, prefers the direct method to write down inventory because it does not call attention to the decline in market value.

Instructions

Answer the following questions:

(a) Is there an ethical issue involved here? Briefly explain.

(b) Is any stakeholder harmed if Krista Mallot's suggestion is used?

(c) What should Harry Fiord do?

WA8-4 The balance sheet valuation of inventory should represent the lower of cost and net realizable value of all inventory owned by a company. The following audit procedures are listed in the external auditor's working papers:

1. Review sales invoices after year end.
2. Review freight documents around year end.
3. Test count a sample of items during the client's physical inventory count and compare the result with the client's count sheets.
4. Review suppliers' invoices and receiving reports both before and after year end.
5. Calculate the gross profit ratio and compare it with the previous year's ratio.
6. During the client's inventory count, select a sample of items from the client's inventory count sheets and count the quantities actually on hand.

Instructions

Give reasons that explain why each of these audit procedures is required.

***WA8-5** Gamble Canada Corporation, a subsidiary of U.S.-based Gamble Texas Corporation, uses the LIFO method for inventory costing. In an effort to lower net income, company president Oscar Gamble tells the plant accountant to take the unusual step of recommending to the purchasing department that it make a large purchase of inventory at year end. The price of the item to be purchased has nearly doubled during the year, and the item represents a major portion of the inventory value.

Instructions

Answer the following questions:

(a) Explain the consequences on the financial statements of the year-end purchase.

(b) Identify the major stakeholders. If the plant accountant recommends the purchase, what are the consequences?

(c) If Gamble Corporation were using the FIFO method of inventory costing, would Oscar Gamble give the same order? Why or why not?

***WA8-6** Harvey Corporation, your client, manufactures paint. The company's president, Andy Harvey, has decided to open a retail store to sell his specialty paint products as well as wallpaper and other supplies that would be purchased from other suppliers. He has asked you for information about the conventional retail method of determining the cost of inventories at the retail store.

Instructions

Prepare a report to the president explaining the retail method of valuing inventories. Your report should include these points:

(a) a description and accounting features of the method

(b) the conditions that may distort the results under the method

(c) a comparison of the advantages of using the retail method to the advantages of using cost methods of inventory pricing

(d) the accounting theory underlying the treatment of net markdowns and net markups under the method

Student Website

www.wiley.com/canada/kieso

Cases

Refer to the Case Primer on the Student Website to help you answer these cases.

CA8-1 Altria Group Inc. is in the consumer packaged goods industry. The company owns 84% of the voting shares of Kraft Foods Inc., and 100% of the voting shares of Philip Morris International Inc., Philip Morris USA Inc., and Philip Morris Capital Corporation. According to the company's annual report, two of the key drivers of growth and long-term shareholder value creation are the company's success at brand building and its dedication to people and commitment to responsibility.

In 2002, 59% of the net revenues and 61% of operating income came from tobacco product sales. Because of the health risks related to the use of tobacco products, the industry is increasingly regulated by government and the company is implicated in substantial tobacco-related litigation.

During 1997 and 1998, the company entered into agreements in the U.S. to settle asserted and unasserted health-care recovery costs and other claims. The agreements, known as the State Settlement Agreements (SSA), impose restrictions on the company mainly in regard to advertising. They also call for payments by the domestic tobacco industry into a fund in the following amounts:

2003	$10.9 billion
2004–2007	$8.4 billion each year
Thereafter	$9.4 billion each year

The fund will be used to settle claims and aid tobacco growers. Each company's share of these payments is based on its market share and Philip Morris records its portion of the settlement costs as cost of goods sold upon shipment. These amounts may increase based on several factors, including inflation and industry volume. In 1999, 2000, and 2001, the company accrued costs of more than $5 billion each year.

Another significant lawsuit, the "Engle Class Action," is still in process. In July 2000, the jury returned a verdict assessing punitive damages against various defendants, and Altria Group was responsible for $74 billion. The company is contesting this and the lawsuit continues. As a result of preliminary judicial stipulations, the company has placed $500 million into a separate interest-bearing escrow account. This money will be kept by the court and distributed to the plaintiffs regardless of the outcome of the trial. The company also placed $1.2 billion into another escrow account, and this amount will be returned to the company if it wins the case.

Instructions

Assume the role of a financial analyst and discuss the related financial reporting issues. Specifically, note alternative accounting treatments for each issue and recommend how each issue should be treated in the financial statements.

CA8-2 Philex Gold Inc. was created in 1996 and is 81%-owned by Philex Mining Corporation. Its shares trade on the TSX Venture Exchange and its objective is to become a substantial low-cost mineral producer in the Philippines. Philex Mining has provided substantial financial support to the company over the past five years as the company is still mainly in the exploration stage. In 2002, the company decommissioned its Bulawan gold mine, which had been in production since 1996. At this point, rehabilitation and reforestation activity is the only activity in the mine.

Over the five-year period, the company carried its gold bullion inventory at net realizable value and recognized revenues on gold sales (net of refining and selling costs) at net realizable value, when the minerals were produced. Gold is a commodity which trades actively and whose price fluctuates according to supply and demand. Below is a chart which shows the price of gold over five recent years.

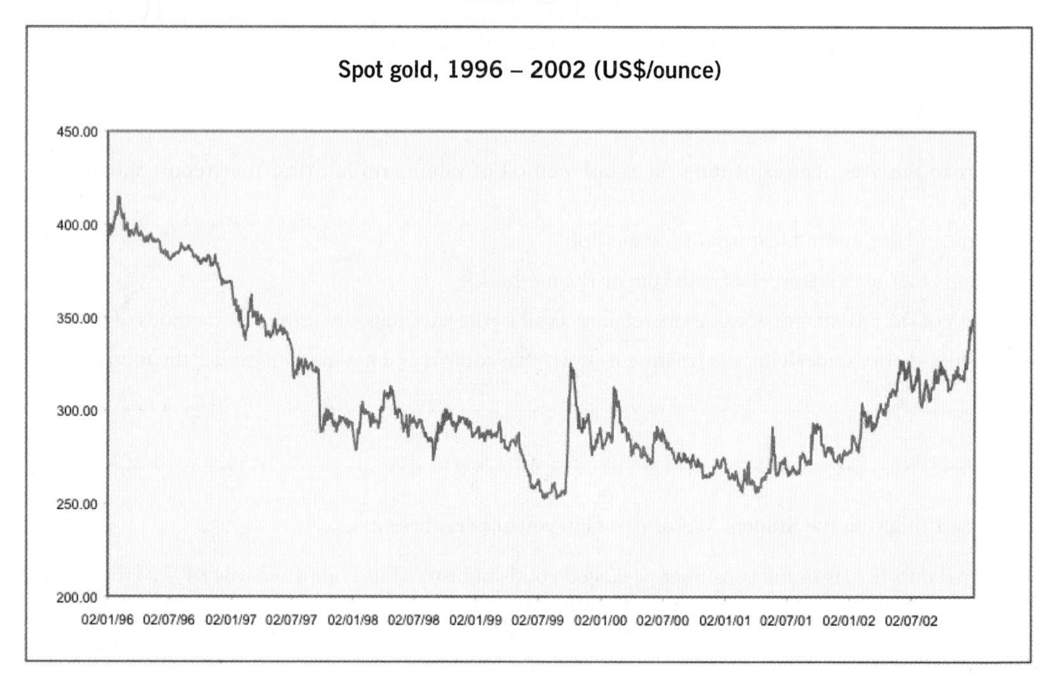

Source: www.gold.org

Instructions

Assume the role of the parent company and assess the financial reporting policies relating to inventory valuation and revenue recognition. Identify any other potential financial reporting issues.

CA8-3 Petro-Canada is one of Canada's largest oil and gas companies, and operates in Canada and internationally. Its shares trade on both the Toronto and New York stock exchanges. The value of the shares rose 88% over a five-year period ending in 2002. Management noted that this growth reflected the company's commitment to creating shareholder value. Natural gas, one of the company's products, is a commodity and its price is therefore affected by supply and demand, which are in turn influenced by weather, political events, and the level of industry inventories.

According to the 2002 annual report, gas prices in 2001 and 2002 were very volatile. Demand decreased due to warmer-than-normal weather conditions and supply increased due to a buildup of gas in storage. These two factors contributed to lower prices. The spot rate for gas declined from $6.57 in 2001 to $4.24 in 2002 (AECO spot price per thousand cubic feet). The company was concerned about continued volatility into 2003 due to the disharmony between the United States and Iraq, as well as a political crisis in Venezuela. The January 2003 cold weather increased demand for natural gas, thus driving prices up.

The company has commitments to purchase natural gas to reduce its exposure to gas price volatility and to manage its fuel costs on fixed-price product sales. It has locked in to buy 600 million cubic feet at $5.99 per thousand cubic feet. Inventory is valued using LIFO and has increased from $455 million to $585 million.

During 2002, Deloitte & Touche LLP became responsible for the audit after Arthur Andersen LLP, the prior auditor, ceased to operate.

Instructions
Adopt the role of Deloitte & Touche LLP and analyze the accounting issues related to the inventory.

CA8-4 Fuego Limited (FL) is a mid-sized business that produces computer paper. During the year, raw material had been increasing significantly in price and FL was finding it difficult to compete since it could not increase its selling prices sufficiently to generate a profit. Its customers, which were primarily "big box" stores (i.e., very large stores that deal with office supplies), threatened to take their business elsewhere if FL did not hold its prices. By year end, the company had significant amounts of inventory and was negotiating with its two largest customers about a price increase. Luckily, raw material prices had begun to decline, making future sales less of a problem, but FL still needed to sell the high-priced inventory on hand in order to at least recover its costs.

Franco Fuego, the company owner, was happy that at least some progress was being made in the discussions and hoped to move the inventory out before year end. Unfortunately, during the night, he was called by the fire department. His warehouse and all the inventory had been burned to the ground. Fire department officials wanted him to see the damages and to ask him a few questions that might help them determine the cause of the fire. Apparently, they had found traces of gasoline in the warehouse. Franco immediately called his insurance company (the inventory and building were fully covered at replacement value as long as there was no foul play).

The insurance company asked whether the company records had also been destroyed. Luckily, Franco kept a backup copy in another location and so he would hopefully be able to help the insurance people determine the value. FL had been using the periodic inventory method and the last count had been at the end of the prior year. While all this was going on, Franco also needed to get draft financial statements to the bank within the next few days since the bank had been monitoring his cash flow situation carefully because his line of credit was almost fully drawn.

Instructions
Adopt the role of Franco Fuego and discuss the financial reporting issues related to the preparation of the current financial statements.

Integrated Case

IC8-1 Bombardier Inc. (BI) is a manufacturer of transportation equipment, including aircraft. It has received significant financing in the past from the Canadian government and is currently in the news asking for an additional $700 million to develop a new line of passenger planes. During the last several years, the company has suffered due to numerous bankruptcies in the aircraft carrier business, which, at least partly, were due to decreased demand for travel after September 11, 2001. In 2004, Paul Tellier, president and CEO, decided to streamline the company and strengthen the balance sheet in the hope of turning the company around.

The company is controlled by the Bombardier family and pays annual dividends. The total debt-to-equity ratio is approximately 7:1—down from approximately 10:1 the prior year. Several of the loan agreements contain debt covenants tied to liquidity and solvency.

The following are excerpts from Bombardier's 2004 annual report:

> **Nature of operations and consolidated financial statement presentation**
> Bombardier Inc. (the "Corporation") is incorporated under the laws of Canada. Bombardier Inc., a diversified manufacturing and services company, is a manufacturer of transportation equipment, including regional and business aircraft and rail transportation equipment. It also provides financial services and asset management in business areas aligned with its core expertise.
>
> Cost of sales – *Aerospace programs*
> Average unit cost for commercial and business aircraft is determined based on the estimated total production costs for a predetermined program quantity. Program quantities are established based on Management's assessment of market conditions and foreseeable demand at the beginning of the production stage for each program, taking into consideration, among other factors, existing firm orders and options.
>
> The average unit cost is recorded to cost of sales at the time of each aircraft delivery. Under the learning curve concept, which anticipates a predictable decrease in unit costs as tasks and production techniques become more efficient through repetition and management action, excess over-average production costs during the early stages of a program are deferred and recovered from sales of aircraft anticipated to be produced later at lower-than-average costs.

Estimates of average unit production costs and of program quantities are an integral component of average cost accounting. Management conducts quarterly reviews as well as a detailed annual review in the fourth quarter, as part of its annual budget process, of its cost estimates and program quantities, and the effect of any revisions are accounted for by way of a cumulative catch-up adjustment to income in the period in which the revision takes place.

Sales incentives

In connection with the sale of new aircraft, the Corporation provides credit guarantees, residual value guarantees and trade-in options to customers. The provisions for losses for credit and residual value guarantees are measured at the time of sale based on the expected net present value of net payments to be made under the guarantees. The provisions for losses for trade-in options are recorded at the amount of the anticipated losses. The Corporation determines expected future payments or losses under the guarantees or trade-in options using, when available, third-party appraisals of expected aircraft value, current credit ratings of guaranteed parties, current and future market conditions, the age and condition of the aircraft and expected availability levels for the aircraft in the market. The provisions are reviewed quarterly and the effect of any revision is recognized in the period in which the revision takes place.

Fractional ownership put options

Under the North American Bombardier Flexjet fractional ownership program, customers purchase fractional shares of a Bombardier business aircraft. The Corporation provides customers with an option to sell back their portion of the aircraft at estimated fair value if the option is exercised within a period of five years from the date of purchase. As at January 31, 2004, the Corporation's commitment to repurchase fractional shares of aircraft based on estimated current fair values totalled $669 million ($985 million as at January 31, 2003).

In addition, certain customers can trade in their fractional shares of aircraft at predetermined amounts for a fractional share of a larger model at predetermined amounts. The total commitment to repurchase fractional shares of aircraft, in exchange for a fractional share of a larger model, was $107 million as at January 31, 2004 ($152 million as at January 31, 2003). The Corporation recorded a $30-million provision as at January 31, 2004 ($32 million as at January 31, 2003) for anticipated losses based on the likelihood that these options will be exercised.

Repurchase obligations

The Corporation has provided certain financing providers and customers, mainly in the transportation segment, the right, under certain conditions, to sell back equipment to the Corporation at predetermined prices. Of the total amount, $224 million as at January 31, 2004 ($233 million as at January 31, 2003) relates to two agreements whereby the Corporation may be required, beginning in 2008, upon customer default on payments to the financing providers, to repurchase the equipment. In addition, on three separate dates, beginning in 2008, the Corporation may also be required to repurchase the equipment. In connection with this commitment, funds have been deposited in a cash collateral account by the customer, which, together with accumulated interest, is expected to entirely cover the Corporation's exposure.

Instructions

Assume the role of the company auditors, Ernst & Young LLP, and analyze the financial reporting issues.

Research and Financial Analysis

RA8-1 Stantec Inc.

Stantec Inc., according to an August 2006 company news release, "provides professional design and consulting services in planning, engineering, architecture, surveying, and project management... from initial concept and financial feasibility to project completion and beyond. Our services are offered through more than 6,000 employees operating out of over 80 locations in North America and the Caribbean."

Stantec's financial statements for its year ended December 31, 2005, are provided in Appendix 5B.

Instructions

(a) Identify the inventory accounts that Stantec reports on its December 31, 2005, balance sheet.

(b) What additional information is provided in the financial statements about this inventory? Taking into account that the *CICA Handbook* Section 3031 requirements did not become effective until 2007, what additional disclosures would you expect Stantec to have to provide in the future?

(c) What amount of cost of goods sold is reported on the statement of income for the year ended December 31, 2005? Explain briefly. What is the company's gross profit percentage for 2005? Compare this with the rate for 2004. Comment briefly. What markup percentage on cost was the company getting in 2005?

(d) How much cash was paid to employees in 2005? Compare this with the cost of goods sold and explain what might cause the difference.

RA8-2 Pacific Safety Products Inc.

Pacific Safety Products Inc., founded in 1984 and headquartered in British Columbia, has as its corporate mission to "bring everyday heroes home safely." According to a recent company news release, it is "an established industry leader in the production, distribution and sale of high performance and high quality safety products...body armor to protect against ballistic, stab and fragmentation threats...and tactical clothing and emergency medical kits." These include bomb and land mine retrieval suits and flame resistant and industrial clothing. The company is engaged in considerable research and development activities, and some of the products that the company developed were featured in the hit movie *Terminator 3: Rise of the Machines*, starring Arnold Schwarzenegger.

Excerpts from the financial statements of Pacific Safety Products (PSP) follow:

CONSOLIDATED BALANCE SHEETS

As at June 30th	2006	2005
ASSETS		
CURRENT ASSETS		
Cash and cash equivalents (note 20)	$ 2,132,886	$ 855,922
Accounts receivable	3,749,043	3,666,650
Inventory (note 4)	4,913,302	4,349,560
Prepaid expenses and deposits	387,654	319,213
Investment tax credits receivable (note 5)	440,263	297,294
Future income taxes recoverable (note 6)	468,656	620,000
Total Current Assets	12,091,804	10,108,639

CONSOLIDATED STATEMENTS OF OPERATIONS AND DEFICIT

For the Years Ended June 30th	2006	2005
SALES (note 17)	$ 32,186,804	$ 16,704,086
COST OF SALES		
Amortization of property, plant and equipment	194,386	178,471
Materials, labour and manufacturing overhead	23,890,824	12,840,795
Total Cost of Sales	24,085,210	13,019,266
GROSS MARGIN	8,101,594	3,684,820

2. SIGNIFICANT ACCOUNTING POLICIES

Inventory
Raw materials are stated at the lower of weighted average cost and replacement cost. Work in process and finished goods are stated at the lower of average cost, which includes direct manufacturing expenses and an allocation of overhead, and net realizable value.

4. INVENTORY

	2006	2005
Raw materials	$ 4,496,851	$ 3,727,471
Work in process	237,312	461,313
Finished goods and samples	179,139	160,776
	$ 4,913,302	$ 4,349,560

Instructions

(a) What type of costs does PSP include in inventory "cost"?

(b) What cost formula (cost flow assumption) does the company use?

(c) How does PSP value its inventory on the balance sheet?

(d) Determine the company's percentages of gross profit on sales and markup on cost for 2005 and 2006. Comment briefly.

(e) Calculate the inventory turnover for the 2006 fiscal year. How old, on average, would you estimate its inventory to be? Comment on any decisions you had to make in calculating the turnover statistic.

(f) PSP manufactures products designed by others to rigid client specifications. The company also develops and manufactures many of its own products, which it protects by patent. Briefly identify how these two processes differ in the type of costs incurred. Do you think all the development and manufacturing costs for its own products are product costs that should be charged to the Inventory account? Explain.

RA8-3 Canadian Tire Corporation, Limited

Refer to the 2005 Annual Report of Canadian Tire Corporation, Limited available on SEDAR (www.sedar.com) or the company's web site (www.canadiantire.ca). Note that the company provides a 10-year financial review at the end of the Annual Report. This summary gives relevant comparative information that is useful for determining trends and predicting the company's future results and position.

Instructions (all amounts in $000)

(a) Prepare three graphs covering the 2001 to 2005 period. The first graph is for net earnings from continuing operations over this five-year period, the second for working capital, and the third for the current ratio. Based on the graphs, predict the values you might expect for the next fiscal period.

(b) Assume that the following errors were discovered after the 2005 financial statements were released:

1. By mistake, invoices for the December 2004 purchases from a major supplier in the amount of $20,000 were not processed through the accounting system until late January 2005, although the ending inventory was correctly stated at year end.
2. At the end of 2005, $10,000 of inventory was excluded from the physical count as it was set aside for delivery to associate dealers. The purchase of this inventory had been correctly recorded in December. The sales invoice to the associate dealers was issued and accounted for in early January 2006 when the delivery was made. (You might want to determine what the company's revenue recognition policy is for shipments of merchandise to dealers.)

(c) Assuming an effective income tax rate of 35%, calculate the correct amount of net earnings from continuing operations, working capital, and the current ratio for all years affected by these errors.

(d) Redraw the trend lines on the graphs developed in part (a).

(e) Do the revised numbers change your expectations for the following year? Comment.

RA8-4 Research

Many companies, such as HydroMississauga and Matsushita Electric of Canada Ltd., have invested in technology to improve their inventory management systems.

Instructions
Research the topic of improvements to inventory management systems, and focus in particular on two examples where companies have been able to change the way they manage this critical asset. Identify what improvements the companies have made. How do these efficiencies affect the balance sheet and income statement, if at all? Be specific.

RA8-5 Magnotta Winery Corporation

Access the annual financial statements of Magnotta Winery Corporation for the year ended January 31, 2006, on the Student Website, SEDAR (www.sedar.com), or the company's website (www.magnotta.com).

Instructions
Refer to these financial statements and the accompanying notes to answer the following questions:

(a) How significant are the inventories relative to total current assets? What categories of inventory does Magnotta Winery report?

(b) Identify all the accounting policies that are the basis for the inventory values reported on the January 31, 2006, balance sheet.

(c) With the release of *CICA Handbook* Section 3031, which became effective in 2007, which of these accounting policies, if any, would you expect to be changed?

(d) What was Magnotta's inventory turnover ratio for the year ended January 31, 2006? What is the average age of the inventory? Comment briefly.

(e) Compare the gross profit ratios for the two most recent years that are reported. Comment briefly.

RA8-6 Sears Canada Inc. versus Hudson's Bay Company

Instructions
From the Student Website, SEDAR (www.sedar.com), or the company websites, access the financial statements of Sears Canada Inc. for its year ended December 31, 2005, and of Hudson's Bay Company for its year ended January 31, 2006. Review the financial statements and answer the following questions:

(a) What is the amount of inventory reported by Sears Canada at December 31, 2005, and by Hudson's Bay at January 31, 2006? What percent of total assets is invested in inventory by each company? How does this compare with the previous year?

(b) Identify the inventory policies for each company that support the inventory values reported on their respective balance sheets.

(c) Calculate and compare the inventory turnover ratios and days to sell inventory for the two companies. If cost of goods sold is not reported, use a surrogate or alternative measure. What choices are there? Identify the limitations of the surrogate you chose, if applicable.

(d) Comment on the results of your calculations in (c) above. Would any differences identified in (b) above help explain differences in the ratios between the two companies?

RA8-7 Research

Identify a company in your local community that develops a product through some form of manufacturing process. Consider a farming operation, a bakery, cement supplier, or other company that converts or assembles inputs to develop a different product.

Instructions
Write a report on the company's inventory. Suggestions: Visit the manufacturing site, view a video of the operation, or speak to company management. Identify what types of costs are incurred in the manufacturing process. Determine which costs are included in inventory cost in the accounting records, and explain why some may be treated as period costs. Does the company use a periodic or a perpetual system? What cost formula does the company use? How does the company determine NRV, or does it?

Food Fortunes

EMPIRE
COMPANY LIMITED

In the 1920s and '30s, when Frank Sobey was expanding his family's grocery store in Nova Scotia, he realized that the company would need a real estate arm to keep control over store locations. This became even more evident through the 1960s and '70s, when large competitors from central Canada could easily win bids for good locations from local developers. "Frank realized he was better off if he bought the site," says Stewart Mahoney, vice-president, treasury and investor relations, at Sobeys' holding company, Empire Company.

Now the Stellarton, Nova Scotia–based Empire Company, which was incorporated in 1983, has three distinct branches: a retail food branch with 71.6% ownership of Sobeys; a real estate branch with 100% ownership of ECL Properties and a 48.3% interest in Crombie REIT, which went public in March 2006; and corporate investments, which include 100% ownership of Empire Theatres, as well as $600 million of investments in "others," says Mahoney. "All the company's various assets and revenues are matched to these three divisions."

Empire is now the largest commercial property owner in Atlantic Canada, with more than 10 million square feet of retail space in 32 enclosed shopping malls, plus several strip malls and big box stores.

The original investment strategy was control, but increasing shareholder value "through income and cash flow growth and equity participation" in other businesses has become a key motivation since then.

Empire's more recent investments include the purchase of Oshawa Foods, creating a national food company with more than 1,300 stores, and the acquisition of 35% of Genstar Development Partnership, a land developer based in Western Canada. Purchased for $29 million, the Genstar shares have since generated more than $100 million in cash returns.

Although Empire does not have a controlling interest in Genstar, it is able to use line-by-line consolidation of the investment on its financial statements. "As they grow, we grow due to our proportionate interest in the company," Mahoney says. ■

Investments

chapter 9

Learning Objectives

After studying this chapter, you should be able to:

1. Explain the difference between strategic and non-strategic investments in financial assets.
2. Define and account for held-to-maturity investments.
3. Identify and account for investments classified as held for trading.
4. Define available-for-sale financial assets and explain how they, and any associated gains and losses, are accounted for and reported.
5. Account for investments in available-for-sale equity instruments.
6. Account for investments in available-for-sale debt instruments.
7. Explain the difference between investments where an investor has no significant influence, has significant influence, or has control, and identify how each type should be accounted for and reported.
8. Explain and apply the equity method of accounting.
9. Explain the basics of consolidation.
10. Identify the differential reporting options available for investments.
11. Explain the objectives of classification, disclosure, and reporting requirements for financial asset investments, and identify several of the major requirements.
12. Compare current Canadian and international GAAP.

Preview of Chapter 9

As the opening vignette implies, companies have different reasons for making long-term investments in other entities. This chapter focuses on the different types of financial asset investments in equity and debt instruments, and how to account for them. In some cases, the nature of the investment determines how it is accounted for and reported, so the classification of these investments is an important first step. This chapter covers investments that are classified as held for trading, held to maturity, or available for sale. The chapter also discusses more strategic investments, such as those where the investor has significant influence over the policies of the investee company or where a parent company actually controls the other company, its subsidiary. The accounting for investments in loans and receivables was covered in Chapter 7.

The chapter is organized as follows:

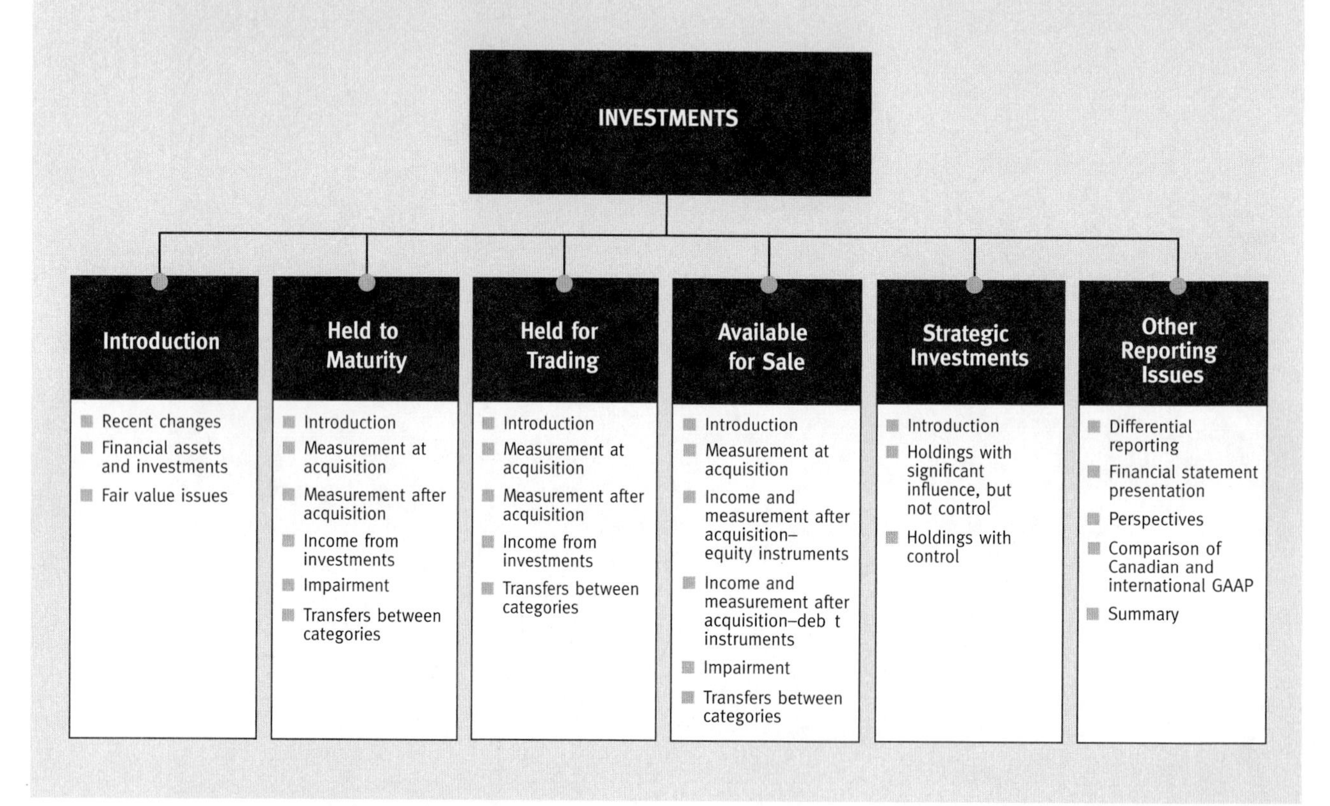

INTRODUCTION

Recent Changes

The deficiencies of the historical cost model have been recognized for a long time, especially in accounting for financial instruments. Because of this, accounting for such instruments has been on the agendas of standard-setting bodies around the world for many years. While many of the inadequacies involved complex issues, such as accounting for derivatives and hedging activities, accounting for ordinary investments in other companies' debt and equity instruments was also at issue.

In its conclusion to the 1997 discussion paper *Accounting for Financial Assets and Financial Liabilities*, a joint committee of the CICA and the International Accounting Standards Committee (now the IASB) strongly favoured a full fair-value model for measuring both primary and derivative instruments. But as there was not enough support to move to a full fair-value model, the AcSB of the CICA eventually issued three *Handbook* sections that substantially harmonized Canadian standards with those of the FASB and IASB. The first three sections in the list that follows became effective in October 2006.[1] Section 3862, effective in October 2007, updates earlier disclosure standards so that they are harmonized with the IASB standards.

Section	*Handbook* Title
1530	Comprehensive Income
3855	Financial Instruments—Recognition and Measurement
3865	Hedges
3862	Financial Instruments—Disclosure

Financial Assets and Investments

The topic of financial instruments is a complex one, but coverage in this chapter is **limited to basic investments in debt and equity instruments.**[2] These represent only some of the broader group of financial assets.

From earlier chapters, we have seen that a **financial asset** is "any asset that is:

(i) cash;

(ii) a contractual right to receive cash or another financial asset from another party;

(iii) a contractual right to exchange financial instruments with another party under conditions that are potentially favourable to the entity; or

(iv) an equity instrument of another entity."[3]

Investors in debt instruments are creditors of the issuing enterprise. Debt instruments include **debt securities** whose prices are normally quoted in an active market such as "investments in government debt, corporate bonds, convertible debt, commercial paper, and securitized debt instruments."[4]

[1] The Canadian standards and the IASB's IAS 39 on financial instruments are much broader in scope than the FASB standards on investments in debt and equity securities.

[2] The topic of derivatives is not included in this chapter. A **derivative** is a financial instrument or other contract that requires little or no initial net investment, that is settled at a future date, and whose value is derived from the level of interest rates, commodity prices, exchange rates, or the level of some other variable. Its value therefore changes as the "underlying" variable changes. Chapter 16 discusses basic contracts such as stock options, rights and warrants, and other derivative instruments. Chapter 7 includes coverage of investments in accounts and notes receivable. Chapters 13 and 14 provide a discussion of financial liabilities, including guarantees, and Chapter 15 reviews the issue of equity securities from the issuing company's perspective. The more complex aspects of financial instruments are left to a course in advanced financial accounting.

[3] *CICA Handbook*, Section 3855.19(b).

[4] *CICA Handbook*, Section 3855.33.

Equity instruments represent ownership interests. Common examples are common, preferred, or other capital stock or shares. They also include rights to acquire or dispose of ownership interests at an agreed-upon or determinable price, such as warrants, rights, and call or put options. An equity instrument is any contract that is evidence of a residual interest in the assets of an entity after deducting all of its liabilities.

Objective 1
Explain the difference between strategic and non-strategic investments in financial assets.

Before looking at how to account for investments, we should understand the **different motivations that companies have for investing** in debt and equity instruments that are issued by other companies. One motivation is **the returns provided by investments** through interest, dividends, or capital appreciation (an increase in the underlying value of the investment). Note that some types of investments provide guaranteed returns (such as term deposits), while others are more risky (such as investments in shares of other companies). Managers may invest for **short-term returns** or **longer-term returns**, depending on their business and whether they need the excess cash for other purposes.

Another reason for investing in equity securities has more to do with **corporate strategy** than returns. Companies may invest in common shares of other companies to influence or control the operations of that company, the **investee**, by exercising their rights as an **investor**. For instance, a strategic investment may give the investing company access to distribution channels or a guaranteed supply of raw materials. The intent is usually to establish a long-term operating relationship between the two entities.

Consider the situation of **Stantec Inc.**, whose financial statements are provided in Appendix 5B. In 2005, Stantec acquired the shares of CPV Group Architects & Engineers Ltd. to strengthen the company's architecture and interior design presence in Canada. Another good example is Montreal-based **Saputo Inc.**'s acquisition of **Molfino Hermanos**, the third-largest dairy processor in Argentina, as part of its strategy to become a world-class cheese company. In the end, however, strategic investments are usually made in order to increase returns to the investor's shareholders.

International Insight

IAS 39 allows a broad group of financial assets to be classified either as a financial asset at fair value through profit or loss, as available for sale, or as held to maturity. U.S. GAAP applies these classifications only to securities.

How investments are accounted for can depend on **the type of instrument** (debt or equity), **management's intent**, which, as noted above, may be quite different from situation to situation, and the **ability to reliably measure the investment's fair value**. The next three sections of this chapter cover straightforward investments in other companies' debt and equity instruments—**situations where the investment does not result in the investor having significant influence or control** over the other company. These investments are classified by accounting standards as either held to maturity, held for trading, or available for sale.

After these sections, strategic investments are reviewed. In these investments, the investor's ownership interest is large enough to give the investor a substantial voice at the investee's boardroom table in decisions about the entity's operations, investments, and financing.

Fair Value Issues

One of the most significant changes in accounting for investments is the requirement to recognize them at their **fair value at acquisition**, and in many cases, again at fair value at each reporting or balance sheet date. What is meant by "fair value"? And what happens to the unrealized holding gains or losses that must be recognized as a consequence?

Fair value is "the amount of the consideration that would be agreed upon in an arm's length transaction between knowledgeable, willing parties who are under no compulsion to act."[5] The best evidence of a financial asset's fair value is a published price quotation in an active market. When there is no active market, other valuation techniques that use mar-

[5] *CICA Handbook*, Section 3855.19(j).

ket-based inputs are used.[6] Unless there is evidence to the contrary, the price paid to acquire an investment is considered to be its fair value.

The price of a debt instrument is usually quoted as a percentage of its par or face value. For example, if a $25,000 face value bond is priced at 99, this means that its fair value is 99% of $25,000, or $24,750. If it is priced at 103.5, it will sell for 103.5% of $25,000, or $25,875. Shares that are traded on a stock exchange are usually quoted at the market price per share in dollars and cents.

How do you determine fair value if an investment's price is not quoted in an active market such as an exchange or by a dealer or broker? If a financial asset is acquired in exchange for non-cash consideration, such as property or services, it may be recognized at the fair value of what is given up. However, clearly determinable values may not be available either for the property or services that are exchanged. In this case, valuation techniques that include information about market conditions that affect the investment are used to estimate the instrument's fair value. The factors that need to be considered include the time value of money, credit risk, indexes of prices of traded equities, market risk premiums, and other market-related information.

Investments in shares are often acquired **on margin**. This means that the investor pays only part of the purchase price to acquire the shares. The rest is financed by the broker. Since the shares legally belong to the investor, the asset is recorded at the full share price and a liability to the broker for the amount that was financed is also recognized.

If financial assets are measured initially at their fair value, how should **transaction costs** directly related to the acquisition—such as fees, commissions, or transfer taxes—be accounted for?[7] The obvious choices are to expense these amounts immediately, or to add them to the cost of the assets acquired, and the answer is—it depends.[8] The accounting standard for each classification of financial asset is explained in the following sections. Regardless of how transaction costs are accounted for at acquisition, transaction costs are **not included** when financial assets are remeasured to their fair value at the balance sheet date.

If a financial instrument is measured at fair value after acquisition, changes in its fair value carrying amount are called **unrealized holding gains or losses**. The change in value is unrealized because it has not been converted to cash or a claim to cash—the asset is still held by the entity. Such gains and losses are only **realized** when the asset is disposed of. Whether the unrealized holding gains or losses are recognized on the income statement or not depends on the classification of the investment.

Illustration 9-1 summarizes the basic approach to accounting for each of the major classifications of non-strategic investments.

---

[6] *CICA Handbook* Section 3855, paragraphs A41 to A65, provides a detailed discussion of fair value measurement considerations.

[7] Brokerage commissions are usually incurred when buying and selling most securities. Commissions vary with the share value and the number of shares/units purchased, but they are often between 1% and 3% of the trade value for smaller trades. For larger trades, the commissions are often substantially lower as a percentage. Discount brokerages offer significant discounts even on smaller trades. Transactions involving mutual funds may have no commission attached to them (no-load funds) but a commission may be charged when the funds are redeemed (back-end commission).

[8] Companies also have a choice of when to recognize (and derecognize) the financial asset. This could be on the trade date, when the commitment is made to buy or sell, or on the settlement date, when the asset is delivered and title is transferred—usually a short time thereafter. When the period between these dates is the standard term for the instrument and the market—termed a **regular-way purchase or sale**—either trade-date or settlement-date accounting may be used. Canadian equities settle in three business days. The same policy is applied consistently to all purchases and sales that belong to the same classification of financial asset and the policy that is chosen is disclosed. This chapter's illustrations assume that trade and settlement dates are the same.

Illustration 9-1
Overview of Accounting for Non-Strategic Investments

	Classification		
	Held to Maturity (HTM)	**Held for Trading (HFT)**	**Available for Sale (AFS)**
Measurement at acquisition	Fair value	Fair value	Fair value
Measurement after acquisition	Amortized cost	Fair value	Fair value (or cost/ amortized cost, if reliable fair value not available)
Transaction costs	Choice: expense immediately or capitalize	Expense immediately	Choice: expense immediately or capitalize
Unrealized holding gains and losses	Not applicable	Recognize in net income	Recognize in OCI; do not recognize in income until realized, or impairment
Impairment losses	Recognize in net income; no reversal permitted	Not applicable	Recognize in net income by transferring unrealized losses from AOCI; no reversal permitted

HELD-TO-MATURITY (HTM) INVESTMENTS

Introduction

Objective 2
Define and account for held-to-maturity investments.

The **held-to-maturity (HTM)** category can only be used for financial assets that have fixed or determinable payments and a fixed maturity date and if the reporting entity has **both (1) the positive intention to hold the investment until its maturity** and **(2) the ability to do so.**[9] Generally, only debt instruments can be classified as this type of investment. A debt investment is not classified as held to maturity if a company intends to hold the financial asset for an undefined period of time or if the issuer can settle the obligation for significantly less than its amortized cost. Likewise, if the investor expects that a sale may be necessary due to changes in interest rates, foreign currency risk, liquidity needs, or other similar reasons, **the investment is not classified as held to maturity.**

Unlike other categories of financial assets, held-to-maturity investments are not accounted for at fair value after acquisition. If management intends to hold the investments to maturity and has no plans to sell them, fair values (selling prices) are not relevant for measuring and evaluating the cash flows associated with them. Therefore, held-to-maturity investments are subsequently measured at their amortized cost. Management reassesses its **intention** and **ability** to hold these investments to maturity at each balance sheet date. Accounting standard setters recognize that fair values are more appropriate measures for most financial assets; thus, the exception to account for them at their amortized cost is allowed **only when these two criteria (i.e., intention and ability to hold to maturity) continue to be met.**

In order to emphasize that this category is very much an exception and to prevent management from choosing accounting treatments based on what it finds most beneficial at a particular time, the classification of investments as held to maturity is further restricted. **An entity is not permitted to classify any financial assets as held to maturity when it has sold or reclassified more than an insignificant amount of held-to-maturity investments before maturity during the current or preceding two fiscal years.** This restriction is not enforced in three situations:

[9] Instruments that meet the definition of loans and receivables are excluded from this classification. Financial assets that meet the HTM definition may also be designated as held for trading or as available for sale when they are first recognized in the books.

1. When the sale or reclassification is so close to the maturity date (e.g., three months) that interest rate changes do not materially affect its fair value
2. When substantially all of the principal that was outstanding at acquisition has been collected
3. When the sale or reclassification is due to a non-recurring, isolated event that is beyond management's ability to anticipate or control[10]

If the disposals or reclassifications are not due to one of these three exceptions, the held-to-maturity classification is **tainted** and **for a period of two years the entity is not permitted to use this classification for any of its financial assets.**

Accounting for held-to-maturity debt investments will be familiar to you. The procedures are almost identical to accounting for long-term notes and loans receivable. You may find it useful to review this section of Chapter 7 before continuing.

Measurement at Acquisition

Like all financial assets, held-to-maturity investments are measured initially at fair value. Companies have two choices in how to account for the transaction costs that they incur in acquiring HTM investments:

1. They can recognize the costs as expenses directly in the income statement.
2. They can add the costs to the initial carrying amount of the asset. In this case, the transaction costs are an adjustment to the premium or discount that is amortized over the investment's life. This requires the effective or yield rate of interest to be recalculated.

The method that management chooses is then applied to all HTM investments and is disclosed.

Measurement after Acquisition

After acquisition, the investment is measured at its **amortized cost**. This is the amount recognized at acquisition reduced by principal repayments, where applicable, plus or minus the cumulative amortization of any discount or premium—i.e., the difference between the initial amount recognized and the maturity value. Impairment charges will also reduce the amortized cost.

Income from Investments Classified as Held to Maturity

Income from debt investments is generally in the form of interest. It can be received in one of two ways, depending on whether the investment is interest-bearing or non-interest-bearing. If it is **interest-bearing**, the party holding the investment on the interest payment date receives all the interest since the last interest payment date. Because debt securities can be bought and sold throughout the year, the practice has developed for the purchaser to pay the seller an amount equal to the interest since the last interest payment date. This interest amount is paid to the seller over and above the agreed exchange price for the investment. If the instrument is **non-interest-bearing**, the price of the bond itself adjusts to its present value at the date of the transaction and no additional amount is paid.

[10] *CICA Handbook*, Section 3855.26. Significance is judged relative to the total amount of investments that are classified as held to maturity.

The total income from an investment is the net cash flow over the time that the investment is held. In the case of financial assets that are held to maturity, the total income is the difference between the principal amount that is received at maturity plus any periodic interest that is received, and the amount paid to acquire the investment including the accrued interest. Because the decision to acquire and hold the investment is based on its yield on the date when it is purchased, the yield rate is also the appropriate rate to measure periodic income over the term that the investment is held.

To illustrate, assume that on January 1, 2008, Robinson Limited pays $92,278 to purchase $100,000 of Chan Corporation 8% bonds.[11] Management determines that this investment meets the criteria for classification as held to maturity. The bonds mature on January 1, 2013, and interest is payable each July 1 and January 1. The discount of $7,722 ($100,000 – $92,278) provides an effective interest rate of 10%. Note that the bond is acquired on an interest payment date and there is therefore no accrued interest for Robinson to acquire and pay for on January 1. Assume Robinson Limited has an August 31 year end.

Robinson's total income is $47,722 over the life of the bonds, calculated as follows:

Cash principal received on maturity of bond	$100,000
Add cash interest received:	
($100,000 × 0.08)/2 × 10 payments	40,000
Less cash paid to acquire the bond	(92,278)
Less cash paid for accrued interest when purchased	-0-
Total income to be recognized	$ 47,722

Because Robinson made the decision to purchase the bond based on its yield, the amount of income that is recognized each period should reflect the yield rate. The **effective interest method** that is used to recognize periodic income results in recognizing a constant yield rate on the investment over the term up to its maturity.

Illustration 9-2 shows the application of the effective interest method to Robinson's investment in the Chan bonds. Note that the method exactly amortizes the discount.

Illustration 9-2

Schedule of Interest Income and Bond Discount Amortization–Effective Interest Method

8% Bonds Purchased to Yield 10%

Date	Cash Received	Interest Income	Bond Discount Amortization	Amortized Cost of Bonds
1/1/08				$ 92,278
7/1/08	$ 4,000[a]	$ 4,614[b]	$ 614[c]	92,892[d]
1/1/09	4,000	4,645	645	93,537
7/1/09	4,000	4,677	677	94,214
1/1/10	4,000	4,711	711	94,925
7/1/10	4,000	4,746	746	95,671

[11] As previously indicated, the value is determined by the investment community and is equal to the present value (PV) of the cash inflows of principal and interest payments on the bond, discounted at the market rate. This is relatively straightforward if the bond is bought/sold on its issue date or on an interest payment due date. At other times, the purchase price of a bond can be estimated as follows:

PV of cash flows on the immediately preceding interest payment date	= $x
Add the increase in PV to date of sale/purchase at yield rate:	
$x × annual yield rate × portion of year since interest payment date	= y
Deduct the cash interest earned since last interest payment date:	
Face value × annual stated rate × portion of year since last interest date	= (z)
Purchase price of a bond bought/sold between interest payment dates:	x + y − z

1/1/11	4,000	4,783	783	96,454
7/1/11	4,000	4,823	823	97,277
1/1/12	4,000	4,864	864	98,141
7/1/12	4,000	4,907	907	99,048
1/1/13	4,000	4,952	952	100,000
	$40,000	$47,722	$7,722	

[a] $4,000 = $100,000 × 0.08 × 6/12
[b] $4,614 = $92,278 × 0.10 × 6/12
[c] $614 = $4,614 − $4,000
[d] $92,892 = $92,278 + $614

The entry to record the purchase of the investment is:

Jan. 1/08	Investment in Chan Corp. Bonds (HTM)	92,278	
	Cash		92,278

A	= L	+	SE
0	0		0

Cash flows: ↓ 92,278 outflow

In practice, **the discount or premium on a bond investment is not usually reported separately**. Instead, a single account is used to record each investment, although a second account could be used to record the discount (or premium) and its amortization.

The journal entry to record the receipt of the first semi-annual interest payment on July 1, 2008 is:

Jul. 1/08	Cash	4,000	
	Investment in Chan Corp. Bonds (HTM)	614	
	Interest Income		4,614

A	= L	+	SE
+4,614			+4,614

Cash flows: ↑ 4,000 inflow

At its year end on August 31, 2008, Robinson recognizes the interest income that has accrued since July 1 and amortizes the discount for the two-month period:

Aug. 31/08	Interest Receivable	1,333	
	Investment in Chan Corp. Bonds (HTM)	215	
	Interest Income		1,548

$4,000 × 2/6 = $1,333
$4,645 × 2/6 = $1,548
$ 645 × 2/6 = $ 215

A	= L	+	SE
+1,548			+1,548

Cash flows: No effect

When the interest payment is received on January 1, 2009, the following entry is made assuming that Robinson does not use reversing entries:

Jan. 1/09	Cash	4,000	
	Investment in Chan Corp. Bonds (HTM)	430	
	Interest Receivable		1,333
	Interest Income		3,097

$ 645 × 4/6 = $ 430
$4,645 × 4/6 = $3,097

A	= L	+	SE
+3,097			+3,097

Cash flows: ↑ 4,000 inflow

Financial Statement Presentation

Illustration 9-3 shows how Robinson Limited reports the items related to its investment in the Chan Corporation bonds in its **August 31, 2008**, financial statements. Note that it is not necessary to state that the bonds are held to maturity on the balance sheet.

Illustration 9-3
Reporting of Held-to-Maturity Investments

BALANCE SHEET	
Current assets	
Interest receivable	$ 1,333
Long-term investments	
Investments in bonds, at amortized cost	$93,107[a]
INCOME STATEMENT	
Other revenue and gains	
Interest income	$ 6,162[b]

[a] $92,278 + $614 + $215 = $93,107
[b] $4,614 + $1,548 = $6,162

Sale of Held-to-Maturity Investments

Assume that Robinson Limited sells its investment in the Chan Corporation bonds on November 1, 2012, at 99¾ plus accrued interest. Interest receivable of $1,333 (2/6 × $4,000) and discount amortization of $317 (2/6 × $952) would have been recognized at the company's August 31, 2012, year end. The following entry is then made on November 1, 2012, to further amortize the discount from September 1 to November 1 and bring the investment to its correct carrying amount at the date of disposal. The discount amortization for this two-month period is $317 (2/6 × $952).

A = L + SE
+317 +317
Cash flows: No effect

Nov. 1/12	Investment in Chan Corp. Bonds (HTM)	317	
	Interest Income		317

The calculation of the realized gain on the sale is explained in Illustration 9-4.

Illustration 9-4
Calculation of Gain on Sale of Bonds

Selling price of bonds ($100,000 × .9975)		$99,750
Less: Carrying amount of bonds on November 1, 2012:		
Amortized cost, July 1, 2012 (see amortization schedule)	$99,048	
Add: Discount amortized for the period July 1, 2012, to November 1, 2012 ($317 to August 31 + $317 from September 1 to November 1)	634	99,682
Gain on sale of bonds		$ 68

The entry to record the sale of the bonds is:

A = L + SE
+1,401 +1,401
Cash flows: ↑ 102,416 inflow

Nov. 1/12	Cash	102,416	
	Interest Receivable		1,333
	Interest Income (2/6 × $4,000)		1,333
	Investment in Chan Corp. Bonds (HTM)		99,682
	Gain on Sale of Bonds (HTM)		68

The credit to Interest Receivable is for the two months of accrued interest at August 31, 2012, and the credit to Interest Income is interest earned from September 1 to November 1, all of which the purchaser pays in cash to Robinson. The debit to Cash is made up of the selling price of the bonds, $99,750, plus the four months of accrued interest, $2,666. The credit to the Investment in Chan Corp. Bonds account is the bonds' carrying amount on the sale date, and the credit to Gain on Sale of Bonds is the excess of the selling price over the bonds' carrying amount or book value.

Remember that selling a held-to-maturity investment before it matures can result in "tainting" all other held-to-maturity investments, with the result that the company is disallowed from using this classification for the next two years. Because the bonds were sold close to their maturity in this case, it is unlikely that this transaction would cause the HTM classification to be tainted.

Impairment of Held-to-Maturity Investments

Investments in financial assets are evaluated at each reporting date to determine if there is any objective evidence that they have suffered **impairment**—a loss in value that is not temporary. A bankruptcy, significant liquidity crisis, or other financial difficulty being experienced by the issuer of the instrument are examples of situations in which a loss in value to the investor may be more than just a short-term fluctuation. In addition, if there are problems in the technological, legal, economic, and/or market environments that the issuer operates in, this too could mean that the carrying amount may not be recoverable.[12]

For held-to-maturity investments, the objective is to determine if it is probable that the investor will be unable to collect all the amounts that are due to the investor according to the contractual terms. If objective evidence supports this conclusion, the investment is impaired and **written down to its fair value and the loss is recognized in net income for the period**. The investment is written down directly, or through the use of a "contra" allowance account. No reversal of the write-down is permitted while the asset is held.

International Insight

Under IAS 39, the investment is written down to the present value of the future cash flows using the original discount rate at acquisition of the instrument. If an event that reduces the impairment occurs after the write-down, the write-down can be reversed.

Transfers between Categories

As indicated above, at each balance sheet date companies are required to reassess their intention and ability to hold investments that they have classified as held to maturity. Entities must have very good reasons for reclassifying an investment; otherwise, they risk tainting the category.

Any investments that do not meet the **intent** and **ability-to-hold** criteria are reclassified as available for sale and are remeasured at their fair value. In situations where the held-to-maturity classification has been tainted due to sales or reclassifications that did not meet a permitted exception, all remaining held-to-maturity investments are reclassified to the available-for-sale category. The difference between the investments' amortized cost and fair value on this date is reported in other comprehensive income. This will be explained more fully in this chapter in the section on available-for-sale investments.

[12] *CICA Handbook*, Section 3855.A67 and A69.

HELD-FOR-TRADING (HFT) INVESTMENTS

Introduction

Objective 3
Identify and account for investments classified as held for trading.

When investments in debt and equity instruments are classified as held for trading, the accounting result closely matches the way the instruments are actually managed. The **held-for-trading (HFT)** category is the **mandatory** classification for financial assets other than loans or receivables, that are acquired to sell in the near term, or as part of a portfolio of managed financial assets with a history of short-term profit-taking. "Trading" in this context means frequent buying and selling, usually to generate profits from short-term differences in price. "Near term" is defined as not more than one year from the date of the financial statements.[13]

Traded securities are often highly marketable, which gives the company the flexibility to liquidate the investments when cash is needed. Specific examples of such investments include short-term paper (certificates of deposit, treasury bills, and commercial paper), debt securities (government and corporate bonds), and equity instruments (preferred and common shares, options, and warrants). While they are similar to the cash equivalents discussed in Chapter 7, these investments may be longer term than cash equivalents and include equity as well as debt and money-market instruments. Such instruments may be described as trading or temporary investments, marketable securities, or investments at fair value with gains and losses to income—there is no requirement to use the held-for-trading classification title.

International Insight

IAS 39 refers to these trading assets as financial assets "at fair value through profit or loss."

Handbook Section 3855 also gives companies an **option to classify almost any financial instrument as held for trading**, as long as the investment is designated as this when it is first recognized. The standard indicates that "designation of a financial instrument as held for trading is not precluded simply because the entity does not intend to sell" it in the short term.[14] Because HFT instruments are carried in the accounts at their fair value and changes in their value are reported in net income, the choice to designate other instruments as held for trading is known as the **fair value option**. Once an instrument is designated in this way, however, the classification cannot be changed.

Investments where management has chosen to apply the fair value option may be short-term (current) or long-term assets. They, too, can be described in a number of ways on the balance sheet including "investments at fair value with gains and losses to income."

Measurement at Acquisition

When investments classified as held for trading are acquired, they are recognized at their fair value. Fair values are readily available for short-term trading investments that must be classified as HFT. In cases where a company has chosen the fair value option, the fair values must be readily available. Unlike held-to-maturity investments, however, **when financial assets are classified as held for trading, all transaction costs must be recognized as expense as they are incurred.**

Measurement after Acquisition

The carrying amount of each held-for-trading investment is adjusted to its current fair value at each reporting date. The resulting unrealized holding gains and losses are reported in net income. A **holding gain or loss** is the net change in an investment's carrying amount

[13] *CICA Handbook*, Section 1508 on Measurement Uncertainty, par. .02.

[14] The exclusions are financial instruments that are not covered by *Handbook* Section 3855, or whose fair value cannot be reliably measured, or if they were not previously classified as held for trading and have been transferred in a related party transaction.

as a result of adjusting it to its new fair value amount (not including any dividend or interest income that has been recognized but not yet received).

Income from Investments Held for Trading

As explained for investments held to maturity, the total income on any investment is always the net cash flow from the investment—the gain or loss on the instrument itself plus any interest or dividend return. Accounting for income on an investment is the art of allocating the total income to specific accounting periods.

For HFT investments, **periodic income** is a combination of the change in an investment's carrying amount plus the interest or dividend income that has been received or is receivable for the period. For many investments classified as HFT, it is not important that interest and dividend income be reported separately from the holding gains or losses. Both are generally accounted for and reported together because this tends to mirror how such investments are managed.

No Separate Reporting of Interest Income

Assume that Investor Inc. acquires a temporary investment in $20,000 face value, 10% Sorfit Ltd. bonds on June 15. The bonds pay interest semi-annually on January 15 and July 15 each year. Investor pays $21,300 for the bonds to yield 8%, and sells the bonds on August 31 for $21,350 when Investor needs the cash for operations.

Illustration 9-5 explains how income is calculated and recorded, assuming there is **no separate reporting of interest income** on the income statement.

Illustration 9-5

Income on an Interest-Bearing Debt Instrument, Interest Income Not Reported Separately

Date	Account	Debit	Credit
June 15	Cost of bonds	$21,300	
	Interest since last interest payment date purchased from seller:		
	$20,000 × 10% × 5/12	833	
	Cash payment	$22,133	
	Temporary Investment in Bonds (HFT)	21,300	
	Interest Receivable	833	
	Cash		22,133
	(To record purchase of Sorfit Ltd. bonds and accrued interest)		
July 15	Cash	1,000	
	Investment Income (HFT)		167
	Interest Receivable		833
	$20,000 × 10% × 6/12 = $1,000		
	(To record receipt of semi-annual interest on Sorfit Ltd. bonds)		
Aug. 31	Selling price of bonds		$21,350
	Interest since last interest payment date sold to purchaser		
	$20,000 × 10% × 1½/12		250
	Cash received from purchaser		$21,600
	Selling price of bonds		$21,350
	Carrying amount of bonds		21,300
	Holding gain on sale of bonds		$ 50
	Cash	21,600	
	Temporary Investment in Bonds (HFT)		21,300
	Investment Income (HFT) ($250 + $50)		300
	(To record sale of bonds, gain and interest accrued since June 15)		

Note that there is no need to use the effective interest method or to amortize any discount or premium on held-for-trading debt instruments if interest income will not be separately reported. Note that the total income reported is \$167 + \$300 = \$467, the net cash flow on the trading transaction. This can also be determined as follows:

Net cash flow:	
Interest received	\$ 1,000
Total cash received on disposition	21,600
Less total cash paid on acquisition	(22,133)
Investment income earned	\$ 467

If Investor Inc. has a June 30 year end, the interest to June 30 must be accrued and the investment must be adjusted to the bond's fair value at June 30. The net amount that results is recognized as investment income. The July 15 and August 31 entries in Illustration 9-5 would then have to take the June 30 year-end entry into account.

For a non-interest-bearing debt investment, the investment income that is earned is the difference between the instrument's purchase price and its maturity value or the proceeds on its disposal. Treasury bills, for example, are usually traded in non-interest-bearing form. Assume that Investor Inc. pays \$19,231 on March 15 for a \$20,000 six-month Treasury bill that matures on September 15. The investment, purchased to yield an 8% return, is designated as a held-for-trading investment. Illustration 9-6 shows how to account for the investment income, assuming that interest income is not reported separately.

Illustration 9-6

Income on a Non-Interest-Bearing Debt Instrument, Interest Income Not Reported Separately

Date	Account	Debit	Credit
Mar. 15	Temporary Investment (HFT)	19,231	
	Cash		19,231
	(To record purchase of a \$20,000, six-month Treasury bill)		
Sept. 15	Cash	20,000	
	Temporary Investment (HFT)		19,231
	Investment Income/Loss (HFT)		769
	(To record the proceeds on maturity of a \$20,000 Treasury bill)		

Note that the investment income, which is entirely interest in this case, is equal to an 8% yield on the amount paid for the investment: \$19,231 × 8% × 6/12 = \$769.

If Investor needed cash prior to September 15 and sold the investment before maturity, the investment income is the difference between its cost and the proceeds on disposal.

Investments in equity securities that are held for trading may pay dividends. These may be recorded separately as dividend income as they are received. If the company does not report interest income separately, it is unlikely that it would report dividend income separately either. Because the holder of the shares on the date of record is entitled to the dividend and this date is generally a few weeks before the paying company mails the dividend cheques, a dividend receivable and the related income may be recognized before the cash is received. When the investment is sold, its cost is removed from the investment account and investment income is recognized.

To demonstrate the accounting for a portfolio of investments classified as held for trading with no separate reporting of interest and dividend income, assume that on December 31, 2008, Western Publishing Corporation provides the information shown in Illustration 9-7 on its held-for-trading investment portfolio. Assume that all investments were acquired in 2008. The investments were recorded at their fair value at acquisition in an account entitled Investments (HFT), and this value is their **carrying amount** on the books before any adjustment.

HFT INVESTMENT PORTFOLIO
December 31, 2008

Investments	Carrying Amount	Fair Value
Burlington Corp. shares	$ 43,860	$ 51,500
Genesta Corp. 8% bonds	184,230	175,200
Warner Ltd. shares	86,360	91,500
Total portfolio	$314,450	$318,200

Adjustment needed to the asset portfolio to bring it to fair value at December 31, 2008: $318,200 − $314,450 = $3,750 debit

Illustration 9-7
Calculation of Fair Value Adjustment–Held-for-Trading Portfolio, December 31, 2008

At December 31, an adjusting entry is made to bring the investment portfolio to its year-end fair value and to record the holding gain. This entry assumes that Western Publishing has one control account in its general ledger for the entire portfolio. It would be equally correct to make a separate entry for each of the three different investments.

		Debit	Credit
Dec. 31/08	Investments (HFT)	3,750	
	Investment Income/Loss (HFT)		3,750

A	= L +	SE
+3,750		+3,750

Cash flows: No effect

The Investment Income/Loss (HFT) account is included in net income on the income statement, and the fair values of the investments at December 31, 2008, now become the carrying amounts on the books. With a fair value measurement approach, the original cost or fair value at acquisition is not relevant.[15]

Now assume that the Genesta Corp. bonds are sold for $174,000 on February 4, 2009, their interest payment date, and that 1,000 shares of Next Ltd. are acquired for their fair value of $49,990 on September 21, 2009.

The entries to record the disposal on February 4 and acquisition on September 21 follow. Note that the bond's carrying amount before the sale is $175,200, its fair value at the last balance sheet date.

		Debit	Credit
Feb. 4/09	Cash	174,000	
	Investment Income/Loss (HFT)	1,200	
	Investments (HFT)		175,200

A	= L +	SE
−1,200		−1,200

Cash flows: ↑ 174,000 inflow

		Debit	Credit
Sept. 21/09	Investments (HFT)	49,990	
	Cash		49,990

A	= L	+ SE
0	0	0

Cash flows: ↓ 49,990 outflow

[15] Certainly the ability of management to earn a return and realize gains on the investments is relevant. In addition, the entity has to keep track in its files of the securities' original cost because only realized gains and losses are taxable or deductible for tax purposes.

Because the gains and losses on investments classified as held for trading are reported in income, the distinction between the portions that are realized and unrealized is blurred. This is not usually an issue, however, particularly for trading securities that are acquired for short-term profit taking.

Illustration 9-8 indicates the carrying amounts and fair values of the portfolio of investments held for trading at December 31, 2009. As Western Publishing prepares financial statements only once a year, the carrying amounts of the Burlington and Warner shares that are still on hand are the fair values reported at December 31, 2008. The carrying amount of the Next Ltd. shares acquired during the year is their fair value at acquisition.

Illustration 9-8
Calculation of Fair Value Adjustment–Held-for-Trading Portfolio, December 31, 2009

HFT INVESTMENT PORTFOLIO
December 31, 2009

Investments	Carrying Amount	Fair Value
Burlington Corp. shares	$ 51,500	$ 50,500
Warner Ltd. shares	91,500	90,100
Next Ltd. shares	49,990	50,600
Total portfolio	$192,990	$191,200

Adjustment needed to the asset portfolio to bring it to fair value at December 31, 2009: $192,990 – $191,200 = $1,790 credit

At December 31, an adjusting entry is made to bring the investments to their year-end fair values.

A	= L +	SE
−1,790		−1,790

Cash flows: No effect

Dec. 31/09	Investment Income/Loss (HFT)	1,790	
	Investments (HFT)		1,790

The investment loss is included in the 2009 income statement, added to the loss recognized on February 4. The portfolio is reported on the 2009 and 2008 balance sheets as follows, assuming the investments were acquired for short-term trading purposes. If management chose the fair value option, designating these investments as held for trading, they could be either long-term or current assets.

	2009	2008
Current assets:		
Temporary investments, at fair value	$191,200	$318,200

Terms other than "temporary investments" may be used, including "short-term investments," "trading securities," or "financial assets at fair value through net income."

Underlying Concept

Investments in financial instruments that are held for trading purposes–and therefore are generally marketable–are reported at fair value because this value is the most relevant.

Separate Reporting of Interest Income

While there is no requirement to distinguish between interest income and the holding gains and losses, a company may choose to report interest separately on its income statement. In this situation, interest income must be determined using the effective interest method, which makes the series of transaction and adjusting entries more complex. To see how this is done, we refer students to the examples of available-for-sale debt investments discussed later in this chapter. The analyses and interest entries are exactly the same, with one exception. With investments classified as available for sale, the holding gains and losses are recognized in other comprehensive income until disposition, **not in net income**. When classified as held for trading, the holding gains and losses are taken **directly to net income**.

Transfers between Categories

Can management change the classification of investments that it has categorized as held for trading, if, for example, it decides to hold an investment until maturity? *Handbook* Section 3855 is very clear on this matter: "An entity should not reclassify a financial instrument into or out of the trading category while it is held."[16] Thus, if the HFT designation is chosen when the instrument is acquired, it cannot be reversed.

AVAILABLE-FOR-SALE (AFS) INVESTMENTS

Introduction

4 Objective
Define available-for-sale financial assets and explain how they, and any associated gains and losses, are accounted for and reported.

This classification is in many ways a default category. **Available-for-sale (AFS)** financial assets are non-derivative assets that are designated as available for sale, or that are not classified as loans and receivables, held-to-maturity investments, or held for trading.[17] The usual sequence in making a classification decision is to determine whether a particular investment is held for short-term trading, held to maturity, whether it qualifies as a loan or receivable, or if the fair value option is chosen. If none of these is appropriate, it falls into the available-for-sale category by default. Use of the category does not mean that the entity intends to sell the investment. As with other classifications, preparers of financial statements may use terms other than "available for sale" to describe this group of financial assets in their financial reports.

Underlying Concept
Fair value is the most appropriate measure for financial assets unless the investor intends to hold the investment to its maturity.

Investments that are classified as available for sale may be **either debt or equity** investments. Although they are usually **measured at fair value**, changes in fair values while the assets are held **are not reported in net income**. Instead, the unrealized holding gains and losses are recognized in other comprehensive income until they are realized.[18] This usually results in income with a lower volatility—with fewer fluctuations—than if the value changes were recognized in the income statement each period.

As explained in Chapter 4, the concept of comprehensive income is new to Canadian financial reporting. Unrealized gains and losses on fair-valued available-for-sale financial instruments are held in accumulated other comprehensive income as a separate component of shareholders' equity until they are realized.

According to *CICA Handbook* Section 1530:

> **Comprehensive income** is the change in equity or net assets of an entity during a period from transactions and events from non-owner sources. Net income is a major component of comprehensive income, with other comprehensive income (OCI) making up the remainder.
>
> **Other comprehensive income (OCI)** comprises revenues, gains, expenses, and losses that accounting standards say are included in comprehensive income, but excluded from net income.
>
> **Accumulated other comprehensive income (AOCI)** is the balance of all past charges and credits to other comprehensive income up to the balance sheet date.

---

[16] Section 3855.80. There is one exception relating to a situation outside the scope of this text.

[17] *CICA Handbook*, Section 3855.19(i).

[18] The unrealized holding gains and losses are recognized in the statement of comprehensive income, net of tax.

Illustration 9-9 shows how these financial statement categories are related.

Illustration 9-9
Net Income, OCI, Comprehensive Income, and AOCI

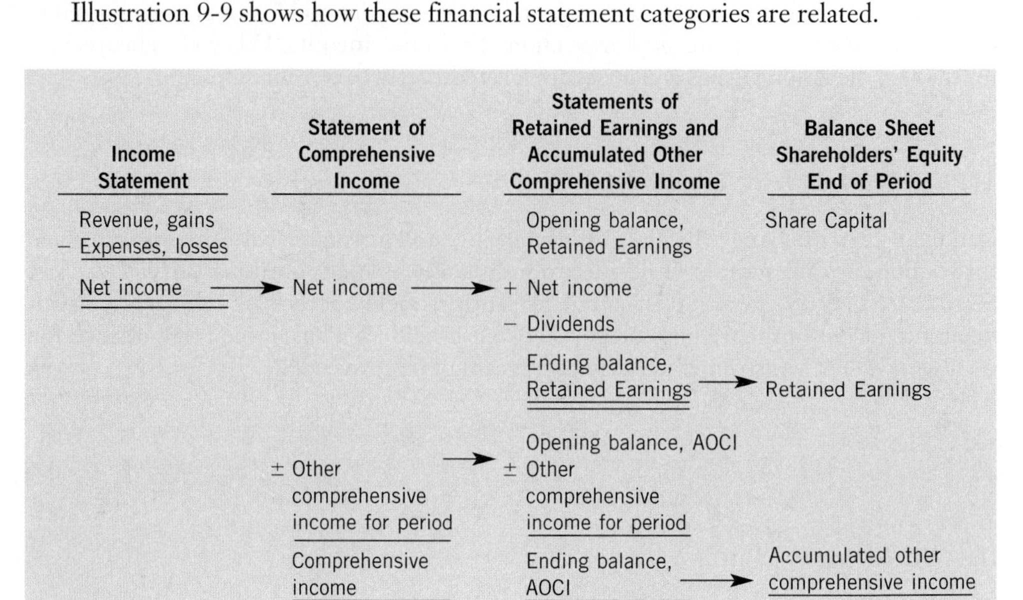

Measurement at Acquisition

Debt and equity investments classified as available for sale are initially recognized at their fair value. Just as they do for investments held to maturity, entities have a choice of how to account for any transaction costs that are incurred when the investment is acquired. They can either recognize all transaction costs in net income as incurred, or add them to the carrying amount of the investment at acquisition. The policy that is chosen is applied to all investments in the AFS category and is disclosed.

Income and Measurement after Acquisition—AFS Equity Instruments

The general rule is that available-for-sale financial assets are measured at fair value. However, when it is not possible to reliably determine fair value, cost or amortized cost is used. This is different from the measurement of a financial instrument classified as held for trading, which is always measured at fair value.

Objective 5
Account for investments in available-for-sale equity instruments.

If an equity investment classified as available for sale **does not have a quoted market price in an active market,** the investment is reported **at cost.** Dividends are recognized as income when received or receivable, and the investment or portfolio of investments continues to be carried and reported at acquisition cost. No gains or losses are recognized until the investment is sold, unless there is a permanent decline in its value. Because unrealized holding gains and losses are not recognized, no entries are made to OCI. This accounting method is relatively straightforward to apply.

Alternatively, equity investments that **have a quoted market price in an active market** are remeasured to their **fair value** at each balance sheet date.[19] As indicated above, unrealized holding gains or losses **are not recognized in net income**, but instead, are

[19] *CICA Handbook* Section 3855.69 indicates that a **quoted market price in an active market** means that "quoted prices reflecting normal market transactions are readily and regularly available from an exchange, dealer, broker, industry group, pricing service or regulatory agency, and those market prices represent actual and regularly occurring market transactions on an arm's length basis."

recognized in other comprehensive income. When the investment is subsequently disposed of (or an impairment in value is recognized), the gains or losses that were previously recognized in OCI are "recycled" (i.e., transferred) out of accumulated other comprehensive income into net income.

To illustrate the remeasurement to fair value, assume that on November 3, 2007, Manitoba Corporation purchases common shares of three companies and classifies them as available for sale. These holdings do not give the company significant influence over the strategic decisions of any of the investee companies. Manitoba pays a commission of $7,500 in acquiring the shares and follows a policy of expensing transaction costs.[20] The purchases are as follows:

	Fair value and cost at acquisition
Nova Industries Ltd.	$259,700
Columbia Soup Corp.	317,500
St. Boniface Pulp Ltd.	141,350
Total	$718,550

The purchase of the investments is recorded as follows:

Nov. 3/07	Investment in Nova Industries	259,700	
	Investment in Columbia Soup	317,500	
	Investment in St. Boniface Pulp	141,350	
	Commissions Expense	7,500	
	Cash		726,050

A = L + SE
−7,500 −7,500

Cash flows: ↓ 726,050 outflow

Alternatively, Manitoba Corporation could use one control account for its available-for-sale investments and a subsidiary ledger to track each investment separately. So that the effect on each investment can be seen, this chapter assumes that control and subsidiary ledgers are not maintained for AFS investments.

On December 6, 2007, Manitoba Corp. receives a cash dividend of $4,200 on its investment in the common shares of Columbia Soup. The cash dividend is recorded as follows:

Dec. 6/07	Cash	4,200	
	Dividend Income		4,200

A = L + SE
+4,200 +4,200

Cash flows: ↑ 4,200 inflow

Illustration 9-10 indicates the costs, carrying amounts, fair values, and unrealized gains and losses at December 31, 2007, for Manitoba's AFS investments.

Illustration 9-10
Schedule of Investments and Holding Gains/Losses–Available-for-Sale Equity Investment Portfolio (2007)

AVAILABLE-FOR-SALE EQUITY INVESTMENT PORTFOLIO
December 31, 2007

Investments	Carrying Amount and Cost	Fair Value	Holding Gain (Loss) for Period
Nova Industries Ltd.	$259,700	$275,000	$ 15,300
Columbia Soup Corp.	317,500	304,000	(13,500)
St. Boniface Pulp Ltd.	141,350	104,000	(37,350)
Total portfolio	$718,550	$683,000	$(35,550)

[20] If the transaction costs were capitalized, instead of expensed, they would be allocated to the individual investments based on their relative fair values.

For Manitoba's portfolio, the gross holding gains are $15,300, and the gross holding losses are $50,850 ($13,500 + $37,350), resulting in a net unrealized loss of $35,550. The fair value of the portfolio is $35,550 less than its carrying amount (and cost, in this first accounting period). The unrealized gains and losses from changes in the fair value of these securities are recorded in a Holding Gain or Loss account and are reported as part of other comprehensive income. In this case, the adjusting entry is as follows.[21] Note that the carrying amount of each investment is adjusted to its fair value at the balance sheet date.

A	= L +	SE
−35,550		−35,550

Cash flows: No effect

Dec. 31/07	Investment in Nova Industries	15,300	
	Holding Loss on Columbia Soup (OCI)	13,500	
	Holding Loss on St. Boniface Pulp (OCI)	37,350	
	Holding Gain on Nova Industries (OCI)		15,300
	Investment in Columbia Soup		13,500
	Investment in St. Boniface Pulp		37,350

A variety of terms may be used to describe the investments on the balance sheet—use of the "available-for-sale" terminology is not required. One presentation that could be used is:

Investments at fair value, with gains and losses in OCI	$683,000

Underlying Concept

When shares of a company have been purchased at various times and at varying costs and only a portion of the holdings are sold, use of an average cost for the disposal is logical, but use of the average cost is no longer a requirement.

Sale of AFS Investments

Now assume that Manitoba sells all of its Nova Industries Ltd. common shares on January 23, 2008, receiving gross proceeds of $287,220.[22] This is $12,220 more than the current carrying amount of the Investment in Nova Industries in the accounts.

While it is possible to record this event using different combinations of entries, the following series of three entries clearly accomplishes what the accounting standard requires:

- The **first entry** adjusts the carrying amount of the investment to its fair value at the date of disposal and captures the holding gain up to that date in OCI.
- The **second entry** removes the carrying amount of the investment from the asset account and records the proceeds on disposal.
- The **third entry** is a **reclassification adjustment** that recycles the holding gain that is now realized from OCI into net income.

Jan. 23/08	Investment in Nova Industries	12,220	
	Holding Gain on Nova Industries (OCI) ($287,220 − $275,000)		12,220

[21] If one control account were used instead, one summary debit to an Unrealized Loss account (OCI) for $35,550 and one credit to the control Investment account for $35,550 would be made. The subsidiary ledger would then be brought up to date for each individual investment. A subsidiary ledger would also likely be used to track the individual components of accumulated other comprehensive income to make it easier to later recycle realized gains and losses to income.

[22] If Manitoba's policy is to expense transaction costs, the gross proceeds received on sale are used in the calculation of the gain or loss and the transaction costs are then expensed. For example, if Manitoba paid transaction costs of $2,800, an additional entry is required to debit Commissions Expense for $2,800 and credit Cash for $2,800. If the policy is to capitalize transaction costs, the net proceeds after deducting such costs are used and no additional entry is needed.

Cash	287,220	
Investment in Nova Industries ($275,000 + $12,220)		287,220
Holding Gain on Nova Industries (OCI)	27,520	
Gain on Sale of Nova Industries		27,520

A = L + SE
+12,220 +12,220

Cash flows: ↑ 287,220 inflow

The amount recycled from OCI to net income is the difference between the investment's cost and the proceeds on disposal ($287,220 − $259,700). It is also the sum of all prior entries to OCI for the Nova Industries shares: a $15,300 gain on December 31, 2007, and a $12,220 gain on January 23, 2008, for a total of $27,520. In effect, the holding gains are taken out of AOCI and are reclassified to net income.

To continue with this example, assume that the information in Illustration 9-11 is provided for Manitoba's available-for-sale portfolio at December 31, 2008.

Illustration 9-11

Calculation of Holding Gain/Loss for Period–Available-for-Sale Equity Investment Portfolio (2008)

AVAILABLE-FOR-SALE EQUITY INVESTMENT PORTFOLIO
December 31, 2008

Investments	Cost	Carrying Amount	Fair Value	Holding Gain (Loss) for Period
Columbia Soup Corp.	$317,500	$304,000	$362,550	$58,550
St. Boniface Pulp Ltd.	141,350	104,000	139,050	35,050
Total portfolio	$458,850	$408,000	$501,600	$93,600

The entry to bring the investments to their fair value at December 31, 2008, is:

Dec. 31/08	Investment in Columbia Soup	58,550	
	Investment in St. Boniface Pulp	35,050	
	Holding Gain on Columbia Soup (OCI)		58,550
	Holding Gain on St. Boniface Pulp (OCI)		35,050

A = L + SE
+93,600 +93,600

Cash flows: No effect

Financial Statement Presentation

Illustration 9-12 indicates how Manitoba Corp.'s December 31, 2008, balance sheet and statements of income, comprehensive income, and changes in accumulated other comprehensive income are reported.

Illustration 9-12

Financial Statement Reporting of Available-for-Sale Investments

BALANCE SHEET
December 31, 2008

Long-term investments (assumed)	
Investments, at fair value with gains and losses in OCI	**$ 501,600**
Shareholders' equity	
Accumulated other comprehensive income	**$ 42,750**

INCOME STATEMENT
Year 2008

Other revenues and gains	
Dividend income	**$ XXX**
Gain on sale of investments in shares	**$ 27,520**

STATEMENT OF COMPREHENSIVE INCOME
Year 2008

Net income (including realized gain)		$ x
Other comprehensive income:		
Holding gains on available-for-sale investments during year ($12,220 + $93,600)	**$105,820**	
Reclassification adjustment for gains included in net income	**(27,520)**	
Other comprehensive income		**78,300**
Comprehensive income		$ x + 78,300

STATEMENT OF CHANGES IN ACCUMULATED OTHER COMPREHENSIVE INCOME
Year 2008

Accumulated other comprehensive income (loss), January 1, 2008	($ 35,550)
Other comprehensive income, 2008	**78,300**
Accumulated other comprehensive income (loss), December 31, 2008	**$ 42,750**

Note that the AOCI at December 31, 2008, can be calculated independently as the difference between the portfolio's carrying amount at that date, $501,600, and the cost of the investments, $458,850. Take your time to be sure you understand the flow of the numbers in this comprehensive example.

Income and Measurement after Acquisition—AFS Debt Instruments

Objective 6
Account for investments in available-for-sale debt instruments.

After they have been acquired, there is another complication with investments in AFS debt instruments. This is because the discount or premium (including any transaction costs that have been capitalized) must be amortized using the effective interest method so that the appropriate amount of interest income is recognized each period.

This has the effect of changing the investment's cost to an amortized cost amount, as well as changing the investment's carrying amount. Information on the amortized cost is kept in supplementary records only—it is not reported on the balance sheet after acquisition. Other than replacing "cost" with "amortized cost," the approach is exactly the same as described above for equity investments: the investments are remeasured and reported at fair value, and the holding gains and losses in value are recorded and reported as an item of other comprehensive income. As is done with equity investments, the accumulated holding gains or losses are removed from other comprehensive income and reported in net income when the asset is disposed of or if it becomes impaired.

Illustration: Single Investment

To illustrate the accounting for available-for-sale debt instruments, assume that a company purchases $100,000, 10%, five-year bonds of Graff Corporation on January 1, 2008, with interest payable on July 1 and January 1. The bonds sell for $108,111, resulting in a bond premium of $8,111 and an effective interest rate of 8%. The company follows a policy of expensing transaction costs as they are incurred.

The entry to record the purchase of the bonds is:

A	= L	+ OE
0	0	0

Cash flows: ↓ 108,111 outflow

Jan. 1/08	Investment in Graff Corp. Bonds	108,111	
	Cash		108,111

Illustration 9-13 shows the effect that the premium amortization has on the interest income that is reported each period. The process is identical to the amortization on investments held to maturity.

Illustration 9-13
Schedule of Interest Income and Bond Premium Amortization–Effective Interest Method

10% BONDS PURCHASED TO YIELD 8%

Date	Cash Received	Interest Income	Bond Premium Amortization	Amortized Cost of Bonds
1/1/08				$108,111
7/1/08	$ 5,000[a]	$ 4,324[b]	$ 676[c]	107,435[d]
1/1/09	5,000	4,297	703	106,732
7/1/09	5,000	4,269	731	106,001
1/1/10	5,000	4,240	760	105,241
7/1/10	5,000	4,210	790	104,451
1/1/11	5,000	4,178	822	103,629
7/1/11	5,000	4,145	855	102,774
1/1/12	5,000	4,111	889	101,885
7/1/12	5,000	4,075	925	100,960
1/1/13	5,000	4,040	960	100,000
	$50,000	$41,889	$8,111	

[a] $5,000 = $100,000 × 0.10 × 6/12
[b] $4,324 = $108,111 × 0.08 × 6/12
[c] $676 = $5,000 − $4,324
[d] $107,435 = $108,111 − $676

The entry to record interest income on the first interest date is:

Jul. 1/08	Cash	5,000	
	Investment in Graff Corp. Bonds		676
	Interest Income		4,324

A = L + SE
+4,324 +4,324
Cash flows: ↑ 5,000 inflow

The company then makes the following entry to recognize interest income at year end:

Dec. 31/08	Interest Receivable	5,000	
	Investment in Graff Corp. Bonds		703
	Interest Income		4,297

A = L + SE
+4,297 +4,297
Cash flows: No effect

As a result, the company reports interest income for 2008 of $8,621 ($4,324 + $4,297).

Assume that at December 31, 2008, the fair value of the Graff Corporation bonds is $105,000. Their carrying amount at this time is $106,732 and the adjustment needed to bring the Investment account to fair value is $1,732:

Original cost and carrying amount of bonds		$108,111
Entries made to Investment in Graff Corp. Bonds account during year when recognizing interest income:		
July 1, 2008	$676 credit	
Dec. 31, 2008	703 credit	(1,379)
Carrying amount before fair value adjustment		106,732
Fair value, December 31, 2008		105,000
Fair value adjustment needed		$ 1,732 credit

There is a holding loss on the bonds of $1,732. This loss is reported as an item of other comprehensive income and it is therefore included in the accumulated other comprehensive income component of shareholders' equity. The entry to adjust the investment to its fair value at December 31, 2008 is:

Dec. 31/08	Holding Loss on Graff Corp. Bonds (OCI)	1,732	
	Investment in Graff Corp. Bonds		1,732

At December 31, 2008, the balance sheet reports:

Long-term Investments (assumed)	
Investment in bonds, at fair value with gains and losses in OCI	$105,000
Shareholders' Equity	
Accumulated other comprehensive income (loss)	$ (1,732)[23]

Illustration: Portfolio of Investments

To illustrate the accounting for a portfolio of investments, assume that Chrona Corporation has two debt securities that are classified as available for sale. Illustration 9-14 provides information on amortized cost, carrying amount, and fair value at December 31, 2009, and the holding gain or loss for the period.

Illustration 9-14
Calculation of Holding Gain/Loss for Period–Available-for-Sale Debt Investment Portfolio (2009)

AVAILABLE-FOR-SALE DEBT INVESTMENT PORTFOLIO
December 31, 2009

Investments	Amortized Cost	Carrying Amount	Fair Value	Holding Gain (Loss) for Period
Watson Corporation 8% bonds	$ 46,201	$ 47,107	$ 51,800	$ 4,693
Sherlock Corporation 10% bonds	197,600	200,000	180,400	(19,600)
Total portfolio	$243,801	$247,107	$232,200	($14,907)

The total fair value of Chrona's available-for-sale portfolio at year end is $232,200 and its carrying amount before its adjustment to year-end fair value is $247,107. Information about the amortized cost is needed only to calculate interest income, and the assumption in this case is that the entry to recognize interest income up to December 31, 2009, has already been made. The entry to bring the investments to fair value is:

Dec. 31/09	Investment in Watson Corp. Bonds	4,693	
	Holding Loss on Sherlock Corp. Bonds (OCI)	19,600	
	Holding Gain on Watson Corp. Bonds (OCI)		4,693
	Investment in Sherlock Corp. Bonds		19,600

As explained earlier, Chrona Corporation may use a control and subsidiary accounts instead of maintaining separate accounts for each investment, as is assumed in this illustration.

[23] This balance can also be determined as the difference between the investment's fair value ($105,000) and amortized cost ($108,000 − $676 − $703 = $106,732) at the balance sheet date.

Sale of Available-for-Sale Investments

When bond investments that are classified as available for sale are sold before their maturity date, an entry has to be made to recognize interest up to the date of disposal. It is important for the interest entry to be made **before the entries to record the disposal**, because the amount of any premium or discount amortization affects the carrying amount of the individual investment. Remember that a bond premium or discount amortization schedule has to be maintained as supplementary information so that the correct amount of interest income can be reported using the effective interest method.

After this, the same three entries that were made for the disposal of AFS equity investments need to be made for AFS debt instruments. To illustrate, assume that Chrona Corporation sold the Watson bonds from Illustration 9-14 on July 1, 2010, for $53,000. After recognizing interest income and amortizing the discount up to the date of disposal, assume that the bond's amortized cost is $46,557 and its carrying amount is $52,156.[24]

The **first entry** recognizes the holding gain that occurred in 2010—the difference between the fair value on disposal and the Watson Corp. bond's carrying amount—and adjusts the investment's carrying amount to the July 1, 2010, fair value. The **second entry** records the disposal of the investment, which is now at its current fair value. The **third entry** transfers or reclassifies the accumulated amount of holding gains on the bond investment from other comprehensive income to a gain account in the income statement. As explained in Illustration 9-15, this is equal to the difference between the investment's amortized cost at the date of disposal and the proceeds that were received.

The three entries are:

Jul. 1/10	Investment in Watson Corp. Bonds	844	
	Holding Gain on Watson Corp. Bonds (OCI)		844
	(Fair value of $53,000 – carrying amount of $52,156)		
	Cash	53,000	
	Investment in Watson Corp. Bonds		53,000
	Holding Gain on Watson Corp. Bonds (OCI)	6,443	
	Gain on Sale of Watson Corp. Bonds		6,443

A = L + SE
+844 +844

Cash flows: ↑ 53,000 inflow

Illustration 9-15 indicates how the realized gain is calculated. Note that it is the amortized cost at the date of disposal that is used, and not the original cost. It could also be calculated as the sum of all previous amounts that have been recognized in OCI as holding gains or losses on the Watson bonds. In our example, however, we do not know how much was recognized as holding gains and losses before December 31, 2009.

Illustration 9-15
Calculation of Realized Gain

Proceeds on disposal of Watson bonds	$53,000
Amortized cost of investment in Watson bonds when sold	46,557
Realized gain on sale of bonds transferred to net income	$ 6,443

Assuming there are no other purchases or sales of available-for-sale investments in 2010, Chrona Corporation prepares the information shown in Illustration 9-16 at year end, December 31, 2010, after adjusting for accrued interest and amortizing the related

[24] This assumes that the discount amortization between January 1, 2010, and July 1, 2010, was $356, increasing the amortized cost from $46,201 to $46,557 and the bond's carrying amount from its December 31, 2009, fair value (and year-end carrying amount) of $51,800 to $52,156.

discount of $600 (assumed). Note that the $600 discount amortization increased both the amortized cost of the investment and the carrying amount since the last balance sheet date by that amount.

Illustration 9-16

Calculation of Holding Gain or Loss for Period–Available-for-Sale Debt Investment Portfolio (2010)

AVAILABLE-FOR-SALE INVESTMENT PORTFOLIO
December 31, 2010

Investments	Amortized Cost	Carrying Amount	Fair Value	Holding Gain (Loss) for Period
	(assumed)	(assumed)		
Sherlock Corporation 10% bonds	$198,200	$181,000	$191,600	$10,600

The entry to record the adjustment of the carrying amount to fair value is:

A	= L +	SE
+10,600		+10,600

Cash flows: No effect

Dec. 31/10	Investment in Sherlock Corp. Bonds	10,600	
	Holding Gain on Sherlock Corp. Bonds (OCI)		10,600

Financial Statement Presentation

Chrona Corporation's December 31, 2010, balance sheet and the 2010 income statement, statement of comprehensive income, and statement of changes in accumulated other comprehensive income contain the items and amounts in Illustration 9-17.

Illustration 9-17

Reporting of Available-for-Sale Investments Carried at Fair Value

BALANCE SHEET
December 31, 2010

Long-term investments (assumed)	
Investment in bonds, at fair value with gains and losses in OCI	**$191,600**
Shareholders' equity	
Accumulated other comprehensive income (loss)	**$ (6,600)**

INCOME STATEMENT
Year 2010

Other revenue and gains	
Interest income, including amortization of discounts (AFS)	**$ XXX**
Gain on sale of investment in bonds (AFS)	**$ 6,443**

STATEMENT OF COMPREHENSIVE INCOME
Year 2010

Net income (including realized gain)		$ x
Other comprehensive income:		
Net holding gains on available-for-sale investments during year ($844 + $10,600)	**$11,444**	
Reclassification adjustment for gains included in net income	**(6,443)**	
Other comprehensive income		**5,001**
Comprehensive income		$ x + 5,001

STATEMENT OF CHANGES IN ACCUMULATED OTHER COMPREHENSIVE INCOME Year 2010	
Accumulated other comprehensive income (loss), January 1, 2010	$(11,601)[25]
Other comprehensive income, 2010	**5,001**
Accumulated other comprehensive income (loss), December 31, 2010	**$ (6,600)**

Impairment of Available-for-Sale Financial Assets

In the same way that it verifies impairment for other financial assets, management determines at each balance sheet date whether there is objective evidence that an available-for-sale investment is impaired. When an investment declines in value below its cost or amortized cost, this is not necessarily evidence of impairment. The decline must be material and prolonged for it to qualify as objective evidence.

For available-for-sale investments **carried at fair value,** decreases in the value of the investments are included in accumulated other comprehensive income (loss) rather than net income. When it is determined that an available-for-sale asset is impaired, the loss must be transferred from AOCI to net income. The impairment loss is calculated as the difference between the current (impaired) fair value of the asset and its acquisition cost (or amortized cost if it is a debt instrument). Impairment losses transferred to net income are not reversed. In other words, if the value of the investment recovers, these gains are recognized and held in AOCI until the investment is disposed of.

For equity investments **carried at cost**, the impairment loss is the difference between the asset's current fair value and its carrying amount on the books. No reversal of this write-down is permitted either.

To illustrate, assume that Strickler Corp. holds an AFS bond investment with a carrying amount of $775,000 and an accumulated loss to date in AOCI of $200,000. The fair value of these securities is now $725,000 and management has objective evidence that the investment's value is impaired.

Assuming that interest income and any discount or premium amortization has already been recognized to date, two entries are now needed. The **first entry** writes the investment down to its current impaired value ($775,000 − $725,000 = $50,000) and recognizes the unrealized decline in value in OCI. The **second entry** transfers the total impairment loss from AOCI to the income statement.

	Dr.	Cr.
Holding Loss on AFS Bond Investments (OCI)	50,000	
Investment in AFS Bond		50,000
(To write down investment to its impaired value)		
Impairment Loss	250,000	
Holding Loss on AFS Bond Investment (OCI)		250,000
(To transfer impairment loss to net income)		

A	= L +	SE
−50,000		−50,000

Cash flows: No effect

A	= L	+ SE
0	0	0

Cash flows: No effect

[25] Accumulated other comprehensive income (loss) at January 1, 2010, is the difference between the amortized cost of the bond investments of $243,801 at December 31, 2009, and the fair value of the bond investments at that date, $232,200. AOCI at December 31, 2010, can be calculated in the same way.

The new carrying amount of the investment is $725,000, and future interest income will be recognized using the original effective interest rate but on this revised amount.

Transfers between Categories

International Insight

The requirements for transfers between categories are consistent with both U.S. and international GAAP.

Financial assets are classified when first acquired and, generally, transfers between categories and changes in the method of accounting for them are not permitted. However, limited reclassification is allowed in the case of a change in circumstance, particularly if it is outside the control and influence of management or owners. When such a change is made, **the income statement effects of the original category are not reversed**. Standards for transfers in and out of the AFS category are summarized first:

Transfer to AFS from HTM: A held-to-maturity investment may be reclassified as available for sale but this could result in questions about management's real intentions for the entire portfolio of held-to-maturity assets. When the HTM portfolio is tainted, either by sales or by reclassification, the entire portfolio is transferred to AFS and remeasured at its fair value.

Transfer from AFS to HTM: Assets may be transferred from AFS to HTM on a discretionary basis if HTM is not tainted, or if the end of the "time out" period has arrived for the tainted HTM portfolio. In this case, the fair value of each asset at the date of transfer becomes its new amortized cost in the held-to-maturity category.

The following two situations are viewed as changes in measurement, not as transfers or changes in classification.

Change from cost (or amortized cost) to fair value basis within the AFS category: If a "quoted market price in an active market" becomes available for an available-for-sale equity investment previously carried on a cost basis, the investment is remeasured from its cost-based carrying amount to its fair value. The resulting holding gain or loss is then recognized in other comprehensive income.

Change from fair value to cost (or amortized cost) basis within the AFS category or to the HTM category: When financial assets that are carried at fair value and have holding gains and losses reported in OCI have to go back to a cost basis, the fair value of the investment is recognized as its new cost or amortized cost on the date when the event occurs. The previously recognized holding gain or loss is amortized from AOCI to net income over its remaining life using the effective interest method. If the investment has no fixed maturity, the gain or loss in AOCI is recognized in net income when the asset is disposed of.[26]

The table in Illustration 9-18 summarizes the accounting treatment for all transfers among the three classifications of financial assets looked at in this chapter.

[26] *CICA Handbook*, Sections 3855.80–.85. This situation may arise in the following circumstances:

1. An active market price for an available-for-sale security carried at fair value is no longer available.
2. There is a change in the entity's intent or ability to hold an investment to maturity—an available-for-sale debt instrument now qualifies as held to maturity.
3. Investments that were previously sent to the "penalty box" due to tainting of the held-to-maturity classification have sat out the required two years and are now eligible for a transfer back to the held-to-maturity category.

Type of Transfer	Measurement Basis	Effect of Transfer on Other Comprehensive Income	Effect of Transfer on Net Income
To and from the HFT category	n/a – reclassification into or out of trading category is not permitted	n/a	n/a
Transfer from held-to-maturity to available-for-sale (or AFS cost-based to AFS FV-based)	Investment is transferred at fair value at the date of transfer	Unrealized gain/loss is recognized in other comprehensive income at the date of transfer	None
Transfer from available-for-sale to held-to-maturity (or AFS FV-based to AFS cost-based)	Investment is transferred at fair value at the date of transfer. This is its new cost or amortized cost	Amortize the unrealized gain/loss in OCI at date of transfer to net income over remaining life of the investment or on disposal if no fixed maturity	None at date of transfer, but over life of investment

Illustration 9-18

Accounting for Transfers between Categories–Summary

STRATEGIC INVESTMENTS

Introduction

Accounting for investments in the common shares of another corporation after acquisition depends mostly on the relationship that the acquisition creates between the investor and the investee. The relationships are classified by the level of influence that is exercised by the investor and this, in turn, is generally related to the degree of share ownership (i.e., more shares usually mean more influence). When the investment is made for strategic purposes, management will want to influence or control the investee's policies. Therefore, the investor is more likely to acquire a higher percentage of the outstanding voting shares.

The levels of interest (i.e., ownership percentage) and the accounting methods for each level are summarized in Illustration 9-19. Note that the percentages given are guidelines rather than rigid standards.

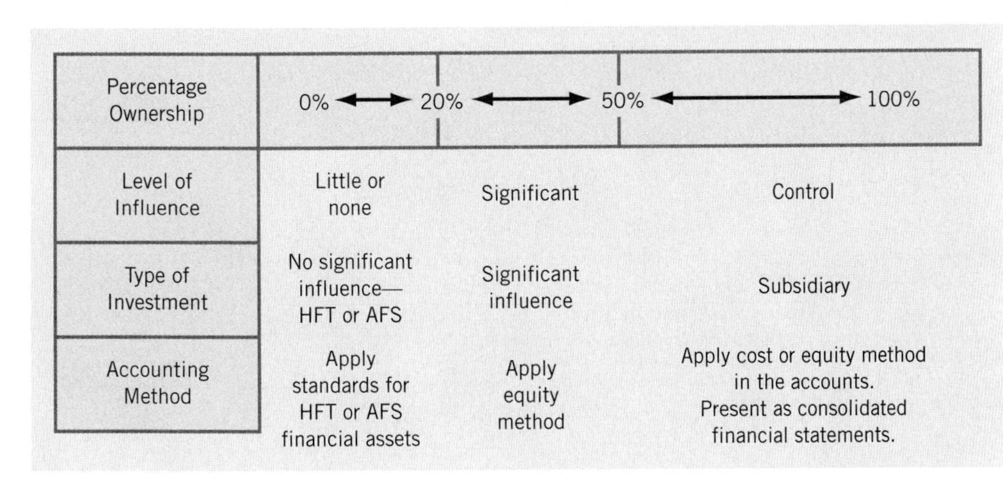

Illustration 9-19

Levels of Influence and Corresponding Accounting Methods

The accounting and reporting for equity investments therefore depend on the level of influence, as explained in Illustration 9-20.[27]

Illustration 9-20
Accounting and Reporting for Equity Investments by Category

Category	Valuation	Unrealized Holding Gains or Losses	Other Income Statement Effects
No significant influence			
1. Available-for-sale	Fair value*	To other comprehensive income and separate component of shareholders' equity (AOCI)	Dividends as received or receivable; gains and losses from sale or impairment
2. Held-for-Trading	Fair value	To net income	Dividends as received or receivable
Significant influence	Equity	Not recognized	Investment income is equal to investor's proportionate share of investee's net income reported (adjusted)
Control: Subsidiary	Consolidation	Not recognized	Line-by-line consolidation of revenues, expenses, gains, and losses

* Unless market prices are not available

Illustration 9-21 presents the holdings of Power Corporation of Canada, controlled by the influential Desmarais family from Quebec. A variety of equity investments are illustrated, from the 100% ownership of Gesca to the 66.4% ownership of Power Financial and through this company to various levels of interest in other Canadian and European enterprises.

Illustration 9-21
Power Corporation of Canada's Empire

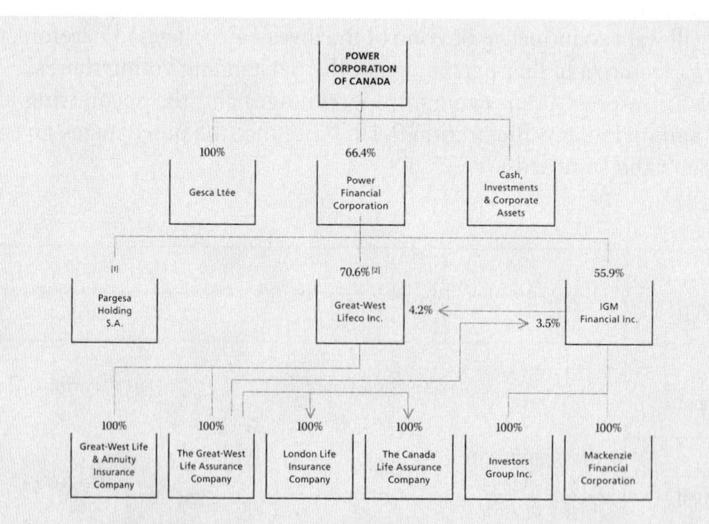

Above percentage denote participating equity interest as at September 30, 2006.
[1] Through its wholly owned subsidiary Power Financial Europe B.V., Power Financial Corporation held a 50 per cent interest in Parjointco N.V. Parjointco held a voting interest of 61.4 per cent and an equity interest of 54.1 per cent in Pargesa Holdings S.A.
[2] 65 per cent direct and indirect voting interest.

[27] Joint ventures are another type of equity investment. Since they can be incorporated companies, they can issue shares. Joint ventures are characterized by **joint control** (versus **unilateral control**). This is usually evidenced through a contractual agreement that states that the venturers (investors) must **share key decision-making**. The accounting method used for joint ventures is the **proportionate consolidation** method (*CICA Handbook*, Section 3055.17). This may change to using the equity method as the IASB changes its standards.

Power Corp. consolidates its subsidiary companies, including Power Financial, and accounts for Power Financial's interest in **Parjointco** by the equity method. Parjointco consolidates its interest in **Pargesa Holding**.

Holdings with Significant Influence, but Not Control

7 Objective
Explain the difference between investments where an investor has no significant influence, has significant influence, or has control, and identify how each type should be accounted for and reported.

When an investor has an interest of less than 20%, **it is presumed that the investor has little or no influence over the investee**. This may not be the case, however. For example, a 16% interest may allow an investor to very significantly influence decisions if the remaining shares are widely held. Alternatively, ownership of 30% of a company's shares may not give an investor company any influence at all if a 70% majority shareholder does not permit any. Therefore, the percentages serve as guidance only.

While an equity interest of less than 50% of an investee corporation does not give an investor legal control, it could give the investor significant influence over the strategic policies of the investee. To provide guidance and an operational definition of **significant influence**, the Accounting Standards Board states that an ability to exercise influence over another company's operating, investing, and financing activities may be indicated in several ways. Examples include the following: representation on the board of directors, participation in policy-making processes, material intercompany transactions, interchange of managerial personnel, or provision of technical information.[28]

To ensure that the significant influence criterion would be applied in a reasonably consistent manner, the standard setters concluded that an investment (direct or indirect) of 20% or more of the voting shares of another company should lead to a presumption that, unless there is evidence to the contrary, an investor has the ability to exercise significant influence over an investee. With less than a 20% voting interest, the assumption is that the investor cannot exercise the required degree of influence, unless the influence is clearly demonstrated.[29]

Equity Method Basics

8 Objective
Explain and apply the equity method of accounting.

When it is evident that there is significant influence—but not control—**the equity method is used**. The investment is initially recorded at the cost of the acquired shares. Subsequently, its carrying amount is adjusted each period for the investor's proportionate share of the changes in the net assets of the investee. The equity method sounds complex at first, but it is only **the accrual basis of accounting applied to investment income**.

Under this method, **the investor recognizes investment income as the investee earns income** by debiting the Investment account and crediting Investment Income. When cash is received from the investment (i.e., the investee pays a dividend on the shares), this converts an asset that has already been recognized—the Investment—to cash. Therefore, Cash is debited and the Investment account is credited.

The investment account changes, in the equity method, to mirror the changes in the investee's book value:

- **When the investee's net assets increase** because it earns income, **the investor increases the carrying amount of its investment** for its proportionate share of the investee's increase in net assets, and also **reports its share of the investee's income as investment income**.
- **When the investee's net assets decrease** because the company pays a dividend, **the investor recognizes the cash received and decreases the carrying amount of the investment** by its share of the decrease in the investee's net assets.

---

[28] *CICA Handbook*, Section 3051.05.

[29] *CICA Handbook*, Section 3051.05.

To illustrate the basics of the equity method, assume that Maxi Corp. purchases a 20% interest in Mini Corp. and has the ability to exercise significant influence over Mini's strategic policies. The entries are shown in Illustration 9-22. Note the effects on the investment account and on the income statement.

Illustration 9-22
Application of the Basics of the Equity Method

On January 2, 2007, Maxi Corp. acquires 48,000 shares (20% of Mini Corp. common shares) at a cost of $10 a share.

Investment in Mini Corp.	480,000	
Cash		480,000

For the year 2007, Mini Corp. reports net income of $200,000; Maxi Corp.'s share is 20%, or $40,000.

Investment in Mini Corp.	40,000	
Investment Income*		40,000

At December 31, 2007, the 48,000 shares of Mini Corp. have a fair value (market price) of $12 a share, or $576,000. The investment value is not considered impaired.

No entry

On January 28, 2008, Mini Corp. announces and pays a cash dividend of $100,000; Maxi Corp. receives 20%, or $20,000.

Cash	20,000	
Investment in Mini Corp.		20,000

For the year 2008, Mini reports a net loss of $50,000; Maxi Corp.'s share is 20%, or $10,000.

Investment Loss*	10,000	
Investment in Mini Corp.		10,000

At December 31, 2008, the 48,000 Mini Corp. shares have a fair value (market price) of $11 a share, or $528,000. The investment value is not considered impaired.

No entry

*This entry is sometimes referred to as the **equity pickup**. The term refers to the fact that the investor is picking up its share of income or loss under the equity method.

Under the equity method, **the accrual basis is applied.** Maxi Corp. therefore reports investment income as Mini Corp. earns income. Revenue recognition is permitted before receiving a dividend, because of the degree of influence that the investor has over the decisions of the investee, including dividend decisions. If the investee company suffers a loss, as Mini Corp. did in 2008, the investor accrues its share of the loss and reduces the carrying amount of its investment.

Underlying Concept

The equity method of accounting results in income statement amounts that more faithfully represent the underlying economic results of the investor company's management decisions.

One of the benefits of this method is that the investor's income statement reports the economics of the situation: if the influence exerted results in the investee performing well, the investor's income statement reflects positive investment income. If the influence results in poor decisions and the investee incurs losses, the investor's income statement reflects its share of the loss. In addition, when the equity method is used the investor cannot manipulate its own income by influencing the timing of a dividend from the investee.

Expanded Illustration of the Equity Method

There are two more complexities in applying the equity method:[30]

[30] A third aspect involves eliminating the effects of unrealized intercompany gains and losses. This and situations where investors pay less for the shares than their proportionate interest in the identifiable net assets of the investee (i.e., "negative goodwill") are topics for an advanced accounting course.

1. Differences between what was originally paid for the investment and the investor's share of the investee's book value need to be identified and accounted for according to the reason for the extra or smaller payment.
2. The major classifications of the income that is reported by the investee at the bottom of its income statement must be retained and reported in the same way on the investor's income statement.

The first item requires an understanding of what the cost of the investment represents. It is unusual for the investor to pay an amount for the investment that is exactly equal to its share of the other company's book value. The excess payment (usually it is extra) could be due to several reasons: there may be unrecorded assets; there may be assets whose fair value is greater than the carrying amount on the investee's books or liabilities whose fair value is less than book value; there may be intangibles, such as goodwill, that the investee company has but which are not recognized in its books; and so on. **Any payment in excess of (or less than) the investor's share of book value is all part of the cost of the investment, and after acquisition, must be accounted for appropriately.**

If the difference is caused by long-lived assets with fair values that are greater than book value, the amount above the asset's book value must be amortized. If it relates to inventory with a fair value in excess of its carrying amount on the investee's books, it must be recognized as an increased expense as the inventory is sold. There may also be assets with fair values that are lower than book value or liabilities with present values higher than book value. **None of these differences are on the investee's records, but they are captured as part of the purchase cost of the investment**, so it is the investment account itself that needs to be adjusted over time.

Because the equity method recognizes and reports the investor's share of the investee company's income, **the type of income that is reported should remain the same**. That is, the portion that is the investor's share of the investee's discontinued operations or extraordinary items is reported separately from the investor's share of income before discontinued operations and extraordinary items. The same principle applies to the investor's portion of the investee's other comprehensive income, changes in accounting policy reported in retained earnings, and capital charges. The requirement is that all of these be reported in the appropriate financial statement of the investor.[31]

To illustrate, assume that on January 1, 2008, Investor Company purchases 250,000 of Investee Company's 1 million outstanding common shares for $8.5 million. Investor has therefore acquired a 25% interest in Investee. The book value of Investee Company (i.e., its net assets) on this date is $30 million and Investor's proportionate share is 25% of this, $7.5 million. Investor Company therefore has paid $1 million in excess of its share of the book value (i.e., $8,500,000 − $7,500,000).

Why did Investor pay $1 million more than its share of Investee's book value? Assume that part of the reason is because Investee's depreciable assets **are undervalued on the books** by $2.4 million. This explains $600,000 ($2,400,000 × 25%) of the excess, as Investor would only pay more in proportion to its ownership interest. Investor Company estimates the remaining life of the depreciable assets to be eight years, so the $600,000 excess payment included in the Investment account will have to be amortized over this period.

The remaining $400,000 is unexplained and therefore is determined to be unrecorded goodwill. Although goodwill has an indefinite life, Investor will have to assess its carrying value each year to determine whether there has been any impairment in its value. This purchase is analyzed in Illustration 9-23.

[31] *CICA Handbook*, Section 3051.09.

Illustration 9-23

Analysis of Acquisition of Significantly Influenced Investee Company

Cost of 25% investment in Investee Co. shares	$8,500,000
25% of book value of Investee Co. represented by investment 25% × $30,000,000	7,500,000
Payment in excess of book value	1,000,000
Fair value allocation to depreciable assets 25% × $2,400,000	600,000
Unexplained excess assumed to be goodwill	$ 400,000
Annual amortization of excess payment for capital assets $600,000/8-year life	$ 75,000

Investee Company later reports net income of $2.8 million for its 2008 fiscal year, including a loss on discontinued operations of $400,000. **Income before discontinued operations** is therefore $3.2 million. Dividends of $1.4 million are also declared and paid by Investee Company on December 31, 2008. To record this, Investor Company's entries for 2008 are as follows:

A	= L	+ SE
0	0	0

Cash flows: ↓ 8,500,000 outflow

January 1, 2008—to record the acquisition of 25% of Investee Co. at cost:		
Investment in Investee Company	8,500,000	
Cash		8,500,000

A	= L	+ SE
0	0	0

Cash flows: ↑ 350,000 inflow

December 31, 2008—to record the receipt of the dividend from Investee Co.:		
Cash	350,000	
Investment in Investee Company ($1,400,000 × 0.25)		350,000

A	= L	+ SE
+700,000		+700,000

Cash flows: No effect

December 31, 2008—to record investment income earned:		
Investment in Investee Company	700,000	
Loss from Discontinued Operations—Investee Company	100,000	
Investment Income		800,000
(Recognition of 25% of Investee Company's income)		

A	= L	+ SE
−75,000		−75,000

Cash flows: No effect

Investment Income	75,000	
Investment in Investee Company		75,000
(Amortization of fair value difference allocated to depreciable capital assets)		

On December 31, Investor Company recognizes its 25% share of Investee Company's net income. Because Investee Company's income includes both continuing and discontinued operation components, 25% of each amount is reported separately by Investor Company. The account Investment in Investee Company is increased for 25% of the increase in Investee's net assets from earning net income (25% × $2,800,000). Furthermore, Investor Company paid more than its share of the book value for Investee Company's net assets and a portion of the excess amount relates to assets that require amortization. The "extra cost" of the depreciable assets to Investor has not been amortized by Investee because Investee only includes amortization on the book value of the assets in its accounts. As a result, the investment income needs to be adjusted for this additional expense that has not been recognized on Investee's books.

Illustration 9-24 shows the calculation of the investment in Investee Company that is presented on Investor Company's December 31, 2008, balance sheet.

Illustration 9-24
Calculation of Investment Carrying Amount

Acquisition cost, January 1, 2008	$8,500,000
Add: 25% of increase in Investee's net assets from earning net income	700,000
Less: 25% of decrease in Investee's net assets from declaration/payment of dividend	(350,000)
Less: Amortization of fair value difference related to depreciable capital assets	(75,000)
Investment in Investee Co, Dec. 31, 2008, at equity	$8,775,000

Impairment in Value

An investment that gives significant influence is assessed at each balance sheet date to determine if there has been a loss in value that is "other than temporary." If this is the case, the carrying amount of the investment is written down to reflect the reduced value and the related loss is reported in net income. No reversal of this loss is permitted even if the value subsequently recovers. The reduced carrying amount is considered to be the investment's new "cost basis."[32]

Disposals and Changes in Classification of Investment

Disposals When an investment accounted for by the equity method is sold, the balance sheet Investment account and the Investment Income account are first brought up to date as at the date of sale. This involves adjusting these accounts for the investor's share of the investee's earnings and changes in book value since the last reporting date. Then the carrying value of the investment is removed from the accounts and the difference between this and the proceeds on disposal is recognized in income as a realized gain or loss. The gain or loss on disposal is reported after income from operations and, unless there is evidence to the contrary, it is included in income before extraordinary items.

Continuing with the example in Illustrations 9-23 and 9-24, assume that Investor Company sold its investment in Investee Company on January 2, 2009, for $9 million. Because the accounts are up to date in this case, the entry to record the sale is:

Cash	9,000,000	
Investment in Investee Company		8,775,000
Gain on Sale of Investment		225,000

A	= L +	SE
+225,000		+225,000

Cash flows: ↑ 9,000,000 inflow

Changes in Classification An investment in the common shares of an investee that has been accounted for as an available-for-sale investment requires a shift to the equity method if the level of ownership or influence increases and becomes **significant** influence. In this case, the carrying amount of the prior investment plus the cost of the additional

[32] *CICA Handbook*, Sections 3051.19 and .20.

purchase is deemed to be the "cost" of all purchases to date. This acquisition cost is used as the basis for analyzing the purchase and in determining whether there are any costs in excess of the investor's share of book value.

Alternatively, if the investor's level of influence falls below the necessary level for continued use of the equity method, a change is made to use the method that is required by the new classification. In this case, the carrying amount of the investment under the equity method when the change in circumstances occurs becomes "cost" if it is to be carried at cost. If it is to be carried at fair value, the investment is adjusted to its fair value at this date.

The equity method is also known as "one-line consolidation" and is applied in ways that are closely related to how consolidation principles are applied. In fact, the equity method "investment income" is the same amount that is needed to increase or decrease the investor's income to the amount that would be reported if the investor had consolidated the results of the investee with those of the investor. Given this similarity, the complexities that result from such investments are left for an advanced accounting course that covers intercorporate investments.

Holdings with Control

Objective 9
Explain the basics of consolidation.

When one corporation acquires a voting interest of more than 50%—a **controlling interest**—in another corporation, the investor corporation is referred to as the **parent** and the investee corporation as the **subsidiary**. Because it holds a majority of the votes at the board of directors meetings of the investee company, the parent company's management virtually controls all the subsidiary's net assets and operations.

An investment in the common shares of a subsidiary is presented as a long-term investment on the separate financial statements of the parent. The investment usually is accounted for by either the equity or cost method on the parent's books. **However, when the parent company prepares its financial statements in accordance with GAAP, it must eliminate the investment and instead report, on a line-by-line basis, all the assets and liabilities of the subsidiary.**

This means that in place of the one-line long-term investment, the parent reports 100% of each of the assets and liabilities over which it has control. Instead of reporting investment income on the income statement, 100% of each of the revenues and expenses reported by the subsidiary is reported on a line-by-line basis with those of the parent company. That is, the parent presents **consolidated financial statements**. This method of reporting an investment in a controlled company is much more informative to the parent company's shareholders than a single-line balance sheet and a single-line income statement account.

The requirement to include 100% of the assets and liabilities and 100% of the revenues, expenses, gains, and losses under the parent's control even when the ownership is less than 100% leads to the recognition of a unique balance sheet and a unique income statement account. These accounts, termed **non-controlling interest** or **minority interest**, represent the percentage of the net assets **not** owned and the percentage of net income that does **not** accrue to the parent company. Treated in the past as non-shareholder claims, non-controlling interest is now being recognized as a legitimate **equity** claim.

Illustration 9-25 summarizes amounts on recent consolidated balance sheets and income statements of **Empire Company Limited**, which, as mentioned in the opening vignette to the chapter, is a diversified Canadian company whose key businesses include food retailing, real estate, and corporate investment activities. The consolidated financial statements include the accounts of all subsidiary companies, including those of **Sobeys Inc.**, which is 70.3%-owned by Empire.

Illustration 9-25

Minority (Non-Controlling) Interest on the Balance Sheet and Income Statement

EMPIRE COMPANY LIMITED
Consolidated Balance Sheets
(in millions)

	May 6, 2006	May 7, 2005
Total assets, including 100% of Sobeys Inc. **assets***	$5,051.5	$4,929.2
Total liabilities, including 100% of Sobeys Inc. **liabilities***	$2,500.9	$2,663.9
Minority interest, including 29.7% of Sobeys Inc. **net assets**	585.4	556.3
Empire Company Limited shareholders' equity	1,965.2	1,709.0
	$5,051.5	$4,929.2

Consolidated Statements of Earnings
(millions)

	Years Ended	
	May 6, 2006 (52 weeks)	May 7, 2005 (53 weeks)
Earnings before minority interest, including 100% of Sobeys Inc. **revenues and expenses***	$363.9	$250.2
Minority interest, including 29.7% of Sobeys Inc. **net earnings**	(67.1)	(63.6)
Net earnings of Empire Company Limited	$296.8	$186.6

*All intercompany assets, liabilities, revenues, and expenses are eliminated.

Underlying Concept

The consolidation of the financial results of different companies follows the economic entity assumption, disregarding the legal boundaries between entities. The key objective is to provide useful information to financial statement users about all the resources under the control of parent company management.

Consolidated financial statements disregard the distinction between separate legal entities and treat the parent and subsidiary corporations as a single economic entity. After acquisition, this means that all intercompany balances and unrealized intercompany gains and losses are eliminated for reporting purposes. An entity cannot report sales or make a profit selling to itself. The subject of when and how to prepare consolidated financial statements is discussed in detail in advanced financial accounting.

What Do the Numbers Mean?

The rules for consolidation seem very straightforward: If a company owns more than 50 percent of another company, it generally should be consolidated. If it owns less than 50 percent, it is generally not consolidated. However, with complex modern business relationships, standard setters realize that this test is too artificial, and that determining who really has control is often based on other factors than share ownership.

In fact, specific guidelines have been developed that force consolidation even though share ownership is not above 50 percent in certain situations. For example, the well-known Enron failure to consolidate three special-purpose entities that were effectively controlled by Enron led to a U.S. $569-million overstatement of income and a U.S. $1.2-billion overstatement of equity. In these three cases, the new GAAP would have led to consolidation. That is, the following factors indicate that consolidation should have occurred: the majority owner of the shares of the special-purpose entity made only a modest investment, Enron received the economic benefits from the activities of the entity, and the substantive risks and rewards related to the special entity's assets and debt rested directly or indirectly with Enron. These arrangements were not unique to Enron! Many companies used non-consolidated special-purpose entities to "window dress" or make their financial statements look better than they really were.

Such actions caused the CICA to issue Accounting Guideline AcG-15 "Consolidation of Variable Interest Entities" (VIEs) to provide guidance on such arrangements—harmonizing the CICA's approach with similar FASB guidance. The guideline requires a company to consolidate a **variable interest entity when the company is the primary beneficiary of such an entity**; that is, when it will absorb a majority of a VIE's expected losses, receive a majority of its expected residual returns, or both. The guideline applies to entities that are established in such a way that control is achieved in other ways than through ownership of voting interests.

OTHER REPORTING ISSUES

The basic issues in accounting for financial asset investments in debt and equity investments have been identified and discussed above. The following additional issues complete the reporting of such assets and are followed by a summary table of the accounting for financial investments in primary debt and equity instruments.

Differential Reporting

Objective 10
Identify the differential reporting options available for investments.

As is also stated in Chapters 2 and 18, and again in Chapter 23, *CICA Handbook* Section 1300, "Differential Reporting," recognizes that there may be situations where the costs associated with providing certain financial information may be greater than the benefits that the information brings to users. For this reason, **when a company is not publicly accountable and its owners unanimously agree, it may choose to follow alternative methods** that are specified by Section 1300.

For such companies, available-for-sale investments that would ordinarily be measured and reported at fair value—not including those with a quoted market price in an active market—may be accounted for instead at cost or amortized cost. As AFS unquoted equity investments are always measured at cost when classified as available for sale, the benefit of this option is really restricted to AFS debt investments.

Accounting for investments in equity securities that give significant influence is another area where qualifying companies may decide to use a simpler method. The allowed alternative is to account for all such investments at cost (instead of using the equity method), and reporting dividends as income.

Qualifying entities may also choose not to consolidate subsidiary companies. The allowed alternative in this case is to account for the investments either under the equity method or at cost.

Companies that select these differential reporting options must also meet strict disclosure requirements.

Financial Statement Presentation

Objective 11
Explain the objectives of classification, disclosure, and reporting requirements for financial asset investments, and identify several of the major requirements.

Investments Held for Trading, Held to Maturity, and Available for Sale

Where should each of these categories of investments be reported on a company's balance sheet? Are they current assets or long-term investments? The reality is that, except for investments held to maturity and some of those classified as held for trading, there is no automatic classification as current or long-term. Held-to-maturity investments, by definition, are **long-term** in nature until 12 months before maturity, when they are generally reclassified as current. Temporary investments in marketable securities that are held for short-term profit taking and therefore automatically classified as held for trading are **current** assets because of management's intention.

However, in situations where management has chosen the fair value option (i.e., it designates investments as held for trading or as available for sale), **intent is not a factor in that choice**. These categories are chosen because of the accounting method that management wants to use for the investments. In these cases, the marketability of the assets and management's intent for them must be assessed. Management's expressed intent should be supported by evidence, such as the history of the company's investment activities, events subsequent to the balance sheet date, and the nature and purpose of the investment. Management considers the following in deciding where these investments are included on the balance sheet:

- **Debt instruments** are classified as current or non-current based on their maturity dates and whether they are expected to be sold or redeemed in the following twelve months.
- **Equity investments** are classified as current if they are available to be used in current operations. Thus, if the invested cash that was used to purchase the equity securities is considered a contingency fund to be used whenever a need arises, then the securities are classified as current.

CICA Handbook Section 3862 presents the disclosure requirements for **financial instruments**, covering a much larger variety of financial statement items than what is seen below. The requirements are extensive and only the major ones are summarized below. Understanding the goal of the disclosure is helpful in determining and even predicting what information is reported.

International Insight

The disclosure requirements for financial assets in *CICA Handbook* Section 3862 are now harmonized with those of IFRS 7.

The objective of the disclosures for **financial asset investments in debt and equity instruments** is to provide information that enables users to evaluate the following:

1. how significant these financial assets are to an entity's financial position and performance
2. the nature and extent of risks that the entity faces as a result of these assets
3. how the entity manages these risks

To meet the first objective, companies are required to present individual amounts for each of the three categories of investments—held for trading, held to maturity, and available for sale—either on the balance sheet or in the related notes. Investments in affiliated companies must be disclosed separately. The investments' fair value is reported along with their carrying amount, where appropriate, and with information about the company's methods of valuation. The amount of net gains or losses from each of these categories is also reported in the same manner, including amounts that have been recognized in and transferred out of other comprehensive income. Companies are also required to report the total interest income on investments that are not classified as held for trading and on impaired financial assets.

Section 3862 also requires that companies report any amounts that resulted when a reclassification led to a change in accounting method from fair value to cost or amortized cost, and that companies disclose information about any financial assets that have been pledged as collateral.

Users must be given a lot of information in order to help them assess the risks facing the entity and how it manages those risks.[33] The types of risk that are associated with financial assets in general—credit, liquidity, and market risk—are discussed more fully in Chapter 16. Entities are required to identify information about their exposure to each type, and how each risk is measured and managed.

In addition to providing such qualitative disclosures, entities must also provide quantitative measures of their exposure to risk and concentrations of it, as well as specific information that is similar to what management uses internally for each major type of risk.

[33] CICA, "Financial Instruments—Disclosures, Section 3862," Exposure Draft, April 2006, par. .31–.42.

Investments Accounted for Using the Equity Method

The significance of an investment to the investor's financial position and operating results generally determines how much disclosure is required. For investments that give significant influence and are accounted for using the equity method, management must report the following:

1. Separate disclosure of the category on the balance sheet or in the notes to the financial statements
2. Separate disclosure of the income from investments that are accounted for using the equity method
3. The difference, if any, between the balance of the investment account and the amount of the investee's net book value, along with an explanation of the accounting treatment being used for the components of the difference

When the financial position and performance of an investment that is accounted for under the equity method is significant to an assessment of the investor, providing supplementary information about the investee's assets, liabilities, and income may be useful. Investments accounted for using the equity method are almost always long-term investments.

Disclosure Example

The Canadian accounting standards that cover financial asset investments have only become mandatory recently, starting with fiscal years beginning on or after October 1, 2006. As a result, Canadian companies were just beginning to apply these standards as the text went to print—too late to include examples of their reporting.

However, Biovail Corporation, a Canadian pharmaceutical company which prepares financial statements under U.S. GAAP as well as Canadian GAAP, reported many of the required disclosures in its U.S.-based statements. Excerpts from these statements for the company's year ended December 31, 2005, are presented in Illustration 9-26. Biovail reports both strategic and non-strategic investments. The company uses consolidation as well as the equity method and reports its available-for-sale securities at fair value with unrealized gains and losses recognized in other comprehensive income or loss.

Illustration 9-26

Financial Reporting and Disclosure of Investments—Biovail Corporation

Student Toolkit—Additional Disclosures

www.wiley.com/canada/kieso

CONSOLIDATED BALANCE SHEETS (partial)

In accordance with United States generally accepted accounting principles
(All dollar amounts expressed in U.S. dollars)

	At December 31	
	2005	2004
ASSETS		
Current		
Cash and cash equivalents	**$445,289**	$ 34,324
Marketable securities	**505**	5,016
Accounts receivable	**132,699**	148,762
Assets of discontinued operation held for sale	**1,893**	—
Inventories	**89,473**	110,154
Deposits and prepaid expenses	**14,923**	16,395
	684,782	314,651
Long-term assets of discontinued operation held for sale	**1,107**	—
Marketable securities	**6,859**	—
Long-term investments	**66,421**	68,046

CONSOLIDATED STATEMENTS OF INCOME (LOSS)

	Years Ended December 31 2005	2004
Operating income	**$301,874**	$221,279
Interest income	**7,175**	1,034
Interest expense	**(37,126)**	(40,104)
Foreign exchange loss	**(1,417)**	(564)
Equity loss	**(1,160)**	(4,179)
Other income (expense)	—	(2,307)
Income (loss) from continuing operations before provision for (recovery of) income taxes	**269,346**	175,159
Provision for (recovery of) income taxes	**22,550**	8,950
Net income (loss) from continuing operations	**246,796**	166,209
Loss from discontinued operation	**(10,575)**	(5,215)
Net income (loss)	**$236,221**	$160,994

CONSOLIDATED STATEMENT OF SHAREHOLDERS' EQUITY

	Deficit	Accumulated other comprehensive income (loss)	Comprehensive income
Balance, December 31, 2004	$(446,684)	$42,082	
Dividends paid	(79,779)	—	
	(526,463)	42,082	
Net income	236,221	—	**$236,221**
Other comprehensive income			
Foreign currency translation adjustment	—	4,597	**4,597**
Unrealized holding gain on available-for-sale investments	—	2,465	**2,465**
Other comprehensive income	—	7,062	**7,062**
Comprehensive income			**$243,283**
Balance, December 31, 2005	$(290,242)	$49,144	

NOTES TO CONSOLIDATED FINANCIAL STATEMENTS

2. SIGNIFICANT ACCOUNTING POLICIES

PRINCIPLES OF CONSOLIDATION

The consolidated financial statements include the accounts of the Company and those of all its wholly-owned and majority-owned subsidiaries. All intercompany transactions and balances have been eliminated.

FAIR VALUE OF FINANCIAL INSTRUMENTS

Fair value of a financial instrument is defined as the amount at which the instrument could be exchanged in a current transaction between willing parties. The estimated fair values of cash equivalents, accounts receivable, accounts payable, accrued liabilities and income taxes payable approximate their carrying values due to their short maturity periods. The fair values of marketable securities, long-term investments, long-term obligations, and derivative financial instruments are based on quoted market prices, if available, or estimated discounted future cash flows.

CASH AND CASH EQUIVALENTS

Cash and cash equivalents include certificates of deposit, treasury bills, investment-grade commercial paper and money market funds with original maturities of 90 days or less when purchased.

MARKETABLE SECURITIES

Marketable securities comprise investment-grade debt securities with original maturities greater than 90 days when purchased and are accounted for as being available-for-sale. These securities are reported at fair value with all unrealized gains and losses recognized in comprehensive income and loss. Realized gains and losses on the sale of these securities are recognized in net income or loss. The amortization of acquisition premiums or discounts is recorded as a deduction from or addition to interest income earned on these securities.

LONG-TERM INVESTMENTS

Long-term investments with determinable market values, where the Company does not have the ability to exercise significant influence, are accounted for as being available-for-sale. These investments are reported at fair value with all unrealized gains and temporary unrealized losses recognized in comprehensive income or loss. Unrealized losses on these investments that are considered to be other-than-temporary are recognized in net income or loss.

Long-term investments without readily determinable market values, where the Company does not have the ability to exercise significant influence, are accounted for using the cost method. Declines in the fair value of these investments below their cost basis that are considered to be other-than-temporary are recognized in net income or loss.

A long-term investment over which the Company has the ability to exercise significant influence is accounted for using the equity method. The Company's share of the losses of this investee is recognized in net income or loss.

On an ongoing basis, the Company evaluates its long-term investments to determine if a decline in fair value is other-than-temporary. Factors that the Company considers include general market conditions, the duration and extent to which the fair value of an investment is below its cost basis and the Company's ability and intent to hold the investment.

8. MARKETABLE SECURITIES

The amortized cost and estimated fair value of marketable securities were as follows:

2005	Amortized cost	Unrealized losses	Fair value
Maturing within one year	$ 511	$ (6)	$ 505
Maturing after one year	6,920	(61)	6,859
	$ 7,431	$ (67)	$ 7,364

11. LONG-TERM INVESTMENTS

	2005	2004
Ethypharm	**$ 30,000**	$ 30,000
Depomed	**26,102**	23,646
Reliant Pharmaceuticals, LLC	**6,259**	8,929
Western Life Sciences Venture Fund	—	872
Other	**4,060**	4,599
	$ 66,421	$ 68,046

ETHYPHARM

In April 2002, the Company invested $67,802,000, including costs of acquisition, to acquire 9,794,118 common shares (15% of the issued and outstanding common shares) of Ethypharm. This investment is being accounted for using the cost method.

In December 2004, the Company recorded a $37,802,000 write-down to the carrying value of its investment in Ethypharm to reflect an other-than-temporary decline in the estimated fair value of this investment. The Company continues to evaluate Ethypharm's financial condition, results of operations and cash flows for additional indications of impairment.

DEPOMED

In July 2002, the Company invested $13,675,000, including costs of acquisition, to acquire 2,465,878 newly issued common shares (15% of the issued and outstanding common shares) of Depomed. In April 2003, in connection with a private placement by Depomed, the Company acquired an additional 1,626,154 common shares of Depomed for $3,533,000. The Company also obtained warrants to acquire 569,154 shares of Depomed, which are exercisable from July 2003 until April 2008 at an exercise price of $2.16 per share. The Company has not exercised these warrants.

The investment in Depomed has been classified as being available-for-sale. At December 31, 2005 and 2004, the Company's investment represented approximately 10% and 12% of the issued and outstanding common shares of Depomed. The Company recorded unrealized holding gains of $2,456,000 and $20,572,000 in 2005 and 2003, respectively, and an unrealized holding loss of $6,916,000 in 2004, in other comprehensive income to reflect changes in the fair value of this investment.

WESTERN LIFE SCIENCES VENTURE FUND

In December 2001, the Company committed to an aggregate capital contribution of approximately $7,790,000 to a limited partnership under the name of Western Life Sciences Venture Fund. The purpose of this fund is to invest in early-stage biotechnology companies. The Company has the exclusive right to negotiate for the distribution, sales, marketing or licensing rights to any products of the investee companies of this fund. This investment is denominated in Canadian dollars and is being accounted for using the equity method.

At December 31, 2005 and 2004, the Company had invested a total of $5,795,000 to acquire Class A units of this fund. At December 31, 2005 and 2004, the Company's investment represented approximately 29% and 28%, respectively, of the total issued and outstanding Class A units. In 2005, 2004 and 2003, the Company's share of the net losses of this fund was $1,160,000, $4,179,000 and $1,010,000, respectively. At December 31, 2005, the Company provided $554,000 for its cumulative share of the net losses of this fund in excess of its investment to date, as the Company has committed to provide additional capital contributions.

Perspectives

To effectively analyze a company's performance and position, it is essential to understand the accounting and reporting for the entity's investments. Some of the key aspects that analysts watch for include the following:

1. Separation of investment results from operating results
2. The relationship between the investment asset and related returns
3. Information that is lost in the process of consolidation

Because the income statement reports on management's performance in operating the company's assets, it is important to separate the results of active operating income from the investment returns, where management's role is more passive. As gains or losses on sales of investments or special dividends can obscure a company's operating performance, these must be separately identified and assessed.

Accounting standards require disclosures that make it possible for a reader to relate the investment category on the balance sheet to the investment income reported on the income statement, and to the holding gains and losses in other comprehensive income.

Understanding the effects of the accounting methods that are used for different categories of investments is a key requirement for the analyst. If an entity has significant investments in companies that are accounted for by the equity method, for example, the analyst needs to be aware that some information is not available because the one-line investment account hides the debt and risk characteristics of the investee company that the entity is exposed to.

Consolidation of subsidiary companies also presents problems. While the financial statements reflect the combined operations of the economic entity, important information is lost through aggregating the parent's results with those of its subsidiaries. This is why segmented information, discussed in Chapter 23, has to be reported in the notes. Analysts also watch for major acquisitions during the current or previous year. The balance sheet contains all the assets of the subsidiary, but the income statement includes only the income earned by the subsidiary since it was acquired by the parent. Any analysis that looks at relationships between income and assets has to adjust for major acquisitions in the period(s) being examined.

Comparison of Canadian and International GAAP

Objective 12
Compare current Canadian and international GAAP.

With recent changes in Canadian accounting standards for financial instruments, there are now few significant differences (at the intermediate level) between Canadian accounting for investments and the international standards. As with other topics, there are differences in vocabulary and guidance, but these do not affect the intent or the outcome of applying the standards.[34] Illustration 9-27 presents the major primary sources of Canadian GAAP and the corresponding international GAAP for investments in primary debt and equity securities of other enterprises.

Illustration 9-27
Primary Sources of GAAP

Canada	International
Section 1530: Comprehensive income	IAS 1: Presentation of financial statements
Section 1590: Subsidiaries	IAS 27: Consolidated and separate financial statements
Section 1600: Consolidated financial statements	IAS 27: Consolidated and separate financial statements IFRS 3: Business combinations
Section 3051: Investments	IAS 28: Investments in associates IAS 36: Impairment of assets
Section 3855: Financial instruments—recognition	IAS 39: Financial instruments: recognition and measurement
Section 3862: Financial instruments—disclosures	IFRS 7: Financial instruments: disclosures
Section 3863: Financial instruments—presentation	IAS 32: Financial instruments: presentation

Non-strategic financial assets: recognition, measurement, and reporting While *CICA Handbook* Section 3855 generally allows any financial asset to be designated as held for trading as long as its fair value can be measured reliably, IAS 39 permits this discretionary classification only when it gives a more relevant measure, when the asset is measured and evaluated internally on a fair value basis, or when this treatment eliminates an accounting mismatch on the income statement.[35] Where Section 3855 permits AFS equity investments to be reported at fair value only when a quoted price is available in an active market, IAS 39 requires all AFS equity investments to be accounted for at fair value unless this value cannot be readily determined. In other words, the two sources use different benchmarks.

Two additional differences reflect a lack of convergence, although the intention in the long term is to have the IASB and Canadian AcSB require the same standard. While they both require that transaction costs on HFT investments be expensed immediately, the AcSB permits a choice of accounting treatment for other classifications. IAS 39 requires that transaction costs for other classifications be capitalized as part of the initial carrying amount of the item. Standards for the measurement of impairment losses are also different, and under IAS 39, impairment losses can be reversed in some circumstances when the impairment loss subsequently decreases. Under Section 3855, no impairment losses are reversed.

Under *Handbook* Section 3855, special conditions for related-party transfers of financial instruments complicate the standards. Neither the FASB nor IASB standards have such related-party conditions. And IAS 39 explicitly covers asset derecognition, a topic not addressed by the Canadian standard.

New *Handbook* Section 3862 and IFRS 7 on disclosure are almost fully converged, although certain paragraphs are different. There are variations in the treatment of asset derecognition and impairment, and there are no differential reporting options in the international standard.

[34] For example, IAS 39 uses the term "financial assets at fair value through profit or loss" for held-for-trading financial assets.

[35] The accounting "mismatch" refers to hedging situations where the changes in fair value are recognized in different accounting periods.

Comprehensive income While current Canadian and international standards are converged, the IASB and FASB are working on a joint project on many aspects of financial statement presentation which may result in short-term differences.

Investments with significant influence Both sets of standards in this area are converged, except for the standards for impairment. The international test for impairment differs from the test in *Handbook* Section 3051, as does the measurement of the loss and ability to subsequently reverse such a charge. Although the AcSB encourages a move to convergence in this area, it may not happen before the changeover date to the IFRSs.

Consolidation In terms of what was discussed about consolidation in Chapter 9, there are no major differences between the Canadian and international standards. This topic, however, and that of the related business combination standards are currently being examined in major projects by FASB and the IASB. The AcSB intends to issue converged standards when these projects are concluded, with an expected effective date in 2009.

Summary

The major primary debt and equity investments and their usual accounting and reporting treatment are summarized in Illustration 9-28.

Illustration 9-28

Summary of Usual Treatment of Major Debt and Equity Investments

Category	Balance Sheet	Income Statement
Held-for-trading (debt and equity investments)	Reported at fair value. Current or non-current assets, depending on nature and intent.	Interest and dividends are recognized as income. (If there is separate reporting of interest, effective interest method is used.) Unrealized holding gains and losses are included in net income.
Available-for-sale (debt and equity investments with quoted market value)	Reported at fair value. Current or non-current assets. Unrealized holding gains and losses are separate component of shareholders' equity (AOCI).	Interest (effective interest method) and dividends are recognized as income. Unrealized holding gains and losses are included in other comprehensive income (OCI).
Available-for-sale (equity investments with no quoted market value)	Reported at cost. Current or non-current assets.	Interest and dividends are recognized as income. Holding gains and losses are recognized only when realized.
Held-to-maturity (debt investments)	Reported at amortized cost. Long-term assets until 12 months to maturity; then current assets.	Interest recognized in income (effective interest method).
Equity method (equity investments)	Originally recognized at cost. Periodically adjusted for investor's share of changes in investee's net assets from earning income and paying dividends. Classified as long-term.	Income is recognized according to the share of the investee's earnings or losses that are reported after the date of investment.
Parent/subsidiary (control)—consolidation	Assets and liabilities of both are added together on line-by-line basis.	Revenues, expenses, gains, and losses are added together on line-by-line basis.

Glossary

www.wiley.com/canada/kieso

Summary of Learning Objectives

1 Explain the difference between strategic and non-strategic investments in financial assets.

Investments in other companies' debt and equity instruments are made for a variety of purposes: to earn a return on surplus cash until it is needed, to benefit from appreciation in the value of the instrument, to be able to influence the strategic decisions of another company so that they benefit the investor, or to control those decisions around the investee's boardroom table. The first two examples are non-strategic in nature, whereas the latter two involve strategies that are used by the investor company's management to plan and operate the business.

2 Define and account for held-to-maturity investments.

Held-to-maturity investments are financial assets with fixed (or determinable) payments and a fixed maturity date that the entity has the intent and ability to hold to maturity. These are investments in debt instruments which are accounted for at amortized cost. No changes in value are recognized unless there is impairment in value. Interest income, recognized using the effective interest method, is recognized in net income.

3 Identify and account for investments classified as held for trading.

For purposes of this chapter, a "trading" financial asset can be one of two types. First, it could be a short-term or temporary investment that is not a loan or receivable, and is acquired mainly in order to sell it in the near term. Secondly, however, it could be any financial asset designated as held for trading by an entity when it is first acquired. The second type exists so that organizations can choose to apply the method of accounting required for these financial assets. Held-for-trading financial assets are accounted for at fair value, with changes in value recognized in net income.

4 Define available-for-sale financial assets and explain how they, and any associated gains and losses, are accounted for and reported.

Available-for-sale investments, a default category, are financial assets that are not classified as loans and receivables, held to maturity, or held for trading. They are accounted for mainly at fair value, with changes in value recognized in other comprehensive income until they are disposed of. On disposal, previously recognized gains or losses are transferred to net income.

5 Account for investments in available-for-sale equity instruments.

Equity instruments classified as available for sale are measured at fair value, with gains and losses recognized in other comprehensive income until the instruments are impaired or sold. Dividends are recognized in net income in the period when they are received or receivable. AFS equity investments that do not have a quoted market price in an active market are accounted for at cost, with no changes in value being recognized unless there is impairment.

6 Account for investments in available-for-sale debt instruments.

Because interest income on AFS investments in debt instruments is accounted for using the effective interest method, accounting for available-for-sale debt investments is more complex. The investment is measured at fair value, with gains and losses recognized in other comprehensive income until the investment is impaired or sold.

KEY TERMS

accumulated other comprehensive income (AOCI), 523
amortized cost, 513
available for sale (AFS), 523
carrying amount, 521
comprehensive income, 523
consolidated financial statements, 542
controlling interest, 542
debt securities, 509
derivative, 509
economic entity, 543
effective interest method, 514
equity instruments, 510
equity method, 537
equity pickup, 538
fair value, 510
fair value option, 518
financial asset, 509
held for trading (HFT), 518
held to maturity (HTM), 512
holding gain or loss, 518
impairment, 517
investee, 510
investor, 510
minority interest, 542
non-controlling interest, 542
on margin, 511
other comprehensive income (OCI), 523
parent, 542
realized, 511
reclassification adjustment, 526
regular-way purchase or sale, 511
significant influence, 537
subsidiary, 542
tainted, 513
transaction costs, 511

7 Explain the difference between investments where an investor has no significant influence, has significant influence, or has control, and identify how each type should be accounted for and reported.

In general, where an investor has less than 20% of the voting shares, it is presumed that the investor has no significant influence over the strategic decisions of the investee. Between 20% and 50%, it is presumed that significant influence can be exercised. When over 50% of the votes are held, the investor can control the strategic decisions made by the board of directors of the investee company. These percentages are not absolute, but guides only—the actual situation is assessed in each case. If there is control, a parent-subsidiary relationship exists and the parent company consolidates the subsidiary when it prepares its GAAP financial statements. If significant influence exists, the equity method is used. If there is no significant influence, the investment is accounted for as an HFT or AFS investment.

8 Explain and apply the equity method of accounting.

Under the equity method, it is acknowledged that there is a substantive economic relationship between the investor and the investee. The investment is originally recorded at cost but is subsequently adjusted each period for changes in the net assets of the investee. That is, the investment's carrying amount is periodically increased (decreased) by the investor's proportionate share of the earnings (losses) of the investee, and is decreased by all dividends received by the investor from the investee. In addition, adjustments are made to investment income and the asset carrying amount for the amortization or realization of any of the fair value differences indicated in the original purchase price. Unrealized gains and losses between the two companies are also eliminated.

9 Explain the basics of consolidation.

Consolidation is a process of substituting the balance in the investment in subsidiary account with 100% of the assets and liabilities of the subsidiary company, line-by-line, and then offsetting this by a non-controlling interest account for the portion of the net assets of the investee company that is not owned by the parent. The parent investor adds all the revenues, expenses, gains, and losses of the investee, on a line-by-line basis, to the same categories of the investor company, again reduced by an account for the non-controlling interest in the investee's income. Any unrealized intercompany gains and losses and intercompany balances are eliminated on consolidation.

10 Identify the differential reporting options available for investments.

Available-for-sale investments that are ordinarily measured at fair value may be accounted for instead at cost or amortized cost, except when they have a quoted market price in an active market. Investments in equity securities that give significant influence may be accounted for at cost, and qualifying entities may also choose not to consolidate subsidiary companies.

11 Explain the objectives of classification, disclosure, and reporting requirements for financial asset investments, and identify several of the major requirements.

Classification as current or long-term assets is based on similar requirements for all assets. The basic question is, "Can and are they expected to be available for operating purposes within one year or the operating cycle if longer?" Disclosure in general is guided by the goal of ensuring that users can assess how significant the financial asset investments are to the financial position and performance of the entity, the risks that the entity is exposed to, and how the risks are managed. Disclosure standards require that investments be identified by category on the balance sheet and that the related amounts of income be reported in net income or other comprehensive income. Entities are required to disclose the amount of realized gains and losses on AFS securities that have been transferred from AOCI to net income, as well as impairment losses and information about transfers between categories of investment. Both qualitative and quantitative information is required about exposure to risk and risk management strategies.

12 Compare current Canadian and international GAAP.

Current standards in Canada are largely aligned with those of the IASB. There are minor differences in the classification and subsequent accounting for some financial assets, and in accounting for transaction costs. The accounting for impairments and derecognition of financial assets are the major differences. An ongoing, joint FASB-IASB project on financial statement presentation will likely result in changes in the basic presentation of financial statement information in the short term. While they will not affect the limited aspects of consolidation that were covered in this chapter, projects on business combinations and consolidation that are currently underway will significantly change the requirements in these areas.

Brief Exercises

(LO 2) BE9-1 Montreal Limited purchased $50,000 of five-year, 9% bonds of Parry Sound Corporation for $46,304, which provide an 11% return, and classified the purchase as a held-to-maturity investment. Prepare Montreal's journal entries for (a) the investment purchase and (b) the receipt of the first year's annual interest and discount amortization.

(LO 2) BE9-2 Mu Corporation purchased $40,000 of five-year, 8% bonds of Phang Inc. for $43,412, which provide a 6% return, and classified the purchase as a held-to-maturity investment. The bonds pay interest semi-annually. Prepare Mu's journal entries for (a) the investment purchase and (b) the receipt of semi-annual interest and premium amortization for the first two interest payments that will be received.

(LO 3) BE9-3 On October 1, Robinson Ltd. purchased bonds with a face value of $20,000 and classified the investment as held for trading. The bonds were priced at $21,100 plus $1,620 for the accrued interest purchased. At December 31, Robinson received in cash the annual interest of $2,000 due December 31, and the bonds' fair value was $21,500. Prepare Robinson's journal entries for (a) the purchase of the investment and accrued interest, (b) the interest received, and (c) the fair value adjustment.

(LO 3) BE9-4 Peaman Corporation purchased 300 common shares of Galactica Inc. as a short-term trading investment for $9,900 on September 8. In December, Galactica declared and paid a cash dividend of $1.75 per share. At year end, December 31, Galactica shares were selling for $35.50 per share. Prepare Peaman Corporation's journal entries to record (a) the purchase of the investment, (b) the dividends received, and (c) the fair value adjustment.

(LO 3) BE9-5 Using the information from BE9-4, assume that the Galactica shares were selling for $31.45 at December 31. Prepare the fair value adjustment required at that date.

(LO 5) BE9-6 Pacioli Corporation purchased 300 common shares of Galetti Inc. for $9,900 and classified them as an available-for-sale investment. During the year, Galetti paid a cash dividend of $3.25 per share. At year end, Galetti shares were selling for $34.50 per share. Prepare Pacioli's journal entries to record (a) the investment purchase, (b) the dividends received, and (c) the fair value adjustment.

(LO 5) BE9-7 Muhammad Corporation has an available-for-sale portfolio of shares with a year-end fair value of $40,000 and a cost of $35,000. Assuming the portfolio's carrying amount is $37,000 before adjustment, prepare the journal entry at year end.

(LO 6) BE9-8 Using the information from BE9-1, assume instead that the bonds were purchased January 1, 2007, and classified as available for sale. Prepare Montreal Limited's journal entries for (a) the purchase of the investment, (b) the receipt of the annual interest on December 31, 2007, and (c) the year-end fair value adjustment. The bonds have a year-end fair value of $47,200.

BE9-9 The following information relates to Cargall Corp. for 2008: net income $800,000; unrealized holding gain of $20,000 related to available-for-sale investments during the year; accumulated other comprehensive income of $60,000 on January 1, 2008. Determine (a) other comprehensive income for 2008, (b) comprehensive income for 2008, and (c) accumulated other comprehensive income at December 31, 2008. **(LO 6)**

BE9-10 Penn Corporation purchased for $300,000 a 25% interest in Teller, Inc. This investment gives Penn significant influence over Teller. During the year, Teller earned net income of $180,000 and paid dividends of $60,000. Assuming the purchase price was equal to 25% of Teller's net book value when it was acquired, prepare Penn's journal entries related to this investment. **(LO 8)**

BE9-11 Khalid Corporation purchased for $630,000 a 30% interest in Mahmood Corporation on January 2, 2008. At that time, the book value of Mahmood's net assets was $1.9 million. Any excess of cost over book value can be attributed to unrecorded intangibles with a useful life of 20 years. Prepare Khalid's December 31, 2008, entry to amortize the excess of cost over book value. **(LO 8)**

Exercises

E9-1 (Investment Classifications) Identify the best classification(s) for each of the securities described below. Each case is independent of the others. **(LO 1)**

1. A bond that will mature in four years was bought one month ago when the price dropped. As soon as the value increases, which is expected next month, it will be sold.
2. Ten percent of the outstanding shares of Farm Corp. were purchased. The company is planning on eventually getting a total of 30% of the outstanding shares.
3. Ten-year bonds were purchased this year. The bonds mature on January 1 of next year.
4. Bonds that will mature in five years are purchased. The company would like to hold them until they mature, but money has been tight recently and the bonds may need to be sold.
5. A bond that matures in 10 years was purchased with money that the company has set aside for an expansion project that is planned for 10 years from now.

E9-2 (Entries for Held-to-Maturity Investments) On January 1, 2008, Dagwood Corp. purchased at par 12% bonds having a maturity value of $300,000. They are dated January 1, 2008, and mature on January 1, 2013, with interest receivable on December 31 of each year. The bonds are classified in the held-to-maturity category. **(LO 2)**

Instructions

(a) Prepare the journal entry to record the bond purchase.

(b) Prepare the journal entry to record the interest received for 2008.

(c) Prepare the journal entry to record the interest received for 2009.

(d) Prepare the journal entry to record the disposal of the bond at maturity.

E9-3 (Entries for Held-to-Maturity Investments) On January 1, 2008, Mo'd Limited paid $322,744.44 for 12% bonds with a maturity value of $300,000. The bonds provide the bondholders with a 10% yield. They are dated January 1, 2008, and mature on January 1, 2013, with interest receivable on December 31 of each year. The bonds are classified in the held-to-maturity category. **(LO 2)**

Instructions

(a) Prepare the journal entry to record the bond purchase.

(b) Prepare a bond amortization schedule.

(c) Prepare the journal entry to record the interest received and the amortization for 2008.

(d) Prepare the journal entry to record the interest received and the amortization for 2009.

(e) Prepare the journal entry to record the disposal of the bond at maturity.

E9-4 (Held-to-Maturity Investments) On January 1, 2008, Phantom Corp. acquires $200,000 of Spiderman Products, Inc. 9% bonds at a price of $185,589. The interest is payable each December 31, and the bonds mature on December 31, 2010. The investment will provide Phantom Corp. with a 12% yield. The bonds are classified as held-to-maturity. **(LO 2)**

Instructions

(a) Prepare a three-year schedule of interest income and bond discount amortization.

(b) Prepare the journal entry for the interest received on December 31, 2009, including the discount amortization.

(c) Prepare the journal entries for the interest received on December 31, 2010, including the discount amortization, and for the maturity of the bond.

(LO 3) **E9-5 (HFT Investments)** On December 31, 2007, Tiger Corp. provided you with the following pre-adjustment information regarding its portfolio of investments held for short-term profit-taking:

	December 31, 2007	
Investments (Trading)	Carrying Amount	Fair Value
Clemson Corp. shares	$20,000	$19,000
Colorin Corp. shares	10,000	9,000
Buffald Ltd. shares	20,000	20,600
Total portfolio	$50,000	$48,600

During 2008, Colorin Corp. shares were sold for $8,200. The fair value of the securities on December 31, 2008, was as follows: Clemson Corp. shares—$20,100; Buffald Ltd. shares—$20,500.

Instructions

(a) Prepare the adjusting journal entry needed on December 31, 2007.

(b) Prepare the journal entry to record the sale of the Colorin Corp. shares during 2008.

(c) Prepare the adjusting journal entry needed on December 31, 2008.

(LO 3) **E9-6 (Investment in Debt Instruments Held for Trading)** Alberta Corp. purchased a $100,000-face-value bond of Myers Corp. on July 31, 2007, for $105,490 plus accrued interest. The bond pays interest annually each November 1 at a rate of 9%. On November 1, 2007, Alberta Corp. received the annual interest. On December 31, 2007, Alberta's year end, a newspaper indicated a market value for these bonds of 104.6. Alberta sold the bonds on January 15, 2008, for $102,600 plus accrued interest. Assume Alberta Corp. does not report interest income separately from gains and losses on these investments.

Instructions

(a) Prepare the journal entries to record the purchase of the bond, the receipt of interest, any adjustments required at year end, and the subsequent sale of the bonds.

(b) How many months were the bonds held by Alberta in 2007? Based on this, how much of the income reported on these bonds should be for interest received? Verify that your answer fits with the income that is reported.

(c) If these bonds were acquired to earn a return on excess funds, did the company meet its objective? If yes, how much return did Alberta Corp. earn while the bonds were held? If not, why not?

(LO 3) **E9-7 (Held-for-Trading Entries)** Lazier Corporation has the following securities in its portfolio of investments classified as held for trading on December 31, 2007:

Investments (Trading)	Carrying Amount (before adjustment)	Fair Value
1,500 shares of David Jones Inc., common	$ 73,500	$ 69,000
5,000 shares of Hearn Corp., common	180,000	174,000
400 shares of Alessandro Inc., preferred	60,000	61,600
	$313,500	$304,600

In 2008, Lazier completed the following securities transactions:

Mar. 1 Sold the 1,500 shares of David Jones Inc. common at $41.50 per share, less fees of $500.
Apr. 1 Bought 700 shares of Oberto Ltd. common at $75 per share, plus fees of $1,300.

Lazier Corporation's portfolio of trading securities appeared as follows on December 31, 2008:

Investments (Trading)	Carrying Amount	Fair Value
5,000 shares of Hearn Corp., common	$174,000	$175,000
700 shares of Oberto Ltd., common	52,500	50,400
400 shares of Alessandro Inc., preferred	61,600	57,000
	$288,100	$282,400

Instructions

Prepare the Lazier Corporation general journal entries for the following:

(a) The December 31, 2007, adjusting entry

(b) The sale of the David Jones Inc. shares

(c) The purchase of the Oberto Ltd. shares

(d) The December 31, 2008, adjusting entry

E9-8 (Entries for Available-for-Sale and Held-for-Trading Equity Investments) The following information is available about Barkley Corp.'s investments at December 31, 2008. This is the first year Barkley has purchased securities for investment purposes. **(LO 3, 5)**

Securities	Cost	Fair Value
3,000 shares of Myers Corporation common shares	$40,000	$48,000
1,000 shares of Cole Inc. preferred shares	25,000	22,000
	$65,000	$70,000

Instructions

(a) Prepare the adjusting entry(ies), if any, at December 31, 2008, assuming the investments are classified as held for trading.

(b) Prepare the adjusting entry(ies), if any, at December 31, 2008, assuming the investments are classified as available for sale.

(c) Discuss how the amounts reported in the financial statements are affected by the choice of classification.

E9-9 (Equity Securities Entries) Arantxa Corporation made the following cash purchases of investments during 2008, the first year in which Arantxa invested in equity securities: **(LO 3, 5)**

1. On January 15, purchased 10,000 shares of Sanchez Corp.'s common shares at $33.50 per share plus commission of $1,980.

2. On April 1, purchased 5,000 shares of Vicario Corp.'s common shares at $52.00 per share plus commission of $3,370.

3. On September 10, purchased 7,000 shares of WTA Corp.'s preferred shares at $26.50 per share plus commission of $4,910.

On May 20, 2008, Arantxa sold 4,000 of the Sanchez common shares at a market price of $35 per share less brokerage commissions of $3,850. The year-end fair values per share were as follows: Sanchez $30; Vicario $55; and WTA $28. In addition, the chief accountant of Arantxa told you that Arantxa Corporation holds these investments with the intention of selling them in order to earn short-term profits from appreciation in their prices.

Instructions

(a) Prepare the journal entries to record the three investments.

(b) Prepare the journal entry for the sale of the 4,000 Sanchez shares on May 20.

(c) Prepare the adjusting entries needed on December 31, 2008.

(d) Repeat parts (a) to (c), assuming the investments will be classified as available for sale. Arantxa's policy is to capitalize transaction costs on the acquisition of AFS investments and reduce the proceeds on disposal.

E9-10 (Available-for-Sale Investments—Entries) On December 31, 2008, Niger Corp. provided you with the following pre-adjustment information for its available-for-sale investments: **(LO 5)**

Investments	Cost and Carrying Amount	Fair Value	Unrealized Gain (Loss)
Sordle Corp. shares	$20,000	$18,500	$(1,500)
Sten Corp. shares	10,000	9,000	(1,000)
British Corp. shares	20,000	20,600	600
Total portfolio	$50,000	$48,100	$(1,900)

During 2009, Sten Corp. shares were sold for $9,400. The fair values of the shares on December 31, 2009, were as follows: Sordle Corp. shares $19,100; British Corp. shares $20,500.

Instructions

(a) Prepare the adjusting journal entry(ies) needed on December 31, 2008.

(b) Prepare the journal entry(ies) to record the sale of the Sten Corp. shares in 2009.

(c) Prepare the adjusting journal entry needed on December 31, 2009.

(d) Early in 2010, an announcement was made that British Corp.'s major patent that was responsible for 75% of its income had lost most of its value due to a technological improvement by a competitor. As a result, British's Corp.'s share price fell to $0.20 per share or $2,000 in total for Niger's holdings. Niger determined that the share value was impaired. Provide the necessary adjusting entry(ies) to recognize these events.

(LO 5) E9-11 **(Available-for-Sale Investment Entries and Financial Statement Presentation)** At December 31, 2008, the available-for-sale equity portfolio of Steffi Inc. was as follows:

Security	Cost and Carrying Amount	Fair Value	Unrealized Gain (Loss)
A	$17,500	$15,000	$(2,500)
B	12,500	14,000	1,500
C	23,000	25,500	2,500
Total	$53,000	$54,500	$ 1,500

On January 20, 2009, Steffi Inc. sold security A for $15,100.

Instructions

(a) Prepare the adjusting entry at December 31, 2008, to adjust the portfolio to fair value.

(b) Show the balance sheet presentation of the investment-related accounts at December 31, 2008. (Ignore notes presentation.)

(c) Prepare the journal entries for the 2009 sale of security A.

(LO 5) E9-12 **(Comprehensive Income Disclosure)** Assume the same information as in E9-11 and that Steffi Inc. reports net income of $120,000 in 2008 and $140,000 in 2009. The adjusting entry to report the portfolio at fair value at the end of 2009 debited the investment portfolio in total by $4,000.

Instructions

(a) Prepare a statement of comprehensive income for 2008, starting with net income.

(b) Prepare a statement of comprehensive income for 2009, starting with net income.

(LO 5) E9-13 **(Available-for-Sale Securities Entries—Buy and Sell)** Hester Corporation has the following securities in its long-term available-for-sale investment portfolio on December 31, 2008:

Investment	Cost and Carrying Amount	Fair Value
1,500 shares of DJ Inc. common	$ 73,500	$ 69,000
5,000 shares of RH Corp. common	180,000	175,000
400 shares of AZ Inc. preferred	60,000	61,600
	$313,500	$305,600

All the investments were purchased in 2008. Hester follows a policy of capitalizing transaction costs on the acquisition of AFS investments and reducing the proceeds on disposal.

In 2009, Hester completed the following transactions:

Mar. 1 Sold the 1,500 shares of DJ Inc. at $45, less fees of $1,200.
Apr. 1 Bought 700 shares of RG Corp. at $75, plus fees of $1,300.

Hester Corporation's portfolio appeared as follows on December 31, 2009:

Investments	Cost	Fair Value
700 shares of RG Corp. common	$ 53,800	$ 50,400
5,000 shares of RH Corp. common	180,000	175,000
400 shares of AZ Inc. preferred	60,000	58,000
	$293,800	$283,400

Instructions

Prepare the general journal entries for Hester for:

1. The 2008 valuation adjusting entry
2. The sale of the DJ Inc. shares
3. The purchase of the RG Corp. shares.
4. The 2009 valuation adjusting entry

E9-14 **(Entries for Available-for-Sale Investments)** Assume the same information as in E9-3 except that the instruments are classified as available for sale. The fair values of the bonds at December 31 of each year are as follows: **(LO 6)**

2008:	$320,500	2011:	$310,000
2009:	$309,000	2012:	$300,000
2010:	$308,000		

Instructions

(a) Prepare the journal entry to record the bond purchase.

(b) Prepare the journal entries to record the interest received and recognition of fair value at December 31, 2008.

(c) Prepare the journal entries to record the interest received and recognition of fair value at December 31, 2009, 2010, 2011, and 2012.

(d) Prepare the journal entry to record the disposal of the bond at maturity.

E9-15 **(Entries for Available-for-Sale Investments)** On January 1, 2009, Jovi Inc. purchased $200,000-face-value 8% bonds of Mercury Ltd. for $184,557. The bonds were purchased to yield 10% interest. Interest is payable semi-annually on July 1 and January 1 and the bonds mature on January 1, 2014. On April 15, 2012, to meet its liquidity needs, Jovi sold the bonds for $189,769 plus accrued interest. **(LO 6)**

Instructions

(a) Prepare the journal entry to record the bond purchase on January 1, 2009. Assume that the bonds are classified as available for sale.

(b) Prepare the amortization schedule for the bonds from the date of purchase to maturity.

(c) Prepare the journal entries to record the semi-annual interest received on July 1, 2009, and December 31, 2009.

(d) The fair values of the Mercury bonds are as follows:

December 31, 2009	$190,449
December 31, 2010	$186,363
December 31, 2011	$185,363

Prepare the necessary adjusting entry to bring the investment to fair value at December 31, 2009, 2010, and 2011. (Hint: You need to take the discount amortization into account).

(e) Prepare the journal entry(ies) to record the events associated with the sale of the bonds on April 15, 2012.

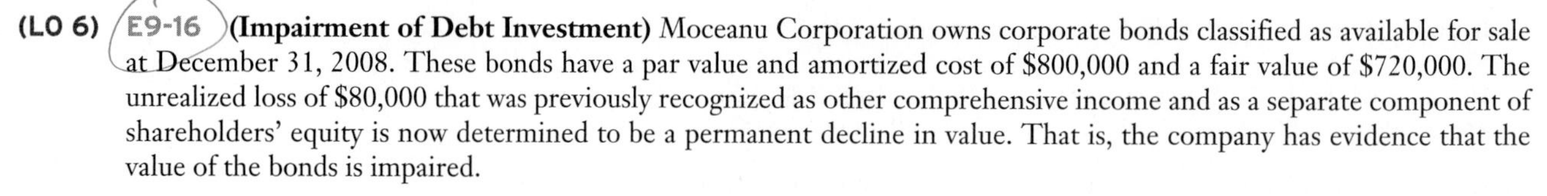

(LO 6) E9-16 (Impairment of Debt Investment) Moceanu Corporation owns corporate bonds classified as available for sale at December 31, 2008. These bonds have a par value and amortized cost of $800,000 and a fair value of $720,000. The unrealized loss of $80,000 that was previously recognized as other comprehensive income and as a separate component of shareholders' equity is now determined to be a permanent decline in value. That is, the company has evidence that the value of the bonds is impaired.

Instructions

(a) Prepare any necessary journal entry(ies) related to the impairment.

(b) What is the new cost basis of the investment? Given that the maturity value of the bonds is $800,000, should Moceanu Corporation accrete (i.e., increase) the difference between the carrying amount and the maturity value over the life of the bonds?

(c) At December 31, 2009, the fair value of the corporate bonds is $760,000. Prepare the entry (if any) to record this information.

(LO 8) E9-17 (Equity Method) Pareau Ltd. invested $1 million in Salut Corp., receiving 25% of its outstanding shares. At the time of the purchase, Salut Corp. had a book value of $3.2 million. Salut Corp. pays out 40% of its net income in dividends each year.

Instructions

Use the information in the following T account for the investment in Salut to answer the following questions:

Investment in Salut Corp.	
1,000,000	
110,000	
	44,000
	15,000

(a) How much was Pareau Ltd.'s share of Salut Corp.'s net income for the year?

(b) How much was Pareau Ltd.'s share of Salut Corp.'s dividends for the year?

(c) How much was Pareau Ltd.'s annual amortization of the excess payment for capital assets?

(d) What was Salut Corp.'s total net income for the year?

(e) What were Salut Corp.'s total dividends for the year?

(f) Assuming that depreciable assets have a remaining useful life of 10 years, how much of the payment in excess of book value was assigned to goodwill?

(LO 5, 8) E9-18 (Journal Entries for Fair Value and Equity Methods) Two independent situations follow:

Situation 1

Conchita Cosmetics acquired 10% of the 200,000 common shares of Martinez Fashion at a total cost of $13 per share on March 18, 2008. On June 30, Martinez declared and paid a $75,000 cash dividend. On December 31, Martinez reported net income of $122,000 for the year. At December 31, the market price of Martinez Fashion was $15 per share. The investment is classified as available for sale.

Situation 2

Monica, Inc. obtained significant influence over the operations of Gurion Corporation by buying 30% of Gurion's 30,000 outstanding common shares at a cost of $9 per share on January 1, 2008. The purchase price of $9 per share did not include any payment in excess of book value or goodwill. On June 15, Gurion declared and paid a cash dividend of $36,000. On December 31, Gurion reported net income of $85,000 for the year.

Instructions

Prepare all necessary journal entries in 2008 for both situations.

(LO 5, 8) E9-19 (Fair Value and Equity Method Compared) Jaycie Inc. acquired 20% of the outstanding common shares of Kulikowski Inc. on December 31, 2007. The purchase price was $1.2 million for 50,000 shares, and is equal to 20% of Kulikowski's book value. Kulikowski declared and paid an $0.85 per share cash dividend on June 30 and again on December 31, 2008. Kulikowski reported net income of $730,000 for 2008. The fair value of Kulikowski's shares was $27 per share at December 31, 2008.

AFS

Instructions

(a) Prepare the journal entries for Jaycie for 2007 and 2008, assuming that Jaycie cannot exercise significant influence over Kulikowski. The investment is classified as available for sale.

(b) Prepare the journal entries for Jaycie for 2007 and 2008, assuming that Jaycie can exercise significant influence over Kulikowski.

(c) What is reported for the investment in Kulikowski shares on the December 31, 2008, balance sheet under each of these methods? What is reported on Jaycie's income statement and statement of comprehensive income in 2008 under each of these methods?

E9-20 (Long-Term Equity Investments and Impairment) On January 1, 2008, Warner Corporation purchased 30% of the common shares of Martz Limited for $180,000. The book value of Martz's net assets was $500,000 on that date. During the year, Martz earned net income of $80,000 and paid dividends of $20,000. Any excess of the purchase cost over Warner's share of Martz's book value is attributable to unrecorded intangibles with a 20-year life. The investment in Martz had a fair value of $185,000 at December 31, 2008. During 2009, Martz incurred a loss of $80,000 and paid no dividends. At December 31, 2009, the fair value of the investment was $140,000. **(LO 5, 6, 8)**

Instructions

(a) Prepare all relevant journal entries related to Warner's investment in Martz for 2008 and 2009, assuming this is its only investment and Warner cannot exercise significant influence over Martz's policies. Warner classifies this investment as available for sale. There is evidence that the decline in Martz's value in 2009 is considered a permanent decline. Illustrate how Other Comprehensive Income is affected in 2008 and 2009.

(b) Prepare all relevant journal entries related to Warner's investment in Martz for 2008 and 2009, assuming this is its only investment and Warner exercises significant influence over Martz's policies. There is evidence that the decline in value in 2009 is considered a permanent decline. Identify any amounts that affect Other Comprehensive Income in 2008 and 2009. Briefly explain.

(c) How would your answer to part (b) be different if you were told that Martz's net income included an extraordinary loss of $10,000 (net of tax).

E9-21 (Determine Proper Income Reporting) The following are two independent situations for you to solve: **(LO 5, 8, 9)**

1. Bacall Inc. received dividends from its common share investments during the year ended December 31, 2008, as follows:
   (a) A cash dividend of $12,000 is received from Sleep Corporation. Bacall owns a 2% interest in Sleep.
   (b) A cash dividend of $60,000 is received from Largo Corporation. Bacall owns a 30% interest in Largo and a majority of Bacall's directors are also directors of Largo Corporation.
   (c) A cash dividend of $72,000 is received from Orient Inc., a subsidiary of Bacall.

   Determine how much dividend income Bacall should report in its 2008 consolidated income statement.
2. On January 3, 2008, Bach Corp. purchased as a long-term (available-for-sale) investment 5,000 common shares of Starr Ltd. for $79 per share, which represents a 2% interest. On December 31, 2008, the shares' market price was $83 per share. On March 3, 2009, Bach sold all 5,000 shares of Starr for $102 per share. Determine the amount of the gain or loss on disposal that should be included in net income in 2009 and in comprehensive income. The investment in Starr Ltd. was Bach Corp.'s only investment.

E9-22 (Equity Method with Cost in Excess of Book Value) On January 1, 2008, Jana Limited purchased 2,500 shares (25%) of the common shares of Novotna Corp. for $355,000. At the date of acquisition, the following additional information relates to the identifiable assets and liabilities of Novotna: **(LO 8)**

	Carrying Amount	Fair Value
Assets not subject to amortization	$ 500,000	$ 500,000
Assets subject to amortization (10 years remaining)	800,000	860,000
Total identifiable assets	1,300,000	1,360,000
Liabilities	100,000	100,000

During 2008, Novotna reported the following information on its income statement:

Income before extraordinary item	$200,000
Extraordinary gain (net of tax)	70,000
Net income	270,000
Dividends declared and paid by Novotna during 2008	120,000

Instructions

(a) Prepare the journal entry to record Jana's purchase of the Novotna shares on January 1, 2008. Assume that any unexplained payment is goodwill.

(b) Prepare the journal entries to record Jana's equity in the net income and dividends of Novotna for 2008. Depreciable assets are amortized on a straight-line basis.

(LO 8) E9-23 (Equity Method with Cost in Excess of Book Value) On January 1, 2008, Strug Inc. purchased 40% of the common shares of Chow Corp. for $400,000. Chow Corp.'s balance sheet reported the following information at the date of acquisition:

Assets not subject to amortization	$200,000
Assets subject to amortization (8 years remaining)	600,000
Liabilities	100,000

Additional information:

1. Both book value and fair value are the same for assets that are not subject to amortization and for the liabilities.
2. The fair value of the assets subject to amortization is $680,000.
3. The company amortizes its capital assets on a straight-line basis.
4. Chow reported net income of $160,000 and declared and paid dividends of $125,000 in 2008.

Instructions

(a) Prepare the journal entry to record Strug's investment in Chow Corp. Assume that any unexplained payment is goodwill.

(b) Prepare the journal entries to record Strug's equity in the net income and dividends of Chow Corp. for 2008.

(c) Assume the same facts as for parts (a) and (b), except that Chow's net income included a loss on discontinued operations of $30,000 (net of tax). Prepare the journal entries to record Strug's equity in the net income of Chow for 2008.

(d) Assume the same facts as above for parts (a) and (b), except that Chow also reports an unrealized gain on available-for-sale investments of $45,000 in Other Comprehensive Income . Explain how your answer to part (b) above would change.

Problems

P9-1 Gypsy Clothing Corp. has the following portfolio of securities classified as held for trading at September 30, 2007, the end of the company's third quarter:

Investment	Cost	Fair Value
5,000 common shares of Alpha Inc.	$225,000	$196,000
3,500 preferred shares of Epsilon Ltd.	133,000	140,000
1,000 common shares of Sigma Supply Inc.	180,000	176,000

On October 10, 2007, the Alpha shares were sold at $57 per share. On November 2, 2007, 3,000 common shares of Gamma Corp. were purchased at $59.50 per share. Gypsy pays a 1% commission on purchases and sales of all securities. At the end of the fourth quarter, on December 31, 2007, the fair values of the shares held were as follows: Epsilon $96,000; Gamma $132,000; and Sigma $193,000. Gypsy Clothing prepares financial statements every quarter.

Instructions

(a) Prepare the journal entries to record the sale, purchase, and adjusting entries related to the portfolio for the fourth quarter of 2007.

(b) Indicate how the investments would be reported on the December 31, 2007, balance sheet. State any assumptions that you have made.

P9-2 The following information relates to the 2008 debt and equity investment transactions of Yellowjackets Ltd. All of the investments have been designated as held for trading. No investments were held at December 31, 2007, and the company only prepares financial statements annually each December 31.

1. On February 1, the company purchased Williams Corp. 12% bonds, with a par value of $500,000, at 106.5 plus accrued interest to yield 10%. Interest is payable April 1 and October 1.

2. On April 1, semi-annual interest was received on the Williams bonds.
3. On July 1, 9% bonds of Saint Inc. were purchased. These bonds, with a par value of $200,000, were purchased at 101 plus accrued interest to yield 8.5%. Interest dates are June 1 and December 1.
4. On August 12, 3,000 shares of Royal Bank of Canada were acquired at a cost of $59 per share. A 1% commission was paid.
5. On September 1, Williams Corp. bonds with a par value of $100,000 were sold at 104 plus accrued interest.
6. On September 28, a dividend of $0.50 per share was received on the Royal Bank shares.
7. On October 1, semi-annual interest was received on the remaining Williams Corp. bonds.
8. On December 1, semi-annual interest was received on the Saint Inc. bonds.
9. On December 28, a dividend of $0.52 per share was received on the Royal Bank shares.
10. On December 31, the following fair values were determined: Williams Corp. bonds 101.75; Saint Inc. bonds 97; Royal Bank shares $60.50.

Instructions

(a) Prepare all journal entries you consider necessary for the above, including year-end adjusting entries at December 31. Yellowjackets Ltd. does not track interest or dividend income separately from gains and losses on its HFT portfolio.

(b) Identify the effect that the transactions for 2008 have on the Yellowjackets Ltd. income statement for that year.

(c) Assume instead that there were HFT investments on hand at December 31, 2007, and that they consisted of shares with a cost of $400,000 and a fair value of $390,000. These non-dividend-paying shares were sold early in 2008 and their original cost was recovered exactly. How would your answer to part (b) be different as a result of this information?

(d) Assume that the Saint Inc. bonds that were purchased on July 1, 2008 were classified as available for sale instead of HFT. Prepare the entries that are required on July 1, December 1, and December 31, 2008, to account for this investment.

P9-3 The following amortization schedule is for an investment in Baker Corp.'s $100,000, five-year bonds with a 7% interest rate and a 5% yield, which were purchased on December 31, 2007, for $108,660:

	Cash Received	Interest Income	Bond Premium Amortized	Amortized Cost of Bonds
Dec. 31, 2007				$108,660
Dec. 31, 2008	$7,000	$5,433	$1,567	107,093
Dec. 31, 2009	7,000	5,354	1,646	105,447
Dec. 31, 2010	7,000	5,272	1,728	103,719
Dec. 31, 2011	7,000	5,186	1,814	101,905
Dec. 31, 2012	7,000	5,095	1,905	100,000

The following schedule presents a comparison of the amortized cost and fair value of the bonds at year end:

	Dec. 31, 2008	Dec. 31, 2009	Dec. 31, 2010	Dec. 31, 2011	Dec. 31, 2012
Amortized cost	$107,093	$105,447	$103,719	$101,905	$100,000
Fair value	$106,500	$107,500	$105,650	$103,000	$100,000

Instructions

(a) Prepare the journal entry to record the purchase of these bonds on December 31, 2007, assuming the bonds are classified as held to maturity.

(b) Prepare the journal entry(ies) related to the held-to-maturity bonds for 2008.

(c) Prepare the journal entry(ies) related to the held-to-maturity bonds for 2010.

(d) Prepare the journal entry(ies), if required, to transfer the bond investment to the available-for-sale category on December 31, 2010, and any entry(ies) that are required on December 31, 2011 and 2012.

(e) Discuss the implications for the company (if any) of reclassifying the investment from held to maturity to available for sale.

(f) Prepare the journal entry(ies) to record the purchase of these bonds, assuming they are classified originally as available for sale.

(g) Prepare the journal entry(ies) related to the available-for-sale bonds for 2008.

(h) Prepare the journal entry(ies) related to the available-for-sale bonds for 2010.

(i) Prepare the journal entry(ies), if required, to transfer the available-for-sale bond investment to the held-to-maturity category on December 31, 2010, and any entry(ies) that are required on December 31, 2011 and 2012.

P9-4 Incognito Corp. has the following securities (all purchased in 2008) in its investment portfolio on December 31, 2008: (1) 3,000 shares of Bush Corp. common shares, which cost $58,500; (2) 10,000 shares of Sanborn Ltd. common shares, which cost $580,000; and (3) 6,000 shares of Abba Corp. preferred shares, which cost $255,000. Their fair market values at the end of 2008 were as follows: Bush Corp. $59,500; Sanborn Ltd. $569,500; and Abba Corp. $254,400.

In 2009, Incognito completed the following transactions:

1. On January 15, sold 3,000 Bush common shares at $23 per share less fees of $1,150.
2. On April 17, purchased 1,000 Tractors Ltd. common shares at $31.50 per share plus fees of $980.

The company adds transaction costs to the cost of acquired investments and deducts them from cash received on the sale of investments. On December 31, 2009, the market values per share of the securities were as follows: Bush $20; Sanborn $62; Abba $40; and Tractors $29. In addition, the accounting supervisor of Incognito tells you that even though all these securities have market values that can be readily determined, Incognito will not actively trade them. Management intends to hold these shares for more than one year and has classified them as available-for-sale investments.

Instructions

(a) Prepare the entries for the sale of the Bush Corp. investment on January 15, 2009.

(b) Prepare the entry to record the Tractors Ltd. share purchase on April 17, 2009.

(c) Calculate the unrealized gains or losses and prepare any required adjusting entry(ies) for Incognito Corp. on December 31, 2009.

(d) Indicate how all amounts will be reported on Incognito's balance sheet, income statement, statement of comprehensive income, and statement of changes in accumulated other comprehensive income for 2009.

P9-5 Big Brother Holdings, Inc. had the following investment portfolio classified as available for sale at January 1, 2007:

Investment	Quantity	Cost per Share	Fair Value at Dec. 31, 2006
Earl Corp.	1,000	$15.00	$11.50
Josie Corp.	900	20.00	16.50
David Corp.	500	9.00	7.20

During 2007, the following transactions took place:

1. On March 1, Josie Corp. paid a $2 per share dividend.
2. On April 30, Big Brother Holdings, Inc. sold 300 shares of David Corp. for $10 per share.
3. On May 15, Big Brother Holdings, Inc. purchased 50 more Earl Corp. shares at $16 per share.
4. At December 31, 2007, the shares had the following market prices per share: Earl Corp. $17; Josie Corp. $19; and David Corp. $8.

During 2008, the following transactions took place:

1. On February 1, Big Brother Holdings, Inc. sold the remaining David Corp. shares for $7 per share.
2. On March 1, Josie Corp. paid a $2 per share dividend.
3. On December 21, Earl Corp. declared a cash dividend of $3 per share to be paid in the next month.
4. At December 31, 2008, the shares had the following market prices per share: Earl Corp. $19; and Josie Corp. $21.

Instructions

(a) Prepare journal entries to record each of the above transactions and year-end events.

(b) Prepare the relevant parts of Big Brother Holdings, Inc.'s 2008 and 2007 comparative balance sheets, income statements, statements of comprehensive income, and statements of changes in accumulated other comprehensive income to show how the investments and related accounts are reported.

P9-6 Alvarez Corp. invested its excess cash in investments classified as available for sale during 2007. As at December 31, 2007, the portfolio consisted of the following common shares:

	Quantity	Cost	Fair Value
Jones, Inc.	1,000 shares	$ 15,000	$ 21,000
Eola Corp.	2,000 shares	50,000	42,000
Yevette Aircraft Ltd.	2,000 shares	72,000	60,000
Total		$137,000	$123,000

Instructions

(a) What should be reported on Alvarez's December 31, 2007, balance sheet for these securities? What should be reported on Alvarez's 2007 income statement and statement of comprehensive income?

(b) On December 31, 2008, Alvarez's available-for-sale portfolio consisted of the following common shares:

	Quantity	Cost	Fair Value
Jones, Inc.	3,000 shares	$ 53,000	$60,000
King Corp.	1,000 shares	16,000	12,000
Yevette Aircraft Ltd.	2,000 shares	72,000	22,000
Total		$141,000	$94,000

During 2008, Alvarez Corp. sold 2,000 shares of Eola Corp. for $38,200 and purchased 2,000 more shares of Jones, Inc. and 1,000 shares of King Corp.

What should be reported on Alvarez's December 31, 2008, balance sheet? What should be reported on Alvarez's 2008 income statement, statement of comprehensive income, and statement of changes in AOCI?

(c) On December 31, 2009, Alvarez's portfolio consisted of the following common shares:

	Quantity	Cost	Fair Value
Yevette Aircraft Ltd.	2,000 shares	$72,000	$82,000
King Corp.	500 shares	8,000	6,000
Total		$80,000	$88,000

During 2009, Alvarez Corp. sold 3,000 shares of Jones, Inc. for $39,900 and 500 shares of King Corp. at a realized loss of $2,700.

What should be reported on Alvarez's December 31, 2009, balance sheet? What should be reported on Alvarez's 2009 income statement, statement of comprehensive income, and statement of changes in AOCI?

(d) In the first quarter of 2010, the market value of King Corp. continued to fall as major customers were lost, and its share price stabilized at $1.00 per share. Alvarez assessed this investment as impaired.

Prepare any entries required to recognize the impairment and explain how this impairment will affect the 2010 balance sheet, income statement, statement of comprehensive income, and statement of changes in AOCI.

P9-7 The following information is from a bond investment amortization schedule. Related fair values are also provided and the company prepares financial statements each December 31. The bonds are classified as available for sale.

	Dec. 31, 2007	Dec. 31, 2008	Dec. 31, 2009	Dec. 31, 2010
Amortized cost	$465,045	$491,150	$519,442	$550,000
Fair value	475,000	499,000	506,000	550,000

Instructions

(a) Indicate whether the bonds were purchased at a discount or at a premium. Explain.

(b) Prepare the entry to adjust the bonds to fair value at December 31, 2008.

(c) Prepare the entry to adjust the bonds to fair value at December 31, 2009.

(d) Prepare all entries that are necessary to record the redemption of the bond at maturity on December 31, 2010.

(e) Assume that management has objective evidence that the investment's value is impaired at December 31, 2009. Prepare all entries that are necessary to record the impairment of the bond at December 31, 2009, and its redemption at maturity on December 31, 2010.

P9-8 Octavio Corp. prepares financial statements annually on December 31, its fiscal year end. At December 31, 2008, the company has the account Investments in its general ledger that contains the following debits for investment purchases, and no credits:

Feb. 1, 2008	Chiang Corp. common shares, no par value, 200 shares	$ 37,400
April 1	Government of Canada bonds, 11%, due April 1, 2018, interest payable April 1 and October 1, 100 bonds of $1,000 par value each	100,000
July 1	Monet Corp. 12% bonds, par $50,000, dated March 1, 2008, purchased at 108 plus accrued interest to yield 11%, interest payable annually on March 1, due on March 1, 2028	56,000
Nov. 1	$60,000, six-month non-interest-bearing Treasury bill that matures on May 1, 2009, bought to yield 10%	57,143

Instructions

(a) Prepare the entry that is necessary to correct any errors in the Investments account. Assume that all the instruments are classified as available for sale.

(b) Prepare the entry(ies) to record any accrued interest and the amortization of any premium or discount on December 31, 2008.

(c) The fair values of the individual securities on December 31, 2008, were:

Chiang Corp. common shares	$ 33,800
Government of Canada bonds	124,700
Monet Corp. bonds	58,600
Treasury bill	58,350

Prepare the entry(ies) that are necessary at December 31, 2008.

(d) During 2009, the following transactions took place:

1. The Treasury bill was sold on February 1, 2009, for $59,600.
2. The Government of Canada bonds were sold on July 1, 2009, for $119,200 plus accrued interest.

Prepare the proper entries to record these transactions.

(e) Using the information from part (d), assume that the Treasury bill was not sold on February 1, 2009, but instead was held until it matured. Give the proper entry to record the disposal of the Treasury bill at maturity.

(f) Explain how your answer to part (c) would change if the company used the differential reporting option. Under what conditions would this be appropriate?

P9-9 Gypsy Corporation reported the following portfolio of investments on its balance sheet at September 30, 2008, its last reporting date:

	Cost	Fair Value
Fogelberg Inc. common (5,000 shares)	$225,000	$200,000
Petra Inc. preferred (3,500 shares)	133,000	140,000
Weisberg Corp. common (1,000 shares)	180,000	179,000

On October 10, 2008, the Fogelberg Inc. shares were sold at $54 per share. In addition, 3,000 shares of Los Tigres Corp. common shares were acquired at $59.50 per share on November 2, 2008. A 1% commission is charged by the company's broker on all transactions and the company's policy is to capitalize all such costs. The December 31, 2008, fair values were as follows: Petra Inc. $96,000; Los Tigres Corp. $132,000; and Weisberg Corp. $193,000. All the investments are classified as available for sale.

Instructions

(a) Prepare the journal entries to record the sale, purchase, and adjusting entries related to the available-for-sale investment portfolio in the last quarter of 2008.

(b) Show how all amounts will be reported on Gypsy Corporation's balance sheet, income statement, statement of comprehensive income, and statement of changes in accumulated other comprehensive income for the quarter ending December 31, 2008.

(c) How would the entries in part (a) change if the securities were classified as trading investments, and how would your answer to part (b) be different?

P9-10 The following information relates to the debt investments of Surin Inc. during a recent year:

1. On February 1, the company purchased Vanessa Corp. 12% bonds with a face value of $500,000 at 100 plus accrued interest. Interest is payable on April 1 and October 1.
2. On April 1, semi-annual interest is received on the Vanessa bonds.
3. On July 1, Chieftains Inc. 9% bonds were purchased. The $200,000-par-value bonds were purchased at 100 plus accrued interest. Interest dates are June 1 and December 1.
4. On September 1, Vanessa Corp. bonds with a par value of $100,000 purchased on February 1 were sold at 99 plus accrued interest.
5. On October 1, semi-annual interest is received on the remaining Vanessa Corp. bonds.
6. On December 1, semi-annual interest is received on the Chieftains Inc. bonds.
7. On December 31, the fair values of the bonds purchased on February 1 and July 1 are 95 and 93, respectively.

Instructions

(a) Prepare any journal entries that you consider necessary, including December 31 year-end entries, assuming the investments are classified as available for sale.

(b) If Surin classified these as held to maturity, explain how the journal entries would differ from the entries in part (a).

(c) If Surin chose the fair value option, explain how the journal entries would differ from the entries in part (a).

(d) For parts (a), (b) and (c), show the December 31 presentation of the balance sheet, income statement, statement of comprehensive income, and statement of changes in accumulated other comprehensive income.

(e) Discuss what factors the company would consider in deciding whether to account for its investments as held for trading, available for sale, or held to maturity.

P9-11 Pacers Corp. is a medium-sized corporation that specializes in quarrying stone for building construction. The company has long dominated the market, and at one time had 70% market penetration. During prosperous years, the company's profits and conservative dividend policy resulted in funds becoming available for outside investment. Over the years, Pacers has had a policy of investing idle cash in equity instruments of other companies. In particular, Pacers has made periodic investments in the company's main supplier, Pierce Industries Limited. Although Pacers currently owns 12% of the outstanding common shares of Pierce, it does not yet have significant influence over the operations of this investee company. Pacers classifies the investment as available for sale.

Cheryl Miller has recently joined Pacers as assistant controller, and her first assignment is to prepare the 2008 year-end adjusting entries for the accounts that are fair-valued for financial reporting purposes. Miller has gathered the following information about Pacers' relevant accounts:

1. In 2008, Pacers acquired shares of Davis Motors Corp. and Smits Electric Ltd. for short-term trading purposes. Pacers purchased 100,000 shares of Davis Motors for $1.4 million and the shares currently have a market value of $1.6 million. Pacers' investment in Smits Electric has not been profitable: the company acquired 50,000 shares of Smits at $20 per share and they currently have a value of $620,000.
2. Before 2008, Pacers invested $22.5 million in Pierce Industries and has not changed its holdings this year. This investment in Pierce Industries was valued at $21.5 million on December 31, 2007. Pacers' 12% ownership of Pierce Industries has a current market value of $22,275,000.

Instructions

(a) Prepare the appropriate adjusting entries for Pacers as at December 31, 2008, to bring both classes of investments to their fair value.

(b) For both categories of investments, describe how the results of the valuation adjustments made in (a) would appear in the body of and/or notes to Pacers' 2008 financial statements.

P9-12 Woolford Corporation has the following portfolio of available-for-sale investments at December 31, 2008:

	Quantity	Percent Interest	Cost per Share	Market Value per Share
Favre Inc.	2,000 shares	8%	$11	$16
Walsh Corp.	5,000 shares	14%	23	17
Dilfer Ltd.	4,000 shares	2%	31	24

Early in 2009, Woolford sold all the Favre Inc. shares for $17 per share, less a 1% commission on the sale. The company follows a policy of expensing transaction costs. On December 31, 2009, Woolford's available-for-sale portfolio consisted of the following common shares:

	Quantity	Percent Interest	Cost	Market Value per Share
Walsh Corp.	5,000 shares	14%	$23	$30
Dilfer Ltd.	4,000 shares	2%	31	23
Conrad Inc.	2,000 shares	1%	25	22

Instructions

(a) What should be reported on Woolford's December 31, 2008, balance sheet for this long-term, available-for-sale portfolio?

(b) What should be reported on Woolford's December 31, 2009, balance sheet for the available-for-sale investments? What should be reported on Woolford's 2009 income statement for the available-for-sale investments?

(c) Prepare Woolford's 2009 statement of comprehensive income.

(d) Assuming that comparative financial statements for 2008 and 2009 are presented in 2009, draft the footnote that is necessary for full disclosure of Woolford's transactions and investments.

P9-13 Fuentes Incorporated is a publicly traded manufacturing company in the technology industry. The company grew rapidly during its first 10 years and made three public offerings during this period. During its rapid growth period, Fuentes acquired common shares in Yukasato Inc. and Dimna Importers.

In 1997, Fuentes acquired 25% of Yukasato's common shares for $588,000 and accounts for this investment using the equity method. The fair value of Yukasato's net assets at the date of purchase is $1.8 million. The excess of the purchase price over the fair value of the net assets relates to assets that are subject to amortization. These assets have a remaining life of 20 years. For its fiscal year ended November 30, 2008, Yukasato Inc. reported net income of $250,000 and paid dividends of $100,000.

In 1999, Fuentes acquired 10% of Dimna Importers' common shares for $204,000 and accounts for this investment as an available-for-sale financial asset.

Fuentes also has a policy of investing idle cash in equity securities to generate short-term profits. The following data are for Fuentes' HFT investment portfolio:

HELD-FOR-TRADING INVESTMENTS
at November 30, 2007

	Cost	Fair Value
Craxi Electric	$326,000	$314,000
Renoir Inc.	184,000	181,000
Seferis Inc.	95,000	98,500
Total	$605,000	$593,500

AVAILABLE-FOR-SALE INVESTMENTS
at November 30, 2007

	Cost	Fair Value
Dimna Importers	$204,000	$198,000

HELD-FOR-TRADING INVESTMENTS
at November 30, 2008

	Cost	Fair Value
Craxi Electric	$326,000	$323,000
Renoir Inc.	184,000	180,000
Mer Limited	105,000	108,000
Total	$615,000	$611,000

AVAILABLE-FOR-SALE INVESTMENTS
at November 30, 2008

	Cost	Fair Value
Dimna Importers	$204,000	$205,000

On November 14, 2008, Tasha Yan was hired by Fuentes as assistant controller. Her first assignment was to prepare the entries to record the November activity and the November 30, 2008 year-end adjusting entries for the current HFT investments and the long-term available-for-sale investment in common shares. Using Fuentes' ledger of investment transactions and the data given above, Yan proposed the following entries and submitted them to Miles O'Brien, controller, for review:

ENTRY 1 (NOVEMBER 8, 2008)

Cash	99,500	
Trading Investments		98,500
Investment Income		1,000

(To record the sale of Seferis Inc. shares for $99,500)

ENTRY 2 (NOVEMBER 26, 2008)

Trading Investments	105,000	
Cash		105,000

(To record the purchase of Mer common shares for $102,200 plus brokerage fees of $2,800)

ENTRY 3 (NOVEMBER 30, 2008)

Investment Income	3,000	
Investment Allowance		3,000

(To recognize a loss equal to the excess of cost over market value of equity securities)

ENTRY 4 (NOVEMBER 30, 2008)

Cash	38,500	
Investment Income		38,500

(To record the following dividends received from investments: Yukasato Inc. $25,000; Dimna Importers $9,000; and Craxi Electric $4,500)

ENTRY 5 (NOVEMBER 30, 2008)

Investment in Yukasato Inc.	62,500	
Investment Income		62,500

(To record share of Yukasato Inc. income under the equity method, $250,000 × 0.25)

Instructions

(a) Are there any differences between the characteristics of held-for-trading and available-for-sale investments in general? Explain. Are there any differences in the specific case of Fuentes Incorporated's investments?

(b) The journal entries proposed by Tasha Yan will establish the value of Fuentes' equity investments to be reported on the company's external financial statements. Review each journal entry and indicate whether or not it is in accordance with the applicable accounting standards. If an entry is incorrect, prepare the correct entry or entries that should have been made.

(c) Because Fuentes owns more than 20% of Yukasato Inc., Miles O'Brien has adopted the equity method to account for this investment. Under what circumstances would it be inappropriate to use the equity method to account for a 25% interest in the common shares of Yukasato Inc.? If the equity method is not appropriate in this case, what method would you recommend? Why?

P9-14 On January 1, 2008, Howard Corporation acquired 10,000 of the 50,000 outstanding common shares of Kline Corp. for $25 per share. The balance sheet of Kline reported the following information at the date of the acquisition:

Assets not subject to amortization	$290,000
Assets subject to amortization	860,000
Liabilities	150,000

Additional information:

1. On the acquisition date, the fair value is the same as the book value for the assets that are not subject to amortization and for the liabilities.

2. On the acquisition date, the fair value of the assets that are subject to amortization is $960,000.
3. Assets that are subject to amortization have a remaining useful life of 8 years as at January 1, 2008.
4. Kline reported 2008 net income of $100,000 and paid dividends of $30,000 in December 2008.
5. Kline's shares had a fair value of $24 per share on December 31, 2008.

Instructions

(a) Prepare the journal entries for Howard Corporation for 2008, assuming that Howard cannot exercise significant influence over Kline and classifies the investment as available for sale.

(b) Prepare the journal entries for Howard Corporation for 2008, assuming that Howard can exercise significant influence over Kline's operations.

(c) How would your answers to parts (a) and (b) change if Howard had acquired the Kline shares on July 2 instead of January 1?

(d) How would your answers to parts (a) and (b) change if the company used differential reporting options?

Writing Assignments

WA9-1 Fran Song looked at the Consolidated Financial Statements of Vixen Manufacturing Limited and shook her head. "I was asked to look at the accounting for Vixen's investments," she said, "but I can't find any investments listed on the balance sheet!" Fran has just begun her work term with Potts and Palmer, a CGA firm in public practice, and she has approached you for help.

Instructions

(a) Explain to Fran what type of investments Vixen likely holds and how they have been accounted for.

(b) Explain the rationale for the reporting standards for this type of investment.

(c) Identify what other evidence there might be on the financial statements that would indicate the existence of this type of investment.

WA9-2 Addison Manufacturing holds a large portfolio of debt and equity securities as an investment. The fair value of the portfolio is greater than its original cost, even though some securities have decreased in value. Ted Abernathy, the financial vice-president, and Donna Nottebart, the controller, are in the process of classifying this securities portfolio in accordance with *CICA Handbook* Section 3855 for the first time. Abernathy wants to classify all investments that have increased in value during the period as held for trading in order to increase net income this year. He wants to classify all the securities that have decreased in value as available for sale (the equity securities) and as held to maturity (the debt securities).

Nottebart disagrees. She wants to classify the investments that have decreased in value as held for trading and those that have increased in value as available for sale (equity) and held to maturity (debt). She argues that the company is having a good earnings year and that recognizing the losses will help to smoothe the income this year. As a result, the company will have built-in gains for future periods when the company may not be as profitable.

Instructions

Answer the following questions.

(a) Will classifying the portfolio as each of them proposes actually have the effect on earnings that they say it will?

(b) Is there anything unethical in what Abernathy or Nottebart are proposing? Who are the stakeholders affected by their proposals?

(c) Identify the options that Addison Manufacturing has in classifying its debt and equity securities. Is there one correct way to do this? Comment.

WA9-3 You have just started working for Andrelli Corp. as part of the controller's group involved in current financial reporting problems. Jackie Franklin, controller for Andrelli, is interested in your accounting background because the company has had a series of financial reporting surprises over the last few years. Recently, the controller learned from the company's auditors that a new *CICA Handbook* standard applies to its financial asset investments. She assumes that you are familiar with these changes in accounting standards as well as other standards relating to investments and asks how the following unrelated situations should be reported in the financial statements.

Situation 1
Temporary investments in the current assets section have a fair value that is $4,200 lower than their cost.

Situation 2
A held-for-trading security whose fair value is currently less than cost is transferred to the available for sale category.

Situation 3
An available-for-sale security whose fair value is currently less than cost is classified as non-current but will be reclassified as current.

Situation 4
A company's portfolio of available-for-sale investments consists of the common shares of one company. At the end of the prior year, the fair value of the investment was 50% of their original cost, and this reduction in market value was reported as an other-than-temporary impairment. However, at the end of the current year, the fair value of the security had increased to twice the original cost.

Situation 5
The company has purchased 20% of the common shares of a supplier and has been able to get three of its nominees elected to the supplier's 10-person board of directors. The supplier reported record earnings of $100,000 this year, but unfortunately was not able to pay out a dividend.

Instructions
What is the effect on the balance sheet and earnings of each of the independent situations above?

WA9-4 On July 1, 2008, Munns Corp. purchased for cash 25% of the outstanding shares of Huber Corporation. Both Munns and Huber have a December 31 year end. Huber Corporation, whose common shares are actively traded on the Toronto Stock Exchange, paid a cash dividend on November 15, 2008, to Munns Corp. and its other shareholders. It also reported net income for 2008 of $920,000.

Instructions
Prepare a one-page memorandum on how Munns Corp. should report the above facts on its December 31, 2008, balance sheet and its 2008 income statement, and also state what additional disclosure might be required in the notes to the financial statements. In your memo, identify and describe the method of valuation that you recommend. If additional information is needed, identify what other information would be necessary or useful. Address your memo to the chief accountant at Munns Corp. and provide reasons for your choices as much as possible.

WA9-5 The Accounting Standards Board issued *CICA Handbook* Section 3855 to specify the recognition and measurement standards for financial instruments. These standards cover the accounting methods and procedures for certain debt and equity instruments. An important part of the statement concerns the classification of investments as held to maturity, available for sale, and held for trading.

Instructions

(a) Why does a company maintain an investment portfolio of held-to-maturity, available-for-sale, and trading securities?

(b) What factors should be considered in determining whether investments should be classified as held to maturity, available for sale, or held for trading? How do these factors affect the accounting treatment for unrealized losses?

Cases

www.wiley.com/canada/kieso

Refer to the Case Primer on the Student Website to help you answer these cases.

CA9-1 Investment Company Limited (ICL) is a private company owned by ten doctors. The objective of the company is to manage the doctors' investment portfolios. It actually began as an investment club ten years ago. At that time, each doctor invested equal amounts of cash and the group met every other week to determine where the money should be invested. Eventually, they decided to incorporate the company and each doctor now owns one-tenth of the voting shares. The company employs two managers who look after the business on a full-time basis and make the investment decisions with input from the owners. Earnings per year after taxes now average $1.5 million. During the year, the following transactions took place:

> Investment A (IA): Purchased common shares of IA for $1 million. IA allows researchers to use expensive lab equipment (which is owned by the company) on a pay-per-use basis. These shares represent 15% of the total outstanding common shares of the company. Because of its percentage ownership, ICL is allowed to appoint one member of IA's board of directors. There are three members on the board. One of the ICL owners has also been hired as a consultant to the company to advise on equipment acquisitions. These shares have not been designated as held for trading and the company is unsure of how long it will keep them. At least two of the owners of the company are interested in holding on to the investments for the longer term as they use the services of IA.
>
> Investment B (IB): Purchased preferred shares of IB representing 25% of the total outstanding shares. The shares will likely be resold within two months, although no decision has yet been made.
>
> Investment C (IC): Purchased 25% interest in voting common shares of IC for $1 million two years ago. The current carrying amount is $950,000 since the company has been in the drug development stage. IC develops drug delivery technology. In the past week, a major drug on which the company has spent large amounts (approximately $10 million) for research and development was declined by the Food and Drug Administration for sale in the United States. Most of the $10 million had previously been capitalized in the financial statements of IC. This is a significant blow to IC as it had been projecting that 50% of its future revenues would come from this drug. IC does not produce financial statements until two months after ICL's year end.

Although the investments have been mainly in private companies so far, the doctors are thinking of revising their investment strategy and investing in more public companies. They feel that the stock market is poised for recovery, and are therefore planning to borrow some funds for investment. The accountant is currently reviewing the above transactions in preparation for a meeting with the bank.

Instructions

Adopt the role of the company's accountant and analyze the financial reporting issues.

CA9-2 CanWest Global Communications Corp. (CWG) owns and operates 16 broadcast television stations and several specialty cable channels, 17 newspapers (including the *National Post*), and many other non-daily publications. It has a 57.6% economic interest in Network TEN (Australia), a 45% interest in TV3 (Republic of Ireland), and 29.9% interest in UTV (Northern Ireland).

According to note 3 to its financial statements, the company owns approximately 15% of the shares and all of the convertible and subordinated debentures of Network TEN. The convertible debentures are convertible into shares which would represent 50% of the total issued shares of the company at the time of conversion. In total, including the debentures, the investment in Network TEN yields a distribution that is equivalent to 57.5% of all distributions paid by Network TEN. CWG has a contractual right to be represented on the board of directors and has appointed three of the board's 13 members.

The investment in TV3 is part of a joint venture agreement with another company. Under the terms of the agreement, control of the company is shared between the two parties.

Although the company has made an attempt to influence the decisions made by UTV management, it has been unsuccessful and does not have any representation on the board of directors.

Investments represent approximately $167 million (approximately 3% of total assets). Even though revenues were up by 17%, net income was only $13 million for the year ended August 31, 2002, down from $47 million the prior year.

Instructions

Adopt the role of a financial analyst and analyze the financial reporting issues.

CA9-3 Fanshaw Bank (FB) made the headlines in newspapers when it announced that it would be restating its financial statements for the year ended October 31, 2007. The restatements were the result of an investigation by the Ontario Securities Commission (OSC) and the Office of the Superintendent of Financial Institutions (OSFI). The investigation uncovered several errors, including the accounting for investments and certain transactions involving mortgage-backed securities (MBS) under GAAP. While the investigation was being completed, the company issued a cautionary press release that advised investors not to rely on the previously issued financial statements.

As a result of the findings, the auditors of the past 35 years were dismissed, as was the bulk of the management team. New internal controls were put in place to ensure that the problem would not happen again. Below are the specific details for two types of transactions that were accounted for incorrectly:

1. Investments in debt securities were initially recorded as held-to-maturity securities as a default designation. The investment would then be left as is or reclassified as either available for sale or held for trading, depending on management's intent. No documentation was prepared.
2. The company entered into transactions called "dollar roll repurchase agreements." Under these agreements, certain securities (MBS) were sold and the company also signed a separate agreement to repurchase the same securities later. All of these were accounted for as secured loans.

Instructions

Adopt the role of one of the members of the investigation team and discuss the issues.

Research and Financial Analysis

RA9-1 Stantec Inc.

Refer to the financial statements of Stantec Inc. for its year ended December 31, 2005, found in Appendix 5B of this text. These financial statements were prepared under the accounting standards in effect in 2005 and therefore do not incorporate the changes in *CICA Handbook* Section 3855.

Instructions

(a) Review Stantec's balance sheet. Identify all financial investments that are reported. You may need to read the notes to the financial statements to get the necessary details.

(b) Does Stantec have any investments in subsidiary companies? Does it own 100% of all its subsidiaries? Can you tell this by looking at the balance sheet? At the income statement?

(c) Does Stantec exercise significant influence over any of its investment holdings? If it does, identify the total investment reported on the December 31, 2005, balance sheet for such investments. Identify the amount of income from these investments that is reported on the 2005 income statement. Comment on the rate of return earned in 2005. How does this compare to 2004?

(d) During 2005, Stantec acquired a subsidiary, The Keith Companies, Inc. Why was this strategic investment made? Was there any "unexplained excess" or goodwill acquired as a result of the price paid for this acquisition? What percentage of the assets from this acquisition is included in Stantec's assets on its December 31, 2005, consolidated balance sheet? What portion of The Keith Companies, Inc. income for the 2005 year is included on Stantec's 2005 consolidated income statement? Comment.

RA9-2 Research Statement Disclosures

CICA Handbook Section 3855, "Financial Instruments—Recognition and Measurement," covers more than the accounting for investments in debt and equity instruments. Beginning with their 2007 financial reports, Canadian companies began to apply this section's provisions.

Instructions

(a) Identify a Canadian company that has applied the requirements of *Handbook* Section 3855.

(b) Identify how the company classified all its investments in debt and equity instruments only, and what accounting policies it applies to each classification.

(c) Does the company report any accumulated other comprehensive income on the balance sheet? If yes, in what amount? What is the source of this balance?

(d) Review the notes to the financial statements and identify all disclosures related to these investments. Do not list the details, but summarize the type of information provided by each disclosure.

RA9-3 Canadian Imperial Bank of Commerce

Refer to the 2006 financial statements and accompanying notes of Canadian Imperial Bank of Commerce (CIBC) that are found on the Student Website or can be accessed through www.sedar.com.

Instructions

(a) What percentage of total assets is held in investments (2006 versus 2005)? Note that CIBC holds a significant loan portfolio also. What is the business reason for holding loans versus securities? Comment on how the investments are classified and presented on the balance sheet.

(b) What percentage of total interest income comes from securities (2006 versus 2005)? Are there any other lines on the income statement relating to securities? What percentage of net income relates to securities (2006 versus 2005)? Calculate an approximate return on the investments in securities. Comment on the return, while looking at the nature of the securities that are being invested in.

(c) Read the notes to the financial statements that are about securities and note the valuation method. Is this consistent with GAAP before the new Section 3855, or with the standards?

(d) Briefly discuss your findings in (c).

RA9-4 Research Issue—Variable Interest Entities (VIEs)

In 2003, the CICA released new Accounting Guideline AcG-15 "Consolidation of Variable Interest Entities." This topic has been high on the agendas of the accounting standard-setting communities around the world—particularly since the fall of Enron in 2001.

Instructions

Research and write a one- to two-page report on variable interest entities. What is a VIE? What is the accounting issue that needs resolution? What is the effect of applying the guideline? That is, how will financial statements differ from what was previously reported? Identify at least one company whose financial statements will be affected and provide numbers to show the size of the impact on the statements.

RA9-5 The Coca-Cola Company and PepsiCo, Inc.

Instructions

Gain access to the 2005 financial statements of The Coca-Cola Company and PepsiCo, Inc. on the Student Website.

(a) Based on the information contained in these financial statements, determine each of the following for each company:

1. Cash used in (for) investing activities during 2005 (from the statement of cash flows)
2. Cash used for acquisitions and investments in unconsolidated affiliates (principally bottling companies) during 2005
3. Total investment in unconsolidated affiliates (or investments and other assets) at December 31, 2005
4. What conclusions about the management of investments can be drawn from these data?

(b) Briefly identify from Coca-Cola's December 31, 2005, balance sheet the investments it reported as being accounted for under the equity method. What is the amount of investments that Coca-Cola reported in its 2005 balance sheet as "cost method investments," and what is the nature of these investments?

(c) In its note number 10 to its Financial Instruments, what total amounts did Coca-Cola report at December 31, 2005, as (1) trading securities, (2) available-for-sale securities, and (3) held-to-maturity securities? What types of investments were included in each category?

Treasures Take Time

Tahera Diamond Corporation recently set a budget of $8 million for 2007 to explore its mining properties in Nunavut. This exploration includes drill testing and soil sample extraction to assess each property's diamond potential.

Tahera has already established one mine in the area—the Jericho Diamond Mine, which is Canada's third and Nunavut's first diamond mine. Jericho started production in 2006 and produced some 275,000 carats by year end.

But, as is true of any natural resource company, a lot of time and money goes into the exploration and development before it can reap such rewards.

After 10 years of exploration programs, feasibility studies, environmental assessments, and efforts to get project approval from the appropriate government and Inuit agencies, the Jericho property was ready to move to the development stage in 2005. Tahera spent approximately $120 million on plant and equipment and development of the mine site, says Andrew Gottwald, vice-president of Finance and Administration, and CFO. "One of the challenges of our property is the location. Mobilization of supplies and equipment by air is costly, causing a heavy reliance on a winter ice road that is available for only a short time in the first quarter of the year. Fuel and explosive inventories for the year are mobilized and stored on site during the winter road season." Development costs include the construction of roads and buildings, and the installation of fuel tanks.

"Exploration costs get capitalized and then eventually, if the property comes to the point where it's developed and mined, that amount gets amortized over the mine life," explains Gottwald. "If it doesn't go that far, it gets written off." Pre-production operating costs that are offset by related revenues are capitalized. Once commercial production is achieved, additional acquisition and development costs are capitalized or expensed, depending on the nature of the item, and any further exploration related to the mine will be expensed. The company expects a mine life of eight years and additional capital purchases during that time to keep the mine operating efficiently. ■

Acquisition of Property, Plant, and Equipment

chapter 10

Learning Objectives

After studying this chapter, you should be able to:

1. Describe the major characteristics of property, plant, and equipment.
2. Identify the costs that are included in the initial valuation of land, buildings, equipment, and similar assets.
3. Describe the accounting issues for self-constructed assets.
4. Identify the costs included in natural resource properties.
5. Describe the accounting issues for interest capitalization.
6. Explain and apply other accounting issues related to the initial measurement of plant assets.
7. Describe and apply the accounting for costs subsequent to acquisition.

After studying Appendix 10A, you should be able to:

8. Calculate the amount of capitalizable interest for projects that have expenditures over a period of time and borrowings from different sources at varying rates.

Preview of Chapter 10

This chapter examines (1) the accounting for costs related to the initial acquisition of property, plant, and equipment, including natural resources, and (2) the treatment of capital asset costs subsequent to acquisition. The amortization (i.e., allocation of long-term plant asset costs to different accounting periods), impairment, and disposal of property, plant, and equipment are presented in Chapter 11, as are the disclosure requirements, analytical issues related to capital assets, and a comparison of Canadian capital asset standards with international requirements. The accounting for long-lived intangible assets is the subject of Chapter 12.

The chapter is organized as follows:

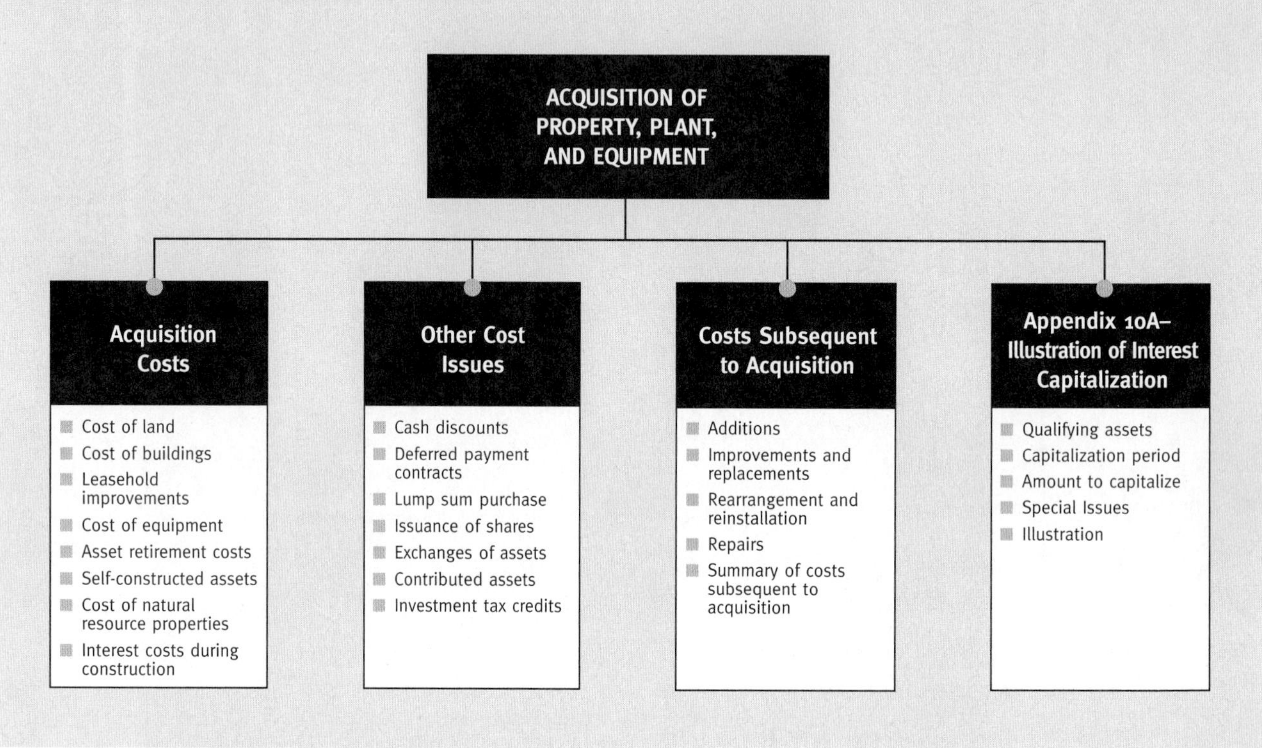

Objective 1
Describe the major characteristics of property, plant, and equipment.

Almost every enterprise, whatever its size or activity, uses long-lived assets. Such long-term resources include both those that have physical substance—property, plant, and equipment—and those without physical substance—intangible assets. This chapter looks at property, plant, and equipment, which are also commonly referred to as tangible capital assets, plant assets, or fixed assets. These terms are used interchangeably by organizations and throughout this textbook. Examples of these assets include land, building structures (offices, factories, warehouses), equipment (machinery, furniture, tools), and natural resource properties.

In the past, the term "depreciation" was used to refer specifically to the amortization of property, plant, and equipment, "depletion" was used for the amortization of natural resource properties, and "amortization" was used for intangibles. While these terms are still common, **amortization** is generally used throughout this text to refer to the allocation of the cost of any long-lived asset to different accounting periods.

The major characteristics of property, plant, and equipment are as follows:

1. **They are acquired and held so that they can be used in operations and are not intended for sale in the ordinary course of business.** Only assets that are used in normal business operations should be classified as property, plant, and equipment.[1]
2. **They are of a long-term nature and are usually amortized.** Property, plant, and equipment provide services over many years. Through periodic amortization charges, the cost of the investment in these assets is assigned to the periods that benefit from using them. The exception is land, which is not amortized unless a material and continual decline in value occurs: for example, if agricultural land becomes less fertile because of poor crop rotation, drought, or soil erosion, it would be worth less to the company.
3. **They possess physical substance.** Property, plant, and equipment are assets that have a physical existence or substance, which makes them different from intangible assets, such as patents or goodwill.

At times there is a fine line between what is categorized as a capital asset and what is categorized as a supply inventory. Assume, for example, that a company has a substantial fleet of trucks (capital assets) and a variety of assets related to the trucks: spare tires, major motor parts, oil and grease, and truck cleaning equipment. What type of asset is each of these? The general approach is to include **in inventory** any spare parts and servicing equipment that have multiple uses and are regularly used and replaced within the accounting period. Major spare parts and standby and servicing equipment that either are useful for more than one period or can be used only with a particular capital asset are classified **as capital assets.**[2]

ACQUISITION COSTS

Historical cost is the usual basis for valuing property, plant, and equipment. **Historical cost is measured by the cash or cash equivalent price of obtaining the asset and bringing it to the location and into the proper condition necessary for its intended use.** The purchase price, freight costs, most provincial sales taxes, and the productive asset's installation costs are considered part of the asset's cost. These costs are allocated to future periods through the amortization process. Any related costs that are incurred after the asset's acquisition, such as additions, improvements, or replacements, are added to the asset's cost **if the asset's service potential is increased.** Otherwise, they are expensed immediately.

International Insight

IAS 16 permits property, plant, and equipment to be revalued to its fair value, which is usually determined by an appraisal based on market-based evidence.

At the acquisition date, cost is the basis that is used for valuation because the cash or cash equivalent price is the best measure of the asset's value at that time. However, there is some disagreement about what to do with changes in value after acquisition. Should the asset value be adjusted to recognize changes in its replacement cost or its fair market value? In Canada today, writing up fixed asset values is considered inappropriate in ordinary circumstances. Although there are minor exceptions (during financial reorganizations, for example), current standards rarely allow something other than historical cost to be used for non-financial assets.

Underlying Concept

Historical costs are **verifiable** and therefore considered more reliable. On the other hand, they do not **faithfully represent** the value of the asset to the business and should therefore be considered less reliable measures. This is an example of a qualitative characteristic trade-off.

The main reasons for this position are (1) at the acquisition date, cost reflects fair value; (2) historical cost involves actual, not hypothetical, transactions, and as a result is more objective; and (3) gains should not be anticipated and recognized before they are realized; that is, before the asset is converted to cash or a claim to cash.

[1] Use in normal business operations includes the production or supply of goods and services, administrative purposes, for rental to others, or for the development, construction, maintenance, or repair of other property, plant, and equipment (*CICA Handbook*, Section 3061.04 [a]).

[2] *CICA Handbook*, Section 3061.04.

Several other valuation methods have been considered and experimented with over the years. These include (1) constant dollar accounting (adjustments for general price-level changes), (2) current cost accounting (adjustments for specific price-level changes), (3) net realizable value, and (4) a combination of constant dollar accounting and current cost or net realizable value.

Cost of Land

Objective 2
Identify the costs that are included in the initial valuation of land, buildings, equipment, and similar assets.

All expenditures that are made to acquire land and make it ready for use are considered part of the land's cost. Land costs typically include (1) the purchase price; (2) closing costs, such as title to the land, legal fees, and recording fees; (3) costs incurred to condition the land for its intended use, such as grading, filling, draining, and clearing; (4) the assumption of any liens, such as taxes in arrears or mortgages or encumbrances on the property; and (5) any additional land improvements that have an indefinite life.

When land has been purchased to construct a building, all costs that are incurred up to the excavation for the new building are considered land costs. **Removal of old buildings, clearing, grading, and filling are considered land costs because these costs are necessary to get the land in condition for its intended purpose**. Any proceeds that are obtained in the process of getting the land ready for its intended use—such as amounts received for salvaged materials from the demolition of an old building or the sale of timber that has been cleared—are treated as reductions in the land cost.

In some cases, the land purchaser becomes responsible for certain obligations on the land, such as back taxes or liens. In these situations, the cost of the land is the cash paid for it, plus the encumbrances. In other words, if the land purchase price is $50,000 cash, but accrued property taxes of $5,000 and liens of $10,000 are required to be paid by the purchaser before title can be transferred, the land cost is $65,000.

Special amounts assessed for local improvements—such as pavements, street lights, and sewers and drainage systems—are usually charged to the Land account because they are relatively permanent and are maintained and replaced by the local government. In addition, it is also proper to charge permanent improvements that are made by the owner, such as landscaping, to the Land account. Improvements with limited lives—such as private driveways, walks, fences, and parking lots—are recorded separately as Land Improvements so they can be amortized over their estimated lives.

Generally, land is considered part of property, plant, and equipment. If the major purpose of acquiring and holding land is speculative, however, it is more appropriate to classify it as an investment. If the land is held by a real estate company for resale, or is held by land developers or subdividers, it is classified as inventory.

In cases where land is held as an investment, what should the accounting treatment be for taxes, insurance, and other direct costs that are incurred while holding the land? Many believe that these costs should be capitalized as part of the land's cost until it is sold and a gain is recognized. This approach is reasonable as long as the total amount that is capitalized is not more than the property's fair value. Such an approach seems justified except in cases where the asset is currently producing revenue, such as with rental property. In this case, such costs are expensed.

International Insight

Under IAS 16, historical cost is the benchmark (i.e., preferred) treatment for property, plant, and equipment. However, it is also allowable to use revalued amounts. If revaluation is used, companies are required to revalue the class of assets regularly.

Cost of Buildings

The cost of buildings includes all expenditures that are directly related to acquiring or constructing them. These costs include (1) materials, labour, and overhead costs that are incurred during construction, and (2) professional fees and building permits. Generally, companies hire contractors to construct their buildings. All costs that are incurred, from excavation to completion, are considered part of the building costs.

One accounting issue relates to the cost of an old building that is on the site of a planned new building. Is the cost to remove the old building a cost of the land or of the new building? The answer is that if land is purchased with an old building on it, then the demolition cost less its salvage value is a cost of getting the land ready for its intended use and relates to the land rather than to the new building. As indicated earlier, all costs of getting an asset ready for its intended use are costs of that asset. On the other hand, if a company razes (tears down) an old building that it owns and previously used in order to raise a new building on the same land, the costs of demolition net of any cost recoveries are included in the cost of disposing of the old building, thus increasing any loss on disposal of the old asset.

Leasehold Improvements

What is the proper accounting for capital expenditures that are made on property that is being leased or rented? Long-term leases ordinarily specify that any **leasehold improvements** revert to the lessor at the end of the lease. If the lessee constructs new buildings on leased land or reconstructs and improves existing buildings, the lessee has the right to use those facilities during the life of the lease, but they become the property of the lessor when the lease expires. The lessee charges the facilities' cost to a separate capital asset account, Leasehold Improvements, and the cost is amortized as an operating expense over the remaining life of the lease or the useful life of the improvements, whichever is shorter.

Cost of Equipment

The term "equipment" in accounting includes delivery equipment, office equipment, machinery, furniture and fixtures, furnishings, factory equipment, and similar tangible capital assets. The cost of such assets includes the purchase price, freight and handling charges that are incurred, insurance on the equipment while it is in transit, the cost of special foundations if they are required, assembling and installation costs, and costs of conducting trial runs. Cost thus includes all reasonable and necessary expenditures that are incurred in acquiring the asset and preparing it for use. The Goods and Services Tax (GST) or Harmonized Sales Tax (HST) that is paid on the acquired assets is treated as an Input Tax Credit, which reduces the amount of GST or HST payable—it does not increase the acquisition cost of the assets.

Asset Retirement Costs

In some industries, when a company acquires and/or uses its long-lived assets, it takes on obligations that need to be met when the assets are eventually retired. For example, a nuclear facility must be decommissioned at the end of its useful life; mine sites must be closed and dismantled and the property must be restored; and landfill sites have significant closure and post-closure costs associated with the end of their operations.

In order to benefit from what these long-lived assets have to offer, entities usually assume responsibility for the costs that are associated with retiring the assets. *CICA Handbook* Section 3110 on "Asset Retirement Obligations" requires companies to recognize the obligation or liability that is associated with the asset's retirement. It is recognized in the period when the legal obligation is created. This may be when the asset is first acquired or during the time when a particular site is mined or garbage landfill site is used.

At the same time that the liability is recorded, the **asset retirement costs** are recognized by "increasing the carrying amount of the related long-lived asset by the same amount as the liability." Although there is a fuller discussion of liability recognition and measurement issues in Chapter 13, students should be aware now that the cost of property, plant, and equipment will often include such a charge when the asset is first acquired. This component of a long-lived asset's cost may change in future periods due to changes in the estimate of the amount and/or timing of the eventual cash flows that will be required to remediate (make good) the asset. Both the original amount that was recognized in the asset's cost and any subsequent revisions are allocated to expense through periodic amortization.

Self-Constructed Assets

Objective 3
Describe the accounting issues for self-constructed assets.

Often, companies construct their own assets. Determining the cost of such machinery, buildings, or other capital assets can be a problem. Without a purchase price or contract price, the company allocates costs and expenses that it incurs to arrive at the cost of the **self-constructed asset**. Materials and direct labour that are used in construction are not difficult to measure; these costs can be traced directly to actual work orders and materials used in the constructed assets.

However, assigning indirect costs of manufacturing creates special problems. These indirect costs, called **overhead** or **burden**, include power, heat, light, insurance, property taxes on factory buildings and equipment, factory supervisory labour, amortization of fixed assets, and supplies. These costs may be handled in one of three ways:

1. **Do not include any fixed overhead costs in the cost of the constructed asset.** The major argument for this treatment is that indirect overhead is generally a fixed cost and assumes that the company's indirect costs will be the same whether the company constructs the asset or not. To charge a portion of the overhead costs in this case to the equipment would reduce current expenses and consequently overstate the current period's income. Therefore, only variable overhead costs that increase as a result of the construction are assigned to the asset cost.

2. **Assign a portion of all overhead to the construction process.** This approach, a full costing concept, assumes that costs attach to all products and assets that are manufactured or constructed. This procedure assigns overhead costs to construction in the same way that they are assigned to normal production. Supporters say that not allocating overhead costs understates the initial cost of the asset and results in an inaccurate future allocation.

3. **Allocate fixed overhead costs based on lost production.** A third alternative is to allocate to the construction project the cost of any reduction in productivity that occurs because the company is devoting its resources to building the asset instead of regular production. This method is attractive as a concept, but it is based on what might have occurred—an opportunity cost concept, which is difficult to measure.

CICA Handbook Section 3061 indicates that the cost of a constructed or developed asset includes direct construction and development costs and "overhead costs directly attributable to the construction or development activity." This guidance allows some flexibility in allocating fixed overhead, but generally a proportionate share of the fixed overhead is assigned to the asset to obtain its cost. This treatment is popular in practice because many entities believe that it leads to a better matching of costs with revenues. If the allocated overhead results in total construction costs being more than the costs that would be charged by an outside independent producer, the excess overhead is recorded instead as a period loss. This prevents a situation from resulting where the asset would be capitalized at more than the expected cash flows to be generated from its use and eventual salvage—its **net recoverable amount**.

Cost of Natural Resource Properties

4 Objective
Identify the costs included in natural resource properties.

Natural resources, which are sometimes called wasting assets, include petroleum, mineral, and timber properties. They are characterized by two main features: (1) complete removal (consumption) of the asset, and (2) replacement of the asset only by an act of nature. Unlike buildings and machinery, natural resources are consumed physically over the period of use and do not retain their original physical characteristics. Regardless, the accounting problems associated with natural resources are similar to those for other tangible capital assets.

Companies often need to spend large amounts to find most types of natural resources, and for every success there are many attempts where nothing is discovered. Furthermore, there are long delays between the time when the costs are incurred and when the benefits are obtained from the extracted resources. The capitalizable costs of natural resource properties relate to four types of activity:

1. Acquisition of properties
2. Exploration
3. Development
4. Restoration

International Insight

The IASB is currently working on a comprehensive project for natural resources that involves national standard setters from Australia, Canada, Norway, and South Africa. The research project is the first step in the development of an approach to resolving accounting issues that are unique to extractive activities.

Costs incurred by a company that are directly identified with these four activities are generally added to the asset cost. In addition, overhead costs that can be directly related to exploration and development activities can also be capitalized, but this does not include general corporate overhead. Production costs are also excluded.

Together, the capitalized costs of acquisition, exploration, development, and restoration make up the **depletion base** of the natural resource. As its name implies, the depletion base is the amount that will subsequently be amortized (through a depletion charge) and form a major portion of the cost of the mined, extracted, or harvested inventory. Through depletion (amortization), the costs of the long-term natural resource capital asset become part of the cost of the inventory that is produced. They are similar to direct materials costs of a manufactured product.

Acquisition Cost

Acquisition cost is the price that is paid to obtain the property rights to search and find an undiscovered natural resource, or the price paid for an already discovered resource. In some cases, property is leased and special royalty payments are paid to the lessor if a productive natural resource is found and is commercially profitable. Generally, the acquisition cost is debited to an account titled Undeveloped or Unproved Property and stays in that account until the results of exploration efforts are known. Timber properties are different, of course, since they are above ground and the extent of the standing timber is already known and proved.

Exploration Costs

After the enterprise has acquired the right to use the property, **exploration costs** are incurred to identify the areas that have potential and to more closely examine areas that have already been identified. Exploration costs include the applicable **operating costs—including depreciation—of equipment and facilities that are used for exploration activities.** The accounting treatment for these costs varies: some firms expense all exploration costs, others only capitalize costs that are directly related to successful projects (**successful efforts approach**), and still others capitalize all these costs whether or not they are related to successful projects (**full cost approach**).[3]

The debate over using the successful efforts approach or the full cost approach is particularly strong in the oil and gas industry. Supporters of the full cost approach believe that unsuccessful ventures are a necessary cost of successful ventures, because the cost of drilling a dry hole is a cost along the way to finding commercially profitable wells. Those who believe that only the costs of successful projects should be capitalized argue that the costs associated with unsuccessful wells do not provide future economic benefits and, therefore, do not meet the definition of an asset. Furthermore, they believe that the only relevant measures for a project are the costs that are **directly related to that project**, and that companies should report any other costs as period charges or expense. They argue that, in applying the full cost approach, an unsuccessful company will end up capitalizing many costs that will make it, over the short term, report the same amount of income as a successful company.

Under both the successful efforts and full cost approaches, exploration costs can be initially capitalized to the Undeveloped or Unproved Property account. If it is determined that the result is not successful and extraction will not be commercially viable, then the two approaches differ in the cost of the natural resource that is reported on the balance sheet. Under **successful efforts**, the costs for unsuccessful exploration activities are charged against earnings; under the **full cost method,** they remain capitalized as part of the cost of the natural resource.[4]

Canadian practice is mixed for the two approaches. Larger companies such as Imperial Oil and Petro-Canada generally use the successful efforts approach. Small to medium-sized companies favour the full cost approach. There are exceptions to this generalization about size: Canadian Natural Resources Ltd. and EnCana Corporation are large companies that use the full cost method. Others, like Paramount Resources Ltd., although relatively small, use the successful efforts method. In the mining industry, more established companies tend to write off exploration costs as they are incurred, while the "juniors" generally defer these costs. The difference in net income under the two methods can be enormous.

Development Costs

International Insight

U.S. GAAP requires that exploration and development costs on resource properties, before the completion of a definitive feasibility study which establishes proven and probable reserves, be expensed as incurred.

Development costs are costs incurred to obtain access to reserves and to provide facilities for extracting, treating, gathering, and storing the resource.[5] These costs include the amortization and operating costs of support equipment (e.g., moveable heavy machinery) and facilities that are needed for development activities. For example, they include such

[3] The CICA's Accounting Guideline 16, "Oil and Gas Accounting—Full Cost," explains the policies and procedures for applying the full cost method of accounting.

[4] At one point, the Securities and Exchange Commission (SEC) in the United States argued in favour of a **reserve recognition accounting (RRA)** method, which it believed would provide more relevant information. Under RRA, as soon as a company discovers oil, the value of the oil is reported on the balance sheet and in the income statement—a current value approach. This method was never fully developed and the SEC subsequently rejected using this method in primary financial statements because of the uncertainty of determining and valuing recoverable quantities of proved oil and gas reserves. Later, the FASB issued *Statement No. 69*, which required current value **disclosures** only. Another current value approach for natural resources in general is **discovery value accounting**. This method debits the resource asset account for increases in the value of natural resources and credits a separate Unrealized Appreciation account in shareholders' equity. As the resource is sold, amounts in the Unrealized Appreciation account are transferred to the income statement as revenue. Application of either RRA or discovery value accounting would make a substantial difference in the balance sheets and income statements of natural resource companies. For example, Atlantic Richfield Co. at one time reported net producing property of U.S. $2.6 billion. If RRA were adopted, the same properties would have been valued at $11.8 billion!

[5] *CICA Handbook*, Accounting Guideline 16.

items as costs incurred to gain access to the resource, drilling costs, tunnels, shafts, and wells that are needed to get to and produce the natural resource. Because machinery and equipment can be moved from one drilling or mining site to another, **their costs are normally capitalized separately** in an account titled Equipment, and only the amortization of the equipment is included in the development cost component of the natural resource as the equipment is used.

In summary, therefore, the preproduction costs that become components of the asset's capital cost and depletion base are based on the approach that is used. Illustration 10-1 summarizes the general flow of costs when the successful efforts method is used. Under the full cost approach, the costs associated with the dry holes, within certain limits, are included as part of the natural resource account on the balance sheet. Accounting for natural resources is complex. Further discussion is reserved for a specialized accounting course.

Illustration 10-1
Flow of Costs: Oil and Gas Industry–Successful Efforts Approach

	Balance Sheet		Income Statement
Activity	Capital Assets	Inventory	
Acquisition costs (AC) incurred	AC		
Exploration costs (EC) incurred	+ EC		
	= Cost of unproved property		
Dry holes drilled	− (AC + EC) of dry holes →		Expense
	= AC + EC of proved resources		
Development costs (DC) incurred	+ DC		
	= AC + EC + DC of proved resources		
Extraction activity			
• depletion of resource	− Depletion →	Depletion expense	
• operating costs incurred		+ Production costs	
Resource sold		− Cost of sales →	Cost of sales
	= Oil & gas property less accumulated depletion	= Oil & gas inventories	

Restoration Costs

As explained above, when the entity is legally responsible for any costs that are associated with the eventual retirement of capital assets, these costs are estimated based on present value concepts and included in the natural resource asset cost and depletion base.

Interest Costs during Construction

5 Objective
Describe the accounting issues for interest capitalization.

Which accounting method is the most appropriate one for interest costs has been a longstanding controversy. Three approaches have been suggested to account for the interest that is incurred in financing the construction or acquisition of property, plant, and equipment:

1. **Do not capitalize interest charges during construction.** Under this approach, interest is considered a cost of financing. The argument is that if the company had used equity financing rather than debt financing, this expense would not have been incurred. The major argument against this approach is that an implicit interest cost is

associated with using cash regardless of its source; in equity financing, there is a real cost to the shareholders, even if there is no contractual claim with interest costs.

International Insight

IAS 23 on borrowing costs recently changed and now requires the capitalization of borrowing costs if they can be attributed directly to the acquisition, construction, or production of a qualifying asset.

2. **Charge construction for the costs of all funds that are used, whether they are identifiable or not.** This method argues that the cost of financing is part of the construction cost, whether by debt, equity, or internal financing. An asset should be charged with all costs that are necessary to get it ready for its intended use. Interest, whether it is actual or imputed, is a cost of building, the same as labour, materials, and overhead. A major criticism of this approach is that imputing a cost of equity capital is subjective and outside the framework of a historical cost system.
3. **Capitalize only the actual interest costs that are incurred during construction.** This approach relies on the historical cost concept where only actual transactions are recorded. It is argued that interest that is incurred is as much a cost of acquiring the asset as the cost of the materials, labour, and other resources that are used. As a result, a company that uses debt financing will have an asset with a higher reported cost than an enterprise that uses equity financing. The results achieved by this approach are considered unsatisfactory by some critics because they hold that an asset's cost should be the same regardless of how it was financed.

International Insight

In the United States, interest must be capitalized for qualifying assets that require a period of time to get them ready for their intended use.

In Canada, capitalization of interest is permitted, but not required. While there is no guidance from CICA, many companies apply the third approach, some using the U.S. standard and others a variation.[6] This position is likely based on two grounds:

1. The third method is consistent with the primary sources of GAAP. The cost principle assumes that "cost" includes all costs that are incurred to acquire the asset and bring it to the condition and location necessary for its intended use. This is an out-of-pocket (i.e., actually incurred) cost and it would have been included as part of the asset's cost if the company had purchased a completed asset from another entity.
2. Wherever a choice of policy is permitted, many companies apply the method that is recognized as GAAP in the United States. The FASB recommends that the actual interest that is incurred during construction be capitalized.

With the recent amendment to international standard IAS 23, which now requires capitalization of borrowing costs for qualifying assets, it is likely that more and more Canadian companies will follow this policy. It is interesting to note that although both the FASB and IASB require capitalization, their approaches to implementation are different, with the result that materially different amounts could be reported.

What Do the Numbers Mean?

Interest capitalization can have a substantial effect on the financial statements. When the earnings of Jim Walter Corporation dropped from $1.51 to $1.17 per share, the building manufacturer looked for ways to regain its profitability and was able to pick up an additional 11 cents per share by capitalizing the interest on coal mining projects and several plants under construction.

How can statement users determine the effect of interest capitalization on a company's bottom line? The amount of interest capitalized in the period has to be disclosed in the notes to the financial statements.[7] For example, Clublink Corporation, a major Canadian owner, operator, and developer of golf clubs across the country, once reported $2,391,000 of capitalized interest, an amount equal to 25 percent of the interest expense deducted on its income statement. The following year's numbers were lower: about 12 percent.

[6] CICA's *Financial Reporting in Canada, 31th Edition* reports that of 200 Canadian companies surveyed, 80 reported having capitalized interest in 2005.

[7] *CICA Handbook*, Section 3850.03.

OTHER COST ISSUES

6 Objective
Explain and apply other accounting issues related to the initial measurement of plant assets.

We have seen that assets are recorded at their initial cost—the amount of cash or cash equivalents paid to acquire the asset. For non-monetary transactions, cost is usually the fair market value of what is given up or received, whichever one is more clearly evident. **Cost and fair market value, however, are sometimes obscured by the process through which an asset is acquired.** As an example, assume that land and buildings are bought together for one price. How are separate costs for the land and buildings determined? Several accounting issues of this nature are examined in the following sections.

Cash Discounts

When cash discounts for prompt payment are offered on purchases of plant assets, how should the discount be reported? If the discount is taken, it is a reduction in the capital asset's purchase price. It is not recognized as a Purchase Discount (see Chapter 8) as purchase discounts relate to inventory purchases that are included in the cost of goods sold. What is not clear, however, is whether a reduction in the asset cost should occur even if the discount is not taken. There are two points of view on this matter.

Under one approach, the net-of-discount amount is considered the asset's cost, **regardless of whether the discount is taken or not.** The rationale for this approach is that an asset's cost is its cash or cash equivalent price. In addition, supporters argue that the terms of cash discounts are so attractive that failure to take them indicates management error or inefficiency. The discount, if it is lost, is the cost of not paying at an earlier date and should be recognized according to its nature as a financing or interest expense.

Supporters of the other approach argue that the discount should not always be deducted from the asset's cost, because the terms may be unfavourable or because it might not be prudent for the company to take the discount. At present, both methods are used in practice. Recognition of the asset at its lower "cash cost" is preferred, at least on conceptual grounds.

Deferred Payment Contracts

Plant assets are often purchased on long-term credit contracts through the use of notes, mortgages, bonds, or equipment obligations. To properly reflect their cost, **assets that are purchased on long-term credit contracts are accounted for at the present value of the consideration that is exchanged** between the contracting parties at the transaction date. For example, a plant asset purchased today in exchange for a $10,000, non-interest-bearing note that is payable four years from now is not recorded at $10,000. The $10,000 note's present value is the transaction's exchange price and the asset's "cash cost." Assuming 12% is an appropriate interest rate to discount this single payment of $10,000 due four years from now, the asset is recognized at a cost of $6,355.20 [$10,000 × 0.63552; see Table A-2 for the present value of a single sum, PV = $10,000 ($PVF_{4,12}$)].

When no interest rate is stated, or if the specified rate is unreasonable, an appropriate interest rate is imputed. The objective is to approximate the interest rate that the buyer and seller would negotiate at arm's length in a similar borrowing transaction. Factors to consider in imputing an interest rate are the borrower's credit rating, the note's amount and maturity date, and prevailing interest rates. **If it can be determined, the acquired asset's cash exchange price is used as the basis for measuring the cost of the asset and identifying the interest element.**

To illustrate, assume that Sutter Corporation purchases a specially built robot spray painter for its production line. The company issues a $100,000, five-year, non-interest-bearing note to Wrigley Robotics Ltd. for the new equipment when the prevailing market interest rate for obligations of this nature is 10%. Sutter is to pay off the note in five $20,000 instalments made at the end of each year. Assume that the fair market value of this specially built robot is not readily determinable and must be approximated by establishing the note's fair value (present value). This calculation and the entries at the purchase and payment dates are as follows:

A = L + SE
+75,816 +75,816

Cash flows: No effect

	At date of purchase	
Equipment	75,816	
Discount on Notes Payable	24,184	
Notes Payable		100,000

Present value of note = $20,000 (PVF – $OA_{5,\ 10\%}$)
= $20,000 (3.79079) (Table A-4)
= $75,816

The difference between the asset's cash cost of $75,816 and the $100,000 cash that is eventually payable is the discount or interest on the $75,816 amount borrowed.

A = L + SE
+7,582 −7,582

Cash flows: No effect

A = L + SE
−20,000 −20,000

Cash flows: ↓ 20,000 outflow

	At end of first year	
Interest Expense	7,582	
Discount on Notes Payable		7,582
Notes Payable	20,000	
Cash		20,000

Interest expense under the effective interest approach is $7,582 [($100,000 − $24,184) × 10%]. The entries at the end of the second year to record interest and to pay off a portion of the note are as follows:

A = L + SE
+6,340 −6,340

Cash flows: No effect

A = L + SE
−20,000 −20,000

Cash flows: ↓ 20,000 outflow

	At end of second year	
Interest Expense	6,340	
Discount on Notes Payable		6,340
Notes Payable	20,000	
Cash		20,000

Interest expense in the second year is determined by applying the 10% interest rate to the net book value of the outstanding Notes Payable, that is, the Notes Payable balance less its contra account, Discount on Notes Payable. At the end of the first year, the Notes Payable account was reduced to $80,000 ($100,000 − $20,000) and the Discount account was reduced to $16,602 ($24,184 − $7,582). The note's net book value, therefore, was $63,398 throughout the second year. The second year's interest expense is calculated as $63,398 × 10%, or $6,340.

If interest is not taken into account in such deferred payment contracts, the asset will be recorded at an amount greater than its fair value. In addition, the interest expense amount that is reported in the income statement will be understated for all periods involved.

Lump Sum Purchase

There is a special problem in determining the cost of capital assets when they are purchased as a group for a single **lump sum price**. When this occurs, and it is not at all unusual, the practice is to allocate the total cost among the various assets based on their relative fair values. The assumption is that costs will vary in direct proportion to their relative values.

Underlying Concept

This is the same principle that is applied to a basket purchase of inventory.

To determine fair value, any of the following might be used: an appraisal for insurance purposes, the assessed valuation for property taxes, or simply an independent appraisal by an engineer or other appraiser.

To illustrate, assume that a company decides to purchase several assets of a smaller company in the same business for a total price of $80,000. The assets purchased are as follows:

	Seller's Book Value	Asset Fair Value
Inventory	$30,000	$ 25,000
Land	20,000	25,000
Building	35,000	50,000
	$85,000	$100,000

The allocation of the $80,000 purchase price based on the relative fair values is shown in Illustration 10-2. Note that the assets' carrying amounts on the seller's books are not representative of their fair values. **They are irrelevant.**

Illustration 10-2

Allocation of Purchase Price–Relative Fair Value Basis

		Asset Cost
Inventory	$\frac{\$25,000}{\$100,000} \times \$80,000 =$	$20,000
Land	$\frac{\$25,000}{\$100,000} \times \$80,000 =$	$20,000
Building	$\frac{\$50,000}{\$100,000} \times \$80,000 =$	$40,000
		$80,000

Issuance of Shares

When property is acquired by issuing securities, such as common shares, the property's cost is measured by the fair value of the shares given or the asset received, whichever one can be measured more reliably. It is not measured by the par, stated, or book value of the shares. **If the shares are actively traded**, the issued shares' market value is a good indicator of the fair value of the property acquired because the shares are a good measure of the current cash equivalent price.[8]

For example, assume that a hardware enterprise decides to purchase land next to its current property in order to expand its carpeting and cabinet operation. Instead of paying

[8] *CICA Handbook* Section 1581 on business combinations provides guidance on using quoted market prices for shares.

cash for the land, it issues to the seller 5,000 no par value common shares with a fair market value of $12 per share. The purchasing company makes the following entry:

A	= L +	SE
+60,000		+60,000

Cash flows: No effect

Land (5,000 × $12)	60,000	
Common Shares		60,000

If the fair value of the shares given up cannot be determined, the fair value of the property should be established and used as the basis for determining the asset's cost and the amount credited to Common Shares.[9]

Exchanges of Assets

When non-monetary assets such as property, plant, and equipment **are acquired for cash or other monetary assets**, the cost of the acquired asset is measured by the fair value (present value) of the cash or other monetary assets that are given up. Monetary assets are "money or claims to future cash flows that are fixed or determinable in amounts and timing by contract or other arrangement."[10] Cash and accounts and notes receivable are the most common types of monetary assets. Non-monetary assets, on the other hand, are assets that are not claims to fixed or determinable cash flows. Examples include inventory, long-lived plant assets, and equity investments in other companies.

When non-monetary assets such as property, plant, and equipment **are disposed of and the company receives monetary assets in exchange**, a gain or loss on disposal is recognized in income. The gain is recognized in income because it is realized—i.e., it has been converted to cash or a claim to cash—and the entity's economic situation has clearly changed in terms of its future cash flows.

However, when an existing **non-monetary asset is exchanged for a new non-monetary asset**, the proper accounting is not necessarily obvious. There are two underlying issues:

1. What should be the cost of the new non-monetary asset that was acquired?
2. Should a gain or loss on disposal be recognized on the non-monetary asset that was given up?

International Insight

The U.S. has harmonized APB Opinion No. 29 with amended IAS 16 to require that exchanges of productive assets be recorded at fair values. Although there is some difference in the terminology that they use, the Canadian, U.S., and international standards are basically converged.

Some argue that the new asset's cost should be determined by its **fair value**, or by the fair value of the asset given up, and that a **gain or loss should be recognized** on the disposal of the old asset. Others believe that the cost of the new asset should be determined by the **book value** of the asset given up, with **no gain or loss recognized**. Still others favour an approach that would **recognize losses** in all cases, but **defer gains** in special situations. In Canada, guidance on non-monetary transactions is found in *CICA Handbook* Section 3831.

Non-monetary transactions, by definition, include both **non-monetary exchanges** and non-monetary non-reciprocal transfers. A non-monetary exchange is an exchange of non-monetary assets (or liabilities or services) for other non-monetary assets (or liabilities or services) with little or no monetary consideration involved. A non-reciprocal transfer is a transfer of an asset (or liability or services) without consideration.[11]

[9] When the shares' market value is used as the basis of valuation, it is important to carefully consider the effect that the issuance of additional shares will have on the existing market price.

[10] *CICA Handbook*, Section 3831.05(d).

[11] *CICA Handbook*, Section 3831.05(f).

General Principle—The Fair Value Standard The general principle is that **non-monetary transactions are accounted for on the same basis as monetary transactions**: thus, the cost of the asset acquired is equal to the fair value of the asset(s) given up or the fair value of the asset acquired, whichever one can be more reliably measured. If the measurements are equally reliable, the fair value of the consideration given up is used. Any gains and losses that result are recognized in income.

International Insight

The FASB standard defines a non-monetary exchange as an exchange where no more than 25 percent of the consideration is monetary. There is no such threshold in the Canadian or international standards, where the economic substance of the transaction has to be assessed.

Why is the accounting like this? Although cash or a claim to cash is not received or is relatively minor in non-monetary exchanges, the earnings process is usually substantially complete. This is because the specific values to the entity of the assets that are received generally are different from the values that are given up. That is, the company's economic circumstances have changed.

The general standard that **non-monetary exchanges be measured at fair value** must be applied, therefore, **unless one or more of the following conditions is true**:

1. The transaction lacks commercial substance.
2. Fair values are not reliably measurable.
3. The exchange transaction was carried out only to facilitate a sale to customers who are not parties to the exchange.

In these situations, the exchange is recorded **at the carrying amount of the asset(s) given up**, including any monetary consideration. Each situation will now be explained in more detail.

1. Transaction Lacks Commercial Substance In following the general standard, the entity basically replaces the carrying value of the asset(s) given up with the fair value of the asset(s) received in exchange, and then reports the difference as a gain (or loss) in net income. Because the underlying economic situation of the company has changed as a result of the transaction—in other words, the transaction has commercial substance—income is permitted to be reported. However, if the company is in the same economic position after the exchange as it was before, there is little or no justification for reporting increased asset values or income.

A transaction has **commercial substance** only if there is a **significant change** in the entity's expected future cash flows. This can be evidenced by a change in either of the following:

1. The configuration of the cash flows underlying the assets that have been exchanged, such as a change in either their expected risk, timing, or amount.
2. The assets' value-in-use or entity-specific value. This relates to an asset's actual value to the specific firm, which means using what the entity expects to gain from having the asset rather than the market's expectations of the asset's value. An example of this would be the value of the cost savings that a company gets from economies of scale that are made possible in the firm by using the asset.

In either case, the change must be significant relative to the fair values of the exchanged assets; significance is often determined by applying professional judgement.

2. Fair Values Are Not Reliably Measurable As might be expected, the exchange cannot be recorded at fair value if the fair value of neither the asset given up nor of the asset received can be reliably measured.

3. Transaction Was Only to Facilitate a Sale to Customers The third exception covers inventory exchanges. Specifically, it applies to when a product or property that is held for sale in the ordinary course of business is exchanged for a product or property that is to be sold in the same line of business in order to facilitate sales to customers who are not parties to the exchange. Consider the case where a company exchanges its inventory items with inventory of another company because of colour, size, and so on in order to meet the immediate needs of a customer. This is a reasonable exception to the use of the fair value rule as the entity's economic situation has not changed as a result of the exchange, the earnings process is not complete, and the company's investment in inventory is not realized until it is sold to the customer. In this case, income is only recognized when the inventory is sold to the customer.

An overriding caution: When an asset is acquired, it cannot be recognized at a higher amount than its fair value at the time of acquisition. In an exchange when the fair value rule cannot be applied, the cost of the new asset is based on the carrying amount of the asset(s) given up. If the carrying amount of the asset(s) given up in the exchange is greater than the fair value of the asset that is received, the new asset is recorded at its lower fair value amount and a loss is recognized.

Accounting for asset exchanges is summarized in Illustration 10-3. This is followed by examples to illustrate the appropriate entries.

Illustration 10-3

Accounting for Asset Exchanges

Does the exchange **(a)** have commercial substance, and **(b)** have determinable fair values, and **(c)** take place other than to facilitate ordinary sales to customers who are not parties to the exchange?

Yes	No
Apply the fair value standard	Exception to the fair value standard
Acquisition cost of asset(s) received = fair value of what is given up or what is acquired, whichever is more reliably measurable.	Acquisition cost of asset(s) received = carrying amount of asset(s) given up.
Difference between book value and fair value of asset(s) given up is recognized in income.	No gain recognized. Loss is recognized only when fair value of asset(s) acquired is less than the carrying amount of the asset(s) given up.

Monetary Exchange of Assets

When assets are exchanged or traded in, the transaction often requires a payment or receipt of cash or some other monetary asset. When the monetary component—or **boot** as it is sometimes called—is significant, the transaction is considered a **monetary exchange,** and the transaction is accounted for at fair values. What proportion is considered significant? This is a matter for professional judgement, but as the percentage gets smaller, the transaction becomes a non-monetary exchange and the need to evaluate whether the transaction has commercial substance increases.

To illustrate a monetary exchange, assume that Information Processing, Inc. trades its used machine for a new model. The machine given up has a book value of $8,000 (original cost $12,000 less $4,000 accumulated amortization) and a fair value of $6,000. It is traded for a new model that has a list price of $16,000. In negotiations with the seller, a trade-in allowance of $9,000 is finally agreed on for the used machine.

Note that the amount agreed on as a **trade-in allowance is not necessarily the used asset's fair value.** In many cases, such as with car dealerships, the trade-in allowance is essentially used to alter the selling price of the new asset without reducing its list price.

The cash payment that is needed and the cost of the new machine are calculated in Illustration 10-4. Because the cash paid is significant relative to the fair value of the total consideration, this is considered a monetary transaction.

Fair value of assets given up:	
Fair value of cash given up—	
List price less trade-in allowance	$16,000 − $9,000 = $ 7,000
Fair value of machine given up	6,000
Cost of new machine = fair value of assets given up	$13,000

Illustration 10-4

Calculation of Cost of New Machine

The journal entry to record this transaction is:

Equipment (new)	13,000	
Accumulated Amortization—Equipment (old)	4,000	
Loss on Disposal of Equipment	2,000	
Equipment (old)		12,000
Cash		7,000

A	= L +	SE
−2,000		−2,000

Cash flows: ↓ 7,000 outflow

The loss on the disposal of the used machine is verified in Illustration 10-5.

Fair value of used machine	$6,000
Book value of used machine	8,000
Loss on disposal of used machine	$2,000

Illustration 10-5

Calculation of Loss on Disposal of Used Machine

Non-Monetary Exchange—Application of Fair Value Standard

To illustrate the general standard for a non-monetary exchange of assets, assume that Cathay Corporation exchanges several used trucks plus cash for vacant land that might be used for a future plant site. The trucks have a combined book value of $42,000 (cost of $64,000 less $22,000 of accumulated amortization). Cathay's purchasing agent, who has had previous dealings in the second-hand market, indicates that the trucks have a fair value of $49,000. In addition to the trucks, Cathay pays $4,000 cash for the land.

This exchange is deemed to be a **non-monetary exchange** and the general fair value standard is applied. The exchange has commercial substance because the pattern and timing of cash flows from the investment in land are very different from those of the trucks. In addition, fair values can be determined and the transaction's purpose was not to facilitate a sale to customers. Assuming that the land's fair value is not known, or its fair value is not as reliable as that of the trucks, the cost of the land is calculated as in Illustration 10-6.

Cost of land = fair value of assets given up:	
Fair value of trucks exchanged	$49,000
Fair value of cash given up	4,000
Acquisition cost of the land	$53,000

Illustration 10-6

Calculation of Land's Acquisition Cost

The journal entry to record the exchange is:

Land	53,000	
Accumulated Amortization—Trucks	22,000	
Trucks		64,000
Cash		4,000
Gain on Disposal of Trucks		7,000

A	= L +	SE
+7,000		+7,000

Cash flows: ↓ 4,000 outflow

The gain is the difference between the fair value of the trucks of $49,000 and their book value of $42,000. It follows that if the fair value of the trucks was $39,000 instead of $49,000, the land's cost is $43,000 ($39,000 + $4,000) and a loss on the exchange of $3,000 ($42,000 – $39,000) is reported. **The accounting is identical to the accounting for a monetary transaction.**

Non-Monetary Exchange—Exception to Fair Value Standard

When an entity **remains in the same economic position after an exchange as before,** recognition of gains cannot be justified. Therefore, the asset acquired is recorded at the book value of the asset given up, and no gain is recognized.

To illustrate, assume Frank Rent-A-Car has an automobile rental fleet of mostly Ford Motor Company products. To offer its customers more choice, Frank's management is interested in increasing the variety of automobiles in its rental fleet by adding numerous General Motors (GM) models. It therefore arranges an exchange with Ned's Rent-A-Car, which owns mainly General Motors vehicles. Under the exchange, a group of Ford automobiles with a fair value of $160,000 and a book value of $135,000 (cost of $150,000 less accumulated depreciation of $15,000) is exchanged for several General Motors models with a fair value of $170,000, and Frank is also required to pay an additional $10,000 cash. As the cash component is a minor portion of the fair value of the total consideration, this is considered a non-monetary exchange.

An assessment of the transaction indicates that the exchange does not have commercial substance. Frank Rent-A-Car's future cash flows (amounts, timing, and risk) are not expected to change significantly as a result of the transaction, and so the company is in substantially the same economic position after the exchange as before. The acquisition cost of the General Motors automobiles is determined as in Illustration 10-7.

Illustration 10-7
Calculation of the Cost of GM Automobiles Acquired

Carrying amount of Ford automobiles given up	$135,000
Carrying amount of cash given up	10,000
Acquisition cost of GM automobiles	$145,000

The entry by Frank to record this transaction is as follows:

A	= L	+ SE
0	0	0

Cash flows: ↓ 10,000 outflow

Automobiles (GM)	145,000	
Accumulated Amortization (Ford)	15,000	
Automobiles (Ford)		150,000
Cash		10,000

Although the increase in value of the Ford vehicles given up (FV of $160,000 – BV of $135,000 = $25,000) is not recognized, it could be thought of as deferred, in which case the acquisition cost of the GM cars could then be calculated in the alternative way shown in Illustration 10-8.

Illustration 10-8
Alternative Measurement of Acquisition Cost

Fair value of GM automobiles	$170,000
Less unrecognized (deferred) gain on Ford automobiles	25,000
Acquisition cost of GM automobiles	$145,000

The "gain" that reduces the new automobiles' cost is essentially recognized through lower depreciation charges as the automobiles are used to generate rental income.

To make it possible for users to understand the effects of non-monetary exchanges on the financial statements, entities must disclose the nature of such transactions, the basis of measurement, and the amount of any resulting gains or losses that are recognized.[12]

Contributed Assets

Companies sometimes receive contributions of assets as donations, gifts, or government grants. Such contributions are referred to as non-reciprocal transfers because they are transfers of assets in one direction only—nothing is given in exchange. Contributions are usually assets (such as cash, securities, land, buildings, or usage of facilities), but they could also be the forgiveness of a debt. If the non-reciprocal transfer is **non-monetary in nature**, the accounting standard is the same as the standard for non-monetary exchanges discussed in the previous section. There are two important issues for non-reciprocal transfers:

1. How should the asset be measured at acquisition?
2. What account should be credited?

When assets are acquired as a donation, a strict cost concept dictates that the asset's acquisition cost is zero. A departure from the cost principle is justified, however, because the only costs that are incurred (legal fees and other relatively minor expenditures) do not form a reasonable basis of accounting for the assets that have been acquired. To record nothing is to ignore the economic realities of an increase in the entity's resources. Therefore, *CICA Handbook* Section 3831 requires **the asset's fair value to be used to establish its "cost" on the books.**

Having established the acquisition cost of the asset, a further question remains about the credit entry in the transaction. Two general approaches have been used to record the credit in this type of transaction:

1. A capital approach: Credit a contributed surplus account, Donated Capital. The increase in assets is viewed as contributed capital rather than as earned revenue. To illustrate, assume a company has recently accepted the donation of land with a fair value of $150,000 from a major shareholder.

   The company makes the following entry:

Land	150,000	
Contributed Surplus—Donated Capital		150,000

A	= L +	SE
+150,000		+150,000

Cash flows: No effect

This approach is only acceptable, however, if the contribution is made by an owner or shareholder. Shareholder contributions of non-monetary assets are rare.

International Insight

The FASB's position is that, in general, companies should recognize contributions as revenues in the period when they are received.

2. An income approach: The contribution is reflected in net income or in other comprehensive income. A contribution by a non-owner meets the definition of an item of **comprehensive income**: a "change in equity (net assets)… from non-owner sources [which] includes all changes in equity during a period except those resulting from investments by owners and distributions to owners."[13] A non-owner contribution, therefore, is included in net income or as an item of other comprehensive income (OCI), the only two components of comprehensive income.

---

[12] *CICA Handbook*, Section 3831.17 and .18.

[13] *CICA Handbook*, Section 1530.03.

Handbook Section 3800 takes the position that government assistance should be recognized in income, either as revenue or as a reduction of expense. If the contributed assets are expected to be used over several future periods, as in the case of a grant for a building or equipment, then the effect on income is spread out over the future periods that benefit from having received the grant. Whether the assets or funds to acquire assets are received from federal, provincial, or municipal governments, existing GAAP requires that recipients defer and recognize the amount that is received over the periods when the related assets are used. This is accomplished by either reducing the asset cost and future amortization by the amount of government assistance received (the **cost reduction method**), or by recording the amount of assistance received as a deferred credit and amortizing it to revenue over the life of the related asset (the **deferral method**).

To illustrate the **cost reduction method**, assume that a company receives a grant of $225,000 from the federal government to upgrade its sewage treatment facility. The entry to record the receipt of the grant under this method is as follows:

A	= L	+ SE
0	0	0

Cash flows: ↑ 225,000 inflow

Cash	225,000	
Equipment		225,000

This results in the equipment being carried on the books **at cost less the related government assistance**. Assuming a 10-year life and straight-line amortization, the annual depreciation expense for the equipment is reduced by $22,500 and net income therefore is increased by this amount each year.

Alternatively, a deferred revenue account can be credited with the grant amount. This amount will then be recognized in income **on the same basis that is used to amortize the underlying asset.** The entries to record the receipt of the grant and its amortization for the first year under the **deferral method** are as follows:

A	= L	+ SE
+225,000	+225,000	

Cash flows: ↑ 225,000 inflow

A	= L	+ SE
	−22,500	+22,500

Cash flows: No effect

Cash	225,000	
Deferred Revenue—Government Grants		225,000
Deferred Revenue—Government Grants	22,500	
Revenue—Government Grants		22,500

A weakness of the cost reduction method is that it reports assets at less than their fair value to the entity. This issue is resolved if the deferral method is used, but this method too has a weakness. The deferral method is not consistent with the conceptual framework because the Deferred Revenue account usually does not meet the definition of a liability.

Note that a donation **of land** by a government cannot be deferred and taken into income over the period it is used because land has an infinite life. Two choices are available in this situation: (1) recognize the full fair value of the land, offset by an equal credit to an other comprehensive income account; or (2) recognize the full fair value of the land, offset by an equal credit to an income statement revenue account.

With the first option, the fair value of the resources that are available to the company is recognized and the contribution is reported in AOCI until the asset is disposed of. New *Handbook* Section 1530, "Comprehensive Income," makes reference to the existence of donations from non-owners as a source of comprehensive income. Under the second option, the value of the land is reported as an asset and the donation is recognized as revenue in net income. The entity is better off as a result of the transaction with non-owners and this is what the income statement is expected to report. Whichever method is adopted, the policy must be disclosed.

Government grants that are awarded to a company **for incurring certain current expenditures**, such as those related to payroll, are recognized in income in the same period as the related expenses. If grants or donations that have been received have a condition attached to them that requires a future event to occur—such as being required to maintain a specified number of employees on the payroll—the contingency is reported in the notes to the financial statements.

Entities are required to provide extensive disclosure about the amounts, terms, and conditions, and accounting treatment they use for government assistance that they have received.[14] This makes it possible for readers to evaluate the effect of such assistance on the entity's financial performance and position.

Although Canadian standards in 2007 are similar to current IFRS, accounting for government grants is one area that is not expected to be converged with the IASB until the changeover to international standards in 2011. Government grants are on the IASB's current agenda, and changes to its existing standards are expected, but not until it comes to terms with related topics dealing with the conceptual framework, non-reciprocal transfers, and obligations related to conditional grants.

International Insight

IASB standards for government grants are expected to change in the near future, resulting in a difference between Canadian standards and IFRS.

Investment Tax Credits

From time to time, federal and provincial governments have tried to stimulate the economy, particularly in areas of high unemployment, by offering special tax advantages to enterprises that invest in specific types of capital assets. The **investment tax credit (ITC)** is one of these incentives. Created by tax legislation, the credit allows enterprises to deduct directly from their income tax liability a specified percentage of the cost of eligible new capital assets. ITCs are also available for specific types of current costs, such as research and development expenditures.

To illustrate, assume that a company purchases an asset for $100,000 and that the asset qualifies for a 10% investment tax credit. If the company has a tax liability of $30,000 before the credit, its tax liability is determined as in Illustration 10-9.

Illustration 10-9

Determination of Tax Liability after an Investment Tax Credit

Taxes payable prior to ITC	$30,000
Less investment tax credit ($100,000 × 10%)	10,000
Final tax liability	$20,000

There has been much debate within the accounting profession about the appropriate way to account for the benefit provided by an investment tax credit. Many believe the ITC is a reduction in the cost of the asset, similar to a purchase discount, and that it should be accounted for over the same period as the life of the related asset; that is, by the cost reduction or deferral approach. Others believe the ITC is a selective reduction in income tax expense in the purchase year. This latter approach—called the **flowthrough approach**—takes the full benefit into income in the year of the asset acquisition by recognizing the full benefit as a reduction in income tax expense. The justification for this treatment is that the tax credit is earned by the act of investment, not by the asset's use or non-use, retention or non-retention.

For its part, the Accounting Standards Board concluded that investment tax credits **are a form of government assistance that should be accounted for on a basis that is**

[14] *CICA Handbook*, Section 3800.18, .22, .24, .26, .29, and .30.

consistent with the accounting for government grants, as described above.[15] That is, the benefit is taken into income on the same basis as the underlying asset, using either the cost reduction or deferral method.

COSTS SUBSEQUENT TO ACQUISITION

Objective 7
Describe and apply the accounting for costs subsequent to acquisition.

After plant assets are installed and ready for use, additional costs are incurred for anything from ordinary repairs to significant additions. The major problem is allocating these costs to the proper accounting periods. **In general, costs that are incurred to achieve greater future benefits are capitalized, whereas expenditures that simply maintain a specific level of service are expensed.** In order for costs to be capitalized, one of four conditions must be present:

1. The asset's life or useful life is increased.
2. The physical output or service capacity of the asset is increased.
3. The quality of the output is improved.
4. The associated operating costs are reduced.[16]

Expenditures that do not increase an asset's service potential are expensed. These include ordinary maintenance or repairs that maintain the asset's existing condition or restore it to normal operating efficiency.

Underlying Concept

Expensing long-lived staplers, pencil sharpeners, and wastebaskets is an application of the materiality constraint.

Most expenditures below an established arbitrary minimum amount are expensed rather than capitalized. Many enterprises adopt a rule that expenditures below, say, \$500, \$10,000, or even higher (depending on the size of the company) are always expensed. Although this treatment may not be correct conceptually, a cost-benefit assessment justifies it.

The distinction between a **capital expenditure** (an asset) and a **revenue expenditure** (an expense) is not always clear-cut, and **this accounting choice can have a significant effect on reported income**. If costs are capitalized as assets on the balance sheet, the income statement is freed from charges that would otherwise reduce the bottom line and earnings per share.

What Do the Numbers Mean?

The "managing" of earnings has been behind many of the well-publicized accounting scandals of recent years. WorldCom executives accounted for billions of dollars of current operating costs as capital additions. Adelphia Communications Corp. aggressively deferred operating items as assets on its balance sheet. Closer to home, Livent has been accused of similar actions in Canada. There is also the case of Toronto-based Atlas Cold Storage Income Trust, the second largest cold storage firm in North America, which announced in 2003 that expenditures of approximately \$3.6 million were inappropriately recorded as additions to capital assets during the previous year. Atlas also adjusted the financial statements of another prior year for an additional \$1.6 million of expenditures that had been recognized as assets. While these examples look like situations where management set out intentionally to exaggerate profits and mislead investors, decisions are made on a daily basis where the distinction between whether an expenditure should be capitalized or expensed is not always clear-cut.

One issue that affects the capitalization decision is determining what counts as a **property unit** that needs to be accounted for. If a fully equipped steamship is considered a property unit, then replacing the engine might be considered an expense. On the other hand, if the ship's engine is considered a property unit, then its replacement would be capitalized. When an item of property, plant, and equipment is made up of significant

[15] *CICA Handbook*, Section 3805.

[16] *CICA Handbook*, Section 3061.26.

separable component parts with useful lives that can be estimated, the cost of each component is recognized separately, as much as it is possible to do so.[17] In most cases, consistent application of a capital/expense policy is more important than trying to provide specific guidelines for each transaction. Generally, four major types of expenditures are incurred for existing assets.

MAJOR TYPES OF EXPENDITURES

Addition Increase or extension of an existing asset.

Improvement and Replacement Substitution of an improved asset for an existing one.

Rearrangement and Reinstallation Movement of an asset from one location to another.

Repairs Expenditures that maintain assets in good operating condition.

Additions

Additions present no major accounting problems. By definition, any **addition to plant assets is capitalized** because a new asset has been created. Adding a wing to a hospital or an air conditioning system to an office, for example, increases the service potential of that facility. Such expenditures are capitalized and are then recognized as expenses in the future periods that benefit from the asset's use.

One problem that does exist in this area is how to account for any changes related to an existing structure as a result of the addition. Is the cost that is incurred to tear down an old wall to make room for an addition a cost of the addition or an expense or loss of the period? Normally, because of practical difficulties in determining the wall's cost, its original carrying amount remains in the accounts, and the cost to tear down the wall is included in the cost of the addition.

Improvements and Replacements

Improvements (often referred to as **betterments**) and **replacements** are substitutions of one asset for another. What is the difference between an improvement and a replacement? An improvement is the substitution of a **better asset** for the one that is currently used (say, a concrete floor substituted for a wooden floor). A replacement, on the other hand, is the substitution of a **similar asset** (a wooden floor for a wooden floor).

Improvements and replacements often result from a general policy to modernize or rehabilitate an older building or piece of equipment. The problem is differentiating between these types of expenditures and normal repairs. Does the expenditure increase the asset's **future service potential**, or does it merely **maintain the existing or original service level**? Service potential is increased when an asset's physical or service capacity is increased, operating costs are reduced, useful life is extended, or the quality of the output is improved. Often, the answer is not clear-cut, and good judgement must be used in order to classify these expenditures.

[17] *CICA Handbook*, Section 3061.30.

If it is determined that the expenditure increases the asset's future service potential and that it should therefore be capitalized, the accounting is handled in one of three ways, depending on the specific circumstances:

1. **Substitution approach.** Conceptually, the substitution approach is always the correct procedure, but it can only be applied if the old asset's carrying amount is known. If that amount can be determined, it is a simple matter to remove the book value of the old asset and replace it with the cost of the new asset. This is easiest to apply when a components approach is used—i.e., when the cost of each component is recognized separately on acquisition.

   To illustrate, assume that Instinct Enterprises Ltd. decides to replace its plumbing pipes. A plumber suggests that the cast iron pipes and copper tubing be replaced by a newly developed plastic tubing. The old pipe and tubing have a book value of $15,000 (cost of $150,000 less accumulated amortization of $135,000), and a scrap value of $1,000. The plastic tubing system has a cost of $125,000. Assuming that Instinct has to pay $124,000 for the new tubing after exchanging the old tubing, the entry is:

A	= L +	SE
−14,000		−14,000

Cash flows: ↓ 124,000 outflow

Plumbing System (new)	125,000	
Accumulated Amortization (old)	135,000	
Loss on Disposal of Plant Assets	14,000	
Plumbing System (old)		150,000
Cash ($125,000 – $1,000)		124,000

   The problem with this approach is the difficulty of determining the old asset's book value. Generally, the parts of a particular asset depreciate at different rates, but often no separate accounting is made. As an example, a truck's tires, motor, and body depreciate at different rates, but most companies use only one amortization rate for the entire truck. Separate amortization rates could be set for each component, but it would be impractical. **If the old asset's carrying amount cannot be determined**, one of the other two approaches is adopted.

2. **Capitalize the new cost.** The justification for capitalizing the improvement or replacement cost is that even though the old asset's carrying amount is not removed from the accounts, enough amortization was taken on the item to reduce the carrying amount almost to zero. Although this assumption may not be true in every case, the differences are often not significant. Improvements are usually treated in this way.

3. **Charge the cost to accumulated amortization**. There are times when the production quantity or quality of the asset itself is not improved, but its useful life is extended. It is common for replacements to extend the asset's useful life but not necessarily improve the quality or quantity of the asset's output. In these circumstances, the expenditure may be debited to Accumulated Amortization rather than to the plant asset account. The theory behind this approach is that the replacement extends the asset's useful life and by doing this recaptures some or all of the past amortization. **The net carrying amount of the asset is the same whether the asset or the accumulated amortization account is debited.**

Rearrangement and Reinstallation

Rearrangement and reinstallation costs that are intended to benefit future periods are different from additions, replacements, and improvements. An example is the rearrangement and reinstallation of a group of machines to facilitate future production. If the original installation cost and the accumulated amortization taken to date can be determined or estimated, the rearrangement and reinstallation cost is handled as a replacement. These amounts, however, are rarely known.

If matching is the main objective, the new costs are capitalized as an asset and amortized over future periods. This is the traditional accounting treatment and it is still acceptable today.

Increasingly, however, accounting standard setters are requiring similar expenditures to be recognized as expenses of the current period. This treatment is more consistent with the asset and liability view of the accounting model set out in *CICA Handbook* Section 1000, which requires an asset to meet the definition of an "economic resource." Capitalizing rearrangement and reinstallation costs as assets comes from a revenue and expense view of the accounting model, where matching is more important.

Repairs

Ordinary repairs are expenditures that are made to maintain plant assets in good operating condition; they are charged to an expense account in the period in which they are incurred based on the argument that this is **the period that receives the primary benefit**. Replacing minor parts, lubricating and adjusting equipment, repainting, and cleaning are examples of maintenance charges that occur regularly and are treated as ordinary operating expenses.

It is often difficult to distinguish a repair from an improvement or replacement. The major consideration is the extent to which the costs that are incurred result in greater future economic benefits. If a **major repair** is made, such as an overhaul where several periods will benefit, the practice has been to account for it as an addition, improvement, or replacement. Some critics, however, argue that costs for planned major expenditures should be expensed as they are incurred unless they represent an additional component or the replacement of an existing component. In other words, if they only restore assets to their original operating condition, an "expense as incurred" approach is justified.

International Insight

SIC 23, an interpretation of IAS 16 on property, plant, and equipment, requires the cost of a major overhaul to be expensed unless the overhauled item has been recognized and depreciated as a separate asset component.

Summary of Costs Subsequent to Acquisition

The schedule in Illustration 10-10 summarizes the accounting treatment for various costs that are incurred after the acquisition of capitalized assets.

Type of Expenditure	Normal Accounting Treatment
Additions	Capitalize cost of addition to asset account.
Improvements and replacements	(a) **Carrying amount known:** Remove cost of and accumulated amortization on old asset, recognizing any gain or loss. Capitalize cost of improvement or replacement. (b) **Carrying amount unknown:** 1. If the asset's useful life is extended, debit accumulated amortization for cost of improvement/replacement. 2. If the quantity or quality of the asset's productivity is increased, capitalize cost of improvement/replacement to asset account.
Rearrangement and reinstallation	(a) If original installation cost is **known**, account for cost of rearrangement/reinstallation as a replacement (carrying value known). (b) If original installation cost is unknown and rearrangement/reinstallation cost is **material** in amount and benefits future periods, capitalize as an asset. (c) If original installation cost is **unknown** and rearrangement/reinstallation cost is **not material or future benefit is questionable**, expense the cost when incurred.

Illustration 10-10

Summary of Costs Subsequent to Acquisition of Property, Plant, and Equipment

Repairs	(a) **Ordinary:** Expense cost of repairs when incurred. (b) **Major:** As appropriate, treat as an addition, improvement, or replacement.

Note: Increasingly, the requirements are moving toward expensing rather than capitalizing unless there is a clear indication that the benefits are greater than the benefits offered by the original asset, the expenditures meet the definition of an asset, and the asset has been recognized and amortized as a separate component.

Imperial Oil Limited, a Canadian integrated oil and gas giant, reported net property, plant, and equipment of U.S. $10,132 million on its December 31, 2005, balance sheet. Illustration 10-11 includes excerpts from Note 1 to Imperial Oil's financial statements that explain the acquisition costs of these assets. The company's primary financial statements are prepared under U.S. GAAP, and a reconciliation is provided of key amounts to Canadian GAAP. One difference relates to the capitalization of interest. Under Canadian standards, companies are not required to capitalize interest related to capital assets under construction. Perhaps because Imperial Oil is very profitable, interest is expensed for Canadian reporting and for Canadian income tax purposes—causing a U.S. $116-million difference in the property, plant, and equipment on its December 31, 2005, balance sheet!

Illustration 10-11
Property, Plant, and Equipment Disclosure

Student Toolkit–Additional Disclosures
www.wiley.com/canada/kieso

NOTES TO CONSOLIDATED FINANCIAL STATEMENTS (excerpts)

Property, plant and equipment

Property, plant and equipment are recorded at cost. Investment tax credits and other similar grants are treated as a reduction of the capitalized cost of the asset to which they apply.

The company uses the successful-efforts method to account for its exploration and development activities. Under this method, costs are accumulated on a field-by-field basis with certain exploratory expenditures and exploratory dry holes being expensed as incurred.

Costs of productive wells and development dry holes are capitalized and amortized on the unit-of-production method for each field. The company uses this accounting policy instead of the full-cost method because it provides a more timely accounting of the success or failure of the company's exploration and production activities.

Maintenance and repair costs, including planned major maintenance, are expensed as incurred. Improvements that increase or prolong the service life or capacity of an asset are capitalized.

Production costs are expensed as incurred. Production involves lifting the oil and gas to the surface and gathering, treating, field processing and field storage of the oil and gas. The production function normally terminates at the outlet valve on the lease or field production storage tank. Production costs are those incurred to operate and maintain the company's wells and related equipment and facilities. They become part of the cost of oil and gas produced. These costs, sometimes referred to as lifting costs, include such items as labour cost to operate the wells and related equipment; repair and maintenance costs on the wells and equipment; materials, supplies and energy costs required to operate the wells and related equipment; and administrative expenses related to the production activity.

Accounting policies for the company's tar sands operation are the same as those described in this summary of significant accounting policies for the company's crude oil and natural gas operations. The capitalization policy for the company's tar sands operation is that acquisition costs are capitalized when incurred. Exploration costs are expensed as incurred. The capitalization of development costs begins only after a determination of proven reserves has been made.

Interest capitalization
Interest costs relating to major capital projects under construction are capitalized as part of property, plant, and equipment. Capitalization of interest ceases when the related asset is substantially complete and ready for its intended use.

Asset retirement obligations and other environmental liabilities
Legal obligations associated with site restoration on the retirement of assets with determinable useful lives are recognized when they are incurred, which is typically at the time the assets are installed. These obligations primarily relate to decommissioning and removal costs of oil and gas wells and related facilities. The obligations are initially measured at fair value and discounted to present value. A corresponding amount equal to that of the initial obligation is added to the capitalized costs of the related asset. Over time the discounted asset retirement obligation amount will be accreted for the change in its present value, and the initial capitalized costs will be depreciated over the useful lives of the related assets.

Summary of Learning Objectives

1 Describe the major characteristics of property, plant, and equipment.

The major characteristics of property, plant, and equipment are: (1) they are acquired for use in operations and not for resale; (2) they are long-term in nature and usually subject to amortization; and (3) they possess physical substance.

2 Identify the costs that are included in the initial valuation of land, buildings, equipment, and similar assets.

Cost of land: Includes all expenditures made to acquire land and to make it ready for use. Land costs typically include the purchase price; closing costs, such as title to the land, legal fees, and registration fees; costs incurred to condition the land for its intended use, such as grading, filling, draining, and clearing; the assumption of any liens, mortgages, or encumbrances on the property; and any additional land improvements that have an indefinite life. Cost of buildings: Includes all expenditures related directly to their acquisition or construction. These costs include materials, labour, and overhead costs that are incurred during construction and professional fees and building permits. Cost of equipment: Includes the purchase price, freight, and handling charges that are incurred; insurance on the equipment while it is in transit; the cost of special foundations if they are required; assembling and installation costs; and the costs of conducting trial runs. In addition, in many cases costs that are associated with asset retirement obligations have to be capitalized and included as part of the asset's cost.

3 Describe the accounting issues for self-constructed assets.

The assignment of indirect costs of manufacturing creates special problems because these costs cannot be traced directly to work and material orders related to the fixed assets that are constructed. These costs might be handled in one of three ways: (1) do not assign any fixed overhead to the cost of the constructed asset, (2) assign a portion of all overhead to the construction process, or (3) allocate the cost based on lost production. The second method is used the most in practice.

4 Identify the costs included in natural resource properties.

There are four types of costs in establishing the cost of natural resource assets such as oil and gas and mining properties: (a) acquisition costs, (b) exploration costs, (c) development costs, and (d) asset retirement costs. In the oil and gas industry, both the full cost method and successful efforts method are acceptable in determining the costs to be capitalized.

5 Describe the accounting issues for interest capitalization.

Companies may choose whether to expense or capitalize interest during the construction of property, plant, and equipment. However, only actual interest (with modifications) may be capitalized. The rationale for capitalization is that, during construction, interest incurred is a necessary cost to acquire the asset, put it in place, and get it ready for use. Also, if the asset had been purchased fully constructed, the manufacturer's costs, such as interest, would make up part of the costs that are recovered in the selling price to the buyer. Any interest cost that is incurred in financing the purchase of an asset that is ready for its intended use should be expensed.

6 Explain and apply other accounting issues related to the initial measurement of plant assets.

The following issues may affect the initial cost of plant assets: *Cash discounts*: Whether or not they are taken, they are generally considered to be a reduction in the asset's cost; cost is the asset's cash or cash equivalent price. *Assets purchased on long-term credit*

Glossary

www.wiley.com/canada/kieso

KEY TERMS

additions, 599
asset retirement costs, 581
betterments, 599
boot, 592
capital approach, 595
capital expenditure, 598
commercial substance, 591
cost reduction method, 596
deferral method, 596
depletion base, 583
development costs, 584
discovery value accounting, 584
exploration costs, 583
fixed assets, 578
flowthrough approach, 597
full cost approach, 58
improvements, 599
income approach, 595
investment tax credit (ITC), 597
leasehold improvements, 581
lump sum price, 589
major repair, 601
monetary assets, 590
natural resources, 583
net recoverable amount, 582
non-monetary assets, 590
non-monetary exchange, 590
non-monetary transaction, 590
non-reciprocal transfers, 595
ordinary repairs, 601
plant assets, 578
property, plant, and equipment, 578
rearrangement and reinstallation costs, 600

contracts: Account for these at the present value of the consideration that is exchanged between the contracting parties. *Lump sum purchase*: Allocate the total cost among the various assets based on their relative fair values. *Issuance of shares*: If the shares are actively traded, the issued shares' market value is a fair indication of the acquired property's cost. If the exchanged shares' market value cannot be determined, the acquired property's fair value is determined and used as the basis for recording the asset's cost and the amount to credit to the common shares. *Exchanges of assets*: When assets are acquired with little or no cash or other monetary assets as part of the consideration, the exchange transaction is accounted for using fair values, with gains/losses recognized in income. Exceptions to this general standard include exchanges which lack commercial substance, where the transaction was undertaken only to facilitate a sale to customers, or when fair values are not reasonably determinable. In these cases, the acquisition cost of the new asset is equal to the carrying amount of the exchanged asset(s). No gains are recognized. *Contributions*: Assets contributed by owners are recognized at their fair value through a credit to Contributed Surplus. Assets contributed by governments are usually recorded at the asset's fair value with a related credit that is taken to income over the same period as the contributed asset is used. *Investment tax credits*: An immediate tax reduction benefit is accounted for in the same way as a government contribution.

7 Describe and apply the accounting for costs subsequent to acquisition.

The accounting treatment of costs that are incurred after acquisition depends on whether the cost is a capital expenditure or a revenue expenditure (i.e., an expense). In general, a capital expenditure—one that results in an increase in the asset's useful life, or in the efficiency of the output obtained from that asset—is charged to the asset account. A revenue expenditure—one that does not increase the asset's future benefits—is expensed immediately. The specific accounting treatment depends on the circumstances.

Appendix 10A

Illustration of Interest Capitalization

8 Objective
Calculate the amount of capitalizable interest for projects that have expenditures over a period of time and borrowings from different sources at varying rates.

Chapter 10 introduced some of the issues for the capitalization of interest during construction. Appendix 10A continues the discussion in more detail and provides an illustration of the application guidance in the FASB's *Statement of Financial Accounting Standards No. 34*, which is often used by Canadian companies. As this text goes to print, the IASB is in process of amending its IAS 23 on borrowing costs to bring it closer to the FASB's SFAS 34 on interest costs. The major change proposed in IAS 23 is to **eliminate the optional treatment of expensing** borrowing costs for the acquisition, construction, or production of a qualifying asset.

While **both standards will require capitalization and their general approach is similar**, there are application differences between SFAS 34 and IAS 23 that could produce different results in practice. These relate to the definitions of borrowing and interest costs, what is included as a qualifying asset, the treatment of income earned on the temporary investment of amounts borrowed, the capitalization rate, and the timing of the beginning and ending of capitalization. At this time, there is no agenda item to deal with these detailed differences. The following discussion of the current U.S. standard highlights the common general approach to interest capitalization.

Three issues need to be considered in implementing this approach:

1. Qualifying assets
2. The capitalization period
3. The amount to capitalize

Qualifying Assets

To qualify for interest capitalization, assets must require an extended time to get them ready for their intended use. Interest costs are capitalized starting with the first expenditure related to the asset, and continuing until the asset is substantially completed and ready for its intended use.

Assets that qualify for interest cost capitalization include assets under construction for an enterprise's own use (including buildings, plants, and large machinery) and assets intended for sale or lease that are constructed or otherwise produced as discrete (i.e., separate) projects (e.g., ships or real estate developments).

Examples of assets that do not qualify for interest capitalization include (1) assets that are in use or ready for their intended use and (2) assets that are not being used in the enterprise's earnings activities and that are not undergoing the activities necessary to get them ready for use, such as land that is not being developed and assets that are not being used because of obsolescence, excess capacity, or needed repairs.

Capitalization Period

The **capitalization period** is the time period during which interest must be capitalized. It begins when three conditions are present:

1. Expenditures for the asset have been made.
2. Activities that are necessary to get the asset ready for its intended use are in progress.
3. Interest cost is being incurred.

Interest capitalization continues as long as these three conditions are present. The capitalization period ends when the asset is substantially complete and ready for its intended use.

Amount to Capitalize

For interest to be capitalized, it must be possible to directly attribute the interest to the project. In addition, the amount that can be charged is limited to the lower of (1) the actual interest cost that is incurred during the period or (2) the avoidable interest. **Avoidable interest** is the amount of interest cost during the period that theoretically could have been avoided if expenditures for the asset had not been made. If the actual interest cost for the period is $90,000 and the avoidable interest is $80,000, only $80,000 is capitalized. Or, if the actual interest cost is $80,000 and the avoidable interest is $90,000, a maximum of $80,000 is capitalized. In no situation can the interest cost include a cost of capital charge for equity financing.

To apply the avoidable interest concept, the potential amount of interest to be capitalized during an accounting period is determined as follows: the **weighted-average accumulated expenditures** for qualifying assets during the period are multiplied by the appropriate interest rate.

Weighted-Average Accumulated Expenditures

In calculating the weighted-average accumulated expenditures, the construction expenditures are weighted by the amount of time (fraction of a year or accounting period) in which interest cost can be incurred on the expenditure. To illustrate, assume a 17-month bridge construction project with current-year payments to the contractor of $240,000 on March 1, $480,000 on July 1, and $360,000 on November 1. The weighted-average accumulated expenditures for the year ended December 31 is calculated as in Illustration 10A-1.

Illustration 10A-1

Calculation of Weighted-Average Accumulated Expenditures

Expenditures			Capitalization		Weighted-Average Accumulated
Date	Amount	×	Period*	=	Expenditures
March 1	$ 240,000		10/12		$200,000
July 1	480,000		6/12		240,000
November 1	360,000		2/12		60,000
	$1,080,000				$500,000

*Months between the date of expenditure and the date when interest capitalization stops or year end arrives, whichever comes first (in this case, December 31)

To calculate the weighted-average accumulated expenditures, the expenditures are weighted by the amount of time that interest cost can be incurred on each one. For the March 1 expenditure, 10 months of interest cost can be associated with the expenditure; for the expenditure on July 1, only 6 months of interest costs can be incurred; and for the expenditure made on November 1, only 2 months of interest cost can be incurred.

Interest Rates

Two principles are used to choose the appropriate interest rates to apply to the weighted-average accumulated expenditures:

1. For the portion of weighted-average accumulated expenditures that is less than or equal to any amounts borrowed specifically to finance construction of the assets, **use the interest rate that was incurred on the specific borrowings**.
2. For the portion of weighted-average accumulated expenditures that is greater than any debt incurred specifically to finance construction of the assets, **use a weighted average of the interest rates incurred on all other outstanding debt during the period.**[18]

Illustration 10A-2 shows the calculation of a weighted-average interest rate for debt that is greater than the amount incurred specifically to finance construction of the assets. It assumes that the principal amounts were outstanding for the full year.

Illustration 10A-2
Calculation of Weighted-Average Interest Rate

	Principal	Interest
12%, two-year note	$ 600,000	$ 72,000
9%, 10-year bonds	2,000,000	180,000
7.5%, 20-year bonds	5,000,000	375,000
	$7,600,000	$627,000

$$\text{Weighted-average interest rate} = \frac{\text{Total interest}}{\text{Total principal}} = \frac{\$627{,}000}{\$7{,}600{,}000} = 8.25\%$$

The avoidable interest in this example, assuming there were no specific borrowings, is the weighted-average amount of accumulated expenditures multiplied by the weighted-average interest rate, or $500,000 × 8.25% = $41,250.

Special Issues Related to Interest Capitalization

Two issues that are related to interest capitalization need special attention:

1. Expenditures for land
2. Interest revenue

Expenditures for Land

When land is purchased with the intention of developing it for a particular use, the interest costs associated with those expenditures may be capitalized. If the land is purchased as

[18] The interest rate to be used may be based exclusively on an average rate of all the borrowings, if desired. Conceptually, however, the specific borrowing rate followed by the average interest rate is preferred. Either method can be used, as SFAS 34 does not provide explicit guidance on this measurement.

a site for a structure (such as a plant site), the interest costs that are capitalized during the construction period are part of the cost of the plant, not of the land. Conversely, if land is being developed to sell it as lots, any capitalized interest cost is part of the developed land's acquisition cost. However, interest costs involved in purchasing land that is held for speculation is not capitalized, because the asset is ready for its intended use.

Interest Revenue

Companies often borrow money to finance the construction of assets and then temporarily invest any excess borrowed funds in interest-bearing securities until the funds are needed to pay for construction. During the early stages of construction, interest revenue that is earned may be more than the interest cost incurred on the borrowed funds. The question is whether it is appropriate to offset interest revenue against interest cost when determining the amount of interest to be capitalized as part of the asset's construction cost.

SFAS 34 generally assumes that short-term investment decisions are not related to the interest incurred as part of the acquisition cost of assets; therefore, interest revenue is usually not netted with capitalized interest. Some critics disagree with this accounting treatment because a company may defer the interest cost but report the interest revenue in the current period.

International Insight

IAS 32 specifies that interest revenue is deducted from the interest cost to be capitalized when income is earned on the temporary investment of funds that were borrowed specifically for the purpose of acquiring a qualifying asset.

Illustration

Assume that on November 1, 2007, Shalla Corporation contracted with Pfeifer Construction Co. Ltd. to have a building constructed for $1.4 million on land costing $100,000. The land is acquired from the contractor and its purchase price is included in the first payment. Shalla made the following payments to the construction company during 2008:

January 1	March 1	May 1	December 31	Total
$210,000	$300,000	$540,000	$450,000	$1,500,000

Construction was completed and the building was ready for occupancy on December 31, 2008. Shalla had the following debt outstanding at December 31, 2008:

Specific Construction Debt	
1. 15%, three-year note to finance construction of the building, dated December 31, 2007, with interest payable annually on December 31	$750,000
Other Debt	
2. 10%, five-year note payable, dated December 31, 2004, with interest payable annually on December 31	$550,000
3. 12%, 10-year bonds issued December 31, 2003, with interest payable annually on December 31	$600,000

The weighted-average accumulated expenditures during 2008 are calculated as in Illustration 10A-3.

Illustration 10A-3
Calculation of Weighted-Average Accumulated Expenditures

Expenditures		×	Current Year Capitalization Period	=	Weighted-Average Accumulated Expenditures
Date	Amount				
Jan. 1	$ 210,000		12/12		$210,000
Mar. 1	300,000		10/12		250,000
May 1	540,000		8/12		360,000
Dec. 31	450,000		0		0
	$1,500,000				$820,000

Note that the expenditure made on December 31, the last day of the year, gets a zero weighting in the calculation, and therefore has no interest cost assigned to it.

Illustration 10A-4 shows the calculation of the avoidable interest.

Illustration 10A-4
Calculation of Avoidable Interest

Weighted-Average Accumulated Expenditures	×	Interest Rate	=	Avoidable Interest
$750,000		0.15 (construction note)		$112,500
70,000[a]		0.1104 (weighted average of other debt)[b]		7,728
$820,000				$120,228

[a]The amount by which the weighted-average accumulated expenditures are greater than the specific construction loan.

[b]Weighted-average interest rate calculation:	Principal	Interest
10%, 5-year note	$ 550,000	$ 55,000
12%, 10-year bonds	600,000	72,000
	$1,150,000	$127,000

$$\text{Weighted-average interest rate} = \frac{\text{Total interest}}{\text{Total principal}} = \frac{\$127,000}{\$1,150,000} = 11.04\%$$

Illustration 10A-5 shows the calculation of the actual interest cost, which is the maximum amount of interest that may be capitalized during 2008.

Illustration 10A-5
Calculation of Actual Interest Cost

Construction note	$750,000 × 0.15 =	$112,500
5-year note	$550,000 × 0.10 =	55,000
10-year bonds	$600,000 × 0.12 =	72,000
Actual interest		$239,500

The interest cost capitalized is $120,228, which is the lesser of the avoidable interest of $120,228 and the actual interest of $239,500.

The journal entries made by Shalla Company during 2008 are as follows:

Tutorial on Interest Capitalization

www.wiley.com/canada/kieso

Jan. 1	Land	100,000	
	Building (or Construction in Process)	110,000	
	Cash		210,000
Mar. 1	Building	300,000	
	Cash		300,000
May 1	Building	540,000	
	Cash		540,000
Dec. 31	Building	450,000	
	Cash		450,000
Dec. 31	Building	120,228	
	Interest Expense		120,228

The capitalized interest of $120,228 will be amortized as part of the asset's depreciation charge—i.e., it will be recognized in expense over the useful life of the asset and not over the term of the debt.

At December 31, 2008, Shalla reports the total amount of interest capitalized in the year in a note to the financial statements. Illustration 10A-6 provides **ClubLink Corporation**'s note to its 2005 financial statements as an example.

Illustration 10A-6

Disclosures Related to Interest Capitalized

CLUBLINK CORPORATION

1. Summary of Significant Accounting policies [excerpt]

Development capital assets include properties under construction or held for future development. ClubLink capitalizes all direct costs relating to the acquisition, development and construction of these properties. ClubLink also capitalizes interest and direct development and management costs to properties under construction.

3. Capital Assets [excerpt]

Interest of $345,000 (2004 – $1,117,000) and direct project development and management costs of $811,000 (2004 – $913,000) have been capitalized during the year to properties under construction.

Glossary

www.wiley.com/canada/kieso

Summary of Learning Objective for Appendix 10A

8. Calculate the amount of capitalizable interest for projects that have expenditures over a period of time and borrowings from different sources at varying rates.

The amount of interest that is capitalized depends on the length of the capitalization period, the amount of avoidable interest, and the weighted-average accumulated expenditures on qualifying assets during the period. The amount is disclosed in the notes to the financial statements.

KEY TERMS

avoidable interest, 606

capitalization period, 606

weighted-average accumulated expenditures, 606

Brief Exercises

Note: All assignment material with an asterisk (*) relates to the appendix to the chapter.

BE10-1 Passos Brothers Inc. purchased land at a price of $57,000. Closing costs were $1,400. An old building was removed at a cost of $28,200. What amount should be recorded as the land cost? **(LO 2)**

BE10-2 Okanagan Utilities Ltd. incurred the following costs in constructing a new maintenance building during the fiscal period. What costs should be included in the cost of the new building? **(LO 2)**

(a) Direct labour, $73,000

(b) Allocation of the president's salary, $54,000

(c) Material purchased for the building, $82,500

(d) Interest on the loan to finance construction until completion, $2,300

(e) Allocation of plant overhead based on labour hours worked on the building, $29,000

(f) Architectural drawings for the building, $7,500

BE10-3 Khan Corporation acquires a coal mine at a cost of $400,000. Development costs that were incurred total $100,000, including $12,300 of depreciation on moveable equipment to construct mine shafts. Based on construction to date, the obligation to restore the property after the mine is exhausted has a present value of $75,000. Prepare the journal entries to record the cost of the natural resource. **(LO 4)**

BE10-4 Junior Oil Corp. purchased the rights to explore a previously undeveloped property in northern Canada at a cost of $20,000. After incurring $80,000 on personnel and transportation costs and another $35,200 on seismic testing, Junior Oil determined that there were economic reserves that could be developed, but no further work was done in this area due to the arrival of winter. What is the effect on Junior's balance sheet and income statement of the expenditures made to date? **(LO 4)**

BE10-5 Chavez Corporation purchased a truck by issuing an $80,000, four-year, non-interest-bearing note to Equinox Inc. The market interest rate for obligations of this nature is 12%. Prepare the journal entry to record the truck purchase. **(LO 6)**

BE10-6 Martin Corporation purchased a truck by issuing an $80,000, 12% note to Equinox Inc. Interest is payable annually and the note is payable in four years. Prepare the journal entry to record the truck purchase. **(LO 6)**

BE10-7 Hamm Inc. purchased land, a building, and equipment from Spamela Corporation for a cash payment of $306,000. The assets' estimated fair values are land $95,000; building $250,000; and equipment $110,000. At what amounts should each of the three assets be recorded? **(LO 6)**

BE10-8 Wizard Corp. obtained land by issuing 2,000 of its no par value common shares. The land was recently appraised at $85,000. The common shares are actively traded at $41 per share. Prepare the journal entry to record the land acquisition. **(LO 6)**

BE10-9 Petri Corporation purchased equipment for an invoice price of $40,000, terms 2/10, n/30. (a) Record the purchase of the equipment and the subsequent payment, assuming the payment was made within the discount period. (b) Repeat (a), but assuming the company's payment missed the discount period. **(LO 6)**

BE10-10 Kristali Corporation traded a used truck (cost $23,000, accumulated amortization $20,700) for another used truck worth $3,700. Kristali also paid $300 cash in the transaction. Prepare the journal entry to record the exchange, assuming the transaction lacks commercial substance. **(LO 6)**

BE10-11 Sloan Ltd. traded a used welding machine (cost $9,000, accumulated amortization $3,000) for office equipment with an estimated fair value of $5,000. Sloan also paid $2,000 cash in the transaction. Prepare the journal entry to record the exchange. The equipment results in different cash flows for Sloan, compared to those the welding machine produced. **(LO 6)**

BE10-12 Bulb Ltd. traded a used truck for a new truck. The used truck cost $30,000 and had accumulated amortization of $27,000. The new truck was worth $35,000. Bulb also made a cash payment of $33,000. Prepare Bulb's entry to record the exchange, and state any assumptions that you have made. **(LO 6)**

BE10-13 Swanson Corp. recently purchased a building to house its manufacturing operations in Moose Jaw for $470,000. The company agreed to lease the land that the building stood on for $14,000 per year from the industrial park owner, and the municipality donated $140,000 to Swanson as an incentive to locate in the area and acquire the building. Prepare entries to record the cash that was exchanged in each of the transactions, assuming the cost reduction method is used. **(LO 6)**

(LO 6) **BE10-14** Use the information for Swanson Corp. in BE10-13. Prepare the entries to record the three cash transactions, assuming the deferral method is used.

(LO 6) **BE10-15** Dubois Inc. received equipment as a donation. The equipment has a fair market value of $55,000. Prepare the journal entry to record the receipt of the equipment under each of the following assumptions:

(a) The equipment was donated by a shareholder.

(b) The equipment was donated by a retired employee.

(LO 7) **BE10-16** Which of the following costs should be expensed when it is incurred?

(a) $13,000 paid to rearrange and reinstall machinery

(b) $200 paid for a tune-up and oil change on a delivery truck

(c) $200,000 paid for an addition to a building

(d) $7,000 paid to replace a wooden floor with a concrete floor

(e) $2,000 paid for a major overhaul that extends the useful life of a truck

(f) $700,000 paid for relocating company headquarters

(LO 5, 8) ***BE10-17** Brent Hill Company is constructing a building. Construction began on February 1 and was completed on December 31. Expenditures were $1.5 million on March 1; $1.2 million on June 1; and $3 million on December 31. Calculate Brent Hill's weighted-average accumulated expenditures that would be used for interest capitalization purposes.

(LO 5, 8) ***BE10-18** Brent Hill Company (see BE10-17) borrowed $1 million on March 1 on a five-year, 12% note to help finance the building construction. In addition, the company had outstanding all year a $2-million, five-year, 13% note payable and a $3.5-million, four-year, 15% note payable. Calculate the weighted-average interest rate that would be used for interest capitalization purposes.

(LO 5, 8) ***BE10-19** Use the information for Brent Hill Company from BE10-17 and BE10-18. Calculate the company's avoidable interest.

Exercises

(LO 2) **E10-1** **(Acquisition Costs of Realty)** The following expenditures and receipts are related to land, land improvements, and buildings that were acquired for use in a business enterprise. The receipts are in parentheses.

(a) Money borrowed to pay a building contractor (signed a note), $(275,000)

(b) A payment for construction from note proceeds, $275,000

(c) The cost of land fill and clearing, $8,000

(d) Delinquent real estate taxes on property, assumed by a purchaser, $7,000

(e) A premium on a six-month insurance policy during construction, $6,000

(f) Refund of one month's insurance premium because construction was completed early, $(1,000)

(g) An architect's fee on a building, $22,000

(h) The cost of real estate purchased as a plant site (land $200,000; building $50,000), $250,000

(i) A commission fee paid to a real estate agency, $9,000

(j) The installation of fences around a property, $4,000

(k) The cost of razing and removing a building, $11,000

(l) Proceeds from the salvage of a demolished building, $(5,000)

(m) Interest paid during construction on money borrowed for construction, $13,000

(n) The cost of parking lots and driveways, $19,000

(o) The cost of trees and shrubbery that were planted, $14,000

(p) Excavation costs for new building, $3,000

(q) The GST on an excavation cost, $180

Instructions

Identify each item by letter and list the items in columnar form, as shown below. Using the column headings that follow, write the letter for each item in the first column and its amount under the column heading where it would be recorded. All receipt amounts should be reported in parentheses. For any amounts that should be entered in the Other Accounts column, also indicate the account title.

Item	Land	Land Improvements	Building	Other Accounts

E10-2 **(Acquisition Costs of Realty)** Glesen Corp. purchased land with two old buildings on it as a factory site for $460,000. The property tax assessment on this property was $350,000: $250,000 for the land and the rest for the buildings. It took six months to tear down the old buildings and construct the factory. **(LO 2)**

The company paid $50,000 to raze the old buildings and sold salvaged lumber and brick for $6,300. Legal fees of $1,850 were paid for title investigation and drawing up the purchase contract. Payment to an engineering firm was made for a land survey, $2,200, and for drawing the factory plans, $82,000. The land survey had to be made before final plans could be drawn. The liability insurance premium that was paid during construction was $900. The contractor's charge for construction was $3,640,000. The company paid the contractor in two instalments: $1,200,000 at the end of three months and $2,440,000 upon completion. Interest costs of $170,000 were incurred to finance the construction.

Instructions

Determine the land and building costs as they should be recorded on the books of Glesen Corp. Assume that the land survey was for the building.

E10-3 **(Purchase and Cost of Self-Constructed Assets)** Wen Corp. both purchases and constructs various equipment that it uses in its operations. The following items are for two different pieces of equipment and were recorded in random order during the calendar year 2008: **(LO 3, 6)**

Purchase	
Cash paid for equipment, including sales tax of $8,000 and GST of $6,000	$114,000
Freight and insurance cost while in transit	2,000
Cost of moving equipment into place at factory	3,100
Wage cost for technicians to test equipment	4,000
Materials cost for testing	500
Insurance premium paid on the equipment during its first year of operation	1,500
Special plumbing fixtures required for new equipment	8,000
Repair cost on equipment incurred in first year of operations	1,300
Cash received from provincial government as incentive to purchase equipment	25,000

Construction	
Material and purchased parts (gross cost $200,000; failed to take 2% cash discount)	$200,000
Imputed interest on funds used during construction (share financing)	14,000
Labour costs	190,000
Overhead costs (fixed $20,000; variable $30,000)	50,000
Profit on self-construction	30,000
Cost of installing equipment	4,400

Instructions

Calculate the total cost for each of these two pieces of equipment. If an item is not capitalized as an equipment cost, indicate how it should be reported.

E10-4 **(Treatment of Various Costs)** Farrey Supply Ltd. is a newly formed corporation that incurred the following expenditures related to land, buildings, machinery, and equipment: **(LO 2, 3, 6)**

Legal fees for title search		$ 520
Architect's fees		2,800
Cash paid for land and dilapidated building on it		112,000
Removal of old building	$20,000	
Less: Salvage	5,500	14,500
Surveying before construction		370
Interest on short-term loans during construction		7,400

Excavation before construction for basement	$ 19,000
Machinery purchased (subject to 2% cash discount, which was not taken)	65,000
Freight on machinery purchased	1,340
Storage charges on machinery, made necessary because building was still under construction when machinery was delivered	2,180
New building constructed (building construction took six months from date of purchase of land and old building)	485,000
Assessment by city for drainage project	1,600
Hauling charges for delivery of machinery from storage to new building	620
Installation of machinery	2,000
Trees, shrubs, and other landscaping after completion of building (permanent in nature)	5,400
Municipal grant to promote locating in the municipality	8,000

Instructions

Determine the amounts that should be included in the cost of land, of buildings, and of machinery and equipment. Assume that Farrey follows a policy of capitalizing interest on self-constructed assets. Indicate how any amounts that are not included in these accounts should be recorded.

(LO 3, 6) **E10-5 (Entries for Asset Acquisition, Including Self-Construction)** The following are transactions related to Hood Limited:

(a) The City of Piedmont gives the company five hectares of land as a plant site. This land's market value is determined to be $81,000.

(b) Hood issues 13,000 no par value common shares in exchange for land and buildings. The property has been appraised at a fair market value of $990,000, of which $180,000 has been allocated to land and $810,000 to buildings. The Hood shares are not listed on any exchange, but a block of 100 shares was sold by a shareholder 12 months ago at $65 per share, and a block of 200 shares was sold by another shareholder 18 months ago at $58 per share.

(c) No entry has been made to remove amounts for machinery constructed during the year that were charged to the accounts Materials, Direct Labour, and Overhead and should have been charged to plant asset accounts. The following information relates to the costs of the machinery that was constructed:

Construction materials used	$15,000
Direct materials used in calibrating the equipment	375
Factory supplies used	900
Direct labour incurred	34,000
Additional overhead (over regular) caused by construction of machinery, excluding factory supplies used	2,700
Fixed overhead rate applied to regular manufacturing operations	60% of direct labour cost
Cost of similar machinery if it had been purchased from outside suppliers	84,000

Instructions

Prepare journal entries on the books of Hood Limited to record these transactions.

(LO 4) **E10-6 (Natural Resource—Minerals)** At the beginning of 2008, Plato Corporation acquired property, including all mineral rights, for $790,000. Of this amount, $80,000 was ascribed to the land itself. Plato, an international player in the mining industry, incurred the following costs during the first six months of the year:

Clearing the trees from the mine site	$ 23,400
Cash received for the timber cleared	1,250
Cost of roads into the mine site	100,000
Mine site office building, to be demolished when the mine is closed	50,000
Purchase of moveable heavy equipment for the above	88,000
Depreciation on heavy equipment used for the costs incurred above	5,800
Allocation of Plato head office costs	14,000
Salary of engineer overseeing above activities	52,000

Instructions

(a) Calculate the amount that should be capitalized to the mining property account. Provide a brief explanation for any amount that you did not include.

(b) Before eventually selling the land, the company has to fill in the hole left by the mining process. It estimates that this will cost $250,000. How would this amount be recorded?

E10-7 **(Natural Resource—Oil)** Oil Products Limited leases property on which oil has been discovered. The lease provides for an immediate payment of $550,000 to the lessor before drilling is begun and an annual rental of $42,000. In addition, the lessee is responsible for cleaning up the waste and debris from drilling and for the costs associated with reconditioning the land for farming when the wells are abandoned. It is estimated that the cleanup and reconditioning obligation has a present value of $31,000. **(LO 4)**

Instructions

Determine the amount that should be capitalized in the Oil Property asset account as a result of the lease agreement.

E10-8 **(Asset Acquisition)** Hayes Industries Corp. purchased the following assets and also constructed a building. All this was done during the current year. **(LO 5, 6, 8)**

Assets 1 and 2

These assets were purchased together for $100,000 cash. The following information was gathered:

Description	Initial Cost on Seller's Books	Amortization to Date on Seller's Books	Book Value on Seller's Books	Appraised Value
Machinery	$100,000	$50,000	$50,000	$90,000
Office Equipment	60,000	10,000	50,000	30,000

Asset 3

This machine was acquired by making a $10,000 down payment and issuing a $30,000, two-year, zero-interest-bearing note. The note is to be paid off in two $15,000 instalments made at the end of the first and second years. It was estimated that the asset could have been purchased outright for $35,000.

Asset 4

A truck was acquired by trading in an older truck that has the same value-in-use. The newer truck has options that will make it more comfortable for the driver; however, the company remains in the same economic position after the exchange as before. Facts concerning the trade-in are as follows:

Cost of truck traded	$100,000
Accumulated amortization to date of sale	40,000
Fair market value of truck traded	80,000
Cash received	10,000
Fair market value of truck acquired	70,000

Asset 5

Office equipment was acquired by issuing 100 shares of no par value common shares. The shares had a market value of $11 per share.

Construction of Building

A building was constructed on land purchased last year at a cost of $150,000. Construction began on February 1 and was completed November 1. The payments to the contractor were as follows:

Date	Payment
Feb. 1	$120,000
June 1	360,000
Sept. 1	480,000
Nov. 1	100,000

To finance construction of the building, a $600,000, 12% construction loan was taken out on February 1. The loan was repaid on November 1. The firm had $200,000 of other outstanding debt during the year at a borrowing rate of 8%.

Instructions

Record the acquisition of each of these assets.

E10-9 **(Acquisition Costs of Trucks)** Jackson Corporation operates a retail computer store. To improve its delivery services to customers, the company purchased four new trucks on April 1, 2008. The terms of acquisition for each truck were as follows: **(LO 6)**

1. Truck #1 had a list price of $17,000 and was acquired for a cash payment of $15,900.

2. Truck #2 had a list price of $18,000 and was acquired for a down payment of $2,000 cash and a non-interest-bearing note with a face amount of $16,000. The note is due April 1, 2009. Jackson would normally have to pay interest at a rate of 10% for such a borrowing, and the dealership has an incremental borrowing rate of 8%.

3. Truck #3 had a list price of $18,000. It was acquired in exchange for a computer system that Jackson carries in inventory. The computer system cost $13,500 and is normally sold by Jackson for $17,100. Jackson uses a perpetual inventory system.

4. Truck #4 had a list price of $16,000. It was acquired in exchange for 1,000 common shares of Jackson Corporation. The common shares are no par value shares with a market value of $15 per share.

Instructions

Prepare the appropriate journal entries for Jackson Corporation for the above transactions. If there is some uncertainty about the amount, give reasons for your choice.

(LO 6) E10-10 (Correction of Improper Cost Entries) Plant acquisitions for selected companies are as follows:

1. Bella Industries Inc. acquired land, buildings, and equipment from a bankrupt company, Torres Co., for a lump sum price of $700,000. At the time of purchase, Torres' assets had the following book and appraisal values:

	Book Value	Appraisal Value
Land	$200,000	$150,000
Buildings	250,000	350,000
Equipment	300,000	300,000

To be conservative, Bella Industries decided to take the lower of the two values for each asset it acquired. The following entry was made:

Land	150,000	
Buildings	250,000	
Equipment	300,000	
Cash		700,000

2. Hari Enterprises purchased store equipment by making a $2,000 cash down payment and signing a $23,000, one-year, 10% note payable. The purchase was recorded as follows:

Store Equipment	27,300	
Cash		2,000
Note Payable		23,000
Interest Payable		2,300

3. Kim Company purchased office equipment for $20,000, terms 2/10, n/30. Because the company intended to take the discount, it made no entry until it paid for the acquisition. The entry was:

Office Equipment	20,000	
Cash		19,600
Purchase Discounts		400

4. Kaiser Inc. recently received land at zero cost from the Village of Chester as an inducement to locate its business in the village. The appraised value of the land was $27,000. The company made no entry to record the land because it had no cost basis.

5. Zimmerman Company built a warehouse for $600,000. It could have contracted out and purchased the building for $740,000. The controller made the following entry:

Warehouse	740,000	
Cash		600,000
Profit on Construction		140,000

Instructions

(a) Prepare the entry that should have been made at the date of each acquisition.

(b) Prepare the correcting entry that is required in each case to correct the accounts. In other words, do not simply reverse the incorrect entry and replace it with the entry in part (a).

(c) List the accounting principle, assumption, or constraint from the conceptual framework that has been violated in each case.

E10-11 (Entries for Equipment Acquisitions) Geddes Engineering Corporation purchased conveyor equipment with a list price of $50,000. Three independent cases that are related to the equipment follow. Assume that the equipment purchases are recorded gross. **(LO 6)**

1. Geddes paid cash for the equipment 15 days after the purchase, along with 6% GST and provincial sales tax of $3,210. The vendor's credit terms were 1/10, n/30.
2. Geddes traded in equipment with a book value of $2,000 (initial cost $40,000), and paid $40,500 in cash one month after the purchase. The old equipment could have been sold for $8,000 at the date of trade, but was accepted for a trade-in allowance of $9,500 on the new equipment.
3. Geddes gave the vendor a $10,000 cash down payment and a 9% note payable with blended principal and interest payments of $20,000 each, due at the end of each of the next two years.

Instructions

(a) Prepare the general journal entries that are required to record the acquisition and payment in each of the three independent cases above. Round to the nearest dollar.

(b) Compare the treatment of the cash discount in item 1 above with the accounting for purchase discounts for inventories using the net method in Chapter 8.

E10-12 (Entries for Acquisition of Assets) Information for Zoe Ltd. follows: **(LO 6)**

1. On July 6, Zoe acquired the plant assets of Desbury Company, which had discontinued operations. The property's appraised value was:

Land	$ 400,000
Building	1,200,000
Machinery and equipment	800,000
Total	$2,400,000

Zoe gave 12,500 of its no par value common shares in exchange. The shares had a market value of $168 per share on the date of the property purchase.

2. Zoe had the following cash expenses between July 6 and December 15, the date when it first occupied the building:

Repairs to building	$105,000
Construction of bases for machinery to be installed later	135,000
Driveways and parking lots	122,000
Remodelling of office space in building, including new partitions and walls	61,000
Special assessment by city on land	18,000

On December 20, Zoe purchased machinery for $260,000, subject to a 2% cash discount, and paid freight on the machinery of $10,500. The machine was dropped while being placed in position, which resulted in repairs costing $12,000. The company paid the supplier within the discount period.

Instructions

(a) Prepare the entries for these transactions on the books of Zoe Ltd.

(b) Prepare the entry for the purchase and payment of the machinery in item 2, assuming the discount was not taken.

E10-13 (Purchase of Equipment with Non-Interest-Bearing Debt) Mohawk Inc. decided to purchase equipment from Central Ontario Industries on January 2, 2008, to expand its production capacity to meet customers' demand for its product. Mohawk issued an $800,000, five-year, non-interest-bearing note to Central Ontario for the new equipment when the prevailing market interest rate for obligations of this nature was 12%. The company will pay off the note in five $160,000 instalments due at the end of each year of the note's life. **(LO 6)**

Instructions

(Round to nearest dollar in all calculations.)

(a) Prepare the journal entry(ies) at the date of purchase.

(b) Prepare the journal entry(ies) at the end of the first year to record the payment and interest, assuming that the company uses the effective interest method.

(c) Prepare the journal entry(ies) at the end of the second year to record the payment and interest.

(d) Assuming that the equipment has a 10-year life and no residual value, prepare the journal entry that is needed to record amortization in the first year. (Straight-line method is used.)

(LO 6) **E10-14 (Purchase of Computer System with Non-Interest-Bearing Debt)** Sparrow Corporation purchased a computer system on December 31, 2007, paying $30,000 down and agreeing to make a further $75,000 payment on December 31, 2010. An interest rate of 10% is implicit in the purchase price. Sparrow uses the effective interest method and has a December 31 year end.

Instructions

(a) Prepare the journal entry(ies) at the purchase date. (Round to two decimal places.)

(b) Prepare any journal entry(ies) required at December 31, 2008, 2009, and 2010.

(LO 6) **E10-15 (Purchase of Equipment with Non-Interest-Bearing Debt)** On September 1, 2008, Reta Corporation purchased equipment for $30,000 by signing a two-year note payable with a face value of $30,000 due on September 1, 2010. The going rate of interest for this level of risk was 8%. The company has a December 31 year end.

Instructions

(a) Calculate the cost of the equipment assuming the note is as follows:

1. An 8% interest-bearing note, with interest due each September 1.
2. A 2% interest-bearing note, with interest due each September 1.
3. A non-interest-bearing note.

(b) Record all journal entries from September 1, 2008, to September 1, 2010, for the three notes in (a). Ignore amortization of the equipment.

(CGA-Canada adapted)

(LO 6) **E10-16 (Asset Exchange, Monetary Transaction)** Cannondale Company purchased an electric wax melter on April 30, 2009, by trading in its old gas model and paying the balance in cash. The following data relate to the purchase:

List price of new melter	$15,800
Cash paid	10,000
Cost of old melter (five-year life, $700 residual value)	11,200
Accumulated amortization on old melter (straight-line)	6,300
Second-hand market value of old melter	5,200

Instructions

Assuming that Cannondale's fiscal year ends on December 31 and amortization has been recorded through December 31, 2008, prepare the journal entry(ies) that are necessary to record this exchange. Give reasons for the accounting treatment you used.

(LO 6) **E10-17 (Non-Monetary Exchange)** Starr Company Limited exchanged equipment that it uses in its manufacturing operations for similar equipment that is used in the operations of Ping Company Limited. Starr also paid Ping $1,500 in cash. The following information pertains to the exchange:

	Starr Co.	Ping Co.
Equipment (cost)	$31,000	$34,000
Accumulated amortization	22,000	16,000
Fair value of equipment	15,500	17,000
Cash paid	1,500	

Instructions

(a) Prepare the journal entries to record the exchange on the books of both companies if the exchange is determined to have commercial substance.

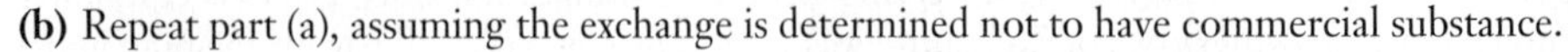

(b) Repeat part (a), assuming the exchange is determined not to have commercial substance.

(c) List some of the factors that the accountant would need to consider in order to determine whether the transaction has commercial substance.

(LO 6) **E10-18 (Non-Monetary Exchanges)** Carver Inc. recently replaced a piece of automatic equipment at a net price of $4,000, f.o.b. factory. The replacement was necessary because one of Carver's customers had accidentally backed his truck into Carver's original equipment and made it inoperable. Because of the accident, the equipment had no resale value to anyone and had to be scrapped. Carver's insurance policy provided for a replacement of Carver's equipment and paid the price of the new equipment directly to the new equipment manufacturer, minus the deductible amount paid to the manufacturer by Carver. The $4,000 that Carver paid was the amount of the deductible that Carver has to pay on any single claim on its insurance policy. The new equipment represents the same value-in-use to Carver. The used equipment had originally cost $65,000. It also had a book value of $45,000 at the time of the accident and a second-hand market value of $50,800 before the accident, based on recent transactions involving similar equipment. Freight and installation charges for the new equipment required Carver to pay an additional $1,100 cash.

Instructions

(a) Prepare the general journal entry to record the transaction to replace the equipment that was destroyed in the accident.

(b) Repeat (a), but assume that the new equipment will result in significant savings to Carver since the new equipment is more efficient and requires less staff time to operate.

E10-19 **(Non-Monetary Exchanges)** Jamil Jonas is an accountant in public practice. Not long ago, Jamil struck a deal with his neighbour Ralph to prepare Ralph's business income tax and GST returns for 2007 in exchange for Ralph's services as a landscaper. Ralph provided labour and used his own equipment to perform landscaping services for Jamil's personal residence for which he would normally charge $500. Jamil would usually charge $650 for the number of hours spent completing Ralph's returns but considers the transaction well worth it since he really dislikes doing his own landscaping. **(LO 6)**

Instructions

How would each party record this transaction? Prepare the journal entries for both Jamil and Ralph's companies.

E10-20 **(Government Assistance)** Lightstone Equipment Ltd. wanted to expand into New Brunswick and was impressed by the provincial government's grant program for new industry. After being sure that it would qualify for the grant program, it purchased property in downtown Saint John on June 15, 2008. The property cost $235,000 and Lightstone spent the next two months gutting the inside of the building and reconstructing the two floors to meet the company's needs. The building has a useful life of 20 years and an estimated residual value of $65,000. In late August, the company moved into the building and began operations. Additional information follows: **(LO 6)**

1. The property was assessed at $195,000, with $145,000 allocated to the land.
2. Architectural drawings and engineering fees related to the construction cost $18,000.
3. The company paid $17,000 to the contractor for gutting the inside of the building and $108,400 for construction.
4. The provincial government contributed $75,000 toward the building costs.

Instructions

(a) Assuming that the company uses the cost reduction method to account for government assistance, answer the following:
1. What is the cost of the building on Lightstone Equipment's balance sheet at August 31, 2008, its fiscal year end?
2. What is the effect of this capital asset on the company's income statement for the company's year ended August 31, 2009?

(b) Assuming the company uses the deferral method to account for government assistance, answer the following:
1. What is the cost of the building on Lightstone Equipment's balance sheet at August 31, 2008?
2. What is the effect of this capital asset on the company's income statement for the company's year ended August 31, 2009?

(c) Compare the balance sheet and income statement presentations for the two alternative treatments for government assistance for the fiscal year ended August 31, 2009.

E10-21 **(Analysis of Subsequent Expenditures)** On January 1, 2008, the accounting records of Robinson Limited included a debit balance of $15 million in the building account and of $12 million in the related accumulated amortization account. The building was purchased in January 1968 for $15 million, and was estimated to have a 50-year useful life with no residual value. Robinson uses the straight-line amortization method for all its property, plant, and equipment. During 2008, the following expenditures relating to the building were made: **(LO 7)**

1. The original roof of the building was removed and replaced with a new roof. The old roof cost $1 million and the new roof cost $2.5 million.
2. The ongoing frequent repairs on the building during the year cost $57,000.
3. The old heating system for the building was replaced with a new system. The new heating system cost $700,000 and is estimated to have a seven-year useful life and no residual value. The cost of the old heating system is unknown.
4. A natural gas explosion caused $44,000 damage to the building. This major repair did not change the estimated useful life of the building.

Instructions
Prepare the journal entries to record the expenditures related to the building during 2008.

(CGA-Canada adapted)

(LO 7) E10-22 (Analysis of Subsequent Expenditures) The following transactions occurred during 2008. Assume that amortization of 10% per year is charged on all machinery and 5% per year on buildings, on a straight-line basis, with no estimated residual value. Assume also that amortization is charged for a full year on all fixed assets that are acquired during the year, and that no amortization is charged on fixed assets that are disposed of during the year.

Jan. 30	A building that cost $132,000 in 1991 was torn down to make room for a new building. The wrecking contractor was paid $5,100 and was permitted to keep all materials salvaged.
Mar. 10	A new part costing $2,900 was purchased and added to a machine that was purchased in 2006 for $16,000. The new part replaced an original machine part, and resulted in a 25% increase in the efficiency of the equipment. The old part's cost was not separable from the original machine's cost.
Mar. 20	A gear broke on a machine that cost $9,000 in 2003, and the gear was replaced at a cost of $85. The replacement does not extend the machine's useful life.
May 18	A special base that was installed for a machine in 2002 when the machine was purchased had to be replaced at a cost of $5,500 because of defective workmanship on the original base. The cost of the machinery was $14,200 in 2002. The cost of the base was $3,500, and this amount was charged to the Machinery account in 2002.
June 23	One of the buildings was repainted at a cost of $6,900. It had not been painted since it was constructed in 2004.

Instructions

(a) Prepare general journal entries for the transactions. (Round to nearest dollar.)

(b) Assume that on March 20, the gear replacement extends the machine's useful life. How would your journal entry change?

(LO 7) E10-23 (Analysis of Subsequent Expenditures) Plant assets often require expenditures subsequent to acquisition. It is important that they be accounted for properly. Any errors will affect both the balance sheets and income statements for several years.

Instructions
For each of the following items, indicate whether the expenditure should be capitalized (C) or expensed (E) in the period when it was incurred:

1. ______ A betterment
2. ______ Replacement of a minor broken part on a machine
3. ______ An expenditure that increases an existing asset's useful life
4. ______ An expenditure that increases the efficiency and effectiveness of a productive asset but does not increase its residual value
5. ______ An expenditure that increases the efficiency and effectiveness of a productive asset and its residual value
6. ______ An expenditure that increases a productive asset's output quality
7. ______ An improvement to a machine that increases its fair market value and its production capacity by 30% without extending the machine's useful life
8. ______ Ordinary repairs
9. ______ An improvement
10. ______ Interest on borrowing that is necessary to finance a major overhaul of machinery that extend its life
11. ______ An expenditure that results in a 10% per year production cost saving
12. ______ Costs of a major overhaul that brings the asset's condition back to "new," with no change in the estimated useful life

(LO 5, 8) *E10-24 (Capitalization of Interest) On December 31, 2007, Omega Inc. borrowed $3 million at 12% payable annually to finance the construction of a new building. In 2008, the company made the following expenditures related to this building: March 1, $360,000; June 1, $600,000; July 1, $1.5 million; December 1, $1.5 million. Additional information follows:

1. Other debt outstanding:
   $4-million, 10-year, 13% bond, dated December 31, 2001, with interest payable annually
   $1.6-million, six-year, 10% note, dated December 31, 2005, with interest payable annually

2. The March 1, 2008, expenditure included land costs of $150,000.
3. Interest revenue earned in 2008 amounted to $49,000.

Instructions

(a) Determine the interest amount that could be capitalized in 2008 in relation to the building construction.

(b) Prepare the journal entry to record the capitalization of interest and the recognition of interest expense, if any, at December 31, 2008.

***E10-25** **(Capitalization of Interest)** The following three situations involve the capitalization of interest: **(LO 5, 8)**

Situation 1
On January 1, 2008, Oksana Inc. signed a fixed-price contract to have Builder Associates construct a major head office facility at a cost of $4 million. It was estimated that it would take three years to complete the project. Also on January 1, 2008, to finance the construction cost, Oksana borrowed $4 million that is repayable in 10 annual instalments of $400,000, plus interest at the rate of 10%. During 2008, Oksana made deposit and progress payments totalling $1.5 million under the contract; and the weighted-average amount of accumulated expenditures was $800,000 for the year. The excess amount of borrowed funds was invested in short-term securities, from which Oksana realized investment income of $250,000.

Situation 2
During 2008, Midori Ito Corporation constructed and manufactured certain assets and incurred the following interest cost in connection with these activities:

	Interest Costs Incurred
Warehouse constructed for Ito's own use	$30,000
Special-order machine for sale to unrelated customer, produced according to customer's specifications	9,000
Inventories routinely manufactured, produced on a repetitive basis	8,000

All of these assets required an extended time period for completion.

Situation 3
Fleming, Inc. has a fiscal year ending April 30. On May 1, 2008, Fleming borrowed $10 million at 11% to finance construction of its own building. Repayments of the loan are to begin the month after the building's completion. During the year ended April 30, 2009, expenditures for the partially completed structure totalled $7 million. These expenditures were incurred evenly throughout the year. Interest that was earned on the part of the loan that was not expended amounted to $650,000 for the year.

Instructions

1. For situation 1, what amount should Oksana report as capitalized interest at December 31, 2008?
2. For situation 2, assuming the effect of interest capitalization is material, what is the total amount of interest costs to be capitalized?
3. For situation 3, how much should be shown as capitalized interest on Fleming's financial statements at April 30, 2009?

(CPA adapted)

Problems

P10-1 At December 31, 2007, certain accounts included in the property, plant, and equipment section of Golden Corporation's balance sheet had the following balances:

Land	$310,000
Buildings	883,000
Leasehold Improvements	705,000
Machinery and Equipment	845,000

During 2008, the following transactions occurred:

1. Land site No. 621 was acquired for $800,000 and a commission of $47,000 to the real estate agent. Costs of $33,500 were incurred to clear the land. In clearing the land, timber and gravel were recovered and sold for $11,000.
2. Land site No. 622, which had a building on it, was acquired for $560,000. The closing statement indicated that the land's assessed tax value was $309,000 and the building value was $102,000. Shortly after acquisition, the building was demolished at a cost of $28,000. A new building was constructed for $340,000 plus the following costs:

Excavation fees	$38,000
Architectural design fees	15,000
Building permit fee	2,500
Imputed interest on funds used during construction (share financing)	8,500

   The building was completed and occupied on September 30, 2008.
3. A third tract of land (No. 623) was acquired for $265,000 and was put on the market for resale.
4. During December 2008, costs of $89,000 were incurred to improve leased office space. The related lease will terminate on December 31, 2010, and is not expected to be renewed.
5. A group of new machines was purchased under a royalty agreement. The terms of the agreement require Golden Corporation to pay royalties based on the units of production for the machines. The machines' invoice price was $111,000; freight costs were $3,300; installation costs were $3,600; and royalty payments for 2008 were $15,300.

Instructions

(a) Prepare a detailed analysis of the changes in each of the following balance sheet accounts for 2008: Land; Leasehold Improvements; Buildings; and Machinery and Equipment. Ignore the related accumulated amortization accounts.

(b) List the items in the situation that were not used to determine the answer to (a) above, and indicate where, or if, these items should be included in Golden's financial statements.

(c) Using the terminology from the conceptual framework in Chapter 2, explain why the items in part (b) were not included in the accounts Land, Leasehold Improvements, Buildings, and Machinery and Equipment.

(AICPA adapted)

P10-2 Selected accounts included in the property, plant, and equipment section of Webb Corporation's balance sheet at December 31, 2007, had the following balances:

Land	$ 300,000
Land Improvements	140,000
Buildings	1,100,000
Machinery and Equipment	960,000

During 2008, the following transactions occurred:

1. A tract of land was acquired for $150,000 as a potential future building site.
2. A plant facility consisting of land and a building was acquired from Knorman Corp. in exchange for 20,000 of Webb's common shares. On the acquisition date, Webb's shares had a closing market price of $37 per share on the Toronto Stock Exchange. The plant facility was carried on Knorman's books at $110,000 for land and $320,000 for the building at the exchange date. Current appraised values for the land and building, respectively, are $230,000 and $690,000.
3. Items of machinery and equipment were purchased at a total cost of $400,000. Additional costs were incurred as follows:

Freight and unloading	$13,000
Sales taxes	20,000
GST	24,000
Installation	26,000

4. Expenditures totalling $95,000 were made for new parking lots, streets, and sidewalks at the corporation's various plant locations. These expenditures had an estimated useful life of 15 years.
5. A machine that cost $80,000 on January 1, 2000, was scrapped on June 30, 2008. Double-declining-balance amortization had been recorded based on a 10-year life.

6. A machine was sold for $20,000 on July 1, 2008. Its original cost was $44,000 on January 1, 2005, and it was amortized on the straight-line basis over an estimated useful life of seven years, assuming a residual value of $2,000.

Instructions

(a) Prepare a detailed analysis of the changes in each of the following balance sheet accounts for 2008: Land, Land Improvements, Buildings, Machinery and Equipment. (Hint: Ignore the related accumulated amortization accounts.)

(b) List the items in the transactions above that were not used to determine the answer to (a), and show the relevant amounts and supporting calculations in good form for each item. In addition, indicate where, or if, these items should be included in Webb's financial statements.

(c) How will the land in item 1 be accounted for when it is used as a building site?

(AICPA adapted)

P10-3 Kiev Corp. was incorporated on January 2, 2008, but was unable to begin manufacturing activities until July 1, 2008, because new factory facilities were not completed until that date. The Land and Building account at December 31, 2008, was as follows:

January 31, 2008	Land and building	$166,000
February 28, 2008	Cost of removal of building	9,800
May 1, 2008	Partial payment of new construction	60,000
May 1, 2008	Legal fees paid	3,770
June 1, 2008	Second payment on new construction	40,000
June 1, 2008	Insurance premium	2,280
June 1, 2008	Special tax assessment	4,000
June 30, 2008	General expenses	36,300
July 1, 2008	Final payment on new construction	40,000
December 31, 2008	Asset write-up	43,800
		405,950
December 31, 2008	Amortization for 2008 at 1%	4,060
Account balance		$401,890

The following additional information needs to be considered:

1. To acquire land and a building, the company paid $80,400 cash and 800 of its no par value, $8, cumulative preferred shares. The fair market value was $107 per share.
2. The costs for removing old buildings amounted to $9,800, and the demolition company kept all the building materials.
3. Legal fees covered the following:

Cost of organization	$ 610
Examination of title covering purchase of land	1,300
Legal work in connection with construction contract	1,860
	$3,770

4. The insurance premium covered the building for a two-year term beginning May 1, 2008.
5. The special tax assessment covered street improvements that are permanent in nature.
6. General expenses covered the following for the period from January 2, 2008, to June 30, 2008:

President's salary	$32,100
Plant superintendent's wages covering supervision of new building	4,200
	$36,300

7. Because of a general increase in construction costs after entering into the building contract, the board of directors increased the building's value by $43,800. It believed that such an increase was justified to reflect the current market at the time when the building was completed. Retained Earnings was credited for this amount.
8. The estimated life of the building is 50 years. The amortization for 2008 was 1% of the asset value (1% of $405,950, or $4,060).

Instructions

Prepare the entries to reallocate the proper balances into Land, Building and Accumulated Amortization accounts at December 31, 2008.

(AICPA adapted)

P10-4 On June 28, 2008, in relocating to a new town, Kerr Corp. purchased a property consisting of two hectares of land and an unused building for $225,000 plus taxes in arrears of $4,500. The company paid a real estate broker's commission of $12,000 and legal fees on the purchase transaction of $6,000. The closing statement indicated that the assessed values for tax purposes were $175,000 for the land and $35,000 for the building. Shortly after acquisition, the building was demolished at a cost of $24,000.

Kerr Corp. then entered into a $1.3-million fixed-price contract with Webb Builders, Inc. on August 1, 2008, for the construction of an office building on this site. The building was completed and occupied on April 29, 2009, as was a separate maintenance building that was constructed by Kerr's employees. Additional costs related to the property included:

Plans, specifications, and blueprints	$25,000
Architects' fees for design and supervision	82,000
Landscaping	42,000
Extras on contract for upgrading of windows	46,000
External signage on the property	23,000
Advertisement in newspaper and on television announcing opening of the building	10,600
Gala opening party for customers, suppliers, and friends of Kerr	18,800
Costs of internal direct labour and materials for maintenance building	67,000
Allocated plant overhead based on direct labour hours worked on maintenance building	10,000
Allocated cost of executive time spent on project	54,000
Interest costs on debt incurred to pay contractor's progress billings up to building completion	63,000
Interest costs on short-term loan to finance maintenance building costs	3,200

As an incentive for Kerr to locate and build in the town, the municipality agreed not to charge its normal building permit fees of approximately $36,000. This amount was included in the $1.3-million contract fee.The building and maintenance building are estimated to have a 40-year life from their dates of completion and will be amortized using the straight-line method.

Kerr has an April 30 year end, and the company accountant is currently analyzing the new Building account that was set up to capture all the expenditures and credits explained above that relate to the property.

Instructions

(a) Prepare a schedule that identifies the costs that would be capitalized and included in the new Building account on the April 30, 2009, balance sheet, assuming the accountant wants to comply with GAAP, but tends to be very conservative in nature; in other words, she does not want to overstate income or assets. Briefly justify your calculations.

(b) Prepare a schedule that identifies the costs that would be capitalized and included in the new Building account on the April 30, 2009, balance sheet, assuming the accountant wants to comply with GAAP, but is aware that Kerr needs to report increased income to support a requested increase in its bank loan next month. Briefly justify your calculations.

(c) Comment on the difference in results for (a) and (b) above. Calculate the total expenses related to the building under both scenarios. What else should be considered in determining the amount to be capitalized?

P10-5 Vidi Corporation made the following purchases related to its property, plant, and equipment during its fiscal year ended December 31, 2008. The company uses the straight-line method of amortization for all its capital assets.

1. In early January, Vidi issued 140,000 common shares with a market value of $6 per share (based on a recent sale of 1,000 shares on the Toronto Stock Exchange) in exchange for property consisting of land and a warehouse. The company's property management division estimated that the market value of the land and warehouse were $600,000 and $300,000, respectively. The seller had advertised a price of $860,000 or best offer for the land and warehouse in a commercial retail magazine. Vidi paid a local real estate broker a finder's fee of $35,000.
2. On March 31, the company acquired equipment on credit. The terms were a $7,000 cash down payment plus payments of $5,000 at the end of each of the next two years. The implicit interest rate was 12%. The equipment's list price was $17,000. Additional costs that were incurred to install the equipment included $1,000 to tear down and replace a wall, and $1,500 to rearrange existing equipment to make room for the new equipment. An additional $500 was spent to repair the equipment after it was dropped during installation.

During the year, the following events also occurred:

3. A new motor was purchased for $50,000 for a large grinding machine (original cost of the machine, $350,000; accumulated amortization at the replacement date, $100,000). The motor will not improve the quality or quantity of production; however, it will extend the grinding machine's useful life from the current 8 years to 10 years.
4. On September 30, the company purchased a small building in a nearby town for $125,000 to use as a display and sales location. The municipal tax assessment indicated that the property was assessed for $95,000, which consists of $68,000 for the building and $27,000 for the land. The building had been empty for six months and required considerable maintenance work before it could be used. The following costs were incurred in 2008: previous owner's unpaid property taxes on the property for the previous year, $900; current year's (2008) taxes, $1,000; reshingling of roof, $2,200; cost of hauling refuse out of the basement, $230; cost of spray cleaning the outside walls and washing windows, $750; cost of painting inside walls, $3,170; and incremental fire and liability insurance of $940 for 15 months.
5. The company completely overhauled the plumbing system in its factory for $55,000. The original plumbing costs were not known.
6. On June 30, the company replaced a freezer with a new one that cost $20,000 cash (market value of $21,000 for the new freezer less trade-in value of old freezer). The cost of the old freezer was $15,000. At the beginning of the year, the company had amortized 60% of the old freezer, that is, 10% per year of use.
7. The company painted the factory exterior at a cost of $12,000.

Instructions

(a) Prepare the journal entries that are required to record the acquisitions and/or costs incurred in the above transactions.

(b) If there are alternative methods to account for any of the transactions, indicate what the alternatives are and your reason for choosing the method that you used.

P10-6 You have been contracted to examine the financial statements of Oilco Limited for the year ending December 31, 2008. Oilco was organized in January 2008 by Mr. Duff and Mr. Henderson, who are the original owners of options to acquire oil leases on 5,000 hectares of land. They paid $1.2 million for the options. Duff and Henderson expected that (1) the oil leases would be acquired by the corporation, and (2) 180,000 common shares of the corporation would subsequently be sold to the public at $20 per share. In February 2008, they exchanged their options plus $400,000 cash and $200,000 of other assets for 75,000 common shares of the corporation. The corporation's board of directors appraised the leases at $2.1 million, basing its appraisal on the price of other parcels that were recently leased in the same area. The options were, therefore, recorded at $900,000 ($2.1 million minus the $1.2-million option price).

The options were exercised (i.e., the land was actually leased) by the corporation in February 2008, before the sale of the common shares to the public in March 2008. Oilco incurred significant exploration costs over the summer, including seismic testing ($32,500), salaries and wages for work crews ($159,000), materials and supplies ($44,400), and vehicle operating costs ($11,900). In addition, Oilco recognized depreciation charges of $23,600 on the equipment that was used in the exploration activity. Leases on approximately 500 hectares of land were eventually abandoned as worthless during the year. Development activities were then postponed until the next spring.

Instructions

(a) 1. What reasoning could Oilco use to support valuing the leases at $2.1 million—the amount of the appraisal by the board of directors?

2. Assuming that the board's appraisal was sincere, what steps could Oilco have taken to strengthen its position to use the $2.1-million value and to provide additional information if questions were asked about a possible overvaluation of the leases?

(b) Determine the balance in the Oil and Gas Property account at December 31, 2008, assuming Oilco uses the successful efforts method of accounting.

(c) Determine the balance in the Oil and Gas Property account at December 31, 2008, assuming Oilco uses the full cost method of accounting. (Assume this is the only venture Oilco is engaged in.)

(d) Determine the balance in the Oil and Gas Property account at December 31, 2008, assuming Oilco expenses all exploration costs as they are incurred.

(e) What effect will the company's choice of method of accounting have on its 2008 financial statements? Comment.

***P10-7** Inglewood Landscaping began constructing a new plant on December 1, 2008. On this date, the company purchased a parcel of land for $184,000 cash. In addition, it paid $2,000 in surveying costs and $4,000 for title transfer fees. An old dwelling on the premises was demolished at a cost of $3,000, with $1,000 being received from the sale of materials.

Architectural plans were also formalized on December 1, 2008, when the architect was paid $30,000. The necessary building permits costing $3,000 were obtained from the city and paid for on December 1 as well. The excavation work began during the first week in December and payments were made to the contractor as follows:

Date of Payment	Amount of Payment
March 1	$240,000
May 1	360,000
July 1	60,000

The building was completed on July 1, 2009.

To finance the plant construction, Inglewood borrowed $600,000 from a bank on December 1, 2008. Inglewood had no other borrowings. The $600,000 was a 10-year loan bearing interest at 10%.

Instructions

(a) Calculate the balance in each of the following accounts at December 31, 2008, and December 31, 2009. Assume that Inglewood follows a policy of capitalizing interest on self-constructed assets.

1. Land

2. Buildings

3. Interest Expense

(b) Identify what the effects would be on Inglewood's financial statements for the years ending December 31, 2008 and 2009, if its policy was to expense all interest costs as they are incurred.

***P10-8** Wordcrafters Inc. is a book distributor that had been operating in its original facility since 1982. The increase in certification programs and continuing education requirements in several professions has contributed to an annual growth rate of 15% for Wordcrafters since 2002. Wordcrafters' original facility became obsolete by early 2008 because of the increased sales volume and the fact that Wordcrafters now carries tapes and disks in addition to books.

On June 1, 2008, Wordcrafters contracted with Favre Construction to have a new building constructed for $5 million on land owned by Wordcrafters. Wordcrafters made the following payments to Favre Construction:

Date	Amount
July 30, 2008	$1,200,000
Jan. 30, 2009	1,500,000
May 30, 2009	1,300,000
Total payments	$4,000,000

Construction was completed and the building was ready for occupancy on May 27, 2009. Wordcrafters had no new borrowings directly associated with the new building but had the following debt outstanding at May 31, 2009, the end of its fiscal year:

14 1/2%, five-year note payable of $2 million, dated April 1, 2005, with interest payable annually on April 1
12%, 10-year bond issue of $3 million sold at par on June 30, 2001, with interest payable annually on June 30

The company follows a policy of capitalizing interest during the construction of major assets.

Instructions

(a) Calculate the weighted-average accumulated expenditures on Wordcrafters' new building during the capitalization period.

(b) Calculate the avoidable interest on Wordcrafters' new building.

(c) Wordcrafters Inc. capitalized some of its interest cost for the year ended May 31, 2009:

1. Identify the item(s) relating to interest costs that must be disclosed in Wordcrafters' financial statements.

2. Calculate the amount of the item(s) that must be disclosed.

(CMA adapted)

P10-9 The production manager of Chesley Corporation wants to acquire a different brand of machine by exchanging the machine that it currently uses in operations for the brand of equipment that others in the industry are using. The brand being used by other companies is more comfortable for the operators because it has different attachments that allow the operators to adjust the controls for a variety of arm and hand positions. The production manager has received the following offers from other companies:

1. Secord Corp. offered to give Chesley a similar machine plus $23,000 in exchange for Chesley's machine.
2. Bateman Corp. offered a straight exchange for a similar machine with essentially the same value-in-use.
3. Shripad Corp. offered to exchange a similar machine with the same value-in-use, but wanted $8,000 cash in addition to Chesley's machine.

The production manager has also contacted Ansong Corporation, a dealer in machines. To obtain a new machine from Ansong, Chesley would have to pay $93,000 and also trade in its old machine. Chesley's equipment has a cost of $160,000, a net book value of $110,000, and a fair value of $92,000. The following table shows the information needed to record the machine exchange between the companies:

	Secord	Bateman	Shripad	Ansong
Machine cost	$120,000	$147,000	$160,000	$130,000
Accumulated amortization	45,000	71,000	75,000	-0-
Fair value	69,000	92,000	100,000	185,000

Instructions

(a) For each of the four independent situations, assume that Chesley accepts the offer. Prepare the journal entries to record the exchange on the books of each company. (Round to the nearest dollar.) When you need to make assumptions for the entries, state the assumptions so that you can justify the entries.

(b) Suggest scenarios or situations where different entries would be appropriate. Prepare the entries for these situations.

P10-10 During the current year, Garrison Construction trades in two relatively new small cranes (cranes no. 6RT and S79) for a larger crane that Garrison expects will be more useful for the particular contracts that the company has to fulfill over the next couple of years. The new crane is acquired from Keillor Manufacturing, which has agreed to take the smaller equipment as trade-ins and also pay $17,500 cash to Garrison. The new crane cost Keillor $165,000 to manufacture and is classified as inventory. The following information is available:

	Garrison Const.	Keillor Mfg.
Cost of crane #6RT	$130,000	
Cost of crane #S79	120,000	
Accumulated amortization, #6RT	15,000	
Accumulated amortization, #S79	18,000	
Fair value, #6RT	120,000	
Fair value, #S79	87,500	
Fair market value of new crane		$190,000
Cash paid		17,500
Cash received	17,500	

Instructions

(a) Assume that this exchange is considered to have commercial substance. Prepare the journal entries on the books of (1) Garrison Construction and (2) Keillor Manufacturing. Keillor uses a perpetual inventory system.

(b) Assume that this exchange is considered to lack commercial substance. Prepare the journal entries on the books of (1) Garrison Construction and (2) Keillor Manufacturing. Keillor uses a perpetual inventory system.

(c) Assume that you have been asked to recommend whether it is more appropriate for the transaction to have commercial substance or not to have commercial substance. Develop arguments that you could present to the controllers of both Garrison Construction and Keillor Manufacturing to justify both alternatives. Which arguments are more persuasive?

P10-11 Zhang Mining Corp. received a $760,000 low bid from a reputable manufacturer for the construction of special production equipment that Zhang needs as part of its expansion program. However, because the company's own plant was not operating at capacity, Zhang decided to use the space available and construct the equipment itself. Zhang recorded the following production costs related to the construction:

Services of consulting engineer	$ 40,000
Work subcontracted	36,000
Materials	280,000
Plant labour normally assigned to production	152,000
Plant labour normally assigned to maintenance	172,000
Total	$680,000

Management prefers to record the equipment cost under the incremental cost method. Approximately 40% of the company's production is devoted to government supply contracts that are all based in some way on cost. The contracts require that any self-constructed equipment be allocated its full share of all costs that are related to its construction.

The following information is also available:

1. The production labour was for partial fabrication of the plant equipment. Skilled personnel were required and were assigned from other projects. The maintenance labour represents idle time of non-production plant employees who would have stayed on the payroll whether or not their services were used.
2. Payroll taxes and employee fringe benefits are approximately 35% of labour costs and are included in the manufacturing overhead cost. Total manufacturing overhead for the year was $6,084,000, which includes the $172,000 of maintenance labour that was used to construct the equipment.
3. Manufacturing overhead is approximately 60% variable and is applied based on production labour costs. Production labour costs for the year for the corporation's normal products totalled $8,286,000.
4. General and administrative expenses include $27,000 of allocated executive salary cost and $13,750 of postage, telephone, supplies, and miscellaneous expenses that have been directly identified with the equipment construction.

Instructions

(a) Prepare a schedule that calculates the amount that should be reported as the full cost of the constructed equipment to meet the government contract requirements. Any supporting calculations should be in good form.

(b) Prepare a schedule calculating the incremental cost of the constructed equipment.

(c) What is the greatest amount that should be capitalized as the equipment cost? Why?

(AICPA adapted)

P10-12 Adamski Corporation manufactures ballet shoes and is experiencing a period of sustained growth. In an effort to expand its production capacity to meet the increased demand for its product, the company recently made several acquisitions of plant and equipment. Tim Mullinger, newly hired with the title Capital Asset Accountant, requested that Walter Kaster, Adamski's controller, review the following transactions:

Transaction 1

On June 1, 2008, Adamski Corporation purchased equipment from Venghaus Corporation. Adamski issued a $20,000, four-year, non-interest-bearing note to Venghaus for the new equipment. Adamski will pay off the note in four equal instalments due at the end of each of the next four years. At the transaction date, the prevailing market interest rate for obligations of this nature was 10%. Freight costs of $425 and installation costs of $500 were incurred in completing this transaction. The new equipment qualifies for a $2,000 government grant.

Transaction 2

On December 1, 2008, Adamski purchased several assets of Haukap Shoes Inc., a small shoe manufacturer whose owner was retiring. The purchase amounted to $210,000 and included the assets in the following list. Adamski engaged the services of Tennyson Appraisal Inc., an independent appraiser, to determine the assets' fair market values, which are also provided.

	Haukap Book Value	Fair Market Value
Inventory	$ 60,000	$ 50,000
Land	40,000	80,000
Building	70,000	120,000
	$170,000	$250,000

During its fiscal year ended May 31, 2009, Adamski incurred $8,000 of interest expense in connection with the financing of these assets.

Transaction 3
On March 1, 2009, Adamski traded in four units of specialized equipment and paid an additional $25,000 cash for a technologically up-to-date machine that should do the same job as the other machines, but much more efficiently and profitably. The equipment that was traded in had a combined carrying amount of $35,000, as Adamski had recorded $45,000 of accumulated amortization against these assets. Adamski's controller and the sales manager of the supplier company agreed that the new equipment had a fair value of $64,000.

Instructions

(a) Tangible capital assets such as land, buildings, and equipment receive special accounting treatment. Describe the major characteristics of these assets that differentiate them from other types of assets.

(b) For each of the three transactions described above, determine the value at which Adamski Corporation should record the acquired assets. Support your calculations with an explanation of the underlying rationale.

(c) The books of Adamski Corporation show the following additional transactions for the fiscal year ended May 31, 2009:

1. Acquisition of a building for speculative purposes
2. Purchase of a two-year insurance policy covering plant equipment
3. Purchase of the rights for the exclusive use of a process used in the manufacture of ballet shoes

For each of these transactions, indicate whether the asset should be classified as an item of property, plant, and equipment. If it should be, explain why. If it should not, explain why not, and identify the proper classification.

(CMA adapted)

P10-13 Donovan Resources Group has been in its plant facility for 15 years. Although the plant is quite functional, numerous repair costs are incurred to keep it in good working order. The book value of the company's plant asset is currently $800,000, calculated as follows:

Original cost	$1,200,000
Accumulated amortization	400,000
	$ 800,000

During the current year, the following expenditures were made to the plant facility:

(a) Because of increased demand for its product, the company increased its plant capacity by building a new addition at a cost of $270,000.

(b) The entire plant was repainted at a cost of $23,000.

(c) The roof was made of asbestos cement slate; for safety purposes, it was removed at a cost of $4,000 and replaced with a wood shingle roof at a cost of $61,000. The original roof's cost had been $40,000 and it was being amortized over an expected life of 20 years.

(d) The electrical system was completely updated at a cost of $22,000. The cost of the old electrical system was not known. It is estimated that the building's useful life will not change as a result of this updating.

(e) A series of major repairs was made at a cost of $47,000, because parts of the wood structure were rotting. The cost of the old wood structure was not known. These extensive repairs are estimated to increase the building's useful life.

Instructions
Indicate how each of these transactions would be recorded in the accounting records.

Writing Assignments

WA10-1 You have been working as a professional accounting trainee for about three months when the accountant for your client, Portables Inc., asks for your input about two transactions that took place in the current year. Portables, Inc., which used to be wholly owned and managed by Angus Dickson, now has 12 shareholders and a sizeable bank loan. Mr. Dickson still owns a majority of the outstanding shares. The accountant is in the process of finalizing the company's financial statements for the year ended June 30, 2008. You are working on the year-end audit and will also prepare the company's tax return.

Situation 1

Management found three suitable sites for a new plant facility, each site with a unique advantage. In order to ensure that there was time to thoroughly investigate the advantages and disadvantages of each site, one-year options were purchased for an amount equal to 6% of the contract price of each site. The costs of the options cannot be applied against the contracts. Before the options expired, one of the sites was purchased at the contract price of $200,000. The option on this site had cost $12,000. The two options that were not exercised had cost $8,000 each.

Instructions

Present arguments in support of recording the land cost at each of the following amounts: (a) $200,000, (b) $212,000, and (c) $228,000. What would you advise?

(AICPA adapted)

Situation 2

Portables, Inc. operates a very successful automobile dealership and has been increasing its real estate holdings. The accountant tells you that the company has just purchased a rental property for $200,000. "The municipal assessment indicates that the land itself is worth about half that amount, but I want you to allocate no more than 10% of the purchase price to the land. We all know that land isn't deductible for tax purposes! The building was in poor condition, so a new roof was put on, a new furnace installed, the structure was completely rewired, and the whole place was painted. These are just maintenance expenses, aren't they?"

You know that recognizing as many expenses as possible for your client will lead to a better tax position for the company, lower cash outflows, and higher share value.

Instructions

Identify the relevant issues and explain how you should handle this situation.

WA10-2 Gomi Medical Labs, Inc. began operations five years ago producing a new type of instrument it hoped to sell to doctors, dentists, and hospitals. The demand for the new instrument was much higher than had been planned for, and the company was unable to produce enough of them to meet demand. The company was manufacturing its product on equipment that had been built at the start of its operations.

To meet demand, more efficient equipment was needed. The company decided to design and build the equipment because the equipment currently available on the market was unsuitable for producing this product.

In 2005, a section of the plant was devoted to developing the new equipment and a special staff was hired. Within six months, a machine, developed at a cost of $714,000, increased production dramatically and reduced labour costs substantially. Thrilled by the new machine's success, the company built three more machines of the same type at a cost of $441,000 each.

Instructions

(a) In general, what costs should be capitalized for self-constructed equipment?

(b) Discuss whether the capitalized cost of self-constructed assets should include the following:

1. The increase in overhead that results from the company's own construction of its fixed assets
2. A proportionate share of overhead on the same basis as what is applied to goods that are manufactured for sale

(c) Discuss the proper accounting treatment of the $273,000 cost amount ($714,000 – $441,000) that was higher for the first machine than the cost of the subsequent machines. This additional cost is not considered as research and development costs.

WA10-3 Investissement-Québec (IQ), the arm of the Quebec government that is responsible for encouraging investment growth in Quebec, announced its support of a new call centre in Montreal in the summer of 2005. IQ announced that Telus, a leading Canadian telecommunications company, would build a $3.5-million call centre that was expected to open in mid-2007. It will be equipped with the most advanced technology available and will employ an "elite team of information technology professionals."

To encourage companies involved in information technologies to locate in the province, IQ offers a 25% tax credit against companies' Quebec income taxes.

Instructions

Prepare a memo that would be suitable to present to the Telus board of directors in which you explain how the receipt of the tax credit is expected to affect Telus's reported total assets and earnings under each of the following independent situations:

(a) Assuming the investment tax credit is based on $2 million of expenditures on IT capital assets. The credit is available in the year the facility opens.

(b) Assuming the investment tax credit is based on creating 150 new jobs for a period of five years. The credit is based on an average wage of $60,000 per employee per year and is available in each of the five years as long as the company has met the eligibility requirements of maintaining the required number of jobs and average wage.

WA10-4 You have two clients in the construction industry that are considering exchanging machinery with each other. Ames Construction has decided to market its services to clients who need major construction projects, but it has a significant inventory of equipment that is more appropriate for smaller home renovations. Johnston Corp.'s strategic plan, on the other hand, has recently changed to focus on home renovations, additions, and repairs. Johnston would like to sell off the equipment it used in constructing larger apartment buildings and condominiums over the past few years and acquire equipment that is more suitable for its new strategy. A deal has been reached between the owner-managers of both companies to exchange a group of machinery and equipment. The details of the transaction are as follows:

	Ames Construction	Johnston Corp.
Original cost	$100,000	$150,000
Accumulated amortization	40,000	80,000
Market value	90,000	120,000
Cash received (paid)	(30,000)	30,000

Instructions

Write a memo to the accountants of both Ames Construction and Johnston Corp. with your recommendation on how this transaction should be recorded on the books of each company. If there are any choices available to them, identify what they are. Be sure to explain the rationale for your recommended treatment.

WA10-5 A machine's invoice price is $40,000. Various other costs relating to the acquisition and installation of the machine—including transportation, electrical wiring, a special base, and so on—amount to $7,500. The machine has an estimated life of 10 years, with no residual value at the end of that period.

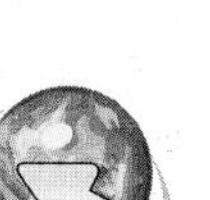

The owner-manager of the company that you work for as an accountant suggests that the incidental costs of $7,500 be charged to expense immediately for the following reasons:

- If the machine is ever sold, these costs cannot be recovered in the sale price.
- The inclusion of the $7,500 in the machinery account on the books will not necessarily result in a closer approximation of this asset's market price over the years, because demand and supply levels could change.
- Charging the $7,500 to expense immediately will reduce income taxes.

Instructions

Prepare a memo to the owner-manager that addresses each of the issues.

(AICPA adapted)

Student Website

www.wiley.com/canada/kieso

Case

Refer to the Case Primer on the Student Website to help you answer these cases.

CA10-1 In 1997, Legacy Hotels Real Estate Investment Trust (LH) was created to hold hotel properties. LH currently holds 22 luxury and first-class hotels in Canada and the United States. The entity is structured as an investment trust, which means that the trust does not pay income taxes on the earnings from the assets that it holds directly; instead, income taxes are paid by the unitholders—those who own ownership units in the trust. The other key feature of the trust is that 85% to 90% of the distributable income is required to be paid to unitholders every year. The units of LH trade on the TSE under the ticker symbol LGY.UN.

Distributable income is calculated as net income before special charges, plus depreciation and amortization less capital replacement reserve and interest on the debentures. LH distributed 127% and 112% of its distributable income in 2002 and 2001, respectively. Management determines the calculation of distributable income since this calculation is not defined by GAAP. As at 2002, Property and Equipment was $1.7 billion compared to $1.9 billion in total assets. Net income for the year was $55 million.

According to the notes to the financial statements, LH capitalizes major renewals and replacements and interest that is incurred during the renovation period of major renovations. Capitalization of interest is based on the borrowing rate of debt for the project or the average cost of borrowing. Maintenance, repairs, and minor renewals and replacements are expensed.

Instructions

Assume the role of PricewaterhouseCoopers LLP, the entity's auditors, and discuss any financial reporting issues.

Integrated Cases

IC10-1 TransAlta Corporation (TC) is a non-regulated power generation and wholesale marketing company. The company had a BBB+ credit rating in 2002 and its goals were stated in its annual report as follows:

- maintain investment-grade credit ratings
- improve interest coverage ratio from 1.4 to between 4 and 6 times
- other goals not specified here

Property, plant, and equipment consist of coal-fired, gas-fired, hydro, and renewable generation assets with a 2002 carrying value of $6 billion (total assets $7.4 billion). The following is an excerpt from the notes to the financial statements:

> The corporation does not provide for the removal costs associated with its hydroelectric generating structures as the costs are not reasonably estimated because of the long service life of these assets. With either maintenance efforts or rebuilding, the water control structures are assumed to be required for the foreseeable future and therefore, no amounts have been provided for site restoration costs for these facilities. Provisions are made for removal of hydro generating equipment.

In August 2000, the company shut down one of its plants due to safety concerns. The plant was repaired and returned to service in June 2001. Under the terms of an agreement related to this plant, the company had been obligated to supply electricity starting in January 2001 unless an unforeseen event prevented the company from fulfilling this liability. If such an unforeseen event occurred, both parties would have to agree that the inability to fulfill the contract was due to an acceptable event. If both parties did not agree, the company would be liable to pay a penalty equal to the cost of obtaining an alternative source of electricity.

The decision went to arbitration in July 2001 and in May 2002, the arbitrator confirmed that the shutdown exempted the company from having to deliver the electricity. The arbitrator did find, however, that the company could have returned the plant to service more quickly and therefore levied a penalty of $39 million on the company. The amount was recorded as an offset to revenues.

In 2001, the company sold its Fort Nelson gas-fired facility, resulting in a gain of $1.3 million after tax. It was not treated as discontinued operations. On August 31, 2000, the company sold its Alberta D&R division, resulting in an after-tax gain of $262.4 million. As part of the agreement, the company must share the benefit or burden of future regulatory decisions affecting the pre-disposition operations. This disposition was treated as a discontinued operation.

In 2002, the Canadian government ratified the Kyoto Protocol, which will make entities that pollute responsible for minimizing their pollution. The additional costs for implementation of the protocol have not been estimated or accrued in TC's financial statements. Some of the power purchase arrangements for the company's coal-fired plants contain provisions that may allow the costs of complying to the Kyoto Protocol to be recovered from the company's customers.

Instructions

Adopt the role of a financial analyst and evaluate the different financial reporting choices that are available to the company for its 2001 and 2002 financial statements.

IC10-2 Eastern Platinum Limited (EPL) is a metals and mineral mining company which is headquartered in Vancouver and whose shares trade on the TSX. Its year end is June 30 and it is audited by Deloitte and Touche LLP.

In April 2005, EPL changed its name from Jonpol Explorations. To date, it has not yet found any economically recoverable reserves. In addition, although it has taken steps to verify the title to mining properties in which it has an interest, these procedures may not guarantee the company's title. According to the financial statements, the properties may be subject to undisclosed prior agreements or transfers, and title may be affected. Mineral properties account for 30% of EPL's total assets, and deferred acquisition costs and intangible assets account for 42%.

According to Note 2 to its financial statements, all costs related to the acquisition, exploration, and development of mineral properties are capitalized. When a property is abandoned, all related costs are written off. The net loss for the period was $2.4 million and the accumulated deficit was $29.5 million. Cash outflows from operation were $162,800 last year and $1,265,254 for the current year. Note 2 states that the amounts shown for mineral properties on the balance sheet do not necessarily represent present or future value and that their recoverability depends on the discovery of economically recoverable reserves, the company's ability to obtain financing, and future profitable productions.

The company also has oil and gas properties and follows the full cost method of accounting for these operations. The full cost method allows all costs related to exploration and development—including asset retirement obligations—to be capitalized. Interest on debt for both productive and unproductive wells is capitalized and the proceeds from dispositions of these properties are applied against the capitalized costs without any gain/loss being recognized. General and administrative costs are not capitalized.

On April 22, 2005, the company acquired all of the issued and outstanding shares of EPHL, another mining company, for a consideration consisting of the issue of 18,750,000 common shares of EPL and $22,595,000 cash (including a refundable value-added tax of $2,800,000). The common shares that were issued were valued at $1.28 per share, which was the average price two days before acquisition, the day of acquisition, and two days later. The shares were trading at 1.96 at the beginning of the fiscal year and 1.48 at the end. The consideration has not yet changed hands as the company is waiting for the South African Department of Minerals and Energy to confirm the transfer of the mineral rights of properties held by EPHL.

After another business combination, EPL paid a success fee of $936,000 to the company that was acquired. The success fee was for the successful completion of the business deal. A director and officer of EPL was also an officer of the acquired company.

Current mineral rights for a significant property—the Mareesburg property—expired on April 29 and the renewal has not been issued even though the company believes it has complied with the regulatory requirements.

Instructions

Assume the role of the auditors and discuss the financial reporting issues for the year ended June 30, 2005.

Research and Financial Analysis

RA10-1 Magna International Inc.

Access the financial statements of Magna International Inc. for the company's year ended December 31, 2005. These are available at www.sedar.com, the company's website, or the Student Website. Review the information that is provided and answer the following questions about the company.

Instructions

(a) What business is Magna International in?

(b) What types of tangible capital assets does Magna report? Do these assets form a significant portion of the company's total assets at December 31, 2005?

(c) Identify all the accounting policies disclosed in the notes to the financial statements that explain how the company determines the cost of its property, plant, and equipment.

(d) How much did Magna spend on new capital asset acquisitions in 2004 and 2005? Identify where the company obtained the funds to invest in these additions.

RA10-2 Intrawest Corporation

Access the financial statements of Intrawest Corporation for the company's year ended June 30, 2006. These are available at www.sedar.com, the company's website, or the Student Website. Review the information that is provided and answer the following questions about the company.

Instructions

(a) What major business(es) is Intrawest Corporation in?

(b) For each major line of business, identify the major categories of assets that you would expect each type of industry to have. List the major categories of assets that Intrawest reports for each line of business.

(c) Do all the company's "Properties" meet the definition of property, plant, and equipment? Discuss.

(d) Ignoring the company's policies on amortization, identify the accounting policies that Intrawest reports for its fixed assets.

(e) If Intrawest had chosen different acceptable accounting policies, would there have been much of an effect on the income that the company reports? Comment.

RA10-3 Sobeys Inc. and Loblaw Companies Limited

Companies in the same line of business usually have similar investments, and capital structures, and an opportunity for similar rates of return. One of the key performance indicators that is used to assess the profitability of companies is the return on assets ratio. This ratio results from two key relationships—the profit margin and the total asset turnover—and in general terms can be written as follows:

Return on assets = Total asset turnover (or Sales ÷ Total assets) × Profit margin (or Income ÷ Sales)

This says that profitability depends directly on how many sales dollars are generated for each dollar invested in assets (total asset turnover) and on how costs are controlled for each dollar of sales (profit margin). An increase in either ratio results in an increase in the return on assets. As property, plant, and equipment is often the largest single asset on the balance sheet, companies need to have strategies to manage their investment in such assets.

Instructions

Access the financial statements of two companies that are in the food distribution business: Sobeys Inc. for the year ended May 6, 2006, and Loblaw Companies Limited for the year ended December 31, 2005. These are available at www.sedar.com, each company's website, or the Student Website. Review the financial statements and answer the following questions.

(a) At each company's year end, determine the percentage of property, plant, and equipment to total assets.

(b) Calculate each company's fixed asset turnover, total asset turnover, and profit margin (using net income) for the most recent year.

(c) Determine the return on assets for each company. Which company is more profitable?

(d) Which company uses its total assets more effectively in generating sales? Its fixed assets?

(e) Are there any differences in accounting policies that might explain the differences in the fixed asset turnover ratios?

(f) Which company has better control over its expenses for each dollar of sales?

(g) Explain why the company with the higher return is more profitable. Does it look like the two companies have different strategies? Comment briefly.

RA10-4 Homburg Invest Inc.

Usually an international comparison assignment involves comparing two similar companies that report under different GAAP. If possible, however, it would be better to compare the same company's financial reports prepared on two different bases. Homburg Invest Inc., a Canadian company, does just that, and notes that the most significant differences relate to its fixed assets.

Instructions

Access the financial statements of Homburg Invest Inc. under both bases of accounting for its year ended December 31, 2005, on SEDAR at www.sedar.com. Review the statements that are presented and answer the following questions.

(a) What business is Homburg Invest Inc. in? What two sets of accounting standards does it report under? Why does the company report under two different sets of generally accepted accounting principles?

(b) Identify the single most significant GAAP difference, and indicate the effect that this has on the income statements. Be specific.

(c) What other GAAP differences are there, if any? What is the effect of these on the income statements?

(d) Which set of financial statements do you think comes closer to meeting the objectives of financial reporting? Discuss briefly.

RA10-5 Research Issue

In groups, and as explained by your instructor, choose eight different companies, taking one company from each of the following industry groups: Consumer products—autos and parts; Consumer products—biotechnology/pharmaceuticals; Film production; Financial services—investment companies and funds; Industrial products—steel; Merchandising—specialty stores; Metals and minerals—integrated mines; and Utilities—telephone utilities. An excellent source is the SEDAR website at www.sedar.com. If you search the database by industry group for financial statements for the most recent 12-month period, you will be able to choose from the large number of public companies on the site.

Instructions

(a) For each company, determine the relative importance of its tangible capital assets to its total assets invested, and the percentage that depreciation or amortization expense is of total expenses.

(b) For each company, determine the percentage of total assets that is financed by long-term debt.

(c) What industries require the highest relative investment in tangible capital assets?

(d) Is there any relationship between the investment in tangible capital property and financing by long-term debt? Comment.

(e) How might the strategies of companies with significant investments in fixed assets or property, plant, and equipment differ from the strategies of companies that have very little investment in such assets?

Rolling Stock

VIA Rail Canada operates 492 intercity trains each week, using a fleet of 75 locomotives and 454 passenger cars to carry more than 4 million passengers a year. These trains run along 12,500 kilometres of track and serve more than 450 Canadian communities. These are no small numbers, and neither are the numbers required to allocate the cost of these trains to the Crown corporation.

Corporate comptroller Anthony Rumjahn says VIA Rail follows the standard accounting theory for amortizing its tangible capital assets, such as the trains. Of the total capital assets of $1,313.3 million, VIA Rail's trains, or "rolling stock," amounted to $746.8 million in 2005. Of that amount, $413.4 million had been amortized to date, leaving a net book value of $333.4 million.

VIA Rail calculates the amortization of tangible capital assets on a "straight-line basis" at rates that are high enough to amortize the cost of the assets, less their residual value, over their estimated lives. The corporation maintains detailed subsidiary records for each car's cost and accumulated depreciation. In the month following the date that the trains are put into service, transfers to specific capital asset accounts are done and amortization is also charged up to the month of disposal, Rumjahn explains. The fleet's economic useful life is calculated after consulting with the engineering group and equipment manufacturers. For the current rolling stock, that number varies from 12 to 30 years.

The trains' purchase price, refurbishment costs, and any other upgrading costs are capitalized if they were incurred to improve the trains' service value or extend their useful lives; otherwise, these costs are expensed. ■

chapter 11

Amortization, Impairment, and Disposition

Learning Objectives

After studying this chapter, you should be able to:

1. Explain the concept of amortization.
2. Identify and explain the factors to consider when determining amortization charges.
3. Calculate amortization charges using the activity, straight-line, and decreasing charge methods and compare the methods.
4. Explain the accounting procedures for depletion of natural resources.
5. Explain the need for special amortization methods and how to apply them.
6. Identify how amortization methods are selected.
7. Explain and apply the accounting procedures for a change in amortization rate.
8. Explain the issues and apply the accounting standards for capital asset impairment.
9. Explain and apply the accounting standards for long-lived assets that will be disposed of through sale.
10. Describe and apply the accounting for the disposal of property, plant, and equipment.
11. Explain how property, plant, and equipment are reported and analyzed.
12. Compare current Canadian and international GAAP.

After studying Appendix 11A, you should be able to:

13. Calculate capital cost allowance in straightforward situations.

Preview of Chapter 11

As the opening vignette shows, capital assets can be a major investment for companies. Given this fact, and given also the alternatives that exist for charging these costs to operations, the potential for impairment in their values, and the argument by some critics that financial statement readers do not need to be concerned with these non-cash expenses, it is important to have a firm understanding of this chapter's topics.

Specifically, this chapter examines the amortization process—the methods of writing off the cost of property, plant, and equipment, and natural resources—and the issues for asset impairment and disposal. In addition, it compares international GAAP and existing Canadian standards. Finally, the appendix outlines key aspects of the capital cost allowance system that is required for income tax purposes.

The chapter is organized as follows:

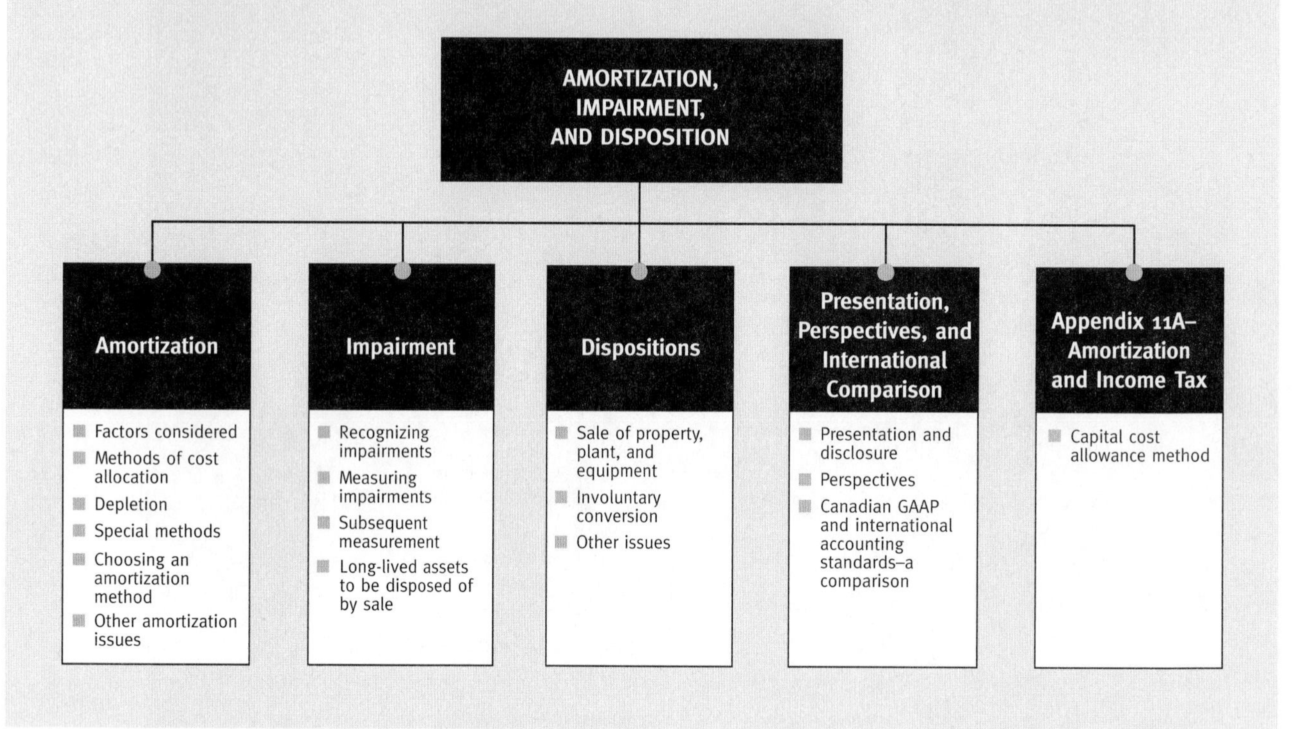

AMORTIZATION—A METHOD OF COST ALLOCATION

Objective 1
Explain the concept of amortization.

At one time or another, most people will purchase and trade in an automobile. In discussions with the automobile dealer, depreciation is a consideration on two points. First, how much has the old car depreciated? That is, what is its trade-in value? Second, how fast will the new car depreciate? That is, what will its trade-in value be? In both cases, depreciation is thought of as a loss in value.

However, to accountants familiar with the historic cost, transactions-based accounting model, **depreciation—or amortization, as it is also called—is not a matter of valuation but a method of cost allocation.** Assets are not amortized based on their decline in market value; rather, an asset's amortization is based on a systematic allocation of its cost to expense.

It is undeniably true that an asset's value changes between the time when it is purchased and the time it is sold or scrapped. A cost allocation approach is used rather than a valuation approach, however, because measuring changes in an asset's value in different periods objectively is often difficult and costly. For this reason, the asset's cost is instead charged to amortization expense over its estimated life and there is no attempt to value the asset at its fair value between acquisition and disposition.

International Insight

IAS 16 permits capital assets to be remeasured to fair value and requires that the amortization for these assets be based on the revalued amount.

Amortization is the charge to income that allocates an asset's cost less salvage or residual value to the periods of service provided by the asset.[1] The *CICA Handbook* indicates that amortization may also be termed "depreciation" or "depletion." In the past, the term **depreciation** was used to refer specifically to the amortization of property, plant, and equipment, **depletion** was used for amortization of natural resource properties, and **amortization** was reserved for intangibles. While these terms are still in common use, "amortization" is used throughout this text to refer to the general process of allocating the cost of long-lived assets to the accounting periods that benefit from their use. "Depletion" has been kept for specific references to natural resource assets.

Underlying Concept

Under the going concern concept, capital assets are expected to be held for use, not for sale; interim market value changes are therefore not considered relevant.

Factors Considered in the Amortization Process

2 Objective

Identify and explain the factors to consider when determining amortization charges.

Three basic questions must be answered before the dollar amount of amortization expense can be determined:

1. What amount of the asset's cost is to be amortized?
2. What is the asset's useful life?
3. What pattern and method of allocating the cost to time periods is the best one for the particular circumstances?

Answering these questions means that several estimates are needed to arrive at the resulting amortization charge. A perfect measure of amortization for each period is not possible, because, except perhaps for the asset's acquisition cost, all the variables in the calculations are estimates.

Amount to Be Amortized

The amount of the asset's cost that is to be amortized—its **amortizable amount**—depends on two factors: the asset's acquisition cost, discussed in Chapter 10, and its residual value. **Residual value** is defined as the estimated net realizable value of an item of property, plant, and equipment **at the end of its useful life to the entity.**[2] It is the amount that the asset is eventually amortized or written down to during its useful life. The residual value is an estimate of the amount that will be recovered from disposal of the asset, and is based as much as possible on the entity's experience with similar assets operating under similar conditions.

Technically, the amortization charge is based on whichever of the following two amounts is greater:

1. The cost less salvage value over the life of the asset
2. The cost less residual value over the asset's useful life

[1] *CICA Handbook*, Section 3061.29.

[2] *CICA Handbook*, Section 3061.12.

Salvage value is the asset's estimated net realizable value **at the end of its life** and is normally an insignificant amount.[3] The purpose of estimating the salvage value is to ensure that the charges that are being made to the income statement as the asset is being used are adequate. For simplicity, the discussions and illustrations that follow consider **cost less residual value** as the amortizable amount.

Illustration 11-1 shows that if an asset has a cost of $10,000 and a residual value of $1,000, only $9,000 of its cost is amortized.

Illustration 11-1
Calculation of Amount to Be Amortized

Original cost	$10,000
Less: residual value	1,000
Amortizable amount	$ 9,000

From a practical standpoint, residual value is often considered to be zero because the amount is immaterial. Some long-lived assets, however, have substantial net realizable values at the end of their useful lives to a specific enterprise. Indeed, companies with similar assets may calculate different amortizable amounts and amortization expense because of differences in how the assets are used and in their estimates of the assets' final values.

Estimate of Useful Life

A capital asset's **useful life** is the period during which the asset is expected to contribute economic benefits to the organization. Useful life can also be stated in terms of the number of units of product or service that the asset is expected to produce or provide to the enterprise.

Useful or service life and physical life are often not the same. A piece of machinery may be physically capable of producing a specific product for many years past its service life in a particular organization, but the equipment may not be used for all of those years. The opening vignette indicates that the "economic useful life" of **VIA Rail**'s fleet is determined through discussions with engineering and manufacturing specialists.

There are many different reasons for disposing of an asset before its physical life is over. New processes or techniques or improved machines may provide the same product or service at lower cost and with higher quality. Changes needed in the product or service itself may shorten an asset's service life. Environmental factors can also influence a decision to retire a particular asset.

Physical factors set the outside limit for an asset's service life. Physical factors relate to such things as decay or wear and tear that result from use of the asset and the passage of time. Whenever the asset's physical nature is the main factor that determines its useful life, maintenance plays a vital role—the better the maintenance, the longer the life of the asset.[4]

Economic factors (e.g., technological or commercial obsolescence) also limit an asset's useful life. Economic or functional factors can be classified into three categories:

1. **Inadequacy** results when an asset stops being useful to an entity because the firm's demands have changed. For example, a company may require a larger building to handle increased production. Although the old building is still in good condition, it may have become inadequate for the enterprise's purposes.

[3] *CICA Handbook*, Section 3061.13 and .28.

[4] The airline industry illustrates the type of problem found in estimations. In the past, aircraft were assumed not to wear out; they just became obsolete. However, some jets have been in service for as long as 20 years, and maintenance of these aircraft has become increasingly expensive. In addition, the public's concern about worn-out aircraft has increased because of much-publicized air disasters. As a result, some airlines are finding it necessary to replace aircraft, not because of obsolescence, but because of physical deterioration.

2. **Supersession** is the replacement of one asset with a more efficient and economical asset. Examples include the replacement of a mainframe computer with a PC network, or the replacement of a Boeing 767 with a Boeing 787.
3. **Obsolescence** is the catch-all category, as it includes any situations that do not fit the categories of inadequacy and supersession.

Because the distinctions among these categories are fuzzy, it is probably best to consider economic factors as a whole instead of trying to make distinctions that are not clear-cut.

An asset's legal life may also limit its useful life to a specific entity. For example, the benefits of leasehold improvements end when the lease term is over.

To illustrate these concepts, consider a new nuclear power plant. Which do you think are the most important factors that determine its useful life: physical factors, economic factors, or its legal life? The limiting factors seem to be (1) ecological considerations, (2) competition from other non-nuclear power sources, and (3) safety concerns. Neither physical nor legal life appear to be primary factors affecting the plant's useful life, although there could be situations where they are.

The problem of estimating service life is difficult; experience and judgement are the main ways of determining service lives. In some cases, arbitrary lives are selected; in others, sophisticated statistical methods are used to establish a useful life for accounting purposes. In many cases, the main basis for estimating an asset's useful life is the enterprise's past experience with similar assets. In an industrial economy such as Canada's, where research and innovation are so prominent, economic and technological factors have as much effect on the service lives of tangible assets as do physical factors, if not more.

What Do the Numbers Mean?

Some companies try to imply that amortization is not a cost. For example, in their press releases they often draw more attention to earnings before interest, taxes, depreciation, and amortization (often referred to as EBITDA) or pro forma earnings other than net income under GAAP. Some companies like the EBITDA figure because it "dresses up" their earnings numbers, and they promote it using the argument that the excluded costs are not operating costs or that amortization and depreciation are non-cash charges. Regardless, when all is said and done, companies must generate enough cash from revenues to cover all their costs, as the amounts that they borrow to finance long-term asset acquisitions have to be repaid. Investors need to understand the differences between these various indicators of financial performance.

Consider **Aliant Inc.**'s review of its results for a recent year. EBITDA was reported at $941.6 million, while net income under GAAP amounted to $177.6 million. In the same year, **Hollinger International Inc.** reported EBITDA of U.S. $111.4 million and a GAAP net loss of U.S. $238.8 million! Because of concerns that investors may be confused or misled by non-GAAP earnings measures, the Canadian Securities Administrators, which is the umbrella group for provincial regulators, issued specific guidance for certain disclosures that are associated with non-GAAP earnings measures. These include requiring that entities present a reconciliation of their non-GAAP measure(s) with audited GAAP results.

While EBITDA and other pro forma reporting have not been prohibited, it appears that the new reporting requirements have made some companies less enthusiastic about reporting these results as prominently as they previously did.

Methods of Cost Allocation (Amortization)

The third factor involved in the amortization decision is the pattern and method of cost allocation. The accounting profession requires that the amortization method be rational and systematic, and that it be used in a "manner appropriate to the nature of an item of property, plant, and equipment with a limited life and its use by the enterprise."[5]

[5] *CICA Handbook*, Section 3061.28.

Underlying Concept

Amortization is an attempt to allocate an asset's cost to the periods that benefit from its use.

A number of amortization methods may be used, classified as follows:

1. Activity methods (units of use or production)
2. Straight-line method
3. Decreasing charge (or accelerated) methods:
   (a) Declining-balance
   (b) Sum-of-the-years'-digits
4. Increasing charge methods
5. Special depreciation methods:
   (a) Group and composite methods
   (b) Hybrid or combination methods[6]

To illustrate the acceptable choices, assume that a company purchases a crane for heavy construction purposes. Illustration 11-2 presents the relevant data on the purchase of the crane.

Illustration 11-2

Data Used to Illustrate Amortization Methods

Cost of crane	$500,000
Estimated useful life in years	5 years
Productive life in hours	30,000 hours
Estimated residual value	$ 50,000

Activity Methods

Objective 3

Calculate amortization charges using the activity, straight-line, and decreasing charge methods and compare the methods.

The **activity method**, sometimes called a variable charge approach, determines amortization **according to usage or productivity** instead of the passage of time. The asset's life is defined in terms of either the output it provides (units it produces), or the input required (the number of hours it operates) to produce the output. Conceptually, a better cost association is established by using an output measure rather than the hours put in, but often the output is not homogeneous or is difficult to measure. In such cases, an input measure, such as machine hours, is an appropriate basis for determining the amortization charge for the accounting period.

The crane poses no particular problem because the usage (hours) is relatively easy to measure. If the crane is used 4,000 hours in the first year, the amortization charge is calculated as in Illustration 11-3.

Illustration 11-3

Amortization Calculation, Activity Method–Crane Example

$$\frac{\text{Cost less residual value}}{\text{Total estimated hours}} = \text{Amortization expense per hour}$$

$$\frac{\$500,000 - \$50,000}{30,000 \text{ hours}} = \$15 \text{ per hour}$$

First year amortization expense: 4,000 hours × $15 = $60,000

[6] Clarence Byrd, Ida Chen, and Joshua Smith, *Financial Reporting in Canada, 2005* (Toronto: CICA, 2005) report that, of the companies surveyed in 2004 that used only one method of amortization, 94% used straight-line, 2% used diminishing-balance (declining-balance), and 4% used the units-of-production method. A small majority of the surveyed companies reported using only one method. Those that used a combination of methods tended to use straight-line and either a units-of-production or diminishing-balance method.

When the asset's utility or usefulness is reduced by usage, activity, or productivity, the activity method is the best at matching costs to the accounting periods that the asset benefits. Companies that adopt this approach will have low amortization during periods of low usage and high charges during high usage.

This method's major limitation is that it is not appropriate in situations where depreciation is a function of time instead of activity. For example, a building usually suffers a great amount of steady deterioration from the weather (a function of time) regardless of how it is used. In addition, when an asset's useful life is affected by economic or functional factors that have nothing to do with its usage, the activity method is much less appropriate. For example, if a company is expanding rapidly, a particular building may soon become obsolete for its intended purpose. The level of activity is irrelevant. Another limitation of using an activity method is that it is often difficult to determine the total units of output or service hours to be received over the useful life of the asset.

Straight-Line Method

Underlying Concept

If the benefits flow evenly over time, there is justification for using the straight-line basis to match the asset's cost with the periods that the asset benefits.

Under the **straight-line method**, depreciation is considered **a function of the passage of time**. This method is widely used in practice because of its simplicity. The straight-line approach is often the most conceptually appropriate, as well. When creeping obsolescence is the main reason for a limited service life, the decline in usefulness may be constant from period to period. The amortization charge for the crane under the straight-line method is calculated in Illustration 11-4.

Illustration 11-4

Amortization Calculation, Straight-Line Method–Crane Example

$$\frac{\text{Cost less residual value}}{\text{Estimated service life}} = \text{Amortization charge}$$

$$\frac{\$500{,}000 - \$50{,}000}{5 \text{ years}} = \$90{,}000$$

The major objection to the straight-line method is that it relies on two questionable assumptions: (1) that the asset's economic usefulness is the same each year, and (2) that maintenance expense is about the same each period (assuming constant revenue flows). If these assumptions are not valid, this method will not give a rational matching of expense with the periods that benefit from the asset.

Another problem with the straight-line method is the distortion that develops in a rate of return analysis (income ÷ assets). Illustration 11-5 indicates how the rate of return increases, assuming constant revenue flows, because the asset's book value decreases. Relying on the increasing trend of the rate of return in such circumstances can be very misleading as a basis for evaluating the success of operations. The increase in the rate of return is only due to the accounting method that is used. It is not due to improvements in underlying economic performance.

Illustration 11-5

Amortization and Rate of Return Analysis–Crane Example

Year	Amortization Expense	Unamortized Asset Balance (net book value)	Income (after amortization expense)	Rate of Return (income ÷ assets)
0		$500,000		
1	$90,000	410,000	$100,000	24.4%
2	90,000	320,000	100,000	31.2%
3	90,000	230,000	100,000	43.5%
4	90,000	140,000	100,000	71.4%
5	90,000	50,000	100,000	200.0%

Decreasing Charge Methods

Underlying Concept

The matching concept does not justify a constant charge to income. If the asset's benefits decline as it gets older, then a decreasing charge to income better matches costs with benefits.

Decreasing charge methods, often called **accelerated amortization** or diminishing-balance methods, create a higher amortization expense in the earlier years and lower charges in later periods. The main justification for this approach is that more amortization is charged in earlier years when the asset offers the greatest benefits. Another argument is that repair and maintenance costs are often higher in later periods, and the accelerated method therefore provides a fairly constant total expense (for amortization plus repairs and maintenance) because the amortization charge is lower in the later periods. When a decreasing charge approach is used by Canadian companies, it is usually a version of what is called the declining-balance method.[7]

Declining-Balance Method The **declining-balance method** uses an amortization rate (expressed as a percentage and called the declining-balance rate) that remains constant throughout the asset's life, assuming there is never a change in estimates. This rate is applied each year to the declining book value (cost less accumulated amortization) to determine amortization expense. The rate is usually calculated as a multiple of the straight-line rate.[8] For example, the double-declining-balance rate for an asset with a 10-year life is 20% (the straight-line rate, which is 100% ÷ 10, or 10%, and multiplied by 2). For an asset with a 20-year life, the triple-declining-balance rate is 15% (the straight-line rate of 100% ÷ 20, or 5%, multiplied by 3), while the double-declining-balance rate would be 10% (100% ÷ 20, or 5%, multiplied by 2).

Unlike other methods, in the declining-balance method **the residual value of the asset is not deducted** in calculating an amortizable amount. Instead, this method applies the appropriate rate to the asset's net book value or carrying amount at the beginning of each period. Since the asset's book value is reduced each period by the amortization charge, the rate is applied to a lower book value each period, resulting in a reduced amortization charge. This process continues until the asset's book value is reduced to its estimated residual value; **when the residual value is reached, there is no more amortization of the asset.**

Illustration 11-6 shows how to apply the **double-declining-balance method**, using the crane example.

---

[7] There is another decreasing charge approach, called the **sum-of-the-years'-digits method**, but it is rarely used in Canada. Under this method, the amortizable amount (i.e., cost less residual value) is multiplied each year by a decreasing fraction. The **denominator** of the fraction equals the sum of the digits of an asset's useful life. For example, the sum of the digits of the life of an asset with a five-year life is 1 + 2 + 3 + 4 + 5 = 15. The **numerator** decreases year by year and the denominator stays constant. Because this is a decreasing charge approach, amortization expense is 5/15 of the amortizable amount in the first year, 4/15 of the amortizable amount in the second year, 3/15 in the third, 2/15 in the fourth, and 1/15 in the fifth year. At the end of the asset's useful life, its net book value should be equal to the estimated residual value. Similarly, for an asset with a 10-year life, the sum of the years' digits, 1 through 10, equals 55. Amortization in the first year is 10/55 of the amortizable amount, in the second year it is 9/55, and so on.

[8] The straight-line rate (%) is equal to 100% divided by the estimated useful life of the asset that is being amortized. A pure form of the declining-balance method (sometimes called the fixed percentage of book value method) has also been suggested as a possibility, but it is not used very much. This approach finds a rate that amortizes the asset exactly to its residual value at the end of its expected useful life. The formula for determining this rate is as follows:

Amortization rate = 1 – [the *n*th root of (Residual value ÷ Acquisition cost)]

The life in years is n. Once the rate is calculated, it is applied to the asset's declining book value from period to period, which means that amortization expense will be lower each subsequent period.

Year	Book Value of Asset, Beginning of Year	Rate on Declining Balance[a]	Amortization Expense	Balance of Accumulated Amortization	Net Book Value, End of Year
1	$500,000	40%	$200,000	$200,000	$300,000
2	300,000	40%	120,000	320,000	180,000
3	180,000	40%	72,000	392,000	108,000
4	108,000	40%	43,200	435,200	64,800
5	64,800	40%	14,800[b]	450,000	50,000

[a] (100% ÷ 5) × 2

[b] Limited to $14,800 because the book value is never reduced below the residual value.

Illustration 11-6
Amortization Calculation, Double-Declining-Balance Method–Crane Example

Increasing Charge Methods

Increasing charge methods, such as **compound interest** and **sinking fund approaches**, produce lower amortization charges in the early years and higher amounts in the later years of an asset's life. The **sinking fund method**, for example, calculates amortization expense as the annual increase in a virtual sinking fund that is designed to accumulate the amortizable amount over the asset's useful life.[9] As the sinking fund increases in size, the amount of the annual increase representing principal and interest also increases.

This method is no longer widely used since few assets provide benefits in such a pattern.

International Insight

IAS 16 identifies only three patterns of allocating depreciable amounts to expense: equal charges, reducing amounts, and amounts that vary with expected use or output.

Depletion

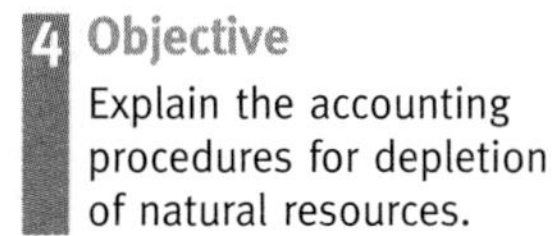

4 Objective

Explain the accounting procedures for depletion of natural resources.

Chapter 10 explains the issues for determining the cost or depletion base of natural resource assets. This cost could include capitalized acquisition, exploration, development, and restoration costs. Because the resource is depleted over time as it is removed, the capitalized costs must be amortized. The amortization, or **depletion expense**, is a product cost, and therefore becomes a direct cost of the minerals or petroleum products that are produced during the period. Illustration 10-1 summarizes this flow of costs for the oil and gas industry.

The accounting problems associated with the depletion of natural resources are similar to the problems encountered with the amortization of other types of property, plant, and equipment. They include:

1. Determining the pattern of depletion (amortization) to be used
2. The difficulty of estimating the asset's useful life

In addition, with natural resource companies there is also the issue of liquidating dividends.

Depletion of Resource Cost

Once the amortizable base amount is established, the next decision is determining how these capitalized costs will be allocated to accounting periods. Normally, **depletion is calculated using an activity approach, such as the units-of-production method**. Using this method, the natural resource's total cost is divided by the estimated recoverable reserves (the number of units that are estimated to be in the resource deposit) to obtain a

[9] This is termed a "virtual" sinking fund because no amounts are actually set aside as they are in a real sinking fund.

cost per unit of product. The cost per unit is then multiplied by the number of units that were extracted during the period to determine the period's depletion.

For example, assume a mining company acquired the right to use 1,000 hectares of land in the Northwest Territories to mine for gold. The lease cost is $50,000; the related exploration costs on the property are $100,000; and development costs incurred in opening the mine are $850,000, all of which have been capitalized. Total costs related to the mine before the first ounce of gold is extracted are, therefore, $1 million. The company estimates that the mine will provide approximately 100,000 ounces of gold. The depletion rate is determined as in Illustration 11-7.

Illustration 11-7
Calculation of Depletion Rate

$$\frac{\text{Total cost} - \text{residual value}}{\text{Total estimated units available}} = \text{Depletion cost per unit}$$

$$\frac{\$1{,}000{,}000}{100{,}000} = \$10 \text{ per ounce}$$

If 25,000 ounces are extracted in the first year, the depletion for the year is $250,000 (25,000 ounces at $10). The entry to record the depletion is:

A	= L	+ SE
0	0	0

Cash flows: No effect

Inventory (Depletion Expense)	250,000	
Accumulated Depletion		250,000

The depletion charge for the extracted resource (in addition to labour and other direct production costs) is initially charged (debited) to inventory. When the resource is sold, the inventory costs are transferred to cost of goods sold and matched with the period's revenue.[10]

The remaining natural resource is reported as part of property, plant, and equipment. The balance sheet presents the property cost and the amount of accumulated depletion entered to date, as follows:

Gold mine (at cost)	$1,000,000	
Less: Accumulated depletion	250,000	$750,000

The equipment used in extracting the resource may also be amortized on a units-of-production basis, especially if the equipment's useful life can be directly assigned to one specific resource deposit. If the equipment is used on more than one job, other cost allocation methods may be more appropriate, such as the straight-line or an accelerated depreciation method.

Estimating Recoverable Reserves

Often, the estimate of recoverable reserves has to be changed either because new information becomes available or because production processes become more sophisticated. Natural resources such as oil and gas deposits and some rare metals have been the greatest

[10] This cost flow is similar to the one for the amortization of factory buildings in a manufacturing company. The initial costs for the building are capitalized in a property, plant, and equipment account, and the amortization of the factory building is then charged to work-in-process inventory as a factory overhead—a conversion cost—as one of the costs of goods manufactured. The amortization thus ends up being charged to the income statement only in the period when the related goods are sold.

challenges. Estimates of these reserves are subject to a significant amount of measurement uncertainty.

This problem and its resolution are the same as those faced in accounting for changes in estimates of the useful lives of plant and equipment. The procedure, explained later in this chapter, is to revise the depletion rate on a prospective basis by dividing the costs remaining on the books less any residual value by the new estimate of the remaining recoverable reserves. This means that a new depletion rate is determined going forward; past depletion is not adjusted. This approach has much merit since the required estimates are so uncertain.

Liquidating Dividends

A company may own a property that it plans to extract natural resources from, and have this as its only major asset. If the company does not expect to purchase more properties, it may decide to distribute back to shareholders their initial capital investment. They do this by paying them dividends that are equal to the accumulated amount of net income (after depletion) **plus the amount of depletion that has been charged**. The major accounting issue is to distinguish between dividends that are a return **of capital** and those that are not. A company issuing a **liquidating dividend** reduces the appropriate Share Capital account for the portion of the dividend that is related to the original investment instead of reducing Retained Earnings, because the dividend is a return of part of the investor's original contribution. Shareholders must be informed about what part of the total dividend is liquidation of capital and what part is a distribution of income or earnings.

To illustrate, assume a mining company has a retained earnings balance of $1,650,000, accumulated depletion on mineral properties of $2.1 million, and common share capital of $5.4 million. The board of directors declares a dividend of $3 per share on the 1 million shares outstanding, indicating that the amount paid out in excess of the retained earnings balance is a return to shareholders of part of their original capital contribution. The entry to record the $3-million dividend is as follows:

Retained Earnings	1,650,000	
Common Shares	1,350,000*	
Cash		3,000,000
*($3,000,000 − $1,650,000)		

A	= L +	SE
−3,000,000		−3,000,000

Cash flows: ↓ 3,000,000 outflow

The $3 dividend represents a $1.65 ($1,650,000/1,000,000) per share **return on investment** and a $1.35 ($1,350,000/1,000,000) per share liquidating dividend, or **return of capital**.

Special Methods of Amortization

5 Objective
Explain the need for special amortization methods and how to apply them.

Sometimes, because the assets have unique characteristics, an enterprise does not choose one of the more common amortization methods. Instead, a company may develop its own special or tailor-made amortization method. GAAP requires only that the method be a rational and systematic approach for allocating the asset's cost over the periods that the asset benefits.

Group and Composite Methods

Amortization is usually applied to a single asset. In some circumstances, however, a company may place related assets (regardless of their type, use, or life) into a single multiple-asset account that is then amortized using one rate. For example, a telecommunications company might amortize telephone poles, microwave systems, or switchboards by groups.

Two methods of amortizing multiple-asset accounts can be used: the group method and the composite method. **The calculations are the same for both:** calculate an average rate and amortize on that basis. The different names for the methods only reflect the degree of similarity of the assets. The **group method** is used when the assets are fairly homogeneous and have approximately the same useful lives. The **composite method** is used when the assets are dissimilar and have different lives. The group method more closely approximates a single-unit cost procedure because the variation from the average is not as great.

To illustrate, assume that a vehicle leasing company amortizes its fleet of cars, trucks, and campers on a composite basis. The amortization rate is determined as in Illustration 11-8.

Illustration 11-8
Amortization Calculation, Composite Basis

Asset	Original Cost	Residual Value	Amortizable Amount	Estimated Life (yrs.)	Amortization per Year (Straight-Line)
Cars	$145,000	$25,000	$120,000	3	$40,000
Trucks	44,000	4,000	40,000	4	10,000
Campers	35,000	5,000	30,000	5	6,000
	$224,000	$34,000	$190,000		$56,000

Composite amortization rate on original cost $= \frac{\$56,000}{\$224,000} = 25\%$

Composite life = (190,000 ÷ 56,000) = 3.39 years

The **composite amortization rate** is determined by dividing the total amortization per year for the collection of assets by their total original cost. If there are no changes in the assets, they will be amortized in the amount of $56,000 per year (the original cost of $224,000 × the composite rate of 25%) until only the residual value remains. It will take the company 3.39 years (the composite life as shown in the illustration) to amortize these assets.

The difference between the group or composite method and the single-unit amortization method is greater when asset retirements occur. When an asset is retired, the resulting gain or loss is buried in the Accumulated Amortization account rather than being recognized separately. This practice is justified because some assets will be retired before the average service life, while others will be retired after the average life. For this reason, **the difference between original cost and cash received is debited to Accumulated Amortization. No gain or loss on disposition is recorded.**

To illustrate, suppose that one of the campers with a cost of $5,000 is sold for $2,600 at the end of the third year. The entry is:

Accumulated Amortization	2,400	
Cash	2,600	
Cars, Trucks, and Campers		5,000

As new assets of the type identified in the group are purchased, there is no need to calculate a new amortization rate—they are amortized using the same group rate. If there are significant changes in the relative weightings of the assets in the group, however, a new group rate would need to be calculated.

A typical financial statement disclosure of the group amortization method is shown in Illustration 11-9 for **Canadian National Railway Company**.

Illustration 11-9

Disclosure of Group Amortization Method

Canadian National Railway Company

Notes to Consolidated Financial Statements, Year Ended December 31, 2005

1 Summary of significant accounting policies (excerpts)

G. Properties

Railroad properties are carried at cost less accumulated depreciation including asset impairment write-downs. Labor, materials and other costs associated with the installation of rail, ties, ballast and other track improvements are capitalized to the extent they meet the Company's minimum threshold for capitalization. Major overhauls and large refurbishments are also capitalized when they result in an extension to the useful life or increase the functionality of the asset. Included in property additions are the costs of developing computer software for internal use. Maintenance costs are expensed as incurred.

The cost of railroad properties, less net salvage value, retired or disposed of in the normal course of business is charged to accumulated depreciation, in accordance with the group method of depreciation.

H. Depreciation

The cost of properties, including those under capital leases, net of asset impairment write-downs, is depreciated on a straight-line basis over their estimated useful lives as follows;

Asset class	Annual rate
Track and roadway	2%
Rolling stock	3%
Buildings	6%
Other	6%

The company follows the group method of depreciation for railroad properties and, as such, conducts comprehensive depreciation studies on a periodic basis to assess the reasonableness of the lives of properties based upon current information and historical activities. Changes in estimated useful lives are accounted for prospectively.

The group or composite method greatly simplifies the bookkeeping process and tends to average out errors caused by over- or under-amortization. As a result, periodic income is not distorted by gains or losses on asset disposals.

Expanded Discussion–Special Amortization Methods

www.wiley.com/canada/kieso

On the other hand, the single-asset approach (1) simplifies the calculation arithmetic; (2) identifies gains and losses on disposal; (3) isolates amortization on idle assets; and (4) represents the best estimate of the amortization of each individual asset. For these reasons, it is most commonly used in practice. Recently support has been increasing in Canada, the United States, and internationally for a **components approach** to depreciation. Under component depreciation, any part or portion of property, plant, and equipment that can be separately identified as an asset is depreciated over its individual expected useful life. For example, a building might be divided into various components such as roof, heating and cooling system, elevator, windows, and so on. The useful life of and amortization charge for each component is then separately determined.

Hybrid or Combination Methods

In addition to the amortization methods described above, companies may develop their own tailor-made methods. One hybrid amortization method that is used by some companies in the steel industry is referred to as the **production variable method**. A specific example of this is a modified units-of-production approach that is used for equipment whose depreciation is a function of physical wear and tear as well as time. The annual charge for amortization is a straight-line amount adjusted by the level of raw steel production. As a result, in some periods the amortization expense is larger than the straight-line amount and in others it is less.

Choosing an Amortization Method

6 **Objective**
Identify how amortization methods are selected.

Which amortization method should be selected, and why? Conceptually, an amortization method is chosen based on which method best matches or correlates the charge to income (i.e., the expense) with the benefits or services that the asset provides to the entity. To determine this, it is necessary to first identify the pattern of benefits to be received. Illustration 11-10 shows possible benefit patterns.

Illustration 11-10
Possible Benefit Patterns for Assets

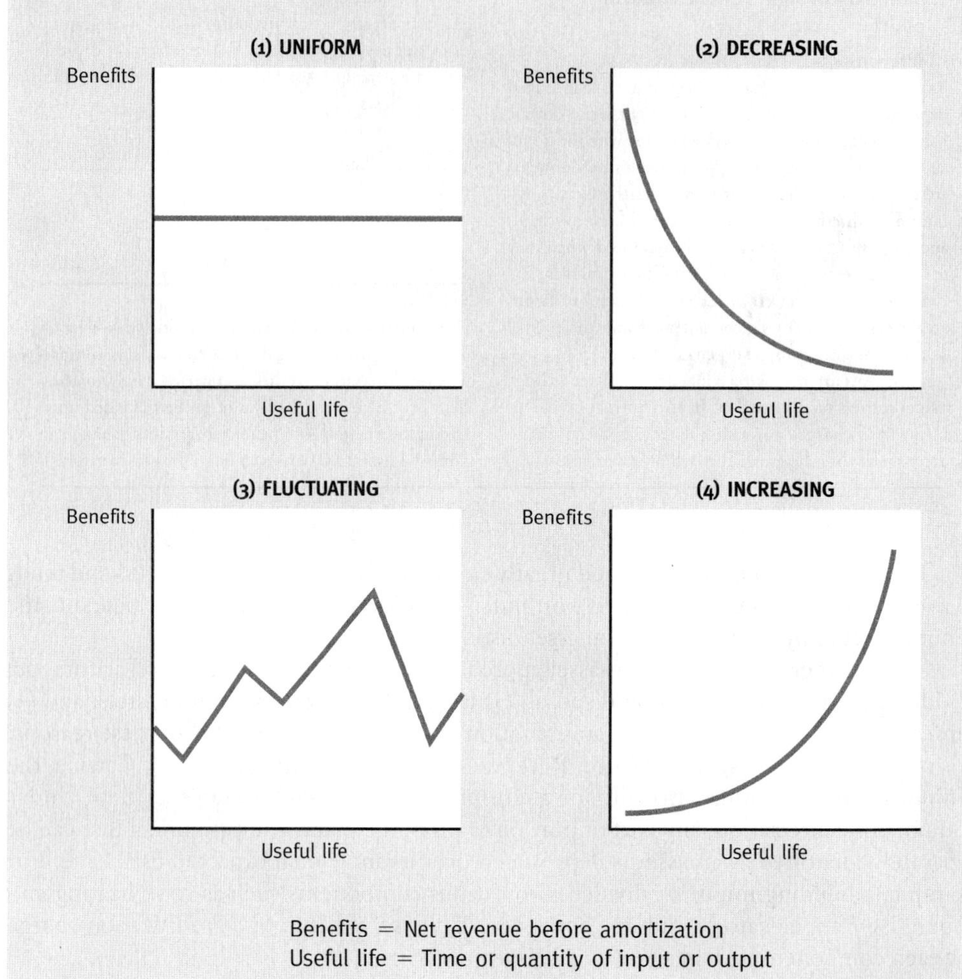

International Insight

In most non-English-speaking nations, companies are not permitted to use one amortization method for financial statements and a different method for tax returns. The financial statements must conform to the tax return.

Pattern (1) is for an asset that provides roughly the same level of benefits in each year of its life. A warehouse could be an example. For such assets, the straight-line method is rational because it results in a constant amortization expense each period. An airplane may be an example of an asset with a decreasing benefit pattern (2). When it is new, it is constantly in service on major routes. As it gets older, its operating efficiency declines—it may be repaired more often and used for more peripheral routes. Amortization expense should therefore decline each year. The use of a truck, in terms of kilometres driven, may fluctuate considerably from period to period, yielding a benefit pattern that varies (3). For such an asset, an activity method rationally matches amortization expense with the asset's benefit pattern. An increasing benefit pattern (4) may result "when an enterprise can price its goods or services so as to obtain a constant rate of return on the investment in the asset."[11] This requires increasing net revenues from the asset's use, which is not a common situation.

[11] *CICA Handbook*, Section 3061.30.

Because it may be difficult in many cases to estimate future revenues, the most important factor in choosing a method may be its **simplicity**. In such cases, it might be argued that the straight-line method of amortization should be used. However, others argue that whatever is used for tax purposes should be used for book purposes because it **eliminates some record-keeping costs**. Because Canadian companies must use the capital cost allowance approach for income tax purposes (discussed in Appendix 11A), they may decide to also use this for financial reporting purposes. This is common for smaller companies. The objectives of financial reporting differ, however, from those of income tax determination, so it is not uncommon for companies to use different methods for tax purposes and for financial reporting. While it is perfectly acceptable to use two different methods since the objectives are different, a consequence of this is that the entity's financial statement amounts for property, plant, and equipment and for income before taxes will be different from the tax basis of capital assets and taxable income. The financial accounting consequences of such differences are examined in Chapter 18.

Underlying Concept

Failing to consider the economic consequences that accounting principles have on companies is a frequent criticism of the accounting profession. However, the neutrality concept requires that the statements be free from bias. And freedom from bias requires that the statements reflect economic reality, even if undesirable effects occur.

Management sometimes appears to choose the method of amortization based on the **perceived economic consequences** of the amounts that will be reported. Companies that want to appear more profitable change from the declining-balance method to a straight-line approach. Because share value tends to be related to reported income, management feels that such a change favourably affects the firm's market value. In fact, research in this area has found just the opposite, with companies that switch to more liberal accounting policies experiencing declines in share values. One rationale is that such changes signal that the company is in trouble and also lead to scepticism about management's attitudes and behaviour.

What Do the Numbers Mean?

Choice of an amortization method affects both the balance sheet (i.e., the carrying amount of property, plant, and equipment) and the income statement (i.e., the amortization expense). It follows, therefore, that various ratios are affected by the choice that is made. These ratios include the rate of return on total assets, debt-to-total assets, and the total asset turnover. Consequently, contractual commitments based on financial statement ratios, such as agreements related to management compensation plans and bond indentures, are potentially important aspects that tend to be considered when choosing an amortization method.

Other Amortization Issues

There remain two additional issues to discuss for amortization:

1. How should amortization be calculated for partial periods?
2. How are revisions in amortization rates handled?

Amortization and Partial Periods

Plant assets are rarely purchased on the first day of a fiscal period or disposed of on the last day of a fiscal period. A practical question therefore is, "How much amortization should be charged for partial periods?"

Assume, for example, that an automated drill machine with a five-year life is purchased for \$45,000 (no residual value) on June 10, 2007. The company's fiscal year ends December 31, and amortization is charged for $6^2/_3$ months during the year. The total amortization for a full year, assuming the straight-line method, is \$9,000 (\$45,000 ÷ 5), and the amortization for the partial year is \$5,000 (\$9,000 × [$6^2/_3$/12]).

Rather than making a precise allocation of cost for a partial period, many companies set a policy to simplify the calculations. For example, amortization may be calculated for the full period on the opening balance in the asset account and no depreciation is charged on acquisitions that occur during the year. Another variation is to charge a full year's amortization on assets that are used for a full year and charge a half-year of amortization in the years of acquisition and disposal. Alternatively, the company may charge a full year's amortization in the year of acquisition and none in the year of disposal.

A company is free to adopt any one of these fractional-year policies in allocating cost to the first and last years of an asset's life, as long as the method is applied consistently. As indicated in the opening vignette, VIA Rail follows a policy of beginning amortization in the month after the train is put into service and continuing it up to the month of disposal. For the illustrations and problem material in this text, amortization is calculated on the basis of the nearest full month, unless something different is stated. Illustration 11-11 shows amortization allocated under five different fractional-year policies using the straight-line method on the automated drill machine purchased for $45,000 on June 10, 2007.

Illustration 11-11
Fractional-Year Amortization Policies

Machine Cost = $45,000	Amortization Allocated per Period Over 5-Year Life*					
Fractional-Year Policy	2007	2008	2009	2010	2011	2012
1. Nearest fraction of a year	$5,000[a]	$9,000	$9,000	$9,000	$9,000	$4,000[b]
2. Nearest full month	5,250[c]	9,000	9,000	9,000	9,000	3,750[d]
3. Half year in period of acquisition and disposal	4,500	9,000	9,000	9,000	9,000	4,500
4. Full year in period of acquisition, none in period of disposal	9,000	9,000	9,000	9,000	9,000	0
5. None in period of acquisition, full year in period of disposal	0	9,000	9,000	9,000	9,000	9,000

[a]6.667/12 ($9,000) [b]5.333/12 ($9,000) [c]7/12 ($9,000) [d]5/12 ($9,000)
*Rounded to nearest dollar

The partial period calculation is relatively simple when the straight-line method is used. But how is partial period amortization handled when an accelerated method is used? To illustrate, assume that an asset was purchased for $10,000 on July 1, 2007, with an estimated useful life of five years. The amortization expense for 2007, 2008, and 2009 using the double-declining-balance method is shown in Illustration 11-12.

Illustration 11-12
Calculation of Partial Period Amortization, Double-Declining-Balance Method

1st full year	(40% × $10,000) =	$4,000
2nd full year	(40% × 6,000) =	2,400
3rd full year	(40% × 3,600) =	1,440
Amortization July 1, 2007, to December 31, 2007:		
	6/12 × $4,000 =	$2,000
Amortization for 2008:		
	6/12 × $4,000 =	$2,000
	6/12 × $2,400 =	1,200
		$3,200
	or ($10,000 − $2,000) × 40% =	$3,200
Amortization for 2009:		
	6/12 × $2,400 =	$1,200
	6/12 × $1,440 =	720
		$1,920
	or ($10,000 − $2,000 − $3,200) × 40% =	$1,920

In calculating amortization expense for partial periods in this example, the amortization charge for a full year was determined first. This amount was then prorated on a straight-line basis between the two accounting periods involved. A simpler approach when using the declining-balance method is to calculate the partial year amortization expense for the acquisition year (e.g., $2,000 for 2007, as shown in the example) and then apply the amortization rate (40%) to the book value at the beginning of each successive year. This is shown in the illustration as the "or" calculations. The charge for each year is the same regardless of the choice of calculation approach.

Revision of Amortization Rates

7 Objective
Explain and apply the accounting procedures for a change in amortization rate.

When a plant asset is purchased, amortization rates are carefully determined based on past experience with similar assets and other pertinent information. Amortization is only an estimate, however, and the expected pattern of consumption of the asset's benefits and estimates of the useful life of property, plant, and equipment and its residual value need to be reviewed regularly. A change in any one of these elements requires that either the amortization method or rate also be changed. Unexpected physical deterioration, unforeseen obsolescence, or changes in the extent or manner in which the asset is used may make the asset's useful life less than what was originally estimated. Improved maintenance procedures, a revision of operating policies, or similar developments may prolong the asset's life beyond the expected period.

For example, assume that machinery that cost $90,000 was estimated originally to have a 20-year life with no residual value and has already been amortized for 10 years. In year 11, it is estimated that its total life is now expected to be 30 years. Amortization has been recorded at the rate of 1/20 of $90,000, or $4,500 per year, by the straight-line method. On the basis of a 30-year life, amortization should have been 1/30 of $90,000, or $3,000 per year. Amortization expense, therefore, has been overstated, and net income understated, for each of the past 10 years. The dollar differences are calculated in Illustration 11-13.

Illustration 11-13
Calculation of Accumulated Difference Due to Revision of Estimate

	Per Year	For Ten Years
Amortization charged per books (1/20 × $90,000)	$4,500	$45,000
Amortization based on a 30-year life (1/30 × $90,000)	3,000	30,000
Excess amortization charged	$1,500	$15,000

Canadian accounting standards **do not permit companies to go back and correct the records** when a change in an estimate is made, **nor to make a "catch-up" adjustment** for the accumulated difference. Section 1506 of the *CICA Handbook* requires instead that the effects of any changes in estimates **be accounted for in the period of change and be applied to future periods**. The reason is that estimates and changes in them are a constant and inherent part of the accounting process. As new information becomes available, it is incorporated into current and future reports.

Therefore, when a change in estimate occurs, no change is made to previously recorded amounts. Instead, a new amortization schedule is prepared for the asset using the unamortized costs that remain on the books, the most recent estimates of the asset's residual value and remaining useful life, and the most appropriate amortization method for the current circumstances. Continuing with our example from the previous illustration, Illustration 11-14 shows the charges for amortization in the current and subsequent periods based on revised calculations, and assuming the straight-line method is still appropriate.

Illustration 11-14

Calculation of Amortization after Revision of Estimated Life

Machinery cost	$90,000
Less: Accumulated amortization to date	45,000
Carrying amount of machinery at end of tenth year	45,000
Less estimated residual value	-0-
Costs to be amortized	$45,000

Revised amortization = $45,000 ÷ 20 years of remaining life = $2,250 per year

The entry to record amortization in each of the remaining 20 years is:

A	= L +	SE
−2,250		−2,250

Cash flows: No effect

Amortization Expense	2,250	
Accumulated Amortization—Machinery		2,250

If the machinery now has an estimated residual value of $5,000 at the end of its revised useful life, the revised amortization rate is $2,000 per year ([$45,000 − $5,000] ÷ 20).

If the double-declining-balance method had been used initially, the change in estimated life would result in a new amortization rate to be applied to the book value in the current (11th) and subsequent years.[12] In this example, a revised remaining life of 20 years results in a revised 5% straight-line and a 10% double-declining rate, which, coincidentally, is the same rate that was used for the first 10 years. As this method ignores residual value in determining amortization expense, a change in residual value is ignored in the revised calculation.

AKITA Drilling Ltd., an oil and gas drilling contractor with operations in northern and western Canada and in Alaska, includes the information in Illustration 11-15 in its notes to a recent financial statement. The information describes the company's change in the estimate of its drilling rigs' useful life.

Illustration 11-15

Change in Estimate of Useful Life

Akita Drilling Limited

Notes to Financial Statements

1. **Summary of Significant Accounting Policies (excerpt)**

Depreciation

Drilling rigs are depreciated using the unit of production method based on an initial estimated life of 2,000 operating days per rig ... [C]ertain large rigs had lives re-estimated to 3,600 operating days per rig. The estimate of 3,600 operating days for specific rigs was based upon these rigs being moved relatively less often than certain smaller capacity rigs thereby encountering less wear and tear than smaller rigs and that AKITA's remaining large rigs were used when AKITA acquired them. If AKITA had adopted the effects of this change in estimate at the beginning of the preceding year, depreciation expense would have been reduced by $246,000 in that year.

[12] To determine the unamortized book value to date when using the double-declining-balance method, the following formula can be used:

Book value = $C(1 - r)^n$, where C = cost of asset; r = amortization rate; and n = number of full years from the asset's acquisition date. For example, if the machinery in the illustration had been amortized using the double-declining-balance method instead of the straight-line method, C = $90,000; r = 2 × (100% ÷ 20) = 10%; and n = 10.

The asset's book value at the end of year 10, therefore, is $\$90,000(1 - 0.10)^{10}$, or $31,381.

IMPAIRMENT

Unlike for current assets, such as inventories, **the lower of cost and market valuation rule does not apply to property, plant, and equipment**. Because current assets are expected to be converted into cash within the operating cycle, it is important to report them on the balance sheet at no more than the net cash that the entity expects to receive from them. Property, plant, and equipment assets, however, are not held to be directly converted into cash, but instead are ordinarily used in operations over the long term. For this reason, the lower of cost and net realizable value is not an appropriate valuation rule for these assets.

8 **Objective**
Explain the issues and apply the accounting standards for capital asset impairment.

Even when long-lived capital assets become partially obsolete, accountants have been reluctant to reduce the assets' carrying amount. They are reluctant because, unlike for inventories, it is difficult to arrive at a fair value to use for property, plant, and equipment that is not subjective and arbitrary. For example, Falconbridge Ltd. had to decide whether all or a part of its property, plant, and equipment in a nickel-mining operation in the Dominican Republic should be written off. The project had been incurring losses because nickel prices were low and operating costs were high. Only if nickel prices increased by approximately 33 percent would the project be reasonably profitable. Whether a write-off was appropriate depended on the future price of nickel. Even if a decision were made to write down the asset, the amount to be written off would not be clear.

Recognizing Impairments

Impairment is a condition that exists when the carrying amount of a long-lived asset that is held for usage is more than its fair value.[13] Various events and changes in circumstances might lead to impairment. Examples include the following:

- A decrease in an asset's market value
- A change in the extent or manner in which an asset is used
- An adverse change in legal factors or in the business environment that affects an asset's value
- An accumulation of costs that is more than the amount that was originally expected to be the cost of acquiring or constructing an asset
- A projection or forecast that demonstrates there will be continuing losses associated with an asset

Underlying Concept
The going concern concept assumes that the entity can recover the cost of the investment in its assets. Under GAAP, the fair value of long-lived assets is not reported, because a going concern (i.e., an operating business) does not plan to sell such assets. However, if the assumption of being able to recover the investment cost is not valid, then a reduction in value should be reported.

If these events or changes in circumstances are significant and indicate that the asset's carrying amount may not be recoverable, a **recoverability test** is used to determine whether impairment has occurred. To do this, an estimate is first made of the future net cash flows that are expected from the use of the asset and its eventual disposition. Then, if the sum of these **undiscounted** expected future cash flows is **less than the asset's carrying amount**, the asset is considered impaired. Conversely, if the sum of the **undiscounted** expected future net cash flows is equal to or greater than the asset's carrying amount, no impairment has occurred.

[13] *CICA Handbook*, Section 3063.03(c). Section 3475 paragraphs .04 to .07 specify that the impairment requirements of Section 3063 also apply to long-lived assets that will be disposed of in a way other than by sale. This includes those that are abandoned or distributed to owners in a spin-off. Until they are abandoned or spun-off, these assets continue to be amortized.

International Insight

An asset's recoverable amount under IAS 36 is the greater of (1) its fair value less costs to sell it and (2) the present value of its estimated future cash flows from use and disposal.

The future cash flows that are associated with a particular long-lived asset are only estimated amounts and, depending on the useful life of the asset, they can extend far into the future. The recoverable amounts, therefore, are **much more difficult to determine than the realizable values of accounts receivable and inventories**. In determining the future cash flows of an asset for the recoverability test, the only amounts that are included are the net cash flows that are directly associated with the asset's use and from its eventual disposal. There are complications when an asset does not generate cash flows independently of other assets. In this case, the individual assets must be combined with others to form an asset group and the recoverability test is applied to the entire asset group.[14]

In short, the recoverability test is essentially a screening device to determine whether an asset is impaired. If the expected future net cash flows from an asset are $400,000 and its carrying amount is $350,000, no impairment has occurred. However, if the expected future net cash flows are $300,000, the asset is considered impaired. The rationale for the recoverability test is the basic assumption that a balance sheet should not report long-lived assets at more than the amount of cash that the entity is expected to recover from that asset.

Measuring Impairments

If the recoverability test indicates that an asset held for use is impaired, the amount of the loss must be calculated. The **impairment loss** is the amount by which the carrying amount of the asset **exceeds its fair value**. Note that this is **not the same thing** as the difference between its carrying amount and its recoverable amount in the recoverability test. **Fair value** is defined as the amount of the consideration that would be agreed upon in an arm's-length transaction between knowledgeable, willing parties who are under no compulsion to act.[15] Fair value is best measured by quoted market prices in active markets, but if there is no active market, other valuation methods are used. The **present value of expected future net cash flows** is considered the next best approach.

To summarize, then, the process of determining an impairment loss involves three steps:

Step 1: Review events or changes in circumstances for possible impairment.

Step 2: If the review indicates potential impairment, apply the recoverability test. If the total expected future net cash flows (undiscounted) from the long-lived asset are less than the carrying amount, the asset is considered impaired.

Step 3: If considered impaired, determine the fair value of the asset based on a method that discounts the future flows to their present value. The impairment loss is the difference between the carrying amount and the fair value.[16]

Illustration One

Assume that a company has equipment that is reviewed for possible impairment because of changes in how the equipment is being used. The asset's carrying amount is $600,000

[14] Section 3063 of the *CICA Handbook* gives extensive application guidance for these complexities.

[15] *CICA Handbook*, Section 3063.03(b).

[16] These general impairment provisions are explained in *Handbook* Section 3063. Impairment provisions for oil and gas assets accounted for using the full cost method are explained in *Accounting Guideline* AcG-16.

($800,000 cost less $200,000 accumulated amortization). The expected future undiscounted net cash flows from the use of the asset and its eventual disposal are estimated to be $650,000. The recoverability test indicates that the $650,000 of expected net cash flows from the asset exceeds its carrying amount of $600,000. As a result, **no impairment is evident**.

Illustration Two

Assume the same facts as above, except that the expected future net cash flows from the equipment are $580,000 instead of $650,000. The recoverability test indicates that the cash flows of $580,000 from the use and disposal of the asset are less than its carrying amount of $600,000. Therefore, the asset is considered impaired. If the asset's market or fair value is $525,000, the impairment loss is calculated as in Illustration 11-16, where Step 3 is applied.

Illustration 11-16
Calculation of Impairment Loss

Carrying amount of the equipment	$600,000
Fair value of equipment	525,000
Loss on impairment	$ 75,000

The entry to record the impairment loss is as follows:

Loss on Impairment	75,000	
Accumulated Amortization		75,000

A	= L +	SE
−75,000		−75,000

Cash flows: No effect

Notice that the entry credits the Accumulated Amortization account rather than the capital asset account itself. Either credit is correct, and both approaches are used in practice. Crediting the Accumulated Amortization account has the advantage of preserving the asset's original cost. The amount of any write-down of a capital asset is charged to expense and disclosed in the same period the impairment is recognized. After the impairment loss is recorded, the amortization method chosen for the asset is reviewed, as are the remaining useful life and residual value. Revised amortization amounts are then determined.

International Insight

International standards require entities to recognize impairment losses on assets that are being carried at cost in the income statement. If the assets are carried at revalued amounts, the asset's impairment is treated as a decrease of the revaluation surplus in equity.

Assuming that the asset continues to be used in operations, the impairment loss is reported as part of income from continuing operations. It is not an extraordinary item. Costs that are associated with an impairment loss are the same costs that would otherwise flow through operations and be reported as part of continuing operations.

A company that recognizes an impairment loss is required to describe the asset, the circumstances that led to the impairment, and the method of determining its fair value. In addition, if the impairment amount is not reported separately on the face of the income statement, the entity must disclose the amount of the loss and where on the income statement it has been reported.

Toromont Industries Inc., a Canadian company that sells, rents, and services mobile equipment and industrial engines and delivers and maintains custom compression systems throughout North America, deducted an "asset impairment charge" of $17.8 million on its 2005 statement of earnings. The information in Illustration 11-17 was provided in Notes 1, 6, and 7 to the company's financial statements for the year ended December 31, 2005. It is clear from these disclosures that the company credited the accumulated depreciation account.

Illustration 11-17
Disclosure of Impairment Loss

Student Toolkit–Additional Disclosures

www.wiley.com/canada/kieso

TOROMONT INDUSTRIES LTD.

1 SIGNIFICANT ACCOUNTING POLICIES

Property, Plant and Equipment

Property, plant and equipment are recorded at cost. Depreciation is recognized principally on a straight-line basis to depreciate the cost of these assets over their estimated useful lives. Estimated useful lives range from 20 to 30 years for buildings, 3 to 10 years for equipment and 20 years for power generation assets.

Impairment of Long-lived Assets

Long-lived assets are reviewed for impairment whenever events or changes in circumstances indicate that the carrying amount may not be recoverable. In cases where the undiscounted expected future cash flows are less than the carrying amount, an impairment loss is recognized. Impairment losses on long-lived assets are measured as the amount by which the carrying value of an asset group exceeds its fair value, as determined by the discounted future cash flows of the asset group.

6 PROPERTY, PLANT AND EQUIPMENT

			2005			2004
	Cost	Accumulated Depreciation	Net Book Value	Cost	Accumulated Depreciation	Net Book Value
Land	$ 37,134	$ –	$ 37,134	$ 35,745	$ –	$ 35,745
Buildings	109,008	33,409	75,599	104,076	27,877	76,199
Equipment	125,840	85,205	40,635	114,489	74,501	39,988
Power generation	44,565	29,680	14,885	44,565	9,686	34,879
	$ 316,547	$ 148,294	$ 168,253	$ 298,875	$ 112,064	$ 186,811

7 IMPAIRMENT OF LONG-LIVED ASSETS

Toromont recently signed a Letter of Intent for a five-year agreement with the Ontario Power Authority. Based on the terms of this agreement, the Company has concluded that the revenues generated will not be sufficient to cover the fixed operating costs and depreciation of the assets. The Company has recorded a pre-tax loss of $17,800 to reflect impairment of these long-lived assets, $11,600 on an after-tax basis. After recording this charge, the net book value of power generation assets was $14,885.

Subsequent Measurement

International Insight

IAS 36 permits write-ups for subsequent recoveries in value when there has been a change in the estimates that are used to determine the asset's recoverable amount.

Once an impairment loss is recorded on an asset that continues to be held for use, the reduced carrying amount **becomes its new cost basis**. To illustrate, assume that at December 31, 2007, equipment with a carrying amount of $500,000 is considered impaired and is written down to its fair value of $400,000. At the end of 2008, the fair value of this asset has increased to $480,000. The asset's carrying amount is not changed to recognize the recovery in its value, but instead it continues to be amortized according to the rate and method that were determined after the impairment was recognized. **The impairment loss is not restored for an asset that is held for use.**[17]

Long-Lived Assets to Be Disposed of by Sale

Objective 9
Explain and apply the accounting standards for long-lived assets that will be disposed of through sale.

What happens if an entity intends to dispose of its long-lived assets by sale instead of continuing to use them? In this case, the asset is classified as **held for sale** and then remeasured at the lower of its carrying amount and fair value less costs to sell—i.e., at its net realizable value. Because the criteria for classifying a long-lived asset as held for sale are very strict, and include the requirement that the asset be disposed of in a short period of time, net realizable value is used in order to provide a better measure of the net cash flows expected from the asset. These criteria were presented in Chapter 4 when discussing the accounting for discontinued operations.

[17] *CICA Handbook*, Section 3063.06. Long-lived assets that are expected to be abandoned or spun off to owners rather than sold have the same impairment test and loss calculation as are used for assets that are held for use.

Assets that are held for sale are not amortized while they are held.[18] The rationale is that it would be inconsistent to apply the concept of amortization to assets that are not in use and are likely to be sold, and to lower of cost and net realizable value valuations. In many respects, **these assets are similar to inventory and are reported at the lower of their carrying amount and net realizable value**. A long-lived asset classified as held for sale will continue to be written down, and further losses will be recognized if the asset's net realizable value continues to drop. Gains (i.e., loss recoveries) are recognized for subsequent increases in net realizable value, but are limited to the amount of the cumulative losses that have already been recognized.

If the long-lived asset is a component of an entity that meets the criteria for being reporting as a discontinued operation, the losses and subsequent recoveries are reported as part of discontinued operations on the income statement. Otherwise, they are reported in income from continuing operations. Regardless, long-lived assets that are classified as held for sale **are reported separately in the balance sheet as long-term assets** unless sold before the financial statements are completed and the proceeds to be received qualify as current assets.[19]

Canam Group Inc., a Quebec-based manufacturing company that specializes in the design, fabrication, and marketing of construction products in Canada, the U.S., and some emerging countries, reported property, plant, and equipment held for sale of $12,992,000 at December 31, 2005, and $9,873,000 one year earlier. Notes 6 and 18 to the company's financial statements, reproduced in Illustration 11-18, provide additional information about these assets.

Illustration 11-18
Disclosures Related to Assets Held for Sale

Canam Group Inc.

6. Assets and Liabilities held for Sale (excerpts)

The company announced the closing of its plants in Columbus, Ohio and in Lafayette, Indiana in 2004 and 2003 respectively. The Company decided to close these plants because of excess production capacity in the joist business in the Midwest region.

Property, plant and equipment held for sale consist mainly of pieces of land, buildings and equipment and are accounted for at the lower of cost and estimated net market value. During fiscal 2005, a decline in value of $918 was recognized ($2,321 in 2004) (note 18).

These assets are being offered for sale based on conditions in their respective real estate markets and it is expected that they will be sold during fiscal 2006. The earnings and cash flows of the two plants located in the United States are included in the Company's current operations and are not considered to be discontinued operations, as the sales territories of these plants are still covered by the Company's other U.S. plants.

18. Expenses Related to Plant Closings

	2005	2004
Severence pay and other expenses	$ 72	$ 798
Impairment of property, plant and equipment held for sale (note 6)	918	2,321
	$990	$3,119

Illustration 11-19 summarizes the key classification and measurement requirements for assets that continue to be held for use and those held for sale. Note that the classification of the asset determines the accounting. These standards are consistent with those in the United States.

[18] *CICA Handbook*, Section 3475.13.

[19] *CICA Handbook*, Section 3475. 33 and .35.

Illustration 11-19
Summary of Long-Lived Assets

	Assets Held for Use	Assets to Be Disposed of by Sale
Handbook:	Section 3063	Section 3475
Classify as:	Held for use	Held for sale
Balance sheet classification:	Property, plant, and equipment	Separately in long-term assets*
Impairment:	Steps 2 and 3: • recoverability • if impaired, write down to fair value No restoration of impairment loss	Carry at lower of carrying amount and net realizable value Remeasure at balance sheet date. Recognize all losses and loss recoveries up to cumulative losses previously recognized
Amortization:	Amortize (reassess rate and method)	No amortization

*Unless the asset is expected to be sold before the financial statements are completed and otherwise meets the definition of a current asset. If so, report it in current assets.

DISPOSITIONS

Sale of Property, Plant, and Equipment

Objective 10
Describe and apply the accounting for the disposal of property, plant, and equipment.

Unless an asset has been classified as held for sale, amortization is taken until the date of disposal, at which time all accounts related to the retired asset are removed. Ideally, on the asset's retirement date, its book value would equal its disposal value, but this is rarely the case. As a result, a gain or loss is usually reported. Why do the amounts differ? Remember that the amortization amount is an estimate of the cost to be allocated to each period; it does not result from a process of valuation. The gain or loss is really a correction of past amortization expense for the years when the capital asset was used. If it had been possible at the time of acquisition to forecast the exact date of disposal and the amount to be realized at disposition, then a better estimate of amortization would have been recorded and no gain or loss would result.

Gains or losses on the retirement of plant assets are shown in the income statement along with other items that arise from ordinary business activities. However, a gain or loss from the disposal of a long-lived asset included in a discontinued business is reported "below the line" with discontinued operations.

To illustrate the disposal of an asset classified as held for use, assume that a machine costing $18,000 has been used for nine years and amortized at a rate of $1,200 per year. If the machine is sold in the middle of the tenth year for $7,000, the entry to record amortization up to the sale date is:

A	=	L	+	SE
−600				−600

Cash flows: No effect

Amortization Expense	600	
Accumulated Amortization—Machinery		600

The entry for the asset's sale is:

Cash	7,000	
Accumulated Amortization—Machinery [($1,200 × 9) + $600]	11,400	
Machinery		18,000
Gain on Disposal of Machinery		400

A	=	L	+	SE
+400				+400

Cash flows: ↑ 7,000 inflow

There is a gain on sale of $400 because the $7,000 of proceeds on disposal of the asset are more than the machinery's book value of $6,600 ($18,000 − $11,400) at the time of sale.

If an asset has previously been classified as held for sale, it is carried at its fair value less costs to sell. In this case, the net proceeds from the sale should therefore be close to the asset's carrying value and it is likely that only minor gains or losses would be recognized when the actual disposal occurs.

Involuntary Conversion

Sometimes an asset's service ends through an involuntary conversion, such as fire, flood, theft, or expropriation. When this happens, the gains or losses are calculated in the same way as they are for any other type of disposal. The only difference is that they may be reported as extraordinary items in the income statement **if the criteria for an extraordinary item are met.**

To illustrate, assume that a company is forced to sell its plant and property that stands directly in the path of a planned major highway. For several years, the provincial government has tried to purchase the land on which the plant stands, but the company has always resisted. The government ultimately exercised its right of eminent domain and its actions have been upheld by the courts. In settlement, the company receives $500,000, which substantially exceeds the $100,000 book value of the plant (cost of $300,000 less accumulated amortization of $200,000) and the $100,000 book value of the land. The following entry is made:

Cash	500,000	
Accumulated Amortization—Plant Assets	200,000	
Plant Assets		300,000
Land		100,000
Gain on Expropriation of Land and Plant Assets		300,000

A	=	L	+	SE
+300,000				+300,000

Cash flows: ↑ 500,000 inflow

A significant gain or loss on this type of unusual, non-recurring transaction that is not a result of management actions is normally shown as an extraordinary item. Similar treatment is given to other types of involuntary conversions assuming that they meet other conditions for extraordinary item treatment. The difference between the amount that is recovered (such as an insurance recovery), if any, and the asset's carrying amount is reported as a gain or loss.

International Insight

International standards do not allow separate presentation of any gains or losses as extraordinary items.

Other Issues

Donations of Capital Assets

In cases where a company donates or contributes a non-monetary asset, the donation is recorded as an expense at the donated asset's fair value. The difference between the asset's fair value and its book value is recognized as a gain or loss. To illustrate, assume that Kline Industries donates land that cost $30,000 and a small building located on the property that cost $95,000, and which has accumulated amortization up to the contribution date of $45,000, to the City of Saskatoon for a city park. Assume the land and building together have a fair value of $110,000. The entry to record the donation is:

A	= L +	SE
−80,000		−80,000

Cash flows: No effect

Contribution (or Donations) Expense	110,000	
Accumulated Amortization—Building	45,000	
Building		95,000
Land		30,000
Gain on Disposal of Land and Building		30,000

Miscellaneous Problems

If an asset is scrapped or abandoned without any cash recovery, the entity recognizes a loss that is equal to the asset's net carrying amount or book value. If the asset has scrap value, the gain or loss is the difference between the asset's scrap value and its book value. If a fully amortized asset is still used, it is kept on the books at its historical cost less its related amortization.

PRESENTATION, PERSPECTIVES, AND INTERNATIONAL COMPARISON

Presentation and Disclosure

Objective 11
Explain how property, plant, and equipment are reported and analyzed.

For each major category of property, plant, and equipment, disclosure is required of the following:

- the cost
- the accumulated amortization, including the amount of any write-downs
- the method of amortization and the amortization rate or period

In addition, disclosure is required of both of the following:

- the net book value of any property, plant, and equipment (including natural resources) that is not currently being amortized because it is under construction or development or because it has been removed from service for an extended period of time
- the amortization expense that has been recognized in the current period's income statement[20]

International Insight

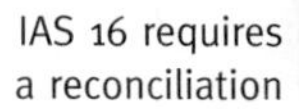

IAS 16 requires a reconciliation of the opening and closing balances in the capital asset accounts, disclosure of the assets' historical cost, and the change in any revaluation surplus.

The requirement for separate disclosure of both the cost and accumulated amortization gives financial statement readers more information than if only the net book value were disclosed. As an example, consider two companies, each having capital assets with a carrying amount of $100,000. The first company's assets cost $1 million and have accumulated amortization of $900,000 charged against them. The second company, on the other hand, has assets with a cost of $105,000, and accumulated amortization of $5,000. With the additional data, information is provided about the size of the original investment in property, plant, and equipment and its relative age. Information about amortization amounts and rates are important disclosures as this is generally the largest non-cash expense that is recognized by most enterprises.

[20] *CICA Handbook*, Section 3061.38 to .40.

General standards of financial statement presentation require entities to disclose whether any assets have been pledged as collateral for liabilities, and if so, what types of assets and to what extent.[21] As these long-lived assets are often used as security for debt instruments, such disclosures are common. Further, whenever a company has a **choice among alternative accounting policies**, the method that was chosen must be reported. Companies in the oil and gas industry, for example, disclose whether they follow the full cost or successful efforts method for their preproduction costs. Additional guidance on financial reporting in this industry is provided by CICA's Accounting Guideline 16 "Oil and Gas Accounting—Full Cost" and U.S. standards. These documents require disclosure about how the entity determines and disposes of costs related to development activities. Some of the most relevant information about natural resource companies is information about their estimated reserves, and whether they are proved or unproved. This information is generally reported as supplementary disclosures outside the summary financial statements.

Student Toolkit–Additional Disclosures

www.wiley.com/canada/kieso

Illustration 11-20 shows the disclosures underlying Canfor Corporation's property, plant, equipment, and timber of $2,211.1 million on its December 31, 2005, balance sheet, and amortization expense of $151.6 million reported on its 2005 income statement.

Illustration 11-20
Disclosures for Property, Plant, and Equipment

NOTES TO THE CONSOLIDATED FINANCIAL STATEMENTS

December 31, 2005

1. SIGNIFICANT ACCOUNTING POLICIES

PROPERTY, PLANT, EQUIPMENT AND TIMBER

Canfor capitalizes the costs of major replacements, extensions and improvements to plant and equipment, together with related interest incurred during the construction period on major projects.

Assets are amortized over the following estimated productive lives:

Buildings	10 to 50 years
Mobile equipment	3 to 20 years
Pulp and kraft paper machinery and equipment	20 years
Sawmill machinery and equipment	5 to 15 years
Oriented strand board machinery and equipment	20 years
Plywood machinery and equipment	5 to 15 years
Logging machinery and equipment	4 to 20 years
Logging roads and bridges	5 to 20 years
Other machinery and equipment	3 to 20 years

Amortization of logging and manufacturing assets is calculated on a unit of production basis. Amortization of plant and equipment not employed in logging and manufacturing is calculated on a straight-line basis. Logging roads are amortized on a basis related to the volume of timber harvested. For those tree farm licenses and timber licenses which are renewable with the Province of British Columbia, amounts capitalized as timber are amortized over the estimated tree growth cycle as volume is harvested. Non-renewable licenses are amortized over the period of the license.

6. PROPERTY, PLANT, EQUIPMENT AND TIMBER

	2005			2004		
(millions of dollars)	Cost	Accumulated Amortization	Net Book Value	Cost	Accumulated Amortization	Net Book Value
Land	$ 24.0	$ -	$ 24.0	$ 22.9	$ -	$ 22.9
Pulp and kraft paper mills	1,260.5	629.8	630.7	1,224.7	590.2	634.5
Sawmills, plywood and oriented strand board plants	1,027.1	338.2	688.9	837.0	315.2	521.8
Logging buildings and equipment	15.4	0.9	14.5	13.0	1.1	11.9
Logging roads and bridges	141.1	92.7	48.4	137.2	76.9	60.3
Other equipment and facilities	42.0	25.3	16.7	37.4	23.3	14.1
Timber	839.9	52.0	787.9	925.3	49.1	876.2
	$ 3,350.0	$ 1,138.9	$ 2,211.1	$ 3,197.5	$ 1,055.8	$ 2,141.7

Included in the above are assets under construction in the amount of $9.7 million (2004 – $85.6 million), which are not being amortized.

[21] *CICA Handbook*, Section 1400.14.

Perspectives

Because property, plant, and equipment and their amortization are so significant on most companies' balance sheets and income statements, it is important to understand the nature of these long-lived assets, and to ensure that management is generating an acceptable rate of return on the investment in them.

Amortization and Replacement of Assets

A common misconception about amortization is that it provides funds to replace capital assets. What makes amortization similar to any other expense is that it reduces net income, but what makes it different is that **it does not involve a current cash outflow**.

To illustrate why amortization does not provide funds for replacing plant assets, assume that a business starts operating with plant assets of $500,000 with a useful life of five years. The company's balance sheet at the beginning of the period is:

Plant assets	$500,000	Owners' equity	$500,000

Now if we assume the enterprise earns no revenue over the five years, the income statements are as follows:

	Year 1	Year 2	Year 3	Year 4	Year 5
Revenue	$ –0–	$ –0–	$ –0–	$ –0–	$ –0–
Amortization	(100,000)	(100,000)	(100,000)	(100,000)	(100,000)
Loss	$(100,000)	$(100,000)	$(100,000)	$(100,000)	$(100,000)

The balance sheet at the end of the five years is:

Plant assets	$–0–	Owners' equity	$–0–

This extreme example shows that amortization in no way provides funds to replace assets. **Funds for the replacement of assets come from new asset inflows represented by revenues** (which are generated through usage of the asset); without the revenues that generate receivables, and ultimately cash, no income is earned and no cash inflow results. If management wants to have a fund available for the replacement of assets, it has to make a separate decision and take steps to set aside cash to accumulate those funds.

Analysis of Property, Plant, and Equipment

Investors are interested in information that tells them how efficiently management uses the long-lived assets it has invested in. Incurring capital costs provides the company with a particular operating capacity and usually creates significant amounts of fixed costs far into the future.

Which ratios provide information about the usage of assets? Assets can be analyzed in terms of both activity (turnover) and profitability. How efficiently a company uses its assets to generate revenue is measured by the **asset turnover ratio**. This ratio is determined by dividing net revenue or sales by average total assets for the period. The resulting number represents the dollars of revenue or sales produced by each dollar invested in assets. **For a particular level of investment in assets, a company that generates more**

revenue per dollar of investment is more efficient and likely to be more profitable. While this may not remain true if the percentage profit on each dollar of revenue is lower than another company's, the asset turnover ratio is one of the key components of return on investment.

To illustrate, the following data will be used from the December 31, 2005, financial statements of H. Paulin & Co., a Canadian manufacturer and distributor of fasteners, fluid system products, automotive parts, and screw machine components. The asset turnover ratio is calculated in Illustration 11-21.

H. PAULIN & CO.
(in thousands)

Sales	$150,170
Total assets, December 31, 2005	92,481
Total assets, December 31, 2004	85,125
Net income	6,020

Illustration 11-21
Asset Turnover Ratio

$$\text{Asset turnover} = \frac{\text{Net revenue}}{\text{Average total assets}}$$

$$= \frac{\$150{,}170}{\dfrac{\$92{,}481 + \$85{,}125}{2}}$$

$$= 1.69$$

The asset turnover ratio shows that H. Paulin & Co. generated $1.69 revenue for each dollar of assets during the 2005 year.

Asset turnover ratios vary considerably among industries. For example, a power utility like TransAlta Corporation has a ratio of 0.36 times, and a grocery chain like Loblaw Companies Limited has a ratio of 2.08 times based on recent financial statements.

Using the profit margin ratio together with the asset turnover ratio makes it possible to determine another ratio, the rate of return earned on total assets. By using the H. Paulin & Co. data shown above, the profit margin ratio and the rate of return on total assets are calculated as in Illustration 11-22.

Illustration 11-22
Profit Margin

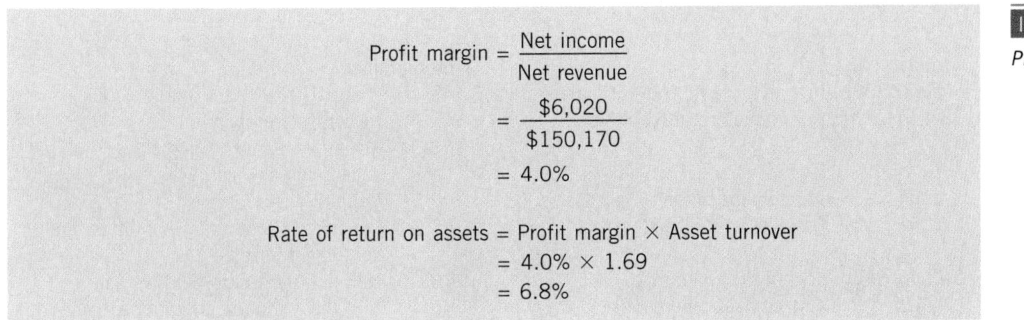

$$\text{Profit margin} = \frac{\text{Net income}}{\text{Net revenue}}$$

$$= \frac{\$6{,}020}{\$150{,}170}$$

$$= 4.0\%$$

$$\text{Rate of return on assets} = \text{Profit margin} \times \text{Asset turnover}$$

$$= 4.0\% \times 1.69$$

$$= 6.8\%$$

The profit margin indicates how much is left over from each sales dollar after all expenses are covered. In the H. Paulin & Co. example, a profit margin of 4.0% indicates that 4.0 cents of profit remained from each $1 of revenue generated. By combining the profit margin with the asset turnover, it is possible to determine the rate of return on assets for the period. This makes intuitive sense. The more revenue that is generated per dollar invested in assets, the better off the company is. Also, the more of each sales dollar that is profit, the better off the company should be. Combined, the ratio provides a measure of the profitability of the company's investment in assets. To the extent that long-lived assets make up a significant portion of total assets, fixed asset management has a definite effect on profitability.

The **rate of return on assets (ROA)** can be directly calculated by dividing net income by average total assets.[22] Continuing with the same example, Illustration 11-23 shows the calculation of this ratio.

Illustration 11-23
Rate of Return on Assets

$$\text{Rate of return on assets} = \frac{\text{Net income}}{\text{Average total assets}} = \frac{\$6,020}{\frac{\$92,481 + \$85,125}{2}} = 6.8\%$$

The 6.8% rate of return calculated in this way is the same as the 6.8% rate calculated by multiplying the profit margin by the asset turnover. The rate of return on assets is a good measure of profitability because it combines the effects of cost control (profit margin) and asset management (asset turnover).

Care must be taken in interpreting the numbers, however. A manager who is interested in reporting a high return on assets ratio can achieve this in the short run by not investing in new plant and equipment and by holding back on expenditures such as those for research and development and employee training—decisions that will result in lower long-term corporate value. In the short run, the result is a higher return on investment because the net income number (the numerator) will be higher and the total asset number (the denominator) lower.

Canadian GAAP and International Accounting Standards—A Comparison

Objective 12
Compare current Canadian and international GAAP.

With a few important exceptions, international standards for property, plant, and equipment are similar to those required by the Accounting Standards Board. Illustration 11-24 identifies the major AcSB standards and the corresponding IASB document.

Illustration 11-24
Primary Sources of GAAP

Canada	International
Section 3061: Property, plant, and equipment Section 3831: Non-monetary transactions	IAS 16: Property, plant, and equipment IAS 40: Investment property SIC-31: Revenue—barter transactions involving advertising services
Section 3063: Impairment of long-lived assets	IAS 36: Impairment of assets
Section 3110: Asset retirement obligations	IAS 37: Provisions, contingent liabilities, and contingent assets
Section 3475: Long-lived assets and discontinued operations	IFRS 5: Non-current assets held for sale and discontinued operations
Section 3800: Government assistance	IAS 20: Accounting for government grants and disclosure of government assistance

[22] A more sophisticated calculation adds back the after-tax interest expense to net income so that the results are not skewed by how the assets are financed. The ratio can then be used more legitimately for intercompany comparisons.

Section 3850: Interest capitalized—disclosure considerations	IAS 23: Borrowing costs
EIC-126: Accounting by mining enterprises for exploration costs AcG-16: Oil and gas accounting—full cost AcG-11: Enterprises in the development stage	IFRS 6: Exploration for and evaluation of mineral resources

The following are significant differences between the current Canadian and international standards:

Fair values permitted. Unlike Section 3061, IAS 16 permits classes of property, plant, and equipment to be revalued to their fair value after acquisition, with changes in value recognized directly in a revaluation surplus account, which is part of shareholders' equity. Amortization is then based on the revalued amount, with the portion associated with the revaluation amount charged against the revaluation surplus instead of income.

There is no separate Canadian standard, apart from Section 3061, that deals with land and/or buildings that are held to earn rentals or for capital appreciation, or both. The IASB, however, has a separate standard (IAS 40) that applies specifically to such assets. IAS 40 permits a fair value measurement model for all investment property, but unlike IAS 16, the changes in fair value are recognized in income rather than a revaluation surplus account.

The AcSB does not expect that there will be convergence with the international standards for these differences until the changeover date, expected to be in 2011.

Impairment. IAS 36 is different from Canadian impairment standards in two major ways. First, under the international standard, the recoverable amount is defined only in terms of fair values and discounted cash flows. There is no recoverability test that uses undiscounted cash flows. The impairment loss is defined as the greater of the difference between the carrying amount and the asset's fair value less disposal costs, or the carrying amount and the present value of the cash flows from use and eventual disposal. Secondly, IAS 36 requires an impairment loss to be reversed when there is a change in any of the estimates that are used to determine the asset's recoverable amount.

The FASB's existing standards are similar to those in Canada. With the FASB and IASB working toward convergence between their requirements, it is unlikely there will be a change in Canada until agreement is reached. This may not happen until close to the changeover date.

Extractive industries. The Canadian standards for companies in the mining and oil and gas industries generally fall under the general requirements of Section 3061 for other property, plant, and equipment. This is not the case internationally where IFRS 6 allows exemptions from its basic requirements in developing an accounting policy for exploration and evaluation assets. The IASB is in the midst of a comprehensive project to research and develop appropriate standards, including the feasibility of a fair value model for such resources. It appears that any changes to Canadian requirements will not occur until close to the changeover date.

Interest costs. IAS 23 has recently been amended to bring the international standard closer to the FASB's requirements.[23] Thus, borrowing costs that can be attributed directly to the acquisition, construction, or production of a qualifying asset must now be capitalized, rather than expensed as they are incurred. The Canadian option of capitalization or expensing is likely to be changed to the international standard on the changeover date.

---

[23] See the introduction to Appendix 10A for differences between the FASB and IFRS requirements in applying this converged approach.

Government assistance. In early 2007, Canadian and international standards on accounting for government assistance are very similar. The IASB, however, is working on a project to reconsider key aspects of IAS 20 and converge its requirements with those of the FASB. Changes that result from this project are likely to cause GAAP differences with the Canadian standard. The project was delayed in 2006 as a result of work on other related projects and, in early 2007, the IASB was expecting a revised IFRS to be issued in 2008. The initial AcSB plan was to adopt the revised IFRS at the changeover date, but it may require earlier convergence.

Non-monetary transactions. The requirements for non-monetary exchanges are very similar, with both sets of standards requiring a fair value measure for exchanges with commercial substance. The IFRS, however, do not specifically cover non-reciprocal transfers. Canadian standards, on the other hand, do not explicitly address barter transactions involving advertising services.

Glossary

www.wiley.com/canada/kieso

Summary of Learning Objectives

1 Explain the concept of amortization.

Amortization is the accounting process of allocating the cost of long-lived assets in a systematic and rational manner to the periods that are expected to benefit from the use of the asset. It is not a process of adjusting assets to their fair values. Amortization is a generic term. The allocation of the cost of intangible capital assets is termed "amortization" as well, while that of property, plant, and equipment is usually referred to as "depreciation." The allocation of capitalized costs of natural resources is termed "depletion."

2 Identify and explain the factors to consider when determining amortization charges.

Three factors involved in determining amortization expense are (1) the amount to be amortized (amortizable amount), (2) the estimated useful life, and (3) the pattern and method of cost allocation to be used.

3 Calculate amortization charges using the activity, straight-line, and decreasing charge methods and compare the methods.

The activity method assumes that the benefits provided by the asset are a function of use or productivity instead of the passage of time. The asset's life is considered in terms of either the output that it provides or an input measure, such as the number of hours it works. The amortization charge per unit of activity (cost less residual value divided by estimated total units of output or input) is determined and multiplied by the units of activity produced or consumed in a period to determine the amortization expense for the period. The straight-line method assumes that an asset provides its benefits as a function of time. As such, cost less residual value is divided by the useful life to determine the amortization expense per period. The straight-line procedure is the most conceptually appropriate when the decline in usefulness is constant from period to period. The decreasing charge method provides for a higher amortization charge in the early years and lower charges in later periods. For this method, a constant rate (e.g., double the straight-line rate) is multiplied by the net book value (cost less accumulated amortization) at the start of the period to determine each period's amortization expense. The main justification for this approach is that the asset provides more benefits in the earlier periods.

KEY TERMS

4 Explain the accounting procedures for depletion of natural resources.

After the depletion base has been established through accounting decisions related to the acquisition, exploration, and development costs of natural resources, these costs are allocated to the natural resources that have been removed. Depletion is normally calculated using the units-of-production method. In this approach, the natural resource's total cost less residual value, if any, is divided by the number of units that are estimated to be in the resource deposit, to obtain a cost per unit of product. The cost per unit is then multiplied by the number of units withdrawn in the period to calculate the depletion expense. Depletion expense is usually added to the cost of the inventory of product removed, similar to the raw material costs incurred in a statement of cost of goods manufactured.

5 Explain the need for special amortization methods and how to apply them.

Two special depreciation methods are the group and composite methods, and hybrid or combination methods. The term "group" refers to a collection of assets that are similar in nature, while "composite" refers to a collection of assets that are dissimilar in nature. The group and composite methods develop one average rate of amortization for all the assets involved and apply this rate as if they were a single asset. The hybrid or combination methods develop an amortization expense that is based on two or more approaches and that suits the specific circumstances of the assets.

6 Identify how amortization methods are selected.

The method chosen should ideally amortize an asset in a pattern and at a rate that correspond to the benefits received from that asset. The accountant uses judgement when selecting and implementing the method that is most appropriate for the circumstances. Tax reporting, simplicity, perceived economic consequences, and impact on ratios are also factors that influence such judgements in practice.

7 Explain and apply the accounting procedures for a change in amortization rate.

Because all the variables in determining amortization are estimates—with the exception, perhaps, of the asset's original cost—it is common for a change in those estimates to result in a change in the depreciation rate. When this or a change in the pattern of asset benefits provided occurs, there is no retroactive change and no catch-up adjustment. The change is accounted for in the current and future periods.

8 Explain the issues and apply the accounting standards for capital asset impairment.

The process to determine an impairment loss is as follows: (1) Review events and changes in circumstances for possible impairment. (2) If events or changes suggest impairment, determine if the sum of the undiscounted expected future net cash flows from the long-lived asset is less than the asset's carrying amount. (3) If it is less, determine the impairment loss by measuring the difference between the asset's carrying amount and its fair value. For assets held for use, the reduced carrying amount of the long-lived asset is considered its new cost basis and no subsequent recovery in value is recognized. Assets to be disposed of other than by sale continue to be classified as held for use, and are amortized until they are disposed of. The same impairment test is then applied and no subsequent increases in value are permitted.

9 Explain and apply the accounting standards for long-lived assets that will be disposed of through sale.

Assets to be disposed of through sale are no longer amortized, but instead are remeasured to their fair value less selling costs at each balance sheet date. Recoveries in

residual value, 639
salvage value, 640
sinking fund method, 645
straight-line method, 643
sum-of-the-years'-digits method, 644
supersession, 641
useful life, 640

value may be recognized to the extent of previous losses. Held for sale items of property, plant, and equipment are separately reported in long-term assets, unless they are to be sold before the financial statements are prepared. In this case, if they otherwise meet the definition of current assets, they are reported in this category.

10 Describe and apply the accounting for the disposal of property, plant, and equipment.

If long-term assets are held and used, amortization continues up to the date of disposal, and then all accounts related to the retired asset are removed from the books. Gains and losses from the disposal of plant assets are shown on the income statement in income before discontinued operations, unless the conditions for reporting as a discontinued operation are met. Gains or losses on involuntary conversions may meet the definition of an extraordinary item. For property, plant, and equipment donated to an organization outside the reporting entity, the donation is reported at its fair value with a gain or loss recognized.

11 Explain how property, plant, and equipment are reported and analyzed.

Wherever there is a choice of accounting methods, the accounting methods applied are reported. Any liability secured by property, plant, equipment, and natural resources is disclosed. Both the assets' carrying value and accumulated amortization are reported. Companies that have significant oil and gas producing activities must provide special additional disclosures about these activities. Analysis may be performed to evaluate the efficiency of use of a company's investment in assets through the calculation and interpretation of the asset turnover rate, the profit margin, and the rate of return on assets.

12 Compare current Canadian and international GAAP.

In most major ways, international and Canadian accounting standards for property, plant, and equipment are similar. Significant differences do exist, however. The differences relate to the IASB option to use fair value measurements for property, plant, and equipment and investment properties; a difference in determining whether an asset is impaired, how the impairment is measured, and the ability to recognize recoveries in value; the standards associated with exploration and evaluation costs in extractive industries; interest capitalization; accounting for government assistance; and non-monetary transactions.

Appendix 11A

AMORTIZATION AND INCOME TAX

Capital Cost Allowance Method

13 Objective
Calculate capital cost allowance in straightforward situations.

For the most part, issues related to the calculation of income taxes are not discussed in a financial accounting course. However, because the concepts of tax depreciation are similar to those of amortization for financial reporting purposes and because the tax method is sometimes adopted for book purposes, an overview of this subject is presented here.

Canadian businesses use the capital cost allowance method to determine amortization in calculating their taxable income and the tax value of assets, regardless of the method that they use for financial reporting purposes. Because companies use this method for tax purposes, some—particularly small businesses—also use it for financial reporting, judging that the benefits of keeping two sets of records, one for financial reporting and one for tax purposes, are less than the costs of doing this.[24] While keeping only one set of records may be expedient, it may not provide a rational allocation of costs in the financial statements. Therefore, many companies keep a record of capital cost allowance for tax purposes and use another method to determine amortization for financial reporting purposes.

The way that the capital cost allowance method works is similar to the declining-balance method covered in the chapter, except for the following:

1. Instead of being labelled amortization or depreciation expense, it is called **capital cost allowance (CCA)**.

2. The *Income Tax Act* (*Income Tax Regulations, Schedule II*) specifies the rate to be used for an asset class. This rate is called the capital cost allowance (CCA) rate. The *Income Tax Act* identifies several different classes of assets and the maximum CCA rate for each class. To determine which class a particular asset falls into, it is necessary to examine the definition of each asset class and the examples given in the Act. Illustration 11A-1 provides examples of various CCA classes, the maximum rate for each, and the types of assets it includes.

Illustration 11A-1
Examples of CCA Classes

Class	Rate	Examples of Assets Included in the Class
1	4%	a bridge, canal, or building, including component parts such as plumbing, elevators, sprinkler systems, etc.
4	6%	railway, tramway, or trolley bus system
6	10%	frame, log, stucco on frame, galvanized iron, or corrugated metal building; greenhouse; oil or water storage tank
8	20%	manufacturing or processing machinery or equipment not included in other specified classes
10	30%	automotive equipment, contractor's movable equipment, including portable camp buildings, processing equipment
16	40%	taxicab, coin-operated video game
33	15%	timber resource property
42	12%	fibre optic cable

Source: Excerpts from Schedule II of the *Income Tax Regulations*

[24] The widespread availability of accounting software capable of maintaining detailed records for property, plant, and equipment, the related amortization expense, and accumulated amortization under a variety of methods has significantly reduced the cost of record keeping and the possibility of errors.

3. CCA is determined separately for each asset class and can be claimed only on year-end amounts in each class. Assuming there have been no net additions (purchases less disposals, if any) to a class during a year, the maximum CCA allowed is the undepreciated capital cost (UCC) at year end multiplied by the CCA rate for the class. In a year when there is a net addition (regardless of when it occurs), the maximum CCA on the net addition is one-half of the allowed CCA rate multiplied by the amount of the net addition. This is usually referred to as the **half-year rule**. The CCA for the net addition plus the CCA on the remaining UCC is the total CCA for the asset class. If there is only one asset in a class, the maximum CCA allowed in the acquisition year is the acquisition cost multiplied by one-half of the CCA rate, even if the asset was purchased one week before year end. No CCA is allowed in the year of disposal for this single asset, even if it was sold just before year end.
4. The government, through the *Income Tax Act*, requires that any benefits that a company receives from government grants and investment tax credits for the purpose of acquiring a capital asset reduce the cost basis of the capital asset for tax purposes. For investment tax credits, the capital cost of the asset and the UCC of the class of asset are reduced in the taxation year following the year of acquisition.
5. CCA can be taken even if it results in a UCC balance that is less than the estimated residual value.
6. Companies are not required to take the maximum rate, or even any CCA, in a particular year, although they normally would as long as they have taxable income. If a company takes less than the maximum CCA in a specific year, it cannot add the remainder to the amount it is claiming in a subsequent year. In every year, the maximum that can be claimed is limited to the UCC times the specified capital cost allowance rate.

To illustrate amortization calculations under the CCA system, assume the following facts for a company's March 28, 2007, acquisition of manufacturing equipment, its only asset in the particular CCA class:

Cost of equipment	$500,000	CCA class	Class 8
Estimated useful life	10 years	CCA rate for Class 8	20%
Estimated residual value	$30,000		

Illustration 11A-2 shows the calculations that are necessary to determine the CCA for the first three years and the UCC at the end of each of the three years.[25]

Illustration 11A-2
CCA Schedule for Equipment

Class 8—20%	CCA	UCC
January 1, 2007		0
Additions during 2007		
Cost of new asset acquisition		$500,000
Disposals during 2007		0
CCA 2007: $500,000 × 1/2 × 20%	$50,000	(50,000)
December 31, 2007		**$450,000**
Additions less disposals, 2008		0
		$450,000

[25] CCA is subject to rules set by government legislation and can therefore change from time to time. Furthermore, various provincial governments can have different rules with regard to determining CCA for purposes of calculating the income on which provincial taxes are based. The examples in this chapter are based on the federal *Income Tax Act* for 2006.

CCA, 2008: $450,000 × 20%	$90,000	(90,000)
December 31, 2008		**$360,000**
Additions less disposals, 2009		0
		$360,000
CCA, 2009: $360,000 × 20%	$72,000	(72,000)
December 31, 2009		**$288,000**

The **undepreciated capital cost (UCC)** at any point in time is known as the capital asset's **tax value**. Note that the capital asset's carrying amount (or net book value) on the balance sheet will be different from its tax value as long as the entity's chosen method of amortization for financial reporting is not the tax method. The significance of this difference to financial reporting is explained in Chapter 18.

Illustration 11A-3 is a continuation of Illustration 11A-2. It incorporates the following complexities:

1. In 2010, the company bought another Class 8 asset for $700,000.
2. In 2011, the company sold for $300,000 the equipment that it purchased in 2007.
3. In 2012, the company sold the remaining Class 8 asset for $500,000. This resulted in no assets remaining in Class 8.

Illustration 11A-3

CCA Schedule for Class 8

Class 8—20%		CCA	UCC
December 31, 2009			**$288,000**
Additions less disposals, 2010			
Cost of new asset			700,000
			$988,000
CCA, 2010			
$288,000 × 20% =	$57,600		
$700,000 × 1/2 × 20% =	70,000	$127,600	(127,600)
December 31, 2010			**$860,400**
Additions less disposals, 2011			
Manufacturing equipment purchased in 2007 (lesser of original cost of $500,000 and proceeds of disposal of $300,000)			(300,000)
			$560,400
CCA, 2011: $560,400 × 20% =		$112,080	(112,080)
December 31, 2011			**$448,320**
Additions less disposals, 2012			
2010 asset acquisition (lesser of original cost of $700,000 and proceeds of disposal of $500,000)			(500,000)
			$ (51,680)
Recaptured CCA, 2012		$ (51,680)	51,680
December 31, 2012			$ 0

Additions to Asset Class

The purchase of another Class 8 asset in 2010 resulted in a **net addition** of $700,000 to the undepreciated capital cost at the end of 2010. Consequently, the balance of the UCC at the end of 2010 prior to determining CCA for the year is made up of this $700,000 plus the $288,000 UCC of the original equipment. The capital cost allowance for 2010 is therefore 20% of $288,000 ($57,600) plus one-half of 20% of the net addition of $700,000 ($70,000) for a total of $127,600.

If a government grant of $35,000 had been received in 2010 to help finance the acquisition of this asset, the addition in 2010 would be reported net of the government grant—i.e., at $700,000 − $35,000 = $665,000. If the 2010 acquisition were eligible instead for an investment tax credit (ITC) of $35,000, the tax legislation specifies that the ITC should reduce the asset's capital cost and the UCC of the class of assets **in the year following** the year of acquisition.[26] Assuming the Class 8 asset acquired in 2010 in Illustration 11A-3 was eligible for a $35,000 ITC, the $700,000 addition is recognized in 2010, and the UCC is reduced by the $35,000 ITC in 2011 along with the $300,000 proceeds on the original manufacturing equipment. The CCA claimed in 2011 is reduced accordingly.

Retirements from an Asset Class, Continuation of Class

While the CCA class is increased by the cost of additions, it is usually reduced **by the proceeds on the asset's disposal**, not by the asset's cost. However, if the proceeds on disposal are greater than the asset's original capital cost, the class is reduced by the cost only. There is a good reason for this. If the proceeds on disposal are greater than the original cost, there is a capital gain on the disposal. Capital gains are taxed separately from ordinary business income in the tax system; thus, the portion that is a capital gain must be identified as being that. This leaves only the cost to be deducted from the CCA class. It is not common for depreciable assets to be sold at amounts in excess of their cost, but when this does occur it is important to separate out the portion that is a capital gain.

In 2011, the original manufacturing equipment is sold for $300,000. Since this is less than its $500,000 capital cost, there is no capital gain on disposal. Therefore, Class 8 is reduced by the proceeds on disposal of $300,000, and the CCA for the year is calculated on the remaining balance in the class.

Retirements from an Asset Class, Elimination of Class

When an asset's disposal eliminates the asset class, either because there are no more assets remaining in the class or because the disposal results in the elimination of the UCC balance of the class, the following may result:

1. There may be a recapture of capital cost allowance, with or without a capital gain.
2. There may be a terminal loss, with or without a capital gain. This occurs only when the last asset in the class is disposed of and an undepreciated capital cost balance still exists in the class after deducting the appropriate amount on the asset disposal.

The amount of proceeds, the asset's original cost, and the balance of the undepreciated capital cost for the class must be examined to determine which of these results occurs.

A **recapture** of capital cost allowance occurs when, after deducting the appropriate amount from the class on disposal of an asset, a negative amount is left as the UCC balance. The negative balance is the amount of CCA that must be recaptured and included in the calculation of taxable income in the year, and is taxed at the normal income tax rates. In effect, when this situation occurs, it suggests that too much CCA was deducted throughout the lives of the assets, and the taxing of the recaptured capital cost allowance therefore adjusts for this. This is what occurred in 2012 in our example. When the proceeds of disposal were deducted from the UCC, the UCC became negative. The excess of $51,680 is therefore included in taxable income in 2012.

---

[26] The rationale is that the ITC is not calculated until after the company's year end, when the tax return is completed and filed.

As indicated above, if an asset is sold for more than its cost, a **capital gain** results. This may occur whether or not the class is eliminated. For tax purposes, a capital gain is treated differently from a recapture of capital cost allowance. Essentially, the **taxable** capital gain (i.e., the amount subject to tax) is only a portion of the capital gain as defined above.[27] The taxable capital gain is included with other taxable income.

If the Class 8 asset purchased in 2010 had been sold in 2012 for $750,000, a capital gain and a recapture of capital cost allowance would have resulted. The capital gain would be $50,000, but only 50% or $25,000 would be the taxable capital gain. In this case, Class 8 would be reduced by $700,000 and the recapture would be $251,680 ($700,000 less the $448,320 UCC).

A **terminal loss** occurs when a positive balance remains in the class after the appropriate reduction is made to the CCA class from the disposal of the last asset. This remaining balance is a terminal loss that is deductible in full when calculating taxable income for the period. If the remaining equipment had been sold in 2012 for $300,000, a terminal loss of $148,320 would have resulted (the UCC of $448,320 less the $300,000 proceeds).

This example illustrating the basic calculations of capital gains, taxable capital gains, recaptured capital cost allowance, and terminal losses has necessarily been oversimplified. In essence, the tax rate on taxable capital gains is specified by tax law, which may change from time to time and have implications in terms of other considerations (e.g., a refundable dividend tax on hand). Similarly, the tax rate that applies to recaptured CCA is affected by the particular circumstances of the type of taxable income that is being reported, of which the recaptured amount is a component. These and other technical aspects, including definitions, are beyond the scope of this text. The reader is warned that specialist knowledge of tax laws is often required to determine income taxes payable.

International Insight

In Switzerland, amortization in the financial statements is the same as that on the tax returns. As a consequence, companies may amortize as much as 80 percent of the cost of assets in the first year.

Summary of Learning Objective for Appendix 11A

13 Calculate capital cost allowance in straightforward situations.

Capital cost allowance is the term used for amortization when calculating taxable income in income tax returns. The mechanics of the CCA method are similar to those of the declining-balance method except that rates are specified for asset classes and the amount claimed is based on year-end balances. The half-year rule is applied to net additions in the year, which means that only 50% of the normal rate is permitted. For an asset class, retirements are accounted for under specific rules that govern the determination of taxable income. Capital gains will occur if the proceeds on disposal exceed the asset's original cost. When an asset class is eliminated, a terminal loss or recapture of capital cost allowance can occur. When a CCA class ends in a negative balance, a recapture of CCA occurs.

Glossary

www.wiley.com/canada/kieso

KEY TERMS

capital cost allowance (CCA), 671
capital cost allowance method, 671
capital gain, 675
half-year rule, 672
net addition, 673
recapture, 674
tax value, 673
terminal loss, 675
undepreciated capital cost (UCC), 673

[27] The percentage of the capital gain that is taxable has varied in recent years. In 2006, the inclusion rate—the portion taxable—was 50%.

Note: All assignment material with an asterisk (*) relates to the appendix to the chapter.

Brief Exercises

(LO 3) **BE11-1** Castle Corporation purchased a truck at the beginning of 2008 for $54,000. The truck is estimated to have a residual value of $2,000 and a useful life of 250,000 kilometres. It was driven 43,000 kilometres in 2008 and 60,000 kilometres in 2009. Calculate amortization expense for 2008 and 2009.

(LO 3, 6) **BE11-2** Cheetah Ltd. purchased machinery on January 1, 2008, for $70,000. The machinery is estimated to have a residual value of $6,000 after a useful life of eight years. (a) Calculate the 2008 amortization expense using the straight-line method. (b) Calculate the 2008 amortization expense using the straight-line method, but assuming the machinery was purchased on September 1, 2008.

(LO 3, 6) **BE11-3** Use the information for Cheetah Ltd. in BE11-2. (a) Calculate the 2008 amortization expense using the sum-of-the-years'-digits method. (b) Calculate the 2008 amortization expense using the sum-of-the-years'-digits method, but assuming the machinery was purchased on April 1, 2008.

(LO 3, 6) **BE11-4** Use the information for Cheetah Ltd. in BE11-2. (a) Calculate the 2008 amortization expense using the double-declining-balance method. (b) Calculate the 2008 amortization expense using the double-declining-balance method, but assuming the machinery was purchased on October 1, 2008.

(LO 2) **BE11-5** Garfield Corp. purchased a machine on July 1, 2007, for $25,000. Garfield paid $200 in title fees and a legal fee of $125 related to the machine. In addition, Garfield paid $500 of shipping charges for delivery, and $475 was paid to a local contractor to build and wire a platform for the machine on the plant floor. The machine has an estimated useful life of six years and residual value of $3,000. Determine the amortizable amount of Garfield's new machine. Garfield uses straight-line amortization.

(LO 4) **BE11-6** Khan Corporation acquires a coal mine at a cost of $400,000. Capitalized development costs total $100,000. After the mine is exhausted, $75,000 will be spent to restore the property, after which it can be sold for $160,000. Khan estimates that 4,000 tonnes of coal can be extracted. Assuming that 700 tonnes are extracted in the first year, prepare the journal entry to record depletion.

(LO 5) **BE11-7** Battlesport Inc. owns the following assets:

Asset	Cost	Residual Value	Estimated Useful Life
A	$70,000	$17,000	10 years
B	50,000	10,000	15 years
C	82,000	14,000	12 years

Calculate the composite amortization rate and the composite life of Battlesport's assets.

(LO 7) **BE11-8** Mystic Limited purchased a computer for $7,000 on January 1, 2007. Straight-line amortization is used for the computer, based on a five-year life and $1,000 residual value. In 2009, the estimates are revised. Mystic now feels the computer will be used until December 31, 2010, when it can be sold for $500. Calculate the 2009 amortization.

(LO 8) **BE11-9** Dinoland Corp. owns machinery that cost $900,000 and has accumulated amortization of $360,000. The expected future net cash flows from the use of the asset are expected to be $500,000. The equipment's fair value is $400,000. Prepare the journal entry, if any, to record the impairment loss.

(LO 8) **BE11-10** Use the information for Dinoland Corp. given in BE11-9. By the end of the following year, the machinery's fair value has increased to $490,000. Assuming the machinery continues to be used in production, prepare the journal entry required, if any, to record the increase in its fair value.

(LO 10) **BE11-11** Simcoe City Corporation owns machinery that cost $20,000 when purchased on January 1, 2005. Amortization has been recorded at a rate of $3,000 per year, resulting in a balance in accumulated amortization of $9,000 at December 31, 2007. The machinery is sold on September 1, 2008, for $10,500. Prepare journal entries to (a) update amortization for 2008 and (b) record the sale.

(LO 10) **BE11-12** Use the information presented for Simcoe City Corporation in BE11-11, but assume the machinery is sold for $5,200 instead of $10,500. Prepare journal entries to (a) update amortization for 2008 and (b) record the sale.

BE11-13 In its 2005 annual report, Ortiz Limited reports beginning-of-the-year total assets of U.S. $1,923 million, end-of-the-year total assets of U.S. $2,487 million, total revenue of U.S. $2,687 million, and net income of U.S. $52 million. (a) Calculate Ortiz's asset turnover ratio. (b) Calculate Ortiz's profit margin. (c) Calculate Ortiz's rate of return on assets, (1) using the asset turnover and profit margin, and (2) using net income. **(LO 11)**

***BE11-14** Timecap Limited purchased an asset at a cost of $54,000 on March 1, 2008. The asset has a useful life of eight years and an estimated residual value of $4,000. For tax purposes, the asset belongs in CCA Class 8, with a rate of 20%. Calculate the CCA for each year, 2008 to 2011, assuming this is the only asset in Class 8. **(LO 13)**

Exercises

E11-1 **(Match Amortization Method with Assets)** The following assets have been acquired by various companies over the past year: **(LO 1, 6)**

1. Boardroom table and chairs for a corporate head office
2. Dental equipment in a new dental clinic
3. Long-haul trucks for a trucking business
4. Weight and aerobic equipment in a new health club facility
5. Classroom computers in a new community college

Instructions

For each long-lived asset listed above, (a) identify the factors to consider in establishing the useful life of the asset, and (b) recommend the pattern of amortization that most closely represents the pattern of economic benefits received by the entity that owns the asset, and defend your position.

E11-2 **(Terminology, Calculations—SL, DDB)** Shih-Shan Corp. acquired a property on September 15, 2007, for $235,000, paying $2,000 in transfer taxes and a $1,500 real estate fee. Based on the provincial assessment information, 75% of the property's value was related to the building and 25% to the land. It is estimated that the building, with proper maintenance, will last for 35 years, at which time it will be torn down. Shih-Shan, however, expects to use it for 10 years only as it is not expected to suit the company's purposes after that. The company should be able to sell the property for $95,000 at that time, with $40,000 of this amount being for the land. **(LO 2, 3, 6)**

Instructions

Assuming a December 31 year end, identify all of the following:

(a) the building's cost
(b) the building's amortizable amount
(c) the building's useful life
(d) amortization expense for 2007, assuming the straight-line method
(e) amortization expense for 2008, assuming the double-declining-balance method
(f) the building's carrying amount at December 31, 2008, assuming the double-declining-balance method

E11-3 **(Amortization Calculations—SL, DDB)** Deluxe Company Ltd. purchases equipment on January 1, 2008, at a cost of $469,000. The asset is expected to have a service life of 12 years and a residual value of $40,000. **(LO 3)**

Instructions

(a) Calculate the amount of amortization for each of 2008, 2009, and 2010 using the straight-line method.
(b) Calculate the amount of amortization for each of 2008, 2009, and 2010 using the double-declining-balance method. (In performing your calculations, round percentages to the nearest one-hundredth and round answers to the nearest dollar.)

E11-4 **(Amortization—Conceptual Understanding)** Chesley Company Ltd. acquired a plant asset at the beginning of Year 1. The asset has an estimated service life of five years. An employee has prepared amortization schedules for this asset using two different methods to compare the results of using one method with the results of using the other. Assume that the following schedules have been correctly prepared for this asset using (1) the straight-line method and (2) the double-declining-balance method. **(LO 3)**

Year	Straight-line	Double-Declining-Balance
1	$12,000	$30,000
2	12,000	18,000
3	12,000	10,800
4	12,000	1,200
5	12,000	0
Total	$60,000	$60,000

Instructions
Answer the following questions.

(a) What is the cost of the asset that is being amortized?

(b) What amount, if any, was used in the amortization calculations for the residual value for this asset?

(c) Which method will produce the higher net income in Year 1?

(d) Which method will produce the higher charge to income in Year 4?

(e) Which method will produce the higher book value for the asset at the end of Year 3?

(f) Which method will produce the higher cash flow in Year 1? In Year 4?

(g) If the asset is sold at the end of Year 3, which method would yield the higher gain (or lower loss) on disposal of the asset?

(LO 3, 6) E11-5 **(Amortization Calculations—SL, DDB; Partial Periods)** Judds Corporation purchased a new plant asset on April 1, 2008, at a cost of $841,000. It was estimated to have a service life of 20 years and a residual value of $67,280. Judds' accounting period is the calendar year.

Instructions

(a) Calculate the amortization for this asset for 2008 and 2009 using the straight-line method.

(b) Calculate the amortization for this asset for 2008 and 2009 using the double-declining-balance method.

(LO 3, 6, 13) E11-6 **(Amortization Calculations—Four Methods; Partial Periods)** Parish Corporation purchased a new machine for its assembly process on August 1, 2008. The cost of this machine was $127,900. The company estimated that the machine will have a trade-in value of $14,069 at the end of its service life. Its useful life was estimated to be five years and its working hours were estimated to be 21,000 hours. Parish's year end is December 31.

Instructions
Calculate the amortization expense under each of the following:

(a) straight-line amortization for 2008

(b) the activity method for 2008, assuming that machine usage was 800 hours

(c) the double-declining-balance method for 2009

*__(d)__ the capital cost allowance method for 2008 and 2009 using a CCA rate of 25%

(LO 3, 6) E11-7 **(Amortization Calculations—Five Methods)** Seceda Furnace Corp. purchased machinery for $315,000 on May 1, 2007. It is estimated that it will have a useful life of 10 years, residual value of $15,000, production of 240,000 units, and 25,000 working hours. During 2008, Seceda Corp. uses the machinery for 2,650 hours and the machinery produces 25,500 units.

Instructions
From the information given, calculate the amortization charge for 2008 under each of the following methods, assuming Seceda has a December 31 year end. (Round to three decimal places.)

(a) Straight-line

(b) Units-of-output

(c) Working hours

(d) Declining-balance, using a 20% rate

(e) Sum-of-the-years'-digits

E11-8 (Different Methods of Amortization) Jackson Industries Ltd. presents you with the following information: **(LO 3, 6)**

Description	Date Purchased	Cost	Residual Value	Life in Years	Amortization Method	Accumulated Amortization to Dec. 31, 2007	Amortization for 2008
Machine A	Dec. 2, 2006	$142,500	$16,000	10	(a)	$39,900	(b)
Machine B	Aug. 15, 2005	(c)	21,000	5	SL	29,000	(d)
Machine C	July 21, 2004	75,400	23,500	8	DDB	(e)	(f)

Instructions

Complete the table for the year ended December 31, 2008. The company amortizes all assets for a half-year in the year of acquisition and the year of disposal.

E11-9 (Amortization for Fractional Periods) On March 10, 2009, Lotus Limited sold equipment that it purchased for $192,000 on August 20, 2002. It was originally estimated that the equipment would have a life of 12 years and a residual value of $16,800 at the end of that time, and amortization has been calculated on that basis. The company uses the straight-line method of amortization. **(LO 6)**

Instructions

(a) Calculate the amortization charge on this equipment for 2002 and for 2009, and the total charge for the period from 2003 to 2008, inclusive, under each of the following six assumptions for partial periods:

1. Amortization is calculated for the exact period of time during which the asset is owned. (Use 365 days for your base.)
2. Amortization is calculated for the full year on the January 1 balance in the asset account.
3. Amortization is calculated for the full year on the December 31 balance in the asset account.
4. Amortization for a half-year is charged on plant assets that are acquired or disposed of during the year.
5. Amortization is calculated on additions from the beginning of the month following their acquisition and on disposals to the beginning of the month following the disposal.
6. Amortization is calculated for a full period on all assets in use for over a half-year, and no amortization is charged on assets in use for less than a half-year. (Use 365 days for your base.)

(b) Briefly evaluate the above methods in terms of basic accounting theory and how simple they are to apply.

E11-10 (Depletion Calculations—Timber) Stanislaw Timber Inc. owns 9,000 hectares of timberland purchased in 1996 at a cost of $1,400 per hectare. At the time of purchase, the land without the timber was valued at $420 per hectare. In 1997, Stanislaw built fire lanes and roads, with a life of 30 years, at a cost of $84,000 and separately capitalized these costs. Every year, Stanislaw sprays to prevent disease at a cost of $3,000 per year and spends $7,000 to maintain the fire lanes and roads. During 1998, Stanislaw selectively logged and sold 700,000 cubic metres of the estimated 3.5 million cubic metres of timber. In 1999, Stanislaw planted new seedlings to replace the cut trees at a cost of $100,000. **(LO 4)**

Instructions

(a) Determine the depletion charge and the portion of depletion included in the cost of timber sold for 1998.

(b) Stanislaw has not logged since 1998. Assuming that Stanislaw logged and sold 900,000 cubic metres of timber in 2009, and the timber cruise (i.e., the appraiser) had estimated a total resource of 5 million cubic metres, determine the cost of timber sold that relates to the depletion for 2009.

(c) How would Stanislaw account for the maintenance costs of the fire lanes and roads and the spraying of the timberland?

(d) Discuss the amortization methods that Stanislaw could use to amortize the cost of the fire lanes and roads.

E11-11 (Depletion Calculations—Oil) Sunglee Drilling Limited leases property on which oil has been discovered. Wells on this property produced 18,000 barrels of oil during the current year and it was sold at an average of $15 per barrel. The total oil resources of this property are estimated to be 250,000 barrels. **(LO 4)**

The lease provided for an immediate payment of $500,000 to the lessor before drilling began and an annual rental of $31,500. Development costs of $625,000 were incurred before any oil was produced, and Sunglee follows a policy of capitalizing these preproduction costs. The lease also specified that each year the lessor would be paid a premium of 5% of the sales price of every barrel of oil that was removed. In addition, the lessee is to clean up all the waste and debris from drilling and to pay the costs of reconditioning the land for farming when the wells are abandoned. It is estimated that the present value of the obligations for the existing wells is $30,000.

Instructions

(a) From the information given, provide the journal entry made by Sunglee Drilling Limited to record depletion for the current year.

(b) Assuming that the oil property was acquired at the beginning of the current year, provide the entry to record the acquisition of the asset and the annual rental payment.

(LO 4) E11-12 **(Depletion Calculations—Timber)** Forda Lumber Inc. owns a 7,000-hectare timber tract that it purchased in 2001 at a cost of $1,300 per hectare. At the time of purchase, the land was estimated to have a value of $300 per hectare without the timber. Forda Lumber Inc. has not logged this tract since it was purchased. In 2008, Forda had the timber cruised (appraised). The cruise estimated that each hectare contained 8,000 cubic metres of timber. In 2008, Forda built 10 kilometres of roads at a cost of $7,840 per kilometre. After the roads were completed, Forda logged and sold 3,500 trees containing 850,000 cubic metres of timber.

Instructions

(a) Determine the cost of timber sold that relates to depletion for 2008.

(b) Assuming that Forda amortizes the logging roads based on the amount of timber that has been cut, determine the amortization expense for 2008.

(c) If Forda plants five seedlings at a cost of $4 per seedling for each tree that is cut, how should Forda treat the reforestation costs?

(LO 4) E11-13 **(Depletion Calculations—Mining)** Belinda Mining Corp. purchased a mining property on February 1, 2008, at a cost of $1,250,000. The company estimated that a total of 80,000 tonnes of mineral was available for mining. Because of strict environmental protection laws, the company is required to restore the property to its previous state after the natural resource has been removed, and it estimates the present value of this restoration obligation at $90,000 based on mining to date. Belinda believes it will be able to sell the property afterwards for $100,000. Developmental costs of $200,000 were incurred before Belinda was able to extract any of the ore. Belinda capitalizes these costs as part of the natural resource. In 2008, 30,000 tonnes were removed, and 22,000 tonnes were sold.

In 2009, a geological survey increased the estimate of the volume of total ore in the mine to 112,000 tonnes. Revised estimates also put the present value of land reclamation and restoration costs for the existing mine at $150,000. In 2009, 25,000 tonnes were mined and 27,000 tonnes sold.

Instructions

Do the following, rounding your answers to two decimal places.

(a) Calculate the following information for 2008: (1) the depletion cost per tonne mined in 2008; (2) the total depletion cost in cost of goods sold in 2008.

(b) Assume that Belinda uses the FIFO cost flow assumption. Calculate the following information for 2009: (1) the depletion cost per tonne mined in 2009; (2) the total depletion cost in cost of goods sold in 2009.

(LO 2, 7, 10) E11-14 **(Amortization Calculation—Replacement, Trade-in)** Zidek Corporation bought a machine on June 1, 2005, for $31,000, f.o.b. the place of manufacture. Freight costs were $200, and $500 was spent to install it. The machine's useful life was estimated at 10 years, with a residual value of $2,500.

On June 1, 2006, a part that was designed to reduce the machine's operating costs was added to the machine and cost $1,980. On June 1, 2009, the company bought a new machine with a larger capacity for $35,000, delivered. A trade-in value was received on the old machine equal to its fair market value of $20,000. Removing the old machine from the plant cost $75, and installing the new one cost $1,500. It was estimated that the new machine would have a useful life of 10 years, with a residual value of $4,000.

Instructions

Assuming that amortization is calculated on the straight-line basis, determine the amount of any gain or loss on the disposal of the first machine on June 1, 2009, and the amount of amortization that should be provided during the company's fiscal year which begins on June 1, 2009.

(LO 5) E11-15 **(Composite Amortization)** Information follows for Nguyen Manufacturing Corporation:

Asset	Cost	Estimated Residual Value	Estimated Life (in years)
A	$25,500	$4,500	8
B	36,600	2,800	10
C	46,000	3,200	7
D	19,700	500	6
E	13,500	1,000	9

Instructions

(a) Calculate the rate of amortization per year to be applied to the plant assets under the composite method, and calculate the composite life of the plant assets.

(b) Prepare the adjusting entry that is necessary at year end to record amortization for a year.

(c) Prepare the entry to record the sale of asset D for cash of $1,100. Assume that it was used for six years, and amortization was entered under the composite method.

(d) In the same year as asset D was sold, it was replaced by asset F at a cost of $25,000. Record the purchase of asset F and prepare the adjusting entry that is necessary at year end to record amortization for the current year.

E11-16 **(Amortization—Change in Estimate)** Machinery purchased for $60,000 by Cheng Corp. in 2004 was originally estimated to have an eight-year life with a residual value of $4,000. Amortization has been entered for five years on this basis. In 2009, it is determined that the total estimated life (including 2009) should have been 10 years with a residual value of $4,500 at the end of that time. Assume straight-line amortization. **(LO 7)**

Instructions

(a) Prepare the entry that is required to correct the prior years' amortization, if any.

(b) Prepare the entry to record amortization for 2009.

(c) Repeat part (b) assuming Cheng Corp. uses the double-declining-balance method of amortization.

E11-17 **(Amortization Calculation—Addition, Change in Estimate)** In 1980, Applied Science Limited completed the construction of a building at a cost of $2 million and occupied it in January 1981. It was estimated that the building would have a useful life of 50 years and a residual value of $500,000. **(LO 7)**

Early in 1991, an addition to the building was constructed at a cost of $700,000. At that time, no changes were expected in its useful life, but the residual value with the addition was estimated to increase by $100,000. The addition would not be of economic use to the company beyond the life of the original structure.

In 2009, as a result of a thorough review of its amortization policies, company management determined that the original life of the building should have been estimated at 40 years. Because the district where the building is has been going through a large-scale renewal, with older buildings being torn down and new ones built, it is now expected that the company's building and addition are unlikely to have any residual value at the end of the 40-year period.

Instructions

(a) Using the straight-line method, calculate the annual amortization that would have been charged from 1981 through 1990.

(b) Calculate the annual amortization that would have been charged from 1991 through 2008.

(c) Prepare the entry, if necessary, to adjust the account balances because of the revision of the estimated life in 2009.

(d) Calculate the annual amortization to be charged beginning with 2009.

E11-18 **(Amortization Replacement—Change in Estimate)** Orel Limited constructed a building at a cost of $2.9 million and has occupied it since January 1988. It was estimated at that time that its life would be 40 years, with no residual value. In January 2008, a new roof was installed at a cost of $380,000, and it was estimated then that the building would have a useful life of 23 years from that date. The cost of the old roof was $160,000. **(LO 7)**

Instructions

(a) What amount of amortization was charged annually from the years 1988 through 2007? (Assume straight-line amortization.)

(b) What entry should be made in 2008 to record the roof replacement?

(c) Prepare the entry in January 2008 to record the revision in the building's estimated life, if necessary.

(d) What amount of amortization should be charged for the year 2008?

E11-19 **(Error Analysis and Amortization)** Devereaux Company Ltd. shows the following entries in its Equipment account for 2008; all amounts are based on historical cost. **(LO 2, 3)**

Equipment

Date	Description	Amount	Date	Description	Amount
1/1	Balance	134,750	6/30	Cost of equipment sold (purchased prior to 2008)	23,000
8/10	Purchases	32,000			
8/12	Freight on equipment purchased	700			
8/25	Installation costs	2,700			
11/10	Repairs	500			

Instructions

(a) Prepare any correcting entries that are necessary.

(b) Assuming that amortization is to be charged for a full year on the ending balance in the asset account, calculate the proper amortization charge for 2008 under both methods listed below. Assume an estimated life of 10 years, with no residual value. The machinery included in the January 1, 2008, Equipment balance was purchased in 2006.

1. Straight-line
2. Declining-balance (assume twice the straight-line rate)

(LO 8) E11-20 (Impairment) The information that follows relates to equipment owned by Gobi Limited at December 31, 2008:

Cost	$9,000,000
Accumulated amortization to date	1,000,000
Expected future net cash flows	7,000,000
Fair value	6,200,000

Assume that Gobi will continue to use this asset in the future. As at December 31, 2008, the equipment has a remaining useful life of four years. Gobi uses the straight-line method of amortization.

Instructions

(a) Prepare the journal entry, if any, to record the impairment of the asset at December 31, 2008.

(b) Prepare the journal entry, if any, to record amortization expense for 2009.

(c) The equipment's fair value at December 31, 2009, is $6.3 million. Prepare the journal entry, if any, to record this increase in fair value.

(LO 9) E11-21 (Impairment) Assume the same information as in E11-20, except that at December 31, 2008, Gobi discontinues use of the equipment and intends to dispose of it in the coming year by selling it to a competitor. It is expected that the disposal cost will be $50,000.

Instructions

(a) Prepare the journal entry, if any, to record the impairment of the asset at December 31, 2008.

(b) Prepare the journal entry, if any, to record amortization expense for 2009.

(c) Assume that the asset was not sold by December 31, 2009. The equipment's fair value on this date is $6.3 million. Prepare the journal entry, if any, to record this increase in fair value. It is expected that the cost of disposal is still $50,000.

(d) Identify where, and at what amount, this asset will be reported on the December 31, 2009, balance sheet.

(LO 8) E11-22 (Impairment) The management of Luis Inc. was discussing whether certain equipment should be written down as a charge to current operations because of obsolescence. The assets had a cost of $900,000, and amortization of $400,000 had been taken to December 31, 2008. On December 31, 2008, management projected the future net cash flows from this equipment to be $300,000 and its fair value to be $230,000. The company intends to use this equipment in the future.

Instructions

(a) Prepare the journal entry, if any, to record the impairment at December 31, 2008.

(b) Where should the gain or loss on the write-down, if any, be reported in the income statement?

(c) At December 31, 2009, the equipment's fair value increased to $260,000. Prepare the journal entry, if any, to record this increase in fair value.

(d) Assume instead that the future net cash flows from the equipment on December 31, 2008, were expected to be $510,000 and its fair value was $450,000 on this date. Prepare the journal entry, if any, to record the impairment at December 31, 2008.

(e) Assume instead that the future net cash flows from the equipment are $45,000 per year for each of the next 10 years and that there is no active market for the equipment. Luis Inc. uses a 10% discount rate on its cash flow estimates. Prepare the journal entry, if any, to record impairment at December 31, 2008.

(f) Discuss why impairment is tested using undiscounted future cash flows rather than the present value of future cash flows.

E11-23 (Entries for Disposition of Assets) On December 31, 2008, Travis Inc. owns a machine with a carrying amount of $940,000. The original cost and accumulated amortization for the machine at this date are as follows: **(LO 10)**

Machine	$1,300,000
Accumulated amortization	360,000
	$ 940,000

Amortization is calculated at $60,000 per year on a straight-line basis.

Instructions

A set of independent situations follows. For each situation, indicate the journal entry to record the transaction. Make sure that amortization entries are made to update the machine's book value before its disposal.

(a) A fire completely destroys the machine on August 31, 2009. An insurance settlement of $430,000 was received for this casualty. Assume the settlement was received immediately.

(b) On April 1, 2009, Travis sold the machine for $1,040,000 to Yoakam Company.

(c) On July 31, 2009, the company donated this machine to the Mountain City Council. The machine's fair market value at the time of the donation was estimated to be $1.1 million.

E11-24 (Disposition of Assets) On April 1, 2008, Estefan Corp. was awarded $460,000 cash as compensation for the forced sale of its land and building, which were directly in the path of a new highway. The land and building cost $60,000 and $280,000, respectively, when they were acquired. At April 1, 2008, the accumulated amortization for the building amounted to $165,000. On August 1, 2008, Estefan purchased a piece of replacement property for cash. The new land cost $160,000 and the new building cost $410,000. **(LO 10)**

Instructions

(a) Prepare the journal entries to record the transactions on April 1 and August 1, 2008.

(b) How would the transaction be shown on the income statement for 2008?

E11-25 (Ratio Analysis) The 2006 annual report of Boutahar Inc. contains the following information (in thousands): **(LO 10)**

	April 27, 2006	April 28, 2005
Total assets	$1,071,348	$ 787,167
Total liabilities	626,178	410,044
Consolidated sales	3,374,463	2,443,592
Net earnings	66,234	49,062

Instructions

(a) Calculate the following ratios for Boutahar Inc. for 2006:

1. Asset turnover ratio
2. Rate of return on assets
3. Profit margin on sales

(b) How can the asset turnover ratio be used to calculate the rate of return on assets?

(c) Briefly comment on the results for the ratios calculated in part (a).

***E11-26 (CCA)** During 2008, Frum Limited sold its only Class 3 asset. At the time of sale, the balance of the undepreciated capital cost for this class was $37,450. The asset originally cost $129,500. **(LO 13)**

Instructions

(a) Indicate what the amounts would be for recaptured CCA, capital gains, and terminal losses, if any, assuming the asset was sold for proceeds of (1) $132,700, (2) $51,000, and (3) $22,000.

(b) Assume the tax rates are scheduled to increase for 2008. What strategy could Frum Limited use to reduce its taxes payable that are due to the recapture on the disposal of the asset?

(LO 13) *E11-27 **(Book vs. Tax Amortization)** Chunmei Inc. purchased computer equipment on March 1, 2007, for $31,000. The computer equipment has a useful life of five years and a residual value of $1,000. Chunmei uses a double-declining-balance method of amortization for this type of capital asset. For tax purposes, the computer is assigned to Class 10 with a 30% rate.

Instructions

(a) Prepare a schedule of amortization covering 2007, 2008, and 2009 for financial reporting purposes for the new asset purchase. The company follows a policy of taking a full year's amortization in the year of purchase and none in the year of disposal.

(b) Prepare a schedule of CCA and UCC for this asset covering 2007, 2008, and 2009, assuming it is the only Class 10 asset owned by Chunmei.

(c) How much amortization is deducted over the three-year period on the financial statements? In determining taxable income? What is the carrying amount of the computer equipment on the December 31, 2009, balance sheet? What is the tax value of the computer equipment at December 31, 2009?

Problems

P11-1 Onyx Corp. purchased Machine no. 201 on May 1, 2008. The following information relating to Machine no. 201 was gathered at the end of May:

Price	$73,500
Credit terms	2/10, n/30
Freight-in costs	$ 970
Preparation and installation costs	$ 3,800
Labour costs during regular production operations	$10,500

It was expected that the machine could be used for 10 years, after which the residual value would be zero. Onyx intends to use the machine for only eight years, however, and expects to then be able to sell it for $1,200. The invoice for Machine no. 201 was paid May 5, 2008. Onyx has a September 30 year end.

Instructions

(a) Calculate the amortization expense for the years indicated using the following methods. (Round to the nearest dollar.)

1. Straight-line method for the fiscal years ended September 30, 2008 and 2009
2. Double-declining-balance method for the fiscal years ended September 30, 2008 and 2009

***(b)** Calculate the capital cost allowance for the 2008 and 2009 tax returns, assuming a CCA class with a rate of 25%.

(c) The president of Onyx tells you that because the company is a new organization, she expects it will be several years before production and sales reach optimum levels. She asks you to recommend an amortization method that will allocate less of the company's amortization expense to the early years and more to later years of the assets' lives. Which method would you recommend? Explain.

(d) In your answer to part (c) above, how would cash flows to the new company be affected by the choice of amortization method? How would current and potential creditors interpret the choice of amortization method?

P11-2 On June 15, 2005, a second-hand machine was purchased for $77,000. Before being put into service, the equipment was overhauled at a cost of $5,200, and additional costs of $400 for direct material and $800 for direct labour were paid in fine-tuning the controls. The machine has an estimated residual value of $5,000 at the end of its five-year useful life. The machine is expected to operate for 100,000 hours before it will be replaced and is expected to produce 1.2 million units in this time. Operating data for the next five fiscal years are as follows:

Year	Hours of Operation	Units Produced
2005	10,000	115,000
2006	25,000	310,000
2007	25,000	294,000
2008	30,000	363,000
2009	10,000	118,000

The company has an October 31 year end.

Instructions

(a) Calculate the amortization charges for each fiscal year under each of the following amortization methods:

1. Straight-line method
2. Activity method: based on output
3. Activity method: based on input
4. Double-declining-balance method
***5.** CCA, Class 8, 20%

(b) What is the carrying amount of the machine on the October 31, 2008, balance sheet under the first four methods above?

***(c)** Compare your answers in (b) with the asset's tax value at the same date.

(d) What happens if the actual hours of operation or units produced do not correspond to the numbers that were estimated in setting the rate?

P11-3 Goran Tool Corp. records amortization annually at the end of the year. Its policy is to take a full year's amortization on all assets that are used throughout the year and amortization for half a year on all machines that are acquired or disposed of during the year. The amortization rate for the machinery is 10% applied on a straight-line basis, with no estimated scrap or residual value.

The balance of the Machinery account at the beginning of 2008 was $172,300; the Accumulated Amortization on Machinery account had a balance of $72,900. The machinery accounts were affected by the following transactions that occurred in 2008:

Jan. 15 Machine no. 38, which cost $9,600 when it was acquired on June 3, 2001, was retired and sold as scrap metal for $600.

Feb. 27 Machine no. 81 was purchased. The fair market value of this machine was $12,500. It replaced two machines, nos. 12 and 27, which were traded in on the new machine. Machine no. 12 was acquired on February 4, 1996, at a cost of $5,500 and was still carried in the accounts although it was fully depreciated and not in use. Machine no. 27 was acquired on June 11, 2001, at a cost of $8,200. In addition to these two used machines, $9,000 was paid in cash.

Apr. 7 Machine no. 54 was equipped with electric controls at a cost of $940. This machine, originally equipped with simple hand controls, was purchased on December 11, 2004, for $1,800. The new electric controls can be attached to any one of several machines in the shop.

12 Machine no. 24 was repaired at a cost of $720 after a fire caused by a short circuit in the wiring burned out the motor and damaged certain essential parts.

July 22 Machines 25, 26, and 41 were sold for $3,100 cash. The purchase dates and cost of these machines were as follows:

No. 25	May 8, 2000	$4,000
No. 26	May 8, 2000	3,200
No. 41	June 1, 2002	2,800

Instructions

(a) Record each transaction in general journal form.

(b) Calculate and record amortization for the year. None of the machines currently included in the balance of the account were acquired before January 1, 1999.

P11-4 On January 1, 2008, Dayan Corporation, a small manufacturer of machine tools, acquired new industrial equipment for $1.1 million. The new equipment had a useful life of five years and the residual value was estimated to be $50,000. Dayan estimates that the new equipment can produce 12,000 machine tools in its first year. It estimates that production will decline by 1,000 units per year over the remaining useful life of the equipment.

The following amortization methods may be used: (1) straight-line, (2) double-declining-balance; and (3) units-of-output. For tax purposes, the CCA class is Class 10—30%.

Instructions

(a) Which of the three amortization methods would maximize net income for financial statement reporting purposes for the three-year period ending December 31, 2010? Prepare a schedule showing the amount of accumulated amortization at December 31, 2010, under the method you chose.

***(b)** Over the same three-year period, how much capital cost allowance would have been written off for tax purposes?

(c) Prepare a graph that covers the five-year period and has separate chart lines for each of the three amortization methods and for the CCA method. Which pattern of amortization do you feel best reflects the benefits that are provided by the new equipment? Explain briefly.

P11-5 The following data relate to the Plant Assets account of Fiedler Inc. at December 31, 2007:

	A	B	C	D
Original cost	$35,000	$51,000	$80,000	$80,000
Year purchased	2002	2003	2004	2006
Useful life	10 years	15,000 hours	15 years	10 years
Residual value	$3,100	$3,000	$5,000	$5,000
Amortization method	straight-line	activity	straight-line	double-declining
Accumulated amortization through 2007[a]	$15,950	$35,200	$15,000	$16,000

[a]In the year an asset is purchased, Fiedler does not record any amortization expense on the asset. In the year an asset is retired or traded in, Fiedler takes a full year's amortization on the asset.

The following transactions occurred during 2008:

1. On May 5, Asset A was sold for $13,000 cash. The company's bookkeeper recorded this retirement as follows:

Cash	13,000	
Asset A		13,000

2. On December 31, it was determined that Asset B had been used 2,100 hours during 2008.
3. On December 31, before calculating amortization expense on Asset C, Fiedler management decided that Asset C's remaining useful life should be nine years as of year end.
4. On December 31, it was discovered that a plant asset purchased in 2007 had been expensed completely in that year. The asset cost $22,000 and had a useful life of 10 years when it was acquired and had no residual value. Management has decided to use the double-declining-balance method for this asset, which can be referred to as "Asset E."

Instructions

Prepare the necessary correcting entries for the year 2008 and any additional entries that are needed to record the appropriate amortization expense on each of the assets.

P11-6 Soon after December 31, 2008, the auditor of Qing Manufacturing Corp. asked the company to prepare an amortization schedule for semi trucks that showed the additions, retirements, amortization, and other data that affected the company's income in the four-year period from 2005 to 2008, inclusive. The following data were obtained.

Balance of Semi Trucks account, January 1, 2005:	
Truck no. 1, purchased Jan. 1, 2002, cost	$18,000
Truck no. 2, purchased July 1, 2002, cost	22,000
Truck no. 3, purchased Jan. 1, 2004, cost	30,000
Truck no. 4, purchased July 1, 2004, cost	24,000
Balance, January 1, 2005	$94,000

The account Semi Trucks—Accumulated Amortization had a correct balance of $30,200 on January 1, 2005 (includes amortization on the four trucks from the respective dates of purchase, based on a five-year life, no residual value). No charges had been made against the account before January 1, 2005.

Transactions between January 1, 2005, and December 31, 2008, and their record in the ledger were as follows:

July 1, 2005 Truck no. 3 was traded for a larger one (no. 5). The agreed purchase price (fair market value) was $34,000. Qing Manufacturing paid the automobile dealer $15,000 cash on the transaction. The entry was a debit to Semi Trucks and a credit to Cash, $15,000.

Jan. 1, 2006 Truck no. 1 was sold for $3,500 cash. The entry was a debit to Cash and a credit to Semi Trucks, $3,500.

July 1, 2007 A new truck (no. 6) was acquired for $36,000 cash and was charged at that amount to the Semi Trucks account. (Assume truck no. 2 was not retired.)

July 1, 2007 Truck no. 4 was so badly damaged in an accident that it was sold as scrap for $700 cash. Qing Manufacturing received $2,500 from the insurance company. The entry made by the bookkeeper was a debit to Cash, $3,200, and credits to Miscellaneous Income, $700, and Semi Trucks, $2,500.

Entries for amortization were made at the close of each year as follows: 2005, $20,300; 2006, $21,100; 2007, $24,450; 2008, $27,800.

Instructions

(a) For each of the four years, calculate separately the increase or decrease in net income that is due to the company's errors in determining or entering amortization or in recording transactions affecting the trucks. Ignore income tax considerations.

(b) Prepare one compound journal entry as at December 31, 2008, to adjust the Semi Trucks account to reflect the correct balances according to your schedule, and assuming that the books have not been closed for 2008.

P11-7 Linda Monkland established Monkland Ltd. in mid-2007 as the sole shareholder. The accounts on June 30, 2008, the company's year end, just prior to preparing the required adjusting entries, were as follows:

Current assets		$100,000
Capital assets		
Land	$40,000	
Building	90,000	
Equipment	50,000	180,000
Current liabilities		40,000
Long-term bank loan		120,000
Share capital		90,000
Net income prior to amortization		30,000

All the capital assets were acquired and put into operation in early July 2007. Estimates and usage information on these assets were as follows:

Building:	25-year life, $15,000 residual value
Equipment:	Five-year life, 15,000 hours of use, $5,000 residual value. The equipment was used for 1,000 hours in 2007 and 1,400 hours in 2008 up to June 30.

Linda Monkland is now considering which amortization method or methods would be appropriate. She has narrowed the choices down for the building to the straight-line or double-declining-balance method, and for the equipment to the straight-line, double-declining-balance, or activity method. She has requested your advice and recommendation. In discussions with her, the following concerns were raised:

1. The company acquires goods from suppliers with terms of 2/10, n/30. The suppliers have indicated that these terms will continue as long as the current ratio does not fall below 2 to 1. If the ratio falls lower, no purchase discounts will be given.
2. The bank will continue the loan from year to year as long as the ratio of long-term debt to total assets does not exceed 46%.
3. Linda Monkland has contracted with the company's manager to pay him a bonus equal to 50% of any net income in excess of $14,000. She prefers to minimize or pay no bonus as long as conditions of agreements with suppliers and the bank can be met.
4. In order to provide a strong signal to attract potential investors to join her in the company, Ms. Monkland believes that a rate of return on total assets of at least 5% must be achieved.

Instructions

(a) Prepare a report for Linda Monkland that (1) presents tables, (2) analyzes the situation, (3) provides a recommendation on which method or methods should be used, and (4) justifies your recommendation by considering her concerns and the requirement that the method(s) used be considered generally acceptable accounting principle(s).

(b) What other factors should you discuss with Ms. Monkland to help her in choosing appropriate amortization methods for her business?

(c) Do any ethical issues arise if an amortization method is chosen in order to manipulate the financial results in a way that will satisfy the constraints listed above? Explain.

P11-8 Wright Mining Ltd. purchased a tract of land for $610,000. After incurring exploration costs of $95,000, the company estimated that the tract will yield 120,000 tonnes of ore having enough mineral content to make mining and processing profitable. It is further estimated that 6,000 tonnes of ore will be mined in the first and last years and 12,000 tonnes every year in between. The land is expected to have a residual value of $30,000.

The company built necessary bunkhouses and sheds on the site at a cost of $39,000. It estimated that these structures would have a physical life of 15 years but, because they must be dismantled if they are to be moved, they have no residual value. The company does not intend to use the buildings elsewhere. Mining machinery installed at the mine was purchased second-hand at a cost of $56,000. This machinery cost the former owner $100,000 and was 50% depreciated when it was purchased. Wright Mining estimated that about half of this machinery will still be useful when the present mineral resources are exhausted but that dismantling and removing them would cost about as much as they are worth at that time. The company does not intend to use the machinery elsewhere. The remaining machinery is expected to last until about one-half the present estimated mineral ore has been removed and will then be worthless. Cost is to be allocated equally between these two classes of machinery.

Wright also spent another $71,000 in opening up the mine so that the ore could be extracted and removed for shipping. The company estimates that the site reclamation and restoration costs that the company is responsible for by contract when the mine is depleted have a present value of $39,900. Wright follows a policy of expensing exploration costs and capitalizing development costs.

Instructions

(a) As chief accountant for the company, you are to prepare a schedule that shows the estimated depletion and amortization costs for each year of the mine's expected life.

(b) Prepare the journal entry(ies) to record the transactions for the acquisition of the mining property and related assets during the first year. Also prepare entries to record amortization and depletion for the first year. Assume that actual production was 7,000 tonnes. Nothing occurred during the year to cause the company engineers to change their estimates of either the mineral resources or the life of the structures and equipment.

(c) Assume that 6,500 tonnes of product were processed and sold during the first year of the mine's expected life. Identify all costs mentioned above that will be included in the first-year income statement of Wright Mining Ltd.

P11-9 Copernicus Logging and Lumber Inc. owns 3,000 hectares of timberland on the north side of a mountain in western Canada. It purchased the tract in 1988 at a cost of $550 per hectare, and began selectively logging it in 2007. In May 2007, a forest fire destroyed most of the timber on the tract. In addition, the logging roads, built at a cost of $150,000, were destroyed, as was logging equipment that had a net book value of $300,000.

At the time of the fire, Copernicus had logged 20% of the estimated 500,000 cubic metres of timber. Before the fire, Copernicus estimated that the land would have a value of $200 per hectare after the timber was harvested. Copernicus includes the logging roads in the depletion base.

Copernicus estimates that it will take three years to salvage the burned timber at a cost of $700,000, and that the burned timber can be sold for pulp wood at an estimated price of $3 per cubic metre. The land value is unknown, but until it will grow vegetation again—which scientists say may be as long as 50 to 100 years—the value is nominal.

Instructions

(a) Determine the depletion cost per cubic metre for the timber that was harvested before the fire.

(b) Prepare the journal entry to record the depletion before the fire.

(c) Determine the amount of the estimated loss before income taxes and show how the losses of roads, machinery, and timber and the timber salvage value should be reported in the financial statements of Copernicus for the year ended December 31, 2007.

P11-10 Western Paper Products Ltd. purchased 10,000 hectares of forested timberland in March 2008. The company paid $1,700 per hectare for this land, which was higher than the $800 per hectare that most farmers were paying for cleared land. During April, May, June, and July 2008, Western cut enough timber to build roads using moveable equipment that it purchased on April 1, 2008. The cost of the roads was $195,000, and the cost of the equipment was $189,000; the equipment was expected to have a $9,000 residual value and would be used for the next 15 years. Western selected the straight-line method of amortization for the moveable equipment. The company began actively harvesting timber in August and by December had harvested and sold 472,500 cubic metres of timber of the estimated 6,750,000 cubic metres available for cutting.

In March 2009, Western planted new seedlings in the harvested area. The cost of planting these seedlings was $120,000. In addition, Western spent $8,000 in road maintenance and $6,000 for pest spraying during 2009. The road maintenance and spraying are annual costs. During 2009, Western harvested and sold 774,000 cubic metres of timber of the estimated 6,450,000 cubic metres that was then available for cutting.

In March 2010, Western again planted new seedlings at a cost of $150,000, and also spent $15,000 on road maintenance and pest spraying. During 2010, the company harvested and sold 650,000 cubic metres of timber of the estimated 6.5 million cubic metres available for cutting.

Instructions

(a) Calculate the amount of amortization and depletion expense for each of the three years. Assume that the roads are usable only for logging and therefore are included in the depletion base.

(b) Identify all costs above that will be included on the income statement of Western Paper Products Ltd. for each of the three years.

P11-11 Release Corporation uses special strapping equipment in its packaging business. The equipment was purchased in January 2007 for $8.6 million and had an estimated useful life of nine years with no residual value. In early April 2008, a part costing $969,000 and designed to increase the efficiency of the machinery was added. The machine's estimated useful life did not change with this addition. By December 31, 2008, new technology had been introduced that would speed up the obsolescence of Release's equipment. Release's controller estimates that expected future net cash flows on the equipment will be $5.5 million and that the fair value of the equipment is $4.6 million. Release intends to continue using the equipment, but estimates that its remaining useful life is now four years. Release uses straight-line amortization.

Instructions

(a) Prepare the journal entry, if any, to record the impairment at December 31, 2008.

(b) Prepare any journal entries for the equipment at December 31, 2009. The fair value of the equipment at December 31, 2009, is estimated to be $5 million.

(c) Repeat the requirements for (a) and (b), assuming that Release intends to dispose of the equipment, but continues to use it while it waits for a satisfactory offer, and that it has not been disposed of as of December 31, 2009.

(d) Repeat the requirements for (a) and (b), assuming that Release designates the equipment as "held for sale." Due to matters beyond Release's control, a potential sale falls through in 2009 and the equipment is still on hand at December 31, 2009.

(e) For each situation in (b), (c), and (d), indicate where the equipment will be reported on the December 31, 2008 and 2009, balance sheets.

P11-12 The following is a schedule of property dispositions for Tomasino Corp.:

SCHEDULE OF PROPERTY DISPOSITIONS

	Cost	Accumulated Amortization	Cash Proceeds	Fair Market Value	Nature of Disposition
Land	$40,000	—	$31,000	$31,000	Expropriation
Building	15,000	—	3,600	—	Demolition
Warehouse	70,000	$11,000	74,000	74,000	Destruction by fire
Machine	8,000	3,200	900	7,200	Trade-in
Furniture	10,000	7,850	—	3,100	Contribution
Automobile	8,000	3,460	2,960	2,960	Sale

The following additional information is available:

Land
On February 15, land that was being held mainly as an investment was expropriated by the city. On March 31, another parcel of unimproved land to be held as an investment was purchased at a cost of $35,000.

Building
On April 2, land and a building were purchased at a total cost of $75,000, of which 20% was allocated to the building on the corporate books. The real estate was acquired with the intention of demolishing the building, which was done in November. Cash proceeds that were received in November were the net proceeds from the building demolition.

Warehouse
On June 30, the warehouse was destroyed by fire. The warehouse had been purchased January 2, 1994, and accumulated amortization of $11,000 had been reported. On December 27, the insurance proceeds and other funds were used to purchase a replacement warehouse at a cost of $90,000.

Machine
On December 26, the machine was exchanged for another machine having a fair market value of $6,300. Cash of $900 was also received as part of the deal.

Furniture

On August 15, furniture was contributed to a registered charitable organization. No other contributions were made or pledged during the year.

Automobile

On November 3, the automobile was sold to Una Guillen, a shareholder.

Instructions

Indicate how these items would be reported on the income statement of Tomasino Corp.

(AICPA adapted)

P11-13 Huston Corporation, a manufacturer of steel products, began operations on October 1, 2006. Huston's accounting department has begun preparing the capital asset and amortization schedule that follows. You have been asked to assist in completing this schedule. In addition to determining that the data already on the schedule are correct, you have obtained the following information from the company's records and personnel:

1. Amortization is calculated from the first day of the month of acquisition to the first day of the month of disposition.
2. Land A and Building A were acquired together for $820,000. At the time of acquisition, the land had an appraised value of $90,000 and the building had an appraised value of $810,000.
3. Land B was acquired on October 2, 2006, in exchange for 2,500 newly issued common shares. At the date of acquisition, the shares had a fair value of $30 each. During October 2006, Huston paid $16,000 to demolish an existing building on this land so that it could construct a new building.
4. Construction of Building B on the newly acquired land began on October 1, 2007. By September 30, 2008, Huston had paid $320,000 of the estimated total construction costs of $450,000. It is estimated that the building will be completed and occupied by July 2009.
5. Certain equipment was donated to the corporation by a local university. An independent appraisal of the equipment when it was donated estimated its fair market value at $30,000 and the residual value at $3,000.
6. Machinery A's total cost of $164,900 includes an installation expense of $600 and normal repairs and maintenance of $14,900. Its residual value is estimated at $6,000. Machinery A was sold on February 1, 2008.
7. On October 1, 2007, Machinery B was acquired with a down payment of $5,740 and the remaining payments to be made in 11 annual instalments of $6,000 each, beginning October 1, 2007. The prevailing interest rate was 8%. The following data were determined from present-value tables and are rounded:

PV of $1 at 8%		PV of an Ordinary Annuity of $1 at 8%	
10 years	0.463	10 years	6.710
11 years	0.429	11 years	7.139
15 years	0.315	15 years	8.559

HUSTON CORPORATION
Capital Asset and Amortization Schedule
For Fiscal Years Ended September 30, 2007, and September 30, 2008

Assets	Acquisition Date	Cost	Residual Value	Amortization Method	Estimated Life in Years	Amortization Expense, Year Ended September 30 2007	2008
Land A	Oct. 1, 2006	$ (1)	N/A	N/A	N/A	N/A	N/A
Building A	Oct. 1, 2006	(2)	$40,000	Straight-line	(3)	$17,450	(4)
Land B	Oct. 2, 2006	(5)	N/A	N/A	N/A	N/A	N/A
Building B	Under Construction	$320,000 to date	—	Straight-line	30	—	(6)
Donated Equipment	Oct. 2, 2006	(7)	3,000	150% declining-balance	10	(8)	(9)
Machinery A	Oct. 2, 2006	(10)	6,000	Double-declining-balance	8	(11)	(12)
Machinery B	Oct. 1, 2007	(13)	—	Straight-line	20	—	(14)

N/A = Not applicable

Instructions

For each numbered item in the schedule, give the correct amount. Round each answer to the nearest dollar.

P11-14 **Situation 1:** Zitar Corporation purchased electrical equipment at a cost of $12,400 on June 2, 2004. From 2004 through 2007, the equipment was amortized on a straight-line basis, under the assumption that it would have a 10-year useful life and a $2,400 residual value. After more experience and before recording 2008's amortization, Zitar revised its estimate of the machine's useful life downward from a total of 10 years to eight years, and revised the estimated residual value to $2,000.

On April 29, 2009, after recording part of a year's amortization for 2009, the company traded in the equipment on a newer model, and received a $4,000 trade-in allowance although its fair value was only $2,800. The new asset had a list price of $15,300 and the supplier accepted $11,300 cash for the balance. The new equipment was amortized on a straight-line basis, assuming a seven-year useful life and a $1,300 residual value.

Situation 2: Boda Limited acquired a truck to deliver and install its specialized products at the customer's site. The vehicle's list price was $45,000, but customization added another $10,000 of costs. Boda took delivery of the truck on September 30, 2008, with a down payment of $5,000, signing a four-year, 8% note for the remainder, payable in equal payments of $14,496 beginning September 30, 2009.

Boda expected the truck to be usable for 500 deliveries and installations. After that, the product's technology would have changed and made the vehicle obsolete. In late July 2011, the truck was destroyed when a concrete garage collapsed. Boda used the truck for 45 deliveries in 2008, 125 in 2009, 134 in 2010, and 79 in 2011. The company received a cheque for $12,000 from the insurance company and paid what remained on the note.

Situation 3: A group of new machines was purchased on February 17, 2008, under a royalty agreement with the following terms: The purchaser, Townsand Corp., is to pay a royalty of $1 to the machinery supplier for each unit of product that is produced by the machines each year. The machines are expected to produce 200,000 units over their useful lives. The invoice price of the machines was $75,000, freight costs were $2,000, unloading charges were $1,500, and royalty payments for 2008 were $13,000.

Townsand uses the units-of-production method to amortize its machinery.

Instructions

(a) For situation 1, determine the amount of amortization expense reported by Zitar for each fiscal year for the years ending December 31, 2004, to December 31, 2009.

(b) For situation 2, prepare all entries that are needed to record the events and activities related to the truck, including the amortization expense on the truck each year. Assume that Boda uses an activity approach to amortize the truck, and bases it on deliveries.

(c) For situation 3, prepare journal entries to record the purchase of the new machines, the related amortization for 2008, and the royalty payment.

***P11-15** Taber Limited reports the following information in its tax files covering the five-year period from 2005 to 2009. All assets are Class 10 with a 30% maximum CCA rate.

2005	Purchased assets A, B, and C for $20,000, $8,000, and $1,200 respectively.
2006	Sold asset B for $7,000; bought asset D for $4,800.
2007	Purchased asset E for $5,000; received an investment tax credit of $1,000.
2008	Sold asset A for $9,900 and asset C for $1,800.
2009	Asset D was destroyed by fire and was uninsured; asset E was sold to an employee for $500.

Instructions

(a) Prepare a capital cost allowance schedule for Class 10 assets covering the 2005 to 2009 period.

(b) Identify any capital gains, terminal losses, or recapture of CCA and indicate how each would be taxed.

***P11-16** Quadros Limited was attracted to the Town of LePage by the town's municipal industry commission. LePage donated a plant site to Quadros, and the provincial government provided $180,000 toward the cost of the new manufacturing facility. The total cost of plant construction came to $380,000 and it was ready for use in early October 2008. Quadros expects the plant to have a useful life of 15 years before it becomes obsolete and is demolished. The company uses the straight-line method of amortization for buildings and is required to include the plant in Class 6 (10% rate) for tax purposes.

Instructions

(a) Prepare the entry(ies) that are required in 2008 to record the payment to the contractor for the building and the receipt of the provincial government assistance. Assume that the company treats the assistance as a reduction of the asset's cost. Also prepare any adjusting entries that are needed at the company's year ends, December 31, 2008 and 2009.

(b) Repeat (a), but assume instead that the company treats the government assistance as a deferred credit.

(c) If Quadros reports 2009 income of $79,000 before amortization on the plant and government assistance, what income before tax will the company report assuming (a) above? Assuming (b) above?

(d) What is the building's tax value at December 31, 2009?

Writing Assignments

WA11-1 Prophet Manufacturing Limited was organized January 1, 2008. During 2008, it used the straight-line method of amortizing its plant assets in its reports to management.

As the company's controller, on November 8 you are having a conference with Prophet's officers to discuss the amortization method to be used for income tax and for reporting to shareholders. Fred Peretti, president of Prophet, has suggested using a new method which he feels is more suitable than the straight-line method for the company's current needs during what he foresees will be a period of rapid expansion of production and capacity. The following is an example in which the proposed method is applied to a capital asset with an original cost of $248,000, an estimated useful life of five years, and a residual value of approximately $8,000:

Year	Years of Life Used	Fraction Rate	Amortization Expense	Accumulated Amortization at Year End	Book Value at Year End
1	1	1/15	$16,000	$ 16,000	$232,000
2	2	2/15	32,000	48,000	200,000
3	3	3/15	48,000	96,000	152,000
4	4	4/15	64,000	160,000	88,000
5	5	5/15	80,000	240,000	8,000

The president favours the new method because of the following claims that he has heard about it:

1. It will increase the funds that are recovered during the years near the end of the assets' useful life when maintenance and replacement disbursements are high.
2. It will result in increased write-offs in later years when the company is likely to be in a better operating position.

Instructions

Draft a response to Fred Peretti that explains the purpose of amortization, and whether the method that has been suggested qualifies as a generally accepted accounting method under GAAP. Identify the circumstances, if any, that would make using the method reasonable and those, if any, that would make using it unreasonable. Also respond to his statement that amortization charges recover or create funds.

WA11-2 Billy Williams, HK Corporation's controller, is concerned that net income may be lower this year. He is afraid that upper-level management might recommend cost reductions by laying off accounting staff, himself included. Williams knows that amortization is a major expense for HK. The company currently uses the same method for financial reporting as it uses for tax purposes—i.e., a declining-balance method—and he is thinking of changing to the straight-line method.

Williams does not want to highlight the increase in net income that would result from this change. He thinks, "Why don't I just increase the estimated useful lives and the residual values of the property, plant, and equipment? They are only estimates anyway. This will decrease amortization expense and increase income. I may be able to save my job and those of my staff."

Instructions

Discuss. Make sure that you identify the objectives of amortization, who the stakeholders are in this situation, what disclosures are required by GAAP, whether any ethical issues are involved, and what Williams should do.

WA11-3 Recently, Brunet Company Ltd. experienced a strike that affected several of its operating plants. The company president indicated that it was not appropriate to report amortization expense during this period because the equipment did not depreciate and an improper matching of costs and revenues would result. She based her position on the following points:

1. It is inappropriate to charge a period with costs when there are no related revenues arising from production in that period.
2. The basic factor of amortization in this instance is wear and tear, and because equipment was idle, there was no wear and tear.

Instructions
Comment on the president's arguments.

WA11-4 Carnago Corporation manufactures home electrical appliances. Company engineers have designed a new type of blender that, thanks to a few attachments, will perform more functions than any other blender currently on the market. Demand for the new blender can be projected with reasonable probability. In order to manufacture the blenders, Carnago needs a specialized machine that is not available from outside sources. It has therefore decided to make the machine in Carnago's own plant.

Instructions
Write a report to Carnago's corporate accountant on the factors that need to be considered in determining an appropriate amortization method for the specialized machine. Be sure to include a discussion of the effect that the projected demand in units for the new blenders (which may be steady, decreasing, or increasing) will have on this decision.

WA11-5 Puma Paper Company Ltd. operates a 300-tonnes-per-day kraft pulp mill and four sawmills in New Brunswick. The company is expanding its pulp mill facilities to a capacity of 1,000 tonnes per day and plans to replace three of its older, less efficient sawmills with an expanded facility. One of the mills to be replaced did not operate for most of 2008 (current year), and there are no plans to reopen it before the new sawmill facility becomes operational.

In reviewing the amortization rates and in discussing the residual values of the sawmills that were to be replaced, it was noted that if present amortization rates were not adjusted, substantial amounts of plant costs on these three mills would not be depreciated by the time the new mill is operational.

Instructions
What is the proper accounting for the four sawmills at the end of 2008?

WA11-6 As a cost accountant for Digby Cannery Inc., you have been approached by Merle Morash, canning room supervisor, about the costs that were charged to his department for 2007. In particular, he is concerned about the line item amortization. Morash is very proud of the excellent condition of his canning room equipment. He has always been vigilant about keeping all equipment serviced and well oiled. He is sure that the large amount of amortization that was charged is a mistake; it does not at all reflect the cost of the minimal wear and tear that the machines have experienced over the last year. He believes that the charge should be considerably lower.

The machines being amortized are six automatic canning machines. All were put into use on January 1, 2007. Each cost $469,000, and has a residual value of $40,000 and a useful life of 12 years. Digby depreciates this and similar assets using the double-declining-balance method. Morash has also pointed out that if you used straight-line amortization, the charge to his department would not be so high.

Instructions
Write a memo to Merle Morash to clear up his misunderstanding of the term "amortization." Also, calculate the first year amortization on all machines using both methods. Explain the theoretical justification for double-declining-balance and why, in the long run, the aggregate charge to amortization will be the same under both methods.

Integrated Cases

Refer to the Case Primer on the Student Website to help you answer these cases.

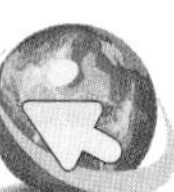
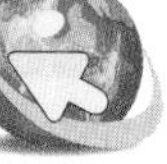

Student Website

www.wiley.com/canada/kieso

IC11-1 ClubLoop Corporation (CL) is a large owner, operator, and developer of golf clubs and resorts. The company is privately owned by several wealthy individuals. During the current year, according to the draft financial statements, revenues increased by 7.2% and net operating income increased by 13% to $22.5 million. Net income dropped from $2.9 million to $822,000. The decrease was largely due to two events, a change in accounting policy and costs related to the settlement of a lawsuit.

One of the company's objectives is to always ensure that capital resources are readily available to meet approved capital expenditures and to take advantage of growth opportunities. According to the draft year-end financial statements, the company has current assets of $12 million and current liabilities of $28 million, resulting in a working capital deficit. Included in the current liabilities are long-term debts that are currently due. The company is working with the related financial institutions to renew or replace these facilities. CL has received unsolicited expressions of interest from several financial institutions concerning these facilities and management believes that these facilities will be replaced—hopefully before the current financial statements are issued.

The company owns most of the land on which CL's golf courses are developed. Currently, the company follows a rigorous "weed and feed" program in order to keep the grass on the golf courses in top shape. The chemicals in these fertilizers, herbicides, and insecticides are felt by some people in the local community to be toxic to the environment. The company has met with several community groups and has agreed to study the issue further. In a current meeting of the board of directors, the CEO committed the company to spending $1 million to limit any potential damage. As at year end, none of this amount has yet been spent. There is a concern that the community groups are going to launch a lawsuit and the company feels that this move will help CL's position if there ends up being a lawsuit. Part of the money is for landscaping to limit the spread of the sprayed chemicals and part of it is for advertising to promote the company as a good corporate citizen.

The company is currently developing new golf courses. All direct costs related to the acquisition, development, and construction of these properties, including interest and management costs, are capitalized. For one of the new locations, which was just purchased and developed in the current year, the company has run into a small problem. After CL spent several million dollars on development, the planned golf course is being blocked by environmentalist groups. The costs to develop the land have been capitalized as previously mentioned, on the basis that they would be recoverable from future membership revenues. However, the company has now decided to sell the land to a real estate developer.

CL's stock-based compensation plan consists of stock options. The company does not recognize any expense for this plan when stock options are issued to employees. It has been the policy of the company to repurchase any shares issued under these stock option plans, although this year the company has indicated that it might not do this since it is planning to redesign the stock-based compensation system.

On July 1, CRA issued notices of assessment to the company regarding a dispute over the recognition of revenues. Although the outcome of an appeal of the assessment cannot be determined, the company believes that it will owe $8.7 million if its appeal is unsuccessful.

Instructions

Adopt the role of the company's auditor and prepare an analysis of the financial reporting issues. (Hint: If there are issues here that are new, use the conceptual framework to help you support your analysis with solid reasoning.)

IC11-2 Talisman Energy Inc. (TE) is an international company whose main business activities include the exploration, development, production, and marketing of crude oil, natural gas, and natural gas liquids. Its strategy is to continue to develop its North American gas business while at the same time expanding internationally. Wherever it makes sense to do so, the company owns and operates key assets and infrastructure and plans to grow through exploration and acquisition.

On October 20, 2002, the company announced that it had entered into an agreement to sell its controversial stake in Sudan. Although the company felt that the investment was a good one (the Sudan operations were profitable), it feared that shareholders were getting tired of the controversy surrounding the political conflict in Sudan. The sale is conditional upon obtaining certain governmental and consortium member consents. TE expects a gain on sale of $351 million. Revenues and costs have not been segregated in the financial statements.

During the year, the company was also forced to lower its previously announced 2003 growth targets. This caused some concern in the marketplace and resulted in investors questioning whether the company could meet its new targets on a going-forward basis.

TE follows what is known as the successful efforts method of accounting for exploration and development costs. Under this method, the costs related to drilling exploratory wells are written off to "dry hole expense" when they are determined to be unsuccessful. Until that time, they are included in property, plant, and equipment as non-depleted capital. As at December 31, 2002, costs related to exploration wells included in non-depleted capital were 3% ($309 million) of property, plant, and equipment. Dry hole expense was $174 million, with net income being $524 million. Note that the alternative treatment—full cost accounting—capitalizes all related costs as property, plant, and equipment, even the costs that are related to unsuccessful wells.

TE monitors its reserves, and reserve estimates are made using available geological and reservoir data, as well as production performance data. The reserves impact the income statement through depletion charges since property, plant, and equipment that relate to oil and gas production are amortized using the units-of-production method over proved, developed reserves. Currently, $1.2 billion of the capital assets are not subject to depletion since they are not yet in the production phase.

Revenues are recognized using the entitlement method, which means that the sales value of the production is recognized as revenue when produced.

Instructions

Adopt the role of company management and discuss the financial reporting issues.

Research and Financial Analysis

RA11-1 Canadian Tire Corporation, Limited

Canadian Tire Corporation, Limited is one of Canada's best-known retailers. Obtain a copy of Canadian Tire's financial statements for the year ended December 31, 2005, either through the Student Website or through SEDAR at www.sedar.com. To answer the following questions, you may also want to include the Ten Year Financial Review that is produced as supplementary information in the annual report.

Instructions

(a) How significant is Canadian Tire's investment in property, plant, and equipment compared to its investment in other assets? Compare this with sample companies in other industries, such as financial services, utilities, and technology. Comment.

(b) Calculate the company's total asset turnover for 2003, 2004, and 2005.

(c) Calculate the company's profit margin for the same three years.

(d) Calculate the company's return on assets for the same three years by using the ratios calculated in (b) and (c) above.

(e) Based on your calculations in (d), suggest ways in which Canadian Tire might increase the return that it earns on its investment in assets.

RA11-2 McDonald's Corporation

McDonald's Corporation is the largest and best-known global food service retailer, with more than 30,000 restaurants in over 100 countries. The company's system-wide sales in 2005 approached U.S. $50 billion. Information related to its property and equipment, taken from the company's financial statements, follows:

MCDONALD'S CORPORATION

Significant Accounting Policies—Property and Equipment. Property and equipment are stated at cost, with depreciation and amortization provided using the straight-line method over the following estimated useful lives: buildings—up to 40 years; leasehold improvements—the lesser of useful lives of assets or lease terms which generally include option periods; and equipment—3 to 12 years.

Property and Equipment (in millions of $U.S.)	Dec. 31, 2005	Dec. 31, 2004
Land	$ 4,486.9	$ 4,661.1
Buildings and improvements on owned land	10,104.5	10,260.3
Buildings and improvements on leased land	10,243.9	10,520.7
Equipment, signs, and seating	4,468.1	4,426.1
Other	593.7	639.6
	29,897.2	30,507.8
Accumulated depreciation and amortization	(9,989.2)	(9,804.7)
Net property and equipment	$19,908.0	$20,703.1

Depreciation and amortization expense was (in millions): 2005—$1,186.7; 2004—$1,138.3; 2003—$1,113.3.

Other information (in millions of $U.S.)	2005	2004	2003
Cash provided by operations	$4,336.8	$3,903.6	$3,268.8
Capital expenditures	$1,606.8	$1,419.3	$1,307.4
Free cash flow	$2,730.0	$2,484.3	$1,961.4
Cash provided by operations as a percent of capital expenditures	144%	141%	141%

Instructions

(a) What method of amortization is used by McDonald's? Does this method seem appropriate for the types of assets that McDonald's has? Comment.

(b) Does depreciation and amortization expense cause cash flows from operations to increase? Explain.

(c) What is "free cash flow"? What is its significance?

(d) Comment on the level of McDonald's cash flows from operations.

RA11-3 Canadian National Railway Company and Canadian Pacific Railway Limited

Two well-known company names in the transportation industry in Canada are Canadian National Railway Company and Canadian Pacific Railway Limited. Go to either SEDAR (www.sedar.com) or the Student Website to gain access to the financial statements of these companies for their years ended December 31, 2005.

Instructions

(a) How significant are the investments made by these companies in property, plant, and equipment? Express the size of these investments as a percentage of total assets.

(b) Compare the types of property, plant, and equipment that each company reports.

(c) Do the companies follow similar policies in what they capitalize as part of property, plant, and equipment?

(d) What methods of amortization are used by each company?

(e) For assets that are similar at both companies, compare their useful lives and/or rates of amortization. Are these similar or would applying them result in differences in the reported results for each year? Explain briefly.

RA11-4 Loblaw Companies Limited and Sobeys Inc.

Loblaw Companies Limited and Sobeys Inc. are competitors in the Canadian food industry. Go to either the Student Website or SEDAR (www.sedar.com) to gain access to the financial statements of Loblaw Companies Limited for its year ended December 31, 2005, and Sobeys Inc. for its year ended May 6, 2006.

Instructions

(a) What amount is reported in the balance sheets as property, plant, and equipment (net) of Loblaw Companies at December 31, 2005, and of Sobeys Inc. at May 6, 2006? What percentage of total assets is invested in this type of asset by each company?

(b) What amortization methods are used by Loblaw and Sobeys? What types of property, plant, and equipment do both companies report? Are they similar? Are their amortization policies and rates similar? How much amortization was reported by each company in each of its last two years?

(c) Calculate, compare, and comment on the following ratios for Loblaw and Sobeys for their most recent year:

1. Asset turnover
2. Profit margin on sales
3. Return on assets

(d) What amount was spent by Loblaw in its most recent year for capital expenditures? By Sobeys? Where do you find this information in the financial statements? What amount of interest, if any, was capitalized by each company?

(e) Does either Loblaw or Sobeys mention anything about the impairment of its long-lived assets? Comment.

RA11-5 Homburg Invest Inc.—An International Comparison

Usually an international comparison assignment involves comparing two similar companies that are reporting under different GAAP. If possible, it would be better to compare the same company's financial reports prepared on two different bases. Homburg Invest Inc., a Canadian company, does exactly that, and notes that the most significant differences relate to its fixed assets.

Instructions

Access the financial statements of Homburg Invest Inc. under both bases of accounting for its year ended December 31, 2005, on SEDAR at www.sedar.com. Review the statements and answer the following questions.

(a) What business is Homburg Invest Inc. in? What two sets of accounting standards does it report under?

(b) Identify the single most significant GAAP difference, and what effect this has on the balance sheet, income statement, and statement of cash flows. Be specific.

(c) Calculate the following ratios for the company's year ended December 31, 2005, under both Canadian GAAP and international standards:

1. Total asset turnover

2. Profit margin

3. Return on assets

(d) Comment on the results obtained in part (c). In your opinion, which set of ratios provides a better assessment of the company's profitability? Explain.

(e) Based on your findings, write a short memo to the chief financial officer of a Canadian company in the same business as Homburg. You need to alert its CFO to the possible effects that the company will experience when Canadian financial accounting requirements are changed to international standards, which is expected to occur in 2011.

RA11-6 Research Topic

A topic that concerns not-for-profit organizations and relates to their long-lived assets is the matter of "deferred maintenance." Canadian schools and universities in particular are concerned with this issue.

Instructions

(a) Research the topic of deferred maintenance well enough so that you understand the term. Explain the concept in 50 words or less.

(b) Interview the chief financial officer of your school, university, or other not-for-profit or government organization to discuss the issue. Can you determine from an organization's financial statements if it has a deferred maintenance problem? Should you be able to? Discuss.

The Intangible Value of Exposure

With the availability of music to download free off the Internet, record companies have complained loudly about copyright infringement and the threat to their businesses. But at least one music industry executive is not worried about this. Craig Horton is the director of publishing at Nettwerk One Music (Canada) Limited, a division of Vancouver-based music producer Nettwerk. He represents songwriters, and exploits their copyrights through CD sales, Internet streaming, podcasts, downloads, ringtones, and the use of their music in film, television, and commercials.

While CD sales have decreased in recent years, film and television companies and advertising agencies have become more interested in the music they include in their productions, and may look to the Internet to find new talent, and thus increase the value of the songwriter's copyright. "Songs earn a specific income from record sales. The Canadian rate is eight and a half cents per track," Horton says. "But when it comes to use in TV, film, or commercials, you can attach any value to that song. We're really ramping up this side of the business." Of the hundred or so Nettwerk staff members in Vancouver, London, Hamburg, New York, Nashville, Boston, and Los Angeles, seven work exclusively on negotiating synchronization rights, the right to use the song in a production. "Music has increasingly become important in television shows and films. Every movie that comes out, one of the first things they think about is the film's soundtrack and the soundtrack album," Horton says, adding that this is another offshoot in negotiating copyright since it involves a whole other set of rights and another revenue stream.

chapter 12

Goodwill and Other Intangible Assets

Learning Objectives

After studying this chapter, you should be able to:

1. Define and describe the characteristics of intangible assets.
2. Identify the recognition and measurement requirements for purchased intangible assets and internally developed intangible assets.
3. Explain how identifiable intangibles are valued after acquisition.
4. Identify and explain the accounting for specific types of intangible assets.
5. Explain the concept of goodwill and apply the accounting procedures for recording goodwill at acquisition and subsequently.
6. Account for intangible asset impairments.
7. Differentiate between research expenditures and development expenditures, and describe and explain the rationale for the accounting for them.
8. Identify other examples of internally developed intangibles and the accounting requirements for them.
9. Identify the disclosure requirements for intangibles and the issues in analyzing this asset category.
10. Compare current Canadian and international GAAP.

After studying the appendix to this chapter, you should be able to:

11. Explain and apply basic approaches to valuing goodwill.

Preview of Chapter 12

As the opening vignette shows, technology is one factor that plays a major role in the growth of intangible asset values for companies and in the risks associated with them. Indeed, because of the growth of the information age, the accounting for and reporting of intangible assets has become increasingly important. This chapter therefore explains the basic conceptual and reporting issues related to intangible assets.

It is organized as follows:

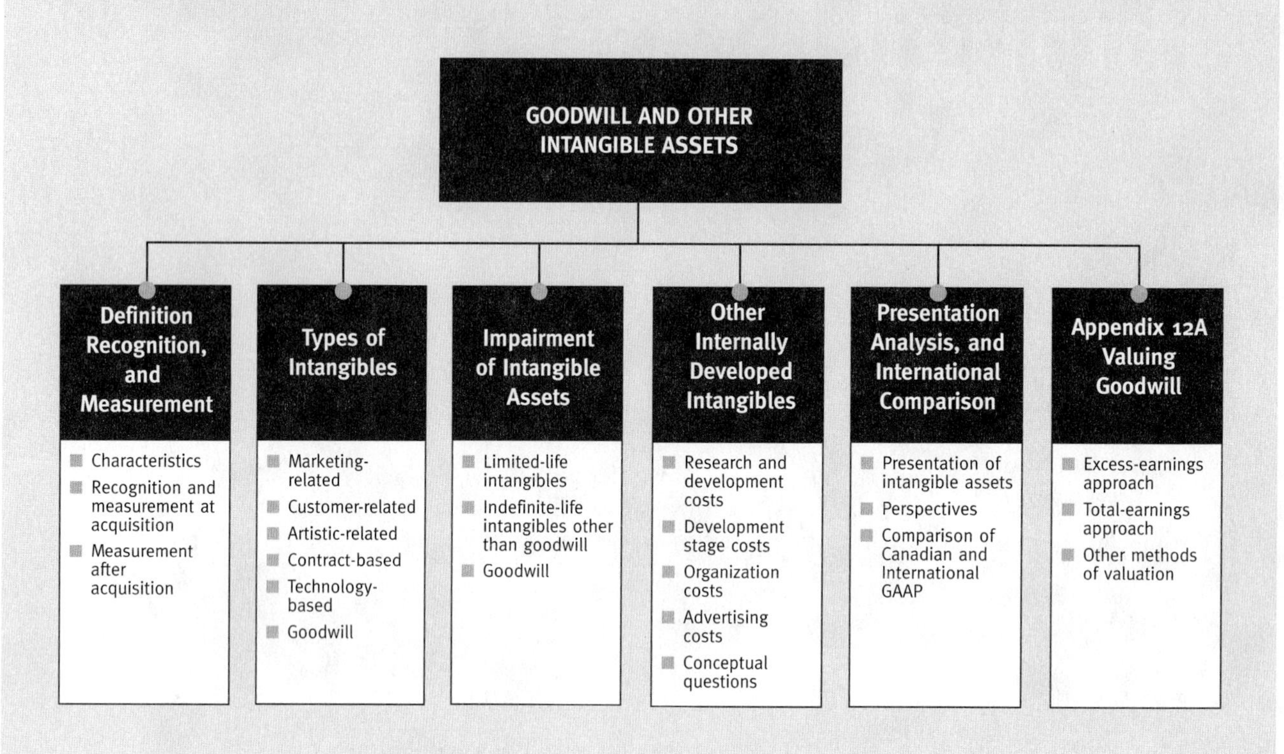

DEFINITION, RECOGNITION, AND MEASUREMENT OF INTANGIBLE ASSETS

Characteristics

Objective 1
Define and describe the characteristics of intangible assets.

Roots Canada's most important asset is not store fixtures—it's the brand image. The major asset of Coca-Cola is not its plant facilities—it's the secret formula for making Coke. Sympatico's most important asset is not its Internet connection equipment—it's the subscriber base. We have an economy that is increasingly dominated by information and service providers, and their major assets are often intangible in nature. Identifying and measuring these intangibles is often difficult, and as a result many intangibles have not been captured on companies' balance sheets.

What are intangible assets? Broadly defined, **intangible assets** are assets that lack physical substance and are not financial assets.[1] These characteristics can be explained as follows:

1. **They lack physical substance.** Unlike for tangible assets such as property, plant, and equipment, the value of intangible assets comes from the rights and privileges that are granted to the company using them.
2. **They are not financial instruments.** Assets such as bank deposits, accounts receivable, and long-term investments in bonds and shares may lack physical substance, but they are not classified as intangible assets. They are financial instruments and their value comes from the right (or claim) to receive cash or cash equivalents in the future. Intangible assets do not provide any such right or claim.

International Insight

IAS 38 defines an intangible asset as an identifiable non-monetary asset without physical substance.

In most cases, intangible assets provide benefits over a period of years. As a result, they are normally classified as long-term assets. Examples of intangibles under this definition include such widely varied assets as patents, copyrights, franchises or licensing agreements, trademarks or trade names, secret formulas, computer software, goodwill, technological know-how, superior management, prepayments, and some development costs. Specific intangibles are discussed later in the chapter.

Recognition and Measurement at Acquisition

Purchased Intangibles

2 Objective
Identify the recognition and measurement requirements for purchased intangible assets and internally developed intangible assets.

Intangible assets that are purchased from another party are **measured at cost**. Cost includes the acquisition cost and all expenditures that are necessary to make the intangible asset ready for its intended use—for example, the purchase price, legal fees, and other incidental expenses. Cost, as was seen in earlier chapters, is the cash cost. If there are delayed payment terms, any portion of the payments that represents interest is recognized as a financing expense rather than as part of the capitalized asset cost. If the intangible asset is acquired for shares or in exchange for other non-monetary assets, the **cost of the intangible is the fair value of the consideration given or the fair value of the intangible received, whichever one can be measured more reliably**.

When several intangibles, or a combination of intangibles and tangibles, are bought in a "basket purchase," the cost is allocated based on fair values. The cost principle essentially applies to purchased intangibles in the same way as it does to purchased tangible assets.

Underlying Concept

The basic attributes of intangibles, the uncertainty of their future benefits, and their uniqueness have discouraged valuing them at more than their cost.

When an enterprise purchases intangible assets as single assets, the accounting is straightforward. When they are acquired as part of a group of assets, however, such as in a business combination, the entity must determine whether the intangible assets should be separately recognized, and to what extent, or if they are considered a part of goodwill. A **business combination** occurs when one entity acquires control over the net assets of another business either by acquiring the net assets directly or by acquiring the equity interests that give control over the net assets. In either case, the purchase price is allocated among all the assets and liabilities to which a value can be attributed—the company's **identifiable net assets**—and any unidentified excess is recognized as goodwill.[2]

International Insight

IAS 38 allows intangibles that can be traded in an active market to be revalued periodically to fair value.

[1] *CICA Handbook*, Section 3062.05(c).

[2] If the net assets are acquired directly, the purchase price is allocated directly to the individual assets and liabilities that have been acquired. If control over the assets is acquired through the acquisition of voting shares, the purchase price is allocated to the identifiable assets and liabilities through the consolidation process.

Identifiable intangibles must have at least one of the following characteristics:

1. they result from contractual or other legal rights,
2. they are intangible assets that can be identified because they can be separated from the entity and sold, transferred, licensed, rented, or exchanged.[3]

For example, the right to lease space at favourable rates arises from contractual arrangements and the right may or may not be transferable to others. A subscription list of a newspaper or successful magazine has value in contributing to future revenue streams and is saleable. These are examples of identifiable intangibles that are given separate recognition.

Goodwill and other intangibles, on the other hand, are not separable from the rest of the entity, and control over the future benefits does not result from contractual or legal rights. For example, the synergies of a combined sales force or a superior management team can be identified as an intangible that has value, but the inability to separate these benefits from the entity in order to exchange them with others or the inability to control the benefits through contractual or other legal rights means that they cannot be recognized as separate identifiable intangibles. They are therefore considered part of goodwill.

While it is important to distinguish one identifiable intangible from another, financial reporting objectives are not well met if every identifiable intangible is recognized separately. At a minimum, the ones that have similar characteristics (such as continuity, stability, and risk) are grouped and recognized together. Because knowledge-based and high-technology companies with large investments in "soft" intangible assets are an important part of our modern economy, how accounting treats such intangibles is a major issue.

Lastly, as occurs for other long-lived assets, when direct costs are incurred after acquisition of the intangible asset in order to enhance its service potential, these costs are accounted for as betterments and are capitalized.

Internally Developed Intangibles

Costs that a company incurs internally to create intangible assets are **generally expensed as they are incurred**. Thus, even though a company may incur substantial research costs that result in its eventually being granted a patent, these costs are expensed as they are incurred. However, the direct costs of obtaining the intangible asset, such as legal costs, are capitalized.

Various reasons are given for this approach. The main argument relates to the uncertainty, **at the time when the research expenditures are made,** of the future benefits that will be had from these expenditures. Supporters argue that the costs that are incurred internally to create such intangibles as patents and brand names have no relationship to their real value, and it is difficult to associate the incurred costs with specific intangible assets. Expensing these costs, therefore, is appropriate. If future benefits are reasonably assured and other aspects of the definition of an asset are met when the costs are incurred, both the direct development costs and overhead costs that can be attributed directly to the development activity are capitalized.[4] Such assets are known as **internally developed intangibles**.

Deferred Charges

A variety of other current expenditures are made with the intention of providing the enterprise with future benefits. In such situations, arguments have been made to defer the costs' recognition as expense until the future benefits are received. Over the last 25 years or so, with the shift toward an accounting model that focuses on asset and liability definition, it has become less acceptable to recognize deferred charges as assets unless the resulting

[3] *CICA Handbook*, Section 1581.48.

[4] *CICA Handbook*, Section 3062.07.

costs meet the definition and recognition requirements of Section 1000, Financial Statement Concepts.[5] Accounting standards continue to be tightened so that the capitalization of deferred costs is only permitted when specific requirements are met.

For the discussion that follows, intangibles are classified into intangible assets that are specifically identifiable, goodwill-type intangible assets, and other internally developed intangibles. The accounting treatment of these three types of intangible assets is shown in Illustration 12-1.

Illustration 12-1

Accounting for the Acquisition Costs of Intangibles

	Manner Acquired	
Type of Intangible	Purchased	Internally Created
Identifiable	Capitalize	Expense, except certain costs
Goodwill-type	Capitalize	Expense
Other internally developed	Capitalize restricted amounts	Capitalize restricted amounts

Measurement after Acquisition

3 Objective
Explain how identifiable intangibles are valued after acquisition.

As has been suggested above, intangibles are a diverse mix of assets. Some intangibles have values based on rights that are given legally by contract, statute, or similar means. Examples include a Tim Hortons franchise or licences granted by government to cable companies. Some of these rights have finite or limited legal lives that can be easily renewed; others have lives that are not renewable, and others are renewable only at a significant cost. Some may be granted in perpetuity and be saleable, while others may not be exchangeable. Internally developed intangibles, such as some customer lists and databases, have a wide range of useful lives, including in some cases indefinite lives if the asset is maintained. An **indefinite life** does not mean "infinite"—that the asset will last forever; rather, it means that there are no legal, regulatory, contractual, competitive, economic, or other factors that appear to limit its useful life to the entity.[6]

International Insight

IAS 38 specifies that intangibles have an indefinite life if there is no foreseeable limit to the period over which the asset is expected to generate net cash flows.

Accounting standards used to require all intangibles to be amortized as they are used over a period of not more than 40 years. While this simplified the accounting, the reality is that intangibles are diverse, and the approach to their valuation after acquisition should be based on their specific characteristics. Under current standards, if an intangible asset has a finite useful life, it is amortized over that useful life. If instead the intangible has an indefinite life and gives no indication of impairment, no amortization is taken. Financial reporting is better served by retaining the asset in the accounts until the asset is determined to be impaired or its life becomes limited.

Limited-Life Intangibles

An intangible asset with a finite or limited life is amortized by systematic charges to expense over its useful life. The useful life should cover the periods over which these assets will contribute to cash flows. The factors to consider in determining the useful life are similar to the factors for long-lived property, plant, and equipment:

1. The expected use of the asset by the entity, and the expected useful life of other assets that may affect the useful life of the intangible asset (such as mineral rights to depleting assets).

[5] *CICA Handbook* Section 1000.29 defines assets as economic resources that are controlled by an entity as a result of past transactions or events and from which future economic benefits may be obtained. Many accountants argue that because deferred charges cannot be considered economic resources, they should not be given asset status.

[6] *CICA Handbook*, Section 3062.15.

2. Any legal, regulatory, or contractual provisions that may either limit the useful life or allow renewal or extension of the asset's legal or contractual life without the entity's having to pay a substantial cost.
3. The effects of obsolescence, demand, competition, and other economic factors. Examples include the stability of the industry, known technological advances, and legislative action that results in an uncertain or changing regulatory environment.
4. The level of maintenance expenditure that is needed to obtain the expected future cash flows from the asset.[7]

Amortization expense for a limited-life intangible asset should ideally reflect the pattern in which the asset's economic benefits are used up, if that pattern can be reliably determined. For example, assume that Second Wave, Inc. has purchased a licence to manufacture a limited quantity of a gene product called Mega. The cost of the licence is amortized following the pattern of production of Mega. If the pattern cannot be determined, the straight-line method is used. (For the assignment material, assume use of the straight-line method unless stated otherwise.) The amortization charges are usually shown **as expenses**, and the credits are made to **separate accumulated amortization accounts**. Note that in the Second Wave, Inc. example, the amortization is an inventoriable cost that is expensed on the income statement as part of cost of goods sold when the product is sold.

The amount to amortize for an intangible asset is its cost less residual value. Uncertainties about residual values for intangibles are greater than they are for items of property, plant, and equipment. Because of this, an intangible asset's residual value is assumed to be zero. There may be a residual value if the asset is expected to have use to another entity and a third party commits to purchase the asset at the end of its useful life, or if there is an observable market for the asset that is expected to still exist at the end of its useful life to the entity.[8]

What happens if a limited-life intangible asset's useful life changes? When this occurs, the remaining carrying amount is amortized over the revised remaining useful life. As explained later in the chapter, limited-life intangibles are also evaluated for impairment **on the same basis as items of property, plant, and equipment**.

Indefinite-Life Intangibles

An intangible asset with an indefinite life **is not amortized**. For example, assume that Double Clik, Inc. acquires a trademark that is used to distinguish a leading consumer product from other such products. The trademark is renewable every 10 years at minimal cost. All evidence indicates that this trademark product will generate cash flows for an indefinite period of time. In this case, the trademark has an indefinite life because it is expected to contribute to cash flows indefinitely.

Indefinite-life intangibles should be tested for impairment at least annually. **The impairment requirements for intangibles with an indefinite life are different** than the ones that are used for limited-life intangibles and property, plant, and equipment.

Illustration 12-2 summarizes the accounting treatment for intangible assets after acquisition.

Illustration 12-2
Accounting Treatment of Intangible Assets after Acquisition

Type of Intangible	Amortization	Impairment Test
Limited-life	Over useful life	Same test as for property, plant, and equipment
Indefinite-life	Do not amortize	A different test, based on fair values

[7] *CICA Handbook*, Section 3062.15.

[8] *CICA Handbook*, Section 3062.13.

TYPES OF INTANGIBLES

4 Objective
Identify and explain the accounting for specific types of intangible assets.

The many different types of intangibles are often classified into the following six major categories:[9]

1. Marketing-related intangible assets
2. Customer-related intangible assets
3. Artistic-related intangible assets
4. Contract-based intangible assets
5. Technology-based intangible assets
6. Goodwill

Marketing-Related Intangible Assets

Marketing-related intangible assets are used mainly in the marketing or promotion of products or services. Examples are trademarks or trade names, newspaper mastheads, Internet domain names, and non-competition agreements.

A very common form of marketing-related intangible asset is a trademark. A **trademark**, **trade name**, or **brand name** is a word, symbol, or design, or combination of these, that is used to distinguish the goods or services of one person or entity from those of others in the marketplace. The right to use a trademark, trade name, or brand name in Canada is granted by the federal government and the registration system is administered by its Trademarks Office.[10] In order to obtain and maintain this right, the owner must have made prior and continuing use of it. Trade names like Kraft Dinner, Pepsi-Cola, and Kleenex and brand names such as President's Choice create immediate product recognition in our minds, which makes them more marketable. Company names themselves also identify qualities and characteristics that the companies have worked hard and spent much on developing.[11]

If a mark or name is **purchased**, its capitalizable cost is the purchase price and other direct costs of acquisition. If it is **developed** by the enterprise itself and its future benefits to the company are reasonably assured, the costs that are capitalized include lawyers' fees, registration fees, design costs, consulting fees, successful legal defence costs, expenditures related to securing the mark or name, direct development costs, and overhead costs that are directly related to its development. When a trademark, trade name, or brand name's total cost is insignificant or if future benefits are uncertain at the time when the costs are incurred, they are expensed rather than capitalized.

What Do the Numbers Mean?

Hoping to promote the management of brands in the same financially robust way as other long-term investments, **Brand Finance plc** and **Ceteris**, in collaboration with the Institute of Communications and Advertising, published a report titled *Canada's Most Valuable Brands 2005* in early 2006. The study used a "royalty relief" approach to value the brands of major companies; that is, the authors determined how much a company would have to pay to license the brand from a third party, and the brand's value is the present value of that hypothetical stream of payments.

[9] This classification framework is used in "Business Combinations," *CICA Handbook* Section 1581, Appendix A.

[10] Canadian Intellectual Property Office: <http://strategis.ic.gc.ca>.

[11] To illustrate how various intangibles might arise from a specific product, consider what the creators of the highly successful game Trivial Pursuit did to protect their creation. First, they copyrighted the 6,000 questions that are at the heart of the game. Then they shielded the Trivial Pursuit name by applying for a registered trademark. As a third mode of protection, the creators obtained a design patent on the playing board's design because it represents a unique graphic creation.

The most valuable Canadian brand, according to this report, belongs to the Royal Bank of Canada, with an estimated worth of over $4.5 billion. Other major Canadian banks were numbers 4, 5, 6, and 7 on the list. The RBC brand, however, does not appear as an asset on the Royal Bank's balance sheet. Why not? Brand value is a function of marketing, advertising, and public relations spending, including customer loyalty and retention programs, which all result in increased volume of business, retail sales, and shipments. This type of cost is expensed as it is incurred because it cannot be directly related to future benefits.

Brand Finance contends that "long-term investment decisions about future promotional expenditures, and the host of other activities that combine to build brand value" are better made when management can articulate the arguments in financial terms, as is done for most other investments.

Trademark registrations in Canada last for 15 years, and are renewable at a reasonable cost. Although the legal life of such assets **may be unlimited**, in practice they may only provide benefits to the enterprise over a **finite** period. Trademarks can, however, be determined to provide benefits to an enterprise indefinitely. A brand such as Coca-Cola, worth billions of dollars, may reasonably be determined to have an indefinite useful life. In this case, the intangible asset is not amortized.

Customer-Related Intangible Assets

International Insight

IAS 38 specifies that internally generated brands, mastheads, publishing titles, customer lists, and other items that are similar in substance shall not be recognized as intangible assets.

Customer-related intangible assets result from interactions with outside parties. Examples are customer lists, order or production backlogs, and both contractual and non-contractual customer relationships.

To illustrate, assume that We-Market Inc. acquires the customer list of a large newspaper for $6 million on January 1, 2008. The customer list is a database that includes names, contact information, order history, and demographic information for a list of customers. We-Market expects to benefit from the information on the acquired list for three years, and it believes that these benefits will be spread evenly over the three years. In this case, the customer list is a limited-life intangible that should be amortized on a straight-line basis over the three-year period.

The entries to record the purchase of the customer list and its amortization at the end of each year are as follows:

A	= L	+ SE
0	0	0

Cash flows: ↓ 6,000,000 outflow

January 1, 2008		
Customer List	6,000,000	
Cash		6,000,000
(To record purchase of customer list)		

A	= L	+ SE
−2,000,000		−2,000,000

Cash flows: No effect

December 31, 2008, 2009, 2010		
Amortization Expense—Customer List	2,000,000	
Accumulated Amortization—Customer List		2,000,000
(To record amortization expense)		

This example assumes that the customer list has no residual value. But what if We-Market determines that it can sell the list for $60,000 to another company at the end of three years? In that case, the residual value is subtracted from the cost in order to determine the amortizable amount. A residual value of zero is assumed *unless* the asset's useful life to the entity is less than the economic life and there is reliable evidence about the existence and amount of residual value.[12]

[12] *CICA Handbook*, Section 3062.13.

Artistic-Related Intangible Assets

Artistic-related intangible assets involve ownership rights to plays, literary works, musical works, pictures, photographs, and video and audiovisual material. These ownership rights are protected by copyrights.

A **copyright** is the exclusive right to copy a creative work or allow someone else to do so. It is a federally granted right that applies to all original literary, dramatic, musical, and artistic works, whatever the mode or form of expression. A copyright is acquired automatically when an original work is created, but it can also be registered with the Copyright Office. The right is granted for the life of the creator plus 50 years, and gives the owner or heirs the exclusive right to reproduce, sell, communicate, or translate an artistic or published work. Copyrights are not renewable. Like trade names, they may be assigned or sold to other individuals.[13] The costs of acquiring and defending a copyright may be capitalized, but research costs that are associated with them are expensed as they are incurred.

Generally, the copyright's useful life is shorter than its legal life. Determining its useful life depends on the unique facts and circumstances of each case. Consumer habits, market trends, and prior experience all play a part, as indicated in the opening story to this chapter. Because it is so difficult to determine how many periods will benefit from a copyright, companies normally choose to write these costs off over a fairly short period of time. Amortization of the copyright is then charged to the years in which the benefits are expected to be received.

Copyrights can be valuable. **Really Useful Group** is a company that consists of copyrights on the musicals of Andrew Lloyd Webber, including *Cats*, *Phantom of the Opera*, *Jesus Christ Superstar*, and others. It has few hard assets, yet has been valued at more than U.S. $300 million. The **Walt Disney Company** once faced the loss of its copyright on Mickey Mouse, a loss which could have affected sales of billions of dollars of Mickey-related goods and services, including theme parks. This copyright was so valuable that Disney and many other big entertainment companies fought all the way to the Supreme Court of the United States—and won, getting an extension of copyright lives from 50 to 70 years!

Contract-Based Intangible Assets

Contract-based intangible assets are the value of rights that come from contractual arrangements. Examples are licensing arrangements, leaseholds, construction permits, broadcast rights, and service or supply contracts. A very common form of contract-based intangible asset is a franchise.

When you drive down the street in an automobile purchased from a **Toyota** dealer, fill your tank at the corner **Petro-Canada** station, grab a coffee at **Tim Hortons**, eat lunch at **McDonald's**, cool off with a **Baskin-Robbins** cone, work at a **Coca-Cola** bottling plant, live in a home purchased through a **Royal Le Page** real estate broker, or vacation at a **Holiday Inn** resort, you are dealing with franchises. A **franchise** is a contractual arrangement under which the franchisor grants the franchisee the right to sell certain products or services, to use certain trademarks, trade names, or brands, or to perform certain functions, usually within a designated geographic area. **Licensing agreements** work in a similar way.

After having developed a unique concept or product, the franchisor protects it through a patent, copyright, trademark, or trade name. The franchisee then acquires the right to exploit the franchisor's idea or product by signing a franchise agreement. Another type of franchise is the arrangement that is commonly entered into by a municipality or other government body and a business enterprise that uses public property. In this case, a privately owned enterprise is given permission to use public property in performing its services.

---

[13] Canadian Intellectual Property Office site: <http://strategis.ic.gc.ca>.

Examples are the use of public waterways for a ferry service, the use of public land for telephone or electric lines, the use of city streets for a bus line, or the use of the airwaves for radio or TV broadcasting. Such operating rights are frequently referred to as **licences** or **permits**, and are obtained through agreements with government departments or agencies.

Franchises and licences may be granted for a definite period of time, for an indefinite period of time, or in perpetuity. The enterprise that acquires the franchise or licence recognizes an intangible asset account titled either Franchise or Licence on its books as soon as there are costs (such as a lump sum payment in advance or legal fees and other expenditures) that are identified with the acquisition of the operating right. The cost of a franchise or licence **with a limited life** is amortized over the lesser of its legal or useful life. A franchise **with an indefinite life, or a perpetual franchise**, is amortized if its **useful life** is deemed to be limited. Otherwise, it is not amortized and continues to be carried at cost.

Annual payments made under a franchise agreement are entered as operating expenses in the period in which they are incurred. They do not represent an asset to the enterprise since they do not relate to future rights.

Another contract-related intangible asset is a **leasehold**: a contractual understanding between a lessor (property owner) and a lessee (property renter) that grants the lessee the right to use specific property, owned by the lessor, for a certain period of time in return for specific cash payments that are generally periodic. In most cases, the periodic rent is included as an expense on the lessee's books.

If the rent for the lease period is paid in advance, or if a lump sum payment is made in advance in addition to periodic rental payments, the **lease prepayments** are allocated as rent expense to the proper periods. By making such advance payments, the lessee purchases the exclusive right to use the property for an extended period of time. These prepayments are usually reported as a prepaid expense or deferred charge rather than as an identifiable intangible asset, even though they meet the definition of an intangible asset.

Leasehold improvements—i.e., improvements that are made to leased property by the lessee—become assets of the lessor at the end of the lease. These are usually recognized and accounted for as property, plant, and equipment rather than as intangible assets.

Underlying Concept

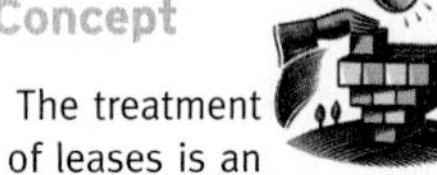

The treatment of leases is an example of the importance of asset definition. The definition of an asset does not require the lessee to obtain ownership but it does require that the asset's benefits flow to and be under the control of the entity.

Special accounting is required in situations where the contract results in a **capital lease**. This happens when the lease agreement transfers substantially all the benefits and risks associated with property ownership to the lessee so that the economic effect on both parties is similar to that of an instalment sale and purchase. In this case, the lease is capitalized as a tangible asset rather than as an intangible, and the present value of the future lease payments is recognized as a long-term liability. Such a lease is referred to as a **capital lease**, and is covered more fully in Chapter 20.

Technology-Based Intangible Assets

Technology-based intangible assets relate to innovations or technological advances. Examples are technology and trade secrets that are granted protection by the federal government's Patent Office. Patents are granted for products and processes that are new, workable, and ingenious. A **patent** gives the holder the right to exclude others from making, selling, or using a product or process for a period of 20 years from the date of application. Fortunes can be made by holding patents, as companies such as **RIM**, **Bombardier**, **IMAX**, **Polaroid**, and **Xerox** can attest.[14]

---

[14] Consider the opposite result: Sir Alexander Fleming, who discovered penicillin, decided not to use a patent to protect his discovery. He hoped that companies would produce it more quickly to help save sufferers. Companies, however, refused to develop it because they did not have the protection of a patent and, therefore, were afraid to make the investment.

If a patent is purchased from an inventor or other owner, the purchase price represents its cost. Other costs that are incurred in connection with securing a patent, as well as legal fees and other unrecovered costs of a successful lawsuit to protect the patent, can be capitalized as part of the patent cost. Research and development costs related to developing a product, process, or idea that is subsequently patented, however, are usually expensed as they are incurred. A more complete discussion of accounting for research and development costs is found later in this chapter.

The cost of a patent is amortized over its legal life or its useful life to the entity, whichever is shorter. If a patent is owned from the date it is granted, and it is expected to be useful during its entire legal life, it is amortized over 20 years. If it appears that it will be useful for a shorter period of time, its cost is amortized to expense over that shorter period.

Changing demand, new inventions replacing old ones, inadequacy, and other factors often limit the useful life of a patent to less than its legal life. For example, the useful life of patents in the pharmaceutical and drug industry is often less than the legal life because of the testing and approval period that follows their issuance. A typical drug patent has five to 11 years knocked off its 20-year legal life. Why? Because a drug manufacturer spends one to four years on animal tests, four to six years on human tests, and two to three years for government agencies to review the tests—all after the patent is issued but before the product goes on the pharmacist's shelves.

Legal fees and other costs that are associated with a successful defence of a patent are capitalized as part of the asset's cost because lawsuits establish the legal rights of the patent holder. Such costs are amortized along with other acquisition costs over the remaining useful life of the patent.

Ideally, patent amortization should follow a pattern that is consistent with the benefits that are received, if that pattern can be reliably determined. This could be based on time or on units produced. To illustrate, assume that on January 1, 2008, Harcott Ltd. either pays $180,000 to acquire a patent or incurs $180,000 in legal costs to successfully defend an internally developed patent. Further, assume that the patent has a remaining useful life of 12 years and is amortized on a straight-line basis. The entries to record the $180,000 expenditure and the amortization at the end of each year are as follows:

January 1, 2008		
Patents	180,000	
Cash		180,000
(To record expenditure related to patent)		
December 31, 2008		
Patent Amortization Expense	15,000	
Accumulated Amortization, Patents		15,000
(To record amortization of patent)		

A	=	L	+	SE
0		0		0

Cash flows: ↓ 180,000 outflow

A	=	L	+	SE
−15,000				−15,000

Cash flows: No effect

Although a patent's useful life may be limited by its legal life, small modifications or additions may lead to a new patent and an extension of the life of the old patent. In this case, the entity can apply the unamortized costs of the old patent to the new patent if the new patent provides essentially the same benefits. Alternatively, if a patent's value is reduced because, for example, demand drops for the product, the asset should be tested for impairment. [15]

[15] Eli Lilly's well-known drug Prozac, which is used to treat depression, accounted for 43% of the company's U.S. sales in 1998. The patent on Prozac expired in 2001 and the company was unable to extend its protection with a second-use patent for the use of Prozac to treat appetite disorders. Sales of Prozac went down substantially in 2001 as generic equivalents entered the market.

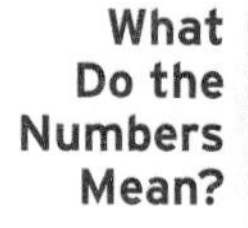

Coca-Cola has managed to keep the recipe for the world's best-selling soft drink under wraps for more than 100 years. How has it done so? The company offers almost no information about its lifeblood. The only written copy of the formula is in a bank vault in Atlanta, Georgia. This handwritten sheet is not available to anyone except by vote of the Coca-Cola board of directors.

Why is science unable to offer some clues? Coke contains 17 to 18 ingredients. These include the usual caramel colour and corn syrup, as well as a blend of oils known as 7X—rumoured to be a mix of orange, lemon, cinnamon, and others. Distilling natural products like these is complicated since they are made of thousands of compounds. Although the original formula contained trace amounts of cocaine, this is one ingredient that you will no longer find in today's Coke. When was it removed? That is a secret, too. Some experts indicate that the power of this formula and related brand image account for almost 95 percent of Coke's U.S. $150 billion share value.

Source: Adapted from Reed Tucker, "How Has Coke's Formula Stayed a Secret?" *Fortune* (July 24, 2000), p. 42.

Another common technology-based intangible relates to **computer software costs**, either for internal use or for sale as a product. Costs that are incurred in the development of software as a product **for external use** are discussed under research and development costs later in this chapter. The accounting for "costs of activities directly attributable to the development, betterment or acquisition of computer software **for internal use**" is covered by the same capitalization criteria required for goodwill and other intangible assets.[16] This means that the cost of purchased software and the direct costs and overhead costs that can be attributed directly to the development of software for internal use may be recognized as intangible assets—provided future benefits are reasonably assured. The cost of any modifications to the computer software can only be capitalized when they meet the definition of a betterment.

What about the costs that a company incurs in developing its own website? The Emerging Issues Committee of the CICA concluded in EIC-118 that the **costs incurred in developing a website** were varied, and that the accounting treatment should be contingent on the type of activity. In general, costs that are incurred in the planning stage, costs to convert existing content to the new system, and regular operating costs should be expensed as they are incurred. On the other hand, costs that are incurred in the website application and infrastructure development stage and expenditures to develop the initial graphics that provide the overall design of the web page should be capitalized. In general, the principles that underlie the recognition and measurement criteria for tangible and intangible long-lived assets are applied here as well.

Goodwill

Objective 5
Explain the concept of goodwill and apply the accounting procedures for recording goodwill at acquisition and subsequently.

Although companies are permitted to capitalize certain costs that are incurred in order to develop identifiable assets such as patents and copyrights, the amounts that are capitalized are generally not significant. Material amounts of intangible assets are recorded, however, when companies purchase intangible assets, and particularly in situations where another business is being purchased, usually referred to as a business combination.

In a business combination, the cost of acquiring the business is assigned first to the identifiable tangible and intangible assets that are acquired and the liabilities that are assumed. The remainder is recorded in an intangible asset account called Goodwill. **Goodwill** is the excess of the purchase cost of a company over the fair value of the identifiable assets acquired

[16] *CICA Handbook*, EIC-86.

and liabilities assumed.[17] Goodwill is often referred to as the most intangible of the intangibles. It is an unidentified excess, and it can only be calculated in relation to the business as a whole. The only way it can be sold is to sell the business.

Recognition of Internally Generated Goodwill

Goodwill that is generated internally is not capitalized in the accounts. Measuring the components of goodwill is simply too complex and associating any costs with future benefits is too difficult. Indeed, the future benefits of goodwill may have no relationship to the costs that were incurred in its development. To add to the mystery, goodwill may even exist when there have been no specific costs to develop it. In addition, because no objective transaction with outside parties has taken place, a great deal of subjectivity—even misrepresentation—might be involved in trying to measure it.

Recognition of Purchased Goodwill

For accounting purposes, goodwill is only recognized when a business combination occurs, because the value of goodwill cannot be separated from a business as a whole. The problem of determining the proper amount to allocate to identifiable intangible assets in a business combination is complex because of the many different types of intangibles that might be acquired. Because goodwill is a residual amount, every dollar that is allocated to other assets, including identifiable intangible assets, is one less dollar assigned to goodwill.

Underlying Concept

Capitalizing goodwill only when it is purchased in an arm's-length transaction and not capitalizing any goodwill that is generated internally is another example of reliability winning out over relevance.

To illustrate, assume that Multi-Diversified, Inc. decides that it needs a parts division to supplement its existing tractor distributorship. The president of Multi-Diversified is interested in buying Tractorling Ltd., a small concern near Toronto that has an established reputation and is looking for a merger candidate. Illustration 12-3 shows Tractorling's balance sheet.

Illustration 12-3
Tractorling Ltd. Balance Sheet

TRACTORLING LTD.
Balance Sheet
December 31, 2007

Assets		Equities	
Cash	$ 25,000	Current liabilities	$ 55,000
Receivables	35,000	Share capital	100,000
Inventories	42,000	Retained earnings	100,000
Property, plant, and equipment, net	153,000		
Total assets	$255,000	Total equities	$255,000

After considerable negotiation, Tractorling Ltd.'s shareholders decide to accept Multi-Diversified's offer of $400,000. What is the value of the goodwill, if any?

The answer is not obvious. The fair values of Tractorling's identifiable assets are not disclosed in its cost-based balance sheet. It is likely, though, that as the negotiations progressed, Multi-Diversified had a detailed investigation done of Tractorling's underlying assets to determine their fair values. Such an investigation may be done through a purchase audit by Multi-Diversified's auditors, or an independent appraisal from some other source. Illustration 12-4 shows the results.

[17] When changes to the business combinations standards (in Exposure Draft form in early 2007) are approved by the IASB and the FASB, the definition of goodwill is likely to change. As this text went to print, the FASB and the IASB were continuing discussions on what the appropriate measurement attributes are for assets acquired, liabilities assumed, and non-controlling interests in a less-than-100-percent acquisition. A finalized standard may not be effective until 2009.

Illustration 12-4
Fair Values of Tractorling Ltd.'s Identifiable Net Assets

Fair Values, December 31, 2007	
Cash	$ 25,000
Receivables	35,000
Inventories	62,000
Property, plant, and equipment, net	265,000
Patents	18,000
Liabilities	(55,000)
Fair value of identifiable net assets	$350,000

Differences between the current fair value and carrying amount are more common among long-term assets, although there can also be significant differences in the current asset category. Cash is obviously not a problem in terms of its value and receivables are normally fairly close to their current valuation, although adjustments do sometimes need to be made because of inadequate bad debt provisions. The fair values of liabilities also are usually close to their recorded book values. However, if interest rates have changed since long-term liabilities were incurred, their current value, which is determined using current interest rates, may be quite different from their carrying amount. A careful analysis must also be done to ensure that there are no unrecorded liabilities.

Returning to our example, the $20,000 difference between the fair value and carrying amount of Tractorling's inventories ($62,000 – $42,000) could be due to several factors. One explanation might be that Tractorling acquired significant inventories when the prices were lower and uses specific identification or an average cost valuation, in which ending inventory is made up of inventory at older costs.

For their part, the values of long-lived assets such as property, plant, and equipment and intangibles will, in many cases, have increased substantially over the years. Any difference could also be due to inaccurate estimates of useful lives or residual values, a policy of continually expensing small expenditures (say, amounts less than $1,000), or substantial increases in replacement costs. Alternatively, there may be assets that have not been recognized in the company's books. In Tractorling's case, land had been acquired many years ago and its fair value had increased significantly, and internally developed patents had not been recognized in the accounts, yet they have a fair value of $18,000.

Since the fair value of the identifiable net assets is determined to be $350,000, why would Multi-Diversified pay $400,000? The seller might point to the company's established reputation, good credit rating, its top management team, well-trained employees, and so on as factors that make the value of the business as a going concern greater than $350,000. At the same time, Multi-Diversified places a premium on the future earning power of these attributes as well as the enterprise's basic asset structure today. At this point in the negotiations, the company's fair value, and price, can be due to many factors; the most important is probably sheer skill at the bargaining table.[18]

Until new accounting standards are agreed on for business combinations, the difference in our example between the cost of the acquisition of $400,000 and the fair value of the identifiable net assets of $350,000 is labelled goodwill.[19] Goodwill is viewed as one or a group of unidentifiable values plus the value of the identifiable intangibles that do not meet the criteria for separate recognition. The procedure for valuation, shown in

[18] Sometimes the excess that is paid is really due to the purchaser's stubbornness or ego, that is, to wanting the business at any price. In this situation, the price paid in excess of the business's fair value should be recognized as a loss.

[19] As indicated in footnote 17, the FASB, IASB, and AcSB in Canada have been working on new harmonized standards for business combinations. In Canada, this will result eventually in new *Handbook* Section 1582. The final standards may not be effective until 2009.

Illustration 12-5, is referred to as a master valuation approach, because goodwill is assumed to cover all the values that cannot be specifically associated with any identifiable tangible or intangible asset.

Purchase price of $400,000 assigned to		
	Cash	$ 25,000
	Receivables	35,000
	Inventories	62,000
	Property, plant, and equipment	265,000
	Patents	18,000
	Liabilities	(55,000)
	Fair value of identifiable net assets	350,000
	Purchase price	400,000
	Value assigned to goodwill	$ 50,000

Illustration 12-5
Determination of Goodwill–Master Valuation Approach

Multi-Diversified's entry to record the purchase of Tractorling's net assets is as follows:[20]

Cash	25,000	
Receivables	35,000	
Inventories	62,000	
Property, plant, and equipment	265,000	
Patents	18,000	
Goodwill	50,000	
Liabilities		55,000
Cash		400,000

A = L + SE
+55,000 +55,000

Cash flows: ↓ 375,000 outflow

Bargain Purchase

A **bargain purchase**, resulting in what is sometimes called **negative goodwill**, arises when the fair value of the identifiable net assets that are acquired is higher than the purchase price, the fair value of the consideration transferred for those net assets. This situation is a result of market imperfection (a poor decision by the seller) because the seller would be better off to sell the assets individually than in total. However, situations do occur when the amount paid is less than the value of the identifiable net assets that are acquired, and this requires that a "credit" be accounted for.

How should this credit be handled in the accounts? Should it be taken to retained earnings directly, to the income statement in the year of purchase, or amortized to income over a reasonable future period? The accounting standards over the past thirty years have taken a variety of approaches to this "bonus," which shows the difficulty there has been in coming to terms with its conceptual nature. The current standard requires that the excess be used to reduce the amounts that are assigned to other assets that were acquired in the purchase and that are generally non-financial in nature. If their values are reduced to zero and some of the excess still remains, the excess amount is recognized as an extraordinary

[20] If Multi-Diversified purchased all of Tractorling's shares instead of the net assets directly, the entry would be:

Investment in Shares of Tractorling	400,000	
Cash		400,000

When Multi-Diversified prepares consolidated financial statements, the Investment account is removed from the balance sheet and is replaced with the underlying assets and liabilities that the Investment balance represents. Regardless of the transaction's legal form, the goodwill appears on the investor's balance sheet.

gain.[21] While some critics do not agree with the recognition of a gain **on the purchase of assets**, this treatment appears to be a practical approach to a situation that rarely occurs. Further discussion of this issue is left to an advanced course in financial accounting.

Valuation after Acquisition

International Insight

Standard setters have had difficulty determining the most appropriate method. Until recently, companies in the UK were allowed to write off goodwill immediately against equity. In 1998, UK companies were required to capitalize and amortize goodwill. With the move to IFRS, they now apply a non-amortization and test-for-impairment policy.

Once goodwill has been recognized in the accounts, how should it be treated in subsequent periods? Three basic approaches have been suggested:

1. **Charge goodwill off immediately to expense.** Because goodwill is not separable and distinct from the business as a whole as other assets are, supporters of this approach say that goodwill demands special treatment. They justify an immediate write-off on the grounds that it makes the accounting for purchased goodwill and goodwill that is created internally consistent, since goodwill created internally does not appear as an asset.

   They further argue that amortization of purchased goodwill leads to double counting, because net income is reduced by amortization of the purchased goodwill as well as by the internal expenditure that is made to maintain or increase its value. Perhaps the best rationale for charging goodwill against income directly is that identifying the periods over which the future benefits are to be received is so difficult that the result is purely arbitrary.

2. **Amortize goodwill over its useful life.** Others believe that goodwill has value when it is acquired, but that its value eventually disappears and it is appropriate that the asset be charged to expense over the periods that are affected. Supporters of this view argue that, to the extent that goodwill represents a wasting asset, this method provides a better matching of the costs of the benefits to revenues than other methods, even though the useful life may be difficult to determine.

3. **Retain goodwill indefinitely unless a reduction in value occurs.** Others believe that goodwill can have an indefinite life and should be retained as an asset until a decline in value occurs. They contend that some form of goodwill should always be an asset since internal goodwill is being expensed to maintain or enhance the purchased goodwill. In addition, unless there is sufficient evidence that a decline in value has occurred, a write-off of goodwill is arbitrary and leads to distortions in net income.

Before 2002, companies were required to amortize goodwill over a period not longer than 40 years. This has changed. Goodwill that is acquired in a business combination **is now considered to have an indefinite life and is no longer amortized**. The standard setters' position is that investors generally do not find the amortization charge helpful in evaluating an entity's performance. In addition, although goodwill may decrease over time, predicting the actual life of goodwill and an appropriate pattern of amortization is extremely difficult. For these reasons, **income statements are not charged with any costs of goodwill unless it is determined that the goodwill has been impaired**.

The Accounting Standards Board decided that **non-amortization of goodwill combined with an adequate impairment test** provides the most useful financial information to the investment community. With no amortization of goodwill, it has therefore now become management's responsibility to ensure that the carrying value of this intangible asset is tested for impairment.

---

[21] The AcSB, FASB, and IASB have all tentatively agreed as part of a joint project on business combinations that this excess amount should be recognized as a gain and included in net income. This standard is expected to be finalized in late 2007, but may not be effective until 2009. See FASB Project Update on "Business Combinations: Applying the Acquisition Method—Joint Project of the IASB and FASB," November 27, 2006, and AcSB Exposure Draft on "Business Combinations, August 2005."

The method of accounting for goodwill can have a significant effect on the income statement of a company because goodwill is often a major asset on its balance sheet. Quebecor Inc., for example, recently reported income of $91.9 million. **If the accounting standard for goodwill had not changed**, the company would have had an additional $123.3 million of amortization expense (after tax and non-controlling interest) related to goodwill and reported a loss of $31.4 million. In addition, because companies were also required to review their existing goodwill and recognize any impairments as an adjustment to their opening balance of retained earnings when the new standard was first applied, Quebecor recognized a goodwill impairment loss of $2.163 billion—a charge that bypassed the income statement completely!

What Do the Numbers Mean?

IMPAIRMENT OF INTANGIBLE ASSETS

6 Objective
Account for intangible asset impairments.

In some cases, the carrying amount of a long-lived asset—whether it is property, plant, and equipment or an intangible—is greater than its fair value, and an **impairment** in its value has therefore occurred. This may require a write-down of its carrying amount and the recognition of an impairment loss.

Impairment of Limited-Life Intangibles

The standards that apply to impairments of **long-lived tangible assets** also apply to **limited-life intangibles.**[22] As indicated in Chapter 11, long-lived assets that a company intends to hold and use are reviewed for impairment whenever events or changes in circumstances indicate that **the carrying amount of the assets may not be recoverable**. This is Step 1. In Step 2, which is the **recoverability test**, the company estimates the future net cash flows that it expects to have from using the asset and from its eventual disposal. If the sum of the **undiscounted** expected future net cash inflows is less than the carrying amount of the asset, an impairment loss must be measured and recognized. Otherwise, no impairment loss is recognized.[23] The impairment loss, calculated in Step 3, is the amount by which the carrying amount of the asset fails the **fair value test**—i.e., the amount by which the carrying amount is greater than the asset's fair value. Because a fair value measure for many intangibles is often not available, companies discount the expected cash flows to estimate the asset's fair value. As with other impairments, the loss is usually reported as part of income from continuing operations.

To illustrate, assume that an enterprise has a patent on a process to extract oil from shale rock. Unfortunately, reduced oil prices have made the shale oil technology somewhat unprofitable, and the patent has provided little income to date. As a result, a recoverability test is performed, and it is found that the expected future net cash flows from this patent are $3.5 million. On the company's books, however, the patent has a carrying amount of $6 million. Because the net recoverable amount of $3.5 million is less than the carrying amount of $6 million, an impairment loss must be measured and recognized. Discounting the expected future net cash flows at the market rate of interest, the fair value of the patent is estimated to be $2 million. The impairment loss calculation—based on fair values—is shown in Illustration 12-6.

[22] *CICA Handbook*, Section 3062.18.

[23] *CICA Handbook*, Section 3063.04 and .05.

Illustration 12-6
Calculation of Loss on Impairment of Patent

Carrying amount of patent	$6,000,000
Fair value (based on discounted cash flows)	2,000,000
Loss on impairment	$4,000,000

The entry to record this loss is:

A	= L +	SE
−4,000,000		−4,000,000

Cash flows: No effect

Loss on Impairment	4,000,000	
Accumulated Amortization, Patents		4,000,000

International Insight

IAS 36 requires that the impairment loss be reversed if in the future there are changes in any of the estimates that were used to determine the loss.

After the impairment is recognized, the patent's reduced carrying amount is its new cost basis. The patent's revised net book value is then amortized over its useful life or legal life, whichever is shorter. If oil prices increase in subsequent periods and the patent's net recoverable amount fully recovers from the impairment, **the entity is not permitted to restore the previously recognized impairment loss.**

Impairment of Indefinite-Life Intangibles Other Than Goodwill

With the exception of goodwill, indefinite-life intangibles should be tested for impairment at least annually, or more often if changes in circumstances indicate that an asset may be impaired.[24] The impairment test for an indefinite-life asset other than goodwill is the **fair value test**. This test compares the fair value of the intangible asset with the asset's carrying amount. If its fair value is less than the carrying amount, an impairment loss is recognized. Why is there a different standard for indefinite-life intangibles? This one-step test is used because it would be relatively easy for many indefinite-life assets to meet the recoverability test—that is, the cash flows would extend many years into the future. **As a result, the recoverability test is not used.**

To illustrate, assume that a company purchases a broadcast licence for $2.1 million, and that the licence is renewable every 10 years if the company provides appropriate service and does not violate the rules and regulations of the Canadian Radio-television and Telecommunications Commission (CRTC). The licence is then renewed with the CRTC twice at a minimal cost, and because cash flows are expected to last indefinitely, the licence is therefore reported as an indefinite-life intangible asset. Assume that the CRTC later decides to no longer renew broadcast licences, but to auction them off to the highest bidder. With two years remaining in the life of the existing licence, the company now performs an impairment test and determines that the fair value of the intangible asset is $750,000. As shown in Illustration 12-7, an impairment loss of $1,350,000 is determined and recorded in the accounts.

Illustration 12-7
Calculation of Loss on Impairment of Broadcast Licence

Carrying amount of broadcast licence	$2,100,000
Fair value of broadcast licence	750,000
Loss on impairment	$1,350,000

[24] Entities that qualify for differential reporting under *CICA Handbook* Section 1300 may choose to test for impairment only when an event or circumstance occurs that indicates that the asset's carrying value may not be recoverable (*CICA Handbook*, Section 3062.59).

The company may either set up and credit an accumulated amortization account for the licence or credit the asset account itself. The licence will now be reported at $750,000, its fair value. Even if the value of the licence increases in the remaining two years, restoration of the previously recognized impairment loss is not permitted.[25]

Impairment of Goodwill

Entities are required to test goodwill for impairment at least once a year unless specific criteria are met that indicate there is a remote possibility of an impairment in value.[26] The impairment rule for goodwill is a **two-step process that is only used for this unique type of asset**:

1. Compare the fair value of the reporting unit[27] against its carrying amount including goodwill. If the fair value of the reporting unit is more than its book value, there is no goodwill impairment and nothing further is required. If the fair value is less than the carrying amount of the unit, a second step is needed.
2. The second step determines if goodwill is impaired by:
   (a) calculating its implied current fair value, and
   (b) comparing this fair value with its carrying amount.

   Its implied current fair value is calculated by comparing the fair value of the reporting unit as a whole with the fair value of its identifiable net assets. If the goodwill's current fair value is more than its book value, no adjustment is necessary. If it is less than its carrying amount, there is an impairment.

To illustrate, assume that Coburg Corporation has three divisions. One division, Pritt Products, was purchased four years ago for $2 million and has been identified as a reporting unit. Unfortunately, it has experienced operating losses over the last three quarters and management is reviewing the reporting unit to determine whether there has been an impairment of goodwill. The carrying amounts of Pritt Division's net assets, including the associated goodwill of $900,000, are listed in Illustration 12-8.

Cash	$ 200,000
Receivables	300,000
Inventory	700,000
Property, plant, and equipment, (net)	800,000
Goodwill	900,000
Less: Accounts and notes payable	(500,000)
Net assets, at carrying amounts	$2,400,000

Illustration 12-8

Pritt Reporting Unit–Carrying Amount of Net Assets Including Goodwill

The fair value of the Pritt Division reporting unit as a whole is estimated to be $2.8 million. As a result, Step 1 indicates that no impairment is evident because the fair value of the division is greater than the book value of the net assets.

[25] *CICA Handbook*, Section 3062.21.

[26] *CICA Handbook*, Section 3062.39. Section 3062.55 indicates that an entity that qualifies for differential reporting under *CICA Handbook* Section 1300 is not required to test annually. Instead, an impairment test is required only when an event or circumstance occurs that indicates that the fair value of a reporting unit may be less than its carrying amount.

[27] Section 3062.05(d) defines a **reporting unit** as the same level or one level below an operating segment, as defined in *CICA Handbook* Section 1701 on Segment Disclosures. "A component of an operating segment is a reporting unit when the component constitutes a business for which discrete financial information is available and segment management regularly reviews the operating results of that component."

However, if the fair value of Pritt Division is $1.9 million—i.e., less than the carrying amount of the net assets—**the second step must be taken** to determine whether goodwill has been impaired. Assume that the carrying amounts of the identifiable net assets (i.e., excluding goodwill) are equal to their fair values. The implied fair value of the goodwill in this case is $400,000, as calculated in Illustration 12-9.

Illustration 12-9
Determination of Implied Fair Value of Goodwill

Fair value of Pritt Division	$1,900,000
Fair value of identifiable net assets of Pritt Division ($2,400,000 − $900,000)	1,500,000
Implied fair value of goodwill	$ 400,000

Note that it is the **fair values of the net identifiable assets** that are used in this calculation. This makes intuitive sense. **There is goodwill only if** the value of a company or reporting unit is greater than the fair value of the individual net assets that make up the company.

The implied current value of the goodwill is then compared with the recorded goodwill to determine whether an impairment loss exists, as Illustration 12-10 shows.

Illustration 12-10
Measurement of Goodwill Impairment

Carrying amount of goodwill	$900,000
Implied value of goodwill	400,000
Impairment loss	$500,000

The entry to record the impairment is:

A	= L +	SE
−500,000		−500,000

Cash flows: No effect

Loss on Impairment of Goodwill	500,000	
Goodwill		500,000

Illustration 12-11 summarizes the impairment tests for various intangible assets.

Illustration 12-11
Summary of Intangible Asset Impairment Tests

Type of Intangible Asset	Impairment Test
Limited life	Recoverability test, then fair value test
Indefinite life other than goodwill	Fair value test
Goodwill	Fair value test on reporting unit, then fair value test on implied goodwill

OTHER INTERNALLY DEVELOPED INTANGIBLES

Commonly, the term **deferred charges** is used to describe different types of items that have debit balances, including certain types of intangibles. Intangibles that are sometimes classified as deferred charges include deferred development costs, pre-operating and start-up costs, and organization costs. However, use of the term "deferred charges" should decrease as standard setters back away from recognizing deferred costs as assets unless the resulting costs meet the definition of an asset.[28] And even when they do meet

[28] Clarence Byrd, Ida Chen, and Joshua Smith report in *Financial Reporting in Canada, 2005* (CICA, 2005) that 57% of the companies surveyed in 2004 made reference to a Deferred Charges category on their balance sheets. Section 3070, Deferred Charges, was removed from the *Handbook* in 2005.

the definition, the assets may then more properly be described as internally developed intangibles.

Deferred charges also include such items as debt discount and issue costs as well as long-term prepayments for insurance, rent, taxes, and other down payments. Over time however, the deferred charges classification is expected to be used less and less because legitimate assets tend to fall into another established category of asset.

As part of the process of harmonizing with international standards, fewer and fewer deferred charges are considered acceptable. Examples of common deferred costs that are still recognized by Canadian GAAP are presented next.

Research and Development Costs

7 **Objective**
Differentiate between research expenditures and development expenditures, and describe and explain the rationale for the accounting for them.

Research and development (R&D) costs are not in themselves intangible assets. The accounting for R&D costs is presented here, however, for two reasons. The first is because research and development activities are often significant and they frequently result in the development of something that is eventually patented or copyrighted—i.e., in the creation of an intangible asset. Examples include a new product, process, idea, formula, composition, or literary work. Secondly, some development costs are capitalized as a type of internally developed intangible asset.

Many businesses spend considerable sums of money on research and development to create new products or processes, to improve present products, and to discover new knowledge that may be valuable at some future date. Illustration 12-12 shows the R&D expenses that were reported by selected Canadian companies with year ends between December 31, 2005, and June 30, 2006.

Illustration 12-12
R&D Expenses

Company	R&D Expenses	% of Revenue
Bioniche Life Sciences Inc.	$12,916 thousand	48.5
Bombardier Inc.	$175.0 million (U.S.)	1.2
MOSAID Technologies Inc.	$14,994 thousand	23.5
Nortel Networks Ltd.	$1,856 million (U.S.)	17.6
QLT Inc.	$74,597 thousand (U.S.)	30.8
Research in Motion Limited	$157,629 thousand (U.S.)	7.6

International Insight
Contrary to Canadian and international standards, all research and development costs are required to be expensed under U.S. GAAP.

There are two difficulties in accounting for research and development expenditures: (1) identifying the costs that are associated with particular activities, projects, or achievements, and (2) determining the amount of the future benefits and length of time over which the benefits may be realized. Because of the uncertainties under the second difficulty, Canadian standards have simplified accounting practice in this area by requiring that **all research costs be charged to expense when they are incurred. Development costs are also expensed when incurred, except in certain very specific circumstances that are carefully defined.**

An exception is permitted to this strict accounting standard if a company acquires **in-process R&D** in a business combination. That is, if one company acquires the business of another company, one of the identifiable assets acquired may be the research work and findings of the acquired company. When the research work and findings meet the requirements for reporting as an asset separate from goodwill, Canadian standards permit this intangible asset to be recognized as an identifiable intangible.

Identifying R&D Activities

To differentiate between research costs and development costs and those that are neither, the following definitions are used:

Research is planned investigation undertaken with the hope of gaining new scientific or technical knowledge and understanding. The investigation may or may not be directed toward a specific practical aim or application.

Development is the translation of research findings or other knowledge into a plan or design for new or substantially improved materials, devices, products, processes, systems, or services prior to the commencement of commercial production or use.[29]

Examples from the *CICA Handbook* of these two types of costs are provided in Illustration 12-13.[30]

Illustration 12-13
Examples of Research and Development Activities

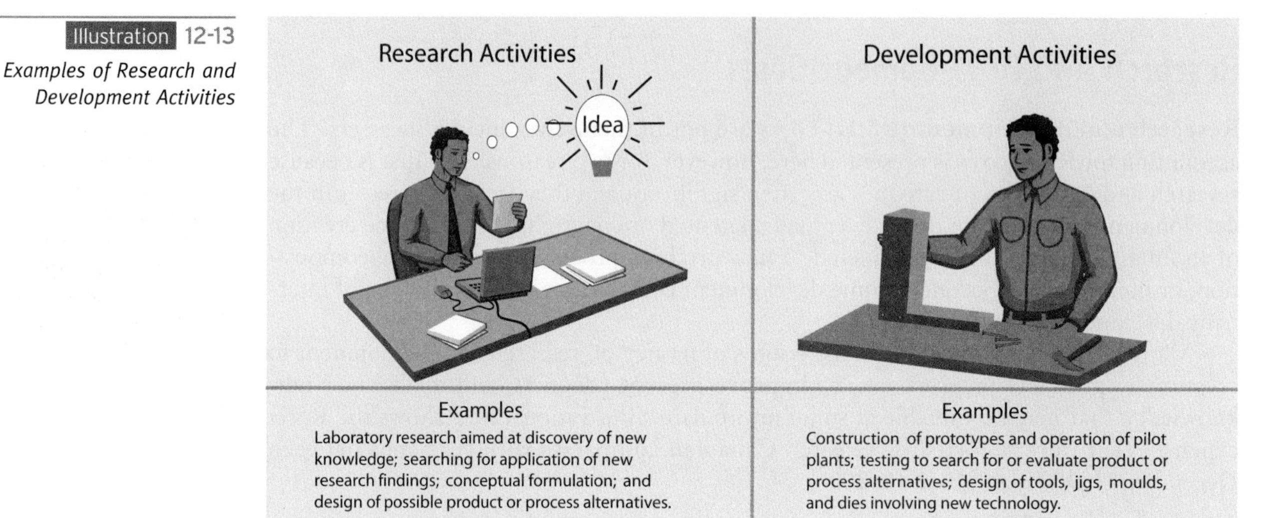

It should be emphasized that R&D activities do not include routine or periodic alterations to existing products, production lines, manufacturing processes, and other ongoing operations, even though these alterations may be improvements. Routine, ongoing efforts to refine, enrich, or improve the qualities of an existing product are not considered R&D activities. R&D costs also do not include expenditures that are related to engineering follow-through, quality control, or troubleshooting during any part of the commercial production phase, nor routine or promotional market research activities.

Trying to distinguish R&D costs from selling and administrative activities can sometimes present a special problem. Ordinary and ongoing market research activities, for example, do not fall under the definition of research and development activities. As indicated earlier in the chapter for website development costs, the principles that underlie the recognition and measurement of tangible and intangible long-lived assets would also be applied to research and development expenditures incurred in selling and administrative activities.

Accounting for R&D Activities

The costs associated with R&D activities are as follows:[31]

1. Materials and services consumed
2. Direct costs of personnel, such as salaries, wages, payroll taxes, and other related costs
3. Amortization of equipment and facilities that are used in R&D activities
4. Amortization of intangibles that are related to R&D activities
5. A reasonable allocation of overhead

[29] *CICA Handbook*, Section 3450.02.

[30] *CICA Handbook*, Section 3450.04 and .05.

[31] *CICA Handbook*, Section 3450.13.

Consistent with (3) above, if a company's R&D activities make use of its own research facility consisting of buildings, laboratories, and equipment that have alternative future uses (in other R&D projects or otherwise), the facility is accounted for as capitalized operational assets. The amortization and other costs that are related to such research facilities are accounted for as R&D expenses.

Sometimes enterprises conduct R&D activities for other entities **under a contractual arrangement**. In this case, the contract usually specifies that all direct costs, certain specific indirect costs, and a profit element should be reimbursed to the enterprise doing the R&D work. Because reimbursement is expected, such R&D costs are recorded as inventory or a receivable. The company that is having the work done for it is the one that reports these costs as R&D activities.

As previously emphasized, when Canadian firms incur research costs, they must write them off as expenses of the period. They also have to expense development costs, **except when all of the following criteria are met**:

1. The product or process is clearly defined and the costs that are attributable to it can be identified.
2. The technical feasibility of the product or process has been established.
3. Management has indicated its intention to produce and market or use the product or process.
4. The future market for the product or process is clearly defined or, if it is to be used internally rather than sold, its usefulness to the enterprise has been established.
5. Adequate resources already exist or are expected to be available to complete the project.

International Insight

IAS 38 also identifies similar circumstances that justify the capitalization and deferral of appropriate development costs. However, current U.S. standards require that all research and developments costs be expensed.

Since all five criteria must be met, this means that an entity is only permitted to defer development costs **when the future benefits are reasonably certain**. Costs that were expensed in previous periods before the criteria were met **are not** restated as assets; and amounts that are greater than the amount that is expected to be recovered from the sale or use of the product or process should not be deferred either.[32] As internally developed intangibles, deferred development costs are amortized to expense, and preferably on a basis that relates to the sale or use of the underlying product or process.

Like other intangibles, unamortized development costs are reviewed at the end of each accounting period. If the criteria that justified deferring the costs are no longer valid, the remaining costs are written off. If the asset's carrying amount is higher than its net recoverable amount, the excess is written off as a charge to the income statement.

To illustrate R&D activities and their related accounting treatment, assume that an enterprise develops, produces, and markets laser machines for medical, industrial, and defence uses. The types of expenditures related to its laser machine activities, along with the recommended accounting treatment, are listed in Illustration 12-14.

Underlying Concept

The requirement that all research and most development costs be expensed as they are incurred is an example of the conflict between relevance and reliability, with this requirement leaning strongly in support of reliability and comparability. The matching of costs with revenues is not as important as ensuring that assets are not overstated.

Illustration 12-14

Sample R&D Expenditures and their Accounting Treatment

Type of Expenditure	Accounting Treatment
1. Construction of long-range research facility (three-storey, 100,000-m² building) for use in current and future projects.	Capitalize and amortize as R&D expense.
2. Acquisition of R&D equipment for use on current project only.	Capitalize and amortize as R&D expense.
3. Purchase of materials to be used on current and future R&D projects.	Inventory and allocate to R&D projects as consumed.
4. Salaries of research staff designing new laser bone scanner.	Expense immediately as research.
5. Research costs incurred under contract for customer and billable monthly.	Expense as operating expense in period of related revenue recognition.

[32] *CICA Handbook*, Section 3450.21 and .23.

6. Material, labour, and overhead costs of prototype laser scanner.	Capitalize as development cost if all criteria are met; otherwise expense.
7. Costs of testing prototype and design modifications.	Capitalize as development cost if all criteria are met; otherwise expense.
8. Legal fees to obtain patent on new laser scanner.	Capitalize as patent and amortize to cost of goods manufactured as used.
9. Executive salaries.	Expense as operating expense (general and administrative).
10. Cost of marketing research related to promotion of new laser scanner.	Expense as operating expense (selling), unless to establish existence and extent of potential market prior to start of commercial production.
11. Engineering costs incurred to advance the laser scanner to full production stage.	Capitalize as development cost if all criteria are met; otherwise expense.
12. Costs of successfully defending patent on laser scanner.	Capitalize as patent and amortize to cost of goods manufactured as used.
13. Commissions to sales staff marketing new laser scanner.	Expense as operating expense (selling).

In the financial statements, disclosure is then made of the total R&D costs that have been charged to expense. Because income tax incentives are associated with this type of activity, it is common for companies to report their R&D expenses net of tax recoveries, either on the face of the income statement or in the notes to the financial statements. Excerpts in Illustration 12-15 from the financial statements of MOSAID Technologies Incorporated for the year ended April 30, 2006, provide a good example of such disclosures.

Illustration 12-15

R&D Disclosures–MOSAID Technologies Incorporated

Student Toolkit–Additional Disclosures

www.wiley.com/canada/kieso

Notes to the Consolidated Financial Statements

Year ended April 30, 2006

(tabular dollar amounts in thousands of Canadian Dollars, except per share amounts)

1. Accounting Policies

Research and development

Research costs are expensed as incurred. Development costs are deferred once technical feasibility has been established and all criteria for deferral under generally accepted accounting principles are met. Such costs are amortized, commencing when the product is released, over the expected life of the product. To date, no development costs have met the criteria for deferral.

Government assistance and investment tax credits

Government assistance and investment tax credits are recorded as a reduction of the related expense or cost of the asset acquired. The benefits are recognized when the Company has complied with the terms and conditions of the approved grant program or applicable tax legislation.

9. Reseach and Development

Investment tax credits were applied to reduce current research and development expenses in the statements of operations and retained earnings as summarized below.

	2006	2005
Total current research and development	**$ 15,518**	$ 7,867
Less: Investment tax credits	**524**	227
Net research and development	**$ 14,994**	$ 7,640

As part of a Research and Development Contribution Agreement with the Government of Canada, the Government contributed $6.2 million, during fiscal years 1999-2001, towards research and development work. The terms of the Agreement require the Company to pay royalties to the government based upon the revenues of the resulting products, for a period extending no later than March 31, 2011. During the year ended April 30, 2006, the Company recorded repayments in the amount of $316,000 (2005 – $71,000). To date, the Company has recorded repayments in the amount of $1,623,000.

The costs of development activities that are **unique to companies in the extractive industries** (prospecting, acquisition of mineral rights, exploration, drilling, mining, and related mineral development) are covered mainly by *CICA Handbook* Section 3061 on property, plant, and equipment. Research and development activities that are similar to those of other industries, however, are governed by the accounting standards in Section 3450.

Many costs have characteristics that are similar to research and development costs. Examples include the costs of companies in a development stage, start-up costs for a new operation, initial operating losses, organization costs, and advertising costs. Explanations of these are provided next.

Development Stage Costs

8 Objective
Identify other examples of internally developed intangibles and the accounting requirements for them.

Companies that are in the development stage face many questions about which costs they should expense and which ones they should capitalize. The general principle is that **the nature of the transaction, not the enterprise's stage of development**, determines the accounting treatment. There are standards for property, plant, and equipment, intangible assets, and research and development activities, and these standards should be followed regardless of how mature the business is. The decision about whether an item is capitalized or expensed is made on the same basis as it is for companies that are not in the development stage.

In addition, CICA's Accounting Guideline 11 "Enterprises in the Development Stage" further clarifies the accounting and reporting practices for such enterprises. It specifies the factors that have to be considered in applying the regular accounting standards as well as specific relevant disclosures that need to be made about significant projects that are under development.

Pre-Operating Costs and Revenues

International Insight

IAS 38 does not permit the capitalization of pre-operating costs.

A specific issue that occurs at the development stage and has been clarified even further is the issue of pre-operating costs. **Pre-operating costs** are costs that are incurred by an entity during the period before it begins commercial operations of a new facility or business. These might include costs incurred for such purposes as employee training and relocation, promotional activities, and the use of materials and supplies. A company may realize small amounts of revenue during this period as well. To what extent should such costs that are not capitalized as part of the cost of a capital asset be deferred?

This issue was dealt with by the Emerging Issues Committee of the CICA. It agreed that an expenditure that is incurred during the pre-operating period can be deferred **if all of the following three criteria are met**:

1. It relates directly to placing the new business into service.
2. It is incremental in nature, and would not have been incurred in the absence of the new business.
3. It is probable that the expenditure is recoverable from the future operations of the new business.[33]

The **pre-operating period** is the period before the new business is ready to begin commercial operations—i.e., the period before it is capable of consistently providing its intended product or service. This period will differ depending on the circumstances and the industry, and should be predefined by management according to either the activity level that is attained or the time period that has passed.

[33] *CICA* EIC-27, Revenues and Expenditures during the Pre-Operating Period.

When the pre-operating period is over, the deferral of expenditures and any offsetting revenues ends, and amortization of the deferred charges begins. The amortization is based on the period and pattern of benefits to be received. A five-year period is assumed to be the likely maximum period for amortization.[34]

To illustrate the types of costs that are permitted to be deferred as pre-operating costs, assume that Canadian-based Hilo Beverage Inc. decides to construct a new plant in Brazil. This is Hilo's first entry into the Brazilian market. As part of its overall strategy, Hilo plans to introduce the company's major Canadian brands into Brazil but have them produced locally. The following are some of the pre-operating costs that might be incurred with these start-up activities:

1. Travel-related costs, costs related to employee salaries, and costs related to feasibility studies, accounting, tax, and government affairs
2. Training of local employees that is related to product, maintenance, computer systems, finance, and operations
3. Recruiting, organizing, and training that is related to establishing a distribution network

Unlike the U.S. and IASB approaches, which call for these costs to be expensed as they are incurred, the Canadian standard specifies that these costs qualify for deferral. They meet the three criteria imposed and are incurred during the predetermined pre-operating period. As work proceeds on a new Canadian standard for internally developed intangible assets, it is likely that pre-operating costs will no longer be permitted to be deferred as assets.

Note, however, that it is not uncommon for development activities to occur at the same time as other activities, such as the acquisition or development of assets, and it is important that the two not be confused. For example, property, plant, and equipment for Hilo's new plant should be capitalized and a careful analysis of costs during the pre-operating period is needed to ensure that all capital asset costs are appropriately accounted for.

Organization Costs

Organization costs are another intangible asset. These are costs that are incurred as part of forming a corporation, such as fees to underwriters (investment bankers) for handling issues of shares or bonds, legal fees, provincial or federal fees of various sorts, and promotional expenditures that are part of the organization of a business.

These items are usually charged to an account called Organization Costs and may be carried as an asset on the balance sheet as expenditures that will benefit the company over its entire life. Because such costs benefit the enterprise for an indefinite period, conceptually they should remain on the balance sheet without being amortized.

Many companies, however, amortize this asset over a short, arbitrary period of time (perhaps up to five years). This is justified on the basis that the corporation's life is indeterminable, the amounts tend not to be significant, or because it is assumed that the early years benefit most from these expenditures.

Advertising Costs

Over the years, PepsiCo has hired various pop stars such as Britney Spears and Beyoncé to advertise its products. How and when should these advertising costs be reported? They could be expensed at a variety of times:

[34] *CICA* EIC-27, Issue 3.

1. When they have completed their singing assignments
2. The first time the advertisement runs
3. Over the estimated useful life of the advertisement
4. In an appropriate way to each of the three periods identified above
5. Over the period that revenues are expected to arise as a result of the advertisement

Because there is no specific Canadian standard on advertising costs, GAAP requires that entities use methods that are consistent with other *Handbook* standards and the conceptual framework. Since future benefits from advertising generally are not defined well enough or cannot be measured with the degree of reliability that is required for these costs to be recognized as an asset, **advertising costs are usually expensed as they are incurred or when the advertising first takes place**. Whichever approach is followed, the results are essentially the same. Tangible assets that are used in advertising, such as billboards or blimps, are recorded as assets because they do have alternative future uses. This approach is generally taken to recording advertising costs because identifying and measuring the future benefits is so difficult.[35]

Conceptual Questions

The requirement that most of the costs that were mentioned above be expensed immediately is a conservative, practical solution that ensures consistency in practice and uniformity among companies. But the practice of immediately writing off expenditures that are made in the expectation of benefiting future periods cannot always be justified on the grounds that it is good accounting theory.

Those who support immediate expensing argue that long-term application of these standards usually makes little difference in terms of its impact on the income statement. They contend, for example, that the amount of R&D cost that is charged to expense in each accounting period would be about the same whether there is immediate expensing or capitalization followed by amortization since most companies are continuously investing in R&D activities. Critics argue, on the other hand, that the balance sheet should report any expenditure that has future benefits as an intangible asset. When a company is not allowed to capitalize any R&D or similar expenditures, this removes from its balance sheet what may be the company's most valuable assets. These decisions represent some of the many trade-offs made between relevance and reliability, and cost-benefit considerations.

PRESENTATION, ANALYSIS, AND INTERNATIONAL COMPARISON

A recent survey indicates that the most common types of intangible assets that are reported, other than goodwill, are broadcast rights, publishing rights, trademarks, patents, licences, customer lists, non-competition agreements, franchises, and purchased R&D.[36] These, along with goodwill, have become an increasingly large proportion of companies' reported assets.

---

[35] This mirrors "Reporting on Advertising Costs," *Statement of Position 93-7* (New York: AICPA, 1993). Note that there are some exceptions to immediate expensing of advertising costs when such costs relate to direct-response advertising, but this subject is beyond the scope of this text.

[36] Clarence Byrd, Ida Chen, and Heather Chapman, *Financial Reporting in Canada, 2000* (CICA, 2000), pp. 284–285 and Clarence Byrd, Ida Chen, and Joshua Smith, *Financial Reporting in Canada, 2005* (CICA, 2005), p. 256.

Presentation of Intangible Assets

Balance Sheet

Objective 9
Identify the disclosure requirements for intangibles and the issues in analyzing this asset category.

On the balance sheet, goodwill is the only intangible that requires separate disclosure as a single line item. Details of the changes in the carrying amount of goodwill that is reported are also required. This includes goodwill that is acquired, write-downs due to impairment, and goodwill that is included in the disposal of any part of a reporting unit. Intangible assets other than goodwill may be aggregated and reported together on the balance sheet with more detailed information provided in a note. For intangibles that are amortized, the amount of such assets that were acquired during the period is disclosed, along with the cost and accumulated amortization for major intangible asset classes and in total. For intangibles that are not amortized, similar disclosures are required, excluding, of course, an amount of accumulated amortization.[37]

Income Statement

For limited-life intangibles, disclosure is required of the amortization methods and rates that were used, as well as the amortization expense that was charged to income for the period. Each goodwill impairment loss is reported separately in the income statement before extraordinary items and discontinued operations, unless the impairment loss is associated with a discontinued operation. In addition, the enterprise must describe the facts and circumstances that led to the impairment; state the amount of the loss, the adjusted carrying amount of goodwill, and which reporting unit (and segment, if applicable) the loss is associated with; and provide an explanation if the loss is an estimate only.

Impairment losses that are associated with other intangibles do not require separate disclosure on the face of the income statement, but the entity must describe each impaired asset, the amount of the loss, where it is reported, and the business segment that is affected.[38]

Illustration of Presentations and Disclosures

Student Toolkit–Additional Disclosures
www.wiley.com/canada/kieso

Excerpts from the financial statements of Dorel Industries Inc. for its year ended December 30, 2005, are provided in Illustration 12-16. This Canadian company designs, manufactures or sources, and markets and distributes a diverse portfolio of consumer products mainly in the United States, Canada, and Europe. Note that the intangibles, including goodwill and deferred charges, make up almost 50 percent of the company's reported assets at December 31, 2005.

It is interesting to read the company's Management Discussion and Analysis in its annual report for this same year. Management identifies the impairment testing of goodwill and certain other indefinite life intangible assets **as one of the four most critical accounting policies**. The company considers that these would "have the most material effect on the financial statements should these policies change or be applied in a different manner."

---

[37] *CICA Handbook*, Section 3062.48 to .51.

[38] *CICA Handbook*, Section 3062.49 to .54.

Illustration 12-16

Balance Sheet Presentation and Related Notes on Intangible Assets

DOREL INDUSTRIES INC.

CONSOLIDATED BALANCE SHEET

AS AT DECEMBER 30, 2005 AND 2004 (All figures in thousands of U.S. dollars)

	2005	2004
ASSETS		
CURRENT ASSETS		
Cash	$ 12,345	$ 11,288
Accounts receivable (Note 5)	287,225	285,207
Income taxes receivable	14,817	7,587
Inventories (Note 6)	279,265	292,991
Prepaid expenses	10,288	12,756
Funds held by ceding insurer (Note 21)	3,647	7,920
Future income taxes (Note 22)	26,060	22,650
	633,647	640,399
PROPERTY, PLANT AND EQUIPMENT (Note 7)	144,248	163,707
DEFERRED CHARGES (Note 8)	15,561	20,983
INTANGIBLE ASSETS (Note 9)	253,245	262,968
GOODWILL (Note 25)	481,518	512,546
OTHER ASSETS (Note 15)	10,750	10,786
ASSETS HELD FOR SALE (Note 3)	3,699	–
	$ 1,542,668	$ 1,611,389

NOTES TO THE CONSOLIDATED FINANCIAL STATEMENTS

AS AT DECEMBER 30, 2005 AND 2004 (All figures in thousands of U.S. dollars, except per share amounts)

NOTE 2 >>> SIGNIFICANT ACCOUNTING POLICIES (*Cont'd*)

Deferred charges

Deferred charges are carried at cost less accumulated amortization.

Research and Development Costs:

The Company incurs costs on activities which relate to research and development of new products. Research costs are expensed as they are incurred. Development costs are also expensed as incurred unless they meet specific criteria related to technical, market and financial feasibility. Deferred development costs are amortized on a straight-line basis over a period of two years.

Financing Costs:

The Company incurred certain costs related to the issue of long-term debt. These amounts are amortized as interest expense on a straight-line basis over the term or life of the related long-term debt.

Goodwill

Goodwill represents the excess of the purchase price over the fair values assigned to identifiable net assets acquired of subsidiary companies. Goodwill, which is not amortized, is tested for impairment annually or more frequently when an event or circumstance occurs that more likely than not reduces the fair value of a reporting unit below its carrying amount.

A two-step impairment test is used to identify potential goodwill impairment and measure the amount of a goodwill impairment loss to be recognized, if any. The fair value of a reporting unit is first compared with its carrying amount, including goodwill, in order to identify a potential impairment. When the fair value of a reporting unit exceeds its carrying amount, goodwill of the reporting unit is considered not to be impaired and the second step of the impairment test is unnecessary. When the carrying amount of a reporting unit exceeds its fair value, the implied fair value of the reporting unit's goodwill is then compared with its carrying amount to measure the amount of the impairment loss, if any. The fair value of a reporting unit is calculated based on discounted cash flows or valuations based on a market approach. When the carrying amount of reporting unit goodwill exceeds the implied fair value of the goodwill, an impairment loss is recognized in an amount equal to the excess.

Intangible Assets

Intangible assets are recorded at cost:

Trademarks

Trademarks acquired as part of business acquisitions are considered to have an indefinite life and are therefore not subject to amortization. They are tested annually for impairment or more frequently when events or changes in circumstances indicate that the trademarks might be impaired. The impairment test compares the carrying amount of the trademarks with its fair value.

Customer Relationships

Customer relationships acquired as part of business acquisitions are amortized on a straight-line basis over a period of 20 to 25 years.

Patents

Patents are amortized on a straight-line basis over their expected useful lives ranging from 1 year to 25 years.

Licences

Certain licences are amortized in proportion to sales of products for which the licences have been acquired, while others are amortized on a straight-line basis over their weighted average expected useful lives of 3 years.

Impairment of Long-Lived Assets

Long-lived assets are tested for recoverability whenever events or changes in circumstances indicate that their carrying amount may not be recoverable. Each quarter-end, the Company assesses its long-lived assets for potential impairment and considers projected future operating results, trends and other circumstances in making such assessments. Impaired assets are written down to estimated fair value, being determined based on discounted cash flows.

NOTE 8 >>> DEFERRED CHARGES

	2005	2004
Development costs	$ 14,402	$ 17,743
Financing costs	843	2,435
Other	316	805
	$ 15,561	$ 20,983

The Company incurred $16,086 (2004 - $18,563) of research and development costs of which $7,945 (2004 - $6,420) were expensed and $8,141 (2004 - $12,143) were deferred. Amortization of deferred development costs and other deferred charges amounted to $10,513 (2004 - $10,105) and $489 (2004 - $138) respectively. The amortization of financing costs included in interest on long-term debt is $1,592 (2004 – $1,578).

NOTE 9 >>> INTANGIBLE ASSETS

	2005		
	Cost	Accumulated Amortization	Net
Trademarks	$ 199,666	$ –	$ 199,666
Customer relationships	49,203	5,114	44,089
Patents	16,116	6,960	9,156
Licences	1,000	666	334
	$ 265,985	$ 12,740	$ 253,245

	2004		
	Cost	Accumulated Amortization	Net
Trademarks	$ 210,658	$ –	$ 210,658
Customer relationships	44,897	3,374	41,523
Patents	15,076	5,100	9,976
Licences	1,000	189	811
	$ 271,631	$ 8,663	$ 262,968

The aggregate amount of amortizable intangible assets acquired amounted to $6,968 (2004 - $3,029) of which $2,755 (2004 – nil) is unpaid at year-end. The aggregate amortization expense of intangible assets amounted to $4,668 (2004 - $3,422).

NOTE 25 >>> SEGMENTED INFORMATION (*Cont'd*)

Goodwill

The continuity of goodwill by industry segment is as follows:

	Total		Juvenile		Home Furnishings		Recreational/Leisure	
	2005	2004	2005	2004	2005	2004	2005	2004
Balance, beginning of year	$ 512,546	$ 353,316	$ 333,781	$ 318,822	$ 31,172	$ 34,494	$ 147,593	$ –
Additions	–	147,593	–	–	–	–	–	147,593
Adjustments	(4,506)	(3,322)	–	–	–	(3,322)	(4,506)	–
Foreign exchange	(26,522)	14,959	(26,522)	14,959	–	–	–	–
Balance, end of year	$ 481,518	$ 512,546	$ 307,259	$ 333,781	$ 31,172	$ 31,172	$ 143,087	$ 147,593

Perspectives

Intellectual Capital and Knowledge Assets

During the 1990s, the conventional financial-accounting model was increasingly criticized for its inability to capture many of the attributes that give a business value. In November 1997, for example, Microsoft had a total book value of U.S. $10.8 billion, while its market capitalization (i.e., the market value of its outstanding shares) was U.S. $166.5 billion. Nortel Networks Corporation traded at a high of $125 per share in mid-2000 although its book value was closer to $5 per share. Why such significant differences?

The answer is that financial accounting is not able to capture and report many of the assets that contribute to future cash flows, and this is seen by some critics as the greatest challenge facing the accounting profession today. Many of the missing values belong to unrecognized, internally developed intangible assets known as **knowledge assets** or **intellectual capital**. These include the value of key personnel—not only Bill Gates, but the many creative and technologically proficient employees in general—the investment in products from research and development and their potential, organizational adaptability, customer retention, strategic direction, brands, flexible and innovative management, customer service capability, and effective advertising programs, to name only some such assets.

Our conventional accounting model, for the most part, captures the results of past transactions. This has been considered a very significant benefit as it is what makes it possible to verify the reported measures and therefore add to the reliability of the financial statements.

In most cases, the intellectual capital and knowledge assets identified above cannot be measured in financial terms with enough reliability to give them accounting recognition. Some cannot be included as assets because of the enterprise's inability to control access to the benefits. Investments that are made in employee education and development, for example, can walk out the door when employees leave the company to work elsewhere.

These indicators of longer-term value that has been created in an organization will ultimately result in realized values through future transactions and, therefore, are relevant information for financial statement readers. Companies increasingly disclose more of this "soft" information in annual reports outside the financial statements, in news releases, and in interviews with market analysts. While some observers believe that standard setters should work to ensure that more of these intangibles are captured on the balance sheet, others believe that new frameworks for reporting performance need to be developed together with—or that they should even replace—the current financial reporting model. Much research is being carried out in the search for solutions to the discrepancies between what gets reported as having value on the financial statements versus what the capital markets perceive as value and is reflected in share prices.

On the other side of the coin, sceptics point to the decline in market value of technology shares in particular, from mid-2000 to mid-2001. Nortel, for example, lost 90 percent of its value over this period, supporting the arguments of many that the historical cost model still has much to recommend it! The "truth," of course, lies somewhere in between. While inflated market values are not reliable enough to support the recognition of previously unrecognized intangible asset value, the historical-cost, transactions-based model certainly fails to capture many of the things that lie at the heart of corporate value. As the accounting community begins to accept the recognition of fair value measures for financial instruments, perhaps this will be followed by the introduction of measurement techniques that are reliable enough to be used for other asset values.

Analysis of Performance

When comparing the operating results of companies—either of one company over time or between companies—it is important to pay close attention to how deferred charges, intangibles, and goodwill have been accounted for. In the United States, accounting standards are much stricter in expensing any costs that do not result in an objectively measurable asset, compared to Canada, where more liberal accounting policies are used.

Note also that the standards for intangibles have changed significantly. The Quebecor Inc. example earlier in the chapter showed the effect that this change in accounting principle had on the company's results. The "big bath" that Quebecor took by writing down goodwill that it had previously reported as an asset means that these asset costs will never flow through the company's income statement, and future operating statements are freed from these costs. In addition, net income for companies with significant investments in goodwill and other indefinite-life intangibles are not comparable to the earnings that these companies reported for the years before the change in policy took effect. For these reasons, it is important to be careful when calculating and interpreting any ratios that include earnings and asset numbers, especially when the results of different years are being compared.

Comparison of Canadian and International GAAP

10 Objective
Compare current Canadian and international GAAP.

With a few specific exceptions, current Canadian standards and international GAAP are converged at the level of detail covered in this chapter. Illustration 12-17 presents the primary sources of GAAP in Canada for intangible assets and the international equivalents.

Illustration 12-17
Primary Sources of GAAP for Intangible Assets

Canada	International
Section 1581: Business combinations	IFRS 3: Business combinations
Section 3062: Goodwill and other intangible assets	IAS 36: Impairment of assets
Section 3063: Impairment of long-lived assets	IAS 38: Intangible assets
Section 3450: Research and development costs	
AcG-11: Enterprises in the development stage	
EIC-27: Revenues and expenditures during the pre-operating period	

The following are significant differences between the current Canadian and international standards:

Business combinations. The Canadian and international standards are converged on aspects of combinations that were covered in this chapter except that IFRS 3 requires any "negative" goodwill from a bargain purchase to be recognized immediately in income.[39]

The IASB, FASB, and AcSB are all working to have a converged standard on business combinations, and it will likely require that all acquired net assets, including goodwill, be measured at fair value; that non-controlling interests be measured at fair value; and that "negative" goodwill from a bargain purchase be recognized in income. These new standards may not be effective until 2009.

Goodwill and other intangible assets. IAS 38 provides more guidance on intangibles than does *Handbook* Section 3062. While the accounting for goodwill is converged, IAS 38 permits intangibles that can be traded in an active market to be remeasured to their fair value. This is not permitted under Canadian standards, and is not likely to be until the changeover date that is expected in 2011.

Impairment models. IAS 36 has a different definition of the reporting unit when it comes to testing for goodwill impairment. It also defines a goodwill impairment loss as the difference between the carrying amount and the recoverable amount of that reporting unit. The impairment tests for other intangibles differ in the same way as they do for property, plant, and equipment, discussed in Chapter 11. That is, IAS 36 does not have a separate recoverability test that compares the carrying amount of the asset with the total undiscounted cash flows that are expected from its use and disposal. IAS 36 also permits subsequent reversal of impairment losses. Harmonization of these differences is expected as part of a longer-term project.

Internally developed intangibles. The AcSB issued a December 2005 Exposure Draft (ED) on internally developed intangibles to amend parts of Sections 1000 and 3062 and bring Canadian practice closer to that of the IASB. The proposed changes to Section 1000 would remove existing paragraphs .26 and .51, which are now sometimes used to justify the recognition of items that do not meet the definition of assets. While IAS 38 does provide clear guidance on what expenditures are recognized as internally developed intangible assets, it also includes blanket restrictions against the recognition of intangibles such as internally developed brands, mastheads, publishing titles, customer lists, and similar items.

Unlike AcG-11 and EIC-27, IAS 38 and the AcSB's ED on internally developed intangibles would not permit development expenditures such as pre-operating costs to be capitalized.

[39] Differences will also arise when less than 100% of a company is acquired.

In early 2007, the AcSB decided to issue a re-exposure draft related to deferral of costs and internally developed intangibles. While it is expected that Canadian standards will definitely move closer to those of the IASB, how this will be accomplished may not be resolved until late in 2007.

Research and development costs. Section 3450 and IAS 38 are converged, except that the international standard allows a periodic revaluation of intangible assets that have active markets. The FASB and IASB are looking at this difference as they work on convergence. The FASB's current standard that all research and development costs be expensed as they are incurred may be relaxed somewhat in the future to permit the capitalization of some development expenditures that have the characteristics and meet the definition of assets.

Summary of Learning Objectives

Student Website

Glossary

www.wiley.com/canada/kieso

KEY TERMS

bargain purchase, 713
brand name, 705
business combination, 701
capital lease, 708
computer software costs, 710
contract-based intangible assets, 707
copyright, 707
customer-related intangible assets, 706
deferred charges, 718
development, 720
fair value test, 715
franchise, 707
goodwill, 710
identifiable intangibles, 702
identifiable net assets, 701
impairment, 715
indefinite life, 703
in-process R&D, 719
intangible assets, 701
intellectual capital, 728
internally developed intangibles, 702
knowledge assets, 728
leasehold, 708
leasehold improvements, 708
lease prepayments, 708
licences, 708
licensing agreements, 707

1 Define and describe the characteristics of intangible assets.

Intangible assets have two main characteristics: (1) they lack physical substance and (2) they are not financial instruments. In most cases, intangible assets provide services over a period of years. As a result, they are normally classified as long-term assets.

2 Identify the recognition and measurement requirements for purchased intangible assets and internally developed intangible assets.

Intangibles, like other non-financial assets, are recorded at cost. When several intangibles, or a combination of intangibles and other assets, are bought in a basket purchase, the cost is allocated based on the relative fair values of the assets. Costs that are incurred to develop an intangible internally are generally expensed immediately because of the uncertainty of the future benefits, and the inability to relate the costs with specific intangible assets. When they are acquired in a business combination, it is necessary that the identifiable intangibles be recognized separately from the goodwill component. Only the intangibles that can be exchanged or whose future benefits can be controlled through contractual or other legal means should be recognized separately as identifiable intangibles. Deferred charges, which are increasingly referred to as internally developed intangibles, are permitted in restricted circumstances where the future benefits that are associated with the incurred costs can be identified.

3 Explain how identifiable intangibles are valued after acquisition.

An intangible with a finite or limited useful life is amortized over its useful life to the entity. Except in unusual and specific circumstances, the residual value is assumed to be zero. The amount to report for amortization expense should reflect the pattern in which the asset is consumed or used up if that pattern can be reliably determined. Otherwise a straight-line approach is used. An intangible with an indefinite life is not amortized until its life is determined to no longer be indefinite. All intangibles are tested for impairment.

4 Identify and explain the accounting for specific types of intangible assets.

Major types of intangibles include the following: (1) marketing-related intangibles that are used in the marketing or promotion of products or services; (2) customer-related intangibles that are a result of interactions with outside parties; (3) artistic-related intangibles that involve ownership rights to such items as plays and literary works; (4) contract-related intangibles that represent the value of rights that arise from contractual arrangements; (5) technology-related intangible assets that relate to innovations or technological advances; and (6) goodwill that arises in business combinations. In addition, a variety of deferred charges are intangible assets; their costs are carried forward to be matched with the revenues of future periods.

5 Explain the concept of goodwill and apply the accounting procedures for recording goodwill at acquisition and subsequently.

Goodwill is unique because, unlike receivables, inventories, and patents that can be sold or exchanged individually in the marketplace, goodwill can be identified only with the business as a whole. Goodwill is a "going concern" valuation and is recorded only when an entire business is purchased. Goodwill that is generated internally is not capitalized in the accounts. A variety of accounting treatments for purchased goodwill have been justified in the past. To calculate goodwill in a 100-percent acquisition, the fair value of the identifiable assets that are acquired and liabilities that are assumed is compared with the purchase price of the acquired business. The difference is goodwill: the excess of cost over the fair value of the identifiable net assets that have been acquired.

6 Account for intangible asset impairments.

An intangible asset is impaired when the carrying amount of the asset exceeds its fair value. Impairment for *limited-life* intangible assets is based first on a recoverability test. If the carrying amount is higher than its net recoverable amount, then an impairment loss must be measured and recognized, based on the asset's fair value. The procedures are the same as for property, plant, and equipment. *Indefinite-life* intangibles use only a fair value test. Goodwill impairments use a two-step process: First, test the fair value of the reporting unit; then apply the fair value test to the implied goodwill.

7 Differentiate between research expenditures and development expenditures, and describe and explain the rationale for the accounting for them.

R&D costs are not in themselves intangible assets, but research and development activities frequently result in the development of something that is patented or copyrighted. Research is planned investigation that is done with the hope of gaining new scientific or technical knowledge and understanding. Development is the translation of research findings or other knowledge into a plan or design for new or substantially improved products or processes prior to commercial production or use. The difficulties in accounting for R&D expenditures are (1) identifying the costs that are associated with particular activities, projects, or achievements; and (2) determining the magnitude of the future benefits and length of time over which such benefits may be realized. Accounting practice requires that all research expenditures be expensed, and that all development costs be expensed except in prescribed circumstances. The circumstances require reasonable assurance that future benefits will be realized.

8 Identify other examples of internally developed intangibles and the accounting requirements for them.

Other internally developed intangible assets include long-term prepayments, organization costs, and deferred charges such as pre-operating costs and advertising costs. In general, only expenditures that are determined to have specific future benefits may be deferred as assets. They are then charged to income as the benefits are realized.

9 Identify the disclosure requirements for intangibles and the issues in analyzing this asset category.

Similar to property, plant, and equipment, the cost and any accumulated amortization is reported on the balance sheet, with separate disclosure of the amortization expense on the income statement. For intangibles that are not amortized, companies must indicate the amount of any impairment losses that have been recognized as well as information about the circumstances that led to the writedown. Goodwill must be separately reported, as are the major classes of intangible assets. Because it is difficult to measure intangibles, some resources, such as intellectual capital, do not get captured on the balance sheet. Other intangibles are recognized, but with a relatively high level of measurement uncertainty. For these reasons and because of recent changes in the accounting policy related to intangibles, care must be taken in the analysis of financial statement information related to earnings and total assets.

10 Compare current Canadian and international GAAP.

In terms of the level of coverage of intangible assets in Chapter 12, there are few differences between current Canadian and international GAAP. Differences do exist in the treatment of "negative" goodwill on a bargain purchase, the treatment of pre-operating costs, what is included as an internally developed intangible, and impairment models for goodwill and other intangibles. In addition, the IASB permits the revaluation of intangible assets where there is an active market; Canadian GAAP does not. The FASB and IASB are working toward convergence, as are the AcSB and IASB.

Appendix 12A

VALUING GOODWILL

Objective 11
Explain and apply basic approaches to valuing goodwill.

In this chapter, we discussed the method of measuring and recording goodwill **as the excess of cost over the fair value of the identifiable net assets that are acquired in a business acquisition**. The determination of a purchase price for a business and the resulting goodwill is an inexact process. As the chapter suggested, it is usually possible to determine the fair value of specifically identifiable assets, but the question remains, "How does a buyer value intangible factors such as superior management, a good credit rating, and so on?"

Excess-Earnings Approach

One widely used method to estimate the amount of goodwill in a business is the **excess-earnings approach**. This approach works as follows:

1. Calculate the average annual "normalized" earnings that the company is expected to earn in the future.
2. Calculate the annual average earnings that the company would be expected to earn if it generated the same return on investment as the average firm in the same industry. The return on investment is the percentage that results when income is divided by the net assets or shareholders' equity invested to generate that income.
3. Calculate the excess annual earnings: the difference between what the firm and the industry are expected to earn in the future. The ability to generate a higher income indicates that the business has an unidentifiable value (intangible asset) that provides this greater earning power. It is this ability to earn a higher rate of return than the industry that is considered to be the heart of what goodwill really is.
4. Estimate the value of the goodwill based on the future stream of excess earnings.

This approach is a systematic and logical way to determine goodwill, as its value is directly related to what makes a company worth more than the sum of its parts. The Tractorling Ltd. example referred to in Illustration 12-4 will be used again now to explain each of the four steps above. We begin with the first step:

1. **Calculate the average annual "normalized" earnings that the company is expected to earn in the future.** Because the past often provides useful information about the future, the past earnings are a good place to start in estimating a company's likely future earnings. Going back three to six years is usually adequate.

   Assume that Tractorling's net income amounts for the last five years and the calculation of the company's average earnings over this period are as in Illustration 12A-1.

Illustration 12A-1

Calculation of Average Past Earnings

EARNINGS HISTORY—TRACTORLING CORPORATION		
2003		$ 60,000
2004		55,000
2005		110,000[a]
2006		70,000
2007		80,000
Total for 5 years		$375,000
Average earnings	$375,000 ÷ 5 years =	$75,000

[a]Includes extraordinary gain of $25,000

Based on the average annual earnings of $75,000 and the fair value of the company's identifiable net assets of $350,000, a rate of return on investment of approximately 21.4% is initially indicated: $75,000 ÷ $350,000. Before we go further, however, we need to know whether $75,000 is representative of Tractorling's **future earnings**. A company's past earnings need to be analyzed to determine whether any adjustments are needed in estimating expected future earnings. This process is often called "normalizing earnings" and the income that results is termed **normalized earnings**.

First, **the accounting policies applied should be consistent with those of the purchaser**. For example, assume that the purchasing company measures earnings using the FIFO cost formula rather than average cost, which Tractorling uses. Further assume that the use of average cost had the effect of reducing Tractorling's net income by $2,000 each year below a FIFO-based net income. In addition, Tractorling uses accelerated amortization while the purchaser uses straight-line. As a result, the reported earnings were $3,000 lower each year than they would have been on a straight-line basis.

Secondly, because the purchaser will pay current prices for the company, **future earnings should be based on the net assets' current fair values** rather than the carrying amount on Tractorling's books. That is, differences between the carrying amounts and fair values of the assets may affect reported earnings in the future. For example, internally developed patent costs not previously recognized as an asset would be recognized on the purchase of Tractorling. This asset will need to be amortized, say, at the rate of $1,000 per year.

Finally, because we are trying to estimate future earnings, **amounts that are not expected to recur should be adjusted out of our calculations**. The 2005 extraordinary gain of $25,000 is an example of such an item. Illustration 12A-2 shows the analysis that can now be made of what the purchaser expects the annual future earnings of Tractorling to be.

Illustration 12A-2

Calculation of Normalized Earnings

Average past earnings of Tractorling (from Illustration 12A-1)		$75,000
Add		
Adjustment for change from average cost to FIFO	$2,000	
Adjustment for change from accelerated to straight-line amortization	3,000	5,000
		80,000
Deduct		
Extraordinary gain ($25,000 ÷ 5)	5,000	
Patent amortization on straight-line basis	1,000	6,000
Expected future earnings of Tractorling		$74,000

Note that it was necessary to divide the extraordinary gain of $25,000 by five years to adjust it correctly. The whole $25,000 was included in the total income earned over the five-year history, but only one-fifth of it, or $5,000, is included in the average annual earnings.[40]

2. **Calculate the annual average earnings that the company would generate if it earned the same return as the average firm in the industry.** Determining the industry's average rate of return earned on net assets requires an analysis of companies that are similar to the enterprise being examined. An industry average may be determined by examining annual reports or data from statistical services. Assume that a rate of 15% is found to be average for companies in Tractorling's industry. **This is the level of earnings that is expected from a company without any goodwill.** In this case, the estimate of what Tractorling's earnings would be if based on the norm for the industry is calculated as in Illustration 12A-3.

Illustration 12A-3
Tractorling's Earnings at the Average Rate for the Industry

Fair value of Tractorling's net identifiable assets	$350,000
Industry average rate of return	15%
Tractorling's earnings if no goodwill	$ 52,500

The net assets' fair value—not their carrying amount—is used to calculate Tractorling's level of earnings at the industry average rate of return. Fair value is used because the cost of the net identifiable assets to any company that is interested in purchasing Tractorling will be their fair value, not their carrying amount on Tractorling's books. This makes fair value the relevant measure.

3. **Calculate the company's excess annual earnings.** The next step is to calculate how much of the company's expected earnings are in excess of the industry norm. This is what gives the company value in excess of the fair value of its identifiable net assets. Tractorling's excess earnings are determined in Illustration 12A-4.

Illustration 12A-4
Calculation of Excess Earnings

Expected future earnings of Tractorling	$74,000
Tractorling's earnings if no goodwill	52,500
Tractorling's excess annual earnings	$21,500

4. **Estimate the value of the goodwill based on the excess earnings.** Because the excess earnings are expected to continue for several years, they are discounted back to their present value to determine how much a purchaser would pay for them now. A discount rate must be chosen, as well as the length of the discount period.

Discount Rate The choice of discount rate is relatively subjective.[41] The lower the discount rate, the higher the goodwill value and vice versa. To illustrate, assume that the

[40] If you find this unclear, try the following approach: Start with the total earnings of $375,000 over the past five years and make the necessary adjustments. First add 5 × $2,000 for the average cost/FIFO adjustment and 5 × $3,000 for the amortization, and then deduct 5 × $1,000 for the patent amortization and $25,000 for the extraordinary gain. The adjusted total five-year earnings of $370,000 are then divided by 5 to get the expected future annual earnings. The result is $74,000.

[41] The following illustration shows how the capitalization or discount rate might be calculated for a small business:

excess earnings of $21,500 are expected to continue indefinitely. If the excess earnings are capitalized at a rate of 25% in perpetuity, for example, the results are as indicated in Illustration 12A-5.

Capitalization at 25%

$$\frac{\text{Excess earnings}}{\text{Capitalization rate}} = \frac{\$21{,}500}{0.25} = \$86{,}000$$

Illustration 12A-5
Capitalization of Excess Earnings at 25% in Perpetuity

As indicated in Illustration 12A-6, if the excess earnings are capitalized in perpetuity at a somewhat lower rate, say 15%, a much higher goodwill figure results.[42]

Capitalization at 15%

$$\frac{\text{Excess earnings}}{\text{Capitalization rate}} = \frac{\$21{,}500}{0.15} = \$143{,}333$$

Illustration 12A-6
Capitalization of Excess Earnings at 15% in Perpetuity

What do these numbers mean? In effect, if a company pays $86,000 over and above the fair value of Tractorling's identifiable net assets because the company generates earnings above the industry norm, and Tractorling actually does generate these excess profits in perpetuity, the $21,500 of extra earnings per year represents a 25% return on the amount invested: i.e., there is a $21,500 return on the $86,000 invested.

If the purchaser invests $143,333 for the goodwill, the extra $21,500 represents a 15% return on investment: $21,500 relative to the $143,333 invested.

Because it is uncertain that excess profits will continue, a conservative rate (higher than the normal rate) tends to be used. Factors that are considered in determining the rate are the stability of past earnings, the speculative nature of the business, and general economic conditions.

Discount Period Determining the period over which excess earnings are expected to continue is perhaps the most difficult problem in estimating goodwill. The perpetuity examples above assume that the excess earnings will last indefinitely. Usually, however, the excess earnings are assumed to last a limited number of years. The earnings are then discounted over that period only.

A Method of Selecting a Capitalization Rate

	%
Long-term Canadian government bond rate	8
Add: Average premium return on small company shares over government bonds	8
Expected total rate of return on small publicly held shares	16
Add: Premium for greater risk and illiquidity	6
Total required expected rate of return, including inflation component	22
Deduct: Consensus long-term inflation expectation	5
Capitalization rate to apply to current earnings	17

From Warren Kissin and Ronald Zulli, "Valuation of a Closely Held Business," *The Journal of Accountancy*, June 1988, p. 42.

[42] Why do we divide by the capitalization or discount rate to arrive at the goodwill amount? Recall that the present value of an ordinary annuity is equal to:

$$P_{\overline{n}|i} = [1 - 1 \div (1 + i)^n] \div i$$

When a number is capitalized in perpetuity, $(1 + i)^n$ becomes so large that $1/(1 + i)^n$ essentially equals zero, which leaves $1/i$ or, as in the case above, $21,500/0.25 or $21,500/0.15.

Assume that the company interested in purchasing Tractorling's business believes that the excess earnings will last only 10 years and, because of general economic uncertainty, chooses 25% as an appropriate rate of return. The present value of a 10-year annuity of excess earnings of $21,500 discounted at 25% is $76,766.[43] This is the amount that a purchaser should be willing to pay above the fair value of the identifiable net assets—i.e., for goodwill—given the assumptions stated.

Total-Earnings Approach

There is another way to estimate goodwill that is similar and that should increase your understanding of the process and the resulting numbers. Under this approach—the **total-earnings approach**—the value of the company as a whole is determined, based on the total expected earnings, not just the excess earnings. The fair value of the identifiable net assets is then deducted from the value of the company as a whole. The difference is goodwill. The calculations under both approaches are provided in Illustration 12A-7, assuming the purchaser is looking for a 15% return on the amounts it will invest in Tractorling, and the earnings are expected to continue into perpetuity.

Illustration 12A-7

Total Earnings Approach to the Calculation of Goodwill

Assumptions:	Expected future earnings		$74,000
	Normal or industry-level earnings		$52,500
	Expected excess future earnings		$21,500
	Discount rate		15%
	Discount period		perpetuity, ∞
Excess-Earnings Approach:	Goodwill	= present value of the annuity of excess future earnings	
		= present value of annuity of $21,500 ($n = \infty$, $i = 0.15$)	
		$= \frac{\$21,500}{0.15}$	= $143,333
Total-Earnings Approach:	Goodwill	= difference between the fair value of the company and the fair value of its identifiable net assets	
	Fair value of company	= present value of the annuity of future earnings	
		= present value of annuity of $74,000 ($n = \infty$, $i = 0.15$)	
		$= \frac{\$74,000}{0.15}$	= $493,333
	Fair value of identifiable net assets	= present value of the annuity of industry-level earnings	
		= present value of annuity of $52,500 ($n = \infty$, $i = 0.15$)	
		$= \frac{\$52,500}{0.15}$	= (350,000)
	Goodwill	=	$143,333

[43] The present value of an annuity of $1 received in a steady stream for 10 years in the future discounted at 25% is $3.57050. The present value of an annuity of $21,500, therefore, is $21,500 × 3.57050 = $76,765.75.

Other Methods of Valuation

There are several other methods of valuing goodwill, some being "quick and dirty" and others very sophisticated. The methods illustrated here are some of the least complex approaches. Others include simply multiplying excess earnings by the number of years that the excess earnings are expected to continue. Often referred to as the **number of years method**, it is used to provide a rough measure of the goodwill factor. The approach has only the advantage of simplicity; it fails to discount the future cash flows and consider the time value of money.

An even simpler method is one that relies on multiples of average yearly earnings that are paid for other companies in the same industry. If Skyward Airlines was recently acquired for five times its average yearly earnings of $50 million, or $250 million, then Worldwide Airways, a close competitor with $80 million in average yearly earnings, would be worth $400 million.

Another method (similar to discounting excess earnings) is the **discounted free cash flow method**, which involves a projection of the company's free cash flow over a long period, typically 10 or 20 years. The method first projects into the future a dozen or so important financial variables, including production, prices, non-cash expenses such as amortization, taxes, and capital outlays—all adjusted for inflation. The objective is to determine the amount of operating cash flow that will be generated over and above the amount needed to maintain existing capacity. The present value of the free cash flow is then calculated. This amount represents the value of the business.

For example, if Magnaputer Ltd. is expected to generate $1 million a year of free cash flow for 20 years, and the buyer's rate-of-return objective is 15%, the buyer would be willing to pay about $6.26 million for Magnaputer. (The present value of $1 million to be received for 20 years discounted at 15% is $6,259,330.) The goodwill, then, is the difference between the $6.26 million and the fair value of the company's identifiable net assets.

In practice, prospective buyers use a variety of methods to produce a valuation curve or range of prices. But the actual price that ends up being paid may be more a factor of the buyer's or seller's ego and horse-trading acumen.

Valuation of a business and its inherent goodwill is at best a highly uncertain process.[44] The estimated value of goodwill depends on a number of factors, all of which are tenuous and subject to bargaining.

Summary of Learning Objective for Appendix 12A

Student Website

Glossary

www.wiley.com/canada/kieso

11 Explain and apply basic approaches to valuing goodwill.

One method of valuing goodwill is the excess-earnings approach. Using this approach, the total future (normalized) earnings that the company is expected to generate is calculated. The next step is to calculate the average earnings that would be generated on net assets in that industry. The difference between what the firm earns and earnings at the industry rate is referred to as the excess earnings. This excess earning power indicates that there are unidentifiable underlying asset values that result in the higher than average earnings. Finding the value of goodwill is a matter of discounting these excess future earnings to their present value. Another method involves determining the total value of the business by capitalizing total earnings, and then deducting the fair values of the identifiable net assets. The number-of-years

KEY TERMS

discounted free cash flow method, 739
excess-earnings approach, 734
normalized earnings, 735
number of years method, 739
total-earnings approach, 738

[44] Business valuation is a specialist field. The Canadian Institute of Chartered Business Valuators (CICBV) oversees the granting of the specialist designation, Chartered Business Valuator (CBV), to professionals who meet the education, experience, and examination requirements.

method of valuing goodwill, which simply multiplies the excess earnings by the number of years of expected excess earnings, is used to provide a rough measure of goodwill. Another method of valuing goodwill is the discounted free cash flow method, which projects the future operating cash that will be generated over and above the amount needed to maintain current operating levels. The present value of the free cash flows is today's value of the firm.

Brief Exercises

(LO 3) **BE12-1** Lichano Corporation purchases a patent from MacAskill Corp. on January 1, 2008, for $87,000. The patent has a remaining legal life of 16 years. Lichano feels the patent will be useful for 10 years. Prepare Lichano's journal entries to record the patent purchase and 2008 amortization.

(LO 2, 3) **BE12-2** Use the information in BE12-1 and assume that at January 1, 2010, the carrying amount of the patent on Lichano's books is $69,600. In January, Lichano spends $26,000 successfully defending a patent suit. Lichano still feels the patent will be useful until the end of 2017. Prepare the journal entries to record the $26,000 expenditure and 2010 amortization.

(LO 2, 3) **BE12-3** Stauder, Inc. spent $72,000 in legal fees while developing the trade name of its new product, the Mean Bean Machine. Prepare the journal entries to record the $72,000 expenditure and the first year of amortization, assuming a useful life of eight years.

(LO 3) **BE12-4** Molinier Corporation obtained a franchise from Monteverde Products Inc. for a cash payment of $110,000 on April 1. The franchise grants Molinier the right to sell certain products and services for a period of 12 years. Prepare Molinier's April 1 journal entry and December 31 adjusting entry.

(LO 2, 3) **BE12-5** Lager Industries Ltd. had one patent recorded on its books as at January 1, 2008. This patent had a book value of $265,000 and a remaining useful life of eight years. During 2008, Lager incurred research costs of $106,000 and brought a patent infringement suit against a competitor. On December 1, 2008, Lager received the good news that its patent was valid and that its competitor could not use the process Lager had patented. The company incurred $96,000 to defend this patent. At what amount should patent(s) be reported on the December 31, 2008, balance sheet, assuming monthly straight-line amortization of patents?

(LO 2) **BE12-6** Wiggens Industries Ltd. acquired two copyrights during 2008. One copyright was on a textbook that was developed internally at a cost of $10,000. This textbook is estimated to have a useful life of three years from September 1, 2008, the date it was published. The second copyright is for a history research textbook and was purchased from University Press on December 1, 2008, for $19,400. This textbook has an indefinite useful life. How should these two copyrights be reported on Wiggens' balance sheet as at December 31, 2008?

(LO 2) **BE12-7** HTM Ltd. decided that it needed to update its computer programs for its supplier relationships. It purchased an off-the-shelf program and modified it internally to link it to HTM's other programs. The following costs may be relevant to the accounting for the new software:

Net carrying amount of old software	$1,100
Purchase price of new software	5,900
Direct cost of internal programmer's time spent on conversion	1,720

Prepare journal entries to record the software replacement.

(LO 2) **BE12-8** Dayon Corporation purchased a trade name, customer list, and manufacturing equipment for a lump sum of $740,000. The fair market values of each asset are $250,000, $290,000 and $320,000, respectively. Prepare the journal entry to record the purchase of the various assets.

(LO 2) **BE12-9** SunKissed Valley Inc. purchased an Internet domain name by issuing a $220,000, five-year, 12%, non-interest-bearing note to Moodie Corp. The note is repayable in five annual payments of $44,000 each. Prepare the journal entry to record the purchase of the intangible asset.

BE12-10 Indicate whether the following items are capitalized or expensed in the current year: **(LO 2, 5 7, 8)**

(a) The purchase cost of a patent from a competitor

(b) Product research costs

(c) Organization costs

(d) Costs that are incurred internally to create goodwill

BE12-11 Earthworm Corp. has capitalized software costs of $820,000 on a product to be sold externally. During its first year, sales of this product totalled $480,000. Earthworm expects to earn $1,140,000 in additional future revenue from this product, which is estimated to have an economic life of four years. Calculate the amount of software amortization, assuming that amortization is based on the pattern in which Earthworm receives benefits from the software program. **(LO 3)**

BE12-12 On September 1, 2008, Dunvegan Corporation acquired Edinburgh Enterprises for a cash payment of $763,000. At the time of purchase, Edinburgh's balance sheet showed assets of $850,000, liabilities of $430,000, and owners' equity of $420,000. The fair value of Edinburgh's assets is estimated to be $1,080,000. (a) Calculate the amount of goodwill acquired by Dunvegan. (b) Prepare the December 31 entry to record amortization, if any, based on a 10-year life. **(LO 5)**

BE12-13 Nagadya Corporation owns a licence that has a carrying amount of $330,000. Nagadya expects future net cash flows from this patent to total $335,000. The patent's fair value is $250,000. Prepare Nagadya's journal entry, if necessary, to record the impairment loss. **(LO 6)**

BE12-14 Use the information in BE12-13 and assume that the licence was granted in perpetuity and has an indefinite life. Prepare Nagadya's journal entry, if necessary, to record the impairment loss. **(LO 6)**

BE12-15 Evans Corporation purchased Filo Company three years ago and recorded goodwill of $455,000 at that time. The carrying amount of the goodwill today is $395,000. The Filo Division's net assets, including the goodwill, have a carrying amount of $845,000. Evans estimates that the fair value of the Filo Division is $745,000 and that the division's fair value of identifiable net assets is $570,000. Prepare Evans' journal entry, if necessary, to record an impairment of goodwill. **(LO 6)**

BE12-16 Use the information in BE12-15 and assume instead that the fair value of the Filo Division's identifiable net assets is $330,000. Prepare Evans' journal entry, if necessary, to record an impairment of goodwill. **(LO 6)**

BE12-17 Sutherland Corporation incurred the following costs in 2008: **(LO 7)**

Cost of laboratory research aimed at discovery of new knowledge	$160,000
Cost of testing in search of product alternatives	260,000
Cost of engineering activity required to advance the design of a product to the manufacturing stage	210,000
	$630,000

Prepare the necessary 2008 journal entry for Sutherland.

BE12-18 Peacock Corporation began operations in early 2008. The corporation incurred $92,000 of costs for fees to underwriters, legal fees, provincial incorporation fees, and promotional expenditures during its formation. Prepare journal entries to record the $92,000 expenditure and 2008 amortization. If this is applicable, assume a full year of amortization based on a five-year life. **(LO 8)**

***BE12-19** Nigel Corporation is interested in purchasing Lau Car Company Ltd. The total of Lau's net income amounts over the last five years is $670,000. During one of those years, Lau reported an extraordinary gain of $94,000. The fair value of Lau's net identifiable assets is $660,000. A normal rate of return is 15%, and Nigel wants to capitalize excess earnings at 20%. Calculate the estimated value of Lau's goodwill. **(LO 11)**

Exercises

E12-1 **(Classification Issues—Intangibles)** The following is a list of items that could be included in the intangible assets section of the balance sheet: **(LO 2, 4 7, 8)**

1. An investment in a subsidiary company
2. Timberland

3. The cost of an engineering activity that is required to advance a product's design to the manufacturing stage
4. A lease prepayment (six months of rent paid in advance)
5. The cost of equipment obtained under a capital lease
6. The cost of searching for applications for new research findings
7. Costs incurred in forming a corporation
8. Operating losses incurred in the start-up of a business
9. Training costs incurred in the start-up of a new operation
10. The purchase cost of a franchise
11. Goodwill generated internally
12. The cost of testing in the search for product alternatives
13. Goodwill acquired in the purchase of a business
14. The cost of developing a patent
15. The cost of purchasing a patent from an inventor
16. Legal costs incurred in securing a patent
17. Unrecovered costs of a successful legal suit to protect the patent
18. The cost of conceptual formulation of possible product alternatives
19. The cost of purchasing a copyright
20. Product development costs
21. Long-term receivables
22. The cost of developing a trademark
23. The cost of purchasing a trademark
24. The cost of an annual update on payroll software
25. The estimated fair value of rights to advertising for a top hockey player in Canada

Instructions

(a) Indicate which items on the list would be reported as intangible assets on the balance sheet.

(b) Indicate how, if at all, the items that are not reportable as intangible assets would be reported in the financial statements.

(LO 2, 4, 8) E12-2 **(Classification Issues—Intangibles)** Selected account information follows for Richmond Inc. as of December 31, 2008. All the accounts have debit balances.

Cable Television Franchises
Music Copyrights
Research Costs
Goodwill
Cash
Discount on Notes Payable
Accounts Receivable
Property, Plant, and Equipment
Leasehold Improvements
Annual Franchise Fee Paid
In-Process Research and Development Acquired in a Business Combination
Film Contract Rights
Customer Lists
Prepaid Expenses
Covenants Not to Compete
Brand Names
Notes Receivable
Investments in Affiliated Companies
Organization Cost
Land
Excess of Purchase Price over Fair Value of Identifiable Net Assets, X Corp.

Instructions

Identify which items should be classified as intangible assets. For the items that are not classified as intangible assets, indicate where they would be reported in the financial statements.

E12-3 (Classification Issues—Intangibles) Borbely Inc. has the following amounts included in its general ledger at December 31, 2008: **(LO 2, 4 7, 8)**

Organization costs	$ 24,000
Trademarks	15,500
Discount on bonds payable	43,000
Deposits with advertising agency for ads to promote goodwill of company	10,000
Excess of cost over fair value of identifiable net assets of acquired subsidiary	75,000
Cost of equipment acquired for research and development projects; the equipment has an alternative future use	105,000
Costs of developing a secret formula for a product that is expected to be marketed for at least 20 years	80,000
Payment for a favourable lease; lease term of 10 years	25,000

Instructions

(a) Based on the information, calculate the total amount for Borbely to report as intangible assets on its balance sheet at December 31, 2008.

(b) If an item should not to be included in intangible assets, explain the proper treatment for reporting it.

E12-4 (Intangible Amortization) Selected information follows for Brown Corporation for three independent situations: **(LO 3)**

1. Brown purchased a patent from Bakhshi Co. for $1.4 million on January 1, 2006. The patent expires on January 1, 2016, and Brown is amortizing it over the 10 years remaining in its legal life. During 2008, Brown determined that the patent's economic benefits would not last longer than six years from the date of acquisition.
2. Brown bought a perpetual franchise from Carmody Inc. on January 1, 2007, for $490,000. Its carrying amount on Carmody's books at January 1, 2007, was $590,000. Assume that Brown can only provide evidence of clearly identifiable cash flows for 25 years, but thinks it could have value for up to 60 years.
3. On January 1, 2004, Brown incurred organization costs of $275,000. Brown is amortizing these costs over five years.

Instructions

(a) In situation 1, what amount should be reported in the balance sheet for the patent, net of accumulated amortization, at December 31, 2008?

(b) In situation 2, what amount of amortization expense should be reported for the year ended December 31, 2008?

(c) In situation 3, what amount, if any, should be reported as unamortized organization costs as at December 31, 2008?

E12-5 (Correct Intangible Asset Account) As the recently appointed auditor for Farber Corporation, you have been asked to examine selected accounts before the six-month financial statements of June 30, 2008, are prepared. The controller for Farber Corporation mentions that only one account is kept for intangible assets. The entries in Intangible Assets since January 1, 2008, are as follows: **(LO 2, 4, 8)**

INTANGIBLE ASSETS

			Debit	Credit	Balance
Jan.	4	Research costs	1,010,000		1,010,000
	5	Legal costs to obtain patent	75,000		1,085,000
	31	Payment of seven months' rent on property leased by Farber (Feb. to Aug.)	91,000		1,176,000
Feb.	11	Proceeds from issue of common shares		260,000	916,000
Mar.	31	Unamortized bond discount on bonds payable due March 31, 2028	84,000		1,000,000
Apr.	30	Promotional expenses related to start-up of business	207,000		1,207,000
June	30	Operating losses for first six months	316,000		1,523,000

Instructions

Prepare the entry or entries that are necessary to correct this account. Assume that the patent has a useful life of 10 years.

E12-6 (Recognition and Amortization of Intangibles) Glesen Limited organized late in 2007 and set up a single account for all intangible assets. The following summary shows the entries in 2008 (all debits) that have been recorded in Intangible Assets since then: **(LO 2, 3)**

Jan. 2	Purchased patent (8-year life)	$ 372,000
Apr. 1	Purchased goodwill (indefinite life)	440,000
July 1	Purchased franchise with 10-year life; expiration date July 1, 2018	460,000
Aug. 1	Payment for copyright (5-year life)	196,000
Sept. 1	Research and development costs	239,000
		$1,707,000

Instructions

Prepare the necessary entries to clear the Intangible Assets account and to set up separate accounts for distinct types of intangibles. Make the entries as at December 31, 2008, and record any necessary amortization so that all balances are accurate as at that date.

(LO 4) **E12-7 (Correct Asset Account)** Sunrise Corporation hired a new bookkeeper at the beginning of the month. The bookkeeper was unsure of how to record transactions for a variety of capital assets. As a result, all the capital asset transactions were recorded in the same account, as follows:

	Capital Assets		Land	
Transaction #	Debit	Credit	Debit	Credit
1	66,000			
2	47,700			
3	11,000			
4	40,000			
5	111,000			
6	2,900			
7		47,500		
8	12,200			
9	4,400			
10		33,000		
Balance	214,700		40,000	

Transaction #:

1. Sunrise purchased a patent for $66,000.
2. Sunrise repaired the roof on the building at a cost of $47,700. The expenditure extended the useful life of the building by five more years.
3. Frequent ongoing repairs and maintenance costs were incurred for $11,000.
4. Sunrise acquired another business and paid $40,000 for goodwill.
5. As a result of a rare spring flood, a loss of $111,000 was sustained on the building. There was no insurance coverage for this type of loss.
6. Sunrise paid the local government $2,900 for the annual business licence.
7. Land acquird in a previous year that was originally purchased for $40,000 was sold for $47,500.
8. Sunrise paid $12,200 in legal fees in a successful defence related to the patent acquired in transaction 1.
9. Sunrise paid insurance costs of $4,400 on capital assets.
10. The bookkeeper recorded the adjusting entry for amortization of $33,000.

Instructions

Prepare the correcting entry(ies) that are necessary to properly classify and correct the capital asset transactions.

(CGA Canada, adapted)

(LO 2, 3) **E12-8 (Accounting for Trade Name)** In early January 2008, Crystal Corporation applied for and received a trade name, incurring legal costs of $24,000. In January 2009, Crystal incurred $14,800 of legal fees in a successful defence of its trade name.

Instructions

(a) Identify the variables that must be considered in determining the appropriate amortization period for this trade name.

(b) Calculate amortization for 2008; book value at December 31, 2008; amortization for 2009; and book value at December 31, 2009, if the company amortizes the trade name over its 15-year legal life.

(c) Repeat part (b), assuming a useful life of five years.

E12-9 **(Accounting for Lease Transaction)** Benet Inc. leases an old building that it intends to improve and use as a warehouse. To obtain the lease, the company paid a bonus of $81,000. Annual rental for the six-year lease period is $132,000. There is no option to renew the lease or right to purchase the property. **(LO 3, 4)**

After the lease is obtained, improvements costing $164,000 are made. The building has an estimated remaining useful life of 17 years.

Instructions

(a) What is the annual lease or rent expense to Benet Inc.?

(b) What amount of annual amortization should Benet record, if any, on a straight-line basis?

(c) How would the various amounts be reported on Benet Inc.'s financial statements?

E12-10 **(Accounting for Organization Costs)** Greeley Corporation was organized in 2007 and began operations at the beginning of 2008. The company is involved in interior design consulting services. The following costs were incurred before the start of operations: **(LO 8)**

Legal fees for organization of the company	$24,000
Improvements to leased offices before occupancy	31,000
Costs of meetings of incorporators to discuss organization activities	8,500
Provincial filing fees to incorporate	1,400
	$64,900

Instructions

(a) Calculate the total amount of organization costs incurred by Greeley.

(b) Prepare a summary journal entry to record the $64,900 of expenditures.

(c) What are the different time periods that Greeley Corporation could consider for amortizing the organization costs?

E12-11 **(Accounting for Patents, Franchises, and R&D)** Lowell Corp. has provided the following information on its intangible assets: **(LO 3, 4, 7)**

1. A patent was purchased from Marvin Inc. for $2.4 million on January 1, 2008. Lowell estimated the patent's remaining useful life to be 10 years. The patent was carried in Marvin's accounting records at a net book value of $2.7 million when Marvin sold it to Lowell.
2. During 2009, a franchise was purchased from Burr Ltd. for $580,000. As part of the deal, Burr must also be paid 5% of revenue from the franchise operations. Revenue from the franchise for 2009 was $2.9 million. Lowell estimates the franchise's useful life to be 10 years and takes a full year's amortization in the year of purchase.
3. Lowell incurred the following research and development costs in 2009:

Materials and equipment	$143,000
Personnel	212,000
Indirect costs	110,000
	$465,000

On January 1, 2009, because of recent events in the field, Lowell estimates that the remaining life of the patent purchased on January 1, 2008, is only five years from January 1, 2009.

Instructions

(a) Prepare a schedule showing the intangibles section of Lowell's balance sheet at December 31, 2009. Show supporting calculations in good form.

(b) Prepare a schedule showing the income statement effect for the year ended December 31, 2009, as a result of the facts above. Show supporting calculations in good form.

(AICPA adapted)

(LO 3, 4, 7) E12-12 **(Accounting for Patents)** During 2004, Weinstein Corporation spent $170,000 on research and development costs. As a result, a new product called the New Age Piano was patented at additional legal and other costs of $18,000. The patent obtained on October 1, 2004, had a legal life of 20 years and a useful life of 10 years.

Instructions

(a) Prepare all journal entries required in 2004 and 2005 as a result of the transactions.

(b) On June 1, 2006, Weinstein spent $9,480 to successfully prosecute a patent infringement. As a result, the estimate of useful life was extended to 12 years from June 1, 2006. Prepare all journal entries required in 2006 and 2007.

(c) In 2008, Weinstein determined that a competitor's product would make the New Age Piano obsolete and the patent worthless by December 31, 2009. Prepare all journal entries required in 2008 and 2009.

(LO 3, 6) E12-13 **(Accounting for Patents)** Tona Industries Ltd. has the following patents on its December 31, 2009, balance sheet:

Patent Item	Initial Cost	Date Acquired	Useful Life at Date Acquired
Patent A	$35,600	Mar. 1, 2006	17 years
Patent B	$15,000	July 1, 2007	10 years
Patent C	$24,400	Sept. 1, 2008	4 years

The following events occurred during the year ended December 31, 2010:

1. Research and development costs of $251,700 were incurred during the year.
2. Patent D was purchased on July 1 for $36,480. This patent has a useful life of 9.5 years.
3. As a result of reduced demand for certain products that are protected by Patent B, there may be an impairment of Patent B's value at December 31, 2010. The controller for Tona estimates the future cash flows from Patent B will be as follows:

For the Year Ended	Future Cash Flows
Dec. 31, 2011	$2,600
Dec. 31, 2012	2,600
Dec. 31, 2013	2,600

The proper discount rate to be used for these flows is 8%. (Assume that the cash flows occur at the end of the year.)

Instructions

(a) Calculate the total carrying amount of Tona's patents on its December 31, 2009, balance sheet.

(b) Calculate the total carrying amount of Tona's patents on its December 31, 2010, balance sheet.

(LO 5) E12-14 **(Accounting for Goodwill)** Fred Moss, owner of Moss Interiors Inc., is negotiating for the purchase of Zweifel Galleries Ltd. The condensed balance sheet of Zweifel follows in an abbreviated form:

ZWEIFEL GALLERIES LTD.
Balance Sheet
As at December 31, 2008

Assets		**Liabilities and Shareholders' Equity**		
Cash	$112,000	Accounts payable		$ 62,000
Land	70,000	Long-term notes payable		329,000
Building (net)	224,000	Total liabilities		391,000
Equipment (net)	175,000	Common shares	$200,000	
Copyright (net)	35,000	Retained earnings	25,000	225,000
Total assets	$616,000	Total liabilities and shareholders' equity		$616,000

Moss and Zweifel agree that land is undervalued by $30,000 and equipment is overvalued by $7,000. Zweifel agrees to sell the gallery to Moss for $365,000.

Instructions

Prepare the entry to record the purchase of the gallery's net assets on Moss's books.

E12-15 (Accounting for Goodwill) On July 1, 2008, Bing Corporation purchased the net assets of Young Company by paying $250,000 cash and issuing a $100,000 note payable to Young Company. At July 1, 2008, the balance sheet of Young Company was as follows: **(LO 5, 6)**

Cash	$ 50,000	Accounts payable	$200,000
Receivables	90,000	Young, capital	235,000
Inventory	100,000		$435,000
Land	40,000		
Buildings (net)	75,000		
Equipment (net)	70,000		
Trademarks (net)	10,000		
	$435,000		

The recorded amounts all approximate current values except for land (worth $60,000), inventory (worth $125,000), and trademarks (worthless). The receivables are shown net of an allowance for doubtful accounts of $12,000. The amounts for buildings, equipment, and trademarks are shown net of accumulated amortization of $14,000, $23,000 and $47,000, respectively.

Instructions

(a) Prepare the July 1, 2008, entry for Bing Corporation to record the purchase.

(b) Assume that Bing tested its goodwill for impairment on December 31, 2009, and determined that it had an implied value of $55,000. Prepare the entry, if any, on December 31, 2009.

(c) Repeat part (a), assuming that the purchase price was only the cash payment of $250,000.

E12-16 (Intangible Impairment) The following information is for a copyright owned by La Mare Corp. at December 31, 2008: **(LO 6)**

Cost	$8,600,000
Carrying amount	4,300,000
Expected future net cash flows	4,000,000
Fair value	3,200,000

Assume that La Mare Corp. will continue to use this copyright in the future. As at December 31, 2008, the copyright is estimated to have a remaining useful life of 10 years.

Instructions

(a) Prepare the journal entry, if any, to record the asset's impairment at December 31, 2008.

(b) Prepare the journal entry to record amortization expense for 2009 related to the copyright.

(c) The copyright's fair value at December 31, 2009, is $3.4 million. Prepare the journal entry, if any, that is necessary to record the increase in fair value.

(d) Using the information from part (a), discuss whether the copyright would be amortized in 2008 before the impairment test. Would the asset be tested for impairment before or after amortizing the copyright?

E12-17 (Accounting for Intangibles) Argot Corporation was organized on July 1, 2007, and provided you with the following information: **(LO 4, 5, 6, 8)**

1. Purchased a franchise for $42,000 on July 2, 2007. The rights to the franchise expire on July 2, 2012, and cannot be renewed. The franchise is expected to be profitable over this entire period.
2. A provincial incorporation fee of $2,000 and related legal fees associated with organizing the company of $5,000 were expensed when they were incurred in 2007.
3. Purchased a patent on January 2, 2008, for $90,000. It is estimated to have a 10-year life.
4. Costs incurred to develop a secret formula were $92,000 as at March 1, 2008. The formula has an indefinite life.
5. On March 30, 2008, Argot Corporation purchased a small manufacturing concern for $730,000. The fair value of the company's identifiable net assets acquired was $520,000.
6. On June 29, 2008, legal fees for the successful defence of the patent purchased in January were $11,900.
7. Research costs incurred in 2008 were $130,000.

Instructions

(a) Prepare the journal entries to record the transactions described in 2007 and 2008, as well as any adjusting entries required at December 31, 2007 and 2008. If necessary, assume a five-year life for any intangible whose useful life is not given.

(b) At December 31, 2008, an impairment test is performed on the franchise purchased in 2007. It is estimated that the net cash flows to be received from the franchise will be $25,000, and its fair value is $13,000. Calculate the amount of impairment, if any, to be recorded on December 31, 2008. Prepare any necessary journal entries.

(c) Prepare the Intangible Assets section of the balance sheet for Argot Corporation at December 31, 2008.

(LO 8) E12-18 **(Goodwill Impairment)** The following is net asset information (including associated goodwill of $200 million) for the Solar Division of Claus, Inc.:

SOLAR DIVISION
Net Assets
as of December 31, 2008

(in millions)	Book Value	Fair Value
Cash	$ 50	$ 50
Receivables	216	159
Property, plant, and equipment (net)	2,618	2,817
Goodwill	206	
Less: Notes payable	(2,700)	(2,700)
Net assets	$ 390	

The purpose of this division (also identified as a reporting unit) is to develop a nuclear-powered aircraft. If successful, travelling delays that are associated with refuelling could be greatly reduced. Many other benefits would also occur. To date, management has not had much success and is deciding whether a writedown is appropriate at this time. Management estimates its future net cash flows from the project to be $400 million. Management has also received an offer to purchase the division for $346 million.

Instructions

(a) Prepare the journal entry, if any, to record the impairment at December 31, 2008.

(b) At December 31, 2009, it is estimated that the division's fair value increased to $400 million. Prepare the journal entry, if any, to record this increase in fair value.

(LO 3, 7) E12-19 **(Accounting for R&D Costs)** From time to time, Gators Corp. embarks on a research program when a special project seems to offer possibilities. In 2008, the company expended $325,000 on a research project, but by the end of 2008 it was impossible to determine whether any benefit would come from it.

Instructions

(a) What account should be charged for the $325,000, and how should it be shown in the financial statements?

(b) The project is completed in 2009, and a successful patent is obtained. The research costs to complete the project are $125,000. The administrative and legal expenses incurred in obtaining patent number 472-1001-84 in 2009 total $20,000. The patent has an expected useful life of five years. Record these costs in journal entry form. Also, record patent amortization for a full year in 2009.

(c) In 2010, the company successfully defended the patent in lengthy litigation at a cost of $48,200. The victory extended the patent's life to December 31, 2017. What is the proper way to account for this cost? Also, record patent amortization (full year) in 2010.

(d) Additional engineering and consulting costs were incurred in 2010. These costs were necessary to advance a product design to the manufacturing stage and totalled $60,000. The costs improved the product design considerably. Discuss the proper accounting treatment for these costs.

(LO 7) E12-20 **(Accounting for R&D Costs)** Timothy Corp. incurred the following costs during 2008 in connection with its research and development activities:

Cost of acquired equipment that will have alternative uses in future research and development projects over the next five years (straight-line amortization used)	$280,000
Materials consumed in research projects	59,000
Materials consumed in the development of a product committed for manufacturing in first quarter 2009	27,000
Consulting fees paid to outsiders for research and development projects, including $4,500 for advice related to the $27,000 of materials used above	100,000
Personnel costs of persons involved in research and development projects	128,000
Indirect costs reasonably allocated to research and development projects	50,000
Materials purchased for future research and development projects	34,000

Instructions

Calculate the amount to be reported as research and development expense by Timothy on its income statement for 2008. Assume the equipment is purchased at the beginning of the year.

E12-21 (Accounting for R&D Costs) The following are four independent situations involving research and development costs: **(LO 7)**

1. During 2008, Sisco Corp. incurred the following costs:

Research and development services performed by Miles Limited for Sisco	$354,000
Testing for evaluation of new products	300,000
Laboratory research aimed at discovery of new knowledge	437,000

2. Odo Corp. incurred the following costs during the year ended December 31, 2008:

Design, construction, and testing of pre-production prototypes and models	$298,000
Routine, ongoing efforts to refine, enrich, or otherwise improve the qualities of an existing product	289,000
Quality control during commercial production, including routine product testing	300,000
Laboratory research aimed at the discovery of new knowledge	428,000

3. Quark Ltd. incurred costs in 2008 as follows:

Equipment acquired for use in various research and development projects	$900,000
Amortization on the equipment above	250,000
Materials used in R&D	309,000
Compensation costs of personnel in R&D	416,000
Outside consulting fees for R&D work	229,000
Indirect costs appropriately allocated to R&D	288,000

4. Julian Inc. incurred the following costs during the year ended December 31, 2008:

Laboratory research aimed at the discovery of new knowledge	$209,000
Radical modification to the formula of a chemical product	195,000
Research and development costs that are reimbursable under a contract to perform research and development for Bashir Inc.	360,000
Testing for the evaluation of new products	226,000

Instructions

(a) In situation 1, how much research and development expense should Sisco Corp. report for the year ended December 31, 2008?

(b) In situation 2, what is the total amount to be classified and expensed as research and development for 2008?

(c) In situation 3, what is the total amount of research and development expense that should be reported in Quark's 2008 income statement?

(d) In situation 4, what is the total amount to be classified and expensed as research and development for 2008?

E12-22 (Accounting for R&D Costs) During 2007, Saskatchewan Enterprises Ltd. spent $5.2 million developing a new software product called Dover. Of this amount, $2.5 million was spent before establishing that the product was technologically feasible. Dover was completed by December 31, 2007 and will be marketed to third parties. Saskatchewan expects a useful life of eight years for this product, with total revenues of $16 million. During 2008, Saskatchewan realized revenues of $3.2 million from sales of Dover. **(LO 7)**

Instructions

(a) Prepare the journal entries that are required in 2007 to record the above.

(b) Prepare the entry to record amortization at December 31, 2008.

(c) At what amount should the software costs be reported in the December 31, 2008, balance sheet? Could the net realizable value of this asset at December 31, 2008, affect your answer? Explain briefly.

(LO 11) ***E12-23 (Calculate Normalized Earnings)** Amanjeet Corporation's pre-tax accounting income of $850,000 for the year 2008 included the following items:

Amortization of identifiable intangibles	$ 87,000
Amortization of building	130,000
Loss from discontinued operations	44,000
Extraordinary gains	162,000
Profit-sharing payments to employees	65,000

Ewing Industries Ltd. would like to purchase Amanjeet Corporation. In trying to measure Amanjeet's normalized earnings for 2008, Ewing determines that the building's fair value is triple the book value and that its remaining economic life is double the life that Amanjeet is using. Ewing would continue the profit-sharing payments to employees, with the payments being based on income from continuing operations before amortization.

Instructions

Calculate the 2008 normalized earnings amount of Amanjeet Corporation that Ewing would need to determine so that it could calculate goodwill.

(LO 11) ***E12-24 (Calculate Goodwill)** Net income figures for Alberta Ltd. are as follows:

2004—$78,000	2007—$86,000
2005—$52,000	2008—$77,000
2006—$81,000	

Future income is expected to continue at the average of the past five years. The company's identifiable net assets are appraised at $460,000 on December 31, 2008. This business is to be acquired by Mooney Corp. early in 2009. The normal rate of return on net assets for the industry is 7%.

Instructions

What amount should be paid for goodwill, and for the company as a whole, if:

(a) goodwill is equal to average excess earnings capitalized at 25%?

(b) a perpetual 15% return is expected on the total investment in the company?

(c) goodwill is equal to five years of excess earnings?

(d) goodwill is equal to the present value of five years of excess earnings capitalized at 18%?

(LO 11) ***E12-25 (Calculate Goodwill)** Xiaofei Corporation is interested in acquiring Richmond Plastics Limited. Richmond has determined that its excess earnings have averaged approximately $150,000 and feels that such an amount should be capitalized over an unlimited period at a 20% rate. Xiaofei feels that because of increased competition, the excess earnings of Richmond Plastics will continue for seven years at the most and that a 15% discount rate is appropriate.

Instructions

(a) How far apart are the positions of these two parties?

(b) Is there really a difference in the two approaches being used by the parties to evaluate Richmond Plastics' goodwill? Explain.

(LO 11) ***E12-26 (Calculate Goodwill)** As the president of Manitoba Recording Corp., you are considering purchasing Moose Jaw CD Corp., whose balance sheet is summarized as follows:

Current assets	$ 300,000	Current liabilities	$ 300,000
Plant and equipment (net)	700,000	Long-term liabilities	500,000
Other assets	300,000	Common shares	400,000
		Retained earnings	100,000
Total	$1,300,000	Total	$1,300,000

The current assets' fair value is $250,000 higher than its carrying amount because of inventory undervaluation. All other assets and liabilities have book values that approximate their fair value. The normal rate of return on net assets for the industry is 15%. The expected annual earnings for Moose Jaw CD Corp. are $140,000.

Instructions

Assuming that the excess earnings are expected to continue for five years, how much would you be willing to pay for goodwill, and for the company? (Estimate goodwill by the present value method.)

***E12-27** **(Calculate Fair Value of Identifiable Assets)** Hartley Inc. bought a business that is expected to give a 20% annual rate of return on the investment. Of the total amount paid for the business, $80,000 was deemed to be goodwill, and the rest was attributed to the identifiable net assets. **(LO 11)**

Hartley Inc. estimated that the annual future earnings of the new business would be equal to the average ordinary earnings per year of the business over the past four years. The total net income over the past four years was $380,000. This amount included an extraordinary loss of $35,000 in one year and an extraordinary gain of $115,000 in one of the other three years.

Instructions

Calculate the fair value of the identifiable net assets that Hartley Inc. purchased in this transaction.

Problems

P12-1 Esplanade Corp. incorporated on June 28, 2007, and set up a single account for all its intangible assets. The following summary discloses the debit entries that were recorded during 2007 and 2008 in that account:

INTANGIBLE ASSETS

July 1, 2007	8-year franchise; expiration date of June 30, 2015	$ 48,000
Oct. 1	Advance payment on leasehold (2-year lease)	28,000
Dec. 31	Net loss for 2007 including incorporation fee, $1,000; related legal fees of organizing, $5,000; expenses of recruiting and training staff for start-up of new business, $3,800	16,000
Feb. 15, 2008	Patent purchased (10-year life)	75,500
Mar. 1	Direct costs of acquiring a 5-year licensing agreement	76,500
Apr. 1	Goodwill purchased (indefinite life)	307,400
June 1	Legal fee for successful defence of patent (see above)	13,350
Dec. 31	Costs of research department for year	160,000
Dec. 31	Royalties paid under licensing agreement (see above)	2,350

The new business started up on July 2, 2007. No amortization was recorded for 2007 or 2008. The goodwill purchased on April 1, 2008, includes in-process research and development valued at $200,000. The company estimates that this amount will help it generate revenues over a 10-year period.

Instructions

Prepare the necessary entries to clear the Intangible Assets account and to set up separate accounts for distinct types of intangibles. Make the entries as at December 31, 2008, and record any necessary amortization so that all balances are appropriate as at that date. State any assumptions that you need to make to support your entries.

P12-2 Ankara Laboratories holds a valuable patent (No. 758-6002-1A) on a precipitator that prevents certain types of air pollution. Ankara does not manufacture or sell the products and processes that it develops. Its approach is to first conduct research and develop products and processes, and then patent them and assign the patents to manufacturers on a royalty basis. Occasionally, it sells a patent. The history of Ankara patent number 758-6002-1A is as follows:

Date	Activity	Cost
1998–1999	Research conducted to develop precipitator	$384,000
Jan. 2000	Design and construction of prototype	88,600
Mar. 2000	Testing of models	42,000
Jan. 2001	Fees paid to engineers and lawyers to prepare patent application; patent granted July 1, 2001	62,850
Nov. 2002	Engineering activity necessary to advance the precipitator design to the manufacturing stage	90,000
Dec. 2003	Legal fees paid to successfully defend precipitator patent	36,700
Apr. 2004	Research aimed at modifying the patented precipitator design	43,000
July 2008	Legal fees paid in unsuccessful patent infringement suit against a competitor	34,000

Ankara assumed a useful life of 17 years when it received the initial precipitator patent. In early 2006, it revised its useful life estimate downward to five remaining years. Amortization is calculated for a full year if the cost is incurred before July 1; if the cost is incurred after June 30, no amortization is taken for the year. The company's year end is December 31.

Instructions

(a) Calculate the carrying amount of patent No. 758-6002-1A on each of the following dates: December 31, 2001; December 31, 2005; and December 31, 2008.

(b) Due to the unsuccessful patent infringement suit in July 2008, Ankara estimates that future cash flows expected from using the patent are only $15,000 and that the patent has a fair value of $10,000. Prepare the journal entry, if any, to record the patent's impairment at December 31, 2008.

P12-3 Information for Haerhpin Corporation's intangible assets follows:

1. On January 1, 2008, Haerhpin signed an agreement to operate as a franchisee of Hsian Copy Service, Inc. for an initial franchise fee of $75,000. Of this amount, $15,000 was paid when the agreement was signed and the balance is payable in four annual payments of $15,000 each, beginning January 1, 2009. The agreement provides that the down payment is not refundable and no future services are required of the franchisor. The present value at January 1, 2008, of the four annual payments discounted at 14% (the implicit rate for a loan of this type) is $43,700. The agreement also provides that 5% of the franchisee's revenue must be paid to the franchisor each year. Haerhpin's revenue from the franchise for 2008 was $950,000. Haerhpin estimates that the franchise's useful life will be 10 years. (Hint: Refer to Appendix 6A to determine the proper accounting treatment for the franchise fee and payments.)
2. Haerhpin incurred $65,000 of experimental costs in its laboratory to develop a patent, and the patent was granted on January 2, 2008. Legal fees and other costs of patent registration totalled $13,600. Haerhpin estimates that the useful life of the patent will be eight years.
3. A trademark was purchased from Shanghai Company for $32,000 on July 1, 2005. Expenditures to successfully defend the trademark in litigation totalled $8,160 and were paid on July 1, 2008. Haerhpin estimates that the trademark's useful life will be 20 years from the acquisition date.

Instructions

(a) Prepare a schedule showing the intangible assets section of Haerhpin's balance sheet at December 31, 2008. Show supporting calculations in good form.

(b) Prepare a schedule showing all expenses resulting from the transactions that would appear on Haerhpin's income statement for the year ended December 31, 2008. Show supporting calculations in good form.

(AICPA adapted)

P12-4 Alberta Matt's Golf Inc. was formed on July 1, 2006, when Matt Magilke purchased Old Master Golf Corporation. Old Master provides video golf instruction at kiosks in shopping malls. Magilke's plan is to make the instruction business part of his golf equipment and accessory stores. Magilke paid $750,000 cash for Old Master. At the time of purchase, Old Master's balance sheet reported assets of $650,000 and liabilities of $200,000 (so shareholders' equity was $450,000). The fair value of Old Master's assets was estimated to be $800,000. Included in the assets was the Old Master trade name with a fair value of $10,000 and a copyright on some instructional books with a fair value of $20,000. The trade name had a remaining life of five years and can be renewed indefinitely at nominal cost. The copyright had a remaining life of 40 years.

Instructions

(a) Prepare the intangible assets section of Alberta Matt's Golf Inc. at December 31, 2006. How much amortization expense is included in Alberta Matt's income for the year ended December 31, 2006? Show all supporting calculations.

(b) Prepare the journal entry to record the amortization expense for 2007. Prepare the intangible assets section of Alberta Matt's Golf Inc. at December 31, 2007. (No impairments need to be recorded in 2007).

(c) At the end of 2008, Magilke is evaluating the results of the instructional business. Due to fierce competition from Internet sites and television (e.g., the Golf Channel), the Old Master reporting unit has been losing money. Its book value is now $500,000 and its fair value is $430,000. The implied value of goodwill is $80,000. Magilke has collected the following information about the company's intangible assets:

Intangible Asset	Expected Cash Flows (undiscounted)	Fair Value
Trade name	$ 9,000	$ 3,000
Copyright	30,000	25,000

Prepare the required journal entries, if any, to record impairments on Alberta Matt's intangible assets. (Assume that any amortization for 2008 has been recorded.) Show supporting calculations.

P12-5 The following information is for the intangible assets of Goldberg Products Limited:

	Renewable Licence	Goodwill	Purchased Patent Costs
Original cost at Jan. 1, 2008	$100,000	$280,000	$48,000
Useful life at Jan. 1, 2008 (estimated)	Indefinite	Indefinite	6 years
Implied fair value, Dec. 31, 2008	$ 95,000	$200,000	$38,000
Implied fair value, Dec. 31, 2009	$ 97,000	$210,000	$32,000
Implied fair value, Dec. 31, 2010	$101,000	$220,000	$14,600
Net recoverable amount, Dec. 31, 2008	$105,000	N/A	$41,500
Net recoverable amount, Dec. 31, 2009	$108,000	N/A	$37,000
Net recoverable amount, Dec. 31, 2010	$120,000	N/A	$17,000

Just before Goldberg's 2007 fiscal year end at December 31, 2007, the company acquired the three intangible assets identified above in a business combination. In early 2009, the company incurred $6,000 of legal costs in successfully defending the rights to the patent. One year later, in early 2010, Goldberg discovered that a competitor had developed a product that would eventually make the company's patent obsolete. Goldberg decided that the patent had only two years of useful life remaining, with no residual value. The company uses straight-line amortization.

Instructions

(a) Prepare all journal entries that are required for the period from January 1, 2008, to December 31, 2010.

(b) Prepare the balance sheet disclosures that are required at December 31, 2008, 2009, and 2010. Identify the items, if any, that require separate disclosure.

(c) Identify all amounts that will be included on the company's income statements for 2008, 2009, and 2010. Also identify the items, if any, that require separate disclosure.

(d) Discuss how frequently impairment tests should be done for the three assets shown above.

P12-6 In late July 2007, Mehta Ltd. paid $3 million to acquire all of the net assets of Sawatzky Corp., which then became a division of Mehta. Sawatzky reported the following balance sheet at the time of acquisition:

Current assets	$ 830,000	Current liabilities	$ 600,000
Non-current assets	2,670,000	Long-term liabilities	530,000
		Shareholders' equity	2,370,000
	$3,500,000		$3,500,000

It was determined at the date of the purchase that the fair value of the identifiable net assets of Sawatzky was $2,610,000. Over the next six months of operations, the new division had operating losses. In addition, it now appears that it will generate substantial losses for the foreseeable future. At December 31, 2007, the Sawatzky Division reports the following balance sheet information:

Current assets	$ 462,000
Non-current assets (including goodwill recognized in purchase)	2,400,000
Current liabilities	(703,500)
Long-term liabilities	(530,000)
Net assets	$1,628,500

It is determined that the fair value of the Sawatzky Division is $1,850,000. The recorded amount for Sawatzky's net assets (excluding goodwill) is the same as their fair value, except for property, plant, and equipment, which has a fair value $130,000 above the carrying amount.

Instructions

(a) Calculate the amount of goodwill if any, that should be recognized, in late July 2007.

(b) Determine the impairment loss, if any, to be recognized on December 31, 2007.

(c) Assume that the fair value of the Sawatzky Division is $1.5 million instead of $1,850,000 on December 31, 2007. Determine the impairment loss, if any, that should be recognized on December 31, 2007.

(d) Prepare the journal entry to record the impairment loss, if any, in (b) and (c) and indicate where the loss would be reported in the income statement.

P12-7 Sato Corporation was incorporated on January 3, 2007. The corporation's financial statements for its first year of operations were not examined by a public accountant. You have been engaged to audit the financial statements for the year ended December 31, 2008, and your audit is almost complete. The corporation's trial balance is as follows:

SATO CORPORATION
Trial Balance
December 31, 2008

	Debit	Credit
Cash	$ 47,000	
Accounts Receivable	73,000	
Allowance for Doubtful Accounts		$ 1,460
Inventories	50,200	
Machinery	82,000	
Equipment	37,000	
Accumulated Amortization		26,200
Patents	128,200	
Leasehold Improvements	36,100	
Prepaid Expenses	13,000	
Goodwill	30,000	
Licensing Agreement No. 1	60,000	
Licensing Agreement No. 2	56,000	
Accounts Payable		73,000
Unearned Revenue		17,280
Common Shares		300,000
Retained Earnings, January 1, 2008		159,060
Sales		720,000
Cost of Goods Sold	475,000	
Selling and General Expenses	180,000	
Interest Expense	9,500	
Extraordinary Losses	20,000	
Totals	$1,297,000	$1,297,000

The following information is for accounts that may still need adjustment:

1. Patents for Sato's manufacturing process were acquired on January 2, 2008, at a cost of $93,500. An additional $34,700 was spent in December 2008 to improve machinery covered by the patents and was charged to the Patents account. Amortization on fixed assets was properly recorded for 2008 in accordance with Sato's practice, which is to take a full year of amortization for property on hand at June 30. No other amortization was recorded. Sato uses the straight-line method for all amortization and amortizes its patents over their legal life, which was 17 years when the patent was granted. Accumulate all amortization expense in one income statement account.
2. At December 31, 2008, management determined that the net future cash flows that are expected from use of the patent would be $80,000, and that the resale value of the patent on this date was approximately $55,000.
3. On January 3, 2007, Sato purchased licensing agreement No. 1, which management believed had an unlimited useful life. Licences similar to this are frequently bought and sold. Sato could only clearly identify cash flows from agreement No. 1 for 18 years. After the 18 years, further cash flows are still possible, but are uncertain. The balance in the Licensing Agreement No. 1 account includes the agreement's purchase price of $57,000 and expenses of $3,000 related to the acquisition. On January 1, 2008, Sato purchased licensing agreement No. 2, which has a life expectancy of 10 years. The balance in the Licensing Agreement No. 2 account includes its $54,000 purchase price and $6,000 in acquisition expenses, but it has been reduced by a credit of $4,000 for the advance collection of 2009 revenue from the agreement. In late December 2007, an explosion caused a permanent 70% reduction in the expected revenue-producing value of licensing agreement No. 1. In January 2009, a flood caused additional damage that rendered the agreement worthless.
4. The balance in the Goodwill account results from legal expenses of $30,000 that were incurred for Sato's incorporation on January 3, 2007. Although management assumes that the $30,000 cost will benefit the entire life of the organization, it decided late in 2008 that these costs should be amortized over a limited life of 30 years. No entry has been made yet.

5. The Leasehold Improvements account includes the following: (a) There is a $15,000 cost of improvements that Sato made to premises that it leases as a tenant. The improvements were made in January 2007 and have a useful life of 12 years. (b) Movable assembly-line equipment costing $15,000 was installed in the leased premises in December 2008. (c) Real estate taxes of $6,100 were paid by Sato in 2008, but they should have been paid by the landlord under the terms of the lease agreement.

   Sato paid its rent in full during 2008. A 10-year non-renewable lease was signed January 3, 2007, for the leased building that Sato used in manufacturing operations. No amortization has been recorded on any amounts related to the lease or improvements.

Instructions

(a) Prepare an eight-column work sheet to adjust the accounts that require adjustment and include columns for an income statement and a balance sheet. A separate account should be used for the accumulation of each type of amortization. Formal adjusting journal entries and financial statements are not required.

(b) Prepare Sato's balance sheet and income statement for the year ended December 31, 2008, in proper form.

(AICPA adapted)

P12-8 Six examples follow of purchased intangible assets. They are reported on the consolidated balance sheet of Hamm Enterprises Limited and include information about their useful and legal lives.

Intangible 1a is the trade name for one of the company's subsidiaries. The trade name has a remaining legal life of 16 years, but it can be renewed indefinitely at a very low cost. The subsidiary has grown quickly, has been very successful, and its name is well known to Canadian consumers. Hamm management has concluded that it can identify positive cash flows from the use of the trade name for another 25 years, and assumes the cash flows will continue even longer.

Intangible 1b is the trade name as identified in 1a, but assume instead that Hamm Enterprises expects to sell this subsidiary in three years since the subsidiary operates in an area that is not part of Hamm's core activities.

Intangible 2 is a licence granted by the federal government to Hamm that allows Hamm to provide essential services to a key military installation overseas. The licence expires in five years, but is renewable indefinitely at little cost. Because of the profitability associated with this licence, Hamm expects to renew it indefinitely. The licence is very marketable, and will generate cash flows indefinitely.

Intangible 3 is a magazine subscription list. Hamm expects to use this subscriber list to generate revenues and cash flows for at least 25 years. It has determined the cash flow potential of this intangible by analyzing the subscribers' renewal history, the behaviour of the group of subscribers, and their responses to questionnaires.

Intangible 4 is a non-competition covenant. Hamm acquired this intangible asset when the company bought out a major owner-managed competitor. The seller signed a contract in which he agreed not to set up or work for another business that was in direct or indirect competition with Hamm. The projected cash flows resulting from this agreement are expected to continue for at least 25 years.

Intangible 5 is medical files. One of Hamm's subsidiary companies owns several medical clinics. A recent purchase of a retiring doctor's practice required a significant payment for the practice's medical files and clients. Hamm considers that this base will benefit the business for as long as it exists, providing cash flows indefinitely.

Intangible 6 is a favourable lease. Hamm acquired a sublease on a large warehouse property that requires annual rentals that are 50% below competitive rates in the area. The lease extends for 35 years.

Instructions

For each intangible asset and situation described above, do the following:

(a) Identify the appropriate method of accounting for the asset subsequent to acquisition, and justify your answer.

(b) Provide an example of a specific situation that would cause you to test the intangible asset for impairment.

P12-9 Chengwei Inc. is a large, publicly held corporation. The following are six selected expenditures that were made by the company during the current fiscal year ended April 30, 2008. The proper accounting treatment of these transactions must be determined in order to ensure that Chengwei's annual financial statements are prepared in accordance with generally accepted accounting principles.

1. Chengwei spent $3 million on a program that is designed to improve relations with its dealers. Dealers responded well to the project and Chengwei's management believes that it will therefore result in significant future benefits. The program was conducted during the fourth quarter of the current fiscal year.

2. A pilot plant was constructed during 2007–08 at a cost of $5.5 million to test a new production process. The plant will be operated for approximately five years. After the five years, the company will make a decision about the economic value of the process. The pilot plant is too small for commercial production, so it will be dismantled when the test is over.
3. During the year, Chengwei began a new manufacturing operation in Newfoundland, its first plant east of Montreal. To get the plant into operation, the following costs were incurred: (a) $100,000 to make the building fully wheelchair-accessible; (b) $41,600 to outfit the new employees with Chengwei uniforms; (c) $12,700 for the reception to introduce the company to others in the industrial mall where the plant is located; and (d) $64,400 in payroll costs for the new employees while they were being trained.
4. Chengwei purchased Eagle Company for $6 million cash in early August 2007. The fair value of Eagle's net identifiable assets was $5.2 million.
5. The company spent $14 million on advertising during the year: $2.5 million was spent in April 2008 to introduce a new product to be released during the first quarter of the 2009 fiscal year; $200,000 was used to advertise the opening of the new plant in Newfoundland; and $5 million was spent on the company product catalogue for the 2008 calendar year. The remaining expenditures were for recurring advertising and promotion coverage.
6. During the first six months of the 2007–08 fiscal year, $400,000 was expended for legal work on a successful patent application. The patent became effective in November 2007. The patent's legal life is 20 years and its economic life is expected to be approximately 10 years.

Instructions

For each of the six items presented, determine and justify the following:

(a) The amount, if any, that should be capitalized and included on Chengwei's statement of financial position prepared as at April 30, 2008.

(b) The amount that should be included in Chengwei's statement of income for the year ended April 30, 2008.

(CMA adapted)

P12-10 During 2006, Moss Tools Ltd. purchased a building site for its product development laboratory at a cost of $69,000. Construction of the building was started in 2006. The building was completed in late December 2007 at a cost of $290,000 and placed in service on January 2, 2008. The building's estimated useful life for amortization purposes is 20 years. The straight-line method of amortization is used and there is no estimated residual value. After the building went into service, several projects were begun and many are still in process.

Management estimates that about 50% of the development projects will result in long-term benefits (i.e., at least 10 years) to the corporation. The other projects either benefited the current period or were abandoned before completion. A summary of the different projects, their number, and the direct costs that were incurred for development activities in 2008 appears in the following table.

Upon recommendation of the research and development group, Moss Tools Ltd. acquired a patent for manufacturing rights at a cost of $98,000. The patent was acquired on April 1, 2007, and has an economic life of 10 years.

	Number of Projects	Salaries and Employee Benefits	Other Expenses (Excluding Building Amortization Charges)
Development of viable products (management intent and capability criteria are met)	15	$ 90,000	$56,000
Abandoned projects or projects that benefit the current period only	10	76,000	15,000
Projects in process—results uncertain	5	45,000	12,000
Total	30	$211,000	$83,000

Instructions

(a) If generally accepted accounting principles are followed, how should the items above that relate to product development activities be reported on the company's income statement and balance sheet at December 31, 2008? Be sure to give account titles and amounts, and briefly justify your presentation.

(b) Outline the criteria that would have to be met for any costs to qualify as deferred development costs.

(CMA adapted)

***P12-11** Beauchesne Inc. has recently become interested in acquiring a South American plant to handle many of its production functions in that market. One possible candidate is De Fuentes SA, a closely held corporation, whose owners have decided to sell their business if a proper settlement can be obtained. De Fuentes' balance sheet is as follows:

Current assets	$150,000
Investments	50,000
Plant assets (net)	400,000
Total assets	$600,000
Current liabilities	$ 80,000
Long-term debt	100,000
Share capital	220,000
Retained earnings	200,000
Total equities	$600,000

Beauchesne has hired Yardon Appraisal Corporation to determine the proper price to pay for De Fuentes SA The appraisal firm finds that the investments have a fair market value of $155,000 and that inventory is understated by $80,000. All other assets and liabilities have book values that approximate their fair values. An examination of the company's income for the last four years indicates that the net income has steadily increased. In 2008, the company had a net operating income of $105,000, and this income should increase by 20% each year over the next four years. Beauchesne believes that a normal return in this type of business is 15% on net assets. The asset investment in the South American plant is expected to stay the same for the next four years.

Instructions

(a) Yardon Appraisal Corporation has indicated that the company's fair value can be estimated in several ways. Prepare estimates of the value of De Fuentes SA, with the value based on each of the following independent assumptions:

1. Goodwill is based on the purchase of average excess earnings over the next four years.
2. Goodwill is equal to the capitalization of average excess earnings of De Fuentes SA at 24%.
3. Goodwill is equal to the present value of the average excess earnings over the next four years discounted at 15%.
4. The value of the business is based on the capitalization of future excess earnings of De Fuentes SA at 16%.

(b) De Fuentes SA is willing to sell the business for $1 million. What advice should Yardon Appraisal give Beauchesne in regard to this offer?

(c) If Beauchesne were to pay $970,000 to purchase the assets and assume the liabilities of De Fuentes SA, how would this transaction be reflected on Beauchesne's books?

***P12-12** The president of Birch Corp., Joyce Pollachek, is thinking of purchasing Balloon Bunch Corporation. She thinks that the offer sounds fair but she wants to consult a professional accountant to be sure. Balloon Bunch Corporation is asking for $78,000 in excess of the fair value of the identifiable net assets. Balloon Bunch's net income figures for the last five years are as follows:

2004—$64,000	2007—$80,000
2005—$50,000	2008—$70,000
2006—$81,000	

The company's identifiable net assets were appraised at $400,000 on December 31, 2008.

You have done some initial research on the balloon industry and discovered that the normal rate of return on identifiable net assets is 13%. After analyzing such variables as the stability of past earnings, the nature of the business, and general economic conditions, you have decided that the average excess earnings for the last five years should be capitalized at 25% and that the excess earnings will continue for about five more years. Further research led you to discover that the Happy Balloon Corporation, a competitor of similar size and profitability, was recently sold for $540,000, six times its average yearly earnings of $90,000.

Instructions

(a) Prepare a schedule that includes the calculation of Balloon Bunch Corporation's goodwill and purchase price under at least three methods.

(b) Write a letter to Joyce Pollachek that includes all of the following:

1. An explanation of the nature of goodwill

2. An explanation of the different acceptable methods of determining the fair value of goodwill. (Include with your explanation of the different methods the rationale for how each method arrives at a goodwill value.)
3. Advice for Joyce Pollachek on how to determine her purchase price.

Writing Assignments

WA12-1 After securing lease commitments from several major stores, Kolber Shopping Centres Ltd. was organized and the company built a shopping centre in a growing suburb. The shopping centre would have opened on schedule on January 1, 2008, if it had not been struck by a severe flood in December. Instead it opened for business on October 1, 2008, and all of the additional construction costs that were incurred as a result of the flood were covered by insurance.

In July 2007, in anticipation of the scheduled January opening, permanent employees were hired to promote the shopping centre, obtain tenants for the remaining unleased space, and manage the property.

A summary of some of the costs incurred in 2007 and the first nine months of 2008 follows:

	2007	January 1, 2008 through September 30, 2008
Interest on mortgage bonds	$720,000	$540,000
Cost of obtaining tenants	300,000	360,000
Promotional advertising	540,000	557,000

The promotional advertising campaign was designed to familiarize shoppers with the centre. If the company had known in time that the centre would not open until October 2008, the 2007 expenditure for promotional advertising would not have been made. The advertising had to be repeated in 2008.

All of the tenants who had leased space in the shopping centre at the time of the flood accepted the October occupancy date on condition that the monthly rental charges for the first nine months of 2008 be cancelled.

Instructions

Explain how each of the costs for 2007 and the first nine months of 2008 should be treated in the accounts of the shopping centre corporation. Give the reasons for each treatment.

(AICPA adapted)

WA12-2 Waveland Corporation's research and development department has an idea for a project that it believes will lead to a new product that would be very profitable for the company. Following company policy, the department requests approval for the project from Waveland Corporation's controller, Ron Santo.

Santo recognizes that corporate profits have been down lately and is hesitant to approve a project that will incur significant expenses that cannot be capitalized under *CICA Handbook* Section 3450 on Research and Development Costs. He knows that if Waveland Corporation contracts out the work to an outside firm and obtains a patent for the process, the company can purchase the patent from the outside firm and record the expenditure as an asset. Santo also knows that Waveland's own R&D department is first-rate, and he is confident that it can do the work well.

Instructions

Advise Ron Santo on what he should do. Ensure that your answer identifies who the stakeholders are in this situation and what the ethical issues are.

WA12-3 On June 30, 2007, your client, Bearcat Limited, was granted two patents for plastic cartons that it had been producing and marketing profitably for the past three years. One patent covers the manufacturing process and the other covers related products.

Bearcat executives tell you that these patents represent the most significant breakthrough in the industry in the past 30 years. The products have been marketed under the registered trademarks Evertight, Duratainer, and Sealrite. Licences under the patents have already been granted by your client to other manufacturers in Canada and abroad and are producing substantial royalties.

On July 1, Bearcat began patent infringement actions against several companies whose names you recognize as substantial and prominent competitors. Bearcat's management is optimistic that these suits will result in a permanent injunction against the manufacture and sale of the infringing products and collection of damages for loss of profits caused by the alleged infringement.

The financial vice-president has suggested that the patents be recorded at the discounted value of expected net royalty receipts.

Instructions

(a) What is the meaning of "discounted value of expected net receipts"? Explain.

(b) How would the value in (a) be calculated for net royalty receipts?

(c) What is the GAAP basis of valuation for Bearcat's patents? Give supporting reasons for this basis.

(d) What basis of valuation is supported in IAS 38, the IASB's standard on intangible assets?

(e) Assuming there are no practical problems in implementing the basis, and ignoring generally accepted accounting principles, what is the preferred basis of valuation for patents? Explain.

(f) What would be the preferred theoretical basis of amortization? Explain. What is Canadian GAAP for this? What does IAS 38 say?

(g) What recognition, if any, should be made of the infringement litigation in the financial statements for the year ending September 30, 2007? Discuss.

(AICPA adapted)

WA12-4 Echo Corp., a retail propane gas distributor, has increased its annual sales volume to a level that is three times greater than the annual sales of a dealer that it purchased in 2005 in order to begin operations. The board of directors of Echo Corp. recently received an offer to negotiate the sale of the company to a large competitor. As a result, the majority of the board wants to increase the stated value of goodwill on the balance sheet to reflect the larger sales volume that it developed through intensive promotion and the product's current market price. A few of the board members, however, would prefer to eliminate goodwill from the balance sheet altogether in order to prevent possible misinterpretations. Goodwill was recorded properly in 2005.

Instructions

(a) Discuss the meaning of the term "goodwill."

***(b)** List the techniques that are used to calculate an estimated value for goodwill in negotiations to purchase a going concern.

(c) Why are the book and fair values of Echo Corp.'s goodwill different?

(d) Discuss the appropriateness of each of the following:

1. Increasing the stated value of goodwill prior to the negotiations
2. Eliminating goodwill completely from the balance sheet

(AICPA adapted)

WA12-5 Nova Jones Ltd. is developing a revolutionary new product. A new division of the company was formed to develop, manufacture, and market this new product. As at year end (December 31, 2008), the new product had not yet been manufactured for resale; however, a prototype unit was built and was in operation. Throughout 2008, the new division incurred costs. These costs included design and engineering studies, prototype manufacturing costs, administrative expenses (including salaries of administrative personnel), and market research costs. In addition, approximately $900,000 in equipment (estimated useful life of 10 years) was purchased to develop and manufacture the new product. Approximately $315,000 of this equipment was built specifically for the design development of the new product; the remaining $585,000 of equipment was used to manufacture the pre-production prototype and will be used to manufacture the new product once it is in commercial production.

Instructions

(a) How are research and development defined in *CICA Handbook* Section 3450?

(b) Briefly state the practical and conceptual reasons for the conclusions that the Accounting Standards Board reached on accounting and reporting practices for research and development costs.

(c) In accordance with Section 3450, how should the various Nova Jones expenditures described above be recorded on the company's financial statements for the year ended December 31, 2008? Provide support for your conclusions.

Case

Refer to the Case Primer on the Student Website to help you answer this case.

CA12-1 Acquisitions Limited (AL) is a privately owned business which operates in the biotechnology business and has recently been on an acquisitions binge. It is now nearing year end and the company has been signalling to its bankers that 2007 has been a good year with substantial revenue growth. At present, the controller is preparing the adjustment for the year-end financial statements in preparation for a meeting with the bank next week. The bank is worried that the company has been overpaying for the acquired businesses and wants to be certain that its profitability and cash flows will not be harmed.

The following intangible assets have been acquired in several acquisitions:

Health-care industry contact lists: The company plans to use these lists for sales purposes and expects that it will be able to benefit from the information on the lists for two to three years.

Patents for drug delivery systems: The legal life remaining is 12 years; however, due to the competitive nature of this branch of research, the protection will only last approximately 8 years. The vendor has agreed to buy back the patent for approximately 50% of the value in 5 years. AL has committed to resell.

A trademark for certain over-the-counter allergy drugs. The legal life remaining on the trademark is three years but it is renewable every five years at little cost. AL is planning to add these drugs to its stable of core revenue-producing drugs and has already invested significant amounts in advertising. Research in the area of treating allergies has led AL scientists to believe that there will not be a better drug or cure for allergies in the near to mid term.

AL has also started up a new on-line distribution business. So far, the company has relocated 40 employees, developed a new website/database, and spent significant amounts on training and advertising. It is now December 15 and preparations to get ready have been ongoing for six months. Management originally estimated that it would take seven months to be up and running. AL is already serving its first few customers in the new business although there are still many little problems to work out. It is estimated that the business will break even in about five more months.

Instructions

Adopt the role of the company's auditors and do a critical evaluation of the financial reporting choices that are available to the company.

Integrated Cases

IC12-1 The following is an excerpt from Biovail Corporation's (BC) Annual Report:

> Biovail Corporation is a full-service pharmaceutical company that applies its proprietary drug delivery technologies in developing "oral controlled-release" products throughout North America. Biovail applies its proprietary drug delivery technologies to successful drug compounds that are free of patent protection to develop oral controlled-release pharmaceutical products. Branded oral controlled-release products improve on existing formulations, providing better therapeutic and economic benefits.
>
> Biovail engages in the formulation, clinical testing, registration, manufacturing, sales and marketing of these oral controlled-release products throughout North America. To date, Biovail technologies have been used to develop 18 products that have been sold in more than 55 countries. Biovail's proven technologies are being applied to over 20 new products currently under development.

In 2003 and 2004, several class action lawsuits were launched against the company for misleading investors. Among other things, the lawsuits allege that the company's growth in revenues is mainly due to acquisitions.

On October 1, 2003, a large shipment of the company's Wellbutrin XL drug was involved in a fatal multi-vehicle traffic accident that killed eight people. BC's truck was rear-ended in the accident, suffering $10,000 in damages, but no product spilled on the ground. The shipment was on its way to GlaxoSmithKline. BC stated that it had to take the drug back to the plant for inspection to be on the safe side. The insurance will only cover the actual manufacturing costs estimated at somewhere between $2–$4 million if the entire order were to be destroyed.

The company stated that the loss caused it to miss its expected quarterly profit target. On October 3, the company announced that it would have to lower revenue expectations by up to 22% for the third quarter, citing the traffic accident as contributing significantly to this by about $15–$20 million.

A week later, Banc of America Securities LLC issued a research report that included commentary by three forensic accountants who reviewed BC's financial reporting and raised a list of concerns over "aggressive accounting." As a result of the report, many investors sold their shares, driving the price of stock down significantly. The company responded to the comment in the report by announcing that it was considering a lawsuit against the analyst for what BC termed irresponsible comments.

Other analysts noted that a substantial portion of Biovail's earnings in the first half of the year came from one-time items. Sixty percent of the company's assets are represented by intangibles and goodwill. Net income for the nine months ended September 30, 2003, was approximately U.S. $75 million.

Instructions

Adopt the role of BC's controller and discuss the financial reporting issues.

IC12-2 Dr. Gary Morrow, a former surgeon, is the president and owner of Morrow Medical (MM), a private Ontario company whose focus is on the design and implementation of various medical and pharmaceutical products. With the recent success of various products put to market by MM, Dr. Morrow has decided that this would be a good opportunity to sell his company and retire to the Arizona desert. Dr. Morrow has located a potential buyer of the business and an agreement has been put in place which would see MM being sold at five times the December 31, 2007, net income. The potential buyer is extremely interested in an MM product that is currently in the development stage—the MM Surgical Drill.

During 2007, MM launched into production a special latex glove for use during surgery. This glove is laced with a special anti-bacterial agent, which significantly reduces the risk of infection during surgery. This product had been in the development phase since 2004 and following approval in early 2006 by Health Canada, it was approved for production and use.

Dr. Morrow was pleased with the initial demand for the product after trial runs conducted by surgeons during late 2006. After the success of the trial testing, MM successfully landed contracts with several hospitals in the province and early feedback from hospitals was favourable. Dr. Morrow was surprised, however, with how small the quantity of orders placed by hospitals actually was. He was certain that hospitals would quickly run out of the gloves and was beginning to fear that they would buy a competitor's product.

Since Dr. Morrow wanted to prevent hospitals from buying elsewhere, as it would result in a loss of sales for MM, for each purchase order received from a hospital, Dr. Morrow shipped several more units than were ordered. He was certain that all of the extra inventory would eventually be consumed and this was MM's way of being ahead of hospitals running out of inventory. To prevent hospitals from returning the extra inventory, he allowed them eight months to either pay for the entire shipment or return any unsold gloves in excess of the initial amount that was ordered. In terms of this product, Dr. Morrow's first priority is always getting the product out of the warehouse and into the hospitals. Orders are generally filled and shipped within two days of the receipt of a purchase order. Because MM is dealing with hospitals, there is little concern over collectibility.

During 2005, under the supervision of Dr. Morrow, MM began the research and development of a special surgical drill (the MM Surgical Drill mentioned above) that would allow for more precise handling by surgeons than any other drill currently in the market. The development of this product grew from various market surveys conducted in hospitals throughout Ontario which showed that surgeons were unhappy with the drills that were currently available on the market.

The following costs were incurred in 2007:

Cost of setting up production lab	$ 30,000
Testing of Surgical Drill	$100,000
Design of the moulds involved in Surgical Drill technology	$ 17,500
Testing to evaluate product alternatives	$ 12,000
Marketing and promotion costs in connection with launching the surgical gloves	$ 15,000

Dr. Morrow intends to capitalize all of these costs for the December 31 year end. In addition, $25,000 of tool design costs that were expensed in 2006 will be capitalized in 2007.

MM has the technical resources available to complete the Surgical Drill project and, since testing to date has been successful, management intends to bring this product to market in early 2009. MM has been faced with cash flow problems in the last few months but hopes that once MM is sold, additional funding will be available to see this product into its production stage.

In early 2007, an engineer testing the surgical drill was severely injured as a result of a product malfunction. This glitch was subsequently identified and fixed. MM was recently served with legal papers naming MM responsible for the injuries that were sustained. The claim is for $500,000. MM lawyers' best estimate of what the company will end up paying is $100,000 to $200,000. As the trial does not begin until 2008, MM has no intention of recording this in its December 31, 2007, financial statements.

Instructions

Adopt the role of the auditor hired by MM's potential buyer and analyze the financial reporting issues.

Research and Financial Analysis

RA12-1 Stantec Inc.

Refer to the financial statements and accompanying notes of Stantec Inc. presented in Appendix 5B and answer the following questions.

Instructions

(a) Does Stantec Inc. report any intangible assets (broadly defined) in its 2005 financial statements and accompanying notes? Identify all intangibles, their reported balance sheet amounts at December 31, 2005, and the accounting policies that are applied to these assets.

(b) What was Stantec's opening balance of goodwill for the year ended December 31, 2005? Its ending balance? Reconcile these amounts, clearly explaining the reasons for each change.

(c) Note 2 to the financial statements indicates that the company entered into three business combinations in 2005, and that the acquisition of The Keith Companies, Inc. was the most significant one. Identify, calculating where necessary, the following amounts for the Keith acquisition:

1. The fair value of identifiable net assets
2. The identifiable intangible assets that were acquired
3. The fair value of Keith

RA12-2 Merck and Johnson & Johnson

Merck & Co., Inc. and Johnson & Johnson are two leading producers of health-care products. Each has considerable assets, and each spends considerable funds each year on the development of new products. The development of a new health-care product is often very expensive and risky. New products must often undergo considerable testing before they get approval for distribution to the public. For example, it took Johnson & Johnson four years and U.S. $200 million to develop its 1-DAY ACUVUE contact lenses. The following are some basic data compiled from the financial statements of these two companies:

(in U.S. millions)	Johnson & Johnson	Merck
Total assets	$53,317	$42,573
Total revenue	47,348	22,939
Net income	8,509	5,813
Research and development expense	5,203	4,010
Intangible assets	11,842	2,765

Instructions

(a) What kinds of intangible assets might a health-care products company have? Do investors care about the specific assets that make up these intangibles; that is, would it be perceived differently if all of Merck's intangibles were goodwill rather than patents?

(b) Suppose the president of Merck has come to you for advice. He has noted that by eliminating research and development expenditures, the company could have reported $1.3 billion more in net income. He is frustrated because much of the research never results in a product, or the products take years to develop. He says that shareholders are eager for higher returns, so he is considering eliminating research and development expenditures for at least a couple of years. What would you advise?

(c) The notes to Merck's financial statements indicate that Merck has goodwill of $1.1 billion. Where does recorded goodwill come from? Is it necessarily a good thing to have a lot of goodwill on your books?

RA12-3 Comparative Analysis

Instructions

Go to the SEDAR website (www.sedar.com) and choose two companies from each of four different industry classifications. Choose from a variety of industries such as real estate and construction, foodstores (under merchandising), biotechnology and pharmaceuticals (under consumer products), publishing (under communications and media), etc. From the companies' most recent financial statements, identify the intangibles and deferred charges, the total assets, and the accounting policies for each type of intangible and deferred charge that is reported.

(a) What amounts were reported for intangible assets and deferred charges by each company?

(b) What percentage of total assets does each company have invested in intangible assets and deferred charges?

(c) Does the type of intangible and deferred charge differ depending on the type of industry? Does the relative size of the investment in this category of asset differ among industries? Comment.

(d) List all the intangible assets you identified and the policies used by these companies in amortizing them, if applicable. Do the policies differ by type of intangible? By type of industry?

(e) Are the amounts of accumulated amortization reported by these companies? Have any impairments been reported in the current period? If so, what disclosure was made about the impairment(s)?

RA12-4 Biovail Corporation

Ontario-based Biovail Corporation formulates, clinically tests, registers, manufactures, and markets pharmaceutical products that are mainly intended for the central nervous system, and cardiovascular and pain management.

Instructions

Access Biovail's Canadian GAAP financial statements for the year ended December 31, 2005, either on the Student Website or on SEDAR (www.sedar.com), and then answer the following.

(a) Identify all types of intangibles that are reported by Biovail. You may have to refer to the notes to the financial statements to complete your list. Are intangible assets a significant portion of the company's total assets?

(b) For each intangible asset that you identified, indicate the accounting policy that Biovail follows.

(c) Describe how Biovail management tests for impairment of intangibles.

(d) Does Biovail report any R&D assets? Explain. What were the company's expenditures on R&D for its year ended December 31, 2005?

(e) How does Biovail account for advertising costs?

(f) Read Note 5 to the financial statements and then describe Biovail's transactions and accounting for its acquisition of intangible assets in 2005.

RA12-5 Pacific Safety Products Inc. (PSP)

Pacific Safety Products Inc., based in Kelowna, British Columbia, manufactures, distributes, and sells protective products and accessories for the defence and security market. Its motto is, "We bring everyday heroes home safely."

Instructions

Obtain a copy of PSP's annual report for its year ended June 30, 2006, from the Student Website or from SEDAR (www.sedar.com). Based on the annual report, write a report to a potential investor in PSP that includes the following: (a) a description of the types of intangible assets that PSP deals with, (b) an explanation of the types of transactions that involve the intangible assets, and (c) the effect that these assets and transactions have on the company's financial position and financial performance.

Table A-1

FUTURE VALUE OF 1

(FUTURE VALUE OF A SINGLE SUM)

$$FVF_{n,i} = (1+i)^n$$

(n) periods	2%	$2\frac{1}{2}$%	3%	4%	5%	6%	8%	9%	10%	11%	12%	15%
1	1.02000	1.02500	1.03000	1.04000	1.05000	1.06000	1.08000	1.09000	1.10000	1.11000	1.12000	1.15000
2	1.04040	1.05063	1.06090	1.08160	1.10250	1.12360	1.16640	1.18810	1.21000	1.23210	1.25440	1.32250
3	1.06121	1.07689	1.09273	1.12486	1.15763	1.19102	1.25971	1.29503	1.33100	1.36763	1.40493	1.52088
4	1.08243	1.10381	1.12551	1.16986	1.21551	1.26248	1.36049	1.41158	1.46410	1.51807	1.57352	1.74901
5	1.10408	1.13141	1.15927	1.21665	1.27628	1.33823	1.46933	1.53862	1.61051	1.68506	1.76234	2.01136
6	1.12616	1.15969	1.19405	1.26532	1.34010	1.41852	1.58687	1.67710	1.77156	1.87041	1.97382	2.31306
7	1.14869	1.18869	1.22987	1.31593	1.40710	1.50363	1.71382	1.82804	1.94872	2.07616	2.21068	2.66002
8	1.17166	1.21840	1.26677	1.36857	1.47746	1.59385	1.85093	1.99256	2.14359	2.30454	2.47596	3.05902
9	1.19509	1.24886	1.30477	1.42331	1.55133	1.68948	1.99900	2.17189	2.35795	2.55803	2.77308	3.51788
10	1.21899	1.28008	1.34392	1.48024	1.62889	1.79085	2.15892	2.36736	2.59374	2.83942	3.10585	4.04556
11	1.24337	1.31209	1.38423	1.53945	1.71034	1.89830	2.33164	2.58043	2.85312	3.15176	3.47855	4.65239
12	1.26824	1.34489	1.42576	1.60103	1.79586	2.01220	2.51817	2.81267	3.13843	3.49845	3.89598	5.35025
13	1.29361	1.37851	1.46853	1.66507	1.88565	2.13293	2.71962	3.06581	3.45227	3.88328	4.36349	6.15279
14	1.31948	1.41297	1.51259	1.73168	1.97993	2.26090	2.93719	3.34173	3.79750	4.31044	4.88711	7.07571
15	1.34587	1.44830	1.55797	1.80094	2.07893	2.39656	3.17217	3.64248	4.17725	4.78459	5.47357	8.13706
16	1.37279	1.48451	1.60471	1.87298	2.18287	2.54035	3.42594	3.97031	4.59497	5.31089	6.13039	9.35762
17	1.40024	1.52162	1.65285	1.94790	2.29202	2.69277	3.70002	4.32763	5.05447	5.89509	6.86604	10.76126
18	1.42825	1.55966	1.70243	2.02582	2.40662	2.85434	3.99602	4.71712	5.55992	6.54355	7.68997	12.37545
19	1.45681	1.59865	1.75351	2.10685	2.52695	3.02560	4.31570	5.14166	6.11591	7.26334	8.61276	14.23177
20	1.48595	1.63862	1.80611	2.19112	2.65330	3.20714	4.66096	5.60441	6.72750	8.06231	9.64629	16.36654
21	1.51567	1.67958	1.86029	2.27877	2.78596	3.39956	5.03383	6.10881	7.40025	8.94917	10.80385	18.82152
22	1.54598	1.72157	1.91610	2.36992	2.92526	3.60354	5.43654	6.65860	8.14028	9.93357	12.10031	21.64475
23	1.57690	1.76461	1.97359	2.46472	3.07152	3.81975	5.87146	7.25787	8.95430	11.02627	13.55235	24.89146
24	1.60844	1.80873	2.03279	2.56330	3.22510	4.04893	6.34118	7.91108	9.84973	12.23916	15.17863	28.62518
25	1.64061	1.85394	2.09378	2.66584	3.38635	4.29187	6.84847	8.62308	10.83471	13.58546	17.00000	32.91895
26	1.67342	1.90029	2.15659	2.77247	3.55567	4.54938	7.39635	9.39916	11.91818	15.07986	19.04007	37.85680
27	1.70689	1.94780	2.22129	2.88337	3.73346	4.82235	7.98806	10.24508	13.10999	16.73865	21.32488	43.53532
28	1.74102	1.99650	2.28793	2.99870	3.92013	5.11169	8.62711	11.16714	14.42099	18.57990	23.88387	50.06561
29	1.77584	2.04641	2.35657	3.11865	4.11614	5.41839	9.31727	12.17218	15.86309	20.62369	26.74993	57.57545
30	1.81136	2.09757	2.42726	3.24340	4.32194	5.74349	10.06266	13.26768	17.44940	22.89230	29.95992	66.21177
31	1.84759	2.15001	2.50008	3.37313	4.53804	6.08810	10.86767	14.46177	19.19434	25.41045	33.55511	76.14354
32	1.88454	2.20376	2.57508	3.50806	4.76494	6.45339	11.73708	15.76333	21.11378	28.20560	37.58173	87.56507
33	1.92223	2.25885	2.65234	3.64838	5.00319	6.84059	12.67605	17.18203	23.22515	31.30821	42.09153	100.69983
34	1.96068	2.31532	2.73191	3.79432	5.25335	7.25103	13.69013	18.72841	25.54767	34.75212	47.14252	115.80480
35	1.99989	2.37321	2.81386	3.94609	5.51602	7.68609	14.78534	20.41397	28.10244	38.57485	52.79962	133.17552
36	2.03989	2.43254	2.88928	4.10393	5.79182	8.14725	15.96817	22.25123	30.91268	42.81808	59.13557	153.15185
37	2.08069	2.49335	2.98523	4.26809	6.08141	8.63609	17.24563	24.25384	34.00395	47.52807	66.23184	176.12463
38	2.12230	2.55568	3.07478	4.43881	6.38548	9.15425	18.62528	26.43668	37.40434	52.75616	74.17966	202.54332
39	2.16474	2.61957	3.16703	4.61637	6.70475	9.70351	20.11530	28.81598	41.14479	58.55934	83.08122	232.92482
40	2.20804	2.68506	3.26204	4.80102	7.03999	10.28572	21.72452	31.40942	45.25926	65.00087	93.05097	267.86355

Table A-2

PRESENT VALUE OF 1

(PRESENT VALUE OF A SINGLE SUM)

$$PVF_{n,i} = \frac{1}{(1+i)^n} = (1+i)^{-n}$$

(n) periods	2%	2½%	3%	4%	5%	6%	8%	9%	10%	11%	12%	15%
1	.98039	.97561	.97087	.96156	.95238	.94340	.92593	.91743	.90909	.90090	.89286	.86957
2	.96117	.95181	.94260	.92456	.90703	.89000	.85734	.84168	.82645	.81162	.79719	.75614
3	.94232	.92860	.91514	.88900	.86384	.83962	.79383	.77218	.75132	.73119	.71178	.65752
4	.92385	.90595	.88849	.85480	.82270	.79209	.73503	.70843	.68301	.65873	.63552	.57175
5	.90583	.88385	.86261	.82193	.78353	.74726	.68058	.64993	.62092	.59345	.56743	.49718
6	.88797	.86230	.83748	.79031	.74622	.70496	.63017	.59627	.56447	.53464	.50663	.43233
7	.87056	.84127	.81309	.75992	.71068	.66506	.58349	.54703	.51316	.48166	.45235	.37594
8	.85349	.82075	.78941	.73069	.67684	.62741	.54027	.50187	.46651	.43393	.40388	.32690
9	.83676	.80073	.76642	.70259	.64461	.59190	.50025	.46043	.42410	.39092	.36061	.28426
10	.82035	.78120	.74409	.67556	.61391	.55839	.46319	.42241	.38554	.35218	.32197	.24719
11	.80426	.76214	.72242	.64958	.58468	.52679	.42888	.38753	.35049	.31728	.28748	.21494
12	.78849	.74356	.70138	.62460	.55684	.49697	.39711	.35554	.31863	.28584	.25668	.18691
13	.77303	.72542	.68095	.60057	.53032	.46884	.36770	.32618	.28966	.25751	.22917	.16253
14	.75788	.70773	.66112	.57748	.50507	.44230	.34046	.29925	.26333	.23199	.20462	.14133
15	.74301	.69047	.64186	.55526	.48102	.41727	.31524	.27454	.23939	.20900	.18270	.12289
16	.72845	.67362	.62317	.53391	.45811	.39365	.29189	.25187	.21763	.18829	.16312	.10687
17	.71416	.65720	.60502	.51337	.43630	.37136	.27027	.23107	.19785	.16963	.14564	.09293
18	.70016	.64117	.58739	.49363	.41552	.35034	.25025	.21199	.17986	.15282	.13004	.08081
19	.68643	.62553	.57029	.47464	.39573	.33051	.23171	.19449	.16351	.13768	.11611	.07027
20	.67297	.61027	.55368	.45639	.37689	.31180	.21455	.17843	.14864	.12403	.10367	.06110
21	.65978	.59539	.53755	.43883	.35894	.29416	.19866	.16370	.13513	.11174	.09256	.05313
22	.64684	.58086	.52189	.42196	.34185	.27751	.18394	.15018	.12285	.10067	.08264	.04620
23	.63416	.56670	.50669	.40573	.32557	.26180	.17032	.13778	.11168	.09069	.07379	.04017
24	.62172	.55288	.49193	.39012	.31007	.24698	.15770	.12641	.10153	.08170	.06588	.03493
25	.60953	.53939	.47761	.37512	.29530	.23300	.14602	.11597	.09230	.07361	.05882	.03038
26	.59758	.52623	.46369	.36069	.28124	.21981	.13520	.10639	.08391	.06631	.05252	.02642
27	.58586	.51340	.45019	.34682	.26785	.20737	.12519	.09761	.07628	.05974	.04689	.02297
28	.57437	.50088	.43708	.33348	.25509	.19563	.11591	.08955	.06934	.05382	.04187	.01997
29	.56311	.48866	.42435	.32065	.24295	.18456	.10733	.08216	.06304	.04849	.03738	.01737
30	.55207	.47674	.41199	.30832	.23138	.17411	.09938	.07537	.05731	.04368	.03338	.01510
31	.54125	.46511	.39999	.29646	.22036	.16425	.09202	.06915	.05210	.03935	.02980	.01313
32	.53063	.45377	.38834	.28506	.20987	.15496	.08520	.06344	.04736	.03545	.02661	.01142
33	.52023	.44270	.37703	.27409	.19987	.14619	.07889	.05820	.04306	.03194	.02376	.00993
34	.51003	.43191	.36604	.26355	.19035	.13791	.07305	.05340	.03914	.02878	.02121	.00864
35	.50003	.42137	.35538	.25342	.18129	.13011	.06763	.04899	.03558	.02592	.01894	.00751
36	.49022	.41109	.34503	.24367	.17266	.12274	.06262	.04494	.03235	.02335	.01691	.00653
37	.48061	.40107	.33498	.23430	.16444	.11579	.05799	.04123	.02941	.02104	.01510	.00568
38	.47119	.39128	.32523	.22529	.15661	.10924	.05369	.03783	.02674	.01896	.01348	.00494
39	.46195	.38174	.31575	.21662	.14915	.10306	.04971	.03470	.02430	.01708	.01204	.00429
40	.45289	.37243	.30656	.20829	.14205	.09722	.04603	.03184	.02210	.01538	.01075	.00373

Table A-3

FUTURE VALUE OF AN ORDINARY ANNUITY OF 1

$$FVF\text{-}OA_{n,\,i} = \frac{(1+i)^n - 1}{i}$$

(n) periods	2%	$2\frac{1}{2}$%	3%	4%	5%	6%	8%	9%	10%	11%	12%	15%
1	1.00000	1.00000	1.00000	1.00000	1.00000	1.00000	1.00000	1.00000	1.00000	1.00000	1.00000	1.00000
2	2.02000	2.02500	2.03000	2.04000	2.05000	2.06000	2.08000	2.09000	2.10000	2.11000	2.12000	2.15000
3	3.06040	3.07563	3.09090	3.12160	3.15250	3.18360	3.24640	3.27810	3.31000	3.34210	3.37440	3.47250
4	4.12161	4.15252	4.18363	4.24646	4.31013	4.37462	4.50611	4.57313	4.64100	4.70973	4.77933	4.99338
5	5.20404	5.25633	5.30914	5.41632	5.52563	5.63709	5.86660	5.98471	6.10510	6.22780	6.35285	6.74238
6	6.30812	6.38774	6.46841	6.63298	6.80191	6.97532	7.33592	7.52334	7.71561	7.91286	8.11519	8.75374
7	7.43428	7.54743	7.66246	7.89829	8.14201	8.39384	8.92280	9.20044	9.48717	9.78327	10.08901	11.06680
8	8.58297	8.73612	8.89234	9.21423	9.54911	9.89747	10.63663	11.02847	11.43589	11.85943	12.29969	13.72682
9	9.75463	9.95452	10.15911	10.58280	11.02656	11.49132	12.48756	13.02104	13.57948	14.16397	14.77566	16.78584
10	10.94972	11.20338	11.46338	12.00611	12.57789	13.18079	14.48656	15.19293	15.93743	16.72201	17.54874	20.30372
11	12.16872	12.48347	12.80780	13.48635	14.20679	14.97164	16.64549	17.56029	18.53117	19.56143	20.65458	24.34928
12	13.41209	13.79555	14.19203	15.02581	15.91713	16.86994	18.97713	20.14072	21.38428	22.71319	24.13313	29.00167
13	14.68033	15.14044	15.61779	16.62684	17.71298	18.88214	21.49530	22.95339	24.52271	26.21164	28.02911	34.35192
14	15.97394	16.51895	17.08632	18.29191	19.59863	21.01507	24.21492	26.01919	27.97498	30.09492	32.39260	40.50471
15	17.29342	17.93193	18.59891	20.02359	21.57856	23.27597	27.15211	29.36092	31.77248	34.40536	37.27972	47.58041
16	18.63929	19.38022	20.15688	21.82453	23.65749	25.67253	30.32428	33.00340	35.94973	39.18995	42.75328	55.71747
17	20.01207	20.86473	21.76159	23.69751	25.84037	28.21288	33.75023	36.97371	40.54470	44.50084	48.88367	65.07509
18	21.41231	22.38635	23.41444	25.64541	28.13238	30.90565	37.45024	41.30134	45.59917	50.39593	55.74972	75.83636
19	22.84056	23.94601	25.11687	27.67123	30.53900	33.75999	41.44626	46.01846	51.15909	56.93949	63.43968	88.21181
20	24.29737	25.54466	26.87037	29.77808	33.06595	36.78559	45.76196	51.16012	57.27500	64.20283	72.05244	102.44358
21	25.78332	27.18327	28.67649	31.96920	35.71925	39.99273	50.42292	56.76453	64.00250	72.26514	81.69874	118.81012
22	27.29898	28.86286	30.53678	34.24797	38.50521	43.39229	55.45676	62.87334	71.40275	81.21431	92.50258	137.63164
23	28.84496	30.58443	32.45288	36.61789	41.43048	46.99583	60.89330	69.53194	79.54302	91.14788	104.60289	159.27638
24	30.42186	32.34904	34.42647	39.08260	44.50200	50.81558	66.76476	76.78981	88.49733	102.17415	118.15524	184.16784
25	32.03030	34.15776	36.45926	41.64591	47.72710	54.86451	73.10594	84.70090	98.34706	114.41331	133.33387	212.79302
26	33.67091	36.01171	38.55304	44.31174	51.11345	59.15638	79.95442	93.32398	109.18177	127.99877	150.33393	245.71197
27	35.34432	37.91200	40.70963	47.08421	54.66913	63.70577	87.35077	102.72314	121.09994	143.07864	169.37401	283.56877
28	37.05121	39.85990	42.93092	49.96758	58.40258	68.52811	95.33883	112.96822	134.20994	159.81729	190.69889	327.10408
29	38.79223	41.85630	45.21885	52.96629	62.32271	73.63980	103.96594	124.13536	148.63093	178.39719	214.58275	377.16969
30	40.56808	43.90270	47.57542	56.08494	66.43885	79.05819	113.28321	136.30754	164.49402	199.02088	241.33268	434.74515
31	42.37944	46.00027	50.00268	59.32834	70.76079	84.80168	123.34587	149.57522	181.94343	221.91317	271.29261	500.95692
32	44.22703	48.15028	52.50276	62.70147	75.29883	90.88978	134.21354	164.03699	201.13777	247.32362	304.84772	577.10046
33	46.11157	50.35403	55.07784	66.20953	80.06377	97.34316	145.95062	179.80032	222.25154	275.52922	342.42945	644.66553
34	48.03380	52.61289	57.73018	69.85791	85.06696	104.18376	158.62667	196.98234	245.47670	306.83744	384.52098	765.36535
35	49.99448	54.92821	60.46208	73.65222	90.32031	111.43478	172.31680	215.71076	271.02437	341.58955	431.66350	881.17016
36	51.99437	57.30141	63.27594	77.59831	95.83632	119.12087	187.10215	236.12472	299.12681	380.16441	484.46312	1014.34568
37	54.03425	59.73395	66.17422	81.70225	101.62814	127.26812	203.07032	258.37595	330.03949	422.98249	543.59869	1167.49753
38	56.11494	62.22730	69.15945	85.97034	107.70955	135.90421	220.31595	282.62978	364.04343	470.51056	609.83053	1343.62216
39	58.23724	64.78298	72.23423	90.40915	114.09502	145.05846	238.94122	309.06646	401.44778	523.26673	684.01020	1546.16549
40	60.40198	67.40255	75.40126	95.02552	120.79977	154.76197	259.05652	337.88245	442.59256	581.82607	767.09142	1779.09031

Table A-4

PRESENT VALUE OF AN ORDINARY ANNUITY OF 1

$$PVF-OA_{n,\,i} = \frac{1-\dfrac{1}{(1+i)^n}}{i}$$

(n) periods	2%	2½%	3%	4%	5%	6%	8%	9%	10%	11%	12%	15%
1	.98039	.97561	.97087	.96154	.95238	.94340	.92593	.91743	.90909	.90090	.89286	.86957
2	1.94156	1.92742	1.91347	1.88609	1.85941	1.83339	1.78326	1.75911	1.73554	1.71252	1.69005	1.62571
3	2.88388	2.85602	2.82861	2.77509	2.72325	2.67301	2.57710	2.53130	2.48685	2.44371	2.40183	2.28323
4	3.80773	3.76197	3.71710	3.62990	3.54595	3.46511	3.31213	3.23972	3.16986	3.10245	3.03735	2.85498
5	4.71346	4.64583	4.57971	4.45182	4.32948	4.21236	3.99271	3.88965	3.79079	3.69590	3.60478	3.35216
6	5.60143	5.50813	5.41719	5.24214	5.07569	4.91732	4.62288	4.48592	4.35526	4.23054	4.11141	3.78448
7	6.47199	6.34939	6.23028	6.00205	5.78637	5.58238	5.20637	5.03295	4.86842	4.71220	4.56376	4.16042
8	7.32548	7.17014	7.01969	6.73274	6.46321	6.20979	5.74664	5.53482	5.33493	5.14612	4.96764	4.48732
9	8.16224	7.97087	7.78611	7.43533	7.10782	6.80169	6.24689	5.99525	5.75902	5.53705	5.32825	4.77158
10	8.98259	8.75206	8.53020	8.11090	7.72173	7.36009	6.71008	6.41766	6.14457	5.88923	5.65022	5.01877
11	9.78685	9.51421	9.25262	8.76048	8.30641	7.88687	7.13896	6.80519	6.49506	6.20652	5.93770	5.23371
12	10.57534	10.25776	9.95400	9.38507	8.86325	8.38384	7.53608	7.16073	6.81369	6.49236	6.19437	5.42062
13	11.34837	10.98319	10.63496	9.98565	9.39357	8.85268	7.90378	7.48690	7.10336	6.74987	6.42355	5.58315
14	12.10625	11.69091	11.29607	10.56312	9.89864	9.29498	8.24424	7.78615	7.36669	6.98187	6.62817	5.72448
15	12.84926	12.38138	11.93794	11.11839	10.37966	9.71225	8.55948	8.06069	7.60608	7.19087	6.81086	5.84737
16	13.57771	13.05500	12.56110	11.65230	10.83777	10.10590	8.85137	8.31256	7.82371	7.37916	6.97399	5.95424
17	14.29187	13.71220	13.16612	12.16567	11.27407	10.47726	9.12164	8.54363	8.02155	7.54879	7.11963	6.04716
18	14.99203	14.35336	13.75351	12.65930	11.68959	10.82760	9.37189	8.75563	8.20141	7.70162	7.24967	6.12797
19	15.67846	14.97889	14.32380	13.13394	12.08532	11.15812	9.60360	8.95012	8.36492	7.83929	7.36578	6.19823
20	16.35143	15.58916	14.87747	13.59033	12.46221	11.46992	9.81815	9.12855	8.51356	7.96333	7.46944	6.25933
21	17.01121	16.18455	15.41502	14.02916	12.82115	11.76408	10.01680	9.29224	8.64869	8.07507	7.56200	6.31246
22	17.65805	16.76541	15.93692	14.45112	13.16800	12.04158	10.20074	9.44243	8.77154	8.17574	7.64465	6.35866
23	18.29220	17.33211	16.44361	14.85684	13.48857	12.30338	10.37106	9.58021	8.88322	8.26643	7.71843	6.39884
24	18.91393	17.88499	16.93554	15.24696	13.79864	12.55036	10.52876	9.70661	8.98474	8.34814	7.78432	6.43377
25	19.52346	18.42438	17.41315	15.62208	14.09394	12.78336	10.67478	9.82258	9.07704	8.42174	7.84314	6.46415
26	20.12104	18.95061	17.87684	15.98277	14.37519	13.00317	10.80998	9.92897	9.16095	8.48806	7.89566	6.49056
27	20.70690	19.46401	18.32703	16.32959	14.64303	13.21053	10.93516	10.02658	9.23722	8.45780	7.94255	6.51353
28	21.28127	19.96489	18.76411	16.66306	14.89813	13.40616	11.05108	10.11613	9.30657	8.60162	7.98442	6.53351
29	21.84438	20.45355	19.18845	16.98371	15.14107	13.59072	11.15841	10.19828	9.36961	8.65011	8.02181	6.55088
30	22.39646	20.93029	19.60044	17.29203	15.37245	13.76483	11.25778	10.27365	9.42691	8.69379	8.05518	6.56598
31	22.93770	21.39541	20.00043	17.58849	15.59281	13.92909	11.34980	10.34280	9.47901	8.73315	8.08499	6.57911
32	23.46833	21.84918	20.38877	17.87355	15.80268	14.08404	11.43500	10.40624	9.52638	8.76860	8.11159	6.59053
33	23.98856	22.29188	20.76579	18.14765	16.00255	14.23023	11.51389	10.46444	9.56943	8.80054	8.13535	6.60046
34	24.49859	22.72379	21.13184	18.41120	16.19290	14.36814	11.58693	10.51784	9.60858	8.82932	8.15656	6.60910
35	24.99862	23.14516	21.48722	18.66461	16.37419	14.49825	11.65457	10.56682	9.64416	8.85524	8.17550	6.61661
36	25.48884	23.55625	21.83225	18.90828	16.54685	14.62099	11.71719	10.61176	9.67651	8.87859	8.19241	6.62314
37	25.96945	23.95732	22.16724	19.14258	16.71129	14.73678	11.77518	10.65299	9.70592	8.89963	8.20751	6.62882
38	26.44064	24.34860	22.49246	19.36786	16.86789	14.84602	11.82887	10.69082	9.73265	8.91859	8.22099	6.63375
39	26.90259	24.73034	22.80822	19.58448	17.01704	14.94907	11.87858	10.72552	9.75697	8.93567	8.23303	6.63805
40	27.35548	25.10278	23.11477	19.79277	17.15909	15.04630	11.92461	10.75736	9.77905	8.95105	8.24378	6.64178

Table A-5

PRESENT VALUE OF AN ANNUITY DUE OF 1

$$PVF-AD_{n,\,i} = 1 + \frac{1 - \dfrac{1}{(1+i)^{n-1}}}{i}$$

(n) periods	2%	$2\frac{1}{2}$%	3%	4%	5%	6%	8%	9%	10%	11%	12%	15%
1	1.00000	1.00000	1.00000	1.00000	1.00000	1.00000	1.00000	1.00000	1.00000	1.00000	1.00000	1.00000
2	1.98039	1.97561	1.97087	1.96154	1.95238	1.94340	1.92593	1.91743	1.90909	1.90090	1.89286	1.86957
3	2.94156	2.92742	2.91347	2.88609	2.85941	2.83339	2.78326	2.75911	2.73554	2.71252	2.69005	2.62571
4	3.88388	3.85602	3.82861	3.77509	3.72325	3.67301	3.57710	3.53130	3.48685	3.44371	3.40183	3.28323
5	4.80773	4.76197	4.71710	4.62990	4.54595	4.46511	4.31213	4.23972	4.16986	4.10245	4.03735	3.85498
6	5.71346	5.64583	5.57971	5.45182	5.32948	5.21236	4.99271	4.88965	4.79079	4.69590	4.60478	4.35216
7	6.60143	6.50813	6.41719	6.24214	6.07569	5.91732	5.62288	5.48592	5.35526	5.23054	5.11141	4.78448
8	7.47199	7.34939	7.23028	7.00205	6.78637	6.58238	6.20637	6.03295	5.86842	5.71220	5.56376	5.16042
9	8.32548	8.17014	8.01969	7.73274	7.46321	7.20979	6.74664	6.53482	6.33493	6.14612	5.96764	5.48732
10	9.16224	8.97087	8.78611	8.43533	8.10782	7.80169	7.24689	6.99525	6.75902	6.53705	6.32825	5.77158
11	9.98259	9.75206	9.53020	9.11090	8.72173	8.36009	7.71008	7.41766	7.14457	6.88923	6.65022	6.01877
12	10.78685	10.51421	10.25262	9.76048	9.30641	8.88687	8.13896	7.80519	7.49506	7.20652	6.93770	6.23371
13	11.57534	11.25776	10.95400	10.38507	9.86325	9.38384	8.53608	8.16073	7.81369	7.49236	7.19437	6.42062
14	12.34837	11.98319	11.63496	10.98565	10.39357	9.85268	8.90378	8.48690	8.10336	7.74987	7.42355	6.58315
15	13.10625	12.69091	12.29607	11.56312	10.89864	10.29498	9.24424	8.78615	9.36669	7.98187	7.62817	6.72448
16	13.84926	13.38138	12.93794	12.11839	11.37966	10.71225	9.55948	9.06069	8.60608	8.19087	7.81086	6.84737
17	14.57771	14.05500	13.56110	12.65230	11.83777	11.10590	9.85137	9.31256	8.82371	8.37916	7.97399	6.95424
18	15.29187	14.71220	14.16612	13.16567	12.27407	11.47726	10.12164	9.54363	9.02155	8.54879	8.11963	7.04716
19	15.99203	15.35336	14.75351	13.65930	12.68959	11.82760	10.37189	9.75563	9.20141	8.70162	8.24967	7.12797
20	16.67846	15.97889	15.32380	14.13394	13.08532	12.15812	10.60360	9.95012	9.36492	8.83929	8.36578	7.19823
21	17.35143	16.58916	15.87747	14.59033	13.46221	12.46992	10.81815	10.12855	9.51356	8.96333	8.46944	7.25933
22	18.01121	17.18455	16.41502	15.02916	13.82115	12.76408	11.01680	10.29224	9.64869	9.07507	8.56200	7.31246
23	18.65805	17.76541	16.93692	15.45112	14.16300	13.04158	11.20074	10.44243	9.77154	9.17574	8.64465	7.35866
24	19.29220	18.33211	17.44361	15.85684	14.48857	13.30338	11.37106	10.58021	9.88322	9.26643	8.71843	7.39884
25	19.91393	18.88499	17.93554	16.24696	14.79864	13.55036	11.52876	10.70661	9.98474	9.34814	8.78432	7.43377
26	20.52346	19.42438	18.41315	16.62208	15.09394	13.78336	11.67478	10.82258	10.07704	9.42174	8.84314	7.46415
27	21.12104	19.95061	18.87684	16.98277	15.37519	14.00317	11.80998	10.92897	10.16095	9.48806	8.89566	7.49056
28	21.70690	20.46401	19.32703	17.32959	15.64303	14.21053	11.93518	11.02658	10.23722	9.54780	8.94255	7.51353
29	22.28127	20.96489	19.76411	17.66306	15.89813	14.40616	12.05108	11.11613	10.30657	9.60162	8.98442	7.53351
30	22.84438	21.45355	20.18845	17.98371	16.14107	14.59072	12.15841	11.19828	10.36961	9.65011	9.02181	7.55088
31	23.39646	21.93029	20.60044	18.29203	16.37245	14.76483	12.25778	11.27365	10.42691	9.69379	9.05518	7.56598
32	23.93770	22.39541	21.00043	18.58849	16.59281	14.92909	12.34980	11,34280	10.47901	9.73315	9.08499	7.57911
33	24.46833	22.84918	21.38877	18.87355	16.80268	15.08404	12.43500	11.40624	10.52638	9.76860	9.11159	7.59053
34	24.98856	23.29188	21.76579	19.14765	17.00255	15.23023	12.51389	11.46444	10.56943	9.80054	9.13535	7.60046
35	25.49859	23.72379	22.13184	19.41120	17.19290	15.36814	12.58693	11.51784	10.60858	9.82932	9.15656	7.60910
36	25.99862	24.14516	22.48722	19.66461	17.37419	15.49825	12.65457	11.56682	10.64416	9.85524	9.17550	7.61661
37	26.48884	24.55625	22.83225	19.90828	17.54685	15.62099	12.71719	11.61176	10.67651	9.87859	9.19241	7.62314
38	26.96945	24.95732	23.16724	20.14258	17.71129	15.73678	12.77518	11.65299	10.70592	9.89963	9.20751	7.62882
39	27.44064	25.34860	23.49246	20.36786	17.86789	15.84602	12.82887	11.69082	10.73265	9.91859	9.22099	7.63375
40	27.90259	25.73034	23.80822	20.58448	18.01704	15.94907	12.87858	11.72552	10.75697	9.93567	9.23303	7.63805

COMPANY INDEX

SUBJECT INDEX

PHOTO CREDITS

Logos are provided courtesy of the respective companies and are used with permission.

Page 2: PhotoDisc/Getty Images.
Page 32: Courtesy WestJet Airlines.
Page 76: Courtesy Alberta Computer Cable.
Page 138: Courtesy Vancity.
Page 198: Courtesy Stantec.
Page 288: Courtesy Cogeco Cable.
Page 352: Digital Vision.
Page 424: Courtesy Brock's.
Page 506: Courtesy Empire Company Limited.
Page 576: Courtesy Tahera Diamond Corporation.
Page 636: Steven J. Brown.
Page 698: Courtesy Netwerk.